ORGANIZATIONAL BEHAVIOUR

UNDERSTANDING AND
MANAGING LIFE AT WORK

ORGANIZATIONAL
BEHAVIOUR

FIFTH
EDITION

GARY JOHNS | ALAN M. SAKS
Concordia University | York University

Toronto

Canadian Cataloguing in Publication Data

Johns, Gary, 1946-
    Organizational behaviour: understanding and managing life at work

5th ed.
ISBN 0-201-64381-2

1. Organizational behaviour. I. Saks, Alan M. (Alan Michael), 1960-   . II. Title.

HD58.7.J63 2001   658.4   C00.930355-3

0-201-64381-2

Vice President, Editorial Director: Michael Young
Acquisitions Editor: Mike Ryan
Marketing Manager: James Buchanan
Developmental Editor: Suzanne Schaan
Production Editor: Mary Ann McCutcheon
Copy Editor: Rohini Herbert
Production Coordinator: Deborah Starks
Page Layout: Hermia Chung
Permissions Research: Susan Wallace-Cox
Photo Research: Alene McNeill
Art Direction: Mary Opper
Interior and Cover Design: Julia Hall
Cover Image: Sandra Dionisi

4 5   05 04 03 02

Printed and bound in United States

For my parents, Bill and Jean.   **Gary Johns**

For my parents, Simon and Renee, and my wife, Kelly.   **Alan M. Saks**

Brief Contents

Contents

Part 3
Social Behaviour and Organizational Processes   201

■ **In Focus**
Absence Cultures—
Norms in Action 213

■ **You Be the
Manager**
San Diego Zoo 223

■ **Global Focus**
Cultural Values and
Globalized Self-
Managed Work
Teams 229

■ **The Manager's
Notebook**
San Diego Zoo 231

■ **In Focus**
Socialization and
Culture at
Quad/Graphics 255

■ **In Focus**
Company's Beer
Commercials Mimic
Its Corporate
Culture 258

■ **You Be the
Manager**
Maintaining the
Culture at the Magic
Kingdom 261

■ **The Manager's
Notebook**
Maintaining the
Culture at the Magic
Kingdom 265

■ **You Be the
Manager**
Managers at
Domino's Go to Boot
Camp to Become
Better Leaders 282

■ **In Focus**
Leadership and
Employee Creativity
291

■ **In Focus**
Leadership
Development and
the Bottom Line at
General Motors 297

Contents

■ **You Be the Manager**
Turning Decision Making into a Science at General Electric Mortgage Insurance 347

■ **Global Focus**
Cultural Differences in Risky Decision Making 355

■ **In Focus**
Brainstorming at IDEO 365

■ **The Manager's Notebook**
Turning Decision Making into a Science at General Electric Mortgage Insurance 368

■ **In Focus**
Empowerment at Delta Hotels and Resorts 384

Part 4
The Total Organization 449

■ **You Be the Manager**
Organizational Structure and Service Excellence
463

■ **Global Focus**
Bureaucracy, Japanese Style: New United Motor Manufacturing, Inc.
468

■ **In Focus**
The Multifirm Spherical Network
471

■ **The Manager's Notebook**
Organizational Structure and Service Excellence
479

■ **In Focus**
Coping with Changes at Boeing 490

■ **Global Focus**
Global Strategic Alliance to Develop New Computer Chip Leads to Cross-Cultural Confusion
501

Preface

In writing this book we have been guided by two goals. First, we wish to convey the genuine excitement inherent in the subject of organizational behaviour. Second, we want the presentation of the material to have both academic and practical integrity, acknowledging the debt of the field to both behavioural science research and organizational practice. To put this another way, we wanted to develop a book that would be useful, as well as enjoyable to read, without oversimplifying key subjects on the premise that this somehow makes them easier to understand.

New to the Fifth Edition

One important change to the fifth edition of *Organizational Behaviour* can be seen on the cover—the addition of Alan Saks as a co-author. An enthusiastic adopter of previous editions, Alan brings added research breadth and practical experience to the text.

The fifth edition of *Organizational Behaviour* adds substantial new content, features, and pedagogy while remaining faithful to the general format and structure of the fourth edition. One of the first things that previous users of the text will notice is that this edition is shorter than the previous edition, with 16 rather than 18 chapters. Chapter 2 from the fourth edition ("Finding Out About Organizational Behaviour") has been moved to an appendix and is now called "Research in Organizational Behaviour." Given the changing nature of organizations, the traditional chapter on careers (Chapter 18 of the fourth edition) has been removed from the text, but the material on mentoring has been retained and can now be found in Chapter 8, "Social Influence, Socialization, and Culture." Other career-relevant material is now dispersed throughout the text.

We have also made a number of minor changes in the order or placement of several topics. For example, we reversed the order of the two major topics in Chapter 2, so that personality is now followed by learning. We made this change to better reflect the notion that people enter organizations with certain personalities and dispositions that precede their organization learning experiences. We moved the material on organizational commitment to Chapter 4, "Values, Attitudes, and Work Behaviour," so that it now follows the discussion of job satisfaction; we also moved the material on goal setting to Chapter 5, "Theories of Work Motivation."

While the major topics of the fourth edition remain, we have added new content to reflect recent research as well as new and emerging themes in the organizational behaviour literature. Major new coverage includes the following topics:

- what employees learn (Chapter 2)
- organizational learning practices, including training and formal learning, informal learning, and the work environment (Chapter 2)
- social learning theory, including modelling, self-efficacy, and self-management (Chapter 2)
- person perception and trust, with a related "In Focus" box, "The Effect of a Performance Appraisal System on Trust Toward Management" (Chapter 3)
- changes in the workplace and employee commitment (Chapter 4)
- employee stock ownership programs (Chapter 6)
- telecommuting (Chapter 6)
- what a team is (Chapter 7)

- psychological contract, socialization tactics, and proactive socialization (Chapter 8)
- developmental leadership, including leader member exchange theory, empowerment, self-management, persuasion and negotiation, and emotional intelligence (Chapter 9)
- global and strategic leadership (Chapter 9)
- gender differences in communication (Chapter 10)
- sexual harassment, including a "You Be the Manager" feature and experiential exercise (Chapter 12), plus coverage of harassment as a stressor (Chapter 13)
- work/life programs (Chapter 13)
- virtual, modular, and boundaryless organizations (Chapter 14)

We have updated many other areas throughout the text with the most current and recent research from both the practising management literature, the popular and business press, and the academic literature. We have also replaced the content of most of the features. The fifth edition contains eleven new chapter-opening vignettes, sixteen new "In Focus" boxes, seven new "Global Focus" boxes, and fourteen new "You Be the Manager" features. These features have been carefully chosen to represent current and exciting examples of organizational behaviour. Of those examples that we have retained from the fourth edition, many of them have been updated with more recent events (e.g., the Hubble telescope vignette in Chapter 11 and the Saturn vignette in Chapter 15) and up-to-date research (e.g., Chapter 13 "In Focus" box on gender differences in salary negotiation).

Finally, in the end-of-chapter material, eleven new cases and seven new experiential exercises have been added. We have also added three new features: an integrative case, case incidents, and integrative discussion questions (see "Pedagogical Features" below for more information).

General Content and Writing Style

Organizational Behaviour, Fifth Edition, is comprehensive; the material included is authoritative and up-to-date, reflecting current research and practical concerns. Both traditional subjects (such as expectancy theory) and newer topics (such as trust, global leadership, and sexual harassment) are addressed. Balanced treatment is provided to micro topics (covered in the earlier chapters) and macro topics (covered in the later chapters).

Although *Organizational Behaviour* is comprehensive, we have avoided the temptation to include too many concepts, theories, and ideas. Rather than comprising a long laundry list of marginally related concepts, each chapter is organized in interlocked topics. The topics are actively interrelated and are treated in enough detail to ensure understanding. Special attention has been devoted to the flow and sequencing of the topics.

The writing style is personal and conversational. Excessive use of jargon is avoided, and important ideas are well defined and illustrated. Special attention has been paid to consistency of terminology throughout the book. We have tried to foster critical thinking about the concepts under discussion by using devices such as asking the reader questions in the body of the text.

Believing that a well-tailored example can illuminate the most complex concept, we have used examples liberally throughout the text to clarify the points under consideration. The reader is not left wondering how a key idea applies to the world of organizations. The book is illustrated with exhibits, cartoons, and excerpts from the business press, such as *Canadian Business* and the *Globe and*

Mail, to enhance the flow of the material and reinforce the relevance of the examples for the student.

We have treated the subject matter generically, recognizing that organizational behaviour occurs in all organizations. The reader will find examples, cases, "In Focus" selections, and "You Be the Manager" features drawn from a variety of settings, including large and small businesses, high technology firms, hospitals, schools, and the military. In addition, care has been taken to demonstrate that the material covered is relevant to various levels and jobs within these organizations.

Organization

Organizational Behaviour is organized in a simple but effective building-block manner. "Part One: An Introduction" defines organizational behaviour, discusses the nature of organizations, introduces the concept of management, and reviews contemporary management concerns. "Part Two: Individual Behaviour" covers the topics of personality, learning, perception, attribution, diversity, attitudes, job satisfaction, organizational commitment, and motivation. "Part Three: Social Behaviour and Organizational Processes" discusses groups, teamwork, socialization, culture, leadership, communication, decision making, power, politics, ethics, conflict, negotiation, and stress. "Part Four: The Total Organization" considers organizational structure, environment, strategy, technology, change, and innovation.

Some instructors may prefer to revise the order in which their students read particular chapters, and they can accomplish this easily. However, Chapter 5, "Theories of Work Motivation," should be read before Chapter 6, "Motivation in Practice." Also, Chapter 14, "Organizational Structure," should be read before Chapter 15, "Environment, Strategy, and Technology." The book has been designed to be used in either a quarter or semester course.

Major Themes and Content

In preparing the fifth edition of *Organizational Behaviour,* we concentrated on developing several themes that are current in contemporary organizational life. This development included adding new content, expanding previous coverage, and addressing the themes throughout the text to enhance integration.

The **global aspects of organizational life** continue to receive strong treatment in this edition to enable students to become more comfortable and more competent in dealing with people from other cultures. Major sections on this theme appear in Chapters 4, 5, 9, and 10, which deal respectively with values, motivation, leadership, and communication. Pedagogical support for the global theme includes new chapter-opening vignettes (Chapters 1, 10, and 12), many boxed "Global Focus" features (Chapters 1, 2, 4, 6, 7, 10, 11, 14, 15, and 16), and a "You Be the Manager" feature (Chapter 4). It also includes two experiential exercises (Chapters 4 and 10) and two cases (Chapters 1 and 6).

The changing nature of workplace demographics and a need to provide a welcoming work environment for all organizational members has led to explicit coverage of **workforce diversity.** The major treatment of this topic occurs in Chapter 3 in the context of interpersonal perception and attribution. Additional treatment occurs in the context of motivation (Chapter 5) and communication (Chapter 10). Pedagogical support for the diversity theme can be found in the "You Be the Manager" feature in Chapter 3. We also see it in some "In Focus" selections (e.g., Chapter 13), a chapter-opening vignette (Chapter 3), and two exercises (Chapters 3 and 4).

Contemporary organizations are focusing more and more on **teamwork**. This has led to expanded coverage of teams and the most recent research findings on team characteristics and group effectiveness (Chapter 7). Pedagogical backup for the teamwork theme includes a new chapter opening vignette (Chapter 7), a "You Be the Manager" feature (Chapter 7), as well as "In Focus" selections (Chapters 5 and 7), a "Global Focus" selection (Chapter 7), and a case study and case incident (Chapter 7). In addition, two experiential exercises (Chapters 7 and 11) discuss aspects of teamwork.

Many organizations continue to undergo major change and transformation. Interrelated topics involving organizational change such as **reengineering, downsizing, advanced technology,** and **total quality management** continue to receive detailed coverage and are the focus of another theme highlighted in this edition. Coverage of reengineering can be found in Chapter 16 and related coverage on downsizing can be found in Chapter 14. Total quality management is covered in some detail in Chapters 6 and 16. Although principal coverage of advanced technology is seen in Chapter 15, the role of technology in communication and decision making can also be found in Chapters 10 and 11, where e-mail, electronic groups, electronic brainstorming, and company television networks are covered. New material has been added on telecommuting (Chapter 7) as well as sections on virtual, modular, and boundaryless organizational structures (Chapter 14). Pedagogical backup for the change theme includes two chapter opening vignettes (Chapters 1 and 16), five "You Be the Manager" features (Chapters 1, 6, 10, 15, and 16), three "In Focus" selections (Chapters 4, 6, and 15), four case studies (Chapters 8, 14, 15, and 16), two case incidents (Chapters 2 and 16), and the Integrative Case.

Finally, the fifth edition of *Organizational Behaviour* reflects the continuing role of **ethics** in organizational decision making. The major formal coverage of ethics is included in Chapter 12 with power and politics. The material has been expanded to cover unethical behaviour and sexual harassment. Pedagogical support for the ethics theme can be found in several chapter-opening vignettes (Chapters 11 and 12), a number of "Ethical Focus" features (Chapters 5, 12, and 13), and an experiential exercise (Chapter 12). Case studies are particularly good vehicles for examining the complexity surrounding ethical issues, and the cases for Chapters 1, 4, and 12 concern explicit ethical dilemmas.

Pedagogical Features

The fifth edition's pedagogical features are designed to complement, supplement, and reinforce the textual material. More specifically, they are designed to promote self-awareness, critical thinking, and an appreciation of how the subject matter applies in actual organizations. The fifth edition of *Organizational Behaviour* includes all of the features found in the previous edition as well as three new pedagogical features: integrative discussion questions, case incidents, and an integrative case.

- All chapters begin with a short **Opening Vignette** chosen to stimulate interest in the chapter's subject matter. All of these vignettes concern real people in real organizations. Each vignette is carefully analyzed at several points in the chapter to illustrate the ideas under consideration. For example, Chapter 8 begins with a discussion of the socialization process at Trilogy Software Inc. This vignette is then used as an example at other points throughout the chapter.

- Each chapter opens with several **Learning Objectives** to help focus the student's attention on the chapter's subject matter.

- In each chapter, students encounter a **"You Be the Manager"** feature that invites them to stop and reflect on the relevance of the material they are studying to a real problem in a real organization. Venues range from Continental Airlines (Chapter 1) to the San Diego Zoo (Chapter 7). Problems range from improving customer service (Chapters 1 and 14) to dealing with allegations of sexual harassment (Chapter 13). At the end of each chapter, **"The Manager's Notebook"** offers some observations about the problem and reveals what the organization actually did.

- All chapters contain **"In Focus," "Global Focus,"** or **"Ethical Focus"** selections that illustrate or supplement the textual material with material from the practicing management literature (e.g., *Fortune*, the *Wall Street Journal*), the research literature (e.g., the *Academy of Management Journal*), and the popular press (e.g., *Globe and Mail*). They are chosen to exemplify real-world problems and practices as they relate to organizational behaviour.

- **Key terms** in each chapter are set in boldface type when they are discussed in the body of the text and are defined in the margin in a **Running Glossary.** To help students find the definitions they need, key terms are highlighted in the index, with page references for definitions also in boldface.

- Each chapter concludes with a **Summary** and **Discussion Questions**. New to the fifth edition, two questions per chapter are **Integrative Discussion Questions**, which are indicated by the  icon. While the traditional discussion questions deal with issues within each chapter, the integrative discussion questions require the student to relate and integrate the material in a current chapter with concepts and theories from previous chapters. For example, one of the questions in the chapter on power, politics, and ethics (Chapter 12) requires students to use the material on organizational learning practices (Chapter 2), models of attitude change (Chapter 4), and contributors to organizational culture (Chapter 8) in order to understand how an organization can create a workplace where ethical behaviour is the norm. Thus, this feature is designed to facilitate student integration of different concepts and theories throughout the text.

- Each chapter includes an **Experiential Exercise**. These exercises span individual self-assessment, role plays, and group activities. To increase confidence in the feedback students receive, the self-assessments generally have a research base.

- A **Case Study** is found in each chapter. The cases are of medium length, allowing great flexibility in tailoring the use of them to one's personal instructional style. We have selected cases that require active analysis and decision making, not simply passive description. Cases span important topics in contemporary organizations such as doing global business (Chapter 1), introducing teams (Chapter 7), and changing corporate culture (Chapter 8).

- As a complement to the case study in each chapter, we have added **Case Incidents**. Case incidents are shorter than the case studies and are designed to focus on a particular topic within a chapter. Because they are short (one or two paragraphs) and deal with realistic scenarios of organizational life, they enable an instructor to quickly generate class discussion on a key theme within each chapter. They can be used at the beginning of a class to introduce a topic and to stimulate student thinking and interest, during the class when a particular topic is being discussed, or at the end of a class when the focus turns to the application of the text material.

- Also new to the fifth edition is an **Integrative Case**. The integrative case is presented at the end of Part 1. Unlike the case studies, which focus only on the material in each chapter, the integrative case requires students to use the material throughout the text in order to understand the case material. Integrative case questions can be found at the end of each of the four sections of the text. The questions deal with the main issues and themes of the chapters within each section. This enables students to gain an increasing awareness and understanding of the case material upon completion of each section of the text. Answering the case questions requires the integration of

material from the chapters within each section as well as successive sections of the text. Therefore, upon completion of the text and the integrative case questions, the student will have acquired a comprehensive understanding of the case through the integration of issues pertaining to individual behaviour, social behaviour and organizational processes, and the total organization.

Supplements for the Instructor

Instructor's Resource Manual. Written by the text authors to ensure close coordination with the book, this extensive manual includes chapter objectives, a chapter outline, answers to all of the text questions and cases, supplemental lecture material, video case teaching notes, and teaching notes for each chapter.

Test Item File. This test bank includes about 1,700 questions, including a mix of factual and application questions. Multiple-choice, true/false, and short answer formats are provided.

Test Manager. This test-generating and grading software allows instructors to assemble their own customized tests from the items included in the test item file.

CBC Videos. This collection of video cases includes segments from CBC's *Venture*. Written cases and questions to accompany the segments can be found on the Companion Web Site, and both the cases and answers to the questions are provided in the Instructor's Resource Manual.

Electronic Transparencies. Each chapter of the text is outlined in a series of PowerPoint slides, which include key points, figures and tables. The transparencies include detailed teaching notes, accessed through PowerPoint's "notes" function.

Supplement for the Student

Companion Web Site. Found at **www.pearsoned.ca/johns**, this Web site acts as an online Study Guide. It includes chapter summaries, self-tests, and CBC video cases, as well as Web links and search tools.

Acknowledgments

Books are not written in a vacuum. In writing *Organizational Behaviour*, Fifth Edition, we have profited from the advice and support of a number of individuals. This is our chance to say thank you.

First, we would like to thank our reviewers for this edition, who provided us with a wealth of insights about how to improve the text: Robert Atkin, University of Pittsburgh; Richard Blackburn, University of North Carolina–Chapel Hill; Claude Dupuis, University of Calgary; Steve Harvey, Bishop's University; James King, Samford University; Robert Loo, University of Lethbridge; Kathy Ready, University of Wisconsin–Eau Clair; Kim Richter, Kwantlen University College; Yaghoub Shafai, Dalhousie University; K. Douglas Smith, Kwantlen University College; Richard Weiss, University of Delaware; Jerry P. White, University of Western Ontario.

The team at Pearson Education Canada have provided great support, dedication, and commitment for this project. In particular, we thank our Acquisitions Editor, Mike Ryan, whose enthusiasm and belief in this project was instrumental in getting it off the ground and guiding it to its completion. We would also like to thank our Developmental Editor, Suzanne Schaan, who is largely responsible for keeping this project on track and making sure that all of the many pieces of this text are in place. We also thank our Supervising Editor, Mary Ann J. McCutcheon, for her efforts in managing the editing process.

We would also like to express our appreciation to those individuals who assisted us during the writing of this text. We thank our research assistants, Dara Potton and Cindy Hutchinson, who spent many hours in the library tracking down and photocopying articles for us. We would also like to express our appreciation to Helena Merriam and the Resource Centre of the Human Resources Professionals Association of Ontario (HRPAO). The Resource Centre, along with Helena's generous help, provided us with a wealth of information that contributed to the writing of this text.

Finally, each of us wish to give thanks to those in our lives who have contributed to our work and the writing of this text:

I (Gary Johns) am grateful to my Concordia University Management Department colleagues for their interest, support, and ideas. Additionally, I would like to thank my students over the years. In one way or another, many of their questions, comments, challenges, and suggestions are reflected in the book. Also, thanks to all my colleagues who have taken time to suggest ideas for the book when we have met at professional conferences. Finally, thanks to Monika Jörg for her enthusiasm, humour, and support.

I (Alan Saks) would like to express my appreciation to my parents, Renee and Simon Saks, who have provided me with continuous support throughout my education and career and celebrated every step along the way. I also wish to thank my wife, Kelly, who has with great patience and encouragement travelled with me on this long journey. Although she did not write a single word in this book, in many ways her contribution to it is as significant as mine. This book is dedicated to her and my parents.

Gary Johns   Alan M. Saks

The Pearson Education Canada

The Pearson Education Canada

companion Website...

Your Internet companion to the most exciting, state-of-the-art educational tools on the Web!

The Prentice Hall Canada Companion Website is easy to navigate and is organized to correspond to the chapters in this textbook. The Companion Website is comprised of four distinct, functional features:

1) **Customized Online Resources**

2) **Online Study Guide**

3) **Reference Material**

4) **Communication**

Explore the four areas in this Companion Website. Students and distance learners will discover resources for indepth study, research and communication, empowering them in their quest for greater knowledge and maximizing their potential for success in the course.

A NEW WAY TO DELIVER EDUCATIONAL CONTENT

1) Customized Online Resources

Our Companion Websites provide instructors and students with a range of options to access, view, and exchange content.

- Syllabus Builder provides instructors with the option to create online classes and construct an online syllabus linked to specific modules in the Companion Website.

- Mailing lists enable instructors and students to receive customized promotional literature.

- Preferences enable students to customize the sending of results to various recipients, and also to customize how the material is sent, e.g., as html, text, or as an attachment.

- Help includes an evaluation of the user's system and a tune-up area that makes updating browsers and plug-ins easier. This new feature will enhance the user's experience with Companion Websites.

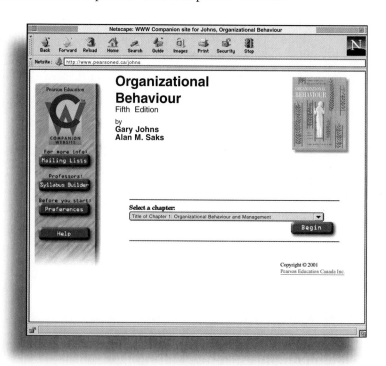

2) Online Study Guide

An Interactive Study Guide forms the core of the student learning experience in the Companion Website. Self-testing modules, organized by text chapter, include multiple choice, true/false, and short essay questions. They provide students with the ability to send answers to our grader and receive instant feedback on their progress through our Results Reporter. Students can check suggested answers after submitting their problems.

3) Reference Material

Reference material broadens text coverage with up-to-date resources for learning. Special **CBC Video Case Studies** provide instructors and students with interesting video segments and stimulting cases for discussion. **Web Destinations** provides direct links to websites relevant to the subject matter in each chapter. **Net News** (**Internet Newsgroups**) are a fundamental source of information about a discipline, containing a wealth of brief, opinionated postings. **Net Search** simplifies key term search using Internet search engines.

4) Communication

Companion Websites contain the communication tools necessary to deliver courses in a **Distance Learning** environment. **Message Board** allows users to post messages and check back periodically for responses. **Live Chat** allows users to discuss course topics in real time, and enables professors to host online classes.

Communication facilities of Companion Websites provide a key element for distributed learning environments. There are two types of communication facilities currently in use in Companion Websites:

- **Message Board** – this module takes advantage of browser technology, providing the users of each Companion Website with a national newsgroup to post and reply to relevant course topics.

- **Live Chat** – enables instructor-led group activities in real time. Using our chat client, instructors can display Website content while students participate in the discussion.

Chapter 1

Multiple Choice

True/False

Short Essay

CBC Video Cases

Destinations

Net News

Net Search

Update

Message Board

Help

Preferences

Feedback

Undock

Companion Websites are currently available for numerous Pearson Education Canada books, including

- Dessler, Cole, and Sutherland, *Human Resources Management in Canada*, Canadian Seventh Edition
- Robbins, Coulter, and Stuart-Kotze, *Management*, Canadian Sixth Edition
- Tuckwell, *Canadian Advertising in Action*, Fifth Edition

Note: CW content will vary slightly from site to site depending on discipline requirements.

The Companion Website can be found at:
www.pearsoned.ca/johns

Pearson Education Canada

26 Prince Andrew Place
Don Mills, Ontario M3C 2T8
To order:
Call: 1-800-567-3800
Fax: 1-800-263-7733

For samples:
Call: 1-800-850-5813
Fax: (416) 447-2819
E-mail: phcinfo_pubcanada@pearsoned.com

Part 1

An Introduction

Organizational Behaviour and Management

DAIMLERCHRYSLER When Chrysler, the third largest carmaker in the United States, and Daimler-Benz announced a $48 billion unprecedented global merger of their companies, they made history by becoming the largest ever industrial merger. Although nobody saw it coming, after the deal was struck by Chrysler Chairman Robert Eaton and Daimler-Benz Chairman Jürgen Schrempp, it was described as a brilliant marriage of opportunity. Daimler-Benz and Chrysler have combined revenues of $130 billion, and the new company DaimlerChrysler has a total of 440,000 employees and is now Europe's largest industrial company and the world's fourth-largest carmaker. In addition to cars and trucks, DaimlerChrysler also makes Airbuses, trains, and ocean-liner engines.

Daimler
Chrysler

According to the Chairmen of both companies, consolidation of the automobile industry was inevitable, given the excess capacity in the world. Both realized the possibilities and opportunities that a partnership could bring. Chrysler makes moderately priced cars and light trucks while Daimler makes luxury cars and heavy trucks; Chrysler's strength is in design and product development, and Daimler-Benz is strong in engineering and technology; Chrysler has a large market share in North America but is weak in Europe; Daimler is the opposite. Chrysler can help Daimler sell its products in the United States and provide logistical and service support for Mercedes-Benz, and Daimler can help Chrysler increase sales in Europe as well as South America, where its truck position is strong. There will also be new opportunities for Chrysler products in Australia and South Africa.

However, integrating two companies that are divided by geography, language, tradition, and national culture is not easy. The potential for conflict and con-

The $48-billion global merger between Chrysler and Daimler-Benz that resulted in DaimlerChrysler has been described as a brilliant marriage of opportunity.

frontation is great. For example, shortly before DaimlerChrysler opened on the New York Stock Exchange, the two companies could not agree on whether the new company would use American- or European-size business cards. To lessen the difficulty of the adjustment period, managers and employees spent a good deal of time getting to know each other during the first year of the merger. German teams spent time in Detroit where they surprised their American counterparts with their skill speaking English, not to mention their knowledge of the lyrics to rock-and-roll oldies at a piano bar.

Meanwhile, the American employees are learning to speak German and attended training on the basics of German social and business etiquette, during which they discovered some German cultural eccentricities, such as eating hamburgers with knives and forks and calling cellular phones "handies." The German employees have been attending cultural awareness seminars on "USA and Germany: Similarities and Differences in Business Life," where they have discovered that the Americans shake hands less and are not allowed to compliment female business colleagues.

When it comes to working together, both sides are learning that they have different styles of decision making. The American style is more fast paced and trial-and-error experimentation compared with the German's painstaking planning and precise implementation. As a result, the Germans perceive the Americans as totally chaotic, and the Americans perceive the Germans as stubborn militarists. In an attempt to find some common ground, the Americans are trying to make more specific plans, and the Germans are experimenting more quickly.

The merger, however, has not been easy or welcomed by everyone. In fact, since the merger, more than a half dozen senior American executives have

DaimlerChrysler
www.daimlerchrysler.com

Learning Objectives

After reading Chapter 1, you should be able to:

1   Define organizations and describe their basic characteristics.

2   Explain the concept of organizational behaviour and describe the goals of the field.

3   Contrast the classical viewpoint of management with that which the human relations movement advocated.

4   Describe the contemporary contingency approach to management.

5   Explain what managers do—their roles, activities, agendas for action, and thought processes.

6   Describe the societal and global trends that are shaping contemporary management concerns.

quit, morale in the old Chrysler headquarters is reported to be low, and some American executives feel that Eaton's announcement of his plans to retire as co-chairman within three years has surrendered Chrysler's power base and undercut their influence. One unhappy employee in Detroit was quoted as saying, "The Germanization has begun."

Many mergers fail because of a clash of organizational cultures. In the case of DaimlerChrysler, success will require much more than the integration of organizational cultures, it also requires an integration of national cultures. In fact, reporters at a news conference are reported to have angered co-chairman Schrempp when they asked about a trans-Atlantic culture clash, and the defections of seven top executives from Chrysler, including two top engineers who are now working at Ford, and three top public relations executives who have gone to General Motors. The defections have raised concerns that DaimlerChrysler could be losing the very talent that made Chrysler so successful.

To make the merger a success, DaimlerChrysler faces enormous logistical and managerial obstacles. According to their own study of cross-border partnerships, 70 percent of all mergers fail. In the end, it will be up to management and effective leadership to make the deal a success. The stress of trying to do so has already taken its toll on top managers. Meanwhile, sales and profit figures continue to be impressive, as do the forecasts and financial outlook for the future, as Mercedes and Chrysler vehicles continue to roll off the same assembly lines.[1]

What we have here is a dramatic example of worklife and management—just what this book is about. Admittedly, this example is more dramatic than most in that it concerns issues of leadership, strategy, change, and culture. It raises some very interesting questions: Why would two large and successful companies from different parts of the world choose to become partners? What are the implications of their partnership? What will be required to make it a success? This book will help you uncover the answers to these questions.

In this chapter, we will define organizations and organizational behaviour and examine its relationship to management. We will explore historical and contemporary approaches to management and consider what managers do and how they think. The chapter concludes with some issues of concern to contemporary managers.

What Are Organizations?

This book is about what happens in organizations. **Organizations** are social inventions for accomplishing common goals through group effort. DaimlerChrysler is obviously an organization, but so are the Vancouver Canucks, CNN, Blue Rodeo, and a college sorority or fraternity.

Organizations. Social inventions for accomplishing common goals through group effort.

Social Inventions

When we say that organizations are social inventions, we mean that their essential characteristic is the coordinated presence of *people*, not necessarily things. DaimlerChrysler owns a lot of things, such as factories, equipment, and offices. However, you are probably aware that through advanced information technology and contracting out work, some contemporary organizations make and sell products, such as computers or clothes, without owning much of anything. Also, many service organizations, such as consulting firms, have little physical capital. Still, these organizations have people, people who present both opportunities and challenges. *The field of organizational behaviour is about understanding people and managing them to work effectively.*

Goal Accomplishment

Individuals are assembled into organizations for a reason. The organizations mentioned above have the very basic goals of selling cars, delivering news, and winning hockey games. Nonprofit organizations have goals such as saving souls, promoting the arts, helping the needy, or educating people. Virtually all organizations have *survival* as a goal. Despite this, consider the list of organizations that have failed to survive: Eastern Airlines, Gimbel's, Child World, and a ton of American savings and loan companies. *The field of organizational behaviour is concerned with how organizations can survive and adapt to change.* Certain behaviours are necessary for survival and adaptation. People have to

- be motivated to join and remain in the organization;
- carry out their basic work reliably, in terms of productivity, quality, and service; and
- be flexible and innovative.[2]

The field of organizational behaviour is concerned with all these basic activities. Innovation and flexibility, which provide for adaptation to change, are especially important for contemporary organizations. Management guru Tom Peters has gone so far as to advise firms to "Get Innovative or Get Dead."[3] The merger of Chrysler and Daimler-Benz is a good example of how organizations change to become more effective and improve their chances of survival.

Tom Peters
www.tompeters.com/training/

Group Effort

The final component of our definition of organizations is that they are based on group effort. At its most general level, this means that organizations depend on

A football team is an organization that accomplishes common goals through team effort.

ACT UP
www.actupny.org

Organizational behaviour. The attitudes and behaviours of individuals and groups in organizations.

There are a variety of different organizations in which individuals work together to accomplish goals through group effort. Though the motivation of Greenpeace may differ from that of ACT UP, both groups strive for survival and goal accomplishment.

interaction and coordination among people to accomplish their goals. Much of the intellectual and physical work done in organizations is quite literally performed by groups, whether they are permanent work teams or short-term project teams. Also, informal grouping occurs in all organizations because friendships develop and individuals form informal alliances to accomplish work. The quality of this informal contact in terms of communication and morale can have a strong impact on goal achievement. For all these reasons, *the field of organizational behaviour is concerned with how to get people to practise effective teamwork.*

Now that we have reviewed the basic characteristics of organizations, let us look more directly at the meaning and scope of organizational behaviour.

What Is Organizational Behaviour?

Organizational behaviour refers to the attitudes and behaviours of individuals and groups in organizations. The discipline of organizational behaviour systematically studies these attitudes and behaviours and provides insight about effectively managing and changing them. It also studies how organizations can be structured more effectively and how events in their external environments affect organizations. Those who study organizational behaviour are interested in attitudes—how satisfied people are with their jobs, how committed they feel to the goals of the organization, or how supportive they are of promoting women or minorities into management positions. Behaviours like cooperation, conflict, innovation, resignation, or ethical lapses are important areas of study in the field of organizational behaviour.

Using an organizational behaviour perspective, reconsider the DaimlerChrysler vignette that opened the chapter. The immediate question is: *What are the implications of the merger and what will be required to make it a success?* Although we will not answer this question directly, we can pose some subsidiary questions highlighting some of the topics that the field of organizational behaviour covers, which we will explore in later chapters.

- What will employees and managers at DaimlerChrysler be required to learn, and how will this learning take place? Learning has become very important in today's rapidly changing world, where continuous learning has become a way of life. Chapter 2 deals with theories of learning and the learning process in organizations.

- Why do the American employees perceive the Germans as "stubborn militarists," and the German employees perceive the Americans as "totally chaotic," and what are the implications of these perceptions? Perceptions are important because people base their actions on their interpretation of reality that is based on their perceptions. Chapter 3 explores the perceptual process and biases in person perception.

- What are the differences between American and German cultural values, and what effect will this have on management practices and employee attitudes and behaviours? Understanding cultural value differences is important for developing globally diverse employees and adjusting management practices across cultures. Chapter 4 focuses on cultural values and the implications of this for importing and exporting management theory and practice.

- What factors will be considered in the formation of teams at DaimlerChrysler? How will new teams be designed, and will they be effective? More and more organizations are using teams and as a result their effectiveness will affect an organization's success. The process of group development and the characteristics of effective teams are covered in Chapter 7.

- How will the cultures of the two corporations be integrated, and what will be the new culture of DaimlerChrysler? Strong cultures have been shown to have a number of advantages that can influence an organization's financial success. How cultures are built and maintained is covered in Chapter 8.

- What style of leadership will be required at DaimlerChrysler, and will leaders have to change their style to become more effective leaders? Leadership is one of the most important ingredients for an organization's success, and the success or failure of DaimlerChrysler will, in large part, be in the hands of its leaders. As you will learn in Chapter 9, the field of organizational behaviour has a longstanding interest in leadership.

- How will DaimlerChrysler communicate with employees and managers who speak different languages and work in different countries? Communication is the process of exchanging information, and effective organizational communication is essential for organizational competitiveness. Communication is the focus of Chapter 10.

- How will Robert Eaton's retirement affect the power of American executives, and why are they so worried about a power imbalance? Power and politics are a natural part of organizational life and are the focus of Chapter 12.

- What role did the environment play in the DaimlerChrysler merger, and why was a merger chosen as a strategic response? How the external environment affects what happens in organizations is the focus of Chapter 15.

- How will the changes at DaimlerChrysler be implemented, and will the process be successful? Organizational change has become a necessary part of organizational survival, and what is most important for success is how the change is managed. Chapter 16 focuses on the organizational change process and organizational development.

These questions provide a good overview of some issues that those in the field of organizational behaviour study. Accurate answers to these questions would go a long way toward explaining why the events in the vignette transpired and suggesting future management actions. Analysis followed by action is what organizational behaviour is all about.

Why Study Organizational Behaviour?

Why should you attempt to read and understand the material in *Organizational Behaviour*?

Organizational Behaviour Is Interesting

At its core, organizational behaviour is interesting because it is about people and human nature. Why did Jürgen Schrempp and Robert Eaton agree to the DaimlerChrysler merger, and why did some of Chrysler's executives quit and accept positions at Ford and General Motors? These questions are interesting—even if you do not care about automobiles—because these leaders did something that will impact the lives of many people both inside and outside of DaimlerChrysler.

Organizational behaviour includes interesting examples of success as well as failure. Later in the text, we will study a company that has to bar employees from starting work too early (Lincoln Electric), a company with strong values for treating people and the environment with respect (Husky Injection Molding Systems), and a company that has had to change its management, structure, and technology in response to changing market forces and declining performance (McDonald's). All these companies are extremely successful, and organizational behaviour helps explain why.

Organizational behaviour does not have to be exotic to be interesting. Anyone who has negotiated with a recalcitrant bureaucrat or had a really excellent boss has probably wondered what made them behave the way they did. Organizational behaviour provides the tools to find out why.

Organizational Behaviour Is Important

Looking through the lens of other disciplines, it would be possible to frame the DaimlerChrysler merger in terms of economics, finance, or marketing. Notice, however, that underlying all these perspectives, it was *still* about organizational behaviour. What happens in organizations often has a profound impact on people. At DaimlerChrysler, several senior American executives quit their jobs, and employees have had to learn about their new partners' cultures and how to compromise. It is clear that the impact of organizational behaviour does not stop at the walls of the organization. The consumers of an organization's products and services are also affected. The DaimlerChrysler merger will result in greater product availability throughout the world. Thus, organizational behaviour is important to managers, employees, and consumers; and understanding it can make us more effective managers, employees, or consumers.

We sometimes fail to appreciate that there is tremendous variation in organizational behaviour. For example, skilled salespeople in insurance or real estate make many, many more sales than some of their peers. Similarly, for every Greenpeace or Sierra Club, there are dozens of failed organizations that were dedicated to saving the environment. The field of organizational behaviour is concerned with explaining these differences and using the explanations to improve organizational effectiveness and efficiency.

Organizational Behaviour Makes a Difference

By now it is probably apparent to you that organizational behaviour can have a powerful influence on the attitudes and behaviours of individuals in organiza-

Greenpeace International
www.greenpeace.org

tions. But can it also have an impact on an organization's effectiveness and the bottom line? In 1995, Mark Huselid conducted an important study on the impact of high-performance work practices and demonstrated that organizational behaviour can impact corporate financial performance.[4] Huselid identified two major dimensions of high performance work practices that he called *employee skills and organizational structures* and *employee motivation*. Employee skills and organizational structures are practices that enhance employees' knowledge and skills, such as quality of worklife programs, incentive plans, and regular attitude surveys. Employee motivation refers to practices that recognize and reinforce desirable employee behaviours, such as formal performance appraisals and linking appraisals to compensation.

Huselid found that these practices impact organizational outcomes, such as lower employee turnover, higher productivity, and an organization's financial performance. In the last several years, an increasing number of studies have confirmed the existence of linkages between organizational behaviour and corporate performance and success.[5]

In his book, *Competitive Advantage Through People*, Jeffrey Pfeffer argues that organizations can no longer achieve a competitive advantage through the traditional sources of success, such as technology, regulated markets, access to financial resources, and economies of scale.[6] Today, the main factor that differentiates organizations is the workforce, and the most successful organizations are those that effectively manage their employees. In other words, sustained competitive advantage and organizational effectiveness are increasingly related to management and organizational behaviour. On the basis of a review of the popular

Jeffrey Pfeffer
www.pfdf.org/leaderbooks/pfeffer/

---

in focus ⟶   Company Takes a Run at Boosting Corporate Spirit

JG Wentworth, which has offices in Philadelphia, PA, and Fort Lee, NJ, is a small financial services company that wanted to uplift company spirit and improve employee fitness. The company, a niche lender, has tried various employee incentive programs, including offering trips for whitewater rafting or to Washington, on the basis of different company goals. But the idea of a corporate marathon program has turned out to be the most successful.

Employees were offered an all-expenses-paid trip to the Los Angeles Marathon if they finished a four-month training program. Employees who often work 10- or 12-hour days, met several times a week at 5 a.m. for runs either in Central Park in New York or along the Schuylkill River in Philadelphia. On the weekends, they would meet for two- to three-hour runs.

"It's amazing how quickly you become friends with people that you run with almost every day, especially when it's cold outside and it's six o'clock in the morning," says Al Nickelberry, director of sales and a 20-year marathoner who helped set up the company's training regimen.

Although 5 a.m. training runs and workers limping around the office with sore knees may not seem like morale boosters, company officials say the marathon program has improved company loy-

alty, led employees to work longer hours, and created a more relaxed workplace.

"When people are healthier, they work better and they enjoy their lives more," says Michael Goodman, Wentworth's executive vice-president. "Because of this, we're a better company." According to vice-president Randi Sellari, "People want to come into work. They have company loyalty, where they didn't have it before. People are talking about the company; they are motivated. I see people staying later."

Forty-six workers of the 250-person staff started the program, and 29 completed the program and got the free trip and ran in the marathon. Even nonrunners got into the spirit by cheering on the marathoners and hosting pasta dinners and a welcome-home party.

The marathon program was so successful that Wentworth is doing it again. The company is giving away free trips to the London Marathon for employees who earn points by running a series of training races. If 50 people qualify for the marathon and the company reaches certain sales targets, the entire staff will get a free trip to England.

Source: Excerpted from Brown, J. (1999, April 8). Company takes a run at boosting corporate spirit. *The Globe and Mail*, p.B9. (Associated Press, Philadelphia).

and academic literature, Pfeffer identified 16 practices of companies that are effective through their management of people. Many of these practices, such as incentive pay, participation and empowerment, teams, job redesign, and training and skill development, are important topics in organizational behaviour and are discussed in this book. Pfeffer's work helps to point out that not only is organizational behaviour interesting and important, but it can also make a difference in the effectiveness and success of organizations.

For a unique example of organizational behaviour and the success of an organization, see "In Focus: *Company Takes a Run at Boosting Corporate Spirit.*"

How Much Do You Know about Organizational Behaviour?

Although this is probably your first formal course in organizational behaviour, you already have a number of opinions about the subject. To illustrate this, consider whether the following statements are true or false. Please jot down a one-sentence rationale for your answer. There are no tricks involved!

1. Workers who are more satisfied with their jobs tend to be much more productive than those who are less satisfied.
2. Effective organizational leaders tend to possess identical personality traits.
3. Nearly all workers prefer stimulating, challenging jobs.
4. Managers have a very accurate idea about how much their peers and superiors are paid.
5. Workers have a very accurate idea about how often they are absent from work.
6. Pay is the best way to motivate employees and improve job performance.

Now that you have your answers, do one more thing. Assume that the correct answer is opposite to the one you have given, that is, if your answer is "true" for a statement, assume that it is actually false, and vice versa. Now, give a one-sentence rationale why this opposite answer could also be correct.

Each of these statements concerns the behaviour of people in organizations. Furthermore, each statement has important implications for the functioning of organizations. If satisfied workers are indeed more productive, organizations might sensibly invest considerable time, energy, and money in fostering satisfaction. Similarly, if most employees prefer stimulating jobs, there are many jobs that could benefit from upgrading. In this book, we will investigate the extent to which statements such as these are true or false and why they are true or false.

The answers to this quiz may be surprising. Substantial research indicates that each of the statements in the quiz is essentially false. Of course, there are exceptions, but in general, researchers have found that satisfied workers are not more productive, the personalities of effective leaders vary a fair amount, many people prefer routine jobs, managers are not well informed about the pay of their peers and superiors, workers underestimate their own absenteeism, and pay is not always the most effective way to motivate workers and improve productivity. However, you should not jump to unwarranted conclusions based on the inaccuracy of these statements until we determine *why* they tend to be incorrect. There are good reasons for an organization to attempt to satisfy its employees. Also, we can predict who might prefer challenging jobs and who will be motivated by pay. We will discuss these issues in more detail in later chapters.

Experience indicates that people are amazingly good at giving sensible reasons as to why the same statement is either true or false. Thus, satisfied workers are productive because they identify with their work or because they are repaying the organization for satisfactory employment conditions. Conversely, workers are satisfied because they have developed rewarding social contacts in the workplace, but these relationships interfere with productivity. The ease with which people can generate such contradictory responses suggests that "common sense" develops through unsystematic and incomplete experiences with organizational behaviour.

However, because common sense and opinions about organizational behaviour do affect management practice, practice should be based on informed opinion and systematic study. To learn more about how to study organizational behaviour, see the Appendix. Now, let us consider the goals of organizational behaviour.

Goals of the Field

Like any discipline, the field of organizational behaviour has a number of commonly agreed on goals. Chief among these are effectively predicting, explaining, and managing behaviour that occurs in organizations. For example, in Chapter 6 we will discuss the factors that predict which reward systems are most effective in motivating employees. Then, we will explain the reasons for this effectiveness and describe how managers can implement effective reward systems.

Predicting Organizational Behaviour

Predicting the behaviour of others is an essential requirement for everyday life, both inside and outside of organizations. Our lives are made considerably easier by our ability to anticipate when our friends will get angry, when our professors will respond favourably to a completed assignment, and when salespeople and politicians are telling us the truth about a new product or the state of the nation. In organizations, there is considerable interest in predicting when people will make ethical decisions, create innovative products, or engage in sexual harassment.

The very regularity of behaviour in organizations permits the prediction of its future occurrence. However, untutored predictions of organizational behaviour are not always as accurate. Through systematic study, the field of organizational behaviour provides a scientific foundation that helps improve predictions of organizational events. Of course, being able to predict organizational behaviour does not guarantee that we can explain the reason for the behaviour and develop an effective strategy to manage it. This brings us to the second goal of the field.

Explaining Organizational Behaviour

Another goal of organizational behaviour is explanation of events in organizations—why do they occur? Prediction and explanation are not synonymous. Ancient societies were capable of predicting the regular setting of the sun but were unable to explain where it went or why it went there. In general, accurate prediction precedes explanation. Thus, the very regularity of the sun's disappearance gave some clues about why it was disappearing.

Organizational behaviour is especially interested in determining why people are more or less motivated, satisfied, or prone to resign. Explaining events is more complicated than predicting them. For one thing, a particular behaviour could have multiple causes. People may resign their jobs because they are dissatisfied with their pay, because they are discriminated against, or because they have failed to respond appropriately to an organizational crisis. An organization that finds itself with a "turnover problem" is going to have to find out why this is happening before it can put an effective correction into place. This behaviour could have many different causes, each of which would require a specific solution. Furthermore, explanation is also complicated by the fact that the underlying causes of some event or behaviour can change over time. For example, the reasons people quit may vary greatly depending on the overall economy and whether there is high or low unemployment in the field in question. Throughout the book, we will consider material that should improve your grasp of organizational behaviour. The ability to understand behaviour is a necessary prerequisite for effectively managing it.

Managing Organizational Behaviour

Management. The art of getting things accomplished in organizations through others.

Management is defined as the art of getting things accomplished in organizations. Managers acquire, allocate, and utilize physical and human resources to accomplish goals.[7] The definition does not include a prescription about how to get things accomplished. As we proceed through the text, you will learn that a variety of management styles might be effective depending on the situation at hand.

If behaviour can be predicted and explained, it can often be controlled or managed. That is, if we truly understand the reasons for high-quality service, ethical behaviour, or anything else, we can often take sensible action to manage it effectively. If prediction and explanation constitute analysis, then management constitutes action. Unfortunately, we see all too many cases in which managers act without analysis, looking for a quick fix to problems. The result is often disaster. The point is not to overanalyze a problem. Rather, it is to approach a problem with a systematic understanding of behavioural science.

Now that we have covered predicting, explaining, and managing organizational behaviour, let us apply this knowledge. Read the case about Continental Airlines in the You Be the Manager feature and answer the questions. At the end of the chapter, find out what Continental did in The Manager's Notebook. This is not a test, but rather an exercise to improve critical thinking, analytical skills, and management skills. Pause and reflect on these application features as you encounter them in each chapter.

Continental Airlines
www.continental.com

Early Prescriptions Concerning Management

For many years, experts interested in organizations were concerned with prescribing the "correct" way to manage an organization to achieve its goals. There were two basic phases to this prescription, which experts often call the classical view and the human relations view. A summary of these viewpoints will illustrate how the history of management thought and organizational behaviour developed.

The Classical View and Bureaucracy

Most of the major advocates of the classical viewpoint were experienced managers or consultants who took the time to write down their thoughts on organizing. For the most part, this activity occurred in the early 1900s. The classical writers acquired their experience in military settings, mining operations, and factories that produced everything from cars to candy. Prominent names include Henri Fayol, General Motors executive James D. Mooney, and consultant

you be the manager

Turnaround at Continental Airlines

The airline had little to be respected for. It had gone through 10 presidents in 10 years. It had basement-level job satisfaction.

In 1994, a number of Continental Airlines mechanics ripped the logos off their uniforms so if they ran errands after work, they would not be identified as the airline's employees. Pilots and flight attendants would slink to the back of crew buses on their way to hotels. Top executives fended off complaints and ribbings at holiday parties, family reunions, you name it. "This airline was probably, candidly, one of the least respected airlines in corporate America," says Ned Walker, vice-president of corporate communications. "You could not get any worse than Continental in 1994."

The situation was like being trapped in an endless holding pattern in rocky weather with only bad coffee and stale peanuts—Hell. To try to rectify the dismal state of affairs that was now Continental Airlines, a new management team was brought on board in late 1994. CEO Gordon Bethune became president at Continental in 1994, and by the end of the year, he had become Chairman and CEO and had let go nearly every vice-president in the company.

The new management team put together a multidimensional plan called Go Forward that became the new flight itinerary for the airline. Central to the plan was the concept of Working Together which included employee involvement, incentive plans, and new channels of communication.

The former head of human resources along with a group of employees literally torched the 800-page corporate policy and procedure book in front of employees, managers, and executives in the company parking lot. This signalled a new attitude toward employee involvement. A task force was struck, including 25 employees from all divisions and levels of the company to create a new policy. The result was a streamlined, 80-page book that was much more user-friendly and was mailed to every employee's home.

Employees were paid a flat $65 for each month that Continental ranked in the top five of the Department of Transportation's on-time performance ratings. Employees helped Continental into the top-five rankings nine times—and received an extra $585 each in reward money. Similar performance incentives were introduced throughout the company. Reservation agents receive bonuses on the basis of responsiveness and the number of completed calls. As a result, the proportion of customer-reservation calls answered within 20 seconds jumped from 20 percent to more than 90 percent, the best rate in the industry. As well, in 1995 the company's profit-sharing paid out for the first time in 10 years. In 1996, employees actually doubled their profit-sharing numbers.

New channels of communication have also been developed in order to ensure that employees read, hear, watch, debate, and question just about everything that goes on in their company. Among the new channels of communication are company newsletters; bright blue and yellow bulletin boards located in the break room of every office in every city in the world in which Continental has operations; employee meetings hosted by the company CEO and president as well as open-house sessions at headquarters; and toll-free numbers for employee suggestions and comments. Since its inception, employees have offered more than 16,000 suggestions for change.

What do you think about the changes made at Continental?

1. Explain the role of organizational behaviour in predicting, explaining, and managing the problems at Continental Airlines.

2. What effect do you think these changes had on the attitudes and behaviour of Continental employees and the organization?

To find out the results of Continental's program, see The Manager's Notebook at the end of the chapter.

Source: Excerpted from Flynn, G. (1997, July). A flight plan for success. *Workforce*, pp. 72-78.

Classical viewpoint. An early prescription on management that advocated high specialization of labour, intensive coordination, and centralized decision making.

Scientific Management. Frederick Taylor's system for using research to determine the optimum degree of specialization and standardization of work tasks.

Scientific Management
centralohio.thesource.net/Files/
ran950823.html

Bureaucracy. Max Weber's ideal type of organization that included a strict chain of command, detailed rules, high specialization, centralized power, and selection and promotion based on technical competence.

Hawthorne studies. Research conducted at the Hawthorne plant of Western Electric in the 1920s and 1930s that illustrated how psychological and social processes affect productivity and work adjustment.

Lyndall Urwick.[8] Although exceptions existed, the **classical viewpoint** tended to advocate a very high degree of specialization of labour and a very high degree of coordination. Each department was to tend to its own affairs, with centralized decision making from upper management providing coordination. To maintain control, the classical view suggested that managers have fairly few subordinates, except for lower-level jobs, where machine pacing might substitute for close supervision.

Frederick Taylor (1856–1915), the father of **Scientific Management**, was also a contributor to the classical school, although he was mainly concerned with job design and the structure of work on the shop floor.[9] Rather than informal "rules of thumb" for job design, Taylor's Scientific Management advocated the use of careful research to determine the optimum degree of specialization and standardization. Also, he supported the development of written instructions that clearly defined work procedures, and he encouraged supervisors to standardize workers' movements and breaks for maximum efficiency. Taylor even extended Scientific Management to the supervisor's job, advocating "functional foremanship," whereby supervisors would specialize in particular functions. For example, one might become a specialist in training workers, while another might fulfill the role of a disciplinarian.

The practising managers and consultants had an academic ally in Max Weber (1864–1920), the distinguished German social theorist. Weber made the term "bureaucracy" famous by advocating it as a means of rationally managing complex organizations. During Weber's lifetime, managers were certainly in need of advice. In this time of industrial growth and development, most management was by intuition, and nepotism and favouritism were rampant. According to Weber, a **bureaucracy** has the following qualities:

- A strict chain of command in which each member reports to only a single superior.
- Criteria for selection and promotion based on impersonal technical skills rather than nepotism or favouritism.
- A set of detailed rules, regulations, and procedures ensuring that the job gets done regardless of who the specific worker is.
- The use of strict specialization to match duties with technical competence.
- The centralization of power at the top of the organization.[10]

Weber saw bureaucracy as an "ideal type" or theoretical model that would standardize behaviour in organizations and provide workers with security and a sense of purpose. Jobs would be performed as intended rather than following the whims of the specific role occupant; in exchange for this conformity, workers would have a fair chance of being promoted and rising in the power structure. Rules, regulations, and a clear-cut chain of command that further clarified required behaviour provided the workers' with a sense of security.

Even during this period, some observers, such as the "business philosopher" Mary Parker Follett (1868–1933), noted that the classical view of management seemed to take for granted an essential conflict of interest between managers and employees.[11] This sentiment found expression in the human relations movement.

The Human Relations Movement and a Critique of Bureaucracy

The human relations movement generally began with the famous **Hawthorne studies** of the 1920s and 1930s.[12] These studies, conducted at the Hawthorne plant of Western Electric near Chicago, began in the strict tradition of industrial engineering. They were concerned with the impact of fatigue, rest pauses, and lighting on productivity. However, during the course of the studies, the researchers (among others, Harvard University's Elton Mayo and Fritz Roethlisberger and Hawthorne's William J. Dickson) began to notice the effects of psychological and social processes on productivity and work adjustment. This impact suggested that there could be dysfunctional aspects to how work was organized. One obvious sign was resistance to management through strong informal group mechanisms like norms that limited productivity to less than what management wanted.

After World War II, a number of theorists and researchers, who were mostly academics, took up the theme begun at Hawthorne. Prominent names included Chris Argyris, Alvin Gouldner, and Rensis Likert. The **human relations movement** called attention to certain dysfunctional aspects of classical management and bureaucracy and advocated more people-oriented styles of management that catered more to the social and psychological needs of employees. This critique of bureaucracy addressed several specific problems:

Human relations movement. A critique of classical management and bureaucracy that advocated management styles that were more participative and oriented toward employee needs.

- Strict specialization is incompatible with human needs for growth and achievement.[13] This can lead to employee alienation from the organization and its clients.

- Strong centralization and reliance on formal authority often fail to take advantage of the creative ideas and knowledge of lower-level members, who are often closer to the customer.[14] As a result, the organization will fail to learn from its mistakes, which threatens innovation and adaptation. Resistance to change will occur as a matter of course.

- Strict, impersonal rules lead members to adopt the minimum acceptable level of performance that the rules specify.[15] If a rule states that employees must process at least eight claims a day, eight claims will become the norm, even though higher performance levels are possible.

- Strong specialization causes employees to lose sight of the overall goals of the organization.[16] Forms, procedures, and required signatures become ends in themselves, divorced from the true needs of customers, clients, and other departments in the organization. This is the "red-tape mentality" that we sometimes observe in bureaucracies.

Obviously, not all bureaucratic organizations have these problems. However, they were common enough that human relations advocates and others began to call for the adoption of more flexible systems of management and the design of more interesting jobs. They also advocated open communication, more employee participation in decision making, and less rigid, more decentralized forms of control.

Contemporary Management—The Contingency Approach

How has the apparent tension between the classical approach and the human relations approach been resolved? First, contemporary scholars and managers recognize the merits of both approaches. The classical advocates pointed out the critical role of control and coordination in getting organizations to achieve their goals. The human relationists pointed out the dangers of certain forms of control and coordination and addressed the need for flexibility and adaptability. Second, as we will study in later chapters, contemporary scholars have learned that management approaches need to be tailored to fit the situation. For example, we would generally manage a payroll department more bureaucratically than a research and development department. Getting out a payroll every week is a routine task with no margin for error. Research requires creativity that is fostered by a more flexible work environment.

Reconsider the 10 questions we posed earlier about the DaimlerChrysler merger. Answering these questions is not an easy task, partly because human nature is so complex. This complexity means that an organizational behaviour text cannot be a "cookbook." In what follows, you will not find formulas to improve job satisfaction or service quality with one cup of leadership style and two cups of group dynamics. We have not discovered a simple set of laws of organizational behaviour that you can memorize and then retrieve when necessary to solve any organizational problem. It is this "quick fix" mentality that produces simplistic and costly management fads and fashions.[17]

There is a growing body of research and management experience to help sort out the complexities of what happens in organizations. However, the general answer to many of the questions we will pose in the following chapters is: "It depends." Which leadership style is most effective? This depends on the characteristics of the leader, those of the people being led, and what the leader is trying to achieve. Will an increase in pay lead to an increase in performance? This depends on who is getting the increase and the exact reason for the increase. These dependencies are called contingencies. The **contingency approach** to management recognizes that there is no one best way to manage; rather, an appropriate style depends on the demands of the situation. Thus, the effectiveness of a leadership style is contingent on the abilities of the followers, and the consequence of a pay increase is partly contingent on the need for money. Contingencies illustrate the complexity of organizational behaviour and show why we should study it systematically. Throughout the text we will discuss organizational behaviour with the contingency approach in mind.

Contingency approach. An approach to management that recognizes that there is no one best way to manage, and that an appropriate management style depends on the demands of the situation.

What Do Managers Do?

Organizational behaviour is not just for managers or aspiring managers. As we noted earlier, a good understanding of the field can be useful for consumers or anyone else who has to interact with organizations or get things done through them. Nevertheless, many readers of this text have an interest in management as a potential career. Managers can have a strong impact on what happens in and to organizations. They both influence and are influenced by organizational behaviour, and the net result can have important consequences for organizational effectiveness.

There is no shortage of texts and popular press books oriented toward what managers *should* do. However, the field of organizational behaviour is also concerned with what really happens in organizations. Let us look at several research studies that explore what managers *do* do. This provides a context for appreciating the usefulness of understanding organizational behaviour.

Managerial Roles

Henry Mintzberg Study
sol.brunel.ac.uk/bola/mintzberg/

Canadian management theorist Henry Mintzberg conducted an in-depth study of the behaviour of several managers.[18] The study earned him a Ph.D. from the Massachusetts Institute of Technology (MIT) in 1968. In the Appendix, we discuss how he conducted the study and some of its more basic findings. Here, however, we are concerned with Mintzberg's discovery of a rather complex set of roles played by the managers: figurehead, leader, liaison person, monitor, disseminator, spokesperson, entrepreneur, disturbance handler, resource allocator, and negotiator. These roles are summarized in Exhibit 1.1.

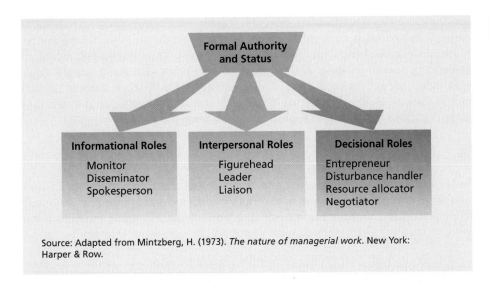

Source: Adapted from Mintzberg, H. (1973). *The nature of managerial work*. New York: Harper & Row.

Exhibit 1.1
Mintzberg's managerial roles.

Interpersonal Roles. Interpersonal roles are expected behaviours that have to do with establishing and maintaining interpersonal relations. In the *figurehead role*, the manager serves as a symbol of his or her organization rather than an active decision maker. Examples of the figurehead role are making a speech to a trade group, entertaining clients, or signing legal documents. In the *leadership role*, the manager selects, mentors, rewards, and disciplines subordinates. In the *liaison role*, the manager maintains horizontal contacts inside or outside the organization. This might include discussing a project with a colleague in another department or touching base with an embassy delegate of a country where one hopes to do future business.

Informational Roles. These roles are concerned with various ways the manager receives and transmits information. In the *monitor role*, the manager scans the internal and external environments of the firm to follow current performance and to keep himself informed of new ideas and trends. For example, the head of Research and Development might attend a professional engineering conference. In the *disseminator role*, managers send information on both facts and preferences to others. For example, the R&D head might summarize what she learned at the conference in an electronic mail message to subordinates. The *spokesperson role* concerns mainly sending messages into the organization's external environment, for example, drafting an annual report to stockholders or giving an interview to the press.

Decisional Roles. The final set of managerial roles Mintzberg discussed deals with decision making. In the *entrepreneur role,* the manager turns problems and opportunities into plans for improved changes. This might include suggesting a new product or service that will please customers. In the *disturbance handler role,* the manager deals with problems stemming from subordinate conflicts and addresses threats to resources and turf. In their *resource allocation roles,* managers decide how to deploy time, money, personnel, and other critical resources. Finally, in their *negotiator roles,* managers conduct major negotiations with other organizations or individuals. The agreement hammered out between Daimler-Benz Chairman Jürgen Schrempp and Chrysler Chairman Robert Eaton is a good example of management's negotiation role.

Of course, the relative importance of these roles will vary with management level and organizational technology.[19] First level supervisors do more disturbance handling and less figureheading. Still, Mintzberg's major contribution to organizational behaviour is to highlight the *complexity* of the roles managers are required to play and the variety of skills they require for effectiveness, including leadership, communication, and negotiation. His work also illustrates the complex balancing act managers face when they must play different roles for different audiences. A good grasp of organizational behaviour is at the heart of acquiring these skills and performing this balancing act.

Managerial Activities

Fred Luthans, Richard Hodgetts, and Stuart Rosenkrantz studied the behaviour of a large number of managers in a variety of different kinds of organizations.[20] They determined that the managers engage in four basic types of activities:

- *Routine communication.* This includes the formal sending and receiving of information (as in meetings) and handling paperwork.
- *Traditional management.* Planning, decision making, and controlling are the primary types of traditional management.
- *Networking.* Networking consists of interacting with people outside of the organization and informal socializing and politicking with insiders.
- *Human resource management.* This includes motivating and reinforcing, disciplining and punishing, managing conflict, staffing, and training and developing subordinates.

Exhibit 1.2 summarizes these managerial activities and shows how a sample of 248 managers divided their time and effort, as determined by research observers (discipline and punishment were done in private and were not open to observation). Perhaps the most striking observation about this figure is how all these managerial activities involve dealing with people.

One of Luthans and colleagues' most fascinating findings is how emphasis on these various activities correlated with managerial success. If we define success as moving up the ranks of the organization quickly, networking proved to be critical. The people who were promoted quickly tended to do more networking (politicking, socializing, and making contacts) and less human resource management

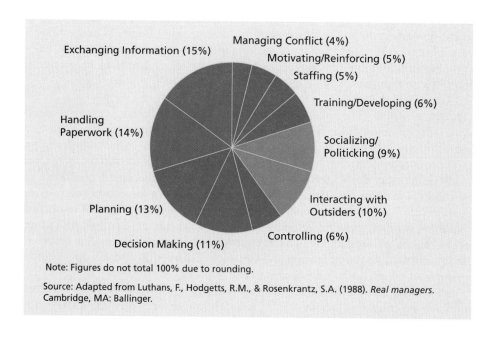

Note: Figures do not total 100% due to rounding.

Source: Adapted from Luthans, F., Hodgetts, R.M., & Rosenkrantz, S.A. (1988). *Real managers.* Cambridge, MA: Ballinger.

Exhibit 1.2
Summary of managerial activities.

than the averages in Exhibit 1.2. If we define success in terms of unit effectiveness and subordinate satisfaction and commitment, the more successful managers were those who devoted more time and effort to human resource management and less to networking than the averages in the exhibit. A good understanding of organizational behaviour should help you manage this tradeoff more effectively, reconciling the realities of organizational politics with the demands of accomplishing things through others.

Managerial Agendas

John Kotter studied the behaviour patterns of a number of successful general managers.[21] Although he found some differences among them, he also found a strong pattern of similarities that he grouped into the categories of agenda setting, networking, and agenda implementation.

Agenda Setting. Kotter's managers, given their positions, all gradually developed agendas of what they wanted to accomplish for the organization. Many began these agendas even before they assumed their positions. These agendas were almost always informal and unwritten, and they were much more concerned with "people issues" and less numerical than most formal strategic plans. The managers based their agendas on wide-ranging informal discussions with a wide variety of people.

Networking. Kotter's managers established a wide formal and informal network of key people both inside and outside of their organizations. Insiders included peers, subordinates, and bosses, but they also extended to these people's subordinates and bosses. Outsiders included customers, suppliers, competitors, government officials, and the press. This network provided managers with information and established cooperative relationships relevant to their agendas. Formal hiring, firing, and reassigning shaped the network, but so did informal liaisons in which they created dependencies by doing favours for others.

Agenda Implementation. The managers used networks to implement the agendas. They would go *anywhere* in the network for help—up or down, in or out of

Dell Computers
www.dell.com

John Kotter's research of successful business managers showed that exemplary managers practise agenda setting, networking, and agenda implementation. Michael Dell, of Dell Computers, is an example of such a manager.

the organization. In addition, they employed a wide range of influence tactics, from direct orders to subtle language and stories that conveyed their message indirectly.

The theme that runs through Kotters's findings is the high degree of informal interaction and concern with people issues that were necessary for the managers to achieve their agendas. To be sure, the managers used their formal organizational power, but they often found themselves dependent on people over whom they wielded no power. An understanding of organizational behaviour helps to recognize and manage these realities.

Managerial Minds

In contrast to how managers act, which is the focus of the previous section, Herbert Simon and Daniel Isenberg have both explored how managers think.[22] Although they offer a wealth of observations, we will concentrate here on a specific issue that each examined in independent research—managerial intuition.

Some people think that organizational behaviour and its implications for management are just common sense. However, careful observers of successful managers have often noted that intuition seems to guide many of their actions. Isenberg's research suggests that experienced managers use intuition in several ways:

- to sense that a problem exists;
- to perform well-learned mental tasks rapidly (e.g., sizing up a written contract);
- to synthesize isolated pieces of information and data; and
- to doublecheck more formal or mechanical analyses ("Do these projections look correct?").

Does the use of intuition mean that managerial thinking is random, irrational, or undisciplined? Both Simon and Isenberg say no. In fact, both strongly dispute the idea that intuition is the opposite of rationality or that intuitive means unanalytical. Rather, good intuition is problem identification and problem solving based on a long history of systematic education and experience that enables the manager to locate problems within a network of previously acquired information. The theories, research, and management practices that we cover in organizational behaviour will contribute to your own information network and give you better managerial intuition about decisions like the merger between Chrysler and Daimler-Benz.

International Managers

The research we discussed above describes how managers act and think in North America. Would managers in other global locations act and think the same way? Up to a point, the answer is probably yes. After all, we are dealing here with some very basic managerial behaviours and thought processes. However, the style in which managers do what they do and the emphasis given to various activities will vary greatly across cultures because of cross-cultural variations in values that affect both managers' and subordinates' expectations about interpersonal interaction. This is why after the DaimlerChrysler merger, many Americans began taking German lessons and the Germans attended training on cultural awareness.[23] Thus, in Chapter 5 we will study cross-cultural differences in motivation, and in Chapter 10 we will explore how communication varies across cultures.

Geert Hofstede has done pioneering work on cross-cultural differences in values that we will study in Chapter 4. Hofstede provides some interesting observa-

International managers must adapt to cross-cultural differences to successfully interact with potential clients and overseas affiliates.

tions about how these value differences promote contrasts in the general role that managers play across cultures.[24] He asserts that managers are cultural heroes and even a distinct social class in North America, where individualism is treasured. In contrast, Germany tends to worship engineers and have fewer managerial types. In Japan, managers are required to pay obsessive attention to group solidarity rather than to star subordinates. In the Netherlands, managers are supposed to exhibit modesty and strive for consensus. In the family-run businesses of Taiwan and Singapore, "professional" management, North American style, is greatly downplayed. To find out more about how management styles differ across cultures, see "Global Focus: *Management European Style*."

The contrasts that Hofstede raises are fascinating because the technical requirements for accomplishing goals are actually the same across cultures. It is only the *behavioural* requirements that differ. Thus, national culture is one of the most important contingency variables in organizational behaviour. The appropriateness of various leadership styles, motivation techniques, and communication methods depends on where one is in the world.

Some Contemporary Management Concerns

To conclude the chapter, we will examine briefly a few issues with which managers are currently concerned. As with previous sections, our goal is to illustrate how the field of organizational behaviour can help you understand and manage these issues.

Diversity—Local and Global

The demographics of the North American population and workforce are changing, and as a result, both the labour force and customers are becoming increasingly culturally diverse. Contributing to this is the increased movement of women into paid employment, as well as immigration patterns. In the past decade, the minority population in California grew by 61 percent.[25] In Canada, visible minorities are the fastest growing segment of the population.[26] The annual report of Employment and Immigration Canada (1992) has projected that two-thirds of today's new entrants to the Canadian labour force will be women, visible minorities, aboriginal people, and persons with disabilities.[27] Native-born

global focus → Management European Style

Do European managers manage differently from Japanese or North American managers? Roland Calori and Bruno Dufour think so. They conducted extensive interviews with 52 top executives from some of western Europe's major "blue chip" firms. Their findings indicate that there are common management philosophies and practices which can be described as a European management style.

On the basis of their interviews, they identified a consensus with regard to four common characteristics of management in Europe. First, they found a greater orientation toward people. Compared with their American or Japanese counterparts, European executives believe they share a common inclination toward the fulfillment of people. In European firms, outsiders are tolerated, and conformity is less accentuated.

A second characteristic of European management is a higher level of internal negotiation. European managers spend a lot of time negotiating inside the firm, between different levels of management, between management and workers, with trade unions, and between headquarters and subsidiaries. As a consequence, they have developed particular skills in negotiation. In American firms, decision making is usually in the hands of the boss, top-down, and quicker than in Europe, and the values of the companies are the values of the top management team. In Japan, decision making follows a consensual process; the boss has power but uses it in a delicate way. Some ideas come from the shop floor, but when decisions are made at the top, everyone agrees. In Europe, the top management has power, but they have to consult, discuss, negotiate, and convince far more than their American and Japanese counterparts have to. As a result, it takes more time to get things done in Europe than in the United States or in Japan.

A third characteristic is greater skill at managing international diversity. European managers have an ability to recognize diversity. They respect and appreciate international diversity and have developed a particular skill in managing it. European firms accept the risk of intercultural management, they respect the host country, they are less imperialistic than the Americans and the Japanese, who still have a tendency to export their models. The Japanese have a tendency to reproduce Japanese management and they also try to reproduce their corporate culture. The American companies try to reproduce their corporate culture by authority of the top management and by procedures. The European tendency to adapt to foreign management practices and markets leads to more decentralization of foreign operations.

A final characteristic of European management is that managers are capable of managing between extremes. Management philosophies and practices in the United States and Japan are often characterized as two extremes on several dimensions, such as the short-term profit orientation of the Americans and the long-term growth orientation of the Japanese. The European management style is much more balanced, half-way between the American and the Japanese models of management. For example, European companies seem to balance individualism and the collective.

These four characteristics of European management are consistent with each other. Managing international diversity and managing between extremes result from the diversity of the European context. The orientation toward people and internal negotiation result from the common history and culture in which economic and social policies, laws, and educational systems are embedded. Such characteristics are valued by top managers, and they seem to fit in the European context, yet they have not proved to be the most successful worldwide.

Source: Excerpted from Calori, R., & Dufour, B. (1995). Management European style. *Academy of Management Executive*, 9, pp. 71-73.

Caucasian North Americans frequently find themselves working with people whose ethnic backgrounds are very different from their own.

Diversity of age is also having an impact in organizations. As a simple example, perhaps you have observed people of various ages working in fast food restaurants that were at one time staffed solely by young people. Both the re-entry of retired people into the workforce and the trend to remove vertical layers in organizations have contributed to much more intergenerational contact in the workplace than was common in the past, so has the rapid promotion of young technical experts in jobs where knowledge is more critical than long experience.[28]

Diversity is also coming to the fore as many organizations realize that they have not treated certain segments of the population, such as women, homosexuals, and the disabled, fairly in many aspects of employment and that organizations have to be able to get the best from *everyone* in order to be truly competitive. Although legal pressures (such as the Americans with Disabilities Act and the Family Leave Act) have contributed to this awareness, general social pressure, especially from customers and clients, has also done so.

Americans with Disabilities Act
www.ada-infonet.org/

Finally, diversity issues are having an increasing impact as organizations "go global." Multinational expansion, strategic alliances, and joint ventures increasingly require employees and managers to come into contact with their counterparts from other cultures, much like the American and German employees have done at DaimlerChryser. Although many of these people have an interest in North American consumer goods and entertainment, it is naive to assume that business values are rapidly converging on some North American model. As a result, North American organizations that operate in other countries need to understand how the workforce and customers in those countries are diverse and culturally different.

What does diversity have to do with organizational behaviour? The field has long been concerned with stereotypes, conflict, cooperation, and teamwork. These are just some of the factors that managers must manage effectively for organizations to benefit from the considerable opportunities that a diverse workforce affords.

Structural Changes in Work Arrangements

Downsizing, restructuring, re-engineering, and outsourcing have had a profound effect on North American and European organizations in the past 10 years or so. Companies such as General Motors, IBM, and Digital Equipment each have laid off thousands of workers. These companies have eliminated high paying manufacturing jobs and once-secure middle-management jobs. As well, there has been a major structural change in work arrangements. Full-time, full-year permanent jobs are being replaced by part-time work and temporary or contract work. It is expected that these work arrangements will become the future standard forms of work,[29] and they will influence the employee-organization relationship.[30]

Surveys suggest that the consequences of these events have been decreased trust, morale, commitment and shifting loyalties. While people remain attached to the work they do, they are much less attached to their employers. A survey by the Families and Work Institute found that 57 percent of respondents strongly agreed that they always tried to do their jobs well, but only 28 percent strongly agreed that they would work harder to help their employer succeed.[31] Other results from this survey are shown in Exhibit 1.3. As you can see, open communication and impact on family life have become critical factors in job choice and are much more important than salary or company size. Another survey by Hay Research for Management found a marked decrease in the attitudes of middle managers toward their employing firms.[32]

The field of organizational behaviour offers many potential solutions to such morale problems. To take just one example, research shows that a remarkable number of organizations failed to adequately communicate their plans to either the victims or the survivors of restructuring.[33] Communication is an important topic in organizational behaviour, and we will study it.

Most observers feel that the forces that led to restructuring have ended the days of joining an organization in one's 20s and staying there until retirement. A succession of jobs with a succession of employers, going where one's skills are needed, is an increasingly common scenario. This means that people will have to look out for their own careers and be able to adapt to a larger variety of people and larger mix of corporate cultures. A good grasp of organizational behaviour can help prepare you for that challenge.

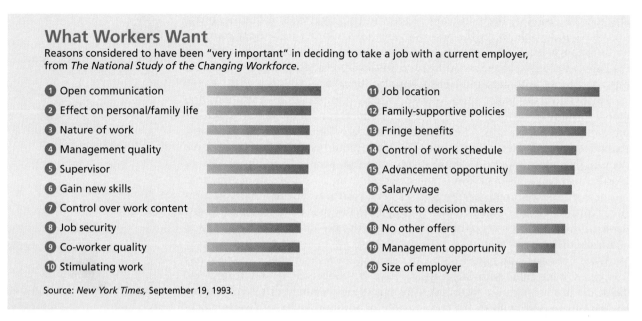

What Workers Want

Reasons considered to have been "very important" in deciding to take a job with a current employer, from *The National Study of the Changing Workforce*.

① Open communication	⑪ Job location
② Effect on personal/family life	⑫ Family-supportive policies
③ Nature of work	⑬ Fringe benefits
④ Management quality	⑭ Control of work schedule
⑤ Supervisor	⑮ Advancement opportunity
⑥ Gain new skills	⑯ Salary/wage
⑦ Control over work content	⑰ Access to decision makers
⑧ Job security	⑱ No other offers
⑨ Co-worker quality	⑲ Management opportunity
⑩ Stimulating work	⑳ Size of employer

Source: *New York Times,* September 19, 1993.

Exhibit 1.3
Factors that influence job choice.

The National Study of the Changing Workforce
www.uaw.org/publications/wash_report/3814/wr381405.html

A Focus on Quality, Speed, and Flexibility

Intense competition for customers, both locally and globally, has given rise to a strong emphasis on quality, both for products and services. Correctly identifying customer needs and satisfying them before, during, and after the sale (whether the consumer purchased a car or health care) are now seen as key competitive advantages. To obtain these advantages, many organizations have begun to pursue programs to achieve continuous improvement in the quality of an organization's products and/or services.

Quality can be very generally defined as everything from speedy delivery to producing goods or services in an environmentally friendly manner. For example, AT&T used its quality program to radically reduce paper pollution in its operations. Other firms with notable quality efforts include Cadillac, Xerox, FedEx, and Motorola.[34] Quality tactics include extensive training, frequent measurement of quality indicators, meticulous attention to work processes, and an emphasis on preventing (rather than correcting) service or production errors. Maine's L.L. Bean mail order clothing and camping operation claims to have shipped 500,000 orders without an error over a period of several months.

Closely allied with quality is speed. Lenscrafters makes glasses "in about an hour," and Dominos became famous for speedy pizza delivery. Local car dealers now do on-the-spot oil changes. Previously, you had to make an appointment days in advance. Perhaps even more important than this external manifestation of speed is the behind-the-scene speed that has reduced the cycle time for getting new products to the market. Firms such as Benetton and The Limited can move new fashions into stores in a couple of months instead of a couple of years, the former norm. American automakers are beginning to approach the Japanese standards for getting a new car design in the showroom in three years instead of five. Such speed can prove to be a real competitive advantage. Sega successfully challenged Nintendo in the video game market by being the first to launch a 16-bit system.

Finally, in addition to improving quality and speed, flexibility on the part of employees and organizations is also an important competitive advantage. Organizations today must operate in increasingly uncertain, turbulent, and chaotic environments that are being driven by the technological revolution and increasing globalization. For some organizations, the competition has become so fierce that it has been referred to as hypercompetition. Hypercompetitive environments are characterized by constant change and high levels of uncertainty. In order to survive in such an environment, organizations need to be flexible so that they can rapidly respond to changing conditions. Thus, organizations will require multiskilled workers, as well as new organizational structures, cultures, and leaders, to build an organization with strategic flexibility to survive and compete in the 21st century.[35]

What does the passion for quality, speed and flexibility have to do with organizational behaviour? For one thing, all require a high degree of employee *involvement* and *commitment*. Often, this means that management must give employees the power to make on-the-spot decisions that were previously reserved for managers. In addition, quality, speed and flexibility all require a high degree of *teamwork* between both individuals and groups who might have some natural tendency to be uncooperative (such as the engineers and accountants involved in car design). The field of organizational behaviour is deeply concerned with such issues.

We hope this brief discussion of several issues that are of concern to managers has reinforced your awareness of using organizational behaviour to better understand and manage life at work. These concerns permeate today's workplace, and we will cover them in more detail throughout the book.

the manager's notebook
Turnaround at Continental Airlines

1. The application of the goals of organizational behaviour of predicting, explaining, and managing behaviour can be used to understand the problems and changes at Continental. At Continental, we can predict employees' negative attitudes and poor customer service. In fact, customers learnt to expect bad service when they flew with Continental. Explanation can help us better understand employees' attitudes and behaviour. A lack of trust and respect between employees and management appears to have created negative attitudes toward the company and an unmotivated workforce. The public also appears to have developed a lack of respect for the airline. As well, employees are not motivated to improve their behaviour and have little input and involvement in how things are done in the organization. Having predicted and explained employee attitudes and behaviour, can it be managed? Continental has implemented programs to improve trust and respect between employees and management and to increase employee attitudes and motivation. New channels of communication have been developed to allow employees greater input and involvement in the company, and incentive programs have been implemented to improve employee motivation.

2. By all accounts, Continental has experienced a major turnaround. After being ranked last among the big 10 airlines in 1993 and 1994, it now earns consistently high ratings. In 1997, for the second consecutive year, Continental was ranked as the number 1 major airline in customer satisfaction for flights of 500 miles or more. The achievement in quality translates into equally impressive monetary figures. In 1995, the company made a profit of $224 million, and in 1996, it more than doubled that. The two years represent the most profitable years in the airline's 63-year history. Just as important is the new attitude of Continental's employees. After a decade-long dip, morale is back up. Employees no longer cringe when their airline is mentioned. In fact, in 1999, Continental was named by *Fortune* magazine as one of the "100 Best Companies" to work for. Not surprisingly, employees no longer rip the logos off their shirts, and sales of Continental logo items at the company store are up 400 percent!

Summary

- Organizations are social inventions for accomplishing common goals through group effort.

- Organizational behaviour refers to the attitudes and behaviours of individuals and groups in an organizational context. The field of organizational behaviour systematically studies these attitudes and behaviours and provides advice about how organizations can manage them effectively. The goals of the field include the prediction, explanation, and management of organizational behaviour.

- Management is the art of getting things accomplished in organizations through others. It consists of acquiring, allocating, and utilizing physical and human resources to accomplish goals.

- The classical view of management advocated a high degree of employee specialization and a high degree of coordination of this labour from the top of the organization. Taylor's Scientific Management and Weber's views on bureaucracy are in line with the classical position.

- The human relations movement pointed out the "people problems" that the classical management style sometimes provoked and advocated more interesting job design, more employee participation in decisions, and less centralized control.

- The contemporary contingency approach to management suggests that the most effective management styles and organizational designs are dependent on the demands of the situation.

- Research on what managers do shows that they fulfill interpersonal, informational, and decisional roles. Important activities include routine communication, traditional management, networking, and human resource management. Managers pursue agendas through networking and use intuition to guide decision making. The demands on managers vary across cultures. A good grasp of organizational behaviour is essential for effective management.

Discussion Questions

1. What are your goals in studying organizational behaviour? What practical advantages might this study have for you?

2. Consider absence from work as an example of organizational behaviour. What are some of the factors that might *predict* who will tend to be absent from work? How might you *explain* absence from work? What are some techniques that organizations use to *manage* absence?

3. Describe the assumptions about organizational behaviour that are reflected in television shows, such as situation comedies and police dramas. How accurate are these portrayals? Do they influence our thinking about what occurs in organizations?

4. To demonstrate that you grasp the idea of contingencies in organizational behaviour, consider how closely managers should supervise the work of their subordinates. What are some factors on which closeness of supervision might be contingent?

5. Management is the art of getting things accomplished in organizations through others. Given this definition, what are some factors that make management a difficult, or at least a challenging, occupation?

6. Use the contingency approach to describe a task or an organizational department where a more classical management style might be effective. Then, do the same for a task or department where the human relations style would be effective.

7. Give an example each of a managerial *figurehead* role, *negotiator* role, and *disseminator* role.

8. Why do studies of managerial behaviour reveal the importance of networking?

9. What are some of the demands that increased workforce diversity and increased global operations make on managers? What are some of the opportunities that these trends offer to managers?

Experiential Exercise

Good Job, Bad Job

The purpose of this exercise is to help you get acquainted with some of your classmates by learning something about their experiences with work and organizations. To do this, we will focus on an important and traditional topic in organizational behaviour—what makes people satisfied or dissatisfied with their jobs (a topic that we will cover in detail in Chapter 4).

1. Students should break into learning groups of four to six people. Each group should choose a recording secretary.

2. In each group, members should take turns introducing themselves and then describing to the others either the best job or the worst job that they have ever had. Take particular care to explain why this particular job was either satisfying or dissatisfying. For example, did factors such as pay, co-workers, boss, or the work itself affect your level of satisfaction? The recording secretary should make a list of the jobs group members held, noting which were "good" and which were "bad." (15 minutes)

3. Using the information from Step 2, each group should develop a profile of four or five characteristics that seem to contribute to dissatisfaction in a job and four or five that contribute to satisfaction in a job. In other words, are there some common experiences among the group members? (10 minutes)

4. Each group should write its "good job" and "bad job" characteristics on the board. (3 minutes)

5. The class should reconvene, and each group's recording secretary should report on the specific jobs the group considered good or bad. The instructor will discuss the profiles on the board, noting similarities and differences. Other issues worth probing are behavioural consequences of job attitudes (e.g., quitting) and differences of opinion within the groups (e.g., one person's bad job might have seemed attractive to someone else). (15 minutes)

Experiential Exercise

OB on TV

The purpose of this exercise is to explore the portrayal of organizational behaviour on television. Most experts on the function of TV as a communication medium agree on two points. First, although TV may present an inaccurate or distorted view of many specific events, the overall content of TV programming does accurately reflect the general values and concerns of society. Second, experts generally agree that TV has the power to shape the attitudes and expectations of viewers. If this is so, we should pay some attention to the portrayal of work and organizational behaviour on TV.

Prepare this exercise before its assigned class:

1. Choose a prime time TV show that interests you. (This means a show that begins between 8 p.m. and 10 p.m. in your viewing area. If your schedule prohibits this, choose another time.) The show in question could be a comedy, a drama, or a documentary, for example, *Ally McBeal* or *NYPD Blue*. Your instructor may give you some more specific instructions about what to watch.

2. On a piece of paper, list the name of the program and its date and time of broadcast. Write the answers to the following questions during or immediately following the broadcast:

   a. What industry is the primary focus of the program? Use the following list to categorize your answer: agriculture; mining; construction; manufacturing; transportation; communication; wholesale trade; retail trade; finance; service; public administration. (Examples of service industries include hotel, health, law, education, newspaper, entertainment, and private investigation. Examples of public administration include justice, police work, and national security.)

   b. What industries or occupations are of secondary focus in the program?

   c. What exact job categories or occupational roles do the main characters in the program play? Use this list to categorize your answers: managerial; clerical; professional; sales; service; craftsperson; machine operator; labourer; lawbreaker; military personnel; customer/patient/client; housework.

   d. Write several paragraphs describing how organizational life is portrayed in the program. For example, is it fun or boring? Does it involve conflict or cooperation? Are people treated fairly? Do they seem motivated? Is work life stressful?

   e. What aspects of the TV portrayal of organizational behaviour do you think were realistic? Which were unrealistic?

3. Be prepared to discuss your findings in class. Your instructor will have some research information about how organizational life has actually been portrayed on TV over the years.

Source: Inspired by the research of Leah Vande Berg and Nick Trujillo, as reported in: Vande Berg, L., & Trujillo, N. (1989). *Organizational life on television.* Norwood, NJ: Ablex.

Case Incident

The Birthday Party

A couple of months ago, on a Saturday, Jennifer organized a 50th-birthday party for her mother. She worked for several months arranging the party and getting her family to agree to the arrangements. She lined up the restaurant at which the party would be held. She arranged the group gifts, prepared for the follow-up party to be held at her house, the whole works. It was going to be a special day for Jennifer, her mother, and everyone else involved. Early on that Saturday morning, Jennifer received a call from her boss and was told that she had to come to work that day. When she began to describe her plans for the day, she was cut off and told, "The board doesn't want excuses. The board wants work." The

50th birthday party was held, but without Jennifer present. She spent the whole Saturday at work. According to Jennifer, it was not even an emergency that led her to be called in.

1. What does this incident tell you about organizational behaviour at Jennifer's organization (e.g., personality, perceptions, leadership, culture, power)?

2. How can organizational behaviour help to predict and explain Jennifer's and her boss's behaviour? What advice would you give to Jennifer and her boss in terms of managing organizational behaviour?

Source: Powell, G. N. (1998). The abusive organization. *Academy of Management Executive*, 12, pp. 95-96.

Case Study

Grappling with Graft

The air-conditioning was on in the hotel room, but Chris Algimontas could not stop sweating. Here he was on his first sales trip to the Middle East, about to lose a $2.7-million deal. And the public works minister's assistant had just asked for a payoff.

Algimontas, 38, was vice-president of sales for Certec Ltd., a high-tech firm that designed computerized traffic-flow management systems for large cities. The modernizing Middle East was a potentially rich market for the company, and Algimontas knew it would be a feather in his cap if he could land this contract.

Certec had hired a local law firm to act as its agent, but Algimontas decided to negotiate the final contract details directly with the ministry of public works. All the company's systems were custom designed, and Algimontas knew the government would be making its decision as much on the basis of Certec's ability to provide personal attention as on price.

Algimontas arrived in the capital late on a Wednesday afternoon and met with the ministry's technical advisers on Thursday. They were clearly impressed with the plans the company had presented months earlier. Algimontas was able to resolve the few questions they had with a few faxes from Certec's head office.

Then came his final negotiating session with the minister's adviser, an immaculately dressed man in his mid-30s. Surprisingly, he showed little interest in discussing the contract. He and Algimontas talked about everything—flight times to London, Canadian winters—but price. Algimontas was relieved when the adviser finally said, "Save your numbers for this evening. We'll talk business over dinner."

The dinner went flawlessly. The adviser negotiated only $75,000 off the contract price. In fact, he showed more enthusiasm comparing notes on their undergraduate days when he discovered that he and Algimontas had graduated from Ivy League universities in the United States.

The two spent the rest of the evening touring the city in a limousine and visiting illegal nightclubs. By 2 a.m. they were firmly cemented by the bonds of alcohol and their distant collegiate past. Algimontas was sure he had clinched the deal. But just as the limo pulled up to Algimontas's hotel, the adviser turned to him, flashed his most charming smile and said, "Oh yes, I forgot to check, but you did include the normal commission for government personnel in your price, didn't you? The Germans and Italians did."

Alarm bells went off in Algimontas's head. "Commission?" he thought, "what commission?" He told the adviser he would check and get back to him the next day.

After a sleepless night, Algimontas phoned Certec's local agent. The lawyer just said, "It is pretty standard procedure. I think about $12,000 is right for a contract this size. You can funnel it through our legal fee, if you want. That is what most of our clients do."

Algimontas was horrified. He had always made it a point to act ethically in all his business dealings, but he did not want to lose such a lucrative contract either. Besides, $12,000 was such a small price to pay.

Should Algimontas take the moral high road and refuse to pay the bribe? Or should he just pay it and chalk it up to local customs? Better yet, is there a way he can avoid paying the bribe and still manage to salvage the deal?

Source: Excerpted from (1990, September) Grappling with graft. *Canadian Business*, p. 103ff.

1. Comment on Chris Algimontas's performance in each of Mintzberg's managerial roles. How effective is his performance in each of these roles?

2. What are some of the cross-cultural differences that Algimontas encounters? How do these differences influence the behaviour of Algimontas and his contacts in the Middle East?

3. Is there anything that Algimontas could have done prior to his trip in order to predict, explain, and manage the situation?

4. Is it ethical for the minister's adviser to request the commission? Is it ethical for Algimontas to pay it? Is the lawyer's advice ethical? What should Algimontas do, and why? What would you do?

Integrative Case: Ace Technology

The meeting ran an hour overtime, and Bill was glad it did. The senior managers finally reached a consensus on the strategy for Ace Technology. The consensus was a critical milestone for the company and set the stage for a number of important change strategies. The task ahead was to make these plans a reality.

A critical topic in the planning session was the antiquated compensation programs. The senior managers agreed that the compensation programs were too complicated and conflicted with the key themes of the company's new strategy. The base pay program emphasized the hierarchy of the organization and was not customer focused. The incentive plans were tied to individual accountability rather than group effort. The recognition programs were too limited in both who was selected and who used them.

Change needed to happen quickly if Ace Technology was going to regain its market leadership. Bill knew that changing the compensation plans was going to be very challenging, but it was too important to be delayed.

As he entered his office, Bill thought, "What do I do now?"

Bill called his management team together to discuss linking human resources programs to the organization's new business strategy. He reviewed the changing conditions in the business environment and the rise of new competitive forces. Although there were many opinions, few team members disagreed about the need to change.

Bill reviewed the mission, vision, and values of the company. Although his staff members had heard this before, Bill outlined the company's strategy against the critical success factors. Bill's team began to see the pay program in context of the new strategy. The team members were able to examine what programs support or defend the new goals. Their discussion consumed most of the three-hour meeting.

Other Ace Technology executives met and conducted intense discussions with their own staff as well. Afterward, Bill and the other executives met to discuss what they had found. Bill summarized the comments he heard from each executive and offered a set of "action themes" that would be important for focusing their initiatives. The executives were making real progress on developing concrete action plans and employees were becoming genuinely excited about the new direction. But, the executives knew the excitement would not be sustained unless the plans could be reinforced.

At the next meeting of Ace Technology's senior management team, the firm's new strategic plan was finalized. The executives identified several common themes in the firm's strategy and established eight critical success factors. These factors are:

- Be more responsive and valuable to our customers than to our competitors.
- Manage costs so that pricing can be lower than our primary competitors' but the firm remains financially strong.
- Continue to seek ways to improve processes of the organization and transfer knowledge across all areas.
- Create a work environment where people feel valued for their contributions.
- Continue to advance the technology and capabilities of our products through research and development.
- Give the customer the products and services they need, when they need them.
- Provide such high-quality products and services that our customers have confidence in our organization.
- Continue to seek ways to be more attractive in the marketplace.

These critical success factors summarized many management initiatives that were in place for years. In light of the eight factors, the executives saw that Ace's success rested on shareholders, customers and employees. Although these were not new concepts, the list strengthened the understanding of what the company needed to do.

Bill then led the executive team in a discussion about action needed. Once the group found key behaviours, Bill used the desired behaviours as the foundation for developing a reward strategy and determining what programs needed to be developed or changed. He also saw how these desired behaviours could serve to refocus other human resources and management initiatives.

The key behaviours the executive team finally developed are:

- Focus on the customers and treat them as we want to be treated.
- Take the initiative to do what needs to be done, for our customers and for ourselves.
- Utilize resources in a responsible manner, and find ways to improve efficiency.
- Continue to increase knowledge and job capabilities.
- Be innovative and resourceful in how to approach work. Experiment with new methods, learn from these experiences, and share the knowledge with others.
- Work as a team with a high degree of mutual respect and collaboration.
- Fulfill the commitment to achieve desired results for the customer and the company.

The executive team realized these actions would need to be modified to fit its specific units. Andrea would need to integrate them differently in Operations than Frank would in Finance. Regardless of the interpretation, the actions provided the missing link between strategy and action.

As Bill and the executives worked on the reward strategy, it became clear that the program did not need to be complicated—the value would be in its simplicity. The group also tried to use many of the programs already in place, making minor modifications. It wanted a flexible reward strategy that could change over time.

The Ace Technology Overall Reward Strategy

Because people are critical to Ace Technology's competitiveness, it is essential that we create a link between the strategy of the company and employee action, between company competitiveness and employee contributions, between the well being of the company and personal well being. As the company prospers, so will our employees. As we face challenging times in the marketplace, we will meet competitive demands effectively. Our reward systems will provide an integrated set of programs in which all members will participate. With such a program, we are demonstrating that Ace Technology is its people, and the people are the company.

Base Compensation

The base pay program will support Ace's ability to acquire and develop superior talent by emphasizing critical competencies. There will be core competencies that reflect the shared values of the company and competencies that focus on the unique requirements of each major functional area. These competencies will be the measuring stick for managing performance, directing careers, investing in training and development, and providing competitive compensation. The base pay levels will be parallel to the median of the market where we compete for talent and business. We will make special provisions for specific functions that are in high demand. Compensation growth will be based on demonstrated competencies that improve the firm's performance and competitiveness.

Variable Compensation

Variable pay programs will focus specific performance requirements for the organization. The purpose of the variable pay program will be to create a clear and significant stake for each individual in the performance of his or her business unit and the company. Cash compensation will emphasize short-term performance requirements and the measures will link directly to the strategic goals of the company. The variable plans primarily will emphasize team performance. Individual incentives will be used if they are clearly aligned with Ace's strategy. In addition, the company will make use of stock options and restricted stock to provide selected people with a meaningful stake in the future of the company. In combination, these variable pay programs will encourage and reinforce desired performance.

Recognition Management

Recognizing and rewarding employee contributions are essential to this organization. The firm will provide and promote a series of formal recognition programs that will reward the contributions of employees. Managers can supplement these specific programs with practices that are of particular relevance to their business units. Business units will focus their recognition process on the contributions of individuals and teams. Recognition will not emphasize high-expense items, except in extraordinary cases. Instead, through a combination of special events, poster boards, newsletters, public meetings, and private discussions, individuals will be appreciated for their contributions. Senior management's role will be to recognize and reward those who do a particularly good job at recognizing others. Ace Technology will continue to make recognition something special.

Several weeks after the reward strategy was developed, human resources managers presented an evaluation of the reward systems to Ace's executives. Managers' opinions differed on whether reward systems would impact behaviour.

Many believed that change would cause disruption and were concerned about the impact. As the discussion unfolded, it became apparent to the group that to do nothing, or make only incremental efforts would have a more negative impact than making a mistake. The firm's new strategy depended on a difference in how employees were rewarded. The executives decided implementation needed to move in stages and be supported by improvements in information availability. The new reward systems will need to support the firm's new strategy directly—by following the changes in some areas or by serving as a catalyst for change in other areas.

In short, Ace Technology determined the following action plan:

- The company wide performance sharing program (i.e., profit sharing) will be eliminated and the dollars will be channeled to support unit-based incentive plans. The reallocation will create a strong line of sight between actions and results with a focus on growth, productivity, cost reductions, delivery performance, and other key success factors.

- Unit-based incentive plans will be developed for all critical functional areas. The incentives will emphasize teams. The measures will use a balanced scorecard approach, emphasizing issues relevant to the unit. The new plan will enhance teamwork, drive a customer focus deep into the organization, and clearly define the commitment to performance.

- The current recognition program will be revamped, providing more opportunities for recognition. A set of tiers will be developed, providing a variety of involvement and reward opportunities. Further, the executive team will review these programs regularly and become active at cross-function events. The emphasis of the recognition program will be innovation, initiative, and outstanding customer service. The program will be transformed from a "nice thing to do" to one that is clearly aligned with desired behaviours.

- The base pay program will shift from being based solely on the market to a combination of competencies and market. The program will emphasize developing a series of career levels tied to the requirements of each major operating unit. Pay opportunities will be tied to career pay bands and increases will be a function of competencies. This will clearly emphasize increasing knowledge, taking responsibility and initiative for personal development, and fulfilling commitments. The base pay program will directly reflect what is important to the company and the employees.

The presentation and discussion demonstrated the group's commitment to link the company's rewards to the critical success factors. Further, the proposed reward programs would form a system of rewards where each element was integrated with the others. The attention was not only on the results but on the process as well.

Source: Thomas B. Wilson. (1998, Summer) Reward strategy—Time to rethink the methods and the messages. *ACA Journal*, pp. 63-69.

Questions

1. What are some organizational behaviour topics and issues that relate to the circumstances at Ace Technology?

2. Discuss the relevance of each of the goals of organizational behaviour for Ace Technology. What does the company want to predict, explain, and manage?

3. Consider Bill's role as a manager in terms of Mintzberg's managerial roles. What roles does he exhibit and how effective is he in performing these roles?

4. What are some of the implications of the events in the case for individuals, groups, and the organization?

Part 2

Individual Behaviour

Chapter 2

Personality and Learning

MOTOROLA Motorola, based in Schaumburg, Illinois, produces semiconductors, microprocessors, and communications equipment. The company is big, old, and well established. As you probably know, many big, old, and well-established firms have had a very difficult time changing to meet the strong competitive demands of today's global business climate. Not Motorola. The firm has learnt how to couple aggressive research and develop-

Motorola

ment with a fanatical concern for manufacturing quality. As a result, Motorola is the worldwide market leader in pagers, two-way radios, and cellular phones. It is the recipient of a Malcolm Baldridge National Quality Award, publicly striving for "six sigma quality," only 3.4 defects per million parts produced.

What do you think is the secret of Motorola's success? According to a research team that spent six weeks camped out at Motorola, this is a company that gives more than lip service to training its employees. In fact, Motorola's policy of guaranteeing 40 hours of training each year to every employee secures its status as a "learning organization."

Motorola was one of seven manufacturing firms whose learning cultures were studied to identify the traits of a "teaching firm." A teaching firm is one that creates an environment in which teaching and learning are institutionally and culturally embedded in the organization. At Motorola, one of the things observed by the research team was a rich interplay between formal training and informal learning back on the job. In fact, the research team calculated that every hour of formal training yielded a four-hour spillover of informal learning.

But how does this spillover occur? One example provided by Motorola's manager of learning research and evaluation goes something like this: When workers attempt to apply to their jobs something they have learned in a formal

The ongoing success of Motorola can be partly credited to a company culture that encourages formal and informal learning.

training session, sometimes the new information does not quite fit, even though it seems to make good sense. In such cases, workers may figure out together how the new information or technique can be incorporated into the existing work routine. Or sometimes, they change work processes to accommodate their new ideas. As these new ideas and new work processes take shape, new learning occurs. Thus, training and informal learning at Motorola are dynamically linked in ways that nourish one another.

The research team also noted a number of instances where informal learning appeared to be taking place at Motorola with no connection to formal training at all. One of these was during assembly-line shift changes, where work shifts overlapped by a half-hour or more. During that time, the departing workers and supervisors would update the next shift on any problems that had occurred. During these updates, they would discuss probable causes and solutions. Among the many and various informal learning opportunities that the research team observed at Motorola, these shift-change discussions appeared to be some of the very richest.

To say that this kind of informal learning at Motorola just happens would be to deny management some of the credit it deserves for having created an environment that is conducive to informal learning. By making a rather big deal of its 40-hour training commitment, the company has attempted to create the expectation that workers will find ways to apply to their jobs the lessons they learn in formal training. Moreover, work teams at the company have been granted a certain amount of autonomy to modify work processes when they believe they have found a better way of doing things. At Motorola, formal training and informal learning are just part of the job.[1]

Motorola
www.motorola.com

Learning Objectives

After reading Chapter 2, you should be able to:

1 Define personality and discuss its general role in influencing organizational behaviour.

2 Discuss the "Big Five" dimensions of personality.

3 Discuss the organizational consequences of differences in locus of control, self-monitoring, and self-esteem.

4 Define learning and understand what is learned in organizations and its general role in influencing organizational behaviour.

5 Differentiate between positive and negative reinforcements and explain how to use them effectively.

6 Explain when to use immediate versus delayed reinforcement and when to use continuous versus partial reinforcement.

7 Distinguish between extinction and punishment and explain how to punish effectively.

8 Explain social learning theory.

9 Discuss organizational learning practices.

Learning is a critical requirement for effective organizational behaviour, and as you have probably heard, in order for organizations to remain competitive in today's rapidly changing environment, employee learning must be continuous and life-long. As you can tell from the opening vignette, this is something that Motorola has clearly mastered. But how has Motorola created a "learning organization" in which formal training and informal learning have become a regular part of employees' worklife? In this chapter we will focus on the learning process and see how effective learning in organizations can be encouraged. While learning is necessary for the acquisition of new skills and behaviours, studies in organizational behaviour have shown that behaviour is also a function of people's personalities. Therefore, we begin this chapter by considering personality and organizational behaviour.

What Is Personality?

The notion of personality permeates thought and discussion in our culture. We are bombarded with information about "personalities" in the print and broadcast media. We are sometimes promised exciting introductions to people with "nice" personalities. We occasionally meet people who seem to have "no personality." But exactly what *is* personality?

Personality is the relatively stable set of psychological characteristics that influences the way an individual interacts with his or her environment. An individual's personality summarizes his or her personal style of dealing with the world. You have certainly noticed differences in personal style on the part of your parents, friends, professors, bosses, and subordinates. It is reflected in the distinctive way that they react to people, situations, and problems.

Where does personality come from? Personality consists of a number of dimensions and traits that are determined in a complex way by genetic predisposi-

Personality. The relatively stable set of psychological characteristics that influences the way an individual interacts with his or her environment.

tion and one's long-term learning history. Although personality is relatively stable, it is certainly susceptible to change through adult learning experience.

Personality and Organizational Behaviour

Because of measurement problems, personality has a rather rocky history in organizational behaviour. However, advances in measurement and trends in organizations have prompted renewed interest. For example, increased emphasis on service jobs with customer contact, concern about ethics and integrity, and contemporary interest in teamwork and cooperation, all point to the potential contribution of personality.[2]

A few words of caution about personality. First, although we often use labels such as "high self-esteem" to describe people, we always should remember that people have a *variety* of personality characteristics. Excessive typing of people does not help us to appreciate their unique potential to contribute to an organization. Second, as we will see, some personality characteristics are useful in certain organizational situations. However, there is no one best personality, and managers need to appreciate the advantages of employee diversity. A key concept here is *fit*, putting the right person in the right job or exposing different employees to different management styles. Finally, we often tend to exaggerate the impact of personality on organizational behaviour. Personality will have the most impact in "weak" situations. These are situations with loosely defined roles, few rules, and weak reinforcement and punishment contingencies. For example, consider a newly formed volunteer community organization. In "strong" situations with more defined roles, rules, and contingencies, personality should have less impact.[3] For example, consider routine military operations.

In what follows, we discuss five general personality dimensions. Then, we cover three personality characteristics with special relevance to organizational behaviour. Later in the text, we will explore the impact of other personality characteristics on job satisfaction, motivation, ethics, organizational politics, and stress.

The "Big Five" Dimensions of Personality

People are unique, people are complex, and there are literally hundreds of adjectives that we can use to reflect this unique complexity. Yet, over the years, psychologists have discovered that there are about five basic but general dimensions that describe personality. These "Big Five" dimensions are summarized in Exhibit 2.1 along with some illustrative traits.[4] The dimensions are:

- *Extraversion*—this is the extent to which a person is outgoing versus shy. High extraverts enjoy social situations, while those low on this dimension (introverts) avoid them.

- *Emotional stability*—the degree to which a person has appropriate emotional control. People with high emotional stability are self-confident and have high self-esteem. Those with lower emotional stability tend toward self-doubt and depression.

- *Agreeableness*—the extent to which a person is friendly and approachable. More agreeable people are warm and considerate. Less agreeable people tend to be cold and aloof.

- *Conscientiousness*—the degree to which a person is responsible and achievement oriented. More conscientious people are dependable and positively motivated. Less conscientious people are unreliable.

- *Openness to experience*—the extent to which a person thinks flexibly and is receptive to new ideas. More open people tend toward creativity and innovation. Less open people favour the status quo.

These dimensions are relatively independent. That is, you could be higher or lower in any combination of dimensions. Also, they tend to hold up well cross-culturally. Thus, people in different cultures use these same dimensions when describing the personalities of friends and acquaintances. There is also evidence that the "Big Five" traits have a genetic basis.[5]

Research has begun to link these personality dimensions to organizational behaviour. First, there is evidence that each of the "Big Five" dimensions is related to job performance.[6] Generally, traits like those in the top half of Exhibit 2.1 lead to better job performance. One review found that high extraversion was important for managers and salespeople and that high conscientiousness facilitated performance for all occupations.[7] Another suggests that conscientiousness is related to retention and attendance at work and is also an important antidote for counterproductive behaviours such as theft, absenteeism, and disciplinary problems.[8] Extraversion has also been found to be related to absenteeism but in a positive direction. In other words, extraverts tend to be absent more often than introverts.[9] As proof of our earlier discussion about situational constraints, one study showed that elevated conscientiousness and extraversion contributed more to managerial performance for managers who had more autonomy in the way they handled their jobs.[10]

Finally, a recent study on the "Big Five" and career success found that the "Big Five" traits were significantly related to both intrinsic (job satisfaction) and extrinsic (income and occupational status) career success. In particular, high conscientiousness was associated with both intrinsic and extrinsic career success, and low neuroticism (i.e., emotional stability), low agreeableness, and high extraversion were also associated with extrinsic success. Perhaps most interesting is that the personality traits were related to career success even when the influence of general mental ability has been taken into account, and both childhood and adult measures of personality predicted career success during adulthood over a period of 50 years. Thus, the results of this study suggest that the effects of personality traits on career success are relatively enduring.[11]

As noted earlier, the "Big Five" personality dimensions are basic and general. We now turn to several more specific personality characteristics that influence organizational behaviour.

Locus of Control

Consider the following comparison. Laurie and Stan are both management trainees in large banks. However, they have rather different expectations regarding their futures. Laurie has just enrolled in an evening Master of Business Administration (MBA) program in a nearby university. Although some of her

Exhibit 2.1
The "Big Five" personality dimensions.

Extraversion	Emotional Stability	Agreeableness	Conscientiousness	Openness to Experience
Sociable, Talkative vs. Withdrawn, Shy	Stable, Confident vs. Depressed, Anxious	Tolerant, Cooperative vs. Cold, Rude	Dependable, Responsible vs. Careless, Impulsive	Curious, Original vs. Dull, Unimaginative

MBA courses are not immediately applicable to her job, Laurie feels that she must be prepared for greater responsibility as she moves up in the bank hierarchy. Laurie is convinced that she will achieve promotions because she studies hard, works hard, and does her job properly. She feels that an individual makes her own way in the world, and that she can control her own destiny. She is certain that she can someday be the president of the bank if she really wants to be. Her personal motto is: "I can do it."

Stan, on the other hand, sees no use in pursuing additional education beyond his bachelor's degree. According to him, such activities just do not pay off. People who get promoted are just plain lucky or have special connections, and further academic preparation or hard work has nothing to do with it. Stan feels that it is impossible to predict his own future but knows that the world is pretty unfair.

Laurie and Stan differ on a personality dimension called **locus of control**. This variable refers to individuals' beliefs about the *location* of the factors that control their behaviour. At one end of the continuum are high internals (like Laurie) who believe that the opportunity to control their own behaviour rests within themselves. At the other end of the continuum are high externals (like Stan) who believe that external forces determine their behaviour. Not surprisingly, compared with internals, externals see the world as an unpredictable, chancy place in which luck, fate, or powerful people control their destinies.[12] (See Exhibit 2.2.)

Internals tend to see stronger links between the effort they put into their jobs and the performance level that they achieve. In addition, they perceive to a greater degree than externals that the organization will notice high performance and reward it.[13] Since internals believe that their work behaviour will influence the rewards they achieve, they are more likely to be aware of and take advantage of information that will enable them to perform effectively.[14]

Research shows that locus of control influences organizational behaviour in a variety of occupational settings. For example, in one of the author's research with customer service representatives and teachers, people who felt that they had internal control over their health were absent less than health externals. In another study, more internal CEOs engaged in greater business risk, pursued more product-market innovation, and led rather than followed competition.[15]

Evidently, because they perceive themselves as being able to control what happens to them, people who are high on internal control are more satisfied with their jobs, earn more money, and achieve higher organizational positions.[16] In addition, they seem to perceive less stress, to cope with stress better, and to engage in more careful career planning.[17]

How should people with various levels of locus of control be managed to enable them to excel? Tellingly, research shows that internals are not necessarily better performers than externals. Rather, internals seem to perform better on jobs that require initiative and innovation, while externals do better on more routine role assignments.[18] Thus, one might look for an internal to staff a startup operation and an external to fill a well-established post. On the one hand, externals seem to prefer somewhat more directive supervision.[19] On the other hand, participation might be more appropriate for an internal subordinate.

Self-Monitoring

We are sure that you have known people who tend to "wear their hearts on their sleeves." These are people who act like they feel and say what they think in spite of their social surroundings. We are also sure that you have known people who are a lot more sensitive to their social surroundings, a lot more likely to fit what they say and do to the nature of those surroundings, regardless of how they think

Self Test of Locus of Control
www.queendom.com/lc.html

Locus of control. A set of beliefs about whether one's behaviour is controlled mainly by internal or external forces.

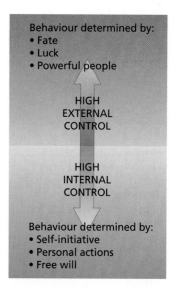

Behaviour determined by:
• Fate
• Luck
• Powerful people

HIGH
EXTERNAL
CONTROL

HIGH
INTERNAL
CONTROL

Behaviour determined by:
• Self-initiative
• Personal actions
• Free will

Exhibit 2.2
The internal/external locus of control continuum.

Self-monitoring. The extent to which people observe and regulate how they appear and behave in social settings and relationships.

or feel. What we have here is a contrast in **self-monitoring,** which is the extent to which people observe and regulate how they appear and behave in social settings and relationships.[20] The people who "wear their hearts on their sleeves" are low self-monitors. They are not so concerned with scoping out and fitting in with those around them. Their opposites are high self-monitors who take great care to observe and control the images that they project. In this sense, high self-monitors behave somewhat like actors. In particular, high self-monitors tend to show concern for socially appropriate behaviour, tune in to social cues, and regulate their behaviour according to these cues.

How does self-monitoring affect organizational behaviour?[21] For one thing, high self-monitors might tend to gravitate toward jobs that require, by their nature, a degree of role-playing. Sales, law, public relations, and politics are examples. In such jobs, ability to adapt to one's clients and contacts is critical; so are communication skills and persuasive abilities, characteristics that high self-monitors frequently exhibit. A couple of studies show that managers are inclined to be higher self-monitors than nonmanagers in the same organization. Promotion in the management ranks is often a function of subjective performance appraisals, and the ability to read and conform to the boss's expectations can be critical for advancement.

One interesting study found that field representatives for a prominent franchise organization were rated as higher performers if they were high self-monitors. This position required the representatives to mediate among many competing interests, including those of the corporation, franchisees, and suppliers. Thus, the ability to adjust successfully to completing social demands, a strength of high self-monitors, came in very handy in this role.[22] In another study that tracked the careers of a sample of master's of business administration graduates, high self-monitors were more likely to change employers and locations and to receive more promotions than low self-monitors. Thus, the ability to regulate and adapt one's behaviour in social situations and to manage the impressions others form of them appears to be a career advantage for high self-monitors.[23]

In social settings that require a lot of verbal interaction, high self-monitors tend to emerge as leaders. Furthermore, they seem to have the behavioural flexibility to adjust their leadership style to the demands of the situation (i.e., friendly versus directive).[24] Again, we see the ability to read and adapt to the social environment.

Are high self-monitors always at an organizational advantage? Not likely. They are unlikely to feel comfortable in ambiguous social settings where it is hard to determine exactly what behaviours are socially appropriate. Dealing with unfamiliar cultures (national or corporate) might provoke stress. Also, some roles require people to go against the grain or really stand up for what they truly believe in. Thus, high self-monitoring types would seem to be weak innovators and would have difficulty resisting social pressure.

Self-Esteem

How well do you like yourself? This is the essence of the personality characteristic called self-esteem. More formally, **self-esteem** is the degree to which a person has a positive self-evaluation. People with high self-esteem have favourable self-images. People with low self-esteem have unfavourable self-images. They also tend to be uncertain about the correctness of their opinions, attitudes, and behaviours. In general, people tend to be highly motivated to protect themselves from threats to their self-esteem.

One of the most interesting differences between people with high and low self-esteem has to do with the *plasticity* of their thoughts and behaviour. People with low self-esteem tend to be more susceptible to external and social influences

Self-esteem. The degree to which a person has a positive self-evaluation.

than those who have high self-esteem, that is, they are more pliable. Thus, events and people in the organizational environment have more impact on the beliefs and actions of employees with low self-esteem. This occurs because, being unsure of their own views and behaviour, they are more likely to look to others for information and confirmation. In addition, people who have low self-esteem seek social approval from others, approval that they might gain from adopting others' views. Finally, people with low self-esteem are more likely than those with higher self-esteem to take negative feedback personally. This will induce change, but this change is not always for the better.[25]

Overall, there is not a consistent relationship between self-esteem and performance. However, employees with low self-esteem tend to react badly to negative feedback—it lowers their subsequent performance.[26] This means that managers should be especially cautious when using negative reinforcement and punishment, as discussed later in this chapter, with subordinates with low self-esteem. If external causes are thought to be responsible for a performance problem, this should be made very clear. Also, managers should direct criticism at the performance difficulty and not at the person. As we will explain shortly, modeling the correct behaviour should be especially effective with employees with low self-esteem. Finally, organizations should try to avoid assigning those with low self-esteem to jobs (such as life insurance sales) that inherently provide a lot of negative feedback.

People with low self-esteem do not react well to ambiguous and stressful situations. Being sensitive to their social environment, they tend to perceive more stress and to cope less well with it.[27] It is probably wise to avoid placing people with very low self-esteem in jobs with competing role demands. For example, first-level supervisors can face competing demands from above and below.

Can a person have too much self-esteem? Probably. Excessive concern for maintaining self-esteem can damage negotiating skills and inhibit people from seeking the help of others. Also, excessive self-confidence can lead people to avoid searching for information that is critical to the solution of a problem or avoid information that threatens their self-image.[28] A little more subtly, the increased plasticity that comes from depressed self-esteem can actually be beneficial when adaptability and openness to external information are useful. Also, those with lower self-esteem are quite willing to imitate credible models, and they respond well to mentoring.

Despite a possible downside to excessive self-esteem, organizations will generally benefit from a workforce with high self-esteem. Such people tend to make more fulfilling career decisions, they exhibit higher job satisfaction, and they are generally more resilient to the strains of everyday worklife.[29] What can organizations do to bolster self-esteem? Opportunity for participation in decision making, autonomy, and interesting work have been fairly consistently found to be positively correlated with self-esteem.[30] Also, organizations should avoid creating a culture with excessive and petty work rules that signal employees that they are incompetent or untrustworthy.[31]

In conclusion, you should understand that because of experiences and factors in the work environment, personality is not the only factor that influences behaviour. Furthermore, learning experiences can not only change behaviour but can also shape one's personality. Let us examine the concept of learning.

What Is Learning?

Learning occurs when practice or experience leads to a relatively permanent change in behaviour potential. The words *practice* or *experience* rule out view-

Learning. A relatively permanent change in behaviour potential that occurs due to practice or experience.

ing behavioural changes caused by factors like drug intake or biological maturation as learning. One does not learn to be relaxed after taking a tranquilizer, and a boy does not suddenly learn to be a bass singer at the age of 14. The practice or experience that prompts learning stems from an environment that gives feedback concerning the consequences of behaviour.

B.F Skinner and Behaviour
129.7.160.115/inst5931/behaviorism.
html

In the 1930s, psychologist B. F. Skinner investigated the behaviour of rats confined in a box containing a lever that delivered food pellets when pulled. Initially, the rats ignored the lever, but at some point they would accidentally operate it and a pellet would appear. Over time, the rats gradually acquired the lever-pulling response as a means of obtaining food. In other words, they *learned* to pull the lever. The kind of learning Skinner studied is called *operant* learning because the subject learns to operate on the environment to achieve certain consequences. The rats learned to operate the lever to achieve food. Notice that operantly learned behaviour is controlled by the consequences that follow it. These consequences usually depend on the behaviour, and this connection is what is learned. For example, salespeople learn effective sales techniques to achieve commissions and avoid criticism from their managers. The consequences of commissions and criticism depend on which sales behaviours salespeople exhibit.

Besides directly experiencing consequences, humans can learn by observing the behaviour of others. This form of learning is called social learning. Generally, social learning involves examining the behaviour of others, seeing what consequences they experience, and thinking about what might happen if we act the same way. If we expect favourable consequences, we might imitate the behaviour. In training, the rookie salesperson might be required to make calls with a seasoned sales veteran. By simply observing the veteran in action, the rookie will probably acquire considerable skill without yet having personally made a sale. Obviously, operant learning theory and social learning theory complement each other in explaining organizational behaviour.[32] Now let us take a look at what people learn in organizations.

What Do Employees Learn?

Before we discuss how people learn, it is important to consider what it is that employees learn in organizations. Learning in organizations can be understood in terms of taxonomies which indicate what employees learn, how they learn, and different learning experiences. The "what" aspect of learning can be described as learning content, of which there are four primary categories: practical, intrapersonal, interpersonal, and cultural awareness.[33]

Practical skills involve job-specific skills, knowledge, and technical competence. For example, at Motorola, employees learn new information and work techniques that are incorporated into their existing work routines. Employees frequently learn new skills and technologies to continually improve performance and to keep organizations competitive. Constant improvement has become a major goal in many organizations today, and training can give an organization a competitive advantage.[34]

Intrapersonal skills involve skills such as problem solving, critical thinking, learning about alternative work processes, and risk taking. At Motorola, employees not only learn new technical skills, but they also figure out how new information and techniques can be incorporated into the existing work routine. Employees also change work processes to accommodate new ideas, and during shift changes, they discuss probable causes and solutions to various problems.

Interpersonal learning involves interactive skills, such as communicating, teamwork, and conflict resolution. Later in this book, we will discuss how groups are becoming the major building blocks of organizations and the importance of

global focus→   CP Hotels Goes Global

William Cornelius Van Horne, the man who built the legendary Banff Springs hotel in 1888, summed up his ambition in a single sentence: "If we can't export the scenery, we'll import the tourists." Van Horne was head of the Canadian Pacific Railway Company when the last spike of Canada's first transcontinental train track was hammered into place. His strategy worked, and the Banff Springs flourished. CP has since built or bought other opulent resorts across Canada, many of which are historic properties, like Toronto's Royal York Hotel and Quebec City's Chateau Frontenac. But as any Canadian knows, the northern climate has its limitations. Freezing temperatures and driving snow are generally bad for tourism.

Bill Fatt knows. That's why the trim 47-year-old chairman and CEO of Canadian Pacific Hotels Corporation is on a mission to turn the company's low season into a high one. He has begun by purchasing some scenery in the sunny spots of the south—namely, New York-based Princess Hotels International Inc., which owned seven resorts in the United States, Mexico, Bermuda, and Barbados. The $540-million acquisition established the Toronto-based CP Hotels as the fourth-largest destination resort operator in North America, while confirming its position as one of the most prized divisions of the Canadian Pacific Ltd. of Calgary, Canada's largest conglomerate. Fatt has made it clear that while the history of CP Hotels is in Canada, its future lies beyond its borders.

All this sounds perfectly reasonable—which is probably why analysts love the deal. There is only one problem. While CP has been enormously successful on its home turf, it now has to export that success to countries with different histories and ways of working from its own. That may be more of a challenge than Fatt thinks.

The Canadian hotelier is now working on exporting his company's "culture," including its emphasis on communication, to its southern resorts.

Fatt believes his customers will receive better service if the rank and file in Mexico, Barbados, and elsewhere are indoctrinated with the CP philosophy. "Three things are important in the hotel business," he says. "Location, product and service. The Princess properties are in great locations, and the product, by and large, is good. We need to work on service." The workers will go through a four-part program that involves training in customer service and recognition of outstanding work.

Despite Fatt's optimism, it remains to be seen how successful that cultural integration will be. Work habits tend to be socially ingrained. It is not the sort of thing that can be changed with a 30-minute video. But they can try. Fatt believes a series of videos they showed on their tour this past September "worked well to start a sense of employee motivation."

However, when Four Seasons opened hotels in Indonesia, they found that training local staff was a major challenge due to training, communication, and cultural barriers. In fact, virtually none of the applicants spoke English, and many did not have any concept about world cuisine and western customs. Because of the culture-based differences, new hires had to be trained in the specifics of western culture as well as English and communication skills. This proved to be especially challenging because traditional corporate training methods that were geared to young Americans with a college education proved useless for the native workers. As a result, they had to find new ways to combine the training needs of the local culture with the high standards of the company's corporate culture.

Sources: Excerpted from Verburg, P. (1999, February 12). New kid on the beach. *Canadian Business*, pp. 52-56; Solomon, C. M. (1997, March). When training doesn't translate. *Workforce*, 76(3), pp. 40-43.

effective communication. As noted above, employees at Motorola frequently communicate with each other when implementing new technologies and teams of employees work together to modify work processes. When General Motors opened a new team-based truck plant in Fort Wayne, Indiana, workers and management received intensive training in group problem solving and interpersonal dynamics.[35]

Finally, cultural awareness involves the social norms of organizations, understanding company goals, business operations, and company expectations and priorities. All employees need to learn the cultural norms and expectations of their organizations in order to function as effective organizational members. For an

CP Hotels
www.cp.ca/cp/e/div/05_cph.htm

example of cultural awareness learning, see "Global Focus: *CP Hotels Goes Global.*"

Now that we have considered the content of learning in organizations, let us now turn to how people learn.

Increasing the Probability of Behaviour

One of the most important consequences that promote behaviour is reinforcement. **Reinforcement** is the process by which stimuli strengthen behaviours. Thus, a *reinforcer* is a stimulus that follows some behaviour and increases or maintains the probability of that behaviour. The sales commissions and criticism mentioned earlier are reinforcers. In each case, reinforcement serves to strengthen behaviours, such as proper sales techniques, that fulfill organizational goals. In general, organizations are interested in maintaining or increasing the probability of behaviours such as correct performance, prompt attendance, and accurate decision making. As we shall see, positive reinforcers work by their application to a situation, while negative reinforcers work by their removal from a situation.

Reinforcement. The process by which stimuli strengthen behaviours.

Positive Reinforcement

Positive reinforcement increases or maintains the probability of some behaviour by the *application* or *addition* of a stimulus to the situation in question. Such a stimulus is a positive reinforcer. In the basic Skinnerian learning situation described earlier, we can assume that reinforcement occurred because the probability of the lever operation increased over time. We can further assume that the food pellets were positive reinforcers because they were introduced after the lever was pulled.

Positive reinforcement. The application or addition of a stimulus that increases or maintains the probability of some behaviour.

Consider the experienced securities analyst who tends to read a particular set of financial newspapers regularly. If we had been able to observe the development of this reading habit, we might have found that it occurred as the result of a series of successful business decisions. That is, the analyst learns to scan those papers whose reading is positively reinforced by subsequent successful decisions. In this example, something is added to the situation (favourable decisions) that increases the probability of certain behaviour (selective reading). Also, the appearance of the reinforcer is dependent or contingent on the occurrence of that behaviour.

In general, positive reinforcers tend to be pleasant things, such as food, praise, money, or business success. However, the intrinsic character of stimuli do not determine whether they are positive reinforcers, and pleasant stimuli are not positive reinforcers when considered in the abstract. Whether or not something is a positive reinforcer depends only on whether it increases or maintains the occurrence of some behaviour by its application. Thus, it is improbable that the Christmas turkey employers give to all the employees of a manufacturing plant positively reinforces anything. The only behaviour which the receipt of the turkey is contingent on is being employed by the company during the third week of December. It is unlikely that the turkey increases the probability that employees will remain for another year or work harder.

Negative Reinforcement

Negative reinforcement increases or maintains the probability of some behaviour by the *removal* of a stimulus from the situation in question. Also, negative reinforcement occurs when a response *prevents* some event or stimulus from occurring. In each case, the removed or prevented stimulus is a *negative reinforcer.* Negative

Negative reinforcement. The removal of a stimulus that, in turn, increases or maintains the probability of some behaviour.

reinforcers are usually aversive or unpleasant stimuli, and it stands to reason that we will learn to repeat behaviours that remove or prevent these stimuli.

Let us repeat this point because it frequently confuses students of organizational behaviour: Negative reinforcers *increase* the probability of behaviour. Suppose we rig a cage with an electrified floor so that it provides a mild shock to its inhabitant. In addition, we install a lever that will turn off the electricity. On the first few trials, a rat put in the cage will become very upset when shocked. Sooner or later, however, it will accidentally operate the lever and turn off the current. Gradually, the rat will learn to operate the lever as soon as it feels the shock. The shock serves as a negative reinforcer for the lever pulling, increasing the probability of the behaviour by its removal.

Managers who continually nag their subordinates unless they work hard are attempting to use negative reinforcement. The only way subordinates can stop the aversive nagging is to work hard and be diligent. The nagging maintains the probability of productive responses by its removal. In this situation, subordinates often get pretty good at anticipating the onset of nagging by the look on the boss's face. This look serves as a signal that they can avoid the nagging altogether if they work harder.

Negative reinforcers generally tend to be unpleasant things, such as shock, nagging, or threat of fines. Again, however, negative reinforcers are defined only by what they do and how they work, not by their unpleasantness. Above, we indicated that nagging could serve as a negative reinforcer to increase the probability of productive responses. However, nagging could also serve as a positive reinforcer to increase the probability of unproductive responses if a subordinate has a need for attention and nagging is the only attention the manager provides. In the first case, nagging was a negative reinforcer—it was terminated following productive responses. In the second case, nagging was a positive reinforcer—it was applied following unproductive responses. In both cases, the responses increased in probability.

Organizational Errors Involving Reinforcement

Experience indicates that managers sometimes make errors in trying to use reinforcement. The most common errors are confusing rewards with reinforcers, neglecting diversity in preferences for reinforcers, and neglecting important sources of reinforcement.

Confusing Rewards with Reinforcers.   Organizations and individual managers frequently "reward" workers with things such as pay, promotions, fringe benefits, paid vacations, overtime work, and the opportunity to perform challenging tasks. Such rewards can fail to serve as reinforcers, however, because organizations do not make them contingent on specific behaviours that are of interest to the organization, such as attendance, innovation, or productivity. For example, many organizations assign overtime work on the basis of seniority, rather than performance or good attendance, even when the union contract does not require it. Although the opportunity to earn extra money might have strong potential as a reinforcer, it is seldom made contingent on some desired behaviour.

For another example of a "lost" reinforcer, take an advertising manager whose graphic artist has trouble meeting deadlines for the completion of projects. When the artist completed his work on an especially crucial sales presentation well before the deadline, the manager waited until a slack period two weeks later to reward him with an afternoon off work. Not only did the manager fail to specify why she was granting the time off, but during the two-week interval, the artist failed to complete two other projects on time! The long period of time between the good performance and the reward destroyed any contingent reinforcing effects, and one might suspect that, if anything, the tardy completions were more likely reinforced.

Neglecting Diversity in Preferences for Reinforcers. Organizations often fail to appreciate individual differences in preferences for reinforcers. In this case, even if managers administer rewards after a desired behaviour, they might fail to have a reinforcing effect. Intuitively, it seems questionable to reinforce a workaholic's extra effort with time off from work, yet such a strategy is fairly common. A more appropriate reinforcer might be the assignment of some challenging task, such as work on a very demanding key project. Some labour contracts include clauses that dictate that supervisors assign overtime to the workers who have the greatest seniority. Not surprisingly, high-seniority workers are often the best paid and the least in need of the extra pay available through overtime. Even if it is administered so that the best-performing high-seniority workers get the overtime, such a strategy might not prove reinforcing—the usual time off might be preferred over extra money.

Managers should carefully explore the possible range of stimuli under their control (such as task assignment and time off from work) for their applicability as reinforcers for particular subordinates. Furthermore, organizations should attempt to administer their formal rewards (such as pay and promotions) to capitalize on their reinforcing effects for various individuals.

Neglecting Important Sources of Reinforcement. There are many reinforcers of organizational behaviour that are not especially obvious. While concentrating on potential reinforcers of a formal nature, such as pay or promotions, organizations and their managers often neglect those which are administered by co-workers or intrinsic to the jobs being performed. Many managers cannot understand why a worker would persist in potentially dangerous horseplay despite threats of a pay penalty or dismissal. Frequently, such activity is positively reinforced by the attention provided by the joker's co-workers. In fact, on a particularly boring job, even such threats might act as positive reinforcers for horseplay by relieving the boredom, especially if the threats are never carried out.

One very important source of reinforcement that managers often ignore is that which accompanies the successful performance of tasks. This reinforcement is available on jobs that provide *feedback* concerning the adequacy of performance. On some jobs, feedback contingent on performance is readily available. Doctors can observe the success of their treatment by observing the progress of their patients' health, and mechanics can take the cars they repair for a test drive. In other cases, organizations must design some special feedback mechanism into the job.

A related source of feedback that many organizations neglect is recognition. In fact, all 35 of the best companies to work for in Canada have some form of public recognition or awards program for their top performers. For example, Canadian Tire's head office has a Wall of Winners, which displays photographs of exceptional customer service. At Fidelity Investments Canada Ltd., up to five employees are honoured each quarter for outstanding performance. They receive $500, a letter of recognition and a lunch. Once a year the "best of the best" receives $1,000.[36] Mary Kay Cosmetics, a Dallas-based firm with 300,000 salespeople and $613 million in sales, uses a variety of forms of recognition to reinforce performance in sales and recruiting. These include various pins, sashes, and badges, as well as pink Cadillacs and coveted five-star vacations. Although some of these things have monetary value, it is their *symbolic* value in denoting various levels of achievement that is especially reinforcing. The company confers much of this recognition at a glitzy Dallas convention with over 30,000 in atten-

Canadian Tire
www.canadiantire.ca

Mary Kay Cosmetics
www.marykay.com

Mary Kay Cosmetics uses a variety of forms of recognition to reinforce performance in sales and recruiting.

dance. Good performers thus serve as models for others. Remember, this is a labour force that might not attain a lot of recognition in other life spheres.[37]

Reinforcement Strategies

What is the best way to administer reinforcers? Should we apply a reinforcer immediately after the behaviour of interest occurs, or should we wait for some period of time? Should we reinforce every correct behaviour, or should we reinforce only a portion of correct responses?

To obtain the *fast acquisition* of some response, continuous and immediate reinforcement should be used—that is, the reinforcer should be applied every time the behaviour of interest occurs, and it should be applied without delay after each occurrence. Many conditions exist, in which the fast acquisition of responses is desirable. These include correcting the behaviour of "problem" employees, training employees for emergency operations, and dealing with unsafe work behaviours. Consider the otherwise excellent performer who tends to be late for work. Under pressure to demote or fire this good worker, the boss might sensibly attempt to positively reinforce instances of prompt attendance with compliments and encouragement. To modify the subordinate's behaviour as quickly as possible, the supervisor might station herself near the office door each morning to supply these reinforcers regularly and immediately.

You might wonder when one would not want to use a continuous, immediate reinforcement strategy to mould organizational behaviour. Put simply, behaviour that individuals learn under such conditions tends not to persist when reinforcement is made less frequently or stopped. Intuitively, this should not be surprising. For example, under normal conditions, operating the power switch on your stereo system is continuously and immediately reinforced by music. If the system develops a short circuit and fails to produce music, your switch-operating behaviour will cease very quickly. In the example in the preceding paragraph, the need for fast learning justified the use of continuous, immediate reinforcement. Under more typical circumstances, we would hope that prompt attendance could occur without such close attention.

Behaviour tends to be *persistent* when it is learned under conditions of partial and delayed reinforcement. That is, it will tend to persist under reduced or terminated reinforcement when not every instance of the behaviour is reinforced

Exhibit 2.3
Summary of reinforcement
strategies and their effects.

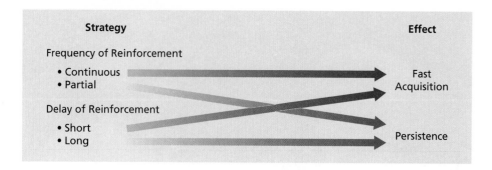

during learning or when some time period elapses between its enactment and re-inforcement. In most cases, the supervisor who wishes to reinforce prompt attendance knows that he will not be able to stand by the shop door every morning to compliment his crew's timely entry. Given this constraint, the supervisor should compliment prompt attendance occasionally, perhaps later in the day. This should increase the persistence of promptness and reduce the subordinates' reliance on the boss's monitoring.

To repeat, continuous, immediate reinforcement facilitates fast learning, and delayed, partial reinforcement facilitates persistent learning (Exhibit 2.3). Notice that it is impossible to maximize both speed and persistence with a single reinforcement strategy. Also, many responses in our everyday lives cannot be continuously and immediately reinforced, so in many cases it pays to sacrifice some speed in learning to prepare the learner for this fact of life. All this suggests that managers have to tailor reinforcement strategies to the needs of the situation. Often, managers must alter the strategies over time to achieve effective learning and maintenance of behaviour. For example, the manager training a new subordinate should probably use a reinforcement strategy that is fairly continuous and immediate (whatever the reinforcer). Looking over the subordinate's shoulder to obtain the fast acquisition of behaviour is appropriate. Gradually, however, the supervisor should probably reduce the frequency of reinforcement and perhaps build some delay into its presentation to reduce the subordinate's dependency on his or her attention.

Reducing the Probability of Behaviour

Thus far in our discussion of learning, we have been interested in *increasing* the probability of various work behaviours, such as attendance or good performance. Both positive and negative reinforcement can accomplish this goal. However, in many cases, we encounter learned behaviours that we wish to *stop* from occurring. Such behaviours are detrimental to the operation of the organization and could be detrimental to the health or safety of an individual employee.

There are two strategies that can reduce the probability of learned behaviour: extinction and punishment.

Extinction

Extinction. The gradual dissipation of behaviour following the termination of reinforcement.

Extinction simply involves terminating the reinforcement that is maintaining some unwanted behaviour. If the behaviour is not reinforced, it will gradually dissipate or be extinguished.

Consider the case of a bright, young marketing expert who was headed for the "fast track" in his organization. Although his boss, the vice-president of marketing, was considering him for promotion, the young expert had developed a very disruptive habit—the tendency to play comedian during department meetings. The vice-president observed that this wisecracking was reinforced by the appreciative laughs of two other department members. He proceeded to enlist their aid to extinguish the joking. After the vice-president explained the problem to them, they agreed to ignore the disruptive one-liners and puns. At the same time, the vice-president took special pains to positively reinforce constructive comments by the young marketer. Very quickly, joking was extinguished, and the young man's future with the company improved.[38]

This example illustrates that extinction works best when coupled with the reinforcement of some desired substitute behaviour. Remember that behaviours that have been learned under delayed or partial reinforcement schedules are more difficult to extinguish than those learned under continuous, immediate reinforcement. Ironically, it would be harder to extinguish the joke-telling behaviour of a partially successful committee member than of one who was always successful at getting a laugh.

Punishment

Punishment involves following an unwanted behaviour with some unpleasant, aversive stimulus. In theory, this should reduce the probability of the response when the actor learns that the behaviour leads to unwanted consequences. Notice the difference between punishment and negative reinforcement. In negative reinforcement a nasty stimulus is *removed* following some behaviour, increasing the probability of that behaviour. With punishment, a nasty stimulus is *applied* after some behaviour, *decreasing* the probability of that behaviour. If a boss criticizes her secretary after seeing the secretary use the office phone for personal calls, we expect to see less of this activity in the future. Exhibit 2.4 compares punishment with reinforcement and extinction.

> **Punishment.** The application of an aversive stimulus following some behaviour designed to decrease the probability of that behaviour.

Using Punishment Effectively

In theory, punishment should be useful for eliminating unwanted behaviour. After all, it seems unreasonable to repeat actions that cause us trouble. Unfortunately, punishment has some unique characteristics that often limit its effectiveness in stopping unwanted activity. First of all, while punishment provides a clear signal as to which activities are inappropriate, it does not by itself demonstrate which activities should *replace* the punished response. Reconsider the executive who chastises her secretary for making personal calls at the office. If the secretary makes personal calls only when she has caught up on her work, she might legitimately wonder what she is supposed to be doing during her occasional free time. If the boss fails to provide substitute activities, the message contained in the punishment might be lost.

Both positive and negative reinforcers specify which behaviours are appropriate. Punishment indicates only what is not appropriate. Since no reinforced substitute behaviour is provided, punishment only temporarily suppresses the unwanted response. When surveillance is removed, the response will tend to recur. Constant monitoring is very time consuming, and individuals become amazingly adept at learning when they can get away with the forbidden activity. The secretary will soon learn when she can make personal calls without detection. The moral here is clear: *Provide an acceptable alternative for the punished response.*

A second difficulty with punishment is that it has a tendency to provoke a strong emotional reaction on the part of the punished individual.[39] This is especially likely when the punishment is delivered in anger or perceived to be unfair. Managers who try overly hard to be patient with subordinates and then finally

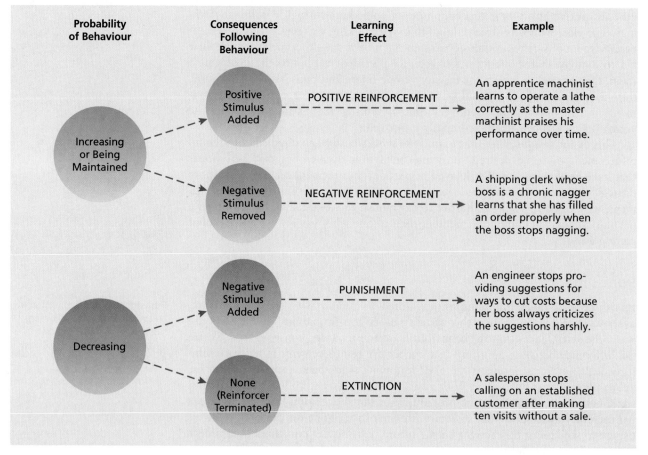

Exhibit 2.4
Summary of learning effects.

Tampa Electric Co.
www.teco.net/TampaElectric.html

blow up risk overemotional reactions. So do those who tolerate unwanted behaviour on the part of their subordinates and then impulsively decide to make an example of one individual by punishing him or her. Managers should be sure that their own emotions are under control before punishing, and they should generally avoid punishment in front of observers.[40] Because of the emotional problems involved in the use of punishment, some organizations, such as Tampa Electric Company and Union Carbide, have downplayed its use in discipline systems. They give employees who have committed infractions *paid* time off to think about their problems.

In addition to providing correct alternative responses and limiting the emotions involved in punishment, there are several other principles that can increase the effectiveness of punishment.

- *Make sure the chosen punishment is truly aversive.* Organizations frequently "punish" chronically absent employees by making them take several days off work. Managers sometimes "punish" ineffective performers by requiring them to work overtime, which allows them to earn extra pay. In both cases, the presumed punishment might actually act as a positive reinforcer for the unwanted behaviour.

- *Punish immediately.* Managers frequently overlook early instances of rule violations or ineffective performance, hoping that things will "work out."[41] This only allows these behaviours to gain strength through repetition. If immediate punishment is difficult to apply, the manager should delay action until a more appropriate time and then reinstate the circumstances surrounding the problem behaviour. For example, the bank manager who observes her teller exhibiting inappropriate behaviour might ask this person to remain after work. She should then carry out punishment at the teller's window rather than in her office, perhaps demonstrating correct procedures and role playing a customer to allow the subordinate to practise them.

■ *Do not reward unwanted behaviours before or after punishment.* Many supervisors join in horseplay with their subordinates until they feel it is time to get some work done. Then, unexpectedly, they do an about-face and punish those who are still "goofing around." Sometimes, managers feel guilty about punishing their subordinates for some rule infraction and then quickly attempt to make up with displays of good-natured sympathy or affection. For example, the boss who criticizes her secretary for personal calls might show up an hour later with a gift of flowers. Such actions present subordinates with extremely confusing signals about how they should behave, since the manager could be inadvertently reinforcing the very response that he or she wants to terminate.

■ *Do not inadvertently punish desirable behaviour.* This happens commonly in organizations (see the cartoon). The manager who does not use all his capital budget for a given fiscal year might have the department's budget for the next year reduced, punishing the prudence of his subordinates. Government employees who "blow the whistle" on wasteful or inefficient practices might find themselves demoted.[42] University professors who are considered excellent teachers might be assigned to onerous, time-consuming duty on a curriculum committee, cutting into their class preparation time.

In summary, punishment can be an effective means of stopping undesirable behaviour. However, managers must apply it very carefully and deliberately in order to achieve this effectiveness. In general, reinforcing correct behaviours and extinguishing unwanted responses are safer strategies for managers than the frequent use of punishment.

SUNTOON by Jim Phillips

FITCHLY... THAT PRODUCT YOU CAME UP WITH IS GREAT... UH... I GUESS NOW WE CAN LAY YOU OFF... RESEARCH & DEVELOPMENT

Social Learning Theory

It has perhaps occurred to you that learning sometimes takes place in organizations without the conscious control of positive and negative reinforcers by managers. For instance, after experiencing just a couple of executive committee meetings, a newly promoted vice-president might look like an "old pro," bringing appropriate materials to the meeting, asking questions in an approved style, and so on. How can we account for such learning?

As we indicated earlier, in addition to learning by directly experiencing the consequences of our behaviour, humans also learn by interacting with and observing the behaviour of others. This form of learning is called social learning. According to Albert Bandura, who is largely responsible for the development of social learning theory, learning is the result of a number of factors interacting with each other.[43] Humans have cognitive and personal capabilities that play an important role in learning. There are three important components of social learning theory, and they include modeling, self-efficacy, and self-management.

Albert Bandura and Theory
www.ship.edu/~cgboeree/
bandura.html

Modeling

Modeling is the process of imitating the behaviour of others. With modeling, learning occurs by observing or imagining the behaviour of others, rather than through direct personal experience.[44] Thus, the new vice-president doubtless modeled his or her behaviour on that of the more experienced peers on the executive committee. But has reinforcement occurred here? It is *self-reinforcement* that

Modeling. The process of imitating the behaviour of others.

occurs in the modeling process. For one thing, it is reinforcing to acquire an understanding of others who are viewed positively. In addition, we are able to imagine the reinforcers that the model experiences coming our way when we imitate his or her behaviour. Surely, this is why we imitate the behaviour of sports heroes and entertainers, a fact that advertisers capitalize on when they choose them to endorse products. In any event, modeling is an important aspect of social learning theory.

What kinds of models are likely to provoke the greatest degree of imitation? In general, attractive, credible, competent, high-status people stand a good chance of being imitated. In addition, it is important that the model's behaviour provoke consequences that are seen as positive and successful by the observer. Finally, it helps if the model's behaviour is vivid and memorable—bores do not make good models.[45] In business schools, it is not unusual to find students who have developed philosophies or approaches that are modeled on credible, successful, high-profile business leaders. Current examples include Microsoft's Bill Gates and Disney's Michael Eisner, both of whom have been the object of extensive coverage in the business and popular press.

The extent of modeling as a means of learning in organizations suggests that managers should pay more attention to the process. For one thing, managers who operate on a principle of "do as I say, not as I do" will find that what they do is more likely to be imitated, including undesirable behaviours, such as expense account abuse. Also, in the absence of credible management models, workers might imitate dysfunctional peer behaviour if peers meet the criteria for strong models. See In Focus: *Modeling Antisocial Behaviour in the Workplace*. On a more positive note, well-designed performance appraisal and reward systems permit organizations to publicize the kind of organizational behaviour that should be imitated.

Self-Efficacy

Self-efficacy. Beliefs people have about their ability to successfully perform a specific task.

While modeling may have helped the vice-president learn how to behave in an executive committee meeting, you might have wondered what made him so confident? Was he not worried that he would fail and full of self-doubt? Such beliefs are known as self-efficacy. **Self-efficacy** refers to beliefs people have about their ability to successfully perform a specific task. It is a cognitive belief that is task specific. Therefore, unlike self-esteem, self-efficacy is not a stable or general personality trait. People can have different self-efficacy beliefs for each task they encounter. For example, the vice-president might have strong self-efficacy for conducting an executive committee meeting but low self-efficacy for writing an organizational behaviour textbook![46]

Because self-efficacy is a cognitive belief, it can be changed and modified in response to different sources of information. In addition to the observation of models, self-efficacy is also influenced by one's experiences performing the task in question, verbal persuasion and social influence of others, and one's physiological or emotional state. Thus, the self-efficacy of the vice-president could have been strengthened by observing the behaviour of others during meetings, encouragement from peers that he will do a great job, and perhaps by his own sense of comfort and relaxation rather than anxiety and stress while attending meetings. Finally, his mastery displayed during the meeting is likely to further strengthen his self-efficacy.

Self-efficacy is a critical component of behaviour that can influence the activities people choose to perform, the amount of effort and persistence devoted to a task, affective and stress reactions, and performance outcomes.[47] In the case of the vice-president, his strong sense of self-efficacy obviously contributed to his ability to perform like an "old pro" at the meeting. Self-efficacy is also a key factor in training. In fact, research on training has shown that the effectiveness of

in focus → Modeling Antisocial Behaviour in the Workplace

Recent reports of antisocial behaviour in the workplace, such as sexual harassment, employee theft, insubordination, sabotage, and violence, indicate that it has become a serious problem in organizations. The term antisocial behaviour is used to describe a range of negative behaviours, including acts that can cause harm to individuals and the property of organizations. In order to understand and prevent antisocial behaviour in organizations, it is necessary to identify the causes of it. Many people believe that antisocial behaviour is an individual-level phenomenon. In other words, the cause of antisocial behaviour rests primarily within the individual and is due to antisocial predispositions, such as personality traits or characteristics.

However, according to Sandra Robinson and Anne O'Leary-Kelly, antisocial behaviour might also be shaped by the group context in which one works and through social learning. They argued that in group settings individuals observe the behaviour of other group members who serve as role models. If group members serve as models of antisocial behaviour then other group members are likely to exhibit antisocial behaviour. Thus, the antisocial behaviour of individuals might be a result of the antisocial behaviour of other group members and the role-modeling process.

Robinson and O'Leary-Kelly conducted a study to examine how individuals' antisocial behaviours at work can be shaped by the antisocial behaviour of co-workers. The study included 35 work groups in 20 different organizations. The results indicated that the antisocial behaviour of a work group was a significant predictor of an individual's antisocial workplace behaviour. This relationship was strongest in groups in which there was a climate of antisocial behaviour, the longer an individual had been a member of the group, and in groups where group members must rely on each other for task accomplishment. They also found that the likelihood of punishment weakened the relationship between antisocial group behaviour and individual antisocial behaviour.

The results of this study demonstrate that individuals' antisocial behaviour in the workplace can be shaped, in part, through the process of observation and modeling. As a result, antisocial behaviour in the workplace can become what the authors refer to as "socially contagious."

Sources: Robinson, S. L., & O'Leary-Kelly, A. M. (1998). Monkey see, monkey do: The influence of work groups on the antisocial behavior of employees. *Academy of Management Journal*, 41, pp. 658-672.; Robinson, S. L., & O'Leary-Kelly, A. M. (1996). Monkey see, monkey do: The role of role models in predicting workplace aggression. *Academy of Management Best Papers Proceedings*, 41, pp. 284-287; Goulet, L.R. (1997). Modeling aggression in the workplace: The role of role models. *Academy of Management Executive*, 11, pp. 84-85.

training programs is partly due to the strengthening of trainees' self-efficacy to perform the task they are being trained to do.[48]

Self-Management

In much of this chapter, we have been concerned with how organizations and individual managers can use learning principles to manage the behaviour of organizational members. However, according to social learning theory, employees can use learning principles to manage their *own* behaviour, making external control less necessary. This process is called **self-management**.[49]

How can self-management occur? You will recall that modeling involved factors such as observation, imagination, imitation, and self-reinforcement. Individuals can use these and similar techniques in an intentional way to control their own behaviour. The basic process involves observing one's own behaviour, comparing the behaviour with a standard, and rewarding oneself if the behaviour meets the standard.[50]

To illustrate some specific self-management techniques, consider the executive who finds that he is taking too much work home to do in the evenings and over weekends. While his peers seem to have most evenings and weekends free, his own family is ready to disown him due to lack of attention! What can he do?[51]

■ *Collect self-observation data.* This involves collecting objective data about one's own behaviour. For example, the executive might keep a log of phone

Self-management. The use of learning principles to manage one's own behaviour.

calls and other interruptions for a few days if he suspects that these contribute to his inefficiency.

- *Observe models.* The executive might examine the time-management skills of his peers to find someone successful to imitate.

- *Set goals.* The executive might set specific short-term goals to reduce telephone interruptions and unscheduled personal visits, enlisting the aid of his secretary and using self-observation data to monitor his progress. Longer-term goals might involve four free nights a week and no more than four hours of work on weekends.

- *Rehearse.* The executive might anticipate that he will have to educate his co-workers about his reduced availability. So as not to offend them, he might practise explaining the reason for his revised accessibility.

- *Reinforce oneself.* The executive might promise himself a weekend at the beach with his family the first time he gets his take-home workload down to his target level.

One western state used a self-management program to improve work attendance among unionized maintenance employees. Those who had used over half their sick leave were invited by the human resource department to participate in an eight-week program with the following features:

- Discussion of general reasons for use of sick leave. High on the list were transportation problems, family difficulties, and problems with supervisors and co-workers.

- Self-assessment of personal reasons for absence and development of personal coping strategies.

- Goal setting to engage in behaviours that should improve attendance (short-term goals) and to improve attendance by a specific amount (long-term goal).

- Self-observation using charts and diaries. Employees recorded their own attendance, reasons for missing work, and steps they took to get to work.

- Identification of specific reinforcers and punishers to be self-administered for reaching or not reaching goals.

Compared with a control group, the employees who were exposed to the program achieved a significant improvement in attendance, and they also felt more confident that they would be able to come to work when confronted with various obstacles to attendance.[52] Self-management programs are frequently successful in positively changing work behaviour.

In the next section, we will look at a number of other organizational learning practices.

Organizational Learning Practices

We began our discussion of learning by describing learning content, and then we focused on how people learn. In this final section, we review a number of organizational learning practices, including an application of operant learning called organizational behaviour modification, training and formal learning, informal learning, and the role of the work environment. Before continuing, consider "You be the Manager: *Safety Is First at Georgia-Pacific.*"

Organizational Behaviour Modification

Organizational behaviour modification. The systematic use of learning principles to influence organizational behaviour.

Most reinforcement occurs naturally, rather than as the result of a conscious attempt to manage behaviour. **Organizational behaviour modification** (O.B. Mod.)

you be the manager

Safety Is First at Georgia-Pacific

How do you think Georgia-Pacific changed its employees' old habits and assumptions? You be the manager.

The forest-products business is definitely not about glamour. Paper mills, sawmills, and plywood factories are dangerous places, full of constant deafening noise, gargantuan razor-toothed blades, long chutes loaded with rumbling tons of lumber, and giant vats full of boiling water and caustic chemicals under tons of pressure. People working around all that stuff tend to sweat a lot.

People used to bleed a lot, too. At one time, the 241 plants and mills operated by Georgia-Pacific, the Atlanta-based forest products giant with $13 billion in annual revenues and more than 47,000 employees, had an unenviable safety record, pretty bad even for a notoriously hazardous industry. There were nine serious injuries per 100 employees each year, and 26 workers had lost their lives on the job between 1986 and 1990.

If the cause of these accidents and injuries was the equipment, then the problem would have been easy to fix. However, most mistakes in any industry are not caused by the nature of the equipment itself—such as the 55-inch knife blade that, whirling like a giant's pencil sharpener, peels a 30-year-old tree down to thin air in just eight seconds. Rather, the trouble comes from people's attitudes and behaviour—for instance, hauling that blade around without wearing protective gloves or trying to clean it while it is running. Workers routinely attempted both procedures in the past, often with bloody results.

Georgia-Pacific people are a little sheepish when they talk about it now, but a macho factor operated in the past as well. Before 1990, workers whose parents and grandparents had toiled in the same mills and factories sometimes took deadly chances as a way of proving their mettle. The biggest challenge, therefore, was to change people's old habits and assumptions. But how? You be the manager.

1. What are some learning practices that Georgia-Pacific could use to change its employees' attitudes and behaviour toward workplace safety?

2. What effect do you think changing its employees' behaviour had on Georgia-Pacific's safety record?

To find out what Georgia-Pacific did and the effect it had on its safety record, see The Manager's Notebook.

Source: Excerpted from A. Fisher. (1997, September 8). Danger zone. *Fortune*, pp. 165-167.

involves the systematic use of learning principles to influence organizational behaviour. In this section, we will describe researchers' attempts to scientifically monitor practical applications of O.B. Mod. In each case, a firm attempted to positively reinforce employee behaviours that were of interest to the organization. In general, research supports the effectiveness of such programs. In fact, a recent review of O.B. Mod. research found that it has a significant positive effect on task performance and the effects are stronger in manufacturing than in service organizations. The results also indicated that both financial and nonfinancial interventions have positive effects.[53]

Georgia-Pacific
www.gp.com

Reinforcing Attendance. A manufacturing company was interested in improving the attendance of its employees. Workers in four sections served as control subjects who did not participate in the program, while those in another section were confronted with the following behaviour modification plan:

Each day that an employee comes to work on time, he is allowed to choose a card from a deck of playing cards. At the end of the five-day week, he will have five cards or a normal poker hand. The highest hand wins $20. There will be eight winners, one for approximately each department.[54]

Supervisors were in charge of monitoring attendance, passing out the cards, and posting on a large chart the poker hands held by subordinates as the week progressed. Over four months, the attendance rate increased by 18 percent for workers exposed to the behaviour modification plan, while the attendance rate for control workers actually decreased somewhat.

Reinforcing Workplace Safety. A second example of the use of organizational behaviour modification involves the reinforcement of safe working behaviour in a food-manufacturing plant. At first glance, accidents appeared to be chance events or wholly under the control of factors such as equipment failures. However, the researchers felt that accidents could be reduced if specific safe working practices could be identified and reinforced. These practices were identified with the help of past accident reports and advice from supervisors. Systematic observation of working behaviour indicated that employees followed safe practices only about 74 percent of the time. A brief slide show was prepared to illustrate safe versus unsafe job behaviours. Then, two reinforcers of safe practices were introduced into the workplace. The first consisted of a feedback chart that was conspicuously posted in the workplace to indicate the percentage of safe behaviours observers noted. This chart included the percentages achieved in observational sessions before the slide show, as well as those achieved every three days after the slide show. A second source of reinforcement was supervisors who were encouraged to praise instances of safe performance that they observed. These interventions were successful in raising the percentage of safe working practices to around 97 percent almost immediately. When the reinforcers were terminated, the percentage of safe practices quickly returned to the level before the reinforcement was introduced. (See Exhibit 2.5.)[55]

Training and Formal Learning

Training is one of the most common and important types of formal learning in organizations. **Training** refers to planned organizational activities that are designed to facilitate knowledge and skill acquisition and the learning of important job-related behaviours.[56] It is reported that companies in the United States spend up to $50 billion a year on formal training programs and $180 billion a year for on-the-job training.[57] Many companies, such as Motorola and Saturn, have a policy of guaranteeing employees a certain number of hours of training each year. The Bank of Montreal built a $50 million learning centre and by end of 1995 averaged 5.4 training days per employee.[58]

While training is one of the most important and costly forms of learning used by organizations, there are two limitations of training. First, most training programs only focus on the practical dimension of the learning content.[59] As a result, other forms of learning are required for the learning of other content areas. Second, although organizations spend a great deal of money investing in training programs, research has shown that much of this investment is wasted because employees do not apply what they learn in training to the job. This problem is called transfer of training and is often due to a work environment that does not support learning. Reports of transfer of training have been as low as 10 percent of training investments.[60] Therefore, to fully understand learning in organizations, it is necessary to consider informal learning and the work environment in addition to training and formal learning.

Training. Planned organizational activities that are designed to facilitate knowledge and skill acquisition and the learning of important job-related behaviours.

Bank of Montreal
www.bankofmontreal.com

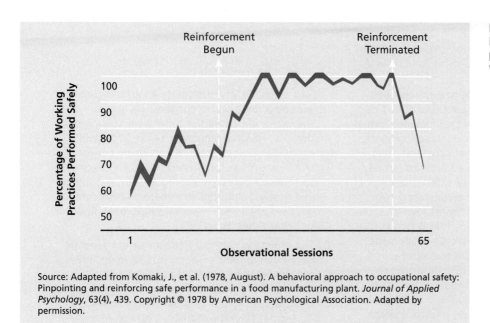

Source: Adapted from Komaki, J., et al. (1978, August). A behavioral approach to occupational safety: Pinpointing and reinforcing safe performance in a food manufacturing plant. *Journal of Applied Psychology*, 63(4), 439. Copyright © 1978 by American Psychological Association. Adapted by permission.

Exhibit 2.5
Percentage of safe working practices achieved with and without reinforcement.

Informal Learning

Compared with formal learning, **informal learning** refers to experiences that are not planned and designed by the organization. As a result, they tend to be more spontaneous, immediate, and task specific than formal learning experiences. It is reported that up to 70 percent of learning in organizations takes place informally.[61] Examples of informal learning include a senior employee showing a new employee how to use a machine, meetings in which team members discuss how to solve work problems, observation of peers and supervisors, receiving and giving feedback, and shift changes.[62]

At Motorola, for example, workers and supervisors update workers on the next shift on problems and discuss probable causes and solutions, and work teams modify work processes when they learn new and better ways of doing their work. Informal learning is not only important because it contributes to learning in all four of the content areas but also because it reinforces formal learning, and research has shown that informal learning is positively related to production performance.[63]

Informal learning. Learning experiences that are not planned and designed by the organization.

The Work Environment

So far, we have noted that learning at Motorola involves both formal and informal practices. At this point you may be wondering how Motorola is able to achieve such a high level of learning. The answer is an environment in which teaching and learning are institutionally and culturally embedded in the organization.[64] This is what is known as a **continuous-learning work environment**.

J. Bruce Tracey, Scott Tannenbaum, and Michael Kavanagh defined a continuous-learning work environment as "one in which organizational members share perceptions and expectations that learning is an important part of everyday work life." As well, "knowledge and skill acquisition are supported by social interaction and work relationships." They studied the work environment in 52 stores of a large supermarket chain. Over 500 store managers attended a three-day training program on supervisory behaviour and skills that included interpersonal skills, such as customer and employee relations, and various administrative procedures. The results indicated that supervisors' transfer of training skills and behaviours

Continuous-learning work environment. A work environment in which learning is considered to be an important part of everyday worklife.

the manager's
notebook
the manager's notebook   Safety Is First at Georgia-Pacific

1. The work at Georgia-Pacific has not changed, but the way people think about it and do it has, thanks to a safety program that includes formal training, safety meetings, videotapes, rewards, and a work environment that constantly reinforces workplace safety. In addition to formal training sessions and weekly safety meetings at all its plants, Georgia-Pacific constantly hammers home its "safety first" message. Thus, one of the most important things that Georgia-Pacific did was to create a work environment that reinforces the importance of safety. Exhortations about safety turn up on every available surface, in the form of posters, stickers (often on hardhats), buttons, T-shirts, and jackets. At division meetings, internal memos, and management speeches, the first thing on the agenda is always safety. The company's TV network and videos are also used to teach safety behaviour. The SafeTV network beams question-and-answer sessions via satellite to about 350 Georgia-Pacific sites around the United States. It also produces and distributes documentary videos for use in safety meetings at the plants. Success stories describe near misses and ways of avoiding accidents, such as how not to get crushed by a 2,800-pound lift truck. Near-miss reports are also written out on index cards, faxed all over the company, and posted on bulletin boards just inside plant entrances. Georgia-Pacific also uses rewards and positive reinforcement to reinforce safety. Supervisors and managers are evaluated, and compensated, on the basis of how they do in four areas. Safety—formerly an afterthought, with no impact on paycheques—is now one of the four and carries the same weight as production. To reinforce employee safety behaviour, every plant keeps track of how many consecutive hours it has functioned without an injury, and those figures are posted at plant entrances and widely publicized elsewhere. Punishment has also been used—workers have been fired for ignoring safety rules.

2. The effects of Georgia-Pacific's safety program have been dramatic—accidents have declined, and productivity has increased. For several years running, it has recorded the best safety record in the industry, and its sawmills are now about 70% safer than the industry average. In a one-year period, 80% of its plants operated without any injuries at all. Best of all, nobody died anywhere. The company's mill in Brunswick, GA, a vast, hot, clamorous place that produces more fluff pulp (the stuff in disposable diapers, among other things) than anywhere else in the world, now records injuries of 0.7 per 100 workers annually. This is about one-third the injury rate at the average bank where the scariest piece of machinery is most likely the photocopier. Georgia-Pacific's safety crusade has worked so well that the company has begun applying the same principles to improving other areas of its business, including quality and customer service.

Source: Excerpted from Fisher, A. (1997, September 8). Danger zone. *Fortune*, pp. 165-167.

were strongly influenced by their work environment. In other words, a continuous-learning work environment was a major factor that contributed to supervisors' learning and behaviour.[65]

The results of this study help us to better understand learning at Motorola. Review the chapter opening vignette and consider some of the signs of a continuous-learning environment at Motorola. For example, consider the interactions and communications among employees. Employees regularly work together to find new and better ways of performing their jobs and exchange information about work problems and solutions. Consider the message that Motorola sends to employees through its commitment to training. Motorola's guarantee of 40 hours of training each year sends a strong message to employees that learning is important and valued by the organization. Finally, consider the extent to which innovation is encouraged and supported by providing work teams with autonomy to modify work processes when they believe they have found a better way of doing things. Clearly, learning at Motorola is encouraged and supported by a continuous-learning work environment and is a good example of an organization that is committed to providing its employees with continuous learning experiences.[66]

Summary

- Personality is the relatively stable set of psychological characteristics that influences the way that we interact with our environment. It has more impact on behaviour in weak situations than in strong situations.

- Research reveals that there are five basic dimensions to personality—extraversion, emotional stability, agreeableness, conscientiousness, and openness to experience.

- Personality characteristics of particular importance for organizational behaviour include locus of control, self-monitoring, and self-esteem. In general, managers should try to match their management styles and work assignments to the personalities of their staff.

- Learning occurs when practice or experience leads to a relatively permanent change in behaviour potential. The content of learning in organizations consists of practical, intrapersonal, and interpersonal skills and cultural awareness. Operant learning occurs as a function of the consequences of behaviour. Social learning involves observation of others' behaviour, self-efficacy, and self-management.

- If some behaviour is occurring regularly or increasing in probability, you can assume that it is being reinforced. The consequence that is maintaining the behaviour is the reinforcer. If the reinforcer is added to the situation following the behaviour, it is a positive reinforcer. These are usually pleasant consequences. If the reinforcer is removed from the situation following the behaviour, it is a negative reinforcer. These are typically unpleasant stimuli.

- Behaviour is learned quickly when it is reinforced immediately and continuously. Behaviour tends to be persistent under reduced or terminated reinforcement when it is learned under conditions of delayed and/or partial reinforcement.

- If some behaviour decreases in probability, you can assume that it is being either extinguished or punished. If the behaviour is followed by no observable consequence, it is being extinguished, that is, some reinforcer that was maintaining the behaviour has been terminated. If the behaviour is followed by the application of some unpleasant consequence, it is being punished.

- Modeling, an example of social learning, is the process of imitating others. Models are most likely to be imitated when they are high in status, attractive, competent, credible, successful, and vivid.

- Self-efficacy is the belief that one can successfully perform a specific task and is influenced by performance on the task, observation of others performing the task, verbal persuasion, and emotional arousal.

- Self-management occurs when people use learning principles to manage their own behaviour, thus reducing the need for external control. Aspects of self-management include collecting self-observation data, observing models, goal setting, rehearsing, and using self-reinforcement.

- Organizational learning practices include organizational behaviour modification, formal training, informal learning, and a continuous-learning work environment.

- Organizational behaviour modification is the systematic use of learning principles to influence organizational behaviour. Companies have successfully used it to improve employees' attendance and to reinforce workplace safety.

Discussion Questions

1. Suppose that you are the manager of two subordinates, one of whom has an internal locus of control and the other has an external locus of control. Describe the leadership tactics that you would use with each subordinate. Contrast the management styles that you would employ for subordinates with high versus low self-esteem.

2. Consider some examples of behaviour that you repeat fairly regularly (such as studying or going to work every morning). What are the positive and negative reinforcers that maintain this behaviour?

3. We pointed out that managers frequently resort to punishing ineffective behaviour. What are some of the practical demands of the typical manager's job that lead to this state of affairs?

4. Discuss a situation that you have observed in which the use of punishment was ineffective in terminating some unwanted behaviour. Why was punishment ineffective in this case?

5. Describe a situation in which you think an employer could use organizational behaviour modification to improve or correct employee behaviour. Can you anticipate any dangers in using this approach?

6. A supervisor in a textile factory observes that one of her subordinates is violating a safety rule that

could result in severe injury. What combination of reinforcement, punishment, extinction, and social learning could she use to correct this behaviour?

? 7. Refer to the material in Chapter 1 on Mintzberg's managerial roles and consider how personality might be a factor in how effectively a manager performs each role. Discuss the relationship among the Big Five personality dimensions, locus of control, self-monitoring, and self-esteem with each of the managerial roles.

? 8. Discuss how each of the organizational learning practices discussed in the chapter can be used by organizations to deal effectively with the contemporary management concerns discussed in Chapter 1 (i.e., Diversity — Local and Global, Structural Changes in Work Arrangements, and A Focus on Quality, Speed, and Flexibility).

Experiential Exercise

Locus of Control

Want to test your locus of control? Just answer the 16 questions below as frankly as possible using the following response scale:

1–Disagree very much   4–Agree slightly
2–Disagree moderately   5–Agree moderately
3–Disagree slightly   6–Agree very much

____ 1. A job is what you make of it.

____ 2. On most jobs, people can pretty much accomplish whatever they set out to accomplish.

____ 3. If you know what you want out of a job, you can find a job that gives it to you.

____ 4. If employees are unhappy with a decision made by their boss, they should do something about it.

____ 5. Getting the job you want is mostly a matter of luck.

____ 6. Making money is primarily a matter of good fortune.

____ 7. Most people are capable of doing their jobs well if they make the effort.

____ 8. In order to get a really good job, you need to have family members or friends in high places.

____ 9. Promotions are usually a matter of good fortune.

____ 10. When it comes to landing a really good job, who you know is more important than what you know.

____ 11. Promotions are given to employees who perform well on the job.

____ 12. To make a lot of money you have to know the right people.

____ 13. It takes a lot of luck to be an outstanding employee on most jobs.

____ 14. People who perform their jobs well generally get rewarded for it.

____ 15. Most employees have more influence on their supervisors than they think they do.

____ 16. The main difference between people who make a lot of money and people who make a little money is luck.

Scoring and Interpretation

You have just completed the Work Locus of Control Scale developed by Paul Spector. To score your scale, first subtract your responses to questions 1, 2, 3, 4, 7, 11, 14, and 15 from 7. For example, if you gave a response of 3 to question 1, give yourself a 4 (7 minus 3). Then add up your resulting scores to all 16 items. Your total should be somewhere between 16 and 96. The lower your score, the more *internal* you are—you see what happens to you to be a result of your own actions and initiative. The higher your score, the more *external* you are—you see what happens to you to be a result of luck, chance, or connections. The average score of 1,165 people in a variety of occupations was 38. Thus, these people tended to see themselves as somewhat more internal than external. In this research, internals tended to report more job satisfaction, more influence at work, and less role stress.

Source: Spector, P. (1988). Development of the Work Locus of Control Scale. *Journal of Occupational Psychology*, 61, pp. 335–340.

Case Incident

Courier Cats

In order to stay competitive, many organizations have to regularly upgrade their computer technology. This was certainly the case for Courier Cats, a small but profitable courier firm. In order to improve the delivery and tracking of parcels, the company decided to invest in a new software program. It was expected that the new software would not only allow the company to expand its business, but it would also improve the quality of service. Because the new software was much more complex and sophisticated than what the company had been using, employees attended a one-day seminar to learn how to use the new system. However, six months after the system was implemented, most employees were still using the old system. Some employees refused to use the new software, while others did not think they would ever be able to learn how to use it.

1. Why do you think that the employees did not use the new software?

2. What are some of the implications that stem from operant learning and social learning theory for increasing the probability that the employees will use the new software?

Case Study

Denver Department Stores

(A)

In the early spring, Jim Barton was evaluating the decline in sales volume experienced by the four departments he supervised in the main store of Denver Department Stores, a Colorado retail chain. Barton was at a loss as to how to improve sales. He attributed the slowdown in sales to the current economic downturn affecting the entire nation. However, Barton's supervisor, Mr. Cornwall, pointed out that some of the other departments in the store had experienced a 15 percent gain over the previous year. Mr. Cornwall added that Barton was expected to have his departments up to par with the others in a short period of time.

Background

Jim Barton had been supervisor of the sporting goods, hardware, housewares, and toy departments in the main store of Denver Department Stores for three of the ten years he had worked for the chain. The four departments were situated adjacent to each other on the ground floor of the store. Each department had a head sales clerk who reported to Barton on merchandise storage and presentation, special orders, and general department upkeep. The head sales clerks were all full-time, long-term employees of Denver Department Stores, having an average of about eight years' experience with the chain. The head clerks were also expected to train the people in the department they supervised. The rest of the staff in each department was made up of part-time employees who lived in or near Denver. Most of the part-time people were students at nearby universities who worked to finance their education. In addition, there were two or three home-makers who worked about 10 hours a week in the evenings.

All sales personnel at Denver Department Stores were paid strictly on an hourly basis. Beginning pay was just slightly over the minimum wage and raises were given on the basis of length of employment and work performance evaluations. The salespeople in the housewares and sporting goods departments were paid about $1.00 an hour more than the clerks in the other departments because it was thought that more sales ability and experience were needed in dealing with the people who shopped for items found in those departments.

As a general rule, the head sales clerk in each department did not actively sell but kept the department well stocked and presentable and trained and evaluated sales personnel. The part-time employees did most of the clerical and sales work. The role of the sales clerk was seen as one of answering customer questions and ringing up the sale rather than actively selling the merchandise except in the two previously mentioned departments where a little more active selling was done.

The sales clerks in Barton's departments seemed to get along well with each other. The four department heads usually ate lunch together. If business was brisk in one department and slow in another, the salespeople in the slower area would assist in the busy department. Male clerks often helped female clerks unload heavy merchandise carts. Store procedure was that whenever a cash register was low on change, a clerk would go to a master till in the stationery department to get more. Barton's departments, however, usually supplied each other with change, thus avoiding the longer walk to the master till.

Barton's immediate supervisor, Mr. Cornwall, had the reputation of being a skilled merchandiser and in the past had initiated many ideas to increase the sales volume of the store. Some of the longer-term employees said that Mr. Cornwall was very impatient and that he sometimes was rude to his subordinates while discussing merchandising problems with them.

The store manager, Mr. Blanding, had been with Denver Department Stores for 20 years and would be retiring in a few years. Earlier in his career Mr. Blanding had taken an active part in the merchandising aspect of the store, but recently, he had delegated most of the merchandising and sales responsibilities to Mr. Cornwall.

Situation

Because of Mr. Cornwall's concern, Barton consulted with his department supervisors about the reason for the declining sales volume. The consensus reached was that the level of customer traffic had not been adequate to allow the departments to achieve a high sales volume. When Barton presented his problem to Mr. Cornwall, Cornwall concluded that since customer traffic could not be controlled and since the departments had been adequately stocked throughout the year, the improvement in sales would have to be a result of increased effort on the part of the clerks in each department. Cornwall added that if sales did not improve soon, the hours of both the full- and part-time sales clerks would have to be cut back. Later, Barton found out that Mr. Cornwall had sent a letter around to each department informing employees of the possibility of fewer hours if sales did not improve.

A few days after Barton received the assignment to increase sales in his department, Mr. Cornwall called him into his office again and suggested that each salesperson carry a personal tally card to record daily sales. Each clerk would record his or her sales, and at the end of the day, the personal sales tally card would be totaled. Cornwall said that by reviewing the cards over a period of time, he would be able to determine who were the "deadwood" and who were the real producers. The clerks were to be told about the purpose of the tally card, and that those clerks who had low sales tallies would have their hours cut back.

Barton told Mr. Cornwall he wanted to consider this program and also discuss it with the head salespeople before implementing it. He told Mr. Cornwall that the next day was his day off, but that when he returned to work the day after, he would discuss this proposal with the head sales clerks.

(B)

On returning to the store after his day off, Barton was surprised to see each of his salespeople carrying a daily tally sheet. When he asked Mr. Cornwall why the program had been adopted so quickly, Mr. Cornwall replied that when it came to improvement of sales, no delay could be tolerated. Barton wondered what effect the new program would have on the personnel in each of his departments.

Before reading Part C of the case, answer these questions:

1. At the beginning of the case, exactly what is the problem facing this branch of Denver Department Stores? What are the various possible reasons for this problem?

2. What are the strengths and weaknesses of the various personnel mentioned in the case (Mr. Cornwall, Barton, the clerks)?

3. In learning theory terms, describe precisely the system that Mr. Cornwall implemented. What are its possible strengths and weaknesses?

4. Predict in detail what you think will happen. To do so, you may wish to consider the various employee behaviours that are necessary for the store to function effectively.

(C)

When Mr. Cornwall issued the tally cards to Barton's salespeople, the head sales clerks failed to fill them out. Two of the head clerks had lost their tally cards when Mr. Cornwall came by later in the day to see how the program was progressing. Mr. Cornwall issued the two head clerks new cards and told them that if they did not "shape up" he would see some "new faces" in the departments.

The part-time salespeople filled out the cards completely, writing down every sale. The rumor that those clerks who had low sales tallies would have their hours cut spread rapidly. Soon the clerks became much more active and aggressive in their sales efforts. Customers were often approached more than once by different clerks in each department. One elderly lady complained that while making her way to the restroom in the back of the hardware department she was asked by four clerks if she needed assistance in making a selection.

When Barton returned the day after the institution of the program, the head sales clerks asked him about the new pro-

gram. Barton replied that they had no alternative but to follow Mr. Cornwall's orders or quit. Later that afternoon, the head clerks were seen discussing the situation on their regular break. After the break, the head clerks began waiting on customers and filling out their sales tally cards.

Not long after the adoption of the program, the stock rooms began to look cluttered. Unloaded carts lined the aisles of the stock room. The shelves on the sales floor were slowly emptied and remained poorly stocked. Sales of items that had a large retail value were especially sought after, and the head sales clerks were often seen dusting and rearranging these more expensive items. The head clerks' tally sheets always had the greatest amount of sales when the clerks compared sheets at the end of each day. (Barton collected them daily and delivered them to Mr. Cornwall.) The friendly conversations among salespeople and between clerks and customers were shortened, and sales were rung up on the cash register and completed in a much shorter time. Breaks were no longer taken as groups, and when they were taken, they seemed to be much shorter than before.

When sales activity was slow in one department, clerks would migrate to other departments where there were more customers. Sometimes conflicts between clerks arose because of competition for sales. In one instance, the head clerk of the hardware department interrupted a part-time clerk from the toy department who was demonstrating a large and expensive table saw to a customer. The head clerk of the hardware department introduced himself as the hardware specialist and sent the toy department clerk back to his own department.

Often customers asked for items which were not on the shelves of the sales floor. When the clerk looked for the item, it was found on the carts which jammed the stock room aisles. Some customers were told the item they desired was not in stock and later the clerk would find it on a cart in the stock room.

When Barton reported his observations of these situations to Mr. Cornwall, he was told that it was a result of the clerks' adjusting to the new program and to not worry about it. Mr. Cornwall pointed out, however, that sales volume had still not improved. He further noted that the sum of all sales reported on the tally sheets was often $500 to $600 more than total department sales according to the cash register.

A few weeks after the introduction of the tally card system, Mr. Cornwall walked through the hardware department and stopped beside three carts of merchandise left in the aisle of the stock room from the morning of the day before. He talked to the head clerk in an impatient tone and asked him why the carts were not unloaded. The clerk replied that if Mr. Cornwall had any questions about the department, he should ask Barton. Mr. Cornwall picked up the telephone and angrily dialed Barton's office. Barton told him that the handling of merchandise had been preempted by the emphasis on the tally card system of recording sales. Mr. Cornwall slammed down the receiver and stormed out of the department.

That afternoon, at Barton's request, Mr. Blanding, Mr. Cornwall, and Barton visited the four departments. After talking with some of the salespeople, Mr. Blanding sent a memo announcing that the tally card program would be discontinued immediately.

After the program had been terminated, sales clerks still took their breaks separately and conversations seemed to be limited to only the essential topics needed to run the department. Barton and the head sales clerks did not talk as freely as they had before, and some of the head clerks said that Barton had failed to represent their best interests to Mr. Cornwall. Some of the clerks said they thought the tally card system was Barton's idea. The part-time people resumed the major portion of the sales and clerical jobs, and the head clerks returned to merchandising. Sales volume in the departments did not improve.

5. What behaviours were reinforced, extinguished, and punished by the system that Mr. Cornwall implemented?

6. Consider the role of the situation and personality before and after the implementation of the tally card program. How do you account for the change in the salesperson's behaviour, and what does it say about the effects of personality?

7. Are there any conditions under which the tally system might have been effective?

8. What are some alternative methods by which sales might have been increased?

9. Summarize the mistakes Mr. Cornwall made in attempting to improve sales.

From J.B. Richie & P. Thompson (1984). *Organization and people: Readings, cases, and exercises in organizational behavior*, 3rd ed. St. Paul, MN: West.

Chapter 3

Perception, Attribution, and Judgment of Others

PRICE WATERHOUSE AND ANN HOPKINS Price Waterhouse is a large public accounting and management consulting firm with an international presence. Several years ago, Ann Hopkins took a job as a manager in the firm's management consulting operation. During the next five years, she proceeded to bring in over $30 million in new business. Finally, she was nominated for partnership in the firm, along with 87 other employees, all of them men. Among the 88 nominees, Hopkins ranked number one in generating new business, and she had more billable hours than any of them in the previous fiscal year. This is one of the chief roles of a partner and a very important consideration for partnership in accounting and consulting firms. At the time of the Hopkins nomination, only seven of the 662 Price Waterhouse partners were women.

> Price
> Waterhouse
> and
> Ann Hopkins

Especially in an accounting firm, Ann Hopkins' ability to generate revenue was hard to dispute. However, opposition to the Hopkins partnership soon surfaced. Thirty-two existing partners offered comments on the Hopkins nomination. Thirteen were supportive, eight claimed to have no informed opinion, and three suggested that she be put on hold. Eight partners felt that she should be denied partnership. Most of the opposition centred on her interpersonal skills, which, opponents said, were aggressive and abrasive. Some partners claimed that she was "too macho" and needed to enroll in a "charm school." Others complained about her swearing. Even one of her supporters advised her to walk, talk, and dress in a more feminine manner.

Half the nominees achieved partnership status. Ann Hopkins was not among them. When she failed to be nominated the next year, she resigned. She subse-

Ann Hopkins fell victim to gender stereotyping when she failed to be selected for partnership status with Price Waterhouse. Are women still expected to conform to a feminine stereotype?

quently filed a suit claiming sex discrimination under Title VII of the Civil Rights Act. A U.S. District Court ruled that Hopkins had been a victim of sex discrimination. In rendering its verdict, the court explicitly recognized that Hopkins had been the victim of a gender stereotype by failing to conform to stereotyped expectations of how a woman should act. The court ordered that she receive $371,000 in back pay and, in a very unusual decision, ruled that Hopkins be admitted into partnership at Price Waterhouse.[1]

Why was Ann Hopkins denied partnership in spite of her financial performance? Why did Price Waterhouse have so few women partners? And what exactly is a gender stereotype? These are the kinds of questions that we will attempt to answer in this chapter. First, we will define perception and examine how various aspects of the perceiver, the object or person being perceived, and the situation influence perception. Following this, we will present a model of the perceptual process, and we will consider some of the perceptual tendencies that we employ in forming impressions of people and attributing causes to their behaviour. Finally, we will examine the role of perception in achieving a diverse workforce, trust, selection interviewing, and performance appraisal. In general, you will learn that perception and attribution influence who gets into organizations, how they are treated as members, and how they interpret this treatment.

What Is Perception?

Perception is the process of interpreting the messages of our senses to provide order and meaning to the environment. Perception helps sort out and organize the complex and varied input received by our senses of sight, smell, touch, taste,

Title VII of Civil Rights Act
www.dol.gov/dol/oasam/public/
regs/statutes/2000e-16.htm

PricewaterhouseCoopers
www.pwcglobal.com

Perception. The process of interpreting the messages of our senses to provide order and meaning to the environment.

Learning Objectives

After reading Chapter 3, you should be able to:

1 Define perception and discuss some of the general factors that influence perception.

2 Explain some basic biases in person perception.

3 Describe how people form attributions about the causes of behaviour.

4 Discuss various biases in attribution.

5 Appreciate the concepts of workforce diversity and valuing diversity.

6 Discuss how racial, ethnic, gender, and age stereotypes affect organizational behaviour.

7 Define trust perceptions and discuss how organizations can foster employee perceptions of trust.

8 Discuss how perception affects the outcomes of selection interviews and performance appraisals.

and hearing. The key word in this definition is *interpreting*. People frequently base their actions on the interpretation of reality that their perceptual system provides, rather than reality itself. If you perceive your pay to be very low, you might seek employment in another firm. The reality—that you are the best-paid person in your department—will not matter if you are unaware of the fact. However, to go a step further, you might be aware that you are the best-paid person and *still* perceive your pay as low in comparison with that of the president of Apple Computer or your ostentatious next-door neighbour.

Some of the most important perceptions that influence organizational behaviour are the perceptions that organizational members have of each other. Because of this, we will concentrate on person perception in this chapter.

Apple Computers
www.apple.com

Components of Perception

Perception has three components—a perceiver, a target that is being perceived, and some situational context in which the perception is occurring. Each of these components influences the perceiver's impression or interpretation of the target (Exhibit 3.1).

The Perceiver

The perceiver's experience, needs, and emotions can affect his or her perceptions of a target.

One of the most important characteristics of the perceiver that influences his or her impressions of a target is experience. Past experiences lead the perceiver to develop expectations, and these expectations affect current perceptions. An interesting example of the influence of experience on perception is shown in Exhibit 3.2. It illustrates the perceptions of 268 managerial personnel in a Fortune 500 company concerning the influence of race and gender on promotion opportunities. As you can see, Caucasian men were much less likely to perceive

Fortune 500
www.fortune.com/fortune/
fortune500

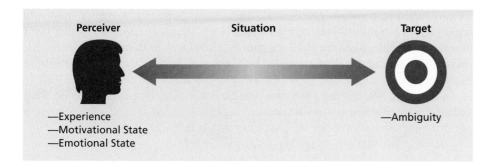

Exhibit 3.1
Factors that influence
perception.

race or gender barriers to promotion than were Caucasian women, non-Caucasian men, and non-Caucasian women.[2] Remember, these people were ostensibly viewing the same "objective" promotion system.

Frequently, our needs unconsciously influence our perceptions by causing us to perceive what we wish to perceive. Research has demonstrated that perceivers who have been deprived of food will tend to "see" more edible things in ambiguous pictures than will well-fed observers. Similarly, lonely college students might misperceive the most innocent actions of members of the opposite sex as indicating interest in them.

Emotions, such as anger, happiness, or fear, can influence our perceptions. We have all had the experience of misperceiving the innocent comment of a friend or acquaintance when we were angry. For example, a worker who is upset about not getting a promotion might perceive the consolation provided by a co-worker as gloating condescension. On the other hand, consider the worker who does get a promotion. He is so happy that he fails to notice how upset his co-worker is because she was not the one promoted.

In some cases, our perceptual system serves to defend us against unpleasant emotions. This phenomenon is **perceptual defence.** We have all experienced cases in which we "see what we want to see" or "hear what we want to hear." In many of these instances, our perceptual system is working to ensure that we do not see or hear things that are threatening.

Perceptual defence. The tendency for the perceptual system to defend the perceiver against unpleasant emotions.

The Target

Perception involves interpretation and the addition of meaning to the target, and ambiguous targets are especially susceptible to interpretation and addition. Perceivers have a need to resolve such ambiguities. You might be tempted to believe that providing more information about the target will necessarily improve perceptual accuracy. Unfortunately, this is not always the case. Writing clearer

	Caucasian Men (N = 123)	Caucasian Women (N = 76)	Non-Caucasian Men (N = 52)	Non-Caucasian Women (N = 17)
Race	26	62	75	76
Gender	31	87	71	82

Note: Table values are the percentages saying that race or gender was important or very important. N = number of cases.

Source: Cox, T. Jr. (1993). *Cultural diversity in organizations: Theory, research, & practice.* San Francisco: Berrett-Koehler, p. 119.

Exhibit 3.2
Ratings of the perceived importance of race and gender for promotion opportunity in executive jobs.

memos might not always get the message across. Similarly, assigning minority workers to a prejudiced manager will not always improve his or her perceptions of their true abilities. As we shall see shortly, the perceiver does not or cannot always use all the information provided by the target. In these cases, a reduction in ambiguity might not be accompanied by greater accuracy.

In the Price Waterhouse case, the billable hours Ann Hopkins achieved were unambiguous. Rather, the resistance to Hopkins centred around social skills, a performance dimension open to a lot more interpretation.

The Situation

Every instance of perception occurs in some situational context, and this context can affect what one perceives. The most important effect that the situation can have is to add information about the target. Imagine a casual critical comment about your performance from your boss the week before she is to decide whether or not you will be promoted. You will likely perceive this comment very differently from how you would if you were not up for promotion. Also, a worker might perceive a racial joke overheard on the job very differently before and after racial strife has occurred in the plant. In both these examples, the perceiver and the target are the same, but the perception of the target changes with the situation. To her detractors, Ann Hopkins' interpersonal style might have been acceptable in some other occupational role, such as a bartender or welder!

A Model of the Perceptual Process

Jerome Bruner and Theory
www.gwu.edu/~tip/bruner.html

Exactly how does the perceiver go about putting together the information contained in the target and the situation to form a picture of the target? Respected psychologist Jerome Bruner has developed a model of the perceptual process that can provide a useful framework for this discussion.[3] According to Bruner, when the perceiver encounters an unfamiliar target, the perceiver is very open to the informational cues contained in the target and the situation surrounding it. In this unfamiliar state, the perceiver really needs information on which to base perceptions of the target and will actively seek out cues to resolve this ambiguity. Gradually, the perceiver encounters some familiar cues (note the role of the perceiver's experience here) that enable her to make a crude categorization of the target. At this point, the cue search becomes less open and more selective. The perceiver begins to search out cues that confirm the categorization of the target. As this categorization becomes stronger, the perceiver actively ignores or even distorts cues that violate initial perceptions. (See the left side of Exhibit 3.3.) This does not mean that an early categorization cannot be changed. It does mean, however, that it will take a good many contradictory cues before one recategorizes the target, and that these cues will have to overcome the expectations that have been developed.

Let us clarify your understanding of Bruner's perceptual model with an example, shown on the right side of Exhibit 3.3. Imagine that a woman who works as an engineer for a large aircraft company is trying to size up a newly hired co-worker. Since he is an unfamiliar target, she will probably be especially open to any cues that might provide information about him. In the course of her cue search, she discovers that he has a Master's degree in aeronautical engineering from Stanford University, and that he graduated with top grades. These are familiar cues because she knows that Stanford is a top school in the field, and she has worked with many excellent Stanford graduates. She then proceeds to categorize her new co-worker as a "good man" with "great potential." With these

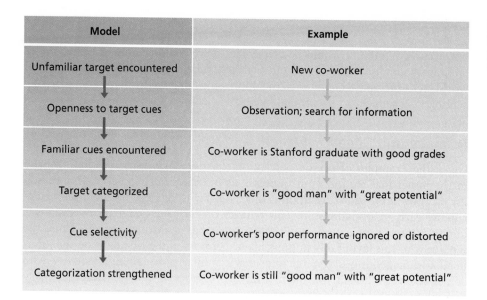

Model	Example
Unfamiliar target encountered	New co-worker
Openness to target cues	Observation; search for information
Familiar cues encountered	Co-worker is Stanford graduate with good grades
Target categorized	Co-worker is "good man" with "great potential"
Cue selectivity	Co-worker's poor performance ignored or distorted
Categorization strengthened	Co-worker is still "good man" with "great potential"

Exhibit 3.3
Bruner's model of the perceptual process and an example.

perceptions, she takes a special interest in observing his performance, which is good for several months. This increases the strength of her initial categorization. Gradually, however, the engineer's performance deteriorates for some reason, and his work becomes less and less satisfactory. This is clear to everyone except the other engineer, who continues to see him as adequate and excuses his most obvious errors as stemming from external factors beyond his control.

Selectivity. Perception is selective. Perceivers do not use all the available cues, and those they use are thus given special emphasis. The established engineer was especially interested in the new recruit's academic credentials and his job performance. A different observer might be interested in different cues but would doubtless be just as selective in forming an impression of the target. This selectivity means that our perception is efficient, and this efficiency can both aid and hinder our perceptual accuracy. The engineer in the above example, in concentrating on her new co-worker's academic background, probably ignored other cues that might have predicted the subsequent performance problem.

Constancy. Bruner's model and the accompanying example also illustrate that our perceptual system works to paint a constant and consistent picture of the target. Perceptual *constancy* refers to the tendency for the target to be perceived in the same way over time or across situations. We have all had the experience of "getting off on the wrong foot" with a teacher or a boss and finding it difficult to change their constant perception of us. The engineer's image of the new co-worker's performance remained constant despite objective reality.

Consistency. Perceptual *consistency* refers to the tendency to select, ignore, and distort cues in such a manner that they fit together to form a homogeneous image of the target. We strive for consistency in our perception of people. We do not tend to see the same person as both good and bad or dependable and untrustworthy. For the engineer, consistency demanded that a Stanford graduate be a good performer. Often, we distort cues that are discrepant with our general image of a person to make the cues consistent with this image.

In the next section, we consider some specific perceptual biases that contribute to selectivity, constancy, and consistency in our perception of people.

Some Basic Biases in Person Perception

For accuracy's sake, it would be convenient if we could encounter others under laboratory conditions, in a vacuum or a test tube, as it were. Because the real world lacks such ideal conditions, the impressions that we form of others are susceptible to a number of perceptual biases.

Primacy and Recency Effects

Given the examples of person perception that we have discussed thus far, you might gather that we form our impressions of others fairly quickly. One reason for this fast impression formation is our tendency to rely on the cues that we encounter early in a relationship. This reliance on early cues or first impressions is known as the **primacy effect**. Primacy often has a lasting impact. Thus, the worker who can favourably impress his or her boss in the first days on the job is in an advantageous position due to primacy. Similarly, the labour negotiator who comes across as "tough" on the first day of contract talks might find this image difficult to shake as the talks continue. Primacy is a form of selectivity, and its lasting effects illustrate the operation of constancy. Sometimes, a **recency effect** occurs in which people give undue weight to the cues they encountered most recently. In other words, last impressions count most. Landing a big contract today might be perceived as excusing a whole year's bad sales performance.

> **Primacy effect.** The tendency for a perceiver to rely on early cues or first impressions.

> **Recency effect.** The tendency for a perceiver to rely on recent cues or last impressions.

Reliance on Central Traits

Even though perceivers tend to rely on early information when developing their perceptions, these early cues do not receive equal weight. People tend to organize their perceptions around **central traits**, personal characteristics of the target that are of special interest to them. In developing her perceptions of her new co-worker, the experienced engineer seemed to organize her impressions around the trait of intellectual capacity. The centrality of traits depends on the perceiver's interests and the situation. Thus, not all engineers would organize their perceptions of the new worker around his intellectual abilities, and the established engineer might not use this trait as a central factor in forming impressions of the people she meets at a party.

Central traits often have a very powerful influence on our perceptions of others. Physical appearance is a common central trait in work settings. Research shows an overwhelming tendency for those who are "beautiful" to also be perceived as "good," especially when it comes to judgments about their social competence.[4] Ann Hopkins evidently paid the price here, since the partners associated her "unfeminine" appearance with negative opinions about her interpersonal skills. In general, research shows that conventionally attractive people are more likely than unattractive people to be hired, given good performance evaluations, and promoted.[5] (See "In Focus: *Attractiveness Pays Off, But It Pays Off Better for Men.*")

> **Central traits.** Personal characteristics of a target person that are of particular interest to a perceiver.

Implicit Personality Theories

Each of us has an implicit personal "theory" about which personality characteristics go together. These are called **implicit personality theories**. Perhaps you expect hardworking people to also be honest. Perhaps you feel that people of average intelligence tend to be most friendly. To the extent that such implicit theories are inaccurate, they provide a basis for misunderstanding.[6] The employee who assumes that her very formal boss is also insensitive might be reluctant to discuss a work-related problem with him that could be solved fairly easily.

> **Implicit personality theories.** Personal theories that people have about which personality characteristics go together.

in focus ➔))   Attractiveness Pays Off, But It Pays Off Better for Men

Consistent with evidence that physical attractiveness is related to obtaining employment and promotion, more attractive employees also have been found to enjoy more economic success in their careers. The research so far suggests that attractiveness is more consistently related to economic success for men than for women. Roszell, Kennedy, and Grabb (1989) examined the relationship of attractiveness to income attainment for over 1,000 Canadians. Attractive persons earned higher annual salaries than less attractive persons. With each increase in rated attractiveness on a five-point scale of attractiveness, the 1981 annual income of the respondent increased by $1,988. After controlling for respondent gender, the gender composition of the job, and 1979 salary, this figure dropped to $1,046 but was still statistically significant. This relationship was found for men, older employees, and those engaged in male-dominated occupations, but not for women, younger employees, and those in female-dominated occupations.

Two studies at the University of Pittsburgh have provided further evidence that good looks pay. In one study, Good, Olson, and Frieze (1986) used height, weight, and body mass (weight relative to height) as indicators of physical attractiveness. They surveyed over 2,000 MBA graduates of the University of Pittsburgh who graduated between 1973 and 1982. For men, weight but not height was found to predict starting salary, and both height and weight predicted the current (1983) salary. However, neither of these variables predicted the starting and current salary of the women in the sample. For each one-inch increase in height, the salary of the men was $600 higher.

Overweight men earned $4,000 less in salary than those of normal weight.

In another study, Frieze, Olson, and Russell (1991) asked a group of people with corporate management experience to rate the physical attractiveness of 700 MBA graduates on a five-point scale. The starting salaries of male graduates receiving the highest attractiveness rating were approximately $5,000 a year more than those receiving the lowest attractiveness rating. After five years, those receiving the highest rating earned $10,000 more than those receiving the lowest rating. Attractiveness had no impact on starting salaries of women but was related to later salaries, although not as strongly as for men. For each increment in attractiveness on the five-point scale, women earned $2,000 more in salary five years later.

Finally, a more recent study looked at the careers of 2,500 law students from a prestigious law school in the United States. An independent panel of raters rated the students' appearance on a scale from one to five. Five years after graduation, those of above-average attractiveness were earning eight to nine percent more than those with below-average attractiveness. After 15 years, those of above-average appearance were earning 12 to 13 percent more.

Source: Excerpted from Stone, E. F., Stone D. L., &. Dipboye, R. L. (1992). Stigmas in organizations: Race, handicaps, and physical unattractiveness. In: K. Kelley (Ed.), *Issues, theory, and research in industrial/organizational psychology*. New York: Elsevier, pp. 419–420; McFarland, J. (1996, January 23). The ugly truth: Looks count. *The Globe and Mail*, p. B12.

Projection

In the absence of information to the contrary, and sometimes in spite of it, people often assume that others are like themselves. This tendency to attribute one's own thoughts and feelings to others is called **projection**. In some cases, projection is an efficient and sensible perceptual strategy. After all, people with similar backgrounds or interests often *do* think and feel similarly. Thus, it is not unreasonable for a capitalistic businessperson to assume that other businesspeople favour the free enterprise system and disapprove of government intervention in this system. However, projection can also lead to perceptual difficulties. The chairperson who feels that an issue has been resolved and perceives committee members to feel the same way might be very surprised when a vote is taken. The honest warehouse manager who perceives others as honest might find stock disappearing. In the case of threatening or undesirable characteristics, projection can serve as a form of perceptual defence. The dishonest worker might say, "Sure

Projection. The tendency for perceivers to attribute their own thoughts and feelings to others.

I steal from the company, but so does everyone else." Such perceptions can be used to justify the perceiver's thievery.

Stereotyping

One way to form a consistent impression of other people is simply to assume that they have certain characteristics by virtue of some category that they fall into. This perceptual tendency is known as **stereotyping,** or the tendency to generalize about people in a social category and ignore variations among them. Categories on which people might base a stereotype include race, age, gender, ethnic background, social class, occupation, and so on.[7] There are three specific aspects to stereotyping.[8]

- We distinguish some category of people (college professors).
- We assume that the individuals in this category have certain traits (absent-minded, disorganized, ivory-tower mentality).
- We perceive that everyone in this category possesses these traits ("All my professors this year will be absent-minded, disorganized, and have an ivory-tower mentality.")

People can evoke stereotypes with incredibly little information. In a "first impressions" study, the mere designation of a woman as preferring to be addressed as Ms. led to her being perceived as more masculine, more achievement oriented, and less likeable than those who preferred the traditional titles Miss or Mrs.[9]

Not all stereotypes are unfavourable. You probably hold favourable stereotypes of the social categories of which you are a member, such as student. However, these stereotypes are often less well developed and less rigid than others you hold. Stereotypes help us develop impressions of ambiguous targets, and we are usually pretty familiar with the people in our own groups. In addition, this contact helps us appreciate individual differences among group members, and such differences work against the development of stereotypes.

Language can be easily twisted to turn neutral or even favourable information into a basis for unfavourable stereotypes. For example, if British people do tend to be reserved, it is fairly easy to interpret this reserve as snobbishness. Similarly, if women who achieve executive positions have had to be assertive, it is easy to interpret this assertiveness as pushiness.

Knowing a person's occupation or field of study, we often make assumptions about his or her behaviour and personality. Accountants might be stereotyped as compulsive, precise, and one-dimensional, while engineers might be perceived as cold and calculating. Reflect on your own stereotypes of psychology or computer science students.

On the average, not all stereotypes are inaccurate. You probably hold fairly correct stereotypes about the educational level of the typical college professor and the on-the-job demeanour of the typical telephone operator. These accurate stereotypes ease the task of developing perceptions of others. However, it is probably safe to say that most stereotypes are inaccurate, especially when we use them to develop perceptions of specific individuals. This follows from the fact that stereotypes are most likely to develop when we do not have good information about a particular group.

This raises an interesting question: If many stereotypes are inaccurate, why do they persist?[10] After all, reliance on inaccurate information to develop our perceptions would seem to be punishing in the long run. In fact, a couple of factors work to *reinforce* inaccurate stereotypes. For one thing, even incorrect stereotypes help us process information about others quickly and efficiently.

you be the manager

Changing Perceptions and Keeping Women at Procter & Gamble Co.

Until recently, no woman sat on P&G's executive committee, and few of its executives were female.

For years, Procter & Gamble has used its marketing expertise to sell some of the world's best-known brands to women. It was far less successful in bringing women into its own management ranks and keeping them. Women were leaving the company at an alarming rate. In 1991, a study of employee turnover uncovered that two of every three good performers who quit the company were women. And because P&G only promotes from within, retention was a critical issue. However, female employees noticed that there were not a lot of women who had families moving up.

In 1993, a task force of seasoned brand managers attacked the problem. In exit interviews, many women said they were leaving to spend more time with family. But the task force nonetheless decided to survey women that P&G regretted losing.

The results were surprising. Of 50 women, only two had dropped out of the workforce. They had not left to be stay-at-home mothers. Instead, they went to other high-profile, high-stress jobs, working more hours than when they were at P&G. In addition, half the women were stunned to hear that P&G considered them a "regrettable loss." This was a huge red flag.

For the first time, it was clear that P&G's gender problem was rooted in the company's insular culture. Few corporate cultures are as dominant as the "Procter Way." "It's such a strong culture, they really want sameness," said a former brand assistant. "The way women think and the way we do business has some inherently different qualities to it...In retrospect, there was a gender aspect to the culture that was not intentional, but was very, very real."

What should P&G do to stem the tide of women leaving the company? You be the manager.

1. Do you think that perceptions played a role in the small number of women in management positions and the high rate of turnover? What are the perceptions of female employees? What are the perceptions of management regarding the career goals and exodus of female employees?

2. What are some of the things that P&G can do to change perceptions and lower the rate of female turnover?

To find out what Procter & Gamble did, consult The Manager's Notebook at the end of the chapter.

Source: Excerpted from T. Parker-Pope. (1998, September 9). Inside P&G, a pitch to keep women employees. *Wall Street Journal*, pp. B1, B6.

Sometimes, it is easier for the perceiver to rely on an inaccurate stereotype than it is to discover the true nature of the target. The male manager who is required to recommend one of his 20 subordinates for a promotion might find it easier to automatically rule out promoting a woman than to carefully evaluate all his subordinates, regardless of gender. Second, inaccurate stereotypes are often reinforced by selective perception and the selective application of language that was discussed above. The Hispanic worker who stereotypes all non-Hispanic managers as unfair might be on the lookout for behaviours to confirm these stereotypes and fail to notice examples of fair and friendly treatment. If such treatment *is* noticed, it might be perceived as patronizing rather than helpful.

Later, we will cover gender, age, racial, and ethnic stereotypes at work. For now, consider You Be the Manager.

Procter & Gamble
www.pg.com

Attribution: Perceiving Causes and Motives

Attribution. The process by which causes or motives are assigned to explain people's behaviour.

Thus far, we have considered a general model of perception and discussed some specific perceptual tendencies that operate as we form impressions of others. We will now consider a further aspect of impression formation—how we perceive people's motives. **Attribution** is the process by which we assign causes or motives to explain people's behaviour. The attribution process is important because many rewards and punishments in organizations are based on judgments about what really caused a target person to behave in a certain way.

In making attributions about behaviour, an important goal is to determine whether the behaviour is caused by dispositional or situational factors. **Dispositional attributions** suggest that some personality or intellectual characteristic unique to the person is responsible for the behaviour, and that the behaviour thus reflects the "true person." If we explain a behaviour as a function of intelligence, greed, friendliness, or laziness we are making dispositional attributions. In general, the business press attributed the turnaround of the Chrysler Corporation to Lee Iacocca's leadership skills and market savvy, not to government loan guarantees or an improving economy.

Dispositional attributions. Explanations for behaviour based on an actor's personality or intellect.

Situational attributions suggest that the external situation or environment in which the target person exists was responsible for the behaviour, and that the person might have had little control over the behaviour. If we explain behaviour as a function of bad weather, good luck, proper tools, or poor advice, we are making situational attributions.

Situational attributions. Explanations for behaviour based on an actor's external situation or environment.

Obviously, it would be nice to be able to read minds in order to understand people's motives. Since we cannot do this, we are forced to rely on external cues and make inferences from these cues. Research indicates that as we gain experience with the behaviour of a target person, three implicit questions guide our decisions as to whether we should attribute the behaviour to dispositional or situational causes.[11]

- Does the person engage in the behaviour regularly and consistently? (**Consistency cues**)
- Do most people engage in the behaviour, or is it unique to this person? (**Consensus cues**)

Unusual behaviours provide us with more information about a person's motives than do conforming behaviours.

- Does the person engage in the behaviour in many situations, or is it distinctive to one situation? (**Distinctiveness cues**)

Let us examine consistency, consensus, and distinctiveness cues in more detail.

Consistency Cues

Unless we see clear evidence of external constraints that force a behaviour to occur, we tend to perceive behaviour that a person performs regularly as indicative of his or her true motives. In other words, high consistency leads to dispositional attributions. Thus, one might assume that the professor who has generous office hours and is always there for consultation really cares about his students. Similarly, we are likely to make dispositional attributions about workers who are consistently good or poor performers, perhaps perceiving the former as "dedicated" and the latter as "lazy." When behaviour occurs inconsistently, we begin to consider situational attributions. For example, if a person's performance cycles between mediocre and excellent, we might look to variations in workload to explain the cycles.

Consistency cues. Attribution cues that reflect how consistently a person engages in some behaviour over time.

Consensus Cues

In general, acts that deviate from social expectations provide us with more information about the actor's motives than conforming behaviours do. Thus, unusual, low-consensus behaviour leads to more dispositional attributions than typical, high-consensus behaviour. The person who acts differently from the majority is seen as revealing more of his or her true motives. Ann Hopkins' detractors viewed her failure to act stereotypically feminine as a character flaw. The informational effects of low-consensus behaviour are magnified when the actor is expected to suffer negative consequences because of the deviance. Consider the job applicant who makes favourable statements about the role of big business in society while being interviewed for a job at General Motors. Such statements are so predictable in this situation that the interviewer can place little confidence in what they really indicate about the candidate's true feelings and motives. On the other hand, imagine an applicant who makes critical comments about big business in the same situation. Such comments are hardly expected and could clearly lead to rejection. In this case, the interviewer would be more confident about the applicant's true disposition regarding big business.

A corollary to this suggests that we place more emphasis on people's private actions than their public actions when assessing their motives.[12] When our actions are not open to public scrutiny, we are more likely to act out our genuine motives and feelings. Thus, we place more emphasis on a co-worker's private statements about his boss than we do on his public relations with the boss.

Consensus cues. Attribution cues that reflect how a person's behaviour compares with that of others.

General Motors
www.gm.com

Distinctiveness Cues

When a behaviour occurs across a variety of situations, it lacks distinctiveness, and the observer is prone to provide a dispositional attribution about its cause. We reason that the behaviour reflects a person's true motives if it "stands up" in a variety of environments. Thus, the professor who has generous office hours, stays after class to talk to students, and attends student functions is seen as truly student oriented. The worker whose performance was good in his first job as well as several subsequent jobs is perceived as having real ability. When a behaviour is highly distinctive, in that it occurs in only one situation, we are likely to assume

Distinctiveness cues. Attribution cues that reflect the extent to which a person engages in some behaviour across a variety of situations.

that some aspect of the situation caused the behaviour. If the only student-oriented behaviour that we observe is generous office hours, we assume that they are dictated by department policy. If a worker performed well on only one job, back in 1985, we suspect that his uncle owns the company!

Attribution in Action

Frequently, observers of real life behaviour have information at hand about consistency, consensus, and distinctiveness. Let us take an example that shows how the observer puts such information together in forming attributions. At the same time, the example will serve to review the previous discussion. Imagine that Smith, Jones, and Kelley are employees who work in separate firms. Each is absent from work today, and a manager must develop an attribution about the cause in order to decide which personnel action is warranted.

- *Smith*—Smith is absent a lot, his peers are seldom absent, and he was absent a lot in his previous job.
- *Jones*—Jones is absent a lot, her peers are also absent a lot, but she was almost never absent in her previous job.
- *Kelley*—Kelley is seldom absent, his co-workers are seldom absent, and he was seldom absent in his previous job.

Just what kind of attributions are managers likely to make regarding the absences of Smith, Jones, and Kelley? Smith's absence is highly consistent, it is a low-consensus behaviour, and it is not distinctive, since he was absent in his previous job. As shown in Exhibit 3.4, this combination of cues is very likely to prompt a dispositional explanation, perhaps that Smith is lazy or irresponsible. Jones is also absent consistently, but it is high-consensus behaviour, in that her peers also exhibit absence. In addition, the behaviour is highly distinctive—she is absent only on this job. As indicated, this combination of cues will usually result in a situational attribution, perhaps that working conditions are terrible, or that the boss is nasty. Finally, Kelley's absence is inconsistent. In addition, it is similar to that of co-workers and not distinctive, in that he was inconsistently absent on his previous job as well. As shown, this combination of cues suggests that some temporary, short-term situational factor causes his absence. It is possible that a sick child occasionally requires him to stay home.

Biases in Attribution

As the preceding section indicates, observers often operate in a rational, logical manner in forming attributions about behaviour. The various cue combinations and the resulting attributions have a sensible appearance. This does not mean

Exhibit 3.4
Cue combinations and
resulting attributions.

	Consistency	Consensus	Distinctiveness	Likely Attribution
Smith	High	Low	Low	Disposition
Jones	High	High	High	Situation
Kelley	Low	High	Low	Temporary Situation

that such attributions are always correct, but that they do represent good bets about why some behaviour occurred. Having made this observation, it would be naive to assume that attributions are always free from bias or error. Earlier, we discussed a number of very basic perceptual biases, and it stands to reason that the complex task of attribution would also be open to bias. Let us consider the fundamental attribution error, actor-observer effect, and self-serving bias.[13]

Fundamental Attribution Error. Suppose you make a mistake in attributing a cause to someone else's behaviour. Would you be likely to err on the side of a dispositional cause or a situational cause? Substantial evidence indicates that when we make judgments about the behaviour of people other than ourselves, we tend to overemphasize dispositional explanations at the expense of situational explanations. This is called the **fundamental attribution error.**[14] For example, some Price Waterhouse partners evidently saw Ann Hopkins as having a flawed personality and discounted the situational impact of her minority status in the firm.

Why does the fundamental attribution error occur? For one thing, we often discount the strong effects that social roles can have on behaviour. We might see bankers as truly conservative people because we ignore the fact that their occupational role and their employer dictate that they act conservatively. Second, many people whom we observe are seen in rather constrained, constant situations (at work, or at school) that reduce our appreciation of how their behaviour can vary in other situations. Thus, we fail to realize that the observed behaviour is distinctive to a particular situation. That conservative banker might actually be a weekend skydiver!

The fundamental attribution error can lead to problems for the managers of poorly performing subordinates. It suggests that dispositional explanations for the poor performance will sometimes be made even when situational factors are the true cause. Laziness or low aptitude might be cited, while poor training or a bad sales territory are ignored. However, this is less likely when the manager has had actual experience in performing the subordinate's job and is thus aware of situational roadblocks to good performance.[15]

Actor-Observer Effect. It is not surprising that actors and observers often view the causes for the actor's behaviour very differently. This difference in attributional perspectives is called the **actor-observer effect.**[16] Specifically, while the observer might be busy committing the fundamental attribution error, the actor might be emphasizing the role of the situation in explaining his or her own behaviour. Thus, as actors, we are often particularly sensitive to those environmental events that led us to be late or absent. As observers of the same behaviour in others, we are more likely to invoke dispositional causes.

We see some of the most striking examples of this effect in cases of illegal behaviour, such as price fixing and the bribery of government officials. The perpetrators and those close to them often cite stiff competition or management pressure as causes of their ethical lapses. Observers see the perpetrators as immoral or unintelligent.[17]

Why are actors prone to attribute much of their own behaviour to situational causes? First, they might be more aware than observers of the constraints and advantages that the environment offered. At the same time, they are aware of their private thoughts, feelings, and intentions regarding the behaviour, all of which might be unknown to the observer. Thus, I might know that I sincerely wanted to get to the meeting on time, that I left home extra early, and that the accident that delayed me was truly unusual. My boss might be unaware of all of this information and figure that I am unreliable.

Fundamental attribution error. The tendency to overemphasize dispositional explanations for behaviour at the expense of situational explanations.

Actor-observer effect. The propensity for actors and observers to view the causes of the actor's behaviour differently.

Self-serving bias. The tendency to take credit for successful outcomes and to deny responsibility for failures.

Self-Serving Bias. It has probably already occurred to you that certain forms of attributions have the capacity to make us feel good or bad about ourselves. In fact, people have a tendency to take credit and responsibility for successful outcomes of their behaviour and to deny credit and responsibility for failures.[18] This tendency is called **self-serving bias,** and it is interesting because it suggests that people will explain the very same behaviour differently on the basis of events that happened *after* the behaviour occurred. If the vice-president of marketing champions a product that turns out to be a sales success, she might attribute this to her retailing savvy. If the very same marketing process leads to failure, she might attribute this to the poor performance of the marketing research firm that she used. Notice that the self-serving bias can overcome the tendency for actors to attribute their behaviour to situational factors. In this example, the vice-president invokes a dispositional explanation ("I'm an intelligent, competent person") when the behaviour is successful.

Self-serving bias can reflect intentional self-promotion or excuse making. However, again, it is possible that it reflects unique information on the part of the actor. Especially when behaviour has negative consequences, the actor might scan the environment and find situational causes for the failure.[19]

To review the basics of attribution, people often use consistency, consensus, and distinctiveness cues in a sensible and rational manner when trying to explain some observed behaviour. However, the fundamental attribution error suggests that observers are often overly ready to invoke dispositional explanations for the behaviour of actors. The actor-observer effect suggests that the actor is more ready to attribute his or her own behaviour to situational factors. Given the self-serving bias, this is especially likely if the behaviour is unsuccessful.

Person Perception and Workforce Diversity

The realities of workforce diversity have become an important factor for many organizations in recent years. **Workforce diversity** refers to differences among employees or potential recruits in characteristics, such as gender, race, age, religion, cultural background, physical ability, and sexual orientation. The interest in diversity stems from at least two broad facts. First, the North American workforce is becoming more diverse. Second, there is growing recognition that many organizations have not successfully managed workforce diversity.

Workforce diversity. Differences among recruits and employees in characteristics, such as gender, race, age, religion, cultural background, physical ability, and sexual orientation.

Workplace Diversity
www.diversityinc.com/

The Changing Workplace

As we mentioned in Chapter 1, the composition of the North American labour force is changing.[20] Thirty years ago, it was mainly Caucasian and mainly male. Now, changing immigration patterns, the ageing of baby boomers, and the increasing movement of women into paid employment make for a lot more variety. People of Asian and Hispanic background have become a growing segment of the labour pool. Immigrants from all parts of the world to Canada are making the Canadian population and labour force increasingly multicultural/multiethnic. Not only is the labour pool changing, but many organizations are seeking to recruit more representatively from this pool so that they employ people who reflect their customer base—to better mirror their markets. This is especially true in the growing service sector, where contact between organizational members and customers is very direct.

The changing employment pool is not the only factor that has prompted interest in diversity issues. Globalization, mergers, and strategic alliances mean that many employees are required to interact with people from substantially different national or corporate cultures. Compounding all this is an increased emphasis on teamwork as a means of job design and quality enhancement. How can a diverse group of individuals work well together?

Valuing Diversity

In the past, organizations were thought to be doing the right thing if they merely tolerated diversity, that is, if they engaged in fair hiring and employment practices with respect to women and minorities. Firms were considered to be doing especially well if they assisted these people to "fit into" the mainstream corporate culture by "fixing" what was different about them.[21] For example, women managers were sometimes given assertiveness training to enable them to be as hard-nosed and aggressive as their male counterparts!

Recently, some have argued that organizations should *value* diversity, not just tolerate it or try to blend everyone into a narrow mainstream. To be sure, a critical motive is the basic fairness of valuing diversity. However, there is increasing awareness that diversity and its proper management can yield strategic and competitive advantages. These advantages include the potential for improved problem solving and creativity when diverse perspectives are brought to bear on an organizational problem, such as product or service quality. They also include improved recruiting and marketing when the firm's human resources profile matches that of the labour pool and customer base (see Exhibit 3.5). The results of a recent study indicate that more organizations are adopting diversity as part of their corporate strategy in order to improve their competitiveness in global markets.[22]

The Urban Institute
www.urban.org

Stereotypes and Workforce Diversity

If there is a single concept that serves as a barrier to valuing diversity, it is the stereotype. Let us examine several workplace stereotypes and their consequences. Common workplace stereotypes are based on gender, age, race, and ethnicity.

Racial and Ethnic Stereotypes. Racial and ethnic stereotypes are pervasive, persistent, frequently negative, and often self-contradictory. Most of us hold at least some stereotypical views of other races or cultures. Over the years, such stereotypes exhibit remarkable stability unless some major event, such as a war, intervenes to change them. Then, former allies can acquire negative attributes in short order.

Personal experience is unnecessary for such stereotype formation. In one study, people were asked to describe the traits of a number of ethnic groups, including several fictional ones. Although they had never met a Danerian, a Pirenian, or a Wallonian, this did not inhibit them from assigning traits, and those they assigned were usually unfavourable![23] Such stereotypes often contain contradictory elements. A common reaction is to describe a particular group as being too lazy, while at the same time criticizing it for taking one's job opportunities away.

There is a remarkable shortage of serious research into racial and ethnic matters in organizations.[24] Nevertheless, what follows is a sample of some typical findings. Just getting in the door can be a problem. For example:

Hewlett-Packard CEO Carly Fiorina, Citigroup CFO Heidi Miller, Morgan Stanley Dean Witter Internet analyst Mary Meeker, Ogilvy & Mather CEO Shelly Lazarus, and eBay CEO Meg Whitman were recently ranked by *Fortune* magazine as the five most powerful women in American business.

The Urban Institute sent out teams of black and white job applicants with equal credentials. The men applied for the same entry-level jobs in Chicago and Washington, D.C., within hours of each other. They were the same age and physical size, had identical education and work experience, and shared similar personalities. Yet in almost 20% of the 476 audits, whites advanced farther in the hiring process, researchers found.[25]

Exhibit 3.5
Competitive advantages to valuing and managing a diverse workforce.

1. Cost Argument	As organizations become more diverse, the cost of a poor job in integrating workers will increase. Those who handle this well will thus create cost advantages over those who don't.
2. Resource-Acquisition Argument	Companies develop reputations on favourability as prospective employers for women and ethnic minorities. Those with the best reputations for managing diversity will win the competition for the best personnel. As the labour pool shrinks and changes composition, this edge will become increasingly important.
3. Marketing Argument	For multinational organizations, the insight and cultural sensitivity that members with roots in other countries bring to the marketing effort should improve these efforts in important ways. The same rationale applies to marketing to subpopulations within domestic operations.
4. Creativity Argument	Diversity of perspectives and less emphasis on conformity to norms of the past (which characterize the modern approach to management of diversity) should improve the level of creativity.
5. Problem-Solving Argument	Heterogeneity in decision and problem solving groups potentially produces better decisions through a wider range of perspectives and more thorough critical analysis of issues.
6. System Flexibility Argument	An implication of the multicultural model for managing diversity is that the system will become less determinant, less standardized, and therefore more fluid. The increased fluidity should create greater flexibility to react to environmental changes (i.e., reactions should be faster and at less cost).

Source: Cox, T.H., & Blake, S. (1991, August). Managing cultural diversity: Implications for organizational competitiveness. *Academy of Management Executive*, 47, pp. 45–56.

Even after getting in the door, career tracking based on racial or ethnic stereotypes is common. For instance, one study found that a stereotype that "African Americans can't handle pressure" was partially responsible for a lack of acceptance of African Americans in managerial roles.[26] Many companies have promoted African American executives to positions having to do with affirmative action, diversity, or urban affairs in spite of their extensive credentials in other substantive areas of business. Similarly, the stereotype of Asian Americans as technical wizards has interfered with their opportunity to ascend to high general management positions.[27]

Attributions can play an important role in determining how job performance is interpreted. For example, one study found that good performance on the part of African American managers was seen to be due to help from others (a situational attribution), while good performance by Caucasian managers was seen to be due to their effort and abilities (a dispositional attribution).[28]

Finally, racial and ethnic stereotypes are also important in the context of the increasing globalization of business. In one study, researchers asked American business students to describe Japanese and American managers along a number of dimensions. The students viewed Japanese managers as having more productive subordinates and being better overall managers. However, the students preferred to work for an American manager.[29] One can wonder how such students will respond to international assignments. Of course, all groups have stereotypes of each other. Japanese stereotypes of Americans probably contribute to Americans not being promoted above a certain level in Japanese firms.

Gender Stereotypes. One of the most problematic stereotypes for organizations is the gender stereotype. Considering their numbers in the workforce, women are severely underrepresented in managerial and administrative jobs. Although women now occupy a significant and growing proportion of entry- and mid-level management positions, this is not the case for top-level positions, as women currently occupy less than five percent of executive positions.[30] There is evidence that gender stereotypes are partially responsible for discouraging women from business careers and blocking their ascent to managerial positions. This underrepresentation of women managers and administrators happens because stereotypes of women do not correspond especially well with stereotypes of businesspeople or managers.

What is the nature of gender stereotypes? A series of studies has had managers describe men in general, women in general, and typical "successful middle managers." These studies have determined that successful middle managers are perceived as having traits and attitudes that are similar to those generally ascribed to men,[31] that is, successful managers are seen as more similar to men in qualities such as leadership ability, competitiveness, self-confidence, ambitiousness, and objectivity. Thus, stereotypes of successful middle managers do not correspond to stereotypes of women. The trend over time in the results of these studies contains some bad news and some good news. The bad news is that *male* managers today hold the same dysfunctional stereotypes about women and management that they held in the early 1970s when researchers conducted the first of these studies. At that time, women managers held the same stereotypes as the men. The good news is that the recent research shows a shift by the women—they now see successful middle managers as possessing attitudes and characteristics that describe *both* men and women in general.[32]

Granting that gender stereotypes exist, do they lead to biased human resource decisions? The answer would appear to be yes. In a typical study, researchers asked male bank supervisors to make hypothetical decisions about workers who were described equivalently except for gender.[33] Women were discriminated against for promotion to a branch manager's position. They were also discriminated against when they requested to attend a professional development conference. In addition, female supervisors were less likely than their male counterparts to receive support for their request that a problem employee be fired. In one case, bias worked to *favour* women. The bank supervisors were more likely to approve a request for a leave of absence to care for one's children when it came from a female. This finding is similar to others that show gender stereotypes tend to favour women when they are being considered for "women's" jobs (such as secretary) or for "women's" tasks (such as supervising other women).[34]

In general, research suggests that the above findings are fairly typical. Women suffer from a stereotype that is detrimental to their hiring, development, promotion, and salaries. Women managers are also more likely than men managers to have to make off-the-job sacrifices and compromises in family life to maintain their careers.[35] However, there is growing evidence that the detrimental effects of such stereotypes are reduced or removed when decision makers have good information about the qualifications and performance of particular women and an accurate picture of the job that they are applying for or seeking promotion into.[36] In particular, several field studies reveal convincingly that women do not generally suffer from gender stereotypes in *performance evaluations* that their supervisors provide.[37] This is not altogether surprising. As we noted earlier, stereotypes help us process information in ambiguous situations. To the extent that we have good information on which to base our perceptions of people, reliance on stereotypes is less necessary. Day-to-day performance is often fairly easy to observe, and gender stereotypes do not intrude on evaluations. On the other hand, hiring and promotion decisions might confront managers with ambiguous targets or situations and prompt them to resort to gender stereotypes in forming impressions.

What about Ann Hopkins? Was she simply an exception to the general rule that women do not suffer in performance appraisals? Probably not. When women make up a very *small* proportion of an employee group (15–20 percent) they tend to suffer a "tokenism" effect that exaggerates the effect of stereotypes.[38] You will recall that Price Waterhouse had only seven women out of 662 partners and that Ann Hopkins was the only woman out of 88 partner nominees. Under such circumstances, research shows that women's performance appraisals suffer.[39] Evidently people view token women as less capable of doing a "man's" job. Also, Ann Hopkins' nomination was not a routine performance appraisal but an evaluation for promotability as well. More subjective criteria and people who were not well acquainted with Hopkins were implicated in this decision.

Age Stereotypes. Another kind of stereotype that presents problems for organizations is the age stereotype. Knowing that a person falls into a certain age range, we have a tendency to make certain assumptions about the person's physical, psychological, and intellectual capabilities.

What is the nature of work-related age stereotypes? Older workers are seen as having less *capacity for performance*. They tend to be viewed as less productive, creative, logical, and capable of performing under pressure than younger workers. In addition, older workers are seen as having less *potential for development*. Compared with younger workers, they are considered more rigid and dogmatic and less adaptable to new corporate cultures. Not all stereotypes of older workers are negative, however. They tend to be perceived as more honest, dependable, and trustworthy (in short, more *stable*). In general, these stereotypes are held by both younger and older individuals.[40] It is worth noting that these stereotypes are essentially inaccurate. For example, age seldom limits the capacity for development until postemployment years.[41] Also, research shows that age and performance are unrelated.[42]

Again, the relevant question arises: Do age stereotypes affect human resource decisions? It would appear that such stereotypes can affect decisions regarding hiring, promotion, and skills development. In one study, researchers had university students make hypothetical recommendations regarding younger and older male workers. An older man was less likely to be hired for a finance job that required rapid, high-risk decisions. An older man was considered less promotable for a marketing position that required creative solutions to difficult problems. Finally, an older worker was less likely to be permitted to attend a conference on advanced production systems.[43] These decisions reflect the stereotypes of the older worker depicted above, and they are doubtless indicative of the tendency for older employees to be laid off during corporate restructuring. Again, however, we should recognize that age stereotypes may have less impact on human resource decisions when managers have good information about the capacities of the particular employee in question.

Managing Diversity with Stereotype Reduction

Given the prevalence of the stereotypes noted above, valuing diversity is not something that occurs automatically. Rather, diversity needs to be *managed* to have a positive impact on work behaviour. Management can use a number of strategies to help reduce the effects of workplace stereotypes.[44]

- Select enough minority members to get them beyond token status. When this happens, the majority starts to look at individual accomplishments, rather than group membership, because they can see variation in the behaviour of the minority.

- Encourage teamwork that brings minority and majority members together.

- Ensure that those making career decisions about employees have accurate information about them rather than having to rely on hearsay and second-hand opinion.

- Train people to be aware of stereotypes.

Training is the most widely used tool for instituting the management of diversity. Most training begins by illustrating the value of diversity and increasing the awareness of stereotypes.

> Among the many companies who have made extensive use of such training are McDonnell Douglas, Hewlett-Packard, and Ortho Pharmaceuticals. McDonnell Douglas has a program ("Woman-Wise and Business Savvy") focusing on gender differences in work-related behaviours. It uses same-gender group meetings and mixed-gender role plays. At its manufacturing plant in San Diego, Hewlett-Packard conducted training on cultural differences between Anglo-Americans and Mexican, Indochinese, and Filipinos. Much of the content focused on cultural differences in communication styles. In one of the most thorough training efforts to date, Ortho Pharmaceuticals started its three-day training with small groups (10–12) of senior managers and eventually trained managers at every level of the company.[45]

Other firms with well-developed diversity training programs include Avon, G.E. Silicones, U.S. West Telecommunications, and Mariott International Inc.

Asset recognition training is one form of training that goes beyond group differences and emphasizes individual uniqueness.[46] In this training, people record on worksheets their own personal knowledge, insights, and experiences. Then, in small groups, each person's unique assets and potential contributions to his or her work group and the organization are identified. Focusing on the individual and going beyond his or her current work role expertise fosters appreciation for diversity. Notice how this training counteracts the perceptual narrowing we described in Bruner's model.

There is as yet little hard research on the success of diversity training programs. However, there is some anecdotal evidence that these programs can actually cause disruption and bad feelings when all they do is get people to open up and generate stereotypes and then send them back to work.[47] Awareness training should be accompanied by skills training that is relevant to the particular needs of the organization. This might include training in resolving intercultural conflict, team building, handling a charge of sexual harassment, or learning a second language. Hewlett-Packard is a company that soon realized that awareness training was not enough. Such training now constitutes only one of nine diversity training modules of this type.[48]

Basic awareness and skills training are not the only components of managing diversity. Organizations must use a number of other tactics. In future chapters, we will consider the following:

- Comprehensive attitude change programs that focus on diversity (Chapter 4).

- Recognizing diversity in employee needs and motives (Chapter 5).

- Using alternative working schedules to offer employees flexibility (Chapter 6).

- Using employee surveys to foster better communication (Chapters 10 and 16).

Avon
www.avon.com

To overcome stereotypes and achieve a diverse workforce, we have to select people on the basis of their talents and appraise their performance fairly. These activities are also important because they can influence employees' perceptions of trust toward management. Let us look at the role of perception in these three areas.

Person Perception and Trust

Do you trust your boss? This is a question that more and more people are asking themselves today. In the last several years, the importance of trust in organizations has become especially evident in the face of major organizational changes that have left many people frustrated and out of work. Not surprisingly, employee trust toward management is reported to be on the decline.[49] One survey found that 47 percent of those who responded agreed that a lack of trust is a problem in their organization. In another survey, 40 percent indicated that they do not believe what management says.[50] A decline in trust can be a serious problem because trust perceptions influence organizational processes and outcomes, such as sales levels, net profits, and employee turnover.[51]

While most of us have some basic understanding of what trust means, most definitions of **trust** refer to it as a willingness to be vulnerable and to take risks with respect to the actions of another party.[52] More specifically, "trust is a psychological state comprising the intention to accept vulnerability based upon positive expectations of the intentions or behaviour of another."[53] Trust perceptions toward management are based on three distinct perceptions: ability, benevolence, and integrity.[54] Ability refers to employee perceptions regarding managements' competence and skills. Benevolence refers to the extent that employees perceive management as caring and concerned for their interests and willing to do good for them. Integrity refers to employee perceptions that management adheres to and behaves according to a set of values and principles that the trustor finds acceptable. The combination of these three factors influences perceptions of trust.

Keeping in mind that trust refers to a willingness to be vulnerable to the actions of others, how trusting would you be if you perceived your boss to be incompetent, unconcerned about your welfare, and/or driven by a set of values that you find unacceptable? Not surprisingly, higher perceptions of management ability, benevolence, and integrity are associated with greater perceptions of trust.

A good example of an organization where perceptions of trust are strong is Beth Israel Hospital in Boston. This is an organization where employees accept the organization's values and principles and where there exists a long history of dealing with employees in a fair and even-handed manner. Hospital leaders act as facilitators rather than bosses, and they have earned credibility with employees. As well, there exists a common philosophy of patient care and worklife throughout the hospital. The hospital also believes strongly that patient care is influenced by how well it cares for its people.[55]

How does trust develop in an organization like Beth Israel Hospital? Because each of the three factors discussed above is related to trust, actions that change employee perceptions of them are likely to change perceptions of trust. One of the things that Beth Israel Hospital has done is to implement a program known as the Scanlon Plan (see Chapter 6). This involved communicating with employees, providing opportunities to solve problems and sharing hospital gains with employees.

With the current trends in the composition of the workforce along with increased workplace diversity and the continued changes in the structure of organizations, the importance of trust is likely to increase in the coming years.[56] Therefore, organizations will have to find ways to improve and maintain high

Trust. A psychological state in which one has a willingness to be vulnerable and to take risks with respect to the actions of another party.

Beth Israel Hospital
www.bidmc.harvard.edu/

in focus → The Effect of a Performance Appraisal System on Trust Toward Management

What can managers do to improve trust in their organization? According to Roger Mayer and James Davis, one answer to this question is a performance appraisal system that is perceived by employees as fair and accurate. They conducted an interesting study that tested the effects of a new performance appraisal system on trust toward top management.

Employees who worked in a small nonunionized manufacturing firm in the plastics industry perceived the organization's current appraisal system as unacceptable. The main reasons for this were because the system did not accurately measure employee job performance, and there was no relationship between performance and rewards. The authors hypothesized that replacing the old system with a new system that would more accurately measure performance and link it to rewards would be perceived by employees as more acceptable and would increase their perceptions of management ability, benevolence, integrity, and trust.

The new performance appraisal system included a self-appraisal form for employees and required

supervisors and employees to meet and discuss the ratings, and supervisors had to discuss expected behaviours and outcomes that were the basis for the evaluation. Employees would then receive pay increases on the basis of their evaluation. Some employees were assigned to receive the new system, and others continued to receive the old system.

The results indicated that employees who received the new system perceived it to be more accurate. The new performance appraisal also produced a significant increase in trust toward top management over time, compared with the group of employees that did not receive the new system. As well, the effect of the appraisal system on perceptions of trust was fully explained by the three trustworthiness factors of ability, benevolence, and integrity.

Source: Based on Mayer, R. C., & Davis, J. H. (1999). The effect of the performance appraisal system on trust for management: A field quasi-experiment. *Journal of Applied Psychology, 84,* pp. 123-136.

levels of trust. For an example of how an organization used performance appraisals to increase trust toward management, see "In Focus: *The Effect of a Performance Appraisal System on Trust Toward Management.*"

Person Perception in the Selection Interview

You have probably had the pleasure (or displeasure!) of sitting through one or more job interviews in your life. After all, the interview is one of the most common organizational selection devices, applied with equal opportunity to applicants for everything from the janitorial staff to the executive suite. With our futures on the line, we would like to think that the interview is a fair and accurate selection device, but is it? Research shows that the interview is a valid selection device, although it is far from perfectly accurate, especially when the interviewer conducts it in an unstructured, free-form format. Validity improves whenever interviewers use a guide to order and organize their questions and impressions.[57]

What factors threaten the validity of the interview? To consider the most obvious problem first, applicants are usually motivated to present an especially favourable impression of themselves. As our discussion of the perception of people implies, it is difficult enough to gain a clear picture of another individual without having to cope with active deception! A couple of the perceptual tendencies that we already discussed in this chapter can also operate in the interview. For one thing, there is evidence that interviewers compare applicants with a stereotype of the ideal applicant.[58] In and of itself, this is not a bad thing. However, this ideal stereotype must be accurate, and this requires a clear understanding of the nature of the job in question and the kind of person who can do well in this job. This is a tall order, especially for the interviewer who is hiring

The interview is a difficult setting in which to form accurate impressions about a candidate. Interview validity increases when interviews are more structured and interviewers ask a set of predetermined questions.

Exhibit 3.6
Two examples of contrast effects.

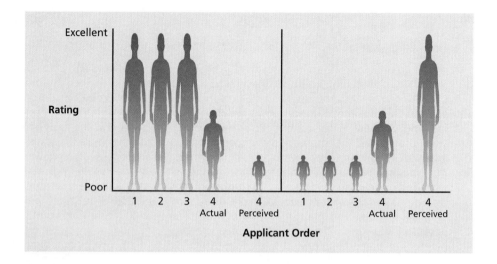

Contrast effects. Previously interviewed job applicants affect an interviewer's perception of a current applicant, leading to an exaggeration of differences between applicants.

applicants for a wide variety of jobs. Second, interviewers have a tendency to exhibit primacy reactions.[59] Minimally, this means that information the interviewer acquired early in the interview will have an undue impact on the final decision. However, it also means that information the interviewer obtained *before* the interview (for instance, by scanning an application form or resumé) can have an exaggerated influence on the interview outcome.

A couple of perceptual tendencies that we have not discussed are also at work in interviews. First, interviewers have a tendency to underweight positive information about the applicant.[60] This tendency means that negative information has undue impact on the decision.[61] It might occur because interviewers get more feedback about unsuccessful hiring than successful hiring ("Why did you send me that idiot?"). It might also happen because positive information is not perceived as telling the interviewer much, since the candidate is motivated to put up a good front. In addition, **contrast effects** sometimes occur in the interview.[62] This means that the applicants who have been interviewed earlier affect the interviewer's perception of a current applicant, leading to an exaggeration of differences between applicants. For example, if the interviewer has seen two excellent candidates and then encounters an average candidate, she might rate this person lower than if he had been preceded by two average applicants (see Exhibit 3.6.). This is an example of the impact of the situation on perception.

It is clear that the interview constitutes a fairly difficult setting in which to form accurate impressions about others. It is of short duration, a lot of information is generated, and the applicant is motivated to present a favourable image. Thus, interviewers often adopt "perceptual crutches" that hinder accurate perception. Earlier, we noted that unstructured interviews are less valid than structured interviews where the interviewer scores the applicant's responses to a predetermined series of questions. This form of interview probably reduces information overload and ensures that applicants can be more easily compared, since they have all responded to an identical sequence of questions.[63]

Person Perception and Performance Appraisal

Once a person is hired, however imperfectly, further perceptual tasks confront organization members. Specifically, the organization will want some index of the person's job performance for decisions regarding pay raises, promotions, transfers, and training needs.

Objective and Subjective Measures

It is possible to find objective measures of performance for certain aspects of some jobs. These are measures that do not involve a substantial degree of human judgment. Ann Hopkins' billable hours are one such measure. In general, though, as we move up the organizational hierarchy, it becomes more difficult to find objective indicators of performance. Thus, it is often hard to find quantifiable evidence of a manager's success or failure. When objective indicators of performance do exist, they are often contaminated by situational factors. For example, it might be very difficult to compare the dollar sales of a snowmobile salesperson whose territory covers Maryland and Virginia with one whose territory is northern Ontario. Also, while dollar sales might be a good indicator of current sales performance, it says little about a person's capacity for promotion to district sales manager.

Because of the difficulties that objective performance indicators present, organizations must often rely on subjective measures of effectiveness, usually provided by managers. However, the manager is confronted by a number of perceptual roadblocks. He or she might not be in a position to observe many instances of effective and ineffective performance. This is especially likely when the subordinate's job activities cannot be monitored directly. For example, a police sergeant cannot ride around in six squad cars at the same time, and a telephone company supervisor cannot visit customers' homes or climb telephone poles with all his or her installers. Such situations mean that the target (the subordinate's performance) is frequently ambiguous, and we have seen that the perceptual system resolves ambiguities in an efficient but often inaccurate manner. Even when performance is observable, employees often alter their behaviour so that they look good when their manager is around.

Rater Errors

Subjective performance appraisal is susceptible to some of the perceptual biases we discussed earlier—primacy, recency, and stereotypes. In addition, a number of other perceptual tendencies occur in performance evaluation. They are often called rater errors. One interrelated set of these tendencies includes leniency, harshness, and central tendency (Exhibit 3.7). **Leniency** refers to the tendency to perceive the performance of one's ratees as especially good, while **harshness** is the

Leniency. The tendency to perceive the job performance of ratees as especially good.

Harshness. The tendency to perceive the job performance of ratees as especially ineffective.

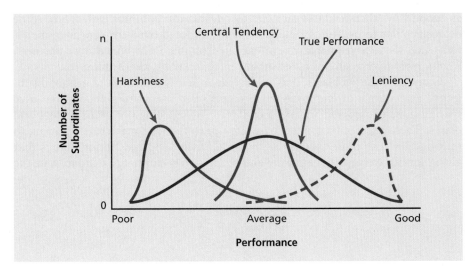

Exhibit 3.7
Leniency, harshness, and central tendency rater errors.

Central tendency. The tendency to assign most ratees to middle-range job performance categories.

tendency to see their performance as especially ineffective. Lenient raters tend to give "good" ratings, and harsh raters tend to give "bad" ratings. Professors with reputations as easy graders or tough graders exemplify these types of raters. **Central tendency** involves assigning most ratees to a middle-range performance category—the extremes of the rating categories are not used. The professor who assigns 80 percent of her students C's is committing this error. Each of these three rating tendencies is probably partially a function of the rater's personal experiences. For example, the manager who has had an especially good group of subordinates might respond with special harshness when management transfers him to supervise a group of slightly less able workers. It is worth noting that not all instances of leniency, harshness, and central tendency necessarily represent perceptual errors. In some cases, raters intentionally commit these errors, even though they have accurate perceptions of workers' performance. For example, a manager might use leniency or central tendency in performance reviews so that his subordinates do not react negatively to his evaluation.

Halo effect. The rating of an individual on one trait or characteristic tends to colour ratings on other traits or characteristics.

Another perceptual error that is frequently committed by performance raters is called the **halo effect**.[64] The halo effect occurs when the observer allows the rating of an individual on one trait or characteristic to colour the ratings on other traits or characteristics. For example, in a teacher evaluation system, a student might perceive his instructor as a nice person, and this might favourably influence his perception of the instructor's knowledge of the material and speed in returning exams and papers. Similarly, a manager might rate a subordinate as frequently late for work, and this might in turn lead her to devalue the subordinate's productivity and quality of work. As these examples illustrate, halo can work either for or against the ratee. In both cases, the rater fails to perceive differences *within* ratees. The halo effect tends to be organized around central traits that the rater considers important. The student feels that being nice is an especially important quality, while the manager places special emphasis on promptness. Ratings on these characteristics then affect the rater's perceptions of other characteristics.

Similar-to-me effect. A rater gives more favourable evaluations to people who are similar to the rater in terms of background or attitudes.

The **similar-to-me effect** is an additional rater error that may, in part, reflect perceptual bias. The rater tends to give more favourable evaluations to people who are similar to the rater in terms of background or attitudes. For example, the manager with an MBA degree who comes from an upper-middle-class family might perceive a similar subordinate as a good performer even though the person is only average. Similarly, a rater might overestimate the performance of an individual who holds similar religious and political views. Such reactions probably stem from a tendency to view our own performance, attitudes, and background as "good." We then tend to generalize this evaluation to others who are, to some degree, similar to us. Ann Hopkins probably suffered from the similar-to-me effect when she received negative evaluations from the Price Waterhouse partners. Raters with diverse subordinates should be especially wary of this error.

Given all these problems, it should be clear that it is difficult to get good subjective evaluations of employee performance. Because of this, human resource specialists have explored various techniques for reducing perceptual errors and biases. There has been a tendency to attempt to reduce rater errors by going to rating scales with more specific behavioural labels. The assumption here is that giving specific examples of effective and ineffective performance will facilitate the

Exhibit 3.8
Behaviourally anchored scale for rating customer service.

Could be expected to exchange a blouse purchased in a distant town and to impress the customer so much that she would buy three dresses and three pairs of shoes.

Could be expected to smooth things over beautifully with an irate customer who returned a sweater with a hole in it and turn her into a satisfied customer.

Could be expected to be friendly and tactful and to agree to reline a coat for a customer who wants a new coat because the lining had worn out in "only" two years.

Could be expected to courteously exchange a pair of gloves that are too small.

Could be expected to handle the after-Christmas rush of refunds and exchanges in a reasonable manner.

Could be expected to make a refund for a sweater only if the customer insists.

Could be expected to be quite abrupt with customers who want to exchange merchandise for a different colour or style.

Could be expected to tell a customer that a "six-week-old" order could not be changed even though the merchandise had actually been ordered only two weeks previously.

Could be expected to tell a customer who tried to return a shirt bought in Hawaii that a store in the States had no use for a Hawaiian shirt.

Source: Campbell, J.P., Dunnette, M.D., Lawler, E.E., III, & Weick, K.E., Jr. (1970). *Managerial behavior, performance, and effectiveness*. New York: McGraw-Hill.

rater's perceptual processes and recall. Exhibit 3.8 shows a behaviourally anchored rating scale that gives very specific behavioural examples (from top to bottom) of good, average, and poor customer service. It was developed for the J.C. Penney Company. With such an aid, the rater might be less likely to be susceptible to perceptual errors when completing the rating task, although the evidence for this is mixed.[65]

J.C. Penney Co.
www.jcpenney.net/

the manager's notebook

Changing Perceptions and Keeping Women at Procter & Gamble Co.

1. Perceptions were very much an important factor contributing to the turnover problem at Procter & Gamble. First, female employees perceived the organization as unconcerned, uncaring, and unwilling to promote them to management and executive positions. In the eyes of female employees, they were not valued by the organization. Certainly, the lack of females in management positions and the organization's failure to do anything to advance their careers contributed to these perceptions. What is perhaps most interesting is how the organization perceived the loss of female employees as "regrettable" and how this very response "stunned" those who had left. There seems to be some inaccuracy in how female employees perceived the organization and how the organization perceived their female employees. For example, until the organization conducted a survey of female employees, there was a perception that they left P&G to spend more time with their families, leading one to suspect that female employees at P&G had been stereotyped in a way that prevented them from being promoted to management ranks. Thus, it would appear that inaccurate perceptions and gender stereotyping were partly responsible for the lack of females in management positions and their high rate of turnover.

2. One of the most important programs that P&G implemented was a program called "Mentoring Up," which turned the mentoring concept on its head by having junior women "mentor" senior men on issues affecting women. The idea meant that the women of P&G would set out to change the P&G culture literally one manager—and one man—at a time. The second thing that P&G did was to make it clear to its female employees that they could have a career at the company. They set goals for women in management including a goal of 40% women at each level of brand management by the year 2005. They also designed female-friendly benefits, and launched an internal "advertising campaign" to convince women that they could succeed at P&G. Women now account for nearly a third of the vice-presidents and general managers in the company's advertising and brand management ranks. As well, some of the company's most important businesses are run by female vice-presidents and general managers, and they continue to rise through the ranks. Women now represent 31% of general managers. The company's highest ranking women, a senior vice-president, became the first woman on P&G's executive committee. In addition, the company was singled out by a women's advocacy group as one of the country's best companies for promoting women. The high turnover rate of women has also dropped and is now on par with that of men, and internal P&G surveys show women's job satisfaction is up 25%.

Source: Excerpted from Parker-Pope, T. (1998, September 9). Inside P&G, a pitch to keep women employees. *The Wall Street Journal*, p. B1, B6.

Summary

- Perception involves interpreting the input from our senses to provide meaning to our environment, and any instance of perception involves a perceiver, a target, and a situational context. The experience, needs, and emotions of the perceiver affect perception, as does the ambiguity of the target.

- Bruner's model of the perceptual process suggests that we are very receptive to cues provided by the target and the situation when we encounter an unfamiliar target. However, as we discover familiar cues, we quickly categorize the target and process other cues to maintain a consistent and constant picture of the target. When the target is a person, this drive for constancy and consistency is revealed in a number of specific perceptual biases, including primacy, recency, implicit personality theory, reliance on central traits, projection, and stereotyping. Gender, age, race, and ethnic stereotypes are especially problematic for organizations.

- Attribution is the process of assigning causes or motives to people's behaviour. The observer is often interested in determining whether the behaviour is due to dispositional (internal) or situational (external) causes. Behaviour is likely to be attributed to the disposition of the actor when the behaviour (1) is performed consistently, (2) differs from that exhibited by other people, and (3) occurs in a variety of situations or environments. An opposite set of cues will prompt a situational attribution. Observers are biased toward making dispositional attributions, while actors are more likely to explain their own behaviour in situational terms, especially when its outcomes are unfavourable.

- The changing nature of the workplace has highlighted the advantages of valuing and managing employee diversity. Organizations can use a number of tactics, including training, to combat stereotypes that threaten diversity efforts.

- Perceptions of trust involve a willingness to be vulnerable and to take risks with respect to the actions of another party. Trust perceptions toward management are based on perceptions of ability, benevolence, and integrity.

- Judging the suitability of job applicants in an interview and appraising job performance are especially difficult perceptual tasks, in part because the target is motivated to convey a good impression. In addition, interviewers and performance raters exhibit a number of perceptual tendencies that are reflected in inaccurate judgments, including contrast effects, leniency, harshness, central tendency, halo, and similar-to-me effects.

Discussion Questions

1. Discuss how differences in the experiences of students and professors might affect their perceptions of students' written work and class comments.

2. Discuss the occupational stereotypes that you hold of computer programmers, the clergy, truck drivers, bartenders, and bankers. How do you think these stereotypes have developed? Has an occupational stereotype ever caused you to commit a socially embarrassing error when meeting someone for the first time?

3. Use Bruner's perceptual model (Exhibit 3.3) to explain why performance appraisals and interviewers' judgments are frequently inaccurate.

4. Discuss the assertion that "the perception of reality is more important than reality itself" in the context of organizations.

5. Suppose an employee does a particularly poor job on an assigned project. Discuss the attribution process that this person's manager will use to form judgments about this poor performance. Be sure to discuss how the manager will use consistency, consensus, and distinctiveness cues.

6. A study of small business failures found that owners generally cited factors such as economic depression or strong competition as causes. However, creditors of these failed businesses were much more likely to cite ineffective management. What attribution bias is indicated by these findings? Why do you think the difference in attribution occurs?

7. Discuss the factors that make it difficult for employment interviewers to form accurate perceptions of interviewees. Explain why a gender or racial stereotype might be more likely to affect a hiring decision than a performance appraisal decision.

8. List several advantages for an organization that hires and effectively manages a diverse workforce.

9. Describe how the principles of operant and social learning theory can be used to manage workplace diversity and reduce the effects of workplace stereotypes. How can the organizational learning practices described in Chapter 2 be used for managing diversity and stereotype reduction?

10. Consider how the four basic types of managerial activities described in Chapter 1 (i.e., routine communication, traditional management, networking, and human resource management) can influence employees' perceptions of trust and result in either low or high trust perceptions. How should managers perform each of these activities in order to improve their employees' perceptions of trust?

Experiential Exercise

Beliefs about Older Workers

The following items are an attempt to assess the attitudes people have about older workers. The statements cover many different opposing points of view; you may find yourself agreeing strongly with some of the statements, disagreeing just as strongly with others, and perhaps uncertain about others.

Using the numbers from 1 to 5 on the rating scale, mark your personal opinion about each statement in the blank space next to each statement. Remember, give your personal opinion according to how much you agree or disagree with each item.

Read each statement carefully. Indicate the response that best tells how you feel about each statement in the space provided. In all cases, older refers to those who are 50 years of age or older.

—1—	—2—	—3—	—4—	—5—
Strongly agree	Agree	Neither agree nor disagre	Disagree	Strongly disagree

____ 1. Older employees have *fewer accidents* on the job.

____ 2. Most companies are *unfair* to older employees.

____ 3. Older employees are *harder to train* for jobs.

____ 4. Older employees are *absent more often* than younger employees.

____ 5. Younger employees have more *serious accidents* than older workers.

____ 6. If two workers had similar skills, I'd *pick the older worker to work with me*.

____ 7. *Occupational diseases* are more likely to occur among younger employees.

____ 8. Older employees usually turn out work of *higher quality*.

____ 9. Older employees are *grouchier* on the job.

____ 10. Younger workers are *more cooperative* on the job.

____ 11. Older workers are more *dependable*.

____ 12. Most older workers cannot keep up with the *speed of modern industry*.

____ 13. Older employees are *most loyal* to the company.

____ 14. Older workers *resist change* and are *too set in their ways*.

____ 15. Younger workers are more interested than older workers in *challenging jobs*.

____ 16. Older worker can *learn new skill*s as easily as other employees.

____ 17. Older employees are *better* employees.

____ 18. Older employees *do not want* jobs with *increased responsibilities*.

____ 19. Older workers are not interested in *learning new skills*.

____ 20. Older employees should '*step aside*' (take a less demanding job) to give younger employees advancement opportunities.

____ 21. The majority of older employees would *quit work* if they could *afford* it.

____ 22. Older workers are usually *outgoing and friendly* at work.

____ 23. Older workers prefer *less challenging jobs* than those they held *when* they were *younger*.

____ 24. It is a *better investment* to *train younger workers* rather than older workers.

____ 25. Older employees in our department *work just as hard* as anyone else.

____ 26. Given a choice, I would not work with an older worker on a daily basis.

____ 27. A person's *performance declines significantly* with age.

Scoring and Interpretation

The scale you have just completed measures your attitudes toward older workers. To score your beliefs about older workers, subtract your responses to each of the following items from 6: 1, 2, 5, 6, 7, 8, 11, 13, 16, 17, 22, and 25. For example, if you put 2 for item 1, give yourself a 4 (6 minus 2). Then simply add up your resulting responses to all 27 items. Your score should fall somewhere between 27 and 135. Low scores indicate an overall negative belief about older workers, while high scores indicate positive beliefs. Thus, the higher your score, the more favourable are your attitudes toward older workers.

Research on older workers has generally found that a negative stereotype of older workers exists in organizations. The danger of this is that it can lead to negative attitudes and discriminatory behaviour toward older workers.

A recent study of 179 employees from three organizations obtained scores that ranged from 54 to 118. The average score was 90, which indicated somewhat positive beliefs about older workers. As reported in other studies, older workers had more positive beliefs about older workers than younger workers. However, younger workers who had more interactions with older workers were found to have more positive beliefs about older workers.

To facilitate discussion, the instructor might have students write their score, age, and how often they come in contact with older workers (daily, several times a week, once a week, or monthly) on pieces of paper. Working in groups and using calculators, the class can compute the class average. On the basis of the distribution of age and contact with older workers in the class, create two age groups (young and older) and two contact with older worker groups (low and high), and calculate the average of these groups. Also, a distribution of the scores might be posted on the board.

Source: Hassell, B. L., & Perrewe, P. L. (1995). An examination of beliefs about older workers: Do stereotypes still exist? *Journal of Organizational Behavior*, 16, pp. 457-468.

Case Incident

Evaluating Gregory

After six months in her new position as manager, Nina was faced with the task of having to conduct performance reviews of her staff. She was worried because she had never done performance reviews and was not sure how to do them. However, in order to ease her way into it, she decided to start with Gregory. Gregory was a recent hire in her department, and Nina felt that he was the most attractive-looking guy she had hired since she became manager. She felt it would be easy to evaluate his performance.

1. According to Bruner's model of the perceptual process, discuss how Nina's perception of Gregory might influence her evaluation of his performance.

2. What are some person perception biases that Nina might make when evaluating Gregory's performance, and how can they be prevented?

Case Study

The Review Session

Jack Adams's mind wandered as he sat outside Bill Squire's office awaiting his yearly performance review ...

Well, it's 8:25. Five more minutes to go. Fifteen years with the company, and this new district manager, Squire, couldn't even call and request this meeting personally. These annual performance appraisals are tough enough, and here I've got a bad sales record for the past 12 months. Surely he'll be able to understand that the sales decreases were a result of the new territory assignments. Two major accounts taken away—not to mention all of the smaller ones. It took me years to develop those accounts and now someone else reaps the benefits. I know my capabilities, I work hard. Next thing you know, Squire will probably tell me to stop playing golf with the customers from my old accounts. Who was it that thought this territory reorganization would be an improvement anyway? So what if some of the reps increased their sales records? Come to think of it, I was kind of surprised that the rep over in the eastern counties increased his sales by over 30 percent. Wonder how he did it. Well, no concern of mine. Somehow in the next 60 minutes I'll have to make Squire understand my 18% deficit. This is ridiculous. I've met this guy twice ...

Meanwhile, inside his office, Bill Squire glanced at his watch, which read 8:30. Doubting that his salesman Adams would be on time, he glanced over the data sheets nervously ...

Certainly hope this meeting doesn't take more than half an hour. So much work to do today. I waited years for this promotion—just never knew it would be so much work. Incredible! Sometimes the other sales managers seem so calm. Bet they're faking it. Now I've got these darn performance appraisals to do. Lucky for me I've got these computer printouts. Let's see ... who is this guy? Adams, huh? Eighteen percent below quota. Well, he'll have to explain that! Isn't he that tall redheaded guy? I suppose it would be easier if I'd had more chance to meet him. Well, these printouts will have to suffice. Actually, look at this—overall district sales are way up. This Adams is one of four whose sales are down. I'm sure he'll think of something real creative to explain this. Some of these reps just never learn that sales is just a matter of sweat and blood—good old-fashioned work. These printouts always tell the final story ...

At 8:40, Bill Squire buzzed his secretary. "Arlene, is Adams ... ah, let's see ... Jack Adams here yet?"

"Yes, he is, Mr. Squire," replied Arlene from the outside office. "He's been here for sometime now."

With some hesitation, Bill Squire asked his secretary to send Jack Adams in.

Squire [shaking hands]: Good morning, Jack. I hope this meeting doesn't interrupt your appointment schedule. I made it early in the morning, figuring your clients don't do business before 10 anyway.

Adams: No Bill, this time is just fine. [Looks around the office.] You've made some changes in here since Mike (Jack Adams's former sales manager) changed jobs.

Squire: Yeah, I prefer things simple. I think it's more in line with the company's new efficiency image. We want the customers to realize we're always on our toes, right?

Adams [quietly]: Sure thing.

At this point, Bill Squire got up from his chair and walked to a table nearby and poured himself a glass of water. Returning to his desk, he picked up the computer printout lying in front of him.

Squire [clearing his voice]: Well, Jack, we better get to it, right? What I've got here is a printout of all sales personnel in my district for the past 12 months. Have you seen any of this information?

Adams: Well, I've seem some of it and …

Squire [interrupting]: Good, then you probably realize we've got a problem here. Over the past year your performance has been 18 percent below the quota that was established for you. You're one of the four reps whose performance is poor. Thirteen other reps beat their quota. Have you had any problems that I'm not aware of?

Jack Adams was now looking out a window beside Bill Squire's desk. His palms were moist and his lips dry. He tried to put his thoughts together, but his mind just seemed to race.

Squire: Jack, did …?

Adams: Yeah, yeah—I heard you. [Folds his arms.] You know, Bill, you're new to this district, and perhaps there is something you need to realize. I've worked for this company for 15 years and I think, if you check the records, I've always been a pretty good sales rep—no, I'd say one of the best. I work hard. I get along great with my customers and …

Squire: Jack, now that you mention it, I had a complaint about you a couple of weeks ago. Kathy Burgess in purchasing at McGabe Company wrote me a letter saying you hadn't been in contact with them for over a month. Andy, who used to have that account, visited them weekly. How can you hope to make the quota if you don't make contact with the customer?

Adams: Andy had that account when the territory was one-third as big and …

Squire: All right, Jack, I realize the territory reassignments have affected reps a little bit …

Adams [excitedly]: A *little* bit …

Squire [raising his hand]: Hold on, hold on—let me finish. As I was saying, the territory reassignments have meant adjusting. But, Jack, that means hard work—you know, good old-fashioned effort. Come on now, Jack, have you been giving it your best shot? Are you sure there isn't something personal going on? Everything okay at home? I'm just trying to be helpful—open up a little bit.

Jack felt a lot of pressure in the back of his neck. His face felt flushed. Open up, he thought to himself, I don't even know this guy. This is what I get after 15 years. He breathed deeply.

Adams [calmly]: Couldn't we try this again. I may have had more trouble than others with the change in territories … [pause] … I guess it's possible. But maybe, just maybe, the reassignment *did* affect me more than some other reps—maybe I didn't get a fair shake … maybe …

Squire [frustrated]: Back to that again, Jack? [Picks up the printout] Let's look at the *facts*. You can't avoid these figures, Jack!

At this point Jack rose from his chair. His knees were trembling as he walked toward Bill Squire's desk. Leaning over the desk, Jack spoke firmly, "I don't give a damn about your figures." He turned and walked out of the office. From outside, Bill heard a door slam. Noticing that his watch read 8:57, Bill sighed. He thought, at least it didn't take over a half hour. Lots of work to do today. (Bill picks up the computer printout.) It'll be nice to talk to these 13 reps. They know what sales and hard work are all about. (He shakes his head.) If only Jack had been able to open up …

Source: This case was prepared by Professor Brendan D. Bannister and Carol A. Pilo, Northeastern University. Copyright © 1984 by Brendan D. Bannister.

1. Describe Jack Adams's perception of Bill Squire, and Bill Squire's perception of Jack Adams. How do they differ from their own self-perceptions?

2. What are some of the reasons for Jack's and Bill's perceptions of each other? Are there any person perception biases that might have influenced their perceptions?

3. Describe Jack's and Bill's attributions regarding Jack's poor sales record. Why are they different, and is there evidence of any attribution biases? Using the three cues of consistency, consensus, and distinctiveness, what is the most likely attribution for Jack's poor sales record?

4. Explain how Jack's and Bill's perceptions and attributions influence their behaviour during the performance review and the outcome.

5. Refer to Bruner's model of the perceptual process to explain Jack's and Bill's perceptions before and after the performance review. Is there anything that either of them could have done to change their perceptions of each other during the review session?

6. Comment on Bill Squire's approach to conducting the performance review and the effect it had on his perceptions of Jack. If he had conducted the performance session differently, would it have changed his perceptions of Jack and the outcome? What should he have done?

7. What advice would you give Bill Squire?

Chapter 4

Values, Attitudes, and Work Behaviour

**Husky
Injection
Molding
Systems Ltd.**

HUSKY INJECTION MOLDING SYSTEMS LTD.
Ontario-based Husky Injection Molding Systems Ltd.
manufactures injection moulding equipment—
high-tech beasts resembling immense waffle irons
that pump out everything from yogurt containers
to car bumpers. More than 90% of its machinery
is exported to 80 countries, with some 3,600
Husky machines now operating globally. Husky
employs 3,000 people in 27 countries.

The company has been growing at 25% per annum for a decade, its sales
soaring from $72 million (U.S.) in 1985 to $700 million. Husky is on its way to
becoming one of the five companies dominating the injection-moulding machinery market and aims to achieve more than $1 billion a year in sales. Husky
alone is credited, in large measure, for Canada's shift from a trade deficit to a
surplus position in plastics machinery.

By now you may be wondering how Husky has achieved such a stellar record
of financial success. The answer is a strong value system that it lives consistently and brings to life in its buildings, its employees, and its products. At
Husky, treating people and the environment with respect is paramount, and
when it comes to labour-management relations, Husky is clearly no ordinary
company.

According to Husky president and founder Robert Schad, Husky is a company
with a conscience and one that is built on values. Those values are apparent
as soon as you arrive at Husky's 21.5-hectare headquarters and manufacturing
plant in Bolton, Ontario, just north of Toronto, where everything is spotlessly
clean and well lit. Manufacturing areas are bright and air-conditioned, and the
walls, even in washrooms, are adorned with framed nature paintings, photos,
or prints. Books on wildlife greet visitors in the waiting rooms. In the cafeterias,

President and founder Robert Schad of Husky Injection Molding Systems Ltd. has built an organization with strong values of environmental responsibility, health and humanity, and egalitarianism.

Husky Injection Molding
Systems Ltd
www.husky.on.ca/home.htm

World Wildlife Fund
www.wwf.org/

staff dine on organic, vegetarian meals, served hot and subsidized by the company. Herbal teas are free. Candy, doughnuts, and vending machines are nonexistent. The entire building is smoke free, and signs about nutrition are everywhere. In addition to the fitness centre, a medical doctor, nurse, naturopath, chiropractor, and massage therapist are on site most days, and employees receive a $500 annual benefit for vitamins. Husky nurtures the mind as well as the body, paying 100% of tuition and book costs for employees who attend university or college.

The firm's governing ethos is strict egalitarianism. Executives use the same parking lot, dining room, and washrooms as everyone else. No titles denoting position are posted. Offices for executives are small and spartan. Casual dress is de rigueur. Employees with children can bring them to Husky's 15,500-square-foot, $5-million child-care centre considered to be a model of contemporary day care.

In keeping with Husky's concern for environmental responsibility, it recycles 95% of its industrial, office, and food waste, uses electric rather than gas-powered fork lifts, and is moving to ammonia-cooled air-conditioning systems. In addition, 5% of after-tax company profits goes to charities and environmental causes, such as the World Wildlife Fund and the Canadian College of Naturopathic Medicine. Husky recently introduced a program that allows employees to earn company shares by helping the environment and community through activities such as walking to work, photocopying on both sides of the paper, and coaching a sports team.

Other benefits are less visible, but no less tangible, including Husky's profit-sharing and share-purchasing plans. About 25% of the shares are held by

Learning Objectives

After reading Chapter 4, you should be able to:

1 Define values and discuss the implications of cross-cultural variation in values for organizational behaviour.

2 Define attitudes and explain how people develop and change attitudes.

3 Explain the concept of job satisfaction and discuss some of its key contributors.

4 Discuss the roles of discrepancy, fairness, and disposition in promoting job satisfaction.

5 Outline the various consequences of job satisfaction and explain the relationship between job satisfaction and mental health, absenteeism, turnover, performance, and organizational citizenship behaviour.

6 Differentiate affective, continuance, and normative commitment and explain how organizations can foster commitment and the impact of changes in the workplace on employee commitment.

employees, and each Husky employee receives a bonus based on a percentage of the company's net earnings. Employee salaries are at the high end of the industry scale. Workers sit on five resource management teams that keep company expenditures under control. As well, a rotating employee council allows workers—from shop-floor machinists to accountants—to meet monthly with the president and voice concerns that are often acted on.

These benefits have allowed Husky to attract the best people and to keep them productive, happy, and proud of where they work. As well, Husky's emphasis on health and humanity pays concrete dividends. The rate of absenteeism is 2.4 days per year per employee; that compares with nine days elsewhere in the manufacturing sector. The company spends $153.70 per employee on drugs, versus the sectoral average of $495.02. There are also lower Workers' Compensation Board claims and more accident-free days. Husky even earns more than $800,000 a year recycling waste.

Husky recently exported its healthy habits and concern for the environment to rural Vermont, where it has built a new $80 million manufacturing plant. Speaking at the plant opening, Schad told the audience, "We don't want to build molds and machines, we want to build a company that's a role model for lasting business success based on our values." The Governor of the state of Vermont described it this way: "This is the most remarkable plant in the state of Vermont, and it may be the most remarkable plant in the United States...It's a corporate example of how to do business."[1]

Would you be happy working at Husky? This would probably be influenced by your values and attitudes, important topics that we will cover in this chapter. Our discussion of values will be particularly oriented toward cross-cultural variations in values and their implications for organizational behaviour. Our discussion of attitudes will cover attitude formation and change. Two critical attitudes are job satisfaction and organizational commitment. We will consider the causes and consequences of both.

What Are Values?

Values. A broad tendency to prefer certain states of affairs over others.

We might define **values** as "a broad tendency to prefer certain states of affairs over others."[2] The *preference* aspect of this definition means that values have to do with feelings and emotions, with what we consider good and bad. The feelings or emotions inherent in values are motivational, since they signal the attractive aspects of our environment that we should seek and the unattractive aspects that we should avoid or change. The words *broad tendency* in this definition mean that values are very general emotional orientations, and that they do not predict behaviour in specific situations very well. Knowing that a person generally embraces the values that support capitalism does not tell us much about how he or she will respond to a homeless person on the street this afternoon.

It is useful to classify values into several categories: intellectual, economic, aesthetic, social, political, and religious.[3] Not everyone holds the same values. Managers might value high productivity (an economic value), while union officials might be more concerned with enlightened supervision and full employment (social values). Husky holds stronger social and health values than the typical organization. We learn values through the reinforcement processes we discussed in Chapter 2. Most are socially reinforced by parents, teachers, and representatives of religions. In fact, our entire social system is designed to teach and reinforce the values deemed appropriate by our society.

To firm up your understanding of values and their impact on organizational behaviour, let us examine some occupational differences in values and see how work values differ across cultures.

Occupational Differences in Values

Members of different occupational groups espouse different values. A research program showed that university professors, city police officers, oil company salespeople, and entrepreneurs had values that distinguished them as groups from the general population.[4] For example, the professors valued "equal opportunity for all" more highly than the average American does. On the other hand, the salespeople and entrepreneurs ranked social values (peace, equality, freedom) lower than the average American does. Value differences such as these might be partially responsible for the occupational stereotypes that we discussed in Chapter 3. Further, these differences can cause conflict between organizations and within organizations when members of different occupations are required to interact with each other. For instance, doctors frequently report that their social values are at odds with the economic values of hospital administrators. In general, a good "fit" between the values of supervisors and subordinates promotes subordinate satisfaction and commitment.[5] There is also evidence that a good "fit" between an individual's values and the values of his/her organization (person-organization fit) also enhances job attitudes and behaviors.[6]

Do differences in occupational values develop after a person enters an occupation, or do such differences cause people to gravitate to certain occupations? Given the fact that values are relatively stable, and that many values are acquired early in life, it would appear that people choose occupations that correspond to their values.[7]

Values Across Cultures

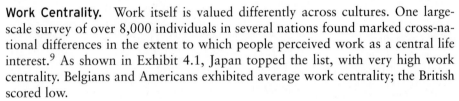

Ben & Jerry's
www.benjerry.com

It is by now a cliché to observe that business has become global in its scope—Ben & Jerry's goes to Russia; Japanese cars dot American roads; Mickey Mouse invades Japan and France; McDonald's opens in Moscow; Europe reduces internal trade barriers. All this activity obscures just how difficult it can be to forge business links across cultures. For example, research shows that anywhere from 16 to 40 percent of managers who receive foreign assignments terminate them early because they perform poorly or do not adjust to the culture.[8] Similarly, a lengthy history of failed business negotiations is attributable to a lack of understanding of cross-cultural differences. At the root of many of these problems might be a lack of appreciation of basic differences in work-related values across cultures. On the other hand, consider the opportunities for organizations that are globally adept (and for graduating students who are cross-culturally sensitive!).

Work Centrality. Work itself is valued differently across cultures. One large-scale survey of over 8,000 individuals in several nations found marked cross-national differences in the extent to which people perceived work as a central life interest.[9] As shown in Exhibit 4.1, Japan topped the list, with very high work centrality. Belgians and Americans exhibited average work centrality; the British scored low.

One question in the survey asked respondents whether they would continue working if they won a large amount of money in a lottery. As you might imagine, those with more central interest in work were more likely to report that they would continue working despite the new-found wealth.

The survey also found that people for whom work was a central life interest tended to work longer hours. This illustrates how cross-cultural differences in work centrality can lead to adjustment problems for foreign employees and managers. Imagine the unprepared British executive who is posted to Japan only to find that Japanese managers commonly work late and then socialize with co-workers or customers long into the night. In Japan, this is all part of the job, often to the chagrin of the lonely spouse. On the other hand, consider the

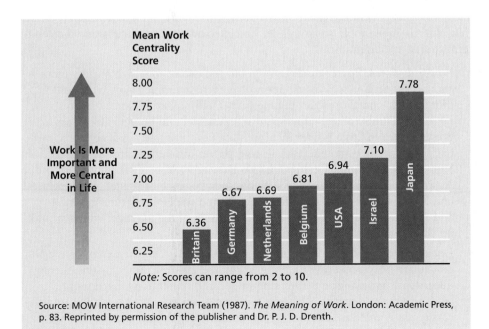

Note: Scores can range from 2 to 10.

Source: MOW International Research Team (1987). *The Meaning of Work.* London: Academic Press, p. 83. Reprinted by permission of the publisher and Dr. P. J. D. Drenth.

Exhibit 4.1
Work centrality across cultures.

In Japan, socializing with colleagues is often part of the job, reflecting the high centrality of work in Japanese values.

Japanese executive posted to Britain who finds out that an evening at the pub is *not* viewed as an extension of the day at the office and not a place to continue talking business.

Hofstede's Study. In one of the most ambitious survey programs ever, Dutch social scientist Geert Hofstede questioned over 116,000 IBM employees located in 40 countries about their work-related values.[10] (There were 20 different language versions of the questionnaire.) Virtually everyone in the corporation participated, from blue-collar workers to top executives. When Hofstede analyzed the results, he discovered four basic dimensions along which work-related values differed across cultures: power distance, uncertainty avoidance, masculinity/femininity, and individualism/collectivism. Subsequent work with Canadian Michael Bond that catered more to Eastern cultures resulted in a fifth dimension, the long-term/short-term orientation.[11]

Power distance. The extent to which an unequal distribution of power is accepted by society members.

- *Power distance.* **Power distance** refers to the extent to which society members accept an unequal distribution of power, including those who hold more power and those who hold less. In small power distance cultures, inequality is minimized, superiors are accessible, and power differences are downplayed. In large power distance societies, inequality is accepted as natural, superiors are inaccessible, and power differences are highlighted. Small power distance societies include Denmark, New Zealand, Israel, and Austria. Large power distance societies include the Philippines, Venezuela, and Mexico. Out of 40 societies, Canada and the United States rank 14 and 15, falling on the low power distance side of the average, which would be 20.

Uncertainty avoidance. The extent to which people are uncomfortable with uncertain and ambiguous situations.

- *Uncertainty avoidance.* **Uncertainty avoidance** refers to the extent to which people are uncomfortable with uncertain and ambiguous situations. Strong uncertainty avoidance cultures stress rules and regulations, hard work, conformity, and security. Cultures with weak uncertainty avoidance are less concerned with rules, conformity, and security, and hard work is not seen as a virtue. However, risk taking is valued. Strong uncertainty avoidance cultures include Japan, Greece, and Portugal. Weak uncertainty avoidance cultures include Singapore, Denmark, and Sweden. On uncertainty avoidance, the United States and Canada are well below average, ranking 9 and 10 out of 40.

■ *Masculinity/femininity.* More masculine cultures clearly differentiate gender roles, support the dominance of men, and stress economic performance. More feminine cultures accept fluid gender roles, stress sexual equality, and stress quality of life. In Hofstede's research, Japan is the most masculine society, followed by Austria, Mexico, and Venezuela. The Scandinavian countries are the most feminine. Canada ranks about mid-pack, and the United States is fairly masculine, falling about halfway between Canada and Japan.

■ *Individualism/collectivism.* More **individualistic** societies tend to stress independence, individual initiative, and privacy. More **collective** cultures favour interdependence and loyalty to one's family or clan. The United States, Australia, Great Britain, and Canada are among the most individualistic societies. Venezuela, Columbia, and Pakistan are among the most collective, with Japan falling about mid-pack.

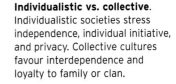

Individualistic vs. collective. Individualistic societies stress independence, individual initiative, and privacy. Collective cultures favour interdependence and loyalty to family or clan.

■ *Long-term/short-term orientation.* Cultures with a long-term orientation tend to stress persistence, perseverance, thrift, and close attention to status differences. Cultures with a short-term orientation stress personal steadiness and stability, face-saving, and social niceties. China, Hong Kong, Taiwan, Japan, and South Korea tend to be characterized by a long-term orientation. The United States, Canada, Great Britain, Zimbabwe, and Nigeria are more short-term oriented. Hofstede and Bond argue that the long-term orientation, in part, explains prolific East Asian entrepreneurship.

Exhibit 4.2 compares the United States, Canada, Mexico, Japan, and West Africa on Hofstede's value dimensions. Note that the profiles for Canada and the United States are very similar, but they differ considerably from that of Mexico. You might want to consider the implications of this for enhanced free trade among the three countries.

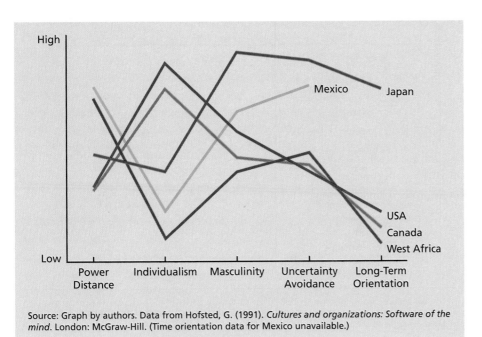

Exhibit 4.2
Cross-cultural value comparisons.

Source: Graph by authors. Data from Hofsted, G. (1991). *Cultures and organizations: Software of the mind.* London: McGraw-Hill. (Time orientation data for Mexico unavailable.)

Hofstede has produced a number of interesting "cultural maps" that show how countries and regions cluster together on pairs of cultural dimensions. The map in Exhibit 4.3 shows the relationship between power distance and degree of individualism. As you can see, these two values tend to be related. Cultures that are more individualistic tend to downplay power differences, while those that are more collectivistic tend to accentuate power differences.

Implications of Cultural Variation

Exporting OB Theories. An important message from the cross-cultural study of values is that organizational behaviour theories, research, and practices from North America might not translate well to other societies, even the one located just south of Texas.[12] The basic questions (How should I lead? How should we make this decision?) remain the same. It is just the *answers* that differ. For example, North American managers tend to encourage a moderate degree of participation in work decisions by subordinates. This corresponds to the fairly low degree of power distance valued here. Trying to translate this leadership style to

Exhibit 4.3
Power distance and individualism values for various countries and regions.

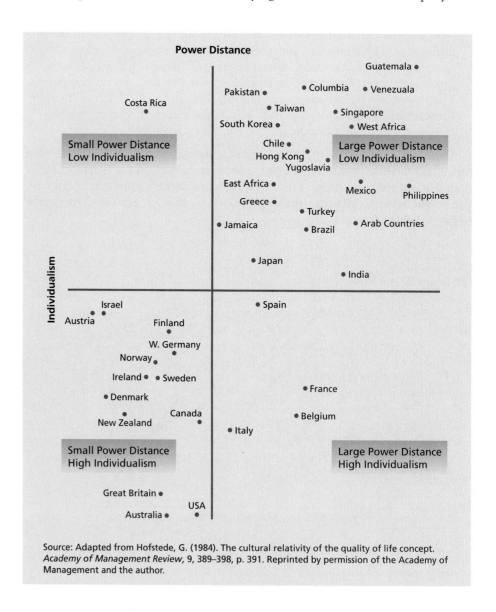

Source: Adapted from Hofstede, G. (1984). The cultural relativity of the quality of life concept. *Academy of Management Review*, 9, 389–398, p. 391. Reprinted by permission of the Academy of Management and the author.

cultures that value high power distance might prove unwise. In these cultures, people might be more comfortable deferring to the boss's decision. Thus, it is unlikely that Husky could translate their low power distance and egalitarianism style to all overseas locations. Similarly, in individualistic North America, calling attention to one's accomplishments is expected and often rewarded in organizations. In more collective Asian or South American cultures, individual success might be devalued, and it might make sense to reward groups rather than individuals. Finally, in extremely masculine cultures, integrating women into management positions might require special sensitivity and timing.

Successful firms have learned to blend the values of their headquarters' corporate culture with those of the host nation in overseas operations. In other words, they export an overall philosophy, while tailoring it to local customs and values. For example, U.S.-based National Semiconductor tends to stress very systematic technical decision making. The Israeli culture tends to be very informal and more collective than that in the United States. In its Israeli operations, the firm has developed a decision-making process that is systematic but team oriented and participative, meeting corporate needs but respecting local values.[13]

Importing OB Theories. Not all theories and practices that concern organizational behaviour are perfected in North America or even in the West. The most obvious examples are the "Japanese management" techniques, such as quality circles, total quality management, and just-in-time production. Although there are success stories of importing these techniques from Japan to North America, there are also numerous examples of difficulties and failure, especially in manufacturing firms. Many of the problems seem to stem from basic value differences between Japan and North America.

Although they are generally successful operations, the pace of work required has led to employee complaints in the plants of Mazda, Nissan, and Honda. Similarly, the quest for continuous improvement and the heavy reliance on employee suggestions for improvement has had a mixed reaction.[14] Leading American companies receive about two suggestions a year from each employee, while the Japanese operations of these auto makers receive between 39 (Nissan) and 127 (Mazda) per employee per year![15] In Japan, cultural values have traditionally dictated a fairly high degree of employment security. Thus, working at a fast pace and providing suggestions for improvement will not put one out of a job. American workers are uncertain about this.

Many of the Japanese-inspired means of organizing work are team oriented. Since Japan has fairly collective cultural values, submerging one's own interests in those of the team is natural. Although employers have successfully used teams in North America, as you will see in Chapter 7, our more individualistic culture would suggest that more careful selection of team members is necessary.

Understanding cultural value differences can enable organizations to successfully import management practices by tailoring the practice to the home culture's concerns. For example, the innovative General Motors Saturn plant in Spring Hill, Tennessee, (discussed in detail in Chapter 15) effectively guarantees lifetime employment to 80 percent of the workforce to ensure that its Japanese-inspired practices are palatable to American employees.

Appreciating Global Customers. An appreciation of cross-cultural differences in values is essential to understanding the needs and tastes of customers or clients around the world. Once relegated to the status of a marketing problem, it is now clear that such understanding fundamentally has to do with organizational behaviour. Errors occur with regularity. For instance, the initial French response to the Euro Disney theme park was less enthusiastic than Disney management

Samsung Electronics
www.samsungelectronics.com/
index.html

expected, probably due, in part, to a failure to truly appreciate French tastes in food, lifestyle, and organized entertainment. Samsung, South Korea's largest company, recalled a calendar featuring models displaying its products that was destined for overseas customers. Some Americans were offended by Miss July's see-through blouse.

Appreciating the values of global customers is also important when the customers enter your own culture. Many firms have profited from an understanding of the increasing ethnic diversity in the United States and Canada.

In this regard, pause for a moment and consider the You Be the Manager feature.

Developing Global Employees. Success in translating management practices to other cultures, importing practices developed elsewhere, and appreciating global customers are not things that happen by accident. Rather, companies need to select, train, and develop employees to have a much better appreciation of differences in cultural values and the implications of these differences for behaviour in organizations.

you be the manager

West Coast Builders and Realtors Cater to Asian Cultural Values

With the large number of Asian immigrants relocating to North America, companies have had to adapt cultural strategies to win in the fiercely competitive market.

Among the 19 Asian countries on the Pacific Rim, North America has been particularly enriched in recent years by newcomers from Hong Kong, Taiwan, Korea, the Philippines, Vietnam, and Japan. According to the Census Bureau, Asians comprise the fastest growing, best educated, and most affluent cultural group in the United States. Given its proximity and climate, the west coast of the United States and Canada has become an attractive location for immigrants from Asia. This influx has been especially advantageous to California's home builders and realtors, including Kathryn Thompson Development Company, Kaufman and Broad Home Corporation, and The William Lyon Company. In an era of recessionary

sales, Asians and Asian Americans comprise 30 to 40 percent of California's home buyers.

In a fiercely competitive market, home builders and realtors gradually realized that they were uncertain about Asian cultural values. For example, they were not used to the involvement of older family members (such as grandparents) in the buying process and the predilection of some Asian cultures to avoid certain unlucky colors and numbers (e.g., street addresses). Furthermore, they did not understand the Chinese concept of *feng shui* which dictates that a house design should follow certain principles to maintain harmony and good luck. Put yourself in the shoes of these builders and realtors. You realize that your construction firm can gain a competitive advantage by catering better to Asian clients. What would you do?

1. Design a plan to better inform your employees about Asian cultural values. Who should be involved?

2. What general lessons about the globalization of business are apparent from this case?

To find out what the California real estate firms did, see The Manager's Notebook at the end of the chapter.

Source: Adapted from Forsberg, M. (1993, May). Cultural training improves relations with Asian clients. *Personnel Journal*, pp. 79–89.

Gillette
www.gillette.com

Gillette is recognized as having one of the best of such programs. The firm produces razor blades, pens (PaperMate), and electrical appliances (Braun) in 28 countries and markets them in more than 200. Over 25 years, it has built a global management team by using a variety of tactics. These include the following:

- Hiring local people as managers outside the United States
- Finding key talent among overseas students studying in North American universities
- Moving managers to posts in other countries to sharpen their international exposure
- Rewarding managers with extensive international experience by putting them in charge of new international markets or joint ventures (such as one in China)
- Bringing groups of young international management trainees to one of three international headquarters (Boston, Singapore, or London) for 18 months of intensive development.[16]

Other firms use different techniques for developing an international perspective. To get their designers to better appreciate the values of the North American market, Japanese car makers, including Nissan and Toyota, have opened design studios in California. The top ranks of Detroit's automakers, once the bastion of mid-westerners, are now liberally filled with Europeans or those with European experience. This has led to improved overall performance and the development of cars that are more suitable for worldwide export. Korea's Samsung now sends about 400 of its most promising young employees overseas for a year to simply immerse themselves in the values of another culture (as one executive put it, "to goof off at the mall"). The company feels that this will pay long-term dividends in terms of international competition.[17]

As you proceed through the text, you will encounter further discussion about the impact of cultural values on organizational behaviour. Now, let us examine attitudes and see how they are related to values.

What Are Attitudes?

An **attitude** is a fairly stable emotional tendency to respond consistently to some specific object, situation, person, or category of people. First, notice that attitudes involve *emotions* directed toward *specific* targets. If I inquire about your attitude toward your boss, you will probably tell me something about how well you *like* him or her. This illustrates the emotional aspect of attitudes. Attitudes are also much more specific than values, which dictate only broad preferences. For example, you could value working quite highly but still dislike your specific job.

The definition states that attitudes are *relatively stable*. Under normal circumstances, if you truly dislike Mexican food or your boss today, you will probably dislike them tomorrow. Of course, some attitudes are less strongly held than others and are thus more open to change. If your negative attitude toward Mexican cuisine stems only from a couple of fast food experiences, I might be able to improve it greatly by exposing you to a home-cooked Mexican meal. This provides you with some new information.

Our definition indicates that attitudes are *tendencies to respond* to the target of the attitude. Thus, attitudes often influence our behaviour toward some object, situation, person, or group:

Attitude ⟶ Behaviour

Attitude. A fairly stable emotional tendency to respond consistently to some specific object, situation, person, or category of people.

This is hardly surprising. If you truly dislike Mexican food, I would not expect to see you eating it. By the same token, if you like your boss, it would not be surprising to hear you speaking well of him:

Dislike Mexican Food → Don't Eat Mexican Food

Like Boss → Praise Boss

Of course, not everyone who likes the boss goes around praising him in public for fear of being seen as too political. Similarly, people who dislike the boss do not always engage in public criticism for fear of retaliation. These examples indicate that attitudes are not always consistent with behaviour, and that attitudes provide useful information over and above the actions that we can observe.

Attitude Formation

Where do attitudes come from? Put simply, attitudes are a function of what we think and what we feel, that is, attitudes are the product of a related belief and value. If you believe that your boss is consultative, and you value consultation, we can conclude that you might have a favourable attitude toward the boss. We can represent this relationship in the form of a simple syllogism.[18] For example:

If the boss is consultative, (Belief)

And consultation is good, (Value)

Then the boss is good. (Attitude)

Given this point of view, we can now expand the attitude model presented earlier to include the thinking and feeling aspects of attitudes represented by beliefs and values:

BELIEF + VALUE ⇒ ATTITUDE → BEHAVIOUR

Thus, we can imagine the following sequence of ideas in the case of a person experiencing work-family conflict:

"My job is interfering with my family life." (Belief)

"I dislike anything that hurts my family." (Value)

"I dislike my job." (Attitude)

"I'll search for another job." (Behaviour)

In attempting to understand attitudes, it is important to distinguish between their belief components and their value components. For example, consider the manager of a manufacturing plant that is plagued by low-quality production. Working backward through our attitude model, the manager might assume that low quality is caused by "poor attitudes" toward quality on the part of the workforce. Are such "poor attitudes" likely to stem from the employees' values or their beliefs about quality? Either might be true. First, the workforce might *value* high quality but *believe* that it is impossible to achieve. Beliefs of this nature might include: "My performance depends on the performance of my work group. My equipment is unreliable." On the other hand, the workforce might *believe* that it can turn out high-quality work but not *value* high quality: "I value a lack of fatigue more than I value making a buck for the company. I value social interaction on the job more than I value attention to quality."

The kind of administrative action that might be necessary to change the workforce's attitudes toward quality depends on the accurate assessment of these beliefs and values. For example, if the beliefs listed above appear to limit quality, management will have to carefully explore the basis for these beliefs (Is equipment really unreliable?). On the other hand, if values appear to be the problem, a different intervention might be called for, such as attempting to hire workers whose value systems correspond more closely to the desired corporate culture.

Changing Attitudes

In our everyday lives, we frequently try to change other people's attitudes. By presenting ourselves in a favourable light (putting our best foot forward), we attempt to get others to develop favourable attitudes toward us. By arguing the case for some attitude we hold, we attempt to get others to embrace this attitude. Thus, it should not surprise us that organizations are also involved in the modification and management of attitudes. Some examples of cases in which management might desire attitude change include the following:

- Attitudes toward workforce diversity
- Attitudes toward ethical business practices
- Attitudes toward anticipated changes, such as the introduction of new technology or total quality management
- Attitudes toward safety practices and the use of safety equipment

Most attempts at attitude change are initiated by a communicator who tries to use persuasion of some form to modify the beliefs or values of an audience that supports a currently held attitude. For example, management might hold a seminar to persuade managers to value workforce diversity, or it might develop a training program to change attitudes toward workplace safety. Persuasion that is designed to modify or emphasize values is usually emotionally oriented. A safety message that concentrates on a dead worker's weeping, destitute family exemplifies this approach. Persuasion that is slanted toward modifying certain beliefs is usually rationally oriented. A safety message that tries to convince workers that hard-hats and safety glasses are not uncomfortable to wear reveals this angle. You have probably seen both these approaches used in AIDS and antismoking campaigns.

These examples represent the traditional approach to most organizational attitude-change programs, that is, they first try to change beliefs and/or values, in order to change attitudes and behaviour. This involves moving from left to right in our attitude model:

Changed Beliefs and/or Values ⟶

Changed Attitudes ⟶ Changed Behaviour

However, cognitive dissonance theory suggests an alternative approach. **Cognitive dissonance** refers to a feeling of tension experienced when certain cognitions are contradictory or inconsistent with each other (i.e., dissonant). Cognitions are simply thoughts or knowledge that people have about their own beliefs, values, attitudes, and behaviour. Therefore, would it be sensible to change a person's behaviour *first*, with the assumption that the person would realign his or her attitudes to support this behaviour? Dissonance theory suggests that engaging in behaviour that is not supported by our attitudes might indeed lead us to change our attitudes to reduce the tension produced by inconsistency. Researchers have observed such effects in studies where people had to role-play behaviours that were inconsistent with their attitudes.[19]

Arnold Goldstein and Melvin Sorcher argue that the traditional view of attitude change has not always proven effective in organizations (Exhibit 4.4).[20] They suggest that attempts to use persuasion to change beliefs and values often

Cognitive dissonance. A feeling of tension experienced when certain cognitions are contradictory or inconsistent with each other.

Exhibit 4.4
Models of attitude change.

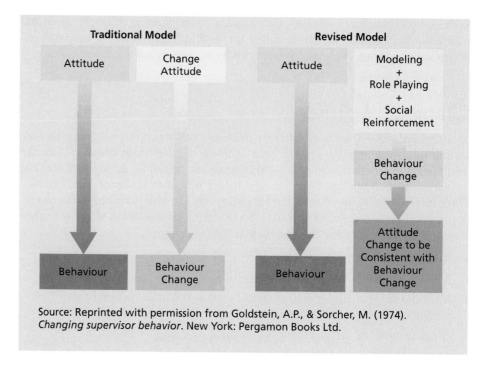

Source: Reprinted with permission from Goldstein, A.P., & Sorcher, M. (1974). *Changing supervisor behavior*. New York: Pergamon Books Ltd.

fail to lead to attitude change because the audience is unable to see how the new beliefs or values will be applicable to their on-the-job behaviour. For example, trainees might learn that people with various ethnic backgrounds have different styles of communication but not understand how to apply this knowledge to dealing with the different people on the job. To deal with this problem, Goldstein and Sorcher suggest that individuals should be taught specific *behaviours* they can apply on the job that correspond to the desired attitude change. When the trainees find these behaviours are successful in carrying out their daily activities, dissonance theory suggests that attitudes will change to correspond to the newly learned behaviours. To teach the new behaviours, Goldstein and Sorcher recommend three techniques:

- *Modeling of correct behaviours.* Videotapes are usually employed for this purpose.
- *Role-playing of correct behaviours by trainees.* In this phase, trainees get a chance to actually *practise* the desired behaviours.
- *Social reinforcement of role-played behaviours.* Trainers and fellow trainees provide reinforcement (usually praise) for correct role-playing performance.

The revised model of attitude change that Goldstein and Sorcher suggest is shown in the right portion of Exhibit 4.4. Organizations such as Agway, AT&T, IBM, and General Electric have applied these techniques with success. Experts recommend them highly for cross-cultural training programs because the trainees actually get a chance to practise social skills useful in other cultures.[21]

AT&T
www.att.com

What Is Job Satisfaction?

Job satisfaction. A collection of attitudes that workers have about their jobs.

Job satisfaction refers to a collection of attitudes that workers have about their jobs. We can differentiate at least two aspects of satisfaction. The first of these is facet satisfaction, the tendency for an employee to be more or less satisfied with various facets of the job. The notion of facet satisfaction is especially obvious when we hear someone say, "I love my work but hate my boss" or "This place pays lousy, but the people I work with are great." Both these statements represent different attitudes toward separate facets of the speakers' jobs. Research suggests that the most relevant attitudes toward jobs are contained in a rather small group of facets: the work itself, pay, promotions, recognition, benefits, working conditions, supervision, co-workers, and organizational policy.[22]

In addition to facet satisfaction, we can also conceive of overall satisfaction, an overall or summary, indicator of a person's attitude toward his or her job that cuts across the various facets.[23] The statement, "On the whole, I really like my job, although a couple of aspects could stand some improvement," is indicative of the nature of overall satisfaction. In a sense, overall satisfaction is an average or total of the attitudes individuals hold toward various facets of the job. Thus, two workers might express the same level of overall satisfaction for different reasons. Specifically, they would have offsetting attitudes toward various facets of the job.

The most popular measure of job satisfaction is the *Job Descriptive Index* (JDI).[24] This questionnaire is designed around five facets of satisfaction. Employees are asked to respond "yes," "no," or "?" (cannot decide) in describing whether a particular word or phrase is descriptive of particular facets of their jobs. Exhibit 4.5 shows some sample JDI items under each facet, scored in the "satisfied" direction. A scoring system is available to provide an index of satisfaction for each facet. In addition, an overall measure of satisfaction can be calculated by adding the separate facet indexes.

Another carefully constructed measure of satisfaction, using a somewhat different set of facets, is the *Minnesota Satisfaction Questionnaire* (MSQ).[25] On this measure, respondents indicate how happy they are with various aspects of their job on a scale ranging from "very satisfied" to "very dissatisfied." Sample items from the short form of the MSQ include:

- The competence of my supervisor in making decisions
- The way my job provides for steady employment
- The chance to do things for other people
- My pay and the amount of work I do

Work
- N Routine
- Y Creative
- N Tiresome
- Y Gives sense of accomplishment

People
- Y Stimulating
- Y Ambitious
- N Talk too much
- N Hard to meet

Promotions
- Y Good opportunity for advancement
- Y Promotion on ability
- N Dead-end job
- N Unfair promotion policy

Supervision
- Y Asks my advice
- Y Praises good work
- N Doesn't supervise enough
- Y Tells me where I stand

Pay
- Y Income adequate for normal expenses
- N Bad
- N Less than I deserve
- Y Highly paid

Exhibit 4.5
Sample items from the Job Descriptive Index with "satisfied" responses.

Source: The Job Descriptive Index, revised 1985, is copyrighted by Bowling Green State University. The complete forms, scoring key, instructions, and norms can be obtained from the Department of Psychology, Bowling Green State University, Bowling Green, Ohio, 43404. Reprinted with permission.

global focus→))   Unhappy in Japan

Those vaunted workers who powered Japan Inc.'s postwar economic miracle have grown alienated and burnt out, according to Chicago-based International Survey Research (ISR). Only 44% of 8,600 Japanese respondents answered favourably recently when ISR asked: " Taking everything into account, how satisfied are you with your company as an employer?"

The surprisingly downbeat reaction thrust Japan to the bottom of the industrialized world's morale heap. Workers in the United States, Britain, Switzerland, Canada, Mexico, and Germany all responded more positively. Details are grim: A mere 33% of Japanese workers judge their companies well managed, down from 45% in 1985. About six out of ten believe their work is not fairly evaluated, and only 37% think they are equitably paid.

John Stanek, CEO of the research firm, believes that the disenchantment is a "textbook example of a broken contract." Japanese workers have long endured horrendous commutes, endless hours, and miserable working conditions in return for guarantees of life-long work. But when their country's economy tanked in the 1990s, the government, unions, and companies failed to deploy a safety net to protect the vulnerable workforce.

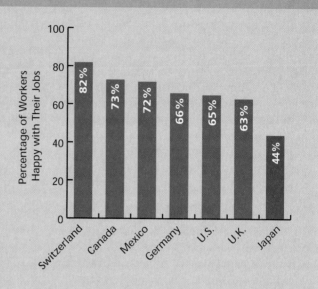

When asked if they liked their jobs, Japan's workers were found to be the grumpiest in the developed world.

Excerpted from Grant, L. (1997, January 13). Unhappy in Japan. *Fortune*, p.142.

Scoring the responses to these items provides an index of overall satisfaction as well as satisfaction on the facets on which the MSQ is based.

A number of firms, including Sears, Marriott, and Maryland's Preston Trucking, make extensive use of employee attitude surveys. We will cover the details of such surveys in Chapter 10 when we explore communication and in Chapter 16 when we cover organizational change and development. For now, consider the job satisfaction of employees around the world in "Global Focus: *Unhappy in Japan.*"

What Determines Job Satisfaction?

When workers on a variety of jobs complete the JDI or the MSQ, we often find differences in the average scores across jobs. Of course, we could almost expect such differences. The various jobs might differ objectively in the facets that contribute to satisfaction. Thus, you would not be astonished to learn that a corporate vice-president was more satisfied with her job than a janitor in the same company. Of greater interest is the fact that we frequently find decided differences in job satisfaction expressed by individuals performing the same job in a given organization. For example, two nurses who work side by side might indicate radically different satisfaction in response to the MSQ item "The chance to do things for other people." How does this happen?

Discrepancy

You will recall that attitudes, such as job satisfaction, are the product of associated beliefs and values. It would appear that these two factors operate to cause differences in job satisfaction even when jobs are identical. First, workers might differ in their beliefs about the job in question, that is, they might differ in their *perceptions* concerning the actual nature of the job. For example, one of the nurses might perceive that most of her working time is devoted to direct patient care, while the other might perceive that most of her time is spent on administrative functions. To the extent that they both value patient care, the former nurse should be more satisfied with this aspect of the job than the latter nurse. Second, even if individuals perceive their jobs as equivalent, they might differ in what they *want* from the jobs. Such desires are preferences that are dictated, in part, by the workers' value systems. Thus, if the two nurses perceive their opportunities to engage in direct patient care as high, the one who values this activity more will be more satisfied with the patient care aspect of work. The **discrepancy theory** of job satisfaction asserts that satisfaction is a function of the discrepancy between the job outcomes people want and the outcomes that they perceive they obtain.[26] The individual who desires a job entailing interaction with the public but who is required to sit alone in an office should be dissatisfied with this aspect of the job. In general, employees who have more of their job-related desires met will report more overall job satisfaction.

Discrepancy theory. A theory that job satisfaction stems from the discrepancy between the job outcomes wanted and the outcomes that are perceived to be obtained.

Fairness

In addition to the discrepancy between the outcomes people receive and those they desire, the other factor that determines job satisfaction is fairness. Issues of fairness affect both what people want from their jobs and how they react to the inevitable discrepancies of organizational life. As we will see, there are two basic kinds of fairness. Distributive fairness has to do with the outcomes we receive, and procedural fairness concerns the process that led to those outcomes.

Distributive Fairness. **Distributive fairness** (often called distributive justice) occurs when people receive what they think they deserve from their jobs, that is, it involves the ultimate *distribution* of work rewards and resources. Above, we indicated that what people want from their jobs is a partial function of their value systems. In fact, however, there are practical limitations to this notion. You might value money and the luxurious lifestyle that it can buy very highly, but this does not suggest that you expect to receive a salary of $200,000 a year. In the case of many job facets, individuals want "what's fair." And how do we develop our conception of what is fair? **Equity theory** states that the inputs that people perceive themselves as investing in a job and the outcomes that the job provides are compared against the inputs and outcomes of some other relevant person or group.[27] Equity will be perceived when the following distribution ratios exist:

Distributive fairness. Fairness that occurs when people receive what they think they deserve from their jobs.

$$\frac{\text{My outcomes}}{\text{My inputs}} = \frac{\text{Other's outcomes}}{\text{Other's inputs}}$$

Equity theory. A theory that job satisfaction stems from a comparison of the inputs one invests in a job and the outcomes one receives in comparison with the inputs and outcomes of another person or group.

In these ratios, **inputs** consist of anything that individuals consider relevant to their exchange with the organization, anything that they give up, offer, or trade to their organization. These might include factors such as education, training, seniority, hard work, and high-quality work. **Outcomes** are those factors that the organization distributes to employees in return for their inputs. The most relevant outcomes are represented by the job facets we discussed earlier—pay, promotions, supervision, the nature of the work, and so on. The "other" in the ratio

Inputs. Anything that people give up, offer, or trade to their organization in exchange for outcomes.

Outcomes. Factors that an organization distributes to employees in exchange for their inputs.

above might be a co-worker performing the same job, a number of co-workers, or even one's conception of all the individuals in one's occupation.[28] For example, the president of the Ford Motor Company probably compares his outcome/input ratio with those that he assumes exist for the presidents of General Motors and DaimlerChrysler. You probably compare your outcome/input ratio in your organizational behaviour class with that of one or more fellow students.

Equity theory has important implications for job satisfaction. First, inequity itself is a dissatisfying state of affairs, especially when we ourselves are on the "short end of the stick." For example, suppose you see the hours spent studying as your main input to your organizational behaviour class and the final grade as an important outcome. Imagine that a friend in the class is your comparison person. Under these conditions, the following situations appear equitable and should not provoke dissatisfaction on your part:

$$\frac{\textbf{You}}{\text{C grade}}{50 \text{ hours}} \quad \frac{\textbf{Friend}}{\text{A grade}}{100 \text{ hours}} \quad \text{or} \quad \frac{\textbf{You}}{\text{A grade}}{60 \text{ hours}} \quad \frac{\textbf{Friend}}{\text{C grade}}{30 \text{ hours}}$$

In each of these cases, a "fair" relationship seems to exist between study time and grades distributed. Now consider the following relationships:

$$\frac{\textbf{You}}{\text{C grade}}{100 \text{ hours}} \quad \frac{\textbf{Friend}}{\text{A grade}}{50 \text{ hours}} \quad \text{or} \quad \frac{\textbf{You}}{\text{A grade}}{30 \text{ hours}} \quad \frac{\textbf{Friend}}{\text{C grade}}{60 \text{ hours}}$$

In each of these situations, an unfair connection appears to exist between study time and grades received, and you should perceive inequity. However, the situation on the left, in which you put in more work for a lower grade, should be most likely to prompt dissatisfaction. This is a "short end of the stick" situation. Conditions such as this often lead to dissatisfaction in organizational life. For example, the employee who frequently remains on the job after regular hours (input) and receives no special praise or extra pay (outcome) might perceive inequity and feel dissatisfied. Similarly, the teacher who obtains a Master's degree (input) and receives no extra compensation (outcome) might react the same way if others have been rewarded for achieving extra education. Equity considerations also have an indirect effect on job satisfaction by influencing what people want from their jobs. If you study 100 hours while the rest of the students average 50 hours, you will expect a higher grade than the class average.

In summary, the equitable distribution of work outcomes contributes to job satisfaction by providing for feelings of distributive fairness. However, let us remember our earlier discussion of cross-cultural differences in values. The equity concept suggests that outcomes should be tied to individual contributions or inputs. This corresponds well with the individualistic North American culture. In more collective cultures, *equality* of outcomes might produce more feeling of distributive fairness. In more feminine cultures, allocating outcomes according to *need* (rather than performance) might provide for distributive fairness.

Procedural fairness. Fairness that occurs when the process used to determine work outcomes is seen as reasonable.

Procedural Fairness. **Procedural fairness** (often called procedural justice) occurs when individuals see the process used to determine outcomes as reasonable, that is, rather than involving the actual distribution of resources or rewards, it is concerned with how these outcomes are decided and allocated. An example will illustrate the difference between distributive and procedural fairness. Out of the blue, Greg's boss tells him that she has completed his performance evaluation and that he will receive a healthy pay raise starting next month. Greg has been working very hard, and he is pleased with the pay raise (distributive fairness). However, he is vaguely unhappy about the fact that all this occurred without his participation. Where he used to work, the employee and the boss would complete independent performance evaluation forms and then sit down and discuss their differences. This provided good feedback for the employee. Greg wonders how his peers who got less generous raises are reacting to the boss's style.

Procedural fairness is particularly relevant to outcomes such as performance evaluations, pay raises, promotions, layoffs, and work assignments. In allocating such outcomes, the following factors contribute to perceptions of procedural fairness.[29] The allocator

- gives adequate reasons for the decisions she takes;
- follows consistent procedures over time and across people;
- uses accurate information and appears unbiased;
- allows two-way communication during the allocation process; and
- welcomes appeals of the procedure or allocation.

As you might imagine, procedural fairness seems especially likely to provoke dissatisfaction when people also see distributive fairness as being low.[30] One view notes that dissatisfaction will be "maximized when people believe that they *would* have obtained better outcomes if the decision maker had used other procedures that *should* have been implemented."[31] (Students who receive lower grades than their friends will recognize the wisdom of this observation!) Thus, Greg, mentioned above, will probably not react too badly to the lack of consultation, while his peers who did not receive large raises might strongly resent the process that the boss used.

Disposition

Could your personality contribute to your feelings of job satisfaction? This is the essential question guiding recent research on the relationship between disposition and job satisfaction. Underlying the previous discussion is the obvious implication that job satisfaction can be increased by changing the work environment to increase fairness and decrease the discrepancy between what an individual wants and what the job offers. Underlying the dispositional view of job satisfaction is the idea that some people are *predisposed* by virtue of their personalities to be more or less satisfied despite changes in discrepancy or fairness.

Some of the research that suggests disposition contributes to job satisfaction is fascinating. Although each of these studies has some problems, as a group they point to a missing dispositional link.[32] For example:

- Identical twins raised apart from early childhood tend to have similar levels of job satisfaction.
- Job satisfaction tends to be fairly stable over time, even when changes in employer occur.
- Disposition measured early in adolescence is correlated with one's job satisfaction as a mature adult.

Taken together, these findings suggest that some personality characteristics originating in genetics or early learning contribute to adult job satisfaction.

Recent research on disposition and job satisfaction has centred around a couple of personality traits. One of these is the general tendency for a person to respond negatively or positively to the environment. The other concerns the dysfunctional thought process that characterizes depression—thoughts that one must be perfect, and that one depends on others for feelings of self-worth. Research shows that negativity and such dysfunctional thought processes threaten people's feeling of well being and provoke job dissatisfaction.[33]

Optimists with more realistic thinking processes are more likely to be satisfied. Research also shows that people who are intrinsically more positive are better decision makers and have better interpersonal skills.[34]

Exhibit 4.6 summarizes what research has to say about the determinants of job satisfaction. To recapitulate, satisfaction is a function of certain dispositional factors and the discrepancy between the job outcomes a person wants and the outcomes that a person perceives she has received. More specifically, people experience greater satisfaction when they meet or exceed the job outcomes they want; perceive the job outcomes they receive as equitable compared with those others receive; and believe that fair procedures determine job outcomes. The outcomes that people want from a job are a function of their personal value systems, moderated by equity considerations. The outcomes that people perceive themselves as receiving from the job represent their beliefs about the nature of that job. Again, we see that job satisfaction represents a set of attitudes about the job stemming from the beliefs and values of the person.

Key Contributors to Job Satisfaction

From what we have said thus far, you might expect that job satisfaction is a highly personal experience. While this is essentially true, we can make some general statements about the facets that seem to contribute the most to feelings of job satisfaction for most North American workers. These include mentally challenging work, high pay, promotions, and friendly or helpful colleagues.[35]

Mentally Challenging Work. This is work that tests employees' skills and abilities and allows them to set their own working pace. Employees usually perceive such work as personally involving and important. It also provides the worker with clear feedback regarding performance. Of course, some types of work can be too challenging, and this can result in feelings of failure and reduced satisfaction. In addition, some employees seem to prefer repetitive, unchallenging work that makes few demands on them.

High Pay. It should not surprise you that pay and satisfaction are positively related. Employee job satisfaction at Husky is probably partly due to industry high salaries as well as bonuses received as part of the company's profit-sharing plan. However, not everyone is equally desirous of money, and some people are cer-

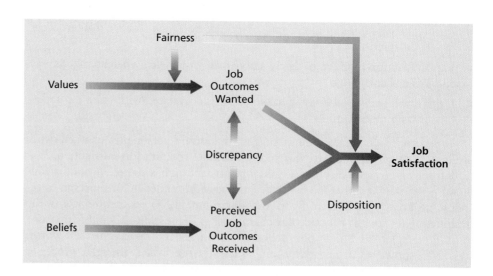

Exhibit 4.6
How discrepancy, fairness, and disposition affect job satisfaction.

tainly willing to accept less responsibility or fewer working hours for lower pay. Individual differences in preferences for pay are especially obvious in the case of reactions to overtime work. In most companies, one finds a group of employees who are especially anxious to earn extra money through overtime and another group that actively avoids overtime work.

Promotions. The ready availability of promotions that management administers according to a fair system contributes to job satisfaction. Ample opportunity for promotion is an important contributor to job satisfaction because promotions contain a number of valued signals about a person's self-worth. Some of these signals may be material (such as an accompanying raise), while others are of a social nature (recognition within the organization and increased prestige in the community). Of course, there are cultural and individual differences in what people see as constituting a fair promotion system. Some employees might prefer a strict seniority system, while others might wish for a system based strictly on job performance. Many of today's flatter, "downsized" organizations no longer offer the promotion opportunities of the past. Well-run firms have offset this by designing lateral moves that provide for challenging work.

People. It should not surprise you that friendly, considerate, good-natured superiors and co-workers contribute to job satisfaction. There is, however, another aspect to interpersonal relationships on the job that contributes to job satisfaction. Specifically, we tend to be satisfied in the presence of people who help us attain job outcomes that we value. Such outcomes might include doing our work better or more easily, obtaining a raise or promotion, or even staying alive. For example, a company of soldiers in battle might be less concerned with how friendly their commanding officer is than with how competently he is able to act to keep them from being overrun by the enemy. Similarly, an aggressive young executive might like a considerate boss but prefer even more a boss who can clarify her work objectives and reward her for attaining them. The friendliness aspect of interpersonal relationships seems most important in lower-level jobs with clear duties and various dead-end jobs. As jobs become more complex, pay is tied to performance, or promotion opportunities increase, the ability of others to help us do our work well contributes more to job satisfaction.

Consequences of Job Satisfaction

If you have to spend eight hours a day five days a week on the job, it would obviously be worthwhile for you to have favourable attitudes toward that job. Thus, job satisfaction is an attitude worthy of interest in and of itself. However, job satisfaction also has important personal and organizational consequences beyond mere happiness with the job. Xerox, Levi Strauss, and Michigan office equipment maker Steelcase are firms that have maintained a competitive advantage by paying particular attention to employee satisfaction. Lately, Sears has also been paying attention to employee satisfaction and its relation to customer satisfaction. (See "In Focus: *Employee Satisfaction Means Customer Satisfaction and Profits at Sears.*")

Levi Strauss & Co.
www.levistrauss.com

Mental Health and Off-the-Job Satisfaction

Can your job drive you crazy? Phrased more formally, can job dissatisfaction promote psychological disturbance? It would appear that more satisfied workers do tend to be psychologically healthier.[36] In addition, positive attitudes toward one's job are often associated with positive attitudes toward one's life in general,[37] that is, satisfied workers tend to report satisfaction with various nonwork aspects of their lives. Of course, the actual causality in these findings can be ambiguous. For example, an individual could become psychologically disturbed because of off-the-job factors and *then* encounter problems on the job due to this disturbance, leading to dissatisfaction. However, to the extent that job satisfaction does contribute to mental health and general life satisfaction, this probably happens because of self-esteem; that is, people feel a sense of accomplishment and worth in performing a satisfying job, and this feeling spills over into their off-job life.

Absence from Work

At Husky Injection Molding Systems, the rate of absenteeism is much lower than at other organizations. This is no small feat, as absenteeism is an expensive behaviour in North America. One estimate pegs the annual American cost up to $46 billion and the Canadian cost up to $10 billion and on the rise.[38] Such costs are attributable to "sick" pay, lost productivity, and chronic overstaffing to compensate for absentees. Many more days are lost to absenteeism than to strikes and other industrial disputes. Is some of this absenteeism the product of job dissatisfaction? The research literature is fairly firm.[39] From it, we can draw the following conclusions.

---

in focus → Employee Satisfaction Means Customer Satisfaction and Profits at Sears

As part of their organizational transformation plan, Sears theorized that things like employee attitudes and whether customers see their stores as fun places to shop were directly linked to financial performance. This led to the development of a business model that would track success in many areas, including management behaviour, employee attitudes, customer satisfaction, and financial performance.

To track and measure the outcomes of the business model, they developed a highly effective and world-class index called the employee-customer-profit model. It comprises six measurements: one measure for a compelling place to work, two for a compelling place to shop, and three for a compelling place to invest. By means of an ongoing process of data collection, analysis, modeling, and experimentation, the Total Performance Indicators (TPI) show Sears how well it is doing with customers, employees, and investors.

In an elaborate 800-store study of employee attitudes recently conducted by Sears, researchers found there is a direct correlation between employee satisfaction and profitability.

Stores with higher satisfaction scores perform better financially than those with lower scores.

Sears found that if positive employee attitudes on 10 essential factors—including workload, treatment by bosses, and so forth—increase by 5 percent, then customer satisfaction will jump 1.3 percent, leading to a 0.5 percentage-point rise in revenue.

Sears' customer satisfaction ratings began creeping upward in 1993, measured against their leading competitors. A *Fortune* magazine survey published in February 1997 showed Sears' customer satisfaction jumped 5.6 percent from 1995 to 1996, more than twice as much as any other retailer surveyed. In 1996 and 1997, its customer satisfaction scores rose two more percentage points, placing it at parity with its target competition.

Employee satisfaction scores also increased during that period. The employee satisfaction score is now 69.5 and has risen 1.5 percent in the past year and a half alone. In addition, the company's turnover rate has plummeted from 100 percent to 66 percent—the bulk of the turnover being in the part-time hourly ranks. For salaried personnel, turnover is about 20 percent.

For Sears—with annual revenues of approximately $44 billion—these improvements in attitudes amount to more than $200 million in additional revenues for the company each year!

Source: Excerpted from Laabs, J. (1999, March). The HR side of Sears' comeback. *Workforce*, 78(3), pp. 24-29.

- Speaking generally, the association between job satisfaction and absenteeism is fairly small.

- The satisfaction facet that is the best predictor of absenteeism is the content of the work itself.

- Job satisfaction is a better predictor of how *often* employees are absent rather than how many *days* they are absent. In other words, it is associated more with frequency of absenteeism than with time lost.

Why is the relationship between absenteeism and job satisfaction not stronger? Several factors probably constrain the ability of many people to convert their like or dislike of work into corresponding attendance patterns.

- Some absence is simply unavoidable because of illness, weather conditions, or day-care problems. Thus, some very happy employees will occasionally be absent owing to circumstances beyond their control.

- Opportunities for off-the-job satisfaction on a missed day may vary. Thus, you might love your job but love skiing or sailing even more. In this case, you might skip work while a dissatisfied person who has nothing better to do shows up.

- Some organizations have attendance control policies that can influence absence more than satisfaction does. In a company that refuses to pay workers for missed days (typical of many hourly paid situations), absence may be more related to economic needs than to dissatisfaction. The unhappy worker who absolutely needs money will probably show up for work. By the same token, dissatisfied and satisfied workers might be equally responsive to threats of dismissal if they are absent.

- On many jobs, it might be unclear to employees how much absenteeism is reasonable or sensible. With a lack of company guidelines, workers might look to the behaviour of their peers for a norm to guide their behaviour. This norm and its corresponding "absence culture" might have a stronger effect than the individual employee's satisfaction with his or her job.[40]

Research regarding the connection between job satisfaction and absence has some interesting implications for managing absenteeism. For one thing, general increases in job satisfaction will probably have little effect on absence levels, unless this satisfaction stems mainly from a revision in job content (a topic that we will consider in Chapter 6). In addition, a high frequency of short-term absence spells is probably a better indicator of an "attitude problem" than a few long spells of time lost. The latter pattern is more likely to reflect medical problems or family demands than job dissatisfaction.

Turnover

Turnover refers to resignation from an organization, and it can be incredibly expensive. For example, it costs several thousand dollars to replace a nurse or a bank teller who resigns. As we move up the organizational hierarchy, or into technologically complex jobs, such costs escalate dramatically. For example, it costs millions of dollars to hire and train a single military fighter pilot. Estimates of turnover costs usually include the price of hiring, training, and developing to proficiency a replacement employee. Such figures probably underestimate the true costs of turnover, however, because they do not include intangible costs, such as work group disruption or the loss of employees who informally acquire special skills and knowledge over time on a job. All this would not be so bad if turnover were concentrated among poorer performers. Unfortunately, this is not always the case. In one study, 23 percent of scientists and engineers who left an organization were among the top 10 percent of performers.[41]

What is the relationship between job satisfaction and turnover? Research indicates a moderately strong connection,[42] that is, less-satisfied workers are more likely to quit. Thus, it is not surprising that Husky has a low turnover rate. However, the relationship between the attitude (job satisfaction) and the behaviour in question (turnover) is far from perfect. This is because a number of steps intervene between being dissatisfied and actually leaving (Exhibit 4.7). At each of these steps, the dissatisfied individual might decide that it is too much trouble to proceed further or that resignation would be an unwise move. A few comments on some of the steps that we see in the model in Exhibit 4.7 are appropriate.[43]

Step 2: Certain individuals might be highly dissatisfied with their jobs but do not even think of quitting. Bad experiences with previous job searches or a poor self-image might not even permit *fantasies* about quitting.

Step 3: One key factor affecting this step is the labour market situation.[44] Under conditions of high unemployment, the dissatisfied worker might evaluate the chances of finding another decent job at nearly zero. The cost of quitting also receives serious consideration here. You might hate your job but have to remain in it because it provides excellent health benefits for your family.

Step 7: It is probably safe to assume that comparisons of alternative jobs with one's present job involve equity considerations, that is, the job seeker compares the inputs and outcomes of his or her present job with those that are anticipated on alternative jobs. If the comparison favours the alternative, the person will intend to resign.

Step 8: Substantial research indicates that stated intentions to quit are better predictors of turnover than is job satisfaction.[45] Intentions to quit are "closer" to an actual behaviour—quitting—than is job satisfaction. Such intentions take into account a number of factors that do not influence satisfaction, and they represent very specific attitudes about *quitting* rather than more general attitudes about the job.

Performance

For many years, the literature targeted at practising managers was filled with articles extolling the virtues of the human relations approach. In a nutshell, this ap-

Exhibit 4.7
Decision process between job dissatisfaction and turnover.

1. Job dissatisfaction experienced

2. Think of quitting

3. Evaluation of expected usefulness of searching for new job and cost of quitting

4. Intention to search for alternatives

5. Search for alternatives

6. Evaluation of alternatives

7. Comparison of alternatives vs. present job

8. Intention to quit or stay

9. Quit or stay

Source: From Mobley, W. H. (1977, April). Intermediate linkages in the relationship between job satisfaction and employee turnover. *Journal of Applied Psychology*, 62(2). Copyright 1977 by the American Psychological Association. Adapted by permission of the author.

proach suggested that considerate, humane supervision and expressing interest in the personal needs of employees were useful ways to manage. Such a management style was not advocated on sheer humanitarian grounds, however. Each article usually indicated that such a style would pay off with increased performance on the part of the work force. Thus, good human relations were seen as a good motivational strategy:

Good Human Relations → Job Satisfaction → Performance

That is, the literature assumed that good human relations would lead to job satisfaction, and that satisfaction would, in turn, stimulate high performance. In discussing the causes of job satisfaction, we have pointed out that certain human relations practices do lead to increased satisfaction. But, does high satisfaction (however achieved) lead to high performance? Formally stated, this viewpoint is called the **"satisfaction causes performance" hypothesis.**

From the quiz in Chapter 1, you will recall that satisfied workers are not generally much more productive than dissatisfied workers. In fact, a large body of research shows that the relationship between satisfaction and performance is positive but usually very low and often inconsistent.[46] Why is this correlation between job attitudes and job behaviour so low? Intuition suggests that we might work harder to pay back the organization for a satisfying job. However, intuition also suggests that we might be so busy enjoying our satisfying job that we have little *time* to be productive. For example, satisfying co-workers and a pleasant superior might lead us to devote more time to social interactions than to work. These contradictory intuitions provoke suspicion that the "satisfaction causes performance" hypothesis might be incorrect.

In recent years, the "satisfaction causes performance" hypothesis has been replaced by the so-called **"performance causes satisfaction" hypothesis,** which asserts that it is high performance that leads to high satisfaction.[47] On the face of it, this viewpoint seems rather curious. How does performance lead to satisfaction? Specifically, performance would seem to lead to satisfaction when the performance is *followed by rewards*, that is:

Performance → Rewards → Job Satisfaction

For example, if you study hard for a midterm exam and are rewarded with a good grade, you should be satisfied with at least some aspects of the course. In this case, your performance would be related to your satisfaction because the performance was rewarded. Similarly, if a supermarket manager increases his store's sales by 30 percent (performance) and is then promoted to district manager (reward), this should increase his job satisfaction. Again, in cases like this, performance and satisfaction should be fairly closely related.

Now for a final crucial question: If performance does cause satisfaction, why do so many studies show a very low relationship between the two variables? Put very simply, many organizations do not do a very good job of tying rewards to performance. In many cases, especially high productivity is not followed by a promotion, extra pay, or assignment to a more interesting task. For example, you have probably experienced doing what you thought was a good job in a course only to receive a mediocre grade. It is doubtful that such an outcome will cause you to be happy with the course. In summary, simply increasing employees' satisfaction should not cause them to perform better.

Organizational Citizenship Behaviour

Despite the authors' best efforts in the previous section, you might well be saying to yourself, "Wait a minute. Somehow, some way, job satisfaction has to have some impact on the extent to which employees will 'go the extra mile' or the

"Satisfaction causes performance" hypothesis. An assumption that high job satisfaction leads to high job performance.

"Performance causes satisfaction" hypothesis. An assumption that high job performance leads to high job satisfaction.

When one worker voluntarily helps out another, it is an example of organizational citizenship, which positively affects organizational effectiveness.

Organizational citizenship behaviour. Voluntary, informal behaviour that contributes to organizational effectiveness.

extent to which they'll cooperate to get the job done." In fact, you could be correct. Recent theory and research suggest that although job satisfaction is not closely related to formal performance measures, it is more strongly related to the informal "citizenship" aspects of organizational membership.[48] **Organizational citizenship behaviour** (OCB) is voluntary, informal behaviour that contributes to organizational effectiveness.[49] In many cases, the formal performance evaluation system does not detect and reward it.

An example of OCB should clarify the concept. You are struggling to master a particularly difficult piece of software and making the attendant noises of discouragement. A colleague at the next desk, busy on her own rush job, comes over and offers assistance. Irritated with the software, you are not even very grateful at first, but within 10 minutes you have solved the problem with her help. Notice the defining characteristics of this example of OCB:

- The behaviour is voluntary. It is not included in her job description.
- The behaviour is spontaneous. Someone did not order or suggest it.
- The behaviour contributes to organizational effectiveness. It extends beyond simply doing you a personal favour.
- The behaviour is unlikely to be explicitly picked up and rewarded by the performance evaluation system, especially since it is not part of the job description.

What are the various forms that OCB might take? As the software example indicates, one prominent form is *helping* behaviour, offering assistance to others. Another might be *conscientiousness* to the details of work, including getting in on the snowiest day of the year and not wasting organizational resources. A third form of OCB involves being a *good sport* when the inevitable frustrations of organizational life crop up—not everyone can have the best office or the best parking spot. A final form of OCB is *courtesy and cooperation*.[50] Examples might include warning the photocopy unit about a big job that is on the way or delaying one's own work to assist a colleague on a rush job.

Just how does job satisfaction contribute to OCB? Fairness seems to be the key.[51] Although distributive fairness (especially in terms of pay) is important, procedural fairness on the part of one's boss seems especially critical.[52] If the boss strays from the prescriptions for procedural fairness we gave earlier, OCB can suffer. If one feels unfairly treated, it might be difficult to lower formal performance for fear of dire consequences. It might be much easier to withdraw the less visible, informal activities that make up OCB. On the other hand, fair treatment and its resulting satisfaction might be reciprocated with OCB, a truly personalized input.

It is interesting that OCB is also influenced by employees' mood at work. People in a pleasant, relaxed, optimistic mood are more likely to provide special assistance to others.[53] Some of this research is based on studies with salespeople, and we are sure it is obvious to you how OCB would make customer service more competitive. Given the pleasant atmosphere at Husky, we would expect much OCB in the firm.

Another important attitude that also predicts organizational citizenship behaviour is organizational commitment. With this in mind, let us look at organizational commitment.

What Is Organizational Commitment?

Organizational commitment is an attitude that reflects the strength of the linkage between an employee and an organization. This linkage has implications for whether someone tends to remain in an organization. As shown in Exhibit 4.8, workers' attitudes toward their job and organization are both important and have changed over the last several decades.

Researchers John Meyer and Natalie Allen have identified three very different types of organizational commitment:[54]

- **Affective commitment** is commitment based on a person's identification and involvement with an organization. People with high affective commitment stay with an organization because they *want* to. Employees at Husky have high affective commitment. They participate in rotating council meetings where they make suggestions for improvements and they are proud of where they work.

Organizational commitment. An attitude that reflects the strength of the linkage between an employee and an organization.

Affective commitment. Commitment based on identification and involvement with an organization.

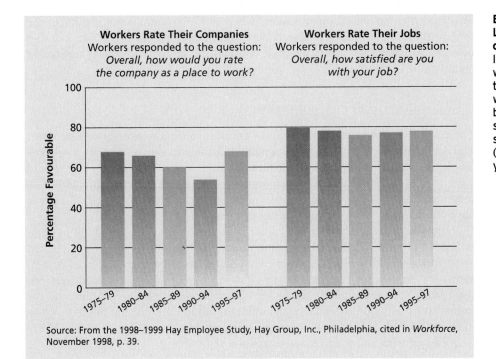

Workers Rate Their Companies
Workers responded to the question:
Overall, how would you rate the company as a place to work?

Workers Rate Their Jobs
Workers responded to the question:
Overall, how satisfied are you with your job?

Percentage Favourable

1975–79 1980–84 1985–89 1990–94 1995–97   1975–79 1980–84 1985–89 1990–94 1995–97

Source: From the 1998–1999 Hay Employee Study, Hay Group, Inc., Philadelphia, cited in *Workforce*, November 1998, p. 39.

Exhibit 4.8
Levels of job satisfaction and organizational commitment. In the past 22 years, workers' satisfaction with their companies as a place to work (left) has gone down, but is on the rise again. The same is true with employees' satisfaction with their jobs (right). While it took a hit in years past, it's now rising.

Continuance commitment.
Commitment based on the costs that would be incurred in leaving an organization.

Normative commitment.
Commitment based on ideology or a feeling of obligation to an organization.

- **Continuance commitment** is commitment based on the costs that would be incurred in leaving an organization. People with high continuance commitment stay with an organization because they *have* to.
- **Normative commitment** is commitment based on ideology or a feeling of obligation to an organization. People with high normative commitment stay with an organization because they think that they *should* do so.

A recent development in the commitment literature is that employees can be committed not only to their organization but also to various constituencies within and outside the organization. For example, each type of commitment could also apply to one's work team, union, or profession.[55]

Key Contributors to Organizational Commitment

As you might expect, the causes of the three forms of commitment tend to differ. Far and away the best predictor of affective commitment is interesting, satisfying work of the type found in enriched jobs (Chapter 6).[56] One mistake that organizations sometimes make is starting employees out in unchallenging jobs so that they do not make any serious errors. This can have a negative impact on affective commitment. Role clarity and having one's expectations met after being hired also contribute to affective commitment.[57]

Continuance commitment occurs when people feel that leaving the organization will result in personal sacrifice, and they perceive that good alternative employment is lacking. Building up "side bets" in pension funds, obtaining rapid promotion, or being well integrated into the community where the firm is located can lock employees into organizations even though they would rather go elsewhere. Not surprisingly, continuance commitment increases with the time a person is employed by his or her organization.[58]

Normative commitment ("I *should* stay here") can be fostered by benefits that build a sense of obligation to the organization. These might include tuition reimbursements or special training that enhances one's skills. Strong identification with an organization's product or service ("I should stay here because the Sierra Club is doing important work") can also foster normative commitment. Finally, certain socialization practices (Chapter 8) that emphasize loyalty to the organization can stimulate normative commitment. For example, sports coaches often haze players who miss practice to stress the importance of loyalty to the team.

Consequences of Organizational Commitment

There is good evidence that all forms of commitment reduce turnover intentions and actual turnover.[59] Organizations plagued with turnover problems among key employees should look carefully at tactics that foster commitment. This would seem to be especially sensible when turnover gets so bad that it threatens customer service. Many service organizations (e.g., restaurants and hotels), however, have traditionally accepted high turnover rates.

Organizations should take care, though, in their targeting of the kind of commitment to boost. Research shows that affective commitment is positively related to performance. However, continuance commitment is *negatively* related to performance, something you might have observed in dealing with burnt-out bureaucrats.[60] An especially bad combination for both the employee and the organization is high continuance commitment coupled with low affective commitment—people locked into organizations that they detest. This happened very frequently during the most recent recession.

Is there a downside to organizational commitment? Very high levels of commitment can cause conflicts between family life and worklife. Also, very high levels of commitment have often been implicated in unethical and illegal behaviour, including a General Electric price-fixing conspiracy and illegal payoffs made by some Lockheed employees. Finally, high levels of commitment to a particular *form or style* of organization can cause a lack of innovation and lead to resistance when a change in the culture is necessary.[61]

General Electric
www.ge.com

Changes in the Workplace and Employee Commitment

Organizations around the globe are experiencing unprecedented change as a result of shifts in workforce demographics, technological innovations, and global competition.[62] In an era of layoffs, downsizing, outsourcing, restructuring, and reengineering, there is evidence that employees are losing commitment to their organizations.[63] People often view their careers as a series of jobs with a variety of potential employers, or they even see themselves as freelancers rather than having a series of jobs in one organization. Because of the consequences of employee commitment for individuals and organizations, it is important to understand how these changes might impact employee commitment.

John Meyer, Natalie Allen, and Laryssa Topolnytsky have studied commitment in a changing world of work, and they noted that changes in the workplace on employee commitment can be seen in three main areas:[64]

- *Changes in the nature of employees' commitment to the organization.* Changes in the workplace can have an impact on all three types of organizational commitment. Depending on the nature of the changes and how they are managed, employees' levels of affective, continuance, and normative commitment can increase or decrease. Whatever the case, the commitment profiles of employees' following a change will be different from what they were prior to the change, and maintaining high levels of affective commitment will be particularly challenging. Changes that are made in the organization's best interest but are detrimental to employees' well being are most likely to damage affective commitment.

- *Changes in the focus of employees' commitment.* As mentioned earlier, the focus of the three types of commitment can include entities other than the organization. Thus, employees generally have multiple commitments. In particular, employee commitment can be directed to others within the organization, such as subunits or divisions, teams, the "new" organization, as well as entities outside the organization, such as one's occupation, career, and union. Therefore, it should not be surprising that changes in the workplace might alter the focus of employees' commitments both within and outside of the organization. For example, as organizations increase in size following mergers and acquisitions, employees are likely to shift their commitment to smaller organizational units, such as their particular division, branch, or team. As well, changes that threaten employees' future in the organization might result in a shift in commitment to entities outside the organization, such as one's profession, occupation, or personal career.

- *The multiplicity of employer–employee relationships within organizations.* As organizations attempt to cope and adapt to rapid change, they need to be flexible enough to shrink and expand their workforce, and at the same time, they need a workforce that is flexible enough to get any job done. This creates a potential conflict as employees who do not have a guarantee of job security may be unwilling to be as flexible as the organization would like or to have a strong affective commitment toward the organization. A

the manager's
notebook

the manager's notebook — West Coast Builders and Realtors Cater to Asian Cultural Values

1. Many firms have exposed their employees to training seminars in which consultants familiarize them with Asian cultural values and practices. Although the sales staff is the most obvious choice for training, some firms have trained senior managers, designers, and architects as well. Such training should cover value differences, but it should also use role-playing and other techniques to teach appropriate behaviour, such as how to shake hands or exchange business cards. It should also teach participants to understand the cultural diversity that distinguishes the various Asian countries.

2. This case reminds us that the globalization of business does not just affect what goes on in or between global firms. It also affects the interface between the firm and its clients. Organizations often anticipate cultural differences when they go into another culture to do business. They are less sensitive to such differences when people from another culture come into the firm's traditional home markets. Training seminars can sensitize employees to the cultural distinctiveness of the firm's various clients.

potential solution to this problem is for organizations to have different relationships with employees and employee groups. For example, an organization might have a group of core employees who perform the key operations required for organizational success. It would be important for this group of employees to have a high level of affective organizational commitment. Other employee groups would consist of those with contractual arrangements or individuals hired on a temporary basis who do not perform the core tasks and whose commitment to the organization is not as important. The idea of a multiplicity of employee–organization relationships enables organizations to have a flexible workforce and at the same time foster a high level of affective commitment among a core group of employees.

In summary, changes in the workplace are having an impact on the nature of employee commitment and employee–employer relationships. It is, therefore, important that organizations understand how changes in the workplace can change the profile and focus of employees' commitment and the impact this can have on employee behaviour and organizational success.

Summary

- Values are broad preferences for particular states of affairs. Values tend to differ across occupational groups and across cultures.

- Critical cross-cultural dimensions of values include power distance, uncertainty avoidance, masculinity/femininity, individualism/collectivism, and time orientation.

- Differences in values across cultures set constraints on the export and import of organizational behaviour theories and management practices. They also have implications for satisfy-

ing global customers and developing globally aware employees.

- Attitudes are a function of what we think about the world (our beliefs) and how we feel about the world (our values). Attitudes are important because they influence how we behave, although we have discussed several factors that reduce the correspondence between our attitudes and behaviours.

- Dissonance theory suggests that attitudes can be changed by getting people to enact desired behaviours that are incompatible with their attitudes.

- Job satisfaction is an especially important attitude for organizations. Satisfaction is a function of the discrepancy between what individuals want from their jobs and what they perceive that they obtain, taking into account distributive and procedural fairness. Dispositional factors also seem to influence job satisfaction. Factors such as challenging work, high pay, promotion opportunities, and friendly, helpful co-workers contribute to job satisfaction. Job satisfaction is important because it may promote mental health and reduce expensive turnover. Satisfied workers are not necessarily much better performers, since good performance might not lead to the acquisition of satisfying rewards. However, satisfied workers might be better organizational citizens.

■ Organizational commitment is an attitude that reflects the strength of the linkage between an employee and an organization. Affective commitment is based on a person's identification with an organization. Continuance commitment is based on the costs of leaving an organization. Normative commitment is based on ideology or feelings of obligation. Changes in the workplace can change the nature and focus of employee commitment as well as employer-employee relationships.

Discussion Questions

1. What are some of the conditions under which a person's attitudes might not predict his or her work behaviour?

2. Many organizations use diversity training to promote favourable attitudes among employees who differ in gender, age, race, ethnicity, or sexual orientation. Given our discussion of attitude change, what factors would improve the success of such efforts? Could behaviour change foster attitude change?

3. Discuss the pros and cons of the argument, "Organizations should do everything they can to enhance the job satisfaction and organizational commitment of their employees."

4. Using the model of the turnover process in Exhibit 4.7, explain why a very dissatisfied worker might not quit his or her job. Explain why workers who are very satisfied with their jobs might not be better performers than those who are less satisfied.

5. Use equity theory to explain why a dentist who earns $100,000 a year might be more dissatisfied

with her job than a factory worker who earns $40,000.

6. Mexico has a fairly high power distance culture, while the United States and Canada have lower power distance cultures. Discuss how effective management techniques might vary between Mexico and its neighbours to the north.

7. Describe some job aspects that might contribute to job satisfaction for a person in a more collective culture. Do the same for a person in a more individualistic culture.

8. Give an example of an employee who is experiencing distributive fairness but not procedural fairness. Give an example of an employee who is experiencing procedural fairness but not distributive fairness.

9. What role do perceptions play in the determination of job satisfaction? Refer to the components of perception in Chapter 3 and describe how perception plays a role in the determination of job satisfaction according to discrepancy theory, equity theory, and dispositions. How can perceptions be changed in order to increase job satisfaction?

10. Does personality influence values and job attitudes? Discuss how the Big Five personality dimensions, locus of control, self-monitoring, and self-esteem might influence occupational choice, job satisfaction, and organizational commitment (affective, continuance, and normative). If personality influences job satisfaction and organizational commitment, how can organizations foster high levels of these attitudes?

Experiential Exercise

Cultural-Diversity Quiz

This quiz will give you an idea of how much you already know about cultural diversity. In some cases, there is more than one correct response to each question.

_____ 1. On average, how long do native-born Americans maintain eye contact?
  a. 1 second
  b. 15 seconds
  c. 30 seconds

_____ 2. True or false: One of the few universal ways to motivate workers, regardless of cultural background, is through the prospect of a promotion.

_____ 3. Learning to speak a few words of the language of immigrant clients, customers, and workers is:
    a. Generally a good idea as the effort communicates respect for the other person
    b. Generally not a good idea because they might feel patronized
    c. Generally not a good idea because they might be offended if a mistake is made in vocabulary or pronunciation

_____ 4. True or false: North American culture has no unique characteristics; it is composed only of individual features brought from other countries.

_____ 5. When communicating across language barriers, using the written word:
    a. Should be avoided; it can insult the immigrant or international visitor's intelligence
    b. Can be helpful; it is usually easier to read English than to hear it
    c. Can be confusing; it is usually easier to hear English than to read it

_____ 6. True or false: Behaving formally around immigrant colleagues, clients, and workers—that is, using last names, observing strict rules of etiquette—is generally not a good idea as it gives the impression of coldness and superiority.

_____ 7. In times of crisis, the immigrant's ability to speak English:
    a. Diminishes because of stress
    b. Stays the same
    c. Improves because of the necessity of coping with the crisis
    d. Completely disappears

_____ 8. The number of languages spoken in the United States today is:
    a. 0–10
    b. 10–50
    c. 50–100
    d. 100+

_____ 9. True or false: Immigrant families in the United States largely make decisions as individuals and have generally abandoned the practice of making decisions as a group.

_____ 10. When you have difficulty understanding someone with a foreign accent:
    a. It probably means that he or she cannot understand you either.
    b. It probably means that he or she is recently arrived in your country.
    c. It is helpful if you listen to all that he or she has to say before interrupting, as the meaning might become clear in the context of the conversation.

    d. It is helpful for you to try to guess what the speaker is saying and to speak for him or her so as to minimize the risk of embarrassment.

_____ 11. When an Asian client begins to give you vague answers before closing a deal, saying things like "It will take time to decide," or "We'll see," the best thing to do is:
    a. Back off a bit, he or she may be trying to say "no" without offending you.
    b. Supply more information and data about your service or product, especially in writing.
    c. Push for a "close." His or her vagueness is probably a manipulative tactic.
    d. State clearly and strongly that you are dissatisfied with his or her reaction so as to avoid any misunderstanding.

_____ 12. Apparent rudeness and abruptness in immigrants is often due to:
    a. Lack of facility with the English language
    b. A difference in cultural style
    c. Differing tone of voice

_____ 13. True or false: Many immigrant and ethnic cultures place greater importance on how something is said (body language and tone of voice) than on the words themselves.

_____ 14. The avoidance of public embarrassment (loss of face) is of central concern to which of the following cultures?
    a. Hispanic
    b. Mainstream American
    c. Asian
    d. Middle-Eastern

_____ 15. True or false: One of the few universals in etiquette is that everyone likes to be complimented in front of others.

_____ 16. In a customer-service situation, when communicating to a decision maker through a child who is functioning as interpreter, it is best to:
    a. Look at the child as you speak so that he or she will be certain to understand you.
    b. Look at the decision maker.
    c. Look back and forth between the two.

_____ 17. Which of the following statements is (are) true?
    a. Most Asian workers like it when the boss rolls up his or her sleeves to work beside employees.
    b. Taking independent initiative on tasks is valued in most workplaces throughout the world.
    c. Many immigrant workers are reluctant to complain to the boss as they feel it is a sign of disrespect.
    d. Asians are quick to praise superiors to their face in an attempt to show respect.

____ 18. True or false: The "V" sign for victory is a universal gesture of good will and triumph.

____ 19. Which of the following statements is (are) true?
   a. It is inappropriate to touch Asians on the hand.
   b. Middle-Eastern men stand very close as a means of dominating the conversation.
   c. Mexican men will hold another man's lapel during a conversation as a sign of good communication.

____ 20. Building relationships slowly when doing business with Hispanics is:
   a. A bad idea; if you do not move things along, they will go elsewhere
   b. A bad idea; they will expect native-born professionals to move quickly, so will be disoriented if you do not
   c. A good idea; it may take longer, but the trust you build will be well worth the effort

Scoring and Interpretation

Below are the correct answers to each of the 20 questions in the Cultural-Diversity Quiz. To score your quiz, simply add up the number of correct answers. If your score is above 15, you are quite knowledgeable about cultural diversity. If your score is below 15, you need to improve your knowledge of cultural diversity.
1. a 2. False 3. A 4. False 5. b 6. False 7. a 8. d 9. False 10. c 11. a 12. a, b, and c 13. True 14. a, c, and d 15. False 16. b 17. c 18. False 19. c 20. c

Reprinted with permission from Sondra B. Thiederman. *Profiting in America's multicultural workplace: How to do business across cultural lines.* Lexington Books, an imprint of Macmillan, Inc. Copyright © by Sondra Thiederman.

Case Incident

How Much Do You Get Paid?

Joan had been working as a reporter for a large television network for seven years. She was an experienced and hard-working reporter who had won many awards over the years for her outstanding work. The work was exciting and challenging, and at $75,000 a year plus benefits she felt well paid and satisfied. Then she found out that two recent graduates from one of the best schools of journalism in the United States had just been hired by her network at a starting salary of $80,000. Further, two other reporters who worked with Joan and had similar track records had just received job offers from American networks and were being offered $150,000 plus $10,000 for every award won for their reporting.

1. According to equity theory, how will these incidents influence Joan's job satisfaction and behaviour?

2. What should Joan do in response to her situation? What should her organization do?

Case Study

The Well-Paid Receptionist

Harvey Finley did a quick doubletake when he caught a glimpse of the figure representing Ms. Brannen's salary on the year-end printout. A hurried call to payroll confirmed it. Yes, his receptionist had been paid $127,614.21 for her services last year. As he sat in stunned silence, he had the sudden realization that since his firm was doing so well this year, she would earn at least 10 to 15 percent more money during the current fiscal year. This was a shock, indeed.

Background

Harvey began his career as a service technician for a major manufacturer of copy machines. He received rather extensive technical training, but his duties were limited to performing routine, on-site maintenance and service for customers. After a year's experience as a service technician, he asked for and received a promotion to sales representative. In this capacity, he established many favourable contacts in the business community of Troupville and the surrounding towns. He began to think seriously about capitalizing on his success by opening his own business.

Then, seven years ago, he decided to take the plunge and start his own firm. He was tired of selling for someone else. When he mentioned his plan to his friends, they all expressed serious doubts; Troupville, a city of approximately 35,000 people located in the deep South, had just begun to recover from a severe recession. The painful memories of the layoffs, bankruptcies, and plummeting real estate values were too recent and vivid to be forgotten.

Undeterred by the sceptics, Harvey was optimistic that Troupville's slow recovery would soon become a boom. Even though his firm would certainly have to be started on a shoestring, Harvey thought his sales experience and technical competence would enable him to survive what was sure to be a difficult beginning. He was nervous but excited when he signed the lease on the first little building. A lifelong dream was either about to be realized or dashed forever. Troupville Business Systems was born.

While he had managed to borrow, rent, lease, or subcontract for almost everything that was absolutely necessary, he did need one employee immediately. Of course, he hoped the business would expand rapidly, and that he would soon have a complete and competent staff. But until he could be sure that some revenue would be generated, he thought he could get by with one person who would be a combination receptionist/secretary and general assistant.

The typical salary for such a position in the area was about $30,000 per year; for Harvey, this was a major expense. Nevertheless, he placed what he thought was a well-worded ad in the "Help Wanted" section of the local newspaper. There were five applicants, four of whom just did not seem quite right for the position he envisioned. The fifth applicant, Ms. Cathy Brannen, was absolutely captivating.

Ms. Brannen was 27 years old with one child. Her resume showed that she had graduated from a two-year office administration program at a state university. She had worked for only two employers following graduation, one for five years and the most recent for two years. Since returning to her hometown of Troupville two months ago, following her divorce, she had not been able to find suitable employment.

From the moment she sat down for the interview, Harvey and Ms. Brannen seemed to be on exactly the same wavelength. She was very articulate, obviously quite bright, and, most importantly, very enthusiastic about assisting with the start-up of the new venture. She seemed to be exactly the sort of person Harvey had envisioned when he first began to think seriously about taking the plunge. He resisted the temptation to offer her the job on the spot, but ended the hour-long interview by telling her that he would check her references and contact her again very soon.

Telephone calls to her two former employers convinced Harvey that he had actually underestimated Ms. Brannen's suitability for the position. Each one said without equivocation that she was the best employee he had ever had in any position. Both former employers concluded the conversation by saying they would rehire her in a minute if she were still available. The only bit of disturbing information gleaned from these two calls was the fact that her annual salary had risen to $32,900 in her last job. Although Harvey thought that the cost of living was probably a bit higher in Houston, where she had last worked, he was not sure she would react favourably to the $30,000 offer he was planning to make. However, he was determined that somehow, Cathy Brannen would be his first employee.

Ms. Brannen seemed quite pleased when Harvey telephoned her at home that same evening. She said she would be delighted to meet him at the office the next morning to discuss the position more fully.

Cathy Brannen was obviously very enthusiastic about the job as outlined in the meeting. She asked all the right questions, responded quickly and articulately to every query posed to her, and seemed ready to accept the position even before the offer was extended. When Harvey finally got around to mentioning the salary, there was a slight change in Cathy's eager expression. She stiffened. Since Harvey realized that salary might be a problem, he decided to offer Cathy an incentive of sorts in addition to the $30,000 annual salary. He told her that he realized his salary offer was lower than the amount she had earned on her last job. And, he told her, he understood that a definite disadvantage of working for a new firm was the complete absence of financial security. Although he was extremely reluctant to guarantee a larger salary because of his own uncertainty regarding the future, he offered her a sales override in the amount of two percent of sales. He explained that she would largely determine the success or failure of the firm. She needed to represent the firm in the finest possible manner to potential customers who telephoned and to those who walked in the front door. For this reason, the sales override seemed to be an appropriate addition to her straight salary. It would provide her with incentive to take an active interest in the firm.

Cathy accepted the offer immediately. Even though she was expecting a salary offer of $32,500, she hoped the sales override might make up the difference. "Who knows," she thought, "two percent of sales may amount to big money someday." It did not, however, seem very likely at the time.

Troupville Business Systems began as a very small distributor of copy machines. The original business plan was just to sell copy machines and provide routine, on-site service. More extensive on-site service and repairs requiring that a machine be removed from a customer's premise were to be provided by a regional distributor located in a major city approximately 100 miles from Troupville.

Troupville Business Systems did well from the start. Several important changes were made in the services the firm offered during the first year. Harvey soon found that there was a greater demand for the leasing of copy machines, particularly the large expensive models which he originally planned to sell. He also soon discovered that his customers wanted to be able to contract directly with his firm for all their service needs. Merely guaranteeing that he could get the machines serviced was not sufficient in the eyes of potential customers. In attempting to accommodate the market, he developed a complete service facility and began to offer leasing options on all models. These changes in the business all occurred during the first year. Growth during that year was steady but not spectacular. While sales continued to grow steadily the second year, it was early in the third year that Harvey made what turned out to be his best decision. He entered the computer business.

Harvey had purchased a personal computer soon after Troupville Business Systems was founded. The machine and its capabilities fascinated him, although he knew virtually nothing about computers. He was soon a member of a local users club, was subscribing to all the magazines, and was taking evening computer courses at the local university—in short, he became a computer buff. Harvey recognized the business potential of the rapidly growing personal computer market, but he did not believe that his original business was sufficiently stable to introduce a new product line just yet.

During his third year of operations, he decided the time was right to enter the computer business. He added to his product line a number of personal computers popular with small businesses in the area. This key decision caused a virtual explosion in the growth of his firm. Several key positions were added, including that of a comptroller. By the fourth year of operations, computers produced by several other manufacturers had been added to Harvey's product line, and he had developed the capability of providing complete service for all products carried. His computer enterprise was not limited to business customers, because he quickly developed a significant walk-in retail trade. Rapid growth continued unabated.

During the first seven years of the company's existence, Cathy Brannen had proven truly indispensable. Her performance exceeded Harvey's highest expectations. Although her official position remained that of secretary/receptionist, she took it on herself to learn about each new product or service. During the early years, Harvey often thought that she did a better job than he did whenever a potential customer called in his absence. Even after he acquired a qualified sales staff, Harvey had no concerns when Cathy had to field questions from a potential customer because a regular salesperson was not available. The customer never realized that the professional young lady capably handling all inquiries was "only" the receptionist.

Cathy began performing fewer sales functions because of the increased number of professional salespersons, but her secretarial duties had expanded tremendously. She was still Harvey's secretary, and she continued to answer virtually every telephone call coming into the business. Since her office was in an open area, she still was the first to greet many visitors.

Cathy took a word-processing course at a local business school shortly after joining the firm. As she began working with Harvey's first personal computer, she, too, developed into a computer aficionado and became the best computer operator in the firm.

The Current Situation

Harvey was shaken by the realization that Cathy Brannen had been paid over $127,000 last year. As he wondered what, if anything, should be done about her earnings, he began to reflect on the previous seven years.

Success had come almost overnight. It seemed as though Troupville Business Systems could do nothing wrong. The workforce had grown at a rate of approximately 15 percent per year since the third year of operations. Seventeen people were now employed by the firm. While Harvey did acknowledge that some of this success was due to being in the right place at the right time, he also had reason to be proud of the choices he had made. Time had proven that all his major decisions had been correct. He also could not overestimate Cathy's contribution to the success of the firm. Yes, certainly, one of the most important days in the life of the firm was the day when Cathy responded to his ad in the newspaper.

Success had brought with it the ever-increasing demands on his time. He had never worked so hard, but the rewards were certainly forthcoming. First, there was the new Jaguar, then the new home on Country Club Drive, the vacation home on the coast, the European trips... Yes, success was wonderful.

During these years Cathy, too, had prospered. Harvey had not thought much about it, but he did remember making a joking comment the first day she drove her new Mercedes to work. He also remembered commenting on her mink coat at the company banquet last December. Cathy had been dazzling.

Now that Harvey realized what he was paying Cathy, he was greatly disturbed. She was making almost twice as much money as anyone else in the firm with the exception of himself. The best salesman had earned an amount in the low nineties last year. His top managers were paid salaries ranging from the high sixties to the mid-seventies. The average salary in the area for executive secretaries was now probably between $30,000 and $35,000 per year. A good receptionist could be hired for under $35,000, and yet Cathy had been paid $127,614.21 last year. The sales override had certainly enabled Cathy to share in the firm's success. Yes, indeed.

As Harvey thought more and more about the situation, he kept returning to the same conclusion. He felt something had to be done about her compensation. It was just too far out of line with other salaries in the firm. Although Harvey was drawing over $200,000 per year in salary and had built an equity in the business of more than $1 million, these facts did not seem relevant as he pondered what to do. It seemed likely that a number of other employees did know about Cathy's compensation level. Harvey wondered why no one ever mentioned it. Even the comptroller never mentioned Cathy's compensation. This did seem quite odd to Harvey, as the comptroller, Frank Bain, knew that Harvey did not even attempt to keep up with the financial details. He relied on Frank to bring important matters to his attention.

With no idea of how to approach this problem, Harvey decided to begin by making a list of alternatives. He got out a piece of paper and, as he stared at the blank lines, overheard Cathy's cheerful exchange with a customer in the next room.

Source: Case prepared by Roland B. Cousins, LaGrange College. Management cooperated in the field research for this case, which was written solely for the purpose of stimulating student discussion. All individuals and incidents are real, but names and data have been disguised at the request of the organization. From the *Case Research Journal*, Spring 1992, pp. 74–79. Copyright the *Case Research Journal* and Roland B. Cousins.

1. Use the ideas of distributive fairness and equity theory to explain why Harvey Finley thinks he pays Cathy Brannen too much.

2. Use the ideas of distributive fairness and equity theory to explain why Cathy Brannen might feel that her pay is fair.

3. What are the likely consequences for job satisfaction, organizational commitment, and behaviour if Ms. Brannen's pay level is truly known to other organizational members? Use equity theory to support your answer.

4. Suppose that you had been in Mr. Finley's position at the time that he hired Ms. Brannen. What would you have done differently to avoid the current situation while still attracting her to join the fledgling firm?

5. What ethical or moral issue does this case raise?

6. What should Mr. Finley do now? Be sure to consider procedural fairness in framing your answer.

Chapter 5

Theories of Work Motivation

Starbucks

STARBUCKS Employees at Starbucks Coffee Co., the world's largest chain of coffee shops, do not just serve up coffee to customers. Rather, these partners, as they are called, are actively involved in the company and are credited with finding new and innovative ways to cut costs and save the company money and increase sales. Their efforts appear to be making a difference. Starbucks stock is up more than 800 percent since the company went public in 1992, and sales and profits have been growing more than 50% a year. There are more than 1,700 Starbucks stores worldwide, including stores in Tokyo, Singapore, and Great Britain, and new stores open almost every day. Starbucks stores can be found in almost every major metropolitan area in the United States, and its blend of coffee is available in restaurants, hotels, offices, and airlines not to mention a Starbucks brand of coffee ice cream and compact discs. No wonder retail sales exceeded $966 million in 1997!

Some might argue that Starbucks' chairman and CEO Howard Schultz, who purchased the company for $4 million in 1987, was in the right place at the right time. After all, 10 years ago a coffee shop was, well, just a place to get a coffee, not somewhere you would go to relax and hang out with a "cuppa-joe." However, take a closer look inside Starbuck's, and what you see will surprise you. Rated as one of *Fortune* magazine's "100 Best Companies to Work for in America," Starbucks' mission statement includes providing a great work environment, treating people with respect and dignity, and making all employees partners. Key to this objective is Starbucks' "special blend" of employee benefits and an innovative work/life program.

Employees first must learn about the company's obsession for quality and customer service. Starbucks' employee training program requires employees

A stock option plan, recognition programs, and a comprehensive work/life benefits program have helped Starbucks create an inspired, enthusiastic, and motivated workforce.

to complete five classes during their first six weeks with the company on topics such as "Brewing the Perfect Cup," "Retail Sales," "Coffee Knowledge," and "Customer Service." Employees are also taught relaxation techniques and on-the-job interpersonal relations.

The hourly pay of Starbucks employees is better than other entry-level food service jobs. But the real difference is the company's "bean stock" program, a stock-option plan that makes every employee of Starbucks a partner and links employee contributions to company profits. Starbucks became one of the first service companies to offer stock options. All employees from top management down are awarded stock options. Beginning in 1991, each employee was awarded stock options worth 12% of their base pay, which has since risen to 14%, thanks to healthy profits. In addition, recognition programs reward outstanding achievement for upholding Starbucks' mission and goals.

Another important ingredient in Starbucks' special blend is a comprehensive work/life benefits program that includes on-site fitness services, and educational support for child care and elder care. All employees who work a minimum of 20 hours a week are entitled to universal benefits packages, including full medical and dental coverage, vision care, disability and life insurance—perks that are usually reserved only for those in the managerial ranks.

To stay attuned to the needs and desires of employees, Starbucks conducts regular opinion surveys and open forums in order to be able to provide programs that address employees' life stages and personal needs. For example, in response to the growing number of employees who were starting families, Starbucks offered flexible work schedules. As well, a number of "nontraditional"

Starbucks Coffee Co.
www.starbucks.com

Learning Objectives

After reading Chapter 5, you should be able to:

1 Define motivation, discuss its basic properties, and distinguish it from performance.

2 Compare and contrast intrinsic and extrinsic motivation.

3 Explain and discuss the managerial implications of need theories of motivation.

4 Explain and discuss the managerial implications of expectancy theory.

5 Explain and discuss the managerial implications of equity theory.

6 Explain and discuss the managerial implications of goal setting theory.

7 Discuss the cross-cultural limitations of theories of motivation.

8 Summarize the relationship among the various theories of motivation, performance, and job satisfaction.

benefits have been designed including a program that links employees with similar interests and hobbies. The objective is to provide a range of work/life solutions that meet the multiple life demands of employees.

The Starbucks' formula appears to be straightforward: Take care of your people, they will take care of your customers, and the bottom line will grow. What is not so straightforward is the creation of an inspired, enthusiastic, and motivated workforce that shares a common purpose, is treated like business partners, and shares the rewards of the company's success. Is it any wonder that Starbucks has met its goal of becoming a $1 billion company![1]

How would *you* like to work at Starbucks? What underlying philosophy of motivation is Starbucks using? Who would be susceptible to this kind of motivation? These are some of the questions that this chapter will explore.

First, we will define motivation and distinguish it from performance. After this, we will describe several popular theories of work motivation and contrast them. Then we will explore whether these theories translate across cultures. Finally, we will present a model that links motivation, performance, and job satisfaction.

Why Study Motivation?

Why should you study motivation? Motivation is one of the most traditional topics in organizational behaviour, and it has interested managers, researchers, teachers, and sports coaches for years. However, a good case can be made that motivation has become even more important in contemporary organizations. Much of this is a result of the need for increased productivity to be globally competitive (as at Starbucks). It is also a result of the rapid changes that contemporary organizations are undergoing. Stable systems of rules, regulations, and procedures that once guided behaviour are being replaced by requirements for flexibility and attention to customers that necessitate higher levels of initiative. This initiative depends on motivation.

What would a good motivation theory look like? In fact, as we shall see, there is no single all-purpose motivation theory. Rather, we will consider several theories that serve somewhat different purposes. In combination, though, a good set of theories should recognize human diversity and consider that the same conditions will not motivate everyone. Also, a good set of theories should be able to explain how it is that some people seem to be self-motivated, while others seem to require external motivation. Finally, a good set of theories should recognize the social aspect of human beings—people's motivation is often affected by how they see others being treated. Before getting to our theories, let us define motivation more precisely.

What Is Motivation?

The term *motivation* is not easy to define. However, from an organization's perspective, when we speak of a person as being motivated, we usually mean that the person works "hard," "keeps at" his or her work, and directs his or her behaviour toward appropriate outcomes.

Basic Characteristics of Motivation

We can formally define **motivation** as the extent to which persistent effort is directed toward a goal.[2]

Motivation. The extent to which persistent effort is directed toward a goal.

Effort. The first aspect of motivation is the strength of the person's work-related behaviour or the amount of *effort* the person exhibits on the job. Clearly, this involves different kinds of activities on different kinds of jobs. A loading dock worker might exhibit greater effort by carrying heavier crates, while a researcher might reveal greater effort by searching out an article in some obscure foreign technical journal. Both are exerting effort in a manner appropriate to their jobs.

Persistence. The second characteristic of motivation is the *persistence* that individuals exhibit in applying effort to their work tasks. The organization would not be likely to think of the loading dock worker who stacks the heaviest crates for two hours and then goofs off for six hours as especially highly motivated. Similarly, the researcher who makes an important discovery early in her career and then rests on her laurels for five years would not be considered especially highly motivated. In each case, workers have not been persistent in the application of their effort.

Direction. Effort and persistence refer mainly to the quantity of work an individual produces. Of equal importance is the quality of a person's work. Thus, the third characteristic of motivation is the *direction* of the person's work-related behaviour. In other words, do workers channel persistent effort in a direction that benefits the organization? Employers expect motivated stockbrokers to advise their clients of good investment opportunities and motivated software designers to design software, not play computer games. These correct decisions increase the probability that persistent effort is actually translated into accepted organizational outcomes. Thus, motivation means working smart as well as working hard.

Goals. Ultimately, all motivated behaviour has some goal or objective toward which it is directed. We have presented the preceding discussion from an organizational perspective, that is, we assume that motivated people act to enhance organizational objectives. In this case, employee goals might include high productivity, good attendance, or creative decisions. Of course, employees can also be motivated by goals that are contrary to the objectives of the organization, including absenteeism, sabotage, and embezzlement. In these cases, they are channeling their persistent efforts in directions that are dysfunctional for the organization.

Extrinsic and Intrinsic Motivation

Some hold the view that people are motivated by factors in the external environment (such as supervision or pay), while others believe that people can, in some sense, be self-motivated without the application of these external factors. You might have experienced this distinction. As a worker, you might recall tasks that you enthusiastically performed simply for the sake of doing them and others that you performed only to keep your job or placate your boss.

Experts in organizational behaviour distinguish between intrinsic and extrinsic motivation. At the outset, we should emphasize that there is only weak consensus concerning the exact definitions of these concepts and even weaker agreement about whether we should label specific motivators as intrinsic or extrinsic.[3] However, the following definitions and examples seem to capture the distinction fairly well.

Intrinsic motivation. Motivation that stems from the direct relationship between the worker and the task; it is usually self-applied.

Intrinsic motivation stems from the direct relationship between the worker and the task and is usually self-applied. Feelings of achievement, accomplishment, challenge, and competence derived from performing one's job are examples of intrinsic motivators, as is sheer interest in the job itself. Off the job, avid participation in sports and hobbies is often intrinsically motivated.

Extrinsic motivation. Motivation that stems from the work environment external to the task; it is usually applied by others.

Extrinsic motivation stems from the work environment external to the task and is usually applied by someone other than the person being motivated. Pay, fringe benefits, company policies, and various forms of supervision are examples of extrinsic motivators.

Obviously, employers cannot package all conceivable motivators as neatly as these definitions suggest. For example, a promotion or a compliment might be applied by the boss but might also be a clear signal of achievement and competence. Thus, some potential motivators have both extrinsic and intrinsic qualities.

Despite the fact that the distinction between intrinsic and extrinsic motivation is fuzzy, many theories of motivation implicitly make the distinction. However, the relationship between intrinsic and extrinsic motivators has been the subject of a great deal of debate.[4] Some research studies have reached the conclusion that the availability of extrinsic motivators can reduce the intrinsic motivation stemming from the task itself.[5] The notion is that when extrinsic rewards depend on performance, the valence of intrinsic rewards decreases. Proponents of this view have suggested that making extrinsic rewards contingent on performance makes individuals feel less competent and less in control of their own behaviour,[6] that is, they come to believe that their performance is controlled by the environment, and that they perform well only because of the money. Thus, intrinsic motivation suffers. However, a recent review of research in this area reached the conclusion that the negative effect of extrinsic rewards on intrinsic motivation occurs only under very limited conditions that are easily avoidable.[7] As well, in organizational settings in which individuals see extrinsic rewards as symbols of success and as signals of what to do to achieve future rewards, they increase their task performance.[8] Thus, it is safe to assume that both kinds of rewards are important and compatible in enhancing work motivation.

Motivation and Performance

At this point, you might well be saying, "Wait a minute, I know many people who are 'highly motivated' but just don't seem to perform well. They work long and hard, but they just don't measure up." This is certainly a sensible observation, and it points to the important distinction between motivation and performance. **Performance** can be defined as the extent to which an organizational member contributes to achieving the objectives of the organization.

Some of the factors that contribute to individual performance in organizations are shown in Exhibit 5.1.[9] While motivation clearly contributes to performance, the relationship is not one-to-one because a number of other factors intervene. Thus, it is certainly possible for performance to be low even when a person is highly motivated—low aptitude, weak skills, poor understanding of the task, or chance can damage the performance of the most highly motivated individual. Of course, an opposite effect is also conceivable. An individual with rather marginal motivation might understand the task so well that some compensation occurs—what little effort the individual makes is expended very efficiently in terms of goal accomplishment. Also, a person with weak motivation might perform well because of some luck or chance factor that boosts performance. Thus, it is no wonder that workers sometimes complain that they receive lower performance ratings than colleagues who "don't work as hard."

In this chapter, we will concentrate on the motivational components of performance, rather than the other determinants in Exhibit 5.1. However, the moral here should be clear: We cannot consider motivation in isolation; high motivation will not result in high performance if employees lack basic aptitudes and skills, do not understand their jobs, or encounter unavoidable obstacles over which they have no control. Contemporary management techniques, such as total quality management, simply will not *work* if employees are deficient in reading, math, and technical skills.[10]

Need Theories of Work Motivation

The first three theories of motivation that we will consider are **need theories**. These theories attempt to specify the kinds of needs people have and the conditions under which they will be motivated to satisfy these needs in a way that contributes to performance. Needs are physiological and psychological wants or desires that individuals can satisfy by acquiring certain incentives or achieving particular goals. It is the behaviour stimulated by this acquisition process that reveals the motivational character of needs:

$$\text{NEEDS} \longrightarrow \text{BEHAVIOUR} \longrightarrow \text{INCENTIVES AND GOALS}$$

Notice that need theories are concerned with *what* motivates workers (needs and their associated incentives or goals). They can be contrasted with *process theories*, which are concerned with exactly *how* various factors motivate people. Need and process theories are complementary rather than contradictory. Thus, a need theory might contend that money can be an important motivator (what), and a process theory might explain the actual mechanics by which money motivates (how).[11] In this section, we will examine three prominent need theories of motivation.

Maslow's Hierarchy of Needs

Abraham Maslow was a psychologist who, over a number of years, developed and refined a general theory of human motivation.[12] According to Maslow, humans

Performance. The extent to which an organizational member contributes to achieving the objectives of the organization.

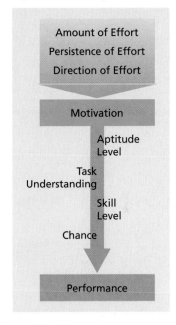

Exhibit 5.1
Factors contributing to individual job performance.

Need theories. Motivation theories that specify the kinds of needs people have and the conditions under which they will be motivated to satisfy these needs in a way that contributes to performance.

have five sets of needs that are arranged in a hierarchy, beginning with the most basic and compelling needs (see the left side of Exhibit 5.2). These needs include:

1. *Physiological needs.* These include the needs that must be satisfied for the person to survive, such as food, water, oxygen, and shelter. Organizational factors that might satisfy these needs include the minimum pay necessary for survival and working conditions that promote existence.

2. *Safety needs.* These include needs for security, stability, freedom from anxiety, and a structured and ordered environment. Organizational conditions that might meet these needs include safe working conditions, fair and sensible rules and regulations, job security, a comfortable work environment, pension and insurance plans, pay above the minimum needed for survival, and freedom to unionize.

3. *Belongingness needs.* These include needs for social interaction, affection, love, companionship, and friendship. Organizational factors that might meet these needs include the opportunity to interact with others on the job, friendly and supportive supervision, opportunity for teamwork, and opportunity to develop new social relationships.

4. *Esteem needs.* These include needs for feelings of adequacy, competence, independence, strength, and confidence, and the appreciation and recognition of these characteristics by others. Organizational factors that might satisfy these needs include the opportunity to master tasks leading to feelings of achievement and responsibility. Also, awards, promotions, prestigious job titles, professional recognition, and the like might satisfy these needs when they are felt to be truly deserved.

5. *Self-actualization needs.* These needs are the most difficult to define. They involve the desire to develop one's true potential as an individual to the fullest extent and to express one's skills, talents, and emotions in a manner that is most personally fulfilling. Maslow suggests that self-actualizing people have clear perceptions of reality, accept themselves and others, and are independent, creative, and appreciative of the world around them. Organizational conditions that might provide self-actualization include absorbing jobs with the potential for creativity and growth as well as a relaxation of structure to permit self-development and personal progression.

Maslow's hierarchy of needs. A five-level hierarchical need theory of motivation that specifies that the lowest-level unsatisfied need has the greatest motivating potential.

Given the fact that individuals may harbour these needs, in what sense do they form the basis of a theory of motivation, that is, what exactly is the motivational premise of **Maslow's hierarchy of needs**? Put simply, the lowest-level unsatisfied need category has the greatest motivating potential. Thus, none of the

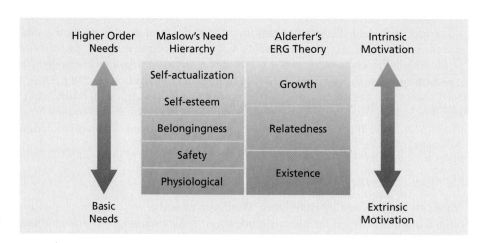

Exhibit 5.2
Relationship between Maslow and Alderfer need theories.

needs is a "best" motivator; motivation depends on the person's position in the need hierarchy. According to Maslow, individuals are motivated to satisfy their physiological needs before they reveal an interest in safety needs, and safety must be satisfied before social needs become motivational, and so on. When a need is unsatisfied, it exerts a powerful effect on the individual's thinking and behaviour, and this is the sense in which needs are motivational. However, when needs at a particular level of the hierarchy are satisfied, the individual turns his or her attention to the next higher level. Notice the clear implication here that a *satisfied need is no longer an effective motivator*. Once one has adequate physiological resources and feels safe and secure, one does not seek more of the factors that met these needs but looks elsewhere for gratification. According to Maslow, the single exception to this rule involves self-actualization needs. He felt that these were "growth" needs that become stronger as they are gratified.

Individuals who are in the lower-level need categories (physiological, safety, and belongingness) seem to be the most susceptible to extrinsic motivation, its exact form corresponding to the need that is most pressing. Observe that money and money substitutes (e.g., insurance and pension plans) figure heavily here. However, as individuals progress up the hierarchy, and higher-order needs (esteem and self-actualization) become prominent, intrinsic motivation comes into play. Here, employers must design work to encourage people to "motivate themselves."

Alderfer's ERG Theory

Clayton Alderfer developed another need-based theory, called **ERG theory**.[13] It streamlines Maslow's need classifications and makes some different assumptions about the relationship between needs and motivation. The name ERG stems from Alderfer's compression of Maslow's five-category need system into three categories—existence, relatedness, and growth needs:

ERG theory. A three-level hierarchical need theory of motivation (existence, relatedness, growth) that allows for movement up and down the hierarchy.

1. *Existence needs*. These are needs that are satisfied by some material substance or condition. As such, they correspond closely to Maslow's physiological needs and to those safety needs that are satisfied by material conditions rather than interpersonal relations. These include the need for food, shelter, pay, and safe working conditions.

2. *Relatedness needs*. These are needs that are satisfied by open communication and the exchange of thoughts and feelings with other organizational members. They correspond fairly closely to Maslow's belongingness needs and to those esteem needs that involve feedback from others. However, Alderfer stresses that relatedness needs are satisfied by open, accurate, honest interaction rather than by uncritical pleasantness.

3. *Growth needs*. These are needs that are fulfilled by strong personal involvement in the work setting. They involve the full utilization of one's skills and abilities and the creative development of new skills and abilities. Growth needs correspond to Maslow's need for self-actualization and the aspects of his esteem needs that concern achievement and responsibility.

As you can see in Exhibit 5.2, Alderfer's need classification system does not represent a radical departure from that of Maslow. In addition, Alderfer agrees with Maslow that as lower-level needs are satisfied, the desire to have higher-level needs satisfied will increase. Thus, as existence needs are fulfilled, relatedness needs gain motivational power. Alderfer explains this by arguing that as more "concrete" needs are satisfied, energy can be directed toward satisfying less concrete needs. Finally, Alderfer agrees with Maslow that the least concrete needs—growth needs—become *more* compelling and *more* desired as they are fulfilled.

It is, of course, the differences between ERG theory and the need hierarchy that represent Alderfer's contribution to the understanding of motivation. First, unlike the need hierarchy, ERG theory does not assume that a lower-level need *must* be gratified before a less concrete need becomes operative. Thus, ERG theory does not propose a rigid hierarchy of needs, and some individuals, owing to background and experience, might seek relatedness or growth even though their existence needs are ungratified. Hence, ERG theory seems to account for a wide variety of individual differences in motive structure. Second, ERG theory assumes that if the higher-level needs are ungratified, individuals will increase their desire for the gratification of lower-level needs. Notice that this represents a *radical* departure from Maslow. According to Maslow, if esteem needs are strong but ungratified, a person will not revert to an interest in belongingness needs because these have necessarily already been gratified. (Remember, he argues that satisfied needs are not motivational.) According to Alderfer, however, the frustration of higher-order needs will lead workers to regress to a more concrete need category. For example, the software designer who is unable to establish rewarding social relationships with superiors or co-workers might increase his interest in fulfilling existence needs, perhaps by seeking a pay increase. Thus, according to Alderfer, an apparently satisfied need can act as a motivator by substituting for an unsatisfied need.

Given the preceding description of ERG theory, we can identify its two major motivational premises as follows: *The more lower-level needs are gratified, the more higher-level need satisfaction is desired; the less higher-level needs are gratified, the more lower-level need satisfaction is desired.*

McClelland's Theory of Needs

McClelland's theory of needs. A nonhierarchical need theory of motivation that outlines the conditions under which certain needs result in particular patterns of motivation.

Psychologist David McClelland has spent several decades studying the human need structure and its implications for motivation. According to **McClelland's theory of needs,** needs reflect relatively stable personality characteristics that one acquires through early life experiences and exposure to selected aspects of one's society. Unlike Maslow and Alderfer, McClelland has not been interested in specifying a hierarchical relationship among needs. Rather, he has been more concerned with the specific behavioural consequences of needs. In other words, under what conditions are certain needs likely to result in particular patterns of motivation? The three needs that McClelland studied most have special relevance for organizational behaviour—needs for achievement, affiliation, and power.[14]

Need for achievement. A strong desire to perform challenging tasks well.

Individuals who are high in **need for achievement** (*n* Ach) have a strong desire to perform challenging tasks well. More specifically, they exhibit the following characteristics:

- *A preference for situations in which personal responsibility can be taken for outcomes.* Those high in *n* Ach do not prefer situations in which outcomes are determined by chance because success in such situations does not provide an experience of achievement.

- *A tendency to set moderately difficult goals that provide for calculated risks.* Success with easy goals will provide little sense of achievement, while extremely difficult goals might never be reached. The calculation of successful risks is stimulating to the high-*n* Ach person.

- *A desire for performance feedback.* Such feedback permits individuals with high *n* Ach to modify their goal attainment strategies to ensure success and signals them when success has been reached.[15]

People who are high in *n* Ach are concerned with bettering their own performance or that of others. They are often concerned with innovation and long-term goal involvement. However, these things are not done to please others or to damage the interests of others. Rather, they are done because they are *intrinsically* satisfying. Thus, n Ach would appear to be an example of a growth or self-actualization need.

People who are high in **need for affiliation** (n Aff) have a strong desire to establish and maintain friendly, compatible interpersonal relationships. In other words, they like to like others, and they want others to like them! More specifically, they have an ability to learn social networking quickly and a tendency to communicate frequently with others, either face-to-face, by telephone, or by letter. Also, they prefer to avoid conflict and competition with others, and they sometimes exhibit strong conformity to the wishes of their friends. The n Aff motive is obviously an example of a belongingness or relatedness need.

People who are high in **need for power** (n Pow) strongly desire to have influence over others. In other words, they wish to make a significant impact or impression on them. People who are high in n Pow seek out social settings in which they can be influential. When in small groups, they act in a "high-profile," attention-getting manner. There is some tendency for those who are high in n Pow to advocate risky positions. Also, some people who are high in n Pow show a strong concern for personal prestige. The need for power is a complex need because power can be used in a variety of ways, some of which serve the power seeker and some of which serve other people or the organization. However, n Pow seems to correspond most closely to Maslow's self-esteem need.

McClelland predicts that people will be motivated to seek out and perform well in jobs that match their needs. Thus, people with high n Ach should be strongly motivated by sales jobs or entrepreneurial positions, such as running a small business. Such jobs offer the feedback, personal responsibility, and opportunity to set goals, as noted above. People who are high in n Aff will be motivated by jobs such as social work or customer relations because these jobs have as a primary task establishing good relations with others. Finally, high n Pow will result in high motivation on jobs that enable one to have a strong impact on others, jobs such as journalism and management. In fact, McClelland has found that the most effective managers have a low need for affiliation, a high need for power, and the ability to direct power toward organizational goals.[16] (We will study this further in Chapter 12.)

Research Support for Need Theories

Measuring peoples' needs and the extent to which they have these needs fulfilled has proven to be a difficult task. Thus, the need theories are not especially easy to test. Nevertheless, we can draw some conclusions about their usefulness.

Maslow's need hierarchy suggests two main hypotheses. First, specific needs should cluster into the five main need categories that Maslow proposes. Second, as the needs in a given category are satisfied, they should become less important, while the needs in the adjacent higher-need category should become more important. This second hypothesis captures the progressive, hierarchical aspect of the theory. In general, research support for both these hypotheses is weak or negative. This is probably a function of the rigidity of the theory, which suggests that most people experience the same needs in the same hierarchical order. However, in this research, there is fair support for a simpler two-level need hierarchy comprising the needs toward the top and the bottom of Maslow's hierarchy.[17]

This latter finding provides some indirect encouragement for the compressed need hierarchy found in Alderfer's ERG theory. Several tests indicate fairly good support for many of the predictions generated by the theory, including expected changes in need strength. Particularly interesting is the confirmation that the

Need for affiliation. A strong desire to establish and maintain friendly, compatible interpersonal relationships.

Need for power. A strong desire to influence others, making a significant impact or impression.

frustration of relatedness needs increases the strength of existence needs.[18] The simplicity and flexibility of ERG theory seem to capture the human need structure better than the greater complexity and rigidity of Maslow's theory.

McClelland's need theory has generated a wealth of predictions about many aspects of human motivation. Recently, researchers have tested more and more of these predictions in organizational settings, and the results are generally supportive of the idea that particular needs are motivational when the work setting permits the satisfaction of these needs.[19]

Managerial Implications of Need Theories

The need theories have some important things to say about managerial attempts to motivate employees.

Appreciate Diversity. The lack of support for the fairly rigid need hierarchy suggests that managers must be adept at evaluating the needs of individual employees and offering incentives or goals that correspond to their own needs. Unfounded stereotypes about the needs of the "typical" employee and naive assumptions about the universality of need satisfaction are bound to reduce the effectiveness of chosen motivational strategies. The best salesperson might not make the best sales manager! The needs of a young recent college graduate probably differ from those of an older employee preparing for retirement. One of the most important aspects of Starbucks work/life benefits program is that it surveys employees to find out what their needs are and then offers programs that meet those needs.

Appreciate Intrinsic Motivation. The need theories also serve the valuable function of alerting managers to the existence of higher-order needs (whatever specific label we apply to them). The recognition of these needs in many employees is important for two key reasons. One of the basic conditions for organizational survival is the expression of some creative and innovative behaviour on the part of members. Such behaviour seems most likely to occur during the pursuit of higher-order need fulfillment, and ignorance of this factor can cause the demotivation of the people who have the most to offer the organization. Second, observation and research evidence support Alderfer's idea that the frustration of higher-order needs prompts demands for greater satisfaction of lower-order needs. This can lead to a vicious motivational circle, that is, because the factors that gratify lower-level needs are fairly easy to administer (e.g., pay and fringe benefits), management has grown to rely on them to motivate employees. In turn, some employees, deprived of higher-order need gratification, come to expect more and more of these extrinsic factors in exchange for their services. Thus, a circle of deprivation, regression, and temporary gratification continues at great cost to the organization.[20]

How can organizations benefit from the intrinsic motivation that is inherent in strong higher-order needs? First, such needs will fail to develop for most employees unless lower-level needs are reasonably well gratified.[21] Thus, very poor pay, job insecurity, and unsafe working conditions will preoccupy most workers at the expense of higher-order outcomes. Second, if basic needs are met, jobs can be "enriched" to be more stimulating and challenging and to provide feelings of responsibility and achievement. We will discuss this process fully in the next chapter. Finally, organizations could pay more attention to designing career paths that enable interested workers to progress through a series of jobs that continue to challenge their higher-order needs. Individual managers could also assign tasks to subordinates with this goal in mind.

Process Theories of Work Motivation

In contrast to need theories of motivation, which concentrate on *what* motivates people, **process theories** concentrate on *how* motivation occurs. In this section, we will examine three important process theories—expectancy theory, equity theory, and goal setting theory.

Process theories. Motivation theories that specify the details of how motivation occurs.

Expectancy Theory

The basic idea underlying **expectancy theory** is the belief that motivation is determined by the outcomes that people expect to occur as a result of their actions on the job. Psychologist Victor Vroom is usually credited with developing the first complete version of expectancy theory and applying it to the work setting.[22] The basic components of Vroom's theory are shown in Exhibit 5.3:

Expectancy theory. A process theory that states that motivation is determined by the outcomes that people expect to occur as a result of their actions on the job.

- **Outcomes** are the consequences that may follow certain work behaviours. First-level outcomes are of particular interest to the organization; for example, high productivity versus average productivity, illustrated in Exhibit 5.3, or good attendance versus poor attendance. Expectancy theory is concerned with specifying how an employee might attempt to choose one first-level outcome instead of another. Second-level outcomes are consequences that follow the attainment of a particular first-level outcome. Contrasted with first-level outcomes, second-level outcomes are most personally relevant to the individual worker and might involve amount of pay, sense of accomplishment, acceptance by peers, fatigue, and so on.

Outcomes. Consequences that follow work behaviour.

- **Instrumentality** is the probability that a particular first-level outcome (such as high productivity) will be followed by a particular second-level outcome (such as pay). For example, a bank teller might figure that the odds are 50 – 50 (instrumentality = .5) that a good performance rating will result in a pay raise.

Instrumentality. The probability that a particular first-level outcome will be followed by a particular second-level outcome.

- **Valence** is the expected value of outcomes, the extent to which they are attractive or unattractive to the individual. Thus, good pay, peer acceptance, the chance of being fired, or any other second-level outcome might be more or less attractive to particular workers. According to Vroom, the valence of first-level outcomes is the sum of products of the associated second-level outcomes and their instrumentalities, that is,

Valence. The expected value of work outcomes; the extent to which they are attractive or unattractive.

$$\text{the valence of a particular first-level outcome} = \Sigma \text{ instrumentalities} \times \text{second-level valences.}$$

In other words, the valence of a first-level outcome depends on the extent to which it leads to favourable second-level outcomes.

- **Expectancy** is the probability that the worker can actually achieve a particular first-level outcome. For example, a machinist might be absolutely certain (expectancy = 1.0) that she can perform at an average level (producing 15 units a day) but less certain (expectancy = .6) that she can perform at a high level (producing 20 units a day).

Expectancy. The probability that a particular first-level outcome can be achieved.

- **Force** is the end product of the other components of the theory. It represents the relative degree of effort that will be directed toward various first-level outcomes. According to Vroom, the force directed toward a first-level outcome is a product of the valence of that outcome and the expectancy that it can be achieved. Thus,

Force. The effort directed toward a first-level outcome.

$$\text{force} = \text{first-level valence} \times \text{expectancy.}$$

We can expect an individual's effort to be directed toward the first-level outcome that has the largest force product. Notice that no matter how valent a particular first-level outcome might be, a person will not be motivated to achieve it if the expectancy of accomplishment approaches zero.

Believe it or not, the mechanics of expectancy theory can be distilled into a couple of simple sentences! In fact, these sentences nicely capture the premises of the theory: *People will be motivated to perform in those work activities that they find attractive and that they feel they can accomplish. The attractiveness of various work activities depends on the extent to which they lead to favourable personal consequences.*

It is extremely important to understand that expectancy theory is based on the perceptions of the individual worker. Thus, expectancies, valences, instrumentalities, and relevant second-level outcomes depend on the perceptual system of the person whose motivation we are analyzing. For example, two employees per-

Exhibit 5.3
A hypothetical expectancy model (E = Expectancy, I = Instrumentality, V = Valence).

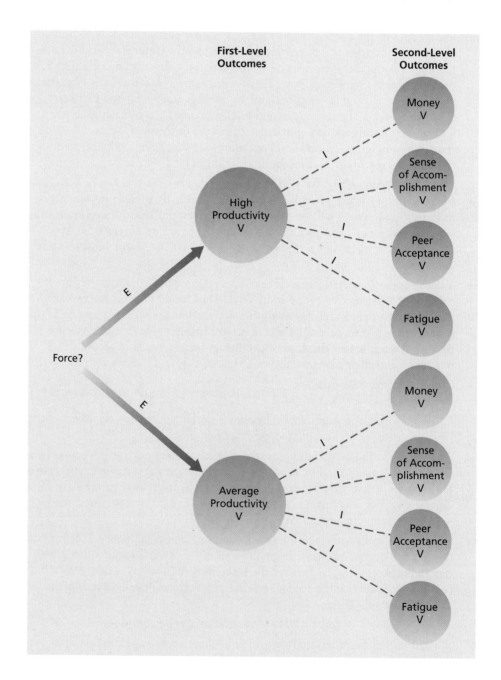

forming the same job might attach different valences to money, differ in their perceptions of the instrumentality of performance for obtaining high pay, and differ in their expectations of being able to perform at a high level. Therefore, they would likely exhibit different patterns of motivation.

Although expectancy theory does not concern itself directly with the distinction between extrinsic and intrinsic motivators, it can handle any form of second-level outcome that has relevance for the person in question. Thus, some people might find second-level outcomes of an intrinsic nature, such as feeling good about performing a task well, positively valent. Others might find extrinsic outcomes, such as high pay, positively valent.

To firm up your understanding of expectancy theory, consider Tony Angelas, a middle manager in a firm that operates a chain of retail stores (Exhibit 5.4). Second-level outcomes that are relevant to him include the opportunity to obtain a raise and the chance to receive a promotion. The promotion is more highly valent to Tony than the raise (7 versus 5 on a scale of 10) because the promotion means more money *and* increased prestige. Tony figures that if he can perform at a very high level in the next few months, the odds are six in ten that he will receive a raise. Thus, the instrumentality of high performance for obtaining a raise is .6. Promotions are harder to come by, and Tony figures the odds at .3 if he performs well. The instrumentality of average performance for achieving these favourable second-level outcomes is a good bit lower (.2 for the raise and only .1 for the promotion). Recall that the valence of a first-level outcome is the sum of the products of second-level outcomes and their instrumentalities. Thus, the valence of high performance for Tony is $(5 \times .6) + (7 \times .3) = 5.1$. Similarly, the valence of average performance is $(5 \times .2) + (7 \times .1) = 1.7$. We can conclude that high performance is more valent for Tony than average performance.

Does this mean that Tony will necessarily try to perform at a high level in the next few months? To determine this, we must take into account his expectancy that he can actually achieve the competing first-level outcomes. As shown in Exhibit 5.4, Tony is absolutely certain that he can perform at an average level (expectancy = 1.0) but much less certain (.3) that he can sustain high performance. Force is a product of these expectancies and the valence of their respective first-level outcomes. Thus, the force associated with high performance is $.3 \times 5.1 = 1.53$, while that associated with average performance is $1.0 \times 1.7 = 1.70$. As a result, although high performance is attractive to Tony, he will probably perform at an average level.

With all this complicated figuring, you might be thinking "Look, would Tony really do all this calculation to decide his motivational strategy? Do people actually think this way?" The answer to these questions is probably no. Rather, the argument is that people *implicitly* take expectancy, valence, and instrumentality into account as they go about their daily business of being motivated. If you reflect for a moment on your behaviour at work or school, you will realize that you have certain expectancies about what you can accomplish, the chances that these accomplishments will lead to certain other outcomes, and the value of these outcomes for you.

Research Support for Expectancy Theory

Tests have provided moderately favourable support for expectancy theory.[23] In particular, there is especially good evidence that the valence of first-level outcomes depends on the extent to which they lead to favourable second-level consequences. We must recognize, however, that the sheer complexity of expectancy theory makes it difficult to test. We have already suggested that people are not used to *thinking* in expectancy terminology. Thus, some research studies show

Exhibit 5.4
Expectancy model for Tony
Angelas (E = Expectancy,
I = Instrumentality,
V = Valence).

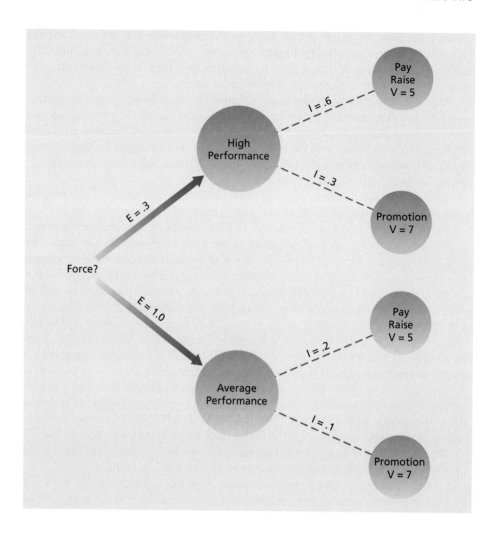

that individuals have a difficult time discriminating between instrumentalities and second-level valences. Despite this and other technical problems, experts in motivation generally accept expectancy theory.

Managerial Implications of Expectancy Theory

The motivational practices suggested by expectancy theory involve "juggling the numbers" that individuals attach to expectancies, instrumentalities, and valences.

Boost Expectancies. One of the most basic things managers can do is ensure that their subordinates *expect* to be able to achieve first-level outcomes that are of interest to the organization. No matter how positively valent high productivity or good attendance might be, the force equation suggests that workers will not pursue these goals if expectancy is low. Low expectancies can take many forms, but a few examples will suffice to make the point.

- Employees might feel that poor equipment, poor tools, or lazy co-workers impede their work progress.

- Employees might not understand what the organization considers to be good performance or see how they can achieve it.

- If performance is evaluated by a subjective supervisory rating, employees might see the process as capricious and arbitrary, not understanding how to obtain a good rating.

Although the specific solutions to these problems vary, expectancies can usually be enhanced by providing proper equipment and training, demonstrating correct work procedures, carefully explaining how performance is evaluated, and listening to employee performance problems. The point of all this is to clarify the path to beneficial first-level outcomes. At Starbucks, employees receive extensive training that should result in high expectancies in areas such as product quality and customer service.

Clarify Reward Contingencies. Managers should also attempt to ensure that the paths between first- and second-level outcomes are clear. Employees should be convinced that first-level outcomes desired by the organization are clearly *instrumental* in obtaining positive second-level outcomes and avoiding negative outcomes. If a manager has a policy of recommending good performers for promotion, she should spell out this policy. Similarly, if managers desire regular attendance, they should clarify the consequences of good and poor attendance. To ensure that instrumentalities are strongly established, they should be clearly stated and then acted on by the manager. Managers should also attempt to provide stimulating, challenging tasks for workers who appear to be interested in such work. On such tasks, the instrumentality of good performance for feelings of achievement, accomplishment, and competence is almost necessarily high. The ready availability of intrinsic motivation reduces the need for the manager to constantly monitor and clarify instrumentalities.[24]

Appreciate Diverse Needs. Obviously, it might be difficult for managers to change the valences that subordinates attach to second-level outcomes. Individual preferences for high pay, promotion, interesting work, and so on are the product of a long history of development and unlikely to change rapidly. However, managers would do well to analyze the diverse preferences of particular subordinates and attempt to design individualized "motivational packages" to meet their needs. Of course, all concerned must perceive such packages to be fair. Let us examine another process theory that is concerned specifically with the motivational consequences of fairness.

Equity Theory

In Chapter 4, we discussed the role of **equity theory** in explaining job satisfaction. To review, the theory asserts that workers compare the inputs that they invest in their jobs and the outcomes that they receive against the inputs and outcomes of some other relevant person or group. When these ratios are equal, the worker should feel that a fair and equitable exchange exists with the employing organization. Such fair exchange contributes to job satisfaction. When the ratios are unequal, workers perceive inequity, and they should experience job dissatisfaction, at least if the exchange puts the worker at a disadvantage vis-à-vis others.

But in what sense is equity theory a theory of motivation? Put simply, *individuals are motivated to maintain an equitable exchange relationship.* Inequity is unpleasant and tension producing, and people will devote considerable energy to reducing inequity and achieving equity. What tactics can do this? Psychologist J. Stacey Adams has suggested the following possibilities:

- Perceptually distort one's own inputs or outcomes.
- Perceptually distort the inputs or outcomes of the comparison person or of the group.
- Choose another comparison person or group.
- Alter one's inputs or alter one's outcomes.
- Leave the exchange relationship.[25]

Equity theory. A process theory that states that motivation stems from a comparison of the inputs one invests in a job and the outcomes one receives in comparison with the inputs and outcomes of another person or group.

Notice that the first three tactics for reducing inequity are essentially psychological, while the last two involve overt behaviour.

To clarify the motivational implications of equity theory, consider Terry, a middle manager in a consumer products company. He has five years' work experience and an MBA degree and considers himself a good performer. His salary is $75,000 a year. Terry finds out that Maxine, a co-worker with whom he identifies closely, makes the same salary he does. However, she has only a Bachelor's degree and one year of experience, and he sees her performance as average rather than good. Thus, from Terry's perspective, the following outcome/input ratios exist:

$$\frac{\text{TERRY } \$75{,}000}{\text{Good performance, MBA, 5 years}} \neq \frac{\text{MAXINE } \$75{,}000}{\text{Average performance, Bachelor's, 1 year}}$$

In Terry's view, he is underpaid and should be experiencing inequity. What might he do to resolve this inequity? Psychologically, he might distort the outcomes that he is receiving, rationalizing that he is due for a certain promotion that will bring his pay into line with his inputs. Behaviourally, he might try to increase his outcomes (by seeking an immediate raise) or reduce his inputs. Input reduction could include a decrease in work effort or perhaps excessive absenteeism. Finally, Terry might resign from the organization to take what he perceives to be a more equitable job somewhere else.

Let us reverse the coin and assume that Maxine views the exchange relationship identically to Terry—same inputs, same outcomes. Notice that she too should be experiencing inequity, this time from relative overpayment. It does not take a genius to understand that Maxine would be unlikely to seek equity by marching into the boss's office and demanding a pay cut. However, she might well attempt to increase her inputs by working harder or enrolling in an MBA program. Alternatively, she might distort her view of Terry's performance to make it seem closer to her own. As this example implies, equity theory is somewhat vague about just when individuals will employ various inequity reduction strategies.

Gender and Equity. As an addendum to the previous example, it is extremely interesting to learn that both women and men have some tendency to choose same-sex comparison persons, that is, when judging the fairness of the outcomes that they receive, men tend to compare themselves with other men, and women tend to compare themselves with other women. This might provide a partial explanation for why women are paid less than men, even for the same job. If women restrict their equity comparisons to (lesser paid) women, they are less likely to be motivated to correct what we observers see as wage inequities.[26]

Research Support for Equity Theory. Most research on equity theory has been restricted to economic outcomes and has concentrated on the alteration of inputs and outcomes as a means of reducing inequity. In general, this research is very supportive of the theory when inequity occurs because of *underpayment*.[27] For example, when workers are underpaid on an hourly basis, they tend to lower their inputs by producing less work. This brings inputs in line with (low) outcomes. Also, when workers are underpaid on a piece-rate basis (e.g., paid $1 for each market research interview conducted), they tend to produce a high volume of low-quality work. This enables them to raise their outcomes to achieve equity. Finally, there is also evidence that underpayment inequity leads to resignation. Presumably, some underpaid workers thus seek equity in another organizational setting.

The theory's predictions regarding *overpayment* inequity have received less support.[28] The theory suggests that such inequity can be reduced behaviourally by increasing inputs or by reducing one's outcomes. The weak support for these strategies suggests either that people tolerate overpayment more than underpayment, or that they use perceptual distortion to reduce overpayment inequity.

Managerial Implications of Equity Theory. The most straightforward implication of equity theory is that perceived underpayment will have a variety of negative motivational consequences for the organization, including low productivity, low quality, theft, and/or turnover. (See "Ethical Focus: *Inequity and Employee Theft.*") On the other hand, attempting to solve organizational problems through overpayment (disguised bribery) might not have the intended motivational effect. The trick here is to strike an equitable balance.

But how can such a balance be struck? Managers must understand that feelings about equity stem from a *perceptual* social comparison process in which the worker "controls the equation," that is, employees decide what are considered relevant inputs, outcomes, and comparison persons, and management must be sensitive to these decisions. For example, offering the outcome of more interesting work might not redress inequity if better pay is considered a more relevant outcome. Similarly, basing pay only on performance might not be perceived as equitable if employees consider seniority an important job input.

Understanding the role of comparison people is especially crucial.[29] Even if the best engineer in the design department earns $2,000 more than anyone else in the department, she might still have feelings of inequity if she compares her salary with that of more prosperous colleagues in *other* companies. Awareness of the comparison people chosen by workers might suggest strategies for reducing felt inequity. Perhaps the company will have to pay even more to retain its star engineer. Equity is achieved at Starbucks by treating all employees as partners who are equal participants in the company's "bean stock" and work/life programs.

Goal Setting Theory

One of the basic characteristics of all organizations is that they have goals. At the beginning of this chapter, individual performance was defined as the extent to which a member contributes to the attainment of these goals or objectives. Thus, if employees are to achieve acceptable performance, some method of translating organizational goals into individual goals must be implemented.

Unfortunately, there is ample reason to believe that personal performance goals are vague or nonexistent for many organizational members. Employees frequently report that their role in the organization is unclear, or that they do not really know what their boss expects of them. Even in cases in which performance goals would seem to be obvious because of the nature of the task (e.g., filling packing crates to the maximum to avoid excessive freight charges), employees might be ignorant of their current performance. This suggests that the implicit performance goals simply are not making an impression.

The notion of **goal setting** as a motivator has been around for a long time. However, theoretical developments and some very practical research demonstrations have begun to suggest just when and how goal setting can be effective.[30]

Goal setting. A motivational technique that uses specific, challenging, and acceptable goals and provides feedback to enhance performance.

What Kinds of Goals Are Motivational?

A large body of evidence suggests that goals are most motivational when they are *specific*, *challenging*, and *accepted* by organizational members. In addition, *feedback* about progress toward goal attainment should be provided.[31]

Goal Specificity. Specific goals are goals that specify an exact level of achievement for people to accomplish in a particular time frame. For example, "I will

in focus → Inequity and Employee Theft

In a survey conducted by the London House publishing firm and the Food Marketing Institute, supermarket employees admitted that they stole an average of $168 worth of merchandise a year. This figure was substantially higher than in previous years' surveys. The most popular products were meat, cheese, cigarettes, and beauty and health-care items. Some of this theft is probably due to feelings of exploitation in employees. Equity theory predicts that underpayment inequity can be resolved by increasing one's outcomes. Theft could be an informal mechanism for doing this. As one survey respondent noted, "During the last couple of years, the company has kept raising the standards and cutting back on the hours allotted to keeping those standards up. If you don't work *off the clock*, the job won't get done. Some people steal as a way to get even."

Psychologist Jerald Greenberg studied employee theft in manufacturing plants before, during, and after the imposition of a temporary 10-week pay cut that was necessitated by a loss of orders. In line with equity theory predictions, he found that theft increased greatly during the rollback and then returned to previous levels once normal pay levels were reinstituted. Greenberg also found that the increase in theft was less pronounced in a plant where management provided an honest and caring explanation for the pay cuts. Perceptions that management was trying to act ethically despite the need for the cuts reduced feelings of inequity.

Sources: London House/Food Marketing Institute (1992). *Third annual report on employee theft in the supermarket industry*. Rosemont, IL: London House; Greenberg, J. (1990). Employee theft as a reaction to underpayment inequity: The hidden cost of pay cuts. *Journal of Applied Psychology, 75*, pp. 561–568.

Food Marketing Institute
www.fmi.org/

enroll in five courses next semester and achieve a *B* or better in each course" is a specific goal. Similarly, "I will increase my net sales by 20 percent in the coming business quarter" is a specific goal. On the other hand, "I will do my best" is not a specific goal, since level of achievement and time frame are both vague.

Goal Challenge. Obviously, specific goals that are especially easy to achieve will not motivate effective performance. However, goal challenge is a much more personal matter than goal specificity, since it depends on the experience and basic skills of the organizational member. One thing is certain, however—when goals become so difficult that they are perceived as *impossible* to achieve, they will lose their potential to motivate. Thus, goal challenge is best when it is pegged to the competence of individual workers and increased as the particular task is mastered. One practical way to do this is to base initial goals on past performance. For example, an academic counsellor might encourage a *D* student to set a goal of achieving *C*s in the coming semester and encourage a *C* student to set a goal of achieving *B*s. Similarly, a sales manager might ask a new salesperson to try to increase his sales by 5 percent in the next quarter and ask an experienced salesperson to try to increase her sales by 10 percent.

Goal Acceptance. Specific, challenging goals must be accepted by the individual if the goals are to have effective motivational properties. In a sense, goals really are not goals unless they are consciously accepted. In a following section, we will discuss some factors that affect goal acceptance.

Goal Feedback. Specific, challenging, accepted goals have the most beneficial effect when they are accompanied by ongoing feedback that enables the person to compare current performance with the goal. This is why a schedule of tasks to be completed often motivates goal accomplishment. Progress against the schedule provides feedback.

Enhancing Goal Acceptance

It has probably not escaped you that the requirements for goal challenge and goal acceptance seem potentially incompatible. After all, you might be quite amenable to accepting an easy goal but balk at accepting a tough one. Thus, it is important to consider some of the factors that might affect the acceptance of challenging, specific goals, including participation, rewards, and management support.

Participation. It seems reasonable that organizational members should be more accepting of goals that are set with their participation than of those simply handed down by their superior. Sensible as this sounds, the research evidence on the effects of participation is very mixed—sometimes participation in goal setting increases performance, and sometimes it does not.[32] If goal acceptance is a potential *problem,* participation might prove beneficial.[33] When a climate of distrust between superiors and subordinates exists, or when participation provides information that assists in the establishment of fair, realistic goals, then it should facilitate performance. On the other hand, when subordinates trust their boss, and when the boss has a good understanding of the capability of the subordinates, participation might be quite unnecessary for acceptance.[34] It is interesting that research shows participation can increase performance by increasing the *difficulty* of the goals that employees adopt.[35] This might occur because participation induces competition or a feeling of team spirit among members of the work unit that leads them to exceed the goal expectations of the supervisor.

Rewards. Will the promise of extrinsic rewards (such as money) for goal accomplishment increase the acceptance of goals? Probably, but there is plenty of evidence that goal setting has led to performance increases *without* the introduction of monetary incentives for goal accomplishment. One reason for this might be that many ambitious goals involve no more than doing the job as it was designed to be done in the first place. For example, encouraging employees to pack crates or load trucks to within 5 percent of their maximum capacity does not really involve a greater expenditure of effort or more work. It simply requires more attention to detail. Goal setting should, however, be compatible with any system to tie pay to performance that already exists for the job in question.

Supportiveness. There is considerable agreement about one factor that will *reduce* the acceptance of specific, challenging performance goals. When supervisors behave in a coercive manner to encourage goal accomplishment, they can badly damage employee commitment to the goal. For goal setting to work properly, supervisors must demonstrate a desire to assist employees in goal accomplishment and behave supportively if failure occurs, even adjusting the goal downward if it proves to be unrealistically high. Threat and punishment in response to failure will be extremely counterproductive.[36]

Research Support for and Managerial Implications of Goal Setting Theory

Goal setting has led to increased performance on a wide variety of tasks, including servicing drink machines, entering data, selling, and typing text. Studies reveal that the positive results of goal setting are not short lived—they persist over a long enough time to have practical value.[37]

A good example of research and the application of goal setting theory occurred at Weyerhaeuser Company. Weyerhaeuser Company is a large forest products firm headquartered in Tacoma, Washington. Weyerhaeuser faced a problem that commonly crops up in production operations—the underutilization of expensive resources. The problem centred on the truck drivers who hauled logs from the forest to a company sawmill. The drivers, who also loaded the trucks, were unionized and paid on an hourly basis. Management determined that the trucks were averaging only about 60 percent of their legal weight capacity. This extreme

Weyerhaeuser Co.
www.weyerhaeuser.com

Drivers at Weyerhaeuser Company were assigned a specific, challenging performance goal of loading their trucks to 94 percent of legal weight capacity.

underloading was very undesirable because extra trucks, extra drivers, and extra diesel fuel were necessary to transport a given amount of timber.

Management was convinced that it could improve the situation if the drivers could be motivated to pay more attention to their loading procedures. Because logs differ in diameter and length, a full load could vary between 60 and 120 logs. Thus, the drivers had to exercise judgment in the loading process. Although a scale was available at the loading point, the drivers did not seem to be making good use of it.

With the union's cooperation, the drivers were assigned a specific, challenging performance goal of loading their trucks to 94 percent of legal weight capacity. Before setting this goal, management simply asked the drivers to do their best to maximize their weight. The results? Over the first several weeks, load capacity gradually increased to over 90 percent and remained at this high level for seven years! In the first nine months alone, the company accountants conservatively estimated the savings at $250,000. These results were achieved without driver participation in setting the goal and without monetary incentives for goal accomplishment. Drivers evidently found the 94 percent goal motivating in and of itself; they frequently recorded their weights in informal competition with other drivers.[38]

As this example demonstrates, the managerial implications of goal setting theory are straightforward: Set specific and challenging goals and provide ongoing feedback so that individuals can compare their performance with the goal. While goals can be motivational in certain circumstances, they obviously have some limitations. For example, the performance impact of goal setting is strongest for simpler jobs rather than more complex jobs, such as scientific and engineering work. In the next chapter, we will discuss a more elaborate application of goal setting theory, called "management by objectives." For now, see the In Focus feature for a consideration of the effects of group goal setting.

Do Motivation Theories Translate Across Cultures?

Are the motivation theories that we have been considering in this chapter culture bound, that is, do they apply only to North America, where they were developed?

in focus → Does Group Goal Setting Improve Group Performance?

While the motivational effects of individual goal setting on performance have been known for many years, much less is known about the effects of group goal setting. This is an important topic as the work in organizations is increasingly being performed by groups of workers. Many types of groups are now quite common in organizations. Given that all groups exist for the purpose of accomplishing goals, the effect of group goals on motivation and group performance is a new and important topic in the area of work motivation. Goals will increasingly be used to motivate groups in addition to individuals. But are group goals also motivational, and will they improve the performance of groups?

In order to answer this question, Anne O'Leary-Kelly, Joseph Martocchio, and Dwight Frink reviewed 29 group goal setting studies that tested the effect of group goals on group performance. Consistent with the results of research on individual goal setting, they found a strong effect for group goals. Groups that set goals performed significantly better than groups that did not set goals. The effect of group goal setting on group performance was similar to the effect of individual goal setting.

The authors also found that the positive effect of group goals on group performance was more likely in groups that set specific goals. Specific goals are particularly important for groups because multiple or competing goals can lead to ambiguity about acceptable performance standards. They also found some evidence that group goals are more effective when the group participates in setting the goals.

While these results confirm the importance of group goal setting, it is important to realize that factors associated with the group context, such as group cohesiveness and social loafing, can also influence group effort and persistence. In addition, the type of task that the group performs might also be an important factor. Group goals might be more or less effective for groups that work interdependently compared with those in which group members work alone. Therefore, compared with individual goal setting, group goal setting and its effect on group performance is much more complex.

Source: Adapted from O'Leary-Kelly, A. M., Martocchio, J. J., & Frink, D. D. (1994). A review of the influence of group goals on group performance. *Academy of Management Journal*, 37, pp. 1285-1301.

The answer to this question is important for North American organizations that must understand motivational patterns in their international operations. It is also important to foreign managers, who are often exposed to North American theory and practice as part of their training and development.

It is safe to assume that most theories that revolve around human needs will come up against cultural limitations to their generality. For example, both Maslow and Alderfer suggest that people pass through a social stage (belongingness, relatedness) on their way to a higher-level personal growth or self-actualization stage. However, as we discussed in the previous chapter, it is well established that there are international differences in the extent to which societies value a more collective or a more individualistic approach to life.[39] In individualistic societies (e.g., the United States, Canada, Great Britain, Australia), people tend to value individual initiative, privacy, and taking care of oneself. In more collective societies (e.g., Mexico, Singapore, Pakistan), more closely knit social bonds are observed, in which members of one's in-group (family, clan, organization) are expected to take care of each other in exchange for strong loyalty to the in-group.[40] This suggests that there might be no superiority to self-actualization as a motive in more collective cultures. In some cases, for example, appealing to employee loyalty might prove more motivational than the opportunity for self-expression because it relates to strong belongingness needs that stem from cultural values. Also, cultures differ in the extent to which they value achievement as it is defined in North America, and conceptions of achievement might be more group oriented in collective cultures than in individualistic North America. Similarly, the whole concept of intrinsic motivation might be more relevant to wealthy societies than to the developing societies.

Cultures differ in how they define achievement. In collective societies where group solidarity is dominant, achievement may be more group oriented than in individualistic societies.

Turning to equity theory, we noted earlier that people should be appropriately motivated when outcomes received "match" job inputs. Thus, higher producers are likely to expect superior outcomes compared with lower producers. This is only one way to allocate rewards, however, and it is one that is most likely to be endorsed in individualistic cultures. In collective cultures, there is a tendency to favour reward allocation based on equality rather than equity.[41] In other words, everyone should receive the same outcomes despite individual differences in productivity, and group solidarity is a dominant motive. Trying to motivate employees with a "fair" reward system might backfire if your definition of fairness is equity and theirs is equality.

Because of its flexibility, expectancy theory is very effective when applied cross-culturally. The theory allows for the possibility that there may be cross-cultural differences in the expectancy that effort will result in high performance. It also allows for the fact that work outcomes (such as social acceptance versus individual recognition) may have different valences across cultures.[42]

Finally, setting specific and challenging goals should also be motivational when applied cross-culturally. However, to be effective, careful attention will be required to adjust the goal-setting process in different cultures. For example, individual goals are not likely to be accepted or motivational in collectivist cultures. Therefore, group rather than individual goals should be used in collectivist cultures. Power distance is also likely to be important in the goal-setting process. In cultures where power distance is large, it would be expected that goals be assigned by superiors. However, in some small power distance cultures in which power differences are downplayed, participative goal setting would be more appropriate. One limitation to the positive impact of goal setting might occur in those (mainly Far-Eastern) cultures in which saving face is important, that is, a specific and challenging goal may not be very motivating if it suggests that failure could occur and if it results in a negative reaction. This would seem to be especially bad if it were in the context of the less-than-preferred individual goal setting. Failure in the face of a very specific goal could lead to loss of face. As well, in the so-called "being-oriented" cultures where people work only as much as needed in order to live and avoid continuous work, there tends to be some resistance to goal setting.[43]

International management expert Nancy Adler has exemplified how cultural blinders often lead to motivational errors:

> International management literature is replete with examples of overgeneralization, due to the dominance of American reward structures. For example,... raising the salaries of a particular group of Mexican workers motivated them to work *fewer,* not more, hours. As the Mexicans explained, "We can now make enough money to live and enjoy life [one of their primary values] in less time than previously. Now, we do not have to work so many hours." In another example, an expatriate manager in Japan decided to promote one of his Japanese sales representatives to manager (a status reward). To the surprise of the expatriate boss, the promotion diminished the new Japanese manager's performance. Why? Japanese have a high need for harmony—to fit in with their colleagues. The promotion, an individualistic reward, separated the new manager from his colleagues, embarrassed him, and therefore diminished his motivation to work.[44]

A primary theme running through this discussion is that appreciating cultural diversity is critical in maximizing motivation. Now that we have covered the various motivation theories, let us use them to evaluate an actual motivation program. Please consult "You Be the Manager: *The New Incentive Program at Wesco Distribution.*"

Wesco Distribution Inc.
www.wescodist.com

you be the manager

The New Incentive Program at Wesco Distribution

> Wesco offers its employees a unique mix of bonuses and commissions tied to the company's top and bottom lines.

Not long ago, Wesco Distribution Inc., an electrical-supplies distributor based in Pittsburgh, was a money-losing unit of Westinghouse Electric Corp. Its staff was demoralized, turnover was high, and the company was adrift. Today, Wesco is thriving, largely due to an aggressive incentive plan that was implemented after the company's ownership changed hands.

To repair the damage quickly and create some forward momentum, the new management team decided to give employees a cut of profits and reward them for increasing net income year over year. Wesco offers its employees a unique mix of bonuses and commissions tied to the company's top and bottom lines. The new system holds risks for employees who do not meet profitability goals, but it also offers huge rewards for aggressive salespeople.

As a starting point, Wesco offers salespeople whose expenses are paid by the company a 12.5% commission on the annual gross profit of their sales. Salespeople who pay their own expenses are entitled to 18% of the gross profit their annual sales bring. For salespeople in the 18% category, Wesco also pays bonuses, capped at $10,000, for exceeding the total profit their sales generated the previous year. One Wesco salesman earned a bundle when he landed a multimillion-dollar contract with the federal government to provide an electric power generation system for the U.S. peacekeeping force in Bosnia.

However, the new system also carries its share of dangers for employees who do not have the drive needed to keep leaping over profitability hurdles. Wesco keeps a close eye on sales performance by grading it on a quarterly basis. Salespeople are paid a monthly advance of about $2,500 to $3,000 against their commission; those who do not cover their advance at the end of a quarter are fired or transferred to a less demanding position. But effective salespeople willing to put in the 60 to 70 hours a week their jobs demand say they are happy at Wesco.

So far, the numbers have proved the program a success. In 1993, when the New York investment bank Clayton, Dubilier & Rice bought Wesco from Westinghouse for $340 million, the company was losing money. Wesco showed a slight profit in 1994 and then went firmly into the black in 1995 with a profit of $25 million. Last year, boosted by a string of acquisitions in 1995, Wesco earned a profit of $32.5 million on sales of $2.3 billion.

At the same time, average annual compensation for the top performers in Wesco's 1,100-member sales force has climbed to more than $140,000 from about $70,000 in 1993. Among the company's 320 branch managers, average annual compensation at the most profitable branches has climbed to $160,000 from about $100,000 in 1993. And the turnover rate is 11%, the company's lowest in 15 years and less than half of what it was before Wesco was sold.

Use the questions below to frame your opinion about the motivational effectiveness of the new incentive program.

1. Use expectancy and goal setting theories to evaluate the strengths and weaknesses of the program.

2. How could equity considerations influence employee receptiveness to the program?

For some commentary on Wesco's incentive program, see The Manager's Notebook at the end of the chapter.

Source: Excerpted from O'Brien, T. L. (1997, April 10). Reaping the rewards. *The Wall Street Journal*, R9.

Putting It All Together: Integrating Theories of Work Motivation

In this chapter, we have presented several theories of work motivation and attempted to distinguish between motivation and performance. In Chapter 4, we discussed the relationship between job performance and job satisfaction. At this point, it seems appropriate to review just how all these concepts fit together. Exhibit 5.5 presents a model that integrates these relationships.

Each of the theories helps us to understand the motivational process. First, in order for individuals to obtain rewards, they must achieve designated levels of performance. We know from earlier in this chapter that performance is a function of motivation as well as other factors such as aptitude, skill, understanding, and chance. In terms of motivation, we are concerned with the amount, persistence, and direction of effort. Therefore, Boxes 1 through 5 explain these relationships.

Perceptions of expectancy and instrumentality (expectancy theory) relate to all three components of motivation (*Box 1*). In other words, individuals direct their effort toward a particular first-level outcome (expectancy) and increase the amount and persistence of effort to the extent that they believe it will result in second-level outcomes (instrumentality). Goal setting theory (*Box 2*) indicates that specific and challenging goals will have a positive effect on amount, persistence, and direction of effort. Goal specificity should also strengthen both expectancy and instrumentality connections. The individual will have a clear picture of a first-level outcome to which her effort should be directed and greater certainty about the consequences of achieving this outcome.

Boxes 3 through 5 illustrate that motivation (*Box 3*) will be translated into good performance (*Box 5*) if the worker has the aptitude and skills relevant to the job and if the worker understands the task (*Box 4*). Chance can also help to translate motivation into good performance. If these conditions are not met, high motivation will not result in good performance. For example, consider a hospital nurse who exhibits tremendous motivation but does not know how to use a syringe properly and is confused about her tasks and responsibilities. Clearly, such an individual will perform poorly in spite of high motivation. It is at this link between motivation and performance that observers frequently make judgments about the motivation of workers. Thus, the head nurse might judge the nurse as having "high" but "misdirected" motivation because the nurse is directing persistent effort in a way that does not help the hospital achieve its goals. This portion of the model is essentially the same as the relationships in Exhibit 5.1.

Exhibit 5.5
Integrative Model of Motivation Theories

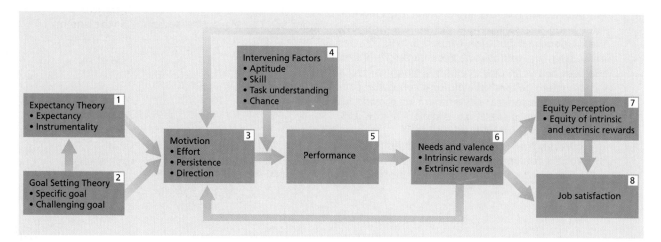

Second, a particular level of performance (*Box 5*) will be followed by certain outcomes. To the extent that performance is followed by outcomes that fulfill individual needs (need theory) and are positively valent second-level outcomes (expectancy theory), they can be considered rewards for good performance (*Box 6*). In general, the connection between performance and the occurrence of intrinsic rewards should be strong and reliable because such rewards are self-administered. For example, the nurse who assists several very sick patients back to health is almost certain to feel a sense of competence and achievement because such feelings stem directly from the job. On the other hand, the connection between performance and extrinsic rewards might be much less reliable because the occurrence of such rewards depends on the actions of management. Thus, the head nurse might or might not recommend attendance at a nursing conference (an extrinsic fringe benefit) for the good performance.

Third, to the extent that the rewards fulfill individual needs (need theory), then they will be motivational as depicted by the path from rewards (*Box 6*) to motivation (*Box 3*). In addition, the rewards that individuals receive are also the outcomes of the equity theory equation and will be used by individuals to form perceptions of equity (*Box 7*). Perceptions of equity also influence motivation (*Box 3*) and job satisfaction (*Box 8*). You will recall that this relationship be-

the manager's notebook
The New Incentive Program at Wesco Distribution

Wesco's new strategy is in tune with new practices for compensating salespeople. While most companies once tied commissions solely to the amount of business captured by a salesperson or a branch office, a growing number are now paying attention to the bottom line and compensating their sales force on the basis of the profitability of new contracts. Wesco's incentive program is unusual, in that it builds a real element of risk into pay—employees could make more or less commissions on the basis of the plan they choose, and failure to cover their advances can mean being fired or transferred.

Let us put the incentive program through a motivation theory audit:

1. In expectancy theory terms, sales and exceeding one's total profit from the previous year are first-level outcomes. Sales commissions and the bonus are second-level outcomes. The commission and bonus are clearly large enough to get employees' attention (12.5% or 18% commission and up to $10,000 bonus), and it should be highly valent. Also, the instrumentality connection between sales and one's commission and bonus is clear and obvious, being spelled out by a formula. Potential problems centre on the expectancy that employees would be able to exceed their previous year's sales, cover their advances, and work the required 60 to 70 hours a week to do so. Outstanding management support would be necessary, as would some sales training geared toward improving sales. Also,

factors beyond the employees' control, such as the economy, could adversely affect profit growth and thus damage expectancy. In goal setting theory terms, the goals of exceeding one's sales each year and covering advances are very specific and probably challenging to most of the sales force which should prove to be highly motivational.

2. From an equity theory perspective, the outcomes that employees receive are a direct result of their inputs. In other words, one's commission and bonus are the result of one's sales. However, when considering the social comparison component of equity theory, a couple of potential problems could result in perceptions of inequity and reduced motivation. First, because of the requirement to leap profitability hurdles and cover advances, employees may feel that they are being treated unfairly, compared with how they were treated under the previous system which did not penalize them for not covering their advance or increasing their sales. Second, because employees who pay their own expenses receive a higher percent of commission and are also eligible for a bonus in comparison with salespersons whose expenses are paid by the company, there is the potential for some salespersons to earn more money for doing the same amount of sales. Large differences in compensation between the two plans might lead to some perceptions of inequity.

tween job outcomes, equity, and job satisfaction was discussed in Chapter 4. According to equity theory, individuals in a state of equity have high job satisfaction. Individuals who are in a state of inequity experience job dissatisfaction. Also recall that in Chapter 4, we emphasized that job satisfaction does not lead to good performance. Conversely, good performance leads to job satisfaction if that performance is rewarded.

In summary, each theory of motivation helps us to understand a different part of the motivational process. Understanding how the different theories of motivation can be integrated brings us to the topic of the next chapter—practical methods of motivation that apply the theories we have been studying in this chapter.

Summary

- Motivation is the extent to which persistent effort is directed toward a goal. Intrinsic motivation stems from the direct relationship between the worker and the task and is usually self-applied. Extrinsic motivation stems from the environment surrounding the task and is applied by others. Performance is the extent to which an organizational member contributes to achieving the objectives of the organization. It is influenced by motivation but also by aptitudes, skills, task understanding, and chance factors.

- Need theories propose that motivation will occur when employee behaviour can be directed toward goals or incentives that satisfy personal wants or desires. The three need theories discussed were Maslow's need hierarchy, Alderfer's ERG theory, and McClelland's theory of needs for achievement, affiliation, and power. Maslow and Alderfer have concentrated on the hierarchical arrangement of needs and the distinction between intrinsic and extrinsic motivation. McClelland has focused on the conditions under which particular need patterns stimulate high motivation.

- Process theories attempt to explain how motivation occurs rather than what specific factors are motivational. Expectancy theory argues that people will be motivated to engage in work activities that they find attractive and that they feel they can accomplish. The attractiveness of these activities depends on the extent to which they lead to favourable personal consequences. Equity theory states that workers compare the inputs that they apply to their jobs and the outcomes that they achieve from their jobs with the inputs and outcomes of others. When these outcome/input ratios are unequal, inequity exists, and workers will be motivated to restore equity.

- Goal setting theory states that goals are motivational when they are specific, challenging, and ac-

ceptable to workers. In some cases, companies can facilitate acceptance of goals through employee participation in goal setting and by financial incentives for goal attainment, but freedom from coercion and punishment seems to be the key factor in achieving goal acceptance.

Discussion Questions

1. Many millionaires continue to work long, hard hours, sometimes even beyond the usual age of retirement. Use the ideas developed in the chapter to speculate about the reasons for this motivational pattern. Is the acquisition of wealth still a motivator for these individuals?

2. Discuss a time when you were highly motivated to perform well (at work, at school, in a sports contest) but performed poorly in spite of your high motivation. How do you know that your motivation was really high? What factors interfered with good performance? What did you learn from this experience?

3. Use Maslow's hierarchy of needs and Alderfer's ERG theory to explain why assembly line workers and executive vice-presidents might be susceptible to different forms of motivation.

4. Colleen is high in need for achievement, Eugene is high in need for power, and Max is high in need for affiliation. They are thinking about starting a business partnership. To maximize the motivation of each, what business should they go into, and who should assume which roles or jobs?

5. Reconsider the case of Tony Angelas, which was used to illustrate expectancy theory. Imagine that you are Tony's boss and you think that he can be motivated to perform at a high level. Suppose you cannot modify second-level outcomes or their va-

lences, but you can affect expectancies and instrumentalities. What would you do to motivate Tony? Prove that you have succeeded by recalculating the force equations to demonstrate that Tony will now perform at a high level.

6. Debate the following statements: Of all the motivational theories we discussed in this chapter, goal setting is the simplest to implement. Goal setting is no more than doing what a good manager should be doing anyway.

7. More and more people are doing freelance contract work from their homes rather than being employed "permanently" by an organization. Speculate about the motivational dynamics of this.

8. Critique the following assertion: People are basically the same. Thus, the motivation theories discussed in the chapter apply equally around the globe.

[?] 9. Refer to the cross cultural dimensions of values described in Chapter 4 (i.e., work centrality, power distance, uncertainty avoidance, masculinity/feminity, individualism/collectivism, and long-term/short-term orientation) and discuss the implications of each value for exporting the work motivation theories across cultures. Based on your analysis, how useful are the theories described in this chapter for understanding and managing motivation across cultures? What are the implications?

[?] 10. Consider the basic characteristics of motivation in relation to operant learning and social learning theory. What are the implications of operant learning and social learning theory for motivation, and how do they compare to the theories of work motivation described in this chapter?

Experiential Exercise

What Are Your Needs?

What are your needs and what will motivate you?

Think about your future career. Think about the ideal job you would like to have. What matters the most to you? What matters the least to you? Listed below are three groups of work-related characteristics. Rank each group separately from 5 for the most important to 1 for the least important.

Career

Rank this Group from 5 (Most) to 1 (Least)

_____ 1 My co-workers will be very friendly.

_____ 2 The company will protect me from harassment by customers, fellow employees, and supervisors.

_____ 3 The working conditions will protect me from bad weather.

_____ 4 The work will be creative and challenging.

_____ 5 My supervisor will recognize the value of my work and praise me for it.

Rank this Group from 5 (Most) to 1 (Least)

_____ 6 I will be able to participate in decision making.

_____ 7 The company will sponsor social activities both on and off the job.

_____ 8 The pay and fringe benefits will be good.

_____ 9 There will be good opportunities for promotion to a higher status job.

_____ 10 The company will work hard to maintain safe working conditions.

Rank this Group from 5 (Most) to 1 (Least)

_____ 11 I will get along well with my supervisor.

_____ 12 There will be a merit pay system based on performance.

_____ 13 The company will provide a cafeteria for its employees.

_____ 14 The work itself will have a flexible schedule, and I will have a lot of autonomy.

_____ 15 There will be excellent job security.

Think about your current job (or if you do not have one right now, think about the last job you had). What are the best things about this job? What are the worst things about the job? Listed below are three groups of characteristics about jobs. Rank each group separately from 5 for the best thing to 1 for the worst thing.

Current Job

Rank this Group from 5 (Best) to 1 (Worst)

_____ 1 My co-workers are very friendly.

_____ 2 The company protects me from harassment by customers, fellow employees, and supervisors.

_____ 3 The working conditions protect me from bad weather.

_____ 4 The work is creative and challenging.

_____ 5 My supervisor recognizes the value of my work and praises me for it.

Rank this Group from 5 (Best) to 1 (Worst)

_____ 6 I am able to participate in decision making.

_____ 7 The company sponsors social activities both on and off the job.

_____ 8 The pay and fringe benefits are good.

_____ 9 There are good opportunities for promotion to a higher status job.

_____ 10 The company works hard to maintain safe working conditions.

Rank this Group from 5 (Best) to 1 (Worst)

_____ 11 I get along well with my supervisor.

_____ 12 There is a merit pay system based on performance.

_____ 13 The company provides a cafeteria for its employees.

_____ 14 The work itself has a flexible schedule and I have a lot of autonomy.

_____ 15 There is excellent job security.

Scoring and Interpretation

The items in this list represent the five levels of needs found in Maslow's hierarchy of needs. Each of the groups of five has an item which refers to one of Maslow's needs as applied to the workplace. Use the number in the left-hand column to sort out the items. Add the scores together for each level of the hierarchy.

The instrument also differentiates between your needs as they exist as an ideal and the way in which your current employer is meeting your needs. These are also scored separately.

Your Career: What Is Your Hierarchy of Needs?

Self-actualization: Add together the ranks for items 4, 6, and 14

(4)   +   (6)   +   (14)   =

Self-esteem: Add together the ranks for items 5, 9, and 12

(5)   +   (9)   +   (12)   =

Belongingness: Add together the ranks for items 1, 7, and 11

(1)   +   (7)   +   (11)   =

Safety: Add together the ranks for items 2, 10, and 15

(2)   +   (10)   +   (15)   =

Physiological: Add together the ranks for items 3, 8, and 13

(3)   +   (8)   +   (13)   =

Current Job: How Are Your Needs Being Met?

Self-actualization: Add together the ranks for items 4, 6, and 14

(4)   +   (6)   +   (14)   =

Self-esteem: Add together the ranks for items 5, 9, and 12

(5)   +   (9)   +   (12)   =

Belongingness: Add together the ranks for items 1, 7, and 11

(1)   +   (7)   +   (11)   =

Safety: Add together the ranks for items 2, 10, and 15

(2)   +   (10)   +   (15)   =

Physiological: Add together the ranks for items 3, 8, and 13

(3)   +   (8)   +   (13)   =

TABLE OF RESULTS		
Hierarchy of Needs	Your Career	Current Job
Self-actualization		
Self-esteem		
Social		
Security		
Physiological		

Analyze your results by comparing your career needs with those in your current job.

1. What is your strongest need? Is it being met in your current job?

2. What differences exist between your career needs and your current job?

3. According to Maslow's need hierarchy theory, what should your current or future employer do to motivate you?

Source: R. Hoffman, & F. Ruemper (1997). What matters in a job? In: *Organizational behavior: Canadian cases and exercises*, 3rd ed. Toronto: Captus Press.

Case Incident

Mayfield Department Stores

As competition in the retail market began to heat up, it became necessary to find ways to motivate the sales staff of Mayfield Department Stores in order to increase sales. Therefore, a motivational program was developed with the help of a consulting firm. Employees were informed that each month employees in the department with the highest sales would have a chance to win a trip to Florida. At the end of the year, the names of all employees in those departments that had the highest sales for at least one month would have their name entered into a draw, and then three names would be chosen to win a one-week trip to Florida paid for by Mayfield.

1. According to need theories of motivation and goal setting theory, will this program be motivational?

2. Discuss the motivational potential of this program according to expectancy theory. Will the program motivate the sales staff and improve sales?

Case Study

Striking Oil

Bruce Spiece frowned and stared out the window of his high-rise office. He had a problem. A *real* problem. In business school at SMU, he had learned that the recognition of a problem was the first step in finding its solution. In this case, he was not so sure.

Spiece was the human resources director for Petrolin, a medium-size, Dallas-based oil company. The problem Spiece faced involved Petrolin's experienced earth scientists. Earth scientists are the professionals who do the "brain work" involved in discovering and extracting oil and gas from the depths of the earth. They include geologists, geophysicists, and petroleum engineers. Underlining the risky nature of oil exploration, Spiece half-jokingly described their work this way: "Geologists guess where the oil is, geophysicists guess what's between the surface and the oil, and petroleum engineers guess how to get the oil out. If they all guess right, we make profits."

With increased domestic oil exploration, earth science graduates became the "bonus babies" of the industry. New BSc's in petroleum engineering were now receiving offers near $70,000, with graduates in geology and geophysics following close behind. Spiece's problem was not connected with the high demand for, and high salaries offered to, new graduates; rather, increasing turnover among Petrolin's experienced earth scientists was troubling him. In the past year, 15 percent of the company's earth scientists had resigned. Most were joining very small independent oil companies. Virtually all these resignees had been employees with five to 15 years' experience, and constituted the very core of Petrolin's exploration staff.

Spiece knew that his problem was not unique. It had begun several years earlier with the major oil companies—the big, publicly traded firms such as Exxon, Amoco,

Chevron, and Shell. The practical aspects of oil exploration and extraction are complex, and several years of experience are necessary before new graduates become full-fledged professionals. Thus, the majors, as well as medium-size firms such as Petrolin, provided training for earth scientists in the entire oil industry. Only the intermediate and major companies had the resources necessary to carry out this development. With the increase in domestic drilling following the oil embargo, many small independent oil companies had stepped up activities or entered the field. With no training resources and an immediate need for experienced earth scientists, these firms had resorted to "raiding" the majors and medium-sized firms for seasoned personnel. Unfortunately, "veterans" were already in short supply—a slowdown in oil exploration in the 1960s had made the earth sciences relatively unattractive to university students at that time.

Some independents used "headhunting" agencies, and Spiece had heard horror stories of telephone calls echoing up and down the corridors of corporate geology departments as aggressive recruiters contacted one professional after another. Similarly, he knew that some headhunters became regulars at restaurants and cocktail lounges frequented by earth scientists, hoping to forge an "accidental" contact. As a result of this aggressive recruiting, all oil firms were experiencing an unacceptable level of turnover among experienced earth scientists. Just when the need for them was greatest, the experienced personnel of geology and engineering departments were being depleted, only to be made up with high-priced new graduates. Also, Spiece was convinced that some resignees were taking inside information about drilling prospects to the smaller competitors.

Why would an experienced earth scientist forsake the security, prestige, and large support staff of a major or intermediate oil company to join a small independent? Spiece recalled an exit interview he had conducted a week ago with Virginia Knox, a veteran Petrolin geologist who was moving to a small Houston independent. Knox had received her geology degree from an Oklahoma university in 1986 and started her career in Shell Oil. She had been with Petrolin since 1992. Spiece began by asking Virginia Knox why she was leaving Petrolin after eight successful years, hoping against hope to hear an answer he had not heard before.

"Money," Virginia Knox responded, "money and opportunity. Look, Mr. Spiece, after 14 years in the oil business, I'm making $75,000, while you're bringing in bonus babies still wet behind the ears at $70,000. That just isn't right. The company I'm going to is paying me $90,000 and giving me a company car. In addition, I'll get a one percent override on everything I find."

Spiece cringed mentally at the word *override*. An override was a royalty paid on the gross revenues of any producing well developed by the geologist. Thus, Virginia Knox would receive one percent of the revenues of any oil she discovered for the independent. The independents had been using this incentive in their raiding efforts, and rumour was that some defectors from the larger firms had become millionaires due to overrides.

"I'm also excited by the work I'll be doing at the new company," continued Virginia Knox. "I'll be prospecting my own wells, with a two- or three-person team. Here at Petrolin we have dozens of geologists doing the same work I do, and it takes forever to get approval to drill."

Spiece understood Knox's point. The majors and intermediates tended to concentrate on the larger and more remote oil fields. Because drilling in such locations required substantial investment, several levels of management scrutinized drilling proposals very cautiously. The independents generally tended to stick to better-known territory, and geologists frequently took their proposals straight to the company president (usually a "shirt-sleeves" type) for consideration.

Spiece tried his best to discourage Virginia Knox's resignation.

"Look, Ms. Knox, I can understand some of the attraction you see in going to a small indepedent. But I think you should be aware of what you're in for. There's no support staff there, and you'll find yourself having to do routine work that you haven't done in years—the stuff our bonus babies do for you here. Also, in that environment you're going to stagnate professionally. Here, we've got a large staff with varied backgrounds, and people are coming in from the universities all the time. This keeps you fresh and current. And don't forget the pressure-cooker atmosphere at the independents. You're on call all the time, you're responsible for the prospects, and you can't take a vacation in the middle of a project. Here, you have others to rely on. And finally, don't expect any regular pay raises at the independent. They're generous up front, but stingy afterwards except for the override. And, personally, I think the value of overrides is rated too highly. You know as well as I do that only 10 percent of all prospects yield oil, and the independents are working smaller fields than we are here."

Virginia Knox had thanked Spiece for his advice and emphasized that she had nothing but the highest regard for Petrolin. But she insisted that her resignation was final.

Bruce Spiece continued to stare out his office window, wondering how the turnover among the experienced Petrolin earth scientists could be reduced. Salary increases were not out of the question, but it was generally agreed that other employees would react negatively to such a move. Middle managers, marketing personnel, and employees who negotiated oil field leases were already incredulous of the salaries accorded to the bonus babies. For larger firms such as Petrolin, overrides were difficult to consider. Because such firms concentrated on bigger, more complex oil prospects, large teams of earth scientists worked together on exploration projects. With such teams, it was hard to decide exactly who deserved how much of a royalty on any given oil strike. Perhaps company cars or large cash bonuses based on exceptional individual performance would help to retain the experienced personnel. Spiece just was not sure.

1. Describe Virginia Knox's motivation toward her job at the time of her resignation. Be specific as to her intrinsic and extrinsic motivation.

2. Speculate about Virginia Knox's need structure. Does her job at Petrolin suit her need structure? Use Maslow's need hierarchy theory and Alderfer's ERG theory to explain Virginia Knox's motivation to resign. What does McClelland's theory of needs say about Virginia Knox's motivational state?

3. Use equity and expectancy theory to analyze Virginia Knox's motivation to resign and to seek a job with a small independent oil firm. Could the turnover problem have been predicted on the basis of these theories? What does each theory suggest as the best approach for dealing with the turnover problem at Petrolin?

4. How might the turnover problem at Petrolin been prevented if the company had acted earlier?

5. Use your understanding of motivation theories to explain how Bruce Spiece might have changed Virginia's mind during the exit interview.

6. What should Bruce Spiece do now?

Source: Case by Gary Johns with some background from Alexander Stuart. (1980, October 6) Manhunt in the oil fields. *Fortune*, pp. 82-86.

Chapter 6

Motivation in Practice

Lincoln Electric Company

LINCOLN ELECTRIC COMPANY On the surface, the Lincoln Electric Company might look like a motivational disaster. The firm, located near Cleveland, Ohio, offers employees no paid sick days and no paid holidays. Lincoln employees have to pay their own health insurance, and overtime work and unexpected job reassignments are mandatory. If older workers lower their productivity they receive less pay. Management does not take seniority into account in promotions. Lincoln managers receive no executive "perks"—no cars, no executive dining room, no club memberships, no management seminars, and no reserved parking.

Despite these apparently draconian policies, Lincoln has become something of a mecca for visiting managers (from Ford, GM, TRW, 3M, Motorola, and McDonnell Douglas), who flock to Cleveland to learn something about motivation. Lincoln is the world's largest producer of arc welding equipment, and it also makes electric motors. The firm has turned a handsome profit every quarter for over 50 years and has not laid anyone off for over 40 years. Employee turnover is extremely low, and Lincoln workers are estimated to be roughly twice as productive as other manufacturing workers. This productivity is an important key to Lincoln's success because it is not dealing in high-tech products, and it does not compete strongly on price.

What is the secret to Lincoln's motivational success? In a word, *money*. Lots of it. Lincoln Electric offers what some say are the best paid factory jobs in the world. At the core of the system is an intricate piece-rate pay plan that rewards workers for what they produce and a merit-based profit-sharing plan that provides a yearly bonus. This bonus, which can approach 100% of regular earnings, is also allocated on merit to managers and staff. The average production

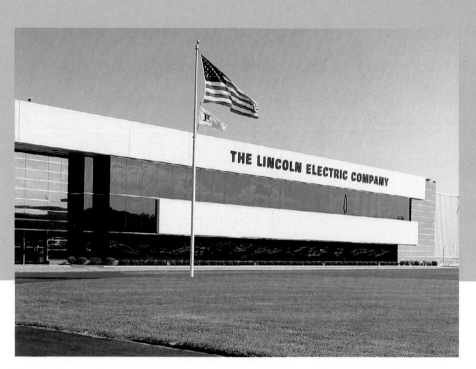

The Lincoln Electric Company near Cleveland, Ohio, is exemplary in employee motivation.

Lincoln Electric Co.
www.lincolnelectric.com

worker has earned $45,000 in recent years, with some earning well over $85,000! If workers think up a way to increase productivity, the company does not adjust the piece-rate to cap potential wages. Also, they cannot work themselves out of a job, since Lincoln has a no-layoff policy. Effectively, this amounts to lifetime employment. Employees are so keen to get working that the company enforces a policy prohibiting them from coming in too early. When the company had its first big hiring in years, it received 27,000 applications.

Life at Lincoln is not for everyone. Some managers would resent the lack of perks. Some new production workers cannot take the fast pace and quit shortly after hiring. Many never even apply because of Lincoln's nonunion status.[1]

Notice the motivational strategies that Lincoln Electric employs—a piece-rate pay plan, a merit-based profit-sharing plan, an annual bonus, and a no-layoff policy. In this chapter, we will discuss four motivational techniques—money, job enrichment, management by objectives, and alternative working schedules. In each case, we will consider the practical problems that are involved in implementation. The chapter will conclude with a discussion of the role of motivation in total quality management.

Money as a Motivator

The money that employees receive in exchange for organizational membership is in reality a package made up of pay and various fringe benefits that have dollar values, such as insurance plans, sick leave, and vacation time. Here, we shall be concerned with the motivational characteristics of pay itself.

According to Maslow and Alderfer, pay should prove especially motivational to people who have strong lower-level needs. For these people, pay can be ex-

Learning Objectives

After reading Chapter 6, you should be able to:

1 Discuss how to tie pay to performance on production jobs and the difficulties of wage incentive plans.

2 Explain how to tie pay to performance on white-collar jobs and the difficulties of merit pay plans.

3 Understand how to use pay to motivate teamwork.

4 Describe the details of the Job Characteristics Model.

5 Discuss the motivational properties of job enrichment.

6 Understand the connection between goal setting and Management by Objectives.

7 Explain how alternative work schedules respect employee diversity.

8 Review the motivational aspects of total quality management.

changed for food, shelter, and other necessities of life. However, suppose you receive a healthy pay raise. Doubtless, this raise will enable you to purchase food and shelter, but it might also demonstrate that your boss cares about you, give you prestige among friends and family, and signal your competence as a worker. Thus, using need hierarchy terminology, pay can also function to satisfy social, self-esteem, and self-actualization needs. If pay has this capacity to fulfill a variety of needs, then it should have especially good potential as a motivator. How can this potential be realized? Expectancy theory provides the clearest answer to this question. According to expectancy theory, if pay can satisfy a variety of

THE WALL STREET JOURNAL

"Well, it sure seems to me that a $4 million a year pitcher should be able to strike out a $1.2 million a year hitter once in a while!"

Source: The Wall Street Journal, July 21, 1993.

global focus → Bus Drivers in Singapore Receive Bonus for Safe Driving

Bus driver Fang Chain Poh is now $780 better off because he takes road safety very seriously. "When a passenger gets on my bus, it is my job to make sure he gets down in one piece and has a good journey. So I always get enough sleep to drive carefully," he said.

Mr. Fang, 37, who has 17 years of experience, is one of more than 4,700 or 88 percent of Singapore Bus Service drivers who received between $200 and $780 each for having maintained good safety records for a six-month period. A total of $3.5 million was given out in all.

This is the second time the Singapore Bus Service is giving out cash awards under the safe driving scheme that was introduced last year. For each week that a driver stays free of accidents and traffic offences, he gets $10. If he can keep it this way for six months, there is an additional bonus of $500 in store.

About 4,000 or 76 percent of the drivers qualified for the bonus this time, up 9 percentage points compared with the first six-month period. Singapore Bus Service chairman Hung Khim presented the cheque for $3.5 million to five drivers, chosen to represent each of the depots at the launch of the Safety Awareness for Excellence (SAFE) Week.

Mr. Fang, who also received the maximum amount of $780 the first time round, said: "Money or no money, bus drivers must always be careful when on the road. But, of course, the extra money is a good way to encourage drivers."

At the ceremony, Mr. Wong told the drivers that the accident rate for last year had fallen to 0.87 accidents for every 100,000 km travelled, compared with the previous rate of 0.95 the previous year. For the first five months of the current year, the number was 0.76 accidents for every 100,000 km.

"I do recognize that about two-thirds of the accidents involving our buses are caused by other road users. Having said that, many accidents are also a result of negligence, inattentiveness, or poor judgment on the part of our drivers," he said.

Source: Excerpted from Kaur, Karamjit. (1997, July 8). More than 4,700 SBS drivers get $3.5m for safe driving. *The Straits Times*, p.3.

needs, it should be highly valent, and it should be a good motivator to the extent that *it is clearly tied to performance*. But is it likely to be as effective across cultures? Lincoln Electric's incentive program did not work when the company tried it in Germany.[2] To find out more about money as a motivator in different cultures, see "Global Focus: *Bus Drivers in Singapore Receive Bonus for Safe Driving*."

Linking Pay to Performance on Production Jobs

The prototype of all schemes to link pay to performance on production jobs is piece-rate. In its pure form, **piece-rate** is set up so that individual workers are paid a certain sum of money for each unit of production they complete. For example, sewing machine operators might be paid two dollars for each dress stitched, or punch press operators might be paid a few cents for each piece of metal fabricated. More common than pure piece-rate is a system whereby workers are paid a basic hourly wage and paid a piece-rate differential on top of this hourly wage. For example, a forge operator might be paid eight dollars an hour plus 30 cents for each unit he produces. In some cases, of course, it is very difficult to measure the productivity of an individual worker because of the nature of the production process. Under these circumstances, group incentives are sometimes employed. For example, workers in a steel mill might be paid an hourly wage and a monthly bonus for each ton of steel produced over some minimum quota. These various schemes to link pay to performance on production jobs are called **wage incentive plans**.

Compared with straight hourly pay, the introduction of wage incentives usually leads to substantial increases in productivity.[3] One review reports a median productivity improvement of 30 percent following the installation of piece-rate

Piece-rate. A pay system in which individual workers are paid a certain sum of money for each unit of production completed.

Wage incentive plans. Various systems that link pay to performance on production jobs.

Wage incentive programs that link pay to performance on production jobs have been shown to improve employee productivity.

pay, an increase not matched by goal setting or job enrichment.[4] Also, a study of 400 manufacturing companies found that those with wage incentive plans achieved 43 to 64 percent greater productivity than those without such plans.[5] Lincoln Electric is a good example of a successful firm that uses a wage incentive plan. Other examples include Steelcase, the Michigan manufacturer of office furniture, and Nucor, a steel producer. In fact, however, not as many organizations use wage incentives as we might expect. What accounts for this relatively low utilization of a motivational system that has proven results?[6]

Potential Problems with Wage Incentives

Despite their theoretical and practical attractiveness, wage incentives have some potential problems when they are not managed with care.

Lowered Quality. It is sometimes argued that wage incentives can increase productivity at the expense of quality. While this may be true in some cases, it does not require particular ingenuity to devise a system to monitor and maintain quality in manufacturing. However, the quality issue can be a problem when employers use incentives to motivate faster "people processing," such as conducting consumer interviews on the street or in stores. Here, quality control is more difficult. At Lincoln Electric, employees are only paid for work that meets quality standards.

Differential Opportunity. A threat to the establishment of wage incentives exists when workers have differential opportunities to produce at a high level. If the supply of raw materials or the quality of production equipment varies from workplace to workplace, some workers will be at an unfair disadvantage under an incentive system. In expectancy theory terminology, workers will differ in the expectancy that they can produce at a high level. Employees at Lincoln Electric have the opportunity to produce at whatever level they choose.

Reduced Cooperation. Wage incentives that reward individual productivity might decrease cooperation among workers. For example, to maintain a high wage rate, machinists might hoard raw materials or refuse to engage in peripheral tasks, such as keeping the shop clean or unloading supplies. Consider what happened when Solar Press, an Illinois printing and packaging company, installed a team wage incentive.

> It wasn't long before both managers and employees began to spot problems. Because of the pressure to produce, teams did not perform regular maintenance on the equipment, so machines broke down more often than before. When people found better or faster ways to do things, some hoarded them from fellow employees for fear of reducing the amount of their own payments. Others grumbled that work assignments were not fairly distributed, that some jobs demanded more work than others. They did, but the system did not take this into account.[7]

At Lincoln Electric, however, employees are motivated to cooperate because they all reap the benefits of company profits and they receive "report-card" evaluations that include cooperation.

Incompatible Job Design. In some cases, the way jobs are designed can make it very difficult to install wage incentives. On an assembly line, it is almost impossible to identify and reward individual contributions to productivity. As pointed out above, wage incentive systems can be designed to reward team productivity in such a circumstance. However, as the size of the team *increases,* the relationship between any individual's productivity and his or her pay *decreases.* For example, the impact of your productivity in a team of two is much greater than the impact of this productivity in a team of 10—as team size increases, the linkage between your performance and your pay is erased, removing the intended incentive effect. At Lincoln Electric, employees are paid according to what they produce.

Restriction of Productivity. A chief psychological impediment to the use of wage incentives is the tendency for workers to restrict productivity. This restriction is illustrated graphically in Exhibit 6.1. Under normal circumstances, without wage incentives, we can often expect productivity to be distributed in a "bell-shaped" manner—a few workers are especially low producers, a few are especially high producers, and most produce in the middle range. When wage incentives are introduced, however, workers sometimes come to an informal agreement about what constitutes a fair day's work and artificially limit their output accordingly. In many cases, this **restriction of productivity** can decrease the expected benefits of the incentive system, as in Exhibit 6.1.

Why does restriction often occur under wage incentive systems? Sometimes, it happens because workers feel that increased productivity due to the incentive will lead to reductions in the workforce. More frequently, however, employees

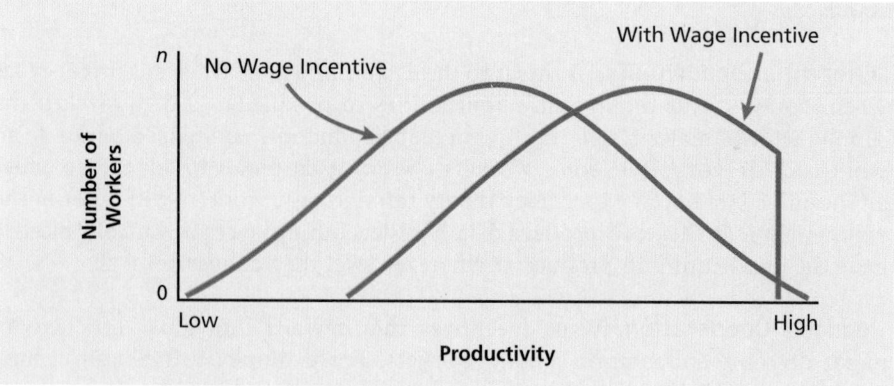

Restriction of productivity. The artificial limitation of work output that can occur under wage incentive plans.

Exhibit 6.1
Hypothetical productivity distributions, with and without wage incentives, when incentives promote restriction.

fear that if they produce at an especially high level, an employer will reduce the rate of payment to cut labour costs. In the early days of industrialization, when unions were nonexistent or weak, this happened. Engineers studied workers under normal circumstances, and management would set a payment rate for each unit of productivity. When management introduced the incentive system, workers employed legitimate shortcuts that they had learnt on the job to produce at a higher rate than expected. In response to this, management simply changed the rate to require more output for a given amount of pay! Stories of such rate-cutting are often passed down from one generation of workers to another in support of restricting output under incentive systems. As you might expect, restriction seems less likely when a climate of trust and a history of good relations exist between employees and management as is the case at Lincoln Electric.

Linking Pay to Performance on White-Collar Jobs

Compared with production jobs, white-collar jobs (including clerical, professional, and managerial) frequently offer fewer objective performance criteria to which pay can be tied. To be sure, company presidents are often paid annual bonuses that are tied to the profitability of the firm, and salespeople are frequently paid commissions on sales. However, trustworthy objective indicators of individual performance for the majority of white-collar jobs are often difficult to find. Thus, performance in many such jobs is evaluated by the subjective judgment of the performer's manager.

Attempts to link pay to performance on white-collar jobs are often called **merit pay plans**. Just as straight piece-rate is the prototype for most wage incentive plans, there is also a prototype for most merit pay plans: Periodically (usually yearly), managers are required to evaluate the performance of subordinates on some form of rating scale or by means of a written description of performance. Using these evaluations, the managers then recommend that some amount of merit pay be awarded to individuals over and above their basic salaries. This pay is usually incorporated into the subsequent year's salary cheques. Since the indicators of good performance on some white-collar jobs (especially managerial jobs) can be unclear or highly subjective, merit pay can provide an especially tangible signal that the organization considers an employee's performance "on track."

Individuals who see a strong link between rewards and performance tend to perform better.[8] In addition, white-collar workers (especially managers) particularly support the notion that performance should be an important determinant of pay.[9] Thus, merit pay plans are employed with a much greater frequency than wage incentive plans. Despite the fact that merit pay can stimulate effective performance, substantial support exists for the idea of merit pay, and most organizations claim to provide merit pay, it appears that many of these systems now in use are *ineffective*. Many individuals who work under such plans do not perceive a link between their job performance and their pay. There is also evidence that pay is, in fact, *not* related to performance under some merit plans.[10] Adding more evidence of ineffectiveness are studies that track pay increases over time. For example, one study of managers showed that pay increases in a given year were often uncorrelated with pay increases in adjacent years.[11] From what we know about the consistency of human performance, such a result seems unlikely if organizations are truly tying pay to performance. In most organizations, seniority, number of subordinates, and job level account for more variation in pay than performance does. Of course, some organizations do hold the line. HBO, Inc., the entertainment company, is one firm that seriously tries to maintain the link between pay and performance.

Merit pay plans. Systems that attempt to link pay to performance on white-collar jobs.

At one time, pay incentives and rewards were reserved for those in upper management positions. However, organizations are increasingly adopting pay-for-performance programs that offer incentives to the entire workforce. Bonuses and incentives are making up an increasing proportion of employees' pay.

In the United States, approximately 34% of 383 major companies surveyed offer formal bonus plans to hourly workers, and nearly two-thirds do so for salaried employees. In Canada, 70% of companies offer incentives, such as cash bonuses, lump sums, profit-sharing, and productivity gainsharing, to nonmanagement employees. The variable pay of executives in 1998 was approximately 26% of base pay, and 7.4% for nonexecutives.[12] However, as discussed below, these programs are not without problems. In fact, in recent years there has been an increasing number of bonus disputes over unpaid or underpaid bonuses that are winding up in the courts.[13]

Potential Problems with Merit Pay Plans

As with wage incentive plans, merit pay plans have several potential problems if employers do not manage them carefully.

Low Discrimination. One reason that many merit pay plans fail to achieve their intended effect is that managers might be unable or unwilling to discriminate between good performers and poor performers. In Chapter 3, we pointed out that subjective evaluations of performance can be difficult to make and are often distorted by a number of perceptual errors. In the absence of performance rating systems designed to control these problems, managers might feel that the only fair response is to rate most employees as equal performers. Good rating systems are rarely employed. Surveys show consistent dissatisfaction with both giving and receiving performance evaluations.[14] Even when managers feel capable of clearly discriminating between good and poor performers, they might be reluctant to do so. If the performance evaluation system does not assist the manager in giving feedback about his or her decisions to subordinates, the equalization strategy might be employed to prevent conflicts with them or among them. If there are true performance differences among subordinates, equalization overrewards poorer performers and underrewards better performers.[15]

Small Increases. A second threat to the effectiveness of merit pay plans exists when merit increases are simply too small to be effective motivators. In this case, even if rewards are carefully tied to performance and managers do a good job of discriminating between more and less effective performers, the intended motivational effects of pay increases might not be realized. Ironically, some firms all but abandon merit when inflation soars or when they encounter economic difficulties. Just when high motivation is needed, the motivational impact of merit pay is removed. Sometimes, a reasonable amount of merit pay is provided, but its motivational impact is reduced because it is spread out over a year or because the organization fails to communicate how much of a raise is for merit and how much is for cost of living. To overcome this visibility problem, some firms have replaced conventional merit pay with a **lump sum bonus** that is paid out all at one time and not built into base pay. Such bonuses get people's attention!

When merit pay makes up a substantial portion of the compensation package, management has to take extreme care to ensure that it ties the merit pay to performance criteria that truly benefit the organization. Otherwise, employees could be motivated to earn their yearly bonus at the expense of long-term organizational goals.

Pay Secrecy. A final threat to the effectiveness of merit pay plans is the extreme secrecy that surrounds salaries in most organizations. It has long been a princi-

Lump sum bonus. Merit pay that is awarded in a single payment and not built into base pay.

ple of human resource management that salaries are confidential information, and management frequently implores employees who receive merit increases not to discuss these increases with their co-workers. Notice the implication of such secrecy for merit pay plans: Even if merit pay is administered fairly, contingent on performance, and generous, employees might remain ignorant of these facts because they have no way of comparing their own merit treatment with that of others. In consequence, such secrecy might severely damage the motivational impact of a well-designed merit plan. Rather incredibly, many organizations fail to inform employees about the average raise received by those doing similar work.

Given this extreme secrecy, you might expect that employees would profess profound ignorance about the salaries of other organizational members. In fact, this is not true—in the absence of better information, employees are inclined to "invent" salaries for other members. Unfortunately, this invention seems to reduce both satisfaction and motivation. Specifically, several studies have shown that managers have a tendency to overestimate the pay of their subordinates and their peers and underestimate the pay of their superiors (see Exhibit 6.2).[16] In general, these tendencies will reduce satisfaction with pay, damage perceptions of the linkage between performance and rewards, and reduce the valence of promotion to a higher level of management.

An interesting experiment examined the effects of pay disclosure on the performance and satisfaction of pharmaceutical salespeople who operated under a merit pay system.

At the time of a regularly scheduled district sales meeting, each of the 14 managers in the experimental group presented to his subordinates the new open salary administration program. The salesmen were given the individual low, overall average, and individual high merit raise amounts for the previous year. The raises ranged from no raise to $75 a month, with a company average of $43. Raises were classified according to district, region, and company increases in pay. Likewise, salary levels (low, average, and high) were given for salesmen on the basis of their years with the company (1 to 5; 5 to 10; 10 to 20; and more than 20 years). Specific individual names and base salaries were not disclosed to the salesmen. However, this information could be obtained from the supervisor. Each salesman's performance evaluation was also made available by the district manager for review by his other salesmen.[17]

After the pay disclosure was implemented, salespeople in the experimental group revealed significant increases in performance and satisfaction with pay. However, since performance consisted of supervisory ratings, it is possible that supervisors felt pressured to give better ratings under the open pay system, in

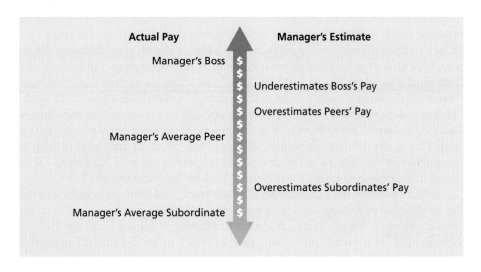

Exhibit 6.2
Manager's estimates of pay earned by boss, peers, and subordinates.

which their actions were open to scrutiny. This, of course, raises an important point. If performance evaluation systems are inadequate and poorly justified, a more open pay policy will simply expose the inadequacy of the merit system and lead managers to evaluate performance in a manner that reduces conflict. Unfortunately, this might be why most organizations maintain relative secrecy concerning pay. One exception is Next Computers, which has a completely open salary system. Although many public and civil service jobs have open pay systems, most make little pretence of paying for performance.

Using Pay to Motivate Teamwork

Some of the dysfunctional aspects of wage incentives and merit pay stem from their highly individual orientations. People sometimes end up pursuing their own agendas (and pay) at the expense of the goals of their work group, department, or organization. As a result, some firms have either replaced or supplemented individual incentive pay with plans designed to foster more cooperation and teamwork.[18] Notice that each of the plans we discuss below has a somewhat different motivational focus. Organizations have to choose pay plans that support their strategic needs. To begin thinking about strategic needs and pay, consider the You Be the Manager feature, "*First Marathon's 'Eat-What-You-Kill' Compensation Philosophy.*"

Profit sharing. The return of some company profit to employees in the form of a cash bonus or a retirement supplement.

Profit Sharing and Employee Stock Ownership Plans (ESOPs). Profit sharing is one of the most commonly used group-oriented incentive systems. In years in which the firm makes a profit, some of this is returned to employees in the form of a bonus, sometimes in cash and sometimes in a deferred retirement fund. Such money is surely welcome, and it might reinforce some identification with the organization. However, it is unlikely that profit sharing, as normally practised, is highly motivational. Its greatest problem is that too many factors beyond the control of the workforce (such as the general economy) can affect profits no matter how well people perform their jobs. Also, in a large firm, it is difficult to see the impact of one's own actions on profits. For example, for two years after Chrysler Corporation's first profit-sharing payment, the company made no payments. And with a workforce of 63,000, one's impact on profits would be completely obscure.

Profit sharing seems to work best in smaller firms that regularly turn a handsome profit and then distribute this profit according to merit. Lincoln Electric uses this strategy.

Employee stock ownership plans (ESOPs). Incentive plans that allow employees to own a set amount of a company's shares and provide employees with a stake in the company's future earnings and success.

In recent years, **employee stock ownership plans (ESOPs)** have also become a popular group-oriented incentive. These plans allow employees to own a set amount of the company's shares. Employees are often allowed to purchase shares at a fixed price and some organizations match employee contributions. ESOPs provide employees with a stake in a company's future earnings and success. It is estimated that more than 14 million people in 15,000 companies in the United States participate in some sort of stock ownership plan.[19] In Canada, 19 of the 35 best companies to work for offer stock options to a majority of their employees. For example, at the Royal Bank of Canada, 90 percent of employees are enrolled in a share ownership plan that matches 50 cents for every dollar an employee invests up to 6 percent of their salary. At PCI Constructors in Edmonton, only employees are permitted to own company stocks.[20]

Other examples include Starbucks' "bean stock" program. Starbucks was one of the first service companies to offer stock options to all employees from top management on down. And as discussed in Chapter 4, Husky Injection Molding Systems Ltd. has a share-purchasing plan in which approximately 25 percent of

First Marathon's "Eat-What-You-Kill" Compensation Philosophy

At First Marathon you are compensated strictly on the amount of money you bring into the company.

Lawrence Bloomberg, founder and CEO of First Marathon Inc., built First Marathon into the largest independent broker in Canada by lavishly rewarding star performers who operated on their own with little hand holding or supervision. Bloomberg compensated his staff strictly on the amount of money they brought into the house. If you were really hot, you could walk away with a $7-million pay packet, as Bloomberg did six years ago. If you were cold, you would find yourself looking for another job.

The system might seem crude, but it produced results. First Marathon was a small player that served the institutional market and not the small retail investor. Instead of specializing in large-cap stocks, a field dominated by the established brokerage houses, First Marathon targeted the up-and-comers that they did not understand. Its small-cap research quickly gained a reputation as some of the best in Canada. Commissions soared from $10 million in 1984, the year the company went public, to more than $100 million in 1996. The firm provided the brains behind a number of successful ventures, including initial public offerings for mining giants Barrick Gold Corp. and Franco-Nevada Mining Corp. Ltd.

But over the past few years, First Marathon lost its magic touch and has hit the wall. The lean mean brokerage is too small to compete for the big deals with the brokerage arms of the big banks, and it is in danger of losing its small-cap niche to a new horde of hungry boutiques. Even

though the firm is financially healthy, the company's precarious position is hurting business.

One idea that Bloomberg talks about enthusiastically is starting a merchant bank that would act as a source of cash for promising young companies. The only problem is that the Big Five banks are already doing the same thing. He is also keen on building up First Marathon's mutual fund operation. The company launched six new funds during the past couple of years to complement its former world-beater, the Marathon Equity Fund. But the First Marathon funds have not been posting stellar performance numbers. And with only $118 million in assets under management—almost $100 million less than it had under administration last year—the brokerage is going to have to invest huge amounts of attention and money to build the business.

Whatever route First Marathon follows, it is in for a seismic shift in its culture. Instead of concentrating its research on small up-and-coming companies, the brokerage is devoting more time and attention to following Canada's established large-cap companies.

Will First Marathon also have to change its "eat-what-you-kill" compensation philosophy? You be the manager.

1. What do you think about First Marathon's "eat-what-you-kill" compensation philosophy? What does it tell you about the use of pay to motivate employees and a company's growth and success?

2. Do you think that First Marathon should change its compensation plan? What changes would you make and why?

To find out what First Marathon did, see The Manager's Notebook at the end of the chapter.

Sources: Excerpted from Harris, J. (1999, January 29). Running scared. *Canadian Business*, pp. 67-72. Information on "pool system" came from: Critchley, B. (1999, January 12). Fee pool is team builder, says firm: First Marathon abandons "eat what you kill" philosophy. *Financial Post*, p.D2.

---

the company's shares are held by employees. Employees at Husky can earn company shares by doing things that help the environment and community.

Employee stock options are believed to increase employees' loyalty and motivation because it aligns their goals and interests with those of the organization and creates a sense of legal and psychological ownership. There is some evidence that ESOPs can improve employee retention and profitability.[21] However, like profit sharing these programs work best in small organizations that regularly turn a profit. In larger organizations it is more difficult for employees to see the connection between their efforts and company profits because many factors can influence the value of a company's stock besides employee effort and performance.

Gainsharing. **Gainsharing** plans are group incentive plans that are based on improved productivity or performance over which the workforce has some control.[22] This often includes reductions in the cost of labour, material, or supplies. When measured costs decrease, the company pays a monthly bonus according to a predetermined formula that shares this "gain" between employees and the firm. For example, a plan installed by Canadian pulp and paper producer Fraser, Inc. rewards employees for low scrap and low steam usage during production. The plan sidesteps the cost of steam generation and the international price for paper, things over which the workforce lacks control.[23]

Gainsharing plans have usually been installed using committees that include extensive workforce participation. This builds trust and commitment to the formulas that are used to convert gains into bonuses. Also, most plans include all members of the work unit, including production people, managers, and support staff.

The most common gainsharing plan is the Scanlon Plan, developed by union leader Joe Scanlon in the 1930s.[24] The plan stresses participatory management and joint problem solving between employees and managers, but it also stresses using the pay system to reward employees for this cooperative behaviour. Thus, pay is used to align company and employee goals. The Scanlon Plan has been used successfully by many small family-owned manufacturing firms. Also, in recent years, many large corporations (e.g., General Electric, Motorola, Carrier, Dana) have installed Scanlon-like plans in some manufacturing plants.[25] The turnaround of the motorcycle producer Harley-Davidson is, in part, attributed to the institution of gainsharing. In general, productivity improvements following the introduction of Scanlon-type plans support the motivational impact of this group wage incentive.[26] However, perception that the plan is fair is critical.[27]

Gainsharing. A group pay incentive plan based on productivity or performance improvements over which the workforce has some control.

At Quebec's Bell Helicopter Textron plant, skill-based pay encourages flexibility in the aircraft assemblers' work assignments and provides them with an overall picture of the work process.

Skill-Based Pay. The idea behind **skill-based pay** (also called pay for knowledge) is to motivate employees to learn a wide variety of work tasks, irrespective of the job that they might be doing at any given time. The more skills that are acquired, the higher the person's pay.[28] Companies use skill-based pay to encourage employee flexibility in task assignments and to give them a broader picture of the work process. It is especially useful on self-managed teams (Chapter 7), in which employees divide up the work as they see fit. It is also useful in flexible manufacturing (Chapter 15), in which rapid changes in job demands can occur. Quebec's Bell Helicopter Textron plant uses skill-based pay for its aircraft assemblers to enhance their flexibility.

Training costs can be high with a skill-based pay system. Also, when the system is in place, it has to be used. Sometimes, managers want to keep employees on a task they are good at rather than letting them acquire new skills. However, skill-based programs can have positive consequences. A recent study on the effects of a skill-based pay system in a large organization that manufactures vehicle safety systems reported an increase in productivity, lower labour costs per part, and a reduction in scrap following implementation of a skill-based pay program.[29]

Exhibit 6.3 compares the various pay plans that organizations use to motivate teamwork.

Skill-based pay. A system in which people are paid according to the number of job skills they have acquired.

Bell Helicopter Textron
www.bhti.com

Exhibit 6.3
Characteristics of team-oriented incentive plans.

PLAN TYPE	HOW IT WORKS	WHAT IT REQUIRES TO BE EFFECTIVE	ADVANTAGES	DISADVANTAGES
Profit sharing and employee stock ownership	Employees receive a varying annual bonus based on corporate profits and/or can purchase a certain amount of the company's shares. Payments can be made in cash or deferred into a retirement fund.	• Participating employees collectively must be able to influence profits. • Owners must value employees' contributions enough to be willing to share profits and ownership.	• The incentive formula is simple and easy to communicate. • The plan is guaranteed to be affordable: It pays only when the firm is sufficiently profitable. • It unites the financial interests of owners and employees.	• Annual payments may lead employers to ignore long-term performance. • Factors beyond the employee's control can influence profits. • The plan forces private companies to open their books.
Gain sharing	When a unit beats predetermined performance targets, all members get bonuses. Objectives often include better productivity, quality, and customer service.	• Objectives must be measurable. • Management must encourage employee involvement. • Employees must have a high degree of trust in management.	• The plan enhances coordination and teamwork. • Employees learn more about the business and focus on objectives. • Employees work harder and smarter.	• Plans that focus only on productivity may lead employees to ignore other important objectives, such as quality. • The company may have to pay bonuses even when unprofitable.
Skill-based pay	An employee's salary or wage rises with the number of tasks he or she can do, regardless of the job performed.	• Skills must be identified and assigned a pay grade. • The company must have well-developed employee assessment and training procedures.	• By increasing flexibility, the plan lets the company operate with a leaner staff. • The plan gives workers a broader perspective, making them more adept at problem solving.	• Most employees will learn all applicable skills, raising labour costs. • Training costs are high.

Source: Perry, N.J. (1988, December 19). Here come richer, riskier pay plans. *Fortune*, 50–58, p. 52.

Job Design as a Motivator

If the use of money as a motivator is primarily an attempt to capitalize on extrinsic motivation, current approaches to using job design as a motivator represent an attempt to capitalize on intrinsic motivation. In essence, the current goal of job design is to identify the characteristics that make some tasks more motivating than others and to capture these characteristics in the design of jobs.

Traditional Views of Job Design

From the advent of the Industrial Revolution until the 1960s, the prevailing philosophy regarding the design of most nonmanagerial jobs was job simplification. The historical roots of job simplification are found in social, economic, and technological forces that existed even before the Industrial Revolution. This preindustrial period was characterized by increasing urbanization and the growth of a free market economy, which prompted a demand for manufactured goods. Thus, a division of labour within society occurred, and specialized industrial concerns, using newly developed machinery, emerged to meet this demand. With complex machinery and an uneducated, untrained work force, these organizations recognized that *specialization* was the key to efficient productivity. If the production of an object could be broken down into very basic, simple steps, even an uneducated and minimally trained worker could contribute his or her share by mastering one of these steps.

The zenith of job simplification occurred in the early 1900s when industrial engineer Frederick Winslow Taylor presented the industrial community with his principles of Scientific Management.[30] From Chapter 1 you will recall that Taylor advocated extreme division of labour and specialization, even extending to the specialization of supervisors in roles such as trainer, disciplinarian, and so on. Also, he advocated careful standardization and regulation of work activities and rest pauses. Intuitively, jobs designed according to the principles of scientific management do not seem intrinsically motivating. The motivational strategies that management used during this period consisted of close supervision and the use of piece-rate pay. It would be a historical disservice to conclude that job simplification was unwelcomed by workers, who were mostly nonunionized, uneducated, and fighting to fulfill their basic needs. Such simplification helped them to achieve a reasonable standard of living. However, in recent years, with a better-educated workforce whose basic needs are fairly well met, behavioural scientists have begun to question the impact of job simplification on performance, customer satisfaction, and the quality of working life.

Job Scope and Motivation

Job scope can be defined as the breadth and depth of a job.[31] Breadth refers to the number of different activities performed on the job, while depth refers to the degree of discretion or control the worker has over how these tasks are performed. "Broad" jobs require workers to *do* a number of different tasks, while "deep" jobs emphasize freedom in *planning* how to do the work.

As shown in Exhibit 6.4, jobs that have great breadth and depth are called high-scope jobs. A professor's job is a good example of a high-scope job. It is broad because it involves the performance of a number of different tasks, such as teaching, grading, doing research, writing, and participating in committees. It is also deep because there is considerable discretion in how academics perform these tasks. In general, professors have a fair amount of freedom to choose a particular teaching style, grading format, and research area. Similarly, management jobs are high-scope jobs. Managers perform a wide variety of activities (supervi-

In his classic film *Modern Times*, Charlie Chaplin performed a typical low-scope job working on an assembly line.

sion, training, performance evaluation, report writing) and have some discretion over how they accomplish these activities.

The classic example of a low-scope job is the traditional assembly line job. This job is both "shallow" and "narrow" in the sense that a single task (such as bolting on car wheels) is performed repetitively and ritually, with no discretion as to method. Traditional views of job design were attempts to construct low-scope jobs in which workers specialized in a single task.

Occasionally, we encounter jobs that have high breadth but little depth or vice versa. For motivational purposes, we can also consider these jobs relatively low in scope. For example, a utility worker on an assembly line fills in for absent workers on various parts of the line. While this job involves the performance of a number of tasks, it involves little discretion as to when or how the worker performs the tasks. On the other hand, some jobs involve a fair amount of discretion over a single, narrowly defined task. For example, quality control inspectors

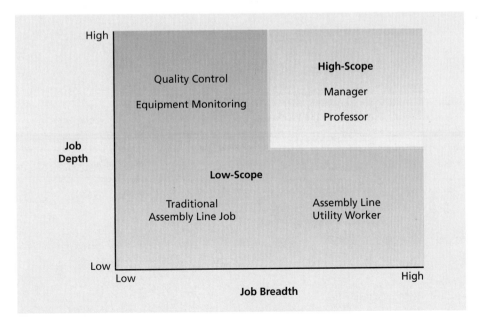

Exhibit 6.4
Job scope as a function of job depth and job breadth.

perform a single, repetitive task, but they might be required to exercise a fair degree of judgment in performing this task. Similarly, workers who monitor the performance of equipment (such as in a nuclear power plant) might perform a single task but again be required to exercise considerable discretion when a problem arises.

The motivational theories we discussed in the previous chapter suggest that high-scope jobs (*both* broad and deep) should provide more intrinsic motivation than low-scope jobs. Maslow's need hierarchy and ERG theory both seem to indicate that people can fulfill higher-order needs by the opportunity to perform high-scope jobs. Expectancy theory suggests that high-scope jobs can provide intrinsic motivation if the outcomes derived from such jobs are attractive.

The Job Characteristics Model

The concept of job scope provides an easy-to-understand introduction to why some jobs seem more intrinsically motivating than others. However, we can find a more rigorous delineation of the motivational properties of jobs in the Job Characteristics Model that J. Richard Hackman and Greg Oldham developed (Exhibit 6.5).[32] As you can observe, the Job Characteristics Model proposes that there are several "core" job characteristics that have a certain psychological impact on workers. In turn, the psychological states induced by the nature of the job lead to certain outcomes that are relevant to the worker and the organization. Finally, several other factors (moderators) influence the extent to which these relationships hold true.

Core Job Characteristics. The Job Characteristics Model shows that there are five core job characteristics that have particularly strong potential to affect

Exhibit 6.5
The Job Characteristics
Model.

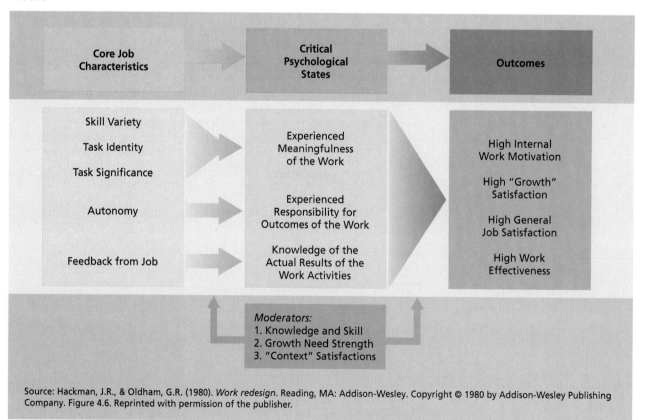

Source: Hackman, J.R., & Oldham, G.R. (1980). *Work redesign*. Reading, MA: Addison-Wesley. Copyright © 1980 by Addison-Wesley Publishing Company. Figure 4.6. Reprinted with permission of the publisher.

worker motivation: skill variety, task identity, task significance, autonomy, and job feedback. These characteristics are described in detail in Exhibit 6.6. In general, higher levels of these characteristics should lead to the favourable outcomes shown in Exhibit 6.5. Notice that **skill variety**, the opportunity to do a variety of job activities using various skills and talents, corresponds fairly closely to the notion of job breadth we discussed earlier. **Autonomy**, the freedom to schedule one's own work activities and decide work procedures, corresponds to job depth. However, Hackman and Oldham recognized that one could have a high degree of control over a variety of skills that were perceived as meaningless or fragmented. Thus, the concepts of task significance and task identity are introduced. **Task significance** is the impact that a job has on others. **Task identity** is the extent to which a job involves doing a complete piece of work, from beginning to end. In addition, they recognized that **feedback**, information about one's performance effectiveness, is also essential for high intrinsic motivation. People are not motivated for long if they do not know how well they are doing.

Hackman and Oldham developed a questionnaire called the Job Diagnostic Survey (JDS) to measure the core characteristics of jobs. The JDS requires job holders to report the amount of the various core characteristics contained in their

Skill variety. The opportunity to do a variety of job activities using various skills and talents.

Autonomy. The freedom to schedule one's own work activities and decide work procedures.

Task significance. The impact that a job has on other people.

Task identity. The extent to which a job involves doing a complete piece of work, from beginning to end.

Feedback. Information about the effectiveness of one's work performance.

Exhibit 6.6
Core job characteristics and example.

1. **Skill variety:** The degree to which a job requires a variety of different activities in carrying out the work, involving the use of a number of different skills and talents of the person.
High variety: The owner-operator of a garage who does electrical repair, rebuilds engines, does body work, and interacts with customers.
Low variety: A body shop worker who sprays paint eight hours a day.

2. **Task identity:** The degree to which a job requires completion of a "whole" and identifiable piece of work, that is, doing a job from beginning to end with a visible outcome.
High identity: A cabinet maker who designs a piece of furniture, selects the wood, builds the object, and finishes it to perfection.
Low identity: A worker in a furniture factory who operates a lathe solely to make table legs.

3. **Task significance:** The degree to which a job has substantial impact on the lives of other people, whether those people are in the immediate organization or in the world at large.
High significance: Nursing the sick in a hospital intensive care unit.
Low significance: Sweeping hospital floors.

4. **Autonomy:** The degree to which the job provides substantial freedom, independence, and discretion to the individual in scheduling the work and determining the procedures to be used in carrying it out.
High autonomy: A telephone installer who schedules his or her own work for the day, makes visits without supervision, and decides on the most effective techniques for a particular installation.
Low autonomy: A telephone operator who must handle calls as they come according to a routine, highly specified procedure.

5. **Job feedback:** The degree to which carrying out the work activities required by the job provides the individual with direct and clear information about the effectiveness of his or her performance.
High feedback: An electronics factory worker who assembles a radio and then tests it to determine if it operates properly.
Low feedback: An electronics factory worker who assembles a radio and then routes it to a quality control inspector who tests it for proper operation and makes needed adjustments.

Source: Definitions from Hackman, J.R., & Oldham, G.R. (1980). The properties of motivating jobs. *Work redesign.* Reading, MA: Addison-Wesley. Copyright © 1980 by Addison-Wesley Publishing Company, Reading, Massachusetts. Reprinted by permission of the publisher. Examples by authors.

Exhibit 6.7
Levels of core job
characteristics for managers
and keypunchers.

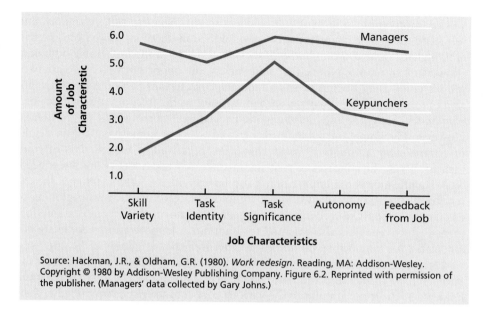

Source: Hackman, J.R., & Oldham, G.R. (1980). *Work redesign.* Reading, MA: Addison-Wesley.
Copyright © 1980 by Addison-Wesley Publishing Company. Figure 6.2. Reprinted with permission of
the publisher. (Managers' data collected by Gary Johns.)

jobs. From these reports, we can construct profiles to compare the motivational
properties of various jobs. For example, Exhibit 6.7 shows JDS profiles for lower-
level managers in a utility company (collected by one of the authors) and those
for keypunchers in another firm (reported by Hackman and Oldham). While the
managers perform a full range of managerial duties, the keypunchers perform a
highly regulated job—anonymous work from various departments is assigned to
them by a supervisor, and their output is verified for accuracy by others. Not surprisingly, the JDS profiles reveal that the managerial jobs are consistently higher
on the core characteristics than are the keypunching jobs.

According to Hackman and Oldham, an overall measure of the motivating
potential of a job can be calculated by the following formula:

$$\begin{matrix} \text{Motivating} \\ \text{potential} \\ \text{score} \end{matrix} = \frac{\overset{\text{Skill}}{\text{variety}} + \overset{\text{Task}}{\text{identity}} + \overset{\text{Task}}{\text{significance}}}{3} \times \text{Autonomy} \times \text{Job feedback}$$

Since the JDS measures the job characteristics on seven-point scales, a motivating potential score could theoretically range from 1 to 343. For example, the
motivating potential score for the keypunchers' jobs shown in Exhibit 6.6 is 20,
while that for the managers' jobs is 159. Thus, the managers are more likely than
the keypunchers to be motivated by the job itself. The average motivating potential score for 6,930 employees on 876 jobs has been calculated at 128.[33]

Critical Psychological States. Why should jobs that are higher on the core characteristics be intrinsically motivating? What is their psychological impact?
Hackman and Oldham argue that work will be intrinsically motivating when it is
perceived as *meaningful,* when the worker feels *responsible* for the outcomes of
the work, and when the worker has *knowledge* about his or her work progress.
As shown in Exhibit 6.5, the Job Characteristics Model proposes that the core job
characteristics affect meaningfulness, responsibility, and knowledge of results in a
systematic manner. When an individual uses a variety of skills to do a "whole" job
that is perceived as significant to others, he or she perceives the work as meaningful. When a person has autonomy to organize and perform the job as he or she
sees fit, the person feels personally responsible for the outcome of the work.
Finally, when the job provides feedback about performance, the worker will have
knowledge of the results of this opportunity to exercise responsibility.

Outcomes. The presence of the critical psychological states leads to a number of outcomes that are relevant to both the individual and the organization. Chief among these is high intrinsic motivation. When the worker is truly in control of a challenging job that provides good feedback about performance, the key prerequisites for intrinsic motivation are present. The relationship between the work and the worker is emphasized, and the worker is able to draw motivation from the job itself. This will result in high-quality productivity. By the same token, workers will report satisfaction with higher-order needs (growth needs) and general satisfaction with the job itself. This should lead to reduced absenteeism and turnover. In fact, the results of one study indicated that job characteristics predicted absenteeism up to 6 years after the job characteristics were assessed. Among the five job characteristics, skill variety, task identity, and autonomy were negatively and consistently related to absenteeism.[34]

Moderators. Hackman and Oldham recognize that jobs that are high in motivating potential do not *always* lead to favourable outcomes. Thus, as shown in Exhibit 6.5, they propose certain moderator or contingency variables (Chapter 1) that intervene between job characteristics and outcomes. One of these is the job-relevant knowledge and skill of the worker. Put simply, workers with weak knowledge and skills should not respond favourably to jobs that are high in motivating potential, since such jobs will prove too demanding. Another proposed moderator is **growth need strength,** which refers to the extent to which people desire to achieve higher-order need satisfaction by performing their jobs. Hackman and Oldham argue that those with high growth needs should be most responsive to challenging work. Finally, they argue that workers who are dissatisfied with the context factors surrounding the job (such as pay, supervision, and company policy) will be less responsive to challenging work than those who are reasonably satisfied with context factors.

Growth need strength. The extent to which people desire to achieve higher-order need satisfaction by performing their jobs.

In tests of the Job Characteristics Model, researchers usually require workers to describe their jobs by means of the JDS and then measure their reactions to these jobs. Although there is some discrepancy regarding the relative importance of the various core characteristics, these tests have generally been very supportive of the basic prediction of the model—workers tend to respond more favourably to jobs that are higher in motivating potential.[35] Where the model seems to falter is in its predictions about growth needs and context satisfaction. Evidence that these factors influence reactions to job design is weak or contradictory.[36]

Job Enrichment

Job enrichment is the design of jobs to enhance intrinsic motivation and the quality of working life. In general, enrichment involves increasing the motivating potential of jobs via the arrangement of their core characteristics. There are no hard and fast rules for the enrichment of jobs. Specific enrichment procedures depend on a careful diagnosis of the work to be accomplished, the available technology, and the organizational context in which enrichment is to take place. However, many job enrichment schemes combine tasks, establish client relationships, reduce supervision, form teams, or make feedback more direct.[37]

Job enrichment. The design of jobs to enhance intrinsic motivation and the quality of working life.

- *Combining tasks.* This involves assigning tasks that might be performed by different workers to a single individual. For example, in a furniture factory a lathe operator, an assembler, a sander, and a stainer might become four "chair makers"; each worker would then do all four tasks. Such a strategy should increase the variety of skills employed and might contribute to task identity as each worker approaches doing a unified job from start to finish.

Duncan Hines Ltd.
www.duncanhines.com

- *Establishing external client relationships.* This involves putting employees in touch with people outside the organization who depend on their products or services. Such a strategy might involve the use of new (interpersonal) skills, increase the identity and significance of the job, and increase feedback about one's performance. Consider this example:

    At the Duncan Hines angel food cake factory in Jackson, Tennessee, the line workers are given letters from customers who have problems with the product. One factory hand called up a customer whose angel food cake did not rise and helped figure out why by asking such questions as "How long did you beat the mix?" and "At what temperature did you bake it?" Says [Procter & Gamble CEO]: "What we've said to the workers is, this is the only place we make angel food cake, and you're responsible for it, and if you want to talk to the consumer, we'd like you to talk to the consumer."[38]

- *Establishing internal client relationships.* This involves putting employees in touch with people who depend on their products or services within the organization. For example, billers and expediters in a manufacturing firm might be assigned permanently to certain salespeople, rather than working on any salesperson's order as it comes in. The advantages are similar to those mentioned for establishing external client relationships.

- *Reducing supervision or reliance on others.* The goal here is to increase autonomy and control over one's own work. For example, management might permit clerical employees to check their own work for errors instead of having someone else do it. Similarly, firms might allow workers to order needed supplies or contract for outside services up to some dollar amount without obtaining permission.

- *Forming work teams.* Management can use this format as an alternative to a sequence of "small" jobs that individual workers perform when a product or service is too large or complex for one person to complete alone. For example, social workers with particular skills might operate as a true team to assist a particular client, rather than passing the client from person to person. Similarly, stable teams can form to construct an entire product, such as a car or boat, in lieu of an assembly-line approach. Such approaches should lead to the formal and informal development of a variety of skills and increase the identity of the job.

- *Making feedback more direct.* This technique is usually used in conjunction with other job design aspects that permit workers to be identified with their "own" product or service. For example, an electronics firm might have assemblers "sign" their output on a tag that includes an address and toll-free phone number. If a customer encounters problems, he or she contacts the assembler directly. In Sweden, workers who build trucks by team assembly are responsible for service and warranty work on "their" trucks that are sold locally.

Potential Problems with Job Enrichment

Despite the theoretical attractiveness of job enrichment as a motivational strategy, and despite the fact that many organizations have experimented with such programs, enrichment can encounter a number of challenging problems.

Poor Diagnosis. Problems with job enrichment can occur when it is instituted without a careful diagnosis of the needs of the organization and the particular jobs in question. Some enrichment attempts might be half-hearted tactical exercises that really do not increase the motivating potential of the job adequately. An especially likely error here is increasing job breadth (variety), while leaving the other crucial core characteristics unchanged. Thus, workers are simply given *more* boring, fragmented, routine tasks to do, such as bolting intake manifolds and water pumps onto engines. On the other side of the coin, in their zeal to use enrichment as a cure-all, organizations might attempt to enrich jobs that are already perceived as too rich by their incumbents. This has happened in some "downsized" firms in which the remaining managers have been assigned too many extra responsibilities.

Lack of Desire or Skill. Put simply, some workers do not *desire* enriched jobs. Almost by definition, enrichment places greater demands on workers, and some might not relish this extra responsibility. Even when people have no basic objections to enrichment in theory, they might lack the skills and competence necessary to perform enriched jobs effectively. Thus, for some poorly educated or trained workforces, enrichment might entail substantial training costs. In addition, it might be difficult to train some workers in certain skills required by enriched jobs, such as social skills. For example, part of the job enrichment scheme at a Philips television manufacturing plant in Holland required TV assemblers to initiate contacts with high-status staff members in other departments when they encountered problems. This is an example of the establishment of an internal client relationship, and many workers found this job requirement threatening.[39]

Demand for Rewards. Occasionally, workers who experience job enrichment ask that greater extrinsic rewards, such as pay, accompany their redesigned jobs. Most frequently, this desire is probably prompted by the fact that such jobs require the development of new skills and entail greater responsibility. For example, one enrichment exercise for clerical jobs in a U.S. government agency encountered this reaction.[40] Sometimes, such requests are motivated by the wish to share in the financial benefits of a successful enrichment exercise. In one documented case, workers with radically enriched jobs in a General Foods dog food plant in Topeka sought a financial bonus based on the system's success.[41] Equity in action!

Union Resistance. Traditionally, North American unions have not been enthusiastic about job enrichment. In part, this is due to a historical focus on negotiating with management about easily quantified extrinsic motivators, such as money, rather than the soft stuff of job design. Also, unions have tended to equate the narrow division of labour with preserving jobs for their members. Faced with global competition, the need for flexibility, and the need for employee initiative to foster quality, companies and unions have begun to dismantle restrictive contract provisions regarding job design. Fewer job classifications mean more opportunities for flexibility by combining tasks and using team approaches.

Supervisory Resistance. Even when enrichment schemes are carefully implemented to truly enhance the motivating potential of deserving jobs, they might fail because of their unanticipated impact on other jobs or other parts of the organizational system. A key problem here concerns the supervisors of the workers whose jobs have been enriched. By definition, enrichment increases the autonomy of employees. Unfortunately, such a change might "disenrich" the boss's job, a consequence that will hardly facilitate the smooth implementation of the job redesign. Some organizations have responded to this problem by effectively doing away with direct supervision of workers performing enriched jobs. Others use the supervisor as a trainer and developer of individuals on enriched jobs. Enrichment can increase the need for this supervisory function.

Management by Objectives

In Chapter 5, we discussed goal setting theory which states that a specific, challenging goal is established to solve a particular performance problem. In this basic form, goal setting is rather lacking in the potential to assist in employee development over time. Usually, management makes no particular provisions for counseling employees in goal accomplishment or for changing goals in some systematic manner as the need arises. It might also occur to you that certain jobs require the simultaneous accomplishment of *several* goals, and that superiors and subordinates might differ in the importance that they attach to these goals or disagree about how to evaluate goal accomplishment. This is particularly likely in the more complex jobs that exist at higher levels in the organization, such as management jobs and staff jobs (e.g., the human resource department or the research and development department).

Management by Objectives (MBO) is an elaborate, systematic, ongoing management program to facilitate goal establishment, goal accomplishment, and employee development.[42] The concept was developed by management theorist Peter Drucker. The objectives in MBO are simply another label for goals. In a well-designed MBO program, objectives for the organization as a whole are developed by top management and diffused down through the organization through the MBO process. In this manner, organizational objectives are translated into specific behavioural objectives for individual members. Our primary focus here is with the nature of the interaction between superiors and individual subordinates in an MBO program. Although there are many variations on the MBO theme, most superior-subordinate interactions share the following similarities:

1. The superior meets with individual subordinates to develop and agree on subordinate objectives for the coming months. These objectives usually involve both current job performance and personal development that may prepare the subordinate to perform other tasks or seek promotion. The objectives are made as specific as possible and quantified, if feasible, to assist in subsequent evaluation of accomplishment. Time frames for accomplishment are specified, and the objectives may be given priority according to their agreed importance. The methods to achieve the objectives might or might not be topics of discussion. Objectives, time frames, and priorities are put in writing.

2. There are periodic meetings to monitor subordinate progress in achieving objectives. During these meetings, people can modify objectives if new needs or problems are encountered.

3. An appraisal meeting is held to evaluate the extent to which the agreed objectives have been achieved. Special emphasis is placed on diagnosing the reasons for success or failure so that the meeting serves as a learning experience for both parties.

4. The MBO cycle is repeated.

An example of a simple MBO objectives form is shown in Exhibit 6.8. Plant manager John Atkins has met with company president Freda Cranford and agreed on eight objectives for the coming months. Notice that these objectives are specific and in most cases quantified. Objectives 7 and 8 are personal development objectives, while the others are performance objectives. The objectives have been given "A" priority or "B" priority (column 2) and a specific deadline for accomplishment (column 3). In his own role as a manager, Atkins would probably use some of these objectives as a basis for establishing the objectives of his subordinates. Thus, objectives 1 through 6 would become the basis of even more specific goals for the production manager, the shipping manager, and the human

Management by Objectives (MBO). An elaborate, systematic, ongoing program designed to facilitate goal establishment, goal accomplishment, and employee development.

Exhibit 6.8
A simple format for recording objectives in an MBO program.

Manager's job title			
John Atkins	7/2	PLANT MANAGER	
Prepared by the Manager	Date	Managerial Job Objectives	
F. W. Cranford	7/2	PRESIDENT	
Reviewed by Supervisor	Date	Supervisor's Job Title	

Statement of Objectives	Priority	Deadline	Outcomes or Results
1. To Increase Deliveries to 98% of All Scheduled Delivery Dates	A	6/31	
2. To Reduce Waste and Spoilage to 3% of All Raw Materials Used	A	6/31	
3. To Reduce Lost Time Due to Accidents to 100 Person-Days/Year	B	2/1	
4. To Reduce Operating Cost to 10% Below Budget	A	1/15	
5. To Install a Quality Control Radioisotope System at a Cost of Less Than $53,000	A	3/15	
6. To Improve Production Scheduling and Preventative Maintenance so as to Increase Machine Utilization Time to 95% of Capacity	B	10/1	
7. To Complete the UCLA Executive Program This Year	A	6/31	
8. To Teach a Production Management Course in University Extension	B	6/31	

Source: Adapted from Raia, A. P. (1974). *Managing by objectives*. Glenview, IL: Scott, Foresman, © 1974, p. 60. Reprinted by permission.

resource manager who report to Atkins. Thus, the MBO program diffuses a goal orientation throughout the organization.

Over the years, a wide variety of organizations have implemented MBO, including Kodak Australasia, Paul Revere Life, the U.S. Air Force, and the Colorado State Patrol. Overall, the research evidence shows clear productivity gains.[43] However, a number of factors are associated with the failure of MBO programs. For one thing, MBO is an elaborate, difficult, time-consuming process, and its implementation must have the full commitment of top management. One careful review showed a 56 percent average gain in productivity for programs with high top management commitment and a 6 percent gain for those with low commitment.[44] If such commitment is absent, managers at lower levels simply go through the motions of practising MBO. At the very least, this reaction will lead to the haphazard specification of objectives and thus subvert the very core of MBO—goal setting. A frequent symptom of this degeneration is the complaint that MBO is "just a bunch of paperwork."[45] Indeed, at this stage, it is!

Even with the best of intentions, setting specific, quantified objectives can be a difficult process. This might lead to an overemphasis on measurable objectives at the expense of more qualitative objectives. For example, it might be much easier to agree on production goals than on goals that involve subordinate development, although both might be equally important. Also, excessive short-term orientation can be a problem with MBO. Finally, even if reasonable objectives are established, MBO can still be subverted if the performance review becomes an exercise in browbeating or punishing employees for failure to achieve objectives.[46]

Alternative Working Schedules as Motivators for a Diverse Workforce

Most North Americans work a five-day week of approximately 40 hours—the "nine-to-five grind." However, many organizations have begun to experiment with modifying these traditional working schedules. The purpose of these modifications is not to motivate people to work harder and thus produce direct performance benefits. Rather, the purpose is to meet diverse workforce needs and promote job satisfaction. In turn, this should facilitate recruiting the best personnel and reduce costly absenteeism and turnover.

Flex-Time

Flex-time. An alternative work schedule in which arrival and quitting times are flexible.

One alternative to traditional working schedules is **flex-time,** which was first introduced on a large scale in Europe. In its most simple and common form, management requires employees to report for work on each working day and work a given number of hours. However, the times at which they arrive and leave are flexible, as long as they are present during certain core times. For example, companies might permit employees to begin their day anytime after 7 a.m. and work until 6 p.m., as long as they put in eight hours and are present during the core times of 9:15 until noon and 2 until 4:15 (Exhibit 6.9). Other systems permit employees to tally hours on a weekly or monthly basis, although they are still usually required to be present during the core time of each working day.[47]

Flex-time is obviously well suited to meeting the needs of a diverse workforce, since it allows employees to tailor arrival and departure times to their own transportation and child-care situation. It should reduce absenteeism, since employees can handle personal matters during conventional business hours.[48] Also, flexible working hours connote a degree of prestige and trust that is usually reserved for executives and professionals.

When jobs are highly interdependent, such as on an assembly line, flex-time becomes an unlikely strategy. To cite an even more extreme example, we simply

"Am I interested in an alternative work arrangement? Yes, I'd like to telecommute from a computer-equipped hot tub on flextime."

Source: David Harbaugh

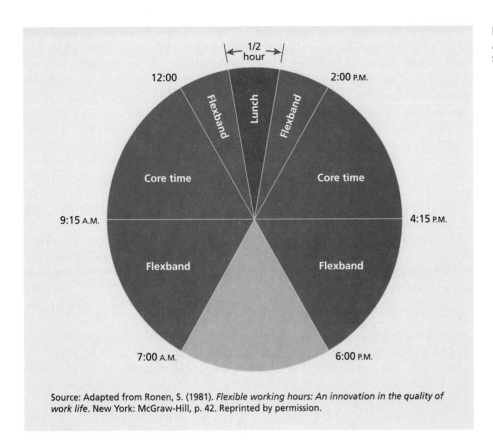

Source: Adapted from Ronen, S. (1981). *Flexible working hours: An innovation in the quality of work life.* New York: McGraw-Hill, p. 42. Reprinted by permission.

Exhibit 6.9
An example of a flex-time schedule.

cannot have members of a hospital operating room team showing up for work whenever it suits them! In addition, flex-time might lead to problems in achieving adequate supervisory coverage. For these reasons, not surprisingly, flex-time is most frequently implemented in office environments. For instance, in a bank, the core hours might be when the bank is open to the public.

Although flex-time has generally been limited to white-collar personnel, it has been applied in a variety of organizations, including insurance companies (Metropolitan Life), financial institutions (Boston's State Street Bank), and government offices (many American states, Canadian and American civil service). As we noted in Chapter 5, Starbucks offers flex-time to all its employees. According to a recent survey, 66% of organizations offered flexible work schedules.[49]

Although the quality of the research on flex-time varies, we can draw a number of conclusions.[50] First, employees who work under flex-time almost always prefer the system to fixed hours. In addition, work attitudes generally become more positive, and employers report minimal abuse of the arrangement. When measured, absenteeism and tardiness have often shown decreases following the introduction of flex-time, and first-line supervisors and managers are usually positively inclined toward the system. Interestingly, slight productivity gains are often reported under flex-time, probably due to better use of scarce resources or equipment rather than to increased motivation. In fact, a recent review of research on flex-time concluded that it has a positive effect on productivity, job satisfaction, satisfaction with work schedule, and employee absenteeism.[51]

Compressed Workweek

A second alternative to traditional working schedules is the **compressed workweek.** This system compresses the hours worked each week into fewer days. The

Compressed workweek. An alternative work schedule in which employees work fewer than the normal five days a week but still put in a normal number of hours per week.

most common compressed workweek is the 4–40 system, in which employees work four 10-hour days each week rather than the traditional five eight-hour days. Thus, the organization or department might operate Monday through Thursday or Tuesday through Friday, although rotation schemes that keep the organization open five days a week are also employed.[52] Printer Quad/Graphics uses a 3–36 system with three 12-hour days a week.

Like flex-time, the shorter workweek might be expected to reduce absenteeism because employees can pursue personal business or family matters in what had been working time. In addition, the 4–40 schedule reduces commuting costs and time by 20 percent and provides an extra day a week for leisure or family pursuits. Although the longer workday could pose a problem for single parents, a working couple with staggered off-days could actually provide their own child care on two of five "working" days.

Technical roadblocks to the implementation of the 4–40 workweek include the possibility of reduced customer service and the negative effects of fatigue that can accompany longer working days. The latter problem is likely to be especially acute when the work is strenuous.

Although research on the effects of the four-day week is less extensive than that for flex-time, a couple of conclusions do stand out.[53] First, people who have experienced the four-day system seem to *like* it. Sometimes this liking is accompanied by increased job satisfaction, but the effect might be short-lived.[54] In many cases, the impact of the compressed workweek might be better for family life than for work life. Second, workers have often reported an increase in fatigue following the introduction of the compressed week. This might be responsible for the uneven impact of the system on absenteeism, sometimes decreasing it and sometimes not. Potential gains in attendance might be nullified as workers take an occasional day off to recuperate from fatigue.[55] Finally, the more sophisticated research studies do not report lasting changes in productivity due to the short workweek.[56] According to the most recent review of research on the compressed workweek, there is a positive effect on job satisfaction and satisfaciton with work schedule but not for absenteeism or productivity.[57]

Job Sharing

Job sharing. An alternative work schedule in which two part-time employees divide the work of a full-time job.

Job sharing occurs when two part-time employees divide the work (and perhaps the benefits) of a full-time job.[58] The two can share all aspects of the job equally, or some kind of complementary arrangement can occur in which one party does some tasks and the co-holder does other tasks.

Job sharing is obviously attractive to people who want to spend more time with small children or sick elders than a conventional five-day-a-week routine permits. By the same token, it can enable organizations to attract and/or retain highly capable employees who might otherwise decide against full-time employment.

There is virtually no hard research on job sharing. However, anecdotal reports suggest that the job sharers must make a concerted effort to communicate well with each other as well as with superiors, co-workers, and clients. Such communication is greatly facilitated by contemporary computer technology and voice mail. However, coordination problems are bound to occur if there is not adequate communication. Also, problems with performance appraisal can occur when two individuals share one job.

Telecommuting

Telecommuting. A system by which employees are able to work at home but stay in touch with their offices through the use of communications technology, such as a computer network, voice mail, and electronic messages.

In recent years, an increasing number of organizations have begun to consider the concept of telecommuting. By **telecommuting**, employees are able to work at

An increasing number of companies are providing their employees with the opportunity to work at home and stay in touch with their offices through the use of communication technology.

home but stay in touch with their offices through the use of communications technology, such as a computer network, voice mail, and electronic messages.[59] Like the other types of alternative working arrangements, telecommuting provides workers with greater flexibility in their work schedules.

Many companies first began implementing telecommuting in response to the Clean Air Act and the Americans with Disabilities act in the United States as well as employee requests for more flexible work arrangements.[60] With the growth in communication technologies, however, other factors have also influenced the spread of telecommuting. For example, telecommuting is changing the way that organizations recruit and hire people. With telecommuting as an option, companies can now hire the best person for a job regardless of where they live in the world, through *distant staffing*.[61] Distant staffing enables employees to work for a company without ever having to come into the office or even be in the same country!

Today, it is estimated that approximately 11 million North Americans are telecommuting, and 51 percent of North American companies offer some form of telecommuting including 1 in 4 Fortune 1000 companies.[62] Companies such as Arden Hills, Control Data, and Northern Telecom who are reliant on communication technology have been at the forefront of telecommuting.[63] At Northern Telecom, where close to 5,000 employees are full-time telecommuters, the company supplies employees with a complete home office set-up that includes a computer, furniture, a data link, telephone lines, a printer, and a fax machine.[64]

The large telecommunications company Pacific Bell realized the possibilities of telecommuting during the Los Angeles Olympics, when it was adopted as a temporary measure to avoid the horrendous automotive gridlock that was expected when the games visitors were added to the city's already clogged freeways. Shortly thereafter, Pacific Bell implemented a pilot project to examine telecommuting, using 100 volunteer managers. On hearing about the project, 400 other managers developed informal arrangements with their bosses to begin telecommuting. Necessity was added to popularity when a large earthquake struck the San Francisco area in the fall of 1989. With the Bay Bridge damaged, leading to impossibly long commutes, the value of telecommuting in times of emergency was obvious.[65]

Although research on telecommuting is limited, it is believed to have a number of advantages for employees and organizations. Organizations benefit from

Pacific Bell
www.pacbell.com

lower costs as a result of a reduction in turnover and the need for less office space and equipment and can attract employees who see it as a desirable benefit.[66] On the basis of a survey of over 3,000 Pacific Bell managers, telecommuting was expected to increase job satisfaction and productivity and decrease stress. Many felt that telecommuting would enhance productivity because of fewer interruptions (i.e., less unscheduled informal communication), and there is some evidence that telecommuting does increase employee productivity.[67] As well, managers linked stress reduction to the opportunity to avoid grinding commutes in urban areas. In fact, the results of a recent survey found that telecommuting did have a positive effect on productivity, flexibility, and work/life balance.[68]

Some negative aspects of telecommuting, although not strongly endorsed, centred on its potential damage to informal communication. These included decreased visibility when promotions were considered, problems in handling rush projects, and workload spillover for nontelecommuters.[69] Other potential problems with telecommuting include distractions in the home environment, feelings of isolation, and overwork. As a result, telecommuting failures have been reported to be as high as 50 percent.[70]

Despite the potential benefits and the growing popularity of telecommuting, many companies are hesitant to implement telecommuting programs because of concerns about trust and control. Many managers are uncomfortable with the prospect of not being able to keep an eye on their employees while they work.[71] Therefore, it is important that there exists a strong perception of trust between employees and management as well as careful planning and clear guidelines before an organization implements a telecommuting program.

Total Quality Management and Motivation

As the earlier sections illustrate, organizations have a lot of options when it comes to using money, job design, goal setting, and work scheduling as motivators. Confused about when to do what? The concepts of *fit* and *balance* can help resolve this confusion. First, the motivational systems chosen should have a good fit with the strategic goals of the organization. Ultimately, speed, quality, and volume of output involve some tradeoffs, and we will not achieve one of these outcomes if we reward another. Second, balance among the components of a motivational system is critical. Job design and work schedules must allow employees to achieve the goals that are set, and the reward system needs to be directed toward this achievement. Let us examine motivational fit and balance in the context of total quality management.

Total quality management (TQM) is a systematic attempt to achieve continuous improvement in the quality of an organization's products and/or services. Quality is defined very broadly to include things such as reliability of performance, ease of use, timely delivery, and value-for-money. A number of characteristics typical of TQM are relevant to our current topic of motivation.[72] These include:

- *An obsession with customer satisfaction.* These customers can be both external customers (e.g., American Express cardholders) and internal customers (e.g., American Express service offices are the customers of the firm's MIS department).

- *A concern for good relations with suppliers.* Suppliers are seen as an integral aspect to achieving high quality, not simply a source of the lowest-priced supply.

- *A search for continuous improvement of processes.* Organizations achieve high quality with meticulous attention to *how* a product or service reaches a

Total quality management (TQM). A systematic attempt to achieve continuous improvement in the quality of an organization's products and/or services.

customer. Federal Express satisfies customers with fast, reliable delivery. It makes money by understanding *how* to do this at a low cost.

■ *The prevention (not just detection) of quality errors.* Rather than fixing things after they go wrong, attention to processes enables organizations to design errors out of the production phase of the product or service.

■ *Frequent measurement and assessment.* Customer needs, customer satisfaction, supplier performance, competitor performance, and internal processes are all rigorously tracked and analyzed.

■ *Extensive training.* Employee training is seen as an investment and as necessary to support the other TQM initiatives.

■ *High employee involvement and teamwork.* The basic philosophy here is that *all* employees at all levels can contribute to delivering high-quality products or services by working together.

Now, let us see how the motivation techniques that we have discussed are related to TQM. How, in practice, do they "fit" with this management philosophy? Several of the examples below are from winners of the United States government's Malcolm Baldrige National Quality Award.[73]

TQM and Goal Setting/MBO

"Continuous improvement" does not sound like a very specific goal! However, everything about TQM, except its general definition, places a high premium on specific goal setting.

Many firms pursuing quality begin at the top using a process called benchmarking to develop quality goals. **Benchmarking** is a systematic process for examining the products, services, and work processes of firms that are recognized as illustrating the best practices for organizational improvement.[74] In other words, it is recognized that quality goals have to be set using information from the organizations that are really *good* at the practice in question. This assures that the goals are challenging but also attainable.

Competitive benchmarking uses firms in the same industry as standards for comparison. Because dealing with competitors is a sensitive issue, this is sometimes done through trade groups that collect and share information anonymously. For example, there is a competitive benchmarking agreement among semiconductor manufacturers (e.g., Intel, DEC, Texas Instruments) and telecommunications competitors (e.g., Bell Atlantic, AT&T, GTE). *Generic benchmarking* looks for the best practices regardless of industry as long as they can be translated into one's own firm. For instance, Xerox visited L.L. Bean (the Maine clothing and outdoors mail-order company) to learn about its excellent warehousing, materials handling, and order filling.[75]

Quality-oriented firms often include quality goals as part of the performance appraisal process. For example, at Westinghouse Commercial Nuclear Fuel Division, quality improvement is explicitly included in an MBO program. Since feedback is necessary for goal achievement, these firms are very active in surveying customers, suppliers, and their own employees for relevant performance information. Personnel are also trained to collect and interpret quality data in their own domain. Many organizations use goal setting to motivate quality performances from their suppliers, setting explicit standards rather than waiting to see what comes through the door. Ford Motor Company has been a pioneer in this area, especially in assisting its suppliers to achieve its standards by doing things such as giving engineering support.

Benchmarking. A systematic process for examining the products, services, and work processes of firms that are recognized as illustrating the best practices for organizational improvement.

TQM and Job Design

One aspect of TQM concerns streamlining processes, where possible, so that there are fewer opportunities for things to go wrong in the production of a completed product or service. On the surface, this might look like bad news for interesting jobs. However, many firms with successful TQM programs have accompanied process simplification with the empowerment of the workforce. **Empowerment** entails giving people the authority, opportunity, and motivation to take initiative and solve organizational problems. In TQM, this often involves the use of job enrichment techniques (see "In-Focus: *New Manufacturing Processes and Job Design*). For instance, inspection of one's own work (direct feedback) is very common, as is increased autonomy to solve customer service problems expediently. For example, at Motorola, sales representatives have the authority to replace defective products even six years after their purchase. Putting "inside" employees into contact with customers is common in quality-oriented firms, thus enhancing external client relationships for the employee and providing a conduit for information from the customer. For example, employees of Lexus, Toyota's luxury car division, call several purchasers each month to find out how their cars are performing. Things can also work in the other direction. Some firms empower lower-level employees to go to suppliers to sort out quality problems. Finally, many companies have used the problem-solving capabilities inherent in teamwork to foster quality. Baldrige Award winner Cadillac employs semi-autonomous work teams. In each of these cases, companies have modified job design to empower employees to prevent or solve quality problems.

Empowerment. Giving people the authority, opportunity, and motivation to take initiative and solve organizational problems.

Xerox Business Products
www.xerox.com

TQM and Money

Successful quality-oriented firms go to a lot of trouble to balance individual rewards with team-oriented rewards.[76] This recognizes the fact that individuals can contribute to quality, but that job designs often dictate teamwork. Xerox Business Products and Systems uses gainsharing to reward teamwork. At Federal Express and Cadillac, managers can make instant cash awards to recognize special contributions to quality. New Balance, the athletic shoe maker, eliminated piece-rate pay and installed a team approach that bases 70 percent of pay on quality and 30 percent on volume. Skill-based pay seems like a natural for TQM, given the system's emphasis on training.

Firms that pursue quality also put a lot of emphasis on nonmonetary recognition, targeting higher order needs such as self-esteem. For instance, at AMP of Canada, a manufacturer of electric connecting products, teams that have made process improvements showcase them to co-workers in a trade-fair-like setting.

Some observers have gone so far as to argue that traditional individually oriented performance appraisal is at odds with the emphasis on processes and teamwork that characterize TQM. Appraisal of teams using customer (internal or external) input is one alternative.[77]

TQM and Alternative Working Schedules

The application of alternative work schedules requires very careful consideration in the context of TQM, especially in the domain of customer satisfaction. For example, the introduction of flex-time means that either internal or external customers might be deprived of the timely advice or attention of a key organizational member who has not arrived for work yet or who has left "early." Flex-time can also play havoc with the operation of work teams. The compressed workweek

in focus → New Manufacturing Processes and Job Design

During the last decade there have been major changes taking place in manufacturing. The traditional practices epitomized by mass production are giving way to a new paradigm. Practices such as "lean production," "world class manufacturing," "integrated manufacturing," "time-based flexible manufacturing," and "new wave manufacturing" represent new manufacturing approaches that are aimed at making organizations more competitive.

These new approaches to manufacturing are designed to provide increased responsiveness to customer demands, by controlling costs and simultaneously improving quality and tailoring output more specifically to customer requirements. To accomplish this, they rely heavily on enabling technologies and techniques such as just-in-time (JIT) and total quality management (TQM).

A key question raised in the implementation of these approaches is whether they are sufficient in themselves to realize new competitive goals or whether wider individual and organizational change is also necessary. Of particular concern is the role of employees and the design of their work. In other words, do employee roles need to change in order for these new manufacturing approaches to be successful, and do their jobs need to be redesigned?

In order to answer this question, Sharon Parker, Toby Wall, and Paul Jackson conducted two studies to examine the implementation of new production practices. They argued that the successful implementation of new manufacturing practices requires that production employees develop a broader role orientation that involves a concern for high product quality, customer satisfaction, working as part of a team, and understanding the importance of gaining and using a wide range of skills and knowledge required to perform effectively. Furthermore, the development of such a broader role orientation requires an increase in job autonomy.

To investigate the effects of job autonomy on production employees' role orientation, the authors conducted two studies on new manufactur-

ing initiatives. The first study involved the implementation of a JIT-TQM initiative that did not involve any change in employees' autonomy in the assembly section of a company that designs and manufactures vehicle seats and seat mechanisms for car manufacturers in the United Kingdom and Europe. The second study involved the introduction of a JIT-TQM initiative that was accompanied by enhanced autonomy in the production department of an American-owned electronics company in the United Kingdom that designed and produced control equipment for use in process industries. Autonomous work teams were formed and multiskilled employees were given the authority to manage day-to-day activities involved in meeting production targets and the responsibility for testing and quality inspection.

The results indicated that employees in the first study who did not experience a change in autonomy did not develop a broader and more proactive role orientation. In fact, they attached less importance to various skills and types of knowledge that would enable high performance. Employees in the second study whose job autonomy was enhanced developed a broader and more flexible role orientation. Overall, the adoption of the JIT-TQM initiative in this company was very successful. Lead times were reduced from 14 weeks to two days; inventory costs were reduced to 20 percent of the initial costs; delivery integrity (meeting customer delivery dates) was improved from 50 percent to 97 percent, and quality (monitored in terms of zero-defect boards and quality yield) was substantially improved.

The results of this research demonstrate that the implementation of new manufacturing practices requires that production employees develop a broader and more flexible role orientation, and this requires that such initiatives also involve work redesign and job enrichment.

Source: Excerpted from Parker, S. K., Wall, T. D., & Jackson, P. R. (1997). "That's not my job": Developing flexible employee work orientations. *Academy of Management Journal*, 40, pp. 899-929.

can present even greater problems, since key personnel could be unavailable for a whole day. Job sharing can be particularly worrisome in terms of perceptions of service quality. One manager in a computer service company reported that clients sometimes prefer one job sharer to another or feel that their account is not receiving the full attention of a single service representative.[78] Telecommuting can cause communication problems between telecommuters and those in the office, and teamwork on the job may suffer.[79]

How can one deal with these problems? Balance among the motivational strategies and adherence to other TQM principles often shows the way. For example, organizations can redesign jobs using cross-training so that even with flex-time there is always someone capable present. Finally, again in line with the TQM emphasis on training, organizations can train people to use alternative work schedules appropriately. DuPont and Corning extend this training right down to the employee level (e.g., how to design a backup schedule) rather than simply training managers.

the manager's notebook
First Marathon's "Eat-What-You-Kill" Compensation Philosophy

1. While some may find First Marathon's compensation plan to be crude, one has to consider the nature of the work and employees, as well as the organization itself. The organization was a new player in a very competitive business. The lavish reward system seems to have been a key factor in helping First Marathon become Canada's largest independent broker. The nature of the work was also well suited for this type of compensation system. Employees work on their own, and the more money they make for the company, the more they make for themselves. Finally, the company attracted top-notch entrepreneurs keen on making the big score. Thus, First Marathon's "eat-what-you-kill" compensation philosophy was a perfect fit for the organization, the work, and the employees. However, given the organization's current position in the industry and its changing focus, is this still the best compensation philosophy?

2. On the way out is the lone wolf "eat-what-you-kill philosophy" that Bloomberg spent years espousing. There will be no more $7-million salaries under its new compensation system.

Instead, First Marathon decided to instill a more team-oriented system in which people get paid for their contribution to a group effort. According to investment banking chief Peter Jones, "If you're trying to do more business with larger-cap companies, which we are, then you are competing for business with bank-owned brokerages, which will have a team of people covering that client. That makes a direct-drive compensation system much more difficult to work." A new system that is similar to that used by First Marathon's larger competitors was approved by the company's directors. The new system is refereed to as a "pool system." Under this system, the fees earned are tossed into a pool, and at the end of each quarter, the amount is divided up among the members of a department. This compensation plan is expected to be more effective for team building and cooperation as well as for establishing long-term relationships with clients. The criteria used to allocate the pool includes teamwork and cooperation as well as working on longer-term projects.

Summary

- Money should be most effective as a motivator when it is made contingent on performance. Schemes to link pay to performance on production jobs are called wage incentive plans. Piece-rate, in which workers are paid a certain amount of money for each item produced, is the prototype of all wage incentive plans. In general, wage incentives increase productivity, but their introduction can be accompanied by a number of problems, one of which is the restriction of production. Attempts to link pay to performance on white-collar jobs are called merit pay plans. Evidence suggests that many merit pay plans are less effective than they could be because merit pay is inadequate, performance ratings are mistrusted, or extreme secrecy about pay levels prevails. Compensation plans to enhance teamwork include profit sharing, employee stock ownership, gainsharing, and skill-based pay.

- Recent views advocate increasing the scope (breadth and depth) of jobs to capitalize on their inherent motivational properties, as opposed to the job simplification of the past. The Job Characteristics Model by Hackman and Oldham suggests that jobs have five core characteristics that affect their motivating potential: skill variety, task identity, task significance, autonomy, and feedback. When jobs are high in these characteristics, favourable motivational and attitudinal consequences should occur. Job enrichment involves designing jobs to enhance intrinsic motivation and the quality of working life. Some specific enrichment techniques include combining tasks, establishing client relationships, reducing supervision and reliance on others, forming work teams, and making feedback more direct.

- Management by Objectives (MBO) is an elaborate goal-setting and evaluation process that organizations typically use for management jobs. Objectives for the organization as a whole are developed by top management and diffused down through the organization and translated into specific behavioural objectives for individual members.

- Some organizations have adopted alternative working schedules, such as flex-time, compressed workweek, job sharing, or telecommuting, with expectations of motivational benefits. Although these schemes should have little effect on productivity, they have the potential to reduce absenteeism and turnover and enhance the quality of working life for a diverse workforce.

- Total quality management is a systematic attempt to achieve continuous improvement in the quality of an organization's products and/or services. It includes great concern with customer satisfaction, supplier relations, continuous process improvement, error prevention, measurement, training, and employee involvement. Effective TQM programs mix and balance the motivation techniques we discussed in this chapter to ensure the implementation of TQM principles.

Discussion Questions

1. Describe some jobs for which you think it would be difficult to link pay to performance. What is it about these jobs that provokes this difficulty?

2. Imagine two insurance companies that have merit pay plans for salaried white-collar personnel. In one organization, the plan truly rewards good performers, while in the other it does not. Both companies decide to make salaries completely public. What will be the consequences of such a change for each company? (Be specific, using concepts such as expectancy, instrumentality, job satisfaction, and turnover.)

3. You are, of course, familiar with the annual lists of the world's 10 worst-dressed people or the 10 worst movies. Here's a new one: A job enrichment consultant has developed a list of the 10 worst jobs, which includes a highway toll collector, pool typist, bank guard, and automatic elevator operator. Use the five core job characteristics to describe each of these jobs. Could you enrich any of these jobs? How? Which should be completely automated? Can you add some jobs to the list?

4. What are the essential distinctions between gain-sharing, profit sharing and employee stock ownership?

5. Some observers have argued that the jobs of the President of the United States and the Prime Minister of Canada are "too big" for one person to perform adequately. This probably means that the jobs are perceived as having too much scope or being too enriched. Use the Job Characteristics Model to explore the accuracy of this contention.

6. Imagine an office setting in which a change to either a four-day week, flex-time or telecommuting would appear to be equally feasible to introduce. What would be the pros and cons of each system? How would factors such as the nature of the business, the age of the workforce, and the average commuting distance affect the choice of systems?

7. How is the concept of workforce diversity related to the motivational techniques discussed in the chapter?

8. Discuss how organizations can realize the total quality management principle of strong attention to customer satisfaction with the motivational techniques that we have covered.

9. Merit pay plans often require that managers conduct performance evaluations of their employees in order to determine the amount of merit pay awarded. Discuss some of the perceptual problems and biases described in Chapter 3 that could create problems for a merit pay plan.

What can be done to improve performance evaluations and the success of merit pay plans?

? 10. Using each of the motivation theories described in Chapter 5, explain how job design and job enrichment can be motivational. According to each theory, when is job design and job enrichment most likely to be effective for motivating workers?

Experiential Exercise

Choose Your Job

People differ in the kinds of jobs they prefer. The following questions give you a chance to consider just what it is about a job that is most important to *you*. For each question, indicate the extent to which you would prefer Job A or Job B if you had to make a choice between them. In answering, assume that everything else about the two jobs is the same except the characteristics being compared. There are no "correct" answers. Just give your personal choice.

Scoring and Interpretation

These questions make up the growth need strength measure from J. Richard Hackman and Greg Oldham's Job Diagnostic Survey. To determine your own growth need strength, first subtract your responses on items 2, 3, 4, 6, 8, and 9 from 6. Then, add up the resulting scores on all 12 items and divide the total by 12. This is your growth need strength score. It should fall somewhere between 1 and 5.

People with high growth needs have a strong desire to obtain growth satisfaction from their jobs. The average growth

—1— Strongly Prefer A	—2— Slightly Prefer A	—3— Neutral	—4— Slightly Prefer B	—5— Strongly Prefer B

	JOB A	JOB B
_____	1. A job where the pay is very good.	A job where there is considerable opportunity to be creative and innovative.
_____	2. A job where you are often required to make important decisions.	A job with many pleasant people to work with.
_____	3. A job in which greater responsibility is given to those who do the best work.	A job in which greater responsibility is given to loyal employees who have the most seniority.
_____	4. A job in an organization which is in financial trouble—and might have to close down within the year.	A job in which you are not allowed to have any say whatever in how your work is scheduled, or in the procedures to be used in carrying it out.
_____	5. A very routine job.	A job where your co-workers are not very friendly.
_____	6. A job with a supervisor who is often very critical of you and your work in front of other people.	A job which prevents you from using a number of skills that you worked hard to develop.
_____	7. A job with a supervisor who respects you and treats you fairly.	A job which provides constant opportunities for you to learn new and interesting things.
_____	8. A job where there is a real chance you could be laid off.	A job with very little chance to do challenging work.
_____	9. A job in which there is a real chance for you to develop new skills and advance in the organization.	A job which provides lots of vacation time and an excellent fringe benefit package.
_____	10. A job with little freedom and independence to do your work in the way you think best.	A job where the working conditions are poor.
_____	11. A job with very satisfying teamwork.	A job which allows you to use your skills and abilities to the fullest extent.
_____	12. A job which offers little or no challenge.	A job which requires you to be completely isolated from co-workers.

score for thousands of individuals employed in a wide variety of jobs is 4.23. Here are some other growth need norms based on occupation, education, and age.[80]

4.46 White-collar	4.92 Sales
4.00 Blue-collar	4.13 Machine trades
4.92 Middle managers	4.16 Construction
4.62 First-line managers	4.02 High school graduates
4.76 Professional and technical	4.72 University graduates
4.18 Clerical	4.01 Under age 20
	4.25 Ages 20–29

Source: Hackman, J. R., & Oldham, G. R. (1974). *The Job Diagnostic Survey: An instrument for the diagnosis of jobs and the evaluation of job redesign projects.* Yale University Department of Administrative Sciences Technical Report No. 4.

Case Incident

The Junior Accountant

After graduating from business school, Sabrita received a job offer from a large accounting firm to work as a junior accountant. She was ranked in the top 10 and could not be happier. During the first six months, however, Sabrita began to reconsider her decision to join a large firm. This is how she described her job: Every day her supervisor brought several files for her to audit. He told her exactly in what order to do them and how to plan her day and work. At the end of the day, the supervisor would return to pick up the completed files. The supervisor collected the files from several other junior accountants, and then put them all together and completed the audit himself. The supervisor would then meet the client to review and discuss the audit. Sabrita did not ever meet the clients, and her supervisor never talked about his meeting with them or the final report. Sabrita felt very discouraged and wanted to quit.

1. Based on the Job Characteristics Model, describe the job characteristics and critical psychological states of Sabrita's job.

2. How would you redesign Sabrita's job to increase its motivating potential?

Case Study

Chang Koh Metal Ptd. Ltd. in China

Chang Koh Metal Engineering Ptd. Ltd. was founded in 1982 by Teo Kai San, a first generation Straits-born Chinese. The company's operations were in the production of metal-stamping precision parts. In 1993, the company expanded its operations by establishing a plant in Putian, China, which was the area of China from which Teo Kai San's parents had emigrated. The founder's son, Andrew Teo, was appointed as general manager. Andrew was 29 years old and had an en-

gineering degree from the National University of Singapore. Prior to joining his father's company, Andrew had worked for an American multinational company in Singapore and had progressed to the rank of line manager, a position with substantial authority and responsibility. Andrew joined his father's company because he felt that his success in the multinational was a sign of his skills, indicating that he deserved a senior position in his father's company on the basis of merit rather than family connections. He also felt that the systems and practices he learned there would enable him to bring more updated management practices to Chang Koh Metal.

Since Andrew's father believed it was important to have in a position of authority a person who was knowledgeable about the local area, he appointed a relative from Putian, Jian Wei, as the plant manager to assist Andrew in the plant's operations. A primary reason for choosing China as the site for a plant was the belief that Singaporean Chinese should find it easy to work with the Chinese in China. After all, the two groups shared a common cultural heritage. The other advantages were the readily available supply of labour—Singapore was experiencing full employment, and the company found it difficult to recruit qualified production workers—and the lower operating costs. After a year in China, however, Andrew was not sure the plan to venture there was wise. Although the labour costs were much lower than in Singapore, productivity was disappointing, and a number of management and labour problems had arisen, which he felt were frustrating his efforts to control the plant efficiently.

Staffing Procedure

Andrew had learned from his previous work experience that it was important to hire the right people with the appropriate qualifications and place them in the positions to which they were best suited in order to ensure smooth operations. But his efforts were hindered by Jian Wei's peculiar hiring practices. To fill open positions, Jian Wei would contact city officials and friends and relatives and ask them for recommendations on who to hire. Most of the time the people hired did not have the skills needed to perform the tasks for which they were hired. Andrew vigorously protested against Jian Wei's practices and instituted formalized procedures to follow in recruitment and selection that called for systematic advertising of positions, evaluation of candidates, and hiring based on qualifications. Jian Wei became upset because he argued that his practices were necessary as a way to keep the channels of communication and mutual exchange open with important officials because the company might need their help in future business dealings. This disagreement created tension between the two men.

Productivity and Quality Issues

The plant in China employed about 150 workers. Andrew adopted the same salary system as he had seen used by his former employer and paid these workers a fixed salary based on the number of hours worked. However, their productivity rates were very low, and the workers demonstrated very little commitment to meeting the company's goals. After three months, Andrew scrapped the salary system and instead instituted a piece-rate system in which the workers were paid a minimum base salary supplemented by an incremental rate for each unit produced above a certain number. In other words, if the workers produced at or below the minimum production standard for the day, they received the minimum wage. If they produced above that rate, they received additional money for each extra piece produced.

For the following two months, Andrew was proud of his innovative management as the results were impressive. Company productivity targets were met, the workers were exerting themselves energetically, and they were even willing to work overtime at the same rate as the usual work day in order to make extra money. However, within a short period of time, he began to receive several complaints from customers about the low quality of the goods they were receiving from the company. Parts that should have been rejected were instead shipped to customers.

In response, Andrew had the quality control and manufacturing specifications printed on large posters and posted around the plant for all to see. He set up a quality control department and implemented 100 percent quality checks. However, all these efforts failed to stop poor-quality products from reaching the customers. As he investigated, he discovered that those in the quality control department were inspecting the parts, but they were passing almost everything that they inspected. He held a training session for the quality control inspectors, pointed out defective parts to them, and had them demonstrate to him that they could distinguish poor quality from good quality. Since it was clear that they could do so, he sent them back to the production floor, convinced that they would now begin to perform as a true quality control unit. Yet within a short period of time it became apparent that the unit was not doing the job any better than before the training session.

Andrew expressed his frustration to Jian Wei and demanded that he take action to improve the situation. Jian Wei protested that the quality control members' actions were completely understandable—they knew that rejected parts would not be added to the total that would count toward the incentive rate compensation and would therefore reduce the wages production workers would receive. They would not take money out of the pockets of the production workers. Andrew felt that the quality control workers should be shown that failure to act would take money out of their own pockets, so he suggested that a system of demerit points be set up for the quality control employees which would lead to deductions from their wages. However, Jian Wei strongly disagreed with the idea, arguing that it was unfair to penalize these employees for doing what they believed was right. Finally, a compromise was reached in which more supervisors were hired for the quality control department to provide closer supervision of the workers. In addition, Andrew arranged to have all final products shipped to Singapore for final inspection before being sent out to customers.

Rules and Regulations

About 15 technicians were responsible for the maintenance of machinery. At any one time, one machine would be set aside for maintenance work. Ninety percent of the time, a machine that was designated as "in maintenance" actually sat unused. To Andrew's dismay, he found that the technicians regularly used the "in maintenance" machine to do moonlighting work to make extra income. To Andrew, this practice was a clear violation of company rules and regulations, a fact that warranted dismissal of the supervisor of the technicians, who had not only condoned the activity but had actually participated in it. Jian Wei supported the employees. He argued that the machine would have been left idle anyway so what was the harm? All activities were conducted outside normal working hours and the technicians' jobs were not being neglected. No additional costs were incurred by the factory, except in the operation of the machine. Jian Wei thought that, as boss, Andrew needed to show much more understanding and sensitivity to the issue than he had. It was unfair to single one person out for punishment, especially when the company had not suffered any losses. In addition, Jian Wei was dismayed to hear Andrew talk about dismissing an employee. He said that such practice just was not done in China—no true Chinese person would think about removing a person's "iron rice bowl." Reluctantly, Andrew agreed to Jian Wei's recommendation to resolve the issue by transferring the technicians' supervisor to another department.

Problems like these made Andrew very doubtful that the operation in China could ever be turned into a profitable venture. His father had been willing to grant Andrew some time to get the plant up and running before he expected results, but now he was starting to ask questions about why the plant was still losing money and why no trend in the direction of profitability was evident in the financial performance figures. He had recently asked Andrew to come up with a concrete plan to turn the situation around. Andrew was wondering what he could do.

1. Comment on the fixed salary system that Andrew adopted from his former employer. Why was this system not effective for motivating the plant workers?

2. Do you think that scrapping the fixed salary system and replacing it with the piece-rate system was a good idea? What are some of the strengths and weaknesses of the piece-rate system?

3. Why was Andrew unsuccessful in his efforts to improve product quality? Do you think that a system of demerit points and wage deductions of the quality control workers would have been effective? Will more supervisors in the quality control department and shipping products to Singapore for final inspection solve the problem? What do you think would be an effective way to improve product quality?

4. Were cross-cultural differences a factor in the effectiveness of the salary systems? How effective do you think each system would have been if the plant was located in North America?

5. Discuss the potential effects of implementing an MBO program in the plant. Do you think it

would improve productivity and solve some of the problems?

6. Are there any conditions under which the piece-rate system might have been more effective?

7. What are some alternative ways to use pay to motivate the workers at the plant? Are there alternatives to the piece-rate system and how effective are

they likely to be? What does this case say about using money as a motivator?

8. What should Andrew do now?

Source: Begley, Thomas (1998), in Gary Oddou and Mark Mendenhall (eds.), *Cases in international organizational behaviour*. Malden, MA: Blackwell.

Integrative Case: Ace Technology

At the end of Chapter 1 you were introduced to the Ace Technology Integrative Case. It focused on issues pertaining to managerial roles and organizational behaviour in general. You were also asked to consider the implications of the events at Ace Technology for individuals, groups, and the organization. Now that you have completed Part 2 of the text and the chapters on Individual Behaviour, you can return to the Ace Technology Integrative Case and focus on issues related to learning, job attitudes, motivation, pay systems, and incentive plans by answering the following questions.

Questions

1. What behaviours are employees at Ace Technology expected to learn?

2. Describe the reward and reinforcement strategies being used to change employees' behaviour at Ace Technology. Do you think that employees will change their behaviour? Why or why not?

3. Discuss the implications of the new strategy and compensation program for employee job satisfaction in terms of equity theory and distributive and procedural fairness. How will the new system impact distributive and procedural fairness?

4. What are the differences between Ace Technology's "antiquated" and new compensation programs? Consider the implications and effectiveness of the new compensation program according to Maslow's and Alderfer's need theories, expectancy theory, and goal setting theory. What are the advantages and disadvantages of the new program according to each theory?

5. How is money being used to motivate employees at Ace Technology? What other programs might be useful for improving employee motivation?

6. Describe the incentive plans being considered by Ace Technology. What are the potential problems with these incentive plans, and how effective do you think they will be for motivating employees and implementing the new strategy?

Social Behaviour and Organizational Processes

Chapter 7

Groups
and Teamwork

DIAMOND PACKAGING SERVICES DIVISION Four assembly lines roll until midnight at Diamond Packaging Services Division without a supervisor in sight. Instead, about 20 temporary workers take direction from a team of 11 full-time colleagues. They operate multiple packaging assembly lines without direct supervision or management support. The team decides who will fold cartons and who will fill boxes. The team tracks product quality and profit, and the team decides when to call it a night.

> Diamond
> Packaging
> Services
> Division

The team approach, which Diamond began developing in 1995, has boosted employee satisfaction and increased the company's productivity, quality, and sales. It also helped the company win the 1998 RIT/*USA Today* Quality Cup for small business.

"I've never seen a team so absolutely autonomous," marvelled Janet Barnard, a Quality Cup judge and professor at the Rochester Institute of Technology College of Business. "They were head and shoulders above all the nominees I saw."

Diamond Packaging, a family business since 1973, created the Packaging Services Division (PSD) in 1989 to fill the cardboard boxes it made. But PSD broke off in 1994 to become an independent profit centre. Manager Kirsten Voss knew she had to change the top-down management structure to survive. PSD's business is based on getting last-minute jobs from clients, such as Westwood-Squibb and Polaroid, that need extra help packaging their pharmaceutical or photographic products. There is no time to work through long management chains. "We have to be flexible and responsive," says Voss, who employs 45 people. "We couldn't do this without teams."

To motivate the teams, PSD also created a daily scorecard that each assembly line on each shift uses. It measures performance in five areas: profit (maximum

TEAM DAILY SCORES	Jones		Nordale		Westwood Spec Comm		Westwood Per Sun Ultralight	Marking		Label Set Mystic			Shipping Eagles	TOTAL
	1st	2nd	1st	2nd	1st	2nd		1st	2nd					
MON. 20	80	NA	90	110	110	95	90	110	120	NA			120	98

Self-managed work teams at Diamond Packaging Services Division have improved employee satisfaction and increased company productivity, quality, and sales.

45 points), quality (35), cleanliness (20), training (15), and safety (5). For every 100 points scored, a $5 token is set aside. When employees earn $1,000, the money is divided among the full-time employees. "It makes everyone really aware of what we're doing," says Anne Faulhaber, who posts scores for everyone to see. "It's more rewarding."

Teams also set a weekly scorecard goal for themselves—and decide how they will be rewarded if they meet it. For example, if the average weekly score for all shifts reached 110, all shifts can leave an hour early on Friday, with pay. "It becomes very clear what the objective is," Voss says. "That drives not just production but quality, training, and safety."

Since the team scorecards started in 1996, employees have developed three times as many job skills. Everyone has a training and development plan. Employees can get points for their scorecards if they turn in ideas on how to improve operations. The number of ideas is up 52%.

The average score per card increased from 86 to 94, and employees are on pace to exceed 100. As well, employees earned twice as much reward money, $5,220, and are on pace to earn $8,200 this year. Customer complaints have fallen by 25%, and PSD, which was not profitable in 1995, increased profits 350% from 1996 to 1997. PSD's revenue also jumped from $2.4 million in 1996 to $3.4 million in 1997. However, the number of late deliveries—four—did not increase. And so far this year, no deliveries have been missed.

"Whether they are thinking about how to prevent errors or how to be better tomorrow, they are always making small, incremental improvements each day," Voss says. "You have an incentive now," says Floyd Reeves, at a machine that

Learning Objectives

After reading Chapter 7, you should be able to:

1 Define groups, distinguish between formal and informal groups, and discuss the factors that lead to group formation.

2 Discuss group development.

3 Explain how group size and member diversity influence what occurs in groups.

4 Review how norms, roles, and status affect group interaction.

5 Discuss the causes and consequences of group cohesiveness.

6 Explain the dynamics of social loafing.

7 Discuss how to design and support self-managed teams.

8 Explain the logic behind cross-functional teams and describe how they can operate effectively.

will slip plastic sleeves over 25,000 film canisters before midnight. "You get to make more decisions."[1]

This excerpt from *USA Today* shows how critical groups or teams are in determining organizational success. In this chapter, we will define the term group and discuss the nature of formal groups and informal groups in organizations. After this, we will present the details of group formation and development. Then, we will consider how groups differ from one another structurally and explore the consequences of these differences. We will also cover the problem of social loafing. Finally, we will examine teams and how to design effective work teams.

What Is a Group?

Group. Two or more people interacting interdependently to achieve a common goal.

We use the word "group" rather casually in everyday discourse—special-interest group, ethnic group, and others. However, for behavioural scientists, a **group** consists of two or more people interacting interdependently to achieve a common goal.

Interaction is the most basic aspect of a group—it suggests who is in the group and who is not. The interaction of group members need not be face-to-face, and it need not be verbal. For example, employees who "telecommute" can be part of their work group at the office even though they live miles away and communicate with a modem. Also, the impromptu group that forms to pass water buckets to fight a fire need not speak to meet the requirement of interaction. Interdependence simply means that group members rely to some degree on each other to accomplish goals. Ten individuals who independently throw buckets of water on a fire do not constitute a true group. Finally, all groups have one or more goals that their members seek to achieve. These goals can range from having fun to marketing a new product to achieving world peace.

Group memberships are very important for two reasons. First, groups exert a tremendous influence on us. They are the social mechanisms by which we acquire many beliefs, values, attitudes, and behaviours. Group membership is also important because groups provide a context in which *we* are able to exert influence on *others*.

Formal work groups are groups that organizations establish to facilitate the achievement of organizational goals. They are intentionally designed to channel individual effort in an appropriate direction. The most common formal group consists of a superior and the subordinates who report to that superior. In a manufacturing company, one such group might consist of a production manager and the six shift supervisors who report to him. In turn, the shift supervisors head work groups composed of themselves and their respective subordinates. Thus, the hierarchy of most organizations is a series of formal interlocked work groups. As the Diamond Packaging case shows, all this direct supervision is not always necessary. Nevertheless, Diamond Packaging's self-managed teams are still formal work groups.

Other types of formal work groups include task forces and committees. *Task forces* are temporary groups that meet to achieve particular goals or to solve particular problems, such as suggesting productivity improvements. *Committees* are usually permanent groups that handle recurrent assignments outside the usual work group structures. For example, a firm might have a standing committee on equal employment opportunity.

It is safe to say that early writers about management and organization felt that their work was done when they had described an organization's formal groups. After all, such groups had management's seal of approval and could be illustrated in black and white on an organizational chart. What more was there to say about grouping? In fact, you probably recognize how incomplete this view is. In addition to formal groups sanctioned by management to achieve organizational goals, informal grouping occurs in all organizations. **Informal groups** are groups that emerge naturally in response to the common interests of organizational members. They are seldom sanctioned by the organization, and their membership often cuts across formal groups. Informal groups can either help or hurt an organization, depending on their norms for behaviour. We will consider this in detail later.

Formal work groups. Groups that are established by organizations to facilitate the achievement of organizational goals.

Informal groups. Groups that emerge naturally in response to the common interests of organizational members.

Group Formation

To orient ourselves to the role of groups, it is useful to consider the factors that lead to group formation. In the case of informal groups, we are concerned with the factors that prompt their emergence in the formal work setting. In the case of formal groups, we are interested in the factors that lead organizations to form such groups and the ease with which the groups can be maintained and managed. The formation of both types of groups is affected by opportunity for interaction, potential for goal accomplishment, and the personal characteristics of group members.

Opportunity for Interaction

One obvious prerequisite for group formation is opportunity for interaction. When people are able to interact with one another, they are able to recognize that they might have common goals that they can achieve through dependence on each other.[2] For example, "inside" employees (such as headquarters technical advisors) often develop more informal solidarity than "outside" employees (such as technicians who visit clients) because they are in more constant interaction. Similarly, organizations are adept at using open-plan offices, face-to-face meetings, and electronic networks to bolster formal work groups.

Potential for Goal Accomplishment

Potential for goal accomplishment is another factor that contributes to group formation and maintenance. Physical goals (such as building a bridge) or intellectual goals (such as designing a bridge) are often accomplished most efficiently by the careful division of labour among groups. Groups can also achieve social-emotional goals, such as self-esteem and security. Informally, strangers might band together during a natural disaster, or employees might band together to protest the firing of a co-worker. Formally, organizations might use decision-making groups to spread the risk associated with a tough decision.

Members' Personal Characteristics

Finally, personal characteristics can influence group formation and maintenance. When it comes to attitudes, there is plenty of evidence that "birds of a feather flock together," that is, people with similar attitudes (such as satisfaction with their job) tend to gravitate together.[3] When it comes to personality characteristics, similar people are often attracted to each other, but opposites sometimes attract.[4] For example, dominant people might seek the company of submissive people. We are speaking here mainly of informal attraction and grouping. When organizations staff formal working groups, they often assign people with different but complementary skills, attitudes, or personalities to the group. A tight-fisted, practical accountant might be included to offset an impulsive, creative marketer.

Group Development

Even relatively simple groups are actually complex social devices that require a fair amount of negotiation and trial-and-error before individual members begin to function as a true group. While employees often know each other before new teams are formed, simple familiarity does not replace the necessity for team development.

Typical Stages of Group Development

Leaders and trainers have observed that many groups develop through a series of stages over time.[5] Each stage presents the members with a series of challenges

Exhibit 7.1
Stages of group development.

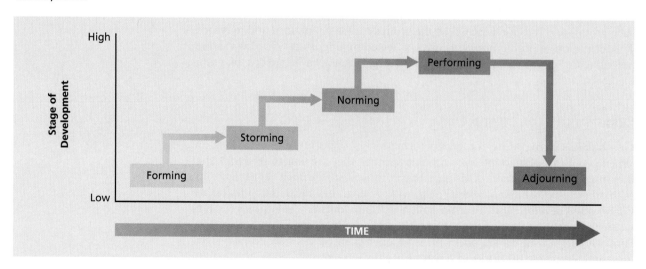

they must master in order to achieve the next stage. These stages (forming, storming, norming, performing, and adjourning) are presented in Exhibit 7.1.

Forming. At this early stage, group members try to orient themselves by "testing the waters." What are we doing here? What are the others like? What is our purpose? The situation is often ambiguous, and members are aware of their dependency on each other.

Storming. At this second stage, conflict often emerges. Confrontation and criticism occur as members determine whether they will go along with the way the group is developing. Sorting out roles and responsibilities is often at issue here. Problems are more likely to happen earlier, rather than later, in group development.

Norming. At this stage, members resolve the issues that provoked the storming, and they develop social consensus. Compromise is often necessary. Interdependence is recognized, norms are agreed to, and the group becomes more cohesive (we will study these processes later). Information and opinions flow freely.

Performing. With its social structure sorted out, the group devotes its energies toward task accomplishment. Achievement, creativity, and mutual assistance are prominent themes of this stage.

Adjourning. Some groups, such as task forces and design project teams, have a definite life span and disperse after achieving their goals. Also, some groups disperse when corporate layoffs and downsizing occur. At this adjourning stage, rites and rituals that affirm the group's previous successful development are common (such as ceremonies and parties). Members often exhibit emotional support for each other.[6]

The stages model is a good tool for monitoring and troubleshooting how groups are developing. However, it is very important to understand that not all groups go through these stages of development. The process applies mainly to new groups that have never met before. Well-acquainted task forces and committees can short-circuit these stages when they have a new problem to work out.[7] Also, some organizational settings are so structured that storming and norming are unnecessary for even strangers to coalesce into a team. For example, most commercial airline cockpit crews perform effectively even though they can be made up of virtual strangers who meet just before takeoff.[8]

Punctuated Equilibrium

When groups have a specific deadline by which to complete some problem-solving task, we can often observe a very different development sequence from that described above. Connie Gersick, whose research uncovered this sequence, describes it as a **punctuated equilibrium model** of group development.[9] Equilibrium means stability, and the research revealed apparent stretches of group stability punctuated by a critical first meeting, a midpoint change in group activity, and a rush to task completion. Along with many real-world work groups, Gersick studied student groups doing class projects, to see if this sequence of events sounded familiar.

Punctuated equilibrium model. A model of group development that describes how groups with deadlines are affected by their first meetings and crucial midpoint transitions.

Phase 1. Phase 1 begins with the first meeting and continues until the midpoint in the group's existence. The very first meeting is critical in setting the agenda for what will happen in the remainder of this phase. Assumptions, approaches, and precedents that members develop in the first meeting end up dominating the first

Exhibit 7.2
The punctuated equilibrium model of group development for two groups.

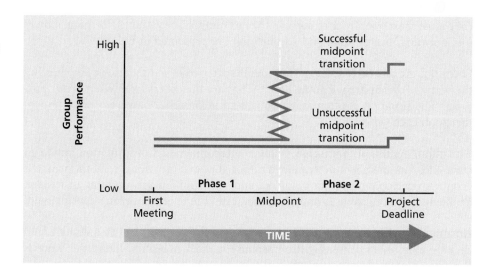

half of the group's life. Although it gathers information and holds meetings, the group makes little visible progress toward the goal.

Midpoint Transition. The midpoint transition occurs at almost exactly the halfway point in time toward the group's deadline. For instance, if the group has a two-month deadline, the transition will occur at about one month. The transition marks a change in the group's approach, and how the group manages it is critical for the group to show progress. The need to move forward is apparent, and the group may seek outside advice. This transition may consolidate previously acquired information or even mark a completely new approach, but it crystallizes the group's activities for Phase 2 just like the first meeting did for Phase 1.

Phase 2. For better or for worse, decisions and approaches adopted at the midpoint get played out in Phase 2. It concludes with a final meeting that reveals a burst of activity and a concern for how outsiders will evaluate the product.

Exhibit 7.2 shows how the punctuated equilibrium model works for groups that successfully or unsuccessfully manage the midpoint transition.

What advice does the punctuated equilibrium model offer for managing product development teams, advertising groups, or class project groups?[10]

- Prepare carefully for the first meeting. What is decided here will strongly determine what happens in the rest of Phase 1.
- As long as people are working, do not look for radical progress during Phase 1.
- Manage the midpoint transition carefully. Evaluate the strengths and weaknesses of the ideas that people generated in Phase 1. Clarify any questions with whoever is commissioning your work. Recognize that a fundamental change in approach must occur here for progress to occur. Essential issues are not likely to "work themselves out" during Phase 2.
- Be sure adequate resources are available to actually execute the Phase 2 plan.
- Resist deadline changes. These could damage the midpoint transition.

Group Structure and Its Consequences

You are no doubt aware that groups frequently seem to differ from one another. The differences that are most obvious might include the way members interact with one another, how members feel about the group, and how the group performs. It is often possible to trace these differences in interaction, feelings, and performance back to how the group is organized.

Group structure refers to the characteristics of the stable social organization of a group, the way a group is "put together." The most basic structural characteristics along which groups vary are size and member diversity. Other structural characteristics are the expectations that members have about each other's behaviour (norms), agreements about "who does what" in the group (roles), the rewards and prestige allocated to various group members (status), and how attractive the group is to its members (cohesiveness).

Group Size

Of one thing we can be certain—the smallest possible group consists of two people, such as a superior and a particular subordinate. It is possible to engage in much theoretical nit picking about just what constitutes an upper limit on group size. However, given the definition of group that we presented earlier, it would seem that congressional or parliamentary size (300 to 400 members) is somewhere close to this limit. In practice, most work groups, including task forces and committees, usually have between three and 20 members.

Size and Satisfaction. The more the merrier? In theory, yes. In fact, however, members of larger groups rather consistently report less satisfaction with group membership than those who find themselves in smaller groups.[11] What accounts for this apparent contradiction?

For one thing, as opportunities for friendship increase, the chance to work on and develop these opportunities might decrease owing to the sheer time and energy required. In addition, larger groups, in incorporating more members with different viewpoints, might prompt conflict and dissension, which work against member satisfaction. As group size increases, the time available for verbal participation by each member decreases. Also, many people are inhibited about participating in larger groups.[12] To the extent that individuals value such participation, dissatisfaction will again be the outcome. Finally, in larger groups, individual members identify less easily with the success and accomplishments of the group. For example, a particular member of a four-person cancer research team should be able to identify his or her personal contributions to a research breakthrough more easily than can a member of a 20-person team.

Size and Performance. Satisfaction aside, do large groups perform tasks better than small groups? This question has great relevance to practical organizational decisions: How many people should a bank assign to evaluate loan applications? How many carpenters should a construction company assign to build a garage? If a school system decides to implement team teaching, how big should the teams be? The answers to these and similar questions depend on the exact task that the group needs to accomplish and on what we mean by good performance.[13]

Some tasks are **additive tasks.** This means that we can predict potential performance by adding the performances of individual group members together. For example, moving a heavy stone is an additive task, and it is possible to estimate the potential productivity of a group of labourers by summing up the forces that they are able to exert. Similarly, building a garage is an additive task, and we can estimate potential speed of construction by adding the efforts of individual carpenters. Thus, for additive tasks, the potential performance of the group increases with group size.

Some tasks are **disjunctive.** This means that the potential performance of the group depends on the performance of its *best member*. For example, suppose that

Additive tasks. Tasks in which group performance is dependent on the sum of the performance of individual group members.

Disjunctive tasks. Tasks in which group performance is dependent on the performance of the best group member.

a research team is looking for a single error in a complicated computer program. In this case, the performance of the team might hinge on its containing at least one bright, attentive, logical-minded individual. Obviously, the potential performance of groups doing disjunctive tasks also increases with group size because the probability that the group includes a superior performer is greater.

We use the term "potential performance" consistently in the preceding two paragraphs for the following reason: As groups performing tasks get bigger, they tend to suffer from process losses.[14] **Process losses** are performance difficulties that stem from the problems of motivating and coordinating larger groups. Even with good intentions, problems of communication and decision making increase with size—imagine 50 carpenters trying to build a house. Thus, actual performance = potential performance – process losses.

These points are summarized in Exhibit 7.3. As you can see in part (a), both potential performance and process losses increase with group size for additive and disjunctive tasks. The net effect is shown in part (b), which demonstrates that actual performance increases with size up to a point and then falls off. Part (c) shows that the *average* performance of group members decreases as size gets bigger. Thus, up to a point, larger groups might perform better as groups, but their individual members would be less efficient.

We should note one other kind of task. **Conjunctive tasks** are those in which the performance of the group is limited by its *poorest performer*. For example, an

Process losses. Group performance difficulties stemming from the problems of motivating and coordinating larger groups.

Conjunctive tasks. Tasks in which group performance is limited by the performance of the poorest group member.

Exhibit 7.3
Relationships among group size, productivity, and process losses.

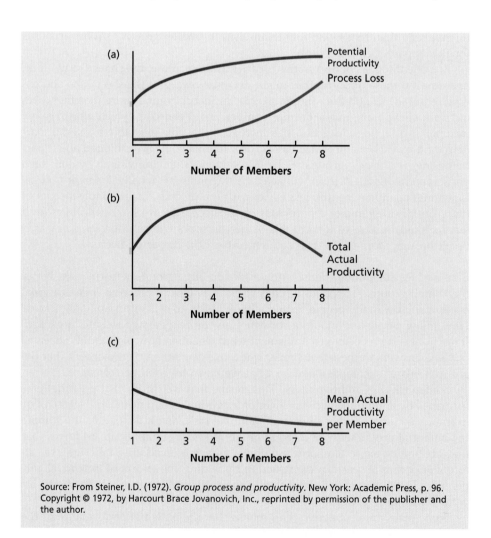

Source: From Steiner, I.D. (1972). *Group process and productivity*. New York: Academic Press, p. 96. Copyright © 1972, by Harcourt Brace Jovanovich, Inc., reprinted by permission of the publisher and the author.

assembly-line operation is limited by its weakest link. Also, if team teaching is the technique used to train workers how to perform a complicated, sequential job, one poor teacher in the sequence will severely damage the effectiveness of the team. Both the potential and actual performance of conjunctive tasks would decrease as group size increases because the probability of including a weak link in the group goes up.

In summary, for additive and disjunctive tasks, larger groups might perform better up to a point, but at increasing costs to the efficiency of individual members. By any standard, performance on purely conjunctive tasks should decrease as group size increases.

Diversity of Group Membership

Imagine an eight member product development task force composed exclusively of 30-something white males of basically Western European heritage. Then imagine another task force with 50% men and 50% women, from eight different ethnic or racial backgrounds, and an age range from 25 to 55. The first group is obviously homogeneous in its membership, while the latter is heterogeneous or diverse. Which task force do you think would develop more quickly as a group? Which would be most creative?

There is a very large body of research, most of it conducted in the laboratory, on the impact of group composition. We know much less about this impact (especially cultural mix) in functioning work groups. Nevertheless, the state of the art looks something like this.[15] Group diversity has a strong impact on interaction patterns—more diverse groups have a more difficult time communicating effectively and becoming cohesive (we will study cohesiveness in more detail shortly). This means that diverse groups might tend to take longer to do their forming, storming, and norming.[16] Once they do develop, more and less diverse groups are equally productive. However, diverse groups sometimes perform better when the task requires cognitive, creativity-demanding tasks and problem solving rather than more routine work because members consider a broader array of ideas.[17]

All this speaks well for the concepts of valuing and managing diversity, which we discussed in Chapter 3. When management values and manages diversity, it offsets some of the initial process loss costs of diversity and capitalizes on its benefits for team performance.

Group Norms

Social **norms** are collective expectations that members of social units have regarding the behaviour of each other. As such, they are codes of conduct that specify what individuals ought and ought not to do or standards against which we evaluate the appropriateness of behaviour.

Norms. Collective expectations that members of social units have regarding the behaviour of each other.

Much normative influence is unconscious, and we are often aware of such influence only in special circumstances, such as when we see children struggling to master adult norms or foreigners sparring with the norms of our culture. We also become conscious of norms when we encounter ones that seem to conflict with each other ("Get ahead," but "Don't step on others") or when we enter new social situations. For instance, the first day on a new job, workers frequently search for cues about what is considered proper office etiquette: Should I call the boss "mister"? Can I personalize my work space?

Norm Development. *Why* do norms develop? The most important function that norms serve is to provide regularity and predictability to behaviour. This consistency provides important psychological security and permits us to carry out our daily business with minimal disruption.

What do norms develop *about*? Norms develop to regulate behaviours that are considered at least marginally important to their supporters. For example, managers are more likely to adopt norms regarding the performance and attendance of subordinates than norms concerning how workers personalize and decorate their offices. In general, less deviation is accepted from norms that concern more important behaviours. Groups frequently develop norms that correspond to their goals to aid in goal attainment.

How do norms develop? As we discussed in Chapter 4, individuals develop attitudes as a function of a related belief and value. In many cases, their attitudes affect their behaviour. When the members of a group *share* related beliefs and values, we can expect them to share consequent attitudes. These shared attitudes then form the basis for norms.[18] Notice that it really does not make sense to talk about "my personal norm." Norms are *collectively* held expectations, depending on two or more people for their existence. However, norms can be targeted at a single individual. For example, work groups frequently develop shared expectations about how their bosses should behave.

Why do individuals tend to comply with norms? Much compliance occurs simply because the norm corresponds to privately held attitudes. This is the case with true supporters of the norm. In addition, even when norms support trivial social niceties (such as when to shake hands or when to look serious), they often save time and prevent social confusion. Most interesting, however, is the case in which individuals comply with norms that *go against* their privately held attitudes and opinions. For example, couples without religious convictions frequently get married in religious services, and people who hate neckties often wear them to work. In short, groups have an extraordinary range of rewards and punishments available to induce conformity to norms. In the next chapter, we will examine this process in detail.

Some Typical Norms. There are some classes of norms that seem to crop up in most organizations and affect the behaviour of members. They include the following:

- *Loyalty norms.* Groups and organizations frequently attempt to exact a strong degree of commitment and loyalty from their members. In the military, these norms are formalized with specific sanctions to be applied to traitors and deserters. In most other cases, loyalty norms tend to be informal. Managers frequently perceive that they must work late, come in on weekends, and accept transfers to other cities in order to prove their loyalty to the company and to their peers.

- *Dress norms.* Social norms frequently dictate the kind of clothing people wear to work.[19] Again, military and quasimilitary organizations tend to invoke formal norms that support polished buttons and razor-sharp creases. Even in organizations that have adopted casual dress policies, employees often express considerable concern about what they wear at work. Such is the power of social norms.

- *Reward allocation norms.* There are at least four norms that might dictate how rewards, such as pay, promotions, and informal favours, could be allocated in organizations:
  a. Equity—reward according to inputs, such as effort, performance, or seniority.
  b. Equality—reward everyone equally.
  c. Reciprocity—reward people the way they reward you.
  d. Social responsibility—reward those who truly need the reward.[20]

Officially, of course, most organizations tend to stress allocation according to some combination of equity and equality norms—give employees what they deserve, and no favouritism.

■ *Performance norms.* The performance of organizational members might be as much a function of social expectations as it is of inherent ability, personal motivation, or technology.[21] Work groups provide their members with potent cues about what an appropriate level of performance is. New group members are alert for these cues: Is it all right to take a break now? Under what circumstances can I be absent from work without being punished? (See "In Focus: *Absence Cultures—Norms in Action.*") Of course, the official organizational norms that managers send to subordinates usually favour high performance. However, work groups often establish their own informal performance norms, such as those that restrict productivity under a piece-rate pay system.

Roles

Roles are positions in a group that have a set of expected behaviours attached to them. Thus, in a sense, roles represent "packages" of norms that apply to particular group members. As we implied in the previous section, many norms apply to all group members in order to be sure that they engage in *similar* behaviours (such as restricting productivity or dressing a certain way). However, the development of roles is indicative of the fact that group members might also be required to act *differently* from one another. For example, in a committee meeting, not every member is required to function as a secretary or a chairperson, and these become specific roles that are fulfilled by particular people.

Roles. Positions in a group that have a set of expected behaviours attached to them.

---

in focus → Absence Cultures—Norms in Action

On first thought, you might assume that absenteeism from work is a pretty individualized behaviour, a product of random sickness or of personal job dissatisfaction. Although these factors contribute to absenteeism, there is growing evidence that group norms also have a strong impact on how much work people miss.

We can see cross-national differences in absenteeism. Traditionally, absence has been rather high in Italy and England, lower in the United States and Canada, and lower yet in Japan and Switzerland. Clearly, these differences are not due to sickness, but rather to differences in cultural values about the legitimacy of taking time off work. These differences get reflected in work group norms.

Within the same country and company, we can still see group differences in absenteeism. A company that one of the authors studied had four plants that made the same products and had identical human resource policies. Despite this, one plant had a 12 percent absence rate while another had a rate of 5 percent. Within one plant, some departments had virtually no absence while others approached 25 percent!

Moving to the small group level, the author also studied small customer service groups in a utility company. Despite all doing the same work in the same firm, there were again striking cross-group differences in absenteeism, ranging from 1 to 13 percent.

These normative differences in absenteeism across groups are called *absence cultures.* How do they develop? People tend to adjust their own absence behaviour to what they see as typical of their group. Then, other factors come into play. In the utility company study, the groups that monitored each others' behaviour more closely had lower absence. A Canadian study found that air-traffic controllers traded off calling in sick so that their colleagues could replace them at double overtime. An English study found that industrial workers actually posted "absence schedules" so that they could take time off without things getting out of hand! All these are examples of norms in action.

Source: Johns, G. (1994, July). *Medical, ethical, and cultural constraints on work absence and attendance.* Presentation made at the 23rd International Congress of Applied Psychology, Madrid, Spain.

In organizations, we find two basic kinds of roles. First, we can identify designated or assigned roles. These are roles that are formally prescribed by an organization as a means of dividing labour and responsibility to facilitate task achievement. In general, assigned roles indicate "who does what" and "who can tell others what to do." In a manufacturing organization, labels that we might apply to formal roles include president, engineer, machinist, manager, and subordinate. In addition to assigned roles, we invariably see the development of emergent roles. These are roles that develop naturally to meet the social-emotional needs of group members or to assist in formal job accomplishment. The class clown and the office gossip fulfill emergent social-emotional roles, while an "old pro" might emerge to assist new group members learn their jobs. Other emergent roles might be assumed by informal leaders or by scapegoats who are the targets of group hostility.

Role ambiguity. Lack of clarity of job goals or methods.

Role Ambiguity. **Role ambiguity** exists when the goals of one's job or the methods of performing it are unclear. Ambiguity might be characterized by confusion about how performance is evaluated, how good performance can be achieved, or what the limits of one's authority and responsibility are.

Exhibit 7.4 shows a model of the process that is involved in assuming an organizational role. As you can see, certain organizational factors lead role senders (such as managers) to develop role expectations and "send" roles to focal people (such as subordinates). The focal person "receives" the role and then tries to engage in behaviour to fulfill the role. This model reveals a variety of elements that can lead to ambiguity.

- *Organizational factors.* Some roles seem inherently ambiguous because of their function in the organization. For example, middle management roles might fail to provide the "big picture" that upper management roles do. Also middle management roles do not require the attention to supervision necessary in lower management roles.

- *The role sender.* Role senders might have unclear expectations of a focal person. Even when the sender has specific role expectations, they might be ineffectively sent to the focal person. A weak orientation session, vague performance reviews, or inconsistent feedback and discipline may send ambiguous role messages to subordinates.

- *The focal person.* Even role expectations that are clearly developed and sent might not be fully digested by the focal person. This is especially true when he or she is new to the role. Ambiguity tends to decrease as length of time in the job role increases.[22]

Exhibit 7.4
A model of the role assumption process.

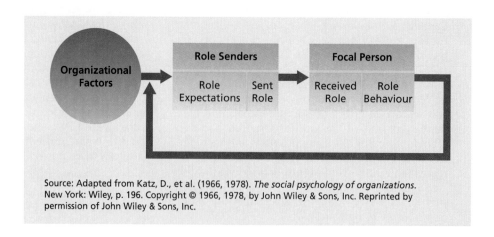

Source: Adapted from Katz, D., et al. (1966, 1978). *The social psychology of organizations.* New York: Wiley, p. 196. Copyright © 1966, 1978, by John Wiley & Sons, Inc. Reprinted by permission of John Wiley & Sons, Inc.

What are the practical consequences of role ambiguity? The most frequent outcomes appear to be job stress, dissatisfaction, reduced organizational commitment, and intentions to quit.[23] Managers can do much to reduce unnecessary role ambiguity by providing clear performance expectations and performance feedback, especially for new employees and for those in more intrinsically ambiguous jobs.

Role Conflict. Role conflict exists when an individual is faced with incompatible role expectations. Conflict can be distinguished from ambiguity, in that role expectations might be crystal clear but incompatible in the sense that they are mutually exclusive, cannot be fulfilled simultaneously, or do not suit the role occupant.

- **Intrasender role conflict** occurs when a single role sender provides incompatible role expectations to the role occupant. For example, a manager might tell a subordinate to take it easy and not work so hard, while delivering yet another batch of reports that requires immediate attention. This form of role conflict seems especially likely to also provoke ambiguity.

- If two or more role senders differ in their expectations for a role occupant, **intersender role conflict** can develop. Boundary role occupants who straddle the boundary between the organization and its clients or customers are especially likely to encounter this form of conflict. Intersender conflict can also stem exclusively from within the organization. The classic example here is the first-level supervisor, who serves as the interface between "management" and "the workers." From above, the supervisor might be pressured to get the work out and keep the troops in line. From below, he or she might be encouraged to behave in a considerate and friendly manner.

- Organizational members necessarily play several roles at one time, especially if we include roles external to the organization. Often, the expectations inherent in these several roles are incompatible, and **interrole conflict** results.[24] One person, for example, might fulfill the roles of a functional expert in marketing, head of the market research group, subordinate to the vice-president of marketing, and member of a product development task force. This is obviously a busy person, and competing demands for her time are a frequent symptom of interrole conflict.

- Even when role demands are clear and otherwise congruent, they might be incompatible with the personality or skills of the role occupant—thus, **person-role conflict** results.[25] Many examples of "whistle blowing" are signals of person-role conflict. The organization has demanded some role behaviour that the occupant considers unethical.

As with role ambiguity, the most consistent consequences of role conflict are job dissatisfaction, stress reactions, lowered organizational commitment, and turnover intentions.[26] Managers can help prevent subordinate role conflict by avoiding self-contradictory messages, conferring with other role senders, being sensitive to multiple role demands, and fitting the right person to the right role.

Status

Status is the rank, social position, or prestige accorded to group members. Put another way, it represents the group's *evaluation* of a member. Just *what* is evaluated depends on the status system in question. However, when a status system works smoothly, the group will exhibit clear norms about who should be awarded higher or lower status.

Role conflict. A condition of being faced with incompatible role expectations.

Intrasender role conflict. A single role sender provides incompatible role expectations to a role occupant.

Intersender role conflict. Two or more role senders provide a role occupant with incompatible expectations.

Interrole conflict. Several roles held by a role occupant involve incompatible expectations.

Person-role conflict. Role demands call for behaviour that is incompatible with the personality or skills of a role occupant.

Status. The rank, social position, or prestige accorded to group members.

Formal Status Systems. All organizations have both formal and informal status systems. Since formal systems are most obvious to observers, let us begin there. The formal status system represents management's attempt to publicly identify those people who have higher status than others. It is so obvious because this identification is implemented by the application of *status symbols* that are tangible indicators of status. Status symbols might include titles, particular working relationships, the pay package, the work schedule, and the physical working environment. Just what are the criteria for achieving formal organizational status? One criterion is often seniority in one's work group. Employees who have been with the group longer might acquire the privilege of choosing day shift work or a more favourable office location. Even more important than seniority, however, is one's assigned role in the organization, one's job. Because they perform different jobs, secretaries, labourers, supervisors, and executives acquire different statuses. Organizations often go to great pains to tie status symbols to assigned roles.

Why do organizations go to all this trouble to differentiate status? For one thing, status and the symbols connected to it serve as powerful magnets to induce members to aspire to higher organizational positions (recall Maslow's need for self-esteem). Second, status differentiation reinforces the authority hierarchy in work groups and in the organization as a whole, since people *pay attention* to high-status individuals.

The differences in formal status that exist within organizations usually carry over to the evaluation of the status of occupations by the public at large. Thus, doctors have more prestige than nurses in the community, just as they do in the hospital. Exhibit 7.5 summarizes ratings of occupational prestige from a number of cross-national surveys. In general, surveys of this nature show remarkable stability over time and good agreement across cultures. In addition, people who themselves differ in status tend to agree very closely in their ratings of the prestige of various occupations.[27] Thus, status judgments of the public at large are influenced by some of the same factors that indirectly lead to formal status differences in organizations—the skill, training, and education of the people being judged.

Informal Status Systems. In addition to formal status systems, one can detect informal status systems in organizations. Such systems are not well advertised, and they might lack the conspicuous symbols and systematic support that people usually accord the formal system. Nevertheless, they can operate just as effectively. Sometimes, job performance is a basis for the acquisition of informal status. The "power hitters" on a baseball team or the "cool heads" in a hospital emergency unit might be highly evaluated by co-workers for their ability to assist in task accomplishment. Some managers who perform well early in their careers are identified as "fast trackers" and given special job assignments that correspond to their elevated status. Just as frequently, though, informal status is linked to factors other than job performance, such as gender or race. For example, the man who takes a day off work to care for a sick child may be praised as a model father. The woman who does the same may be questioned about her work commitment.

Consequences of Status Differences. Status differences have a paradoxical effect on communication patterns. Most people like to communicate with others at their own status or higher, rather than with people who are below them.[28] The result should be a tendency for communication to move up the status hierarchy. However, if status differences are large, people can be inhibited from communicating upward. These opposing effects mean that much communication gets stalled.

Exhibit 7.5
Standard prestige scores for various occupations.

78	College and university teachers; physicians
72	Architects; lawyers
70	Dentists
69	Chemists
67	Bank officers and financial managers
66	Psychologists; airplane pilots; chemical and mechanical engineers
63	Controllers and treasurers
62	Accountants
60	Clergymen; economists
57	Elementary school teachers
56	Stock and bond salesmen; painters and sculptors
55	Office managers; draftsmen
54	Librarians; registered nurses
52	Sales managers (non-retail); actors
51	Computer programmers
50	Radio and television announcers; airline stewardesses
49	Real estate agents and brokers
48	Bank tellers
45	Musicians and composers
44	Insurance agents, brokers, and underwriters
43	Automobile mechanics
40	Farmers; policemen and detectives
39	Foremen
38	Receptionists
37	Air traffic controllers
34	Funeral directors
33	Mail carriers; truck drivers
31	File clerks
23	Bartenders; waiters
22	Garage workers and gas station attendants
14	Newsboys
13	Garbage collectors

Note: Scores can range from 92 to –2. They are derived from studies of occupational prestige carried out in many countries around the world and applied to the 1970 U.S. Census Detailed Occupational Classifications. This is why some labels are sex-typed.

Source: From Donald J. Treiman, *Occupational prestige in comparative perspective*, pp. 306–315. Copyright © 1977 by Academic Press, Inc. Reprinted by permission of the author and the publisher.

Status also affects the amount of various group members' communication and their influence in group affairs. As you might guess, higher-status members do more talking and have more influence.[29] Some of the most convincing evidence comes from studies of jury deliberations, in which jurors with higher-social status (such as managers and professionals) participate more and have more effect on the verdict.[30] Thus, if the plant superintendent, the production manager, and a production supervisor make the rounds on an assembly line, we can offer a pretty good guess about who will do the most talking. Unfortunately, there is no guarantee that the highest-status person is the most knowledgeable about the problem at hand!

Reducing Status Barriers. Although status differences can be powerful motivators, their tendency to inhibit the free flow of communication has led many organizations to downplay status differentiation by doing away with questionable status symbols. The goal is to foster a culture of teamwork and cooperation across the ranks. The high-tech culture of Silicon Valley has always been pretty egalitarian and lacking in conspicuous status symbols, but even old-line industries are getting on the bandwagon. For example, Union Carbide's Connecticut headquarters has equal-sized offices and no executive dining rooms or parking

Saturn Inc.
www.saturncars.com/index.html

lots. At GM's Saturn plant, the big boss wears the same gear as the line workers, and the executive team at Levi Strauss & Co. wears examples of its own informal clothing line. At Maritime Life Assurance Co. a spectacular ninth-floor ocean view of the Northwest Arm was made into an elegant, wood-panelled cafeteria for employees instead of executive offices.[31]

Some organizations employ phony or misguided attempts to bridge the status barrier. Some examples of "casual Friday" policies (wearing casual clothes on Fridays) only underline status differences the rest of the week if no other cultural changes are made.

Many observers note that e-mail networks have leveled status barriers.[32] High-speed transmission, direct access, and the opportunity to avoid live confrontation often encourage lower-status parties to communicate directly with organizational VIPs. This has even been seen in the rank-conscious military.

Group Cohesiveness

Group cohesiveness. The degree to which a group is especially attractive to its members.

Group cohesiveness is a critical property of groups. Cohesive groups are those that are especially attractive to their members. Because of this attractiveness, members are especially desirous of staying in the group and tend to describe the group in favourable terms.[33]

The arch-stereotype of a cohesive group is the major league baseball team that begins September looking like a good bet to win its division and get into the World Series. On the field we see well-oiled, precision teamwork. In the clubhouse, all is sweetness and joviality, and interviewed players tell the world how fine it is to be playing with "a great bunch of guys."

Cohesiveness is a relative, rather than absolute, property of groups. While some groups are more cohesive than others, there is no objective line between cohesive and noncohesive groups. Thus, we will use the adjective *cohesive* to refer to groups that are more attractive than average for their members.

Factors Influencing Cohesiveness

What makes some groups more cohesive than others? Important factors include threat, competition, success, member diversity, group size, and toughness of initiation.

Threat and Competition. External threat to the survival of the group increases cohesiveness in a wide variety of situations.[34] As an example, consider the wrangling, uncoordinated corporate board of directors that quickly forms a united front in the face of a takeover bid. Honest competition with another group can also promote cohesiveness.[35] This is the case with the World Series contenders.

Why do groups often become more cohesive in response to threat or competition? They probably feel a need to improve communication and coordination so that they can better cope with the situation at hand. Members now perceive the group as more attractive because it is seen as capable of doing what has to be done to ward off threat or to win. There are, of course, limits to this. Under *extreme* threat or very *unbalanced* competition, increased cohesiveness will serve little purpose. For example, the partners in a firm faced with certain financial disaster would be unlikely to exhibit cohesiveness because it would do nothing to combat the severe threat.

Success. It should come as no surprise that a group becomes more attractive to its members when it has successfully accomplished some important goal, such as defending itself against threat or winning a prize.[36] By the same token, cohesiveness will decrease after failure, although there may be "misery loves company" exceptions. The situation for competition is shown graphically in Exhibit 7.6. Fit-Rite Jeans owns two small clothing stores (A and B) in a large city. To boost sales, it holds a contest between the two stores, offering $150 worth of merchandise to each employee of the store that achieves the highest sales during the next business quarter. Before the competition begins, the staff of each store is equally cohesive. As we suggested above, when competition begins, both groups become more cohesive. The members become more cooperative with each other, and in each store there is much talk about "we" versus "they." At the end of the quarter, store A wins the prize and becomes yet more cohesive. The group is especially attractive to its members because it has succeeded in the attainment of a desired goal. On the other hand, cohesiveness plummets in the losing store B—the group has become less attractive to its members.

Member Diversity. Earlier, we pointed out that groups that are diverse in terms of gender, age, and race can have a harder time developing cohesiveness than more homogeneous groups. However, if the group is especially interested in accomplishing some particular task, its success in performing the task will often outweigh member similarity in determining cohesiveness.[37] For example, one study found no relationship between cohesiveness and similarity of age or education for industrial work groups.[38] Another found that the cohesiveness of groups composed of African American and Caucasian southern soldiers was dependent on successful task accomplishment rather than racial composition.[39]

Size. Other things being equal, bigger groups should have a more difficult time becoming and staying cohesive. In general, such groups should have a more difficult time agreeing on goals and more problems communicating and coordinating effort to achieve these goals. Earlier, we pointed out that large groups frequently divide into subgroups. Clearly, such subgrouping is contrary to the cohesiveness of the larger group.

Toughness of Initiation. Despite its rigorous admissions policies, the Harvard Business School does not lack applicants. Similarly, exclusive yacht and golf clubs might have waiting lists for membership extending several years into the future.

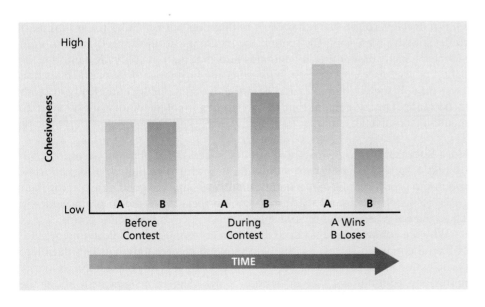

Exhibit 7.6
Competition, success, and cohesiveness.

All this suggests that groups that are tough to get into should be more attractive than those that are easy to join.[40] This is well known in the armed forces, where rigorous physical training and stressful "survival schools" precede entry into elite units, such as the Special Forces or the Rangers.

Sun Microsystems is a firm with extremely rigorous selection procedures, often exposing job applicants to between four and seven interviews with up to 20 interviewers.[41] Catalytica, Inc., a Mountain View, California, high-tech up-and-comer that specializes in pollution control, also uses tough selection to foster cohesiveness that involves grilling applicants for days at a time.[42]

Consequences of Cohesiveness

From the previous section, it should be clear that managers or group members might be able to influence the level of cohesiveness of work groups by using competition or threat, varying group size or composition, or manipulating membership requirements. The question remains, however, as to whether *more* or *less* cohesiveness is a desirable group property. This, of course, depends on the consequences of group cohesiveness and who is doing the judging.

More Participation in Group Activities. Because cohesive groups are attractive to their membership, members should be especially motivated to participate (in several senses of the word) in group activities. For one thing, because members wish to remain in the group, voluntary turnover from cohesive groups should be low. For another, members like being with each other; therefore, absence should be lower than that exhibited by less cohesive groups. In a third sense, participation should be reflected in a high degree of communication within the group as members strive to cooperate with and assist each other. In addition, this communication might well be of a more friendly and supportive nature, depending on the key goals of the group.[43]

More Conformity. Because they are so attractive and coordinated, cohesive groups are well equipped to supply information, rewards, and punishment to individual members. These factors take on special significance when they are administered by those who hold a special interest for us. Thus, highly cohesive groups are in a superb position to induce conformity to group norms.

Members of cohesive groups are especially motivated to engage in activities that will *keep* the group cohesive. Chief among these activities is applying pressure to deviants to get them to comply with group norms. Cohesive groups react to deviants by increasing the amount of communication directed at these individuals.[44] Such communication contains information to help the deviant "see the light," as well as veiled threats about what might happen if he or she does not. Over time, if such communication is ineffective in inducing conformity, it tends to decrease. This is a signal that the group has isolated the deviant member to maintain cohesiveness among the majority.

More Success. Above, we pointed out that successful goal accomplishment contributes to group cohesiveness. However, it is also true that cohesiveness contributes to group success—in general, cohesive groups are good at achieving their goals. Research has found that group cohesiveness is related to performance.[45] Thus, there is a reciprocal relationship between success and cohesiveness.

Why are cohesive groups effective at goal accomplishment? Probably because of the other consequences of cohesiveness we discussed above. A high degree of participation and communication, coupled with active conformity to group norms and commitment, should ensure a high degree of agreement about the goals the group is pursuing and the methods it is using to achieve these goals. Thus, coordinated effort pays dividends to the group.

Since cohesiveness contributes to goal accomplishment, should managers attempt to increase the cohesiveness of work groups by juggling the factors that influence cohesiveness? To answer this question, we must emphasize that cohesive groups are especially effective at accomplishing *their own* goals. If these goals happen to correspond with those of the organization, increased cohesiveness should have substantial benefits for group performance. If not, organizational effectiveness might be threatened. In fact, a recent study found that group cohesiveness was related to the productivity of paper-machine work crews that accepted the goals of the organization. Cohesiveness did not improve productivity in work crews that did not accept the goals of the organization.[46] One large-scale study of industrial work groups reached the following conclusions:

- In highly cohesive groups, the productivity of individual group members tends to be fairly similar to that of other members. In less cohesive groups there is more variation in productivity.

- Highly cohesive groups tend to be *more* or *less* productive than less cohesive groups.[47]

These two facts are shown graphically in Exhibit 7.7. The lower variability of productivity in more cohesive groups stems from the power of such groups to induce conformity. To the extent that work groups have productivity norms, more cohesive groups should be better able to enforce them. Furthermore, if cohesive groups accept organizational norms regarding productivity, they should be highly productive. If cohesive groups reject such norms, they are especially effective in limiting productivity.

One other factor that influences the impact of cohesiveness on productivity is the extent to which the task really requires interdependence and cooperation among group members (e.g., a football team versus a golf team). Cohesiveness is more likely to pay off when the task requires more interdependence.[48]

In summary, cohesive groups tend to be successful in accomplishing what they wish to accomplish. In a good labour relations climate, group cohesiveness on interdependent tasks should contribute to high productivity. If the climate is marked by tension and disagreement, cohesive groups might pursue goals that result in low productivity.

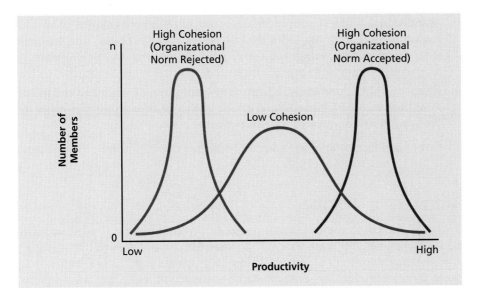

Exhibit 7.7
Hypothetical productivity curves for groups varying in cohesiveness.

Social Loafing

Have you ever participated in a group project at work or school in which you did not contribute as much as you could have because other people were there to take up the slack? Or have you ever reduced your effort in a group project because you felt that others were not pulling their weight? If so, you have been guilty of social loafing. **Social loafing** is the tendency that people have to withhold physical or intellectual effort when they are performing in a group task.[49] The implication is that they would work harder if they were alone rather than part of the group. Earlier we said that process losses in groups could be due to coordination problems or to motivation problems. Social loafing is a motivation problem.

People working in groups often feel trapped in a social dilemma, in that something that might benefit them individually—slacking off in the group—will result in poor group performance if everybody behaves the same way. Social loafers resolve the dilemma in a way that hurts organizational goal accomplishment. Notice that the tendency for social loafing is probably more pronounced in individualistic North America that in more collective and group-oriented cultures.

As the questions above suggest, social loafing has two different forms. In the *free rider effect*, people lower their effort to get a free ride at the expense of their fellow group members. In the *sucker effect*, people lower their effort because of the feeling that others are free riding, that is, they are trying to restore equity in the group. You can probably imagine a scenario in which the free riders start slacking off and then the suckers follow suit. Group performance suffers badly.

What are some ways to counteract social loafing?[50]

- *Make individual performance more visible.* Where appropriate, the simplest way to do this is to keep the group small in size. Then, individual contributions are less likely to be hidden. Posting performance levels and making presentations of one's accomplishments can also facilitate visibility.

- *Make sure that the work is interesting.* If the work is involving, intrinsic motivation should counteract social loafing.

- *Increase feelings of indispensability.* Group members might slack off because they feel that their inputs are unnecessary for group success. This can be counteracted by using training and the status system to provide group members with unique inputs (e.g., having one person master computer graphics programs).

- *Increase performance feedback.* Some social loafing happens because groups or individual members simply are not aware of their performance. Increased feedback, as appropriate, from the boss, peers, and customers (internal or external) should encourage self-correction. Group members might require assertiveness training to provide each other with authentic feedback.

- *Reward group performance.* Members are more likely to monitor and maximize their own performance (and attend to that of their colleagues) when the group receives rewards for effectiveness.

Before our discussion of work teams, pause and consider You Be the Manager.

Social loafing. The tendency to withhold physical or intellectual effort when performing a group task.

What Is a Team?

We began this chapter with a simple question: "What is a group?" Now you may be asking yourself, "What is a team?" Some writers have suggested that a "team" is something more than a "group". They suggest that a group becomes a team when there exists a strong sense of shared commitment, and when a synergy de-

The
bioclimatic
zones of the
San Diego Zoo
pose a unique
challenge for
the zoo's
managers.

California's San Diego Zoo is considered to be one of the world's premier zoological parks, long noted for its innovative exhibition techniques. In line with its goals of educating the public about conservation and providing an enjoyable experience for visitors, the zoo started to develop a series of bioclimatic zones that immersed visitors in the native habitat of animals and plants rather than having them view them from a distance. For example, in the Tiger River zone, plants, animals, birds, and visitors comingle much more than in a traditional exhibit.

The development of the bioclimatic zones presented zoo management with a problem. In the old days, when plants, animals, and visitors were more separated, it was easy to figure out who was responsible for what; gardeners, animal keepers, maintenance people, and construction people all had their own "territories," but they were professional, not geographic. Under the new zone system, all these functions became much more interdependent. For example, now some of the plants are there to be eaten by animals, not just admired! Zoo management wondered if jobs and work could be reorganized to better correspond to the new system of bioclimatic zones.

1. How can extreme separation between jobs sometimes hurt organizational effectiveness, including customer service?

2. What should zoo management do to better align its human resources with the new zone system?

To find out what the San Diego zoo did, see The Manager's Notebook at the end of the chapter.

Source: Adapted from Caudron, S. (1993, December). Are self-directed teams right for your company? *Personnel Journal*, pp. 76–84.

velops such that the group's efforts are greater than the sum of its parts.[51] While such differences might be evident in some instances, our definition of a group is sufficient to describe most teams that can be found in organizations. The term "team" is generally used to describe "groups" in organizational settings. Therefore, for our purposes in this chapter, we use the terms interchangeably.

In recent years, many organizations like Diamond Packaging have begun to use team-based work arrangements. Other well known examples include GM's Saturn Plant, Rubbermaid, Xerox, Federal Express, and General Electric to name just a few. It has been estimated that 80% of organizations with 100 or more employees now use some form of teams, and more than 50% of all organizations in the United States are exploring team-based work systems.[52] Thus, it should not be surprising that teams have become the major building blocks of organizations and are now quite common in North America.[53] The reasons for this vary but in many cases, it is an attempt to improve efficiency, quality, customer satisfaction, innovation, and/or the speed of production.

Consider the case of Diamond Packaging that began this chapter. The company had to become more flexible and responsive in order to survive in a business that is based on getting last-minute jobs from clients. This required a shift from a traditional top-down management structure to a team approach that enabled the company to improve productivity, quality, sales, and customer satisfaction.

San Diego Zoo
www.sandiegozoo.com

These results are consistent with research that has shown improvements in organizational performance in terms of both efficiency and quality as a result of team-based work arrangements.[54]

With the increasing popularity of work teams in organizations and evidence of their potential for substantial improvements in productivity, many researchers have begun to study the characteristics of effective work teams.[55] Knowledge along these lines can have important practical implications on how to design effective work teams in organizations. In the remainder of this chapter, we will focus on the characteristics and design of effective teams, with special emphasis on self-managing and cross-functional work teams.

Designing Effective Work Teams

The double-edged nature of group cohesiveness suggests that a delicate balance of factors dictates whether a work group is effective or ineffective. In turn, this raises the idea that organizations should pay considerable attention to how work groups are designed and managed. At first, the notion of designing a work group might seem strange. After all, don't work groups just "happen" in response to the demands of the organization's goals or technology? While these factors surely set some limits on how groups are organized and managed, organizations are finding that there is still plenty of scope for creativity in work group design.

A good model for thinking about the design of effective work groups is to consider a successful sports team, whether professional or amateur. In most cases, such teams are small groups made up of highly skilled individuals who are able to meld these skills into a cohesive effort. The task they are performing is intrinsically motivating and provides very direct feedback. If there are status differences on the team, the basis for these differences is contribution to the team, not some extraneous factor. The team shows an obsessive concern with obtaining the right personnel, relying on tryouts or player drafts, and the team is "coached," not supervised. With this informal model in mind, let us examine the concept of group effectiveness more closely.

J. Richard Hackman of Harvard University (co-developer of the Job Characteristics Model, Chapter 6) has written extensively about work group effec-

"NO, BUT I THINK I COULD LEARN TO BE A TEAM PLAYER."

tiveness.[56] According to Hackman, a work group is effective when (1) its physical or intellectual output is acceptable to management and to the other parts of the organization that use this output, (2) group members' needs are satisfied rather than frustrated by the group, and (3) the group experience enables members to *continue* to work together.

What leads to group effectiveness? In colloquial language, we might say "sweat, smarts, and style." More formally, Hackman notes that group effectiveness occurs when high effort is directed toward the group's task, when great knowledge and skill are directed toward the task, and when the group adopts sensible strategies for accomplishing its goals. And just how does an organization achieve this? As with Diamond Packaging, there is growing awareness in many organizations that the answer is self-managed work teams.

Self-Managed Work Teams

Although the exact details vary tremendously, **self-managed work teams** generally provide their members with the opportunity to do challenging work under reduced supervision. Other labels that we often apply to such groups are autonomous, semiautonomous, and self-regulated. The general idea, which is more important than the label, is that the groups tend to regulate much of their own members' behaviour. Much interest in such teams has been spurred by the success of teams in Japanese industry.

Critical to the success of self-managed teams are the nature of the task, the composition of the group, and various support mechanisms.[57] Notice that many of the suggestions that follow should improve coordination and discourage social loafing.

Self-managed work teams. Work groups that have the opportunity to do challenging work under reduced supervision.

Tasks for Self-Managed Teams. Experts agree that tasks assigned to self-managed work teams should be complex and challenging, requiring high interdependence among team members for accomplishment. In general, these tasks should have the qualities of enriched jobs, which we described in Chapter 6. Thus, teams should see the task as significant, they should perform the task from beginning to end, and they should use a variety of skills. The point here is that self-managed teams have to have something useful to self-manage, and it is fairly complex tasks that capitalize on the diverse knowledge and skills of a group. Taking a bunch of olive stuffers on a food-processing assembly line, putting them in distinctive jumpsuits, calling them the Olive Squad, and telling them to self-manage will be unlikely to yield dividends in terms of effort expended or brainpower employed. The basic task will still be boring!

Outside the complexity requirement, the actual range of tasks for which organizations have used self-managed teams is wide, spanning both blue- and white-collar jobs. In the white-collar domain, complex service and design jobs seem especially conducive to self-management. Organizations such as 3M, Aetna Life & Casualty, and Federal Express make extensive use of teams. At Federal Express, for example, self-managed back-office clerical teams are credited with improving billing accuracy and reducing lost packages for a savings of millions of dollars.[58]

3M
www.3m.com

In the blue-collar domain, Kodak, General Mills, GM's Saturn plant, and Chaparral Steel of Midlothian, Texas, make extensive use of self-managed work groups. In general, these groups are responsible for dividing labour among various subtasks as they see fit and making a variety of decisions about matters that impinge on the group. When a work site is formed from scratch and lacks an existing culture, the range of these activities can be very broad. Consider the self-managed teams formed in a new English confectionery plant.

Production employees worked in groups of 8 to 12 people, all of whom were expected to carry out each of eight types of jobs involved in the production process. Group members were collectively responsible for allocating jobs among themselves, reaching production targets and meeting quality and hygiene standards, solving local production problems, recording production data for information systems, organizing breaks, ordering and collecting raw materials and delivering finished goods to stores, calling for engineering support, and training new recruits. They also participated in selecting new employees. Within each group, individuals had considerable control over the amount of variety they experienced by rotating their tasks, and each production group was responsible for one product line. Group members interacted informally throughout the working day but made the most important decisions—for example, regarding job allocation—at formal weekly group meetings where performance was also discussed.[59]

Corning, Inc. opened a ceramic filter plant in Blacksburg, Virginia, that is organized along similar principles. Autonomous, flexible teams resulted in outstanding profitability.

If a theme runs through this discussion of tasks for self-managed teams, it is the breakdown of traditional, conventional, specialized *roles* in the group. Group members adopt roles that will make the group effective, not ones that are simply related to a narrow specialty. Exhibit 7.8 shows the results of a survey of American firms indicating the extent of tasks performed by self-managing teams.

Corning Inc.
www.corning.com

Composition of Self-Managed Teams. How should organizations assemble self-managed teams to ensure effectiveness? "Stable, small, and smart" might be a fast answer.[60]

- *Stability.* Self-managed teams require considerable interaction and high cohesiveness among their members. This, in turn, requires understanding and trust. To achieve this, group membership must be fairly stable. Rotating members into and out of the group will cause it to fail to develop a true group identity.[61]

- *Size.* In keeping with the demands of the task, self-managed teams should be as small as is feasible. The goal here is to keep coordination problems and social loafing to a minimum. These negative factors can be a problem for all

Exhibit 7.8
Functions performed by self-managed teams.

	All Sizes*		Number of Employees			
		100–499	500–999	1,000–2,499	2,500–9,999	10,000 or More
Set Work Schedules	69%	69%	63%	74%	64%	66%
Deal Directly with External Customers	59%	60%	63%	47%	43%	49%
Set Production Quotas/Performance Targets	57%	57%	70%	49%	59%	57%
Training	55%	55%	48%	63%	53%	64%
Purchase Equipment or Services	47%	48%	52%	35%	32%	41%
Deal with Vendors/Suppliers	46%	45%	56%	47%	47%	44%
Performance Appraisals	37%	36%	37%	44%	42%	33%
Budgeting	35%	33%	52%	42%	34%	33%
Hiring	29%	28%	41%	30%	25%	26%
Firing	21%	21%	26%	19%	13%	10%

*Refers to U.S. organizations with 100 or more employees.
Source: Gordon, J. (1992, October). Work teams: How far have they come? *Training*, pp. 59-65.

groups, but they can be especially difficult for self-managed groups. This is because reduced supervision means that there is no boss to coordinate the group's activities and search out social loafers who do not do their share.

- *Expertise.* It goes without saying that group members should have a high level of expertise about the task at hand. Everybody does not have to know everything, but the group as a *whole* should be very knowledgeable about the task. Again, reduced supervision discourages "running to the boss" when problems arise, but the group must have the resources to successfully solve these problems. One set of skills that all members should probably possess to some degree is *social skills.* Understanding how to talk things out, communicate effectively, and resolve conflict is especially important for self-managed groups.

- *Diversity.* Put simply, a team should have members who are similar enough to work well together and diverse enough to bring a variety of perspectives and skills to the task at hand. A product planning group consisting exclusively of new, male MBAs might work well together but lack the different perspectives that are necessary for creativity.

One way of maintaining appropriate group composition might be to let the group choose its own members, as occurred at the confectionery plant we discussed above. In the GM Saturn start-up, a panel of union and management members evaluated applications for all blue- and white-collar jobs, paying particular attention to social skills.[62] A potential problem with having a group choose its own members is that the group might use some irrelevant criterion (such as race or gender) to unfairly exclude others. Thus, human resources department oversight is necessary, as are very clear selection criteria (in terms of behaviours, skills, and credentials). The selection stage is critical, since some studies (including the one in the confectionary plant) have shown elevated turnover in self-managed teams.[63] "Fit" is important, and well worth expending the extra effort to find the right people.

The theme running through this discussion of team composition favours *high cohesiveness* and the development of group *norms* that stress group effectiveness.

Supporting Self-Managed Teams. A number of support factors can assist self-managed teams in becoming and staying effective. Reports of problems with teams can usually be traced back to inadequate support.

- *Training.* In almost every conceivable instance, members of self-managed teams will require extensive training. At Saturn, for example, new workers receive five full days of training, a figure unheard of in the traditional American auto industry. The kind of training depends on the exact job design and on the needs of the workforce. However some common areas include:
  - *Technical training.* This might include math, computer use, or any tasks that a supervisor formerly handled. Cross-training in the specialties of other teammates is common.
  - *Social skills.* Assertiveness, problem solving, and routine dispute resolution are skills that help the team operate smoothly.
  - *Language skills.* This can be important for ethnically diverse teams. Good communication is critical on self-managed teams.
  - *Business training.* Some firms provide basic elements of finance, accounting, and production so that employees can better grasp how their team's work fits into the larger picture.

  At Diamond Packaging, employees have developed three times as many job skills under the team approach, and all employees have a training and development plan.

■ *Rewards.* The general rule here is to try to tie rewards to team accomplishment rather than to individual accomplishment while still providing team members with some individual performance feedback. Diamond Packaging evaluates team performance and rewards teams with cash awards. Teams also set goals for themselves and decide how they will be rewarded if they meet them. Gainsharing, profit sharing, and skill-based pay (Chapter 6) all seem to be compatible reward systems for a team environment. Skill-based pay is especially attractive because it rewards the acquisition of multiple skills that can support the team. To provide individual performance feedback, some firms have experimented with peer (e.g., team member) performance appraisal. Many have also done away with status symbols that are unrelated to group effectiveness (such as reserved parking and dining areas).

■ *Management.* Self-management will not receive the best support when managers feel threatened and see it as reducing their own power or promotion opportunities. Some schooled in the traditional role of manager may simply not adapt. Those who do can serve important functions by mediating relations *between* teams and by dealing with union concerns, since unions are often worried about the cross-functional job sharing in self-management.

A study found that the most effective managers in a self-management environment encouraged groups to observe, evaluate, and reinforce their own task behaviour.[64] This suggests that coaching teams to be independent enhances their effectiveness.[65] At Diamond Packaging, the work teams are responsible for many decisions as well as tracking product quality and profit without direct supervision.

Exhibit 7.9 summarizes the factors that influence work group effectiveness. Michael Campion and his colleagues have studied team characteristics and group effectiveness in teams of professional and nonprofessional workers.[66] Their results provide strong support for many of the relationships shown in Exhibit 7.9. For example, they found that task characteristics were related to most measures of group effectiveness including productivity, team member satisfaction, and manager and employee judgements of group effectiveness. Group composition characteristics were related to only a few of the effectiveness measures. In particular, teams perceived as too large for their tasks were rated as less effective than teams perceived as an appropriate size or too small. Managerial support was re-

Exhibit 7.9
Factors influencing work group effectiveness.

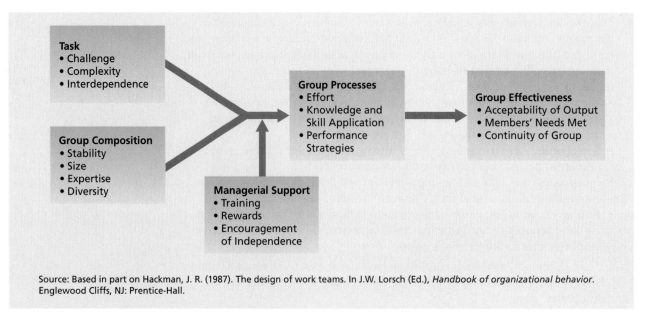

Source: Based in part on Hackman, J. R. (1987). The design of work teams. In J.W. Lorsch (Ed.), *Handbook of organizational behavior.* Englewood Cliffs, NJ: Prentice-Hall.

lated to many of the measures of effectiveness and was found to be one of the best predictors of group performance in another recent study.[67] Campion and colleagues found that group processes were the best predictors of group effectiveness which is consistent with Exhibit 7.9. Overall, research has shown improvements in team productivity, quality, customer satisfaction, and safety following the implementation of self-managed work teams.[68]

Finally, in keeping with some of the issues introduced in earlier chapters, you might be wondering what role values play in the use and effectiveness of self-managed work teams in different cultures. To find out, check out "Global Focus: *Cultural Values and Globalized Self-Managed Work Teams.*"

Sara Lee Corp.
www.saralee.com

global focus→ Cultural Values and Globalized Self-Managed Work Teams

The use of teams and self-managed work teams (SMWT) in North America is now quite common. Thus, it should come as no surprise that North American–based multinational firms have begun using self-managed work teams in their foreign facilities. For example, the Goodyear Tire & Rubber Company has begun SMWT initiatives in Europe, Latin America, and Asia; the Sara Lee Corporation currently uses SMWTs in Puerto Rico and Mexico; and Texas Instruments Malaysia has arranged the majority of its workforce into SMWTs. These are examples of what has been referred to as globalized SMWTs.

But will these globalized SMWTs be accepted and effective in all cultures? According to Bradley Kirkman and Debra Shapiro, cultural values can influence resistance to SMWTs and their effectiveness. They argue that differences in cultural values can be an important factor when considering whether employees' will resist either the process of self-management and/or collaborative teamwork. For example, because people from "individualistic" cultures are more concerned with their own welfare over the interests of their group or organization, they are more likely to resist teams than individuals from collective cultures who value the welfare of the group over the individual.

Kirkman and Shapiro identified three cultural values that can affect resistance to self-management: power distance, doing-versus-being orientation, and determinism versus free will. Employees from high power distance cultures, such as the Philippines, Venezuela, and India, expect managers to lead and are uncomfortable with the delegation of discretionary decisions and the role ambiguity that can result from new tasks. As a result, management approaches such as self-management that provide employees with more autonomy and responsibility are likely to be resisted by employees in high power distance cultures.

The extent to which one engages in work versus nonwork activities is a cultural value known as a "doing-versus-being" orientation. People from doing-oriented cultures stress accomplishments, work hard to achieve goals, and maximize work. In contrast, individuals from being-oriented cultures stress release, work only as much as needed to be able to live, and avoid continuous work. Mexico and Malaysia are examples of being-oriented cultures, and the United States is an example of a doing-oriented culture. Self-management activities revolve around setting goals and continuous work which is consistent with a doing orientation and inconsistent with a being orientation. Therefore, individuals from being-oriented cultures are likely to resist self-management.

Determinism versus free will has to do with whether individuals feel that their actions are governed primarily by external forces (deterministic cultures) or believe that they alone control their actions (free will cultures). Deterministic cultures include Malaysia and Indonesia, and free will cultures include Australia, Canada, and the United States. Because self-management involves activities associated with changing one's environment and its outcomes, individuals from deterministic cultures who believe they have very little control over their environment are likely to resist self-management.

Thus, individuals from some cultures are likely to be more receptive to SMWTs, while others are likely to be more resistant, depending on their cultural values. Because resistance to SMWTs can negatively impact group effectiveness, cultural values need to be considered when designing and implementing SMWTs. Having an understanding of how cultural values influence resistance should enable managers to design interventions that may facilitate employee support for SMWTs and to better match the form or operational characteristics of SMWTs to team members' cultural values.

Source: Based on Kirkman, B. L., & Shapiro, D. L. (1997). The impact of cultural values on employee resistance to teams: Toward a model of globalized self-managing work team effectiveness. *Academy of Management Review*, 22, pp. 730-757.

Cross-functional teams. Work groups that bring people with different functional specialties together to better invent, design, or deliver a product or service.

Thermos
www.thermos.com

Cross-Functional Teams

To close the chapter, let us look at another kind of team that contemporary organizations are using with increasing frequency. **Cross-functional teams** bring people with different functional specialties together to better invent, design, or deliver a product or service.

A cross-functional team might be self-managed and permanent if it is doing a recurrent task that is not too complex. For example, UPS and Times Mirror have multiskilled sales teams that sell and deliver products and services. If the task is complex and unique (such as designing a car), cross-functional teams require formal leadership, and their lives will generally be limited to the life of the specific project. In both cases, the "cross-functional" label means such diverse specialties are necessary so that cross-training is not feasible. People have to be experts in their own area but able to cooperate with others.

Cross-functional teams, which have been used in service industries such as banking and hospitals, are probably best known for their successes in product development.[69]

- Rubbermaid, which was named by *Fortune* as one of America's Most Admired Companies, uses teams to invent and design a remarkable variety of innovative household products. They introduce more than 365 products a year!

- Thermos used a team to invent a very successful ecologically friendly electric barbecue grill. It sped to the market in record time.

- The auto industry has embraced cross-functional teams to reduce the cycle time needed to design new cars. Particular beneficiaries have been the Dodge Viper sports car and Ford's newest Mustang. Even venerable Rolls-Royce is using such teams.

The general goals of using cross-functional teams include some combination of innovation, speed, and quality that come from early coordination among the various specialties. We can see their value by looking at the traditional way auto manufacturers have designed cars in North America.[70] First, stylists determine what the car will look like and then pass their design on to engineering, which develops mechanical specifications and blueprints. In turn, manufacturing must then consider how to construct what stylists and engineers have designed. Somewhere down the line, marketing and accounting get their say. This process leads to problems. One link in the chain might have a difficult time understanding what the previous link meant. Worse, one department might resist the ideas of another simply because they "were not invented here." The result of all this is slow, expensive development and early quality problems. In contrast, the cross-functional approach gets all the specialties working together from day one. A complex project, such as a car design, might have over 30 cross-functional teams working at the same time.

The speed factor can be dramatic. Manufacturers have reduced the development of a new car model from five years to around three. Boeing used a cross-functional team to reduce certain design analyses from two weeks to only a few minutes.

Principles for Effectiveness. Recent research has discovered a number of factors that contribute to the effectiveness of cross-functional teams.[71]

- *Composition.* All relevant specialties are obviously necessary, and effective teams are sure not to overlook anyone. Auto companies put labour representatives on car design teams to warn of assembly problems. On the Mustang and Thermos projects, the companies included outside suppliers.

- *Superordinate goals.* **Superordinate goals** are attractive outcomes that can only be achieved by collaboration. They override detailed functional objectives that might be in conflict (e.g., finance versus design). On the Mustang project, the superordinate goal was to keep the legendary name alive in the face of corporate cost cutters.

- *Physical proximity.* Team members have to be relocated close to each other to facilitate informal contact. Mustang used a former furniture warehouse in Allen Park, Michigan, to house its teams.

- *Autonomy.* Cross-functional teams need some autonomy from the larger organization, and functional specialists need some authority to commit their function to project decisions. This prevents meddling or "micromanaging" by upper level or functional managers.

- *Rules and procedures.* Although petty rules and procedures are to be avoided, some basic decision procedures must be laid down to prevent anarchy. On the Mustang project, it was agreed that a single manufacturing person would have a veto over radical body changes.

- *Leadership.* Because of the potential for conflict, cross-functional team leaders need especially strong people skills in addition to task expertise. The "tough engineer" who headed the Mustang project succeeded in developing his people skills for that task.

We will consider other material relevant to cross-functional teams when we cover conflict management and organizational design.

Superordinate goals. Attractive outcomes that can only be achieved by collaboration.

---

the manager's notebook

San Diego Zoo

The San Diego zoo experience shows that self-managed teams are appropriate for service jobs as well as in manufacturing environments.

1. Extreme separation between job duties and functions (the zoo has 97 job classifications) can lead to a lack of cooperation and gaps in performance. The gardener who fails to pick up a piece of trash ("let the groundskeeper do it") or the maintenance worker who ignores a bird in distress ("that's the keeper's job") are not performing optimally. Unfortunately, the extreme separation of job functions often leads to this isolation.

2. The zoo formed self-managed work teams to oversee the various zones. The one for Tiger River has seven people, including specialists in birds, animals, gardening, construction, and maintenance. They are cross-trained to assist each other, have their own budget, and jointly maintain the zone. Both job satisfaction and visitor service have improved under the system.

Summary

- A group consists of two or more people interacting interdependently to achieve a common goal. The formation and maintenance of groups depend on opportunity for interaction, potential for goal accomplishment, and the personal characteristics of members.

- Some groups go through a series of developmental stages: Forming, storming, norming, performing, and adjourning. However, the punctuated equilibrium model stresses an important first meeting, a period of little apparent progress, a critical midpoint transition, and a phase of goal-directed activity.

- As groups get bigger, they provide less opportunity for member satisfaction. When tasks are additive (performance depends on the addition of individual effort) or disjunctive (performance depends on that of the best member), larger groups should perform better than smaller groups if the group can avoid process losses due to poor communication and motivation. When tasks are conjunctive (performance is limited by the weakest member), performance decreases as the group gets bigger because the chance of adding a weak member increases.

- Norms are expectations that group members have about each other's behaviour. They provide consistency to behaviour and develop as a function of shared attitudes. In organizations, both formal and informal norms often develop to control loyalty, dress, reward allocation, and performance.

- Roles are positions in a group that have associated with them a set of expected behaviours. Role ambiguity refers to a lack of clarity of job goals or methods. Role conflict exists when an individual is faced with incompatible role expectations, and it can take four forms: intrasender, intersender, interrole, and person-role. Both ambiguity and conflict have been shown to provoke job dissatisfaction, stress, and lowered commitment.

- Status is the rank or prestige that a group accords its members. Formal status systems use status symbols to reinforce the authority hierarchy and reward progression up the hierarchy. Informal status systems also operate in organizations, though they might lack conspicuous status symbols. Although status differences are motivational, they also lead to communication barriers.

- Cohesive groups are especially attractive to their members. Threat, competition, success, and small size contribute to cohesiveness, as does a tough initiation into the group. The consequences of cohesiveness include increased participation in group affairs, improved communication, and increased conformity. Cohesive groups are especially effective in accomplishing their own goals, which might or might not be those of the organization.

- Social loafing occurs when people withhold effort when performing a group task. This is less likely when individual performance is visible, the task is interesting, there is good performance feedback, and the organization rewards group achievement.

- Members of self-managed work teams do challenging work under reduced supervision. For greatest effectiveness, such teams should be stable, small, well trained, and moderately diverse in membership. Group-oriented rewards are most appropriate.

- Cross-functional teams bring people with different functional specialties together to better invent, design, or deliver a product or service. They

should have diverse membership, a superordinate goal, some basic decision rules, and a fair degree of autonomy. Members should work in the same physical location, and leaders require people skills as well as task skills.

Discussion Questions

1. Describe the kind of skills that you would look for in members of self-managed teams. Explain your choices.

2. Debate: Effective teamwork is more difficult for individualistic Americans, Canadians, and Australians than for more collectivist Japanese.

3. Consider a large office in an insurance firm that consists of clerks, secretaries, and claims processors. Suppose that several informal friendship groups have formed on the basis of proximity and attitude similarity. Discuss the potential pros and cons of these groups for the organization. Does the existence of such informal groups make special demands on office managers? Should organizations try to prevent the development of such groups?

4. Suppose that a group of United Nations representatives from various countries forms to draft a resolution regarding world hunger. Is this an additive, disjunctive, or conjunctive task? What kinds of process losses would such a group be likely to suffer? Can you offer a prediction about the size of this group and its performance?

5. Explain how a cross-functional team could contribute to product or service quality. Explain how one could contribute to speeding up product design.

6. Mark Allen, a representative for an international engineering company, is a very religious person and an elder in his church. Mark's direct superior has instructed him to use "any legal means" to sell a large construction project to a foreign government. The vice-president of international operations had informed Mark that he could offer a generous "kickback" to government officials to clinch the deal, although such practices are illegal. Discuss the three kinds of role conflict that Mark is experiencing.

7. Some organizations have made concerted efforts to do away with many of the status symbols associated with differences in organizational rank. All

employees park in the same lot, eat in the same dining room, and have similar offices and privileges. Discuss the pros and cons of such a strategy. How might such a change affect organizational communications?

8. You are an executive in a consumer products corporation. The president assigns you to form a task force to develop new marketing strategies for the organization. You are permitted to choose its members. What things would you do to make this group as cohesive as possible? What are the dangers of group cohesiveness for the group itself and for the organization of which the group is a part?

9. What role do perceptions play in group development? Refer to the perceptual process and biases in Chapter 3 and discuss the implications for each stage of group development. What are the implications for improving the development of groups?

10. How can groups be motivated? Consider the implications of each of the work motivation theories described in Chapter 5. What do the theories tell us about how to motivate groups?

Experiential Exercise

NASA

The purpose of this exercise is to compare individual and group problem solving and to explore the group dynamics that occur in a problem-solving session. It can also be used in conjunction with Chapter 11. The instructor will begin by forming groups of four to seven members.

The situation described in this problem is based on actual cases in which men and women lived or died, depending on the survival decisions they made. Your "life" or "death" will depend on how well your group can share its present knowledge of a relatively unfamiliar problem, so that the group can make decisions which will lead to your survival.

The Problem

You are a member of a space crew originally scheduled to rendezvous with a mother ship on the lighted surface of the moon. Due to mechanical difficulties, however, your ship was forced to land at a spot some 200 miles from the rendezvous point. During landing, much of the equipment aboard was damaged, and, because survival depends on reaching the mother ship, the most critical items available must be chosen for the 200-mile trip. On the next page are listed the fifteen items left intact and undamaged after the landing. Your task is to rank them in terms of their importance to your crew in reaching the rendezvous point. In the first column (step 1) place the number 1 by the most important item, the number 2 by the second most important, and

so on, through number 15, the least important. You have fifteen minutes to complete this phase of the exercise.

After the individual rankings are completed, participants should be formed into groups having from four to seven members. Each group should then rank the fifteen items as a team. This group ranking should be a general consensus after a discussion of the issues, not just the average of each individual ranking. While it is unlikely that everyone will agree exactly on the group ranking, an effort should be made to reach at least a decision that everyone can live with. It is important to treat differences of opinion as a means of gathering more information and clarifying issues and as an incentive to force the group to seek better alternatives. The group ranking should be listed in the second column (step 2). The third phase of the exercise consists of the instructor providing the expert's rankings, which should be entered in the third column (step 3). Each participant should compute the difference between the individual ranking (step 1) and the expert's ranking (step 3), and between the group ranking (step 2) and the expert's ranking (step 3). Then add the two "difference" columns—the smaller of the score, the closer the ranking is to the view of the experts.

Source: Teleometrics International.

Discussion

The instructor will summarize the results on the board for each group, including (a) average individual accuracy score, (b) group accuracy score, (c) gain or loss between the average individual score and the group score, and (d) the lowest individual score (i.e., the best score) in each group.

The following questions will help guide the discussion:

1. As a group task, is the NASA exercise an additive, disjunctive, or conjunctive task?

2. What would be the impact of group size on performance in this task?

3. Did any norms develop in your group that guided how information was exchanged or how the decision was reached?

4. Did any special roles emerge in your group? These could include a leader, a secretary, an "expert," a critic, or a humorist. How did these roles contribute to or hinder group performance?

5. Consider the factors that contribute to effective self-managed teams. How do they pertain to a group's performance on this exercise?

6. How would group diversity help or hinder performance on the exercise?

Case Incident

The Group Assignment

Janet never liked working on group assignments; however, this time she thought it would be different because she knew most of the people in her group. However, it was not long before things started going badly. After the first meeting, the

NASA tally sheet

Items	Step 1 Your individual ranking	Step 2 The team's ranking	Step 3 Survival expert's ranking	Step 4 Difference between Step 1 & 3	Step 5 Difference between Step 2 & 3
Box of matches					
Food concentrate					
50 feet of nylon rope					
Parachute silk					
Portable heating unit					
Two .45 calibre pistols					
One case dehydrated milk					
Two 100-lb. tanks of oxygen					
Stellar map (of the moon's constellation)					
Life raft					
Magnetic compass					
5 gallons of water					
Signal flares					
First aid kit containing injection needles					
Solar-powered FM receiver-transmitter					
Total					

(The lower the score the better) | Your score | Team score |

group could not agree when to meet again. When they finally did agree to meet, nobody had done anything, and the assignment was due in two weeks. The group then agreed to meet again the next day to figure out what to do. However, two of the group members did not show up. The following week Janet tried in vain to arrange for another meeting, but the other group members said they were too busy, and that it would be best to divide the assignment up and have each member work on a section. The night before the assignment was due the group members met to give Janet their work. Finally, Janet thought, we are making progress. However, when she got home and read what the other members had written she was shocked at how bad it was. Janet spent the rest of the night and early morning doing the whole assignment herself. Once the course ended, Janet never spoke to any of the group members again.

1. Refer to the typical stages of group development and explain the development of Janet's group.

2. To what extent was group cohesiveness a problem in Janet's work group? What might have made the group more cohesive?

Case Study

Levi Strauss & Co.'s Flirtation with Teams

The Levi Strauss & Co. is the largest clothing manufacturer in the United States. It has a long history of being profitable, good to its workers, and charitable to its factory towns. Compared with other companies in the apparel industry, Levi Strauss is known for generous wages and good working conditions. According to CEO Robert Haas, Levi's treatment of its workers and concern for their welfare is far greater than in other companies in the industry.

When other American apparel firms moved their manufacturing offshore, Levi Strauss & Co. maintained a large American manufacturing base and was often ranked as one of the best companies to work for. In fact, in 1997 the company received an award from the United Nations for improving global workplace standards.

Up until 1992, Levi's employees worked on their own operating machines in which they performed a single, specific, and repetitive task, such as sewing zippers or belt loops on jeans. Pay was based on a piece-rate system, in which workers were paid a set amount for each piece of work completed. A worker's productivity and pay was highly dependent on levels of skill, speed, and stamina.

By 1992, however, Levi Strauss & Co. began to feel the pressure of overseas, low-cost competitors, and realized the need to increase productivity and reduce costs in order to remain competitive and keep their North American plants open. The company decided that the best solution was teamwork. In a memo sent to workers, Levi's operations vice-president wrote, "This change will lead to a self-managed work environment that will reduce stress and help employees become more productive." Teamwork was felt to be a humane, safe, and profitable solution that would be consistent with the company's philosophy.

Gone was the old system of performing a single task all the time and the piece-rate system that went with it. Now groups of 10 to 50 workers shared the tasks and would be paid for the total number of trousers that the group completed. The team system was expected to lower the monotony of piece-work by enabling workers to do different tasks and to therefore lower repetitive-stress injuries.

Although employees were given brief seminars and training on team building and problem solving, it was not long before problems began to arise. Top performers complained about their less skilled and slower teammates that caused a decline in their wages. Meanwhile, the wages of lower skilled workers increased. Threats, insults, and group infighting became a regular part of daily work as faster workers tried to rid their group of slower workers. To make matters worse, top performers responded to their lower wages by reducing their productivity. Not surprisingly, employee morale began to deteriorate.

Another problem was that whenever a group member was absent or slow, the rest of the team had to make up for it. This exacerbated the infighting among team members and resulted in excessive peer pressure. In one instance, an enraged worker had to be restrained from throwing a chair at a team member who constantly harassed her about working too slow, and in another incident, a worker threatened to kill a member of her team. An off-duty sheriff's deputy had to be placed at the plant's front entrance.

Because the groups had limited supervision, they had to resolve group problems on their own, and they also divided up the work of absent members themselves. In some plants, team members would chase each other out of the bathroom and nurse's station. Slower teammates were often criticized, needled, and resented by their group. Some could not take the resentment and simply quit. In one group, a member was voted off her team because she planned to have hand surgery.

And although workers were now part of a team system, management was not given guidance on how to implement the system. As a result, each manager had his or her own idea of how the team system should work, including team size, structure, pay formulas, and shop-floor layouts. One former production manager described the situation as worse than chaos and more like hell!

To make matters worse, the team system did not improve the situation for Levi's. Labour and overhead costs increased by up to 25% during the first years of the team system.

Efficiency, based on the quantity of pants produced per hour worked, dropped to 77% of preteam levels. Although productivity began to improve, it is only at 93% of the piecework level. Even in some of the company's best plants, production has fallen and remained at lower levels since the introduction of teams. And although one of the reasons for adopting the team system was to lower the high costs of injuries that resulted from workers pushing themselves to achieve piece-rate goals, these costs continued to rise in many plants even after the team approach was implemented.

Profit margins also began to decline as competitors began offering private-label jeans at two-thirds the price of Levi's, and Levi's market share of men's denim-jeans in the United States fell from 48% in 1990 to 26% in 1997. As costs continued to increase, plant managers were warned that they would face an uncertain future unless they cut costs by 28% by the end of year.

Teams did, however, result in some improvements. For example, the average turnaround time of receiving an order and shipping it was reduced from nine to seven weeks. As well, because the teams were responsible for producing completed pairs of pants, there was less work in process at the end of each day compared with the piece-rate system, where each worker did only one part of the job. And according to CEO Robert Haas, teams allowed workers to manage themselves and to find better and safer ways of working.

Nonetheless, the team system did not help Levi's achieve its objectives. In February 1997, CEO Robert Haas announced that the company would cut its salaried workforce by 20% in the next 12 months. The following November, the company closed 11 factories in the United States and laid off 6,395 workers. In an unusual response to being laid off, one worker described it as a "relief" from the burden and stress that had become part of her job.

In February 1999, as sales of Levi's jeans continued to fall, the company let go another 5,900 or 30% of its workforce of 19,900 in the United States and Canada and announced that it will close 11 of its remaining 22 plants in North America. According to company officials, plant closings might have been sooner and job losses greater if they had not adopted the team system.

Commenting on the team approach, a now retired former manufacturing manager said, "We created a lot of anxiety and pain and suffering in our people, and for what?" According to a production manager who has taken early retirement, "It's just not the same company anymore. The perceived value of the individual and the concern for people just is not there." A veteran worker who has gone back to the old system of doing a single task and is now paid in part for what she produces said, "I hate teams. Levi's is not the place it used to be."

While officials said they plan to stick with the team approach in the remaining American plants, managers say that the team approach is on its way out as they search for other ways to increase productivity, like the old way of doing things.

In recent years, Levi Strauss & Co. has begun to contract out much of its work and now manufactures 45% of its jeans for the American market outside North America, compared with 15% in 1991, and none 10 years ago. Although it remains one of the last major American-based apparel companies with a substantial amount of company-owned production in North America, it now contracts manufacturing in 50 countries worldwide. According to John Ermatinger, president of the company's American division, "Shifting a significant portion of our manufacturing for the American and Canadian markets to contractors throughout the world will give the company greater flexibility to allocate resources and capital to its brands."

1. Discuss the stages of group development and the implications of them for the development of the teams at Levi Strauss.

2. Discuss some of the norms that emerged in the teams. What was their function and how did they influence the behaviour of group members?

3. Discuss the role dynamics that emerged in the groups. Is there any evidence of role ambiguity or role conflict?

4. How cohesive were the groups at Levi Strauss? What factors contribute to the level of cohesiveness?

5. Analyze and evaluate the effectiveness of the teams using the concepts summarized in Exhibit 7.9.

6. The teams were supposed to be self-managing teams. Critique this idea in terms of the principles for effectiveness for such teams given in the text.

7. Do you think it was a good idea for Levi Strauss & Co. to implement a team system? Was it the best solution to deal with increased global competition? Why wasn't the team approach at Levi Strauss & Co. more effective, and with your knowledge of groups, what might you do differently if you had to implement a team system at Levi Strauss?

8. What does the Levi Strauss experience tell us about the use of teams and their effectiveness?

Sources: Gilbert, C. (1998, September). Did modules fail Levi's or did Levi's fail modules? *Apparel Industry Magazine*, pp. 88–92; King, R. T., Jr. (1998, May 20). Levi's factory workers are assigned to teams and morale takes a hit. *The Wall Street Journal*, pp. A1, A6; McFarland, J. (1999, February 23). Levi Strauss slashes 5,900 jobs. *The Globe and Mail*, p. B5; Steinhart, D. (1999, February 23). Levi to shut plants in Cornwall, *U.S. Financial Post*, pp. C1, C9.

Chapter 8

Social Influence, Socialization, and Culture

Trilogy
Software Inc.

TRILOGY SOFTWARE INC. A month into her first job, Lauren Arbittier stood at a roulette wheel at a Las Vegas casino and, egged on by her co-workers and bosses, put down a $2,000 bet. Until she joined Trilogy Software Inc., she never thought of herself as a gambler. "I'm just not someone who throws money around," she says. But then, she had not worked for Joe Liemandt, who put Ms. Arbittier and 35 other new recruits up to the big bet.

Mr. Liemandt is Trilogy's chairman and chief executive officer, an energetic 30-year-old who dropped out of Stanford University in 1990 to start a software company. In building Trilogy to more than $100 million in revenue, he learned the hard way that taking risks and suffering the consequences are a crucial part of business. And he wants new hires to understand the experience firsthand.

In an unusual indoctrination, he puts the company's college recruits through a kind of corporate boot camp, complete with long workouts and little time at home. His goal: To develop creative people who work well in teams, adapt to swift changes in customer demands—and take chances.

Mr. Liemandt and Trilogy need these newcomers to succeed. This year, he hired 300 recent graduates, bringing total employment to 700, in hopes of firing up Trilogy's already rapid growth. As a maker of industry-leading software that helps companies manage product pricing, sales plans, and commissions, he is facing increasing competition from Siebel Systems Inc., which recently made a big acquisition, and SAP AG, the German powerhouse that has started to make some Trilogy-like products. Still, Trilogy's cash flow is abundant, and Mr. Liemandt, in his boot-camp venture at least, is not worrying about the company's bottom line.

New recruits at Trilogy Software Inc. attend Trilogy University, a kind of corporate boot camp, designed to transform them into creative individuals who can work in teams, adapt to changes, and take risks.

Trilogy Software Inc.
www.triolgy.com

To find and attract talented grads, the company spends more than $10,000 per hire on visits to Austin, dinners and outings at 20 universities. Some students have nicknamed Trilogy "The Firm" because its outsized recruiting tactics resemble those of the notorious law firm Bendini, Lambert & Locke in John Grisham's novel.

For three months, Mr. Liemandt is dedicating nearly all his time to training this group. "Trilogy University" classes begin at 8 a.m. and, in the first month, last until midnight. The company caters meals and stocks snack rooms more richly than some convenience stores. It schedules softball games and trips to Austin's nightclubs and even to the beach four hours away.

Though the company pays from $45,000 for recent college graduates to $90,000 for MBAs, few people know exactly what their new jobs will be. In classes led by Mr. Liemandt and seven other Trilogy veterans, everyone learns about programming languages, product plans, and marketing. Trilogy's venture-capital backers talk, and Mr. Liemandt's mother, a company director, drops in to tell a few funny stories about the boss.

In the second week, the hires are divided into 80 teams and given three weeks to complete projects ranging from making an existing Trilogy product run faster to creating new products from scratch. In addition to affecting where each person will end up, the projects offer a short-term reward: Teams that do well will win a two-day trip to Las Vegas. But Mr. Liemandt tells the fresh-faced crowd that effort will not be enough. Projecting a slide that reads, "No Reward for Trying," he warns, "If you set a hard goal and don't make it, you don't win points."

Learning Objectives

After reading Chapter 8, you should be able to:

1. Understand the difference between information dependence and effect dependence.

2. Differentiate compliance, identification, and internalization as motives for social conformity.

3. Describe the factors that influence conformity to social norms.

4. Describe the stages of organizational socialization and some methods of socialization.

5. Define organizational culture and discuss the contributors to a culture.

6. Discuss the assets and liabilities of strong organizational cultures.

7. Review how we can diagnose an organizational culture.

At midnight the day before the projects are due, Trilogy's new hires receive e-mail with their review schedule. The next day Mr. Liemandt arrives in jeans and a checkered shirt with the sleeves rolled up. Through the day, he scoots between three review teams, sometimes pausing only for a few minutes, sometimes taking over the review and grilling team members well beyond the allotted 15 minutes. That evening, two hours before the buses are scheduled to take the winners to two chartered planes to Las Vegas, Mr. Liemandt and his executives gather for a final discussion. Twenty of the 80 projects are deemed failures: some people should be left behind.

A short time later, Mr. Liemandt starts by reading off the names of a few winners. The anxiety is audible. But the group breaks into cheers and applause when he finally announces that everyone will go to Las Vegas. "I know we get up here and preach results are all that matters, and then we have a slide that says, 'Effort doesn't count,'" Mr. Liemandt says. "But you guys delivered a whole lot as a group."

In the wee hours of the next morning, 300 Trilogy employees pour into the Luxor Hotel and Casino. The only event everyone promised to attend was a stop at the roulette wheel scheduled just before they flew home. Enjoying the break, Ms. Arbittier gambles $20 and calls home to brag about winning $9 at the craps table.

The roulette table is another matter. Mr. Liemandt challenges employees to take a $2,000 bet, believing that amount is enough money to convey a sense of pain—and risk—but not enough to cause financial disaster. Trilogy will put up the cash, and losers will have their paycheques reduced by $400 a month for five months.

Ms. Arbittier decides at the last minute to join in. Almost immediately, she starts to question the decision. How will she survive? Altogether, 36 recruits agree to bet, enough to fill all the public spots on the wheel. The bettors gather around the roulette table in a special room for high stakes gamblers, while the others stand outside. Sweating as the dealer drops the ball, Ms. Arbittier struggles for a view. In an instant, the colleague holding number 23 wins $72,000, and Ms. Arbittier is out $2,000.

However, for Ms. Arbittier the payoff came in the eyes of her peers who could not believe she had taken the plunge. Now part of the exclusive "L2K Club," for "lost $2,000," she has a new reputation, a T-shirt, and a glass etching of the roulette event and her number, 35. Still it took her three weeks to work up the nerve to tell her parents about the $2,000—and she did it by e-mail instead of a phone call. "We are known as risk-takers, an important attribute in the high-tech world," she writes. Moreover, the boss knows who she is. "Joe knows every L2K-er pretty well."

Mr. Liemandt is back to his day-to-day job building the company and considering a public offering. Crediting his $9 million training program with keeping retention high, he says only one of the 300 brand-new hires has left. Next year, he wants to bring 1,000 recruits and run them through a similar drill. But he will not set up a project competition. "You can't run the same play twice," he says.[1]

This description of a successful organization raises a number of interesting questions. Why does Trilogy spend so much time and money on training new hires? Do employees actually accept the ideas and values that they encounter in their training? What is the effect of this type of training on employees attitudes and behaviour? These are the kinds of questions that we will probe in this chapter.

First, we will examine the general issue of social influence in organizations, how members have an impact on each other's behaviour and attitudes. Social norms hold an organization together, and conformity to such norms is a product of social influence. Thus, the next section discusses conformity. Following this, we consider the elaborate process of socialization, the learning of the organization's norms and roles. Socialization both contributes to and results from the organizational culture, the final area that we will explore.

Social Influence in Organizations

In the previous chapter, we pointed out that groups exert influence over the attitudes and behaviour of their individual members. As a result of social influence, people often feel or act differently from how they would as independent operators. What accounts for such influence? In short, in many social settings, and especially in groups, people are highly *dependent* on others. This dependence sets the stage for influence to occur.

Information Dependence and Effect Dependence

We are frequently dependent on others for information about the adequacy and appropriateness of our behaviour, thoughts, and feelings. How satisfying is this job of mine? How nice is our boss? How much work should I take home to do over the weekend? Should we protest the bad design at the meeting? Objective, concrete answers to such questions might be hard to come by. Thus, we must often rely on information that others provide.[2] In turn, this **information dependence** gives others the opportunity to influence our thoughts, feelings, and actions via the signals they send to us.[3]

Individuals are often motivated to compare their own thoughts, feelings, and actions with those of others as a means of acquiring information about their adequacy. The effects of social information can be very strong, often exerting as much or more influence over others as objective reality.[4]

As if group members were not busy enough tuning into information provided by the group, they must also be sensitive to the rewards and punishments the group has at its disposal. Thus, individuals are dependent on the *effects* of their behaviour as determined by the rewards and punishments provided by others. **Effect dependence** actually involves two complementary processes. First, the group frequently has a vested interest in how individual members think and act because such matters can affect the goal attainment of the group. Second, the member frequently desires the approval of the group. In combination, these circumstances promote effect dependence.

In organizations, plenty of effects are available to keep individual members "under the influence." Superiors typically have a fair array of rewards and punishments available, including promotions, raises, and the assignment of more or less favourable tasks. At the informal level, the variety of such effects available to co-workers is staggering. They might reward cooperative behaviour with praise, friendship, and a helping hand on the job. Lack of cooperation might result in nagging, harassment, name calling, or social isolation.

> **Information dependence.** Reliance on others for information about how to think, feel, and act.

> **Effect dependence.** Reliance on others due to their capacity to provide rewards and punishment.

Social Influence in Action

One of the most obvious consequences of information and effect dependence is the tendency for group members to conform to the social norms that have been established by the group. In the last chapter, we discussed the development and function of such norms, but we have postponed until now the discussion of why norms are supported. Put simply, much of the information and many of the effects on which group members are dependent are oriented toward enforcing group norms.

Motives for Social Conformity

The fact that Roman Catholic priests conform to the norms of the church hierarchy seems rather different from the case in which convicts conform to norms that prison officials establish. Clearly, the motives for conformity differ in these two cases. What is needed, then, is some system to classify different motives for conformity.[5]

Compliance. **Compliance** is the simplest, most direct motive for conformity to group norms. It occurs because a member wishes to acquire rewards from the group and avoid punishment. As such, it primarily involves effect dependence. Although the complying individual adjusts his or her behaviour to the norm, he or she does not really subscribe to the beliefs, values, and attitudes that underlie the norm. Most convicts conform to formal prison norms out of compliance. Similarly, very young children behave themselves only because of external forces.

> **Compliance.** Conformity to a social norm prompted by the desire to acquire rewards or avoid punishment.

Identification. Some individuals conform because they find other supporters of the norm attractive. In this case, the individual identifies with these supporters and sees himself or herself as similar to them. Although there are elements of effect

Identification. Conformity to a social norm prompted by perceptions that those who promote the norm are attractive or similar to oneself.

dependence here, information dependence is especially important—if someone is basically similar to you, then you will be motivated to rely on them for information about how to think and act. **Identification** as a motive for conformity is often revealed by an imitation process in which established members serve as models for the behaviour of others. For example, a newly promoted executive might attempt to dress and talk like her successful, admired boss. Similarly, as children get older, they might be motivated to behave themselves because such behaviour corresponds to that of an admired parent with whom they are beginning to identify.

Internalization. Some conformity to norms occurs because individuals have truly and wholly accepted the beliefs, values, and attitudes that underlie the norm. As such, **internalization** of the norm has happened, and conformity occurs because it is seen as *right*, not because it achieves rewards, avoids punishment, or pleases others. That is, conformity is due to internal, rather than external, forces. In general, we expect that most religious leaders conform to the norms of their religion for this reason. Similarly, the career army officer might come to support the strict discipline of the military because it seems right and proper, not simply because colleagues support such discipline. In certain organizational settings, some of these motives for conformity are more likely than others. Lauren Arbittier has accepted the values of Trilogy Software. The once cautious spender now considers herself a risk-taker and a member of the exclusive "L2K Club."

Internalization. Conformity to a social norm prompted by true acceptance of the beliefs, values, and attitudes that underlie the norm.

Factors Influencing Conformity to Norms

What determines the extent to which a particular group member will be likely to conform to group norms? Put simply, factors that increase or decrease information and effect dependence should influence the extent of conformity of individual group members.

Publicity. Conformity to group norms is less likely when the behaviour in question is not public. Such a condition reduces effect dependence. For example, suppose an executive group has two equally strong informal norms—not cheating on expense accounts and not leaving the office before six o'clock. Other things being equal, an executive who disagrees with both norms would be more likely to comply with the leaving-time norm than the cheating norm because violation of the former would be more obvious. In some piece-rate pay situations in which groups have developed norms to restrict productivity, workers will lie about their own output to prevent pressure from their co-workers.

Size of the Opposition. Any tendency to "go along with the crowd" is enhanced when the "crowd" is bigger because a large opposition contains more sources of information and more sources of reward and punishment. Research on jury size shows that small juries tend to render less consistent verdicts than large juries.[6] This might stem, in part, from the fact that dissenters in small juries feel freer to stand their ground.

Dissension. Conformity to a norm is also influenced when an individual finds that he or she has a "partner in crime," that is, someone who also rejects the norm. As you might guess, such a condition strongly reduces the subject's tendency to conform. Dissenters provide alternative sources of information to the group consensus and change potential reward and punishment patterns.

The Issue at Hand. The issue in question can also influence conformity. In general, difficult, ambiguous issues increase the tendency toward conformity to group norms. For example, suppose four sales managers are asked to nominate one of their subordinates for promotion to manager. The subordinates are usually on the road, and there has been little opportunity to observe their managerial abilities. If, for some reason, three of the managers favour a particular candidate, it should be difficult for the fourth to dissent, since the choice is difficult and ambiguous.

Status. The relationship between status in the group and conformity is complex but easy to understand. If nonconformity occurs, it should usually occur among two classes of people—high-status members, or low-status members who have been actively rejected by the group (the latter have often been socially isolated or serve as scapegoats). High-status members have often *achieved* their high status because they have generally conformed to group norms. Thus, on an issue chosen at random, it is often safe to predict conformity from such a person. However, high-status members also receive **idiosyncrasy credits** from the group because of their history of conformity. This means that having paid their dues to the group, they are permitted to occasionally deviate without fear of censure.[7] On the other hand, low-status isolates and scapegoats have already rejected the group as a source of information and suffered the negative effects of doing so. Thus, they have little to gain by conforming in a particular case. Finally, low-status members who are striving to become fully integrated into the group (usually *new* members) should reveal a strong tendency to conform, since they are both effect and information dependent (Exhibit 8.1).

Idiosyncrasy credits. Social credits earned from regular conformity to group norms that allow occasional deviance from the norms.

The Subtle Power of Compliance

In many of the examples given in the previous section, especially those dealing with effect dependence, it is obvious that the doubting group member is motivated to conform only in the *compliance* mode, that is, he or she really does not support the belief, value, and attitude structure underlying the norm but conforms simply to avoid trouble or obtain rewards. Of course, this happens all the time. Individuals without religious beliefs or values might agree to be married in a church service to please others. Similarly, a store cashier might verify a credit card purchase by a familiar customer even though he feels that the whole process is a waste of time. These examples of compliance seem trivial enough, but a little compliance can go a long way.

A compliant individual is necessarily *doing* something that is contrary to the way he or she *thinks* or *feels*. As we pointed out in our discussion of attitudes in

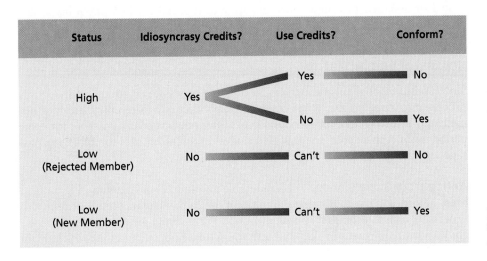

Status	Idiosyncrasy Credits?	Use Credits?	Conform?
High	Yes	Yes	No
		No	Yes
Low (Rejected Member)	No	Can't	No
Low (New Member)	No	Can't	Yes

Exhibit 8.1
Status, idiosyncrasy credits, and conformity.

Chapter 4, such a situation is highly dissonant and arouses a certain tension in the individual. Now, one way to reduce this dissonance is to cease conformity. This is especially likely if the required behaviour is at great variance with one's values or moral standards. However, this might require the person to adopt an isolate or scapegoat role, equally unpleasant prospects. The other method of reducing dissonance is to gradually accept the beliefs, values, and attitudes that support the norm in question. This is more likely when the required behaviour is not so discrepant with one's current value system.

Consider Mark, an idealistic graduate of a college social work program who acquires a job with a social services agency. Mark loves helping people but hates the bureaucratic red tape and reams of paperwork that is necessary to accomplish this goal. However, to acquire the approval of his boss and co-workers and to avoid trouble, he follows the rules to the letter of the law. This is pure compliance. Over time, however, Mark begins to *identify* with his boss and more experienced co-workers because they are in the enviable position of controlling those very rewards and punishments that are so important to him. Obviously, if he is to *be* one of them, he must begin to think and feel like them. Finally, Mark is promoted to a supervisory position, partly because he is so cooperative. Breaking in a new social worker, Mark is heard to say, "Our rules and forms are very important. You don't understand now, but you will." The metamorphosis is complete—Mark has *internalized* the beliefs and values that support the bureaucratic norms of his agency.

Although this story is slightly dramatized, the point that it makes is accurate—simple compliance can set the stage for more complete involvement with organizational norms and roles.

Socialization: Getting (Some) Conformity from Members

Socialization. The process by which people learn the norms and roles that are necessary to function in a group or organization.

The story of Mark, the social worker, in the previous section describes how one individual was socialized into a particular organization. In the chapter opening vignette, we described how new hires are socialized at Trilogy Software. **Socialization** is the process by which people learn the norms and roles that are necessary to function in a group or organization. As we shall see, some of this process might occur before membership formally begins. Furthermore, socialization is an ongoing process by virtue of continuous interaction with others in the workplace. However, there is good reason to believe that socialization is most potent during certain periods of membership transition, such as when one is promoted or assigned to a new work group, and especially when one joins a new organization.[8]

Stages of Socialization

Since organizational socialization is an ongoing process, it is useful to divide this process into three stages.[9] One of these stages occurs before entry, another immediately follows entry, and the last occurs after one has been a member for some period of time. In a sense, the first two stages represent hurdles for achieving passage into the third stage (see Exhibit 8.2).

Anticipatory Socialization. A considerable amount of socialization might occur even before a person becomes a member of a particular organization. This process is called anticipatory socialization. Some anticipatory socialization includes a formal process of skill and attitude acquisition, such as that which might

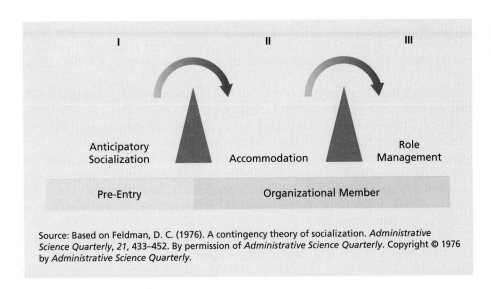

Source: Based on Feldman, D. C. (1976). A contingency theory of socialization. *Administrative Science Quarterly, 21*, 433–452. By permission of *Administrative Science Quarterly*. Copyright © 1976 by *Administrative Science Quarterly*.

Exhibit 8.2
Stages of organizational socialization.

occur by attending university. Other anticipatory socialization might be informal, such as that acquired through a series of summer jobs or even by watching the portrayal of organizational life in television shows and movies. As we shall see shortly, organizations vary in the extent to which they encourage anticipatory socialization in advance of entry. Also, we shall see that not all anticipatory socialization is accurate and useful for the new member.

Accommodation. In the accommodation stage, the new recruit, armed with some expectations about organizational life, encounters the day-to-day reality of this life. Formal aspects of this stage might include orientation programs, training programs (such as that at Trilogy Software), and rotation through various parts of the organization. Informal aspects include getting to know and understand the style and personality of one's boss and co-workers. At this stage, the organization and its experienced members are looking for an acceptable degree of conformity to organizational norms and the gradual acquisition of appropriate role behaviour. At Trilogy Software such behaviours include creativity, working in teams, and risk taking. Recruits, on the other hand, are interested in having their personal needs and expectations fulfilled. If accommodation is reached, the recruit will have complied with critical organizational norms and should begin to identify with experienced organizational members.

Role Management. Having survived the accommodation process and acquired basic role behaviours, the member's attention shifts to fine tuning and actively managing his or her role in the organization. He or she might be expected to exercise some idiosyncrasy credits and modify the role to better serve the organization. This might require forming connections outside the immediate work group. And the organizational member must confront balancing the now-familiar organizational role with nonwork roles and family demands. Each of these experiences provides additional socialization to the role occupant, who might begin to internalize the norms and values that are prominent in the organization.

Now that we have seen a basic sketch of how socialization proceeds, let us look in greater detail at some of the key issues in the process.

The Naive New Member and the Psychological Contract

People seldom join organizations without expectations about what membership will be like. In fact, it is just such expectations that lead them to choose one career or job over another. Management majors have some expectations about what they will be doing when they become management trainees at Citicorp. Similarly, even 18-year-old army recruits have notions about what military life will be like.

Research indicates that people entering organizations hold many expectations that are inaccurate and often unrealistically high.[10] In one study of telephone operators, for example, researchers obtained people's expectations about the nature of the job *before* they started work. They also looked at these employees' perceptions of the actual job shortly *after* they started work. The results indicated that many perceptions were less favourable than expectations. A similar result occurred for students entering an MBA program.[11] Such changes, which are fairly common, support the notion that socialization has an important impact on new organizational members.

Why do new members often have unrealistic expectations about the organizations they join?[12] To some extent, occupational stereotypes, such as those we discussed in Chapter 3, could be responsible. The media often communicate such stereotypes. For example, a person entering nurses' training might have gained some expectations about hospital life from watching *General Hospital*. Those of us who teach might also be guilty of communicating stereotypes. After four years of study, the new management trainee at Citicorp might be dismayed to find that the emphasis is on *trainee* rather than *management!* Finally, unrealistic expectations may also stem from overzealous recruiters who paint rosy pictures in order to attract job candidates to the organization. Taken together, these factors demonstrate the need for socialization.

When people join organizations, they also have ideas about what they expect to receive from the organization and what they plan to give the organization in return. Such perceptions form what is known as the **psychological contract**. A psychological contract refers to beliefs held by employees concerning the reciprocal obligations between them and their organization.[13] For example, an employee might expect to receive rewards and promotions in return for hard work and loyalty.

Unfortunately, psychological contract violations appear to be a common occurrence. One study found that 55% of recent MBA graduates reported that some aspect of their psychological contract had been broken by their employer.[14] Contract violations occur when an employee perceives that his/her organization has failed to fulfill one or more promised obligations of the psychological contract. This often results in feelings of anger and betrayal and can have a negative effect on employees' work attitudes and behaviour.[15]

Why do psychological contract violations occur? As is the case with unrealistic expectations, recruiters are often tempted to promise more than their organization can provide in order to attract the best job applicants. In addition, newcomers often lack sufficient information to form accurate perceptions concerning their psychological contract. As a result, there will be some incongruence or differences in understandings between an employee and the organization about promised obligations. In addition, organizational changes, such as downsizing and restructuring, can cause organizations to knowingly break promises made to an employee that they are either unable or unwilling to keep.[16]

It is therefore important that newcomers develop accurate perceptions in the formation of a psychological contract. Many of the terms of the psychological contract are established during anticipatory socialization. Therefore, organizations need to ensure that truthful and accurate information about promises and obligations is communicated to new members before and after they join an organization. Incongruence and psychological contract violations are less likely in organizations where socialization is intense.[17] This further points to the need for socialization.

Psychological contract. Beliefs held by employees concerning the reciprocal obligations between them and their organization.

The Dilemmas of Socialization

Individuals enter organizations with a unique set of skills, interests, and attitudes. This fact of life poses interesting dilemmas for both the individual and the organization.

On the one hand, new members wish to maintain their individual identity and self-respect by retaining their unique qualities and building on them. On the other hand, they are also anxious to learn the ropes of the organization and use these unique qualities in a manner acceptable to peers and superiors. The organization and its experienced members also face a similar dilemma. On the one hand, new members need some encouragement to support the norms and role requirements of the organization. Without this support, organizational goals will be impossible to achieve because the firm or institution simply will not be *organized*. On the other hand, complete and total allegiance to existing norms and role requirements will render the organization dinosaur-like, unable to adapt to a changing environment. In this case, creative and innovative behaviours on the part of individual members are stifled, and existing norms and roles take on a life of their own.

These, then, are the dilemmas of socialization: How should individuals react to socialization practices? And how can organizations socialize members to an adequate extent without frustrating them or stifling their uniqueness?

From the individual's viewpoint, many people simply avoid joining organizations whose socialization practices are incompatible with their needs. Of course, this can be tricky business, given the inaccurate perceptions of organizational practices that many outsiders hold. Finding themselves at the mercy of socialization that does not meet their needs, individuals might effect a compromise or decide to seek employment elsewhere.

Organizations attempt to solve *their* socialization dilemmas by tailoring socialization methods to their particular needs. Intuitively, this seems reasonable. Somehow, the making of a priest seems different from the making of a stockbroker!

Under some circumstances, organizations are pretty much willing to make do with what they get in terms of recruits, that is, they attempt to build on the characteristics that the person brings into the setting rather than attempting radical socialization. Many volunteer organizations, such as charities and community groups, are like this, since they have little power over recruits. At the other extreme, some organizations have as their goal the radical socialization of members, hoping to strip them of old beliefs, values, and attitudes and get them to internalize new ones. Whether they are successful or not, prisons, mental hospitals, and religious orders have this orientation toward inmates, patients, and novitiates.[18]

Most business organizations tend to fall between these extremes. However, there has been a growing trend toward more extensive and rigorous socialization, especially in firms that are very concerned with quality and customer service. We will explore this later in the context of strong organizational cultures; now let us consider how organizations socialize new members.

Methods of Socialization

For various jobs, organizations differ in terms of *who* does the socializing, *how* it is done, and *how much* is done.

Reliance on External Agents

Organizations differ in the extent to which they make use of other organizations to help socialize their members. For example, hospitals do not develop experienced cardiologists from scratch. Rather, they depend on medical schools to socialize potential doctors in the basic role requirements of being a physician. Similarly, business firms rely on university business schools to send them recruits who think and act in a business-like manner. In this way, a fair degree of anticipatory socialization may exist before a person joins an organization. On the other hand, organizations such as police forces, the military, and religious institutions are less likely to rely on external socializers. Police academies, boot camps, and seminaries are set up as extensions of these organizations to aid in socialization.

Organizations that handle their own socialization are especially interested in maintaining the continuity and stability of job behaviours over a period of time. Conversely, those that rely on external agencies to perform anticipatory socialization are oriented toward maintaining the potential for creative, innovative behaviour on the part of members—there is less "inbreeding." Of course, reliance on external agents might present problems. The engineer who is socialized in university courses to respect design elegance might find it difficult to accept cost restrictions when he or she is employed by an engineering firm. For this reason, organizations that rely heavily on external socialization always supplement it with formal training and orientation or informal on-the-job training.

Realistic Job Previews

We noted earlier that new organizational members often harbour unrealistically inflated expectations about what their jobs will be like. When the job is actually begun, it fails to live up to these expectations, individuals experience "reality shock," and job dissatisfaction results. As a consequence, costly turnover is most likely to occur among newer employees who are unable to survive the discrepancy between expectations and reality. For the organization, this sequence of events represents a failure of socialization.

Realistic job previews. The provision of a balanced, realistic picture of the positive and negative aspects of a job to job applicants.

Obviously, organizations cannot control all sources of unrealistic job expectations, such as those provided by television shows and glorified occupational stereotypes. However, they *can* control those generated during the recruiting process by providing job applicants with realistic job previews. **Realistic job previews** provide a balanced, realistic picture of the positive and negative aspects of the job to job applicants.[19] Thus, they provide "corrective action" to expectations at the anticipatory socialization stage. Exhibit 8.3 compares the realistic job preview process with the traditional preview process that often sets expectations too high by ignoring the negative aspects of the job.

How do organizations design and conduct realistic job previews? Generally, they obtain the views of experienced employees and human resource officers about the positive and negative aspects of the job. Then, they incorporate these views into booklets or videotape presentations for applicants.[20] For example, a video presentation might involve interviews with job incumbents discussing the pros and cons of their jobs. Realistic previews have been designed for jobs as diverse as telephone operator, life insurance salesperson, Marine Corps recruit, and supermarket worker.

Toyota
www.toyota.com

Sometimes realistic previews use simulations to permit applicants to actually sample the work. One at Toyota USA's Georgetown, Kentucky, plant stresses the repetitive nature of the work and the need to be a team player. Applicants to Nissan's Smyrna, Tennessee, plant work many hours without pay to see what the work is really like.

Evidence shows that realistic job previews are effective in reducing expectations and turnover, and improving job performance.[21] What is less clear is exactly why turnover reduction occurs. Reduced expectations and increased job satisfac-

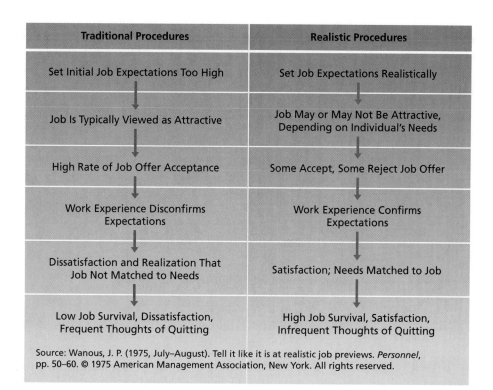

Traditional Procedures	Realistic Procedures
Set Initial Job Expectations Too High	Set Job Expectations Realistically
Job Is Typically Viewed as Attractive	Job May or May Not Be Attractive, Depending on Individual's Needs
High Rate of Job Offer Acceptance	Some Accept, Some Reject Job Offer
Work Experience Disconfirms Expectations	Work Experience Confirms Expectations
Dissatisfaction and Realization That Job Not Matched to Needs	Satisfaction; Needs Matched to Job
Low Job Survival, Dissatisfaction, Frequent Thoughts of Quitting	High Job Survival, Satisfaction, Infrequent Thoughts of Quitting

Source: Wanous, J. P. (1975, July–August). Tell it like it is at realistic job previews. *Personnel*, pp. 50–60. © 1975 American Management Association, New York. All rights reserved.

Exhibit 8.3
Traditional and realistic job previews compared.

tion are part of the answer. Less clear is whether realistic previews cause those not cut out for the job to withdraw from the application process.[22] Although the turnover reductions from realistic previews are small, they can result in substantial financial savings for organizations.[23] Providing realistic job previews can also help prevent psychological contract violations.[24]

Socialization Tactics

While realistic job previews are used primarily during the anticipatory stage of socialization, you might be wondering how organizations socialize newcomers during the encounter stage of socialization. Consider how the new hires are socialized at Trilogy Software. All of them go through training together as a group and attend formal classes at "Trilogy University." They know that their training will last three months, and they are trained by the company chairman and other veterans of the company. Training includes classes in various areas, such as programming languages, product plans, and marketing, followed by group projects that last for three weeks.

Clearly, there is a deliberate, conscious, and structured manner to the socialization of new hires at Trilogy Software. John Van Maanen and Edgar Schein developed a theory of socialization that helps us understand and explain the socialization process that is used at companies like Trilogy Software. They suggested that there are at least six **socialization tactics** that organizations can use to structure the early work experiences of newcomers. Each of the six tactics consists of a bipolar continuum.[25]

First, organizations can use a *collective* or an *individual* socialization tactic. When using the collective tactic, a number of new members are socialized as a group, going through the same experiences and facing the same challenges as is the case at Trilogy Software. Army boot camps, fraternity pledge classes, and training classes for salespeople and airline attendants are also common examples. In contrast, the individual tactic consists of socialization experiences that are tai-

Socialization tactics. The manner in which organizations structure the early work experiences of newcomers.

Some socialization tactics such as debasement and hazing are designed to strip new members of their old beliefs, values, and attitudes and get them to internalize new ones.

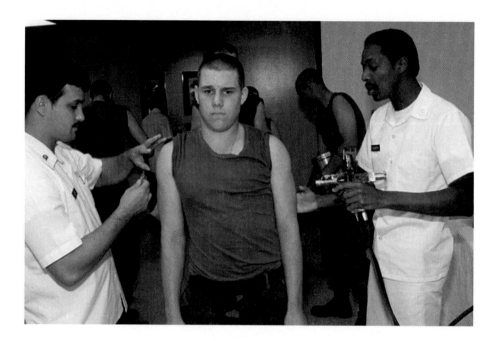

lor-made for each new member. Simple on-the-job training and apprenticeship to develop skilled craftspeople constitute individual socialization.

Socialization tactics can also be *formal* or *informal.* Formal tactics involve segregating newcomers from regular organizational members and providing them with formal learning experiences during the period of socialization. Informal tactics, however, do not distinguish a newcomer from more experienced members and rely more on informal and on-the-job learning. *Sequential* versus *random* tactics have to do with whether there is a clear sequence of steps or stages during the socialization process. With a sequential tactic, there is a fixed sequence of steps leading to the assumption of the role, compared with the random tactic in which there is an ambiguous or changing sequence. Socialization tactics can also be distinguished in terms of the existence of a time frame during which the socialization period lasts. If the socialization tactic is *fixed,* there is a time table for the assumption of the role. For example, at Trilogy Software, the training of new hires lasts for three months. If the tactic is *variable,* then there is no time frame to indicate when the socialization process ends and the newcomer assumes his/her new role. Socialization tactics also vary in terms of whether or not experienced members of the organization participate in the socialization of new members. The *serial* tactic refers to a process where newcomers are socialized by experienced members of the organization as is the case at Trilogy Software. The *disjunctive* tactic refers to a socialization process where role models and experienced organization members do not groom new members or "show them the ropes."

Finally, socialization tactics can be either *investiture* or *divestiture.* Divestiture tactics refer to what is also known as debasement and hazing. This is seen when organizations put new members through a series of experiences that are designed to humble them and strip away some of their initial self-confidence. Debasement is a way of testing the commitment of new members and correcting for faulty anticipatory socialization. Having been humbled and stripped of preconceptions, members are then ready to learn the norms of the organization. An extreme example is the rough treatment and shaved heads of Marine Corps recruits.

Not all debasement experiences are formal. The immediate work group might take it on itself to test the new member through informal hazing. For example, the group might ask a newly hired engineer to explain the plans for an impossible or "nonsense" electrical circuit. Similarly, fellow officers might send the rookie cop in alone to shake down a bar that is frequented by unfriendly bikers. Often, such experiences are designed to illustrate how group members must depend on each other.

Debasement experiences most commonly occur in entry-level jobs, whether blue-collar or white-collar. A new executive vice-president would be unlikely to suffer debasement unless he or she was entering a hostile environment. Sometimes organizations prefer not to use debasement or hazing as part of the socialization of newcomers. Rather, they employ the investiture socialization tactic which affirms the incoming identity and attributes of new hires rather than deny and strip them away. Organizations that carefully select new members for certain attributes and characteristics would be more likely to use this tactic.

Research on the six socialization tactics has found that they can be grouped into two separate patterns of socialization. *Institutionalized socialization* consists of collective, formal, sequential, fixed, serial, and investiture tactics. *Individualized socialization* consists of individual, informal, random, variable, disjunctive, and divestiture tactics. Institutionalized socialization reflects a more structured program of socialization and, as a result, will help reduce newcomers' feelings of uncertainty. On the other hand, individualized socialization reflects a relative absence of structure, and as a result, the early work experiences of newcomers will remain somewhat uncertain.[26]

On the basis of this description, it should be apparent to you that the socialization process at Trilogy Software is highly structured and more institutionalized than individualized. Why do you think that this was the approach used to socialize new hires? Well, just consider the intended outcome of Trilogy's socialization program—creative people who work well in teams, adapt to changes, and take chances. Institutionalized socialization tactics are effective in promoting organizational loyalty, esprit de corps, and uniformity of behaviour among those being socialized. This last characteristic is often very important. No matter where they are in the world, soldiers know whom to salute and how to do it. Similarly, air passengers need not expect any surprises from cabin attendants, thanks to the attendants' institutionalized socialization.

Institutionalized socialization tactics are especially effective in inducing uniform behaviour because there are so many models present who are undergoing the same experience. At Trilogy, new hires are socialized so that their attitudes and behaviour will be consistent with the organization's culture of creativity and risk taking. In addition, the individuals being socialized might pressure each other to toe the line and "do things right." Thus, in institutionalized socialization, one's peers prove to be especially potent sources of information. Consider the pressure and approval of peers at the roulette table during the Trilogy trip to Las Vegas. This follows from our earlier discussion of conformity.

When socialization is individualized, new members are more likely to take on the particular characteristics and style of their socializers. Thus, two newly hired real estate agents who receive on-the-job training from their bosses might soon think and act more like their bosses than like each other. As you can see, uniformity is less likely under individualized socialization.

Institutionalized socialization is always followed up by some individualized socialization as the member joins his or her regular work unit. For example, rookie police officers are routinely partnered with more experienced officers. At this point, they will begin to develop some individuality in the style with which they perform their jobs. This is certainly likely to be the case for the new hires at Trilogy Software once their three months of socialization and training have ended.

Research on socialization tactics tends to support the basic predictions regarding the effects of institutionalized/individualized socialization on newcomers' attitudes and behaviour. As well, institutionalized socialization tactics have been shown to result in lower role ambiguity and conflict, positive job satisfaction and organizational commitment, and lower turnover.[27]

The Role of the Mentor[28]

It should be apparent from our discussion of socialization tactics that supervisors and peers play an important role in the socialization process. While effective relationships between supervisors and subordinates obviously influence the socialization and career success of individuals within an organization, one particularly important relationship is that between a newcomer or apprentice and a mentor. A **mentor** is an older or more senior person in the organization who gives a junior person special attention, such as giving advice and creating opportunities to assist them during the early stages of their career. While someone other than the junior person's boss can serve as a mentor, often the supervisor is in a unique position to provide mentoring. Many research efforts have documented the importance of having a mentor when starting one's career and how it can influence career success.[29] Research on business school graduates has shown that having a mentor early in one's career is associated with increased promotional progress, higher salaries, and more satisfaction with career prospects later in one's career.[30]

Career Functions of Mentoring. A mentor provides many career-enhancing benefits to the young apprentice.[31] These benefits are made possible by the senior person's experience, status, knowledge of how the organization works, and influence with powerful people in the organization. The career functions of mentoring include:

- *Sponsorship*. The mentor might nominate the apprentice for advantageous transfers and promotions.
- *Exposure and visibility*. The mentor might provide opportunities to work with key people and see other parts of the organization.
- *Coaching and feedback*. The mentor might suggest work strategies and identify strengths and weaknesses in the apprentice's performance.
- *Developmental assignments*. Challenging work assignments a mentor can provide will help develop key skills and knowledge that are crucial to career progress.

Peers are infrequently in a position to be able to provide such career functions.

Psychosocial Functions of Mentoring. Besides helping directly with career progress, mentors can provide certain psychosocial functions that are helpful in developing the apprentice's self-confidence, sense of identity, and ability to cope with emotional traumas that can damage a person's effectiveness. These include:

- *Role modeling*. This provides a set of attitudes, values, and behaviours for the junior person to imitate.
- *Acceptance and confirmation*. The mentor can also provide encouragement and support and help the apprentice gain self-confidence.
- *Counseling*. This provides an opportunity to discuss personal concerns and anxieties concerning career prospects, work-family conflicts, and so on.

Can organizations formally assign mentors to apprentices and achieve the career benefits normally associated with more spontaneous informal mentor-

Mentor. An older or more senior person in the organization who gives a junior person special attention, such as giving advice and creating opportunities to assist them during the early stages of their career.

apprentice relationships? A number of organizations have implemented what they see as very successful formal mentorship programs.[32] Limited research on such programs concludes that formal programs are nearly as beneficial as informal relationships and are certainly more beneficial than not having a mentor.[33]

While all mentors, by definition, provide some subset of the career functions, mentors do not always provide these psychosocial functions. A network of close peers can go a long way in providing functions that one's mentor is not able to. People starting their careers should be aware of the importance of these career and psychosocial functions and attempt to establish a social network that will fulfill them. A mentor relationship is usually a key element in this broader set of relationships. To some extent, a supportive and well-connected social network can substitute for not having an effective mentor.[34]

Women and Mentors. One factor that inhibits women's career development, compared with their male counterparts, is the difficulty women have historically faced in establishing an apprentice-mentor relationship with a senior person in the organization.[35] The problem goes well beyond the traditional gender stereotyping we discussed in Chapter 3. It stems from the fact that senior people, who are in the best position to be mentors, are frequently men. A young woman attempting to establish a productive relationship with a senior male associate faces complexities that the male apprentice does not. Part of the problem is the lack of experience many male mentor candidates have in dealing with a woman in roles other than daughter, wife, or lover. Often, a woman's concerns are going to be different from those her male mentor experienced at that stage in his career. As a result, the strategies that he models might have limited relevance to the female apprentice. Perhaps the greatest complexity is associated with fears that their relationship will be perceived as involving sexual intimacy. Concerns about appearances and what others will say can make both people uncomfortable and get in the way of a productive relationship.

Because of these concerns, the prospective female apprentice faces more constraints than her male counterpart. Research has confirmed that cross-gender mentor-apprentice dyads are less likely to get involved in informal after-work social activities. These activities can help apprentices establish relationships with other influential people in a relaxed setting. Research also confirms that apprentices in a cross-gender dyad are less likely to see their mentor as a role model and, thereby, less likely to realize the developmental benefits of an effective model.[36]

How critical is mentoring to a woman's career? The research evidence suggests that mentoring is even more critical to women's career success than it is to men's. Women who make it to executive positions invariably had a mentor along the way. This is true for half to two-thirds of men executives.[37] Thus, for women with these career aspirations, finding a mentor appears to be a difficult but crucial task. The good news here is that there is some evidence that women work harder in an apprentice role and end up being more effective than men apprentices.[38] Also, as time goes on and more women progress into higher organizational levels, more same-gender mentoring relationships will be available for younger women.[39] For women who are unable to find an effective mentor, establishing an informed and supportive social network is a way to obtain some of the career and psychosocial functions we discussed above.

Race, Ethnicity, and Mentoring. Limited racial and ethnic diversity at higher levels of organizations constrain the mentoring opportunities available to younger minority group employees. Research shows that mentors tend to select apprentices who are similar to them in terms of race and nationality as well as gender.[40] While there are exceptions, research confirms that minority apprentices in cross-ethnic group mentoring relationships tend to report less assistance, compared with those with same-race mentors.[41] Cross-race mentoring relationships seem to focus on instrumental or career functions of mentoring (e.g., sponsorship, coaching, and feedback) and provide less psychosocial support functions (e.g., role modeling, counseling) than is generally seen in same-race dyads.[42] Although the increasing diversity of organizations makes this tendency less problematic, it suggests that minority group members should put extra efforts into developing a supportive network of peers who can provide emotional support and role modeling as well as the career functions.

Proactive Socialization

On the basis of what you have read so far in this chapter about the socialization of newcomers, you might have the impression that individuals are at the mercy of organizations in terms of becoming socialized and adjusted. This, however, is not the case. You may recall from Chapter 2, that individuals do not learn only from the actions of those in their environment. Rather, individuals also learn through their interactions and observations of others, and from their own self-management behaviour. In other words, newcomers can be proactive rather than passive during their socialization. **Proactive socialization** refers to the process in which newcomers play an active role in their own socialization through the use of a number of proactive socialization tactics.

One of the most important tactics that newcomers can employ to be proactive during socialization is to request feedback and seek information. Newcomers can acquire important feedback about their job performance and information about their work tasks, role, group, and the organization by requesting feedback, asking questions, and by observing the behaviour of co-workers and supervisors. Research has shown that newcomers' acquisition of information is positively related to their job attitudes and adjustment.[43] As well, the frequency of information seeking has been found to be positively related to task mastery, role clarity, social integration, job satisfaction, and job performance, and negatively related to intentions to leave.[44] To acquire information during socialization, newcomers have been found to rely primarily on observation followed by interpersonal sources. Supervisors are the information source most strongly related to positive socialization outcomes.[45]

In addition to information seeking, there are a number of other tactics that newcomers can use to be proactive during socialization. For example, recall from Chapter 2 that self-management involves the use of learning principles to manage one's own behaviour. Thus, newcomers can manage their own behaviour during socialization through the use of self-management. One study found that newcomers who engaged in self-management behaviour reported lower levels of anxiety and stress during their first month of work, and more positive work outcomes six months later.[46]

Other proactive socialization tactics that have been studied include networking, general socializing, building relationships with one's boss, negotiating job changes, career planning, seeking help or advice, communicating work goals and aspirations, developing skills, and working extra hours. Newcomers use of these proactive socialization tactics have been found to have a positive influence on their socialization.[47] Finally, newcomers can also be proactive by actively seeking a mentor. One study found that some newcomers were more likely to initiate and receive mentoring, and mentoring was positively related to career attainment and success.[48]

One of the goals of socialization is to ensure that new employees learn and understand the key beliefs, values, and assumptions of an organization's culture. With this in mind, consider "In Focus: *Socialization and Culture at Quad/Graphics*."

Proactive socialization. The process through which newcomers play an active role in their own socialization through the use of a number of proactive socialization tactics.

in focus ➠)) Socialization and Culture at Quad/Graphics

Socialization is a way of life for the workers at one of the largest printers in the United States. Quad/Graphics, headquartered in Pewaukee, Wisconsin, employs 10,700 people in 16 plants scattered from Georgia to Japan. The employee-owned company, founded in 1971 by a CEO who regularly peppers workers with e-mail missives he calls "Bonkersville Notes," is growing rapidly. It added 1,800 people in 1997.

But here, the half-day class in Quad Culture and the nine-week Quad Technologies course are not just for newcomers; they are for anyone who wants to go.

"Strictly speaking, 'orientation' is limited to the usual things—signing up for benefits, and teaching safety rules," says Claire Ho, Quad/Graphics' corporate communications manager. "Our concern was, with such a strong corporate culture, how do we continue to demonstrate and communicate this when we're growing so fast and expanding across the country? So we emphasize perpetuating the culture through actions."

Unusual actions, too. Like the navy-blue uniforms—kind of like a gas station attendant's, Ho confesses—that everyone wears, from CEO Harry Quadracci and vice-presidents down to press operators, secretaries, and customer service reps. "The president wears a bow tie with his," Ho says. This custom, in place since 1993, emphasizes the commonality of employee goals. "The uniforms says we're all production workers, no matter what our job," she says. "It really breaks down walls."

Then there are the on-site day-care facilities, medical clinics, and fitness centres (the latter staffed by fitness trainers). The free lawyers the company brings to some locations to help employees with personal legal issues like divorce or property disputes. The every-other-day employee newspaper, 12 to 16 pages long. The discounted bus program for people who commute to Quad/Graphics' mostly rural plants from bigger cities like Milwaukee. And the celebrations—the yearly black-tie affair at the president's house, and the "Bright Lights and Trumpets" ceremonies, complete with class ring and cake, that mark employees' 10-year anniversaries with the company.

These classes and celebrations are Quadracci's way of showing that communicating corporate culture is a priority for all Quad/Graphics employees, not just new hires, Ho says. If this blurs the line between orientation and on-the-job training, well, so be it.

Source: Excerpted from Ganzel, R. (1998, March). Putting out the welcome mat. *Training*, pp. 54-62.

Organizational Culture

The last several pages have been concerned with socialization into an organization. To a large degree, the course of that socialization both depends on and shapes the culture of the organization. Let us examine culture, a concept that has gained the attention of both researchers and practising managers.

Quad/Graphics
www.qg.com

What Is Organizational Culture?

At the outset, we can say that organizational culture is not the easiest concept to define. Informally, culture might be thought of as an organization's style, atmosphere, or personality. This style, atmosphere, or personality is most obvious when we contrast what it must be like to work in various organizations such as IBM, Sears, the U.S. Marine Corps, or the Toronto Blue Jays. Even from their mention in the popular press, we can imagine that these organizations provide very different work environments. Thus, culture provides uniqueness and social identity to organizations.

More formally, **organizational culture** consists of the shared beliefs, values, and assumptions that exist in an organization.[49] In turn, these shared beliefs, values, and assumptions determine the norms that develop and the patterns of behaviour that emerge from these norms. The term *shared* does not necessarily mean that members are in close agreement on these matters, although they might well be. Rather, it means that they have had uniform exposure to them and have

Organizational culture. The shared beliefs, values, and assumptions that exist in an organization.

"Wilkens, the next time we catch you coming to work in a suit and tie,
I'm afraid we're going to have to let you go."

some minimum common understanding of them. Several other characteristics of culture are important.

- Culture represents a true "way of life" for organizational members, who often take its influence for granted. Frequently, an organization's culture becomes obvious only when it is contrasted with that of other organizations or when it undergoes changes.

- Because culture involves basic assumptions, values, and beliefs, it tends to be fairly stable over time. In addition, once a culture is well established, it can persist despite turnover among organizational personnel, providing social continuity.

- The content of a culture can involve matters that are internal to the organization or external. Internally, a culture might support innovation, risk taking, or secrecy of information. Externally, a culture might support "putting the customer first" or behaving unethically toward competitors.

- Culture can have a strong impact on both organizational performance and member satisfaction.

Culture is truly a social variable, reflecting yet another aspect of the kind of social influence that we have been discussing in this chapter. Thus, culture is not simply an automatic consequence of an organization's technology, products, or size. For example, there is some tendency for organizations to become more bureaucratic as they get larger. However, the culture of a particular large organization might support an informal, nonbureaucratic atmosphere.

Can an organization have several cultures? The answer is yes. Often, unique **subcultures** develop that reflect departmental differences or differences in occupation or training.[50] A researcher who studied Silicon Valley computer companies found that technical and professional employees divided into "hardware types" and "software types." In turn, hardware types subdivided into engineers and technicians, and software types subdivided into software engineers and computer scientists. Each group had its own values, beliefs, and assumptions about how to design computer systems.[51] Effective organizations will develop an overarching culture that manages such divisions. For instance, a widely shared norm might exist that, in effect, says, "We fight like hell until a final design is chosen, and then we all pull together."

Subcultures. Smaller cultures that develop within a larger organizational culture that are based on differences in training, occupation, or departmental goals.

The "Strong Culture" Concept

Some cultures have more impact on the behaviour of organizational members than others. In a **strong culture**, the beliefs, values, and assumptions that make up the culture are both intense and pervasive across the organization.[52] In other words, the beliefs, values, and assumptions are strongly supported by the majority of members, even cutting across any subcultures that might exist. Thus, the strong culture provides great consensus concerning "what the organization is about" or what it stands for. In weak cultures, on the other hand, beliefs, values, and assumptions are less strongly ingrained and/or less widely shared across the organization. Weak cultures are thus fragmented and have less impact on organizational members. All organizations have a culture, although it might be hard to detect the details of weak cultures.

To firm up your understanding of strong cultures, let us consider thumbnail sketches of three organizations that are generally agreed to have strong cultures.

- *General Electric.* Under the leadership of CEO Jack Welch, this industrial giant, based in Fairfield, Connecticut, was transformed from a lethargic and inward-looking company to a fleet-of-foot global competitor with an openness to new ideas. GE became known for extremely high performance standards and its goal to be first or second in the world in all its businesses.

- *Southwest Airlines.* This Dallas-based company has turned a consistent profit in the turbulent airline industry by focusing on low-cost, short-distance flights. Southwest is known for fostering a family atmosphere that has inspired extremely high employee motivation and commitment.

- *3M.* This Minneapolis-based company produces tape, adhesives, abrasives, and building materials. The firm is known for its extreme dedication to product innovation. 3M rewards its employees for creativity and risk taking to this end, and accepts failure as part of the game.

Three points are worth emphasizing about these examples of strong cultures. First, an organization need not be big to have a strong culture. If its members

Strong culture. An organizational culture with intense and pervasive beliefs, values, and assumptions.

Southwest Airlines
www.southwest.com

The strong culture of Alliance Atlantis Communications Inc. has helped the company win more than 500 major awards in film and television including the Genie Award for the 1999 Best Motion Picture for its film "Sunshine".

agree strongly about certain beliefs, values, and assumptions, a small business, school, or social service agency can have a strong culture. Second, strong cultures do not necessarily result in blind conformity. For example, the strong culture at 3M supports and rewards *non*conformity in the form of innovation and creativity. Finally, General Electric, Southwest Airlines, and 3M are obviously successful organizations. Do strong cultures always result in organizational success? Before continuing, consider "In Focus: *Company's Beer Commercials Mimic Its Corporate Culture*."

Assets of Strong Cultures

Organizations with strong cultures have several potential advantages over those lacking such a culture.

Coordination. In effective organizations, the right hand (e.g., finance) knows what the left hand (e.g., production) is doing. The overarching values and assumptions of strong cultures can facilitate such communication. In turn, different

---

in focus ➛ ➜ Company's Beer Commercials Mimic Its Corporate Culture

If you think beer commercials depict a phony world in which young people are having way too much fun, drop by Encore Encore Strategic Marketing Ltd. It not only makes beer commercials. It could pass for one.

Its unique corporate culture—which stresses good times, openness, and a healthy dose of hard work—is one reason the small Toronto agency is reeling in some big accounts, to the chagrin of Canada's advertising establishment.

Its most recent victory was scooping the coveted Molson Canadian brand assignment away from MacLaren McCann Canada Inc., which had handled the brand since the sixties. Encore Encore also is in the running for Molson Export and Miller.

Encore Encore's head office, in a converted Victorian-style home in Toronto's upscale Yorkville district, looks ordinary enough from the outside. But its modus operandi is unusual, even in the self-conscious advertising world, where agencies wear their coolness as a badge of honour.

How many agencies have a 1976 Airstream trailer parked out back to serve as an extra office? Or a black Labrador named Phoenix who wanders from room to room, sniffing visitors? Or a vice-president of marketing who, apart from bringing his dog to work, looks like he just returned from the beach?

"Here, anything goes from a what-you-wear standpoint. There's not a lot of rules," explains Robert Peters who co-founded the agency in 1993 and sports a polo shirt, shorts, and tennis shoes (minus socks). Mr. Peters who, in addition to being

a marketer, is an accomplished pianist who plays in Encore Encore's house band and, according to one company employee, asked her to sing along while he played Piano Man on the office piano during her job interview.

"Don't get the idea Encore Encore is all fun and games," says co-founder Brad Weir. "It's very casual, very open, but very get-down serious when business is to be done." Its size (45 employees) and open culture gives it advantages over large agencies, he says. With less bureaucracy, it can react quickly, and clients have access to senior people, not just low-level staffers.

For all the emphasis on fun, employees say 10- or 12-hour days are not uncommon, particularly when big projects come along, such as Molson Canadian. Encore Encore's ads for the beer, which feature the tag line "Here's where we get Canadian," mimic its own culture, offering liberal helpings of young people, rock music, and good times.

Besides its accounts in Canada, Encore Encore does about 25 percent of its work in the United States, for clients such as Molson and Brown-Forman Beverages Worldwide of Louisville, Kentucky, better known as the maker of Jack Daniel's whisky. Encore Encore's owners will not provide precise figures, but they say revenue is between $5 and $10 million. Business will be up about 35 percent this year, they predict.

Source: Excerpted from Heinzl, J. (1999, May 26). At Encore, work is like an ad. *The Globe and Mail*, M1.

parts of the organization can learn from each other and can coordinate their efforts. This is especially important in decentralized, team-oriented organizations.

Comparing the General Motors Saturn organization to established GM divisions provides a good contrast in cultural strength and coordination. Saturn, which has a strong culture oriented toward customer service, received praise from the automotive press for its communication with customers and dealers when inevitable early model quality problems cropped up. When quality problems arose with the new Chevy Camaro and Pontiac Firebird, GM received praise for not shipping defective cars, but it was criticized for not communicating well with customers and dealers.[53] Ironically, GM developed Saturn, in part to serve as a cultural model for the established GM divisions that have long had rather fragmented cultures.

Conflict Resolution. You might be tempted to think that a strong culture would produce strong conflicts within an organization, that is, you might expect the intensity associated with strongly held assumptions and values to lead to friction among organizational members. There might be some truth to this. Nevertheless, sharing core values can be a powerful mechanism that helps to ultimately resolve conflicts, a light in a storm as it were. For example, in a firm with a core value of fanatical customer service, it is still possible for managers to differ about how to handle a particular customer problem. However, the core value will often suggest an appropriate dispute resolution mechanism—"Let's have the person who is closest to the customer make the final decision."

Financial Success. Does a strong culture pay off in terms of dollars and cents, that is, do the assets we discussed above get translated into bottom-line financial success? The answer seems to be yes, as long as the liabilities discussed below can be avoided.

One study of insurance companies found that firms whose managers responded more consistently to a culture survey (thus indicating agreement about the firm's culture) had greater asset and premium growth than those with disagreement.[54] Another study had members of six international accounting firms complete a value survey, the results of which you see in Exhibit 8.4. Because all firms were in the same business, there is some similarity to their value profiles (e.g., attention to detail is valued over innovation). However, close inspection shows that the six firms actually differ a good deal in their value profiles. Firms E and F tended to emphasize the work task values of detail and stability and to deemphasize a team orientation and respect for people. Comparatively, firms A, B, and C tended to emphasize these interpersonal relationship values. The author determined that firms E and F had much higher employee turnover rates, a fact that was estimated to cost each between $6 and $9 million a year, compared with firms A, B, and C.[55]

There is growing consensus that strong cultures contribute to financial success and other indicators of organizational effectiveness *when the culture supports the mission, strategy, and goals of the organization.*[56]

Liabilities of Strong Cultures

On the other side of the coin, strong cultures can be a liability under some circumstances.

Resistance to Change. The mission, strategy, or specific goals of an organization can change in response to external pressures, and a strong culture that was appropriate for past success might not support the new order, that is, the strong

Exhibit 8.4
Scores on organizational
culture values across six
accounting firms.

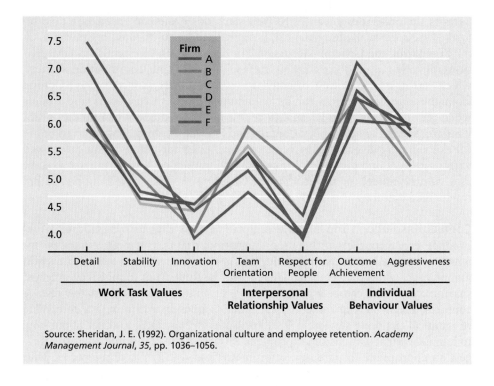

Source: Sheridan, J. E. (1992). Organizational culture and employee retention. *Academy Management Journal, 35*, pp. 1036–1056.

consensus about common values and appropriate behaviour that makes for a strong culture can prove to be very resistant to change. This means that a strong culture can damage a firm's ability to innovate.

An excellent example is the case of IBM. A strong culture dedicated to selling and providing excellent service for mainframe computers contributed to the firm's remarkable success. However, this strong culture also bred strong complacency that damaged the company's ability to compete effectively with smaller, more innovative firms. IBM's strong mainframe culture limited its competitiveness in desktop computing, software development, and systems compatibility.

Culture Clash. Strong cultures can mix as badly as oil and water when a merger or acquisition pushes two of them together under the same corporate banner.[57] Both General Electric and Xerox, large organizations with strong cultures of their own, had less than perfect experiences when they acquired small high-technology Silicon Valley companies with unique cultures. The merger of BankAmerica and Security Pacific resulted in a particularly strong culture clash. In each of these cases, the typical scenario concerns a freewheeling smaller unit confronting a more bureaucratic larger unit.

Pathology. Some strong cultures can threaten organizational effectiveness simply because the cultures are, in some sense, pathological.[58] Such cultures may be based on beliefs, values, and assumptions that support infighting, secrecy, and paranoia, pursuits that hardly leave time for doing business. Here is an example of an unsuccessful semiconductor firm whose culture exhibited considerable paranoia.

> The two founders took all kinds of precautions to prevent their ideas from being stolen. They fragmented jobs and processes so that only a few key people in the company really understood the products. They rarely subcontracted work. And they paid employees very high salaries to give them an incentive to stay with the firm. These three precautions combined to make Paratech's costs among the highest in the industry.[59]

Security Pacific
www.securitypacific.com

you be the manager

Maintaining the Culture at the Magic Kingdom

How does the Walt Disney Company attract and retain service employees and maintain excellent customer service despite low pay, curtailed individuality, rigorous rules, and routine work?

The Walt Disney Company empire includes the Disney Studios, Disneyland Resort in California, the Walt Disney World Resort in Florida, and a lucrative licensing arrangement for products based on Disney characters. There is universal agreement that Disney has been successful, especially in its theme parks and associated resorts, by virtue of an unwavering dedication to excellent customer service.

By all appearances, the task does not seem easy. The workforce is mostly young and not especially well paid. They are particularly likely to be scheduled to work on busy holidays and vacation periods, just when they would like to spend time with friends and family. Much of the work itself is basically routine and boring (try uttering "Welcome, Voyager" with conviction thousands of times a day to the hordes who visit Space Mountain!). Also, Disney has some of the most rigid grooming standards in the industry, forbidding beards, mustaches, and dangling jewellery. The company even provides samples of which basic black shoes are acceptable. The image here is clean-cut and conservative.

If individuality is discouraged, all-American friendliness is encouraged. Employees are expected to be friendly, polite, courteous, and helpful when they are in the presence of customers. They are told that they are players in a live performance and are part of a show in the Magic Kingdom. And all employees are responsible for

making the park guests feel welcomed, special, and happy. Customers must feel that they are in a magical place that is the most wonderful place in the world.

Disney relies heavily on promotion from within, even in its management ranks. Its white-collar turnover is low by any standard, and its turnover rate is well below average for hourly service employees. Disney has been so successful that firms such as General Motors and DuPont have sent executives to Disney-sponsored seminars to understand how Disney has managed to provide guests with such a clean, pleasant, friendly environment for all these years.

So, how does The Walt Disney Company attract and retain service employees despite low pay, curtailed individuality, rigorous rules, and fairly routine work while maintaining excellent customer service? According to some people at Disney, a magic ingredient called "pixie dust" inspires employees to provide first-rate customer service. You be the manager.

1. Is it possible for companies like The Walt Disney Company to find employees who will be dedicated and committed to a strong corporate culture like Disney's? How can The Walt Disney Company make sure that the people they hire will buy into the Disney culture?

2. Is it sufficient to hire the right people at Disney and then expect them to live up to the company's values and provide excellent customer service? What else should Disney do after employees have been hired to ensure that they are dedicated and committed to the Disney philosophy?

To find out Disney's secret, see The Manager's Notebook at the end of the chapter.

Sources: Burka, P. (1988, November 8). What they teach you at Disney U. *Fortune*, Special advertising section; Solomon, C. M. (1989), December). How does Disney do it? *Personnel*, 50–57; Van Maanen, J. V., & Kunda, G. (1989). "Real feelings": Emotional expression and organizational culture. *Research in Organizational Behaviour*, 11, 43–103; Blocklyn, P. L. (1988, December). Making magic: The Disney approach to people management. *Personnel*, pp. 28-35.

Contributors to the Culture

How are cultures built and maintained? In this section, we consider two key factors that contribute to the foundation and continuation of organizational cultures. Before continuing, please consult You Be the Manager.

CEO Frank Stronach of Magna International is a classic example of a founder whose values have shaped the organization's culture.

The Founder's Role. It is certainly possible for cultures to emerge over time without the guidance of a key individual. However, it is remarkable how many cultures, especially strong cultures, reflect the values of an organization's founder.[60] The imprint of Walt Disney on the Disney Company, Sam Walton on Wal-Mart, Ray Kroc on McDonald's, T. J. Watson on IBM, Frank Stronach on Magna International, and Bill Gates on Microsoft is obvious. As we shall see shortly, such imprint is often kept alive through a series of stories about the founder passed on to successive generations of new employees. This provides continuing reinforcement of the firm's core values. In a similar vein, most experts agree that top management strongly shapes the organization's culture. The culture will usually begin to emulate what top management "pays attention to." Sometimes, the culture begun by the founder can cause conflict when top management wishes to see an organization change directions. At Apple Computer, Steven Jobs nurtured a culture based on new technology and new products—innovation was everything. When top management perceived this strategy to be damaging profits, it introduced a series of controls and changes that led to Jobs's resignation as chairman.[61]

Socialization. The precise nature of the socialization process is a key to the culture that emerges in an organization, because socialization is the means by which individuals can learn the culture's beliefs, values, and assumptions. Weak or fragmented cultures often feature haphazard selection and a nearly random series of job assignments that fail to present the new hire with a coherent set of experiences. On the other hand, Richard Pascale of Stanford University notes that organizations with strong cultures go to great pains to expose employees to a careful step-by-step socialization process (Exhibit 8.5).[62]

- *Step 1—Selecting Employees.* New employees are carefully selected to obtain those who will be able to adapt to the existing culture, and realistic job previews are provided to allow candidates to deselect themselves. As an example, Pascale cites Procter & Gamble's series of individual interviews, group interviews, and tests for brand management positions.
- *Step 2—Debasement and Hazing.* Debasement and hazing provoke humility in new hires so that they are open to the norms of the organization.

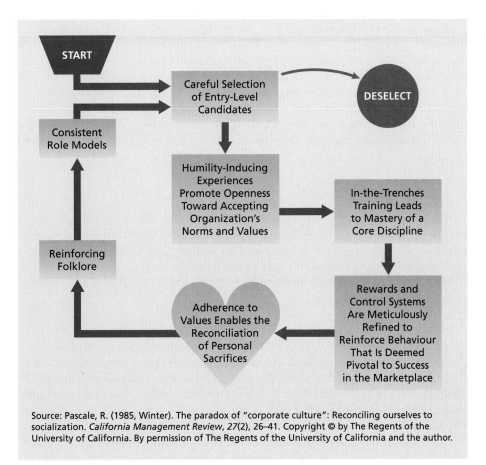

Source: Pascale, R. (1985, Winter). The paradox of "corporate culture": Reconciling ourselves to socialization. *California Management Review, 27*(2), 26–41. Copyright © by The Regents of the University of California. By permission of The Regents of the University of California and the author.

Exhibit 8.5
Socialization steps in strong cultures.

- *Step 3—Training "in the Trenches."* Training begins "in the trenches" so that employees begin to master one of the core areas of the organization. For example, even experienced MBAs will start at the bottom of the professional ladder to ensure that they understand how *this* organization works. At Lincoln Electric, an extremely successful producer of industrial products, new MBAs literally spend eight weeks on the welding line so that they truly come to understand and appreciate Lincoln's unique shopfloor culture. At Trilogy Software, the company chairman dedicates three months to training new employees so they can learn to become creative risk-takers.

- *Step 4—Reward and Promotion.* The reward and promotion system is carefully used to reinforce those employees who perform well in areas that support the goals of the organization.

- *Step 5—Exposure to Core Culture.* Again and again, the culture's core beliefs, values, and assumptions are asserted to provide guidance for member behaviour. This is done to emphasize that the personal sacrifices required by the socialization process have a true purpose.

- *Step 6—Organizational Folklore.* Members are exposed to folklore about the organization, stories that reinforce the nature of the culture. We examine this in more detail below.

- *Step 7—Role Models.* Identifying people as "fast-trackers" provides new members with role models whose actions and views are consistent with the culture. These role models serve as tangible examples for new members to imitate.

Pascale is careful to note that it is the *consistency* among these steps and their mutually reinforcing properties that make for a strong culture. Given that they are socializing theme park employees rather than rocket scientists, it is remarkable how many of these tactics the Disney company (profiled earlier in the You Be the Manager feature) uses. Selection is rigorous, and grooming standards serve as mild debasement. Everyone begins at the bottom of the hierarchy. Pay is low, but promotion is tied to performance. Folklore stresses core values ("Walt's in the park."). Better performers serve as role models at Disney University or in paired training.

Diagnosing a Culture

Earlier, we noted that culture represents a "way of life" for organizational members. Even when the culture is strong, this way of life might be difficult for uninitiated outsiders to read and understand. One way to grasp a culture is to examine the symbols, rituals, and stories that characterize the organization's way of life. For insiders, these symbols, rituals, and stories are mechanisms that teach and reinforce the culture.

Chaparral Steel
www.chaparralsteel.com

Symbols. At the innovative Chaparral Steel Company in Texas, employees have to walk through the human resources department to get to their lockers. Although this facilitates communication, it also serves as a powerful symbol of the importance that the company places on its human resources. For years, IBM's "respect for the individual" held strong symbolic value that was somewhat shaken with its first-ever layoffs. Such symbolism is a strong indicator of corporate culture.[63]

Some executives are particularly skilled at using symbols consciously to reinforce cultural values. CEO Carl Reichardt of Wells Fargo is known as a fanatic cost cutter. According to one story, Reichardt received managers requesting capital budget increases while sitting in a tatty chair. As managers made their cases, Reichardt picked at the chair's exposed stuffing, sending a strong symbolic message of fiscal austerity. This was in case they had missed the message conveyed by having to pay for their own coffee and their own office Christmas decorations![64]

Rituals. Observers have noted how rites, rituals, and ceremonies can convey the essence of a culture.[65] For example, at Tandem, a California computer company, Friday afternoon "popcorn parties" are a regular ritual. (For years, these parties were called "beer busts." We will leave it up to you to decide whether this change of names is symbolic of a major cultural shift!) The parties reinforce a "work hard, play hard" atmosphere and reaffirm the idea that weekly conflicts can be forgotten. The Disney picnics, beach parties, and employee nights are indicative of a peer-oriented, youth-oriented culture. At Mary Kay Cosmetics, elaborate "seminars" with the flavour of a Hollywood premiere combined with a revival meeting are used to make the sales force feel good about themselves and the company. Pink Cadillacs and other extravagant sales awards reinforce the cultural imperative that any Mary Kay woman can be successful. Rituals need not be so exotic to send a cultural message. In some companies, the annual performance review is an act of feedback and development. In others, it might be viewed as an exercise in punishment and debasement.

Stories. As we noted above, the folklore of organizations—stories about past organizational events—is a common aspect of culture. These stories, told repeatedly to successive generations of new employees, are evidently meant to communicate "how things work," whether they are true, false, or a bit of both. Anyone who has spent much time in a particular organization is familiar with such stories, and they often appear to reflect the uniqueness of organizational cultures. However, research indicates that a few common themes underlie many organizational stories.

- Is the big boss human?
- Can the little person rise to the top?
- Will I get fired?
- Will the organization help me when I have to move?
- How will the boss react to mistakes?
- How will the organization deal with obstacles?[66]

Issues of equality, security, and control underlie the stories that pursue these themes. Also, such stories often have a "good" version, in which things turn out well, and a "bad" version, in which things go sour. For example, there is a story that Ray Kroc, McDonald's founder, canceled a franchise after finding a single fly in the restaurant.[67] This is an example of a sour ending to a "how will the boss react to mistakes?" story. Whether the story is true or not, its retelling is indicative of one of the core values of the McDonald's culture—a fanatical dedication to clean premises.

the manager's notebook

Maintaining the Culture at the Magic Kingdom

The Walt Disney Company is an excellent example of how an organization effectively communicates and instills its cultural values. Disney does this through an extensive selection process and an elaborate socialization and training program.

1. Before employees even begin to learn about the Disney way, they must pass through a rigorous selection process. Every applicant for an hourly job at Disney is given an eight-to-ten minute preliminary interview. Because Disney's strong corporate culture is not for everyone, a film is shown to warn job candidates about Disney expectations and the standards of grooming and behaviour. Realistic job previews are used to ensure that new hires have realistic expectations about the work. Applicants who accept Disney's conditions of employment and pass the preliminary interview are then given a 45-minute job interview. Elaborate group selection interviews stress attitudes and personality over academic credentials. During busy periods of the year, such as Christmas and summer vacations, employees from different areas of Disney assist in the hiring of temporary employees. For salaried employees, internal promotion is used to fill 60 to 80 percent of positions, and a very careful and elaborate selection process is used to fill the remaining 20 to 40 percent.

2. Once job applicants are accepted for a job at The Walt Disney Company, they attend "Disney University" and take the Traditions course, which exposes them to the lingo and lore of Disney. In the Disney vocabulary, they are hosts or cast members, not employees, and customers are guests. Similarly, their uniforms are costumes, and they are "on stage" when they are in the public part of the park. There are group tests ("Name the Seven Dwarfs in Snow White") to foster teamwork. Cast members learn that their role in making people happy includes picking up any stray trash and being able to answer any conceivable question a guest asks. When everyone does this, employees serve as role models for each other. After the group training at Disney U., employees are assigned to experienced peers who train them in the techniques of their specific job assignment. This "paired training," along with the Traditions class, is much more extensive than is typical in most service organizations. Thus, guests have little reason to expect poor performance from a new cast member, who has been well versed in Disney's values regarding family entertainment. Cast members who demonstrate outstanding service and the traditional Disney values are acknowledged with company and division awards. In the old days, the cry "Walt's in the park" would motivate cast members to do their very best. Today, Disney U. trainers often exhort students with "Walt's always in the park now." The spirit lives.

Summary

- There are two basic forms of social dependence. Information dependence means that we rely on others for information about how we should think, feel, and act. Effect dependence means that we rely on rewards and punishments provided by others. Both contribute to conformity to norms.

- There are several motives for conformity to social norms. One is compliance, in which conformity occurs mainly to achieve rewards and avoid punishment. It is mostly indicative of effect dependence. Another motive for conformity is identification with other group members. Here, the person sees himself or herself as similar to them and relies on them for information. Finally, conformity may be motivated by the internalization of norms, and the person is no longer conforming simply because of social dependence.

- Conformity to norms is most likely when others will be aware of deviance, when the opposition is large and unanimous, and when the issue at hand is ambiguous. High-status group members have generally achieved their status by conformity to group norms. However, they may deviate on a particular issue by exercising idiosyncrasy credits that they have built up by previous conformity. Low-status members who are new to the group are especially likely to exhibit conformity, while those rejected by the group have nothing to gain by conformity.

- Organizational members learn norm and role requirements through stages of socialization. Some organizations rely on other organizations to do a certain amount of anticipatory socialization, while others handle the process themselves. Some rely on institutionalized socialization tactics, in which new members learn the ropes as a group, while others socialize new members on an individual basis and use more individualized socialization tactics. Also, realistic job previews can help new members cope with initial unrealistic expectations. Mentors can assist new members during socialization and influence their career success, and new members can play an active part in their socialization through the use of proactive socialization tactics.

- Organizational culture consists of the shared beliefs, values, and assumptions that exist in an organization. Subcultures can develop that reflect departmental or occupational differences. In strong cultures, beliefs, values, and assumptions are intense, pervasive, and supported by consensus.

- Potential assets of a strong culture include good coordination, appropriate conflict resolution, and financial success.

- Potential liabilities of a strong culture include inherent pathology, resistance to change, and culture clash when mergers or acquisitions occur.

- An organization's founder and its socialization practices can strongly shape a culture. Symbols, rituals, and stories are often useful in diagnosing a culture.

Discussion Questions

1. Compare and contrast information dependence with effect dependence. Under which conditions should people be especially information dependent? Under which conditions should people be especially effect dependent?

2. Describe an instance of social conformity that you have observed in an organizational setting. Did compliance, identification, or internalization motivate this incident? Were the results beneficial for the organization? Were they beneficial to the individual involved?

3. Imagine that a large organization is charged with making illegal financial contributions to a political campaign. What are the situational factors that might prompt executives to conform to such organizational norms at the expense of societal norms that stand against such behaviour?

4. Consider how you were socialized into the college or university where you are taking your organizational behaviour course. Did you have some unrealistic expectations? Where did your expectations come from? What outside experiences prepared you for college or university? Are you experiencing institutionalized or individualized socialization? What are some proactive socialization tactics that you can employ to facilitate your socialization?

5. What are the pros and cons of providing realistic job previews for a job that is objectively pretty bad?

6. Imagine that you are starting a new business in the retail trade. You are strongly oriented toward providing excellent customer service. What could you do to nurture a strong organizational culture that would support such a mission?

7. Discuss the advantages and disadvantages of developing a strong organizational culture.

8. Discuss some socialization practices that build a strong organizational culture.

?　9. What are the implications of social learning theory for social influence and socialization? Discuss the practical implications of each component of social learning theory (i.e., modeling, self-efficacy, and self-management) for the socialization of new organization members.

?　10. Refer to the models of attitude change described in Chapter 4. What are the implications of each model for changing an organization's culture? If you wanted to change the culture of an organization, what would be the best approach?

Experiential Exercise

The Organizational Culture–Values Survey

The purpose of the Organizational Culture–Values Survey is for you to learn about those values that are most important to you and to develop a values profile of yourself. You can also compare your values with those of a current or previous organization where you were employed. By comparing the rankings of each list you can determine the degree of fit or match between your values and those of the organization.

First, rank the values in the order of most importance to you. Place the number 1 next to the value you feel is most important and the number 16 next to the one you think is least important. Then number the second and fifteenth and so on. Second, do the same thing for your current organization if you are employed or the most recent organization where you were last employed.

Your Values	Organizational Values	Difference
___ Ambition	___ Ambition	___
___ Broadmindedness	___ Broadmindedness	___
___ Competence	___ Competence	___
___ Cheerfulness	___ Cheerfulness	___
___ Cleanliness	___ Cleanliness	___
___ Courage	___ Courage	___
___ Helpfulness	___ Helpfulness	___
___ Honesty	___ Honesty	___
___ Imagination	___ Imagination	___
___ Independence	___ Independence	___
___ Intelligence	___ Intelligence	___
___ Obedience	___ Obedience	___
___ Politeness	___ Politeness	___
___ Responsibility	___ Responsibility	___
___ Self-control	___ Self-control	___
___ Tolerance	___ Tolerance	___

Scoring and Interpretation

Compare your values profile to the values orientation of your organization. For each value, calculate the difference between the two rankings in the space indicated, and then calculate a total difference score. A small difference indicates a better fit or match between your values and those of your organization. Large differences indicate a lack of fit or a mismatch. Research indicates that a good fit or match between an employee's values and those of the organization is positively related to job attitudes and behaviour.

To facilitate class discussion and your understanding of values and organizational culture, consider the following issues.

1. How different are your values from the values of your organization, and what are the implications of this for your job attitudes and behaviour?

2. How can an understanding of the values that are most important to you assist in your decision to join an organization?

3. What are the implications for organizations that hire employees whose values differ from those of the organization, and what should they do about it?

Source: The scale is from Hoffman, R., & Ruemper, F. (1997). *Organizational Behaviour: Canadian Cases and Exercises*, 3rd ed. Toronto: Captus Press Inc.

Case Incident

The Reality Shock

Soon after starting his new job, Jason began to wonder about the challenging work he was supposed to be doing, the great co-workers he was told about, and the ability to attend training and development programs. None of these things seemed to be happening as he had expected. To make matters worse, he had spent most of the first month working on his own and reading about the organization's mission, history, policies, and so on. Jason was beginning to wonder if this was the right job and organization for him. He was feeling very dissatisfied and seriously thinking about quitting.

1. Explain how Jason's anticipatory socialization might be contributing to his disappointment and job attitudes. How might this situation have been prevented?

2. Given Jason's current situation, is there anything the organization can do to prevent Jason from quitting?

Case Study

Changing the Culture at AMR Corp. and American Airlines

Fort Worth-based AMR Corp. and American Airlines are on a roll. In 1998, it had record profits and record revenues. American was the second-largest airline in the world, the most profitable by a wide margin and a market dominator. Travellers were practically fighting for the right to buy tickets, and ticket prices were some of the highest since deregulation 20 years ago. In fact, by virtually every measure, one could fairly say that there had never been a better time in American's history. With all this good news, you would think that new CEO Don Carty would be happy to maintain the status quo.

But the 52-year old, Canadian-born Carty is trying something new, something that has never been done at American. He is trying to change the way the company's 120,000 employees feel about their company. He wants the American of the not-too-distant future to be not only a great airline, but also a great airline to work for.

"American's people have always had great pride in the company, at least when talking to others outside the company. That's a legacy from the days of Mr. C. R.," Carty said, referring to C.R. Smith, American's paternalistic founder, who served as chief executive for 35 years. "But it's really more than that. This company has always had that sense of 'eliteness'."

Unfortunately, Carty said, that sense of being part of an elite, trail-blazing standard-setting company has rarely been translated into the kind of "love" for the company that employees of industry maverick Southwest Airlines, for example, seem to have for their company. "And that is management's fault," he said.

"Even though most of our people are very proud to be a part of this very well-known, well-respected company, some, maybe even most, of our people have just never had a sense that this was a great place to work because they never felt that management cared about them," he said.

So, Carty is trying to change that, to make American—and AMR—a company that its people can love because it is

a company that cares about and responds to their needs. He wants to create a kinder, gentler corporate culture. To that end, he has spent much of his first eight months as CEO preaching to workers and managers alike about the importance of building not only professional skills and competencies, but also the enthusiasm and the love and respect for each other that he believes has been missing within American.

Few within the company doubt Carty's sincerity. But in the minds of some, he still has to overcome his long association with former CEO Robert Crandall, whose success was always shadowed by the deep dislike many employees had for him. "It goes all the way back to C.R. Smith, who while paternalistic and caring in his own way, was very tough and no-nonsense," said Edward Starkman, an analyst at SBC Warburg Dillion Read. "And that attitude was certainly expanded on by both Al Casey and Bob Crandall after C.R. American has always been managed with an 'inside-out approach.' It has done what it has wanted to in order to achieve its corporate goals and has given customers and employees only what management thought they needed in order for the company to achieve its corporate goals." Carty is promoting "a very big change in the fundamental character of the company," Starkman said.

"Personally, I believe Don Carty is sincere," said Rich La Voy, president of the 9,000-member Allied Pilots Association at American. "He is changing the tone of conversations. We have cordial, civil conversations. Nobody is screaming at each other. On that level, the relationship is good and getting better." "I think most everybody involved with him from our organization likes the guy personally. But they also know that he was never more than an arm's length away from every decision ever made up there before. So they're waiting to see if he'll really do what he said."

According to Jack Britain, an associate professor of management at the University of Texas at Dallas and a consultant on managing culture, organizational, and economic change, "There has been such a strong command-and-control culture in that organization that everybody is reluctant to step out and take risks, exercise initiative. If Mr. Carty can, by tweaking the corporate culture there, unlock that potential, then real productivity improvements and service quality improvements can be made. And that, no doubt, would find its way to the company's bottom line."

Indeed, Carty said he believes that employees who are happy and feel secure will deliver better customer service. "Look, I don't think we've focused hard enough on it in the past," he said. "We've talked a lot about the importance of service. We've trained. We've spent a lot of money on training and on the selection of our people. We've paid our people a lot of money."

And although he said he believes American employees deliver better service than the company's domestic competitors, "I don't think we've fully marshalled and harnessed the capability of our people by building the kind of enthusiasm we're capable of building for this company. I believe the employees do love this company and they just want to be turned on," Carty said. He believes that if they can turn on their employees and engender their enthusiasm, "they will help us find ways to provide better service and ways to save money doing it."

For any company that has a reputation for being less than employee-friendly, creating change is a big task. For American, it is a mammoth undertaking, one that will take years to complete, if ever. That is because employee attitudes grow out of a corporate culture that, in many cases, is older than the employees themselves and which has been strongly reinforced over the years.

Carty says he already sees a glimmer of change in employees' attitudes. He cites as evidence the rejection by the airline's 14,000 airport and reservations agents of the Communications Workers of America's effort to unionize them.

"We have been working diligently to create a culture of cooperation and enthusiasm among all employees," Carty said. "I believe the result of this election is a message from our passenger-service agents that we are moving in the right direction."

Yet, Carty said he knows it will take more than talk to make permanent changes to the corporate culture of a company as large, as diverse, and as spread out as American. "The ultimate measure of whether or not we're managing the company consistent with what we say is going to be our behaviour, not our words."

1. Compare and contrast the "old" culture of AMR Corp. and American Airlines and the "new" culture that Don Carty wants to create.

2. Do you think that Don Carty should change the culture at AMR Corp. and American Airlines? Is a change in culture likely to improve employee attitudes and the quality of service? Will it improve productivity?

3. Comment on some of the things that Don Carty is doing to change the culture. How effective do you think his approach is for changing the company's culture?

4. What are some of the major obstacles facing Don Carty in his attempt to change the company's culture?

5. What are some of the things that Don Carty should do in order to change the culture? If it was up to you, would you want to change the culture, and if so, what are some of the things that you would do?

Source: Excerpted from Reed, D. (1999, January 30). Changing the company-worker relationship. *The Gazette*, p.17. (Knight Rider Newspapers).

Chapter 9

Leadership

SOUTHWEST AIRLINES began operations in Dallas in 1971. Within two years, it was turning a profit, and it has done so every year since in a turbulent industry where even its strongest competitors have had many unprofitable years. And thanks to American Airlines closing its hub in Nashville in 1995, Southwest is now the number one carrier in Nashville and the most successful airline in North America. Part of Southwest's success formula has been its ability to exploit profitable market niches. Although the airline has specialized in short-hop, low-fare flights in the southwest states, it has recently begun to expand into long-haul routes and now serves 55 cities. In exchange for the low fares, loyal passengers have been willing to forego onboard food, assigned seating, and baggage forwarding. In turn, this lack of complication allows Southwest to turn flights around at the gate quickly and fly more segments per day. This efficient use of its Boeing 737 aircraft makes Southwest the most efficient, lowest-cost carrier in the industry. Although intelligent operations are part of Southwest's key to success, they would not work without loyalty, commitment, and a corporate culture that stresses customer service, innovation, and "family orientation" among employees. Industry observers are in strong agreement that these competitive advantages are due, in large part, to the leadership of Southwest's founder and CEO Herb Kelleher. Kelleher, a bawdy, fun-loving man with a ready smile, knows many of the company's 29,000 employees personally. Unlike most businesses, Southwest gives priority to employees rather than customers. Southwest does not scrimp on the salaries and benefits of its highly productive employees. Salaries are roughly comparable with other carriers, there is a lucrative profit-sharing program, and training is state-of-the-art. The company, according to the authors of The 100 Best Companies to Work for in America, is one of the 10 best employers.

Southwest Airlines' Herb Kelleher

Southwest Airlines employees credit much of the company's success to the leadership of CEO Herb Kelleher, who supports a corporate culture based on customer service, innovation, and "family orientation" among employees.

Under Kelleher's vision, Southwest hires people for their positive attitudes and cooperative values. Then, it empowers them to do what they have to do to continue to top the Department of Transportation's list for on-time flights and customer satisfaction. For example, check-in personnel can permit customers with restricted-date tickets to fly immediately in the case of family emergencies. Innovative personnel developed a series of amusing games to entertain customers during delays caused by bad weather. The Harley-riding fun-loving Kelleher serves as a strong role model for such actions. At the same time, he clarifies what is important in more serious matters by personally approving all expenses over $1,000 and personally reviewing all pilot performance evaluations, emphasizing the joint importance of low costs and flight safety. The teamwork at Southwest is illustrated by pilots' willingness to load baggage, shuttle wheelchairs, and tidy up planes on layovers.

Some have likened the Southwest employee loyalty to a cult, a comparison that does not bother Kelleher. In a video prepared to rally his troops against a competitive threat from United Airlines to its California shuttle routes, Kelleher combined the style of an evangelist with that of General George Patton.

Recently, Southwest employees paid $60,000 for a humorous full-page ad in *USA Today* to honour Kelleher on Boss's Day. Among other things, they thanked him for singing at their holiday party, but for singing only once a year!

The airline's ad agency recently designed a billboard with the message "Herb Nonstop" to honour him for being named CEO of the Year in *Chief Executive* magazine's survey of American CEOs.[1]

Learning Objectives

After reading Chapter 9, you should be able to:

1 Define and discuss the role of both formal and emergent leadership.

2 Explain and critically evaluate the trait approach to leadership.

3 Explain the concepts of consideration and initiating structure and their consequences.

4 Describe and evaluate Fiedler's Contingency Theory.

5 Describe and evaluate House's Path-Goal Theory.

6 Explain how and when to use participative leadership.

7 Discuss the merits of transformational leadership and charisma.

8 Discuss the merits of developmental leadership.

9 Describe and evaluate global and strategic leadership.

10 Explain the concepts of leadership neutralizers and substitutes.

Herb Kelleher is a case study in successful leadership. But exactly what is leadership, and what makes a leader successful? Would Kelleher be successful in some other leadership situation? These are the kinds of issues that this chapter tackles.

First, we will define leadership and find out if we can identify special leadership traits. After this, we will explore how leaders emerge in groups. Next, we will examine the consequences of various leadership behaviours and examine theories contending that effective leadership depends on the nature of the work situation. Following this are discussions of participation, transformational leadership, developmental leadership, and global and strategic leadership. We will conclude by critically evaluating the importance of leadership in organizations.

What Is Leadership?

A recent issue of *Fortune* magazine illustrates the perceived importance of leadership in business and public affairs. The cover story profiles America's toughest bosses and debates the merits of their tyrannical leadership styles. Another story, about total quality management, stresses the absolute necessity for CEOs to be visibly involved if such programs are to be successful. A recent article in *Report on Business Magazine* suggests that leadership will increasingly make the difference between success and failure for many organizations, and corporations in North America spend approximately $15 billion a year to make their leaders more effective.[2]

Leadership. The influence that particular individuals exert on the goal achievement of others in an organizational context.

Leadership occurs when particular individuals exert influence on the goal achievement of others in an organizational context. Thus, *Fortune* debates the merits of "tough" influence and highlights the necessity of CEO influence in steering TQM efforts. Effective leadership exerts influence in a way that achieves organizational goals by enhancing the productivity, innovation, satisfaction, and commitment of the workforce.

In theory, *any* organizational member can exert influence on other members, thus engaging in leadership. In practice, though, some members are in a better position to be leaders than others. Individuals with titles such as manager, executive, supervisor, and department head occupy formal or assigned leadership roles. As part of these roles they are *expected* to influence others, and they are given specific authority to direct subordinates. Of course, the presence of a formal leadership role is no guarantee that there is leadership. Some managers and supervisors fail to exert any influence on others. These people will usually be judged ineffective leaders. Thus, leadership involves going beyond formal role requirements to influence others.

Individuals might also emerge to occupy informal leadership roles. Since informal leaders do not have formal authority, they must rely on being well liked or being perceived as highly skilled in order to exert influence. In this chapter we will concentrate on formal leadership, although we will consider informal leadership as well.

The (Somewhat Elusive) Search for Leadership Traits

Throughout history, social observers have been fascinated by obvious examples of successful interpersonal influence, whether the consequences of this influence were good, bad, or mixed. Individuals such as Henry Ford, Martin Luther King, Jr., Barbara Jordan, Ralph Nader, and Joan of Arc have been analyzed and reanalyzed to discover what made them leaders and what set them apart from less successful leaders. The implicit assumption here is that those who become leaders and do a good job of it possess a special set of traits that distinguish them from the masses of followers. While philosophers and the popular media have advocated such a position for centuries, trait theories of leadership did not receive serious scientific attention until the 1900s.

Research on Leadership Traits

During World War I the U.S. military recognized that it had a leadership problem. Never before had the country mounted such a massive war effort, and able officers were in short supply. Thus, the search for leadership traits that might be useful in identifying potential officers began. Following the war, and continuing

Saturn chair and president Cynthia Trudell and president and CEO Jacques Bougie of Alcan are examples of effective leaders.

through World War II, this interest expanded to include searching for leadership traits in populations as diverse as school children and business executives. Some studies tried to differentiate traits of leaders and followers, while others were a search for traits that predicted leader effectiveness or distinguished lower-level leaders from higher-level leaders.[3]

Traits. Individual characteristics such as physical attributes, intellectual ability, and personality.

Just what is a trait, anyway? **Traits** are personal characteristics of the individual, including physical characteristics, intellectual ability, and personality. Research has shown that many, many traits are not associated with whether people become leaders or how effective they are. However, research also shows some traits are associated with leadership. There is a list of these traits in Exhibit 9.1.[4] As you might expect, leaders (or more successful leaders) tend to be higher than average on these dimensions, although the connections are not very strong. Notice that the list portrays a high energy person who really wants to have an impact on others but at the same time is smart and stable enough not to abuse his or her power. Interestingly, this is a pretty accurate summary description of Southwest Airlines' Herb Kelleher.

Many prominent firms use personality tests and assessment centres to measure leadership traits when making hiring and promotion decisions. However, there are some aspects to the trait approach that limit its ultimate usefulness.

Limitations of the Trait Approach

Even though some traits appear to be related to leadership, there are several reasons why the trait approach is not the best means of understanding and improving leadership.

In many cases, it is difficult to determine whether traits make the leader or the opportunity for leadership produces the traits. For example, do dominant individuals tend to become leaders, or do employees become more dominant *after* they successfully occupy leadership roles? This distinction is important. If the former is true, we might wish to seek out dominant people and appoint them to leadership roles. If the latter is true, this strategy will not work.

Even if we know that dominance, intelligence, or tallness is associated with effective leadership, we have few clues about what dominant or intelligent or tall people *do* to influence others successfully. As a result, we have little information about how to train and develop leaders and no way to diagnose failures of leadership.

The most crucial problem of the trait approach to leadership is its failure to take into account the *situation* in which leadership occurs. Intuitively, it seems reasonable that top executives and first-level supervisors might require different traits to be successful. Similarly, physical prowess might be useful in directing a logging crew but irrelevant to managing a team of scientists.

Exhibit 9.1
Traits associated with leadership effectiveness.

Intelligence
Energy
Self-confidence
Dominance
Motivation to lead
Emotional stability
Honesty and integrity
Need for achievement

Lessons from Emergent Leadership

The trait approach is mainly concerned with what leaders *bring* to a group setting. The limitations of this approach gradually promoted an interest in what leaders *do* in group settings. Of particular interest were the behaviours of certain group members that caused them to *become* leaders. As we shall see, this study of emergent leadership gives us some good clues about what formally assigned or appointed leaders must do to be effective.

Imagine that a grass-roots organization has assembled to support the election of a local politician to the state legislature. In response to a newspaper ad, 30 individuals show up, all of whom admire Jonathan Greed, the aspiring candidate.

The self-appointed chairperson begins the meeting and asks for volunteers for various subcommittees. The publicity subcommittee sounds interesting, so you volunteer and find yourself with six other volunteers, none of whom knows the others. Your assigned goal is to develop an effective public relations campaign for Greed. From experience, you are aware that someone will emerge to become the leader of this group. Who will it be?

Without even seeing your group interact, we can make a pretty good guess as to who will become the leader. Quite simply, it will be the person who *talks* the most, as long as he or she is perceived as having relevant expertise.[5] Remember, leadership is a form of influence, and one important way to influence the group is speaking a lot. What would the "big talker" talk about? Probably about planning strategy, getting organized, dividing labour, and so on—things to get the task at hand accomplished. We often call such a leader a **task leader** because he or she is most concerned with accomplishing the task at hand.

Suppose the group members are also asked who they *liked* the most in the group. Usually, there will be a fair amount of agreement, and the nominated person might be called the **social-emotional leader**. Social-emotional influence is more subtle than task influence, and it involves reducing tension, patching up disagreements, settling arguments, and maintaining morale.

In many cases, the task and social-emotional leadership roles are performed by the same group member.[6] In some instances, though, two separate leaders emerge to fill these roles. When this happens, these two leaders usually get along well with each other and respect each other's complementary skills.[7]

The emergence of two leadership roles has been noted again and again in a wide variety of groups. This suggests that task leadership and social-emotional leadership are two important functions that must occur in groups. On the one hand, the group must be structured and organized to accomplish its tasks. On the other hand, the group must stick together and function well as a social unit, or the best structure and organization will be useless. Thus, in general, leaders must be concerned with both the social-emotional and task functions. Furthermore, organizations almost never appoint *two* formal leaders to a work group. Thus, the formal appointed leader must often be concerned with juggling the demands of two distinct roles.

There is an important qualifier to the preceding paragraph. It should be obvious that task and social-emotional functions are both especially important in the case of newly developing groups. However, for mature, ongoing groups, one leadership role might be more important than the other. For example, if group members have learned to get along well with each other, the social-emotional role might decrease in importance. Also, the two leadership roles may have different significance in different situations. Suppose a team of geologists is doing a routine series of mineral prospecting studies in a humid, bug-infested jungle. In this case, its leader might be most concerned with monitoring morale and reducing tensions provoked by the uncomfortable conditions. If the team becomes lost, task leadership should become more important—a logical plan for finding the way must be developed.

Task leader. A leader who is concerned with accomplishing a task by organizing others, planning strategy, and dividing labour.

Social-emotional leader. A leader who is concerned with reducing tension, patching up disagreements, settling arguments, and maintaining morale.

The Behaviour of Assigned Leaders

We turn now to the behaviour of assigned or appointed leaders, as opposed to emergent leaders. What are the crucial behaviours such leaders engage in, and how do these behaviours influence subordinate performance and satisfaction? In other words, is there a particular *leadership style* that is more effective than other possible styles?

Consideration and Initiating Structure

The most involved, systematic study of leadership to date was begun at Ohio State University. The Ohio State researchers began by having subordinates describe their superiors along a number of behavioural dimensions. Statistical analyses of these descriptions revealed that they boiled down to two basic kinds of behaviour—consideration and initiating structure.

Consideration is the extent to which a leader is approachable and shows personal concern for subordinates. The considerate leader is seen as friendly, egalitarian, and protective of group welfare. Obviously, consideration is related to the social-emotional function discovered in studies of emergent leadership.

Initiating structure is the degree to which a leader concentrates on group goal attainment. The structuring leader stresses standard procedures, schedules the work to be done, and assigns subordinates to particular tasks. Clearly, initiating structure is related to the task function revealed in studies of emergent leadership.

Theoretically, consideration and initiating structure are not incompatible. Presumably, a leader could be high, low, or average on one or both dimensions. Given our earlier discussion of emergent leadership functions, you might assume that a leader who is high on both dimensions would be the most effective. In the next section, we shall consider this possibility.

The Consequences of Consideration and Structure

The association between leader consideration, leader initiating structure, and subordinate responses has been the subject of hundreds of research studies. At first glance, the results of these studies seem confusing and often contradictory.[8] Sometimes consideration seems to promote satisfaction or high performance, and sometimes it does not. Sometimes structure prompts satisfaction or performance, and sometimes it does not. However, when we consider the particular *situation* in which the leader finds himself or herself, a clearer picture emerges.

- When subordinates are under a high degree of pressure due to deadlines, unclear tasks, or external threat, initiating structure increases satisfaction and performance. (Soldiers stranded behind enemy lines should perform better under directive leadership.)

- When the task itself is intrinsically satisfying, the need for high consideration and high structure is generally reduced. (The teacher who really enjoys teaching should be able to function with less social-emotional support and less direction from the principal.)

- When the goals and methods of performing the job are very clear and certain, consideration should promote subordinate satisfaction, while structure should promote dissatisfaction. (The job of refuse collection is clear in goals and methods. Here, subordinates should appreciate social support but view excessive structure as redundant and unnecessary.)

- When subordinates lack knowledge as to how to perform a job, or the job itself has vague goals or methods, consideration becomes less important, while initiating structure takes on additional importance. (The new astronaut recruit should appreciate direction in learning a complex, unfamiliar job.)[9]

As you can see, the effects of consideration and initiating structure depend on characteristics of the task, the subordinate, and the setting in which work is performed. Thus, the leader who is high in both consideration and structure will not always perform better than other types of leaders.[10] In some cases, one type of behaviour or the other might be unhelpful or even damaging to subordinate performance or satisfaction.

Consideration. The extent to which a leader is approachable and shows personal concern for subordinates.

Initiating structure. The degree to which a leader concentrates on group goal attainment.

Situational Theories of Leadership

We have referred to the potential impact of the situation on leadership effectiveness several times. Specifically, *situation* refers to the *setting* in which influence attempts occur. This setting includes the nature of the subordinates, the nature of the task they are performing, and characteristics of the organization. The two leadership theories below consider situational variables that seem especially likely to influence leadership effectiveness.

Fiedler's Contingency Theory

Fred Fiedler of the University of Washington has spent over three decades developing and refining a situational theory of leadership called **Contingency Theory**.[11] This name stems from the notion that the association between *leadership orientation* and *group effectiveness* is contingent on (depends on) the extent to which the *situation is favourable* for the exertion of influence. In other words, some situations are more favourable for leadership than others, and these situations require different orientations on the part of the leader.

Leadership Orientation. Fiedler has measured leadership orientation by having leaders describe their **Least Preferred Co-Worker (LPC)**. This person may be a current or past co-worker. In either case, it is someone with whom the leader has had a difficult time getting the job done. To obtain an LPC score, the troublesome co-worker is described on eighteen scales of the following nature:

PLEASANT :_ :_ :_ :_ :_ :_ :_ :_ : UNPLEASANT
        8 7 6 5 4 3 2 1

FRIENDLY :_ :_ :_ :_ :_ :_ :_ :_ : UNFRIENDLY
        8 7 6 5 4 3 2 1

The leader who describes the LPC relatively favourably (a high LPC score) can be considered *relationship* oriented, that is, despite the fact that the LPC is or was difficult to work with, the leader can still find positive qualities in him or her. On the other hand, the leader who describes the LPC unfavourably (a low

Contingency Theory. Fred Fiedler's theory that states that the association between leadership orientation and group effectiveness is contingent on how favourable the situation is for exerting influence.

Least Preferred Co-Worker. A current or past co-worker with whom a leader has had a difficult time accomplishing a task.

Situational theories of leadership explain how leadership style must be tailored to the demands of the task and the qualities of subordinates.

LPC score) can be considered *task* oriented. This person allows the low-task competence of the LPC to colour his or her views of the personal qualities of the LPC ("If he's no good at the job, then he's not good, period.").

Fiedler has argued that the LPC score reveals a personality trait that reflects the leader's motivational structure. High LPC leaders are motivated to maintain interpersonal relations, while low LPC leaders are motivated to accomplish the task. Despite the apparent similarity, the LPC score is *not* a measure of consideration or initiating structure. These are observed *behaviours,* while the LPC score is evidently an *attitude* of the leader toward work relationships.

Situational Favourableness. Situational favourableness is the "contingency" part of Contingency Theory, that is, it specifies when a particular LPC orientation should contribute most to group effectiveness. According to Fiedler, a favourable leadership situation exists when the leader has a high degree of control and when the results of this control are very predictable. Factors that affect situational favourableness, in order of importance, are the following:

- *Leader-member relations.* When the relationship between the leader and the group members is good, the leader is in a favourable situation to exert influence. Loyal, supportive subordinates should trust the leader and follow his or her directives with little complaint. A poor relationship should damage the leader's influence and even lead to insubordination or sabotage.

- *Task structure.* When the task at hand is highly structured, the leader should be able to exert considerable influence on the group. Clear goals, clear procedures to achieve these goals, and straightforward performance measures enable the leader to set performance standards and hold subordinates responsible ("Fill 10 of these crates an hour."). When the task is unstructured ("Devise a plan to improve the quality of life in our city."), the leader might be in a poor position to evaluate subordinate work or to prove that her approach is superior to that of the group.

- *Position power.* Position power is formal authority that is granted by the organization to tell others what to do. The more position power the leader holds, the more favourable is the leadership situation. In general, committee chairpersons and leaders in volunteer organizations have weak position power. Managers, supervisors, and military officers have strong position power.

In summary, the situation is most favourable for leadership when leader-member relations are good, the task is structured, and the leader has strong position power—for example, a well-liked army sergeant who is in charge of servicing jeeps in the base motor pool. The situation is least favourable when leader-member relations are poor, the task is unstructured, and the leader has weak position power—for instance, the disliked chairperson of a voluntary homeowner's association who is trying to get agreement on a list of community improvement projects.

The Contingency Model. Under what conditions is one leadership orientation more effective than another? As shown in Exhibit 9.2, we can arrange the possible combinations of situational factors into eight octants, which form a continuum of favourability. The model indicates that a task orientation (low LPC) is most effective when the leadership situation is very favourable (octants I, II, and III) *or* when it is very unfavourable (octant VIII). On the other hand, a relationship orientation (high LPC) is most effective in conditions of medium favourability (octants IV, V, VI, and VII). Why is this so? In essence, Fiedler argues that leaders can "get away" with a task orientation when the situation is favourable—

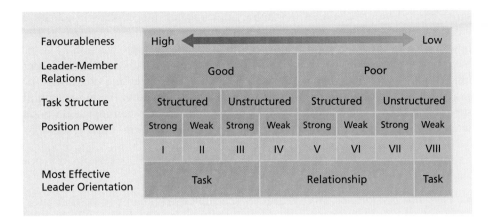

Exhibit 9.2
Predictions of leader
effectiveness from Fiedler's
Contingency Theory of
leadership.

subordinates are "ready" to be influenced. Conversely, when the situation is very unfavourable for leadership, task orientation is necessary to get anything accomplished. In conditions of medium favourability, the boss is faced with some combination of an unclear task or a poor relationship with subordinates. Here, a relationship orientation will help to make the best of a situation that is stress provoking but not impossibly bad.

Evidence and Criticism. The conclusions about leadership effectiveness in Exhibit 9.2 are derived from many studies that Fiedler summarizes.[12] However, the Contingency Theory has been the subject of as much debate as any theory in organizational behaviour.[13] Fiedler's explanation for the superior performance of high LPC leaders in the middle octants is not especially convincing, and the exact meaning of the LPC score is one of the great mysteries of organizational behaviour. It does not seem to be correlated with other personality measures or predictive of specific leader behaviour. It now appears that a major source of the many inconsistent findings regarding Contingency Theory is the small sample sizes that researchers used in many of the studies. Advances in correcting for this problem statistically have led recent reviewers to conclude that there is reasonable support for the theory.[14] However, Fiedler's prescription for task leadership in octant II (good relations, structured task, weak position power) seems contradicted by the evidence, suggesting that his theory needs some adjustment.

House's Path-Goal Theory

Robert House, building on the work of Martin Evans, has proposed a situational theory of leadership—Path-Goal Theory.[15] Unlike Fiedler's Contingency Theory, which relies on the somewhat ambiguous LPC trait, **Path-Goal Theory** is concerned with the situations under which various leader *behaviours* are most effective.

The Theory. Why did House choose the name Path-Goal for his theory? According to House, the most important activities of leaders are those that clarify the paths to various goals of interest to subordinates. Such goals might include a promotion, a sense of accomplishment, or a pleasant work climate. In turn, the opportunity to achieve such goals should promote job satisfaction, leader acceptance, and high effort. Thus, *the effective leader forms a connection between subordinate goals and organizational goals.*

House argues that to provide *job satisfaction* and *leader acceptance*, leader behaviour must be perceived as immediately satisfying or as leading to future

Path-Goal Theory. Robert House's theory concerned with the situations under which various leader behaviours (directive, supportive, participative, achievement-oriented) are most effective.

satisfaction. Leader behaviour that subordinates see as unnecessary or unhelpful will be resented. House contends that to promote subordinate *effort*, leaders must make rewards dependent on performance and ensure that subordinates have a clear picture of how they can achieve these rewards. To do this, the leader might have to provide support through direction, guidance, and coaching. For example, the bank teller who wishes to be promoted to supervisor should exhibit superior effort when his boss promises a recommendation contingent on good work and explains carefully how the teller can do better on his current job.

Leader Behaviour. Path-Goal Theory is concerned with four specific kinds of leader behaviour. These include:

- *Directive behaviour.* Directive leaders schedule work, maintain performance standards, and let subordinates know what is expected of them. This behaviour is essentially identical to initiating structure.

- *Supportive behaviour.* Supportive leaders are friendly, approachable, and concerned with pleasant interpersonal relationships. This behaviour is essentially identical to consideration.

- *Participative behaviour.* Participative leaders consult with subordinates about work-related matters and consider their opinions.

- *Achievement-oriented behaviour.* Achievement-oriented leaders encourage subordinates to exert high effort and strive for a high level of goal accomplishment. They express confidence that subordinates can reach these goals.

According to Path-Goal Theory, the effectiveness of each set of behaviours depends on the situation which the leader encounters.

Situational Factors. Path-Goal Theory has concerned itself with two primary classes of situational factors—subordinate characteristics and environmental factors. Exhibit 9.3 illustrates the role of these situational factors in the theory. Put simply, the impact of leader behaviour on subordinate satisfaction, effort, and acceptance of the leader depends on the nature of the subordinates and the work environment. Let us consider these two situational factors in turn, along with some of the theory's predictions.

According to the theory, different types of subordinates need or prefer different forms of leadership. For example:

- Subordinates who are high need achievers (Chapter 5) should work well under achievement-oriented leadership.

- Subordinates who prefer being told what to do should respond best to a directive leadership style.

- When subordinates feel that they have rather low task abilities, they should appreciate directive leadership and coaching behaviour. When they feel quite

Exhibit 9.3
The Path-Goal Theory of leadership.

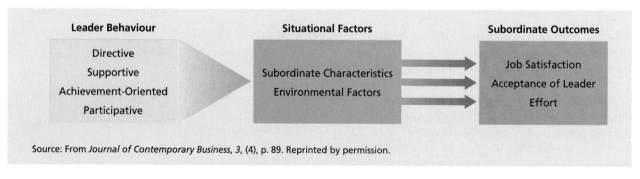

Source: From *Journal of Contemporary Business, 3,* (4), p. 89. Reprinted by permission.

capable of performing the task, they will view such behaviours as unnecessary and irritating.

As you can observe from these examples, leaders might have to tailor their behaviour to the needs, abilities, and personalities of individual employees.

Also, according to the theory, the effectiveness of leadership behaviour depends on the particular work environment. For example:

- When tasks are clear and routine, subordinates should perceive directive leadership as a redundant and unnecessary imposition. This should reduce satisfaction and acceptance of the leader. Similarly, participative leadership would not seem to be useful when tasks are clear, since there is little in which to participate. Obviously, such tasks are most common at lower organizational levels.

- When tasks are challenging but ambiguous, subordinates should appreciate both directive and participative leadership. Such styles should clarify the path to good performance and demonstrate that the leader is concerned with helping subordinates to do a good job. Obviously, such tasks are most common at higher organizational levels.

- Frustrating, dissatisfying jobs should increase subordinate appreciation of supportive behaviour. To some degree, such support should compensate for a disliked job, although it should probably do little to increase effort.

As you can see from these examples of environmental factors, effective leadership should *take advantage of* the motivating and satisfying aspects of jobs while *offsetting or compensating for* those job aspects that demotivate or dissatisfy. At Southwest Airlines, Herb Kelleher has managed to develop an appropriate mix of supportive, achievement-oriented, and participative leadership.

Evidence and Criticism. In general, there is some research support for most of the situational propositions discussed above. In particular, there is substantial evidence that supportive or considerate leader behaviour is most beneficial in supervising routine, frustrating, or dissatisfying jobs and some evidence that directive or structuring leader behaviour is most effective on ambiguous, less-structured jobs.[16] The theory appears to work better in predicting subordinate job satisfaction and acceptance of the leader than in predicting subordinate performance.[17]

Before continuing, pause and consider the "You Be the Manager: *Managers at Domino's Go to Boot Camp to Become Better Leaders.*"

Participative Leadership: Involving Subordinates in Decisions

In the discussion of Path-Goal Theory, we raised the issue of participative leadership. Because this is such an important topic, let us devote further attention to participation.

What Is Participation?

At a very general level, **participative leadership** means involving subordinates in making work-related decisions. The term *involving* is intentionally broad. Participation is not a fixed or absolute property, but a relative concept. This is illustrated in Exhibit 9.4. Here, we see that leaders can vary in the extent to which

Participative leadership.
Involving subordinates in making work-related decisions.

you be the manager

Managers at Domino's Go to Boot Camp to Become Better Leaders

They dress in army fatigues and spend 24 hours a day with each other in the woods.

Fast food outlets like Domino's Pizza require a high degree of standardization in order to respond to many orders that must be completed in a short period of time. The tasks are highly structured and routine and involve taking orders, preparing the orders, and then delivering them. Managers must schedule work, maintain performance standards, and let subordinates know what is expected of them. Many of the employees are young and have minimal education and work experience.

Given the nature of the work and the characteristics of the employees, what type of leadership style and behaviour will be most effective and how should Domino's train its leaders? Management training and leadership development has become big business today with many companies like Domino's spending thousands of dollars to train their managers each year. However, not all managers attend the type of boot camp leadership training that they do at Domino's Pizza. Domino's spends approximately $2,300 for each manager to attend a four-day training program, in which managers, dressed in army fatigues and combat boots, spend 24 hours

a day with each other in the woods, eating, sleeping, and not showering.

Consider the experiences of one group of 18 Domino's managers. Each day began at dawn and ended around 2 a.m. The exercises included a reconnaissance mission in search of enemy troops; raiding the enemy's camp, and showering it with pink paint while screaming and cussing at the top of their lungs and being awakened by the sound of paint balls smashing against their tent in the middle of the night. Many CEOs including Citicorp's John Reed and NationsBank's Hugh McColl attribute their success in the business world to the lessons they learned in the armed forces. Perhaps sending managers like those at Domino's for a few days in a simulated boot camp will make them more effective leaders. But can a few days playing war games with paint-ball rifles make you a better leader? You be the manager.

1. Do you think that this type of boot camp training will make Domino's managers more effective leaders? What do the situational theories of leadership tell us?

2. What are some of the general factors that constrain the transfer of any leadership training to the job?

To find out more about leadership training at Domino's, turn to The Manager's Notebook at the end of the chapter.

Source: Based on Brown, E. (1998, September, 28). War games to make you better at business. *Fortune*, pp. 291–296.

Domino's Pizza
www.dominos.com

they involve subordinates in decision making. Minimally, participation involves obtaining subordinate opinions before making a decision oneself. Maximally, it allows subordinates to make their own decisions within agreed-on limits. As the "area of freedom" on the part of subordinates increases, the leader is behaving in a more participative manner. There is, however, an upper limit to the area of subordinate freedom available under participation. Participative leadership should not be confused with the *abdication* of leadership, which is almost always ineffective.

Participation can involve individual subordinates or the entire group of subordinates that reports to the leader. For example, participation on an individual basis might work best when setting performance goals for particular subordinates, planning subordinate development, or dealing with problem employees. On the other hand, the leader might involve the entire work group in decision making when determining vacation schedules, arranging for telephone coverage during lunch hour, or deciding how to allocate scarce resources, such as travel money or secretarial help. As these examples suggest, the choice of an individual or group participation strategy should be tailored to specific situations.

Potential Advantages of Participative Leadership

Just why might participation be a useful leadership technique? What are its potential advantages?

Motivation. Participation can increase the motivation of subordinates.[18] In some cases, participation permits them to contribute to the establishment of work goals and to decide how they can accomplish these goals. It might also occur to you that participation can increase intrinsic motivation by enriching subordinates' jobs. In Chapter 6, you learned that enriched jobs include high-task variety and increased subordinate autonomy. Participation adds some variety to the job and promotes autonomy by increasing the "area of freedom" (Exhibit 9.4).

Quality. Participation can enhance quality in at least two ways. First, an old saying argues that "two heads are better than one." While this is not always true, there do seem to be many cases in which "two heads" (participation) lead to higher-quality decisions than the leader could make alone.[19] In particular, this is most likely when subordinates have special knowledge to contribute to the decision. In many research and engineering departments, it is common for the professional subordinates to have technical knowledge that is superior to that of their boss. This occurs either because the boss is not a professional or because the boss's knowledge has become outdated. Under these conditions, participation in technical matters should enhance the quality of decisions.

Participation can also enhance quality because high levels of participation often empower employees to take direct action to solve problems without checking every detail with the boss. You will recall from Chapter 6 that empowerment gives employees the authority, opportunity, and motivation to take initiative and solve problems.

Exhibit 9.4
Subordinate participation in decision making can vary.

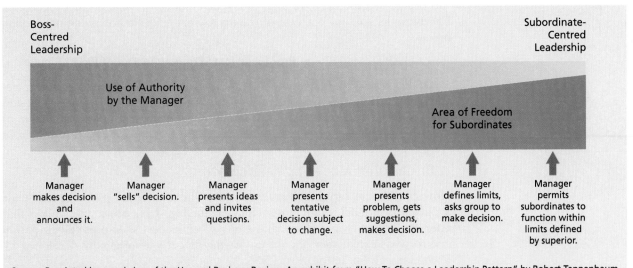

Acceptance. Even when participation does not promote motivation or increase the quality of decisions, it can increase the subordinates' acceptance of decisions. This is especially likely when issues of *fairness* are involved.[20] For example, consider the problems of scheduling vacations or scheduling telephone coverage during lunch hours. Here, the leader could probably make high-quality decisions without involving subordinates. However, the decisions might be totally unacceptable to the employees because they perceive them as unfair. Involving subordinates in decision making could result in solutions of equal quality that do not provoke dissatisfaction. Public commitment and ego involvement probably contribute to the acceptance of such decisions.

Potential Problems of Participative Leadership

You have no doubt learned that every issue in organizational behaviour has two sides. Consider the potential difficulties of participation.

Time and Energy. Participation is not a state of mind. It involves specific behaviours on the part of the leader (soliciting ideas, calling meetings), and these behaviours use time and energy. When a quick decision is needed, participation is not an appropriate leadership strategy. The hospital emergency room is not the place to implement participation on a continuous basis!

Loss of Power. Some leaders feel that a participative style will reduce their power and influence. Sometimes, they respond by asking subordinates to make trivial decisions of the "what colour shall we paint the lounge" type. Clearly, the consequences of such decisions (for motivation, quality, and acceptance) are near-zero. A lack of trust in subordinates and a fear that they will make mistakes is often the hallmark of an insecure manager. On the other hand, the contemporary call for flatter hierarchies and increased teamwork make such sharing of power inevitable.

Lack of Receptivity or Knowledge. Subordinates might not be receptive to participation. When the leader is distrusted, or when a poor labour climate exists, they might resent "having to do management's work." Even when receptive, subordinates might lack the knowledge to contribute effectively to decisions. Usually, this occurs because they are unaware of *external constraints* on their decisions. For example, consider the case of the toy factory with the following production process:

$$\text{PARTS MADE} \longrightarrow \text{PARTS PAINTED} \longrightarrow \text{PARTS ASSEMBLED}$$

In this factory, participation among the paint crew led them to establish elevated production levels that led to problems for the parts makers and toy assemblers. Management was forced to take control of production levels, and most of the painters quit.[21]

A Situational Model of Participation

How can leaders capitalize on the potential advantages of participation while avoiding its pitfalls? Victor Vroom and Arthur Jago have presented a model that attempts to specify in a practical manner when leaders should use participation and to what extent they should use it (the model was originally developed by Vroom and Philip Yetton).[22]

Vroom and Jago begin with the recognition that there are various degrees of participation that a leader can exhibit. For issues involving the entire work group, the following range of behaviours is plausible (A stands for autocratic, C for consultative, and G for group):

AI. You solve the problem or make the decision yourself, using information available to you at the time.

AII. You obtain the necessary information from your subordinates, then decide the solution to the problem yourself. You may or may not tell your subordinates what the problem is in getting the information from them. The role played by your subordinates in making the decision is clearly one of providing the necessary information to you, rather than generating or evaluating alternative solutions.

CI. You share the problem with the relevant subordinates individually, getting their ideas and suggestions without bringing them together as a group. Then you make the decision, which may or may not reflect your subordinates' influence.

CII. You share the problem with your subordinates as a group, obtaining their collective ideas and suggestions. Then you make the decision, which may or may not reflect your subordinates' influence.

GII. You share the problem with your subordinates as a group. Together you generate and evaluate alternatives and attempt to reach agreement (consensus) on a solution. Your role is much like that of chairman. You do not try to influence the group to adopt "your" solution, and you are willing to accept and implement any solution which has the support of the entire group.[23]

Which of these strategies is most effective? According to Vroom and Jago, this depends on the situation or problem at hand. In general, the leader's goal should be to make high-quality decisions to which subordinates will be adequately committed without undue delay. To do this, he or she must consider the questions in Exhibit 9.5. The quality requirement (QR) for a problem might be low if it is very unlikely that a technically bad decision could be made or all feasible alternatives are equal in quality. Otherwise, QR is probably high. The commitment requirement (CR) is likely to be high if subordinates are very concerned about which alternative is chosen or if they will have to actually implement the decision. The problem is structured (ST) when the leader understands the current situation, the desired situation, and how to get from one to the other. Unfamiliarity, uncertainty, and novelty in any of these matters reduces problem structure. The other questions in Exhibit 9.5 are fairly self-explanatory. Notice, however, that all are oriented toward preserving either decision quality or commitment to the decision.

By tracing a problem through the decision tree, the leader encounters the prescribed degree of participation for that problem. In every case, the tree shows the fastest approach possible (i.e., the most autocratic) that still maintains decision quality and commitment. In many cases, if the leader is willing to sacrifice some speed, a more participative approach could stimulate subordinate development (as long as quality or commitment is not threatened).

The original decision model developed by Vroom and Yetton, on which the Vroom and Jago model is based, has substantial research support.[24] Following the model's prescriptions is more likely to lead to successful managerial decisions than unsuccessful decisions. The model has been used frequently in management development seminars.

Does Participation Work?

Now we come to the bottom line—does participative leadership result in beneficial outcomes? There is substantial evidence that employees who have the opportunity

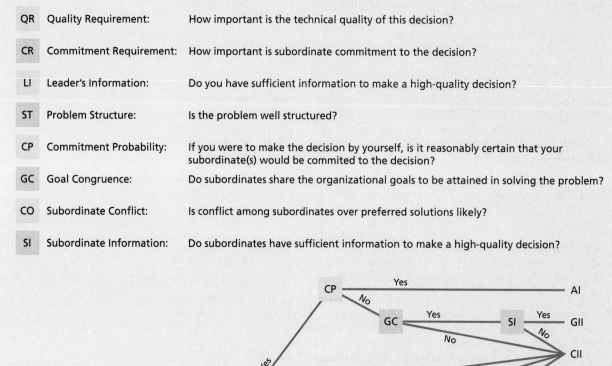

QR	Quality Requirement:	How important is the technical quality of this decision?
CR	Commitment Requirement:	How important is subordinate commitment to the decision?
LI	Leader's Information:	Do you have sufficient information to make a high-quality decision?
ST	Problem Structure:	Is the problem well structured?
CP	Commitment Probability:	If you were to make the decision by yourself, is it reasonably certain that your subordinate(s) would be commited to the decision?
GC	Goal Congruence:	Do subordinates share the organizational goals to be attained in solving the problem?
CO	Subordinate Conflict:	Is conflict among subordinates over preferred solutions likely?
SI	Subordinate Information:	Do subordinates have sufficient information to make a high-quality decision?

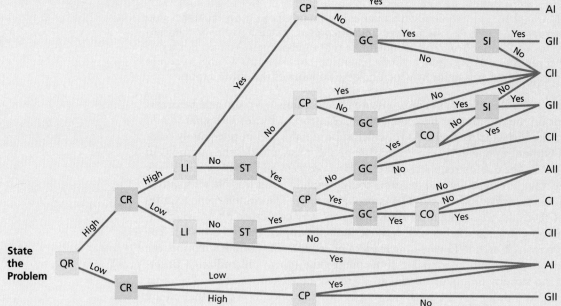

Source: Reprinted from Vroom, V. H., & Jago, A. G. (1988). *The new leadership: Managing participation in organizations.* Englewood Cliffs, NJ: Prentice-Hall. Copyright © 1987 by Vroom, V. H., & Jago, A. G.

Exhibit 9.5
The Vroom and Jago decision tree for participative leadership.

to participate in work-related decisions report more job satisfaction than those who do not. Thus, most workers seem to *prefer* a participative work environment. However, the positive effects of participation on productivity are open to some question. For participation to be translated into higher productivity, it would appear that certain facilitating conditions must exist. Specifically, participation should work best when subordinates feel favourable toward it, when they are intelligent and knowledgeable about the issue at hand, and when the task is complex enough to make participation useful.[25] In general, these conditions are incorporated into the Vroom and Jago model. Like any other leadership strategy, the usefulness of participation depends on the constraints of the situation.

Transformational Leadership and Charisma

Thus far in the chapter, we have been studying various aspects of what we can call transactional leadership. Transactional leadership is leadership that is based on a fairly straightforward exchange between the leader and the followers—subordinates perform well, and the leader rewards them; the leader uses a participatory style, and the subordinates come up with good ideas. Although it might be difficult to do well, such leadership is routine, in the sense that it is directed mainly toward bringing subordinate behaviour in line with organizational goals. However, you might have some more dramatic examples of leadership in mind, examples in which leaders have had a more profound effect on followers by giving them a new vision that instilled true commitment to a project, a department, or an organization. Such leadership is called **transformational leadership** because the leader decisively changes the beliefs and attitudes of followers to correspond to this new vision.[26]

Popular examples of transformational leadership are easy to find—consider Herb Kelleher's founding of Southwest Airlines, Disney CEO Michael Eisner's role in improving Disney's performance, Steven Jobs's vision in bringing the Apple Macintosh to fruition, Mary Ann Lawlor's turnaround of Drake Business Schools, or CEO Jack Welch's ongoing revision of General Electric's strategy. Each of these leaders went beyond a mere institutional figurehead role and even beyond a transactional leadership role to truly transform subordinates' thinking about the nature of their businesses. However, these prominent examples should not obscure the fact that transformational leadership can occur in less visible settings. For example, a new coach might revitalize a sorry peewee soccer team or an energetic new director might turn around a moribund community association using the same types of skills.

But what *are* the skills of these exceptional transformational leaders who encourage considerable effort and dedication on the part of followers? Bernard Bass of the State University of New York at Binghamton has conducted extensive research on transformational leaders.[27] Bass notes that transformational leaders are usually good at the transactional aspects of clarifying paths to goals and rewarding good performance. But he also notes three qualities that set transformational leaders apart from their transactional colleagues: intellectual stimulation, individualized consideration, and charisma.

Transformational leadership. Providing followers with a new vision that instills true commitment.

Intellectual Stimulation

Intellectual stimulation contributes, in part, to the "new vision" aspect of transformational leadership. People are stimulated to think about problems, issues, and strategies in new ways. Often, creativity and novelty are at work here. For example, Steve Jobs was convinced that the Apple Macintosh had to be extremely user friendly. As you might imagine, many of the technical types who wanted to sign on to the Mac project needed to be convinced of the importance of this quality, and Jobs was just the person to do it, raising their consciousness about what it felt like to be a new computer user.

Individualized Consideration

Individualized consideration involves treating subordinates as distinct individuals, indicating concern for their personal development, and serving as a mentor when appropriate. The emphasis is a one-on-one attempt to meet the needs of the individual in question in the context of the overall goal or mission. Bass implies that individualized consideration is particularly striking when military leaders exhibit it because the military culture generally stresses impersonality and "equal" treatment. General Stormin' Norman Schwartzkopf, commander of American troops during the Gulf war, was noted for this. Herb Kelleher's personal knowledge of many Southwest employees illustrates individualized consideration.

Charisma

Charisma. The ability to command strong loyalty and devotion from followers and thus have the potential for strong influence among them.

Charisma is the third, and by far the most important, aspect of transformational leadership. In fact, many authors simply talk about charismatic leadership, although a good case can be made that a person could have charisma without being a leader. **Charisma** is a term stemming from a Greek word meaning *favoured* or *gifted*. Charismatic individuals have been portrayed throughout history as having personal qualities that give them the potential to have extraordinary influence over others. They tend to command strong loyalty and devotion, and this, in turn, inspires enthusiastic dedication and effort directed toward the leader's chosen mission. In terms of the concepts we developed in Chapter 8, followers come to trust and *identify* with charismatic leaders and to *internalize* the values and goals they hold. Charisma provides the *emotional* aspect of transformational leadership.

It appears that the emergence of charisma is a complex function of traits, behaviours, and being in the right place at the right time.[28] Prominent traits include self-confidence, dominance, and a strong conviction in one's beliefs. Charismatics often act to create an impression of personal success and accomplishment. They hold high expectations for follower performance while at the same time expressing confidence in followers' capabilities. This enhances the self-esteem of the followers. The goals set by charismatic leaders often have a moral or ideological flavour to them. In addition, charismatic leaders often emerge to articulate the feelings of followers in times of stress or discord. If these feelings go against an existing power structure, the leader might be perceived as especially courageous.

Kelleher's video challenging his employees to meet the threat posed by United Airlines had moral and ideological overtones. The loyalty and devotion of Southwest Airlines employees to Herb Kelleher is illustrated by the ad of thanks they took out in *USA Today*.

Charisma is an important aspect of transformational leadership. Richard Branson of Virgin Group is a charismatic leader who commands strong loyalty and devotion from his employees.

Virgin Group
www.virgin.com

Charismatic Stages.   One interesting view of the emergence of charisma portrays it as a stage-like process.[29] Although such stages probably do not occur in all instances of charisma, this portrayal does clarify how charisma contributes to transformational leadership.

- In the first stage, the leader carefully evaluates the status quo for opportunities for change. He or she devotes particular attention to assessing subordinate needs and organizational constraints. At the same time, the leader seeks out or even causes deficiencies in the status quo. For example, he or she might commission market research to show a strong demand for a product or service that the organization does not offer.

- In the second stage, the leader formulates a vision or mission that challenges the status quo, but that somehow corresponds to the followers' needs and aspirations. For example, he or she might envision a product that will return the firm to its former eminence as a respected innovator in engineering. At this stage, impression management is important to articulate the vision to followers. Here is where rhetoric, self-confidence, and showing confidence in others come into play. The new mission's ability to change the unsatisfactory status quo is emphasized.

- In the final stage of charismatic emergence, the leader actually gets subordinates to achieve the new vision or mission, often by setting an example of self-sacrifice and flaunting unconventional expertise to build subordinate trust. For example, the leader might work extensive hours, make risky challenges to other organizational members who threaten the mission, and suggest unusual but workable technical solutions.

Charisma has been studied most intensively among political leaders and the leaders of social movements. Winston Churchill, Martin Luther King, Nelson Mandela, and Gandhi appear charismatic. Among American Presidents, one study concludes that Jefferson, Jackson, Lincoln, Kennedy, and Reagan were charismatic, while Coolidge, Harding, and Buchanan were not.[30] Among business leaders, Mary Kay Ash and Lee Iacocca are often cited as charismatic.

In passing, we must also mention that charisma has a dark side, a side that is revealed when charismatics abuse their strong influence over others for purely personal reasons.[31] Such people often exploit the needs of followers to pursue a reckless goal or mission. Adolf Hitler and cult leader David Koresh personify extreme examples of charismatic abuse. We will explore the abuse of power further in Chapter 12.

To summarize, transformational leaders provide intellectual stimulation and individualized consideration to followers. Most importantly, though, they exhibit charisma. The recent research evidence suggests that subordinates perceive such leaders as especially effective in stimulating both satisfaction and effort.[32]

Developmental Leadership

One of the things you might have noticed about the theories of leadership described so far is that there is a clear distinction in most theories between two role players: leaders and followers. Theories of leadership have for the most part treated leadership as a form of control in which leaders use their formal authority and power to command and control the behaviour of their followers. This is especially evident in the transactional theories of leadership such as Path-Goal Theory. As well, Contingency Theory even treats position power as a situational variable that is used to determine the most effective style of leadership. Many of the traditional theories of leadership have as their basis the notion that leadership involves controlling and directing subordinates' behaviour in an effort to achieve compliance.

However, in today's rapidly changing and competitive environment, the traditional control approach to leadership is changing. With an ever-increasing rate of environmental change, global competition, team-based work arrangements, and a more educated and professional workforce, leaders need to be more developmental than controlling. Leaders can no longer simply control and direct the behaviour of employees who are highly educated and who seek greater challenges and opportunities for learning and development. According to General Electric CEO, Jack Welch, "21st century managers will forgo their old powers—to plan, organize, implement, and measure—for new duties: counseling groups, providing resources for them, helping them think for themselves". Thus, future managers need to function as facilitators not as controllers or directors.[33] They need to be developmental leaders.

What is **developmental leadership**? Developmental leadership involves working with organizational members as partners and using persuasion and negotiation rather than formal power and authority to achieve high levels of commitment rather than compliance. The role of the leader is to help individuals develop the capabilities they need to be successful in their jobs and careers and to help the organization achieve its goals. For example, at 3M, top management sees its role as developing and supporting employee initiatives rather directing and controlling them.[34]

An important component of developmental leadership is the nature of the relationship between leaders and employees. One theory of leadership that explains leader-employee relationships is **Leader Member Exchange or LMX Theory**. Unlike other theories of leadership that focus on leader characteristics or the situation, the focus of LMX theory is the dyadic relationship between a leader and an employee. The quality of the relationship that develops between a leader and an employee is expected to influence employee attitudes and behaviour. High-quality relationships or high LMX involves a high degree of mutual influence and obligation as well as trust, loyalty, and respect between a leader and an employee. As well, high LMX leaders provide employees with challenging tasks and opportunities as well as greater latitude and discretion, task-related resources and recognition.[35] Research has found that the quality of LMX is related to a number of important outcomes, including employee job performance, overall satisfaction, satisfaction with supervision, commitment, role conflict, role clarity, and turnover intentions.[36] Thus, high LMX leaders are likely to be particularly effective developmental leaders. For an example of how LMX can influence the development of employee creativity, refer to "In Focus: *Leadership and Employee Creativity*".

In addition to the quality of relationships between leaders and employees, there are a number of other factors that are also important for developmental leadership including self-management, empowerment, persuasion and negotiation, and emotional intelligence.

■ *Self-management.* Recall from Chapter 2 that self-management involves the use of learning principles to manage one's own behaviour. In effect, this allows individuals to control and motivate themselves rather than an external agent, such as a manager. One of the things that developmental leaders do is practise and teach their employees self-management skills. Charles Manz and Henry Sims refer to this type of leader as a superleader because they lead others to lead themselves. In other words, they enable others to become self-leaders who can manage and guide their own behaviour.[37] This leadership quality is especially important for self-managing work teams. In Chapter 7, we noted that the traditional directive role of the manager is

---

Developmental leadership. A style of leadership that involves working with organizational members as partners and using persuasion and negotiation rather than formal power and authority to achieve high levels of commitment rather than compliance.

Leader Member Exchange Theory. A theory of leadership that focuses on the quality of the relationship that develops between a leader and an employee.

in focus → Leadership and Employee Creativity

One of the most important factors for organizational and national competitiveness is an organization's ability to innovate. In order to innovate, however, organizations must be able to tap into the creative potential of their workforce, as individual creativity is the major building block for organizational innovation. Research on leadership has shown that leaders play a key role in obtaining many important outcomes, such as employee job satisfaction, commitment, and performance. But can leadership also be a factor in obtaining employee creativity?

To find out about the role of leadership for creativity, Pamela Tierney, Steven Farmer, and George Graen conducted a study in a large chemical corporation. Participants included 191 full-time employees, including research managers, research assistants, section leaders, project leaders, work group professionals, and work group technicians. They hypothesized that a number of employee and leader characteristics would be related to employee creativity, including cognitive style and intrinsic motivation for creativity.

They also hypothesized that the nature or quality of the relationship between leaders and employees, or what is known as LMX (leader member exchange), would also be related to employee creativity. High-quality relationships or high LMX are characterized by trust, respect, and mutual obligation. Because high LMX leaders encourage risk taking, provide greater job latitude, and provide

employees with opportunities for engaging in challenging and relevant tasks, it was hypothesized that high LMX would be positively related to employee creativity.

The results indicated that the creative output of employees was higher for employees who enjoy creativity-related tasks and have an innovative cognitive style. Creativity was particularly high when both the leader and employee had strong intrinsic motivation for creativity tasks. As expected, high LMX was related to greater creativity. Interestingly, LMX was found to be most important for the creativity of employees who did not have an innovative cognitive style. In other words, the creative output of these employees was greater if they had a high-quality LMX. Employees with an innovative cognitive style were creative regardless of the type of relationship they had with their supervisors.

Thus, the results of this research demonstrate that leaders play an important role in the creative output of their employees, which is a critical requirement for organizational innovation. The authors recommend that organizations interested in promoting creativity should consider providing their leaders with relationship-building training.

Source: Adapted from Tierney, P., Farmer, S. M., & Graen, G. B. (1999). An examination of leadership and employee creativity: The relevance of traits and relationships. *Personnel Psychology*, 52, pp. 591-620.

---

inappropriate for self-managing work teams because the team performs many of the traditional tasks of the leader. Leaders in organizations with self-managing work teams need to encourage and instruct team members in self-management and to become more of a coach and facilitator. Developmental leaders teach, encourage, and reinforce others in the skills of self-management. There is some research evidence that self-management leadership behaviours are positively related to employee job satisfaction and work group effectiveness.[38]

- *Empowerment.* Developmental leaders empower employees and teams by giving them the authority and opportunity to take initiative and solve organizational problems. Thus, developmental leaders transfer some of their power and influence to employees. They realize that not only are employees and work teams capable of taking direct action to solve problems on their own, but that in a rapidly changing and increasingly competitive environment, employees must be empowered in order to solve problems and make decisions as problems arise.

- *Persuasion and negotiation.* The traditional approach to leadership is based on the use of formal power and authority to influence the behaviour of others. How do developmental leaders influence people in organizations?

According to Jay Conger, effective managers today are skilled at constructive persuasion.[39] They influence others to pursue a course of action and a common goal by convincing them of the merits of something rather than ordering, commanding, or directing them to do it. Constructive persuasion involves four components: (1) Building credibility, (2) finding common ground, (3) developing compelling positions and evidence, and (4) connecting emotionally with others. Persuading others to work toward common goals also requires that leaders be skilled negotiators. This means that they ask questions, interact with employees as equals, use reason more than emotion, share information, look for win-win outcomes, and ensure that the process does not degrade those with different views.[40] Developmental leaders influence the behaviour of others by using persuasion and negotiation rather than power and authority.

- *Emotional Intelligence.* Developmental leaders also have a high degree of emotional intelligence. In research that compared top performers with average performers in senior leadership positions, Daniel Goleman found that emotional intelligence was substantially more important than cognitive abilities, and that the most effective leaders have high levels of emotional intelligence. Emotional intelligence consists of the following components:

  1. *Self-awareness:* An understanding of one's strengths, weaknesses, emotions, values, goals, and how one's feelings affect them and others.

  2. *Self-regulation:* This refers to having control over one's feelings and impulses and a propensity for reflection and thoughtfulness.

  3. *Motivation:* Motivation to achieve beyond expectations and a desire for new challenges and a passion for work.

  4. *Empathy:* An ability to sense and understand the feelings, emotions, and views of others.

  5. *Social Skill:* The ability to effectively manage relationships and build networks, and being able to find common ground with different people.[41]

Finally, it is important to realize that all the characteristics and behaviours of developmental leadership can be learned. In fact, an increasing number of managers are realizing that they must change their style of leadership and learn to become developmental leaders rather than traditional control-style leaders.[42] It is also interesting to note that leaders with high emotional intelligence are those who are most likely to have self-management, persuasion, and negotiation skills and to empower others. Fortunately, emotional intelligence can also be learned.[43] Developmental leadership is likely to become a more common form of leadership as it becomes increasingly apparent to managers and leaders that in order for them and their organizations to be successful, they must engender high levels of employee commitment rather than mere compliance.[44] In this way, they can work toward the development of the human capital that will be necessary for organizations to compete in an increasingly competitive and turbulent environment.[45]

Global and Strategic Leadership

In Chapter 1, it was noted that an important contemporary concern of management is global diversity and the global economy. It was also noted that employees and managers are increasingly required to travel to other countries and work with their counterparts in other cultures. In Chapter 4 we noted that many managers terminate foreign assignments because they perform poorly or do not adjust to the culture. With this in mind, you might be wondering what it takes to be a global leader. Many of the traditional theories of leadership were developed during a time when leaders in North America spent most, if not all, of their career working in their country of origin. As a result, traditional theories of leadership do not consider the problems and challenges of global leadership.

Today's leaders must be able to function effectively in the global marketplace. In fact, a recent study on global leaders found that by the year 2015, trade between nations will exceed that within nations. Furthermore, 85% of the American Fortune 500 companies that were surveyed indicated that they do not have an adequate number of executives who are globally competent.[46]

So what is global leadership? **Global leadership** involves having leadership capabilities to function effectively in different cultures and being able to cross language, social, economic, and political borders.

According to Hal Gregersen, Allen Morrison, and Stewart Black who have studied global leadership, global leaders have the following four characteristics:[47]

- *Unbridled inquisitiveness.* Global leaders spend much of their time traveling and working in different cultures which makes business and management both complex and uncertain. They must be able to function effectively in different cultures in which they are required to cross language, social, economic, and political borders. As a result, a key characteristic of global leaders is that they relish the opportunity to see and experience new things. For the global leader, constant learning and inquisitiveness are necessary for success.

- *Personal character.* Personal character consists of two components: an emotional connection to people from different cultures and uncompromising integrity. The ability to connect with others involves a sincere interest and concern for them, and a willingness to listen to and understand others' viewpoints. Global leaders also demonstrate an uncompromising integrity by maintaining high ethical standards and loyalty to their organization's values that results in a high level of trust throughout the organization.

- *Duality.* For global leaders, duality means that they must be able to manage uncertainty and balance global and local tensions. The degree of uncertainty faced by global managers is enormous when you consider that each country and culture has its own unique problems and difficulties. As well, global leaders are able to balance the tensions and dualities of global integration and local demands.

- *Savvy.* Because of the greater challenges and opportunities of global business, global leaders need to have business and organizational savvy. Global business savvy means that global leaders understand the conditions they face in different countries and are able to recognize new market opportunities for their organization's goods and services. Organizational savvy means that global leaders are well informed of their organization's capabilities and international ventures. Organizational savvy is necessary in order to mobilize the organization across cultures, languages, economies, and physical distance.

Earlier in this chapter, we discussed research on leadership traits. By now you might be wondering if global leaders are born or made. According to the authors of the study, the answer is both, that is, "global leaders are born and then made." Individuals with the potential to become global leaders have experience working or living in different cultures, they speak more than one language, and have an aptitude for global business. However, in order to become true global leaders, they require extensive training and development. The development of global leaders consists of four strategies:

- *Travel.* International travel enables future global leaders to experience first hand the culture, economy, politics, and day-to-day life in foreign countries.

Global leadership. A set of leadership capabilities required to function effectively in different cultures and the ability to cross language, social, economic, and political borders.

This also provides opportunities to connect with and understand members of different cultures.

- *Teams.* Working in teams with members of diverse backgrounds and different perspectives requires one to think globally. It also provides additional opportunities to understand the views and perspectives of individuals with diverse backgrounds.

- *Training.* Training programs aid in the development of global leaders by providing instruction on topics such as international and global strategy, business, and ethics, as well as cross-cultural communication and multicultural team leadership. Action learning projects in addition to classroom instruction can help develop global business savvy and duality.

- *Transfers.* The most powerful strategy for developing global leaders is to send them on overseas assignments. Living and working in a foreign country was rated by leaders as the most influential experience in their lives. Transfers enable leaders to develop many of the characteristics that global leaders require to be successful.

In addition to being a global leader, leaders in today's complex and challenging global economy must also be strategic leaders. **Strategic leadership** refers to a leader's "ability to anticipate, envision, maintain flexibility, think strategically, and work with others to initiate changes that will create a viable future for the organization."[48] Strategic leaders can provide an organization with a sustainable competitive advantage by helping their organizations compete in turbulent and unpredictable environments and by exploiting growth opportunities.[49]

According to Duane Ireland and Michael Hitt, there are six components to effective strategic leadership in the 21st century:[50]

- *Determining the firm's purpose or vision.* Strategic leaders must have a clear vision of their organization and its purpose, and provide guidelines for where the firm is going and how it will get there.

- *Exploiting and maintaining core competencies.* Core competencies refer to the resources and capabilities that provide an organization with a competitive advantage. Strategic leaders must be able to develop and exploit their organization's core competencies in new and competitive ways.

- *Developing human capital.* Human capital refers to the knowledge and skills of an organization's workforce. Strategic leaders invest in the education and development of their organization's workforce and view the workforce as a critical resource.

- *Sustaining an effective organizational culture.* As described in Chapter 8, organizational culture refers to the shared beliefs, values, and assumptions that exist in an organization. An organization's culture can be a source of competitive advantage. Therefore, strategic leaders must be able to shape an organization's culture so that it is effective and can provide the organization with a competitive advantage. A major reason for the success of Southwest Airlines is the firm's culture which is, in large part, due to the efforts of CEO Herb Kelleher.

- *Emphasizing ethical practices.* Strategic leaders will establish ethical principles that guide the practices and behaviour of the organization and its members and will develop a culture in which ethical principles and practices are the norm and the foundation for decisions.

- *Establishing balanced organizational controls.* Organizational controls are formal procedures that guide work and organizational activities toward the achievement of performance objectives. Strategic leaders must establish

Strategic leadership. Leadership that involves the ability to anticipate, envision, maintain flexibility, think strategically, and work with others to initiate changes that will create a viable future for the organization.

strategic and financial controls to facilitate flexible, creative, and innovative behaviours.

In addition to these six elements, the authors also recommend that strategic leaders focus on growth opportunities, create, manage, and mobilize knowledge and intellectual capital, be open and honest in their interactions with all the organization's stakeholders, and focus on the future. Accordingly, "strategic leadership may prove to be one of the most critical issues facing organizations. Without effective strategic leadership, the probability that a firm can achieve superior or even satisfactory performance when confronting the challenges of the global economy will be greatly reduced."[51]

In summary, developing global and strategic leaders is becoming an increasingly important concern for organizations around the world. In order to be successful in the global economy, it is critical for an organization to have global and strategic leaders. This means that leaders need to understand what strategic leadership involves and how it can be a competitive advantage in the 21st century. As well, organizations must identify and develop leaders who have the capability to become global leaders. For many organizations, however, this will not be easy as most report that they do not have enough global leaders now or for the future and they do not have a system in place for developing them. Interestingly, this appears to be the case for organizations in all countries, not just those in North America.[52]

George Cohon, senior chairman of McDonald's Restaurants of Canada, is an example of a quintessential global business leader who took McDonald's to Russia.

Gender, Culture, and Leadership Style

Do men and women tend to adopt different leadership styles? Recently, a number of popular books have argued that women leaders tend to be more intuitive, less hierarchically oriented, and more collaborative than their male counterparts. Is this true? Notice that two opposing logics could be at work here. On the one hand, different socialization experiences could lead men and women to learn different ways of exerting influence on others. On the other hand, men and women should be equally capable of gravitating toward the style that is most appropriate in a given setting. This would result in no general difference in style.

A very careful review of the evidence by researchers Alice Eagly and Blair Johnson concludes that there are few differences in leadership style between men and women in organizational settings, with one exception—women have a tendency to be more participative or democratic than men.[53] Interestingly, a recent article in *Fortune* magazine on the 50 most powerful women in American business noted that women leaders are making the business world much less macho. Why is this so? One theory holds that women have better social skills that enable them to successfully manage the give-and-take that participation requires. Another theory holds that women avoid more autocratic styles because they violate gender stereotypes and lead to negative reactions. This might explain why a recent study on gender and leadership found that women are perceived by themselves and their co-workers as performing significantly better as managers than are men.[54] Exhibit 9.6 highlights some of the qualities of successful women executives.

Are various leadership styles equally effective across cultures? Some universality is to be expected. For example, anywhere in the world, it seems to be reasonable to be somewhat more directive with inexperienced and untrained subordinates and to be participative when you are uninformed but your subordinates have expert knowledge.

Still, preferences for style will vary with cultural values. For instance, more directive leadership styles will be more acceptable in cultures that favour rather

Exhibit 9.6
Qualities of successful
women executives.

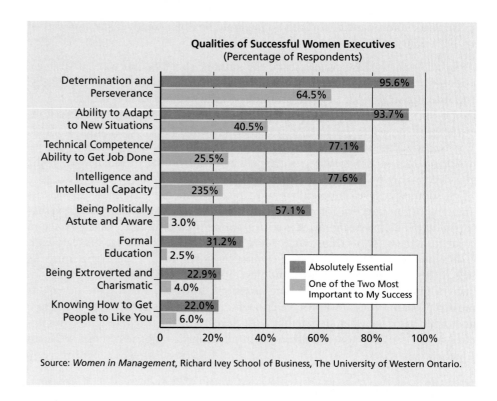

Source: *Women in Management*, Richard Ivey School of Business, The University of Western Ontario.

large power differences, such as those characteristic of some South American countries. On the other hand, more participative approaches seem to have flourished in cultures that are removed from the extremes of both power distance and individualism, such as Japan and some Scandinavian countries. Thus, while cultural values are likely to influence the preference for various leadership styles and behaviours, most empirical research supports the applicability of leadership theories across cultures. As well, some leadership behaviours are universally important across cultures.[55] For example, there is very strong support for the universality of the transactional-transformational leadership paradigm across organizations and cultures.[56]

Does Leadership Matter?

Does leadership really *matter,* that is, does it have a strong influence on the effectiveness of organizations? This might seem like an incredible question after we have devoted so many pages to consideration, initiating structure, situational influence, participation, transformation, LMX, development, global and strategic leadership. However, as you have seen, the study of leadership, despite its great volume, has not produced perfect agreement about what constitutes effective leadership. Perhaps we are tilting at windmills. Maybe leadership just is not important to organizations. Let us examine the pros and cons of this issue, but first consider "In Focus: *Leadership Development and the Bottom Line at General Motors.*"

Pros and Cons of Leader Influence

The notion that leadership is important rests mainly on the premise that special influence is necessary to get things done because we cannot design organizations perfectly and completely. You have probably experienced this phenomenon. The

in focus →)) Leadership Development and the Bottom Line at General Motors

The Service Parts Operations (SPO) is a division of General Motors responsible for getting GM dealers and retailers the parts they need when they need them. The division has 30 warehousing facilities around the world, with a total of 12,350 employees. Over the years, the division improved productivity by changing its systems and processes. Nonetheless, management felt that employees' productivity did not match their potential. In fact, discussions with several major customers as well as a survey of warehousing and parts supplier companies indicated that SPO was not meeting customers' needs; it came in 10th place out of 10 companies surveyed.

The division's General Manager felt that in order to improve productivity, it would be necessary to consider leadership style and supervisory skill. A consulting firm was hired to assess desired management competencies and to design and conduct a leadership development program. However, there was a catch to this initiative: The leadership program would first be conducted at a pilot facility, and changes would have to be measured and shown to be cost effective before the program could be implemented throughout the division.

Managers at the pilot facility attended a two-day assessment to identify strengths and weaknesses of the desired supervisory competencies. Consultant coaches and immediate supervisors helped each manager develop an individualized development plan based on their performance. Using management simulations, the training highlighted coaching, accountability, teamwork, quality, safety, communication, and customer relations.

To evaluate the leadership development intervention, data were collected before and after the program was implemented and compared with data from several other facilities that did not receive the training. The results indicated a number of significant changes. First, there was a positive change in the culture of the leadership team. Compared with the other facilities, the culture improved in areas such as continuous improvement, cooperation between departments, support, and teamwork. Second, the employees' and managers' job satisfaction showed a significant improvement at the pilot facility. Third, while the overall performance of the pilot facility was 15 percent lower than the comparison facilities before the leadership development program, after the initiative, it was better than the other facilities in five key areas: schedule attainment, quality, productivity, health and safety, and absenteeism. In financial terms, this amounted to a 21 percent productivity improvement at the pilot location and nearly $4.4 million savings to its operating budget. This provided strong evidence that the leadership development program was a worthwhile investment.

It was therefore concluded that the leadership development intervention had a positive effect on the leadership culture and resulted in a significant improvement in performance that was far greater than the cost of the program. On the basis of these findings, management decided to implement the leadership development program at other locations in the division.

Source: Based on Davis, S. R., Lucas, J. H., & Marcotte, D. R. (1998, April). GM links better leaders to better business. *Workforce*, 77, pp. 62-68.

university financial office cannot give you a refund until it is approved by the registrar. The registrar cannot approve the refund until it is approved by the professor. And the professor just went on sabbatical to Tasmania! *Here's* a case in which leadership is necessary! In other words, schools, hospitals, and business firms exhibit many loose ends or gaps that can be dealt with only by effective leadership. More specifically:

- Organizations do not have a rule or policy for every contingency. (The boss decides whether a particular absence is legitimate or illegitimate.)
- Organizational environments change, and someone must be responsive to this change. (Leadership is needed to spearhead major changes, such as total quality programs and workforce diversity efforts.)
- Organizational members differ in their needs and goals. (A sensitive manager might be able to motivate one employee with challenging work assignments and another with the promise of a raise in pay.)[57]

Conditions of this nature suggest that there is considerable *latitude* for leadership actions that can help or hinder the organization in achieving its goals.[58]

The notion that leadership is not so important rests mainly on the premise that a number of factors conspire to constrain the influence that individuals in leadership roles might have. In other words, the potential for influence is inhibited, and the leader's latitude is more apparent than real. One author has argued that the following factors limit leader impact:[59]

- In most organizations, rigid selection and promotion policies dictate that those who achieve leadership positions have very similar leadership styles. (If all the managers in a government office behave similarly, they should have similar influence—one manager is easily replaceable by another who should be equally effective.)

- The leader's performance can be strongly affected by external factors beyond his or her control. (The best boss in the company might not be able to overcome subordinates' resentment of the dirty, boring work required by a particular technology.)

Obviously, the argument that leadership matters and the position that leadership does not matter both sound pretty rational. This suggests that both positions may be true under certain circumstances. Let us examine what these circumstances might be.

Leadership Neutralizers and Substitutes

Experts have proposed some interesting ideas in response to the dilemma of whether leadership matters.[60] First, they argue that certain subordinate, task, and organizational characteristics can serve as **neutralizers of leadership.** When these factors are present in the work setting, they reduce the leader's opportunities to exercise influence. In this case, then, leadership might not "matter" because the leader's influence attempts are stymied. When such factors are not present, the leader might have an important effect on subordinate satisfaction and performance. For example, consider the following situations:

- Martin is a petroleum engineer for a major oil company. He is a troubleshooter who deals with company problems around the world, and he is constantly "on the go." He sees his boss about every two months. Martin is very interested in his job, and he does not care about what performance rating or merit raise he receives.

- Shawn is a management trainee in a large insurance company. Her office is beside that of her boss, and she consults with him about ten times a day. Shawn hopes to obtain a good performance rating so that she can receive a lucrative promotion.

Obviously, Shawn's boss is in a better position to exercise influence than Martin's boss. The latter's leadership potential is to some extent neutralized by the fact that he seldom sees Martin and because Martin is unresponsive to the rewards he can provide.

Going a step further, some neutralizers of leadership can actually serve as **substitutes for leadership.** In other words, some subordinate, task, and organizational characteristics might operate to make leadership unnecessary or redundant. While simple neutralizers reduce the *effectiveness* of leadership attempts, substitutes reduce the *necessity* for leadership. For example, consider these situations:

Neutralizers of leadership.
Factors in the work setting that reduce a leader's opportunity to exercise influence.

Substitutes for leadership.
Factors in the work setting that can take the place of active leadership, making it unnecessary or redundant.

- A group of 10 welders and riveters is assembling a large natural gas pipeline. All of them are highly experienced, and they work well together as a friendly, cohesive unit. Their task is clear and unambiguous—assembling 50 yards of pipe each day.

- A group of computer experts has decided to start a new company to design and market software packages. Although they are all technical experts, they know nothing about financing their venture or marketing their proposed products. There is much disagreement about how to establish the new enterprise and how to choose which software to develop.

In which of these situations does leadership seem more necessary? For the pipe crew, the straightforwardness of the task at hand and the friendly, cooperative working relationships could well serve as substitutes for active, formal leadership. We would not be surprised to see the crew work well even if the boss called in sick for several days. On the other hand, the proposed computer firm is begging for leadership. Its goals are unclear, and its founders are unlikely to reach an easy agreement. There are no substitutes for leadership here.

Exhibit 9.7 summarizes a number of potential neutralizers of leadership. In some cases, these neutralizers can also serve as substitutes. In the first example discussed above (Martin versus Shawn), indifference toward rewards and spatial distance were presented as simple neutralizers. These factors reduce the impact of leadership, but they do not reduce the need for leadership. In the second example, a clear task, experienced workers, and a cohesive work group served as substitutes for formal leadership for the pipe crew. The computer group did not have the advantages of these substitutes. Notice that some factors neutralize social-emotional influence, some neutralize task influence, and some neutralize both. For example, highly experienced, knowledgeable subordinates might need little task leadership, but they still require social-emotional support from the leader.

In summary, leadership should "matter" most when neutralizers and substitutes are not present in subordinates' skills and attitudes, task design, or the organizational design. The presence of neutralizers and substitutes should reduce the impact of formal leadership.[61]

Neutralizing Characteristics	Will Neutralize Considerate or Social-Emotional Leadership	Will Neutralize Initiating Structure or Task Leadership
Of Subordinate		
Ability, experience, knowledge		X
Professional orientation	X	X
Indifference toward rewards	X	X
Of Task		
Routine and clear		X
Provides its own feedback		X
Intrinsically satisfying	X	
Of Organization		
Inflexible rules and procedures		X
Cohesive work groups	X	X
Spatial distance between leader and subordinate	X	X

Exhibit 9.7
Neutralizers of leadership.

the manager's notebook

Managers at Dominos Go to Boot Camp to Become Better Leaders

1. One of the objectives of the boot camp training program is to improve managers' teamwork, leadership, and communication skills. Certainly, these are skills that can benefit all leaders. However, situational theories of leadership such as Contingency Theory and Path-Goal Theory indicate that the most effective leadership style and behaviour depend on situational variables, such as task and subordinate characteristics. Given that the style of leadership associated with the military tends to be task oriented and directive, we would not expect it to be effective in all situations. At Dominos, however, Contingency Theory predicts that given a task that is highly structured and managers with high position power, a task-oriented style of leadership would be most effective if leader-member relations are good. However, if leader-member relations are poor, a structured task in which the leader has strong position power calls for a relationship-oriented leadership style. According to Path-Goal Theory, supportive and considerate leader behaviour is most beneficial when supervising routine, frustrating, or dissatisfying jobs. Directive or structuring leader behaviour is most effective for ambiguous, less structured jobs. Thus, it would seem that while some directive leadership might be necessary to ensure that Domino's procedures are being adhered to, especially if leader-member relations are poor, given the routine and structured nature of the work, a considerate leader would be most effective. Thus, it is questionable whether a boot camp military style training program is the most effective for Domino's. But has the training changed the way managers work at Dominos? While most managers have responded positively to their training experience, it is not clear if they have acquired any new abilities. However, some say they are better communicators and have begun cross-training their employees. According to Domino's national director of corporate training, managers are able to link their work experiences to the lessons learned in boot camp.

2. Factors that can inhibit leadership training from being transferred back to the job include (a) one's boss is not receptive to the training, (b) employees are suspicious about the manager's new behaviour, (c) the ultimate purpose of the training is unclear to the manager or to the employees, and (d) no rewards are available for successful change on the job.

Summary

- Leadership occurs when an individual exerts influence on others' goal achievement in an organizational context. Early studies of leadership were concerned with identifying physical, psychological, and intellectual traits that might predict leader effectiveness. While some traits appear weakly related to leadership capacity, there are no traits that guarantee leadership across various situations.

- Studies of emergent leadership have identified two important leadership functions—the task function and the social-emotional function. The former involves helping the group achieve its goals through planning and organizing, while the latter involves resolving disputes and maintaining a pleasant group environment. Explorations of the behaviour of assigned leaders have concentrated on initiating structure and consideration, which are similar to task behaviour and social-emotional behaviour. The effectiveness of consideration and structure depends on the nature of the task and the subordinates.

- We discussed two situational theories of leadership. Fiedler's Contingency Theory suggests that different leadership orientations are necessary, depending on the favourableness of the situation for the leader. Favourableness depends on the structure of the task, the position power of the leader, and the satisfactoriness of the relationship between the leader and the group. Fiedler argues that task-oriented leaders perform best in situations that are either very favourable or very unfavourable. Relationship-oriented leaders are said to perform best in situations of medium favourability. House's Path-Goal Theory suggests that leaders will be most effective when they are able to clarify the paths to various subordinate goals that are also of interest to the organization. According to House, the effectiveness of directive, supportive, participative, and achievement-oriented behaviour depends on the nature of the subordinates and the characteristics of the work environment.

- Participative leader behaviour involves subordinates in work decisions. Participation can increase subordinate motivation and lead to higher-quality and more acceptable decisions. The Vroom and Jago model specifies how much participation is best for various kinds of decisions. Participation works best when subordinates are desirous of participation, when they are intelligent and knowledgeable, and when the task is reasonably complex.

- Transformational leaders modify the beliefs and attitudes of followers to correspond to a new vision. They provide intellectual stimulation and individualized consideration. They also have charisma, the ability to command extraordinary loyalty, dedication, and effort from followers.

- Developmental leaders work with organizational members as partners and use persuasion and negotiation rather than formal power and authority to achieve high levels of commitment. They also empower their employees and teach them how to manage their own behaviour using self-management skills.

- Global leaders can function effectively in different cultures and are characterized by their inquisitiveness, personal character, global business and organizational savvy, and their ability to manage the dualities of global integration and local demands. Strategic leaders initiate changes that enable their organizations to compete in turbulent and uncertain environments.

- Leadership is most important when few neutralizers or substitutes for leadership exist. Neutralizers are factors that make leadership attempts less effective, and substitutes are factors that can act in place of leader influence.

Discussion Questions

1. Name a physical, intellectual, or personality trait that might be associated with effective leadership, and defend your position. Then discuss a situation in which this trait might *not* be associated with effective leadership.

2. Discuss a case of emergent leadership that you have observed. Why did the person in question emerge as a leader? Did he or she fulfill the task role, the social-emotional role, or both?

3. Contrast the relative merits of consideration and initiating structure in the following leadership situations: running the daily operations of a branch bank; commanding an army unit under enemy fire; supervising a group of college students who are performing a hot, dirty, boring summer job. Use House's Path-Goal Theory to support your arguments.

4. Fred Fiedler argues that leader LPC orientation is difficult to change, and that situations should be "engineered" to fit the leader's LPC orientation. Suppose that a relationship-oriented (high LPC) person finds herself assigned to a situation with poor leader-member relations, an unstructured task, and weak position power. What could she do to make the situation more favourable for her relationship-oriented leadership?

5. Describe a situation that would be ideal for having subordinates participate in a work-related decision. Discuss the subordinates, the problem, and the setting. Describe a situation in which participative decision making would be an especially unwise leadership strategy. Why is this so?

6. What are charismatic individuals skilled at doing that gives them extraordinary influence over others? Describe a leadership situation in which a highly charismatic transformational leader would probably *not* be the right person for the job.

7. Discuss the pros and cons of the following statement: All managers should learn to become developmental leaders because developmental leadership is the most effective approach to leadership today.

8. Identify a leader who you think is a global leader and describe the characteristics and behaviours that make that person a global leader. Do you think that global leaders are born or made?

9. Consider the relationship between leadership and organizational culture. Using the approaches to leadership discussed in this chapter (e.g., leadership traits, behaviours, situational theories, participative leadership, development leadership, and LMX theory), describe how a leader can influence the culture of an organization. Based on your analysis, do you think that leaders have a strong influence on an organization's culture?

10. What effect does leadership have on employee motivation? Using each of the theories of motiva-

tion described in Chapter 5, discuss the implications for leadership. In other words, according to each theory, what should a leader do in order to motivate employees?

Experiential Exercise

Leadership Style

Below are three cases in which a leader confronts a problem that requires him or her to make a decision. After reading each case, use your intuition to decide which of Vroom and Jago's five decision strategies (AI, AII, CI, CII, GII) the leader should use. Then reread each case and trace its characteristics through the decision tree shown in Exhibit 9.5. Did your intuitive answers differ from those that the decision tree analysis provides? If so, what factors led to the difference?

Case I

You are the general foreman in charge of a large gang laying an oil pipeline. It is now necessary to estimate your expected rate of progress in order to schedule material deliveries to the next field site.

You know the nature of the terrain you will be traveling and have the historical data needed to compute the mean and variance in the rate of speed over that type of terrain. Given these two variables, it is a simple matter to calculate the earliest and latest times at which materials and support facilities will be needed at the next site. It is important that your estimate be reasonably accurate. Underestimates result in idle foremen and workers, and an overestimate results in tying up materials for a period of time before they are to be used.

Progress has been good, and your five foremen and other members of the gang stand to receive substantial bonuses if the project is completed ahead of schedule.

Case II

You are on the division manager's staff and work on a wide variety of problems of both administrative and technical nature. You have been given the assignment of developing a universal method to be used in each of the five plants in the division for manually reading equipment registers, recording the readings, and transmitting the scorings to a centralized information system. All plants are located in a relatively small geographical region.

Until now, there has been a high error rate in the reading and/or transmittal of the data. Some locations have considerably higher error rates than others, and the methods used to record and transmit the data vary between plants. It is probable, therefore, that part of the error variance is a function of specific local conditions rather than anything else, and this will complicate the establishment of any system common to all plants. You have the information on error rates but no information on the local practices that generate these errors or on the local conditions that necessitate the different practices.

Everyone would benefit from an improvement in the quality of the data, as it is used in a number of important de-

cisions. Your contacts with the plants are through the quality-control supervisors who are responsible for collecting the data. They are a conscientious group committed to doing their jobs well, but they are highly sensitive to interference on the part of higher management in their own operations. Any solution that does not receive the active support of the various plant supervisors is unlikely to reduce the error rate significantly.

Case III

You are the head of a staff unit reporting to the vice-president of finance. He has asked you to provide a report on the firm's current portfolio including recommendations for changes in the selection criteria currently employed. Doubts have been raised about the efficiency of the existing system in the current market conditions, and there is considerable dissatisfaction with prevailing rates of return.

You plan to write the report, but at the moment, you are quite perplexed about the approach to take. Your own speciality is the bond market, and it is clear to you that a detailed knowledge of the equity market, which you lack, would greatly enhance the value of the report. Fortunately, four members of your staff are specialists in different segments of the equity market. Together they possess a vast amount of knowledge about the intricacies of investment. However, they seldom agree on the best way to achieve anything when it comes to the stock market. While they are obviously conscientious as well as knowledgeable, they have major differences when it comes to investment philosophy and strategy.

You have six weeks before the report is due. You have already begun to familiarize yourself with the firm's current portfolio and have been provided by management with a specific set of constraints that any portfolio must satisfy. Your immediate problem is to come up with some alternatives to the firm's present practices and select the most promising for detailed analysis in your report.

Source of Cases: Vroom, V. H., & Yetton, P. W. (1973). *Leadership and decision-making*. Pittsburgh: University of Pittsburgh Press. © 1973 by University of Pittsburgh Press. Reprinted by permission.

Case Incident

The New Leader

Although it was still weeks before Elsa was to be formally appointed as the leader of a newly formed group, she decided to show her boss and the other group members that she was worthy of a promotion. She was going to become the leader of the product development group. The team of young and educated staff would be responsible for developing new and innovative computer software programs. Their first project was to develop new software packages for the airline industry. This would be a challenging opportunity to break into an industry where they had no previous experience. In an effort to show the group her leadership skills and get to know them better, Elsa decided to become very friendly with them. She joked around whenever she had a chance and always asked them to join her for lunch. She also let them know that if they needed to talk she would be in her office where she spent most of her time reading articles about the airline industry. At the end of the month, several of her staff stopped having lunch with her and some were thinking of quitting the group. Elsa was shocked when she overheard some of them saying, "Who does she think she is anyway?" and describing her promotion as a "big mistake."

1. What is the problem with Elsa's approach to leadership? Discuss her leadership style according to Fiedler's Contingency Theory of leadership and her leadership behaviour according to Path-Goal Theory.

2. Given Elsa's situation, should she adopt a transactional or transformational approach to leadership? How effective would transformational leadership be in her situation? Would developmental leadership be effective?

Case Study

L. J. Summers Company

Jon Reese could not think of a time in the history of L.J. Summers Company when there had been as much anticompany sentiment among the workers as had emerged in the past few weeks. He knew that Mr. Summers would place the blame on him for the problems with the production workers because Jon was supposed to be helping Mr. Summers' son, Blaine, to become oriented to his new position. Blaine had only recently taken over as production manager of the company. Blaine was unpopular with most of the workers, but the events of the past weeks had caused him to be resented even more. This resentment had increased to the point that several of the male workers had quit, and all the women in the assembly department had refused to work.

The programs that had caused the resentment among the workers were instituted by Blaine to reduce waste and lower production costs, but they had produced completely opposite results. Jon knew that on Monday morning he would have to explain to Mr. Summers why the workers had reacted as they did, and that he would have to present a plan to resolve the employee problems, reduce waste, and decrease production costs.

Company History

L. J. Summers Company manufactured large sliding doors made of many narrow aluminium panels held together by thick rubber strips, which allowed the door to collapse as it was opened. Some of the doors were as high as 18 feet and were used in buildings to section off large areas. The company had grown rapidly in its early years mainly due to the expansion of the building program of the firm's major customer, which accounted for nearly 90 percent of Summers' business.

When L.J. Summers began the business, his was the only firm that manufactured the large sliding doors. Recently,

however, several other firms had begun to market similar doors. One firm in particular had been bidding to obtain business from Summers' major customer. Fearing that the competitor might be able to underbid his company, Mr. Summers began urging his assistant, Jon, to increase efficiency and cut production costs.

Conditions before the Cost Reduction Programs

A family-type atmosphere had existed at Summers before the cost reduction programs were instituted. There was little direct supervision of the workers from the front office, and no pressure was put on them to meet production standards. Several of the employees worked overtime regularly without supervision. The foremen and workers often played cards together during lunchtime, and company parties after work were common and popular. Mr. Summers was generally on friendly terms with all the employees, although he was known to get angry if something displeased him. He also participated freely in the daily operations of the company.

As Mr. Summers' assistant, Jon was responsible for seeing to it that the company achieved the goals established by Mr. Summers. Jon was considered hard working and persuasive by most of the employees and had a reputation of not giving in easily to employee complaints.

Blaine Summers had only recently become the production manager of Summers. He was in his early 20s, married, and had a good build. Several of the workers commented that Blaine liked to show off his strength in front of others. He was known to be very meticulous about keeping the shop orderly and neat, even to the point of making sure that packing crates were stacked "his way." It was often commented among the other employees how Blaine seemed to be trying to impress his father. Many workers voiced the opinion that the only reason Blaine was production manager was that his father owned the company. They also resented his using company employees and materials to build a swing set for his children and to repair his camper.

Blaine, commenting to Jon one day that the major problem with production was the workers, added that people of such calibre as the Summers' employees did not understand how important cost reduction was, and that they would rather sit around and talk all day than work. Blaine rarely spoke to the workers but left most of the reprimanding and firing up to his assistant, Evelyn Brown.

Summers employed about 70 people to perform the warehousing, assembly, and door-jamb building, as well as the packing and shipping operations done on the doors. Each operation was supervised by a foreman, and crews ranged from three men in warehousing to 25 women in the assembly department. The foremen were usually employees with the most seniority and were responsible for quality and on-time production output. Most of the foremen had good relationships with the workers.

The majority of the work done at Summers consisted of repetitive assembly tasks requiring very little skill or training; for example, in the pinning department the workers operated a punch press, which made holes in the panels. The job consisted of punching the hole and then inserting a metal pin into it. Workers commented that it was very tiring and boring to stand at the press during the whole shift without frequent breaks.

Wages at Summers were considered to be low for the area. The workers griped about the low pay but said that they tried to compensate by taking frequent breaks, working overtime, and "taking small items home at night." Most of the workers who worked overtime were in the door-jamb department, the operation requiring the most skill. Several of these workers either worked very little or slept during overtime hours they reportedly worked.

The majority of the male employees were in their mid-20s; about half of them were unmarried. There was a great turnover among the unmarried male workers. The female employees were either young and single or older married women. The 25 women who worked in production were all in the assembly department under Lela Pims.

The Cost Reduction Programs

Shortly after Mr. Summers began stressing the need to reduce waste and increase production, Blaine called the foremen together and told them that they would be responsible for stricter discipline among the employees. Unless each foreman could reduce waste and improve production in his department, he would either be replaced or receive no pay increases.

The efforts of the foremen to make the workers eliminate wasteful activities and increase output brought immediate resistance and resentment. The employees' reactions were typified by the following comment: "What has gotten into Chuck lately? He's been chewing us out for the same old things we've always done. All he thinks about now is increasing production." Several of the foremen commented that they did not like the front office making them the "bad guys" in the eyes of the workers. The workers did not change their work habits as a result of the pressure put on them by the foremen, but a growing spirit of antagonism between the workers and the foremen was apparent.

After several weeks of no apparent improvement in production, Jon called a meeting with the workers to announce that the plant would go on a four-day, 10-hours-a-day work week in order to reduce operating costs. He stressed that the workers would enjoy having a three-day weekend. This was greeted with enthusiasm by some of the younger employees, but several of the older women complained that the schedule would be too tiring for them, and that they would rather work five days a week. The proposal was voted on and passed by a two-to-one margin. Next Jon stated that all overtime had to be approved in advance by Blaine. Overtime would be allowed only if some specific job had to be finished. Those who had been working overtime protested vigorously, saying that this would only result in lagging behind schedule, but Jon remained firm on this new rule.

Shortly after the meeting, several workers in the door-jamb department made plans to stage a work slowdown so that the department would fall behind schedule and they would have to work overtime to catch up. One of the workers, who had previously been the hardest working in the department, said, "We will tell them that we are working as fast as possible, and that we just can't do as much as we used to in a five-day week. The only thing they could do would be to fire us, and they would never do that." Similar tactics were devised by workers in other departments. Some workers said that if they could not have overtime they would find a better paying job elsewhere.

Blaine, observing what was going on, told Jon, "They think I can't tell that they are staging a slowdown. Well, I simply won't approve any overtime, and after Jack's department gets way behind I'll let him have it for fouling up scheduling."

After a few weeks of continued slowdown, Blaine drew up a set of specific rules, which were posted on the company bulletin board early one Monday morning (see box). This brought immediate criticism from the workers. During the next week, they continued to deliberately violate the posted rules. On Friday, two of the male employees quit because they were penalized for arriving late to work and for "lounging around" during working hours. As they left, they said they would be waiting for their foreman after work to get even with him for turning them in.

Production Shop Regulations

1. Anyone reporting late to work will lose one half hour's pay for each five minutes of lateness. The same applies to punching in after lunch.

2. No one is to leave the machine or post without the permission of the supervisor.

3. Anyone observed not working will be noted, and if sufficient occurrences are counted the employee will be dismissed.

That same day the entire assembly department (all women) staged a work stoppage to protest an action taken against Myrtle King, an employee of the company since the beginning. The action resulted from a run-in she had with Lela Pims, foreman of the assembly department. Myrtle was about 60 years old and had been turned in by Lela for resting too much. Myrtle became furious, saying she could not work 10 hours a day. Several of her friends had organized the work stoppage after Myrtle had been sent home without pay credit for the day. The stoppage was also inspired by some talk among the workers of forming a union. The women seemed to favour this idea more than the men did.

When Blaine found out about the incident, he tried joking with the women and in jest threatened to fire them if they did not begin working again. When he saw he was getting nowhere, he returned to the front office. One of the workers commented, "He thinks he can send us home and push us around and then all he has to do is tell us to go back to work and we will. Well, this place can't operate without us."

Jon soon appeared and called Lela into his office and began talking with her. Later, he persuaded the women to go back to work and told them that there would be a meeting with all the female employees on Monday morning.

Jon wondered what steps he should take to solve the problems at L. J. Summers Company. The efforts of management to increase efficiency and reduce production costs had definitely caused resentment among the workers. Even more disappointing was the fact that the company accountant had just announced that waste and costs had increased since the new programs had been instituted, and the company scheduler reported that Summers was farther behind on shipments than ever before.

1. Discuss the leadership at L. J. Summers Company before the cost reduction program. How does it compare with the leadership after the program? Is the leadership responsible for the problems facing the company?

2. Use House's Path-Goal Theory to analyze the leadership situation confronting the foreman following the cost reduction program. What leadership style does the theory suggest?

3. Use Fiedler's Contingency Theory to analyze the leadership situation following the cost reduction program. What leadership style does the theory suggest?

4. Run the cost reduction program through the Vroom and Jago decision tree (Exhibit 9.5). What level of participation is indicated? How does this compare with the level of participation actually used to implement the program?

5. Discuss the merits of transformational or charismatic leadership at L. J. Summers Company. What about LMX theory and developmental leadership?

6. What do the events in this case say about the effects of leadership on employees and organizations?

7. What do you think Jon Reese should do to resolve the problems, reduce waste, and decrease production costs?

Chapter 10

Communication

CIRQUE DU SOLEIL is no ordinary circus. If you have ever been lucky enough to see a Cirque du Soleil show, you know that it is more sophisticated, more athletically challenging, and more beautiful than your basic elephants-and-clowns Big Top extravaganza. Just as extraordinary is how this global organization so successfully manages its 2,100 employees, who represent 40 different nationalities and more than 15 languages.

Most of the employees are attached to tours, with 500 employees at the company's international headquarters in Montreal, Quebec. The company also has offices in Las Vegas, Amsterdam, Netherlands, and Singapore, and even employees assigned to a permanent office tend to travel a lot. Add to this the company's use of 1,800 temps a year to work as ushers, and security and ticket personnel while on tour, and you have the potential for mayhem.

However, just as impressive as the Cirque du Soleil show is how it uses communication to keep employees informed and involved in the company. Communications play a huge role in letting employees know what jobs are available, encouraging employee feedback, and keeping employees educated about the company.

How is this done? All jobs are posted on the Internet and in company bulletins. If the company needs a secretary in Europe, it will post the job in every project and office it has, even the tour in Hong Kong. An employee-written newspaper flourishes without corporate censorship. A worldwide video club allows employees in different locations around the world to exchange videotapes. Employees in the Las Vegas finance department can tape themselves on the job and swap tapes with workers in the casting department in Montreal to

Effective communication is especially important at Cirque du Soleil, where employees represent 40 different nationalities and speak more than 15 languages.

keep the community feeling close. And if an employee in the secretarial pool at headquarters has never seen a show, she might find herself flying to a tour stop in Chicago.

Communication becomes a global conversation between employees and executives through the company's three publications, *Hand to Hand, The Ball*, and the Nouvel-Expérience. These publications keep employees informed about new projects and tours and provide news from around the globe. One of the publications even has a column called "Culture Shock," in which employees describe their experiences in different countries.

To stay in touch with employees around the world, personnel from human resources travel to different venues to talk to employees one-on-one and to get an idea of what's going on in the everyday life of the company. At Cirque du Soleil, the lines of communication are always open from country to country.[1]

Cirque du Soleil
www.cirquedusoleil.com

Cirque du Soleil is a shining example of the importance of good communication for organizational success. It also illustrates how employees and managers can communicate with each other and the importance of cross-cultural communication.

In this chapter we shall explore these and other aspects of communication in organizations. First, we will define communication and present a model of the communication process and then illustrate the importance of communication. We will investigate superior-subordinate communication, the "grapevine," the verbal and nonverbal language of work, gender differences, and cross-cultural communication. Finally, we will discuss personal and organizational means of improving communication.

Learning Objectives

After reading Chapter 10, you should be able to:

1 Define communication and explain why communication by the strict chain of command is often ineffective.

2 Discuss barriers to effective superior-subordinate communication.

3 Explain the organizational grapevine and discuss its main features.

4 Review the role of both verbal and nonverbal communication at work.

5 Discuss gender differences in communication and how it can cause communication problems.

6 Discuss how communication differs across cultures and how it is influenced by cultural context.

7 Generate some personal approaches to improving communication.

8 Discuss some organizational approaches to improving communication.

What Is Communication?

Communication. The process by which information is exchanged between a sender and a receiver.

Communication is the process by which information is exchanged between a sender and a receiver. This seductively simple definition is broad enough to cover a wide variety of information exchanges. For example, the wall thermostat and the furnace in your house are constantly engaged in communication. The thermostat (sender) tells the furnace (receiver) how hot it should run. In turn, the furnace (sender) gives the thermostat (receiver) feedback about how hot it is running via the room temperature. This ongoing exchange of information contributes to your comfort.

The kind of communication we are concerned with in this chapter is *interpersonal* communication—the exchange of information between people. The simplest prototype for interpersonal communication is a one-on-one exchange between two individuals. Exhibit 10.1 presents a model of the interpersonal communication process and an example of a communication episode between a purchasing manager and her assistant. As you can see, the sender must *encode* his or her thoughts into some form that can be *transmitted* to the receiver. In this case, the manager has chosen to encode her thoughts in writing and transmit them via electronic mail. Alternatively, the manager could have encoded her thoughts in speech and transmitted them via a tape recording or face-to-face. The assistant, as a receiver, must *perceive* the message and accurately decode it to achieve accurate understanding. In this case, the assistant uses a parts catalogue to decode the meaning of an "A–40." To provide *feedback*, the assistant might send the manager a copy of the order form for the flange bolts. Such feedback involves yet another communication episode that tells the original sender that her assistant received and understood the message.

This simple communication model is valuable because it points out the complexity of the communication process and demonstrates a number of points at which errors can occur. Such errors lead to a lack of correspondence between the sender's initial thoughts and the receiver's understanding of the intended message. A slip of the finger on the keyboard can lead to improper encoding. A poor elec-

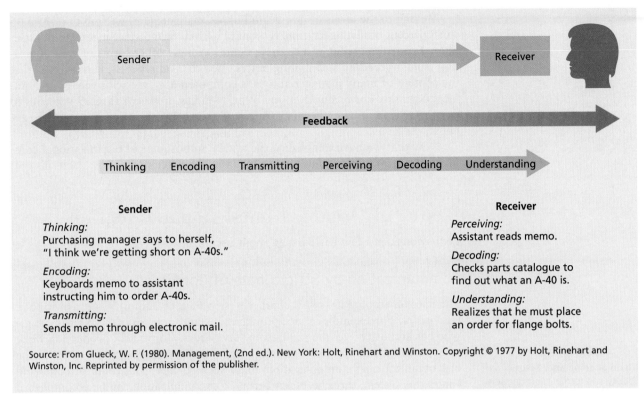

Sender

Thinking:
Purchasing manager says to herself,
"I think we're getting short on A-40s."

Encoding:
Keyboards memo to assistant
instructing him to order A-40s.

Transmitting:
Sends memo through electronic mail.

Receiver

Perceiving:
Assistant reads memo.

Decoding:
Checks parts catalogue to
find out what an A-40 is.

Understanding:
Realizes that he must place
an order for flange bolts.

Source: From Glueck, W. F. (1980). Management, (2nd ed.). New York: Holt, Rinehart and Winston. Copyright © 1977 by Holt, Rinehart and Winston, Inc. Reprinted by permission of the publisher.

Exhibit 10.1
A model of the communication process and an example.

tronic mail system can lead to ineffective transmission. An outdated parts catalogue can result in inaccurate decoding. As you might imagine, encoding and decoding may be prone to even more error when the message is inherently ambiguous or emotional. This is because the two parties may have very different perceptions of the "facts" at hand.

Effective communication occurs when the right people receive the right information in a timely manner. Violating any of these three conditions results in a communication episode that is ineffective.

Effective communication. The right people receive the right information in a timely manner.

The Importance of Communication

A recent large-scale survey by the Families and Work Institute found that the number one factor in influencing respondents' decision to take a job with their current employer was open communication.[2] Global competition, downsizing, and an increased pace of organizational change have all placed a premium on good organizational communication, and this is no doubt reflected in the survey results.

The importance of communication is also revealed by analyses of how organizational members spend their time at work. Careful studies of production workers indicate that they participate in between 16 and 46 communication episodes per hour.[3] Even the low figure of 16 episodes works out to one episode every four minutes.

As we move up the organization's hierarchy, it is evident that more and more time is spent communicating. For first-level supervisors of production jobs, various studies show that 20 to 50 percent of the boss's time at work is spent in verbal communication. When communication through paperwork is added, these figures increase to between 29 and 64 percent.[4]

Moving to the levels of middle and upper management, we find that from 66 to 89 percent of managers' time is spent in verbal (face-to-face meetings and telephone) communication.[5] Since these figures exclude other forms of communication (such as reading and writing letters, memos, and reports), it is obvious that the content of many managerial jobs is composed almost exclusively of communication tasks. For example, in one year, Honda's president gave 99 speeches to employees emphasizing the company's need to excel in the race for lower auto exhaust emissions![6]

Now that we have established the critical importance of organizational communication, let us examine some of its basic characteristics.

Basics of Organizational Communication

Let us consider a few basic issues about organizational communication.

Communication by Strict Chain of Command

The lines on an organizational chart represent lines of authority and reporting relationships. For example, a vice-president has authority over the plant manager, who has authority over the production supervisors. Conversely, production workers report to their supervisors, who report to the plant manager, and so on. In theory, organizational communication could stick to this strict **chain of command.** Under this system, three necessary forms of communication can be accomplished.

Chain of command. Lines of authority and formal reporting relationships.

Downward communication flows from the top of the organization toward the bottom. For example, a vice-president of production might instruct a plant manager to gear up for manufacturing a new product. In turn, the plant manager would provide specifics to supervisors, who would instruct the production workers accordingly.

Downward communication. Information that flows from the top of the organization toward the bottom.

Upward communication flows from the bottom of the organization toward the top. For instance, a research engineer might conceive a new plastic formula with unique properties. She might then pass this on to the research and development manager, who would then inform the relevant vice-president.

Upward communication. Information that flows from the bottom of the organization toward the top.

Horizontal communication occurs between departments or functional units, usually as a means of coordinating effort. Within a strict chain of command, such communication would flow up to and then down from a *common superior*. For example, suppose a salesperson gets an idea for a new product from a customer. To get this idea to the research staff, it would have to be transmitted up to and down from the vice-presidents of marketing and research, the common superiors for these departments.

Horizontal communication. Information that flows between departments or functional units, usually as a means of coordinating effort.

Clearly, a lot of organizational communication does follow the formal lines of authority shown on organizational charts. This is especially true for the examples of upward and downward communication given above—directives and instructions usually pass downward through the chain of command, and ideas and suggestions pass upward. However, the reality of organizational communication shows that the formal chain of command is an incomplete and sometimes ineffective path of communication.

Deficiencies in the Chain of Command

Managers recognize that sticking strictly to the chain of command is often ineffective.

Informal Communication. The chain of command obviously fails to consider *informal* communication between members. In previous chapters, we discussed how informal interaction helps people accomplish their jobs more effectively. The World Wide Video Club is an example of informal communication at Cirque du Soleil. Of course, not all informal communication benefits the organization. An informal grapevine might spread unsavoury, inaccurate rumours across the organization.

Filtering. Getting the right information to the right people is often inhibited by filtering. **Filtering** is the tendency for a message to be watered down or stopped altogether at some point during transmission, and it is something of a double-edged sword. On the one hand, employees are *supposed* to filter information. For example, production workers are not expected to inform their bosses of every trivial event that occurs on the job. Similarly, vice-presidents are not expected to communicate every detail of the management of the company clear to the shop floor. On the other side of the coin, overzealous filtering will preclude the right people from getting the right information, and the organization will suffer accordingly. Upward filtering often occurs because subordinates are afraid that their boss will use the information against them. Downward filtering is often due to time pressures or simple lack of attention to detail, but more sinister motives may be at work. As the old saying goes, "information is power," and some managers filter downward communications to maintain an edge on their subordinates. For example, a manager who feels that an up-and-coming subordinate could be promoted over her might filter crucial information to make the subordinate look bad at a staff meeting.

Obviously, the potential for filtering increases with the number of links in the communication chain. For this reason, organizations establish channels in addition to those revealed in the formal chain of command. For instance, many managers establish an **open door policy** in which any organizational member below them can communicate directly without going through the chain.[7] Such a policy should decrease the upward filtering of sensitive information if subordinates trust the system. To prevent downward filtering, many organizations attempt to communicate directly with potential receivers, bypassing the chain of command. For example, the president of a company might use the public address system to accurately inform employees about intended layoffs. Research has shown that certain types of information are more likely to be filtered than are others, thus indicating the selective need for alternative channels of communication. For example, information that is concerned directly with production might pass down through the hierarchy relatively intact, while that concerned with nonproduction matters (such as a change in the parking regulations) might be subjected to considerable filtering.[8]

Slowness. Even when the chain of command transmits information faithfully, it can be painfully slow. The chain of command can be even slower for horizontal communication between departments, and it is not a good mechanism for reacting quickly to customer problems. Cross-functional teams and employee empowerment, concepts we introduced earlier in the text, have been used to improve communication in these areas by short-circuiting the chain of command.

In summary, informal communication and the recognition of filtering and time constraints guarantee that organizations will develop channels of communication beyond the strict chain of command.

Superior-Subordinate Communication

Superior-subordinate communication consists of the one-to-one exchange of information between a boss and a subordinate. As such, it represents a key element

Filtering. The tendency for a message to be watered down or stopped during transmission.

Open door policy. The opportunity for employees to communicate directly with a manager without going through the chain of command.

Bombardier
www.bombardier.com

in upward and downward communication in organizations. Ideally, such exchange should enable the boss to instruct the subordinate in proper task performance, clarify reward contingencies, and provide social-emotional support. In addition, it should permit the subordinate to ask questions about his or her work role and make suggestions that might further the goals of the company or institution. At Bombardier, supervisors on the shop floor meet with employees every month to discuss production issues and provide feedback.[9]

A survey of 32,000 employees in the United States and Canada asked them to rank their preferred and current sources of organizational information. As Exhibit 10.2 illustrates, the immediate supervisor was the actual source *and* the preferred source of most information.[10] In addition, perceptions that supervisors are good communicators tend to be correlated positively with organizational performance.[11] Thus, any organization would wish to establish good superior-subordinate communication. For an example of how good superior-subordinate communication can help an organization become successful, see "In Focus: *Taking a Walk at Home Depot*."

How Good Is Superior-Subordinate Communication?

The extent to which superiors and subordinates agree about work-related matters and are sensitive to each other's point of view is one index of good communication. Although the parties might "agree to disagree" about certain matters, extreme and persistent perceptual differences are problematic. Research indicates that superiors and subordinates often differ in their perceptions of the following issues:

- How subordinates should and do allocate time
- How long it takes to learn a job
- The importance subordinates attach to pay
- The amount of authority the subordinate has
- The subordinate's skills and abilities
- The subordinate's performance and obstacles to good performance
- The superior's leadership style[12]

Exhibit 10.2
Preferred and current sources of information about organizational issues.

Preferred Ranking	Sources of Information	Current Ranking
1	My immediate supervisor	1
2	Small group meetings	4
3	Top executives	11
4	Employee handbook/other brochures	3
5	Local employee publication	8
6	Orientation program	12
7	Organization-wide employee publication	6
8	Annual state-of-the-business report	7
9	Bulletin boards	5
10	Upward communication program	14
11	The union	9
12	Mass meetings	10
13	Audiovisual programs	15
14	Mass media	13
15	The grapevine	2

Source: Foltz, R. G. (1985). Communication in contemporary organizations. In Reuss, C. & Silvis, D. (Eds.), *Inside organizational communication* (2nd ed.). New York: Longman, p. 10. Copyright © 1985 by Longman Publishing Group. Reprinted with permission of Longman Publishing Group.

in focus ➔))   Taking a Walk at Home Depot

After being fired from their executive positions at a chain of home improvement centres, Bernie Marcus and Arthur Blank decided to pursue their dream: a home improvement store that would be bigger, better, and more exciting than any store of its kind. With $2 million raised by the two partners, the first Home Depot store was opened in Atlanta in 1979. Today, there are 775 Home Depot stores, 160,000 associates, and annual sales of $30 billion in the United States, Canada, and Chile.

One of the most important principles that the co-founders believe has contributed to their success is communication. However, unlike most chairmen and CEOs, Bernie Marcus and Arthur Blank make communication their personal business. In order to have direct contact and face-to-face interaction with the company's store associates, the two co-founders employ a number of unique techniques that they believe are key to the dramatic growth of the company.

In order to communicate with store associates, Marcus and Blank occasionally take a "store walk." A store walk is a visit, often unannounced, to a Home Depot store by the chairman or CEO, a board member, an officer of the company, or a district manager. During these visits, they walk through the store, look at displays and signs, listen in on conversations, and talk to customers. When there are no customers around, they talk to associates, and if a customer needs help, the chairman or CEO will provide it. As well, during a store walk they will meet with 15 to 20 associates and talk about the business without the managers. Sometimes they put on Home Depot orange aprons and work on the floor. Store walks facilitate communication from the top to the bottom of the

organization and are a requirement for executives and the board of directors.

A second communication technique is called "Bernie Road Shows"; these are conducted at least eight times a year. A road show begins with a store walk with senior executives along with merchants, district managers, and officers of the division, during which time they review the merchandising philosophy and concepts. In the evening, Marcus meets with district managers and officers to exchange information and opinions. The managers have "immunity" and can ask any question without fear of negative repercussions. The next day, Marcus will study the issues and provide answers for all the questions, calling a company officer, when necessary, to get an answer. By the time the road show ends, the managers have all the answers to their questions.

Over the years, Marcus and Blank have learned a great deal from talking with associates and managers. Store walks and road shows have helped them make improvements and respond to employees' needs and suggestions. For example, during one store walk, Marcus was introduced to a kitchen designer who was leaving the company because he did not have a retirement plan.

They talked for 45 minutes, and six months later, the company introduced an employee stock ownership plan (ESOP).

Sources: Kennedy, M. (1999, June 24). The sort-of-regular guys behind Home Depot. *Financial Post*, C8; Blank, A. (1999, May 28). They sweat the small stuff. *Canadian Business.* pp.51-56; Excerpt from Bernie Marcus and Arthur Blank with Bob Andelman. *Built from Scratch: How a couple of regular guys grew the Home Depot from nothing to $30 billion*, Published by Times Books, a division of Random House, Inc.

Perceptual differences like this suggest a lack of openness in communication, which might contribute to much role conflict and ambiguity, especially on the part of subordinates. In addition, a lack of openness in communication reduces subordinate job satisfaction.[13]

Barriers to Effective Superior-Subordinate Communication

What causes communication problems between superiors and subordinates? In addition to basic differences in personality (Chapter 2) and perception (Chapter 3), the following factors have been implicated.

Conflicting Role Demands. In the previous chapter, we noted that the leadership role requires superiors to attend to both task and social-emotional functions. That is, the boss must simultaneously direct and control the subordinate's work *and* be attentive to the emotional needs and desires of the subordinate. Many superiors have difficulties balancing these two role demands. For example, consider the following memo from a sales manager to one of the company's younger sales representatives:

> I would like to congratulate you on being named Sales Rep of the Month for March. You can be very proud of this achievement. I now look forward to your increased contribution to our sales efforts, and I hope you can begin to bring some new accounts into the company. After all, new accounts are the key to our success.

In congratulating the young sales rep and in suggesting that he increase his performance in the future, the manager tries to take care of social-emotional business and task business in one memo. Unfortunately, the sales rep might be greatly offended by this communication episode, feeling that it slights his achievement and implies that he has not been pulling his weight in the company. In this case, two separate communiques, one dealing with congratulations and the other with the performance directive, would probably be more effective.

The Mum Effect. Another factor inhibiting effective superior-subordinate communication is the **mum effect**. This distinctive term refers to the tendency to avoid communicating unfavourable news to others.[14] Often, people would rather "keep mum" than convey bad news that might provoke negative reactions on the part of the receiver. For example, physicians are often reluctant to inform patients or their families of the diagnosis of terminal illness.

As the example involving the physician illustrates, the sender need not be *responsible* for the bad news in order for the mum effect to occur. For instance, a structural engineer might be reluctant to tell her boss that there are cracks in the foundation of a building, even though a subcontractor was responsible for the faulty work. It should be obvious, though, that the mum effect is probably even more likely when the sender *is* responsible for the bad news. For example, the nurse who mistakenly administers an incorrect drug dose might be very reluctant to inform the head nurse of her error. Subordinates with strong aspirations for upward mobility are especially likely to encounter communication difficulties with their bosses.[15] This might be due, in part, to the mum effect—employees who desire to impress their bosses to achieve a promotion have strong motives to withhold bad news.[16]

The mum effect does not apply only to subordinates. The boss might be reluctant to transmit bad news downward. In research conducted by one of the authors, it was found that subordinates who had good performance ratings were more likely to be informed of those ratings than subordinates who had bad ratings. Managers evidently avoided communicating bad news for which they were partly responsible, since they themselves had done the performance ratings. Given this, it is not surprising that managers and their subordinates often differ in their perceptions of subordinate performance.[17]

Status Effects. A third factor that might inhibit superior-subordinate communication is the tendency for superiors to *devalue* communication with their subordinates. In Chapter 7, we pointed out that the status of group members affects communication patterns—people reveal a clear desire to communicate with people of a similar or higher status, rather than those of a lower status. From this, it follows that necessary communications with people of lower status, such as one's subordinates, might be viewed negatively. In an interesting study designed to test this proposal, managers were asked to record every communication episode that they engaged in during a week at work.[18] In addition to specifying the method of communication and identifying the other party, they were asked to report their

Mum effect. The tendency to avoid communicating unfavourable news to others.

attitude toward each episode. The results indicated a clear tendency for the managers to react more favourably to episodes with higher-status organizational members than to those involving their subordinates. Subordinates doubtless catch on to such negative reactions and begin to withhold information, a situation that contributes to poor communication.

As we also noted in Chapter 7, many contemporary organizations have downplayed status differences, partly to foster better communication among managers and employees.

Time. A final factor that might lead to poor superior-subordinate communication is the simple constraint of time. This is especially true at lower organizational levels. You will recall that we concluded that first-level supervisors spend between 20 and 50 percent of their working time in verbal communication. Furthermore, these studies reveal that most of this time is spent communicating with subordinates. Now, on the face of it, this seems pretty generous—subordinates may receive up to 50 percent of the boss's time on the job. However, there is a catch here. Remember that many first-level supervisors have more than 20 subordinates reporting to them. Thus, simple division indicates that *each* subordinate might receive less than one percent of the boss's total time on the job each day. Indeed, studies have indicated that superior-subordinate communication on production jobs averages only *four minutes* a day![19] Given this whole string of logic, it is no wonder that managers perceive conversations with subordinates to be more frequent than the subordinates do.[20]

The Grapevine

Just inside the gates of the steel mill where one of the authors used to work there was a large sign that read "X days without a major accident." The sign was revised each day to impress on the workforce the importance of safe working practices. A zero posted on the sign caught one's attention immediately, since this meant that a serious accident or fatality had just occurred. Seeing a zero on entering the mill, workers seldom took more than five minutes to find someone who knew the details. While the victim's name might be unknown, the location and nature of the accident were always accurate, even though the mill was very large and the accident had often occurred on the previous shift. How did this information get around so quickly? It traveled through the "grapevine."

Characteristics of the Grapevine

The **grapevine** is the informal communication network that exists in any organization. As such, the grapevine often cuts across formal lines of communication that are recognized by management. Observation suggests several distinguishing features of grapevine systems:

Grapevine. An organization's informal communication network.

- We generally think of the grapevine as communicating information by word of mouth. However, written notes, electronic mail, and fax messages can contribute to the transmission of information (see the cartoon). For example, a fax operator in the New York office might tell the Zurich office that the chairman's wife just had a baby.

- Organizations often have several grapevine systems, some of which may be loosely coordinated. For instance, a secretary who is part of the "office grapevine" might communicate information to a mail carrier, who passes it on to the "warehouse grapevine."

■ The grapevine may transmit information relevant to the performance of the organization as well as personal gossip.[21] Many times, it is difficult to distinguish between the two: "You won't *believe* who just got fired!"

How accurate is the grapevine? One expert concludes that at least 75 percent of the noncontroversial organizationally related information carried by the grapevine is correct.[22] Personal information and emotionally charged information are most likely to be distorted.

Grapevine information does not run through organizations in a neat chain in which person A tells only person B who tells only person C. Neither does it sweep across the organization like a tidal wave, with each sender telling six or seven others, who each, in turn, transmit the information to six or seven *other* members. Rather, only a proportion of those who receive grapevine news pass it on, with the net effect that more "know" than "tell."[23]

Who Participates in the Grapevine?

Just who is likely to tell, that is, who is likely to be a transmitter of grapevine information? Personality characteristics may play a role. For instance, extroverts might be more likely to pass on information than introverts. Similarly, those who lack self-esteem might pass on information that gives them a personal advantage.

The nature of the information might also influence who chooses to pass it on. In a hospital, the news that a doctor has obtained a substantial cancer research grant might follow a very different path from news involving his affair with a nurse!

Finally, it is obvious that the *physical* location of organizational members is related to their opportunity to both receive and transmit news via the "vine." Occupants of work stations that receive a lot of traffic are good candidates to be grapevine transmitters. A warm control room in a cold plant or an air-conditioned computer room in a sweltering factory might provide their occupants with a steady stream of potential receivers for juicy information. On the other side of

"YOU WOULDN'T WANT TO PUT ANY CLASSIFIED MATERIAL INTO THIS MODEL — IT HAS A GOSSIPING PROGRAM BUILT INTO IT."

Source: (1992, July 13). *Current Contents*, 24(28), p. 6.

the coin, jobs that require movement throughout the organization also give their holders much opportunity to serve as grapevine transmitters. Mail carriers and maintenance personnel are good examples.

Pros and Cons of the Grapevine

Is the grapevine desirable from the organization's point of view or not? For one thing, it can keep employees informed about important organizational matters, such as job security. In some organizations, management is so notoriously lax at this that the grapevine is a regular substitute for formal communication. (As shown in Exhibit 10.2, the grapevine is perceived as the second most common but least preferred source of information!) The grapevine can also provide a test of employee reactions to proposed changes without making formal commitments. Managers have been known to "leak" ideas (such as a change to a four-day workweek) to the grapevine in order to probe their potential acceptance. Anita Roddick, the founder and managing director of The Body Shop, plants ideas with the office gossips in order to tap into the organization's informal networks.[24] Finally, participation in the grapevine can add a little interest and diversion to the work setting.

The grapevine can become a real problem for the organization when it becomes a constant pipeline for rumours. A **rumour** is an unverified belief that is in general circulation.[25] The key word here is *unverified*—although it is possible for a rumour to be true, it is not likely to *remain* true as it runs through the grapevine. Because people cannot verify the information as accurate, rumours are susceptible to severe distortion as they are passed from person to person.

Rumour. An unverified belief that is in general circulation.

Rumours seem to spread fastest and farthest when the information is especially ambiguous, when the content of the rumour is important to those involved, when the rumour seems credible, and when the recipient is anxious.[26]

Increasingly difficult global competition, staff reductions, and restructuring have placed a premium on rumour control. At the same time, organizations should avoid the tendency to be mum about giving bad news. Federal Express used its own TV network to assure its American employees that their jobs were secure when it curtailed its European package delivery operations.

The Verbal Language of Work

A friend of one of the authors just moved into a new neighbourhood. In casual conversation with a neighbour, he mentioned that he was "writing a book on OB." She replied with some enthusiasm, "Oh, that's great. My husband's in obstetrics too!" The author's friend, of course, is a management professor who was writing a book on organizational behaviour. The neighbour's husband was a physician who specialized in delivering babies.

Every student knows what it means to do a little "cramming in the caf" before an exam. Although this phrase might sound vaguely obscene to the uninitiated listener, it reveals how circumstances shape our language and how we often take this shaping for granted. In many jobs, occupations, and organizations we see the development of a specialized language or **jargon** that associates use to communicate with each other. Thus, OB means organizational behaviour to management professors and obstetrics to physicians.

Jargon. Specialized language used by job holders or members of particular occupations or organizations.

Rosabeth Moss Kanter, in studying a large corporation, discovered its attempt to foster COMVOC, or "common vocabulary," among its managers.[27] Here, the goal was to facilitate communication among employees who were often geographically separated, unknown to each other, and "meeting" impersonally through telex or memo. COMVOC provided a common basis for interaction among virtual strangers. In addition, managers developed their own informal supplements to COMVOC. Upward mobility, an especially important topic in the corporation, was reflected in multiple labels for the same concept:

Fast trackers	One performers
High fliers	Boy (girl) wonders
Superstars	Water walkers

While jargon is an efficient means of communicating with peers and provides a touch of status to those who have mastered it, it can also serve as a *barrier* to communicating with others. For example, local jargon might serve as a barrier to clear communication between departments such as sales and engineering. New organizational members often find the use of jargon especially intimidating and confusing.

A second serious problem with the use of jargon is the communication barrier that it presents to those *outside* the organization or profession. Consider the language of the corporate takeover, with its greenmail, poison pills, and white knights! Kanter, the researcher who studied COMVOC in a large corporation, found that wives of male executives could generate a total of 103 unfamiliar terms and phrases that their husbands used in relation to work! Such a situation might contribute to a poor understanding of what the spouse does at work and how work can make such heavy demands on family life.

The Nonverbal Language of Work

Have you ever come away from a conversation having heard one thing yet believing the opposite of what was said? Professors frequently hear students say that they understand a concept but somehow know that they do not. Students often hear professors say, "Come up to my office any time," but somehow know that they do not mean it. How can we account for these messages that we receive in spite of the words we hear? The answer is often nonverbal communication.

Nonverbal communication. The transmission of messages by some medium other than speech or writing.

Nonverbal communication refers to the transmission of messages by some medium other than speech or writing. As indicated above, nonverbal messages can be very powerful, in that they often convey "the real stuff," while words serve as a smoke screen. Raised eyebrows, an emphatic shrug, or an abrupt departure can communicate a lot of information with great economy. The minutes of dramatic meetings (or even verbatim transcripts) can make for extremely boring reading because they are stripped of nonverbal cues. These examples involve the transmission of information by the so-called body language. Below, we consider body language and the manipulation of objects as major forms of nonverbal communication.

Body Language

Body language. Nonverbal communication by means of a sender's bodily motions, facial expressions, or physical location.

Body language is nonverbal communication that occurs by means of the sender's bodily motions and facial expressions or the sender's physical location in relation to the receiver.[28] Although we can communicate a variety of information via body language, two important messages are the extent to which the sender likes and is interested in the receiver and the sender's views concerning the relative status of the sender and the receiver.

In general, senders communicate liking and interest in the receiver when they

- position themselves physically close to the receiver;
- touch the receiver during the interaction;

- maintain eye contact with the receiver;
- lean forward during the interaction; and
- direct the torso toward the receiver.[29]

As you can see, each of these behaviours demonstrates that the sender has genuine consideration for the receiver's point of view.

Senders who feel themselves to be of higher status than the receiver act more *relaxed* than those who perceive themselves to be of lower status. Relaxation is demonstrated by

- the casual, asymmetrical placement of arms and legs;
- a reclining, nonerect seating position; and
- a lack of fidgeting and nervous activity.[30]

In other words, the greater the difference in relaxation between two parties, the more they communicate a status differential to each other.

People often attempt to use nonverbal behaviour to communicate with others, just like they use verbal behaviour. This use could include showing our true feelings, "editing" our feelings, or trying to actively deceive others. It is difficult to regulate nonverbal behaviour when we are feeling very strong emotions. However, people are otherwise pretty good at nonverbal "posing," such as looking relaxed when they are not. On the other hand, observers also show some capacity to detect such posing.[31]

One area in which research shows that body language has an impact is on the outcome of employment interview decisions. Employment interviewers are usually faced with applicants who are motivated to make a good verbal impression. Thus, in accordance with the idea that "the body doesn't lie," interviewers might consciously or unconsciously turn their attention to nonverbal cues on the assumption that they are less likely to be censored than verbal cues. Nonverbal behaviours, such as smiling, gesturing, and maintaining eye contact, have a favourable impact on interviewers when they are not overdone.[32] However, it is unlikely that such body language can overcome bad credentials or poor verbal performance.[33] Rather, increased body language might give the edge to applicants who are otherwise equally well qualified. Remember, in an employment interview, it is not just what you say, but also what you do!

Props, Artifacts, and Costumes

In addition to the use of body language, nonverbal communication can also occur through the use of various objects such as props, artifacts, and costumes.

Office Decor. Consider the manner in which people decorate and arrange their offices. Does this tell visitors anything about the occupant? Does it communicate any useful information? The answer is yes. One typical study found that students would feel more welcome and comfortable in professors' offices when the office was (1) tidy, (2) decorated with posters and plants, and (3) the desk was against the wall instead of between the student and the professor.[34] A neat office evidently signaled that the professor was well organized and had time to talk to them. Perhaps personal decoration signaled, "I'm human." When the desk was against the wall, there was no tangible barrier between the parties. Other research has shown that people who are more outgoing and internally controlled arrange their desks and visitors' chairs in an open and inviting manner.[35] Thus, it appears that visitor responses to variations in office decor have some validity.

The decor and arrangement of furniture in a person's office conveys nonverbal information to visitors.

Does Clothing Communicate? "Wardrobe engineer" John T. Molloy is convinced that the clothing organizational members wear sends clear signals about their competence, seriousness, and promotability, that is, receivers unconsciously attach certain stereotyped meanings to various clothing and then treat the wearer accordingly. For example, Molloy insists that a black raincoat is the kiss of death for an aspiring male executive. He claims that black raincoats signal "lower-middle class," while beige raincoats lead to "executive" treatment both inside and outside the firm. For the same reason, Molloy strongly vetoes sweaters for women executives. Molloy stresses that proper clothing will not make up for a lack of ambition, intelligence, and savvy. Rather, he argues that the wrong clothing will prevent others from detecting these qualities. To this end, he prescribes detailed "business uniforms," the men's built around a conservative suit and the women's around a skirted suit and blouse.[36] The rise in the number of image consultants who help aspiring executives "dress for success" testifies to the popularity of such thinking.

Research reveals that clothing does indeed communicate.[37] Even at the ages of 10 to 12 years, children associate various brand names of jeans with different personality characteristics of the wearer! Such effects persist into adulthood. Researchers' simulations have shown that more masculinely dressed and groomed women are more likely to be selected for executive jobs. However, one study shows that there might be a point at which women's dress becomes "too masculine" and thus damages their prospects.[38] Observers note that women's clothing styles have been of special research interest because there is less of a consensus about just how female executives should dress.

If clothing does indeed communicate, it might do so partly because of the impact it has on the wearer's own self-image. Proper clothing might enhance self-esteem and self-confidence to a noticeable degree. One study contrived to have some student job applicants appear for an interview in street clothes, while others had time to dress in more appropriate formal interview gear. Those who wore more formal clothes felt that they had made a better impression on the interviewer. They also asked for a starting salary that was $4,000 higher than the job seekers who wore street clothes![39]

Gender Differences in Communication

Do men and women communicate differently? According to Deborah Tannen, not only are there gender differences in communication styles, but these differences influence the way that men and women are perceived and treated in the workplace. Gender differences in communication have their origin in childhood. Girls see conversations as a way to develop relationships and networks of connection and intimacy. Boys view conversations as a way for them to achieve status within groups and to maintain independence. Surprisingly, these childhood differences persist and continue in the workplace where they influence who gets recognized and who is valued.[40]

The typical example of how these differences are played out in the workplace is in a business meeting in which a woman comes up with a great suggestion or idea and by the end of the meeting one of her male peers receives the credit for it. Similarly, a woman might have a great idea for a new product but nobody pays any attention to it until a man suggests it.[41] In these instances, what often happens is that a man picks up the idea of a female co-worker and spends more time arguing and talking about it. As a result, he gets heard and he gets the credit.[42]

Gender differences in communication revolve around what Tannen refers to as the "One Up, One Down" position. Men tend to be more sensitive to power dynamics and will use communication as a way to position themselves in a one-up situation and avoid a one-down position. Women are more concerned with rapport building, and they communicate in ways that avoid putting others down. As a result, women often find themselves in a one-down position, which can have a negative effect on the rewards they receive and their careers.[43]

On the basis of her research, Tannen has found that there are a number of key differences in male and female communication styles and rituals that often place women in a one-down position:

- *Getting credit.* Men are more likely to blow their horn about something they have done, compared with women, and as a result, men are more likely to receive credit for their contributions.

- *Confidence and boasting.* Men tend to be more boastful about themselves and their capabilities and minimize their doubts, compared with women, who downplay their certainty. As a result, men tend to be perceived as more confident.

- *Asking questions.* Most people know that men do not like to ask for directions when they are lost. This is because they realize that asking questions can put them in a one-down position and reflect negatively on them. Therefore, men are less likely than women to ask questions in situations that can put them in a one-down position and threaten their independence.

- *Apologies.* Women and men differ in their use of apologies. Women will often say "I'm sorry" as a way of expressing concern, such as when a friend has had a bad day. For women, apologies are part of a ritual that is used to establish rapport. Men, however, avoid such ritual apologies because for them it is a sign of weakness that can place them in a one-down position.

- *Feedback.* Men and women also differ in the way they use feedback. Women will often buffer criticism by beginning with praise as a way to save face for the person receiving the criticism and avoid putting them in a one-down position. Men, however, tend to be much more blunt and straightforward. These differences can lead to misunderstandings as when a man interprets a woman's praise, rather than the criticism, as the main message.

- *Compliments.* If a friend of yours has just completed a class presentation and asks for your thoughts about it, what would you say? Women are more likely to provide a compliment such as "Great presentation" or "Good job." Men, however, are more likely to interpret the question literally and provide a critique, not realizing that all that is expected is a compliment. This is because women exchange compliments as part of a common ritual. In other words, women frequently give compliments and expect to receive them. Men are more concerned with being in a one-up position and placing others in a one-down position, and therefore do not compliment others as frequently.

- *Ritual opposition.* Men often use ritual opposition or fighting as a form of communication and the exchange of ideas. This often takes the form of attacking others' points of view, challenging them in public, and being combative and argumentative. For women, this type of ritual opposition is seen as a personal attack and something to be avoided. Many women have difficulty working in such an environment and tend to come across as insecure and unable to defend their ideas.

- *Managing up and down.* Men and women also differ in the way they communicate with those above and below them in the organizational chain of command. Many women believe that in order to be recognized and rewarded, what matters most is doing a good job. Unfortunately, this is not always the case. What also matters is who you communicate with and what you discuss. Men spend much more time communicating with their superiors and talking about their achievements. Not surprisingly, this type of communication influences who gets recognized and promoted. When in positions of power, women tend to downplay their superiority, leading others to believe that they are not capable of projecting their authority and are incompetent.

- *Indirectness.* What would be your response if your supervisor asked you a relatively simple questions such as, "How would you feel about helping out the human resource department hire a new person for our department?" Would you then think about how you "feel" about helping or would you interpret this as a request to actually do it? In North America, persons in positions of authority are expected to give direct orders when asking subordinates to do something. Women in positions of authority, however, tend to be indirect when giving orders. For instance, in the above example, what is really being said is, "Help the human resource department hire a person for our department." Such indirectness can lead to misunderstandings and be perceived as a lack of appropriate demeanour and confidence.[44]

As the above examples indicate, the differences in communication styles between men and women almost always reflect negatively on women and place them in a one-down position. Does this mean that women should change the way they communicate? Not necessarily. It depends on the person they are communicating with and the situation. For example, the communication styles that women are accustomed to are most appropriate when communicating with other women, and the same goes for men. Problems and misunderstandings arise when those communicating do not understand the rituals and styles of each other. The key, according to Deborah Tannen, is to recognize that people have different linguistic styles and adopt a flexible style so that you can adjust your style, when necessary. For example, men should learn to admit when they make a mistake and women could learn to be more direct when asking subordinates to do something. Being able to use different communication styles will allow one to adjust their style to any given situation. This is not only important when considering gender differences in communication, but it is also important for effective cross-cultural communication, which is our next topic.[45]

Cross-Cultural Communication

Consider a commonplace exchange in the world of international business:

> A Japanese businessman wants to tell his Norwegian client that he is uninterested in a particular sale. To be polite, the Japanese says, "That will be very difficult." The Norwegian interprets the statement to mean that there are still unresolved problems, not that the deal is off. He responds by asking how his company can help solve the problems. The Japanese, believing he has sent the message that there will be no sale, is mystified by the response.[46]

Obviously, ineffective communication has occurred between our international businesspeople, since the Norwegian has not received the right information about the (non)sale. From the Norwegian's point of view, the Japanese has not encoded his message in a clear manner. The Japanese, on the other hand, might criticize the weak decoding skills of his Scandinavian client. Thus, we see that problems in communication across cultures go right to the heart of the communication model that we studied at the beginning of the chapter.

In Chapter 4, we learned that various societies differ in their underlying value systems. In turn, these differences lead to divergent attitudes about a whole host of matters ranging from what it means to be on time for a meeting to how to say "no" to a business deal (as illustrated above). In Chapter 4, we also noted that a surprising number of managers do not work out well in international assignments. Many of these failures stem from problems in cross-cultural communication. Let us examine some important dimensions of such communication.

Language Differences

Communication is generally better between individuals or groups that share similar cultural values. This is all the more so when they share a common language. Thus, despite acknowledged differences in terminology ("lift" versus "elevator," "petrol" versus "gasoline"), language should not be a communication barrier for the American executive who is posted to a British subsidiary. Despite this generality, the role of language in communication involves some subtle ironies. For example, a common language can sometimes cause visitors to misunderstand or be surprised by legitimate cultural differences because they get lulled into complacency. Boarding a Qantas Airlines flight in Australia, one of the authors was attempting to pick up a magazine from a rack in the 747 when he was admonished by a flight attendant with the sharp words "First class, mate." Grinning sheepishly, he headed back to his tourist class seat without the magazine. Wise to the ways of Australia, he was not offended by this display of brash informality. However, a less familiar North American, assuming that "they speak English, they're just like us," might have been less forgiving, attributing the flight attendant's behaviour to a rude personality rather than national style. By the same token, the flight attendant would be surprised to learn that someone might be offended by his words.

As the Qantas example indicates, speaking the same language is no guarantee of perfect communication. In fact, the Norwegian and Japanese businesspeople described above might have negotiated in a common language, such as English. Even then, the Norwegian did not get the message. Speaking generally, however, learning a second language should facilitate cross-cultural communication. This is especially true when the second-language facility provides extra insight into the "communication style" of the other culture. Thus, the Norwegian would profit from understanding that the Japanese have sixteen subtle ways to say no, even if he could not understand the language perfectly.[47] Even though Americans are notoriously adverse to learning a second language, many executives seem to be getting the message in the face of the increasing globalization of business. Although the language of international business is surely gravitating toward English, learning the second language should provide better insight into the nuances of a business partner's culture.

Nonverbal Communication Across Cultures

From our earlier discussion of nonverbal communication, you might be tempted to assume that it would hold up better than verbal communication across cultures. While there are some similarities across cultures in nonverbal communication, there are also many differences. Here are a few examples.

- *Facial expressions.* People are very good at decoding basic, simple emotions in facial expressions, even across cultures. Americans, Japanese, and members of primitive New Guinea tribes can accurately detect anger, surprise, fear, and sadness in the same set of facial photographs.[48] Thus, paying particular attention to the face in cross-cultural encounters will often yield communication dividends. However, this does not always work because some cultures (such as that of Japan) frown on the display of negative facial expressions, no doubt prompting the "inscrutable" label.

- *Gestures.* Except for literal mimicry ("I need food," "Sign here"), gestures do not translate well across cultures. This is because they involve symbolism that is not shared. Most amusing are those cases in which the same gesture has different meanings across cultures:

    In the United States, a raised thumb is used as a signal of approval or approbation, the "thumbs up" signal, but in Greece, it is employed as an insult, often being associated with the expression "katsa pano" or "sit on this." Another example is the ring sign, performed by bringing the tips of the thumb and finger together so that they form a circle. For most English-speaking people it means O.K. and is, in fact, known as the "O.K. gesture." But in some sections of France, the ring means zero or worthless. In English-speaking countries, disagreement is signaled by shaking the head, but in Greece and southern Italy the head-toss is employed to signify "no."[49]

- *Gaze.* There are considerable cross-cultural differences in the extent to which it is considered suitable to look others directly in the eye. Latin Americans and Arabs favour an extended gaze, while Europeans do not. In many parts of the Orient, avoiding eye contact is a means of showing respect. In North America, it often connotes disrespect.

- *Touch.* In some cultures, people tend to stand close to one another when meeting and often touch each other as an adjunct to conversation. This is common in Arab, Latin American, and South European countries. On the other hand, North Europeans and North Americans prefer to "keep their distance."[50]

In an interesting experiment on nonverbal cross-cultural communication, English people received training in social skills that were appropriate to the Arab world. These included standing or sitting close to others and looking into their eyes, coupled with extensive touching, smiling, and handshaking. Experimenters then introduced Arabs to a trained subject and to a control subject who had only been exposed to general information about the Middle East. When asked whom they liked better, the Arabs preferred the people who had received training in their own nonverbal communication style.[51] We can well imagine a business meeting between English and Saudi bankers, both true to their cultures. The Saudis, gazing and touching, finish the meeting wondering why the English are so inattentive and aloof. The English, avoiding eye contact and shrinking from touch, wonder why the Saudis are so aggressive and threatening!

Etiquette and Politeness Across Cultures

Cultures differ considerably in how etiquette and politeness are expressed.[52] Very often, this involves saying things that one does not literally mean. The problem is that the exact form that this takes varies across cultures, and careful decoding is necessary to avoid confusion and embarrassment. Literal decoding will almost always lead to trouble. Consider the North American manager who says to a subordinate, "Would you like to calculate those figures for me?" This is really a mild order, not an opportunity to say no to the boss's "invitation." However, put yourself in the place of a foreign subordinate who has learned that Americans generally speak directly and expect directness in return. Should she say no to the boss?

In some cultures, politeness is expressed with modesty that seems excessive to North Americans. Consider, for example, the Chinese visitor's response to a Canadian who told him that his wife was very attractive. The Chinese modestly responded, "No, no, my wife is ugly." Needless to say, what was said was not what was meant. For another example of high modesty, see "Global Focus: *Chinese Display Modesty Bias in Performance Ratings.*"

In social situations, the Japanese are particularly interested in maintaining feelings of interdependence and harmony. To do this, they use a large number of set phrases or "lubricant expressions" to express sympathy and understanding, soften rejection, say no indirectly, or facilitate apology. To North Europeans and

---

global focus → Chinese Display Modesty Bias in Performance Ratings

One method of attempting to improve communication between managers and employees is to have both parties independently complete a performance appraisal of the employee and then sit down together to try to resolve any discrepancies. Although this common practice is a sensible strategy, studies in North America reveal some tendency for employees to rate their own performance higher than the boss rates it. This is probably a function of self-serving tendencies on the part of the subordinate (Chapter 3), and it can certainly contribute to superior-subordinate conflict.

Would such self-inflated ratings occur in all cultures? Jiing-Lih Farh, Gregory Dobbins, and Bor-Shiuan Cheng reasoned that in the collectivist Chinese culture of Taiwan, inflating one's own individual performance rating would be unlikely. Thus, they compared self- and supervisory ratings of performance for 982 subordinate-supervisor pairs in the Republic of China (Taiwan). Here, sub-

ordinates showed a distinct modesty bias—a tendency to underevaluate their own performance compared with the boss's rating. Consider the communication problems this could pose when a manager from either culture has both Chinese and North American subordinates. Interpreting the meaning of the self-ratings would require true cultural sensitivity.

A related problem is the tendency for Chinese job applicants to minimize their skills and abilities in employment interviews. A careful examination of the applicant's credentials will often show that he or she is being far too modest about past accomplishments.

Source: Adapted from Farh, J. L., Dobbins, G. H., & Cheng, B. S. (1991). Cultural relativity in action: A comparison of self-ratings made by Chinese and U.S. Workers. *Personnel Psychology, 44,* pp. 129–147.

North Americans, who do not understand the purpose of these ritual expressions, they seem at best to be small talk and at worst to be insincere.

> Learning to use lubricant expressions may be as difficult and painful as it is important, particularly in cases where Japanese norms and values are in conflict with those commonly held by Americans. For instance, an American executive who attributes his success in the American business world to his being articulate, assertive, and decisive is likely to feel strong resistance to using softening lubricant expressions, such as, "Well, I'm not really sure about this but ..." or "It's difficult to say exactly but ..." in English *or* in Japanese. The area of apologizing also often raises vehement negative reactions from Americans: "I'm not going to say 'I'm sorry' if I didn't do anything wrong." "They're the ones who are at fault, so why should I apologize?" "It seems almost dishonest to say we're sorry when we aren't." Japanese, however, are more concerned with smoothing relationships and maintaining harmony than with "objective" determination of who is at fault. Thus, there are a number of rhetorical lubricant expressions of apology that are used regardless of whether one is "truly sorry" or "really at fault."[53]

Social Conventions Across Cultures

Over and above the issue of politeness and etiquette, there are a number of social conventions that vary across cultures and can lead to communication problems.[54] We have already alluded to the issue of directness. Especially in business dealings, North Americans tend to favour "getting down to brass tacks" and being specific about the issue at hand. Thus, the uninitiated businessperson might be quite surprised at the rather long period of informal chat that will begin business meetings in the Arab world or the indirectness and vagueness of many Japanese negotiators.

Greetings and how people say hello also vary across cultures and these differences can lead to misunderstandings (Exhibit 10.3). For example, in North America people often greet one another by asking "How are you?" and yet seem uninterested in the response. While this is an acceptable way of saying hello to North Americans, visitors from other cultures find this to be hypocritical. In other cultures, people greet each other by asking, "Where are you going?" Such a question is considered intrusive to North Americans who do not realize that this too is just a way of greeting somebody.[55]

What individuals consider a proper degree of loudness for speech also varies across cultures, and people from "quieter" societies (such as the United Kingdom) might unfairly view those from "louder" societies (such as the Middle East) as pushy or intimidating.

What people consider proper punctuality also varies greatly around the world. In North America and Japan, punctuality at meetings and social engagements is expected and esteemed. In the Arab world and Latin America, being late for a meeting is not viewed negatively. In fact, one study found that being on time for an appointment connoted success in the United States and being *late* connoted success in Brazil.[56] Notice how an American businessperson might decode a Brazilian's lateness as disrespect, while the Brazilian was just trying to make a proper impression.

Exhibit 10.4 shows the results of a study of differences in the pace of life across cultures. It illustrates the accuracy of clocks, the time to walk 100 feet, and the time to get served in a post office. As you can see, Japan is the most time conscious, while Indonesia is quite leisurely. Such differences are especially likely to provoke communication problems when we attribute them to a *person* and ignore the overall influence of the culture.

**Greetings from Around the World:
Cultural Differences in Saying "Hello"**

Culture	Description
Japan	The bow—bending forward and down at the waist.
India	*Namaste*—placing hands at the chest in a praying position and bowing slightly.
Thailand	Wai—same as namaste (India).
Middle East	*Salaam*—used primarily among the older generation. Right hand moves upward, touching first the heart, then the forehead, an then moving up into the air.
Maori tribespeople (New Zealand) and Eskimos	Rubbing noses.
East African tribes	Spitting at each other's feet.
Tibetan tribesmen	Sticking out their tongues at each other.
Bolivia	Handshake accompanied by a hearty clap on the back.
Russia	Friends begin with a handshake and move to a "bear hug."
Latin America	*Abrazo*—embracing with both arms.

Source: Data from R.E. Axtell (1991). *Gestures: The do's and taboos of body language around the world.* New York: Wiley.

Exhibit 10.3
Greetings from around the world: cultural differences in saying "hello".

Finally, nepotism, favouring one's relatives in spite of their qualifications, is generally frowned on in more individualistic societies, such as North America and North Europe. However, in more collective cultures, such as those found in Africa and Latin America, people are expected to help their relatives. Hence, an

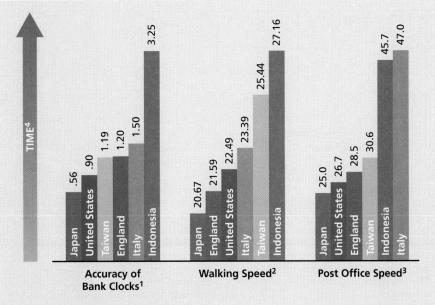

1 Deviations are reported in minutes
2, 3 Speeds are in seconds
4 Smaller numbers indicate more accurate clocks, faster walking speeds, and faster office speeds, respectively

Source: Levine, R., & Wolff, E. (1985, March). Social time: The heartbeat of culture. *Psychology Today*, 28–35.

Exhibit 10.4
Pace of life in six countries.

American manager might view his Nigerian colleague's hiring his own son as irresponsible. The Nigerian might see it as irresponsible *not* to hire his own flesh and blood.

Cultural Context

Cultural context. The cultural information that surrounds a communication episode.

In the previous sections, we provided many examples of communication differences across cultures. Is there some organizing principle underlying these differences, something that helps to summarize them? The concept of cultural context provides a partial answer. **Cultural context** is the cultural information that surrounds a communication episode. It is safe to say that context is always important in accurately decoding a message. Still, as Exhibit 10.5 shows, cultures tend to differ in the importance to which context influences the meaning to be put on communications.[57]

Some cultures, including many Oriental, Latin American, African, and Arab cultures, are high-context cultures. This means that the message contained in communication is strongly influenced by the context in which the message is sent. In high-context cultures, literal interpretations are often incorrect. Examples include those mentioned earlier—the Japanese really meant that the business deal was dead, and the Chinese did not really mean that his wife was unattractive.

Low-context cultures include North America, Australia, Northern Europe (excluding France), and Scandinavia. Here, messages can be interpreted more lit-

Exhibit 10.5
High- versus low-context cultures.

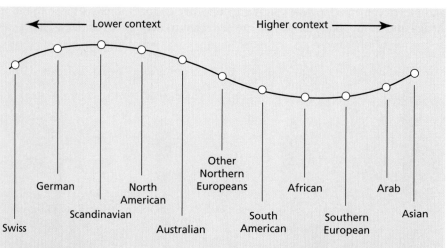

Low-context cultures
(Information must be provided explicitly, usually in words.)

- Less aware of nonverbal cues, environment and situation
- Lack well-developed networks
- Need detailed background information
- Tend to segment and compartmentalize information
- Control information on a "need to know" basis
- Prefer explicit and careful directions from someone who "knows"
- Knowledge is a commodity

High-context cultures
(Most information drawn from surroundings. Very little must be explicit transferred.)

- Nonverbal important
- Information flows freely
- Physical context relied upon for information
- Environment, situation, gestures, mood all taken into account
- Maintain extensive information networks

Source: Donald W. Klopf, *Intercultural Encounters: The Fundamentals of Intercultural Communication.* Englewood, Colorado: Morton Publishing Company, 1995, p. 33.

erally because more meaning resides in the message than in the context in which the communication occurs. The "straight talk" that Americans favour is such an example. However, such straight talk is not any straighter in meaning than that heard in high-context cultures if one also learns to attend to the context when decoding messages.

Differences in the importance of context across cultures have some interesting implications for organizational communication, especially when we consider what might occur during business negotiations. Consider the following:[58]

- People from high-context cultures want to know about you and the company that you represent in great detail. This personal and organizational information provides a context for understanding your messages to them.

- Getting to the point quickly is not a style of communication that people in high-context cultures favour. Longer presentations and meetings allow people to get to know one another and to consider a proposal in a series of stages.

- When communicating with people from a high-context culture, give careful consideration to the age and rank of the communicator. Age and seniority tend to be valued in high-context cultures, and the status of the communicator is an important contextual factor that gives credibility to a message. Younger fast trackers will do fine in low-context cultures where "it's the message that counts."

- Because they tend to devalue cultural context, people from low-context cultures tend to favour very detailed business contracts. For them, the meaning is in the message itself. High-context cultures place less emphasis on lengthy contracts because the context in which the deal is sealed is critical.

Some more general advice for good cross-cultural communication is presented in the next section.

Personal Approaches to Improving Communication

What can you do to improve your own ability to communicate better with your boss, your subordinates, your peers, as well as customers, clients, or suppliers? Good question. More and more people are learning that developing their communication skills is just as sensible as developing their accounting skills, their computer skills, or anything else that will give them an edge in the job market.

Improvements in communication skills are very reinforcing. When you communicate well, people generally respond to you in a positive way, even if they are not totally happy with your message. Poor communication can provoke a negative response that is self-perpetuating, in that it leads to even *poorer* communication. This happens when the other party becomes resistant, defensive, deceptive, or hostile.

Basic Principles of Effective Communication

Let us consider some basic principles of effective face-to-face communication.[59] These principles are basic, in that they apply to upward, downward, horizontal, and outside communication. They generally apply to cross-cultural encounters, as long as they are applied in conjunction with the advice in the following section, "When in Rome..."

Take the Time. Good communication takes time. Managers, in particular, should be aware that status differences, cultural differences, the mum effect, and other barriers mean that they need to devote extra effort to developing good rapport with subordinates. Not taking adequate time often leads to the selection of the wrong communication medium. One of the authors has seen a "don't do this" memo sent to 130 subordinates because two of them committed some offence. Of course, the memo irritated 128 people and the two offenders really did not grasp the problem. The boss should have taken the time to meet face-to-face with the two people in question.

Be Accepting of the Other Person. Try to be accepting of the other person as an individual who has the right to have feelings and perceptions that may differ from your own. You can accept the person even if you are unhappy with something that he or she has done. Having empathy with others (trying to put yourself in their place and see things from their perspective) will increase your acceptance of them. Acting superior or arrogant works against acceptance.

Do Not Confuse the Person with the Problem. Although you should be accepting of others, it is generally useful to be problem oriented rather than person oriented. For example, suppose a subordinate does something that you think might have offended a client. It is probably better to focus on this view of the problem than to impute motives to the subordinate ("Don't you care about the client's needs?"). The focus should be on what the person did, not who the person is. Along these same lines, try to be more descriptive rather than evaluative. Again, focus on what exactly the subordinate did to the client, not how bad the consequences are.

Congruence. A condition in which a person's words, thoughts, feelings, and actions all contain the same message.

Say What You Feel. More specifically, be sure that your words, thoughts, feelings, and actions exhibit **congruence**—that they all contain the same message. A common problem is soft-pedaling bad news, such as saying someone's job is probably secure when you feel that it probably is not. However, congruence can also be a problem with positive messages. Some managers find it notoriously difficult to praise excellent work or even to reinforce routine good performance. Congruence can be thought of as honesty or authenticity, but you should not confuse it with brutal frankness or cruelty. Also, remember that in some high-context cultures, "saying what you feel" is done very indirectly. Still, the words and feelings are congruent in their own context.

Active listening. A technique for improving the accuracy of information reception by paying close attention to the sender.

Listen Actively. Effective communication requires good listening. People who are preoccupied with themselves or who simply hear what they expect to hear are not good listeners. Good listening improves the accuracy of your reception, but it also shows acceptance of the speaker and encourages self-reflection on his or her part. Developing good listening skills can be harder than acquiring good speaking skills. Good listening is not a passive process. Rather, good communicators employ active listening to get the most out of an interaction. Techniques of **active listening** include the following:

- *Watch your body language.* Sit up, lean forward, and maintain eye contact with the speaker. This shows that you are paying attention and are interested in what the speaker is saying (this is another aspect of congruence).

- *Paraphrase what the speaker means.* Reflecting back what the speaker has said shows interest and ensures that you have received the correct message.

- *Show empathy.* When appropriate, show that you understand the feelings that the speaker is trying to convey. A phrase such as "Yes, that client has irritated me, too" might fill the bill.

- *Ask questions.* Have people repeat, clarify, or elaborate what they are saying. Avoid asking leading questions that are designed to pursue some agenda that *you* have.
- *Wait out pauses.* Do not feel pressured to talk when the speaker goes silent. This discourages him or her from elaborating.

Give Timely and Specific Feedback. When you initiate communication to provide others with feedback about their behaviour, do it soon and be explicit. Speed maximizes the reinforcement potential of the message, and explicitness maximizes its usefulness to the recipient. Say *what* was good about the person's presentation to the client, and say it soon.

When in Rome ...

Frankly, you are off to a pretty good start in cross-cultural communication if you can do a careful job of applying the basic communication principles we discussed above. However, people's basic skills sometimes actually *deteriorate* when they get nervous about a cross-cultural encounter. Let us cover a few more principles for those situations.

Assume Differences Until You Know Otherwise. The material we presented earlier on cross-cultural communication and that in Chapter 3 on workforce diversity should sensitize you to the general tendency for cross-cultural differences. In a cross-cultural situation, caution dictates assuming that such differences exist until we are proven wrong. Remember, we have a tendency to project our own feelings and beliefs onto ambiguous targets (Chapter 3), leading us to ignore differences. Be particularly alert when dealing with good English speakers from cultures that emphasize harmony and avoidance of conflict (e.g., Japan). Their good English will tempt you to think that they think like you do, and their good manners will inhibit them from telling you otherwise.

Recognize Differences *Within* Cultures. Appreciating differences between cultures can sometimes blind us to the differences among people within a culture. This, of course, is what stereotypes do (Chapter 3). Remember, your German subordinates will have as many different personalities, skills, and problems as your North American subordinates. Remember that there are occupational and social class differences in other countries just like there are at home, although they can be harder to decipher (this is why one of the authors once shook hands with the chef at a French business school, mistaking him for the dean!).

Watch Your Language (and Theirs). Unless the person with whom you are communicating is very fluent in English, speak particularly clearly, slowly, and simply. Avoid clichés, jargon, and slang. Consider how mystifying phrases such as "I'm all ears," "let's get rolling," and "so long" must be.[60] By the same token, do not assume that those who are facile in your language are smarter, more skilled, or more honest than those who are not.

Organizational Approaches to Improving Communication

In this section, we shall discuss some organizational techniques that can improve communication. We consider other techniques in Chapter 13 (with regard to conflict reduction) and Chapter 16 (with regard to organizational development).

FedEx
www.fedex.com

Information richness. The potential information-carrying capacity of a communication medium.

Before continuing, consider the use of communication at Federal Express in "You Be the Manager: *Communicating Change at Federal Express and Flying Tiger.*"

Choosing the Correct Medium

To communicate effectively, it is important to choose the correct medium to properly convey your intended message. Of particular importance is choosing a medium that can transmit information of appropriate richness. **Information richness** is the potential information-carrying capacity of a communication medium.[61] As you

---

you be the manager
Communicating Change at Federal Express and Flying Tiger

The FedEx management team spent what some might view as an extravagant amount of time and money to communicate with employees.

In December 1988, Federal Express acquired Flying Tiger Line, Inc., its rival in the international air freight business. FedEx senior mangers realized that the organizations' "strategic fit" would mean little if the people in the organizations could not be convinced that the merger made sense. The FedEx credo of "People-Service-Profit" was about to be put to a highly visible test.

As Jim Perkins, senior vice-president for human resources at FedEx said: "We wanted a merger our people would be proud of, to reflect who we are as a company, our people philosophy. We wanted a merger that would bring the merged company on to the FedEx team." Employees throughout the organizations were concerned, however. Careers, loyalty, and years of trust were at stake.

FedEx management did not waste much time. Less than two hours after the Dow Jones wire service announced the merger, FedEx chairman Fred Smith and chief operating officer Jim Barksdale, gave an unscripted, unrehearsed address over the company's satellite television network—FXTV—to 35,000 employees in 800 locations. From the start, Smith and Barksdale described the move as a "merger" and not an "acquisition." The phrasing had symbolic importance to people in both organi-

zations. The choice of terminology "didn't require a lot of debate or discussion," said Carol Presley, senior vice-president for marketing and corporate communications. "We wanted the Flying Tiger people to feel we really did want them."

Still, FedEx employees had serious concerns. Most Flying Tiger employees, for instance, were unionized. Moreover, some had been employed by their company longer than FedEx had been in existence. To FedEx employees, therefore, joining forces with these outsiders could threaten their seniority.

Altogether, the lives—and concerns—of 70,000 people were involved. And the FedEx management team would spend what some might view as an extravagant amount of time and money to communicate—talk and listen—with employees. For months following the merger announcement, questions and answers traveled back and forth, up and down the organization. The means of communication included face-to-face meetings, company publications, videos, and television programs, including the daily company news broadcast, "FX Overnight."

But was it all necessary and worth the expense? You be the manager.

1. How important was it for FedEx to communicate with employees about the merger with Flying Tiger? What do you think about the approach(es) that FedEx used to communicate with employees?

2. What effect do you think the communications had on the employees and the merger?

To find out more about the effect of communication and the FedEx merger, check out The Manager's Notebook at the end of the chapter.

Source: Excerpted from Young, M., & Post, J. E. (1993). Managing to communicate, communicating to manage: How leading companies communicate with employees. *Organizational Dynamics*, 22, pp. 31-43.

can see in Exhibit 10.6, we can rank order various media in terms of their information richness. A face-to-face transmission of information is very high in richness because the sender is personally present, audio and visual channels are used, body language and verbal language are occurring, and feedback to the sender is immediate and ongoing. A telephone conversation is also fairly rich, but it is limited to the audio channel, and it does not permit the observation of body language. At the other extreme, communicating via numeric computer output lacks richness because it is impersonal and uses only numeric language. Feedback on such communication might also be very slow. Returning to the chapter opening vignette, Cirque du Soleil uses mediums that are high in richness (face-to-face talks between employees and personnel from human resources) and low in richness (Internet job postings).

At first thought, always using a rich medium might seem attractive. However, reflection indicates that this is not a good idea. Rich information media can be expensive and time consuming to use, and the messages that they convey can be difficult to send to a large number of receivers. Also, very rich media can inhibit some aspects of communication. For example, research shows that strangers working in face-to-face groups tend to use more inhibited speech than those interacting via computer screens.[62] Also, participation tends to be more equal across group members when they interact via computer, a medium that is richer than a letter (because of fast feedback) but not as rich as the telephone (because of the lack of audio cues). Evidently, people (especially the quiet types) are less likely to censor themselves when they are protected by the distance afforded by the computer.

A good rule to follow is that less routine messages require richer communication media.[63] Memos and written reports are fine for recurrent, noncontroversial, impersonal communication. New news, intended changes, controversial messages, and emotional issues generally call for richer (i.e., face-to-face or video) media.

360 Degree Feedback

Traditionally, employee performance appraisal has been viewed as an exercise in downward communication in which the boss tells the subordinate how he or she is doing. More recently, performance appraisal has become a two-way communication process in which subordinates are also able to have upward impact

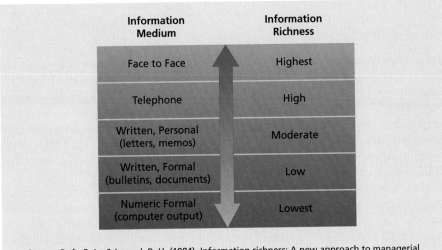

Exhibit 10.6
Communication media and information richness.

Source: Daft, R. L., & Lengel, R. H. (1984). Information richness: A new approach to managerial behavior and organization design. *Research in organizational behavior, 6,* 191–233, p. 196. Reprinted by permission of JAI Press, Inc.

concerning their appraisal. Most recently, some firms have expanded the communication channels in performance appraisal to include not only superior and self-ratings but also ratings by subordinates, peers, and clients or customers. This so-called multisource or **360 degree feedback** is often part of a total quality management system. Firms that have tried it include Honeywell, Sprint, Amoco, and Burger King. At Nebraska's Midlands Community Hospital, patients are incorporated into the process when nurses receive feedback.[64]

The 360 degree system usually focuses on required behavioural competencies rather than bottom-line performance. It is usually used for employee development rather than salary determination. It is possible that the various sources of feedback could contradict each other, and ratees may need some assistance in putting all this input together. However, in a well-designed 360 degree system, the various information sources ideally provide unique data about a person's performance. When supervisors receive performance ratings from multiple subordinates, it is called upward feedback. A recent study on upward feedback over a five-year period found that managers who were initially rated as poor or moderate showed significant improvements in feedback ratings especially when the managers met with their employees to discuss their upward feedback.[65]

Employee Surveys and Survey Feedback

Surveys of the attitudes and opinions of current employees can provide a useful means of upward communication. Since surveys are usually conducted with questionnaires that provide for anonymous responses, employees should feel free to voice their genuine views. A good **employee survey** contains questions that reliably tap employee concerns and also provide information that is useful for practical purposes. Survey specialists must summarize (encode) results in a manner that is easily decoded by management. Surveys are especially useful when they are administered periodically. In this case, managers can detect changes in employee feelings that might deserve attention. For example, a radical decrease in satisfaction with pay might be a precursor of labour troubles and signal needed revision of the compensation package.

When survey results are fed back to employees, along with management responses and any plans for changes, this feedback should enhance downward communication. Survey feedback shows employees that management has heard and considered their comments. Plans for changes in response to survey concerns indicate a commitment to two-way communication.[66]

Suggestion Systems and Query Systems

Suggestion systems are designed to enhance upward communication by soliciting ideas for improved work operations from employees. They represent a formal attempt to encourage useful ideas and prevent their filtering through the chain of command. The simplest example of a suggestion system involves the use of a suggestion box into which employees put written ideas for improvements (usually anonymously). This simple system is usually not very effective, since there is no tangible incentive for making a submission and no clear mechanism to show that management considered a submission.

Much better are programs that *reward* employees for suggestions that are actually adopted and provide feedback as to how management evaluated each suggestion. For simple suggestions a flat fee is usually paid (perhaps $100). For complex suggestions of a technical nature that might result in substantial savings to the firm, a percentage of the anticipated savings is often awarded (perhaps several thousand dollars). An example of such a suggestion might be how to perform machinery maintenance without costly long-term shutdowns. When strong pub-

360 degree feedback. Performance appraisal that uses the input of supervisors, subordinates, peers, and clients or customers of the appraised individual.

Sprint
www.sprint.com

Employee survey. Anonymous questionnaire that enables employees to state their candid opinions and attitudes about an organization and its practices.

Suggestion systems. Programs designed to enhance upward communication by soliciting ideas for improved work operations from employees.

licity follows the adopted suggestions (such as explaining them in the organization's employee newsletter), downward communication is also enhanced, since employees receive information about the kind of innovations desired.

Related to suggestion systems are *query systems* that provide a formal means of answering questions that employees may have about the organization. These systems foster two-way communication and are most effective when questions and answers are widely disseminated. Many organizations have a column of questions and answers in their employee newsletters, the content ranging from questions about benefits to the firm's stock performance.

An interesting type of query system is the anonymous letter. In fact, an increasing number of CEOs are actively soliciting employees' anonymous complaints. The president and chief executive of Browning-Ferris Industries Inc., invites employees to send him unsigned critical questions using an e-mail system that disguises the sender's identity. He then posts the replies on an electronic bulletin board. Anonymous letters have been instrumental in making changes at a number of companies.[67]

Telephone Hotlines and TV Networks

Many organizations have adopted *telephone hotlines* to further communication. Some are actually query systems, in that employees can call in for answers to their questions. For example, C&P Telephone Companies have an interactive system to handle queries about equal employment opportunity and affirmative action. More common are hotlines that use a news format to present company information. News may be presented live at prearranged times or recorded for 24-hour availability. Such hotlines prove especially valuable at times of crisis, such as storms or strikes.[68]

One fast growing technique for promoting good communication is a company-owned television network, such as the one at Ford Motor Company.

> More than 90 major companies in North America have their own TV satellites or cable networks, according to a survey from KJH Communications, an Atlanta consulting firm. The companies use TV for rumour control, to boost workers' involvement, to smooth operations in emergencies, and to cut millions of dollars in travel costs for training and new product briefings.
>
> Ford began with just one monthly news program, but by 1989, it was broadcasting daily. Today, the daily Ford news program—which is broadcast

Many firms have developed their own TV networks to facilitate communication with employees.

Triolgy Software Inc.
www.triolgy.com

each day at 10 a.m. and repeated throughout the day—is watched by 60 percent of blue-collar employees and 40 to 45 percent of white-collar employees, according to internal surveys.[69]

Other prominent firms with their own TV networks include IBM, Federal Express, J.C. Penney, and DaimlerChrysler. DaimlerChrysler uses its system to train mechanics right at their own dealerships.

Management Training

Is good communication a mysterious inherited art, or can bosses be trained to communicate more effectively with subordinates? The evidence suggests that proper training can improve the communication skills of managers. Notice the specific use of the word *skills* here. Vague lectures about the importance of good communication simply do not tell managers *how* to communicate better. However, isolating specific communication skills and giving the boss an opportunity to practice these skills should have positive effects. The manager who has confidence in how to handle delicate matters should be better able to handle the balance between social-emotional and task demands.

Effective training programs often present videotaped models correctly handling a typical communication problem. Managers then role-play the problem and are reinforced by the trainers when they exhibit effective skills. At General Electric, for example, typical communication problems that this kind of training addresses have included discussing undesirable work habits, reviewing work performance, discussing salary changes, and dealing with subordinate-initiated discussions.[70] North Carolina's Center for Creative Leadership incorporates 360 degree feedback data from peers, superiors, and subordinates into its training.

It might seem that training of this nature is essentially focused on downward communication. However, there is much evidence that the disclosure of one's attitudes and feelings promotes reciprocity on the part of the receiver.[71] Thus, the manager who can communicate effectively downward can expect increased upward communication in return.

---

the manager's notebook

Communicating Change at Federal Express and Flying Tiger

1. FedEx's efforts to communicate with employees about the merger may seem extreme, but their approach was not unique among well-managed companies. One of the most significant factors in FedEx's approach to communication was the CEO's leadership and the strong commitment by management to communicate with employees. Managers must be willing to deliver key messages themselves. Managers at FedEx spent a great deal of time talking to employees. They used rich mediums, such as two-way communication and face-to-face meetings. Also important was FedEx's use of technology combined with more personalized approaches of communication. The most effective employee communication programs couple a liberal and imaginative use of high technology, such as FedEx's television network, with a high-touch strategy that involves face-to-face and personalized communications. Managers at FedEx also communicated to employees how the merger will affect them and their jobs, providing a link to the "big picture." Finally, FedEx was quick to communicate the details of the merger with employees. The cost of not communicating in a timely manner could have resulted in disaffection, anger, and loss of trust.

2. FedEx managers considered the effort well worth the expense. In fact, assuaging the concerns proved vital to the achievement of all the objectives that inspired the merger. Chief operating office Jim Barksdale described the payoff: "Placing such an emphasis on internal communication has made us the company we are. We couldn't be anywhere near the size we are, and have the profitablility or the relationship with our employees we have, if we weren't deeply into the business of communicating with people."

Summary

- Communication is the process by which information is exchanged between a sender and a receiver. Organizational members (especially managers) spend a considerable portion of their time communicating. Effective communication involves getting the right information to the right people in a timely manner.

- Although much routine communication can occur via the chain of command, the chain tends to be slow and prone to filtering. It also ignores informal communication.

- Superior-subordinate communication is frequently ineffective. The superior might have difficulty balancing task and social-emotional demands, and both superiors and subordinates might be reluctant to inform each other of bad news (the mum effect). Also, superiors might devalue communicating with subordinates or simply not have enough time to spend interacting with them.

- The grapevine is the organization's informal communication network. Only a portion of people who receive grapevine information pass it on. Key physical locations or jobs that require movement around the organization encourage certain members to pass on information. The grapevine can be useful to the organization, and it often transmits information accurately. However, it becomes problematic when rumours (unverified beliefs) circulate.

- Verbal language that is tailored to the needs of a particular occupation or organization is known as jargon. While jargon aids communication between experienced associates, it can often prove confusing for new organizational members and people outside the organization.

- Nonverbal communication is the transmission of messages by a medium other than speech or writing. One major form is body language, which involves body movement or the placement of the body in relation to the receiver. Much body language is subtle and automatic, communicating factors such as liking, interest, and status differences. Other forms of nonverbal communication involve office decoration, office arrangement, and the clothing worn at work.

- Differences in communication styles between men and women have their origin in childhood but persist and continue in the workplace where they can influence the way men and women are perceived and treated.

- Communication across cultures can be difficult owing to obvious language differences but also to less obvious differences in nonverbal style, social conventions, and matters of etiquette.

- In low-context cultures, individuals can interpret messages more literally than in high-context cultures, where issues surrounding a message are more critical to understanding it.

- Personal approaches to improving communication include taking the time, being accepting of others, concentrating on the problem, saying what you feel, listening actively, and giving timely and specific feedback.

- When communicating cross-culturally, assume cultural differences until you know otherwise, recognize differences within cultures, and use simple language.

- Organizational approaches to improving communication include 360 degree feedback, employee surveys, suggestion and query systems, hotlines and TV networks, and management training. Communicators should select richer media for less routine messages.

Discussion Questions

1. Using Exhibit 10.1 as a guide, describe a communication episode that you have observed in an organization. Who were the sender and receiver? Was the episode effective? Why or why not?

2. Debate: Since more and more global business is being conducted in English, North Americans will not have cross-cultural communication problems in the future.

3. Describe or invent a situation in which communicating strictly by the chain of command would be very ineffective.

4. "It is very difficult to establish good superior-subordinate communication." What evidence would support this position?

5. Discuss the pros and cons of the existence of the grapevine in organizations. Suppose an organization wanted to "kill" the grapevine. How easy do you think this would be?

6. Discuss a case in which you heard one message communicated verbally and "saw" another transmitted nonverbally. What was the content of each message? Which one did you believe?

7. Under what conditions might body language or clothing have a strong communicative effect? When might the effect be weaker?

8. Debate: As more women move into management positions in organizations the gender differences in communication between men and women will eventually disappear and so will communication problems in the future.

? 9. What role do perceptions play in gender differences in communication? Refer to the components of the perceptual system in Chapter 3 and use it to explain how differences in communication styles between men and women can result in misunderstandings and inaccurate perceptions. What effect might these misunderstandings and inaccurate perceptions have on gender stereotypes?

? 10. How does a manager's leadership style affect superior-subordinate communication? Refer to the theories of leadership described in Chapter 9 (e.g., leadership traits, behaviours, situational theories, participative leadership, developmental leadership, and LMX theory) and explain their implications for effective superior-subordinate communication.

Experiential Exercise

Cross-Cultural Confusion

The purpose of this exercise is to find out whether you can diagnose the reasons for the apparent work-related "cross-cultural confusion" illustrated in the three incidents below. In thinking through your diagnosis, you must consider the relative impact of differences in cultural values versus other factors that might have caused the problem.

Working alone, read each incident and rank order the potential explanations given for the problem in terms of their likelihood. Give a rank of 1 to the most likely, 2 to the next most likely, and so on. Also, jot down a brief rationale for your ranking that considers the cultural difference and other factors. Why or why not is a particular explanation correct? Following this, one of two procedures can be used:

1. The instructor can discuss the rankings with the class as a whole.

2. The class can break into small learning groups, discuss each incident, and develop a group ranking for each incident. Following this, the instructor can compare the group rankings and discuss them with the class as a whole.

Your instructor will give you the expert opinion about the explanations for the events, given the cultures involved and the situational factors mentioned in the incidents. Of course, individuals are unique. The correctness of these explanations is based on a "typical" cultural response in the absence of other information.

Incident 1: Who's in Charge?

The president of Janice Tani's firm asked her, as chief executive of the marketing division, and her staff (three male MBAs) to set up and close an important contract with a Japanese firm. He thought his choice especially good as Janice (a Japanese American from California) knew the industry well and could also speak Japanese.

As she and her staff were being introduced, Janice noticed a quizzical look on Mr. Yamamoto's face and heard him repeat "chief executive" to his assistant in an unsure manner. After Janice had presented the merits of the strategy in Japanese, referring to notes provided by her staff, she asked Mr. Yamamoto what he thought. He responded by saying that he needed to discuss some things further with the head of her department. Janice explained that was why she was there. Smiling, Mr. Yamamoto replied that she had done an especially good job of explaining, but that he wanted to talk things over with the person in charge. Beginning to be frustrated, Janice stated that she had authority for her company. Mr. Yamamoto glanced at his assistant, still smiling, and he arranged to meet with Janice at another time.

Why did Mr. Yamamoto keep asking Janice about the executive in charge?

1. He did not really believe that she was actually telling the truth about who she was.

2. He had never heard the term "executive" before and did not understand the meaning of "chief executive."

3. He had never personally dealt with a woman in Janice's position, and her language ability caused him to think of her in another capacity.

4. He really did not like her presentation and did not want to deal with her firm.

5. He was attracted to her and wanted to meet with her alone.

Incident 2: Shaping Up the Office

Ronald, an ambitious young executive, had been sent to take over the Sales branch of his American company in São Paulo, Brazil. He spent a few weeks learning the routines with the departing manager and was somewhat disturbed by the informality and lack of discipline that seemed to characterize the office. People seemed to indulge in excessive socializing, conversations seemed to deal more with personal than business matters, and no one seemed to keep to their set schedules. Once he had formally taken over, he resolved to do something about this general slackness and called the staff together for a general meeting. He told them bluntly that work rates and schedules would have to be adhered to and hoped that a more business-like atmosphere would prevail. Over the next few months, he concentrated on improving office efficiency, offering higher bonuses and incentives to those who worked well and private warnings to those who did not. By the end of the first quarter he felt he had considerably improved the situation and was therefore somewhat surprised to find sales figures had significantly dropped since his takeover.

What reason would you give to Ronald for this drop in sales?

1. He has probably lowered the office morale.

2. The salesmen probably resent his management style and are deliberately trying to make him look bad.

3. The salesmen would probably have responded better to a more participative approach to the problems.

4. Key Brazilian workers lost face through Ronald's actions.

Incident 3: Transmitting Information on Transmission Systems

"Adjustment to Japan has been much easier than I thought," Ted Owens told his wife about a year after their move from the United States. Ted had been sent by an automobile company in Detroit to see if he could establish production facilities for transmission systems that would be built in Japan and imported to the United States. Having been told that negotiations take a long time in Japan, he was not disappointed that it had taken a year for a major meeting to be set up with the key Japanese counterparts. But the Japanese had studied the proposal and were ready to discuss it this morning, and Ted was excited as he left for work. At the meeting, people discussed matters that were already in the written proposal that had been circulated beforehand. Suddenly it occurred to Ted that there was an aspect of quality control inspection that he had left out of the proposal. He knew that the Japanese should know of this concern since it was important to the long-range success of the project. Ted asked the senior person at the meeting if he could speak, apologized for not having already introduced the quality control concern he was about to raise, and then went into his addition to the proposal. His presentation was met with silence, and the meeting was later adjourned without a decision having been made on the whole manufacture-importation program. Since Ted thought that a decision would be made that day, he was puzzled.

What was the reason for Ted's difficulty?

1. Ted had brought up quality control, an issue about which the Japanese are very proud. The Japanese thought that Ted was questioning their commitment to quality control.

2. Ted had brought up an issue on which there had not been prior discussion among the people somehow involved in that specific issue.

3. Ted had asked the senior person about speaking; in actuality, there was a younger person present who was in charge, and Ted should have deferred to this person.

4. Expecting a decision in a year is still unrealistic. Ted should be more patient.

Source: Incidents from Brislin, R. W., Cushner, K., Cherrie, C., & Yong, M. (1986). *Intercultural interactions: A practical guide.* pp. 157–158, 164–165, 172. Copyright © 1986 by Sage Publications, Inc. Reprinted by permission of Sage Publications, Inc.

Case Incident

The 360 Degree Feedback Program

A CEO from a large size manufacturing company attended an executive development conference and heard about 360 degree feedback programs. He liked the idea. At the conference, he heard all about the benefits of 360 degree feedback. He persuaded his senior management that the company should pursue 360 feedback because it would be a lot better than their current annual performance appraisal. He stated, "360 feedback comes directly from people who are in the best positions to evaluate the performance of the people they work with. Supervisors will have more information to support their appraisals of others and, therefore, more leverage to do something about some people's performance. We'll use the 360 feedback to help determine people's merit raises. That way, we'll make sure that people make improvements based on the feedback they received." The CEO asked the human resource management (HRM) department in the company to recruit a consulting firm that specialized in 360 degree feedback. HRM found a firm and then used a small focus group to help customize the firm's 99-item 360 degree survey.

After the first round of 360 degree feedback, almost everyone in the organization, including the CEO was at least a little frustrated or disappointed with the outcomes of the process. People complained about how many surveys they had to fill out and how long the process took. Supervisors felt that many of the 360 ratings were inflated. In short, the data were not worth much. The company was faced with a decision about whether to continue or discontinue the 360 feedback program.

Source: Waldman, D. A., Atwater, L. E., & Antonioni, D. (1998). Has 360 degree feedback gone amok? *Academy of Management Executive,* 12, pp. 86-94.

1. How does 360 degree feedback aim to improve communications in an organization?

2. Why was the 360 degree feedback program described in the case incident unsuccessful? What should the organization do now?

Case Study

"Walk Tall"

Jacobsville is a company town. HAL, the giant of the computer field, has maintained its corporate headquarters and a major production facility here for over 50 years. Many long-time residents of Jacobsville equate success with being a part of the HAL family. Working for HAL has traditionally been like being a member of the family—secure, protected, a bit structured, and quite conservative. "HAL takes care of its own" could well be the company motto. The Human Resources Department has long "waiting lists" of local applicants for positions at HAL.

David Grazinno grew up in Jacobsville, attended the local branch of the state university, and (MBA in hand) landed a much sought after position in the Purchasing Department of HAL.

David is a member of the Component Group. This unit is responsible for purchasing all memory components for the corporation on a world-wide basis. The technology involved in these components is evolving rapidly, so there are constant changes in the specifications regarding purchases.

Historically, Buyers have been promoted to Purchasing from manufacturing areas, clerical, the mail room, etc. However, three years ago, upper level management decided "new blood" was necessary for the Purchasing Department and began actively recruiting college graduates. Almost half the Buyers now have degrees, and they are "fast tracked." Two graduates who have been with HAL about four years have recently been promoted to Senior Buyers.

Mark Mead manages the Component Unit. At 33, he recently completed his MBA through a part-time evening program. Don Clemenski is the Senior Buyer in the unit. He was promoted two months ago, after 11 years in Purchasing. Connie Harris (25) has been in the unit for seven months. She has a bachelor's degree in Business Administration and is considered very sharp. As Senior Buyer, Don is responsible for training new hires.

Mark had been impressed with David's self-assurance (as well as his MBA) when he decided to hire him three months ago. Now, he is not so sure. He decided to speak to his friend, Susan Jones, in Human Resources:

"I'm not sure what's happening with Grazinno; he just doesn't seem to be working out. Initially, he impressed me as a really assertive, take-charge guy. I expected him to be my number one producer in no time. Even though Don was responsible for his training, I asked Connie to show him the ropes. She has caught on so quickly and made such progress in the last few months that I thought those two would really be a dynamic duo. I've tried to convey my concern, but nothing changes. He just isn't living up to specs. Maybe you could find out what it would take to get him moving."

David was eager to talk with someone about the situation. Susan invited him to lunch, where he proceeded to tell her his account of his first few months in Purchasing:

"During my first week on the job, Mark told me that it would be a good idea if I would talk to the three other Purchasing Managers to find out what their departments do. My manager thought that this would be a good way for me to 'get on board.'

"However, getting in touch with a manager is no small task. I paid approximately fifteen visits to each manager's office during the following week and still failed to find any of them at their desks.

"At the end of the following week, Mark asked me how many managers I had talked to. I told him that I didn't get the chance to see any of them. He then became slightly upset and told me that I had to become more aggressive and assertive. He told me that I had to become more of a 'go-getter.' It did not seem to matter to him that I had tried very hard to talk to the other managers.

"During the next two weeks, I noticed that Connie had been acting very peculiar. Every time I asked her a question she became very nervous, abrupt, or she just interrupted me. After three weeks of this very kind treatment, I asked her if the person who trained her had the same kind of foul mouth that she has had with me. She replied that she acted that way because she was busy. I informed her that whether she was busy or not, I was tired of her talking to me like I was something that was stuck on the bottom of her shoe. I told her that henceforth I would not tolerate any more abuse and that I wanted to be treated with the same respect that I treated her with. She took my tongue-lashing like a true champion. For the next month she did not talk to me at all.

"I was beginning to find it very difficult to get in touch with Don, the person who was responsible for training me. The man was rarely in his office. When I did get in touch with him, the encounters were usually very brief. He would give me some work to do, and after quickly giving me some instructions (Don is a very fast talker) he would briskly walk out of my office. I would do as much of the work as I could. When I had to ask Don a question, he would be impossible to find. I would then try to finish the assignment anyway, but because I could not get the help I needed I usually made some mistake. Surprisingly, Don always managed to find me when I made a mistake on work that he had given me.

"When I did make mistakes, Don was very good about reminding me about what an excellent college education I have. He would express amazement that I could not handle the very infrequent assignments that he would dole out to me, given the education I have. Coincidentally, there would usually be several people in close proximity when Don was expressing his amazement with my alleged lack of competence.

"Another favourite tactic Don likes to use was to give me several five-minute assignments. I would go to his office to ask him to give me some work. Don would then give me a task which would take about five to ten minutes to finish. When I completed the task I would go back to Don's office only to find that he was not there. Don's whereabouts would then remain a mystery for two to three hours.

"Toward the end of my second month with the company, I noticed that Mark would be looking at me in a very strange manner when I would be walking down the hallway. It seemed as if he had something on this mind. Finally, he approached me and told me that he would like to see me in his office.

"Mark then prefaced our meeting by telling me that I was acting too quiet and laid back since I was hired. He said that it was okay to be quiet as long as I was quietly being assertive.

"Mark told me that when I walked down the hallway it did not look like I was in a hurry to reach my destination.

"My manager also claimed that many other managers (not just purchasing managers), as well as my co-workers, have commented to him on how quiet and unassertive I seemed to be. Because of reports such as these, he told me that people are starting to get the wrong idea about me. He felt that this should concern me because at HAL you never know who you are going to be working for. Someday a position could be open that I would qualify for. However, the person who is responsible for filling the position may not know anything about me except the way I walk down the hallway (it seems strange that this person would not take the time to find out a little more about me than that).

"Mark also told me that if I wanted to learn the job I should try to hang on to Don's shirttails. He said that Don was a very busy guy and that I just might have to plant myself on his doorstep in order to keep in touch with him. He went on to say that he is aware that work is not always readily available. To remedy this, Mark said that I should be willing "to look under a rock" to find work so that I can keep myself busy.

"Mark expressed surprise at how outgoing and assertive I was when he interviewed me. 'It seems,' he said, 'that you are not the same person that I interviewed.'

"At no point during this wonderful conversation did my manager question my ability. In the past two months, I made two presentations, one to my department and one to my manager's manager. On both occasions, Mark told me that I did an excellent job. He just could not understand why I was not that outgoing all the time.

"On the subject of training (meaning Don), my manager conceded that some people are better teachers than others, but nevertheless I am going to have to be more aggressive in seeking assistance and work. Mark commented that it did not look like I was 'chomping at the bit' to find work.

"Basically, my manager felt that things were not going as planned (what his plans were, if any, I don't know). He said that as of now, on a scale of one to five (five being low), that I would rate a four. He then went on to tell me that a four rating really is not all that bad. In fact, he said that a four rating is quite common for new hires. After all, how could somebody who is new be expected to perform his job that well?"

Source: Jack R. Vivona, in J. L. Frantzve, *Behaving in Organizations: tales from the trenches* (1983). Boston: Allyn and Bacon.

1. How effective is the communication in the Component Group at HAL? Cite specific examples in which effective or ineffective communication occurred.

2. Comment on superior-subordinate communication in the Component Group. Are there perceptual differences between David and Mark that are having an effect on how they communicate? What barriers might be causing communication problems between David and the other members of the Component Group?

3. What are some principles of effective face-to-face communication that might improve communication between David and the other members of the group?

4. To what extent is communication operating through the grapevine in the case? What effect is it having on people's perceptions and behaviour?

5. Comment on the potential usefulness of 360 degree feedback and upward feedback for improving communications in the Component Group.

6. How effective is Mark as a manager?

7. What do you think Mark should do?

8. What should David do?

9. Should the Human Resource Department become involved?

Chapter 11

Decision Making

NASA'S HUBBLE SPACE TELESCOPE In
December of 1993, NASA astronauts successfully
completed what was surely the most complicated
and difficult space flight ever. The flight, which included two lengthy space walks, was made to repair the near-sighted Hubble space telescope.
Hubble, which had been launched into position
three years earlier, had greatly disappointed the
scientific community when the images that it sent
back to earth were immediately recognized to be badly flawed. Although fine
tuning did improve some of the data being generated, the $1.6 billion tele-
scope in no way lived up to its promise as the most complicated and expensive
scientific instrument ever launched into space. The repair improved NASA's
image, which was certainly in need of repair after the original Hubble launch
and the earlier fatal explosion of the Challenger space shuttle.

> NASA's
> Hubble
> Space
> Telescope

The Hubble problem stemmed from an aberration in the telescope's primary
mirror. The mirror, the largest ever constructed, was supplied to NASA by
Perkin-Elmer Corporation of Danbury, Connecticut. The firm had radically underbid competitor Kodak to win the $70 million contract, and this low bid put
the company under extreme pressure to complete the job without a hitch. The
complexity and delicacy of the task were amazing, requiring a wide range of
technicians, engineers, and optical designers. The mirror had to be remarkably
smooth and precisely curved.

The final product *was* remarkably smooth, but it was incorrectly curved.
Subsequent investigation showed that the problem started when technicians
improperly shimmed the $1 million device that guided the polishing of the
mirror with three metal washers worth about 20 cents. There was evidence of
the problem when preliminary grinding of the mirror was completed, but it was

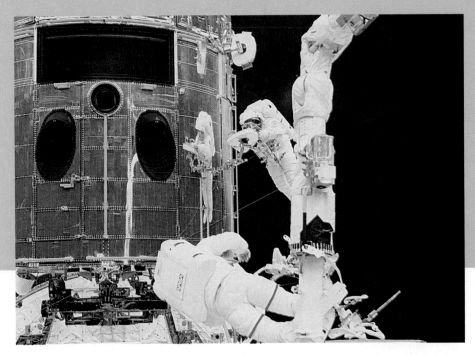

Despite early warnings that the lens of the Hubble space telescope was flawed, NASA launched it anyway, which cost the agency millions of dollars in repairs.

discounted because of the still-rough state of the surface. In subsequent internal tests, as the company did more and more work on the mirror, the aberration was again apparent, but each time it was explained away. The engineer who oversaw the tests was said to be leery of outsiders and rejected pleas for external, independent tests "just to be sure." He claimed that pleas for external testing were rejected due to costs.

A retired Perkin-Elmer optical designer who had been hired as a quality trouble shooter was routinely rebuffed by the lens team for intruding on their turf. When he suggested that arch-competitor Kodak be contracted to make independent tests of the lens, he was branded a traitor. NASA's own quality assurance was minimal due to cash problems.

The flawed lens was launched without a NASA quality signoff. A subsequent federal investigation led to an agreement in which Perkin-Elmer agreed to pay $25 million in exchange for a Justice Department deal to drop potential lawsuits. It is estimated that the problem could have been repaired before the launch for $1.7 million. The complicated NASA repair job was pegged at over $600 million.

In recent years, NASA has made a number of changes in order to prevent future fiascos like the Hubble telescope. Among the changes is an Office of Continual Improvement, a council to act as a steering committee in making policy decisions, quality councils in each of NASA's 10 field centres, teams at all levels that review what NASA is doing and how it is doing it, and independent teams that review projects that run into scheduling or budget problems. In addition, all employees are encouraged to make suggestions for changes.

Perkin-Elmer Corp.
www.perkin-elmer.com

Learning Objectives

After reading Chapter 11, you should be able to:

1 Define decision making and differentiate well-structured and ill-structured problems.

2 Discuss the impact of framing and cognitive biases on the decision process.

3 Explain the process of escalation of commitment to an apparently failing course of action.

4 Compare and contrast perfectly rational decision making with decision making under bounded rationality.

5 Summarize the pros and cons of using groups to make decisions.

6 Explain the groupthink phenomenon.

7 Review how groups handle risk when making decisions.

8 Discuss techniques for improving organizational decision making.

9 Explain the promise and problems of electronic decision-making groups.

Many believe that it will take years for all these changes to be fully implemented, given the strong institutional and cultural traditions of NASA, not to mention some opposition and resistance inside and outside NASA. Others believe that if NASA is to survive, it has no choice but to fully transform itself.

In the meantime, the Hubble telescope now takes dazzling photographs of planets, stars, and galaxies, such as the extraordinary "polar-ring" galaxy located some 130 million light years away! The Hubble recently received a tune-up from the space shuttle Discovery after being disabled for a month and a half. The astronauts spent several days refurbishing the telescope, during which time they replaced many of its old and broken parts and equipped it with new high-tech devices that will keep it running for the next several years.[1]

How could so many smart people make a series of such bad decisions? We will find out in this chapter. First, we will define decision making and present a model of a rational decision-making process. As we work through this model, we shall be especially concerned with the practical limitations of rationality. After this, we will investigate the use of groups to make decisions. Finally, the chapter closes with a description of some techniques to improve decision making.

What Is Decision Making?

Consider the following questions that might arise in a variety of organizational settings:

- How much inventory should our store carry?
- Where should we locate the proposed community mental health centre?

- Should I remain on this job or accept another?
- How many classes of Philosophy 200 should our department offer next semester?
- Should our diplomats attend the summit conference?

Common sense tells us that someone is going to have to do some decision making to answer such questions.

Decision making is the process of developing a commitment to some course of action.[2] Three things are noteworthy about this definition. First, decision making involves making a *choice* among several action alternatives—the store can carry more or less inventory, and the mental health centre can be located at the north or south end of town. Second, decision making is a *process* that involves more than simply the final choice among alternatives—if you decide to accept the offer of a new job, we want to know *how* this decision was reached. Finally, the "commitment" mentioned in the definition usually involves some commitment of *resources*, such as time, money, or personnel—if the store carries a large inventory, it will tie up cash; if the chairperson of Philosophy offers too many introductory classes, he might have no one available to teach a graduate seminar. The Hubble telescope project required a substantial resource commitment.

In addition to conceiving of decision making as the commitment of resources, we can also describe it as a process of problem solving.[3] A **problem** exists when a gap is perceived between some existing state and some desired state. For example, the chairperson of the Philosophy department might observe that there is a projected increase in university enrollment for the upcoming year, and that his course schedule is not completed (existing state). In addition, he might wish to adequately service the new students with Philosophy 200 classes and at the same time satisfy his Dean with a timely, sensible schedule (desired state). In this case, the decision-making process involves the perception of the existing state, the conception of the desired state, and the steps that the chairperson takes to move from one state to the other.

Well-Structured Problems

For a **well-structured problem,** the existing state is clear, the desired state is clear, and how to get from one state to the other is fairly obvious. Intuitively, these problems are simple, and their solutions arouse little controversy. This is because such problems are repetitive and familiar.

- Assistant bank manager—which of these 10 car loan applications should I approve?
- Welfare officer—how much assistance should this client receive?
- Truck driver—how much weight should I carry?

Because decision making takes time and is prone to error, organizations (and individuals) attempt to program the decision making for well-structured problems. A **program** is simply a standardized way of solving a problem. As such, programs short-circuit the decision-making process by enabling the decision maker to go directly from problem identification to solution.

Programs usually go under labels such as *rules, routines, standard operating procedures,* or *rules of thumb.* Sometimes, they come from experience and exist only "in the head." Other programs are more formal. You are probably aware that routine loan applications are "scored" by banks according to a fixed formula that takes into account income, debt, previous credit, and so on. Some programs exist in the form of straightforward rules—"Truck drivers will always carry between 85 and 95 percent of legal weight."

Decision making. The process of developing a commitment to some course of action.

Problem. A perceived gap between an existing state and a desired state.

Well-structured problem. A problem for which the existing state is clear, the desired state is clear, and how to get from one state to another is fairly obvious.

Program. A standardized way of solving a problem.

Many of the problems encountered in organizations are well structured, and programmed decision making provides a useful means of solving these problems. However, programs are only as good as the decision-making process that led to the adoption of the program in the first place. In computer terminology, "garbage in" will result in "garbage out." Another difficulty with decision programs is their tendency to persist even when problem conditions change.

These difficulties of programmed decision making are seen in the ineffective hiring procedures that some firms use. To solve the recurrent problem of choosing employees for lower-level jobs, almost all companies use application forms. These forms are part of a decision program. However, some firms have persisted in asking for information (such as age or marital status) that violates equal employment and human rights legislation or is not job related. Costly lawsuits have resulted. Furthermore, there is seldom evidence that this information is a valid predictor of job performance (garbage in—garbage out).

Ill-Structured Problems

Ill-structured problem. A problem for which the existing and desired states are unclear, and the method of getting to the desired state is unknown.

The extreme example of an **ill-structured problem** is one in which the existing and desired states are unclear, and the method of getting to the desired state (even if clarified) is unknown. For example, a vice-president of marketing might have a vague feeling that the sales of a particular product are too low. However, she might lack precise information about the product's market share (existing state) and the market share of its most successful competitor (ideal state). In addition, she might be unaware of exactly how to increase the sales of this particular product.

Ill-structured problems are generally unique, that is, they are unusual and have not been encountered before. In addition, they tend to be complex and involve a high degree of uncertainty. As a result, they frequently arouse controversy and conflict among the people who are interested in the decision. For example, consider the following:

- Should we vaccinate the population against a new flu strain when the vaccination might have some bad side effects?
- Should we implement a risky attempt to rescue political hostages?
- In which part of the country should we build a new plant?

It should be obvious that ill-structured problems such as these cannot be solved with programmed decisions. Rather, the decision makers must resort to nonprogrammed decision making. This simply means that they are likely to try to gather more information and be more self-consciously analytical in their approach. Ill-structured problems can entail high risk and stimulate strong political considerations. We will concentrate on them in this chapter.

Now that you are familiar with different kinds of problems, consider the You Be the Manager feature.

The Compleat Decision Maker—A Rational Decision-Making Model

Exhibit 11.1 presents a model of the decision process that a rational decision maker might use. When a problem is identified, a search for information is begun. This information clarifies the nature of the problem and suggests alternative solutions. These are carefully evaluated, and the best is chosen for implementation. The implemented solution is then monitored over time to ensure its

Turning Decision Making into a Science at General Electric Mortgage Insurance

GE tackles 8,000 delinquent loans a year.

If you stop making your mortgage payments because of job loss, divorce, illness, etc., chances are you will get a call from someone at General Electric Mortgage Insurance. As one of the largest companies insuring in the event that people stop paying their mortgage,

Employees deal daily with hardship. But it is a business, and profitability relies heavily on the quick decisions of 25 representatives who determine if you are in so deep that the house must be sold or foreclosure initiated, or if, with a little patience, the loan can be "cured," meaning, you get back on your feet and become your old reliable self.

GE has long been frustrated that a handful of representatives have been much better at making such decisions. Each top performer seemed to arrive at decisions differently, yet all had a knack for knowing which loans could be cured.

Such success had always been attributed to experience and gut instinct, an art that could not easily be taught to others. But GE decided it could save millions of dollars if it turned "art into science," says Buz Mertes, vice-president of loss mitigation and customer service.

It took a chance, pulling its most successful representatives off the job for 10 months and putting them in a room where they argued heatedly about what made their decisions superior. The idea was to find ways to accurately predict which home buyers delinquent on their mortgage payments would likely recover and which should sell their houses as soon as possible and to transfer this knowledge to other representatives.

But would it work? Can all the representatives be trained to make decisions like the most successful representatives do? You be the manager.

1. Is it possible to program or standardize the decision making process at GE? Can people be trained to make better decisions?

2. What do you think was the outcome of GE's attempt to find out how successful representatives make decisions?

To find what happened at GE, check The Manager's Notebook at the end of the chapter.

Source: Excerpted from Jones, D. (1998, May 1). GE turns decision-making 'art into science'. *USA Today*, p.5B.

immediate and continued effectiveness. If difficulties occur at any point in the process, repetition or recycling may be effected.

It might occur to you that we have not yet determined exactly what a "rational" decision maker is. Before we discuss the specific steps of the model in detail, let us contrast two forms of rationality.

Perfect versus Bounded Rationality

The prototype for **perfect rationality** is the familiar Economic Person (formerly Economic Man), whom we meet in the first chapter of most introductory textbooks in economics. Economic Person is the perfect, cool, calculating decision maker. More specifically, he or she

- can gather information about problems and solutions without cost and is thus completely informed;
- is perfectly logical—if solution A is preferred over solution B, and B is preferred over C, then A is necessarily preferable to C; and
- has only one criterion for decision making—economic gain.

Perfect rationality. A decision strategy that is completely informed, perfectly logical, and oriented toward economic gain.

Exhibit 11.1
The rational decision-making process.

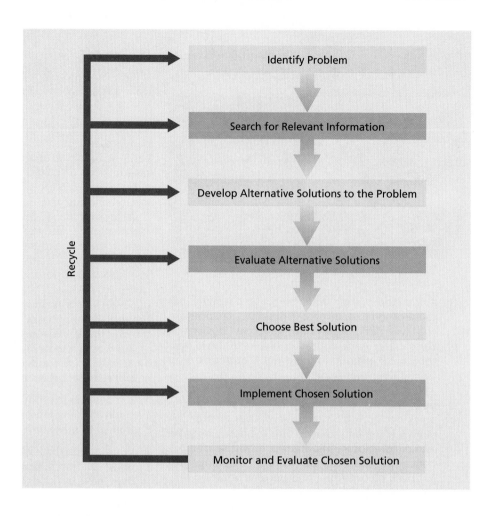

While Economic Person is useful for theoretical purposes, the perfectly rational characteristics embodied in Economic Person do not exist in real decision makers. Nobel Prize winner Herbert Simon recognizes this and suggests that administrators use **bounded rationality** rather than perfect rationality,[4] that is, while they try to act rationally, they are limited in their capacity to acquire and process information. In addition, time constraints and political considerations (such as the need to please others in the organization) act as bounds to rationality.

Framing and cognitive biases both illustrate the operation of bounded rationality. **Framing** refers to the (sometimes subtle) aspects of the presentation of information about a problem that are assumed by decision makers.[5] A frame could include assumptions about the boundaries of a problem, the possible outcomes of a decision, or the reference points used to decide if a decision is successful.[6] As we shall see, how problems and decision alternatives are framed can have a powerful impact on resulting decisions.

Cognitive biases are tendencies to acquire and process information in a particular way that is prone to error (see the cartoon). These biases constitute assumptions and shortcuts that can improve decision-making efficiency, but they frequently lead to serious errors in judgment. We will see how they work, in the following pages.

Problem Identification and Framing

You will recall that a problem exists when a gap occurs between existing and desired conditions. Such gaps might be signaled by dissatisfied customers or vigi-

Bounded rationality. A decision strategy that relies on limited information and that reflects time constraints and political considerations.

Framing. Aspects of the presentation of information about a problem that are assumed by decision makers.

Cognitive biases. Tendencies to acquire and process information in an error-prone way.

"IT'S BEGINNING TO SHOW SOME HUMAN CHARACTERISTICS — FAULTY REASONING, FORGETFULNESS AND REPETITION."

Source: *Current Contents*, July 17, 1989.

lant superiors or subordinates. Similarly, the press might contain articles about legislation or ads for competing products that signal difficulties for the organization. The perfectly rational decision maker, infinitely sensitive and completely informed, should be a great problem identifier. Bounded rationality, however, can lead to the following difficulties in problem identification:[7]

- *Perceptual defence.* In Chapter 3, we pointed out that the perceptual system may act to defend the perceiver against unpleasant perceptions. For example, the documentation on the Hubble mirror fiasco suggests that some Perkin-Elmer employees simply could not see what they did not want to see—that the mirror had a serious aberration.

- *Problem defined in terms of functional specialty.* Selective perception can cause decision makers to view a problem as being in the domain of their own specialty (e.g., marketing) even when some other perspective might be warranted.

- *Problem defined in terms of solution.* This form of jumping to conclusions effectively short-circuits the rational decision-making process. When Coca-Cola changed its time-honoured formula to produce a "new" Coke, it appears that its market share problem was prematurely defined in terms of a particular solution—we need to change our existing product.

- *Problem diagnosed in terms of symptoms.* "What we have here is a morale problem." While this might be true, a concentration on surface symptoms will provide the decision maker with few clues about an adequate solution. The real problem here involves the cause of the morale problem. Low morale due to poor pay suggests different solutions than does low morale due to boring work.

When a problem is identified, it is necessarily framed in some way. Consider how different it is to frame a $10,000 expenditure as a cost (something to be avoided) versus an investment (something to be pursued). Or, consider how different it is to frame a new product introduction as a military campaign against competitors versus a crusade to help customers. Or, consider how a firm might view a new piece of technology as a threat to its business or an opportunity to be exploited. In each case, the facts of the matter might be the same, but the different decision frames might lead to very different decisions.

Rational decision makers should try to be very self-conscious about how they have framed problems ("We have assumed that this is a product innovation problem"). Also, they should try out alternative frames ("Let's imagine that we don't need a new product here."). Finally, decision makers should avoid overarching, universal frames (corporate culture gone wild). While it is a good idea to "put customers first," we do not want to frame every problem as a customer service problem.[8]

Information Search

As you can see in Exhibit 11.1, once a problem is identified, a search for information is instigated. This information search may clarify the nature or extent of the problem and begin to suggest alternative solutions. Again, our perfectly rational Economic Person is in good shape at this second stage of the decision-making process. He or she has free and instantaneous access to all information necessary to clarify the problem and develop alternative solutions. Bounded rationality, however, presents a different picture. Information search might be slow and costly.

Too Little Information. Sometimes, decision makers do not acquire enough information to make a good decision. Several cognitive biases contribute to this. For one thing, people tend to be mentally lazy and use whatever information is most readily available to them. Often, this resides in the memory, and we tend to remember *vivid, recent* events.[9] Although such events might prove irrelevant in the context of the current problem, we curtail information search and rely on familiar experience. The manager who remembers that "the last time we went to an outside supplier for parts, we got burned" may be ignoring the wisdom of contracting out a current order.

Information overload can lead to errors, omissions, delays, and stress.

Another cognitive bias that contributes to incomplete information search is the well-documented tendency for people to be overconfident in their decision making.[10] This difficulty is exacerbated by **confirmation bias,** the tendency to seek out only information that conforms to one's own definition of or solution to a problem. Both these biases can lead people to shirk the acquisition of additional information. The Hubble mirror decision makers avoided outside tests that would have revealed that the early signals of a problem were, in fact, correct. Similarly, in the fatal *Challenger* space launch, only a limited range of data about the impact of temperature on mechanical failure was examined.

Too Much Information. While the bounds of rationality often force us to make decisions with incomplete or imperfect information, *too much* information can also damage the quality of decisions. **Information overload** is the reception of more information than is necessary to make effective decisions. As shown in Exhibit 11.2, advances in technology have made information overload an even greater problem as people now receive more messages and information than ever. According to one study, the average person sends and receives approximately 178 messages a day.[11]

As you might guess, information overload can lead to errors, omissions, delays, and cutting corners.[12] In addition, decision makers facing overload often attempt to use all the information at hand, then get confused and permit low-quality information or irrelevant information to influence their decisions.[13] Perhaps you have experienced this when writing a term paper—trying to incorporate too many references and too many viewpoints into a short paper can lead to a confusing, low-quality end product. More is not necessarily better.

However, decision makers seem to *think* that more is better. In one study, even though information overload resulted in lower-quality decisions, overloaded decision makers were more *satisfied* than those who did not experience overload.[14] Why is this so? For one thing, even if decisions do not improve with additional information, confidence in the decisions may increase ("I did the best I could"). Second, decision makers may fear being "kept in the dark" and associate the

Confirmation bias. The tendency to seek out information that conforms to one's own definition of or solution to a problem.

Information overload. The reception of more information than is necessary to make effective decisions.

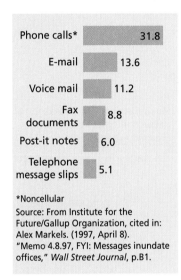

Phone calls*	31.8
E-mail	13.6
Voice mail	11.2
Fax documents	8.8
Post-it notes	6.0
Telephone message slips	5.1

*Noncellular
Source: From Institute for the Future/Gallup Organization, cited in: Alex Markels. (1997, April 8). "Memo 4.8.97, FYI: Messages inundate offices," *Wall Street Journal*, p.B1.

Exhibit 11.2
Average number of messages received daily per employee.

Farcus
by David Waisglass
Gordon Coulthart

WAISGLASS/COULTHART

© 1994 Farcus Cartoons

"Where should I put the really important messages?"

possession of information with power. One research review draws these conclusions about information gathering and use.[15] Managers

- gather much information that has little decision relevance;
- use information that they collected and gathered after a decision in order to justify that decision;
- request information that they do not use;
- request more information, regardless of what is already available; and
- complain that there is not enough information to make a decision even though they ignore available information.

In conclusion, although good information improves decisions, organizational members often obtain more or less information than is necessary for adequate decisions.

Alternative Development, Evaluation, and Choice

Perfectly informed or not, the decision maker can now list alternative solutions to the problem, examine the solutions, and choose the best one. For the perfectly rational, totally informed, ideal decision maker, this is easy. He or she conceives of all alternatives, knows the ultimate value of each alternative, and knows the probability that each alternative will work. In this case, the decision maker can exhibit **maximization**—that is, he or she can choose the alternative with the greatest expected value. Consider a simple example:

Maximization. The choice of the decision alternative with the greatest expected value.

	Ultimate Value	Probability	Expected Value
Alternative 1	$100,000 Profit	.4	$40,000 Profit
Alternative 2	$ 60,000 Profit	.8	$48,000 Profit

Here, the expected value of each alternative is calculated by multiplying its ultimate value by its probability. In this case, the perfectly rational decision maker would choose to implement the second alternative.

Unfortunately, things do not go so smoothly for the decision maker working under bounded rationality. He may not know all alternative solutions, and he might be ignorant of the ultimate values and probabilities of success of those solutions that he knows.

Again, cognitive biases come into play. In particular, people are especially weak intuitive statisticians, and they frequently violate standard statistical principles. For example:[16]

- People avoid incorporating known existing data about the likelihood of events ("base rates") into their decisions. For instance, firms continue to launch novelty food products (e.g., foods squeezed from tubes or foods developed by celebrities) even though they have a very high failure rate in the market.

- Large samples warrant more confidence than small samples. Despite this, data from a couple of (vivid) focus groups might be given more weight than data from a large (but anonymous) national survey.

- Decision makers often overestimate the odds of complex chains of events occurring—the scenario sounds sensible despite being less likely with every added link in the chain. "This product will be successful because the price of oil will fall *and* our competitors won't master the technology *and* free trade laws will be enacted."

- People are poor at revising estimates of probabilities and values as they acquire additional information. A good example is the **anchoring effect,** which illustrates that decision makers do not adjust their estimates enough from some initial estimate that serves as an anchor. For example, in one study, real estate agents allowed the *asking price* of a house to unduly influence their *professional evaluation* of the house.[17]

Anchoring effect. The inadequate adjustment of subsequent estimates from an initial estimate that serves as an anchor.

Making decision makers more accountable can sometimes improve decision making. However, these basic statistical cognitive biases are not generally reduced by accountability.[18]

The perfectly rational decision maker can evaluate alternative solutions against a single criterion—economic gain. The decision maker who is bounded by reality might have to factor in other criteria as well, such as the political acceptability of the solution to other organizational members—will the boss like it? Since these additional criteria have their own values and probabilities, the decision-making task increases in complexity.

The bottom line here is that the decision maker working under bounded rationality frequently "satisfices" rather than maximizes.[19] **Satisficing** means that the decision maker establishes an adequate level of acceptability for a solution and then screens solutions until he or she finds one that exceeds this level. When this occurs, evaluation of alternatives ceases, and the solution is chosen for implementation. For instance, the human resources manager who feels that absenteeism has become too high might choose a somewhat arbitrary acceptable level (e.g., the rate one year earlier), then accept the first solution that seems likely to achieve this level. Few organizations seek to *maximize* attendance.

Satisficing. Establishing an adequate level of acceptability for a solution to a problem and then screening solutions until one that exceeds this level is found.

Risky Business

Choosing between decision alternatives often involves an element of risk, and the research evidence on how people handle such risks is fascinating. Consider this scenario that decision researcher Max Bazerman developed. Which alternative solution would you choose?

> Robert Davis, head of the legal staff of a Fortune 500 company, has delayed making one of the most critical recommendations in the organization's history. The company is faced with a class action suit from a hostile group of consumers. While the organization believes that it is innocent, it realizes that a court may not have the same perspective. The organization is expected to lose $50 million if the suit is lost in court. Davis predicts a 50 percent chance of losing the case. The organization has the option of settling out of court by paying $25 million to the "injured" parties. Davis's senior staff has been collecting information and organizing the case for over six months. It is time for action. What should Davis recommend?

Alternative A   Settle out of court and accept a sure *loss* of $25,000,000,

or

Alternative B   Go to court expecting a 50 percent probability of a $50,000,000 loss.[20]

Notice that these two solutions are functionally equivalent in terms of dollars and cents (50 percent of $50 million = $25 million). Nonetheless, you probably tended to choose alternative B—about 80 percent of students do. Notice also that alternative B is the riskier of the two alternatives, in that it exposes the firm to a *potential* for greater loss.

Now, consider two further descriptions of the alternatives. Which solution would you choose?

Alternative C   Settle out of court and *save* $25,000,000 that could be lost in court,

or

Alternative D   Go to court expecting a 50 percent probability of *saving* $50,000,000.

Again, these two solutions are functionally equivalent in monetary terms (and equivalent to options A and B). Yet, you probably chose solution C—80 percent of students do. Notice that this is the *less* risky alternative, in that the firm is not exposed to a potential $50 million loss.

This is a graphic example of the power of framing. Alternatives A and B frame the problem as a choice between losses, while C and D frame it as a choice between gains or savings. Research by Daniel Kahneman and Amos Tversky shows that when people view a problem as a choice between losses, they tend to make risky decisions, rolling the dice in the face of a sure loss. When people frame the alternatives as a choice between gains they tend to make conservative decisions, protecting the sure win.[21]

It is very important to be aware of what reference point you are using when you frame decision alternatives. It is not necessarily wrong to frame a problem as a choice between losses, but this can contribute to a foolish level of risk taking. The (rescinded) decision to alter Coke's formula, the Iran-Contra affair, and the fatal launch of the space shuttle *Challenger* have all been attributed to perceived choices between losses.[22] In the *Challenger* example, the weather conditions were far from ideal for a launch, but a delay would have led to further technical and political problems for NASA. At least, this is the way the decision makers framed the available alternatives. If the Hubble mirror contractors went so far as to frame the problem, we can bet that they were considering a $1.7 million expenditure to fix the mirror, not saving $25 million in settlement fees.

We should emphasize that learning history can modify these general preferences for or against risk.[23] For example, suppose that a firm has become very successful by virtue of a series of risky decisions and is now faced with sitting on a handsome market share or investing in a product that could boost its share even higher. This win-win scenario would normally provoke conservatism, but the firm's historical success may tempt managers to choose the risky course of action and invest in the new product. Choosing a risky course of action might also be a function of one's culture (see "Global Focus: *Cultural Differences in Risky Decision Making*").

Solution Implementation

When a decision is made to choose a particular solution to a problem, the solution must be implemented. The perfectly rational decision maker will have factored any possible implementation problems into his or her choice of solutions. Of course, the bounded decision maker will attempt to do the same when estimating probabilities of success. However, in organizations, decision makers are often dependent on others to implement their decisions, and it might be difficult to anticipate their ability or motivation to do so.

A good example of implementation problems occurs when products such as cars are designed, engineered, and produced in a lengthy series of stages. For example, engineering might have to implement decisions made by designers, and production planning might have to implement decisions made by engineering. As we noted in Chapter 7, this sequential process frequently leads to confusion, conflict, and delay, unless cross-functional teams are used during the decision-making process. When they work well, such teams are sensitive to implementation problems.

global focus →)) Cultural Differences in Risky Decision Making

When making a decision, who would be greater risk takers—the Americans or the Chinese? If you think it would be people in the United States, then like most people who answered this question in a recent survey, you are wrong. In fact, research on cultural differences in decision making has found just the opposite. In a study by Elke Weber and Christopher Hsee, the Chinese were willing to invest in financial deals that the Americans found too risky.

In order to try to understand these cultural differences, Weber and Hsee conducted a study in which they asked people in the United States, China, Germany, and Poland not only how willing they would be to invest in a set of financial options but also how risky they perceived the options to be. As was the case in the previous study, the Chinese were willing to invest the most money. In addition, they also perceived the lowest amount of risk. The Americans were willing to invest the least amount and perceived the greatest amount of risk. People from Germany and Poland fell somewhere in between. These results suggest that one of the reasons that people from China take greater risks is that they perceive the same risks as smaller than do people from the United States and the other countries. Controlling for cultural differences in perceiving risk, the researchers found that the

Chinese and the Americans were willing to tolerate the same amount of risk; however, the Chinese still considered the financial options to be less risky than did the Americans.

On the basis of these findings, Weber and her colleagues proposed what they call the "cushion hypothesis." They argue that people in collectivist cultures, such as in China, can take greater financial risks because their social networks protect (or "cushion") them from large financial losses. Thus, the Chinese see the risks as lower because they feel they are protected.

The Chinese are also more confident in their judgments than are the Americans. Frank Yates found that people in many Asian countries are more overconfident than people in the United States. However, people in Japan were found to be more similar to people in the United States than to those in other Asian countries. Yates believes that people in countries such as China think about problems differently from people in the United States and Japan. These findings have important practical implications for people who work on international teams and with people from different cultures.

Source: Based on Azar, B. (1999, May). How do different cultures weigh the same decision? *APA Monitor*, p.12.

Solution Evaluation

When the time comes to evaluate the implemented solution, the decision maker is effectively examining the possibility that a new problem has occurred: Does the (new) existing state match the desired state? Has the decision been effective? For all the reasons we stated previously, the perfectly rational decision maker should be able to evaluate the effectiveness of the decision with calm, objective detachment. Again, however, the bounded decision maker might encounter problems at this stage of the process.

Justification. As we said earlier, people tend to be overconfident about the adequacy of their decisions. Thus, substantial dissonance can be aroused when a decision turns out to be faulty. One way to prevent such dissonance is to avoid careful tests of the adequacy of the decision. As a result, many organizations are notoriously lax when it comes to evaluating the effectiveness of expensive training programs or advertising campaigns. If the bad news cannot be avoided, the erring decision maker might devote his or her energy to trying to justify the faulty decision.

The justification of faulty decisions is best seen in the irrational treatment of sunk costs. **Sunk costs** are permanent losses of resources incurred as the result of a decision.[24] The key word here is "permanent." Since these resources have been lost (sunk) due to a past decision, they should not enter into future decisions. Despite this, psychologist Barry Staw has studied how people often "throw good resources after bad," acting as if they can recoup sunk costs. This process

Sunk costs. Permanent losses of resources incurred as the result of a decision.

Escalation of commitment. The tendency to invest additional resources in an apparently failing course of action.

is **escalation of commitment** to an apparently failing course of action, in which the escalation involves devoting more and more resources to actions implied by the decision.[25] For example, suppose an executive authorizes the purchase of several new computers to improve office productivity. The machines turn out to be very unreliable, and they are frequently out of commission for repairs. Perfect rationality suggests admitting to a mistake here. However, the executive might authorize an order for more machines from the same manufacturer to "prove" that he was right all along, hoping to recoup sunk costs with improved productivity from an even greater number of machines.

Dissonance reduction is not the only reason that escalation of commitment to a faulty decision may occur. In addition, a social norm that favours *consistent* behaviour by administrators might be at work.[26] Changing one's mind and reversing previous decisions might be perceived as a sign of weakness, a fate to be avoided at all costs.

Escalation of commitment sometimes happens even when the current decision maker is not responsible for previous sunk costs. For example, politicians might continue an expensive unnecessary public works project that was begun by a previous political administration. Here, dissonance reduction and the appearance of consistency are irrelevant, suggesting some other causes of escalation. For one thing, decision makers might be motivated not to appear wasteful.[27] ("Even though the airport construction is way over budget and flight traffic doesn't justify a new airport, let's finish the thing. Otherwise, the taxpayers will think we've squandered their money.") Also, escalation of commitment might be due to the way in which decision makers frame the problem once some resources have been sunk. Rather than seeing the savings involved in reversing the decision, the problem might be framed as a decision between a sure loss of x dollars (which have been sunk) and an uncertain loss of $x + y$ dollars (maybe the additional investment will succeed). As we noted earlier, when problems are framed this way, people tend to avoid the certain loss and go with the riskier choice, which in this case is escalation.[28]

Escalation can occur in both competitive and noncompetitive situations. Some Wall Street analysts felt that Viacom Inc. paid too much for entertainment giant Paramount in its five-month bidding war with QVC Network. Escalation is frequently seen in competitive bidding. As a noncompetitive example, many respected Wall Street securities analysts advised the purchase of IBM stock even as it was falling lower and lower in response to the firm's difficulties in the early 1990s.

Viacom Inc.
www.viacom.com

There are elements of escalation in the Hubble mirror fiasco. Perkin-Elmer continued to pour money into smoothing the flawed shape of the mirror despite early warnings of the flaw. The company expended effort justifying the questionable test results.

Are there any ways to prevent the tendency to escalate commitment to a failing course of action? Logic and research suggest the following:[29]

- Encourage continuous experimentation with reframing the problem to avoid the decision trap of feeling that more resources *have* to be invested. Shift the frame to saving rather than spending.

- Set specific goals for the project in advance that must be met if more resources are to be invested. This prevents escalation when early results are "unclear."

- Place more emphasis in evaluating managers on *how* they made decisions and less on decision outcomes. This kind of accountability is the sensible way to teach managers not to fear failure.

- Separate initial and subsequent decision making so that individuals who make the initial decision to embark on a course of action are assisted or replaced by others who decide if a course of action should be continued.

It may be tempting to think that using groups to make decisions will reduce the tendency toward escalation. However, research shows that groups are *more* prone than individuals to escalate commitment.[30] Certainly, many of the prominent escalation fiascos have been group decisions.

Hindsight. The careful evaluation of decisions is also inhibited by faulty hindsight. **Hindsight** refers to the tendency to review the decision-making process that we used in order to find out what we did right (in the case of success) or wrong (in the case of failure). While hindsight can prove useful, it often functions as a cognitive bias.

The classic example of hindsight involves the armchair quarterback who "knew" that a chancy intercepted pass in the first quarter was unnecessary because the team won the game anyway! The armchair critic is exhibiting the knew-it-all-along effect. This is the tendency to assume after the fact that we knew all along what the outcome of a decision would be. In effect, our faulty memory adjusts the probabilities that we estimated before making the decision to correspond to what actually happened.[31] This can prove quite dangerous. The money manager who consciously makes a very risky investment that turns out to be successful might revise her memory to assume that the decision was a sure thing. The next time, the now-confident investor might not be so lucky!

Another form of faulty hindsight is the tendency to take personal responsibility for successful decision outcomes while denying responsibility for unsuccessful outcomes.[32] Thus, when things work out well, it is because *we* made a careful, logical decision. When things go poorly, some unexpected *external* factor messed up our sensible decision!

Rational Decision Making—A Summary

The rational decision-making model in Exhibit 11.1 provides a good guide for how many decisions *should* be made but only a partially accurate view of how they *are* made. For complex, unfamiliar decisions, such as choosing an occupation, the rational model provides a pretty good picture of how people actually make decisions.[33] Also, organizational decision makers often follow the rational model when they agree about the goals they are pursuing.[34] On the other hand,

Hindsight. The tendency to review the decision-making process to find what was done right or wrong.

Stage	Perfect Rationality	Bounded Rationality
Problem Identification	Easy, accurate perception of gaps that constitute problems	Perceptual defence; jump to solutions; attention to symptoms rather than problems
Information Search	Free; fast; right amount obtained	Slow; costly; reliance on flawed memory; obtain too little or too much
Development of Alternative Solutions	Can conceive of all	Not all known
Evaluation of Alternative Solutions	Ultimate value of each known; probability of each known; only criterion is economic gain	Potential ignorance of or miscalculation of values and probabilities; criteria include political factors
Solution Choice	Maximizes	Satisfices
Solution Implementation	Considered in evaluation of alternatives	May be difficult owing to reliance on others
Solution Evaluation	Objective, according to previous steps	May involve justification, escalation to recover sunk costs, faulty hindsight

Exhibit 11.3
Perfectly rational decision making contrasted with bounded rationality.

Exhibit 11.4
Summary of cognitive biases in decision making.

- Decision makers tend to be overconfident about the decisions that they make.
- Decision makers tend to seek out information that confirms their own problem definitions and solutions. (Confirmation bias)
- Decision makers tend to remember and incorporate vivid, recent events into their decisions.
- Decision makers fail to incorporate known existing data about the liklihood of events into their decisions.
- Decision makers ignore sample sizes when evaluating samples of information.
- Decision makers overestimate the odds of complex chains of events occurring.
- Decision makers do not adjust estimates enough from some initial estimate that serves as an anchor as they acquire more information. (Anchoring effect)
- Decision makers have difficulty ignoring sunk costs when making subsequent decisions.
- Decision makers overestimate their ability to have predicted events after-the-fact, take responsibility for successful decision outcomes, and deny responsibility for unsuccessful outcomes. (Hindsight)

there is plenty of case study evidence of short-circuiting the rational model in organizational decisions, in part because of the biases we discussed above.[35] Thus, it should not be surprising that a recent study of 356 decisions in medium to large organizations in the United States and Canada found that half the decisions made in organizations fail. These failures were found to be primarily due to the use of poor tactics on the part of managers who impose solutions, limit the search for alternatives, and use power to implement their plans.[36] True experts in a field will also often short-circuit the rational model, using their knowledge base stored in memory to skip steps logically.[37] Exhibit 11.3 summarizes the operation of perfect and bounded rationality at each stage of the decision process. Exhibit 11.4 summarizes the various cognitive biases that we have covered.

Group Decision Making

Many, many organizational decisions are made by groups rather than individuals, especially when problems are ill structured. In this section, we shall consider the advantages and problems of group decision making.

Why Use Groups?

There are a number of reasons for employing groups to make organizational decisions.

Decision Quality. Experts often argue that groups or teams can make higher-quality decisions than individuals. This argument is based on the following three assumptions:

- Groups are *more vigilant* than individuals are—more people are scanning the environment.
- Groups can *generate more ideas* than individuals can.
- Groups can *evaluate ideas better* than individuals can.

At the problem identification and information search stages, vigilance is especially advantageous. A problem that some group members miss might be identified by others. For example, a member of the board of directors might notice a short article in an obscure business publication that has great relevance for the firm. In searching for information to clarify the problem suggested in the article, other members of the board might possess unique information that proves useful.

When it comes to developing alternative solutions, more people should literally have more ideas, if only because someone remembers something that others have forgotten. In addition, members with different backgrounds and experiences may bring different perspectives to the problem. This is why undergraduate students, graduate students, faculty, and administrators are often included on university task forces to improve the library or develop a course evaluation system.

When it comes to evaluating solutions and choosing the best one, groups have the advantage of checks and balances, that is, an extreme position or incorrect notion held by one member should be offset by the pooled judgments of the rest of the group.

These characteristics suggest that groups *should* make higher-quality decisions than individuals can. Shortly, we will find out whether they actually do so.

Decision Acceptance and Commitment. As we pointed out in our discussion of participative leadership in Chapter 9, groups are often used to make decisions on the premise that a decision made in this way will be more acceptable to those involved. Again, there are several assumptions underlying this premise:

- People wish to be involved in decisions that will affect them.
- People will better understand a decision in which they participated.
- People will be more committed to a decision in which they invested personal time and energy.

The acceptability of group decisions is especially useful in dealing with a problem described earlier—getting the decision implemented. If decision makers truly understand the decision and feel committed to it, they should be willing to follow through and see that it is carried out.

Diffusion of Responsibility. High quality and acceptance are sensible reasons for using groups to make decisions. As you may recall from Chapter 9, a somewhat less admirable reason to employ groups is to allow for **diffusion of responsibility** across the members in case the decision turns out poorly. In this case, each member of the group will share part of the burden of the negative consequences, and no one person will be singled out for punishment. Of course, when this happens, individual group members often "abandon ship" and exhibit biased hindsight—"I knew all along that the bid was too high to be accepted, but they made me go along with them."

Diffusion of responsibility. The ability of group members to share the burden of the negative consequences of a poor decision.

Do Groups Actually Make Higher-Quality Decisions Than Individuals Do?

The discussion in the first part of the previous section suggested that groups *should* make higher-quality decisions than individuals do. But *do* they? Is the frequent use of groups to make decisions warranted by evidence? The answer is yes. One review concludes that "groups usually produce more and better solutions to problems than do individuals working alone."[38] Another concludes that group performance is superior to that of the average individual in the group.[39] More specifically, groups should perform better than individuals when

- the group members differ in relevant skills and abilities, as long as they do not differ so much that conflict occurs;
- some division of labour can occur;
- memory for facts is an important issue; and

- individual judgments can be combined by weighting them to reflect the expertise of the various members.[40]

To consolidate your understanding of these conditions, consider a situation that should favour group decision making: A small construction company wishes to bid on a contract to build an apartment complex. The president, the controller, a construction boss, and an engineer work together to formulate the bid. Since they have diverse backgrounds and skills, they divide the task initially. The president reviews recent bids on similar projects in the community; the controller gets estimates on materials costs; the engineer and boss review the blueprints. During this process, each racks his or her brain to recall lessons learned from making previous bids. Finally, they put their information together, and each member voices an opinion about what the bid should be. The president decides to average these opinions to arrive at the actual bid, since each person is equally expert in his or her own area.

Disadvantages of Group Decision Making

Although groups have the ability to develop high-quality, acceptable decisions, there are a number of potential disadvantages to group decision making.

Time. Groups seldom work quickly or efficiently, compared with individuals. This is because of the process losses (Chapter 7) involved in discussion, debate, and coordination. The time problem increases with group size. When the speed of arriving at a solution to a problem is a prime factor, organizations should avoid using groups.

Conflict. Many times, participants in group decisions have their own personal axes to grind or their own resources to protect. When this occurs, decision quality may take a back seat to political wrangling and infighting. In the example about the construction company we presented earlier, the construction boss might see it to his advantage to overestimate the size of the crew required to build the apartments. On the other hand, the controller might make it her personal crusade to pare labour costs. A simple compromise between these two extreme points of view might not result in the highest-quality or most creative decision.

Domination. The advantages of group decision making will seldom be realized if meetings are dominated by a single individual or a small coalition. Even if a dominant person has good information, this style is not likely to lead to group acceptance and commitment. If the dominant person is particularly misinformed, the group decision is very likely to be ineffective.

Groupthink. In retrospect, have you ever been involved in a group decision that you knew was a "loser" but that you felt unable to protest? Perhaps you thought you were the only one who had doubts about the chosen course of action. Perhaps you tried to speak up, but others criticized you for not being on the team. Maybe you found yourself searching for information to confirm that the decision was correct and ignoring evidence that the decision was bad. What was happening? Were you suffering from some strange form of possession? Mind control?

In Chapter 8, we discussed the process of conformity in social settings. As you might expect, conformity can have a strong influence on the decisions that groups make. The most extreme influence is seen when **groupthink** occurs. This happens when group pressures lead to reduced mental efficiency, poor testing of reality, and lax moral judgment.[41] In effect, unanimous acceptance of decisions is stressed over quality of decisions.

Groupthink. The capacity for group pressure to damage the mental efficiency, reality testing, and moral judgment of decision-making groups.

Psychologist Irving Janis, who developed the groupthink concept, felt that high group cohesiveness was at its root. It now appears that other factors might be equally important or more important.[42] These include concern for approval from the group and the isolation of the group from other sources of information. However, the promotion of a particular decision by the group leader appears to be the strongest cause.[43] In any event, Janis provides a detailed list of groupthink symptoms:

- *Illusion of invulnerability.* Members are overconfident and willing to assume great risks. They ignore obvious danger signals.

- *Rationalization.* Problems and counterarguments that members cannot ignore are "rationalized away."

- *Illusion of morality.* The decisions the group adopts are not only perceived as sensible, they are also perceived as *morally* correct.

- *Stereotypes of outsiders.* The group constructs unfavourable stereotypes of those outside the group who are the targets of their decisions.

- *Pressure for conformity.* Members pressure each other to fall in line and conform with the group's views.

- *Self-censorship.* Members convince themselves to avoid voicing opinions contrary to the group.

- *Illusion of unanimity.* Members perceive that unanimous support exists for their chosen course of action.

- *Mindguards.* Some group members may adopt the role of "protecting" the group from information that goes against its decisions.[44]

Obviously, victims of groupthink are operating in an atmosphere of unreality that should lead to low-quality decisions. Groupthink has been implicated in the decision process that led to NASA's fatal launch of *Challenger.*[45] We can also see it in the Hubble mirror decision process.[46] To begin with, a dominant leader in charge of the internal tests appears to have isolated the mirror project team from outside sources of information. Symptoms of groupthink followed: At least three sets of danger signals that the mirror was flawed were ignored or explained away (illusion of invulnerability and rationalization); Kodak was dismissed as too incompetent to test the mirror (stereotype of outsiders); the consultant who suggested that Kodak test the mirror received bitter criticism but still felt he did not protest enough in the end (mindguarding and self-censorship); the defence of the isolated working methods was viewed as more "theological" than technical (illusion of morality).

What can prevent groupthink? Leaders must be careful to avoid exerting undue pressure for a particular decision outcome and concentrate on good decision processes. Also, leaders should establish norms that encourage and even reward responsible dissent, and outside experts should be brought in from time to time to challenge the group's views.[47] Some of the decision-making techniques we discuss later in the chapter should help prevent the tendency as well.

How Do Groups Handle Risk?

Almost by definition, problems that are suitable for group decision making involve some degree of risk and uncertainty. This raises a very important question: Do groups make decisions that are more or less risky than those of individuals? Or will the degree of risk assumed by the group simply equal the average risk preferred by its individual members? The answer here is obviously important. Consider the following scenario:

An accident has just occurred at a nuclear power plant. Several corrections exist, ranging from expensive and safe to low-cost but risky. On the way to an emergency meeting, each nuclear engineer formulates an opinion about what should be done. But what will the group decide?

Conventional wisdom provides few clear predictions about what the group of engineers will decide to do. On the one hand, it is sometimes argued that groups will make riskier decisions than individuals do because there is security in numbers, that is, diffusion of responsibility for a bad decision encourages the group to take greater chances. On the other hand, it is often argued that groups are cautious, with the members checking and balancing each other so much that a conservative outcome is sure to occur. Just contrast the committee-laden civil service with the swashbuckling style of independent operators, such as Ted Turner and Donald Trump!

Risky shift. The tendency for groups to make riskier decisions than the average risk initially advocated by their individual members.

Given this contradiction of common sense, the history of research into group decision making and risk is both interesting and instructive. A Massachusetts Institute of Technology student, J.A.F. Stoner, reported in a Master's thesis that he had discovered clear evidence of a **risky shift** in decision making.[48] Participants in the research reviewed hypothetical cases involving risk, such as those involving career choices or investment decisions. As individuals, they recommended a course of action. Then they were formed into groups, and the groups discussed each case and came to a joint decision. In general, the groups tended to advise riskier courses of action than the average risk initially advocated by their members. This is the risky shift. As studies were conducted by others to explore the reasons for its causes, things got more complicated. For some groups and some decisions, **conservative shifts** were observed. In other words, groups came to decisions that were *less* risky than those of the individual members before interaction.

Conservative shift. The tendency for groups to make less risky decisions than the average risk initially advocated by their individual members.

It is now clear that both risky and conservative shifts are possible, and they occur in a wide variety of real settings, including investment and purchasing decisions. But what determines which kind of shift occurs? A key factor appears to be the initial positions of the group members before they discuss the problem. This is illustrated in Exhibit 11.5. As you can see, when group members are somewhat conservative before interaction (the X's), they tend to exhibit a conservative shift when they discuss the problem. When group members are somewhat risky initially (the ●'s), they exhibit a risky shift after discussion. In other words, *group discussion seems to polarize or exaggerate the initial position of the group*.[49] Returning to the nuclear accident, if the engineers initially prefer a somewhat conservative solution, they should adopt an even more conservative strategy during the meeting.

Why do risky and conservative shifts occur when groups make decisions? Evidence seems to indicate two main factors:[50]

- Group discussion generates ideas and arguments that individual members have not considered before. This information naturally favours the members' initial tendency toward risk or toward conservatism. Since discussion provides "more" and "better" reasons for the initial tendency, the tendency ends up being exaggerated.

- Group members try to present themselves as basically similar to other members but "even better." Thus, they try to one-up others in discussion by adopting a slightly more extreme version of the group's initial stance.

In summary, administrators should be aware of the tendency for group interaction to polarize initial risk levels. If this polarization results from the sensible exchange of information, it might actually improve the group's decision. However, if it results from one-upmanship, it might lead to low-quality decisions.

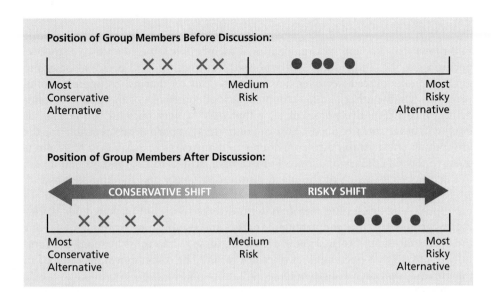

Exhibit 11.5
The dynamics of risky and conservative shifts for two groups.

Improving Decision Making in Organizations

Can the decision making process and its outcomes be improved? One study recently found that managers can improve the success of their decisions by using various tactics, such as making the need for action clear at the outset, setting objectives, carrying out an unrestricted search for solutions, and getting key people to participate.[51] It stands to reason that organizational decision making can improve if decision makers receive encouragement to follow more closely the rational decision-making model shown in Exhibit 11.1. This should help to preclude the various biases and errors that we have alluded to throughout the chapter. Each of the following techniques has this goal.

Training Discussion Leaders

When organizations utilize group decision making, an appointed leader often convenes the group and guides the discussion. The actions of this leader can "make or break" the decision. On the one hand, if the leader behaves autocratically, trying to "sell" a preconceived decision, the advantages of using a group are obliterated, and decision acceptance can suffer. If the leader fails to exert *any* influence, however, the group might develop a low-quality solution that does not meet the needs of the organization. The use of role-playing training to develop these leadership skills has increased the quality and acceptance of group decisions. The following are examples of the skills that people learn in discussion leader training.[52]

- State the problem in a nondefensive, objective manner. Do not suggest solutions or preferences.

- Supply essential facts and clarify any constraints on solutions (e.g., "We can't spend more than $5,000").

- Draw out all group members. Prevent domination by one person, and protect members from being attacked or severely criticized.

- Wait out pauses. Do not make suggestions or ask leading questions.

- Ask stimulating questions that move the discussion forward.

- Summarize and clarify at several points to mark progress.

Stimulating and Managing Controversy

Full-blown conflict among organizational members is hardly conducive to good decision making. Individuals will withhold information, and personal or group goals will take precedence over developing a decision that solves organizational problems. On the other hand, a complete lack of controversy can be equally damaging, since alternative points of view that may be very relevant to the issue at hand will never surface. Such a lack of controversy is partially responsible for the groupthink effect, and it also contributes to many cases of escalation of commitment to flawed courses of action. For example, stifled controversy played a part in the disastrous launch of the space shuttle *Challenger* and the Hubble fiasco.

Research shows a variety of ways to stimulate controversy in decision-making groups—incorporating members with diverse ideas and backgrounds, forming subgroups to "tear the problem apart," and establishing norms that favour the open sharing of information.[53] However, these tactics must be managed carefully to ensure that open conflict does not result. The discussion skills covered in the previous section can help here.

One interesting method of controversy stimulation is the appointment of a **devil's advocate** to challenge existing plans and strategies. The advocate's role is to challenge the weaknesses of the plan or strategy and state why it should not be adopted. For example, a bank might be considering offering an innovative kind of account. Details to be decided include interest rate, required minimum balance, and so on. A committee might be assigned to develop a position paper. Before a decision is made, someone would be assigned to read the paper and "tear it apart," noting potential weaknesses. Thus, a decision is made in full recognition of the pros and cons of the plan.

Evidence indicates that the controversy promoted by the devil's advocate improves decision quality.[54] However, to be effective, the advocate must present his or her views in an objective, unemotional manner.

Traditional Brainstorming

Brainstorming is the "brain child" of a Madison Avenue advertising executive.[55] Its major purpose is to increase the number of creative solution alternatives to problems. Thus, **brainstorming** focuses on the *generation* of ideas rather than the *evaluation* of ideas. If a group generates a large number of ideas, the chance of obtaining a truly creative solution is increased.

Brainstorming was originally conceived as a group technique. It was assumed that in generating ideas, group members could feed off each other's suggestions and be stimulated to offer more creative solutions. To ensure this, the group is encouraged to operate in a free-wheeling, off-the-wall manner. No ideas should be considered too extreme or unusual to be voiced. In addition, no criticism of ideas should be offered, since this can inhibit useful lines of thinking. For instance, an advertising agency might convene a group to generate names for a new toothpaste or soft drink. Similarly, a government agency might convene a group to generate possible solutions for welfare fraud.

Traditional brainstorming has not fulfilled its full creative promise. Research has shown conclusively that individuals working alone tend to generate more ideas than when in groups.[56] In other words, four people working independently (and encouraged to be creative and nonevaluative) will usually generate more ideas than the same people working as a team. Why is this? Likely explanations include inhibition, domination of the group by an ineffective member, or the sheer physical limitations of people trying to talk simultaneously. Later, we will consider an electronic alternative to traditional brainstorming that does increase idea generation. However, as "In Focus: *Brainstorming at IDEO*" illustrates,

Devil's advocate. A person appointed to identify and challenge the weaknesses of a proposed plan or strategy.

Brainstorming. An attempt to increase the number of creative solution alternatives to problems by focusing on idea generation rather than evaluation.

in focus ➤))   Brainstorming at IDEO

IDEO is the biggest product design firm in the United States. Founded in 1978 by David Kelley, it is headquartered in Palo Alto, California, but also has offices in Tokyo, London, Boston, Chicago, and several other cities. Most of its employees are industrial designers and mechanical engineers, serving clients that vary from start-up firms to the Fortune top 50. The range of IDEO's design contributions is immense, spanning laptop computers, sports equipment, and surgical devices. Well-known products include the first Apple Computer mouse, Nike sunglasses, Crest toothpaste tubes, and the Palm V electronic organizer. The company is the winner of many product design awards and is so admired that its clients requested that it offer workshops on innovation and creativity. NEC, Kodak, and Steelcase are among the firms that send employees to these workshops.

IDEO employees feel that an important key to the firm's success is its extensive use of brainstorming to exchange design ideas. The average IDEO engineer participates in 24 brainstorming sessions a year. Sessions last from 45 minutes to two hours and include three to 10 participants with various specialities and skills. "Rules" for brainstorming, prominently displayed on meeting room walls, include (1) one discussion at a time, (2) stay on the topic, (3) build on others' ideas, (4) defer judgment, and (5) encourage wild ideas.

Researchers Robert Sutton and Andrew Hargadon were interested in why IDEO makes such extensive use of group brainstorming, in light of the research showing that the procedure does not result in more ideas being generated than occur when people "brainstorm" alone. What they found was that the procedure results in a number of other important creative and business advantages. In terms of the organizational culture, they found that it helped organizational memory and supported a culture of wisdom, that is, ideas from one session can be used on subsequent unrelated projects, and participants learn to appreciate the good ideas of others. At the individual level, the sessions motivate and stimulate the engineers and allow them to show off their good ideas to their colleagues. Finally, IDEO uses the brainstorming sessions to impress their clients, who really get to see how the design process unfolds. Thus, brainstorming shapes the organizational culture, helps retain good talent, and contributes to client confidence.

Sources: Brown, E. (1999, April 12). A day at innovation university. *Fortune*, pp. 163-165; Sutton, R.I., & Kelley, T.A. (1997, Fall). Creativity doesn't require isolation: Why product designers bring visitors "backstage." *California Management Review*, pp. 75-91; Sutton, R.I., & Hargadon, A. (1996). Brainstorming groups in context: Effectiveness in a product design firm. *Administrative Science Quarterly*, 41, pp. 685-718.

brainstorming can provide advantages that extend beyond the mere number of ideas generated.

Stimulating controversy in groups can generate new ideas and challenge existing plans and strategies.

Nominal Group Technique

The fact that nominal (in name only) brainstorming groups generate more ideas than interacting brainstorming groups gave rise to the **nominal group technique** (NGT) of decision making. Unlike brainstorming, NGT is concerned with both the generation of ideas and the evaluation of these ideas:

> Imagine a meeting room in which seven to 10 individuals are sitting around a table in full view of each other; however, at the beginning of the meeting they do not speak to each other. Instead, each individual is writing ideas on a pad of paper in front of him or her. At the end of five to 10 minutes, a structured sharing of ideas takes place. Each individual, in round-robin fashion, presents one idea from his or her private list. A recorder writes that idea on a flip chart in full view of other members. There is still no discussion at this point of the meeting—only the recording of privately narrated ideas. Round-robin listing continues until all members indicate they have no further ideas to share. Discussion follows during the next phase of the meeting; however, it is structured so that each idea receives attention before independent voting. This is accomplished by asking for clarification, or stating support or non-support of each idea listed on the flip chart. Independent voting then takes place. Each member privately, in writing, selects priorities by rank-ordering (or rating). The group decision is the mathematically pooled outcome of the individual votes.[57]

As you can see, NGT carefully separates the generation of ideas from their evaluation. Ideas are generated nominally (without interaction) to prevent inhibition and conformity. Evaluation permits interaction and discussion, but it occurs in a fairly structured manner to be sure that each idea gets adequate attention. NGT's chief disadvantage would seem to be the time and resources required to assemble the group for face-to-face interaction. The Delphi technique was developed, in part, to overcome this problem.

The Delphi Technique

The **Delphi technique** of decision making was developed at the Rand Corporation to forecast changes in technology. Its name derives from the future-telling ability of the famous Greek Delphic Oracle.[58] Unlike NGT, the Delphi process relies solely on a nominal group—participants do not engage in face-to-face interaction. Thus, it is possible to poll a large number of experts without assembling them in the same place at the same time. We should emphasize that these experts do not actually make a final decision; rather, they provide information for organizational decision makers.

The heart of Delphi is a series of questionnaires sent to respondents. Minimally, there are two waves of questionnaires, but more are not unusual. The first questionnaire is usually general in nature and permits free responses to the problem. For example, suppose the CEO of a large corporation wishes to evaluate and improve the firm's total quality management program. A random sample of managers who have worked closely with TQM would receive an initial questionnaire asking them to list the strengths and weaknesses of the program. The staff would collate the responses and develop a second questionnaire that might share these responses and ask for suggested improvements. A final questionnaire might then be sent asking respondents to rate or rank each improvement. The staff would then merge the ratings or rankings mathematically and present them to the president for consideration.

A chief disadvantage of Delphi is the rather lengthy time frame involved in the questionnaire phases, although fax and e-mail can speed up sending and receiving. In addition, its effectiveness depends on the writing skills of the respondents and their interest in the problem, since they must work on their own rather than as part of an actual group. Despite these problems, Delphi is an efficient method of pooling a large number of expert judgments, while avoiding the problems of conformity and domination that can occur in interacting groups.

Electronic Decision-Making Groups— Promise and Problems

In closing the chapter, let us consider the impact that electronic, computer-mediated information technology has on organizational decision making. You have probably heard of some of the more exotic forms of this technology, such as decision support systems and expert systems. These systems use databases compiled by experts to aid in the diagnosis and solution of problems. Here, we will consider something less exotic but equally interesting, the formation of electronic groups.

Electronic groups are simply decision-making groups whose members are linked together electronically rather than face-to-face. A typical group would interact on an electronic mail network, sending messages with a keyboard and receiving them via a monitor. These messages can be saved in computer memory for future reference.

Contrasting electronic groups with their face-to-face counterparts suggests some of the factors that might influence electronic decisions. For one thing, in electronic groups there is the potential for members to enter information anonymously. And even if contributions are not anonymous, people might *feel* somewhat more anonymous than in a face-to-face group. Second, audiovisual sources of information about how other members feel, expressed in body language and tone of voice, is missing. Finally, in electronic groups, many people can "talk" at the same time. As we will see, these differences affect the social structure of groups and consequently affect their decision making.

Electronic groups. Decision-making groups whose members are linked electronically rather than face-to-face.

Electronic Brainstorming

Some research on electronic groups has concentrated on the idea generation aspect of decision making. **Electronic brainstorming** uses computer-mediated technology to accomplish the same goals as traditional brainstorming, the generation of novel ideas without evaluation. As we noted above, face-to-face interaction actually reduces individual brainstorming performance. But what happens if people brainstorm as an electronic group?

Once over the size of two members, electronic brainstorming groups perform better than face-to-face groups in terms of both quantity and quality of ideas.[59] Also, as electronic groups get larger, they tend to produce more ideas, but the ideas-per-person measure remains stable. In contrast, as face-to-face groups get bigger, fewer and fewer ideas per person are generated (remember social loafing from Chapter 7). What accounts for the success of electronic brainstorming? Reduced inhibition about participating and the ability for people to enter ideas simultaneously without waiting for others seem to be the main reasons. Notice that these factors become especially critical as the group gets bigger. Some organizations have done electronic brainstorming with up to 30-member groups.

Electronic brainstorming. The use of computer-mediated technology to improve traditional brainstorming practices.

Beyond Brainstorming

Other research on electronic groups has gone beyond brainstorming to look at more complex and complete decision tasks that actually require reaching a solution. The results reveal both promise and problems.[60]

Electronic groups tend to be more egalitarian than face-to-face groups, that is, status barriers tend to be broken down, and participation is more evenly distributed among members. In one study of executives, men were five times more likely than women to make an initial decision proposal in a face-to-face meeting.[61] In an electronic meeting, men and women were equally likely to make the first proposal. This egalitarianism is obviously a good thing. On the other hand, electronic communication has also encouraged impulsive, rude messages and the expression of extreme views ("flaming").

For some well-established groups, electronic meetings seem to speed up the decision process. However, for newly formed groups, electronic interaction invariably slows the decision process and leads to difficulty for the group to reach consensus. "Flaming" might be a partial cause, but the lack of verbal and nonverbal cues also makes it difficult to recognize subtle trends toward consensus. This suggests the need for an electronic version of some of the discussion leader skills we listed earlier.

A final trend is the apparent tendency for electronic groups to make more extreme decisions than face-to-face groups, especially when it comes to risk. This trend, if confirmed, is disturbing because we have pointed out that face-to-face groups themselves have problems dealing with risk. Perhaps people feel less accountable for electronic decisions.

The impact of electronic groups on organizational decisions is obviously of importance to managers. Such groups provide great potential for crossing the barriers of time and space to improve group decisions. All the same, it is clear that they add some new complexities to the challenging task of making good decisions.

---

the manager's notebook

Turning Decision Making into a Science at General Electric Mortgage Insurance

1. The types of decisions that GE representatives make can be considered examples of ill-structured problems, that is, the existing and desired states are not always clear, and how to get from one state to the other is not straightforward. Furthermore, such decisions are risky, involve a high degree of uncertainty, and can result in costly errors. Therefore, it can be quite advantageous if programs can be developed to standardize these types of decisions through the use of programs. Programming such decisions can provide a useful means of solving the types of problems that GE representatives must deal with on a regular basis. However, the effectiveness of such programs are only as good as the decision-making process that is used to develop them. Obviously, GE's use of its most successful representatives to develop a program based on how they make superior decisions is the key to the development of a successful programmed decision-making system. Once the system has been developed, other representatives can be trained to use it. This should result in more effective decisions for all users of the system.

2. The group of successful representatives developed a system for accurately predicting which home buyers delinquent on their mortgage payments would be most likely to recover and those that should sell their houses. As a result, GE created a computer program that lets all representatives be equally good at their jobs. The program works much like income tax software, allowing the representatives to respond to a series of questions about a borrower's income, willingness to pay, ZIP code (to determine if houses in the area have depreciated in value), assets and other debts, such as car loans. The new system resulted in avoiding 1,600 foreclosures in its first year, up 43%, and saved GE about $8 million by making decisions more quickly, and by more accurately selecting which loans could be cured. The satisfaction rating from customers—the mortgage lenders that GE insures—rose from 61% to 76%. The program has also been almost perfect at predicting which borrowers, under threat of foreclosure, eventually will agree to pay for default losses and at what percentage. In 1998, GE was awarded the RIT/*USA Today* Quality Cup for service businesses in recognition of the development of the system.

Summary

- Decision making is the process of developing a commitment to some course of action. Alternatively, it is a problem-solving process. A problem exists when a gap is perceived between some existing state and some desired state.

- Some problems are well structured. This means that existing and desired states are clear, as is the means of getting from one state to the other. Well-structured problems are often solved with programs, which simply standardize solutions. Programmed decision making is effective as long as the program is developed rationally and as long as conditions do not change.

- Ill-structured problems contain some combination of an unclear existing state, an unclear desired state, or unclear methods of getting from one state to the other. They tend to be unique and nonrecurrent, and they require nonprogrammed decision making, in which the rational model comes into play.

- Rational decision making includes (1) problem identification, (2) information search, (3) development of alternative solutions, (4) evaluation of alternatives, (5) choice of the best alternative, (6) implementation, and (7) ongoing evaluation of the implemented alternative. The imaginary, perfectly rational decision maker has free and easy access to all relevant information, can process it accurately, and has a single ultimate goal—economic maximization. Real decision makers must suffer from bounded rationality. They do not have free and easy access to information, and the human mind has limited information processing capacity and is susceptible to a variety of cognitive biases. In addition, time constraints and political considerations can outweigh anticipated economic gain. As a result, bounded decision makers usually satisfice (choose a solution that is "good enough") rather than maximize. Perceptual defence, faulty hindsight, attempts to recover sunk costs, inadequate information, and information overload may damage the quality of decisions.

- Groups can often make higher-quality decisions than individuals can because of their vigilance and their potential capacity to generate and evaluate more ideas. Also, group members might accept more readily a decision in which they have been involved. Given the proper problem, groups will frequently make higher-quality decisions than individuals can. However, using groups takes a lot of time and might provoke conflict. In addition, groups might fall prey to groupthink, in which social pressures to conform to a particular decision outweigh rationality. Groups might also make decisions that are more risky or conservative than those of individuals.

- Attempts to improve decision making have involved training discussion leaders, stimulating controversy, brainstorming, the nominal group technique, and the Delphi technique.

- Electronic groups are decision-making groups that interact electronically rather than face-to-face. Electronic brainstorming is effective in generating ideas, and participation in electronic decision making tends to be egalitarian. However, electronic groups can have a hard time reaching consensus, and they tend to make riskier decisions than face-to-face groups.

Discussion Questions

1. The director of an urban hospital feels that there is a turnover problem among the hospital's nurses. About 25 percent of the staff resign each year, leading to high replacement costs and disruption of services. Use the decision model in Exhibit 11.1 to explore how the director might proceed to solve this problem. Discuss probable bounds to the rationality of the director's decision.

2. Describe a decision-making episode (in school, work, or personal life) in which you experienced information overload. How did you respond to this overload? Did it affect the quality of your decision?

3. Many universities must register thousands of students for courses each semester. Is this a well-structured problem or an ill-structured problem? Does it require programmed decisions or nonprogrammed decisions? Elaborate.

4. An auditing team fails to detect a case of embezzlement that has gone on for several months at a bank. How might the team members use hindsight to justify their faulty decisions?

5. A very cohesive planning group for a major oil company is about to develop a long-range strategic plan. The head of the unit is aware of the groupthink problem and wishes to prevent it. What steps should she take?

6. Discuss the implications of diffusion of responsibility, risky shift, and conservative shift for the members of a parole board.

7. Discuss how the concepts of groupthink and escalation of commitment might be related to some cases of unethical decision making (and its cover-up) in business.

8. What are the similarities and differences of the nominal group technique and the Delphi technique? What are the comparative advantages and disadvantages?

9. Consider the role of communication in decision making. Explain how barriers to effective superior-subordinate communication can affect decision making in organizations. How can personal and organizational approaches for improving communication improve decision making?

10. Does group structure influence group decision making? Explain how each of the following structural characteristics might influence group decision quality, acceptance and commitment, and diffusion of responsibility: group size, diversity, norms, roles, status, and cohesiveness.

Experiential Exercise

The New Truck Dilemma

Preparation for Role Playing

The instructor will:

1. Read general instructions to class as a whole.

2. Place data regarding name, length of service, and make and age of truck on chalkboard for ready reference by all.

3. Divide class into groups of six. Any remaining members should be asked to join one of the groups and serve as observers.

4. Assign roles to each group by handing out slips with the names Chris Marshall, Terry, Sal, Jan, Sam, and Charlie. Ask each person to read his or her own role only. Instructions should not be consulted once role playing is begun.

5. Ask the Chris Marshalls to stand up when they have completed reading their instructions.

6. When all Chris Marshalls are standing, ask that each crew member display conspicuously the slip of paper with his or her role name so that Chris can tell who is who.

The Role-Playing Process

1. The instructor will start the role playing with a statement such as the following: "Chris Marshall has asked the crew to wait in the office. Apparently Chris wants to discuss something with the crew. When Chris sits down that will mean he or she has returned. What you say to each other is entirely up to you. Are you ready? All Chris Marshalls please sit down."

2. Role playing proceeds for 25 to 30 minutes. Most groups reach agreement during this interval.

Collection of Results

1. Each supervisor in turn reports his or her crew's solution. The instructor summarizes on the chalkboard by listing the initials of each repair person and indicating with arrows which truck goes to whom.

2. A tabulation should be made of the number of people getting a different truck, the crew members considering the solution unfair, and the supervisor's evaluation of the solution.

Discussion of Results

1. Comparison of solutions will reveal differences in the number of people getting a different truck, who gets the new one, the number dissatisfied, etc. Discuss why the same facts yield different outcomes.

2. The quality of the solution can be measured by the trucks retained. Highest quality would require the poorest truck to be discarded. Evaluate the quality of the solutions achieved.

3. Acceptance is indicated by the low number of dissatisfied repair people. Evaluate solutions achieved on this dimension.

4. List problems that are similar to the new truck problem. See how widely the group will generalize.

General Instructions

This is a role-playing exercise. *Do not read the roles given below until assigned to do so by your instructor!*

Assume that you are a repair person for a large utility. Each day you drive to various locations in the city to do repair work. Each of you drives a small truck and you take pride in keeping it looking good. You have a possessive feeling about your truck and like to keep it in good running order. Naturally, you would like to have a new truck, too, because a new truck gives you a feeling of pride.

Here are some facts about the trucks and the crew that reports to Chris Marshall, the supervisor of repairs:

Terry—17 years with the company, has a 2-year-old Ford
Sal—11 years with the company, has a 5-year-old Dodge
Jan—10 years with the company, has a 4-year-old Ford
Sam—5 years with the company, has a 3-year-old Ford
Charlie—3 years with the company, has a 5-year-old Chevrolet

Most of you do all your driving in the city, but Jan and Sam cover the jobs in the suburbs.

You will be one of the people mentioned above and will be given some further individual instructions. In acting your part in role playing, accept the facts as well as assume the attitude supplied in your specific role. From this point on, let your feelings develop in accordance with the events that transpire in the role-playing process. When facts or events arise that are not covered by the roles, make up things that are consistent with the way it might be in a real-life situation.

When the role playing begins, assume that Chris Marshall called the crew into the repair office.

Role for Chris Marshall, Supervisor. You are the supervisor of a repair crew, each of whom drives a small service truck to and from various jobs. Ever so often you get a new truck to exchange for an old one, and you have the problem of deciding which one of your crew you should give the new truck to. Often there are hard feelings because each person seems to feel entitled to the new truck, so you have a tough time being fair. As a matter of fact, it usually turns out that whatever you decide, most of the crew consider it wrong. You now have to face the issue again because a new truck has just been allocated to you for assignment. The new truck is a Chevrolet.

In order to handle this problem, you have decided to put the decision up to the crew themselves. You will tell them about the new truck and will put the problem in terms of what would be the fairest way to assign the truck. *Do not take a position yourself because you want to do what the crew thinks is most fair.* However, be sure that the group reaches a decision.

Role for Terry. When a new Chevrolet truck becomes available, you think you should get it because you have most seniority and do not like your present truck. Your own car is a Chevrolet, and you prefer a Chevrolet truck such as you drove before you got the Ford.

Role for Sal. You feel you deserve a new truck. Your present truck is old, and since the more senior crew member has a fairly new truck, you should get the next one. You have taken excellent care of your present Dodge and have kept it looking like new. People deserve to be rewarded if they treat a company truck like their own.

Role for Jan. You have to do more driving than most of the other crew because you work in the suburbs. You have a fairly old truck and feel you should have a new one because you do so much driving.

Role for Sam. The heater in your present truck is inadequate. Since Charlie backed into the door of your truck, it has never been repaired to fit right. The door lets in too much cold air, and you attribute your frequent colds to this. You want a warm truck since you have a good deal of driving to do. As long as it has good tires, brakes, and is comfortable, you do not care about its make.

Role for Charlie. You have the poorest truck in the crew. It is five years old, and before you got it, it had been in a bad wreck. It has never been good, and you have put up with it for three years. It is about time you got a good truck to drive, and you feel the next one should be yours. You have a good accident record. The only accident you had was when you sprung the door of Sam's truck when he opened it as you backed out of the garage. You hope the new truck is a Ford, since you prefer to drive one.

Source: Adapted from Maier, N. R. F., & Verser, G. C. (1982). *Psychology in industrial organizations* (5th ed.). Copyright 1982 by Houghton Mifflin Company. Adapted with permission.

Case Incident

The Big Meeting

Larry was about to attend his first meeting since starting his new job. His group was going to meet with the president of the company to make a decision about whether to start testing a new drug on humans. The drug was designed to help people lose weight and was expected to make millions of dollars for the company. Just before the meeting, Larry's supervisor quietly told him that tests on animals have shown that the drug has terrible side effects and has resulted in the death of 15% of the animals tested. He also told Larry that this was known by everybody in the company, and he did not think the drug was ready to be tested on humans.

When the meeting began, the president of the company began to talk about how successful the company has been in the development of new drugs. He told them that the new drug will help millions of people, and that the public has a right to have it as soon as possible. "We have to begin testing immediately," he said, "it is our responsibility to continue our record of success, and our commitment to provide the public with drugs they need and desire. It is the right thing to do." The president then asked if anyone had anything to say before the group made a decision. Nobody said anything. Larry was shocked that his supervisor did not raise the issues he had mentioned to Larry before the meeting. So Larry decided to ask a question. "What about the results of the clinical trials with animals?" "The medical staff don't know what they're talking about," said the president. "They sometimes act like fools with those animals, and they don't know how to make business or management decisions, and that's what we have to do now." The group then unanimously voted to begin testing the drug on humans immediately. Larry could not believe that everybody supported the decision.

1. How rational was the decision to start testing the drug on humans? Is there any evidence of bounded rationality?

2. What are some of the issues in group decision making that might explain the decision to start testing the drug on humans?

Case Study

A New Direction for the Upstage Theatre

The board of the Upstage Theatre Company had assembled to hear the Artistic Director's proposals for the following year's season. Mark Buck, the Artistic Director, had built a reputation on his staging of popular comic seasons, and most members of the board expected a similar proposal this year.

Buck entered the boardroom, and after a few general remarks, began to speak about his plans for the season. As he spoke, the board members began to look at each other with astonishment. Buck was proposing a radical departure for the Theatre, a season of serious works, starting with a Shakespearean tragedy and working up to a piece by Arthur Miller. At the end of this totally unexpected proposal, he looked round at his audience. "Any questions?" he asked rather blandly, while privately enjoying the obvious bewilderment on the part of the board. He loved surprising people!

Jean Carlisle, the chairman of the board, was the only one not surprised by the proposal, as Buck had approached her several weeks ago and dropped some hints about his idea. Buck, she had a shrewd suspicion, was out primarily to promote his own career. Known as a "comedy man" first and foremost, he was in danger of being typecast within the industry. Only by rounding out his production experience could he hope to progress.

Carlisle, however, could see a lot of possibilities in the proposal for a "serious" season, even though she knew it would be dismissed as foolhardy by a number of the established board members. Her involvement with the Upstage Theatre was based on a sincere commitment to the cultural development of the community. Lately, she had been coming under some fire from her family and friends for not urging that more "culturally significant" work be performed by the Theatre. When she had first heard of Buck's proposal, she had decided to support it and had accordingly begun to consider how best to get the board to support it as well.

Now she turned to Robert Ramsay, a board member who had been brought in for his connections with the business community. "Well, Robert, it's an interesting proposal we have in front of us," she said. "What do you think?"

Ramsay, she happened to know, had been considerably embarrassed in front of the board recently, as a result of his inability to raise money for the Theatre. She also knew that much of the resistance to corporate support of the Theatre had come from the fact that its plays were not considered serious enough. Thus, Ramsay, she reasoned, would support the departure proposed by Buck.

This was indeed the case. "I think it's a marvellous idea. And I'm sure it's the kind of season the financial community would support," said Ramsay.

Several others on the board protested strongly against the proposed season. The most vociferous of these was Olaf Vickers, a local playwright of some repute. Vickers had had several of his comedy works performed by the Upstage Theatre Company over the years. The argument presented by Buck, Carlisle, and Ramsay managed to quiet these objections, however, at least to the point where the board voted to examine the marketing and financial implications of the proposal and meet again in two weeks' time.

When the board met again, a month later, the battle lines were more clearly drawn. Olaf Vickers spoke first. "I move that we dismiss the proposal for a 'tragedy' season," he said. "The Theatre has always had a reputation for comic works, and this reputation should not be thrown away lightly. I feel that our artistic director should go back and rethink his proposals."

Jean Carlisle, however, was ready with an answer. "I know how you feel," she said. "But I think we have to consider some other factors, too. For years now our theatre has been losing money, and how long the various arts councils will go on funding us is an open question. As I told you last year, some of the government people are very concerned that we develop more in the way of box office support and outside funding. Now, as I see it, this proposal may give us a chance to do just that. I've asked Mark Buck to do an unofficial survey among the town's theatre community, and I think you'll find the results interesting."

The artistic director now stood up. "We've been able to put together a random sample of theatregoers from the subscription lists of other theatres in town," he said. "I had a couple of people in the administrative office phone these people and do a straw poll survey of their preferences. The results indicate that a majority would patronize a new tragedy season. So I think we can expect some box office support for this proposal."

He sat down amid murmurs from the board members. Carlisle then asked Ramsay to address the meeting. "I've canvassed the business community," he said. "A number of corporations have indicated their interest in supporting a 'serious season' here. I think it's safe to say that we could count on fairly generous corporate support should we decide to go ahead."

A heated debate followed these announcements. While many of the previously uncommitted board members now leaned toward acceptance of the proposed season, a significant minority, lead by Olaf Vickers, opposed it. As the by-laws required a two-thirds majority to approve a policy change, the meeting adjourned without any decision being taken. It was decided to meet again the following week to resolve the crisis, if possible.

During that week, Jean Carlisle paid a visit to Olaf Vickers. After some polite discussion of theatre matters, she came to the point. "You know Olaf," she said sadly, "it's rather a pity you don't support the proposal for a 'serious' season."

"Why's that?" inquired the playwright suspiciously.

"Well," explained Carlisle, "it's just that I was talking to Buck the other day, and he wanted to commission you to write a work to wrap up the season. He says he's sure a serious piece by you would be just the thing to cap the year."

"I'm glad that he at least remembers part of the Theatre's original mandate," growled Vickers. "After all, the Upstage is supposed to be committed to the development of new local authors."

"And it's a commitment he takes very seriously," replied Carlisle. "And so do I, I can assure you. That's why if we were to go ahead with the season he suggests, I would move that your new play be commissioned immediately. I hope we can come to some agreement when we next meet," she added as she rose to go.

"Maybe," Vickers replied thoughtfully.

At the next meeting, Vickers announced that after some thought, he had changed his mind and would now support the new season. Several weeks later, it was announced that as local playwright, he had been asked to write a serious work to be performed as season finale.

Source: Morgan, G. (1989). *Creative organization theory*. Newbury Park, CA: Sage.

1. In the formal sense of the word, what is the general problem facing the board of directors of the Upstage Theatre Company? Is this a well-structured or an ill-structured problem?

2. How have various members of the board framed the problem that the board is wrestling with? What accounts for the differences?

3. To what extent has the board complied with or deviated from the rational decision-making model shown in Exhibit 11.1?

4. Is there any evidence in the case of escalation to a failing course of action? Of groupthink? If so, account for these tendencies.

5. Discuss the merits and demerits of using this particular group to make this particular decision. In general, is this the kind of problem that warrants using a group?

6. The board appears to be on the way to approving a rather risky foray into serious theatre. Use framing to explain this decision, then use group dynamics.

7. In retrospect, can you suggest any improvements that could have been made to the decision process?

Chapter 12

Power, Politics, and Ethics

INTERNATIONAL OLYMPIC COMMITTEE (IOC)
When Juan Antonio Samaranch, the President of the International Olympic Committee (IOC), announced to the world that Nagano, Japan, would host the 1998 Winter Olympic Games, there was joy in Japan and sadness in Salt Lake City, Utah, which lost by only four votes. With the facilities already built, Salt Lake City had been the favourite to win, compared with Nagano, which did not have a single facility built when it made its bid for the games. How then did Salt Lake City lose?

According to a wealthy businessman from Nagano, who played a key role in Nagano's bid for the Olympic games, facilities had very little to do with winning. In an interview with reporter Bob Simon on the television program *60 Minutes*, he stated that Nagano won the games through the development of friendships with members of the IOC. Friendships that he cultivated by visiting 70 countries over a period of three years and by inviting IOC committee members and their families on all-expenses-paid trips to Nagano. It has also been reported that Nagano spent millions of dollars on expensive gifts and lavish entertainment for IOC members as part of its bidding campaign.

Several years later, Juan Antonio Samaranch announced to the world that Salt Lake City would host the 19th Winter Olympic Games in 2002. This time there was joy in Salt Lake City. But what had changed? Did the Salt Lake City Organizing Committee (SLOC) change their strategy? Apparently, they had learned how to play the game.

Three years after Salt Lake City was awarded the 2002 Winter Olympic Games, a Salt Lake City TV station received a document that indicated that

The once proud symbol of the Olympic games has been tarnished as a result of the Salt Lake City bribery scandal and allegations that the International Olympic Committee is plagued by rampant corruption and bribery.

the SLOC paid for a "scholarship" for the daughter of an IOC member. The president of the SLOC then admitted that 13 people, including relatives of IOC members, received a total of $393,871 in financial assistance or scholarships from the committee. Several weeks later the U.S. Justice Department and FBI began an investigation on whether SLOC broke the bribery, fraud, or corruption laws. Salt Lake City's joyous victory was now tainted by allegations of bribery and vote buying and became known as the Salt Lake City bribery scandal. An investigation by the IOC found that cash and gifts worth $100,000 were common in Salt Lake City's bid for the 2002 Winter Olympics. An internal ethics investigation has since condemned the top officials of Salt Lake City's Olympic bid.

For the IOC, this was just the tip of the iceberg. In the weeks and months that followed, it was alleged that the IOC was plagued by rampant corruption and bribery. Revelations were made that IOC members had abused their power and accepted hundreds of thousands of dollars in bribes, gifts, and favours in ex-change for their votes. While the scandal began with Salt Lake City, Olympic hopefuls from around the world began to report of IOC members asking for cash, cars, real estate, and campaign contributions for themselves, as well as medical treatment, college tuition, and jobs for relatives. Suddenly, the Olympic movement found itself in the biggest and worst scandal in its history and its greatest ethics crisis ever.

An IOC investigative committee headed by Montreal lawyer and IOC vice-president Richard Pound was formed to investigate IOC corruption. In March 1999, members of the IOC gathered in Lausanne, Switzerland, behind closed doors to decide the fate of those accused of wrong doing along with a number

Olympic Committee
www.olympic.org

Learning Objectives

After reading Chapter 12, you should be able to:

1   Define power and review the bases of individual power.

2   Explain how people obtain power in organizations.

3   Discuss the concept of empowerment.

4   Review various influence tactics.

5   Provide a profile of power seekers.

6   Explain strategic contingencies and discuss how subunits obtain power.

7   Define organizational politics and discuss its various forms.

8   Define ethics and review the ethical dilemmas that managers face.

9   Define sexual harassment and discuss what organizations can do to prevent it and how they should respond to allegations.

Olympic Scandal
www.npr.org/programs/specials/
ioc/index.html

of reforms that were recommended by the investigative committee. Nine IOC members were censured, six were expelled for corruption, and four resigned. In total, 10 members have been expelled. Several ongoing investigations, not only by the IOC but also by jurisdictions in Australia, Britain, Canada, Japan, Russia, and the United States, could result in more resignations.

In addition, the committee has set in motion a number of reforms including an ethics committee that will police IOC members. As well, IOC members must limit their involvement in the bid process. They can no longer visit bidding cities and cannot be contacted directly by bid committees. A committee has also been formed to recommend changes in the IOC's structure, including the way IOC members are chosen and the bid-selection process.

Members of the IOC also voted overwhelmingly in support of their leader, Juan Antonio Samaranch, who told a group of journalists that the worst scandal in the history of the Olympic movement was now in the past, the result of a handful of bad apples who have been thrown out. Others, however, are not convinced. They see a culture of corruption and greed in which bid-rigging has existed for years, and even those who did not accept bribes knew about it and allowed the corruption to continue.

Others remain sceptical about the changes announced by the IOC and are calling for greater reforms, more accountability, and greater transparency. Some critics have called for the resignation of Juan Antonio Samaranch and the entire IOC membership. Samaranch, who selects all IOC members, flatly rejects the suggestion.

In the meantime, the IOC remains what some have called an autocratic and secretive body that is accountable only to itself and whose books and deliberations are closed to the public and the press, and whose members are still handpicked by Juan Antonio Samaranch.[1]

This vignette illustrates the main themes of this chapter—power, politics, and ethics. First, we shall define power and discuss the bases of individual power. Then we shall examine how people get and use power and who seeks it. After this, we shall explore how organizational subunits, such as particular departments, obtain power, define organizational politics, and explore the relationship of politics to power. Finally, we will look at ethics in organizations and sexual harassment.

At one time, power and politics were not considered polite topics for coverage in organizational behaviour textbooks. At best, they were seen as irrational and, at worst, as evil. Now, though, theorists and researchers recognize what managers have known all along—that power and politics are *natural* expressions of life in organizations. They often develop as a rational response to a complex set of needs and goals, and their expression can be beneficial. However, it can also put a strain on ethical standards, as is the case with the International Olympic Committee and those bidding for the Olympic Games.

What Is Power?

Power is the capacity to influence others who are in a state of dependence. Several points about this definition deserve elaboration. First, notice that power is the *capacity* to influence the behaviour of others. Power is not always exercised.[2] For example, most professors hold a great degree of potential power over students in terms of grades, assignment load, and the ability to embarrass students in class. Under normal circumstances, professors use only a small amount of this power.

Second, the fact that the target of power is dependent on the powerholder does not imply that a poor relationship exists between the two. For instance, your best friend has power to influence your behaviour and attitudes because you are dependent on him or her for friendly reactions and social support. Presumably, you can exert reciprocal influence for similar reasons.

Third, power can flow in any direction in an organization. Often, members at higher organizational levels have more power than those at lower levels. However, in specific cases, reversals can occur. For example, the janitor who finds the president in a compromising position with a secretary might find himself in a powerful position if the president wishes to maintain his reputation in the organization!

Finally, power is a broad concept that applies to both individuals and groups. On the one hand, an individual production manager might exert considerable influence over the supervisors who report to her. On the other, the marketing department at XYZ Foods might be the most powerful department in the company, able to get its way more often than other departments. But from where do the production manager and the marketing department obtain their power? We explore this issue in the following sections. First, we consider individual bases of power. Then we examine how organizational subunits, such as the marketing department, obtain power.

Power. The capacity to influence others who are in a state of dependence.

The Bases of Individual Power

If you wanted to marshal some power to influence others in your organization, where would you get it? As psychologists John French and Bertram Raven explained, power can be found in the *position* that you occupy in the organization or the *resources* that you are able to command.[3] The first base of power, legitimate power, is dependent on one's position or job. The other bases (reward, coercive, referent, and expert power) involve the control of important resources. If

"RELAX, STEVENS, YOU'RE NOT REALLY FIRED. I WAS JUST EXPERIENCING A BRIEF POWER SURGE."

other organizational members do not respect your position or value the resources that you command, they will not be dependent on you, and you will lack the power to influence them.

Legitimate Power

Legitimate power. Power derived from a person's position or job in an organization.

Legitimate power derives from a person's position or job in the organization. It constitutes the organization's judgment about who is formally permitted to influence whom, and it is often called authority. As we move up the organization's hierarchy, we find that members possess more and more legitimate power. In theory, organizational equals (e.g., all vice-presidents) have equal legitimate power. Of course, some people are more likely than others to *invoke* their legitimate power—"Look, *I'm* the boss around here."

Organizations differ greatly in the extent to which they emphasize and reinforce legitimate power. At one extreme is the U.S. Army, which has many levels of command, differentiating uniforms, and rituals (e.g., salutes), all designed to emphasize legitimate power. On the other hand, the academic hierarchy of universities tends to downplay differences in the legitimate power of lecturers, professors, chairpeople, and deans.

When legitimate power works, it often does so because people have been socialized to accept its influence. Experiences with parents, teachers, and law enforcement officials cause members to enter organizations with a degree of readiness to submit to (and exercise) legitimate power. In fact, studies consistently show that employees cite legitimate power as a major reason for following their boss's directives, even across various cultures.[4]

Reward Power

Reward power. Power derived from the ability to provide positive outcomes and prevent negative outcomes.

Reward power means that the powerholder can exert influence by providing positive outcomes and preventing negative outcomes. In general, it corresponds to the concept of positive reinforcement discussed in Chapter 2. Reward power often backs up legitimate power, that is, managers and supervisors are given the chance to recommend raises, do performance evaluations, and assign preferred tasks to subordinates. Of course, *any* organizational member can attempt to exert influence over others with praise, compliments, and flattery, which also constitute rewards.

Coercive Power

Coercive power is available when the powerholder can exert influence using punishment and threat. Like reward power, it is often a support for legitimate power. Supervisors and managers might be permitted to dock pay, assign unfavourable tasks, or block promotions. Despite a strong civil service system, even U.S. government agencies provide their executives with plenty of coercive power.

> **Coercive power.** Power derived from the use of punishment and threat.

Of course, coercive power is not perfectly correlated with legitimate power. Lower-level organizational members can also apply their share of coercion. For example, consider work-to-rule campaigns that slow productivity by adhering religiously to organizational procedures. Cohesive work groups are especially skillful at enforcing such campaigns.

In Chapter 2, we pointed out that the use of punishment to control behaviour is very problematic because of emotional side effects. Thus, it is not surprising that when managers use coercive power, it is generally ineffective and can provoke considerable employee resistance.[5]

Referent Power

Referent power exists when the powerholder is *well liked* by others. It is not surprising that people we like readily influence us. We are prone to consider their points of view, ignore their failures, seek their approval, and use them as role models. In fact, it is often highly dissonant to hold a point of view that is discrepant from that held by someone we like.[6]

> **Referent power.** Power derived from being well liked by others.

Referent power is especially potent for two reasons. First, it stems from *identification* with the powerholder. Thus, it represents a truer or deeper base of power than reward or coercion, which may stimulate mere compliance to achieve rewards or avoid punishment. In this sense, charismatic leaders (Chapter 9) have referent power. Second, *anyone* in the organization may be well liked, irrespective of his or her other bases of power. Thus, referent power is available to everyone from the janitor to the president.

Friendly interpersonal relations often permit influence to extend across the organization, outside the usual channels of legitimate authority, reward, and coercion. For example, a production manager who becomes friendly with the design engineer through participation in a task force might later use this contact to ask for a favour in solving a production problem.

Expert Power

A person has **expert power** when he or she has special information or expertise that the organization values. In any circumstance, we tend to be influenced by experts or by those who perform their jobs well. However, the more crucial and unusual this expertise, the greater is the expert power available. Thus, expert power corresponds to difficulty of replacement. Consider the business school that has one highly published professor who is an internationally known scholar and past presidential cabinet member. Such a person would obviously be difficult to replace and should have much greater expert power than an unpublished lecturer.

> **Expert power.** Power derived from having special information or expertise that is valued by an organization.

One of the most fascinating aspects of expert power occurs when lower-level organizational members accrue it. Many secretaries have acquired expert power

Exhibit 12.1
Employee responses to bases of power.

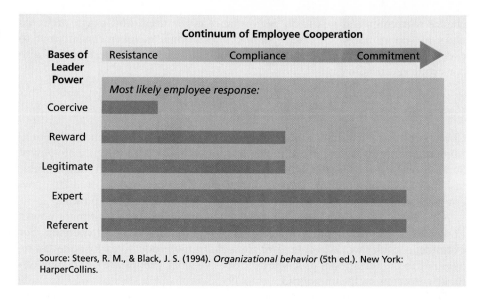

Source: Steers, R. M., & Black, J. S. (1994). *Organizational behavior* (5th ed.). New York: HarperCollins.

through long experience in dealing with clients, keeping records, or sparring with the bureaucracy. Frequently, they have been around longer than those they serve. In this case, it is not unusual for bosses to create special titles and develop new job classifications to reward their expertise and prevent their resignation. FedEx sends a quarterly magazine to 350,000 secretaries in recognition of the power they wield to select a courier.[7]

Expert power is especially common among lower-level members in scientific and technical areas. Consider the solid-state physicist who has just completed her Ph.D. dissertation on a topic of particular interest to her new employer. Although new to the firm, she might have considerable expert power. Put simply, she *knows* more than her boss, whose scientific knowledge in this area is now outdated.

Expert power is a valuable asset for managers. Of all the bases of power, expertise is most consistently associated with subordinate effectiveness.[8] Also, research shows that subordinates perceive women managers as more likely than male managers to be high on expert power.[9] Women often lack easy access to more organizationally based forms of power, and expertise is free for self-development. Thus, being "better" than their male counterparts is one strategy that women managers have used to gain influence.

Exhibit 12.1 summarizes likely employee responses to various bases of managerial power. As you can see, coercion is likely to produce resistance and lack of cooperation. Legitimate power and reward power are likely to produce compliance with the boss's wishes. Referent and expert power are most likely to generate true commitment and enthusiasm for the manager's agenda.

How Do People Obtain Power?

Now that we have discussed the individual bases of power, we can turn to the issue of how people *get* power, that is, how do organizational members obtain promotions to positions of legitimate power, demonstrate their expertise, and get others to like them? And how do they acquire the ability to provide others with rewards and punishment? Rosabeth Moss Kanter, an organizational sociologist, has provided some succinct answers—Do the right things, and cultivate the right people.[10]

Doing the Right Things

According to Kanter, some activities are "righter" than others for obtaining power. She argues that activities lead to power when they are extraordinary, highly visible, and especially relevant to the solution of organizational problems.

Extraordinary Activities. Excellent performance of a routine job might not be enough to obtain power. What one needs is excellent performance in *unusual* or *nonroutine* activities. In the large company that Kanter studied, these activities included occupying new positions, managing substantial changes, and taking great risks. For example, consider the manager who establishes and directs a new TQM program. This is a risky major change that involves the occupancy of a new position. If successful, the manager should acquire substantial power.

Visible Activities. Extraordinary activities will fail to generate power if no one knows about them. People who have an interest in power are especially good at identifying visible activities and publicizing them. The successful marketing executive whose philosophy is profiled in *Fortune* will reap the benefits of power. Similarly, the innovative surgeon whose techniques are reported in the *New England Journal of Medicine* will enhance her influence in the hospital.

Relevant Activities. Extraordinary, visible work may fail to generate power if no one cares. If nobody sees the work as relevant to the solution of important organizational problems, it will not add to one's influence. The English professor who wins two Pulitzer prizes will probably not accrue much power if his small college is financially strapped and hurting for students. He would not be seen as contributing to the solution of pressing organizational problems. As we shall see shortly, being in the right place at the right time is crucial to the acquisition of power. In another college, these extraordinary, visible activities might generate considerable influence.

Cultivating the Right People

An old saying advises, "It's not what you know, it's *who* you know." In reference to power in organizations, there is probably more than a grain of truth to the latter part of this statement. Developing informal relationships with the right people (especially when coupled with doing the right things) can prove a useful means of acquiring power. Kanter suggests that the right people can include organizational subordinates, peers, and superiors. To these, we might add certain crucial outsiders.

Outsiders. Establishing good relationships with key people outside one's organization can lead to increased power within the organization. Sometimes this power is merely a reflection of the status of the outsider, but all the same, it may add to one's internal influence. The assistant director of a hospital who is friendly with the president of the American Medical Association might find herself holding power by association. Cultivating outsiders may also contribute to more tangible sources of power. Organizational members who are on the boards of directors of other companies might acquire critical information about business conditions that they can use in their own firms.

Subordinates. At first blush, it might seem unlikely that power can be enhanced by cultivating relationships with subordinates. However, as Kanter notes, an individual can gain influence if she is closely identified with certain up-and-coming subordinates—"I taught her everything she knows." In academics, some professors are better known for the brilliant Ph.D. students they have supervised than for their own published work. Of course, there is also the possibility that an outstanding subordinate will one day become one's boss! Having cultivated the relationship earlier, one might then be rewarded with special influence.

Cultivating subordinate interests can also provide power when a manager can demonstrate that he or she is backed by a cohesive team. The research director who can oppose a policy change by honestly insisting that "My people won't stand for this" knows that there is strength in numbers.

Peers. Cultivating good relationships with peers is mainly a means of ensuring that nothing gets in the way of one's *future* acquisition of power. As one moves up through the ranks, favours can be asked of former associates, and fears of being "stabbed in the back" for a past misdeed are precluded. Organizations often reward good "team players" with promotions on the assumption that they have demonstrated good interpersonal skills. On the other side of the coin, people often avoid contact with peers whose reputation is seen as questionable.

Superiors. Liaisons with key superiors probably represent the best way of obtaining power through cultivating others. As we discussed in Chapter 8, such superiors are often called mentors or sponsors because of the special interest they show in a promising subordinate. Mentors can provide power in several ways. Obviously, it is useful to be identified as a protégé of someone higher in the organization. More concretely, mentors can provide special information and useful introductions to other "right people."

Empowerment—Putting Power Where It Is Needed

Early organizational theorists used to treat power as something of a fixed quantity: An organization had so much, the people on the top had a lot, and lower-level employees had a little. Our earlier analysis of the more informal sources of power (such as being liked and being an expert) hints at the weakness of this idea.

"... DON'T THINK OF THIS AS YOUR CUBICLE, THINK OF IT AS AN EMPOWERMENT ZONE ..."

Thus, contemporary views of power treat it less as a fixed-sum phenomenon. This is best seen in the concept of **empowerment**, which means giving people the authority, opportunity, and motivation to take initiative to solve organizational problems.[11] We used this concept earlier in the text when discussing total quality management (Chapter 6) and participative and developmental leadership (Chapter 9). Here, we will examine the idea in a little more detail.

In practice, having the authority to solve an organizational problem means having legitimate power. This might be included in a job description, or a boss might delegate it to a subordinate.

Having opportunity usually means freedom from bureaucratic barriers and other system problems that block initiative. In a service encounter, if you have ever heard "Sorry, the computer won't let me do that" or "that's not my job," you have been the victim of limited opportunity. Opportunity also includes any relevant training and information about the impact of one's actions on other parts of the organization.

The motivation part of the empowerment equation suggests selecting for positions people who will be intrinsically motivated by power and opportunity and aligning extrinsic rewards with successful performance. Also, leaders who express confidence in subordinates' abilities (especially transformational leaders, Chapter 9) can contribute to empowerment. A good example occurred when a nay-saying union shop steward, doubting General Electric's commitment to changing its corporate culture, explained a recurrent problem with a supplier's component. His manager, sensing he was correct, chartered a plane, and the subordinate left that same night to visit the supplier and solve the problem.[12] It goes without saying that managers have to be tolerant of occasional mistakes from empowered employees.

In Chapter 2, we discussed self-efficacy in the context of social learning theory. People who are empowered have a strong sense of self-efficacy, the feeling that they are capable of doing their jobs well and "making things happen." Empowering lower-level employees can be critical in service organizations, where providing customers with a good initial encounter or correcting any problems that develop can be essential for repeat business. The Nordstrom store chain is one firm that is known for empowering sales personnel to make on-the-spot adjustments or search out merchandise at other stores. Customers have even had enthusiastic store personnel change flat tires. This dedication to customer service enables Nordstrom to spend only a fraction of the industry average on advertising.

We should emphasize that empowerment does not mean providing employees with a maximum amount of unfettered power. Rather, used properly, empowerment puts power where it is *needed* to make the organization effective. This depends on organizational strategy and customer expectations. The average Taco Bell customer does not expect highly empowered counter personnel who offer to make adjustments to the posted menu—a friendly, fast, efficient encounter will do. On the other hand, the unempowered waiter in a fancy restaurant who is fearful of accommodating reasonable adjustments and substitutions can really irritate customers. Speaking generally, service encounters predicated on high volume and low cost need careful engineering. Those predicated on customized personalized service need more empowered personnel.[13] For a good example of this, see "In Focus: *Empowerment at Delta Hotels and Resorts.*"

Given this discussion, you might wonder whether organizational members could have *too much* power. Exhibit 12.2 nicely illustrates the answer. People are empowered, and should exhibit effective performance, when they have sufficient power to carry out their jobs. Above, we mainly contrasted empowerment with situations in which people had inadequate power for effective performance. However, as the exhibit shows, excessive power can lead to abuse and ineffective

Delta Hotels and Resorts
www.deltahotels.com

in focus → Empowerment at Delta Hotels and Resorts

The senior vice-president of people and quality at Delta Hotels has the job of empowering more than 7,000 employees across North America to make daily business decisions without having to turn to their managers for approval.

"It's always been a company where young people have been expected and encouraged to make decisions based on trust, which is a core value," Bill Pallett says. "In the mid-nineties, it was recognized that we need to formalize it more in terms of an approach as to how we do business."

Through the company's "power to please" program, employees at Delta's 32 properties in Canada have the training and authority to settle a disputed minibar charge or offer a complimentary room if the guest has a reasonable complaint. At Delta, guests do not hear, "I have to talk to my manager about this" or have to wait for a response.

Delta, which is headquartered in Toronto and is a wholly owned subsidiary of Canadian Pacific Hotels Ltd., is on the leading edge of incorporating empowerment into corporate culture.

As a result, Delta's employee turnover rate has dropped, morale has improved, and occupancy rates have risen without having to drop prices to be competitive.

At Delta, empowerment is also a means to delight customers. Employees can take the initiative and, for example, offer flu-stricken guests humidifiers or lemon tea. "The name of the game isn't customer satisfaction, it's customer loyalty. It costs more to go out and get new customers than retain your current customers," Mr. Pallett says.

To support "the power to please" program, Delta has produced an award-winning training video. The company also stands behind its promise that employees receive a certain amount of empowerment training every year; otherwise, workers are entitled to one week's additional pay.

Using the National Quality Institute of Canada's model of excellence to assess each hotel, Delta has found that 95 percent of its employees believe they are truly empowered to make decisions. And employee opinion surveys have a 90 percent satisfaction rating.

Now Delta is talking with other companies in the service industries and the medical sectors about its empowerment program. Is empowerment something companies should consider? "It would be costly not to do," Mr. Pallett says.

Source: Excerpted from (1999, May 31). Delta promotes empowerment. *The Globe and Mail*, C5.

performance. One is reminded of the recurrent and inappropriate use of government aircraft by political bigwigs as an example. As we will see in the following sections, the fact that people can have too much power does not always inhibit them from seeking it anyway!

Exhibit 12.2
Relationship between power and performance.

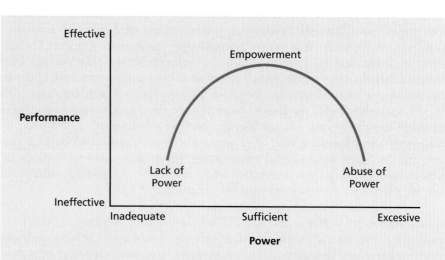

Source: Adapted from Whetten, D. A., & Cameron, K. S. (1995). *Developing management skills*. New York: HarperCollins.

Influence Tactics—Putting Power to Work

As we discussed earlier, power is the potential to influence others. But exactly how does power result in influence? Research has shown that various **influence tactics** convert power into actual influence. These are specific behaviours that power holders use to affect others.[14] These tactics include the following:

- Assertiveness—ordering, nagging, setting deadlines, and verbal confrontation;
- Ingratiation—using flattery and acting friendly, polite, or humble;
- Rationality—using logic, reason, planning, and compromise;
- Exchange—doing favours or offering to trade favours;
- Upward appeal—making formal or informal appeals to organizational superiors for intervention; and
- Coalition formation—seeking united support from other organizational members.

What determines which influence tactics you might use? For one thing, your bases of power.[15] Other things being equal, someone with coercive power might gravitate toward assertiveness, someone with referent power might gravitate toward ingratiation, and someone with expert power might try rationality. Of course, rationality or its appearance is a highly prized quality in organizations, and its use is viewed positively by others. Thus, surveys show that people report trying to use rationality very frequently.

As you can guess, the use of influence tactics is also dependent on just who you are trying to influence—subordinates, peers, or superiors. Subordinates are more likely to be the recipients of assertiveness than peers or superiors. Despite the general popularity of rationality, it is most likely to be directed toward superiors. Exchange, ingratiation, and upward appeal are favoured tactics for influencing both peers and subordinates.[16]

Which influence tactics are most effective? Some of the most interesting research has concerned upward influence attempts directed toward superiors. It shows that, at least for men, using rationality as an influence tactic was associated with receiving better performance evaluations, earning more money, and experiencing less work stress. A particularly ineffective influence style is a "shotgun" style that is high on all tactics with particular emphasis on assertiveness and exchange. In this series of studies, women who used ingratiation as an influence tactic received the highest performance evaluations (from male managers).[17]

Influence tactics. Tactics that are used to convert power into actual influence over others.

Who Wants Power?

Who wants power? At first glance, the answer would seem to be everybody. After all, it is both convenient and rewarding to be able to exert influence over others. Power whisks celebrities to the front of movie lines, gets rock stars the best restaurant tables, and enables executives to shape organizations in their own image. Actually, there are considerable individual differences in the extent to which individuals pursue and enjoy power. On television talk shows, we occasionally see celebrities recount considerable embarrassment over the unwarranted power that public recognition brings.

Earlier we indicated that some people consider power a manifestation of evil. This is due, in no small part, to the historic image of power seekers that some psychologists and political scientists have portrayed. Several aspects of this image are strikingly similar:

- Power seekers are neurotics who are covering up feelings of inferiority.
- Power seekers are striving to compensate for childhood deprivation.
- Power seekers are substituting power for lack of affection.[18]

There can be little doubt that these characteristics do apply to some power seekers. Underlying this negative image of power seeking is the idea that some power seekers feel weak and resort primarily to coercive power to cover up, compensate for, or substitute for this weakness. Power is sought for its own sake and is used irresponsibly to hurt others. Adolf Hitler comes to mind as an extreme example.

But can one use power responsibly to influence others? Psychologist David McClelland says yes. In Chapter 5, we discussed McClelland's research on need for power (n Pow). You will recall that n Pow is the need to have strong influence over others. This need is a reliable personality characteristic—some people have more n Pow than others.[19] Also, just as many women have high n Pow as men.[20] People who are high in n Pow in its "pure" form conform to the negative stereotype depicted above—they are rude, sexually exploitative, abuse alcohol, and show a great concern with status symbols. However, when n Pow is responsible and controlled, these negative properties are not observed. Specifically, McClelland argues that the most effective managers

- have high n Pow;
- use their power to achieve organizational goals;
- adopt a participative or "coaching" leadership style; and
- are relatively unconcerned with how much others like them.

McClelland calls such managers *institutional managers* because they use their power for the good of the institution rather than for self-aggrandizement. They refrain from coercive leadership but do not play favourites, since they are not worried about being well liked. His research reveals that institutional managers are more effective than *personal power managers,* who use their power for personal gain, and *affiliative managers,* who are more concerned with being liked than with exercising power. Exhibit 12.3 shows that institutional managers are generally superior in giving subordinates a sense of responsibility, clarifying organizational priorities, and instilling team spirit.[21] We can conclude that the need for power can be a useful asset, as long as it is not a neurotic expression of perceived weakness.

Finally, what happens when people want power but cannot get it because they are locked in a low-level job or faced with excessive rules and regulations? People react to such powerlessness by trying to gain control, but if they cannot succeed, they feel helpless and become alienated from their work.[22] This is something that empowerment is designed to prevent.

Controlling Strategic Contingencies— How Subunits Obtain Power

Subunit power. The degree of power held by various organizational subunits, such as departments.

Thus far, we have been concerned with the bases of *individual* power and how individual organizational members obtain influence. In this section, we shift our concern to **subunit power.** Most straightforwardly, the term subunit applies to organizational departments. In some cases, subunits could also refer to particular jobs, such as those held by software engineers or environmental lawyers.

How do organizational subunits acquire power, that is, how do they achieve influence that enables them to grow in size, get a bigger share of the budget, obtain better facilities, and have greater impact on decisions? In short, they control

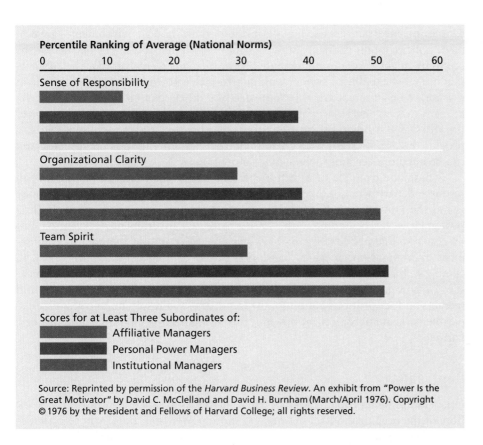

Exhibit 12.3
Responses of subordinates of managers with different motive profiles.

strategic contingencies, which are critical factors affecting organizational effectiveness. This means that the work *other* subunits perform is contingent on the activities and performance of a key subunit. Again, we see the critical role of *dependence* in power relationships. If some subunits are dependent on others for smooth operations (or their very existence), they are susceptible to influence. We turn now to the conditions under which subunits can control strategic contingencies.

Strategic contingencies. Critical factors affecting organizational effectiveness that are controlled by a key subunit.

Scarcity

Differences in subunit power are likely to be magnified when resources become scarce.[23] When there is plenty of budget money or office space or support staff for all subunits, they will seldom waste their energies jockeying for power. If cutbacks occur, however, differences in power will become apparent. For example, well-funded quality-of-worklife programs or organizational development efforts might disappear when economic setbacks occur because the subunits that control them are not essential to the firm's existence.

Subunits tend to acquire power when they are able to *secure* scarce resources that are important to the organization as a whole. One study of a large state university found that the power of academic departments was associated with their ability to obtain funds through consulting contracts and research grants. This mastery over economic resources was more crucial to their power than was the number of undergraduates taught by the department.[24]

Uncertainty

Organizations detest the unknown. Unanticipated events wreak havoc with financial commitments, long-range plans, and tomorrow's operations. The basic sources of uncertainty exist mainly in the organization's environment—government policies might change, sources of supply and demand might dry up, or the economy might take an unanticipated turn. It stands to reason that the subunits that are most capable of coping with uncertainty will tend to acquire power.[25] In a sense, these subunits are able to protect the others from serious problems. By the same token, uncertainty promotes confusion, which permits *changes* in power priorities as the organizational environment changes. Those functions that can provide the organization with greater control over what it finds problematic and can create more certainty will acquire more power.[26]

A dramatic example of a shift in subunit power has occurred for the human resource departments of large corporations during the past 20 years. For many years, the human resource function in most organizations had relatively little power. However, beginning in the 1970s, increased government intervention into human resource policies began. This was especially true in the area of employment discrimination, in which legislation provoked considerable uncertainty. In coming to the rescue, human resource departments acquired a long-awaited measure of power. The uncertainty provoked by downsizing, new technology, and mergers and acquisitions continues the trend, and as a result, human resource departments in many organizations are now recognized to be important strategic partners.

Centrality

Other things being equal, subunits whose activities are most central to the work flow of the organization should acquire more power than those whose activities are more peripheral.[27] A subunit's activities can be central in at least three senses. First, they may influence the work of most other subunits. The finance or accounting department is a good example here—its authority to approve expenses and make payments affects every other department in the firm.

Centrality also exists when a subunit has an especially crucial impact on the quantity or quality of the organization's key product or service. This is one reason for the former low power of human resource departments—their activities were then seen as fairly remote from the primary goals of the organization. Similarly, a production department should have more power than a research and development department that only "fine tunes" existing products.

Finally, a subunit's activities are more central when their impact is more immediate. As an example, consider a large city government that includes a fire department, a police department, and a public works department. The impact of a lapse in fire or police services will be felt more immediately than a lapse in street repairs. This gives the former departments more potential for power acquisition.

Substitutability

A subunit will have relatively little power if others inside or outside the organization can perform its activities. If the subunit's staff is nonsubstitutable, however, it can acquire substantial power.[28] One crucial factor here is the labour market for the specialty performed by the subunit. A change in the labour market can result in a change in the subunit's influence:

> In the 1950s, when there were relatively few engineers to service an expanding American economy, engineers had great prestige and power. They could force employers to provide them with large salaries and benefits, by threatening to withhold their services. By the early 1970s, however, many persons had become engineers and consequently the bargaining power of engineers with employers was practically nil.[29]

In the 1990s there was again a shortage of engineers (and scientists), with a consequent increase in their bargaining power. Precisely in line with the strategic contingencies idea, observers note how this shortage has provided real opportunities for properly trained women and members of minorities to move into positions of power from which they were excluded when there were plenty of white male engineers and scientists to go around.[30]

If the labour market is constant, subunits whose staffs are highly trained in technical areas tend to be less substitutable than those which involve minimal technical expertise. For example, consider the large telephone company that makes extensive use of a computerized management information system. The department in charge of this system might acquire considerable power because its computer analysts perform specialized work that others in the company cannot do. On the other hand, if telephone operators go on strike, management personnel can substitute for them by handling the phones.

Finally, if work can be contracted out, the power of the subunit that usually performs these activities is reduced. Typical examples include temporary office help, off-premises data entry, and contracted maintenance, laboratory, and security services. The subunits that control these activities often lack power because the threat of "going outside" can counter their influence attempts.

Organizational Politics—Using and Abusing Power

In previous pages, we have avoided using the terms *politics* or *political* in describing the acquisition and use of power. This is because not all uses of power constitute politics.

The Basics of Organizational Politics

Organizational politics is the pursuit of self-interest within an organization, whether or not this self-interest corresponds to organizational goals.[31] Frequently, politics involves using means of influence that the organization does not sanction and/or pursuing ends or goals that are not sanctioned by the organization.[32]

We should make several preliminary points about organizational politics. First, political activity is self-conscious and intentional. This separates politics from ignorance or lack of experience with approved means and ends. Second, implicit in all but the mildest examples of politics is the idea of resistance, the idea that political influence would be countered if detected by those with different agendas. Third, we can conceive of politics as either individual activity or subunit activity. Either a person or a whole department could act politically. Finally, it is possible for political activity to have beneficial outcomes for the organization, even though these outcomes are achieved by questionable tactics.

We can explore organizational politics using the means/ends matrix in Exhibit 12.4. It is the association between influence means and influence ends that determines whether activities are political and whether these activities benefit the organization.

- *I. Sanctioned means/sanctioned ends.* Here, power is used routinely to pursue agreed-on goals. Familiar, accepted means of influence are employed to achieve sanctioned outcomes. For example, a manager agrees to recommend a raise for a subordinate if she increases her net sales by 30 percent in the next six months. There is nothing political about this.

Organizational politics. The pursuit of self-interest in an organization, whether or not this self-interest corresponds to organizational goals.

Exhibit 12.4
The dimensions of
organizational politics.

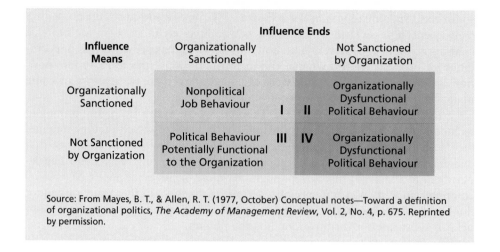

Source: From Mayes, B. T., & Allen, R. T. (1977, October) Conceptual notes—Toward a definition
of organizational politics, *The Academy of Management Review*, Vol. 2, No. 4, p. 675. Reprinted
by permission.

- *II. Sanctioned means/nonsanctioned ends.* In this case, acceptable means of influence are abused to pursue goals that the organization does not approve. For instance, a head nurse agrees to assign a subordinate nurse to a more favourable job if the nurse agrees not to report the superior for stealing medical supplies. While job assignment is often a sanctioned means of influence, covering up theft is not a sanctioned end. This is dysfunctional political behaviour.

- *III. Nonsanctioned means/sanctioned ends.* Here, ends that are useful for the organization are pursued through questionable means. For example, although officials of the Salt Lake City Olympic Committee were pursuing a sanctioned end—the 2002 Winter Olympics—the use of bribery and vote-buying as a means of influence was not sanctioned by the Committee. As well, consider a commercial artist vying with a co-worker to have his proposal accepted for an advertising campaign. Feeling that his proposal is truly better, the artist takes the account executive to dinner, flatters him, and subtly discredits the co-worker's proposal. Currying favour and discrediting others are seldom approved methods of influence. However, if the proposal is really superior, the consequences might be beneficial for the firm. This is obviously a grey area of politics.

- *IV. Nonsanctioned means/nonsanctioned ends.* This quadrant may exemplify the most flagrant abuse of power, since disapproved tactics are used to pursue disapproved outcomes. For example, to increase his personal power, the head of an already overstaffed legal department wishes to increase its size. He intends to hire several of his friends in the process. To do this, he falsifies workload documents and promises special service to the accounting department in exchange for the support of its manager. Members of the IOC who traded their votes for money and gifts is also an example of dysfunctional political behaviour.

We have all seen cases in which politics have been played out publicly in order to "teach someone a lesson." More frequently, though, politicians conceal their activities with a "cover story" or "smoke screen" to make them appear legitimate.[33] Such a tactic will increase the odds of success and avoid punishment from superiors. A common strategy is to cover nonsanctioned means and ends with a cloak of rationality.

Do political activities occur under particular conditions or in particular locations in organizations? Some tentative conclusions include the following:

- Managers report that most political manoeuvring occurs among middle and upper management levels rather than at lower levels.

- Some subunits are more prone to politicking than others. Clear goals and routine tasks (e.g., production) might provoke less political activity than vague goals and complex tasks (e.g., research and development).

- Some issues are more likely than others to stimulate political activity. Budget allocation, reorganization, and personnel changes are likely to be the subjects of politicking. Setting performance standards and purchasing equipment are not.

- In general, scarce resources, uncertainty, and important issues provoke political behaviour.[34]

Returning to the story that began the chapter, it should now be clear that the bidding for the Olympic Games is fraught with a great deal of power and politics. The Olympic games have become a very lucrative business that can add substantially to the host economies. As a result, many committees biding on the games have gone to great lengths in their efforts to win the games by influencing members of the IOC through the development of friendships and offering expensive gifts and large sums of money. Members of the IOC, in turn, used their voting power for their own personal gain. Thus, both parties provide good examples of how influence means and ends operate in the political process.

Machiavellianism—The Harder Side of Politics

Have you ever known people in an organization or another social setting who had the following characteristics?

- Act very much in their own self-interest, even at the expense of others.
- Cool and calculating, especially when others get emotional.
- High self-esteem and self-confidence.
- Form alliances with powerful people to achieve their goals.

These are some of the characteristics of individuals who are high on a personality dimension known as Machiavellianism. **Machiavellianism** is a set of cynical beliefs about human nature, morality, and the permissibility of using various tactics to achieve one's ends. The term derives from the 16th century writings of the Italian civil servant Niccolo Machiavelli, who was concerned with how people achieve social influence and the ability to manipulate others. The degree to which an individual endorses the beliefs of Machiavelli is representative of a stable psychological trait.

Compared with "low Machs," "high Machs" are more likely to advocate the use of lying and deceit to achieve desired goals and to argue that morality can be compromised to fit the situation in question. In addition, high Machs assume that many people are excessively gullible and do not know what is best for themselves. Thus, in interpersonal situations, the high Mach acts in an exceedingly practical manner, assuming that the ends justify the means. Not surprisingly, high Machs tend to be convincing liars and good at "psyching out" competitors by creating diversions. Furthermore, they are quite willing to form coalitions with others to outmanoeuvre or defeat people who get in their way.[35] In summary, high Machs are likely to be enthusiastic organizational politicians.

This discussion of the Machiavellian personality trait probably raises two questions on your part. First, you might wonder, do high Machs feel guilty about the social tactics that they utilize? The answer would appear to be no. Since they are cool and calculating, rather than emotional, high Machs seem to be able to

Machiavellianism. A set of cynical beliefs about human nature, morality, and the permissibility of using various tactics to achieve one's ends.

insulate themselves from the negative social consequences of their tactics. Second, you might wonder how successful high Machs are at manipulating others and why others would tolerate such manipulation. After all, the characteristics we detail above are hardly likely to win a popularity contest, and you might assume that targets of a high Mach's tactics would vigorously resist manipulation by such a person. Again, the high Mach's rationality seems to provide an answer to this question. Put simply, it appears that high Machs are able to accurately identify situations in which their favoured tactics will work. Such situations have the following characteristics:

- The high Mach can deal face-to-face with those he or she is trying to influence.
- The interaction occurs under fairly emotional circumstances.
- The situation is fairly unstructured, with few guidelines for appropriate forms of interaction.[36]

In combination, these characteristics reveal a situation in which the high Mach can use his or her tactics because emotion distracts others. High Machs, by remaining calm and rational, can create a social structure that facilitates their personal goals at the expense of others. Thus, it would appear that high Machs are especially skilled at getting their way when power vacuums or novel situations confront a group, department, or organization. For example, imagine a small family-run manufacturing company whose president dies suddenly without any plans for succession. In this power vacuum, a high Mach vice-president would have an excellent chance of manipulating the choice of a new president. The situation is novel, emotion provoking, and unstructured, since no guidelines for succession exist. In addition, the decision-making body would be small enough for face-to-face influence and coalition formation.

Networking—The Softer Side of Politics

Only a small proportion of the population has the personality profile characteristic of the hardball Machiavellian politician. Despite this, political influence is often necessary to enable organizational members to achieve their goals, especially if these goals involve some degree of change or innovation. Thus, a more common and more subtle form of political behaviour involves networking. **Networking** can be defined as establishing good relations with key organizational members and/or outsiders in order to accomplish one's goals. If these goals are beneficial to the organization, we can describe networking as functional political behaviour. In essence, networking involves developing informal social contacts to enlist the cooperation of others when their support is necessary. Upper-level managers often establish very large political networks both inside and outside the organization (Exhibit 12.5). Lower-level organizational members might have a more restricted network, but the principle remains the same.

Some networking is a function of one's location in the organization's workflow and formal communication channels.[37] A key location provides the opportunity to interact with and establish influence over others. However, individuals can also pursue networking more aggressively. One study of general managers found that they used face-to-face encounters and informal small talk to bolster their political networks. They also did favours for others and stressed the obligations of others to them. Personnel were hired, fired, and transferred to bolster a workable network, and the managers forged connections among network members to create a climate conducive to goal accomplishment.[38]

High-powered executives are not the only people who are concerned about networking. Many telecommuters (Chapter 6) who work at home worry about

Networking. Establishing good relations with key organizational members and/or outsiders in order to accomplish one's goals.

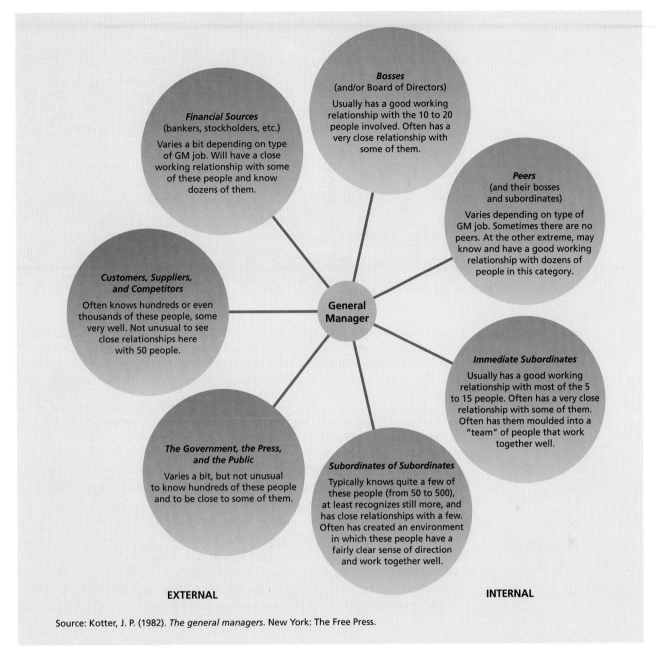

Source: Kotter, J. P. (1982). *The general managers.* New York: The Free Press.

EXTERNAL   INTERNAL

Exhibit 12.5
A typical general manager's network.

being "cut out of the loop" of office influence because they are not physically present for informal office interaction. In turn, they fret that this will damage their promotion opportunities. Successful telecommuters report that they go to extra trouble to keep their bosses and co-workers informed about what they are doing at home, keeping their names visible in the communication network. At Bell Atlantic, they showed their bosses videotapes of their home offices.[39]

Defensiveness—Reactive Politics

So far, our discussion of politics has focused mainly on the proactive pursuit of self-interest. Another form of political behaviour, however, is more reactive, in that it concerns the defence or protection of self-interest. The goal here is to reduce threats to one's own power by avoiding actions that do not suit one's own

political agenda or avoiding blame for events that might threaten one's political capital. Blake Ashforth and Ray Lee describe some tactics for doing both.[40]

Astute organizational politicians are aware that sometimes the best action to take is no action at all. A number of defensive behaviours can accomplish this mission:

- *Stalling.* Moving slowly when someone asks for your cooperation is the most obvious way of avoiding taking action without actually saying no. With time, the demand for cooperation may disappear. The civil service bureaucracy is infamous for stalling on demands from acting governments.

- *Overconforming.* Sticking to the strict letter of your job description or to organizational regulations is a common way to avoid action. The same dedicated politician may be happy to circumvent his job description or organizational regulations when it suits his agenda.

- *Buck passing.* Having someone else take action is an effective way to avoid doing it yourself. Buck passing is especially dysfunctional politics when the politician is best equipped to do the job but worries that it might not turn out successfully ("Let's let the design department get stuck with this turkey.").

Another set of defensive behaviours is oriented around the motto "If you can't avoid action, avoid blame for its consequences." These behaviours include:

- *Buffing.* Buffing is the tactic of carefully documenting information showing that an appropriate course of action was followed. Getting "sign offs," authorizations, and so on are examples. Buffing can be sensible behaviour, but it takes on political overtones when doing the documenting becomes more important than making a good decision. It is clearly dysfunctional politics if it takes the form of fabricating documentation.

- *Scapegoating.* Blaming others when things go wrong is classic political behaviour. Scapegoating works best when you have some power behind you. One study found that when organizations performed poorly, more powerful CEOs stayed in office and the scapegoated managers below them were replaced. Less powerful CEOs were dismissed. [41]

The point of discussing these defensive political tactics has not been to teach you how to do them. Rather, it is to ensure that you recognize them as political behaviour. Many of the tactics are quite mundane, and it is easy to write them off as isolated cases of laziness or some such thing. However, viewing them in context again illustrates the sometimes subtle ways that individuals pursue political self-interest in organizations. Politics, like power, is natural in all organizations. Whether or not politics is functional for the organization depends on the ends that are pursued and the influence means that are used.

Ethics in Organizations

Several years ago, the Johnson & Johnson subsidiary that was responsible for Tylenol quickly and decisively withdrew the product from the market after poison-laced examples of it were discovered. Subsequent to this, Copley Pharmaceutical was criticized for acting slowly to recall tainted drugs, and Syntex and Upjohn were both charged with obscuring negative side effects in newly developed medicines. How can we account for the apparent difference in ethics reflected in the decisions that underpinned these actions?

For our purposes, **ethics** can be defined as systematic thinking about the moral consequences of decisions. Moral consequences can be framed in terms of the potential for harm to any stakeholders in the decision. **Stakeholders** are simply people inside or outside the organization who have a potential to be affected by the decision. This could range from the decision makers themselves to "innocent bystanders."[42] Ethics is a major branch of philosophy, and we will not attempt to describe the various schools of ethical thought. Instead, we will focus on the kinds of ethical issues that organizational decision makers face and some of the factors that stimulate unethical decisions.

Ethics. Systematic thinking about the moral consequences of decisions.

Stakeholders. People inside or outside of an organization who have the potential to be affected by organizational decisions.

Over the years, researchers have conducted a number of surveys to determine managers' views about the ethics of decision making in business.[43] Some striking similarities across studies provide an interesting picture of the popular psychology of business ethics. First, far from being shy about the subject, a large majority agree that unethical practices occur in business. Furthermore, a substantial proportion (between 40 and 90 percent, according to the particular study) report that they have been pressured to compromise their own ethical standards when making organizational decisions. Finally, in line with the concept of self-serving attributions, managers invariably tend to see themselves as having higher ethical standards than their peers and sometimes their superiors.[44] The unpleasant picture emerging here is one where unethical behaviour tempts managers who sometimes succumb, but feel that they still do better than others on moral grounds.

In case you think that students are purer than organizational decision makers, think again. Research is fairly consistent in showing that business students have looser ethical standards than practising managers, at least when responding to written descriptions of ethical issues.[45] Among business students, undergraduates have been found to be more ethical than MBA students.[46] In addition, women have been found to have higher ethical standards than men when evaluating ethical business practices, especially among student samples.[47]

The Nature of Ethical Dilemmas

What are the kinds of ethical dilemmas that most frequently face organizational decision makers? Exhibit 12.6 shows the results of a Conference Board survey of 300 companies around the world. As you can see, conflicts of interest, questionable gift giving, and sexual harassment top the list of ethical concerns (while executive salaries are seen to present fewer problems!). Especially noteworthy is the

Exhibit 12.6
A survey of ethical issues.

The Conference Board asked executives at 300 companies worldwide whether the following constituted ethical issues for business. The percentage of affirmative responses is listed next to the issue.	
Issue	**Percent**
Employee conflicts of interest	91
Inappropriate gifts to corporate personnel	91
Sexual harassment	91
Unauthorized payments	85
Affirmative action	84
Employee privacy	84
Environmental issues	82
Employee health screening	79
Conflicts between company's ethics and foreign business practices	77
Security of company records	76
Workplace safety	76
Advertising content	74
Product safety standards	74
Corporate contributions	68
Shareholder interests	68
Corporate due process	65
Whistleblowing	63
Employment at will	62
Disinvestment	59
Government contract issues	59
Financial and cash management procedures	55
Plant/facility closures and downsizing	55
Political action committees	55
Social issues raised by religious organizations	47
Comparable worth	43
Product pricing	42
Executive salaries	37

Source: From *Corporate ethics,* a Conference Board research report (New York: The Conference Board). Reprinted by permission.

fact that 77 percent of firms report problems in dealing with foreign business practices that are contrary to their own ethical norms. Inappropriate gift giving and receiving were obviously the main concerns in the Salt Lake City bribery scandal in which IOC members exchanged their votes for expensive gifts and large amounts of money.

Ethical issues often tend to be peculiar to the specific domain in which we are usually making decisions. As an example, let us consider the ethical dilemmas that the various subspecialties of marketing face.[48] Among market researchers, telling subjects the true sponsor of the research has been an ongoing topic of debate. Among purchasing managers, where to draw the line in accepting favours (e.g., sports tickets) from vendors poses ethical problems. Among product managers, issues of planned obsolescence, unnecessary packaging, and differential pricing (e.g., charging more in the inner city) raise ethical concerns. When it comes to salespeople, how far to go in enticing customers and how to be fair in expense account use have been prominent ethical themes. Finally, in advertising, the range of ethical issues can (and does) fill books. Consider, for example, the decision to use sexual allure to sell a product.

In contrast to these occupationally specific ethical dilemmas, what are the common themes that run through ethical issues that managers face? An in-depth interview study of an occupationally diverse group of managers discovered seven themes that defined their moral standards for decision making.[49] Here are those themes and some typical examples of associated ethical behaviour:

- *Honest communication.* Evaluate subordinates candidly; advertise and label honestly; do not slant proposals to senior management.

- *Fair treatment.* Pay equitably; respect the sealed bid process; do not give preference to suppliers with political connections; do not use lower-level people as scapegoats (see "Ethical Focus: *Is Integrity Testing Ethical?*").

- *Special consideration.* The "fair treatment" standard can be modified for special cases, such as helping out a long-time employee, giving preference to hiring the disabled, or giving business to a loyal but troubled supplier.

- *Fair competition.* Avoid bribes and kickbacks to obtain business; do not fix prices with competitors.

- *Responsibility to organization.* Act for the good of the organization as a whole, not for self-interest; avoid waste and inefficiency.

- *Corporate social responsibility.* Do not pollute; think about the community impact of plant closures; show concern for employee health and safety.

- *Respect for law.* Legally avoid taxes, do not evade them; do not bribe government inspectors; follow the letter and spirit of labour laws.

Causes of Unethical Behaviour

What are the causes of unethical behaviour? The answer to this question is important so that you can anticipate the circumstances that warrant special vigilance.

Institute for Business Ethics
www.depaul.edu/ethics/

---

ethical focus →)) Is Integrity Testing Ethical?

How would you like to apply for a job and have the recruiter ask you to take a written test that purports to measure your honesty? This is a more and more common occurrence in North American organizations. Estimates suggest that there are somewhere around 5 million integrity tests administered in the United States each year. This testing stems directly from an increasing concern about employee theft and fraud and indirectly from the passage of the Employee Polygraph Protection Act. This act, which effectively prohibits the use of electronic "lie detectors" for selection, prompted increased research into the use of written integrity tests. These tests, much cheaper to administer, have been embraced by many more businesses. There are two basic kinds of integrity tests. Some are straightforward measures of attitudes toward dishonesty that may also ask about past dishonest acts. Surprisingly, faking responses does not seem to be a serious problem. Other integrity tests are less overt in purpose because they measure personality characteristics, such as conscientiousness and reliability. A careful and comprehensive review by Deniz Ones, Chockalingam Viswesvaran, and Frank Schmidt concludes that integrity tests are valid predictors of work behaviour. Although the correlations of the tests scores with theft per se are small, the tests do a pretty good job of predicting a broader class of

counterproductive behaviours that include theft, absenteeism, substance abuse, property damage, and so on. But are such tests ethical? Some observers have criticized the tests on the grounds of invasion of privacy. However, Dan Dalton and Michael Metzger take a different viewpoint. They argue that such tests are ethically questionable because they generate many "false positives," labeling people dishonest who are not dishonest. *All* tests make such classification errors, but they contend that integrity tests are especially prone because true dishonesty is fairly uncommon, and rare events are hard to predict. They further argue that the unfairly rejected applicant is unlikely to be told the true reason due to fear of legal problems.

What do you think about the ethics of integrity testing? Remember, they do predict counterproductive behaviour despite the classification errors.

Sources: Ones, D. S., Viswesvaran, C., & Schmidt, F. L. (1993). Comprehensive meta-analysis of integrity test validities: Findings and implications for personnel selection and theories of job performance. *Journal of Applied Psychology, 78*, pp. 679–703; Dalton, D. R., & Metzger, M. B. (1993). "Integrity testing" for personnel selection: An unsparing perspective. *Journal of Business Ethics, 12*, pp. 147–156; Ones, D. S., Schmidt, F. L., Viswesvaran, C., and Lykken, D. T. (1996). Controversies over integrity testing: Two viewpoints. *Journal of Business and Psychology, 10*, pp. 487-501.

Knowing the causes of unethical behaviour can aid in its prevention. Because the topic is sensitive, you should appreciate that this is not the easiest area to research. The major evidence comes from surveys of executive opinion, case studies of prominent ethical failures, business game simulations, and responses to written scenarios involving ethical dilemmas.

Gain. Although the point might seem mundane, it is critical to recognize the role of temptation in unethical activity. The anticipation of healthy reinforcement for following an unethical course of action, especially if no punishment is expected, should promote unethical decisions.[50] This is, of course, exactly the situation that the IOC members found themselves in, and until the Salt Lake City scandal, no member had ever been expelled. Consider, also, Dennis Levine, the Drexel Burnham Lambert investment banker who was convicted of insider trading in Wall Street's biggest scandal.

> It was just so easy. In seven years I built $39,750 into $11.5 million, and all it took was a 20-second phone call to my offshore bank a couple of times a month—maybe 200 calls total. My account was growing at 125% a year, compounded. Believe me, I felt a rush when I would check the price of one of my stocks on the office Quotron and learn I'd just made several hundred thousand dollars. I was confident that the elaborate veils of secrecy I had created—plus overseas bank-privacy laws—would protect me.[51]

Role Conflict. Many ethical dilemmas that occur in organizations are actually forms of role conflict (Chapter 7) that get resolved in an unethical way. For example, consider the ethical theme of corporate social responsibility we listed above. Here, an executive's role as custodian of the environment (do not pollute) might be at odds with his or her role as a community employer (do not close the plant that pollutes).

A very common form of role conflict that provokes unethical behaviour occurs when our "bureaucratic" role as an organizational employee is at odds with our role as the member of a profession.[52] For example, engineers who in their professional role opposed the fatal launch of the space shuttle *Challenger* due to cold weather were pressured to put on their bureaucratic "manager's hats" and agree to the launch. More recently, both the insurance and brokerage businesses have been rocked by similar ethics problems. Agents and brokers report being pressured as employees to push products that are not in the best interests of their clients. Frequently, reward systems (i.e., the commission structure) heighten the conflict, which then becomes a conflict of interest between self and client.

Competition. Stiff competition for scarce resources can stimulate unethical behaviour. This has been observed in both business game simulations and industry studies of illegal acts, in which trade offences, such as price fixing and monopoly violations, have been shown to increase with industry decline.[53] For example, observers cite a crowded and mature market as one factor prompting price fixing violations in the folding-carton packaging industry.[54] We should note one exception to the "competition stresses ethics" thesis. In cases in which essentially *no* competition exists, there is also a strong temptation to make unethical decisions. This is because the opportunity to make large gains is not offset by market checks and balances. Prominent examples have occurred in the defence industry, in which monopoly contracts to produce military hardware have been accompanied by some remarkable examples of overcharging taxpayers.

Personality. Are there certain types of personalities that are prone to unethical decisions? Perhaps. After all, not all members of the IOC accepted bribes even though they certainly could have. How can we explain why some members acted unethically while others resisted temptation? Business game simulations have shown that people with strong economic value orientations (Chapter 4) are more likely to behave unethically than those with weaker economic values.[55] Also, there are marked individual differences in the degree of sophistication that people use in thinking about moral issues.[56] Other things being equal, it is sensible to expect that people who are more self-conscious about moral matters will be more likely to avoid unethical decisions. Finally, people with a high need for personal power (especially Machiavellians) might be prone to make unethical decisions, using this power to further self-interest rather than for the good of the organization as a whole.

In closing this section, let us recall that we have a tendency to exaggerate the role of dispositional factors, such as personality, in explaining the behaviour of others (Chapter 3). Thus, when we see unethical behaviour, we should look at situational factors, such as competition and the organization's culture, as well as the personality of the actor.

Organizational and Industry Culture. Bart Victor and John Cullen found that there were considerable differences in ethical values across the organizations they studied.[57] These differences involved factors such as consideration for employees, respect for the law, and respect for organizational rules. In addition, there were differences across groups within these organizations. This suggests that aspects of an organization's culture (and its subcultures) can influence ethics. This corresponds to the repeated finding in executive surveys that peer and superior conduct are viewed as strongly influencing ethical behaviour, for good or for bad. The presence of role models helps to shape the culture (Chapter 8). If these models are actually rewarded for unethical behaviour, rather than punished, the development of an unethical culture is likely. In fact, firms convicted of illegal acts often tend to be repeat offenders.[58]

Many critics of the IOC have pointed to its culture as the real problem rather than just a few individuals. They cite years of bribery and corruption that were known by all members and IOC leaders who did nothing about it. Certainly, their failure to punish unethical behaviour must have contributed to a culture in which such behaviour was tolerated and allowed to continue.

The role of culture is also seen in the tendency for firms in certain industries to be convicted of illegal acts, although competition may also play a part. The food, lumber, oil refining, and automobile industries are more prone than others to such problems.[59]

Observers of the folding-carton price fixing scandal we mentioned above note how top managers frequently seemed out of touch with the difficulty of selling boxes in a mature, crowded market. They put in place goal setting and reward systems (e.g., commission forming 60 percent of income) that almost guaranteed unethical decisions, systems that are much more appropriate for products on a growth cycle.[60] In fact, research shows that upper-level managers generally tend to be naive about the extent of ethical lapses in those below them. This can easily contribute to a success-at-any-cost culture.[61]

Finally, a consideration of culture suggests the conditions under which corporate codes of ethics might actually have an impact on decision making. If such codes are specific, tied to the actual business being done, and correspond to the reward system, they should bolster an ethical climate. If vague codes that do not correspond to other cultural elements exist, the negative symbolism might actually damage the ethical climate.

Is Playing Politics Ethical?

Is political activity ethical? It is particularly important to be clear about who the relevant stakeholders are when we decide to act politically. Because politics by definition involves self-interest, it is easy to gloss over others' legitimate interests when playing the game.

Perhaps the most easily identified stakeholders are political opponents, if they exist for the particular political episode in question. For instance, we discussed above several examples of individuals or groups contending for resources or control. Political opponents may invoke very different ethical criteria to justify their actions, and these criteria might be difficult to reconcile.

The larger organization's role as a stakeholder in political activity can itself be ethically complicated. One study found that managers who established a strong political network were most likely to obtain frequent promotions. However, in terms of setting performance standards and developing subordinate satisfaction and commitment, less political managers performed better, using their communication and human resource management skills. In the researchers' words, the political managers were more "successful" but less "effective."[62] However, it would be difficult to question the ethics of the political managers for shortchanging the organization when they were tangibly rewarded for acting politically!

This example raises a third category of stakeholders whose interests we might consider in the political arena—subordinates or co-workers who are affected by political activity. A common instance involves making unreasonable demands on subordinates, as is the case with our next topic, sexual harassment.

Before continuing, consider the You Be the Manager feature.

Sexual Harassment—When Power and Ethics Collide

As indicated in Exhibit 12.6, sexual harassment is near the top of the list of ethical concerns. In recent years, a number of high profile sexual harassment cases have made news headlines and brought increased attention to this problem. For example, a cover story in *Maclean's* reported that sexual harassment and assault in the Canadian Forces is common.[63] In addition to the numerous cases of sexual harassment reported in the American and Canadian military, many organizations including Mitsubishi, Astra, Sears and Roebuck, and Del Laboratories have found themselves in costly litigation cases.[64] The failure of these organizations to effectively respond to charges of sexual harassment has cost them millions of dollars in settlements as well as lower productivity, and increased absenteeism and turnover. Sexual harassment in the U.S. army is reported to cost $250 million a year in lost productivity, absenteeism, and the replacement and transfer of employees.[65] As well, the effects on employees can include decreased morale and job satisfaction, as well as negative effects on psychological and physical well being.[66] There is also some evidence that men who perceive their workplace as hostile toward women and minorities report lower job satisfaction and trust toward their employer.[67]

Although there are many examples of what constitutes sexual harassment, the following is a fairly comprehensive definition:

> The EEOC [Equal Employment Opportunity Commission] regulatory guidelines state that unwelcome sexual advances, requests for sexual favours, and other verbal or physical conduct of a sexual nature constitute sexual harassment when submission to requests for sexual favours is made explicitly or implicitly a term or condition of employment; submission to or rejection of such requests is used as a basis for employment decisions; or such conduct unreasonably interferes with work performance or creates an intimidating, hostile, or offensive work environment. On the basis of these guidelines, current legal frameworks generally support two causes of action that claimants may state: coercion of sexual cooperation by threat of job-related consequences (quid pro quo harassment) and unwanted and offensive sex-related verbal or physical conduct, even absent any job-related threat (hostile work environment).[68]

you be the
manager

Sexual Harassment at Tory Haythe

The events were considered to be inappropriate on the part of the founding and senior American partner, Thomas Haythe, who is one of North America's most successful lawyers.

One of Canada's most prestigious law firms, Tory Tory DesLauriers & Binnington recently celebrated a groundbreaking merger with the equally prestigious New York-based law firm Haythe & Curley to become Tory Haythe. Although small by New York standards with only 75 lawyers, Haythe & Curley also has offices in Beijing and London and has major corporate clients. The merger was celebrated by the two firms with a six-foot long cake that was iced with the Toronto and Manhattan skylines.

The merger was one of three recent major mergers involving Canadian law firms. Such mergers are part of a global trend of law firm mergers in order to meet the national and international demands of clients.

Canadian law students have long considered Tory Tory DesLauriers & Binnington as one of the most desirable firms to work for. The newly formed Tory Haythe has 300 lawyers and is Canada's eighth-largest law firm and is now an even more attractive prospect to aspiring law students.

However, while the cross-border merger was expected to improve the firm's international image, Tory Haythe suddenly found itself trying to avoid a tarnished image. The firms' New York lawyers had flown to Toronto for a two-day working meeting with their Toronto counterparts. The themes of the meeting were professionalism, integrity, and respect.

On Friday night, half way through the meetings, there was a get-together followed by dinners at the Toronto homes of some of the partners of the firm. Afterwards, some of the lawyers went to a Toronto bar for drinks. However, by Saturday morning senior Canadian partner, Les Viner, began to hear about events that happened Friday night, events that were considered to be inappropriate behaviour on the part of the founding and senior American partner, Thomas Haythe, who also happens to be one of North America's most successful lawyers.

The allegations indicated that what happened was not an isolated incident and involved more than one woman. There were also witnesses for most of the events. Apparently, Haythe made sexual advances to several junior and senior Tory Tory lawyers and groped several female lawyers who are reported to have been traumatized by his actions. According to reports in several newspapers, Haythe is rumoured to have touched the women's breasts and genitalia, made lewd comments, and placed at least one woman's hands on his private parts.

By Monday the stories had become so public and pervasive that the firm was faced with the prospect of a very public scandal. The incident received considerable coverage in the media including front page stories and a newspaper war between Canada's two national newspapers. It also sparked a debate in the legal community, which paid close attention to the scandal. Long-time lawyers of the firm were reported to be shocked and appalled at the behaviour exhibited and deeply upset. Suddenly, the firm had to respond to some very serious allegations of sexual harassment. What should they do? How should they respond to the allegations of Haythe's inappropriate behaviour? You be the manager.

1. How can a sexual harassment policy help an organization deal with the kinds of allegations made against Thomas Haythe and what should be included in such policies?

2. What do you think Tory Haythe should do about the allegations regarding Haythe's inappropriate behaviour?

To find out how the firm responded, see The Manager's Notebook at the end of the chapter.

Sources: Church, E. (1999, November 26). Professional mergers can trip on scant scrutiny. *The Globe and Mail*, p. M1; Tesher, E. (1999, November 30). Sexual harassment and power politics. *The Toronto Star*, p. A25; Wente, M. (1999, November 27). Thomas Haythe's foolish choices. *The Globe and Mail*, pp. A1, A25; Fine, S., & Milner, B. (1999, November 27). Medical issue raised in law-firm affair. *The Globe and Mail*, p. A2; Fine, S. (1999, November 25). Senior partner at top law firm fired for sexual harassment. *The Globe and Mail*, pp. A1, A10; Fine, S. (1999, November 26). Inside the fall of Thomas Haythe. *The Globe and Mail*, pp. A1, A2; Sexton, R. (1999, December 4). A 40-year career destroyed in one night. *National Post*, p. B7; Walton, D., & Gibb-Clark, M. (1999, November 26). Shouldn't they know better? *The Globe and Mail*, p. A18; Peirce, E., Smolinski, C. A., & Rosen, B. (1998). Why sexual harassment complaints fall on deaf ears. *Academy of Management Executive*, 12, pp. 41-54.

While few would argue that sexual harassment is a form of unethical behaviour, what does it have to do with power? Sexual harassment is a form of unethical behaviour that stems, in part, from the abuse of power and the perpetuation of a gender power imbalance in the workplace. Managers or supervisors who use their position, reward, or coercive power to request sexual favours, demonstrate verbal or physical conduct of a sexual nature as a condition of employment, or as a basis for employment decisions toward those in less powerful positions, are abusing their power and acting in an unethical manner. While the most severe forms of sexual harassment are committed by supervisors, the most frequent perpetrators are actually co-workers. Although co-workers do not necessarily have the same formal power bases as supervisors, power differences often exist among co-workers and can also play a role in co-worker sexual harassment. Whether the harasser is a supervisor or a co-worker, he/she is likely to be more powerful than the person being harassed.[69] Not surprisingly, the most vulnerable victims of sexual harassment are those who are powerless and cannot afford to lose their jobs.[70]

Sexual harassment is also prevalent in hostile work environments that perpetuate the societal power imbalance between men and women. For example, the higher incidences of sexual harassment reported in military environments are believed to be partly a function of the rigid hierarchy and power differentials in the organization structure.[71] Incidents of sexual harassment and organizational inaction to complaints of sexual harassment are also more likely in male-dominated industries and organizations in which women are powerless and men attempt to execute and secure their dominance and position of power relative to women.[72]

Unfortunately, many organizations are slow to react to complaints of sexual harassment, and many do nothing about it until the complainant has reported it to the EEOC. For example, until recently, the Canadian Forces denied that a problem exists and has been accused of mishandling sexual assault cases.[73] This phenomenon has been referred to as the "deaf ear syndrome," which refers to the "the inaction or complacency of organizations in the face of charges of sexual harassment"[74] A review of organizational inaction in response to sexual harassment allegations found three main reasons to explain why organizations fail to respond: inadequate organizational policies and procedures for managing sexual harassment complaints; defensive managerial reactions and rationalizations for failing to act in the face of complaints; and organizational features that contribute to inertial tendencies (e.g., international companies in the United States have problems managing sexual harassment).[75]

Organizations can effectively deal with allegations of sexual harassment and increase their responsiveness by taking a number of important measures. On the basis of their review of the deaf ear syndrome, Ellen Peirce, Carol Smolinski, and Benson Rosen offer the following recommendations:

- *Examine the characteristics of deaf ear organizations.* Managers should examine their own organizations to determine if they have any of the characteristics that would make them susceptible to the deaf ear syndrome.

- *Foster management support and education.* Sexual harassment training programs are necessary to educate managers on how to respond to complaints in a sensitive and respectful manner.

- *Stay vigilant.* Managers must monitor the work environment and remove displays of a sexual nature and factors that can contribute to a hostile work environment.

- *Take immediate action.* One of the most important things that organizations can do is act immediately to complaints of sexual harassment. Failure to act is likely to result in negative consequences for the organization and the victims of sexual harassment. Organizations considered to be the best places for women to work are known for their swift action and severe handling of harassers.

- *Create a state-of-the-art policy.* Sexual harassment policies and procedures need to clearly define what constitutes sexual harassment and the sanctions that will be brought to bear on those found guilty of sexual harassment behaviour.

- *Establish clear reporting procedures.* User-friendly policies need to be designed so that there are clear procedures for filing complaints and mechanisms in place for the impartial investigation of complaints. The privacy of those involved must also be protected.[76]

In general, organizations that are responsive to complaints of sexual harassment have top management support and commitment, comprehensive education and training programs, continuously monitor the work environment, respond to complaints in a thorough and timely manner, and have clear policies and reporting procedures.[77] An example of such an organization is E. I. Du Pont de Nemours, which has developed a sexual harassment awareness program called *A Matter of Respect*, which includes interactive training programs, peer-level facilitators that are trained to meet with employees who want to talk about sexual harassment, and a 24-hour hotline. As the company has become more international, so has its training on sexual harassment which is now provided in Japan, China, Mexico, and Puerto Rico.[78]

E.I Du Pont de Nemours
www.dupont.com

Employing Ethical Guidelines

During the 1990s, many organizations began to invest in ethical programs. A recent survey of large American organizations reported that 78 percent have codes of ethics, 51 percent have telephone lines for reporting ethical concerns, and 30 percent have offices for dealing with ethics.[79]

A few simple guidelines, regularly used, should help in the ethical screening of decisions. The point is not to paralyze your decision making but to get you to think seriously about the moral implications of your decisions before they are made.[80]

- Identify the stakeholders that will be affected by any decision.
- Identify the costs and benefits of various decision alternatives to these stakeholders.
- Consider the relevant moral expectations that surround a particular decision. These might stem from professional norms, laws, organizational ethics, codes, and principles, such as honest communication and fair treatment.
- Be familiar with the common ethical dilemmas that decision makers face in your specific organizational role or profession.
- Discuss ethical matters with decision stakeholders and others. Do not think ethics without talking about ethics.
- Convert your ethical judgments into appropriate action.

What this advice does is enable you to recognize ethical issues, make ethical judgments, and then convert these judgments into behaviour.[81]

Training and education in ethics have become very popular in North American organizations. Boeing has a noteworthy program in an industry (aerospace) that has seen its share of ethical scandals.

Boeing, which has been singled out for its outstanding internal program for ethics, trains its more than 145,000 employees in ethical values and uses a communication channel that enables employees to report infractions or concerns. A company-created pamphlet entitled "Business Conduct Guidelines" which emphasizes policies on ethics and standards of conduct and compliance is used in the training program. Training includes a videotape customized with an opening message by the general manager of each division. Situations are presented, both dramatic (FBI visits to homes) or routine (exchanges between customers, employees, suppliers, managers, and subordinates). Training is led by a business ethics advisor in each division.[82]

The evidence that exists so far indicates that formal education in ethics does have a positive impact on ethical attitudes.[83]

the manager's notebook

Sexual Harassment at Tory Haythe

1. Organizational inaction in response to sexual harassment complaints is often due to inadequate sexual harassment policies and procedures. Sexual harassment policies and procedures lay the groundwork for identifying what sexual harassment involves and how to report and respond to sexual harassment complaints. Sexual harassment policies should be clearly written and include definitions of sexual harassment with examples of acceptable and unacceptable behaviour as well as user-friendly reporting procedures that are clear and unambiguous. User-friendly policies should include clear procedures for filing complaints, mechanisms for rapid investigation, and provisions for protecting the privacy of accusers and accused. Sanctions should also be clearly indicated. A company's sexual harassment policy indicates top management's conviction that sexual harassment will not be tolerated at any level in the organization and ensures that a mechanism exists so that victims of sexual harassment can register complaints, and that such complaints can be redressed.

   When Tory Tory DesLauriers & Binnington merged with Haythe & Curley, they brought with them a seven-page corporate policy on sexual harassment in the workplace. Their policy indicates their commitment to providing a workplace in which all members are able to work in an environment free from harassment; what harassment means along with examples; what to do in the case of harassment; informal resolution options; and disciplinary and rehabilitative action that can result in the discharge of an employee or partner. Tory Tory DesLauriers & Binnington has long had a zero tolerance atmosphere of sexual harassment. Three years ago the firm held a session to train its members in harassment policy following complaints against its staff members. According to senior Canadian partner Les Viner, Haythe's actions violated the firm's sexual harassment policy.

2. In a recent review of several high-profile sexual harassment cases, it was concluded that the most important thing for an organization to do in response to sexual harassment complaints is to act immediately. In fact, many organizations that are known as best places for women to work have reputations for dealing swiftly and severely with harassers. In the case of Thomas Haythe, he publicly apologized before 250 colleagues for his inappropriate behaviour at a dinner the following evening that was sponsored by the firm. However, within four days following the incident, he was fired from his firm for sexual harassment. Among the American partners of the firm, there was no dissent about taking action against him. All agreed, unanimously, quickly, and decisively, that it was intolerable, and there was no division at all among the men and women in the firm. Senior Canadian partner Les Viner said, "Swift, decisive action was taken because it threatened our core values of professionalism and collegiality and respect." The firm has said that Haythe will not be returning, and that the name of the firm will be changed to reflect his departure. After being removed from his roles and responsibilities in the firm, Haythe went on medical leave and was reported to be undergoing medical assessment for a medical condition that could be a brain tumour.

Summary

- Power is the capacity to influence other people who are in a state of dependence. People have power by virtue of their position in the organization (legitimate power) or by virtue of the resources that they command (reward, coercion, friendship, or expertise).

- People can obtain power by doing the right things and cultivating the right people. Activities that lead to power acquisition need to be extraordinary, visible, and relevant to the needs of the organization. People to cultivate include outsiders, subordinates, peers, and superiors. Managers with high need for power are effective when they use this power to achieve organizational goals.

- Empowerment means giving people the authority, opportunity, and motivation to solve organizational problems. Power is thus located where it is needed to give employees the feeling that they are capable of doing their jobs well.

- Influence tactics are interpersonal strategies that convert power into influence. They include assertiveness, ingratiation, rationality, exchange, upward appeal, and coalition formation. Rationality (logic, reason, planning, compromise) is generally the most efficient tactic.

- Organizational subunits obtain power by controlling strategic contingencies. This means that they are able to affect events that are critical to *other* subunits. Thus, departments that can obtain resources for the organization will acquire power. Similarly, subunits gain power when they are able to reduce uncertainty for the organization, when their function is central to the workflow, and when other subunits or outside contractors cannot perform their tasks.

- Organizational politics occurs when influence means that are not sanctioned by the organization are used or when nonsanctioned ends are pursued. The pursuit of nonsanctioned ends is always dysfunctional, but the organization may benefit when nonsanctioned means are used to achieve approved goals.

- Several political tactics were discussed: Machiavellianism is a set of cynical beliefs about human nature, morality, and the permissibility of using various means to achieve one's ends. Situational morality, lying, and "psyching out" are common tactics. Networking is establishing good relations with key people to accomplish goals. Defensiveness means avoiding taking actions that do not suit one's political agenda and avoiding blame for negative events.

- Ethics is systematic thinking about the moral consequences of decisions. Of particular interest is impact on stakeholders, people who have the potential to be affected by the decision.

- Common themes that run through ethical dilemmas that managers face include honest communication, fair treatment, special consideration, fair competition, responsibility to the organization, social responsibility, and respect for law.

- Causes of unethical behaviour include the potential for great gain, the existence of role conflict, the extremes of business competition (great or none), organizational and industry culture, and certain personality characteristics.

- Sexual harassment is a form of unethical behaviour that stems, in part, from the abuse of power and the perpetuation of a gender imbalance in the workplace.

Discussion Questions

1. Contrast the bases of power available to an army sergeant with those available to the president of a voluntary community association. How would these differences in power bases affect their influence tactics?

2. Are the bases of individual power easily substitutable for each other? Are they equally effective? For example, can coercive power substitute for expert power?

3. Suppose that you are an entrepreneur who has started a new chain of consumer electronic stores. Your competitive edge is to offer excellent customer service. What would you do to empower your employees to help achieve this goal?

4. Imagine that you are on a committee at work or in a group working on a project at school that includes a "high Mach" member. What could you do to neutralize the high Mach's attempts to manipulate the group?

5. Discuss the conditions under which the following subunits of an organization might gain or lose power: Legal department; research and development unit; public relations department. Use the concepts of scarcity, uncertainty, centrality, and substitutability in your answers.

6. Differentiate between power and politics. Give an example of the use of power that is not political.

7. There is a saying that "politics is a way of life in organizations." Do you agree? Is political activity necessary for organizations to function?

8. Is sexual harassment more likely to be a problem in some occupations and types of organizations? Describe those occupations and organizational cultures where sexual harassment is most likely to be a problem. What can be done to prevent sexual harassment in these occupations and organizations?

9. Consider the role of politics and ethics in decision making. How can organizational politics be a source of effective or ineffective decision making in organizations? In what way can the causes of unethical behaviour influence decision making?

10. How can an organization create an ethical workplace where ethical behaviour is the norm? Refer to the organizational learning practices in Chapter 2, the models of attitude change in Chapter 4, and the contributors to organizational culture in Chapter 8 to answer this question.

Experiential Exercise

Is This Sexual Harassment?

Goals

1. To help students to understand what is and what is not sexual harassment on the job.

2. To apply the federal government's sexual harassment guidelines to workplace situations. The Equal Employment Opportunity Commission's guidelines define sexual harassment as:

> "unwelcome sexual advances, requests for sexual favours, and other physical and verbal contact of a sexual nature when it affects the terms of employment under one or more of the following conditions: such an activity is a condition for employment; such an activity is a condition of employment consequences such as promotion, dismissal, or salary increases; such an activity creates a hostile working environment."

Instructions

Given the guidelines, which of the following incidents are examples of sexual harassment? Explain your reasons for your answers. Your instructor will give you the expert opinion on whether or not each incident is an example of sexual harassment.

1. While teaching Gary how to run the new spreadsheet program on the computer, Lois, his supervisor, puts her hand on his shoulder.

2. Julie, the new secretary to the vice-president of manufacturing, frequently has to go out into the plant as part of her job. Several of the machinists have been whistling at her and shouting off-colour remarks as she passes through the shop. One of the other women in the company found Julie crying in the ladies' room after such an incident.

3. Paul and Cynthia, two sales reps, are both married. However, it is well known that they are dating each other outside the office.

4. Jeanne's boss, Tom, frequently asks her out for drinks after work. She goes because both are single and she enjoys his company. On one of these occasions, he asks her out to dinner for the following Saturday evening.

5. Steve's boss, Cathy, frequently makes suggestive comments to him and has even suggested that they meet outside the office. Although at first he ignored these remarks, recently he made it clear to her that he had a steady girlfriend and was not available. When she gave him his performance appraisal, much to his surprise, she cited him for not being a team player.

6. Jackie received a call at work that her father died suddenly. When she went to tell her boss that she had to leave, she burst into tears. He put his arms around her and let her cry on his shoulder.

7. Marge's co-worker, Jerry, frequently tells her what she is wearing is very attractive.

8. While being hired as a secretary, Amanda is told that she may occasionally be expected to accompany the manager on important overnight business trips to handle the clerical duties at these meetings.

9. Joe, an elderly maintenance man, often makes suggestive comments to the young females in the office. His behaviour has been reported to his supervisor several times but it is dismissed as, 'Don't be so sensitive, old Joe doesn't mean any harm."

10. Jennifer frequently wears revealing blouses to the office. Several times she has caught male employees staring at her.

Source: Carol P. Harvey, M. June Allard, *Understanding diversity: Readings, cases, and exercises*. HarperCollins College.

Case Incident

Mr. Nobody

After graduating from university at the top of his class, Jack was ready to set the corporate world on fire. Soon after landing a job in a top brokerage firm, he was determined to move up the corporate ladder as fast as possible. As always, Jack liked to influence people and get them to see and do things his way. Unfortunately, he soon found that nobody really cared about what he had to say, and after a month, his co-workers started avoiding him. Jack could not understand how he went from being so influential in university to a nobody at work.

Questions

1. How would you explain to Jack his lack of power and influence in the organization?

2. What advice would you give Jack on how to obtain power in his organization?

Case Study

Managing the Marketing Department

Richard Walsh's first career had been that of a researcher for a small Midwestern market research firm. He had begun this job with a fresh MBA degree, dividing his time between working long hours, getting married, and starting a family. At the research firm, Walsh was recognized as bright and competent, but he was also seen as somewhat arrogant and egotistical. Walsh liked to flaunt his intellect, and he frequently strung multisyllabic words together as if he were an Oxford University don. He prided himself on keeping up with the latest marketing research techniques emanating from the top universities, and he frequently gave rambling lectures about the virtues or vices of some new technique to the perplexed staff of the firm.

At the age of 37, Richard Walsh made a radical career change. Selling the family home, he and his family moved to the East Coast, and he enrolled in a Ph.D. program at a university with a reasonable reputation. The move had been carefully planned, and the family lived in a small rented apartment and conserved resources to support Richard's endeavour. As a graduate student, he was perceived as fairly intelligent, but argumentative. After three and a half years, Walsh received his Ph.D. degree and took a job as an assistant professor at Collins College. He felt that he could have gone to a much more prestigious school, but he told friends that his wife and children really wanted to return to the Midwest. "Besides, I'll build that place into a powerhouse or else move on to Stanford," he laughed.

When Richard arrived at Collins College, the dean of the business school immediately appointed him coordinator of the marketing area. At the time, faculty at Collins were organized by teaching areas and not separated into formal departments. There were only two other marketing professors, both older individuals who did not hold Ph.D.s, and the dean was eager to put Ph.D.s in the coordination positions to take advantage of their more recent university experience for curriculum development. Both of Walsh's senior colleagues were happy to be relieved of the coordination job since it cut into their consulting time and were very supportive of their new colleague.

Richard took to the coordinator's job with relish. He updated many course descriptions and introduced two new courses in his specialty, marketing research. In addition, he revised the scheduling of the marketing courses, taking pains to incorporate the time preferences of his two senior colleagues. Richard quickly acquired a reputation as an effective if longwinded speaker at faculty meetings, where he showed an impressive command of the language. During his first three years at Collins, his prestige among the faculty was aided considerably by the publication of several works from his Ph.D. dissertation. Two of these were technical notes in prestigious marketing journals, and the other was a monograph put out by an obscure New York publisher. Since the publication efforts of Collins' faculty were almost nil, this activity was noticed. Privately, Richard's two marketing colleagues described the monograph as brilliant, although both admitted they really did not understand it very well.

Richard's fourth year at Collins was an important one for him. He was promoted to associate professor, received tenure, and was appointed chairperson of the newly formed marketing department. The business school at Collins was going to be expanded, and the dean felt that formal departments would be necessary as the school grew in size. Richard's appointment was enthusiastically supported by his two older colleagues, who had consistently deferred to his judgment during his years as coordinator.

The key task of the new department chairperson was to hire additional faculty and to make decisions about the renewal of their contracts. Previously, these tasks had been performed directly by the dean. The dean was particularly interested in increasing the research and publication output of the business school, and Richard readily agreed. "After all," he said, "I'm the only person around here publishing in the top journals. We need more of that."

During the next few years, Collins's chairpersons were generally successful in recruiting new faculty. Most departments hired new Ph.D.s or individuals in the very last stages of their doctoral dissertations. Although they were not from exceptional schools, most turned out to be good teachers and active researchers and publishers. Gradually, the reputation of the Collins business school was increasing.

In the marketing department, Richard Walsh employed a somewhat different recruiting strategy. He tended to hire Ph.D. students who were in the very early phases of their dissertations. They were usually from the better schools, and Richard said that they had great potential for building an "intellectual core" in the department. His senior marketing colleagues agreed. When someone asked Richard how he managed to attract people from the better schools to the relatively modest Collins campus, he replied that he looked for those who were "power stricken." "You'd be surprised what a job offer will do to a poor graduate with a whole dissertation to complete," he grinned.

Some of the new marketing faculty complained that their teaching loads were heavier than they had expected, and that Richard had been vague about this when they were being recruited. In the other departments new recruits were given a reprieve from committees so that they could devote their time to getting their teaching and research off to a good start. Richard, on the other hand, assigned new recruits to several committees so that they could "get the feel of the college."

Over the years, successive new recruits in marketing experienced considerable difficulty in completing their dissertations. Although some surreptitiously looked for jobs elsewhere, they soon learned that it was difficult to obtain another position without having finished their Ph.D.s. Richard was very sympathetic to their difficulties, and he frequently recounted the privations he and his family had endured during his graduate study. In addition, he was always willing to provide frank and lengthy critiques of the dissertation work they had accomplished.

New recruits were hired under two-year contracts, and a decision was made early in the second year as to whether they would be renewed for another two years. Although the chairpersons had the final say in this matter, it was standard practice in all departments to convene a department meeting to evaluate those up for renewal and to vote on renewal decisions. At the first renewal meeting for each candidate, Richard spoke forcefully in favour of contract renewal, citing his or her "great potential." Consistently, the two senior members agreed with Richard, as did the junior members (who were often in the same boat as the person on whom they were voting). Thus, over the years, first renewals occurred in spite of incomplete dissertations.

Second renewal decisions were made early in a faculty member's fourth year at Collins. By this time, most had completed their dissertations or were very close to doing so. Richard's approach to second renewal decisions varied considerably from that used in first renewal decisions. Typically, he began second-renewal meetings with an eloquent speech about maintaining the quality of the department increasing its research and publication efforts. "After all," he said, "we don't want to end up granting tenure to someone who will never publish anything." Invariably, those up for renewal had achieved no publications, and Richard spoke against their renewal. His senior colleagues always agreed, as did all the junior members who were awaiting their own first renewal decisions. This group consistently carried the vote, and no junior member lasted more than four years in the Collins marketing department.

Jack Ross, dean of the school of business at Collins, sat in his office and wondered what to do about the marketing department. During his reign as dean, Ross felt that he had generally been successful in increasing the quality of the school. However, he had gradually come to see the marketing department as a weak link in the chain. Although marketing had hired some promising people, turnover was high because of nonrenewals, and publication productivity was low. Even Richard Walsh had not published anything since his success years ago.

Recently, a delegation of the other chairpersons had complained to Ross that their departments were not receiving enough travel money to cover the presentation of research papers at learned conferences. They had implied (though not said directly) that the marketing department received too much travel money. Ross knew that almost all of the marketing's travel allocation was spent by Richard Walsh, who frequently attended conferences for recruiting purposes. However, the dean had begun to wonder about Walsh's recruiting strategy. For years, he had been unable to hire anyone in his own specialty, marketing research, even though another person in this area was desperately needed. Furthermore, Walsh never seemed to follow up on leads provided by the dean for experienced, well-published marketing professors who might be attracted to Collins.

Jack Ross worried about what he should say to Richard Walsh.

Source: Case prepared by Gary Johns.

1. Is power an issue in *Managing the Marketing Department*? If so, who has power over whom?

2. What bases of individual power does Richard Walsh command?

3. How did Richard Walsh acquire the power he holds?

4. Why did Richard Walsh engage in his unique hiring and contract renewal strategy? What are his motives? Is he a Machiavellian? Does he have a high need for power?

5. Is there evidence of organizational politics in the case? Defend your answer.

6. Is ethics an issue in this case? Explain your answer.

7. What should Dean Ross do about the marketing department?

Chapter 13

Conflict and Stress

ARTHUR ANDERSEN WORLDWIDE is a $9.5 billion organization and the world's largest accounting and consulting firm. In 1989, the accounting firm Arthur Andersen gave the firm's consultants its own business unit, which became known as Andersen Consulting. In an effort to subsidize and nurture the consulting unit, agreements were made to transfer funds between the two divisions that would equalize partner compensation across Andersen Worldwide. This meant that the consultants would receive subsidies from the greater revenues generated by the accounting unit.

> **Arthur Andersen versus Andersen Consulting**

Today, Andersen Consulting has grown to 64,000 employees and 1,038 partners with offices in 46 countries. It is considered to be one of the largest, most successful, and highest-paying consulting firms surpassing major firms, such as McKinsey & Co. It consults with many large global companies, including Royal Dutch Shell, Microsoft Corp., and Dupont Co. One would have thought that such success would be cause for celebration throughout Andersen Worldwide. After all, the 2,600 partners of Andersen Worldwide earn an average of more than $400,000 a year. However, things seemed to have soured between the two units, largely due to a lag in traditional accounting business and the tremendous growth and demand for strategic and technology consulting.

Since 1989, the revenues of Andersen Consulting have quintupled and reached a record $8.3 billion in 1998. As a result, Andersen Consulting now brings in more money than Arthur Andersen. By comparison, Arthur Andersen with 91,000 employees in 79 countries and 1,700 partners, generates $5.2 billion in revenue. Thus, Andersen Consulting has been more prosperous than Arthur Andersen with fewer partners and offices, and its partners earn an average of $50,000 to $100,000 more a year than the partners of Arthur Andersen.

The partners of Andersen Consulting voted to seek an arbitration to resolve a long standing conflict with Arthur Andersen that could effectively break up Andersen Worldwide.

This has caused a considerable amount of conflict between Arthur Andersen and Andersen Consulting. With its growth and increased dealings with large corporations, Andersen Consulting has become a global force with a more powerful role in the firm and a desire to have less to do with its colleagues at Arthur Andersen. In fact, in some cities where the accountants and consultants once shared office space, the consultants have moved out into separate offices. As a result, new consulting partners no longer know the accounting partners, and they rarely socialize. There is also the issue of a clash between two different cultures within one organization and differences in work habits and business philosophy. Andersen Consulting is a large global corporation and considers itself a global entity that has no headquarters. Arthur Andersen is run through local, regional, and foreign offices.

Many believe that the real source of the conflict is money. Andersen Consulting now brings in far more money than Arthur Andersen, and as a result, the transfer payments that were originally used to nurture and subsidize Andersen Consulting are now flowing the other way. The large profits of Andersen Consulting are helping to subsidize the incomes of the accountants to a tune of about $100 million a year which is causing a great deal of resentment among the consultants.

The conflict was exacerbated in 1993 when the partners of Arthur Andersen decided to form its own consulting operation to offer computer consulting services. The partners of Andersen Consulting were outraged that the accounting unit took their money and then built a rival computer- and management-consulting practice. By 1997, the new unit was bringing in $500 million annually and now does about half as much consulting as Andersen Consulting. To make matters worse, the accounting unit has apparently on occasion offered to do

Andersen Consulting
www.andersen.com/

Learning Objectives

After reading Chapter 13, you should be able to:

1 Define interpersonal conflict and review its causes in organizations.

2 Explain the process by which conflict occurs.

3 Discuss the various modes of managing conflict.

4 Review a range of negotiation techniques.

5 Discuss the merits of stimulating conflict.

6 Distinguish among stressors, stress, and stress reactions.

7 Discuss the role that personality plays in stress.

8 Review the sources of stress encountered by various organizational role occupants.

9 Describe behavioural, psychological, and physiological reactions to stress and discuss techniques for reducing or coping with stress.

the same work as their consulting partners for lower fees, and in one case, Andersen Consulting lost a $250,000 job to Arthur Andersen.

Andersen Consulting began complaining about the existence of two competing consulting firms with the Andersen name and the confusion it was causing clients. Clients also began to complain about the conflicts in Andersen Worldwide, and the partners wanted a resolution. To help solve the problem, Andersen executives formed a special committee that was eventually disbanded because it could not reach an agreement. In another attempt to solve the conflict, three top partners were asked to come up with a proposal to settle things once and for all. They came up with a three-step plan that would involve negotiations or a binding decision made by an arbitrator. However, both sides accuse the other of rejecting the proposal.

The chief executive of Andersen Worldwide suggested dividing the firm into five or more business units and combining all the consulting operations under one consulting umbrella. Another plan was to spin off Andersen Consulting into a stock offering. Both plans were rejected by the partners. The managing partner of Arthur Andersen suggested that if the consultants wanted to leave Andersen Worldwide they must pay a steep premium—$10 billion. If they stayed, he suggested that both units be allowed to compete for lucrative technology consulting contracts, and that the transfer payments continue although they might be capped at $180 million a year.

None of this was satisfactory to Andersen Consulting who argued that they are leaving because Arthur Andersen's consulting practice breached an agreement that they would not pursue computer consulting services with companies whose annual revenue was more than $175 million. Andersen Consulting has proposed taking over Arthur Andersen's consulting practice in return for the continuation of the transfer payments. This was unsatisfactory to Arthur Andersen who would lose partners and its control of Andersen Worldwide's governing board of partners, not to mention considerable revenues if it gave up its consulting unit. So the partners of Andersen Consulting voted unanimously to seek an arbitration that would effectively break up Andersen Worldwide. Their lawyers have submitted a breach-of-contract complaint against Arthur Andersen to the arbitration offices of the International Chamber of Commerce in Paris. In response, Arthur Andersen says that Andersen Consulting must pay a $10 billion exit fee plus royalties on technology and the use of the Andersen name if they leave. Officials of Andersen Consulting argue that they do not have to pay an exit fee, and that Arthur Andersen must return the hundreds of millions in transfer payments that they have been receiving from Andersen Consulting.

Andersen Worldwide, the parent of the two units, has responded by filling a $14.6 billion counterclaim against Andersen Consulting. The International Chamber of Commerce in Paris has appointed an attorney to oversee the arbitration who is expected to render a decision sometime this year.[1]

Like power and politics, conflict is a natural occurrence in organizations, although not always in this extreme and open form. Conflict can have benefits, but it can also lead to problems, such as employee stress.

In this chapter, we will define interpersonal conflict, discuss its causes, and examine various ways of handling conflict. We place particular emphasis on negotiation. Then, we will explore organizational stress, noting its causes and the consequences that it can have for both the individual and the organization. Various strategies for reducing or coping with stress will be considered.

What Is Conflict?

Interpersonal conflict is a process that occurs when one person, group, or organizational subunit frustrates the goal attainment of another. Thus, the curator of a museum might be in conflict with the director over the purchase of a particular work of art. Likewise, the entire curatorial staff might be in conflict with the financial staff over cutbacks in acquisition funds.

In its classic form, conflict often involves antagonistic attitudes and behaviours. As for attitudes, the conflicting parties might develop a dislike for each other, see each other as unreasonable, and develop negative stereotypes of their opposites ("Those scientists should get out of the laboratory once in a while."). Antagonistic behaviours might include name calling, sabotage, or even physical aggression. In some organizations, the conflict process is managed in a collaborative way that keeps antagonism at a minimum. In others, conflict is hidden or suppressed and not nearly so obvious (e.g., some gender conflict).[2]

> **Interpersonal conflict.** A process that occurs when one person, group, or organizational subunit frustrates the goal attainment of another.

Causes of Organizational Conflict

It is possible to isolate a number of factors that contribute to organizational conflict.[3]

Group Identification and Intergroup Bias

An especially fascinating line of research has shown how identification with a particular group or class of people can set the stage for organizational conflict. In this research, people have typically assigned people to groups randomly or on the basis of some trivial characteristic, such as eye colour. Even without interaction or cohesion, people have a tendency to develop a more positive view of their own "in-group" (be it a friendship group, a work group, or a department) and a less positive view of the "out-group" of which they are not a member.[4] The ease with which this unwarranted intergroup bias develops is disturbing.

Why does intergroup bias occur? Self-esteem is probably a critical factor. Identifying with the successes of one's own group and disassociating oneself from out-group failures boosts self-esteem and provides comforting feelings of social solidarity. In research by one of the authors, for example, it was found that people felt that their work group's attendance record was superior to that of their occupation in general (and, by extension, other work groups).[5] Attributing positive behaviour to your own work group should contribute to your self-esteem.

In organizations, there are a number of groups or classes with which people might identify. These might be based on personal characteristics (e.g., race or gender), job function (e.g., sales or production), or job level (e.g., manager or non-manager). Furthermore, far from being random or trivial, differences between groups might be accentuated by real differences in power, opportunity, clients serviced, and so on. As indicated in the chapter opening vignette, at Andersen Worldwide, identification is based on being a member of the accounting or consulting group. The best prognosis is that people who identify with some groups will tend to be leery of out-group members. The likelihood of conflict increases as the factors we cover below enter into the relationship between groups.

The increased emphasis on teams in organizations generally places a high premium on getting employees to identify strongly with their team. The prevalence of intergroup bias suggests that organizations will have to pay special attention to managing relationships *between* these teams.

Interdependence

When individuals or subunits are mutually dependent on each other to accomplish *their own* goals, the potential for conflict exists. For example, the sales staff is dependent on the production department for the timely delivery of high-quality products. This is the only way sales can maintain the good will of its customers. On the other hand, production depends on the sales staff to provide routine orders with adequate lead times. Custom-tailored emergency orders will wreak havoc with production schedules and make the production department look bad. In contrast, the sales staff and the office maintenance staff are not highly interdependent. Salespeople are on the road a lot and should not make great demands on maintenance. Conversely, a dirty office probably will not lose a sale!

Interdependence can set the stage for conflict for two reasons. First, it necessitates interaction between the parties so that they can coordinate their interests. Conflict will not develop if the parties can "go it alone." Second, as we noted in the previous chapter, interdependence implies that each party has some *power* over the other. It is relatively easy for one side or the other to abuse its power and create antagonism.

Interdependence does not *always* lead to conflict. In fact, it often provides a good basis for collaboration through mutual assistance. Whether interdependence prompts conflict depends on the presence of other conditions, which we will now consider.

Differences in Power, Status, and Culture

Conflict can erupt when parties differ significantly in power, status, or culture.

Power. If dependence is not mutual, but one way, the potential for conflict increases. If party A needs the collaboration of party B to accomplish its goals, but B does not need A's assistance, antagonism may develop. B has power over A, and A has nothing with which to bargain. A good example is the quality control system in many factories. Production workers might be highly dependent on inspectors to approve their work, but this dependence is not reciprocated. The inspectors might have a separate boss, their own office, and their own circle of friends (other inspectors). In this case, production workers might begin to treat inspectors with hostility, one of the symptoms of conflict.

Status. Status differences provide little impetus for conflict when people of lower status are dependent on those of higher status. This is the way organizations often work, and most members are socialized to expect it. However, because of the design of the work, there are occasions when employees with technically lower status find themselves giving orders to, or controlling the tasks of, higher-status people. The restaurant business provides a good example. In many restaurants, lower-status waiters and waitresses give orders and initiate queries to higher-status cooks or chefs. The latter might come to resent this reversal of usual lines of influence.[6] The advent of the "electronic office" led to similar kinds of conflict. As secretaries mastered the complexities of electronic mail, they found themselves having to educate senior executives about the capabilities and limitations of such systems. Some executives are defensive about this reversal of roles.

Culture. When two or more very different cultures develop in an organization, the clash in beliefs and values can result in overt conflict. Hospital administrators who develop a strong culture centred on efficiency and cost-effectiveness might find themselves in conflict with physicians who share a strong culture based on providing excellent patient care at any cost. A telling case of cultural conflict occurred when Apple Computer expanded and hired professionals away from several companies with their own strong cultures.

Hewlett-Packard
www.hp.com

> During the first couple of years Apple recruited heavily from Hewlett-Packard, National Semiconductor, and Intel, and the habits and differences in style among these companies were reflected in Cupertino. There was a general friction between the rough and tough ways of the semiconductor men (there were few women) and the people who made computers, calculators, and instruments at Hewlett-Packard.... Some of the Hewlett-Packard men began to see themselves as civilizing influences and were horrified at the uncouth rough-and-tumble practices of the brutes from the semiconductor industry.... Many of the men from National Semiconductor and other stern backgrounds harboured a similar contempt for the Hewlett-Packard recruits. They came to look on them as prissy fusspots.[7]

As is evident in the vignette that began this chapter, Andersen Consulting developed its own unique culture with work habits and a business philosophy that made it distinct from Arthur Andersen.

Ambiguity

Ambiguous goals, jurisdictions, or performance criteria can lead to conflict. Under such ambiguity, the formal and informal rules that govern interaction break down. In addition, it might be difficult to accurately assign praise for good outcomes or blame for bad outcomes when it is hard to see who was responsible for what. For example, if sales drop following the introduction of a "new and improved" product, the design group might blame the marketing department for a poor advertising campaign. In response, the marketers might claim that the "improved" product is actually inferior to the old product.

Ambiguous performance criteria are a frequent cause of conflict between superiors and subordinates. The basic scientist who is charged by a chemical company to "discover new knowledge" might react negatively when her boss informs her that her work is inadequate. This rather open-ended assignment is susceptible to a variety of interpretations.

Scarce Resources

In the previous chapter, we pointed out that differences in power are magnified when resources become scarce. This does not occur without a battle, however, and conflict often surfaces in the process of power jockeying. Limited budget money, secretarial support, or computer time can contribute to conflict. Consider the company that installs a new computer for administrative and research purposes. At first, there is plenty of computer time and space for both uses. However, as both factions make more and more use of the computer, access becomes a problem. Conflict may erupt at this point.

Scarcity has a way of turning latent or disguised conflict into overt conflict. Two scientists who do not get along very well may be able to put up a peaceful front until a reduction in laboratory space provokes each to protect his domain. At Andersen Worldwide, a major source of conflict was lucrative consulting contracts that both Arthur Andersen and Andersen Consulting were pursuing.

Types of Conflict

Although a variety of causes contribute to the emergence of organizational conflict, most conflicts boil down to several basic types or combinations of these types. These include disputes over goals, facts, and procedures.[8]

Disputes over goals are very common in organizations. Consider this General Mills general manager for fruit snacks as she reflects on the common conflict between marketing and manufacturing:

> "The goal of the people in the plants is to run lots of cases fast," she says. "Our goal is to constantly bring something new to consumers." The manufacturing people do not like the way she changes the colours of the fruit-snack wrapping and places new prizes, such as glow-in-the-dark sharks, inside the boxes. She argues, "Doing these things is crucial to growing the business."[9]

Disputes over facts very frequently arise in technical situations. Motorola's biggest project, a worldwide cellular phone network, was nearly scuttled by debate over its technical feasibility.

Disputes over procedures generally centre around one party's expectations about how the other party should behave. Matters of ethics (Chapter 12), fairness (Chapter 4), and respecting status hierarchies often fuel procedural conflicts. For example, a well-documented source of conflict between employees and managers has to do with the legitimacy of employee absenteeism and the fairness of management response to it.[10]

Being aware of these different types of conflict should sensitize you to the need to be sure that you understand what a conflict episode is really about. For instance, very basic differences in goals (should we expand the business?) are not necessarily resolvable by clearing up disputes over facts (what is our potential market size?). Also, notice that spillover between domains can occur. For instance, a conflict over facts (which project has more technical merit?) can lead to procedural conflict if one party is seen as trying to unethically sabotage the other's work. When this happens, true conflict resolution can occur only when *all* aspects of the conflict (i.e., both facts and procedures) are dealt with. Finally, one party might frame a conflict as a goal conflict, while the other might see it as a procedural conflict or a conflict over facts. In seeking resolution, it is important to try to see the conflict from your opponent's frame of reference.

The Conflict Process

A number of events occur when one or more of the causes of conflict we noted above takes effect. We will assume here that the conflict in question occurs between groups, such as organizational departments. However, much of this is also relevant to conflict between individuals. Specifically, when conflict begins, we often see the following events transpire:

- "Winning" the conflict becomes more important than developing a good solution to the problem at hand.

- The parties begin to conceal information from each other or to pass distorted information.

- Each group becomes more cohesive. Deviants who speak of conciliation are punished, and strict conformity is expected.

- Contact with the opposite party is discouraged except under formalized, restricted conditions.

- While the opposite party is negatively stereotyped, the image of one's own position is boosted.

- On each side, more aggressive people who are skilled at engaging in conflict may emerge as leaders.[11]

You can certainly see the difficulty here. What begins as a problem of interdependence, ambiguity, or scarcity quickly escalates to the point that the conflict process *itself* becomes an additional problem. The elements of this process then work against the achievement of a peaceful solution. The conflict continues to cycle "on its own steam."

Modes of Managing Conflict

How do you tend to react to conflict situations? Are you aggressive? Do you tend to hide your head in the sand? As conflict expert Kenneth Thomas notes, there are several basic reactions that can be thought of as styles, strategies, or intentions for dealing with conflict. As shown in Exhibit 13.1, these approaches to managing conflict are a function of both how *assertive* you are in trying to satisfy your own or your group's concerns and how *cooperative* you are in trying to satisfy those of the other party or group.[12] It should be emphasized that none of the five styles for dealing with conflict in Exhibit 13.1 is inherently superior. As we will see, each style might have its place given the situation in which the conflict episode occurs.

Exhibit 13.1
Approaches to managing organizational conflict.

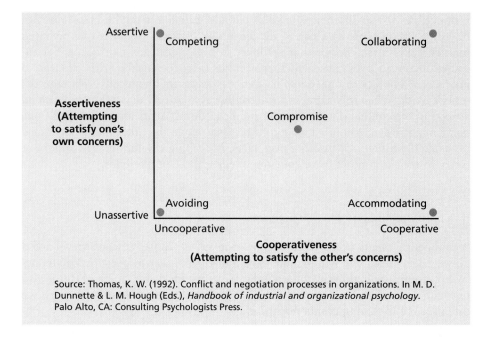

Source: Thomas, K. W. (1992). Conflict and negotiation processes in organizations. In M. D. Dunnette & L. M. Hough (Eds.), *Handbook of industrial and organizational psychology.* Palo Alto, CA: Consulting Psychologists Press.

Avoiding

Avoiding. A conflict management style characterized by low assertiveness of one's own interests and low cooperation with the other party.

The **avoiding** style is characterized by low assertiveness of one's own interests and low cooperation with the other party. This is the "hiding the head in the sand" response. Although avoidance can provide some short-term stress reduction from the rigors of conflict, it does not really change the situation. Thus, its effectiveness is often limited. Some press accounts of IBM's difficulties have suggested that its culture avoided the kind of goal conflict that was necessary to shake its outdated reliance on mainframe computers.

Of course, avoidance does have its place. If the issue is trivial, information is lacking, people need to cool down, or the opponent is very powerful and very hostile, avoidance might be a sensible response.

Accommodating

Accommodating. A conflict management style in which one cooperates with the other party, while not asserting one's own interests.

Cooperating with the other party's wishes while not asserting one's own interests is the hallmark of **accommodating**. The Clinton administration was accused of accommodating the military government of Haiti when it allowed a small band of protestors to turn back an American ship that was acting as an advance guard for the return of the country's deposed president.

If people see accommodation as a sign of weakness, it does not bode well for future interactions. However, it can be an effective reaction when you are wrong, the issue is more important to the other party, or you want to build goodwill.

Competing

Competing. A conflict management style that maximizes assertiveness and minimizes cooperation.

A **competing** style tends to maximize assertiveness for your own position and minimize cooperative responses. In doing so, you tend to frame the conflict in strict win-lose terms. Full priority is given to your own goals, facts, or procedures. Bill Gates, the billionaire chairman of Microsoft, tends to pursue the competing style:

> Gates is famously confrontational. If he strongly disagrees with what you're saying, he is in the habit of blurting out, "That's the stupidest ...thing I've ever

heard!" People tell stories of Gates spraying saliva into the face of some hapless employee as he yells, "This stuff isn't hard! I could do this stuff in a weekend!" What you're supposed to do in a situation like this, as in encounters with grizzly bears, is stand your ground: if you flee, the bear will think you're game and will pursue you, and you can't outrun a bear.[13]

The competing style holds promise when you have a lot of power (e.g., Gates), you are sure of your facts, the situation is truly win-lose, or you will not have to interact with the other party in the future.

Compromise

Compromise combines intermediate levels of assertiveness and cooperation. Thus, it is itself a compromise between pure competition and pure accommodation. In a sense, you attempt to satisfice (Chapter 11) rather than maximize your outcomes and hope that the same occurs for the other party. In the law, a plea-bargain is an example of a compromise between the defending lawyer and the prosecutor.

Compromise. A conflict management style that combines intermediate levels of assertiveness and cooperation.

Compromise places a premium on determining rules of exchange between the two parties. As such, it always contains the seeds for procedural conflict in addition to whatever else is being negotiated. Also, compromise does not always result in the most creative response to conflict. Compromise is not so useful for resolving conflicts that stem from power asymmetry, because the weaker party may have little to offer the stronger party. However, it is a sensible reaction to conflict stemming from scarce resources. Also, it is a good fall-back position if other strategies fail.

Collaborating

In the **collaborating** mode, both assertiveness and cooperation are maximized in the hope that an integrative agreement occurs that fully satisfies the interests of both parties. Emphasis is put on a win-win resolution in which there is no assumption that someone must lose something. Rather, it is assumed that the solution to the conflict can leave both parties in a better condition. Ideally, collaboration occurs as a kind of problem solving exercise (Chapter 11). It probably works best when the conflict is not intense and when each party has information that is useful to the other. Although, effective collaboration can take time and practice to develop, it frequently enhances productivity and achievement.[14]

Collaborating. A conflict management style that maximizes both assertiveness and cooperation.

Some of the most remarkable examples of collaboration in contemporary organizations are those between companies and their suppliers. Traditionally, adversarial competition in which buyers try to squeeze the very lowest price out of suppliers, who are frequently played off against each other, has dominated these relationships. This obviously does not provide much incentive for the perpetually insecure suppliers to invest in improvements dedicated toward a particular buyer.

Things are changing. Honda provides copious engineering advice to its suppliers. One, Donelly Corporation of Holland, Michigan, was chosen to be Honda's exclusive supplier of mirrors for its American-built cars. Donelly built an entirely new plant to make exterior mirrors on the basis of a handshake deal. Motorola does things a little differently with its suppliers, falling somewhere between competing and collaborating. The firm teaches suppliers total quality management practices at its "Motorola University" but then scores the suppliers against each other on frequent report cards that give them feedback for improvement. It also involves them from the beginning of all design projects.[15]

Collaboration also helps to manage conflict within organizations. Our discussion of cross-functional teams in Chapter 7 is a good example. Research

Collaboration can provide unions and management with win-win solutions.

shows that collaboration between organizational departments is particularly important for providing good customer service.[16]

Managing Conflict with Negotiation

The stereotype we have of negotiation is that it is a formal process of bargaining between labour and management or buyer and seller. However, job applicants negotiate for starting salaries, employees negotiate for better job assignments, and people with sick kids negotiate to leave work early. To encompass all these situations, we might define **negotiation** as "a decision-making process among interdependent parties who do not share identical preferences."[17] Negotiation constitutes conflict management, in that it is an attempt either to prevent conflict or to resolve existing conflict.

Negotiation is an attempt to reach a satisfactory exchange among or between the parties. Sometimes, negotiation is very explicit, as in the case of the labour negotiation or the buyer-seller interaction. However, negotiation can also proceed in a very implicit or tacit way.[18] For instance, in trying to get a more interesting job assignment or to take off from work early, the terms of the exchange are not likely to be spelled out very clearly. Still, this is negotiation.

It has become common to distinguish between distributive and integrative negotiation tactics.[19] **Distributive negotiation** assumes a zero-sum, win-lose situation in which a fixed pie is divided up between the parties. If you reexamine Exhibit 13.1, you can imagine that distributive negotiation occurs on the axis between competition and accommodation. In theory, the parties will more or less tend toward some compromise. On the other hand, **integrative negotiation** assumes that mutual problem solving can result in a win-win situation in which the pie is actually enlarged before distribution. Integrative negotiation occurs on the axis between avoiding and collaborating, ideally tending toward the latter.

Distributive and integrative negotiations can take place simultaneously. We will discuss them separately for pedagogical purposes.

Distributive Negotiation Tactics

Distributive negotiation is essentially single-issue negotiation. Many potential conflict situations fit this scenario. For example, suppose you find a used car that

Negotiation. A decision-making process among interdependent parties who do not share identical preferences.

Distributive negotiation. Win-lose negotiation in which a fixed amount of assets is divided between parties.

Integrative negotiation. Win-win negotiation that assumes that mutual problem solving can enlarge the assets to be divided between parties.

you really like. Now, things boil down to price. You want to buy the car for the minimum reasonable price, while the seller wants to get the maximum reasonable price.

The essence of the problem is shown in Exhibit 13.2. Party is a consulting firm who would like to win a contract to do an attitude survey in Other's firm. Party would like to make $90,000 for the job (Party's target) but would settle for $70,000, a figure that provides for minimal acceptable profit (Party's resistance point). Other thinks that the survey could be done for as little as $60,000 (Other's target) but would be willing to spend up to $80,000 for a good job (Other's resistance point). Theoretically, an offer in the Settlement range between $70,000 and $80,000 should clinch the deal, if the negotiators can get into this range. Notice that every dollar that Party earns is a dollar's worth of cost for Other. How will they reach a settlement?[20]

Threats and Promises. Threat consists of implying that you will punish the other party if he or she does not concede to your position. For example, the Other firm might imply that it will terminate its other business with the consulting company if it does not lower its price on the attitude survey job. Promises are pledges that concessions will lead to rewards in the future. For example, Other might promise future consulting contracts if Party agrees to do the survey at a lower price. Of course, the difference between a threat and a promise can be subtle, as when the promise implies a threat if no concession is made.

Threat has some merit as a bargaining tactic if one party has power over the other that corresponds to the nature of the threat, especially if no future negotiations are expected or if the threat can be posed in a civil and subtle way.[21] If power is more balanced and the threat is crude, a counterthreat could scuttle the

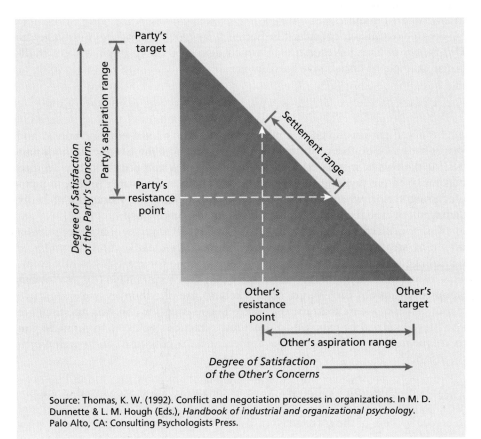

Exhibit 13.2
A model of distributive negotiation.

Source: Thomas, K. W. (1992). Conflict and negotiation processes in organizations. In M. D. Dunnette & L. M. Hough (Eds.), *Handbook of industrial and organizational psychology.* Palo Alto, CA: Consulting Psychologists Press.

negotiations, despite the fact that both parties could be satisfied in the Settlement range. Promises have merit when your side lacks power and anticipates future negotiations with the other side. Both threat and promises work best when they send interpretable signals to the other side about your true position, what really matters to you. Careful timing is critical.

Firmness versus Concessions. How about intransigence—sticking to your target position, offering few concessions, and waiting for the other party to give in? Research shows that such a tactic is likely to be reciprocated by the other party, thus increasing the chances of a deadlock.[22] On the other hand, a series of small concessions early in the negotiation will often be matched. Good negotiators often use face-saving techniques to explain concessions. For example, the consulting firm might claim that it could reduce the cost of the survey by printing it on cheaper paper.

Persuasion. Verbal persuasion or debate is common in negotiations. Often, it takes a two-pronged attack. One prong asserts the technical merits of the party's position. For example, the consulting firm might justify its target price by saying "We have the most qualified staff. We do the most reliable surveys." The other prong asserts the fairness of the target position. Here, the negotiator might make a speech about the expenses the company would incur in doing the survey.

Verbal persuasion is an attempt to change the attitudes of the other party toward your target position. Persuaders are most effective when they are perceived as expert, likable, and unbiased. The obvious problem in distributive negotiations is bias—each party knows the other is self-interested. One way to deal with this is to introduce some unbiased parties. For example, the consulting firm might produce testimony from satisfied survey clients. Also, disputants often bring third parties into negotiations on the assumption that they will process argumentation in an unbiased manner.

Before continuing, consider "In Focus: *Why Do Women Earn Less? Gender Differences in Salary Negotiation,*" which discusses salary negotiation, a traditional example of distributive bargaining.

Integrative Negotiation Tactics

As we noted earlier, integrative negotiation rejects a fixed-pie assumption and strives for collaborative problem solving that advances the interests of both parties. At the outset, it is useful but sobering to realize that people have a decided bias for fixed-pie thinking. A good example is seen in the North American manufacturing sector, where such thinking by both unions and management badly damaged the global competitiveness of manufacturing firms.[23]

Why the bias for fixed-pie thinking? First, integrative negotiation requires a degree of creativity. Most people are not especially creative, and the stress of typical negotiation does not provide the best climate for creativity in any event. This means that many of the role models that negotiators have (e.g., following labour negotiations on TV) are more likely to use distributive than integrative tactics. To complicate matters, if you are negotiating for constituents, they are also more likely to be exposed to distributive tactics and likely to pressure you to use them. Nevertheless, attempts at integrative negotiation can be well worth the effort.[24]

Copious Information Exchange. Most of the information exchanged in distributive bargaining is concerned with attacking the other party's position and trying to persuade them of the correctness of yours. Otherwise, mum's the word. A freer

in focus → Why Do Women Earn Less? Gender Differences in Salary Negotiation

One of the best-documented inequities in the diverse contemporary workplace is the salary gap between men and women. Consistently, studies show that women are paid less, even when sophisticated controls match men and women in terms of education and experience. No single factor is responsible for this salary disparity. Rather, it probably stems from a mixture of biased starting salaries, biased performance evaluations, and the segregation of women into lower-paying jobs.

Cynthia Kay Stevens, Anna Bavetta, and Marilyn Gist were interested in the starting salary part of this equation. First, they reviewed research that suggested men were inclined to use more, or more skillful, tactics in negotiating their starting salaries. In one survey, the men reported receiving an average of $742 more for their negotiation efforts than did women. Stevens, Bavetta, and Gist reasoned that the differential socialization of women and men could result in women either having less tactical understanding of negotiation, being less persistent in negotiation, or being less confident about their ability to negotiate. Thus, they designed three training modules for MBA students.

The first module was oriented toward conveying an understanding of negotiation tactics. After this training, a simulated salary negotiation showed that women negotiated $1,350 less than men! This showed that tactical knowledge was not the problem. Next, half the students were exposed to goal setting training, in which they set specific, challenging goals for salary negotiation (Chapter 5). The other half experienced self-management training in which they also identified obstacles to good negotiation and planned how to overcome them (Chapter 2). A second simulated negotiation revealed that goal setting did not reduce the disparity between men and women, although it helped both groups negotiate higher salaries. The self-management training helped both groups negotiate better salaries, and it erased the difference between men's and women's starting salaries.

A recent review of 21 studies on gender differences in negotiation outcomes found that although men negotiated significantly better outcomes than women, the overall difference between men and women was small. However, the authors note that even small differences in salary and wage negotiations could be perpetuated through subsequent salary increases based on percentage of pay. Furthermore, differences in negotiation outcomes could also be a factor in creating a "glass-ceiling" effect to the extent that women are less effective in negotiating opportunities and positions of power and status. Thus, training programs that enable women to negotiate better starting salaries comparable with men can have short- and long-term benefits.

Source: Adapted from Stevens, C. K., Bavetta, A. G., & Gist, M. E. (1993). Gender differences in the acquisition of salary negotiation skills: The role of goals, self-efficacy, and perceived control. *Journal of Applied Psychology*, 78, pp. 723–735; Stuhlmacher, A.F., and Walters, A.E. (1999). Gender differences in negotiation outcome: A meta-analyses. *Personnel Psychology*, 52, pp. 653–677.

flow of information is critical to finding an integrative settlement. The problem, of course, is that we all tend to be a bit paranoid about information being used against us in bargaining situations. This means that trust must be built slowly. One way to proceed is to give away some noncritical information to the other party to get the ball rolling. As we noted earlier, much negotiation behaviour tends to be reciprocated. Also, ask the other party a lot of questions, and *listen* to their responses. This is at odds with the tell-and-sell approach in most distributive negotiations. If all goes well, both parties will begin to reveal their true interests, not just their current positions.

Framing Differences as Opportunities. Parties in a negotiation often differ in their preferences for everything from the timing of a deal to the degree of risk that each party wants to assume. Traditionally, such differences are framed as barriers to negotiations. However, such differences can often serve as a basis for integrative agreements because, again, they contain information that can telegraph each party's real interests. For instance, imagine that two co-workers are negotiating for the finishing date of a project that they have to complete by a certain deadline. Due to competing demands, one wants to finish it early, and the other wants to just make the deadline. In the course of the discussion, they realize that they can divide the labour such that one begins the project while the other finishes it, satisfying both parties fully (notice that this is not a compromise).

Cutting Costs. If you can somehow cut the costs that the other party associates with an agreement, the chance of an integrative settlement increases. For example, suppose that you are negotiating with your boss for a new, more interesting job assignment, but she does not like the idea because she relies on your excellent skills on your current assignment. By asking good questions (see above), you find out that she is ultimately worried about the job being done properly, not about your leaving it. You take the opportunity to inform her that you have groomed a subordinate to do your current job. This reduces the costs of her letting you assume the new assignment.

Integrative solutions are especially attractive when they reduce costs for *all* parties in a dispute. For example, firms in the computer and acoustics industries have joined together to support basic research on technology of interest to all firms. This reduces costly competition to perfect a technology that all parties need anyway.

Increasing Resources. Increasing available resources is a very literal way of getting around the fixed-pie syndrome. This is not as unlikely as it sounds when you realize that two parties, working together, might have access to twice as many resources as one party. One of the authors once saw two academic departments squabbling to get the approval to recruit one new faculty member for whom there was a budget line. Seeing this as a fixed pie leads to one department winning all or to the impossible compromise of half a recruit for each department. The chairs of the two departments used their *combined* political clout to get the dean to promise that they could also have exclusive access to one budget line the following year. The chairs then flipped a coin to see who would recruit immediately and who would wait a year. This minor compromise on time was less critical than the firm guarantee of a budget line.

Superordinate goals. Attractive outcomes that can be achieved only by collaboration.

Introducing Superordinate Goals. As discussed in Chapter 7, **superordinate goals** are attractive outcomes that can be achieved only by collaboration.[25] Neither party can attain the goal on its own. Superordinate goals probably represent the best example of creativity in integrative negotiation because they change the entire landscape of the negotiation episode.

Given its recent success and merger with Daimler-Benz, you might be surprised to know that Chrysler Corporation almost went broke in 1980. With the prospect of bankruptcy and massive unemployment looming large, the United Auto Workers and Chrysler management collaborated on a scheme to renew the company. This collaboration was far removed from the auto industry's traditional fixed-pie, distributive bargaining.

Third Party Involvement

Sometimes, third parties come into play to intervene between negotiating parties. Often, this happens when the parties reach an impasse. This is, of course, what has happened in the Arthur Andersen versus Andersen Consulting conflict. Another example is when a manager might have to step into a conflict between two subordinates or even between two departments. In other cases, third party involvement exists right from the start of the negotiation. For example, real estate agents serve as an interface between home sellers and buyers.

Mediation. The process of mediation occurs when a neutral third party helps to facilitate a negotiated agreement. Formal mediation has a long history in labour disputes, international relations, and marital counseling. However, by definition, almost any manager might be required to occasionally play an informal mediating role.

What do mediators do?[26] First, almost anything that aids the *process* or *atmosphere* of negotiation can be helpful. Of course, this depends on the exact situation at hand. If there is tension, the mediator might serve as a lightning rod for anger or try to introduce humour. The mediator might try to help the parties clarify their underlying interests, both to themselves and to each other. Occasionally, imposing a deadline or helping the parties deal with their own constituents might be useful. Introducing a problem-solving orientation to move toward more integrative bargaining might be appropriate.

The mediator might also intervene in the *content* of the negotiation, highlighting points of agreement, pointing out new options, or encouraging concessions.

Research shows that mediation has a fairly successful track record in dispute resolution. However, mediators cannot turn water into wine, and the process seems to work best when the conflict is not too intense and the parties are resolved to use negotiation to resolve their conflict. If the mediator is not seen as neutral or if there is dissension in the ranks of each negotiating party, mediation does not work so well.[27]

Arbitration. The process of arbitration occurs when a third party is given the authority to dictate the terms of settlement of a conflict (although there is nonbinding arbitration, which we will not consider here). Although disputing parties sometimes agree to arbitration, it can also be mandated formally by law or informally by upper management or parents. The key point is that negotiation has broken down, and the arbitrator has to make a final distributive allocation—this is not the way to integrative solutions. This is precisely what the arbitrator will be doing when he renders a decision to Andersen Worldwide.

In *conventional arbitration*, the arbitrator can choose any outcome, such as splitting the difference between the two parties. In *final offer arbitration*, each

Superordinate goals represent the best example of creativity in integrative negotiation because they change the entire landscape of the negotiation episode and can be achieved only by collaboration.

party makes a final offer, and the arbitrator chooses one of them. This latter invention was devised to motivate the two parties to make sensible offers that have a chance of being upheld. Also, fear of the all-or-nothing aspect of final arbitration seems to motivate more negotiated agreement.[28]

One of the most commonly arbitrated disputes between employers and employees is dismissal for excessive absenteeism. One study found that the arbitrators sided with the company in over half of such cases, especially when the company could show evidence of a fair and consistently applied absentee policy.[29]

Is All Conflict Bad?

In everyday life, there has traditionally been an emphasis on the negative, dysfunctional aspects of conflict. This is not difficult to understand. Discord between parents and children, severe labour strife, and international disputes are unpleasant experiences. To some degree, this emphasis on the negative aspects of conflict is also characteristic of thinking in organizational behaviour. Recently, though, there has been growing awareness of the potential *benefits* of organizational conflict.

The argument that conflict can be functional rests mainly on the idea that it promotes necessary organizational change. One advocate of this position puts it this way:

$$\text{CONFLICT} \rightarrow \text{CHANGE} \rightarrow \text{ADAPTATION} \rightarrow \text{SURVIVAL}^{\,30}$$

In other words, for organizations to survive, they must adapt to their environments. This requires changes in strategy that may be stimulated through conflict. For example, consider the museum that relies heavily on government funding and consistently mounts exhibits that are appreciated only by "true connoisseurs" of art. Under a severe funding cutback, the museum can survive only if it begins to mount more popular exhibits. Such a change might occur only after much conflict within the board of directors.

Just how does conflict promote change? For one thing, it might bring into consideration new ideas that would not be offered without conflict. In trying to "one up" the opponent, one of the parties might develop a unique idea that the other cannot fail to appreciate. In a related way, conflict might promote change because each party begins to monitor the other's performance more carefully. This search for weaknesses means that it is more difficult to hide errors and problems from the rest of the organization. Such errors and problems (e.g., a failure to make deliveries on time) might be a signal that changes are necessary. Finally, conflict may promote useful change by signaling that a redistribution of power is necessary. Consider the human resource department that must battle with managers to get diversity programs implemented. This conflict might be a clue that some change is due in power priorities. All these outcomes have occurred at Motorola, where conflict is used strategically as a catalyst for change but is not so high that it is completely dysfunctional.

Conflict stimulation. A strategy of increasing conflict in order to motivate change.

All this suggests that there are times when managers might use a strategy of **conflict stimulation** to cause change. But how does a manager know when some conflict might be a good thing? One signal is the existence of a "friendly rut," in which peaceful relationships take precedence over organizational goals. Another signal is seen when parties that should be interacting closely have chosen to withdraw from each other to avoid overt conflict. A third signal occurs when conflict is suppressed or downplayed by denying differences, ignoring controversy, and exaggerating points of agreement.[31]

Logic suggests that the causes of conflict, discussed earlier, such as scarcity and ambiguity, could be manipulated by managers to achieve change.[32] For example, consider the president and the controller of a manufacturing company who felt that the budgets allocated to various departments were not a good reflection of changing priorities. They introduced a zero-base budget that required all departments to justify their needs, regardless of past allocations. Since the departments were required to compete for a scarce resource, considerable conflict developed. It was agreed that this conflict helped to promote needed changes in funding emphasis.

A Model of Stress in Organizations

During the last decade, stress has become a serious concern for individuals and organizations. In fact, the headline of a recent news article on stress referred to excessive stress as "the plague of the 1990s," and a popular business magazine named a special issue "The Limit," in recognition of workers being pushed to the limit like never before at all levels in the workplace.[33] The levels of stress in the workplace today are at an all-time high, and the implications of this are alarming. A recent cover story in *Newsweek* magazine indicated that new research has found that stress not only can cause heart disease and ulcers but can also lead to memory loss, immune deficiency and greater vulnerability to infections, and a particular type of obesity.[34] In addition to the negative effects of stress on the psychological and physical health of employees, it can also result in negative consequences for organizations, including lower productivity, higher rates of turnover, worker conflict, and increased workers' compensation claims and legal expenses.[35] In fact, the direct and indirect costs of stress-related and mental disorders in the United States is estimated to be about $100 billion.[36] The annual cost of time lost due to stress in Canada is $12 billion.[37]

It is easy to imagine situations that must surely prove stressful for organizational members. Baseball players battling for the World Series, the White House staff during the Monica Lewinsky affair, and personnel working in nuclear power plants during emergencies have obviously been exposed to elevated levels of tension. However, these dramatic cases should not obscure the fact that stress can be part of the everyday routine of organizations. In fact, many cases of conflict of the kind we have just been discussing can provoke considerable stress. The model of a stress episode in Exhibit 13.3 can guide our introduction to this topic.[38]

Stressors

Stressors are environmental events or conditions that have the potential to induce stress. There are some conditions that would prove stressful for just about everyone. These include things like extreme heat, extreme cold, isolation, or hostile

Stressors. Environmental events or conditions that have the potential to induce stress.

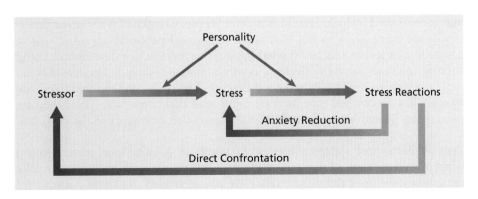

Exhibit 13.3
Model of a stress episode.

people. More interesting is the fact that the individual personality often determines the extent to which a potential stressor becomes a real stressor and actually induces stress.

Stress

Stress. A psychological reaction to the demands inherent in a stressor that has the potential to make a person feel tense or anxious.

Stress is a psychological reaction to the demands inherent in a stressor that has the potential to make a person feel tense or anxious because the person does not feel capable of coping with these demands.[39] Stress is not intrinsically bad. All people require a certain level of stimulation from their environment, and moderate levels of stress can serve this function. In fact, one would wonder about the perceptual accuracy of a person who *never* experienced tension. On the other hand, stress does become a problem when it leads to especially high levels of anxiety and tension.

Stress Reactions

Stress reactions. The behavioural, psychological, and physiological consequences of stress.

Stress reactions are the behavioural, psychological, and physiological consequences of stress. Some of these reactions are essentially passive responses, over which the individual has little direct control, such as elevated blood pressure. Other reactions are active attempts to *cope* with some previous aspect of the stress episode. Exhibit 13.3 indicates that stress reactions that involve coping attempts might be directed toward dealing directly with the stressor or simply reducing the anxiety generated by stress. In general, the former strategy has more potential for effectiveness than the latter because the chances of the stress episode being *terminated* are increased.[40]

Often, reactions that are useful for the individual in dealing with a stress episode may be very costly to the organization. The individual who is conveniently absent from work on the day of a difficult inventory check might prevent personal stress but leave the organization short handed (provoking stress in others). Thus, organizations should be interested in the stress that individual employees experience.

Personality and Stress

Personality (Chapter 2) can have an important influence on the stress experience. As shown in Exhibit 13.3, it can affect both the extent to which potential stressors are perceived as stressful and the types of stress reactions that occur. Let us look at two key personality traits.

Locus of Control. You will recall from Chapter 2 that locus of control concerns people's beliefs about the factors that control their behaviour. Internals believe that they control their own behaviour, while externals believe that their behaviour is controlled by luck, fate, or powerful people. Compared with internals, externals are more likely to feel anxious in the face of potential stressors.[41] Most people like to feel in control of what happens to them, and externals feel less in control. Internals are more likely to confront stressors directly because they assume that this response will make a difference. Externals, on the other hand, are anxious but do not feel that they are masters of their own fate. Thus, they are more prone to simple anxiety-reduction strategies that only work in the short run.

Type A Behaviour Pattern. Interest in the Type A behaviour pattern began when physicians noticed that many sufferers of coronary heart disease, especially those who developed the disease relatively young, tended to exhibit a distinctive pattern of behaviours and emotions.[42] Individuals who exhibit the **Type A behaviour pattern** tend to be aggressive and ambitious. Their hostility is easily aroused, and they feel a great sense of time urgency. They are impatient, competitive, and preoccupied with their work. The Type A individual can be contrasted with the Type B, who does not exhibit these extreme characteristics. Compared with Type B individuals, Type A people report heavier workloads, longer work hours, and more conflicting work demands.[43] Whether or not these reports are accurate, we will see later that such factors turn out to be potent stressors. Thus, either Type A people encounter more stressful situations than Type Bs do, or they perceive themselves as doing so. In turn, Type A individuals are likely to exhibit adverse physiological reactions in response to stress. These include elevated blood pressure, elevated heart rate, and modified blood chemistry. Frustrating, difficult, or competitive events are especially likely to prompt these adverse reactions. In addition, Type A people perform better than Type Bs in situations that call for persistence, endurance, or speed. They can ignore fatigue and distraction to accomplish their goals. Type A individuals seem to have a strong need to control their work environment. This is doubtless a full-time task that stimulates their feelings of time urgency and leads them to overextend themselves physically.[44]

As research has accumulated, it has become increasingly clear that the major component of Type A behaviour that contributes to adverse physiological reactions is hostility and repressed anger. This may also be accompanied by exaggerated cynicism and distrust of others. When these factors are prominent in a particular Type A individual's personality, stress is most likely to take its toll.[45]

> **Type A behaviour pattern.** A personality pattern that includes aggressiveness, ambitiousness, competitiveness, hostility, impatience, and a sense of time urgency.

Stressors in Organizational Life

A recent study found that among a sample of employed Canadians, the most common source of stress is workplace stressors.[46] In this section, we will examine potential stressors in detail. Some stressors can affect almost everyone in any organization, while others seem especially likely to affect people who perform particular roles in organizations.

Executive and Managerial Stressors

Executives and managers make key organizational decisions and direct the work of others. In these capacities, they seem to experience special forms of stress.

Role Overload. **Role overload** occurs when one must perform too many tasks in too short a time period, and it is a common stressor for managers, especially in today's downsized organizations.[47] The open-ended nature of the managerial job is partly responsible for this heavy and protracted workload.[48] Management is an ongoing *process*, and there are few signposts to signify that a task is complete and that rest and relaxation are permitted. Especially when coupled with frequent moves or excessive travel demands, a heavy workload often provokes conflict between the manager's role as an organizational member and his or her role as a spouse or parent. Thus, role overload may provoke stress, at the same time preventing the executive from enjoying the pleasures of life that can reduce stress.

> **Role overload.** The requirement for too many tasks to be performed in too short a time period.

Heavy Responsibility. Not only is the workload of the executive heavy, but it can have extremely important consequences for the organization and its members. A vice-president of labour relations might be in charge of a negotiation strategy that could result in either labour peace or a protracted and bitter strike.

To complicate matters, the personal consequences of an incorrect decision can be staggering. For example, the courts have fined or even jailed executives who have engaged in illegal activities on behalf of their organizations. Finally, executives are responsible for people as well as things, and this influence over the future of others has the potential to induce stress. The executive who must terminate the operation of an unprofitable plant, putting many out of work, or the manager who must fire a subordinate, putting one out of work, might experience guilt and tension.[49]

Operative-Level Stressors

Operatives are individuals who occupy nonprofessional and nonmanagerial positions in organizations. In a manufacturing organization, operatives perform the work on the shop floor and range from skilled craftspeople to unskilled labourers. As is the case with other organizational roles, the occupants of operative positions are sometimes exposed to a special set of stressors.

Poor Physical Working Conditions. Operative-level employees are more likely than managers and professionals to be exposed to physically unpleasant and even dangerous working conditions. Although social sensibility and union activity have improved working conditions over the years, many employees must still face excessive heat, cold, noise, pollution, and the chance of accidents.

Poor Job Design. Although bad job design can provoke stress at any organizational level (executive role overload is an example), lower-level blue- and white-collar jobs are particular culprits. It might seem paradoxical that jobs that are too simple or not challenging enough can act as stressors. However, monotony and boredom can prove extremely frustrating to people who feel capable of handling more complex tasks. In fact, research has found that job scope can be a stressor at levels that are either too low or too high.[50]

According to Robert Karasek's **job demands–job control model**, jobs that make high demands on employees while giving them little control over workplace decisions are especially prone to produce stress and negative stress reactions.[51] High demands might include a hectic work pace, excessive workload, limited time to accomplish tasks, or responsibility for extreme economic loss. Lack of control means limited decision latitude and authority. Jobs that often involve high demand and little control include telephone operators, nurse's aides, assembly line workers, garment stitchers, and bus drivers. As Exhibit 13.4 demonstrates, these jobs fall into a zone of increased risk for heart disease (the area to the right of the dashed curve). Stress might be partially responsible for this elevated risk.

Boundary Role Stressors and Burnout

Boundary roles are positions in which organizational members are required to interact with members of other organizations or with the public. For example, a vice-president of public relations is responsible for representing his or her company to the public. At the operative level, receptionists, salespeople, and installers often interact with customers or suppliers.

Occupants of boundary role positions are especially likely to experience stress as they straddle the imaginary boundary between the organization and its environment. This is yet another form of role conflict in which one's role as an organizational member might be incompatible with the demands made by the public or other organizations. A classic case of boundary role stress involves salespeo-

---

Job demands–job control model. A model that asserts that jobs promote high stress when they make high demands while offering little control over work decisions.

Boundary roles. Positions in which organizational members are required to interact with members of other organizations or with the public.

Exhibit 13.4
Heart disease risk for
various occupations.

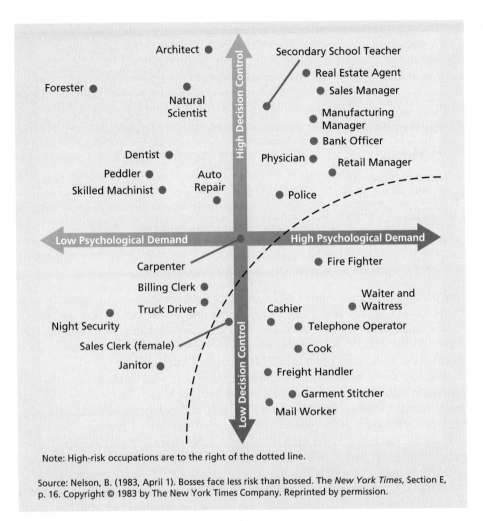

Note: High-risk occupations are to the right of the dotted line.

Source: Nelson, B. (1983, April 1). Bosses face less risk than bossed. The *New York Times*, Section E, p. 16. Copyright © 1983 by The New York Times Company. Reprinted by permission.

ple. In extreme cases, buyers desire fast delivery of a large quantity of custom-tailored products. The salesperson might be tempted to "offer the moon" but is at the same time aware that such an order could place a severe strain on his or her organization's production facilities. Thus, the salesperson is faced with the dilemma of doing his or her primary job (selling), while protecting another function (production) from unreasonable demands that could result in a broken delivery contract.

A particular form of stress experienced by some boundary role occupants is burnout. **Burnout,** as Christina Maslach and Susan Jackson define it, is a combination "of emotional exhaustion, depersonalization, and reduced personal accomplishment that can occur among individuals who work with people in some capacity."[52] Frequently, these other people are organizational clients who require very special attention or who are experiencing severe problems. Thus, teachers, nurses, paramedics, social workers, and police are especially likely candidates for burnout.

Burnout appears to follow a stagelike process that begins with emotional exhaustion (Exhibit 13.5). The person feels fatigued in the morning, drained by the work, and frustrated by the day's events. One way to deal with this extreme exhaustion is to distance oneself from one's clients, the "cause" of the exhaustion. In an extreme form, this might involve treating them like objects and lacking concern for what happens to them. The clients might also be seen as blaming the employee for their problems. Finally, the burnt-out individual develops feelings of

Burnout. Emotional exhaustion, depersonalization, and reduced personal accomplishment among those who work with people.

Exhibit 13.5
The stages of burnout and
their symptoms.

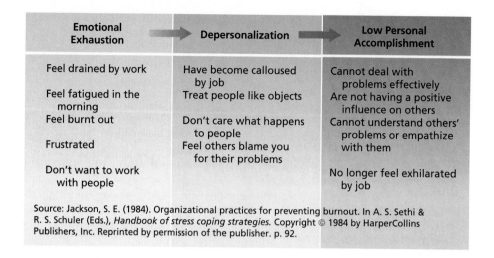

Emotional Exhaustion	Depersonalization	Low Personal Accomplishment
Feel drained by work	Have become calloused by job	Cannot deal with problems effectively
Feel fatigued in the morning	Treat people like objects	Are not having a positive influence on others
Feel burnt out	Don't care what happens to people	Cannot understand others' problems or empathize with them
Frustrated	Feel others blame you for their problems	
Don't want to work with people		No longer feel exhilarated by job

Source: Jackson, S. E. (1984). Organizational practices for preventing burnout. In A. S. Sethi & R. S. Schuler (Eds.), *Handbook of stress coping strategies.* Copyright © 1984 by HarperCollins Publishers, Inc. Reprinted by permission of the publisher. p. 92.

low personal accomplishment—"I can't deal with these people, I'm not helping them, I don't understand them." In fact, because of the exhaustion and depersonalization, there might be more than a grain of truth to those feelings. Although the exact details of this progression are open to some question, these three sets of symptoms paint a reliable picture of burnout.[53]

Burnout seems to be most common among people who entered their jobs with especially high ideals. Their expectations of being able to "change the world" are badly frustrated when they encounter the reality shock of troubled clients (who are often perceived as unappreciative) and the inability of the organization to help them. Teachers get fed up with being disciplinarians, nurses get upset when patients die, and police officers get depressed when they must constantly deal with the "losers" of society.[54]

What are the consequences of burnout? Some individuals bravely pursue a new occupation, often experiencing guilt about not having been able to cope in the old one. Others stay in the same occupation but seek a new job. For instance, the burnt-out nurse might go into nursing education to avoid contact with sick patients. Some people pursue administrative careers in their profession, attempting to "climb above" the source of their difficulties. These people often set cynical examples for idealistic subordinates. Finally, some people stay in their jobs and become part of the legion of "deadwood," collecting their paychecks but doing little to contribute to the mission of the organization. Many "good bureaucrats" seem to choose this route.[55]

Some General Stressors

To conclude our discussion of stressors that people encounter in organizational life, we will consider some that are probably experienced equally by occupants of all roles.

Interpersonal Conflict. From our earlier discussion of interpersonal conflict, you might correctly guess that it can be a potent stressor, especially for those with strong avoidance tendencies. The entire range of conflict, from personality clashes to intergroup strife, is especially likely to cause stress when it leads to real or perceived attacks on our self-esteem or integrity. Although conflict can lead to stress in many settings, outside work, we often have the option of terminating the relationship, of "choosing our friends," as it were. This option is often not available at work.

Work-Family Conflict. A recent study on the costs of work-family conflict found that it is costing Canadian companies at least $2.7 billion a year in lost time, and the Canadian health care system $425 million as a result of increased visits to the doctor to treat problems associated with the conflict.[56]

Two facts of life in contemporary society have increased the stress stemming from the interrole conflict between being a member of one's family and the member of an organization. First, the increase in the number of homes in which both parents work and the increase in the number of single parent families has led to a number of stressors centred around child care. Finding adequate daycare and disputes between partners about sharing child-care responsibilities can prove to be serious stressors.

Second, increased life spans have meant that many people in the prime of their careers find themselves providing support for elderly parents, some of whom may be seriously ill. This inherently stressful elder-care situation is often compounded by feelings of guilt about the need to tend to matters at work.

There is every reason to believe that women are particularly victimized by stress due to work-family conflict, although it is reported to be a rapidly growing problem for men as well.[57] Much anecdotal evidence suggests that women who take time off work to deal with pressing family matters are more likely than men to be labeled disloyal or undedicated to their work. Also, many managers seem to be insensitive to the demands that these basic demographic shifts are making on their subordinates, again compounding the potential for stress.

Job Insecurity and Change. Secure employment is an important goal for almost everyone, and stress may be encountered when it is threatened. During the last decade, organizations have undergone substantial changes that have left many workers unemployed and threatened the security of those who have been fortunate enough to remain in their jobs. The trend toward mergers and consolidations along with reengineering, restructuring, and downsizing has led to increasingly high levels of stress among workers who have either lost their jobs or must live with the threat of more layoffs, the loss of friends and co-workers, and an increased workload. The fear of job loss has become a way of life for employees at all organizational levels.[58]

Police officers must deal with a unique type of on-the-job stress: workplace violence. There has been an upswing in psychological counseling for officers experiencing stress reactions.

At the operative level, unionization has provided a degree of employment security for some, but the vagaries of the economy and the threat of technology and other organizational changes hang heavy over many workers. Among professionals, the very specialization that enables them to obtain satisfactory jobs becomes a millstone whenever social or economic forces change. For example, aerospace scientists and engineers have long been prey to the boom-and-bust nature of their industry. When layoffs occur, these people are often perceived as overqualified or too specialized to easily obtain jobs in related industries. Finally, the executive suite does not escape job insecurity. Recent pressures for corporate performance have made cost cutting a top priority for many companies. One of the surest ways to cut costs in the short run is to reduce executive positions and thus reduce the total management payroll. Many top corporations have greatly thinned their executive ranks in recent years.

Role Ambiguity. We have already noted how role conflict, having to deal with incompatible role expectations, can provoke stress. There is also substantial evidence that role ambiguity can provoke stress.[59] From Chapter 7, you will recall that role ambiguity exists when the goals of one's job or the methods of performing the job are unclear. Such a lack of direction can prove stressful, especially for people who are low in their tolerance for such ambiguity. For example, the president of a manufacturing firm might be instructed by the board of directors to increase profits and cut costs. While this goal seems clear enough, the means by which it can be achieved might be unclear. This ambiguity can be devastating, especially when the organization is doing poorly and no strategy seems to improve things.

Sexual Harassment. In Chapter 12, we discussed sexual harassment in terms of the abuse of power and a form of unethical behaviour. Sexual harassment is also considered to be a major workplace stressor with serious consequences for employees and organizations that are similar to or more negative than other types of job stressors.[60] Sexual harassment in the workplace is now considered to be widespread in both the public and private sector, and most harassment victims are subjected to ongoing harassment and stress.[61] The negative effects of sexual harassment experiences include a decrease in morale, job satisfaction, organizational commitment, and job performance, and an increase in absenteeism, turnover, and job loss. Sexual harassment has also been found to have serious effects on the psychological and physical well being of harassment victims.[62] Victims of sexual harassment experience depression, frustration, nervousness, fa-

Exhibit 13.6
Sources of stress at various points in the organization.

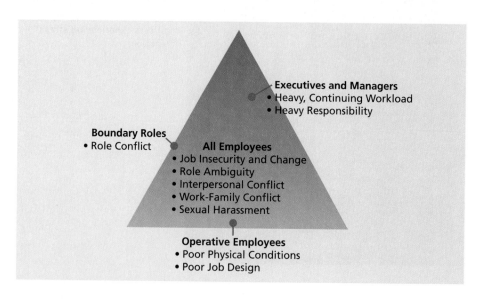

tigue, nausea, hypertension, and symptoms of posttraumatic stress disorder.[63] Organizations in which sexual harassment is most likely to be a problem are those that have a climate that is tolerant of sexual harassment and where women are working in traditional male-dominated jobs and in a male-dominated workplace.[64]

Exhibit 13.6 summarizes the sources of stress at various points in the organization. The "Ethical Focus: *Workplace Violence Is a Source of and Reaction to Stress*" illustrates a contemporary source of stress as well as a reaction to stress, our next topic.

ethical focus →   Workplace Violence Is a Source of and Reaction to Stress

Violence in the workplace has become a serious and global problem. In the United States, an average of 20 people are murdered at work each week, and it is estimated that 1 million workers are assaulted annually. Homicide has become the leading cause of death for women at work and is the third leading cause overall. Violent acts are estimated to cost American employers about $4 billion a year. The rate of assaults against women and men in the workplace in Canada is even higher than in the United States.

On-the-job violence has long been a documented source of stress for police officers. Seeing violence being committed by others, having to resort to deadly force, and even accidentally shooting one's own partner are stressors that are unique to police work. The result can be substance abuse, marital problems, and even the use of violence within the family. Trained to control their emotions on the job, officers can find it difficult to discern an appropriate outlet for the feelings provoked by work violence. As a result, there has been a steady rise in the number of police departments offering psychological counseling for officers who are experiencing stress reactions.

In recent years, it has become apparent that violence on the job is not confined to police work. Violence on the job is also a problem for government workers, teachers, retail sales clerks, real estate agents, airline workers, and in service settings, such as hospitals, nursing homes, and social service agencies. Violence and crime have also become a particular source of stress for delivery people, whether the thing being delivered is mail, pizza, or parcels. Co-workers, customers, patients, and strangers are all potential sources of violence.

Some of the most extreme examples of workplace violence have been the string of mass shootings in American post offices and in Canada where an angry transit employee shot and killed four co-workers. These shootings (only the visible tip of an iceberg of violent acts in the post office) provoked considerable stress among survivors. At Royal Oak, Michigan, for example, a team of 100 mental health volunteers provided extensive crisis inter-

vention counseling. This was followed up by sessions on communication and conflict resolution designed to get at the sources of violence.

While the fear of workplace violence is considered to be a major stressor that can impair employees' capability and willingness to perform their jobs, violence in the workplace can also be a consequence of or reaction to stress. Employees are finding it increasingly difficult to cope with the stress of work, and some are finding themselves at the breaking point. The threat of layoffs and job loss due to restructuring and downsizing combined with the anxiety and pressures of constant change has led to an increasing number of violent acts.

An increasingly common reaction to job-related stress is workplace rage which often takes the form of a screaming fit, tantrums, outbursts, a chair through a window, assaults, or any act or threat of violence. Violence as a reaction to stress is often the result of a sense of injustice or unfair treatment that produces extreme and chronic tension or anxiety. Responsibility for such an emotional state is often placed on the organization or specific managers or bosses who then become the targets of a violent act.

The issue of violence in the workplace is now receiving more attention from employers and governments who must take responsibility for employee safety. In Canada, plans are being made for a federal law on workplace violence that will require employers to perform risk assessments, establish policies for dealing with violence, and report all violent incidents in the workplace. Employers will increasingly be required to take steps to protect their employees against violence in the workplace.

Cole, T. (1999, February). All the rage. *Report on Business Magazine.* pp. 50-57. Fowlie, L. (1999, May 31). Protecting staff from violence. *Financial Post,* p. C15. DeFrank, R. S., & Ivancevich, J. M. (1998). Stress on the job: An executive update. *Academy of Management Executive,* 12, pp. 55-66; Pulley, B. (1994, March 7). Crime becomes occupational hazard of deliverers. The *Wall Street Journal,* p. B1; Braverman, M. (1993, December 12). Violence: the newest worry on the job. *New York Times,* De Angelis, T. (1993, October). Psychologists aid victims of violence in post office. *APA Monitor,* pp. 1, 44, 45.

Reactions to Organizational Stress

In this section, we shall examine the reactions that people who experience organizational stress might exhibit. These reactions can be divided into behavioural, psychological, and physiological responses.

Behavioural Reactions to Stress

Behavioural reactions to stress are overt activities that the stressed individual uses in an attempt to cope with the stress. They include problem solving, withdrawal, and the use of addictive substances.

Problem Solving. In general, problem solving is directed toward terminating the stressor or reducing its potency, not toward simply making the person feel better in the short run. Problem solving is reality oriented, and while it is not always effective in combating the stressor, it reveals flexibility and realistic use of feedback. Most examples of a problem-solving response to stress are undramatic because problem solving is generally the routine, sensible, obvious approach that an objective observer might suggest. Consider the following examples of problem solving.

- *Delegation.* A busy executive reduces her stress-provoking workload by delegating some of her many tasks to a capable subordinate.

- *Time management.* A manager who finds the day too short writes a daily schedule, requires his subordinates to make formal appointments to see him, and instructs his secretary to screen phone calls more selectively.

- *Talking it out.* An engineer who is experiencing stress because of poor communication with her nonengineer superior resolves to sit down with the boss and hammer out an agreement concerning the priorities on a project.

- *Asking for help.* A salesperson who is anxious about his company's ability to fill a difficult order asks the production manager to provide a realistic estimate of the probable delivery date.

- *Searching for alternatives.* A machine operator who finds his monotonous job stress provoking applies for a transfer to a more interesting position for which the pay is identical.

The presence of stress or stressors is implicated in reduced job performance.[65] Notice that these problem-solving responses will often reduce stress and stimulate performance, benefiting both the individual and the organization's bottom line.

Withdrawal. Withdrawal from the stressor is one of the most basic reactions to stress. In organizations, this withdrawal takes the form of absence and turnover. Compared with problem-solving reactions to stress, absenteeism fails to attack the stressor directly. Rather, the absent individual is simply attempting some short-term reduction of the anxiety prompted by the stressor. When the person returns to the job, the stress is still there. From this point of view, absence is a dysfunctional reaction to stress for both the individual and the organization. The same can be said about turnover when a person resigns from a stressful job on the spur of the moment merely to escape stress. However, a good case can be made for a well-planned resignation in which the intent is to assume another job that should be less stressful. This is actually a problem-solving reaction that should benefit both the individual and the organization in the long run. Absence, turnover, and turnover intentions have often been linked with stress and its causes.[66]

Use of Addictive Substances. Smoking, drinking, and drug use represent the least satisfactory behavioural responses to stress for both the individual and the organization. These activities fail to terminate stress episodes, and they leave employees less physically and mentally prepared to perform their jobs. We have all heard of hard-drinking newspaper reporters and advertising executives, and it is tempting to infer that the stress of their boundary role positions is responsible for their drinking. Unfortunately, like these, most reports of the relationship between stress and the use of addictive substances are anecdotal. However, there are indications that cigarette use and alcohol abuse are associated with the presence of work-related stress.[67]

Psychological Reactions to Stress

Psychological reactions to stress primarily involve emotions and thought processes, rather than overt behaviour, although these reactions are frequently revealed in the individual's speech and actions. The most common psychological reaction to stress is the use of defence mechanisms.

Defence mechanisms are psychological attempts to reduce the anxiety associated with stress. Notice that, by definition, defence mechanisms concentrate on *anxiety reduction*, rather than actually confronting or dealing with the stressor. Some common defence mechanisms include the following:

Defence mechanisms.
Psychological attempts to reduce the anxiety associated with stress.

- *Rationalization* is attributing socially acceptable reasons or motives to one's actions so that they will appear reasonable and sensible, at least to oneself. For example, a male nurse who becomes very angry and abusive when learning that he will not be promoted to supervisor might justify his anger by claiming that the head nurse discriminates against men.

- *Projection* is attributing one's own undesirable ideas and motives to others so that they seem less negative. For example, a sales executive who is undergoing conflict about offering a bribe to an official of a foreign government might reason that the official is corrupt.

- *Displacement* is directing feelings of anger at a "safe" target rather than expressing them where they may be punished. For example, a construction worker who is severely criticized by the boss for sloppy workmanship might take out his frustrations in an evening hockey league.

- *Reaction formation* is expressing oneself in a manner that is directly opposite to the way one truly feels, rather than risking negative reactions to one's true position. For example, a low-status member of a committee might vote with the majority on a crucial issue rather than stating his true position and opening himself to attack.

- *Compensation* is applying one's skills in a particular area to make up for failure in another area. For example, a professor who is unable to get her research published might resolve to become a superb teacher.

Is the use of defence mechanisms a good or bad reaction to stress? Used occasionally to temporarily reduce anxiety, they appear to be a useful reaction. For example, the construction worker who displaces aggression in an evening hockey league rather than attacking a frustrating boss might calm down, return to work the next day, and "talk it out" with the boss. Thus, the occasional use of defence mechanisms as short-term anxiety reducers probably benefits both the individual and the organization. In fact, people with "weak defences" can be incapacitated by anxiety and resort to dysfunctional withdrawal or addiction.

When the use of defence mechanisms becomes a chronic reaction to stress, however, the picture changes radically. The problem stems from the very character of defence mechanisms—they simply do not change the objective character of the stressor, and the basic conflict or frustration remains in operation. After some short-term relief from anxiety, the basic problem remains unresolved. In fact, the stress might *increase* with the knowledge that the defence has been essentially ineffective.

Physiological Reactions to Stress

Can work-related stress kill you? This is clearly an important question for organizations, and it is even more important for individuals who experience excessive stress at work. Many studies of physiological reactions to stress have concentrated on the cardiovascular system, specifically on the various risk factors that might prompt heart attacks. For example, there is evidence that work stress is associated with electrocardiogram irregularities and elevated levels of blood pressure, cholesterol, and pulse.[68] Research has found that workplace stress can double the risk of heart attacks.[69] Although dentists probably cause *you* stress, you might be surprised to learn that *they* also suffer from a fairly high rate of physiological problems that might be due to stress. One study found that the difficulties of building a dental practice, the image of the dentist as an inflictor of pain, and a lack of appreciation from patients were related to various cardiovascular risks.[70] Stress has also been associated with the onset of diseases such as respiratory and bacterial infections.[71]

Reducing or Coping with Stress

This chapter would be incomplete without a discussion of personal and organizational strategies that can reduce or cope with stress. Before continuing, consult "You Be the Manager: *Striking a Balance at Steelcase Inc.*"

Job Redesign

Organizations can redesign jobs to reduce their stressful characteristics. In theory, it is possible to redesign jobs anywhere in the organization to this end. Thus, an overloaded executive might be given an assistant to reduce the number of tasks he or she must perform. In practice, most formal job redesign efforts have involved enriching operative-level jobs to make them more stimulating and challenging. As we noted in Chapter 6, this is usually accomplished by giving employees more control over the pace of their work and permitting them to use more of their skills and abilities. Although enrichment often increases job satisfaction and reduces withdrawal, there have been almost no studies of the impact of enrichment on stress reduction or physiological indicators of stress. One exception is a study in the production and packing department of a candy producer that showed distinct improvements in employee mental health after job enrichment.[72] Such tests are important because it is conceivable that job enrichment could provoke stress rather than reduce it. In general, job redesign is an important method of dealing with stress because it attempts to *remove* stressors rather than simply helping employees to *cope with* stressors.

Social Support

Everyday experience suggests to us that the support of others can help us deal with stress. We have all seen children who are facing a tense experience run to an adult for support and comfort, and we have all seen on television the victims of

you be the manager

Striking a Balance at Steelcase Inc.

According to Steelcase Inc. CEO Jim Hackett, it is better to let people feel satisfied in all aspects of their lives than to drive them into the ground.

During the last decade, organizations have undergone dramatic changes that have had a major impact on the lives of their employees. Organizations are demanding more from their employees, who are increasingly being asked to do more with fewer resources. This has had serious consequences for employees and their organizations.

One study recently reported that in Canada, workers have a difficult time juggling their work and family lives, and that this is costing their employers $2.7 billion a year in lost time. This is because workers are visiting their doctors more often in order to treat the problems that result from the conflict and stress associated with trying to balance work and family obligations.

Another study found that Canadians are spending so much time at work that they are stressed for time and do not have enough time to spend with their family and friends as they struggle to balance paid work, unpaid work, and personal lives.

One company that is particularly concerned about the increasing demands and employee stress is Steelcase Inc., the world's largest office furniture maker with about 20,000 employees, $2.7 billion in sales last year and a long list of blue-chip clients. According to CEO Jim Hackett, the high-fliers in Silicon Valley who are making increasing demands on their employees have it all wrong.

Although their stocks have been trading in the stratosphere, while his company's shares are near record lows, he wonders what the demands of work are doing to workers who must constantly turn in 90-hour weeks and give their all to their employers.

"What good is it if you hit your numbers and you ruin lives? There's no social value in an approach like that," says Mr. Hackett, 44, who became president and chief executive officer in 1994. Since becoming CEO at the 87-year old company, Mr. Hackett has led Steelcase through some trying times, including its transition from a family firm to a publicly traded company last year.

Since then, he has watched Steelcase's stock lose about two-thirds its value—to as low as $12.87 after topping $37 in the weeks following the initial public offering. Recently, sales have slumped throughout the industry as Fortune 500 clients, caught in a frenzy of merger activity, have little need to buy new desks or chairs.

As a corporate leader, Mr. Hackett insists it is part of his responsibility to debunk the myth that working harder will always create better results. It is better, he says, to let people feel satisfied in all aspects of their lives than to drive them into the ground.

"We have to know the fuel gauges of our people, and we have to know what is possible and not go beyond those limits," he says. That said, Mr. Hackett concedes that both workers and corporate leaders have to do more and work harder than ever before. But companies must also develop programs and policies to help their people cope with the added demands and the stress that they are bound to create. Mr. Hackett says he feels an obligation to help individuals work more efficiently when they are in their office so that they can better manage their time.

1. What do you think about Mr. Hackett's suggestion that organizations should develop programs to help employees cope with increased work demands?

2. What kinds of programs and policies should companies like Steelcase develop to help employees cope with increased job demands?

To find out more about these issues and the programs developed at Steelcase, refer to The Manager's Notebook at the end of the chapter.

Sources: Church, E. (1999, October 20). Office life matters at Steelcase. *The Globe and Mail*, p. M1; Gibb-Clark, M. (1999, June 4). Work v. family: The $2.7-billion crisis. *The Globe and Mail*, p. M1; Ulrich, D. (1997). *Human Resource Champions*. Boston, MA: Harvard Business School Press; Walton, D. (1999, November 10). Workaholic Canadians starved for time. *The Globe and Mail*, pp. A1, A12; Carey, E. (1999, November 10). All work and no play makes Canadians tense. *The Toronto Star*, p. A10.

Companies are striving to be much more "family friendly" than in past years. Some organizations offer daycare for children of employees.

natural disasters finding solace in others. Although the dynamics of job stress might be more subtle, there is every reason to believe that social support should work the same way for people who experience job stress.

Speaking generally, social support simply refers to having close ties with other people. In turn, these close ties could affect stress by bolstering self-esteem, providing useful information, offering comfort and humour, or even providing material resources (such as a loan). Research evidence shows that the benefits of social support are double barreled. First, people with stronger social networks exhibit better psychological and physical well being. Second, when people encounter stressful events, those with good social networks are likely to cope more positively. Thus, the social network acts as a buffer against stress.[73]

Off the job, individuals might find social support in a spouse, family, or friends. On the job, social support might be available from one's superior or co-workers. Logic and some research evidence suggest that the buffering aspects of social support are most potent when they are directly connected to the source of stress. This means that co-workers and superiors might be the best sources of support for dealing with *work*-related stress. In particular, most managers need better training to recognize subordinate stress symptoms, clarify role requirements, and so on. Unfortunately, some organizational cultures, especially those that are very competitive, do not encourage members to seek support in a direct fashion. In this event, relationships that people develop in professional associations can sometimes serve as an informed source of social support.

"Family Friendly" Human Resource Policies

In order to reduce stress associated with dual careers, child care, and elder care, many organizations are beginning to institute "family friendly" human resources policies.[74] These policies generally include some combination of formalized social support, material support, and increased flexibility to adapt to employee needs.

In the domain of social support, some firms (such as Dow Jones, Atlantic Richfield, and Colgate-Palmolive) distribute newsletters, such as *Work and Family Life,* that deal with work-family issues. Others, such as Lincoln National insurance, have developed company support groups for employees dealing with elder-care problems. Some companies have contracted specialized consultants to provide seminars on elder-care issues.

Colgate-Palmolive
www.colgate.com

A most prominent and welcome form of material support consists of corporate daycare centres. Flexibility (which provides more *control* over family issues) includes flex-time, telecommuting, and job sharing (Chapter 6), as well as family leave policies that allow time off for caring for infants, sick children, and aged dependents. Although many firms boast of having such flexible policies, a common problem is encouraging managers to *use* them in an era of downsizing and lean staffing.

Firms that are noted for their family-friendly human resource policies include Corning, Xerox, IBM, American Express, and US West, a large regional telecommunications company.

Stress Management Programs

Some organizations have experimented with programs designed to help employees "manage" work-related stress. Such programs are also available from independent off-work sources. Some of these programs help physically and mentally healthy workers prevent problems due to stress. Others are therapeutic in nature, aimed at individuals who are already experiencing stress problems. Although the exact content of the programs varies, most involve one or more of the following techniques: meditation; training in muscle-relaxation exercises; biofeedback training to control physiological processes; training in time management; and training to think more positively and realistically about sources of job stress.[75] Although each of these techniques has been useful in reducing anxiety and tension in other contexts, they have only recently been applied in the work setting. Tentative evidence suggests that these applications are useful in reducing physiological arousal, sleep disturbances, and self-reported tension and anxiety.[76]

Work/Life Programs

Many people have argued that a balanced lifestyle that includes a variety of leisure activities combined with a healthy diet and physical exercise can reduce stress and counteract some of the adverse physiological effects of stress. For some organizations, work/life balance programs and quality-of-life benefits have become a strategic retention tool. Employees are increasingly demanding work/life balance benefits, and employers are realizing that by providing them they can increase commitment and reduce turnover. Northern Telecom has a comprehensive work/life balance program that includes family-care leave for the parents of newborns or newly adopted children; retirement investment matching; coffee bars; subsidized gym memberships; sports areas; and meditation and spirituality rooms where employees can relax or observe their religious practices.[77]

An increasing number of organizations are providing work/life programs. For example, Eddie Bauer Inc. offers work/life programs to their employees to help them lead more productive and balanced lives. Workers are encouraged to participate in mental and physical fitness through a variety of programs. Employee assistance programs are also available to help employees manage personal problems, mental and emotional difficulties, alcohol and chemical dependency, as well as legal and financial assistance.[78] At Husky Injection Molding Systems the cafeteria only serves healthy food and at the company's head office in Bolton, Ontario, a naturopath, a chiropractor, a medical doctor, a nurse, and a massage therapist are on staff, and employees are encouraged to use the company's large fitness centre.[79] Starbucks also has a work/life program that includes on-site fitness services.[80] Studies show that fitness training is associated with improved mood, a better self-concept, reduced absenteeism, and reports of better performance. Work/life programs are also believed to result in lower health-care costs. Some of these improvements probably stem from stress reduction.[81]

Eddie Bauer Inc.
www.eddiebauer.com/

the manager's notebook

Striking a Balance at Steelcase Inc.

1. According to Dave Ulrich of the University of Michigan, the major problem facing employees is not so much the increasing demands being made on them but, rather, the lack of resources that they require to cope and manage the increasing demands. As demands made on employees increase, so can employee stress and depression. Ulrich suggests that organizations resolve this problem through the use of a demand/resource framework. The framework indicates that employees will experience stress and depression when the demands being made on them exceed the resources they have to manage them. Therefore, organizations need to find ways to help employees find the right balance between demands and resources. To balance demands and resources, Ulrich suggests three strategies: (1) Find ways to help employees do less by reducing demands (e.g., set priorities among demands, reengineer work processes by streamlining, automating, and simplifying); (2) increase the resources that employees have to do their work (e.g., provide employees with more control over how and when they do their work, provide employees with computers and other technology); and (3) help employees turn demands into resources (e.g., consider the impact of company policies on employees' families, involve employees in key decisions).

2. One of the things that Mr. Hackett emphasizes at Steelcase is a balanced perspective such that one's value does not increase or decrease because of the job they do. In addition to this balanced perspective, Steelcase has tried to make it easier for employees to live healthier lives, even as the demands of their jobs increase. For example, it has adopted a model of more numerous, smaller exercise facilities that enable staff to "sneak away with no hassles" at any time when they have a break in their day. In addition, the company is trying to offer its staff healthy food on site. To discourage consumption of fast food for dinner, it has started a program that lets employees place a dinner order for their family at noon that they can pick up at the end of the day. The employee pays for the meal, but Steelcase provides it at a discount. Mr. Hackett says he is also exploring the idea of providing "restorative sleep" areas for his staff so they can grab a quick nap if they are suffering from jet lag or just need to rejuvenate themselves.

Summary

- Interpersonal conflict is a process that occurs when one person, group, or organizational unit frustrates the goal attainment of another. Such conflict can revolve around facts, procedures, or the goals themselves.

- Causes of conflict include intergroup bias, high interdependence, ambiguous jurisdictions, and scarce resources. Differences in power, status, and culture are also a factor.

- The conflict process includes factors such as the need to win the dispute, withholding information, increased cohesiveness, negative stereotyping of the other party, reduced contact, and emergence of aggressive leaders.

- Modes of managing conflict include avoiding, accommodating, competing, compromise, and collaborating.

- Negotiation is a decision-making process among parties that do not have the same preferences.

- Distributive negotiation essentially attempts to divide up a fixed amount of outcomes. Frequent tactics include threats, promises, firmness, concession making, and persuasion. Integrative negotiation attempts to enlarge the amount of outcomes via collaboration or problem solving. Tactics include exchanging copious information, framing differences as opportunities, cutting costs, increasing resources, and introducing superordinate goals.

- Stressors are environmental conditions that have the potential to induce stress. Stress is a psychological reaction that can prompt tension or anxiety because an individual feels incapable of coping with the demands made by a stressor.

- Personality characteristics can cause some individuals to perceive more stressors than others, experience more stress, and react more negatively to this stress. In particular, people with external locus of control and the Type A behaviour pattern are prone to such reactions. Type A individuals are aggressive, ambitious, and often hostile. They are preoccupied with their work and feel a great sense of time urgency. Hostility is the key factor in physiological risk.

- At the managerial or executive level, common stressors include role overload and high responsibility. At the operative level, poor physical working conditions and underutilization of potential due to poor job design are common stressors. Boundary role occupants often experience stress in the form of conflict between demands from inside the employing organization and demands from outside. Burnout may occur when interaction with clients produces emotional exhaustion, depersonalization, and low accomplishment. Job insecurity and change, role ambiguity, sexual harassment, interpersonal conflict, and work-family conflicts have the potential to induce stress in all organizational members.

- Behavioural reactions to stress include problem solving, withdrawal, and the use of addictive substances. Problem solving is the most effective reaction because it confronts the stressor directly and thus has the potential to terminate the stress episode. The most common psychological reaction to stress is the use of defence mechanisms to temporarily reduce anxiety. The majority of studies on physiological reactions to stress focus on cardiovascular risk factors.

- Strategies that might reduce organizational stress include job redesign, social support, family-friendly human resource policies, stress management programs, and work/life balance programs.

Discussion Questions

1. The manager of a fast food restaurant sees that conflict among the staff is damaging service. How might she implement a superordinate goal to reduce this conflict?

2. The same company hires two finance majors right out of college. Being in a new and unfamiliar environment, they begin their relationship cooperatively. However, over time, they develop a case of deep interpersonal conflict. What factors could account for this?

3. What are some of the factors that make it a real challenge for conflicting parties to develop a collaborative relationship and engage in integrative negotiation?

4. Two social workers just out of college join the same county welfare agency. Both find their case loads very heavy and their roles very ambiguous. One exhibits negative stress reactions, including absence and elevated alcohol use. The other seems to cope very well. Use the stress episode model to explain why this might occur.

5. Imagine that a person who greatly dislikes bureaucracy assumes her first job as an investigator in a very bureaucratic government tax office. Describe the stressors that she might encounter in this situation. Give an example of a problem-solving reaction to this stress. Give an example of a defensive reaction to it.

6. The jobs in the previous two questions are boundary role jobs. Explain this, and describe why boundary roles often prove stressful.

7. Compare and contrast the stressors that might be experienced by an assembly-line worker and the president of a company.

8. Discuss the advantages and disadvantages of hiring employees with Type A personality characteristics.

9. Does personality influence the way individuals manage conflict? Consider the relationship among each of the following personality characteristics and the five approaches to managing organizational conflict described in this chapter: the "Big Five" dimensions of personality, locus of control, self-monitoring, self-esteem, need for power, and machiavellianism.

10. Can leadership be a source of stress in organizations? Refer to the leadership theories described in Chapter 9 (e.g., leadership traits, behaviours, situational theories, participative leadership, developmental leadership, and LMX theory) and explain how leadership can be a source of stress. According to each theory, what can leaders do to reduce stress and help employees cope with it?

Experiental Exercise

Coping with Stress

To what extent does each of the following fit as a description of you? (Circle one number in each line across.)

	Very true	Quite true	Some- what true	Not very true	Not at all true
1. I "roll with the punches" when problems come up.	1	2	3	4	5
2. I spend almost all my time thinking about my work.	5	4	3	2	1
3. I treat other people as individuals and care about their feelings and opinions.	1	2	3	4	5
4. I recognize and accept my own limitations and assets.	1	2	3	4	5
5. There are quite a few people I could describe as "good friends."	1	2	3	4	5
6 I enjoy using my skills and abilities both on and off the job.	1	2	3	4	5
7. I get bored easily.	5	4	3	2	1
8. I enjoy meeting and talking with people who have different ways of thinking about the world.	1	2	3	4	5
9. Often in my job I "bite off more than I can chew."	5	4	3	2	1
10. I'm usually very active on weekends with projects or recreation.	1	2	3	4	5
11. I prefer working with people who are very much like myself.	5	4	3	2	1
12. I work primarily because I have to survive, and not necessarily because I enjoy what I do.	5	4	3	2	1
13. I believe I have a realistic picture of my personal strengths and weakness.	1	2	3	4	5
14. Often I get into arguments with people who don't think my way.	5	4	3	2	1
15. Often I have trouble getting much done on my job.	5	4	3	2	1
16. I'm interested in a lot of different topics.	1	2	3	4	5
17. I get upset when things don't go my way.	5	4	3	2	1
18. Often I'm not sure how I stand on a controversial topic.	5	4	3	2	1
19. I'm usually able to find a way around anything which blocks me from an important goal.	1	2	3	4	5
20. I often disagree with my boss or others at work.	5	4	3	2	1

Scoring and Interpretation

Dr. Alan A. McLean, who developed this checklist, feels that people who cope with stress effectively have five characteristics. First, they know themselves well and accept their own strengths and weaknesses. Second, they have a variety of interests off the job, and they are not total "workaholics." Third, they exhibit a variety of reactions to stress, rather than always getting a headache or always becoming depressed. Fourth, they are accepting of others who have values or styles different from their own. Finally, good copers are active and productive both on and off the job.

Add together the numbers you circled for the four questions contained in each of the five coping scales.

Coping scale	Add together your responses to these questions	Your score (write in)
Knows self	4, 9, 13, 18	_____
Many interests	2, 5, 7, 16	_____
Variety of reactions	1, 11, 17, 19	_____
Accepts other's values	3, 8, 14, 20	_____
Active and productive	6, 10, 12, 15	_____

Then, add the five scores together for your overall total score.

Scores on each of the five areas can vary between 5 and 20. Scores of 12 or above perhaps suggest that it might be useful to direct more attention to the area. The overall total score can range between 20 and 100. Scores of 60 or more may suggest some general difficulty in coping on the dimensions covered.

Source: McLean, A. A. (1979). *Work stress*. Reading, MA: Addison-Wesley, pp. 126–127. Copyright © 1976 by Management Decision Systems, Inc. Reprinted by permission.

Case Incident

Karoshi

Karoshi is Japanese for "death by overwork." This well-documented ailment, in which people develop illnesses from high stress and the pressures of overtime work—with many literally keeling over and dying at their desks, was officially recognized as a fatal illness by the Japanese in 1989. Officially, the first person who died of karoshi was a 48-year old man who typically worked 15-hour days at an Osaka company and had worked 100 hours of overtime every month for a year. Eventually, this overload proved fatal. He died after putting in three consecutive 15-hour days.

Following are two examples of karoshi, whose toll runs to nearly 10,000 deaths each year in Japan.

Shinji Masami, 37, a design engineer at Hino Motors, a large subsidiary of Toyota that produces trucks, had to design parts that fit together well in final assembly. The job was intense and had pressing deadlines. From 1980 through

1986, Masami worked an average of 2,600 hours, about 25 percent more than the average Japanese. Days before his death he complained of severe headaches and abdominal pains. Yet he forced himself to go to work until his last day. He died of brain hemorrhage while at work in the office.

Jun Ishii, 47, a manager of Mitsui's Soviet division, collapsed and died at a business hotel after having spent his last five days escorting Russian visitors to local machine manufacturers. During the 10 months preceding his death, Ishii had made many business trips, totalling 103 days, to the Soviet Union, with little time for rest in between.

1. Do you think that incidents of karoshi like those described in the case incident can become a problem in North America? Does karoshi depend on whether the overtime work is voluntary or involuntary, and is personality a factor?

2. What can organizations in North America do to prevent karoshi?

Source: Babbar, S., & Aspelin, D. J. (1998). The overtime rebellion: Symptom of a bigger problem? *Academy of Management Executive*, 12, pp. 68-76.

Case Study

Kate Cooper

My name is Kate Cooper. I am 31, a registered nurse with a bachelor's degree in nursing and 6 years of supervisory experience. I was charge nurse and then house supervisor in the medical/surgical wing of a large regional medical centre and was in-service director in charge of continuing education and staff development in a geriatric nursing setting. In addition, I have been teaching nursing courses in the night program at a local technical school.

Ready for the next step in my career, I obtained the position of Manager of Adult Services for the twenty-bed adult psychiatric wing at Green Meadows Hospital. Green Meadows was a newly constructed forty-room community hospital for the care of acutely ill psychiatric patients. It was the 23rd facility owned by Southern Hospitals Corporation (SHC), the largest chain of acute-care psychiatric hospitals in the country.

I felt excited about my new position. I saw it as a fine opportunity for career development in nursing, and the possibility of transferring to other facilities in the chain was a definite benefit in my eyes. I had many projects to complete before the planned opening of the hospital in two weeks, and I started my new position with high energy and enthusiasm.

My supervisor, Alan Jones, who hired me, was assistant administrator of the hospital. He had one year of previous experience as director of nursing at a 50-bed acute-care psychiatric hospital. On my first day, he encouraged me to "just dig right in and get started" organizing my department. I asked to see my job description and the hospital policy manual to become familiar with the organization employing me. Alan gave me a job description and explained that I was part of the "start-up" process. At this time there was no human resources handbook for employees.

One condition of employment I stipulated in accepting the job was that I be able to continue my schooling as a part-time graduate student working on my master's degree in nursing education. Alan Jones readily agreed to this condition, stating that he was a strong supporter of continuing education for all managers and staff.

In my opinion, the first week I worked for Green Meadows consisted of many wasted hours. I learned on my own that my main task prior to the opening was to hire the patient-care staff for my 20-bed unit. I tried to line up interviews for nurses and mental health workers, since Alan Jones had told me to "go ahead and hire the personnel you need for your unit."

Peter Smith, manager of the 18-bed chemical dependency unit, had previously worked with Alan Jones at a psychiatric hospital 50 miles from Green Meadows. Peter had been hired by Alan along with two other managers from that location but had not yet arrived at Green Meadows. Peter was hiring staff for his unit, and he told me he wanted to interview the nurses and mental health workers also, since those employees would be working in his unit as well.

This request surprised me. I tried to find an organization chart and asked the hospital administrator, Doug Anderson, in passing one morning if he had one I could see. He jokingly asked me if I was serious. "After all," he said, "I think it is changing every day." I laughed at first, but my amusement was short lived when no chart was forthcoming. Eventually, I came to visualize the organization chart as presented in Case Exhibit 13.1.

Doug Anderson had served as office manager in a small hospital in California. His wife, an occupational therapist, was also a part-time employee at Green Meadows. Two of Doug's hires were a personal friend from California, Leonard Snare, and Leonard's wife. Leonard's sole job qualification was certification to be a psychiatric technician, earned by attending workshops. His wife worked in the business office.

Construction work had progressed, and Green Meadows was ready for staff occupancy one week before the planned hospital opening. Although much remained to be done and things were still confused, I was excited about moving into my new office.

During the previous week Peter and I had hired our initial staff. I was worried my unit would not be ready to receive patients and had written a five-day orientation program specific to the unit that included information I thought my patient-care staff would find beneficial. I shared the orientation outline with Peter, who informed me that he would need two and a half days to teach the new staff members *his* program alone.

I was shocked and angered that he had planned this commitment for my staff. With one week left, both orientation programs could not be completed prior to opening. I asked Peter if his plan had been cleared with Alan Jones. Peter replied with a grin, "Of course. It was his idea." As a result, I sought out Alan and asked if he could meet on some neutral ground with the adult psychiatric and chemical dependency units. I told him that orientation to my department was just as important as orientation to Peter's department. Alan told me that Peter had his program all ready to go and

Case Exhibit 13.1
Green Meadows Hospital
management staff—partial
organizational chart.

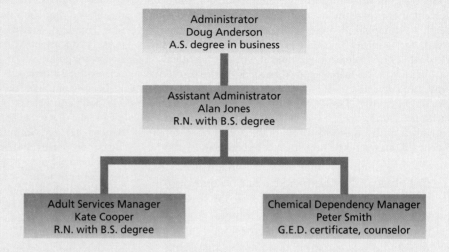

would only need "a couple of days" to present it. All this left me feeling very frustrated.

I had other problems with Alan. Despite his having told me to go ahead and hire the staff nurses and mental health workers, I later discovered he was hiring those people at the same time I was interviewing prospective employees. In addition, Alan had instructed me to assume the role of in-service director and write the staff orientation program. He told me that I would have to be the unit head nurse for the chemical dependency unit, although I told him that I thought the responsibilities would be too great due to my duties as the adult services unit manager. Alan's response to my doubts was his standard one in such situations: "You are tough, and I know you can handle it."

As a result of these and similar interactions with Alan, I became confused and frustrated by his lack of support and his behaviour, which seemed inconsistent with the directions he had given me. I was overwhelmed with the amount of work and responsibility. I was most frustrated and angered when additional tasks were "dumped" on me because I felt I had to complete the extra work as soon as possible in addition to doing my own work on the unit.

Alan apparently had difficult relationships with some other employees as well. Other female managers complained almost from the start that Alan needed to be "put in his place" for his sexist remarks and behaviours. Doug Anderson received reports indicating that Alan's behaviour had been inappropriate on several occasions. Doug also heard second hand that Alan was overstepping his responsibilities as assistant administrator and making policy statements contrary to Doug's positions.

This general employee dissatisfaction continued. Three months after the opening of the hospital, Alan Jones strongly implied that I would have to quit school. He explained that he expected people to be there, saying that "to be a good manager you should be here all the time." I took issue with this and sought Doug Anderson's assistance. Doug had never been informed about my going to school and was unaware that I was even taking classes. Alan alone had approved my return to school to continue my education. Doug's response was simply to encourage me to speak with Alan again and "communicate better with him."

Feeling pressure on several fronts, I reached the limit of my tolerance with Alan Jones and handed in my notice of resignation. Alan Jones subsequently refused to speak with me. The manager of the chemical dependency unit told me that my timing was lousy, accused me of trying to create waves, and said I should put work as a priority over continuing my education.

Source: Case prepared by William E. Stratton, Idaho State University; David Efraty, University of Houston—Downtown; and Kim Jardine. From *Case Research Journal*, Spring 1993. The manager cooperated in the field research for this case, which was written solely for the purpose of stimulating student discussion. All incidents and individuals are real, but the names of persons and of the organization have been disguised. Copyright © 1993 by the *Case Research Journal* and William E. Stratton.

1. What are the various causes of the conflict that can be observed in this case?

2. What approaches does Kate Cooper take to try to manage the conflict she is experiencing?

3. Is Kate experiencing stress? If so, what are its causes?

4. What kinds of stress reactions does Kate exhibit?

5. Evaluate the management style of Alan Jones.

6. What evidence of negotiation is seen in the case? What kind of negotiation *should have* occurred?

Integrative Case: Ace Technology

At the end of Part Two of the text on Individual Behaviour, you answered a number of questions about the Ace Technology Integrative Case that dealt with issues related to learning, job attitudes, motivation, pay systems, and incentive plans. Now that you have completed Part Three of the text and the chapters on Social Behaviour and Organizational Processes, you can return to the Ace Technology Integrative Case and enhance your understanding of some of the main issues associated with social behaviour and organizational processes by answering the following questions.

Questions

1. Discuss the culture at Ace Technology. Would you consider it a strong culture? Why or why not, and what are the implications of this for the new strategy? What effect will the new reward system have on the culture?

2. Consider Bill's leadership style and behaviour in the case. Use Fiedler's Contingency Theory and House's Path-Goal Theory to analyze the leadership situation confronting Bill. What leadership style does each theory suggest?

3. Run the new strategy and compensation plan through the Vroom and Jago decision tree (Exhibit 9.5). What level of participation is indicated?

4. Discuss the merits of transformational or charismatic leadership, LMX theory, and developmental leadership at Ace Technology. What do these theories suggest about the effectiveness of Bill's leadership?

5. Discuss communication at Ace Technology. How is the new strategy and compensation program communicated, and how effective is communication at Ace Technology?

6. Consider the decision-making process at Ace Technology. How was the decision made on the new strategy and compensation program, and how effective was it?

Part 4

The Total Organization

Chapter 14

Organizational Structure

W.L. GORE & ASSOCIATES, INC. Unless you are
an avid hiker or camper, you may not be familiar
with W. L. Gore & Associates, Inc. The firm, based
in Newark, Delaware, is best known for the Gore-
Tex brand fabric, a breathable, waterproof fabric
laminate found in premium outdoor clothing and
space suits. However, Gore also produces other
high-tech products, including electrical cable, vas-
cular grafts and other medical products, and a
wide variety of environmental filters and other industrial products. Founded in
1958 by ex-Dupont R&D chemist Bill Gore in the basement of his home, the
firm has 45 plants worldwide. Its annual revenue is around $1.4 billion, and it
has posted good profits for over 30 years straight.

W.L. Gore & Associates, Inc.

Gore's 6,500 "associates" (not employees) operate under what the company
describes as unmanagement. There are no titles, no bosses, and no budgets.
By extension, there is no hierarchy or formal chain of command, no predetermined channels of communication, and no fixed organizational structure.
People are not hired for a job, but rather, for a commitment. How does any
work get done?

The company has a unique, flat structure that it calls a lattice system in which
an associate assumes responsibility for developing a new product. Then, he or
she has to recruit volunteers from other parts of the company to form a team.
This team could eventually become a plant, which would be divided into
smaller teams that choose their own leaders. Gore intentionally limits plant
size to no more than 200 associates to foster good communication. Each
plant is self-sufficient with its own manufacturing, finance, and research and
development contained within the facility.

W. L. Gore & Associates Inc. has a unique, flat organizational structure called a lattice system, which fosters a creative and energizing work environment and continual innovation.

Instead of bosses, the company has sponsors. New hires are assigned to sponsors who help them understand their commitments and what is required to be successful in those commitments. Another important responsibility of a sponsor is to be a "positive advocate" for new associates. This involves gathering information and feedback about a new associate's personal development and presenting it to a compensation committee. The information is then used to rank all associates within a functional area and to determine their compensation.

How did Gore come up with such a unique structure? The structure is a result of the core values that founder Bill Gore instituted in order to develop a creative and energizing work environment. The key to Gore's success has been continual innovation, which is due, in large part, to the organization's cultural values of fairness, continuous learning, commitment, and consultation.

The lattice structure supports and reinforces the culture in a number of important ways. For example, because there are no formal channels of communication, associates must communicate and consult with each other. In addition, because associates do not have narrowly defined job titles that lock them into specific tasks, they are more likely to take on new and challenging assignments. Thus, the structure helps to foster communication and consultation among associates and in the development of new ideas and commitments.

What is it like to work in a lattice organizational structure, compared with a more traditional hierarchical structure? According to a human resources leader at Gore, "Issuing orders, writing rules, and releasing memos is much easier than trying to obtain buy-in from a group, selling another associate on a new idea, or encouraging and motivating an individual or a team."

W.L. Gore & Associates
www.gore.com

Learning Objectives

After reading Chapter 14, you should be able to:

1 Define organizational structure and explain how it corresponds to division of labour.

2 Discuss the relative merits of various forms of departmentation.

3 Review the more basic and more elaborate means of achieving organizational coordination.

4 Discuss the nature and consequences of traditional structural characteristics.

5 Explain the distinction between organic and mechanistic structures.

6 Discuss the emergence of network, virtual, modular, and boundaryless organizations.

7 Review important considerations concerning downsizing.

The challenges of the lattice system seem to have made a difference. W. L. Gore & Associates have continued to grow and prosper, thanks to their unique structure that fosters a creative work environment and continual innovation. But how do Gore employees feel about working in a "lattice" organizational structure? It appears that the lattice system also fosters positive attitudes. Gore has been ranked in the top 10 on *Fortune* magazine's The 100 Best Companies to Work for in America![1]

Why is W. L. Gore & Associates organized and structured the way it is? And how does its unique organizational structure affect organizational members and the overall effectiveness of the organization? These are the kinds of questions that we shall attempt to answer in this chapter and the next.

First, we will define organizational structure and discuss the methods for dividing labour and forming departments. Then we will consider some methods for coordinating labour as well as traditional structural characteristics and the relationship between size and structure. Finally, we will review some signals of structural problems.

What Is Organizational Structure?

In previous chapters, we were concerned primarily with the bits and pieces that make up organizations. First, we analyzed organizational behaviour from the standpoint of the individual member—how his or her learning, perception, attitudes, and motivation affect behaviour. Then we shifted our analysis to groups and to some of the processes that occur in organizations, including communication, leadership, and decision making. In this chapter we adopt yet another level of analysis by looking at the organization as a whole. Our primary interest is the causes and consequences of organizational structure.

Shortly, we will discuss organizational structure in detail. For now, it is enough to know that it broadly refers to how the organization's individuals and groups are *put together* or *organized* to accomplish work. This is an important issue. An organization could have well-motivated individual members and properly led groups and still fail to fulfill its potential because of the way their efforts are divided and coordinated.

In Chapter 1, we defined organizations as social inventions for accomplishing common goals through group effort. In this chapter and the next, we shall see that organizational structure intervenes between goals and organizational accomplishments and thus influences organizational effectiveness. Among other things, structure affects how effectively and efficiently group effort is coordinated.

To achieve its goals, an organization has to do two very basic things—*divide* labour among its members and then *coordinate* what has been divided. For example, consider how a university divides its labour—some members teach, some run the graduate program, some take care of accounts, and some handle registration. It is simply unlikely that anyone could do *all* these things well. Furthermore, within each of these subunits, labour would be further divided. For example, the registrar's office would include a director, secretaries, clerks, and so on. With all this division, some coordination is obviously necessary.

We can conclude that **organizational structure** is the manner in which an organization divides its labour into specific tasks and achieves coordination among these tasks.[2]

Organizational structure. The manner in which an organization divides its labour into specific tasks and achieves coordination among these tasks.

The Division and Coordination of Labour

Labour must be divided because individuals have physical and intellectual limitations. *Everyone* cannot do *everything*; even if this were possible, tremendous confusion and inefficiency would result. There are two basic dimensions to the division of labour, a vertical dimension and a horizontal dimension. Once labour is divided, it must be coordinated to achieve organizational effectiveness.

Vertical Division of Labour

The vertical division of labour is concerned primarily with apportioning authority for planning and decision making—who gets to tell whom what to do? As we see in Exhibit 14.1, in a manufacturing firm, the vertical division of labour is usually signified by titles, such as president, manager, and supervisor. In a university, it might be denoted by titles, such as president, dean, and chairperson. Organizations differ greatly in the extent to which labour is divided vertically. For example, the U.S. Army has nine levels of command ranging from four-star generals to sergeants. Wal-Mart has five levels between its CEO and its store managers. On the other hand, an automobile dealership might have only two or three levels, and a university would usually fall between the extremes. Separate departments, units, or functions *within* an organization will also often vary in the extent to which they vertically divide labour. A production unit might have several levels of management, ranging from supervisor to general manager. A research unit in the same company might have only two levels of management. A couple of key themes or issues underlie the vertical division of labour.

Autonomy and Control. Holding other factors constant, the domain of decision making and authority is reduced as the number of levels in the hierarchy increases. Put another way, managers have less authority over fewer matters. On the other hand, a flatter hierarchy pushes authority lower and involves people further down the hierarchy in more decisions.

Exhibit 14.1
The dimensions of division of
labour in a manufacturing
firm.

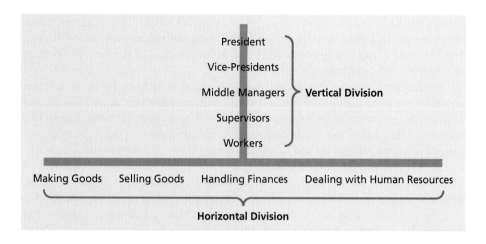

Communication. A second theme underlying the vertical division of labour is communication or coordination between levels. As labour is progressively divided vertically, timely communication and coordination can become harder to achieve. Recall our discussion in Chapter 10 of information filtering as a barrier to communication. As the number of levels in the hierarchy increases, filtering is more likely to occur.

These two themes illustrate that labour must be divided vertically enough to ensure proper control but not so much as to make vertical communication and coordination impossible. The proper degree of such division will vary across organizations and across their functional units.

Horizontal Division of Labour

The horizontal division of labour groups the basic tasks that must be performed into jobs and then into departments so that the organization can achieve its goals. Required workflow is the main basis for this division. The firm schematized in Exhibit 14.1 must produce and sell goods, keep its finances straight, and keep its employees happy. A hospital must admit patients, subject them to lab tests, fix what ails them, and keep them comfortable, all the while staying within its budget. Just as organizations differ in the extent to which they divide labour vertically, they also differ in the extent of horizontal division of labour. In a small business, the owner might be a "jack-of-all-trades," making estimates, delivering the product or service, and keeping the books. As the organization grows, horizontal division of labour is likely, with different groups of employees assigned to perform each of these tasks. Thus, the horizontal division of labour suggests some specialization on the part of the workforce. Up to a point, this increased specialization can promote efficiency. A couple of key themes or issues underlie the horizontal division of labour.

Job Design. The horizontal division of labour is closely tied to our earlier consideration of job design (Chapter 6). An example will clarify this. Suppose that an organization offers a product or service that consists of A work, B work, and C work (e.g., fabrication, inspection, and packaging). There are at least three basic ways in which it might structure these tasks:

- Form an ABC Department in which all workers do ABC work.
- Form an ABC Department in which workers specialize in A work, B work, or C work.
- Form a separate A Department, B Department, and C Department.

There is nothing inherently superior about any of these three designs. Notice, however, that each has implications for the jobs involved and how these jobs are coordinated. The first design provides for enriched jobs in which each worker can coordinate his or her own A work, B work, and C work. It also reduces the need for supervision and allows for self-managed teams. However, this design might require highly trained workers, and it might be impossible if A work, B work, and C work are complex specialties that require (for example) engineering, accounting, and legal skills. The second design involves increased horizontal division of labour in which employees specialize in tasks and in which the coordination of A work, B work, and C work becomes more critical. However, much of this coordination could be handled by properly designing the head of the department's job. Finally, the third design offers the greatest horizontal division of labour in that A work, B work, and C work are actually performed in separate departments. This design provides for great control and accountability for the separate tasks, but it also suggests that someone above the department heads will have to get involved in coordination. There are several lessons here. First, the horizontal division of labour strongly affects job design. Second, it has profound implications for the degree of coordination necessary. Finally, it also has implications for the vertical division of labour and where control over work processes should logically reside.

Differentiation. A second theme occasioned by the horizontal division of labour is related to the first. As organizations engage in increased horizontal division of labour, they usually become more and more differentiated. **Differentiation** is the tendency for managers in separate functions or departments to differ in terms of goals, time spans, and interpersonal styles.[3] In tending to their own domains and problems, managers often develop distinctly different psychological orientations toward the organization and its products or services.

A classic case of differentiation is that which often occurs between marketing managers and those in research and development. The goals of the marketing managers might be external to the organization and oriented toward servicing the marketplace. Those of R&D managers might be oriented more toward excellence in design and state-of-the-art use of materials. While marketing managers want products to sell *now*, R&D managers might feel that "good designs take time." Finally, marketing managers might believe that they can handle dispute resolution with R&D through interpersonal tactics learnt when they were on the sales force ("Let's discuss this over lunch"). R&D managers might feel that "the design data speaks for itself" when a conflict occurs. The essential problem here is that the marketing department and the R&D department *need* each other to do their jobs properly![4] Shortly, we will review some tactics to help achieve necessary coordination.

Differentiation is a natural and necessary consequence of the horizontal division of labour, but it again points to the need for coordination, a topic that we will consider in more detail below. For now, let us examine more closely how organizations can allocate work to departments.

Differentiation. The tendency for managers in separate departments to differ in terms of goals, time spans, and interpersonal styles.

Departmentation

As we suggested above, once basic tasks have been combined into jobs, a question still remains as to how to group these jobs so that they can be managed effectively. The assignment of jobs to departments is called departmentation, and it represents one of the core aspects of the horizontal division of labour. It should be recognized that "department" is a generic term; some organizations use an alternative term, such as unit, group, or division. There are several methods of departmentation, each of which has its strengths and weaknesses.

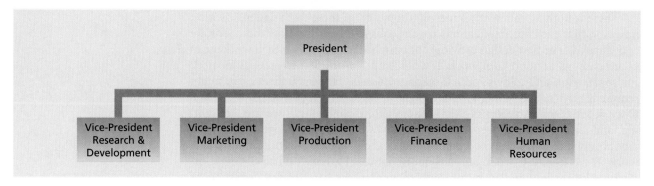

Exhibit 14.2
Functional departmentation.

Functional departmentation.
Employees with closely related skills and responsibilities are assigned to the same department.

Functional Departmentation. This form of organization is basic and familiar. Under **functional departmentation,** employees with closely related skills and responsibilities (functions) are located in the same department (Exhibit 14.2). Thus, those with skills in sales and advertising are assigned to the marketing department, and those with skills in accounting and credit are assigned to the finance department. Under this kind of design, employees are grouped according to the kind of resources they contribute to achieving the overall goals of the organization.[5]

What are the advantages of functional departmentation? The most cited advantage is that of efficiency. When all the engineers are located in an engineering department, rather than scattered throughout the organization, it is easier to be sure that they are neither overloaded nor underloaded with work. Also, support factors, such as reference books, computer terminals, and laboratory space can be allocated more efficiently with less duplication. Some other advantages of functional departmentation include the following:

- Communication within departments should be enhanced, since everyone "speaks the same language."

- Career ladders and training opportunities within the function are enhanced because all parties will share the same view of career progression.

- It should be easier to measure and evaluate the performance of functional specialists when they are all located in the same department.

What are the disadvantages of functional departmentation? Most of them stem from the specialization within departments that occurs in the functional arrangement. As a result, a high degree of differentiation can occur between functional departments. At best, this can lead to poor coordination and slow response to organizational problems. At worst, it can lead to open conflict between departments, in which the needs of clients and customers are ignored. Departmental empires might be built at the expense of pursuing organizational goals.

There is consensus that functional departmentation works best in small to medium-sized firms that offer relatively few product lines or services. It can also be an effective means of organizing the smaller divisions of large corporations. When the scale gets bigger and the output of the organization gets more complex, most firms gravitate toward product departmentation or its variations.

Product departmentation.
Departments are formed on the basis of a particular product, product line, or service.

Product Departmentation. Under **product departmentation,** departments are formed on the basis of a particular product, product line, or service. Each of these departments can operate fairly autonomously because it has its own set of functional specialists dedicated to the output of that department. For example, a computer firm might have a hardware division and a software division, each with its own staff of production people, marketers, and research and development personnel (Exhibit 14.3).

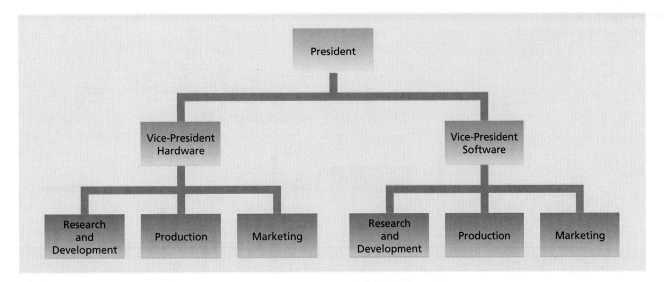

What are the advantages of product departmentation? One key advantage is better coordination among the functional specialists who work on a particular product line. Since their attentions are focused on one product and they have fewer functional peers, fewer barriers to communication should develop. Other advantages include flexibility, since product lines can be added or deleted without great implications for the rest of the organization. Also, product-focused departments can be evaluated as profit centres, since they have independent control over costs and revenues. This is not feasible for most functional departments (e.g., the research and development department does not have revenues). Finally, product departmentation often serves the customer or client better, since the client can see more easily who produced the product (the software group, not Ajax Computers). All in all, product structures have more potential than functional structures for responding to customers in a timely way.

Are there any disadvantages to product departmentation? Professional development might suffer without a critical mass of professionals working in the same place at the same time. Also, economies of scale might be threatened and inefficiency might occur, if relatively autonomous product-oriented departments are not coordinated. R&D personnel in an industrial products division and a consumer products division might work on a similar problem for months without being aware of each other's efforts. Worse, product-oriented departments might actually work at cross purposes.

Matrix Departmentation. The system of **matrix departmentation** is an attempt to capitalize simultaneously on the strengths of both functional and product departmentation.[6] In its most literal form, employees remain tied to a functional department such as marketing or production, but they also report to a product manager who draws on their services (Exhibit 14.4). For example, in a firm in the chemical industry, a marketing expert might matrix with the household cleaning products group.

There are many variations on matrix design. Most of them boil down to what exactly gets crossed with functional areas to form the matrix and the degree of stability of the matrix relationships. For example, besides products, a matrix could be based on geographical regions or projects. For instance, a mechanical engineer in a global engineering company could report both to the mechanical engineering department at world headquarters and the regional manager for Middle East operations. This would probably be a fairly stable arrangement.

Matrix departmentation.
Employees remain members of a functional department while also reporting to a product or project manager.

Exhibit 14.4
Matrix departmentation.

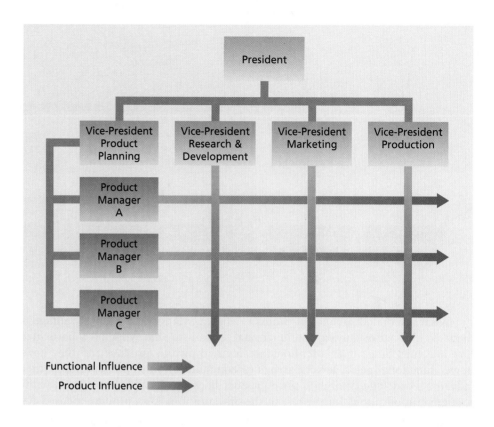

On the other hand, a matrix could be based on shorter-term projects. NASA uses this system, as do many consulting firms and research labs. The cross-functional team that designed the current Ford Mustang (Chapter 7) drew members from various Ford functions (e.g., styling, marketing, engineering) to support this project. When the design was completed, members went on to other assignments.

The matrix system is quite elegant when it works well. Ideally, it provides a degree of *balance* between the abstract demands of the product or project and the people who actually do the work, resulting in a better outcome. Also, it is very flexible. People can be moved around as project flow dictates, and projects, products, or new regions can be added without total restructuring. Being focused on a particular product or project can also lead to better communication among the representatives from the various functional areas (precisely why Ford used a cross-functional team to design the Mustang).

Two interrelated problems threaten the matrix structure. First, there is no guarantee that product or project managers will see eye-to-eye with various functional managers. This can create conflict that reduces the advantages of the matrix. Next, employees assigned to a product or project team in essence report to two managers, their functional manager and their product or project manager. This violation of a classical management principle (every employee should have only one boss) can result in role conflict and stress, especially at performance review time. The upshot of this is that managers need to be well trained under matrix structures. In your authors' opinion, some of the bad press that matrix designs received stems from their early application in technical environments where neither functional mangers nor project managers had well-developed people-management skills.

Other Forms of Departmentation. Several other forms of departmentation also exist.[7] Two of these are simply variations on product departmentation. One is geographic departmentation. Under **geographic departmentation**, relatively

Ford Motor Co.
www.ford.com

Geographic departmentation.
Relatively self-contained units deliver an organization's products or services in a specific geographic territory.

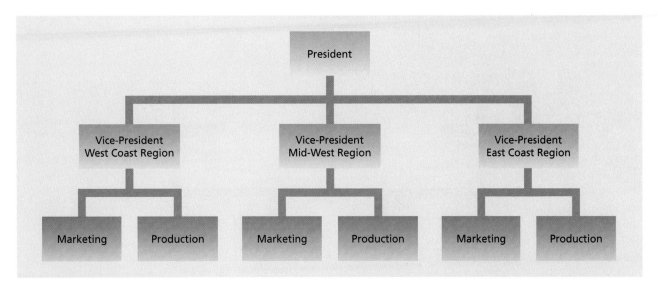

Exhibit 14.5
Geographic departmentation.

self-contained units deliver the organization's products or services in specific geographic territories (Exhibit 14.5). This form of departmentation shortens communication channels, allows the organization to cater to regional tastes, and gives some appearance of local control to clients and customers. National retailers, insurance companies, and oil companies generally exhibit geographic departmentation.

Another form of departmentation closely related to product departmentation is customer departmentation. Under **customer departmentation,** relatively self-contained units deliver the organization's products or services to specific customer groups (Exhibit 14.6). The obvious goal is to provide better service to each customer group through specialization. For example, many banks have commercial lending divisions that are separate from the consumer loan operations. Universities might have separate graduate and undergraduate divisions. An engineering firm might have separate divisions to cater to civilian and military customers. In general, the advantages and disadvantages of geographic and customer departmentation parallel those for product departmentation.

Customer departmentation.
Relatively self-contained units deliver an organization's products or services to specific customer groups.

Finally, we should recognize that few organizations represent "pure" examples of functional, product, geographic, or customer departmentation. It is not unusual to see **hybrid departmentation,** which involves some combination of these structures. For example, a manufacturing firm might retain human resources, finance, and legal services in a functional form at headquarters but use product departmentation to organize separate production and sales staffs for each product. Similarly, McDonald's and Wal-Mart centralize many activities at their respective headquarters but also have geographic divisions that cater to regional tastes and make for efficient distribution. The hybrids attempt to capitalize on the strengths of various structures, while avoiding the weaknesses of others.

Hybrid departmentation. A structure based on some mixture of functional, product, geographic, or customer departmentation.

Basic Methods of Coordinating Divided Labour

When the tasks that will help the organization achieve its goals have been divided among individuals and departments, they must be coordinated so that goal accomplishment is actually realized. We can identify five basic methods of **coordination,** which is a process of facilitating timing, communication, and feedback.[8]

Coordination. A process of facilitating timing, communication, and feedback among work tasks.

Direct Supervision. This is a very traditional form of coordination. Working through the chain of command, designated supervisors or managers coordinate

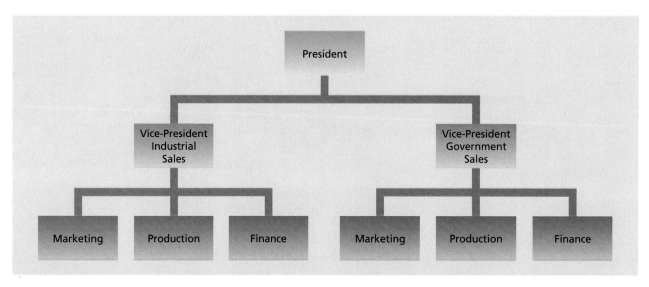

Exhibit 14.6
Customer departmentation.

the work of their subordinates. For instance, a production supervisor coordinates the work of his or her subordinates. In turn, the production superintendent coordinates the activities of all the supervisors. This method of coordination is closely associated with our discussion of leadership in Chapter 9.

Standardization of Work Processes. Some jobs are so routine that the technology itself provides a means of coordination. Little direct supervision is necessary for these jobs to be coordinated. The automobile assembly line provides a good example. When a car comes by, worker X bolts on the left A-frame assembly, and worker Y bolts on the right assembly. These workers do not have to interact, and they require minimal supervision. Work processes can also be standardized by rules and regulations. McDonald's stringent routine for constructing a burger is such an example.

Standardization of Outputs. Even when direct supervision is minimal and work processes are not standardized, coordination can be achieved through the standardization of work outputs. Concern shifts from how the work is done to ensuring that the work meets certain physical or economic standards. For instance, workers in a machine shop might be required to construct complex valves that require a mixture of drilling, lathe work, and finishing. The physical specifications of the valves will dictate how this work is to be coordinated. Standardization of outputs is often used to coordinate the work of separate product or geographic divisions. Frequently, top management assigns each division a profit target. These standards ensure that each division "pulls its weight" in contributing to the overall profit goals. Thus, budgets are a form of standardizing outputs.

Standardization of Skills. Even when work processes and output cannot be standardized, and direct supervision is unfeasible, coordination can be achieved through standardization of skills. This is seen very commonly in the case of technicians and professionals. For example, a large surgery team can often coordinate its work with minimal verbal communication because of its high degree of interlocked training—surgeons, anesthesiologists, and nurses all know what to expect from each other because of their standard training. MBA programs are often designed to provide some standardized skills (e.g., the ability to read a balance sheet) to people with different functional specialties.

Mutual Adjustment. Mutual adjustment relies on informal communication to coordinate tasks. Paradoxically, it is useful for coordinating the most simple and the most complicated divisions of labour. For example, imagine a small florist shop that consists of the owner-operator, a shop assistant, and a delivery person. It is very likely that these individuals will coordinate their work through informal processes, mutually adjusting to each other's needs. At the other extreme, consider the top executive team of virtually any corporation. Such teams are generally composed of people with a variety of skills and backgrounds (e.g., finance, marketing) and tend to be preoccupied with very nonroutine problems. Again, mutual adjustment would be necessary to coordinate their efforts because standardization would be impossible.

Now that we have reviewed the five basic methods of coordinating divided labour, a few comments are in order. First, as we see in Exhibit 14.7, the methods can be crudely ordered in terms of the degree of *discretion* they permit individual workers in terms of task performance. Applied strictly, direct supervision permits little discretion. Standardization of processes and outputs permits successively more discretion. (However, clever workers can "beat" these forms of standardization.) Finally, standardization of skills and mutual adjustment put even more control into the hands of those who are actually doing the work. Obviously, W.L. Gore leans toward the right of the continuum.

Notice that just as division of labour affects the design of jobs, so does the method of coordination employed. As we move from the left side to the right side of the continuum of coordination, there is greater potential for jobs to be designed in an enriched manner. By the same token, an improper coordination strategy can destroy the intrinsic motivation of a job. Traditionally, much work performed by professionals (e.g., scientists and engineers) is coordinated by their own skill standardization. If the manager of a research lab decides to coordinate work with a high degree of direct supervision, the motivating potential of the scientists' jobs might be damaged. *The manager* is doing the work that *they* should be doing.

The use of the various methods of coordination tends to vary across different parts of the organization. These differences in coordination stem from the way labour has been divided. As we noted, upper management relies heavily on mutual adjustment for coordination. Where tasks are more routine, such as in the lower part of the production subunit, we tend to see coordination via direct supervision or standardization of work processes or outputs.[9] Advisory subunits staffed by professionals, such as a legal department or a marketing research group, often rely on a combination of skill standardization and mutual adjustment.

Finally, methods of coordination may change as task demands change. Under peacetime conditions or routine wartime conditions, the army relies heavily on direct supervision through a strict chain of command. However, this method of coordination can prove ineffective for fighting units under heavy fire. Here, we might see a sergeant with a radio instructing a captain where to direct artillery fire. This reversal of the chain of command is indicative of mutual adjustment.

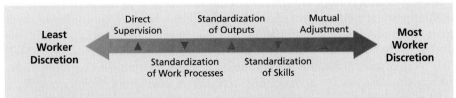

Exhibit 14.7
Methods of coordination as a continuum of worker discretion.

Source: From Mintzberg, H. (1979). *The structuring of organizations: A synthesis of the research.* Englewood Cliffs, NJ: Prentice-Hall, p.198. © 1979. Reprinted by permission of Prentice-Hall, Inc., Englewood Cliffs, NJ.

Similarly, the trend toward self-managed work teams (Chapter 7) downplays direct supervision and focuses on mutual adjustment among team members.

Other Methods of Coordination

The forms of coordination we discussed above are very basic, in that almost every organization uses them. After all, when do we see an organization that *does not* exhibit some supervision, some standardization, and some talking things out? Sometimes, however, coordination problems are such that more customized, elaborate mechanisms are necessary to achieve coordination. This is especially true when we are speaking of lateral coordination across highly differentiated departments. Recall that the managers of such departments might vary greatly in goals, time spans, and interpersonal orientation. Figuratively at least, they often "speak different languages." The process of attaining coordination across differentiated departments usually goes by the special name of **integration**.[10] Good integration achieves coordination without reducing the differences that enable each department to do its own job well.[11] For example, in a high-technology firm, we do not *want* production and engineering to be so cosy that innovative tension is lost.[12]

> **Integration.** The process of attaining coordination across differentiated departments.

In ascending order of elaboration, three methods of achieving integration include the use of liaison roles, task forces, and full-time integrators.[13]

Liaison Roles. A **liaison role** is occupied by a person in one department who is assigned, as part of his or her job, to achieve coordination with another department. In other words, one person serves as a part-time link between two departments. Sometimes the second department might reciprocate by nominating its own liaison person. For example, in a university library, reference librarians might be required to serve as liaison people for certain academic departments or schools. In turn, an academic department might assign a faculty member to "touch base" with its liaison in the library. Sometimes, liaison people might actually be located physically in the corresponding department.

> **Liaison role.** A person is assigned to help achieve coordination between his or her department and another department.

Task Forces and Teams. When coordination problems arise that involve several departments simultaneously, liaison roles are not very effective. **Task forces** are temporary groups set up to solve coordination problems across several departments. Representatives from each department are included on a full-time or part-time basis, but when adequate integration is achieved, the task force is disbanded. Citicorp, Xerox, and Ford are firms that have made extensive use of task forces.

> **Task forces.** Temporary groups set up to solve coordination problems across several departments.

Self-managed and cross-functional teams (Chapter 7) are also an effective means of achieving coordination. Such teams require interaction among employees who might otherwise operate in an independent vacuum. Cross-functional teams are especially useful in achieving coordination for new product development and introduction.

Integrators. **Integrators** are organizational members who are permanently installed between two departments that are in clear need of coordination. In a sense, they are full-time problem solvers. Integrators are especially useful for dealing with conflict between (1) highly interdependent departments, (2) which have very diverse goals and orientations, (3) in a very ambiguous environment. Such a situation occurs in many high-technology companies.[14] For example, a solid-state electronics firm might introduce new products almost every month. This is a real strain on the production department, which might need the assistance of the design scientists to implement a production run. The scientists, on the other hand, rely on production to implement last-minute changes due to the rapidly changing technology. This situation badly requires coordination.

> **Integrators.** Organizational members permanently assigned to facilitate coordination between departments.

Integrators usually report directly to the executive to whom the heads of the two departments report. Ideally, they are rewarded according to the success of both units. A special kind of person is required for this job, since he or she has great responsibility but no direct authority in either department. The integrator must be unbiased, "speak the language" of both departments, and rely heavily on expert power.[15] An engineer with excellent interpersonal skills might be an effective integrator for the electronics firm.

Before continuing, please consider the You Be the Manager.

McDonald's Restaurants
www.mcdonalds.com

you be the manager

Organizational Structure and Service Excellence

At McDonald's, nothing is left to chance or voluntarism, from layout to equipment, to the behaviour of staff.

Many organizations now realize that service quality and excellence can provide them with a competitive advantage. Organizations that can differentiate themselves in terms of unique service activities can also improve their competitiveness. For example, even a bread manufacturer whose product is the same as those of the competitors can have an advantage over them by managing distribution and other service elements more effectively.

Service quality can be understood in terms of a number of key criteria that customers use to evaluate service quality. The criteria include reliability, responsiveness, competence, courtesy, communication, and understanding and knowing the customer. Two companies known for service quality are McDonald's restaurants and Ritz-Carlton Hotels. Interestingly, the approach taken by these two organizations to service excellence is very different. At McDonald's, for example, nothing is left to chance or voluntarism, from layout, to equipment, to the behaviour of the staff. All this is dictated in a detailed operations manual developed at company headquarters. The manual provides instructions for training employees how to pre-

sent themselves, what to say to customers, and how to do their jobs. For example, strict grooming standards require that men keep their hair short and their shoes black and polished, and women are expected to wear hair nets and to use only very light makeup. McDonald's standards and procedures have contributed to the company's worldwide success.

Service excellence is also a major concern for Ritz-Carlton Hotels, a winner of the Baldridge Award for quality. Employees at Ritz-Carlton are part of a team, and they are empowered to do whatever is necessary to satisfy a customer. And depending on the level of the employee, this means spending up to $4,000 to make something right for a customer. Employees and managers at Ritz-Carlton Hotels expect each other to do whatever it takes to delight hotel guests.

Clearly, McDonald's and Ritz-Carlton have different approaches for delivering service excellence, and they also have different organizational structures that are designed to ensure that they meet customers' expectations and provide quality service. Failure to meet customer expectations can be the result of an inadequate organizational structure. For example, the consumer-products company Procter & Gamble Co. had a product departmentation organization structure. In particular, seven sales representatives, known as the Seven Dwarfs, each managed a specific product line, such as laundry detergent. This meant that each sales representative would make separate calls on retailers, and they rarely communicated with each other. As a result, retailers had to order each P&G product separately. Further, because each product line followed its own policies, retailers had to purchase each product according to a particular policy. For example, Tide detergent might be delivered in cases as ordered, but to get a reasonable price for Charmin, each store would have to take a full truckload, even if the product would sit in the retailer's warehouse.

COM DEV, an international manufacturer of space and ground-based wireless communications products located in Cambridge, Ontario, saw its stock soar from $8.25 to $40.25 within 10 months of going public. The future looked bright for the company, which was expected to continue to prosper. However, within just a short period of time, the company's revenue began to decline and its shares began to sharply fall and reached levels below $5. One of the major reasons noted for COM DEV's decline is bungled customer relations and the way the company deals with customers. COM DEV's organizational structure is a classic product departmentation, that is, the company is organized according to separate functions, including an engineering group, a sales group, a marketing group, a manufacturing group, and so on. Unfortunately, this presented problems when dealing with customers and made it difficult to determine who was responsible and accountable for failures in customer service.

Could these companies improve customer service by changing the organizational structure? You be the manager.

1. What are the structural characteristics required for service quality at McDonald's and Ritz-Carlton Hotels?

2. How can Proctor & Gamble Co. and COM DEV change their organizational structures to improve service quality?

To find out more about the structure of these organizations and customer service, see The Manager's Notebook.

Sources: Ritzer. G. (1993). *The McDonaldization of society*. Thousand Oaks, CA: Pine Forge Press; North, D. (1998, December 24; 1999, January 8). Lost in space. *Canadian Business*, pp. 45-48; Narisetti, R. (1997, January 15). Too many choices: P&G, seeing shoppers wee being confused, overhauls marketing. *The Wall Street Journal*, pp. A1, A8; Horwitz, F. M., & Neville, M. A. (1996). Organization design for service excellence: A review of the literature. *Human Resource Management*, 35, pp. 471-492; Schneider, B., & Bowen, D. E. (1995). *Winning the Service Game*. Boston, MA: Harvard Business School Press.

Traditional Structural Characteristics

Every organization is unique in the exact way that it divides and coordinates labour. Few business firms, hospitals, or schools have perfectly identical structures. What is needed, then, is some efficient way to summarize the effects of the vertical and horizontal division of labour and its coordination on the structure of the organization. Over the years, management scholars and practising managers have agreed on a number of characteristics that summarize the structure of organizations.[16]

Span of Control

Span of control. The number of subordinates supervised by a superior.

The **span of control** is the number of subordinates supervised by a superior. There is one essential fact about span of control: The larger the span, the less *potential* there is for coordination by direct supervision. As the span increases, the attention that a supervisor can devote to each subordinate decreases. When work tasks are routine, coordination of labour through standardization of work processes or output often substitutes for direct supervision. Thus, at lower levels in production units, it is not unusual to see spans of control ranging to over 20. In the managerial ranks, tasks are less routine, and adequate time is necessary for informal mutual adjustment. As a result, spans at the upper levels tend to be smaller. Also, at lower organizational levels, workers with only one or a few specialties report to a supervisor. For instance, an office supervisor might supervise only clerks. As we climb the hierarchy, workers with radically different specialties might report to the boss. For example, the president might have to deal with vice-presidents of human resources, finance, production, and marketing. Again, the complexity of this task might dictate smaller spans.[17]

Flat versus Tall

Holding size constant, a **flat organization** has relatively few levels in its hierarchy of authority, while a **tall organization** has many levels. Thus, flatness versus tallness is an index of the vertical division of labour. Again, holding size constant, it should be obvious that flatness and tallness are associated with the average span of control. This is shown in Exhibit 14.8. Both schematized organizations have 31 members. However, the taller one has five hierarchical levels and an average span of two, while the flatter one has three levels and an average span of five. Flatter structures tend to push decision-making powers downward in the organization because a given number of decisions are apportioned among fewer levels. Also, flatter structures generally enhance vertical communication and coordination.

Radical differences in organizational height can exist even within industries. For example, at Ford and GM, the number of levels between the chief executive and plant workers varies between 17 and 22. At Toyota, only seven levels intervene.[18] Some analysts have argued that this reduced height is, in part, responsible for the ability of the Japanese manufacturer to get products to market more quickly. In general, there has been a North American trend toward flatter organizations, especially with downsizing, a topic we will cover shortly.

Formalization

Formalization refers to the extent to which work roles are highly defined by the organization.[19] A very formalized organization tolerates little variability in the way members perform their tasks. Some formalization stems from the nature of the job itself; the work requirements of the assembly line provide a good example of this. More interesting, however, is formalization that stems from rules,

Flat organization. An organization with relatively few levels in its hierarchy of authority.

Tall organization. An organization with relatively many levels in its hierarchy of authority.

Formalization. The extent to which work roles are highly defined by an organization.

Exhibit 14.8
The relationship between span of control and organizational flatness and tallness.

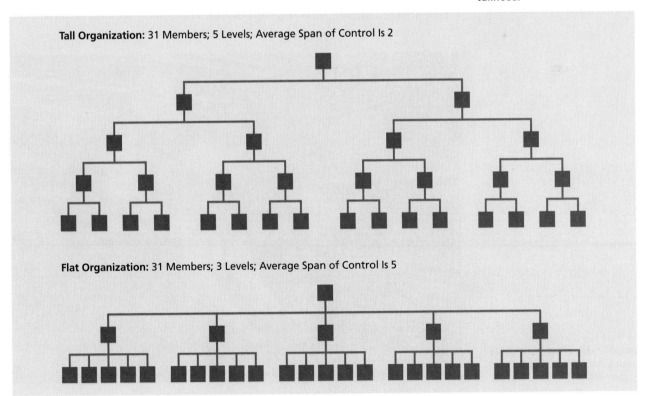

Tall Organization: 31 Members; 5 Levels; Average Span of Control Is 2

Flat Organization: 31 Members; 3 Levels; Average Span of Control Is 5

regulations, and procedures that the firm or institution chooses to implement. Detailed, written job descriptions, thick procedure manuals, and the requirement to "put everything in writing" are evidence of such formalization. Many government organizations use this method of formalization.

Sometimes, formalization seems excessive. Perhaps this is why so many fast food employees ignore the hair-net rule. A U.S. Energy Department document detailing how to change a light bulb in a radioactive area is 317 pages long and specifies duties for 43 people.[20]

Centralization

Centralization. The extent to which decision-making power is localized in a particular part of an organization.

Centralization refers to the extent to which decision-making power is localized in a particular part of the organization. In the most centralized organization, the power for all key decisions would rest in a single individual, such as the president. In a more decentralized organization, decision-making power would be dispersed down through the hierarchy and across departments. One observer suggests that limitations to individual brainpower often prompt decentralization:

> How can the Baghdad salesperson explain the nature of his clients to the Birmingham manager? Sometimes the information can be transmitted to one centre, but a lack of cognitive capacity (brainpower) precludes it from being comprehended there. How can the president of the conglomerate corporation possibly learn about, say, 100 different product lines? Even if a report could be written on each, he would lack the time to study them all.[21]

Of course, the information-processing capacity of executives is not the only factor that dictates degree of centralization. Some organizations consciously pursue a more participative climate through decentralization. Bill Gore thought this way very explicitly. In others, top management might wish to maintain greater control and opt for stronger centralization. One of Ray Kroc's innovations was not to permit *regional* franchises that could grow powerful and challenge the

At Food Lion, buying is centralized, but local managers have autonomy to stay close to customers.

firm's basic principles.[22] The successful North Carolina-based supermarket chain Food Lion has generally decentralized with growth, giving local managers more autonomy in order to stay close to customers and cater to regional differences. However, the buying function and store design and construction have remained centralized to maintain efficiency and contain costs. Also, the lighting of all 1,041 stores in 14 states is centralized with computer control.[23]

Food Lion Inc.
www.foodlion.com

Hewlett-Packard, producer of computers, printers, and interactive video, has long relied on the merits of decentralization to foster high tech innovation and creativity:

> H-P executives have an enviable degree of freedom. For one thing, they are authorized to reinvest the capital their businesses generate. They can attack markets in their own ways, rather than slavishly wait for orders that reduce them to just one part of a grand corporate strategy. Says video products general manager [Jim] Olson: "We don't feel an allegiance to any other part of H-P. We feel an allegiance to the customer."[24]

Degree of centralization should put decision-making power where the best *knowledge* is located. Often, this means decentralizing functions with direct customer contact, while centralizing functions that have a more internal orientation (e.g., MIS).

Complexity

Complexity refers to the extent to which organizations divide labour vertically, horizontally, and geographically.[25] A fairly simple organization will have few management levels (vertical division) and not many separate job titles (horizontal division). In addition, jobs will be grouped into a small number of departments, and work will be performed in only one physical location (geographic division). At the other extreme, a very complex organization will be tall, will have a large number of job titles and departments, and might be spread around the world. The essential characteristic of complexity is *variety*—as the organization becomes more complex, it has more kinds of people performing more kinds of tasks in more places, whether these places are departments or geographic territories.

Complexity. The extent to which an organization divides labour vertically, horizontally, and geographically.

Summarizing Structure—Organic versus Mechanistic

Do the various structural characteristics that we have been reviewing have any natural relationship to one another? Is there any way to summarize how they tend to go together?

If you think back to the very first chapter of the book, you will recall how early prescriptions about management tended to stress employee specialization, along with a very high degree of control and coordination. These themes were common to the classical management theorists, Taylor's Scientific Management, and Weber's bureaucracy. On the other hand, you will also recall how the human relations movement detected some of the problems that specialization and control can lead to—boredom, resentment, and low motivation. Consequently, these human relations advocates favoured more flexible management systems, open communication, employee participation, and so on (See "Global Focus: *Bureaucracy, Japanese Style: New United Motor Manufacturing, Inc.*").

global focus

Bureaucracy, Japanese Style: New United Motor Manufacturing, Inc.

Highly bureaucratic, regimented work environments have often been criticized as being alienating and demotivating. Paul Adler set out to study an apparent exception to this assumption, New United Motor Manufacturing, Inc. (NUMMI). NUMMI is a joint venture between Toyota and General Motors. Located in Fremont, California, it started operation in 1984 and currently produces the Chevrolet Geo Prizm, Toyota Corolla, and Toyota Tacoma pickup truck. The design and operation of NUMMI are based on the Toyota Production System, a "Japanese management" style developed at Toyota's Takaoka plant in Japan. The majority of NUMMI's unionized workforce was employed at a former GM plant on the same site. This plant had a terrible record for quality, productivity, and labour relations. When closed in 1982, it often suffered from absenteeism rates of more than 20 percent on Mondays and Fridays and had hundreds of unresolved grievances. Shortly after going on line, NUMMI achieved higher productivity than any GM plant. The quality of its production, measured by independent standards, was also remarkably high. And what about the workforce? Absenteeism has averaged about 3 percent, turnover is low, grievances are few, and employees report high satisfaction on company attitude surveys. About 90 percent of the workforce participates in the company suggestion system.

This record is somewhat surprising given the extremely mechanistic design and tight work discipline at NUMMI. The jobs are very regimented, even by assembly-line standards. They are very narrow in scope, and most take less than a minute to complete. Gesture-by-gesture standardization is the rule. Formalized procedures exist for ensuring that these work methods are identical across employees and shifts. Job cycle times are very low, although most employees do rotate through two or three jobs on a given day. Penalties for absenteeism are strict.

Adler notes that some critics of Japanese management techniques have cited ultra-Taylorism and "management by stress." Although the jobs at NUMMI are ultra-Tayloristic, Adler found little evidence of management by stress. His research found several reasons for NUMMI's success despite its mostly mechanistic structure. For one thing, the job design at the plant is not handed down by an industrial engineering department, as is typical in most plants. Rather, workers are taught to time their own jobs with stop watches and to compare various procedures in terms of efficiency. In his terms, this is democratic Taylorism rather than despotic Taylorism. If a more efficient process is discovered, it is formalized. Also, management has been effective in instilling a culture that stresses the efficiencies of bureaucracy for manufacturing standardized products while deemphasizing its use as a method of controlling workers. Adler terms the results a "learning bureaucracy," a system in which both employees and managers see the wisdom of continuous improvement and actually have a standardized procedure for achieving it.

Sources: Adler, P. S. (1993). The 'learning bureaucracy': New United Motor Manufacturing, Inc. *Research in Organizational Behaviour*, 15, pp. 111–194; Adler, P. S., & Cole, R. E. (1993, Spring). Designed for learning: A tale of two auto plants. *Sloan Management Review*, pp. 85–94.

Mechanistic structures.
Organizational structures characterized by tallness, specialization, centralization, and formalization.

Organic structures.
Organizational structures characterized by flatness, low specialization, low formalization, and decentralization.

In general, the classical theorists tended to favour **mechanistic structures.**[26] As Exhibit 14.9 demonstrates, these structures tend toward tallness, narrow spans, specialization, high centralization, and high formalization. The other structural and human resources aspects in the exhibit complement these basic structural prescriptions. By analogy, the organization is structured as a mechanical device, each part serving a separate function, each part closely coordinated with the others. Speaking generally, functional structures tend to be rather mechanistic.

We can contrast mechanistic structures with organic structures. As shown in Exhibit 14.9, **organic structures** tend to favour wider spans, fewer authority levels, less specialization, less formalization, and decentralization. Flexibility and informal communication are favoured over rigidity and the strict chain of command. Thus, organic structures are more in line with the dictates of the human relations movement. Speaking generally, the matrix form is organic.

The labels *mechanistic* and *organic* represent theoretical extremes, and structures can and do fall between these extremes. But is one of these structures supe-

Exhibit 14.9
Mechanistic and organic structures.

Organizational Characteristics	Types of Organization Structure	
Index	**Organic**	**Mechanistic**
Span of control	Wide	Narrow
Number of levels of authority	Few	Many
Ratio of administrative to production personnel	High	Low
Range of time span over which an employee can commit resources	Long	Short
Degree of centralization in decision making	Low	High
Proportion of persons in one unit having opportunity to interact with persons in other units	High	Low
Quantity of formal rules	Low	High
Specificity of job goals	Low	High
Specificity of required activities	Low	High
Content of communications	Advice and information	Instructions and decisions
Range of compensation	Narrow	Wide
Range of skill levels	Narrow	Wide
Knowledge-based authority	High	Low
Position-based authority	Low	High

Source: From Seiler, J. A. (1967). *Systems analysis in organizational behavior.* Homewood, IL: Irwin, p. 168. © Richard D. Irwin, Inc. 1967. This exhibit is an adaptation of one prepared by Paul R. Lawrence and Jay W. Lorsch in an unpublished "Working Paper on Scientific Transfer and Organizational Structure," 1963. The latter, in turn, draws heavily on criteria suggested by W. Evans. "Indices of the Hierarchical Structure of Industrial Organizations," *Management Science*, Vol. IX (1963), pp. 468–77, Burns and Stalker, *op. cit.*, and Woodward, *op. cit.*, as well as those suggested by R. H. Hall, "Intraorganizational Structure Variables," *Administrative Science Quarterly*, Vol. IX (1962), pp. 295–308.

rior to the other? To answer this, pause for a moment and consider the structures of a fast-food restaurant chain like McDonald's and the structure of W.L. Gore & Associates discussed in the chapter-opening vignette. At the restaurant level, McDonald's is structured very mechanistically. This structure makes perfect sense for the rather routine task of delivering basic convenience food to thousands of people every day and doing it with uniform quality and speed. Of course, McDonald's headquarters, which deals with less routine tasks (e.g., product development, strategic planning), would be more organically structured. W.L. Gore & Associates develops and manufactures products that are highly dependent on fast-changing high technology. Its founder also despised bureaucracy. An organic structure suits Gore perfectly.

In general, more mechanistic structures are called for when an organization's environment is more stable and its technology is more routine. Organic structures tend to work better when the environment is less stable and the technology is less routine. We will examine these matters in more detail in the next chapter. For now, it is enough to recognize that there is no "one best way" to organize.

Network and Virtual Organizations

Recent years have seen the advent of new, more organic organizational structures. Global competition and deregulation, as well as advances in technology and communications, have motivated these structures. Typically, the removal of unnecessary bureaucracy and the decentralization of decision making result in a more adaptable organization. A more extreme example is the increasing existence of network organizations. In a **network organization,** various functions are coordinated as much by market mechanisms as by managers and formal lines of

Network organization. Liaisons between specialist organizations that rely strongly on market mechanisms for coordination.

authority.[27] That is, emphasis is placed on who can do what most effectively and economically rather than on fixed ties dictated by an organizational chart. All the assets necessary to produce a finished product or service are present in the network as a whole, not held in-house by one firm. Ideally, the network members cooperate, share information, and customize their services to meet the needs of the network.

In stable networks, core firms that are departmentalized by function, product, or some other factor contract out some functions to favoured partners so that they can concentrate on the things that they do best (see the left of Exhibit 14.10). DaimlerChrysler, for instance, has its car seats supplied by an upstream firm that also does all the research associated with seating.

The most interesting networks are dynamic or virtual organizations, such as that illustrated in the right portion of Exhibit 14.10. In a **virtual organization** an alliance of independent companies share skills, costs, and access to one another's markets. Thus, they consist of a network of continually evolving independent companies.[28] A "broker" firm with a good idea invents a network in which a large amount of the work is done by other network partners who might change over time or projects. Each partner in a virtual organization contributes only in its area of core competencies. Contemporary book publishers are good examples. These firms do not employ authors, print books, or distribute books. Rather, they specialize in contracting authors for a particular project, providing developmental assistance, and marketing the final product. Printing, distribution, and some editorial and design work are handled by others in the network. Such networks are not new, as they have been used for years in the fashion and film industries. However, more firms in other industries, such as computers and biotechnology, are now adopting network forms.

As indicated, a key advantage of the network form is its flexibility and adaptability. A virtual organization is even more flexible than a matrix. Networks also allow organizations to specialize in what they do best. In its network, Daimler

Virtual organization. A network of continually evolving independent organizations that share skills, costs, and access to one another's markets.

Exhibit 14.10
Types of network organizations.

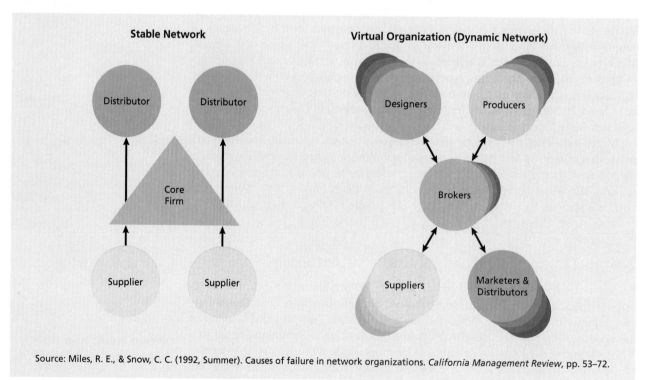

Source: Miles, R. E., & Snow, C. C. (1992, Summer). Causes of failure in network organizations. *California Management Review*, pp. 53–72.

Chrysler has intentionally positioned itself as a car manufacturer, not a car seat manufacturer. In turn, its supplier has a strong incentive to specialize in its product because DaimlerChrysler is a good, stable customer.

Network and virtual organizations face some special problems.[29] Stable networks can deteriorate when the companies dealing with the core firm devote so much of their effort to this firm that they are isolated from normal market demands. This can make them "lazy," resulting in a loss of their technological edge. Virtual organizations lose their organic advantage when they become legalistic, secretive, and too binding of the other partners. The computer industry has experienced this problem with its network arrangements. It is now believed that in order for network organizations to be successful, they must adopt a spherical structure. To find out more, see "In Focus: *The Multifirm Spherical Network.*"

ABB Group
www.abb.com

The Multifirm Spherical Network

Technical and Computer Graphics (TCG), located in Sydney, Australia, a group of small companies that, by practising sophisticated entrepreneurship, project leadership and self-management, has become the largest privately owned computer service business in Australia. It is a highly interactive network of 24 companies with combined annual revenues of approximately $50 million and a staff of about 200. TCG is considered to be one of its country's most significant innovators in portable data terminals, computer graphics, simulators, bar-coding systems, electronic data interchange, electronic identification tags, and other applications of information and communications technology.

Within TCG, new product development (and hence network expansion) is called "triangulation," meaning that it involves a three-cornered partnership among a TCG firm, a similar technology-based firm outside TCG, and a major customer. The triangular product-development process typically involves five key steps: (1) Identify the market niche; (2) find a developmental partner; (3) locate a major customer; (4) involve other TCG firms; and (5) extend the triangle in new directions.

In a multifirm spherical network, such as that used by TCG, every individual is expected to be an entrepreneur and sometime project leader. Moreover, every individual in the various TCG firms works closely, as part of a self-managed team, with other professionals in the network. Although the total network staff of 200 individuals is small by most company comparisons, the organization has global reach. And, perhaps most importantly, TCG has few rules and no pyramidical management hierarchy.

TCG's success, based on the widespread application of technical, entrepreneurial, and self-management skills, provides evidence of how a group of small firms can hook themselves together to form a highly flexible spherical network. But can

this structure work in large companies? The evidence suggests that it can.

A good example of a well-developed, large-company spherical network is that operated by electrical equipment manufacturer ABB (Asea Brown Boveri). Although ABB has over 200,000 employees, all work in small organizational units. The average plant employs fewer than 200 workers, and most of the company's 5,000 profit centres contain only 40 to 50 people. Even though the members of most ABB plants and offices do not directly engage in entrepreneurial activities, they come into contact with both external customers and internal partners through ABB's equivalent of global trading companies, called business areas. Thus, like TCG, virtually every member of the firm is close to the customer and responsive to market developments. ABB also has minimized the amount of rule-guided behaviour among its internal units, substituting instead a series of market-oriented processes and rewards that encourage cooperation and mutually beneficial actions.

The overall success of a spherical network organization hinges on management's' willingness to put people in this type of arrangement and the ability to make such an arrangement work once it has been designed. This requires a human resource management philosophy in which employees act as partners in their own development. Managers, in turn, must not only facilitate employee development but also locate opportunities for employees to apply their continuously expanding knowledge and ability.

Source: Excerpted from Miles, R. E., & Snow, C. C. (1995, Spring). The new network firm: A spherical structure built on a human investment philosophy. *Organizational Dynamics*, pp. 5-18.

The Modular Organization

In today's highly uncertain and fast-changing environment, many organizations are realizing that there are advantages to not becoming a large and vertically integrated bureaucracy. Instead, they focus on a few core activities that they do best, such as designing and marketing computers, and let other companies perform all the other activities. A **modular organization** is an organization that performs a few core functions and outsources noncore activities to specialists and suppliers. Services that are often outsourced include the manufacturing of parts, trucking, catering, data processing, and accounting. Thus, modular organizations are like hubs that are surrounded by networks of suppliers that can be added or removed as needed. And unlike a virtual organization, in which the participating firms give up part of their control and are interdependent, the modular organization maintains complete strategic control. [30]

By outsourcing noncore activities, modular organizations are able to keep unit costs low and develop new products more rapidly. It also allows them to use their capital in areas where they have a competitive advantage, such as design and marketing. This has enabled companies such as Dell Computer and Nike to experience large and rapid growth in a relatively short period of time, as they have not had to invest in fixed assets. Nike and Reebok concentrate on designing and marketing high-tech fashionable sports and fitness footwear. However, Nike has limited production facilities and Reebok does not even own a plant. Both organizations contract out production to suppliers in countries with low-cost labour, such as Taiwan, South Korea, and other Asian countries. [31]

Modular organizations in the electronics industry buy their products already built or they buy the parts from suppliers and then assemble them. Dell Computer, for example, assembles computers from outsourced parts, and this allows them to focus on marketing and service. Because it does not own any plants, Dell can afford to invest in areas such as training salespeople and service technicians.[32] The automotive industry in North America has also begun to be heavily involved in outsourcing and to become increasingly modular. A major player in the outsourcing of auto parts is Magna International which is the world's leading auto-parts supplier. Consider DaimlerChrysler's minivan. Magna designs, engineers, and manufactures a great deal of the vehicle, including the seats, mirrors,

Modular organization. An organization that performs a few core functions and outsources noncore activities to specialists and suppliers.

Dell Computers
www.dell.ca

Nike
www.nike.com

Modular organizational structures enable organizations to keep unit costs low and develop new products rapidly by outsourcing noncore activities and focusing on what they do best.

door panels, locks, and more. An increasing number of auto makers are now outsourcing major parts of their vehicles to parts suppliers like Magna in an effort to improve efficiency and quality. The trend is also catching on Europe and Japan.[33] For example, Toyota has achieved great success by relying on a network of suppliers.[34] Outsourcing is also taking place among auto parts suppliers, as manufacturers of smaller parts are providing the supplies for those who make the larger parts.[35]

Although there are many advantages of the modular organization, they are also some disadvantages. Modular organizations work best when they focus on the right speciality and have good suppliers. Because they are dependent on so many outsiders, it is critical that they find suppliers who are reliable and loyal and can be trusted with trade secrets. Modular organizations also must be careful not to outsource critical technologies, which could diminish future competitive advantages. Another disadvantage of the modular organization is that it decreases the operational control of the organization due its dependence on outsiders.[36]

In summary, the modular organization is a lean and streamlined organizational structure with great flexibility making it particularly well suited to organizations in rapidly changing environments. Many modular organizations have become extremely profitable and competitive. And although modular organizational structures have been most popular in the trendy fast-paced apparel and electronics industries, other industries, such as automotive, steel, chemicals, and photographic equipment, are also becoming more modular.[37]

The Boundaryless Organization

An important outcome of the two basic dimensions to the division and coordination of labour, is that the structure of most organizations consists of a rigid vertical hierarchy and many departments. As a result, traditional organizational structures consist of boundaries or barriers that divide people at different hierarchical levels and separate those in different departments. This can be problematic to the extent that the different levels and departments are interdependent, as is usually the case in most organizations. In other words, the work in one department is dependent on and affects the performance of other departments. Such interdependence often results in open conflict. For example, in organizations with a tall vertical hierarchy, there can be conflict between employees at the lower levels and management in the upper ranks. In organizations with a functional structure, the various departments often do not communicate or coordinate their efforts even though their tasks are interdependent. Thus, the barriers that exist in traditional organizational structures can stifle productivity and innovation.[38]

General Electric's CEO Jack Welch says boundaries are crazy because they separate employees from management, and the organization from its customers and suppliers. In order to remove the vertical and horizontal boundaries in organizations, Jack Welch developed the idea of the boundaryless organization. In a **boundaryless organization**, the boundaries that divide employees, such as hierarchy, job function, and geography, as well as those that distance companies from suppliers and customers are broken down.[39] Thus, a boundaryless organization removes vertical, horizontal, and external barriers so that employees, managers, customers, and suppliers can work together, share ideas, and identify the best ideas for the organization.

What does the structure of a boundaryless organization look like? Instead of being organized around functions with many hierarchical levels, the boundaryless organization is made up of self-managing and cross-functional teams that are

Boundaryless organization. An organization that removes vertical, horizontal, and external barriers so that employees, managers, customers, and suppliers can work together, share ideas, and identify the best ideas for the organization.

organized around core business processes that are critical for satisfying customers, such as new-product development or materials handling. The teams comprise individuals from different functional areas within the organization, as well as customers and suppliers. Each business process has an owner who is in charge of the process and process performance. Thus, the traditional vertical hierarchy is flattened and replaced by layers of teams making the organization look more horizontal than vertical.[40] Information and knowledge can be quickly distributed throughout the organization and directly to where it is needed without first being filtered by a tall vertical hierarchy.[41] Boundaryless organizations are able to achieve greater integration and coordination within the organization and with external stakeholders.

A good example is Chrysler's development of the Neon before the merger with Daimler-Benz. Chrysler wanted to develop a profitable subcompact vehicle, something that it had previously been unable to do. Rather than find a partner as some other automobile makers had done, the company decided to try something new. They involved many internal and external stakeholders including personnel from different functional areas, such as engineering, marketing, purchasing, finance, and labour, as well as suppliers and consumers. By removing the boundaries between these groups and having them work together, the company was able to avoid delays that are often the result of disagreements and misunderstandings. As a result, Chrysler developed the Neon in a record 42 months at a price tag of $1.3 billion. By comparison, Ford spent $2 billion and took five years to develop the money-losing Ford Escort, and GM spent $5 billion and took seven years to develop the Saturn.[42]

While boundaryless organizations have a number of advantages including the ability to adapt to environmental changes, they have a number of disadvantages. For example, it can be difficult to overcome political and authority boundaries, and it can be time consuming to manage the democratic processes required to coordinate the efforts of many stakeholders.[43] Even General Electric realizes that it will take years before being boundaryless becomes natural.[44] Nonetheless, some believe that the boundaryless organization is the perfect organizational structure for the 21st century [45]

In summary, many of the traditional organizational structures are being replaced by more flexible structures that break down external and internal boundaries. Network or virtual organizations and modular organizations represent structures that breakdown or modify external organizational boundaries, and the boundaryless organization is an attempt to remove both external and internal boundaries. For many organizations, traditional organizational structures are no longer effective, and so they must find new ways to structure and coordinate their efforts in order to adapt to environmental changes and to remain competitive.

The Impact of Size

It is perhaps trivial to note that the giant General Motors Corporation is structured differently from a small video rental shop. But exactly how does organizational size (measured by number of employees) affect the structure of organizations?[46]

Size and Structure

In general, large organizations are more complex than small organizations.[47] For example, a small organization is unlikely to have its own legal department or market research group, and these tasks will probably be contracted out. Economies of scale enable large organizations to perform these functions themselves but with a consequent increase in the number of departments and job titles. In turn, this horizontal specialization often stimulates the need for additional complexity in the form of appointing integrators or creating planning departments. As horizontal specialization increases, management levels must be added (making the organization taller) so that spans of control do not get out of hand.[48] To repeat, size is associated with increased complexity.

Complexity means coordination problems, in spite of integrators, planning departments, and the like. This is where other structural characteristics come into play. In general, bigger organizations are less centralized than smaller organizations.[49] In a small company, the president might be involved in all but the least critical decisions. In a large company, the president would be overloaded with such decisions, and they could not be made in a timely manner. In addition, since the large organization will also be taller, top management is often too far removed from the action to make many operating decisions. How is control retained with decentralization? The answer is formalization—large organizations tend to be more formal than small organizations. Rules, regulations, and standard procedures help to ensure that decentralized decisions fall within accepted bounds.

Two further points about the relationship between size and structure should be emphasized. First, you will recall that product departmentation is often preferable to functional departmentation as the organization increases in size. Logically, then, organizations with product departmentation should exhibit more complexity and more decentralization than those with functional departmentation. A careful comparison of Exhibits 14.2 and 14.3 will confirm this logic. In the firm with the product structure, research, production, and marketing are duplicated, increasing complexity. In addition, since each product line is essentially self-contained, decisions can be made at a lower organizational level.

Finally, we should recognize that size is only one determinant of organizational structure. Even at a given size, organizations might require different structures to be maximally effective. In the next chapter, we will examine other determinants of structure, principally environmental pressures and technology.

Exhibit 14.11 summarizes the relationship between size and structural variables.

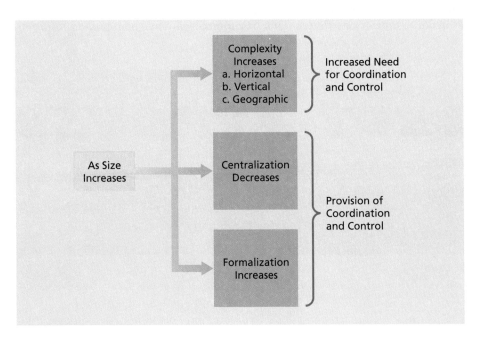

Exhibit 14.11
The relationship between size and structure.

Downsizing

A reduction in workforce size, popularly called downsizing, has been an organizational trend of the 1980s and 1990s. During this period, millions of jobs have disappeared as organizations seek to bolster efficiency and cut costs in an era of global competition, government deregulation, corporate raiding, changing consumer preferences, and advancing technologies.[50] Downsizing has a number of implications for organizational structure.

Downsizing. The intentional reduction in workforce size with the goal of improving organizational efficiency or effectiveness.

Compaq Computers
www.compaq.com

Downsizing and Structure. Downsizing might be formally defined as the intentional reduction in workforce size with the goal of improving organizational efficiency or effectiveness.[51] Notice that this definition does not imply that the organization's fortunes are necessarily in decline, although a shrinking market could motivate downsizing. In fact, Compaq Computer announced substantial downsizing during a year of record revenues and shipments in anticipation of the need to be more competitive in the future.[52]

How should downsizing affect organizational structure? It is tempting to "work backwards" through Exhibit 14.11 and simply say that as size *decreases* the firm should reduce its complexity, centralize, and become less formalized. In the case of a very simple downsizing, this logic might work. However, notice its limitations. First, some of the conditions listed above that often prompt downsizing are *new* conditions, not simply the opposite of the factors that led to organizational growth in the past. For example, deregulation has led to a completely new cast of competitors in the banking and telecommunications industries. Second, the logic of simply working backward through Exhibit 14.11 would assume that downsizing occurs proportionally in all parts of an organization. As you may know, this is not the case. White-collar managerial and staff jobs have been disproportionately reduced in the most recent downsizing, for reasons varying from high salaries to improvements in information technology. The upshot of all this is that a new downsized structure should not necessarily look like a mini version of the old structure.

Downsizing can be accomplished in a variety of ways. Although layoffs have been common, some organizations have relied on hiring freezes and natural attrition. In practice, downsizing is often accompanied by reducing horizontal or vertical complexity. Vertically, management levels have been removed to make organizations flatter. This has sometimes made sense when informa-

Many organizations have not adequately managed the structural and human consequences of downsizing. As a result, reductions in workforce size have tended not to result in long-term cost reductions or improvements in productivity.

tion technology enables the remaining managers to more effectively monitor the performance of their subordinates. Also, self-managed teams (Chapter 7) can act as substitutes for a level of management. Horizontally, functions can be combined (e.g., inspection and quality) or removed altogether by contracting them out.

Problems with Downsizing. Experience and research indicate that many organizations have not done a good job of anticipating and managing the structural and human consequences of downsizing. For instance, when faced with serious decline, organizations have a decided tendency to become more mechanistic, particularly more formalized and centralized.[53] Rules are closely enforced, and higher levels of management take part in more day-to-day decisions. This can be useful to get the organization back on track, but it can also reduce flexibility just when it is needed. A good rule to follow is to avoid unnecessary formalization or centralization of matters that might have a negative impact on customers or clients. In other words, do not allow internal tightening up to damage external relationships.

One downsizing tactic has been to greatly reduce or even to eliminate whole departments of headquarters advisory staff. For instance, a human resource department might be downsized or the legal department eliminated. Many such staff units have become bloated over the years, and they have been known to isolate top management from divisional concerns and to bureaucratize decision making. Thus, downsizing can provoke decentralization, giving line managers more power and speeding up decisions. On the other hand, some firms have eliminated such positions and then turned around and hired consultants to do the same work. Contracting work out can be a viable strategy, but it is clear that some consulting arrangements have proven more expensive than the original in-house unit.[54] A good rule to follow is to think very carefully about the *work* that needs to be done and *who* should do it before downsizing.

A common structural downsizing error has been to flatten organizations by removing management levels without considering the implications for job design and workload. A glance at Exhibit 14.8 illustrates the crux of the problem: If only the management ranks are thinned, managers have larger spans below them and less support above them. This works well if decentralization is called for and if the people in the lower ranks are ready to assume greater decision-making responsibility. It does not work well if managers are overloaded with work or are incapable of delegating to subordinates. Advanced information technology and training can sometimes assist managers in coping with increased spans of control.

Thinking in advance about the structural aspects of downsizing is not a substitute for involving employees in downsizing plans. Surprising people with workforce cuts is very likely to result in low morale, reduced personal productivity, and continuing distrust of management. Some survivors of downsizing have even reported being guilty because they retained their jobs.[55]

In summary, downsizing has the potential to improve organizational effectiveness in certain circumstances, but its impact on structure and morale must be anticipated and managed. Research has shown that contrary to expectations, downsizing does not result in cost reductions in the long run or improvements in productivity. The negative outcomes of downsizing, however, are primarily due to poor implementation, such as a lack of supporting activities. When carefully and properly implemented, downsizing can have positive consequences.[56]

A Footnote: Symptoms of Structural Problems

At the beginning of the chapter, we observed that it is sometimes difficult to appreciate the impact of organizational structure on the behaviour that occurs in organizations. Now that you have been through the basics of structure, your appreciation of this impact should be much improved. Let us conclude the chapter by considering some symptoms of structural problems in organizations.

- *Bad job design.* As we noted at several points, there is a reciprocal relationship between job design and organizational structure. Frequently, improper structural arrangements turn good jobs on paper into poor jobs in practice. A tall structure and narrow span of control in a research and development unit can reduce autonomy and turn exciting jobs into drudgery. An extremely large span of control can overload the most dedicated supervisor.

- *The right hand does not know what the left is doing.* If repeated examples of duplication of effort occur, or if parts of the organization work at cross-purposes, structure is suspect. One author gives the example of one division of a large organization laying off workers while another division was busy recruiting from the same labour pool![57] The general problem here is one of coordination and integration.

- *Persistent conflict between departments.* Managers are often inclined to attribute such conflicts to personality clashes between key personnel in the warring departments. Just as often, a failure of integration is the problem. One clue here is whether the conflict persists even when personnel changes occur.

- *Slow response times.* Ideally, labour is divided and coordinated to do business quickly. Delayed responses might be due to improper structure. Centralization might speed responses when a few decisions about a few products are required (dictating functional departmentation). Decentralization might speed responses when many decisions about many products are required (dictating product departmentation).

- *Decisions made with incomplete information.* In Chapter 11, we noted that managers generally acquire more than enough information to make decisions. After the fact, if we find that decisions have been made with incomplete information, and the information existed somewhere in the organization, structure could be at fault. It is clear that structural deficiencies were, in part, responsible for keeping top NASA administrators unaware of the mechanical problems that contributed to the explosion of the space shuttle *Challenger*.[58] This information was known to NASA personnel, but it did not move up the hierarchy properly.

- *A proliferation of committees.* Committees exist in all organizations, and they often serve as one of the more routine kinds of integrating mechanisms. However, when committee is piled on committee, or when task forces are being formed with great regularity, it is often a sign that the basic structure of the organization is being "patched up" because it does not work well.[59] A structural review might be in order, if too many people are spending too much time in committee meetings.

the manager's notebook

Organizational Structure and Service Excellence

1. Service quality and excellence are, in large part, based on an organization's strategy and how predictable or stable its outputs are. For example, some organizations like McDonald's have stable and predictable outputs and require a high degree of standardization in order to ensure service excellence. Such a "Production Line" approach is characterized by the simplification of tasks, a clear division of labour, and little decision-making discretion on the part of employees. For other organizations, such as Ritz-Carlton Hotels, the outputs are changing and unpredictable, as the outputs required to satisfy each customer can vary. Thus, service excellence involves responding to individual customers' needs. This "Empowerment Approach" of service excellence requires that employees understand and contribute to the organization's performance, are provided with the power to make decisions, information about the organization's performance, and rewards based on organization performance. Each approach has implications for organizational structure. For example, the Empowerment Approach is best suited to organizations with unpredictable outcomes and requires fewer organizational levels or a flatter organizational structure with few levels between top management and front-line employees and smaller units, both of which improve the ease of communication. Less formalization and decentralization of decision making authority is also important in order to empower employees and enable them to make decisions and respond to customer's needs, as is the case for Ritz-Carlton. These characteristics are consistent with an organic organizational structure. Organizations with predictable outputs emphasize standardization and they tend to have taller organizational structures that emphasize standardization of work processes and outputs, direct supervision, and greater formalization and centralization, which is the case for McDonald's. High levels of standardization and formalization helps McDonald's maintain uniform quality standards. These characteristics are consistent with a mechanistic organizational structure.

2. The product and departmentalization organizational structures of Proctor & Gamble and COM DEV made it difficult for them to provide quality service to their customers. As a result, they changed their structures by integrating the different product and department areas into teams that service particular customers. At Proctor & Gamble, there are no longer seven different sales representatives with a specific product line. The so-called Seven Dwarfs have been replaced by teams that consist of salespeople and experts in market research, logistics, shelf management, and manufacturing. The teams work with retailers to design promotions for local shoppers. As well, retailers now deal with only one P&G employee who handles all truck schedules. Trucks now deliver only what is needed on the basis of the retailer's sales. This has saved retailers millions of dollars and improved P&G's relationship with them. As well, surveys have shown that P&G leads all other consumer-goods companies in helping retailers become more efficient. COM DEV changed their structure in order to improve the way they deal with customers. The traditional structure that was organized according to function has been split into a series of units. Each unit now serves a major customer and is responsible for developing business, designing new products, and getting them manufactured and delivered. While COM DEV knows that it will take time to fix its problems, they are starting to see some improvements.

Ritz-Carlton Hotels
www.ritzcarlton.com

Summary

- Organizational structure is the manner in which an organization divides its labour into specific tasks and achieves coordination among these tasks. Labour is divided vertically and horizontally. Vertical division of labour concerns the apportioning of authority. Horizontal division of labour involves designing jobs and grouping them into departments. While functional departmentation locates employees with similar skills in the same department, other forms of departmentation locate employees in accordance with product, geography, or customer requirements.

- Basic methods of coordinating divided labour include direct supervision, standardization of work processes, standardization of outputs, standardization of skills, and mutual adjustment. Workers are permitted more discretion as coordination moves from direct supervision through mutual adjustment. More elaborate methods of coordination are aimed specifically at achieving integration across departments. These include liaison roles, task forces, teams, and integrators.

- Traditional structural characteristics include span of control, flatness versus tallness, formalization, centralization, and complexity. Larger organizations tend to be more complex, more formal, and less centralized than smaller organizations.

- The classical organizational theorists tended to favour mechanistic organizational structures (small spans, tall, formalized, and fairly centralized). The human relations theorists, having noted the flaws of bureaucracy, tended to favour organic structures (larger spans, flat, less formalized, and less centralized). However, there is no one best way to organize, and both mechanistic and organic structures have their places.

- Many of the traditional organizational structures are being replaced by more flexible structures that break down external and internal boundaries. Network or virtual organizations and modular organizations are structures that break down or modify external barriers, and the boundaryless organization removes both internal and external barriers.

- As organizations grow in size they tend to become more complex (vertically, horizontally, geographically), more formalized, and less centralized.

- Downsizing is the intentional reduction in workforce size with the goals of improving organizational efficiency or effectiveness. Sensible downsizing avoids mechanistic tendencies, retains necessary personnel, and respects good job design principles.

- Symptoms of structural problems include poor job design, extreme duplication of effort, conflict between departments, slow responses, too many committees, and decisions made with incomplete information.

Discussion Questions

1. Discuss the division of labour in a college classroom. What methods are used to coordinate this divided labour? Do differences exist between very small and very large classes?

2. Is the departmentation in a small college essentially functional or product oriented? Defend your answer. (*Hint:* In what department will the historians find themselves? In what department will the groundskeepers find themselves?)

3. Which basic method(s) of coordination is (are) most likely to be found in a pure research laboratory? On a football team? In a supermarket?

4. What are the relative merits of mechanistic versus organic structures?

5. Discuss the logic behind the following statement: "We don't want to remove the differentiation that exists between sales and production. What we want to do is achieve integration."

6. As Spinelli Construction Company grew in size, its founder and president, Joe Spinelli, found that he was overloaded with decisions. What two basic structural changes should Spinelli make to rectify this situation without losing control of the company?

7. Describe a situation in which a narrow span of control might be appropriate and contrast it with a situation in which a broad span might be appropriate.

8. Make up a list of criteria that would define a good downsizing effort.

9. How do the structural characteristics of organizations influence leadership, communication, decision making, and power in organizations? Discuss the implications of each of the structural characteristics (i.e., span of control, organization

levels, formalization, centralization, and complexity) for leadership behaviour, communication and decision making processes, and the distribution and use of power in organizations.

? 10. How do the new forms of organizational structure such as virtual, modular, and boundaryless organizations influence the culture of an organization? In other words, what is the relationship between these types of structures and an organization's culture? What is the relationship between these structures and the use and effectiveness of teams?

Experiential Exercise

Organizational Structure Preference Scale

In most organizations, there are differences of opinion and preferences as to how the organization should be structured and how people should conduct themselves. Following are a number of statements concerning these matters. The purpose of this survey is for you to learn about your own preferences about the structure of organizations. Please use the response scale below to indicate the extent to which you agree with each statement.

1 — Disagree strongly
2 — Disagree
3 — Neither agree nor disagree
4 — Agree
5 — Agree strongly

____ 1. I get most of my motivation to work from the job itself rather than from the rewards the company gives me for doing it.

____ 2. I respect my supervisors for what they know rather than for the fact that the company has put them in charge.

____ 3. I work best when things are exciting and filled with energy. I can feel the adrenalin rushing through me and I like it.

____ 4. I like it best if we can play things by ear. Going by the book means you do not have any imagination.

____ 5. People who seek security at work are boring. I don't go to work to plan my retirement.

____ 6. I believe that planning should focus on the short term. Long-term planning is unrealistic. I want to see the results of my plan.

____ 7. Don't give me a detailed job description. Just point me in the general direction and I will figure out what needs to be done.

____ 8. I don't expect to be introduced to new people. If I like their looks, I'll introduce myself.

____ 9. Goals should be set by everyone in the organization. I prefer to achieve my own goals rather than those of someone else.

____ 10. One of the things I prefer most about a job is that it be full of surprises.

____ 11. I like a job that is full of challenges.

____ 12. Organization charts are only needed by people who are already lost.

____ 13. Technology is constantly changing.

____ 14. Supervision and control should be face-to-face.

____ 15. If organizations focus on problem solving, the bottom line will take care of itself.

____ 16. I would never take a job which involved repetitive activities.

____ 17. Organizations are constantly in a state of change. I don't worry about how the players line up.

____ 18. Every decision I make is a new one. I don't look for precedents.

____ 19. When people talk about efficiency, I think they really don't want to do a good job.

____ 20. The people who know the most about the work should be put in charge.

Scoring and Interpretation

To calculate your organizational structure preference score, simply add up your responses to each of the 20 questions. Scores can range from 20 to 100. Your score on this survey indicates your preference for a mechanistic or organic organizational structure. A score of less than 50 indicates a preference for a mechanistic or formal organizational structure. Mechanistic structures tend to favour tallness, narrow spans, specialization, centralization, and formalization. Scores above 50 indicate a preference for a more organic or informal organizational structure. Organic structures tend to favour wider spans, fewer authority levels, less specialization, less formalization, and decentralization. Flexibility and informal communication are favoured over rigidity and the strict chain of command.

Source: "Exercise 20: Mechanistic or Organic Organizational Design" from *Organizational Behaviour: Canadian Cases and Exercises*, 3rd edition, by R. Hoffman and F. Ruemper (Toronto: Captus Press Inc., 1997), pp. 298–299. Reprinted by permission of Captus Press Inc.

Case Incident

Conway Manufacturing

Conway Manufacturing is a large organization that manufactures machine tools that are used by workers in various industries. In recent years, sales of the company's products have begun to fall as a result of increasing competition. Customers have also begun to complain about the quality of Conway's products. In response, Conway decided to design some new high-quality products.

The Research and Development department was asked to develop some new designs for several of Conway's best-selling products. When the Engineering Department looked at the designs, they rejected them outright saying that they were not very good. Engineering then revised the designs and sent them to the Production Department. However, the Production Department responded by sending them back to the Engineering Department insisting that they would be impossible to produce. In the meantime, the Marketing Department had begun a campaign based on the material they had received from the Research and Development Department. One year later, Conway was still no closer to producing new products. In the meantime, more customers were complaining and threatening to find new suppliers, and the competition continued to take more and more of Conway's business.

1. Describe the structure of Conway Manufacturing. What are some of the problems that Conway is having, and is organizational structure a factor?

2. What would be the most effective structure to design new high-quality products in a short period of time?

Case Study

Expansion at Dimitri's Baked Goods Inc.

Dimitri's Baked Goods is a Windsor (Ontario)-based bakery specializing in Macedonian pastries, "zelnik" and "vielnik," sweet and regular bread, and traditional Christmas and Easter cakes. The company employs four sales representatives, two secretaries, and a production staff that varies between 24 and 32 people. The firm also employs a small sales staff of three at its only retail outlet. The pastry, bread, and cakes are distributed all over Ontario and Western Canada. Distribution channels in Eastern Canada are in the process of being established.

Dimitri Leakos started this business in a small shop over 30 years ago. Leakos was not self-employed when he first settled in Canada from the Macedonian region of Greece. Macedonians are proud of their heritage, although they are not well recognized as a distinct ethnic group. The Canadian census did not even list Macedonians or the Macedonian language until 1981. This neglect is the result of the fact that historic Macedonia falls today within three Balkan countries: Bulgaria, Greece, and Yugoslavia. Throughout its recent history, Macedonia has been subjected to external and sometimes divisive control. The first significant immigration to Canada probably came as a result of uprisings against the Ottoman Empire in the early years of the 20th century. Both World Wars led to further waves of immigration. Most Macedonians live in the Toronto-Hamilton area, but a group from one Macedonian village settled in Windsor.

It was important to Leakos that he became established in a Macedonian community, and Windsor provided that for him. At first, he was an employee in a bakery owned by others in order to learn the business and to learn to read and write English. But he always had the need to control his own environment and was motivated more by this need than by any ideas of greater wealth.

Dimitri's Baked Goods began as a small bakery near the tunnel to Detroit. It was close to the downtown area of Windsor and in the heart of the local Macedonian area. He still maintains this original location as a retail sales outlet, although he has had to move his production and distribution to a suburban area where larger quarters were available. Leakos expanded his business to a 3,000 square metre facility on Dougall Avenue.

Dimitri's growth was based on two factors. The first was the growing demand from the Macedonian community for commercially produced versions of ethnic food, which were originally produced at home. While many first-generation Macedonians still do their own baking, the next generation is more inclined to buy it. The second factor was his success in broadening his market beyond its original Macedonian base. This is, by far, the most important cause of his growth. His enthusiastic marketing to non-Macedonians has been enormously successful.

Leakos is the stereotypical workaholic small businessperson. He is the owner, plant manager, production manager, sales supervisor, marketing manager, product development supervisor, and also one of the line workers at Dimitri. These duties force him to work between 12 and 17 hours a day, 7 days a week, but he allows himself to take three-week long vacations spread throughout the year. He is a moderate risk taker who does not undertake new ventures without a great deal of research to prove to himself it will be successful. Once he starts a task, he remains committed to it until it is accomplished. He prefers tasks that provide immediate feedback to those with only long-term prospects. For example, when any of his sophisticated machinery breaks down and engineers are flown in from the manufacturers in Europe, he will spend as much time as possible with them in order to learn how to perform the repairs.

Decision making is extremely centralized at Dimitri's Baked Goods. Leakos has total control over his business. He has been running it this way for three decades with great success and, until recently, he has seen no reason to change. He feels centralization makes his business more flexible because he can act without delay when problems arise.

The structure at Dimitri's is quite informal. Leakos deals with all his employees on an individual basis. The production roles in the bakery vary at different times. Workers are not forced to specialize in one skill. Their work might rotate among packaging, shipping, and maintenance. Only the bakers are somewhat specialized, but they too help to get the goods delivered. The hierarchy is extremely flat and has very little horizontal differentiation. There is a production department, a sales department, two office workers, plus the retail outlet. Leakos handles all the staff functions of personnel, planning, and budgeting. Every employee at Dimitri reports to Leakos. Dimitri has followed this functional structure since the business was first developed.

Because Leakos is the only supervisor at Dimitri's, his practices have defined the supervisory style. He seems to practise an employee-oriented leadership. He helps his people with personal problems, treats them as equals, and avoids punitive actions. Leakos seldom refuses to compromise, nor does he insist on things be done his way. His style is unobtrusive, leading by example rather than by threats. Everyone admires his personal effort on the production floor every day. He is more concerned with results than methods.

Leakos's supervisory methods have developed very high employee morale. As a result of this, there are few grievances and a low turnover rate. Many employees have been with the company for 10 to 15 years. His main problem comes during peak seasons such as Christmas and Easter, when production cannot keep up with demand. At those times, Leakos is forced to hire seasonal staff, and many employees have to work overtime and weekends. Then, Leakos becomes more authoritarian and grievances increase. These holiday work schedules conflict with family and social festivities. Because of his excellent personal relationships with his employees, he is able to keep turnover low, even though these problems arise.

Motivation is often a problem in assembly-line work, and may result in high absenteeism and employee turnover. Leakos uses a strategy of job rotation and job enlargement. This strategy grew naturally from the expansion of the business over the years rather than from any deliberate policy on his part. He has avoided job specialization, only because it was not natural for him to have it. Leakos also understands the need for rewarding desirable behaviour. At Christmas and Easter, when he needs employees to come in on weekends, he rewards them with praise, free coffee and doughnuts, packages of pastry, and legs of lamb to take home to their families. He also has a Christmas bonus program, which he uses to reward those who are willing to work overtime. He schedules a one-week vacation period after the peak Christmas and Easter seasons and again during the first week in August. Leakos is fairly generous with pay and benefits. The production employees are paid about twice the legal minimum wage and get time-and-a-half for overtime. They have all statutory holidays off or are paid overtime for working them. There are three weeks of paid vacation. He provides personal time off with pay for family emergencies and illnesses and is also understanding of the needs of his workers to fulfill family duties. Leakos is very generous when his employees have a wedding or christening in the family.

Almost all the workers at Dimitri's are from the Macedonian community in Windsor and speak Macedonian. Most of them are housewives earning a second income. They are unskilled and have little formal education. At Dimitri's, employees find themselves in a comfortable environment, where they can speak their own language and affiliate with others with similar cultural background and interests. Since the Macedonian community in Windsor is well organized, the employees know each other from outside and see each other on their own time. They all know about upcoming weddings and planned outings to the Boufsko Cello, the Macedonian community park on Lake Erie. Whenever a new position becomes available, the employees are encouraged to spread the word to others in their circle who might be interested.

Sales are now escalating so quickly that production facilities are unable to keep up with demand. Leakos has had to delay his plans to expand into the United States market even though he knows his products are popular in Detroit. The customs officers at the Windsor/Detroit Tunnel tell him they see his cakes and pastry every day (bought in Windsor and carried over the border). Some of his pastries are served in Greek restaurants in downtown Detroit. The Free Trade Agreement with the United States has led him to think that now is the time for a major marketing move into the United States.

Source: R. Hoffman & F. Ruemper. *Organizational behaviour: Canadian cases and exercises*, 3rd ed. Captus Press. Based on original research by Steven Zullo and John Tannis.

1. Draw the existing organization chart for Dimitri's Baked Goods Inc. Describe the structure of the organization using concepts such as span of control, formalization, centralization, and complexity.

2. What form of departmentation does the company rely on? Discuss the advantages and disadvantages of this form of departmentation with reference to the issues mentioned in the case. Consider the appropriateness of other forms of departmentation for the company. What form would be most effective?

3. Use the concept and methods of coordination to analyze the functioning of the organization and the implications of this for expansion.

4. Is the company ready to undertake an expansion? Why or why not?

5. Suggest some alternative organizational structures that might be needed for a successful expansion. Do these alternatives have any potential problems?

6. If the company decides to expand, how will this affect structural characteristics, such as span of control, formalization, centralization, and complexity?

7. How do you think the company should respond to the pressures to expand?

Chapter 15

Environment, Strategy, and Technology

SATURN Saturn was conceived as a totally new corporation, a wholly owned General Motors subsidiary that delivered its first cars in fall 1990. The formerly autonomous division, headquartered in Spring Hill, Tennessee, has its own sales and service operations. At the time, why did GM decide to separate Saturn so decisively from the existing corporate structure, rather than just add yet another product line to its Chevrolet, Oldsmobile, Pontiac, Buick, and Cadillac lines? General Motors insiders and auto industry analysts cited two primary reasons. First, GM badly needed to find ways to cut costs to compete in the small car market, in which estimates suggested that Japanese manufacturers enjoyed a great cost advantage. Second, top GM executives hoped to use the Saturn venture as a testing ground for innovations that could be applied throughout the rest of the organization, especially ones that could get new models to the market more quickly. To accomplish both these goals, the freedom of a completely "fresh start" and the protection autonomy offered seemed to be essential.

With the exception of the use of plastic for vertical body parts, Saturn cars do not represent a radical technical departure for GM. Rather, it is the way in which the cars are built and marketed that is innovative. Extensively trained self-managed work teams assemble the cars, maintain their own equipment, order supplies, set work schedules, and even select new team members. To control quality and reduce transport costs, much subassembly is done by suppliers that are located close to the plant or even within the plant itself, thus fostering a close cooperative arrangement. Parts that do come in from the outside are delivered precisely when they are needed and directly to the location where they are used in assembly. In the marketing domain, dealers are

General
Motors'
Saturn
Venture

General Motors' Saturn was conceived as a totally new corporation with innovations in automobile design, manufacturing, and marketing.

given more exclusive territories than is typical of North American auto manufacturers. As long as they meet stiff requirements in several key areas, they are given substantial autonomy to tailor their operations to local needs.

These changes in manufacturing and marketing are supported by a number of departures from conventional structure, management style, and labour relations practices. Saturn has a flatter management structure than the traditional GM divisions. A computerized "paperless" operation of electronic mail and a single, highly integrated database speed decisions and counter bureaucracy. Finally, GM agreed to a truly ground-breaking labour contract with the United Auto Workers. There are no time clocks, and workers are on salaries, although these salaries average less than industry hourly wages. In addition, restrictive work rules were eliminated to support the team assembly concept. In exchange for these concessions, GM devotes a percentage of the industry hourly wage to performance incentives and a profit-sharing plan for Saturn workers. Also, 80 percent of the workforce is granted what amounts to lifetime employment security. Union representatives sit on planning and organizing committees.

The Saturn project is not as radical as it was planned to be. The company rejected initial ideas for more extensive use of computers and robotics in assembly on the basis of experiences in some other GM plants. Instead, GM placed even more emphasis on developing a motivated workforce. Also, Saturn's initial marketing scheme called for showrooms in malls, dealers without inventories, computerized ordering, and so on. Some of these plans were downscaled, in part because of stringent state regulations about the permitted configuration of car dealerships.

Learning Objectives

After reading Chapter 15, you should be able to:

1   Discuss the components of an organization's external environment.

2   Explain how environmental uncertainty and resource dependence affect what happens in organizations.

3   Understand how organizational structure can serve as a strategic response to environmental demands.

4   Explain how vertical integration, mergers, acquisitions, strategic alliances, interlocking directorates, and the establishment of legitimacy reflect strategic responses.

5   Describe the basic dimensions of organizational technology.

6   Explain how organizations must match organizational structure to technology.

7   Discuss the impact of advanced information technology on job design and organizational structure.

United Auto Workers
www.uaw.org

Has Saturn fulfilled the promise of its multibillion-dollar investment? Early cars suffered from quality glitches that the company attended to quickly, even replacing some faulty cars for free. As a result of such tactics and extremely cooperative dealers (many of whom organize customer picnics and car clinics), intense customer loyalty resulted in Saturn turning a profit three years after the first car rolled off the assembly line. However, the company has been in the red most years and has not recouped the initial investment. Many observers have noted the failure of other parts of GM to embrace the Saturn innovations. The United Auto Workers have consistently resisted Saturn-type labour agreements at any other manufacturing sites. Saturn has been slow to develop new models, and competitors are outpacing the company in terms of technical refinement and safety, even copying some of its "buyer-friendly" sales techniques. Although Saturn buyers have good demographics in terms of income and education, the company has been slow to develop larger sedans, minivans, and sports utility vehicles to offer them. Gaining investment funds for such projects from GM has been difficult because the parent firm has been busy recentralizing much vehicle development and engineering.

Four years after its startup, Saturn became part of the GM Small Car Group. This required Saturn leadership to work even harder to ensure the spirit of the Saturn partnership remained strong. Even though organizational and market changes challenged Saturn's unique culture, the original memorandum of agreement between Saturn and its workers was renewed in late 1999. While the majority of Saturn's workers still believe strongly in the company and its mission, only time will tell if Saturn can continue to resist environmental pressures on its innovative culture.[1]

The Saturn story illustrates some of the major questions that we will consider in this chapter. How does the external environment influence organizations? How can an organization develop a strategy to cope with this environment? And how can technology and other factors be used to implement strategy? In the previous chapter, we concluded that there is no one best way to design an organization. In this chapter, we will see that the proper organizational structure is contingent on environmental, strategic, and technological factors.

The External Environment of Organizations

In previous chapters, we have been concerned primarily with the internal environments of organizations—those events and conditions inside the organization—that affect the attitudes and behaviours of members. In this section, we turn our interest to the impact of the **external environment**—those events and conditions surrounding the organization that influence its activities.

There is ample evidence in everyday life that the external environment has tremendous influence on organizations. The OPEC oil embargo of 1973 and subsequent oil price increases shook North American automobile manufacturers to their foundations. Faced with gasoline shortages, increasing gasoline prices, and rising interest rates, consumers postponed automobile purchases or shifted to more economical foreign vehicles. As a consequence, workers were laid off, plants were closed, and dealerships failed, while the manufacturers scrambled to develop more fuel-efficient smaller cars. The emphasis of advertising strategies changed from styling and comfort to economy and value. Significant portions of the manufacturers' environment (Middle East oil suppliers, American consumers, and Japanese competitors) prompted this radical regrouping.

Environmental conditions change, and by the mid-1980s an international oil surplus pushed gasoline prices down. Consumers responded with increased interest in size, styling, and performance. Auto industry analysts noted that some manufacturers responded to this shift faster than others. Chrysler, trimmed of bureaucracy by its near demise several years earlier, responded quickly and scored a number of marketing coups. General Motors responded less quickly, and the Saturn project was an attempt to enable the company to respond more quickly to environmental trends.

In the new millennium, the auto industry faces accelerated global competition, especially to supply the increasing middle class in the developing countries. Joint ventures and mergers between companies are common. California's legislation requiring zero exhaust emissions from a portion of each manufacturer's cars has prompted experimentation with electric vehicles. As always, the external environment profoundly shapes organizational behaviour.

Organizations as Open Systems

Organizations can be described as open systems. **Open systems** are systems that take inputs from the external environment, transform some of these inputs, and send them back into the external environment as outputs (Exhibit 15.1).[2] Inputs include capital, energy, materials, information, technology, and people; outputs include various products and services. Some inputs are transformed (e.g., raw materials), while other inputs (e.g., skilled craftspeople) assist in the transformation process. Transformation processes may be physical (e.g., manufacturing or surgery), intellectual (e.g., teaching or programming), or even emotional (e.g., psychotherapy). For example, an insurance company imports actuarial experts, information about accidents and mortality, and capital in the form of insurance

External environment. Events and conditions surrounding an organization that influence its activities.

Open systems. Systems that take inputs from the external environment, transform some of them, and send them back into the environment as outputs.

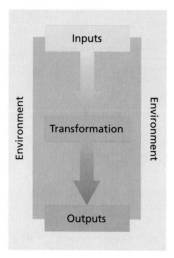

Exhibit 15.1
The organization as an open system.

premiums. Through the application of financial knowledge, it transforms the capital into insurance coverage and investments in areas such as real estate. Universities import seasoned scholars and aspiring students from the environment. Through the teaching process, educated individuals are returned to the community as outputs.

The value of the open systems concept is that it sensitizes us to the need for organizations to cope with the demands of the environment on both the input side and the output side. As we will see, some of this coping involves adaptation to environmental demands. On the other hand, some coping may be oriented toward changing the environment.

First, let us examine the external environment in greater detail.

Components of the External Environment

The external environment of any given organization is obviously a "big" concept. Technically, it involves any person, group, event, or condition outside the direct domain of the organization. For this reason, it is useful to divide the environment into a manageable number of components.[3]

The General Economy. Organizations that survive through selling products or services often suffer from an economic downturn and profit by an upturn. When a downturn occurs, competition for remaining customers increases, and organizations might postpone needed capital improvements. Of course, some organizations thrive under a poor economy, including welfare offices and law firms that deal heavily in bankruptcies. In addition, if a poor economy is accompanied by high unemployment, some organizations might find it opportune to upgrade the quality of their staffs, since they will have an ample selection of candidates.

We see a clear example of the impact of the general economy in the most recent recession. Faced with falling orders (reduced inputs), thousands of organizations engaged in radical downsizing as a means of cutting costs.

Customers. All organizations have potential customers for their products and services. Piano makers have musicians, and consumer activist associations have disgruntled consumers. The customers of universities include not only students, but also the firms that employ their graduates and seek their research assistance. Organizations must be sensitive to changes in customer demands. For example, the small liberal arts college that resists developing a business school might be faced with declining enrollment.

Successful firms are generally highly sensitive to customer reactions. L'Oréal, the world's largest producer of cosmetics, announced that it would no longer test its products on animals in response to customer demand. Taco Bell moved to a nonsmoking environment in its company-owned restaurants as a result of a year-long survey that showed that the majority of both smokers and nonsmokers preferred a smoke-free environment in restaurants.

Suppliers. Organizations are dependent on the environment for supplies that include labour, raw materials, equipment, and component parts. Shortages can cause severe difficulties. For instance, the lack of a local technical school might prove troublesome for an electronics firm that requires skilled labour. Similarly, a strike by a company that supplies component parts might cause the purchaser to shut down its assembly line.

As alluded to earlier in the text, many contemporary firms have changed their strategy for dealing with suppliers. It used to be standard practice to have many of them and to keep them in stiff competition for one's business, mainly by extracting the lowest price. Now, more exclusive relationships with suppliers, on the basis of quality and reliable delivery, are becoming more common. Dell Computer reduced its suppliers from 140 to 80 and its freight carriers from 21 to 3.

Competitors. Environmental competitors vie for resources that include both customers and suppliers.[4] Thus, hospitals compete for patients, and consulting firms compete for clients. Similarly, utility companies compete for coal, and professional baseball teams compete for free agent ballplayers. Successful organizations devote considerable energy to monitoring the activities of competitors.

The computer software industry provides an instructive lesson in how competition can change over time. In the early days of software development (not very long ago!), there were a large number of players in the field, and small companies could find a profitable niche. There was plenty of room for many competitors in what was an essentially technology-driven business. However, the growing domination of Microsoft, which slashed prices and consolidated multiple functions in its programs, has prompted a great number of mergers, acquisitions, and failures among firms dealing in basic consumer software, such as word processing and spreadsheets.[5]

Microsoft
www.microsoft.com

For many organizations today the competition has become so aggressive that their environments have been described as hypercompetitive. Organizations that find themselves in hypercompetitive environments must become extremely flexible in order to respond quickly to changes and cope with hypercompetition.[6]

Social/Political Factors. Organizations cannot ignore the social and political events that occur around them. Changes in public attitudes toward ethnic diversity, the proper age for retirement, or the proper role of big business will soon affect them. Frequently, these attitudes find expression in law through the political process. Thus, organizations must cope with a series of legal regulations that prescribe fair employment practices, proper competitive activities, product safety, and clients' rights.

One example of the impact of social trends on organizations is Wal-Mart's move to ban handgun sales in its stores. Another is the increasing public interest in environmentalism. Many firms have been fairly proactive in their responses. For example, Pacific Gas & Electric works closely with environmental groups and has a dedicated environmentalist on its board. And McDonald's has become a visible proponent of recycling and an active educator of the public on environmental issues.[7]

An example of the conversion of a social trend into political and governmental action is the deregulation of the American and Canadian airline industries. Part of a general trend to reduce federal regulation of business, this action spurred a long series of market entries, fare wars, route wars, mergers, acquisitions, and bankruptcies. Many a harried airline executive felt the target of the ancient Chinese curse "May you live in interesting times"! A similar trend took place in deregulation of financial services. To learn more about the influence of deregulation and the environment, see "In Focus: *Coping with Environmental Changes at Boeing*."

Technology. The environment contains a variety of technologies that are useful for achieving organizational goals. As we shall see, technology refers to ways of doing things, not simply to some form of machinery. The ability to adopt the proper technology should enhance an organization's effectiveness. For a business firm, this might involve the choice of a proper computer system or production technique. For a mental health clinic, it might involve implementing a particular form of psychotherapy that is effective for the kinds of clients serviced.

in focus ➤)))   Coping with Environmental Changes at Boeing

If you have been on an air plane lately, chances are you travelled on a plane that was built by Boeing. Its products carry more than three-quarters of all airborne travellers every day, and it builds most of the new commercial airliners entering service around the world. Boeing is also the largest American exporter as well as the leading supplier to both the Pentagon and NASA and employs some 230,000 workers directly and perhaps three times that many through its related companies.

However, during the last couple of years, Boeing has had more than its share of problems. Massive production problems in 1997 led to the unthinkable shutdown of two assembly lines for a full month and a $1.6 billion charge against earnings. Boeing's operating margins, meanwhile, have continued to shrink, leading to earnings last year of a measly $1.1 billion on revenues of $56.2 billion. What's more, the company has announced that the earnings picture will not brighten much until 2001 at the earliest.

A major problem for Boeing has been an inefficient production process. For example, Boeing's cavernous Boeing 747-400 plant in Everett, Washington, is surprisingly quiet and low tech. There are no flashing lasers or whizzing robots. Just small teams of workers, many wielding nothing more sophisticated than hand tools. It looks, in fact, like a giant version of the repair bay in your neighbourhood service station. The problem is that your humble service station probably operates more efficiently. Every alteration, even a seemingly minor one like moving the location of an emergency flashlight holder, consumes thousands of hours of engineering time, requires hundreds of pages of detailed drawings, and costs hundreds of thousands, if not millions, of dollars to execute.

Boeing executives have known for years—for decades even—that their factories were inefficient, their supply chains tangled, their computer systems outmoded. Ever since the late 1970s they have tried, in a piece-meal fashion, to fix these problems. But they never took the issues seriously, as Boeing managed to prosper even with such archaic methods. The reasons are clear enough. Its major customers—airlines protected by regulation and a free-spending Department of Defence—cared little about price. Then too, Boeing has had no hyperefficient competitor from Japan (or anyplace else) breathing down its neck.

But how the times have changed! The environment in which Boeing does business has undergone such epochal change that now the company is being forced to become more efficient. Airline deregulation is spreading around the globe, the post-Cold War Pentagon has gone on a diet, and

Boeing's only remaining commercial-air plane competitor in passenger jets, Airbus Industrie, a government-subsidized European consortium, is chipping away at Boeing's lead in the marketplace and has successfully wooed several long-time Boeing customers. As well, the airlines have learned to extract huge discounts from aircraft manufacturers by offering long-term deals and then bargaining hard on price.

How has Boeing responded? First, it has radically altered the size and shape of the company. In 1997, it completed a $16.3 billion merger with McDonnell Douglas, a move that eliminated the only other American contender in the commercial aircraft business. That combination came right on the heels of Boeing's $3.1 billion acquisition of the defence and space operations of Rockwell International. Boeing, long an also-ran in defence, is now the largest builder of military aircraft in the world.

Second, the company plans to streamline its inefficient commercial-airline group and totally overhaul and revamp the way it designs and produces air planes. Boeing's time-honoured practices, designed for the pre-deregulation era when airlines blithely passed costs along to passengers, have allowed customers a nearly limitless selection of options for each aircraft ordered. The solution to this morass is to move to more modular manufacturing, offer customers fewer choices, and stop trying to make each plane coming down the line a unique creation. At the core of Boeing's plans to streamline its production processes is a program known as DCAC/MRM, pronounced "DEE-kak M-R-M." The program is so sweeping and so complicated that it has already taken managers two years longer to put it into place than originally anticipated.

Important and costly as production reform is, the program barely begins to address the way workers actually do their jobs on the assembly line. To tackle that challenge, Boeing has come up with another set of initiatives, loosely grouped under the rubric of "lean manufacturing." Guided by consultants, employees huddle in five-day "accelerated improvement workshops," where they brainstorm on how to do their jobs more efficiently.

Employees at the factory that builds wings for the 737s and 747s, for example, have been able to trim production time for some functions from 56 to 28 days—by moving machines, designing new tools, and cutting out unnecessary inventory. Under the most optimistic scenario, the company will have its planned reforms in place by 2001!

Sources: Excerpted from Henkoff, R. (1998, January 12). Boeing's big problem. *Fortune*, pp. 96-103; Labich, K. (1999, March 1). Boeing finally hatches a plan. *Fortune*, pp. 100-106.

An example of the impact of technology on organizational life is the advent of computer-aided design (CAD). With CAD, designers, engineers, and draftspeople can produce quick, accurate drawings via computer. They can store databases and run simulations that produce visual records of the reaction of objects to stress, vibration, and design changes. Some firms have found that CAD reduces design lead times and increases productivity. Others have had a difficult time reorganizing to exploit this technology. In general, CAD has broken down the traditional role differences between designers, engineers, and drawing technicians.

Now that we have outlined the basic components of organizational environments, a few more detailed comments are in order. First, this brief list does not provide a perfect picture of the large number of actual interest groups that can exist in an organization's environment. **Interest groups** are parties or organizations other than direct competitors that have some vested interest in how an organization is managed. For example, Exhibit 15.2 shows the interest groups that surround a small private college. As you can see, our list of six environmental components actually involves quite an array of individuals and agencies with which the college must contend. To complicate matters, some of these individuals and agencies might make competing or conflicting demands on the college. For instance, booster clubs might press the college to allocate more funds to field a winning football team, while scholarship sponsors might insist that the college match their donations for academic purposes.

Such competition for attention from different segments of the environment is not unusual. While antidrug organizations have sometimes supported the screening of employees for drug use, the American Civil Liberties Union has taken a keen interest in the violation of privacy that such tests can involve. Obviously, different interest groups evaluate organizational effectiveness according to different criteria.[8]

Different parts of the organization will often be concerned with different environmental components. For instance, we can expect a marketing department to be tuned in to customer demands and a legal department to be interested in regulations

Interest groups. Parties or organizations other than direct competitors that have some vested interest in how an organization is managed.

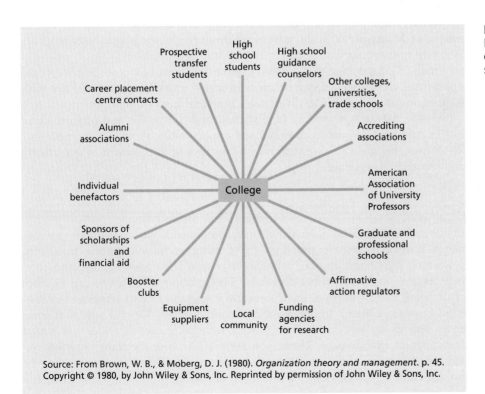

Exhibit 15.2
Interest groups in the external environment of a small private college.

Source: From Brown, W. B., & Moberg, D. J. (1980). *Organization theory and management.* p. 45. Copyright © 1980, by John Wiley & Sons, Inc. Reprinted by permission of John Wiley & Sons, Inc.

stemming from the social/political component. As we indicated in the previous chapter, coordination of this natural division of interests is a crucial concern for all organizations. Also, as environmental demands change, it is important that power shifts occur to allow the appropriate functional units to cope with these demands.

Finally, events in various components of the environment provide both constraints and opportunities for organizations. Although environments with many constraints (e.g., high interest rates, strong competition, and so on) appear pretty hostile, an opportunity in one environmental sector might offset a constraint in another. For example, the firm that is faced with a dwindling customer base might find its salvation by exploiting new technologies that give it an edge in costs or new product development.

The Environment of Saturn

Let us return to the story that began the chapter and analyze some of the environmental components that shaped General Motors' plans regarding the Saturn project. A strong impetus for the Saturn venture was the $2,000 cost advantage per small car that Japanese competitors held at the time. However, cost reductions mean little unless the quality of the Saturn automobile is comparable with that of Japanese makes. To enhance quality, GM exercised particular control over parts suppliers, inducing them to locate within or near the plant to facilitate communication with Saturn engineering and manufacturing personnel.

During the recessionary early 1980s, the general economy faltered, and unions lost considerable bargaining power. Union membership fell, and GM capitalized on changing social attitudes toward unions to forge an innovative contract with the United Auto Workers. However, an interest group, the National Right to Work Legal Defence Foundation, challenged the legality of the contract. This group, which provides legal aid to workers who do not wish to join unions, argued that it was improper for GM to specify the United Auto Workers as a bargaining agent in advance of any workers having been hired.[9] The challenge failed.

Several technological advances were exploited at Saturn, although not as many as GM envisioned at the start of the project. Still, the plastic body parts are innovative, as is a sophisticated paperless database operation.

Finally, GM gambled that it could exploit a segment of customers that would not normally consider a domestic car—dedicated import buyers. It did not wish to develop a new car only to divert sales from existing GM product lines.

Clearly, Saturn is a product of environmental constraints and opportunities. But exactly how do such constraints and opportunities affect the organization? To answer this question, we turn to the concepts of environmental uncertainty and resource dependence.

Environmental Uncertainty

Environmental uncertainty. A condition that exists when the external environment is vague, difficult to diagnose, and unpredictable.

In our earlier discussion of environmental components, we implied that environments have considerable potential for causing confusion among managers. Customers may come and go, suppliers may turn from good to bad, and competitors may make surprising decisions. The resulting uncertainty can be both challenging and frustrating. **Environmental uncertainty** exists when an environment is vague, difficult to diagnose, and unpredictable. We all know that some environments are less certain than others. Your hometown provides you with a fairly certain environment. There, you are familiar with the transportation system, the language, and necessary social conventions. Thrust into the midst of a foreign culture, you encounter a much less certain environment. How to greet a stranger, order a meal, and get around town become significant issues. There is nothing intrinsically bad about this uncertainty. It simply requires you to marshal a particular set of skills in order to be an effective visitor.

Like individuals, organizations can find themselves in more or less certain environments. But just exactly what makes an organizational environment uncertain? Put simply, uncertainty depends on the environment's *complexity* (simple versus complex) and its *rate of change* (static versus dynamic).[10]

- *Simple environment.* A simple environment involves relatively few factors, and these factors are fairly similar to each other. For example, consider the pottery manufacturer that obtains its raw materials from two small firms and sells its entire output to three small pottery outlets.

- *Complex environment.* A complex environment contains a large number of dissimilar factors that affect the organization. For example, the college in Exhibit 15.2 has a more complex environment than the pottery manufacturer. In turn, the Saturn organization has a more complex environment than the college.

- *Static environment.* The components of this environment remain fairly stable over time. The small-town radio station that plays the same music format, relies on the same advertisers, and works under the same FCC regulations year after year has a stable environment. (Of course, no environment is *completely* static; we are speaking in relative terms here.)

- *Dynamic environment.* The components of a highly dynamic environment are in a constant state of change, which is unpredictable and irregular, not cyclical. For example, consider the firm that designs and manufactures microchips for electronics applications. New scientific and technological advances occur rapidly and unpredictably in this field. In addition, customer demands are highly dynamic as firms devise new uses for microchips. A similar dynamic environment faces Saturn, in part owing to the vagaries of the energy situation and in part owing to the fact that marketing automobiles has become an international rather than a national business. For example, fluctuations in the relative value of international currencies can radically alter the cost of competing imported cars quite independently of anything Saturn management does.

As we see in Exhibit 15.3, it is possible to arrange rate of change and complexity in a matrix. A simple/static environment (cell 1) should provoke the least uncertainty, while a dynamic/complex environment (cell 4) should provoke the most. Some research suggests that change has more influence than complexity on uncertainty.[11] Thus, we might expect a static/complex environment (cell 2) to be somewhat more certain than a dynamic/simple environment (cell 3).

Earlier, we stated that different portions of the organization are often interested in different components of the environment. To go a step further, it stands to reason that some aspects of the environment are less certain than others. Thus, some subunits might be faced with more uncertainty than others. For example, the research and development department of a microchip company would seem to face a more uncertain environment than the human resource department.

Increasing uncertainty has several predictable effects on organizations and their decision makers.[12] For one thing, as uncertainty increases, cause-and-effect relationships become less clear. If we are certain that a key competitor will not match our increased advertising budget, we may be confident that our escalated ad campaign will increase our market share. Uncertainty about the competitor's response reduces confidence in this causal inference. Second, environmental uncertainty tends to make priorities harder to agree on, and it often stimulates a fair

Exhibit 15.3
Environmental uncertainty as a function of complexity and rate of change.

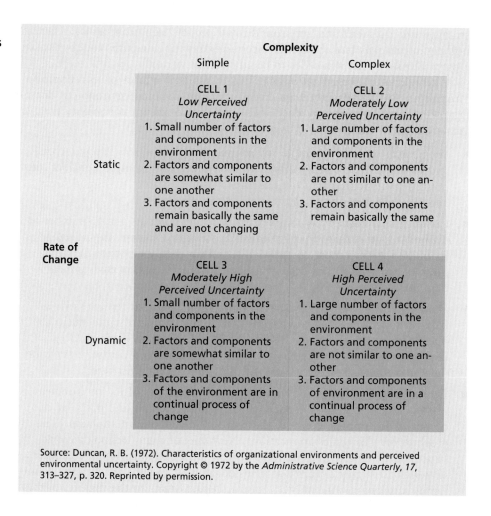

Source: Duncan, R. B. (1972). Characteristics of organizational environments and perceived environmental uncertainty. Copyright © 1972 by the *Administrative Science Quarterly, 17,* 313–327, p. 320. Reprinted by permission.

degree of political jockeying within the organization. To continue the example, if the consequences of increased advertising are unclear, other functional units might see the increased budget allocation as being "up for grabs." Finally, as environmental uncertainty increases, more information must be processed by the organization to make adequate decisions. Environmental scanning, boundary spanning, planning, and formal management information systems will become more prominent.[13] This illustrates that organizations will act to cope with or reduce uncertainty because uncertainty increases the difficulty of decision making and thus threatens organizational effectiveness. Shortly, we will examine in greater detail the means of managing uncertainty. First, we explore another aspect of the impact of the environment on organizations.

Resource Dependence

Earlier, we noted that organizations are open systems that receive inputs from the external environment and transfer outputs into this environment. Many inputs from various components of the environment are valuable resources that are necessary for organizational survival. These include things such as capital, raw materials, and human resources. By the same token, other components of the environment (such as customers) represent valuable resources on the output end of the equation. All this suggests that organizations are in a state of **resource dependence** with regard to their environments.[14] Carefully managing and coping with this resource dependence is a key to survival and success.

Resource dependence. The dependency of organizations on environmental inputs, such as capital, raw materials, and human resources.

Although all organizations are dependent on their environments for resources, some organizations are more dependent than others. This is because some environments have a larger amount of readily accessible resources.[15] A classic case of a highly resource-dependent organization is a newly formed small business. Cautious bank managers, credit-wary suppliers, and a dearth of customers all teach the aspiring owner the meaning of dependence. Also, many organizations in traditional "smokestack" industries encounter a much less munificent environment. Investors are wary, customers are disappearing, and skilled human resources are attracted to situations with better career prospects. Historically, the computer and software industries were located in munificent environments. Capital was readily available, human resources were trained in relevant fields, and new uses for computers were continually being developed. Although this is still to some extent the case, we have already alluded to the shakeout in the market for basic software. The days are gone when business amateurs can develop a new wordprocessing package and become multimillionaires, like the founders of WordPerfect. The big firms have consolidated the market.

Resource dependence can be fairly independent of environmental uncertainty, and dealing with one issue will not necessarily have an effect on the other. For example, although the computer industry generally faces a fairly munificent environment, this environment is uncertain, especially with regard to rate of change. On the other hand, many mature small businesses exist in a fairly certain environment but remain highly resource dependent.

Competitors, regulatory agencies, and various interest groups can have a considerable stake in how an organization obtains and transforms its resources.[16] In effect, the organization might be indirectly resource dependent on these bodies and thus susceptible to a fair degree of social control. For example, Saturn could have begun operations without unionization (the Nissan plant located in Tennessee is not unionized). However, other GM plants are organized by the United Auto Workers. To preclude labour difficulties and ensure the presence of committed human resources, GM agreed to United Auto Workers representation from the outset of the project.

The concept of resource dependence does not mean that organizations are totally at the mercy of their environments. Rather, it means that they must develop strategies for managing both resource dependence and environmental uncertainty.

Strategic Responses to Uncertainty and Resource Dependence

Organizations devote considerable effort to developing and implementing strategies to cope with environmental uncertainty and resource dependence. **Strategy** can be defined as the process by which top executives seek to cope with the constraints and opportunities posed by an organization's environment.

Exhibit 15.4 outlines the nature of the relationship between environment and strategy. At the top, the objective organizational environment is portrayed in terms of uncertainty and available resources, as we discussed above. However, much of the impact that the environment has on organizations is indirect rather than direct, filtered through the perceptual system of managers and other organizational members.[17] By means of the perceptual process we discussed in Chapter 3, personality characteristics and experience may colour managers' perceptions of the environment. For example, the environment might seem much more complex and unstable for a manager who is new to his job than for one who has years of experience. Similarly, the optimistic manager might perceive

Strategy. The process by which top executives seek to cope with the constraints and opportunities that an organization's environment poses.

more resources than the pessimistic manager.[18] It is the perceived environment that comprises the basis for strategy formulation.

Strategy formulation itself involves determining the mission, goals, and objectives of the organization. At the most basic level, for a business firm, this would even involve consideration of just what business the organization should pursue. Then, the organization's orientation toward the perceived environment must be determined. This might range from being defensive and protective of current interests (such as holding market share) to prospecting vigorously for new interests to exploit (such as developing totally new products).[19] There is no single correct strategy along this continuum. Rather, the chosen strategy must correspond to the constraints and opportunities of the environment. Finally, the strategy must be implemented by selecting appropriate managers for the task and employing appropriate techniques as shown in Exhibit 15.4.

Organizational Structure as a Strategic Response

How should organizations be structured to cope with environmental uncertainty? Paul Lawrence and Jay Lorsch of Harvard University have studied this problem.[20]

Lawrence and Lorsch chose for their research more and less successful organizations in three industries—plastics, packaged food products, and paper con-

Exhibit 15.4
Environment, strategy, and
organizational effectiveness.

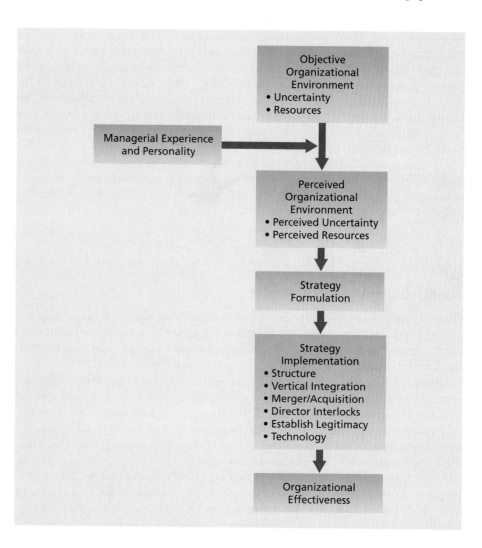

tainers. These industries were chosen intentionally because it was assumed that they faced environments that differed in perceived uncertainty. This was subsequently confirmed by questionnaires and interviews. The environment of the plastics firms was perceived as very uncertain because of rapidly changing scientific knowledge, technology, and customer demands. Decisions had to be made even though feedback about their accuracy often involved considerable delay. At the opposite extreme, the container firms faced an environment that was perceived as much more certain. No major changes in technology had occurred in 20 years, and the name of the game was simply to produce high-quality standardized containers and get them to the customer quickly. The consequences of decisions could be learned in a short period of time. The perceived uncertainty faced by the producers of packaged foods fell between that experienced by the plastics producers and that faced by container firms.

Going a step further, Lawrence and Lorsch also examined the sectors of the environment that were faced by three departments in each company: sales (market environment), production (technical environment), and research (scientific environment). Their findings are shown in Exhibit 15.5. The crucial factor here is the *range* of uncertainty across the subenvironments faced by the various departments. In the container companies, producing, selling, and research (mostly quality control) were all fairly certain activities. In contrast, the range of uncertainty encountered by the plastics firms was quite broad. Research worked in a scientific environment that was extremely uncertain. On the other hand, production faced a technical environment that was a good bit more routine.

When Lawrence and Lorsch examined the attitudes of organizational managers, the impact of perceived environmental uncertainty became apparent. First of all, because the departments of the plastics firms had to cope with sectors of the environment that differed in certainty, the plastics firms tended to be highly differentiated (Chapter 14). Thus, their managers tended to differ rather greatly in terms of goals, interpersonal relationships, and time spans. For example, production managers were interested in immediate, short-term problems, while managers in the research department were concerned with longer-range scientific development. Conversely, the container firms were not highly differentiated because the environmental sectors with which they dealt were more similar in perceived certainty. The food packaging firms were more differentiated than the container firms but less differentiated than the plastic companies.

Because they faced a fairly certain environment and because they were fairly undifferentiated, the container firms had adopted mechanistic structures. The

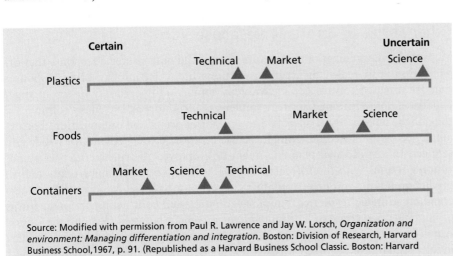

Exhibit 15.5
Relative perceived uncertainty of environmental sectors in the Lawrence and Lorsch study.

Source: Modified with permission from Paul R. Lawrence and Jay W. Lorsch, *Organization and environment: Managing differentiation and integration.* Boston: Division of Research, Harvard Business School,1967, p. 91. (Republished as a Harvard Business School Classic. Boston: Harvard Business School Press,1986).

most successful was organized along strict functional lines and was highly centralized. Coordination was achieved through direct supervision and formalized written schedules. All in all, this container firm conformed closely to the classical prescriptions for structure. At the other extreme, the most successful plastics companies had adopted organic structures. This was the most sensible way to deal with an uncertain environment and high differentiation. Decision-making power was decentralized to locate it where the appropriate knowledge existed. Coordination was achieved through informal mutual adjustment, ad hoc teams that cut across departments, and special integrators who coordinated between departments (Chapter 14). In addition, the departments themselves were structured somewhat differently, research being the most organic and production the least organic.

The Lawrence and Lorsch study is important because it demonstrates a close connection among environment, structure, and effectiveness. However, follow-up research has not been entirely supportive of their findings, and several contradictory studies exist.[21] Despite these spotty research findings, organizations very commonly tailor structure to strategy in coping with the environment.

For example, in order to make the company more flexible and entrepreneurial, McDonald's created a new decentralized regional structure in the United States consisting of regional divisions. Five new regional division heads have been appointed in order to create smaller companies within the larger McDonald's. The divisions have their own staff functions, such as human resources, and a president who is responsible for results. As well, each division has autonomy over things like advertising, restaurant openings, and product development.[22]

Part of the GM Saturn organization's strategy is to reduce the development time for new models. This helps to counteract uncertainty in the marketplace. To implement the strategy, the company opted for a flatter, more organic, less bureaucratic structure for Saturn.

The argument presented so far suggests that strategy always determines structure, rather than the other way around. This is a reasonable conclusion when considering an organization undergoing great change or the formation of a new organization (such as Saturn). However, for ongoing organizations, structure sometimes dictates strategy formulation. For instance, highly complex decentralized structures might dictate strategies that are the product of political bargaining between functional units. More centralized simple structures might produce strategies that appear more rational and less political (although not necessarily superior in effectiveness).[23]

Other Forms of Strategic Response

Variations on organizational structure are not the only strategic response that organizations can make. Structural variations often accompany other responses that are oriented toward coping with environmental uncertainty or resource dependence. Some forms of strategy implementation appear extremely routine, yet they might have a strong effect on the performance of the organization. For example, economic forecasting might be used to predict the demand for goods and services. In turn, formal planning might be employed to synchronize the organization's actions with the forecasts. All this is done to reduce uncertainty and to predict trends in resource availability. Lobbying and public relations are also common strategic responses. Simple negotiating and contracting are other forms of implementing strategy. The innovative agreement between GM and the United Auto Workers regarding Saturn is one such example. General Motors' strategy involved guaranteeing itself a ready supply of flexible labour at somewhat less than the going wage rate at its other plants.

Some more elaborate forms of strategic response are worth a more detailed look. Notice how many of these concern relationships *between* organizations.

Vertical Integration. Many managers live in fear of disruption on the input or output end of their organizations. A lack of raw materials to process or a snag in marketing products or services can threaten the very existence of the organization. One basic way to buffer the organization against such uncertainty over resource control is to use an inventory policy of stockpiling both inputs and outputs. For example, an automaker might stockpile needed parts in advance of an anticipated strike at a supplier. At the same time, it might have 30 days' supply of new cars in its distribution system at all times. Both inventories serve as environmental "shock absorbers." A natural extension of this logic is **vertical integration,** the strategy of formally taking control of sources of supply and distribution.[24] Major oil companies, for instance, are highly vertically integrated, handling their own exploration, drilling, transport, refining, retail sales, and credit. Starbucks, the Seattle-based chain of espresso bars, imports, roasts, and packages its own coffee and refuses to franchise its bars in order to maintain high quality.

Vertical integration can reduce risk for an organization in many cases. However, when the environment becomes very turbulent, it can reduce flexibility and actually increase risk.[25] Managerial inefficiencies can also develop as a result of control and coordination difficulties, and various bureaucratic costs can also result. However, the results of a recent study indicates that the benefits of vertical integration outweigh the costs.[26]

Mergers and Acquisitions. In recent years, we have seen the headlines again and again: MCI WorldCom acquires Sprint Corp.; Canadian National Railway Co. and Burlington Northern Santa Fe Corp. propose to merge into North America's largest freight railway; Air Canada takes over Canadian Airlines; Monsanto Co. and rival Pharmacia & Upjohn sign a merger agreement worth $23.4 billion; America Online proposes a $160 billion takeover of Time Warner Inc. Such mergers of two firms or the acquisition of one firm by another are increasingly common strategic responses. Some mergers and acquisitions are stimulated by simple economies of scale. For example, a motel chain with 100 motels might

Vertical integration. The strategy of formally taking control of sources of organizational supply and distribution.

Mergers of two firms or the acquisition of one firm by another such as Air Canada's acquisition of Canadian Airlines have become increasingly common strategic responses in recent years.

have the same advertising costs as one with 50 motels. Other mergers and acquisitions are pursued for purposes of vertical integration. For instance, a paper manufacturer might purchase a timber company. When mergers and acquisitions occur within the *same* industry, they are being effected partly to reduce the uncertainty prompted by competition. When they occur across *different* industries (a diversification strategy), the goal is often to reduce resource dependence on a particular segment of the environment. A portfolio is created so that if resources become threatened in one part of the environment, the organization can still prosper.[27] This was one motive for Philip Morris to take over food companies such as Kraft. Antismoking sentiments and legislation have provided much uncertainty for the firm's core cigarette business.

One trend in contemporary North America has been mergers between hospitals to avoid duplication and thus cut costs. In the United States, this has been particularly motivated by "managed care" health providers who have insisted that hospitals become more efficient.

Strategic Alliances. We have all heard about bad blood following a merger or acquisition, especially after a hostile takeover. This failure of cultures to integrate smoothly (Chapter 8) is only one reason that mergers that look good from a financial point of view often end up as operational disasters. Is there any way to have the benefits of matrimony without the attendant risks? Increasingly, the answer seems to be **strategic alliances,** that is, actively cooperative relationships between legally separate organizations. The organizations in question retain their own cultures, but true cooperation replaces distrust, competition, or conflict for the project at hand. Properly designed, such alliances reduce risk and uncertainty for all parties, and resource *interdependence* is recognized. The network organization we discussed in the previous chapter is one form of strategic alliance.

Organizations can engage in strategic alliances with competitors, suppliers, customers, and unions.[28] Among competitors, one common alliance is a research and development consortium in which companies band together to support basic research that is relevant for their products. For example, several Canadian producers of audio speakers formed a consortium under the National Research Council to perfect the technology for "smart speakers" that adjust automatically to room configuration. Another common alliance between competitors is the joint venture, in which organizations combine complementary advantages for economic gain or new experience. The Toyota-General Motors joint venture in a California auto plant gave Toyota manufacturing access to the United States and gave GM experience with Japanese management techniques. This experience heavily influenced GM's subsequent decisions about how to structure and manage Saturn.

Strategic alliances with suppliers and customers have a similar theme of reducing friction and building trust and cooperation. At Union Pacific, for example, customers can place orders and track the progress of their own shipments by accessing UP's own mainframe. In manufacturing, it used to be standard procedure to have a number of suppliers that were chosen on the basis of low cost. If one supplier's quality or delivery was poor, it was dropped, and the slack was made up by another. Now it is becoming common for manufacturers to work closely with a small set of stable suppliers to ensure ongoing excellence in quality, delivery, and service. Hewlett-Packard, Ford, and General Motors are notably progressive in this.[29]

Finally, strategic alliances can occur between companies and unions. The innovative Saturn labour contract is just such an example.

Strategic alliances are most successful and stable when the senior managers of the firms meet frequently and when the firms behave "transparently" toward one another, exchanging information quickly and accurately. A prior history of co-

Strategic alliances. Actively cooperative relationships between legally separate organizations.

operation and a feeling that the partner is not taking unfair advantage of the alliance are also important.[30]

Strategic alliances between global partners are increasingly common. Examples include the Ford-Mazda connection, the European Airbus consortium, and a Canon-Olivetti joint venture in copiers. These global alliances can be especially difficult to manage due to cross-cultural differences in expectations. For example, North Americans favour shorter time horizons and a rather direct approach to conflicts. Far Eastern cultures favour longer time horizons and "talking around" overt conflict [31] (see "Global Focus: *Global Strategic Alliance to Develop New Computer Chip Leads to Cross-Cultural Confusion*.")

Siemens AG
www.siemens.com/en/home/

Interlocking Directorates. If we added up all the positions on boards of directors in the country and then added up all the people who serve as directors, the second number would be considerably smaller than the first. This is because of **interlocking directorates,** the condition that is said to exist when one person serves as a director on two or more boards. Such interlocking is legally prohibited when the firms are direct competitors; but as you can imagine, a fine line may exist as to the definition of a direct competitor. Many have recognized that interlocking directorates provide a subtle but effective means of coping with environmental uncertainty and resource dependence. The director's expertise and experience with one organization can provide valuable information for another. Sometimes the value of the interlock is more direct. This is especially true when

Interlocking directorates. A condition existing when one person serves on two or more boards of directors.

---

global focus → Global Strategic Alliance to Develop New Computer Chip Leads to Cross-Cultural Confusion

EAST FISHKILL, N.Y. — Three competing companies from three continents—Siemens AG of Germany, Toshiba Corp. of Japan, and IBM—are trying to develop a revolutionary computer memory chip together. The Triad, as they call themselves, has been working on research at the IBM facility in this small Hudson River Valley town. The undertaking is cutting-edge, both in technology and in the scope of its cross-cultural cooperation.

Initially, some organizers wondered whether more than 100 scientists from competitive, culturally diverse backgrounds could work together on such a large project. They were right to worry.

At East Fishkill, Siemens scientists were shocked to find Toshiba colleagues closing their eyes and seeming to sleep during meetings (a common practice for overworked Japanese managers when talk does not concern them). The Japanese, who normally work in big groups, found it painful to sit in small, individual offices and speak English; some now withdraw when they can into all-Japanese groups. IBMers complained that the Germans plan too much and that the Japanese—who like to review ideas constantly—will not make clear decisions. Suspicions circulate that some researchers are withholding information from the group.

The separation has prevented the hoped-for big creative leaps that researchers call Aha! effects. "I

wish I had a good example of breaking through that and coming up with a great new idea, but unfortunately that hasn't happened very much," says [IBM's Matt] Wordeman. He adds, however, that the engineers themselves are extremely talented, and this has permitted them to overcome disappointments and wasted time, keeping the project on track.

Wordeman and other Triad participants emphasize that despite the huge extra effort required, the project is not in trouble. Work is on schedule—even a bit ahead in part—and they are finding ways to overcome communications problems, they say. Members of all three teams say they have learned huge amounts, both about technology and about cooperating with outsiders.

Cooperative projects of this kind are likely to proliferate, and the reason is money. In business after business, development costs are ballooning, driving more and more cash-strapped companies to look for ways to cooperate with competitors.

Source: Excerpted from Browning, E. S. (1994, May 3). Computer chip project brings rivals together, but the cultures clash. *The Wall Street Journal*, pp. A1, A8.

it is a "vertical interlock" in which one firm provides inputs to or receives outputs from the other (for instance, a director might serve on the board of a steel company and that of an auto producer):

> In addition to reducing uncertainty concerning inputs or outputs, a vertical interlock may also create a more efficient method of dealing with the environment. The outside director might be able not only to obtain the critical input but also to procure favourable treatment, such as a better price, better payment terms, or better delivery schedules. In addition, the search costs or the complexity involved in dealing with the environment may be reduced.[32]

Interlocks can also serve as a means of influencing public opinion about the wealth, status, or social conscience of a particular organization. Highly placed university officials, clergy, and union leaders are effectively board members in their own organizations, and they may be sought as board members by business firms to convey an impression of social responsibility to the wider public.[33] Resources are easier to obtain from a friendly environment than from a hostile environment!

Establishing Legitimacy. It is something of a paradox that environmental uncertainty seems to increase the need to make correct organizational responses but at the same time makes it harder to know which response is correct! One strategic response to this dilemma is to do things that make the organization appear *legitimate* to various constituents.[34] Taking actions that conform to prevailing norms and expectations will often be strategically correct, but equally important, it will have the *appearance* of being strategically correct. In turn, management will appear to be rational, and providers of resources will feel comfortable with the organization's actions.

How can legitimacy be achieved? One way is by association with higher status individuals or organizations. For example, an organization without much established status might put a high-status outsider on its board or form a strategic alliance with a more prestigious partner. Another way is to be seen as doing good deeds in the community. Thus, many companies engage in corporate philanthropy and various charity activities. A third way to achieve legitimacy is to make very visible responses to social trends and legal legislation. For example, many firms have appointed directors of workforce diversity or established official units to deal with implementing the ramifications of the Americans with Disabilities Act. Although such highly visible responses are not the only way to proceed with these matters, they do send obvious signals to external constituents that the organization is meeting social expectations. Probably the most common way of achieving legitimacy is to imitate management practices that other firms have institutionalized.

Attempts to achieve legitimacy can backfire. This is especially evident when management practices from other firms are copied without careful thought. Firms that "got on the bandwagon" of total quality management or downsizing without clear rationale have often had unsuccessful experiences, despite the appearance of following recognized business trends.

The preceding are just a few examples of the kinds of strategic responses that organizations can implement to cope with the environment. Now, let us examine in greater detail another such response—technological choice.

The Technologies of Organizations

The term *technology* brings to mind physical devices, such as turret lathes, handsaws, computers, and electron microscopes. However, as we pointed out earlier, this is an overly narrow view of the concept. To broaden this view, we might define **technology** as the activities, equipment, and knowledge necessary to turn organizational inputs into desired outputs. In a hospital, relevant inputs might include sick patients and naive interns, while desired outputs include well people and experienced doctors. In a steel mill, crucial inputs include scrap metal and energy, while desired outputs consist of finished steel. What technologies should the hospital and the steel mill use to facilitate this transformation? More important for our purposes, do different technologies require different organizational structures to be effective?

The concepts of technology and environment are closely related.[35] The inputs that are transformed by the technology come from various segments of the organization's environment. In turn, the outputs that the technology creates are returned to the environment. In addition, the activities, equipment, and knowledge that constitute the technology itself seldom spring to life within the organization. Rather, they are imported from the technological segment of the environment to meet the organization's needs.

Organizations choose their technologies.[36] In general, this choice will be predicated on a desired strategy. For example, the directors of a university mental health centre might decide that they wish to deal only with students suffering from transitory anxiety or mild neuroses. Given these inputs, certain short-term psychotherapies would constitute a sensible technology. More disturbed students would be referred to clinics that have different strategies and different technologies.

Different parts of the organization rely on different technologies, just as they respond to different aspects of the environment as a whole. For example, the human resource department uses a different technology from the finance department. However, research has often skirted this problem, concentrating on the "core" technology used by the key operating function (e.g., the production department in manufacturing firms).

Basic Dimensions of Technology

Organizational technology has been defined, conceptualized, and measured in literally dozens of different ways.[37] Some analysts have concentrated on degree of automation; others have focused on the degree of discretion granted to workers. Here we will consider other classifications of technologies, specifically those of Charles Perrow and James D. Thompson. These classification schemes are advantageous because we can apply them both to manufacturing firms and to service organizations, such as banks and schools.

Perrow's Routineness. According to Perrow, the key factor that differentiates various technologies is the routineness of the transformation task that confronts the department or organization.[38] **Technological routineness** is a function of two factors:

- *Exceptions.* Is the organization taking in standardized inputs and turning out standardized outputs (few exceptions)? Or is the organization encountering varied inputs or turning out varied outputs (many exceptions)? The technology becomes less routine as exceptions increase.

- *Problems.* When exceptions occur, are the problems easy to analyze or difficult to analyze? That is, can programmed decision making occur, or must workers resort to nonprogrammed decision making? The technology becomes less routine as problems become more difficult to analyze.

As Exhibit 15.6 demonstrates, the exceptions and problems dimensions can be arranged to produce a matrix of technologies. This matrix includes the following technologies:

Technology. The activities, equipment, and knowledge necessary to turn organizational inputs into desired outputs.

Technological routineness. The extent to which exceptions and problems affect the task of converting inputs into outputs.

Exhibit 15.6
Perrow's matrix of
technologies.

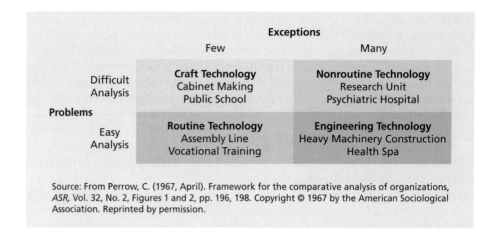

Source: From Perrow, C. (1967, April). Framework for the comparative analysis of organizations, *ASR*, Vol. 32, No. 2, Figures 1 and 2, pp. 196, 198. Copyright © 1967 by the American Sociological Association. Reprinted by permission.

- *Craft technologies* typically deal with fairly standard inputs and outputs. Cabinetmakers use wood to make cabinets, and public schools attempt to educate "typical" students. However, when exceptions are encountered (a special order or a slow learner), analysis of the correct action might be difficult.

- *Routine technologies,* such as assembly-line operations and technical schools, also deal with standardized inputs and outputs. However, when exceptions do occur (a new product line or a new subject to teach), the correct response is fairly obvious.

- *Nonroutine technologies* must deal frequently with exceptional inputs or outputs, and the analysis of these exceptions is often difficult. By definition, research units are set up to deal with difficult, exceptional problems. Similarly, psychiatric hospitals encounter patients with a wide variety of disturbances. Deciding on a proper course of therapy can be problematic.

- *Engineering technologies* encounter many exceptions of input or required output, but these exceptions can be dealt with by using standardized responses. For example, individuals with a wide variety of physical conditions visit health spas, and each has a particular goal (e.g., weight loss, muscle development). Despite this variety, the recommendation of a training regimen for each individual is a fairly easy decision.

From most routine to least routine, we can order Perrow's four technological classifications in the following manner: routine, engineering, craft, nonroutine. Shortly, we will consider which structures are appropriate for these technologies. First, let us examine Thompson's technological classification.

Thompson's Interdependence. In contrast to Perrow, James D. Thompson was interested in the way in which work activities are sequenced or "put together" during the transformation process.[39] A key factor here is **technological interdependence,** the extent to which organizational subunits depend on each other for resources, such as raw materials or information. In order of increasing interdependence, Thompson proposed three classifications of technology (Exhibit 15.7). These classifications are as follows:

Technological interdependence. The extent to which organizational subunits depend on each other for resources, raw materials or information.

Pooled interdependence. A condition in which organizational subunits are dependent on the pooled resources generated by other subunits but are otherwise fairly independent.

- *Mediating technologies* operate under **pooled interdependence.** This means that each unit is to some extent dependent on the pooled resources generated by the other units but is otherwise fairly independent of those units. Thompson gives rather abstract examples, such as banks, which mediate between depositors and borrowers, and post offices, which mediate between the senders and receivers of letters. However, the same argument can be applied more clearly to the branches of banks or post offices. The health of a

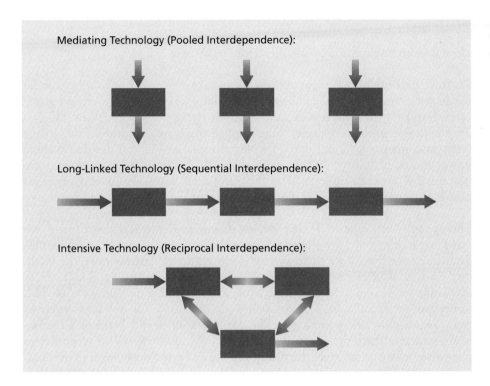

Exhibit 15.7
Thompson's technology
classification.

bank as a whole might depend on the existence of several branches, but these branches operate almost independently of each other. Each has its own borrowers and depositors. Similarly, post office branches are dependent on other branches to forward and receive mail, but this is the limit of their required interaction. A taxi company is another good example of pooled interdependence.

■ *Long-linked technologies* operate under **sequential interdependence.** This means that each unit in the technology is dependent on the activity of the unit that preceded it in a sequence. The transformed product of each unit becomes a resource or raw material for the next unit. Mass production assembly lines are the classic example of long-linked technology. However, many "paper-processing" technologies, such as the claims department of an insurance company, are also sequentially interdependent (claims must be verified before they are adjusted and must be adjusted before they are settled).

Sequential interdependence. A condition in which organizational subunits are dependent on the resources generated by units that precede them in a sequence of work.

■ *Intensive technologies* operate under **reciprocal interdependence.** This means that considerable interplay and mutual feedback must occur between the units performing the task in order to accomplish it properly. This is necessary because each task is unique, and the intensive technology is thus a customized technology. One example might be the technology employed by a multidisciplinary research team. Thompson cites a general hospital as a prime example of intensive technology:

Reciprocal interdependence. A condition in which organizational subunits must engage in considerable interplay and mutual feedback to accomplish a task.

> At any moment an emergency admission may require some combination of dietary, x-ray, laboratory, and housekeeping or hotel services, together with the various medical specialities, pharmaceutical services, occupational therapies, social work services, and spiritual or religious services. Which of these is needed, and when, can be determined only from evidence about the state of the patient.[40]

As technologies become increasingly interdependent, problems of coordination, communication, and decision making increase. To perform effectively, each technology requires a tailored structure to facilitate these tasks.

Structuring to Cope with Technology

How does technology affect organizational structure?

Perrow. According to Perrow, routine technologies should function best under mechanistic structures, while nonroutine technologies call for more organic structures. In the former case, few exceptions to the normal course of events and easily analyzable problems suggest high formalization and centralization. In the latter case, many exceptions and difficult problems suggest that decision-making power should be located "where the action is." The craft and engineering technologies fall between these prescriptions. Research has generally supported his notion that more routine technologies adopt more mechanistic structures.[41]

Thompson. According to Thompson, increasing technological interdependence must be accompanied by increased coordination or integration mechanisms. There is research evidence to support this proposition.[42] Furthermore, the *methods* used to achieve coordination should be reflected in structural differences across the technologies. Mediating technologies, operating only under pooled interdependence, should be able to achieve coordination via standardization of rules, regulations, and procedures. This formalization is indicative of a mechanistic structure (consider banks and the post office). Long-linked technologies must also be structured mechanistically, but the increased demands for coordination prompted by sequential interdependence must be met by planning, scheduling, and meetings. Finally, intensive technologies require intensive coordination, and this is best achieved by mutual adjustment and an organic structure that permits the free and ready flow of information among units.[43]

Woodward. The most famous study of the relationship between technology and structure is that of Joan Woodward. Woodward examined the technology, structure, and organizational effectiveness of 100 firms in South Essex, England.[44] This study is especially interesting because it began as an attempt to test the argument that mechanistic structures will prove most effective in all cases. In brief, this test failed—there was no simple, consistent relationship between organizational structure and effectiveness—and many of the successful firms exhibited organic structures. Woodward then analyzed and classified the technologies of the 80 firms in her sample that had clear-cut, stable production processes. She used the classifications unit, mass, and process production. Some examples of these classifications include the following:

- *Unit* (production of single units or small batches)
  Custom-tailored units
  Prototype production
  Fabrication of large equipment in stages (e.g., locomotives)
  Small batches to order
- *Mass* (production of large batches or mass production)
  Large batches on assembly lines
  Mass production (e.g., bakeries)
- *Process* (input transformed as an ongoing process)
  Chemicals processed in batches
  Continuous-flow production (e.g., gasoline, propane)

From top to bottom, this scale of technology reflects both increasing smoothness of production and increasing impersonalization of task requirements.[45] Less and less personal intervention is necessary as machines control more and more of the work. Woodward's mass technology incorporates aspects of Perrow's routine technology and Thompson's long-linked technology. Her unit technology seems to cover Perrow's craft and engineering technologies and some aspects of Thompson's intensive technology. It is difficult to isolate Woodward's process technology in the Perrow or Thompson classifications.

Now for the key questions. Did organizational structures tend to vary with technology? If so, was this variance related to organizational effectiveness? The answer in both cases is yes. Each of the three technologies tended to have distinctive structures, and the most successful firms had structures that closely approximated the average of their technological groups. For instance, Woodward found that as the production process became smoother, more continuous, and more impersonal, the management of the system took on increasing importance, that is, moving from unit to mass to process, there were more managers relative to workers, more hierarchical levels, and lower labour costs. This is not difficult to understand. Unit production involves custom-tailored craftswork in which the workers can essentially manage their own work activity. However, it is very labour intensive. On the other hand, sophisticated continuous-process systems (such as those used to refine gasoline) take a great amount of management skill and technical attention to start up. Once rolling, a handful of workers can monitor and maintain the system.

Successful firms with unit and process technologies relied on organic structures, while successful firms that engaged in mass production relied on mechanistic structures. For example, the latter firms had more specialization of labour, more controls, and greater formalization (a reliance on written rather than verbal communication). At first glance, it might strike you as unusual that the firms at the extremes of the technology scale (unit and process) both tended to rely on organic structures. However, close consideration of the actual tasks performed under each technology resolves this apparent contradiction. Unit production generally involves custom-building complete units to customer specifications. As such, it relies on skilled labour, teamwork, and coordination by mutual adjustment and standardized skills. The work itself is not machine-paced and is far from mechanistic. At the other extreme, process production is almost totally automated. The workers are essentially skilled technicians who monitor and maintain the system, and they again tend to work in teams. While the machinery itself operates according to a rigid schedule, workers can monitor and maintain it at their own pace. Informal relationships with supervisors replace close control.

Woodward's research is a landmark in demonstrating the general proposition that structure must be tailored to the technology the organization adopts to achieve its strategic goals. Her findings have been replicated and extended by others.[46] However, there have been disconfirming studies, and a constant debate has gone on about the relative importance of organizational size versus technology in determining structure.[47] For an example of how technology can affect organizational structure, please consider the You Be the Manager feature.

Signicast Corp.
www.signicast.com

Saturn. The design of the Saturn organization shows evidence of an attempt to match structure to technology. In Woodward's terms, the core technology at Saturn is obviously mass production. However, some of its unique features, such as building automatic and manual transmissions on the same line to exactly match a car order, mean that the technology is somewhat less routine (in Perrow's terms) than the conventional monolithic assembly line. To take advantage of this, the shopfloor organization, with its work teams and reduced supervision, is more organic than is typical for the North American auto industry. This, then, is also reflected in the managerial and professional ranks, in which the technology for designing cars was modified. Instead of passing designs from department to department (Thompson's sequential interdependence), early involvement of all critical departments was obtained (Thompson's reciprocal interdependence). Again, this points to a more organic structure backed up by sophisticated electronic aids

you be the
manager

Changing the Technology at Signicast Corp.

While the new automated continuous-flow processing technology would contribute to the objectives of speed, low cost, and flexibility, would other changes be necessary?

Signicast Corp., an investment castings manufacturer based in Milwaukee, had a major problem. In 1992, the company was landlocked in its Milwaukee facility. There was absolutely no more room for expansion. "If we wanted to continue to grow—and we very much wanted to—we'd have to buy some land and build," said Robert Schuemann, vice-president of sales and administration. "Why don't we build what we've always wanted? As long as we can start from a blank sheet of paper, we can design the best facility in the world."

So management decided to build a new $12 million automated plant. They began talking to customers to learn how Signicast could improve its investment-castings service, which makes precise metal parts direct to customers' blueprints, such as a kickstand for a Harley-Davidson motorcycle or a part for a John Deere tractor.

Customers' principal concerns were long lead times, unreliable delivery dates, and cost. Accordingly, the new plant would be designed to attack these concerns. The strategy for cutting lead time was to cut throughput-time (the time it takes to make a product from beginning to end). That, in turn, required converting production from batch processing (creating batches of product at intervals) to automated continuous-flow processing. "In a traditional shop, people spend most of their time trying to figure out what to do next," says Terry Lutz, Signicast's president. "With a control system and continuous-flow manufacturing, we're able to get the product to flow to the people. Everybody knows what to do, because that's what comes next." If an order starts

on time, the process ensures it will ship on time, thus providing more reliable delivery dates.

A core group of five executives started planning the new facility to be built in Hartford, about 25 miles northwest of the existing Milwaukee facility. Every Signicast employee had an opportunity to contribute to the new facility. An early decision was made to build the new plant as a small module, designated Hartford 1, that would handle a closely related product mix for which Signicast would develop business. If successful, Signicast would then build a second facility, Hartford 2, and develop a product mix for that module. Each module would be a stand-alone operation.

While the new technology would contribute to the objectives of speed, low cost, and flexibility, would other changes be necessary? Manufacturing throughput-times were to be only three to five days versus approximately 25 days at Milwaukee. Signicast would achieve low costs only if production was right the first time, every time. Thus, the executive team resolved that no space would be allocated to rework. Signicast employees at Milwaukee, working within the batch-processing technology, perform only one highly specialized job consistent with a mechanistic organizational structure. However, management realized that Hartford personnel would have to do more and have more responsibility than their counterparts at Milwaukee.

What else would have to change as result of the new automated and continuous-flow technology and the objectives of low costs, speed, and flexibility? You be the manager.

1. How will the change in technology at Signicast affect organizational structure? Refer to Perrow, Thompson, and Woodward to answer this question.

2. What changes do you think Signicast made in order to tailor the organization's structure to the new technology?

To find out what Signicast did, consult The Manager's Notebook at the end of the chapter.

Source: Based on Nagler, B. (1998, January). Recasting employees into teams. *Workforce*, 77(1), pp. 101-106.

to facilitate coordination and communication. In fact, let us now turn our attention to advanced information technology.

Implications of Advanced Information Technology

In concluding the chapter, let us consider some of the implications that ongoing advances in information technology are having for organizational behaviour. Speaking broadly, **advanced information technology** refers to the generation, aggregation, storage, modification, and speedy transmission of information made possible by the advent of computers and related devices. Information technology is equally applicable in the factory or the office. In the factory, examples include robots, computer numerically controlled machine tools, and automated inventory management. In the office, it covers everything from word processing to electronic mail to automated filing to expert systems. Between the office and the factory, it includes computer-aided design and engineering.

Advanced information technology. The generation, aggregation, storage, modification, and speedy transmission of information made possible by the advent of computers and related devices.

The Two Faces of Advanced Technology

It is important to recognize that there has been much inaccurate hoopla about advanced information technology. This began even before the first mainframe computers were perfected, and it continues today. To exaggerate only slightly, doomsayers have painted a dark picture of job loss and de-skilling, with technology running wild and stifling the human spirit. Opponents of this view (often vendors of hardware and software) have painted a rosy picture of improved productivity, superior decision making, and upgraded, happy employees. It probably does not surprise you that research fails to support either of these extremes as a general state of affairs. In the early days of mainframe batch data processing, de-skilling, job pacing, and loss of routine clerical jobs did occur. However, as we shall see, the consequences of current advanced information technology are much less deterministic.

This discussion of extremes alerts us to a more realistic issue that we might call the "two faces" of technology.[48] This means that a given form of advanced information technology can have exactly *opposite* effects, depending on how it is employed. For example, the same system that is designed to monitor and control employees (say, by counting keystrokes) can also provide feedback and reduce supervision. Additionally, the same technology that can de-skill jobs can build skills *into* jobs. How can these opposite effects occur? They are possible because information technology is so *flexible*. In fact, we are discussing information technology separately from the core technologies discussed earlier because it is so flexible that it can be applied in conjunction with any of them.

The flexibility of information technology means that it is not deterministic of a particular organization structure, or job design. Rather, it gives organizations *choices* about how to organize work. The company that wishes to decentralize can use information technology to provide lower-level employees with data to make decisions. The company that wishes to centralize can use the other face of the same technology to gather information from below to retain control. Such choices are a function of organizational culture and management values rather than inherent in the hardware. They should match the strategy the organization is pursuing, as our discussion of advanced manufacturing will show.

For purposes of discussion, we will distinguish between advanced manufacturing technology and advanced office technology. However, as we shall see, this distinction is artificial, since advanced technology has the capability to link the office more closely to the factory or to clients, customers, and suppliers in the outside environment.

Advanced Manufacturing Technology

Three major trends underlie advanced manufacturing technology.[49] The first is an obvious capitalization on computer intelligence and memory. The second is flexibility, in that the technology can accomplish a changing variety of tasks. This is usually the product of an organizational strategy that favours adaptiveness, small batch production, and fast response. In turn, this strategy follows from attempting to find and exploit short-term "niches" in the marketplace rather than hoping to produce large volumes of the same product year after year. Consider this textile firm:

> Milliken has reduced its average production run from 20,000 to 4,000 yards and can dye lots as small as 1,000 yards. Apparel makers, textile and fibre firms, and retailers have recently joined to launch the so-called Quick Response program, designed to improve the flow of information among the various groups and speed order times. The program's goal is to cut the 66-week cycle from fibre to retail in the United States to 21 weeks.[50]

As a third trend, advanced manufacturing technologies are increasingly being designed to be integrated with *other* advanced technologies that organizations use. For example, the computer-aided design system that is used to design and modify a product can also be used to design, operate, and modify its production process via computer-aided manufacturing programs (the result being a so-called CAD/CAM system). Ultimately, using most of the technologies mentioned here, computer-integrated manufacturing systems (CIM) that integrate and automate all aspects of design, manufacturing, assembly, and inspection can be put in place. In turn, computerized information systems can link these tasks to supply and sales networks. Exhibit 15.8 compares highly flexible manufacturing systems with traditional mass production.[51]

What are the general implications of advanced manufacturing technology for organizational behaviour? Such technology tends to automate the more routine information-processing and decision-making tasks. Depending on job design, what might remain for operators are the more complex, nonroutine tasks—those dealing with system problems and exceptions. In addition, task interdependence tends to increase under advanced technologies. For example, design, manufacturing, and marketing become more reciprocally than sequentially interdependent in a flexible manufacturing system. Finally, let us remember that such advanced technologies are adopted, in part, to cope with a less certain environment. Thus, many advanced technological systems result in nonroutine, highly interdependent tasks that are embedded in an uncertain environment.[52]

Organizational Structure. What are the implications of this shift in technology? As Exhibit 15.8 shows, one effect is a movement toward flatter, more organic structures to capitalize on the technology's flexibility.[53] This corresponds to Woodward's finding that unit technologies require more organic designs than mass technologies, and the adoption of more flexible, short-term production batches is an example of unit technology. The expectation of flatter structures stems from the fact that more highly automated systems will handle information processing and diagnoses that were formerly performed by middle managers. Implications of advanced technology for centralization are interesting. On the one hand, matters such as ordering raw materials and scheduling production

Organizational Characteristic	Flexible Manufacturing	Mass Production
Strategy	• Adapt to environment • Produce small batches • Small inventory, fast turnover • Respond fast	• Buffer against environment • Produce large batches • Large inventory, slow turnover • Respond predictably
Product	• Many variations, variable life cycles	• Few variations, long life cycles
Marketing	• Exploit niche markets	• Cater to mass market
Structure	• Organic, integrated	• Mechanistic, differentiated
Suppliers	• Few, chosen for reliability and responsiveness	• Many, chosen on basis of cost
Jobs	• Flexible jobs; teamwork	• Rigid, specialized jobs; little teamwork

Exhibit 15.8
Flexible manufacturing compared with traditional mass production.

should become more highly centralized. This is both required by the flexibility of the system and permitted by its enhanced information-processing capability. On the other hand, when problems or exceptions occur or when new designs are conceived, decentralization might be called for to locate decision making in the hands of lower-level specialists. However, the whole thrust of advanced technology dictates greater integration among specialities, such as design, engineering, production, and marketing. This might require a retreat from the rigid functional structures (Chapter 14) that are common in manufacturing firms. Minimally, it suggests the increased use of integrators, task forces, planning committees, and other mechanisms that stimulate coordination. One study of 185 firms that adopted advanced manufacturing technology found a general trend toward decentralization with more formalized rules and procedures to ensure coordination and effective exploitation of the technology.[54] However, another recent study on the effects of computer-based technology in manufacturing organizations found that it reduced the number of levels in the hierarchy and centralized operational authority and influence.[55]

Job Design. Advanced manufacturing technology can be expected to affect the design of jobs, and this is where the issue of choice we alluded to earlier clearly comes into play. There is evidence that such technology can reduce worker control over shopfloor jobs and water down existing skills.[56] An example is having skilled machinists operate lathes that have been programmed by a remote technician. However, other choices are possible, including teaching the machinists to program the lathe or at least to edit existing programs for local conditions. The latter approaches have been shown to gain cooperation and commitment to the new technology and to enhance performance.[57] Following this logic, since advanced technology tends to automate routine tasks, operative workers must usually acquire advanced skills (e.g., computer skills). Also, since advanced technology tends to be flexible as well as expensive to operate, workers themselves must be flexible and fast to respond to problems. Extreme division of labour can be counterproductive in advanced technology. For example, operators simply might not be able to wait for someone else to perform routine maintenance and thus might have to have the flexibility to do this themselves. Similarly, traditional distinctions between roles (electrical maintenance versus mechanical maintenance or drafting versus design) begin to blur when the needs for coordination that advanced technology imposes are recognized.

All this points to the design of jobs for advanced manufacturing technology according to the principles of job enrichment we discussed in Chapter 6. In turn, this suggests that proper training is critical and that pay levels should be revised to fit the additional skills and responsibilities prompted by the technology. Many observers have recommended that self-managed teams (Chapter 7) be made responsible for setting up, running, and maintaining the system.[58] In fact, GM has adopted this scheme for the Saturn plant. Such teams permit cross-transfer of skills and provide the cross-task integration that is necessary to keep things working smoothly. The team concept is also applicable to other forms of advanced technology. For example, one company organized its CAD/CAM users into teams composed of two designers, a draftsperson, and a toolmaker.[59]

Advanced Office Technology

As we noted above, the label advanced office technology can be applied sensibly to everything from word processing to exotic expert decision systems. Advanced office technology illustrates the coming together of some combination of three previously separate technologies—computers, office machines, and telecommunications (for example, a word processor combines a computer and a typewriter). The most common basic functions of the technology are the following:[60]

- Text processing
- Communication (e.g., electronic mail, fax)
- Information storage and retrieval
- Analysis and manipulation of information
- Administrative support (e.g., electronic calendars)

As with advanced manufacturing technology, we can point to some environmental and strategic concerns that have stimulated the adoption of advanced office technology, although these concerns are more general. One is obviously the potential for *labour saving*. Consider, for example, word processing (revisions are easy), video conferencing (a trip to the Coast is unnecessary), or spreadsheet analysis (many "What if?" scenarios can be probed by one manager). Another major concern stimulating the adoption of advanced technology is *responsiveness*, both within the organization and also to customers and suppliers. Speed and personalization of response are common goals. Finally, *improved decision making* is a goal of various decision support systems, expert systems, and the like.

The implications of advanced office technology are far reaching. What follows is an illustrative sample, again focusing on organizational structure and job design.

Organizational Structure. At least as it pertains to management jobs, the link between office technology and organizational structure has been dominated by two related issues—the impact of information technology on tallness/flatness and centralization. Regarding tallness and flatness, advanced technology has enabled a reduction in the number of supervisory and middle-management personnel.[61] Fewer supervisors are needed because electronic monitoring and feedback often replace routine supervision, and existing supervisors can handle larger spans of control. With fewer supervisors, fewer middle managers are required. Also, some advanced technology, such as decision support and expert systems, can make up for analyses performed by middle managers. For its size (over 80,000 employees), FedEx is a flat organization, having only five levels. This is due, in part, to advanced electronic communication systems.

Actual research evidence on all this is rather scanty and mainly targeted at the middle-management issue. Although there are reports of staff reductions, it is difficult to know how much of this is a direct result of office technology as opposed to the imposition of flatness to make organizations more responsive to the external environment. Some research points to increased demands on middle-management jobs as larger spans require them to be in charge of more diverse areas and as their performance is more monitorable by top management due to the technology.[62]

The impact of advanced office technology on centralization of decision making is variable, precisely as it should be.[63] Again, the key is the extreme flexibility of information technology. The same systems that allow senior managers to meddle in lower-level operations might enable junior staffers to assemble data and make decisions. Notice, though, that advanced technology does imply a freer, more democratic flow of information and general communication. This suggests that advanced technology enables a wider range of people at more levels to be involved in organizational decision making.[64] Exactly how this capacity gets played out in decision-making practice is most likely a function of strategy and prevailing culture.

Job Design. The impact of advanced office technology on job design and related quality of working life differs considerably with job status. Among clerical and secretarial employees, when jobs have not been lost altogether, there is the potential for de-skilling and reduced motivating potential.[65] A good case in point occurred in many organizations when word processing was introduced. Because the equipment was then expensive, secretarial support was often shifted into word processing pools to make efficient use of the hardware.[66] This frequently resulted in task specialization and a reduction in task identity. However, most observers agree that such technology can actually upgrade skills if it is used to optimal capacity and the work is not highly fragmented.[67] In fact, one study found that the extent to which computers have a positive or negative effect on job characteristics depends on several factors, such as the amount of time spent on computing and noncomputing components of a job, the nature of the work done on the computer, and the nature of the work that is done apart from the computer.[68]

Turning to quality of working life, word processing and related video display work have been known to provoke eyestrain, muscular strain, and stress symptoms. However, proper work station design and work pacing can help cope with these problems. Computer monitoring (such as counting keystrokes or timing the length of phone calls by service workers) has also been linked to stress reactions. However, there are studies that show that such monitoring may be viewed favourably by employees when it is used for job feedback rather than as a basis for punishment.[69]

On the whole, professionals and managers seem to have taken to advanced office technology remarkably well. Routine aspects of such jobs (such as doing tedious calculations) have often been replaced by more cerebral pursuits. One exception may be some semiprofessional jobs, such as drafting, in which de-skilling can occur without thoughtful job redesign.

There are many examples of organizations that have had poor success in introducing advanced technology because they ignored the human dimension. This raises the issue of implementing change in organizations, a concern of the next chapter.

the manager's notebook

Changing the Technology at Signicast Corp.

1. Signicast Corp.'s shift to an automated continuous-flow processing technology is a good example of how a shift in technology can affect organizational structure. According to Perrow, routine technologies should function best under mechanistic structures while nonroutine technologies call for more organic structures. With the new continuous-flow technology, there is likely to be more exceptions and difficult problems compared with the batch-processing technology. Thus, decision-making power should be located "where the action is," and this is most likely to occur in an organic structure. According to Thompson, the continuous-flow technology would result in greater technological interdependence and would require intensive coordination. This would call for greater mutual adjustment and an organic structure for the free and ready flow of information among units. According to Woodward, we would once again expect a more organic structure. Woodward's research showed that successful firms with unit and process technologies relied on organic structures, while successful firms that engaged in mass production relied on mechanistic structures. Because process production is almost totally automated, the workers are usually skilled technicians who monitor and maintain the system, and they tend to also work in teams. As well, informal relationships with supervisors replace close control. Thus, all three theories predict an organic structure in which workers make decisions, coordinate their efforts, and work in teams. Now let us take a look at how the new technology actually changed the structure at Signicast.

2. The basic requirements for new hires at Milwaukee are a high school diploma and a good work ethic. No specific experience is sought because Signicast provides all necessary training. For the 135 new employees at Hartford, however, the same basic requirements were sought plus a team orientation, good trainability, good communication skills, and a willingness to do varied jobs over a 12-hour shift. These skills were now required because of changes in job design and working arrangements. For example, it was decided that employees at Hartford would not operate the same job for more than four to six hours as was the case at Milwaukee. Instead, employees would be cross-trained to do a variety jobs thus enabling them to move elsewhere in the plant to work and perform two or more jobs on a shift. This would make jobs more interesting, teach employees new skills, and reduce injuries. Thus, Hartford was structured so that people would move to the work rather than having the work moved to the people. Employees have the title of technician and operate equipment, inspection devices, and other aspects of the plant, while machines do the heavy grunt work. Signicast also created teams for the Hartford plant. Instructors from a local technical college were brought in to give 10-week team-building courses for two hours a week. The course covered habits, problem solving, team building, diversity, and other issues affecting how workers relate to their co-workers and work, and how they can solve problems as a team. A team consists of everyone on a given 12-hour shift. There are two day-teams (6 a.m. to 6 p.m.) and two night-teams (6 p.m. to 6 a.m.), and each team has its own supervisor. These teams have a large degree of input and impact. Many policies and procedures are put to a vote as to what team members want. Because the supervisor runs the entire plant, he or she has neither the time nor the inclination to do any straw boss-type supervision. Accordingly, empowered workers have to be both motivated and trained to do their jobs not only well but independently. In the end, Signicast was able to build a new kind of workforce along with a new kind of facility because management realized that in addition to technology, changes also had to be made in work arrangements, structure, and job design. The reduced supervision combined with the use of empowered work teams and cross-trained multiskilled employees created a more organic structure that was more suitable to the new automated technology.

Summary

- Organizations are open systems that take inputs from the external environment, transform some of these inputs, and send them back into the environment as outputs. The external environment includes all the events and conditions surrounding the organization that influence this process. Major components of the environment include the economy, customers, suppliers, competitors, social/political factors, and existing technologies.

- One key aspect of the external environment is its uncertainty. More uncertain environments are vague, difficult to diagnose, and unpredictable. Uncertainty is a function of complexity and rate of change. The most uncertain environments are complex and dynamic—they involve a large number of dissimilar components that are changing unpredictably. More certain environments are simple and stable—they involve a few similar components that exhibit little change. As environmental uncertainty increases, cause-effect relationships get harder to diagnose, and agreeing on priorities becomes more difficult because more information must be processed.

- Another key aspect of the external environment is the amount of resources it contains. Some environments are richer or more munificent than others, and all organizations are dependent on their environments for resources.

- Strategy is the process that executives use to cope with the constraints and opportunities posed by the organization's environment, including uncertainty and scarce resources. One critical strategic response involves tailoring the organization's structure to suit the environment. In general, as the Lawrence and Lorsch study demonstrates, mechanistic structures are most suitable for more certain environments, and organic structures are better suited to uncertain environments. Other strategic responses include vertical integration, mergers and acquisitions, strategic alliances, interlocking directorates, establishing legitimacy, and technological choice.

- Technology includes the activities, equipment, and knowledge necessary to turn organizational inputs into desired outputs. One key aspect of technology is the extent of its routineness. A routine technology involves few exceptions to usual inputs or outputs and readily analyzable problems. A nonroutine technology involves many exceptions that are difficult to analyze. Another key aspect of technology is the degree of interdependence that exists between organizational units. This may range from simple pooling of resources, to sequential activities, to complex reciprocal interdependence.

- The most famous study of the relationship between technology and structure was Joan Woodward's. She determined that unit and process technologies performed best under organic structures, while mass production functioned best under a mechanistic structure. In general, less routine technologies and more interdependent technologies call for more organic structures.

- Advanced information technology generates, aggregates, stores, modifies, and speedily transmits information. In the factory, it permits flexible manufacturing that calls for organic structures, enriched jobs, and increased teamwork. In the office and the organization as a whole, the flexibility of advanced information technology means that its effects are highly dependent on management values and culture.

Discussion Questions

1. Construct a diagram of the various interest groups in the external environment of CNN Television. Discuss how some of these interest groups may make competing or contradictory demands on CNN.

2. Give an example of vertical integration. Use the concept of resource dependence to explain why an organization might choose a strategic response of vertical integration.

3. Discuss how interlocking directorates might reduce environmental uncertainty and help manage resource dependence.

4. Explain why organizations operating in more uncertain environments require more organic structures.

5. Distinguish among pooled interdependence, sequential interdependence, and reciprocal interdependence in terms of the key problem each poses for organizational effectiveness.

6. Give an example of unit technology, mass technology, and process technology. For which type of technology are the prescriptions of the classical organizational theorists best suited?

7. Imagine that a company is converting from conventional mass technology to a highly flexible, computerized, integrated production system. List structural and behavioural problems that the company might have to anticipate in making this conversion.

8. Discuss this statement: The effects of advanced information technology on job design and organizational structure are highly predictable.

? 9. Consider the effect of environmental uncertainty and resource dependence on power and politics in organizations. To what extent is subunit power and organizational politics a function of environmental uncertainty and resource dependence? Does environmental uncertainty and resource dependence predict and explain the distribution and use of power and politics in organizations?

? 10. How does technology influence job design? Discuss the effect of technology according to Perrow, Thompson, and Woodward on the following approaches to job design described in Chapter 6: traditional views of job design, the Job Characteristics Model, and job enrichment.

Experiential Exercise

Diagnosing an Organization

The purpose of this exercise is to choose an organization and to diagnose it in terms of the concepts we covered in the chapter. Doing such a diagnosis should enable you to see better how the degree of "fit" among organizational structure, environment, strategy, and technology influences the effectiveness of the organization. The discussion throughout the chapter of the General Motors' Saturn organization provides a general model for the nature of the exercise.

This exercise is suitable for an individual or group project completed outside the class or a class discussion guided by the instructor. In the case of the group project completed outside the class, each group might choose and contact a local organization for information. Alternatively, library resources might be consulted to diagnose a prominent national or international organization. Your instructor might suggest one or more organizations for diagnosis.

1. Discuss in detail the external environment of the chosen organization.

   a) How has the general economy affected this organization recently? Is the organization especially sensitive to swings in the economy?

   b) Who are the organization's key customers? What demands do they make on the organization?

   c) Who are the organization's key suppliers? What impact do they have on the organization?

   d) Who are the organization's important competitors? What threats or opportunities do they pose for the organization?

   e) What general social and political factors (e.g., the law, social trends, environmental concerns) affect the organization in critical ways?

2. Drawing on your answers to question 1, discuss both the degree of environmental uncertainty and the nature of resource dependence the organization faces. Be sure to locate the firm or institution in the appropriate cell of Exhibit 15.3, and defend your answer.

3. What broad strategies (excluding structure) has the organization chosen to cope with its environment?

4. Describe in as much detail as possible the structure of the organization, and explain how this structure represents a strategic response to the demands of the environment. Is this the proper structure for the environment and broad strategies that you described in response to the earlier questions?

   a) How big is the organization?

   b) What form of departmentation is used?

   c) How big are the spans of control?

   d) How tall is the organization?

   e) How much formalization is apparent?

   f) To what extent is the organization centralized?

   g) How complex is the organization?

   h) Where does the organization fall on a continuum from mechanistic to organic?

5. Describe the organization's core technology in terms of routineness (Exhibit 15.6) and interdependence (Exhibit 15.7). Is its structure appropriate for its technology?

6. What impact has advanced information technology had on the organization?

Case Incident

GTE

Telephone operations account for four-fifths of GTE's $20 billion in annual revenues. With deregulation, the telephone business has become intensely competitive, and GTE was looking for ways to both cut costs and improve customer service. Improved service can reduce service costs in the field, improve existing customers' relationships, and attract new customers. The traditional approach to such improvements has been to try to "fine tune" existing procedures in the repair, billing, and marketing departments. However, GTE saw merit in trying to totally reengineer the way customers interacted with the company to make the process more efficient and satisfying, perhaps using some of its own technology.

GTE was using a traditional system in which a customer needing repair service called an operator who took down basic information and then bounced the customer around various departments until someone could solve his or her problem. This system of passing on customers was both expensive and inefficient. What if a single customer wanted to question a bill, obtain a calling card, and report a dial tone problem?

1. Describe the external environment of GTE and the relevant components of it. What influence does the external environment have on GTE?

2. What would you do to improve customer service at GTE and how does advanced information technology provide opportunities for improved customer service?

Sources: Sager, I. (1994). The great equalizer. *Business Week* (Special issue: The Information Revolution). 100–107; Stewart, T. A. (1993, August 23). Reengineering: The hot new management tool. *Fortune*, 41–48; Greengard, S. (1993, December). Reengineering: Out of the rubble. *Personnel Journal*, 48A–48O; Brain Blevins, GTE.

Case Study

Philips NV

Introduction

Established in 1891, the Dutch company Philips NV is one of the world's largest electronics enterprises. Its businesses are grouped into four main divisions: lighting, consumer electronics, professional products, (computers, telecommunications, and medical equipment), and components (including chips). In each of these areas, it ranks alongside the likes of Matsushita, General Electric, Sony, and Siemans as a global competitor. In the late 1980s, the company had several hundred subsidiaries in 60 countries, it operated manufacturing plants in more than 40 countries, it employed approximately 300,000 people, and it manufactured thousands of different products. However, despite its global reach by 1990, Philips was a company in deep trouble. After a decade of deteriorating performance, in 1990 Philips lost $2.2 billion on revenues of $28 billion. A major reason seems to have been the inability of Philips to adapt to the changing competitive conditions in the global electronics industry during the 1970s and 1980s.

Philips' Traditional Organization

To trace the roots of Philips' current troubles, one has to go back to World War II. Until then, the foreign activities of Philips had been run from its head office in Eindhoven. However, during World War II, the Netherlands was occupied by Germany. Cut off from their home base, Philips' various national organizations began to operate independently. In essence, each major national organization developed into a self-contained company with its own manufacturing, marketing, and R&D functions.

Following the war, top management felt that the company could be most successfully rebuilt through its national organizations. There were several reasons for this belief. First, high trade barriers made it logical that self-contained national organizations be established in each major national market. Second, it was felt that strong national organizations would allow Philips to be responsive to local demands in each country in which it competed. And third, given the substantial autonomy that the various national organizations had gained during the war, top management felt that reestablishing centralized control might prove difficult and yield few benefits.

At the same time, top management felt the need for some centralized control over product policy and R&D in order to achieve some coordination between national organizations. Its response was to create a number of worldwide product divisions (of which there were 14 by the mid-1980s). In theory, basic R&D and product development policy were the responsibilities of the product divisions, whereas the national organizations were responsible for day-to-day operations in a particular country. Product strategy in a given country was meant to be determined jointly by consultation between the responsible national organization and the product divisions. It was the national organizations that implemented strategy.

Another major feature of Philips' organization was the dummvirate form of management. In most national organizations, top-management responsibilities and authority were shared by two managers—one responsible for "commercial affairs" and another responsible for "technical activities." This form of management had its origins in the company's founders—Anton and Gerard Philips. Anton was a salesman and Gerard an engineer. Throughout the company, there seemed to be a vigorous, informal competition between technical and sales managers, with each attempting to outperform the other. Anton once noted:

> The technical management and the sales management competed to outperform each other. Production tried to produce so much that sales would not be able to get rid of it; sales tried to sell so much that the factory would not be able to keep up [Aguilar and Yoshino, 1987].

The top decision-making and policy-making body in the company was a 10-person board of management. While board members all shared general management responsibility, they typically maintained a special interest in one of the functional areas of the company (for example, R&D, manufacturing, marketing). Traditionally, most of the members of the management board were Dutch and had come up through the Eindhoven bureaucracy, although most had extensive foreign postings, often as a top manager in one of the company's national organizations.

Environmental Change

From the 1960s onward, a number of significant changes took place in Philips' competitive environment that were to profoundly affect the company. First, due to the efforts of the General Agreement on Tariffs and Trade (GATT), trade barriers fell worldwide. In addition, in Philips' home base,

Europe, the emergence of the European Economic Community, of which the Netherlands was an early member, led to a further reduction in trade barriers between the countries of Western Europe.

Second, during the 1960s and 1970s a number of new competitors emerged in Japan. Taking advantage of the success of GATT in lowering trade barriers, the Japanese companies produced most of their output at home and then exported to the rest of the world. The resulting economies of scale allowed them to drive down unit costs below those achieved by Western competitors, such as Philips, that manufactured in multiple locations. This significantly increased competitive pressures in most of the business areas where Philips competed.

Third, due to technological changes, the cost of R&D and manufacturing increased rapidly. The introduction of transistors and then integrated circuits called for significant capital expenditures in production facilities—often running into hundreds of millions of dollars. To realize scale economies, substantial levels of output had to be achieved. Moreover, the pace of technological change was declining and product life cycles were shortening. This gave companies in the electronics industry less time to recoup their capital investments before new-generation products came along.

Finally, as the world moved from a series of fragmented national markets toward a single global market, uniform global standards for electronic equipment were beginning to emerge. This standardization showed itself most clearly in the videocassette recorder business, where three standards initially battled for dominance—the Betamax standard produced by Sony, the VHS standard produced by Matsushita, and the V2000 standard produced by Philips. The VHS standard was the one most widely accepted by consumers, and the others were eventually abandoned. For Philips and Sony, both of which had invested substantially in their own standard, this was a significant defeat. Philips' attempt to establish its V2000 format as an industry standard was effectively killed off by the decision of its own North American national organization, over the objections of Eindhoven, to manufacture according to the VHS standard.

Organizational and Strategic Change

By the early 1980s, Philips realized that if it was to survive, it would have to restructure its business radically. Its cost structure was high due to the amount of duplication across national organizations, particularly in the area of manufacturing. Moreover, as the V2000 incident demonstrated, the company's attempts to compete effectively were being hindered by the strength and autonomy of its national organizations.

The first attempt at change came in 1982 when Wisse Dekker was appointed CEO. Dekker quickly pushed for manufacturing rationalization, creating international production centres that served a number of national organizations and closing many small inefficient plants. He also pushed Philips to enter into more collaborative arrangements with other electronics firms in order to share the costs and risks of developing new products. In addition, Dekker accelerated a trend that had already begun within the com-

pany to move away from the dual leadership arrangement within national organizations (commercial and technical), replacing this arrangement with a single general manager. Furthermore, Dekker tried to "tilt" Philips' matrix away from national organizations by creating a corporate council where the heads of product divisions would join the heads of the national organizations to discuss issues of importance to both. At the same time, he gave the product divisions more responsibility to determine companywide research and manufacturing activities.

In 1986, Dekker was succeeded by Cor van de Klugt. One of van de Klugt's first actions was to specify that profitability was to be the central criterion for evaluating performance within Philips. The product divisions were given primary responsibility for achieving profits. This was followed in late 1986 by his termination of the U.S. Philips trust, which had been given control of Philips' North American operations during World War II and which still maintained control as of 1986. By terminating the trust, van de Klugt, in theory, reestablished Eindhoven's control over the North American subsidiary. Then, in May 1987, van de Klugt announced a major restructuring of Philips. He designated four product divisions—lighting, consumer electronics, components, and telecommunications and data systems—as "core divisions," the implication being that other activities would be sold off. At the same time he reduced the size of the management board. Its policy-making responsibility was devolved to a new group management committee, comprising the remaining board members plus the heads of the core product divisions. No heads of national organizations were appointed to this body, thereby further tilting power within Philips away from the national organizations toward the product divisions.

Despite these changes, Philips' competitive position continued to deteriorate. Many outside observers attributed this slide to the dead hand of the huge head office bureaucracy at Eindhoven (which comprised more than 3,000 people in 1989). They argued that while van de Klugt had changed the organizational chart, much of this change was superficial. Real power, they argued, still lay with the Eindhoven bureaucracy and their allies in the national organizations. In support of this view, they pointed out that since 1986 Philips' workforce had declined by less than 10 percent, instead of the 30 percent reduction that many analysts were calling for.

Alarmed by a 1989 loss of $1.06 billion, the board forced van de Klugt to resign in May 1990. He was replaced by Jan Timmer. Timmer quickly announced that he would cut Philips's worldwide workforce by 10,000 to 283,000, and launch a $1.4 billion restructuring. Investors were unimpressed—most of them thought that the company needed to lose 40,000 to 50,000 jobs—and reacted by knocking the share price down by 7 percent. Since then, however, Timmer had made some progress. In mid-1991, he sold off Philips's minicomputer division—which at the time was losing $1 million per day—to Digital Equipment. He also announced plans to reduce costs by $1.2 billion by cutting the workforce by 55,000. In addition, he entered into a strategic alliance with Matsushita, the Japanese electronic giant, to manufacture and market the Digital Compact Cassette (DCC).

Source: Charles W.L. Hill, University of Washington. From Gareth Jones. (1993). *Organizational theory: Text and cases*, 2nd ed. Addison Wesley (Reading). Reprinted with permission.

1. Discuss the role the environment played in terms of the strategy and structure of Philips prior to the 1960s.

2. Discuss the environmental components of Philips that have been exerting influence since the 1960s.

3. Apply the concepts of environmental uncertainty, resource dependence, and strategy to the Philips case.

4. Discuss Philips first attempt to cope and change with Wisse Dekker as CEO considering the interplay among strategy, structure, and technology. Why was this program not more successful?

5. Discuss Philips second attempt to cope and change with Cor van de Klugt as CEO again considering the interplay among strategy, structure, and technology. Why was this program not more successful?

6. Discuss Philips third attempt to cope and change with Jan Timmer as CEO again considering the interplay among strategy, structure, and technology. Will this program be more successful than the previous two?

7. Not all efforts at organizational change turn out successfully. What strategic responses were used by Philips to try to cope with environmental uncertainty, and how successful were they? Would other strategic responses have been more successful?

8. Describe the technology of Philips. What role did technology play in the problems experienced by Philips, and how might changes in technology lead to improvements?

Chapter 16

Organizational Change, Development, and Innovation

MCDONALD'S CORP. In 1982, Peters and Waterman published their popular book on management, *In Search of Excellence,* in which McDonald's was noted as one of America's excellent companies. In 1988, a feature article appeared in *Fortune* magazine titled, "The McDonald's Mystique." Below the title, the byline read, "How does this behemoth march on while competitors stumble?" But 10 years later, in March of 1998, a cover story in *Business Week* showed a sad-faced Ronald McDonald on the magazine cover with the caption, "Can It Regain Its Golden Touch?" Oh, how times have changed!

McDonald's Corp.

During the last 10 years, McDonald's share of fast-food sales in the United States has declined almost two percentage points to 16.2 percent even with a 50 percent increase in the number of restaurants. Although revenue and net income have more than tripled since 1987, after five decades of growth, it has begun to stagnate. In fact, while nearly every other top consumer brand has prospered, McDonald's operating profits have not even kept pace with inflation. International earnings growth have also fallen below the company's projections.

Many believe that the root of the problem is McDonald's failure to respond to changing market forces. McDonald's has a long history of tradition and holding the past sacred rather than embracing change. Considered to be one the most insular of large companies around, most of McDonald's top executives have been with the company for decades, and its board of directors is made up of current and former executives, vendors, and service providers. Rather than bring in new leaders when the business needed to change, the company has stuck to its philosophy of the 1950s and 1960s of rewarding and promoting managers who start at a young age and stay for life.

In response to problems related to new product innovation and food quality, McDonald's has embarked on a change program that includes a new custom-order food production system that will make it easier to customize sandwiches, expand the menu, and improve quality.

Among McDonald's many troubles is a dismal record of new product innovation. Its last successful new product was Chicken McNuggets which was launched in 1983. During the 1990s McDonald's spent millions of dollars on test products like carrot sticks, fried chicken, pasta, fajitas, pizza, the low-fat McLean Deluxe, and the much ballyhooed Arch Deluxe. Most of these products are now either off the McDonald's menu or available at only a limited number of restaurants. According to analysts, the new products just did not taste very good.

As well, McDonald's has failed to create new products that appeal to adults. In fact, its core menu has not changed much since the early 1980s. This has led some analysts to conclude that McDonald's has stopped innovating. In fact, it has not been able to grow much beyond its basic formula of burgers and fries.

Another fundamental problem facing McDonald's is the quality of its food. Consumers increasingly are demanding better tasting food and more variety. They are curbing their takeout habits and have become choosier when it comes to spending their fast-food dollars. In one recent poll, both Wendy's and Burger King came out ahead of McDonald's in terms of taste, and in another survey on taste, McDonald's was ranked 87th out of 91 food chains. In another survey, McDonald's received low marks on food quality, value, service, and cleanliness. McDonald's own internal company surveys have found significant dissatisfaction with food quality.

Clearly, the times have changed. With so many fast-food choices available, convenience is no longer enough to be successful. Among the most important factors that consumers today are looking for are quality and taste. However, instead of responding to these changes, McDonald's began a major American expansion that angered franchisees and created an opportunity for its com-

Burger King
www.burgerking.com

Learning Objectives

After reading Chapter 16, you should be able to:

1. Explain the environmental forces that motivate organizational change.

2. Describe the basic change process and the issues that require attention at various stages of change.

3. Explain how organizations can deal with resistance to change.

4. Define organizational development and discuss its general philosophy.

5. Discuss team building, survey feedback, total quality management, and reengineering as organizational development efforts.

6. Discuss the problems involved in evaluating organizational development efforts.

7. Define innovation and discuss the factors that contribute to successful organizational innovation.

8. Understand the factors that help and hurt the diffusion of innovations.

petitors to capture some of McDonald's 42 percent share of the $36 billion fast-food market. Burger King bit into its market share with a better-tasting burger, and Wendy's improved sales, thanks to new stuffed pitas and a spicy chicken sandwich.

In response to its problems and the changing market forces, McDonald's has embarked on a change program that began when Chief Executive Michael R. Quinlan shuffled his American management team. Jack M. Greenberg, McDonald's head of American operations, brought on board a handful of new managers. Then in April of 1998, it was announced that Greenberg would replace Quinlan as CEO, becoming only the fourth CEO in the company's history.

Greenberg has a number of plans to get McDonald's back on track. A new custom-order food production system called "Made for You" has been developed that will make it easier to customize sandwiches, expand the menu by providing greater flexibility, and improve quality by making fresher burgers. Although the McDonald's tradition has been to promote from within, they plan to go outside when there is a need. The best ideas for new products and ideas from any McDonalds will be shared with all stores. In order to spur innovation, there are plans for a program that will encourage and reward new ideas at all levels of the organization.

The company has also adopted a more decentralized regional-management structure to decentralize authority in an effort to revitalize the company's entrepreneurial spirit. The American market has been divided into five regional divisions, with autonomy over advertising, restaurant openings, and product development. Each division is expected to operate as a small company within McDonald's.

For many, Greenberg represents a new era for the world's largest restaurant company. He is admired by franchisees and seen as someone who is visible, approachable, accessible, and involved. Franchisees see a change in management philosophy away from the previous fortress mentality. As unlikely as it may seem to those who have watched McDonald's performance deteriorate and its stock tumble, the company appears to be experiencing a rejuvenation. The new food system is now in 20 percent of American stores, and the company's stock has been climbing with sales and profits on the rise.[1]

This story reflects the themes of our chapter. McDonald's environment changed, and it had to change with it to survive and prosper. This change required innovations in both products and management processes.

In this chapter, we will discuss the concept of organizational change, including the whys and whats of change. Then, we will consider the process by which change occurs and examine problems involved in managing change. Following this, we define organizational development and explore several development strategies as well as innovation, a special class of organizational change.

The Concept of Organizational Change

Common experience indicates that organizations are far from static. Our favourite small restaurant experiences success and expands. We return for a visit to our alma mater and observe a variety of new programs and new buildings. The local Chevy dealer also begins to sell Geos. As consumers, we are aware that such changes may have a profound impact on our satisfaction with the product or service offered. By extension, we can also imagine that these changes have a strong impact on the people who work at the restaurant, university, or car dealership. In and of themselves, such changes are neither good nor bad. Rather, it is the way in which the changes are *implemented* and *managed* that is crucial to both customers and members. This is the focus of the present chapter.

Why Organizations Must Change

All organizations face two basic sources of pressure to change—external sources and internal sources.

In Chapter 15, we pointed out that organizations are open systems that take inputs from the environment, transform some of these inputs, and send them back into the environment as outputs. Most organizations work hard to stabilize their inputs and outputs. For example, a manufacturing firm might use a variety of suppliers to avoid a shortage of raw materials and attempt to turn out quality products to ensure demand. However, there are limits on the extent to which such control over the environment can occur. In this case, environmental changes must be matched by organizational changes, if the organization is to remain effective. For example, consider the successful producer of record turntables in 1970. In only a few years, the turntable market virtually disappeared with the advent of reasonably priced cassette and CD players. If the firm was unable to anticipate this by developing a new product and a market, it surely ceased to exist.

Probably the best recent example of the impact of the external environment in stimulating organizational change is the increased competitiveness of business. Brought on, in part, by a more global economy, deregulation, and advanced technology, businesses have had to become, as the cliché goes, leaner and meaner.

Companies such as IBM and GM have laid off thousands of employees. Many firms did away with layers of middle managers, developing flatter structures so as to be more responsive to competitive demands. Mergers, acquisitions, and joint ventures with foreign firms have become commonplace, as have less adversarial relationships with unions and suppliers. Harley-Davidson was an early player in this game as it came to grips with the threat that Japanese motorcycle producers posed.

Change can also be provoked by forces in the internal environment of the organization. Low productivity, conflict, strikes, sabotage, and high absenteeism and turnover are some of the factors that signal to management that change is necessary. Very often, internal forces for change occur in response to organizational changes that are designed to deal with the external environment. Thus, many mergers and acquisitions that were to bolster the competitiveness of an organization have been followed by cultural conflict between the merged parties. This conflict often stimulates further changes that were not anticipated at the time of the merger.

The discussion of organizational change is traditional in organizational behaviour texts. However, the trends we are discussing here have truly magnified the importance of this topic. In contemporary organizations, much change is led by top management and involves sweeping modifications of a strategy. The entire organization is likely to be affected, and familiar employee values are likely to be challenged.[2]

In spite of these trends toward change, the internal and external environments of various organizations will be more or less dynamic. In responding to this, organizations should differ in the amount of change they exhibit. Exhibit 16.1 shows that organizations in a dynamic environment must generally exhibit more change to be effective than those operating in a more stable environment. Also, change in and of itself is not a good thing, and organizations can exhibit too much change as well as too little. The company that is in constant flux fails to establish the regular patterns of organizational behaviour that are necessary for effectiveness.

What Organizations Can Change

In theory, organizations can change just about any aspect of their operations they wish. Since change is a broad concept, it is useful to identify several specific domains in which modifications can occur. Of course, the choice of *what* to change

Exhibit 16.1
Relationships among environmental change, organizational change, and organizational effectiveness.

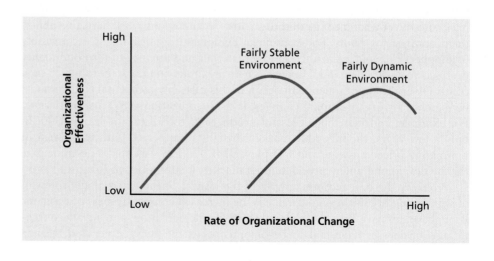

depends on a well-informed analysis of the internal and external forces signaling that change is necessary.[3] Factors that can be changed include:

- *Goals and strategies.* Organizations frequently change the goals and the strategies they use to reach these goals. Expansion, the introduction of new products, and the pursuit of new markets represent such changes.

- *Technology.* Technological changes can vary from minor to major. The introduction of online computer access for employees is a fairly minor change. Moving from a rigid assembly line to flexible manufacturing is a major change. McDonald's new food production system is an example of a change in technology.

- *Job design.* Companies can redesign individual groups of jobs to offer more or less variety, autonomy, identity, significance, and feedback, as we discussed in Chapter 6.

- *Structure.* Organizations can be modified from a functional to a product form or vice versa. Formalization and centralization can be manipulated, as can tallness, spans of control, and networking with other firms. Structural changes also include modifications in rules, policies, and procedures. McDonald's adoption of a more decentralized regional management structure represents a structural change.

- *Processes.* The basic processes by which work is accomplished can be changed. For instance, some stages of a project might be done concurrently rather than sequentially.

- *Culture.* As we discussed in Chapter 8, organizational culture refers to the shared beliefs, values, and assumptions that exist in an organization. An organization's culture has a strong influence on the attitudes and behaviours of organizational members. As a result, one of the most important changes that an organization can make is to change its culture. In fact, culture change is so critical that the main reason reported for the failure of organizational change programs is the failure to change an organization's culture. In addition, because organizational culture is known to be a major factor in providing an organization with a competitive advantage and long-term effectiveness, changing an organization's culture is considered to be a fundamental aspect of organizational change.[4]

- *People.* The membership of an organization can be changed in two senses. First, the actual *content* of the membership can be changed through a revised hiring process. This is often done to introduce "new blood" or to take advantage of the opportunities that a more diverse labour pool offers. Second, the existing membership can be changed in terms of skills and attitudes by various training and development methods.

Two important points should be made about the various areas in which organizations can introduce change. First, a change in one area very often calls for changes in others. Failure to recognize this systemic nature of change can lead to severe problems. For example, consider the functionally organized East Coast chemical firm that decides to expand its operations to the West Coast. To be effective, this goal and strategy change might require some major structural changes, including a more geographic form and decentralization of decision-making power.

Second, changes in goals, strategies, technology, structure, process, job design, and culture almost always require that organizations give serious attention to people changes. As much as possible, necessary skills and favourable attitudes should be fostered *before* these changes are introduced. For example, although providing bank employees with a revised computer system is a fairly minor tech-

nological change, it might provoke anxiety on the part of those whose jobs are affected. Adequate technical training and clear, open communication about the change can do much to alleviate this anxiety.

The Change Process

By definition, change involves a sequence of organizational events or a psychological process that occurs over time. The distinguished psychologist Kurt Lewin has suggested that this sequence or process involves three basic stages—unfreezing, changing, and refreezing.[5]

Unfreezing. The recognition that some current state of affairs is unsatisfactory.

Honda Motor Co.
www.honda.com

Change. The implementation of a program or plan to move the organization and/or its members to a more satisfactory state.

Unfreezing. Unfreezing occurs when recognition exists that some current state of affairs is unsatisfactory. This might involve the realization that the present structure, task design, or technology is ineffective, or that member skills or attitudes are inappropriate. *Crises* are especially likely to stimulate unfreezing. A dramatic drop in sales, a big lawsuit, or an unexpected strike are examples of such crises. At Ontario Hydro, for example, hundreds of managers had to reapply for their own jobs as part of a massive reorganization and culture-change effort. Talk about getting people's attention! A visit to Honda's American motorcycle plant by Harley-Davidson executives shocked them. The plant's great efficiency was obtained without a computer and with very few support staff. The decline of McDonald's share of fast food sales was a key factor in stimulating unfreezing. Of course, unfreezing can also occur without crisis. Employee attitude surveys, customer surveys, and accounting data are often used to anticipate problems and initiate change before crises are reached.

Change. Change occurs when some program or plan is implemented to move the organization and/or its members to a more satisfactory state. The terms *program* and *plan* are used rather loosely here, since some change efforts reveal inadequate planning. Change efforts can range from minor to major. A simple skills training program and a revised hiring procedure constitute fairly minor changes, in which few organizational members are involved. Conversely, major changes that involve many members might include extensive job enrichment, radical restructuring, or serious attempts at empowering the workforce.

Refreezing. When changes occur, the newly developed behaviours, attitudes, or structures must be subjected to **refreezing**, that is, they must become an enduring part of the organization. At this point, the effectiveness of the change can be examined, and the desirability of extending the change further can be considered. It should be emphasized that refreezing is a relative and temporary state of affairs.

Refreezing. The condition that exists when newly developed behaviours, attitudes, or structures become an enduring part of the organization.

Issues in the Change Process

The simple sketch of the change process presented in the preceding section ignores several important issues that organizations must confront during the process. These issues represent problems that must be overcome if the process is to be effective. Exhibit 16.2 illustrates the relationship between the stages of change and these problems, which include diagnosis, resistance, evaluation, and institutionalization.

Diagnosis

Diagnosis is the systematic collection of information relevant to impending organizational change. Initial diagnosis can provide information that contributes to unfreezing by showing that a problem exists. Once unfreezing occurs, further diagnosis can clarify the problem and suggest just what changes should be implemented. It is one thing to feel that "hospital morale has fallen drastically" but quite another to be sure that this is true and to decide what to do about it.

Diagnosis. The systematic collection of information relevant to impending organizational change.

Relatively routine diagnosis might be handled through existing channels. For example, suppose the director of a hospital laboratory believes that many of his lab technicians do not possess adequate technical skills. In conjunction with the hospital human resources manager, the director might arrange for a formal test of these skills. The hospital could devise a training program to correct inadequacies and establish a more stringent selection program to hire better personnel.

For more complex, nonroutine problems, there is considerable merit in seeking out the diagnostic skills of a change agent. **Change agents** are experts in the application of behavioural science knowledge to organizational diagnosis and change. Some large firms have in-house change agents who are available for consultation. In other cases, outside consultants might be brought in. In any event, the change agent brings an independent, objective perspective to the diagnosis, while working with the people who are about to undergo change.

Change agents. Experts in the application of behavioural science knowledge to organizational diagnosis and change.

It is possible to obtain diagnostic information through a combination of observations, interviews, questionnaires, and the scrutiny of records. Attention to the views of customers or clients is critical. As the next section will show, there is usually considerable merit in using questionnaires and interviews to involve

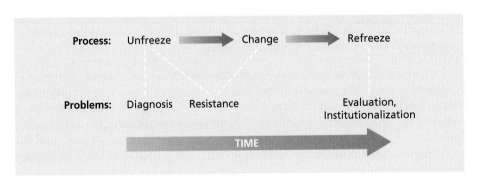

Exhibit 16.2
The change process and change problems.

the intended targets of change in the diagnostic process. The next section will also show why the change agent must be perceived as *trustworthy* by his or her clients.

The importance of careful diagnosis cannot be overemphasized. Proper diagnosis clarifies the problem and suggests *what* should be changed and the proper *strategy* for implementing change without resistance.[6] Unfortunately, many firms have a tendency to imitate the change programs of their competitors or other visible firms, without doing a careful diagnosis of their own specific needs. Similarly, managers sometimes confuse symptoms with underlying problems. This usually leads to trouble.

Resistance

As the saying goes, people are creatures of habit, and change is frequently resisted by those at whom it is targeted. More precisely, people may resist both unfreezing and change. At the unfreezing stage, defence mechanisms (Chapter 13) might be activated to deny or rationalize the signals that change is needed. Even if there is agreement that change is necessary, any specific plan for change might be resisted. This has been commonplace in recent years in American national politics. Although Congress has recognized the need to enhance federal revenues or reduce spending to reduce the budget deficit, many specific plans to do one or both have encountered strong resistance.

Resistance. Overt or covert failure by organizational members to support a change effort.

Causes of Resistance. Resistance to change occurs when people either overtly or covertly fail to support the change effort. Why does such failure of support occur? Several common reasons include the following:[7]

- *Politics and self-interest.* People might feel that they personally will lose status, power, or even their jobs with the advent of the change.

- *Low individual tolerance for change.* Predispositions in personality might make some people uncomfortable with changes in established routines.

- *Misunderstanding.* The reason for the change or the exact course that the change will take might be misunderstood.

- *Lack of trust.* People might clearly understand the arguments being made for change but not trust the motives of those proposing the change.

- *Different assessments of the situation.* The targets of change might sincerely feel that the situation does not warrant the proposed change and that the advocates of change have misread the situation. (At UPS, managers saw the introduction of scanning bar-coded packages as a way to help customers trace goods. Employees saw it as a way to track them and spy on them.[8])

UPS
www.ups.com

- *A resistant organizational culture.* Some organizational cultures have especially stressed and rewarded stability and tradition. Advocates of change in such cultures are viewed as misguided deviants or aberrant outsiders. (When deregulation forced massive changes at AT&T, the resistant traditionalists were labeled "bellheads" by the new guard![9])

Underlying these various reasons for resistance are two major themes: (1) change is unnecessary because there is only a small gap between the organization's current identity and its ideal identity; and (2) change is unobtainable (and threatening) because the gap between the current and ideal identities is too large. Exhibit 16.3 shows that a moderate identity gap is probably most conducive to increased acceptance of change because it unfreezes people, while not provoking maximum resistance.

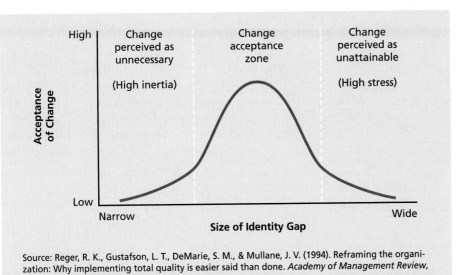

Source: Reger, R. K., Gustafson, L. T., DeMarie, S. M., & Mullane, J. V. (1994). Reframing the organization: Why implementing total quality is easier said than done. *Academy of Management Review*, 19, pp. 565–584.

Exhibit 16.3
Probability of acceptance of change.

Dealing with Resistance.[10] Low tolerance for change is mainly an individual matter, and it can often be overcome with supportive, patient supervision.

If politics and self-interest are at the root of resistance, it might be possible to co-opt the reluctant by giving them a special, desirable role in the change process or by negotiating special incentives for change. For example, consider office computing. Many heads of information services resisted the proliferation of personal computers, feeling that this change would reduce their power as departments moved away from dependence on the mainframe. Some organizations countered this resistance by giving information services control over the purchase, maintenance, and networking of personal computers, providing an incentive for change.

If misunderstanding, lack of trust, or different assessments are provoking resistance, good communication can pay off. Contemporary organizations are learning that obsessive secrecy about strategy and competition can have more internal costs than external benefits. It is particularly critical that lower-level managers understand the diagnosis underlying intended change and the details of the change so that they can convey this information to employees accurately. Springing "secret" changes on employees, especially when these changes involve matters such as workforce reduction, is sure to provoke resistance.

Involving the people who are the targets of change in the change process often reduces their resistance.[11] This is especially appropriate when there is adequate time for participation, when true commitment ("ownership") to the change is critical, and when the people who will be affected by the change have unique knowledge to offer.

Finally, transformational leaders (Chapter 9) are particularly adept at overcoming resistance to change. One way they accomplish this is by "striking while the iron is hot," that is, by being especially sensitive to when followers are *ready* for change. For example, when Lee Iacocca became president of Chrysler, the situation was so bad that employees knew that change would have to occur. The other way is to unfreeze current thinking by installing practices that constantly examine and question the status quo. One research study of CEOs who were transformational leaders noted the following unfreezing practices:[12]

- An atmosphere is established in which dissent is not only tolerated but encouraged. Proposals and ideas are given tough objective reviews, and disagreement is not viewed as disloyalty.

"... BEEN THERE, DONE THAT..."

- The environment is scanned for objective information about the organization's true performance. This might involve putting lots of outsiders on the board of directors or sending technical types out to meet customers.
- Organizational members are sent to other organizations and even other countries to see how things are done elsewhere.
- The organization compares itself along a wide range of criteria *against the competition,* rather than simply comparing its performance against last year's. This avoids complacency.

Transformational leaders are skilled at using the new ideas that stem from these practices to create a revised vision for followers about what the organization can do or be. Often, a radically reshaped culture is the result. In the process, as we suggested in Chapter 9, they are good at inspiring trust and encouraging followers to subordinate their individual self-interests for the good of the organization. This combination of tactics keeps followers within the zone of acceptance shown in Exhibit 16.3.

Evaluation and Institutionalization

It seems only reasonable to evaluate changes to determine whether they accomplished what they were supposed to and whether that accomplishment is now considered adequate. Obviously, objective goals, such as return on investment or market share, might be easiest and most likely to be evaluated. Of course, organizational politics can intrude to cloud even the most objective evaluation.

Organizations are notorious for doing a weak job of evaluating "soft" change programs that involve skills, attitudes, and values. However, it is possible to do a thorough evaluation by considering a range of variables:

- Reactions—did participants like the change program?
- Learning—what was acquired in the program?
- Behaviour—what changes in job behaviour occurred?
- Outcomes—what changes in productivity, absence, etc. occurred?[13]

To some extent, reactions measure resistance, learning reflects change, and behaviour reflects successful refreezing. Outcomes indicate whether refreezing is useful for the organization. Unfortunately, many evaluations of change efforts never go beyond the measurement of reactions. Again, part of the reason for this may be political. The people who propose the change effort fear reprisal if failure occurs.

If the outcome of change is evaluated favourably, the organization will wish to institutionalize that change. This means that the change becomes a permanent part of the organizational system, a social fact that persists over time, despite possible turnover by the members who originally experienced the change.[14]

Logic suggests that it should be fairly easy to institutionalize a change that has been deemed successful. However, we noted that many change efforts go unevaluated or are only weakly evaluated, and without hard proof of success, it is very easy for institutionalization to be rejected by disaffected parties. This is a special problem for extensive, broad-based change programs that call for a large amount of commitment from a variety of parties (e.g., extensive participation, job enrichment, or work restructuring). It is one thing to institutionalize a simple training program but quite another to do the same for complex interventions that can be judged from a variety of perspectives.

Studies of more complex change efforts indicate that a number of factors can inhibit institutionalization. For example, promised extrinsic rewards (such as pay bonuses) might not be developed to accompany changes. Similarly, initial changes might provide intrinsic rewards that create higher expectations that cannot be fulfilled. Institutionalization might also be damaged if new hires are not carefully socialized to understand the unique environment of the changed organization. As turnover occurs naturally, the change effort might backslide. In a similar vein, key management supporters of the change effort might resign or be transferred. Finally, environmental pressures, such as decreased sales or profits, can cause management to regress to more familiar behaviours and abandon change efforts.[15]

It stands to reason that many of the problems of evaluation and institutionalization can be overcome by careful planning and goal setting during the diagnostic stage. In fact, *planning* is a key issue in any change effort. Let us now examine organizational development, a means of effecting planned change. But first, please consult the You Be the Manager feature.

Organizational Development: Planned Organizational Change

Organizational development (OD) is a planned, ongoing effort to change organizations to be more effective and more human. It uses the knowledge of behavioural science to foster a culture of organizational self-examination and readiness for change. A strong emphasis is placed on interpersonal and group processes.[16]

The fact that OD is *planned* distinguishes it from the haphazard, accidental, or routine changes that occur in all organizations. OD efforts tend to be *ongoing* in at least two senses. First, many OD programs extend over a long period of time, involving several distinct phases of activities. Second, if OD becomes institutionalized, continual reexamination and readiness for further change become permanent parts of the culture. In trying to make organizations more *effective* and more *human*, OD gives recognition to the critical link between personal processes, such as leadership, decision making, and communication, and organizational outcomes, such as productivity and efficiency. The fact that OD uses *behavioural science knowledge* distinguishes it from other change strategies that rely solely on principles of accounting, finance, or engineering. However, an OD intervention may also incorporate these principles. OD seeks to modify *cultural norms and roles* so that the organization remains self-conscious and prepared for

Organizational development (OD). A planned, ongoing effort to change organizations to be more effective and more human.

you be the
manager
The Transformation of the Harley-Davidson Motor Company

> The quality of the bikes was so bad it was said that you could tell where a Harley had been parked by the puddle of oil on the pavement.

The Harley-Davidson Motor Company began in 1903 in a shack behind the Davidson brothers' home. Their friend William Harley came up with the original design. In 1906, the company had one full-time employee who had, up to that point, built a total of 50 motor-cycles. This compares with today's production of several hundred bikes per day. However, between the company's 1903 inception and the 1970s, production had rapidly expanded at the expense of quality. AMF, who owned Harley at the time, tripled production to 75,000 units annually over a period of four years. Quality began to deteriorate to the point that more than half the bikes came off the line missing parts. Dealers often had to fix the bikes in order to sell them and Harley earned a reputation for poor quality. The quality of the bikes was so bad that at one point it was said you could tell where a Harley had been parked by the puddle of oil on the pavement. Others joked that Harley owners had to own two bikes—one to ride and one for spare parts!

By the mid-1970s the situation became more critical when Japanese motorcycle makers, such as Honda and Yamaha, aggressively introduced high-quality state-of-the-art heavyweight machines in direct competition to Harley's once-exclusive market known as "Hog Heaven." Harley's share of the heavyweight motorcycle market eroded from 78 percent in 1973 to 31 percent in 1980 to 13 percent in 1983. The number of employees went from a peak of 4,000 in 1980 to 2,200 in 1982.

The Harley engine was also a problem. Not only did it leak oil and vibrate, but it was no match to the flawlessly smooth Japanese bikes

that were more appealing to first-time buyers. The company nearly went bankrupt because of its outdated technology and a badly managed manufacturing process. It became clear that if Harley was going to survive, it would have to improve quality and update the design of its engine.

In 1981, a group of Harley executives purchased the company from AMF and once again an independent Harley-Davidson Motor Co. was in business. With the Japanese still producing better bikes at a lower cost, a group of Harley executives toured Honda's assembly plant in Marysville, Ohio. Harley finally began to understand how the Japanese were beating them. But how should they change, and could they convince employees that they had to play the game the Japanese way?

By the late 1980s, Harley had transformed itself and became a symbol of the classic American turnaround. It has since experienced phenomenal growth. Market share rose to 51 percent by 1990 and to over 60 percent by 1993. Today, Harley-Davidson has more than $1.5 billion in sales and about 56 percent of the American super-heavyweight motorcycle market. Its market share and sales continue to increase in the face of a shrinking market. Its major problem today is that they cannot make enough bikes to meet the demand.

The vice-president of sales sums up his philosophy and that of the Harley-Davidson Motor Company this way: "Success is a journey and not a destination. And the journey is never over." What do you think Harley did as part of its "journey" back from the brink of bankruptcy?

1. What changes do you think Harley made to turn the company around?

2. How do you think Harley was able to overcome resistance to change?

To find out how Harley transformed itself, consult The Manager's Notebook at the end of the chapter.

Sources: Maska, B. S. (1993, August 2). Born to be real. *Industry Week*, 14–18; Slutsker, B. (1993, May 24). Hog wild. *Forbes*, 45–46; Reid, P. C. (1990). *Well made in America*. New York: McGraw-Hill. Quote from Boyd, M. (1993, September). Harley-Davidson Motor Company. *Incentive*, 26–31; Book Excerpt (1989, September 25). How Harley beat back the Japanese. *Fortune*, pp. 160-164; Interview with Richard Teerlink (1995, September). Circles and cycles. *Executive Excellence*, pp. 6- 7; Filipczak, B. (1996, February). Values keep Harley-Davidson on the road to success. *Training*, pp. 38-42; Boehme, C. (1991, November). Harley-Davidson's long marriage of mechanics and art. *World Vision*, pp. 22-27.

adaptation. Finally, a focus on *interpersonal* and *group* processes recognizes that all organizational change affects members, and their cooperation is necessary to implement change.

To summarize the above, we can say that OD recognizes that systematic attitude change must accompany changes in behaviour, whether these behaviour changes are required by revisions in tasks, work processes, organizational structure, or business strategies.

Traditionally, the values and assumptions of OD change agents were decidedly humanistic and democratic. Thus, self-actualization, trust, cooperation, and the open expression of feelings among all organizational members have been viewed as desirable.[17] In recent years, OD practitioners have shown a more active concern with organizational effectiveness and with using development practices to further the strategy of the organization. This joint concern with both people and performance has thus become the credo of many contemporary OD change agents. The focus has shifted from simple humanistic advocacy to generating data or alternatives that allow organizational members to make informed choices.[18]

Some Specific Organizational Development Strategies

The organization that seeks to "develop itself" has recourse to a wide variety of specific techniques, and many have been used in combination. We discussed some of these techniques earlier in the book. For example, job enrichment and management by objectives (Chapter 6) are usually classed as OD efforts, as are diversity training (Chapter 3), self-managed and cross-functional teams (Chapter 7), and empowerment (Chapter 12). In this section, we will discuss four additional OD strategies that illustrate the diversity of the practice. Team building illustrates how work teams can be fine-tuned to work well together. Survey feedback shows how OD can be conceived of as an ongoing applied research effort. Total quality management shows how organizations can prepare themselves for continuous improvement. Finally, reengineering illustrates the radical redesign of organizational processes. The first two methods are limited in scope and are often a part of other change efforts. The second two methods are broader in scope and lead to more sweeping organizational change.

Team Building

Team building attempts to increase the effectiveness of work teams by improving interpersonal processes, goal clarification, and role clarification.[19] (What is our team trying to accomplish, and who is responsible for what?) As such, it can facilitate communication and coordination. The term *team* can refer to intact work groups, special task forces, new work units, or people from various parts of an organization who must work together to achieve a common goal.

Team building usually begins with a diagnostic session, often held away from the workplace, in which the team explores its current level of functioning. The team might use several sources of data to accomplish its diagnosis. Some data might be generated through sensitivity training, outdoor "survival" exercises (see "Global Focus: *Outdoor Training Culture Clash*"), or open-ended discussion sessions. In addition, "hard" data, such as attitude survey results and production figures, might be used. The goal at this stage is to paint a picture of the current strengths and weaknesses of the team. The ideal outcome of the diagnostic

Team building. An effort to increase the effectiveness of work teams by improving interpersonal processes, goal clarification, and role clarification.

global focus → Outdoor Training Culture Clash

Many organizations are investing in outdoor training programs for individual managers, management teams, and work groups. Outdoor training has become one of the most popular techniques for team building.

More than 100 training organizations currently offer some type of outdoor training, also known as adventure or experiential learning. Such programs are designed to develop team and leadership skills through structured outdoor activities, such as rock climbing and white water river rafting, that require participants to learn how to work together as a team.

Participants include such varied groups as Fortune 100 executives, nurses, and civic group volunteers. Some organizations have even developed their own outdoor training programs, and others are sending managers "into the woods" as part of their traditional executive education programs.

But is outdoor training an effective technique for team building in all cultures? There is some evidence that participants from different cultures respond differently to outdoor training. While Canadians behave very much like Americans, British participants perceive the experience as too American and refer to it as "high fives huggy stuff" and "a lot of hooey." Germans also respond this way, and Spanish participants tend to hide.

There is also some evidence that when there is only one or two participants from a particular culture, such as British or German, among a group of

participants that are primarily American, the British and German participants hold back because they do not do things the same way in their culture. However, when they are with their colleagues or with other Europeans, the wall is removed, and they become much more involved in the training experience.

Inspired by productivity improvements as a result of sending more than 50 senior managers through an outdoor training program, CP Hotels invited 21 important international clients to accompany sales representatives on a three-day, $1,500-a-head outdoor training course in Whistler, British Columbia.

While the decision to invite clients from different cultures proved to be a success, particularly with the Japanese, it also showed a need for fine tuning. Some of the Europeans—in particular, the Germans— were uncomfortable with mushy displays of emotion. This has led to the belief that in dealing with some cultures, the program may have to be revised and adapted to the culture. For some cultures, outdoor training will have to remove the "huggy-feely-touchy stuff."

Source: Excerpted from French, C. (1996, August 20). When cultures collide. *The Globe and Mail*, p. C1.

session is a list of needed changes to improve team functioning. Subsequent team-building sessions usually have a decidedly task-oriented slant—How can we actually implement the changes indicated by the diagnosis? Problem solving by subgroups might be used at this stage. Between the diagnostic and follow-up sessions, the change agent might hold confidential interviews with team members to anticipate implementation problems. Throughout, the change agent acts as a catalyst and resource person.

Compaq Canada Inc. sends its employees for team-building at an indoor wilderness corporate training centre that is located in an industrial building in Toronto. Team members participate in exercises, such as scaling a 10.6-metre-high "rock" wall, climbing a steep pole and jumping off, and crossing a "toxic river" which is actually painted on the floor. In order to complete these exercises successfully, employees must learn to work as a team and in the process solve communication problems that they are having on the job. Following the team-building sessions, a detailed action plan is prepared, and follow-up sessions are subsequently held to ensure that the changes are implemented. Since its merger with Digital Equipment Corp., Compaq has been sending teams from all departments in the company and also plans to hold sessions with client companies.[20]

Compaq Canada sends its employees for team-building at an indoor wilderness corporate training centre where they learn to work as a team and to solve communication problems.

When team building is used to develop *new* work teams, the preliminary diagnostic session might involve attempts to clarify expected role relationships and additional training to build trust among team members. In subsequent sessions, the expected task environment might be simulated with role-playing exercises. One company used this integrated approach to develop the management team of a new plant.[21] In the simulation portion of the development, typical problems encountered in opening a new plant were presented to team members via hypothetical in-basket memos and telephone calls. In role-playing the solutions to these problems, they reached agreement about how they would have to work together on the job and gained a clear understanding of each other's competencies. Plant startups were always problem laden, but this was the smoothest in the history of the company.

Team building can also work to facilitate change. Harley-Davidson used it to introduce resistant middle managers to employee-involvement concepts. At Oldsmobile, select dealers who wished to sell the new Aurora had to participate in team building. One goal was to get them to adopt no-haggle pricing policies and not undercut each other's prices. U.S. West Communications used team building to lead a geographically dispersed management group through a stressful downsizing and reorganization.[22]

Ideally, team building is a continuing process that involves regular diagnostic sessions and further development exercises as needed. This permits the team to anticipate new problems and to avoid the tendency to regress to less effective pre-development habits.

Survey Feedback

In bare-bones form, **survey feedback** involves collecting data from organizational members and feeding these data back to them in a series of meetings in which members explore and discuss the data.[23] The purpose of the meetings is to suggest or formulate changes that emerge from the data. In some respects, survey feedback is similar to team building. However, survey feedback places more emphasis on the collection of valid data and less emphasis on the interpersonal

Survey feedback. The collection of data from organizational members and the provision of feedback about the results.

processes of specific work teams. Rather, it tends to focus on the relationship between organizational members and the larger organization.

As its name implies, survey feedback's basic data generally consist of either interviews or questionnaires completed by organizational members. Before data are collected, a number of critical decisions must be made by the change agent and organizational management. First, who should participate in the survey? Sometimes, especially in large organizations, the survey could be restricted to particular departments, jobs, or organizational levels where problems exist. However, most survey feedback efforts attempt to cover the entire organization. This approach recognizes the systemic nature of organizations and permits a comparison of survey results across various subunits.

Second, should questionnaires or interviews be used to gather data? The key issues here are coverage and cost. It is generally conceded that *all* members of a target group should be surveyed. This procedure builds trust and confidence in survey results. If the number of members is small, the change agent could conduct structured interviews with each person. Otherwise, cost considerations dictate the use of a questionnaire. In practice, this is the most typical data-gathering approach.

Finally, what questions should the survey ask? Two approaches are available. Some change agents use prepackaged, standardized surveys, such as the University of Michigan Survey of Organizations.[24] This questionnaire covers areas such as communication and decision-making practices and employee satisfaction. Such questionnaires are usually carefully constructed and permit comparisons with other organizations in which the survey has been conducted. However, there is some danger that prepackaged surveys might neglect critical areas for specific consideration and so many change agents choose to devise their own custom-tailored surveys.

Feedback seems to be most effective when it is presented to natural working units in face-to-face meetings. This method rules out presenting only written feedback or feedback that covers only the organization as a whole. In a manufacturing firm, a natural working unit might consist of a department, such as production or marketing. In a school district, such units might consist of individual schools. Many change agents prefer that the manager of the working unit conduct the feedback meeting. This demonstrates management commitment and acceptance of the data. The change agent attends such meetings and helps facilitate discussion of the data and plans for change.

IBM is one firm that has a very active employee survey program that it administers through its worldwide computerized office information system.[25] Travelling employees can log on and complete the survey wherever they are in the world, and "write in" comments are possible. The computerized format makes it very easy to custom-tailor questions by geographical region or occupational group. Because data collection and processing are part of the same system, analysis and feedback times are very short, sometimes only a matter of days.

Ford Motor Company also has a comprehensive, worldwide employee attitude survey called Ford Pulse.[26] Sixty-five core questions that are linked to strategic issues are always completed by both salaried and hourly employees. Up to 35 supplemental questions are custom-developed to cover local issues. Ford validated the importance of the Pulse results at 147 Ford Credit branches in Canada and the United States. The results showed that branches with higher Pulse scores had higher customer satisfaction, market share, and business volume and lower loan delinquency and employee turnover. The top part of Exhibit 16.4 shows the association between several Pulse dimensions and customer satisfaction with the branch. The lower part shows the association between Pulse scores and market share. These kind of bottom-line results go a long way toward enhancing the

IBM Corp.
www.ibm.com

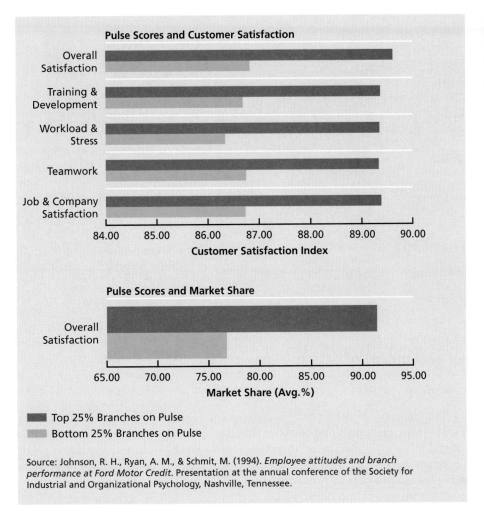

Source: Johnson, R. H., Ryan, A. M., & Schmit, M. (1994). *Employee attitudes and branch performance at Ford Motor Credit*. Presentation at the annual conference of the Society for Industrial and Organizational Psychology, Nashville, Tennessee.

Exhibit 16.4
Relationship between Ford Pulse survey scores and customer satisfaction and market share at Ford Motor Credit branches.

credibility of the survey to managers and underlining the importance of accountability for "people issues."

Total Quality Management

In Chapter 6, you will recall that we defined **total quality management (TQM)** as a systematic attempt to achieve continuous improvement in the quality of an organization's products and/or services. Typical characteristics of TQM programs include an obsession with customer satisfaction; a concern for good relations with suppliers; continuous improvement of work processes; the prevention of quality errors; frequent measurement and assessment; extensive training; and high employee involvement and teamwork. In Chapter 6, we considered the implication of TQM for employee motivation. Here, we will focus more on the broad philosophy of TQM and its relationship to organizational change and development.[27]

Prominent names associated with the quality movement include W. Edwards Deming, Joseph Juran, and Philip Crosby.[28] Although each of these "quality gurus" advocates somewhat different paths to quality, all three are concerned with using teamwork to achieve continuous improvement to please customers. Exhibit 16.5 highlights the key principles underlying customer focus, continuous improvement, and teamwork. In turn, each of these principles is associated with certain practices and specific techniques that typify TQM.

Total quality management (TQM). A systematic attempt to achieve continuous improvement in the quality of an organization's products and/or services.

	Customer Focus	**Continuous Improvement**	**Teamwork**
Principles	Paramount importance of providing products and services that fulfill customer needs; requires organizationwide focus on customers	Consistent customer satisfaction can be attained only through relentless improvement of processes that create products and services	Customer focus and continuous improvement are best achieved by collaboration throughout an organization as well as with customers and suppliers
Practices	Direct customer contact Collecting information about customer needs Using information to design and deliver products and services	Process analysis Reengineering Problem solving Plan/do/check/act	Search for arrangements that benefit all units involved in a process Formation of various types of teams Group skills training
Techniques	Customer surveys and focus groups Quality function deployment (translates customer information into product specifications)	Flowcharts Pareto analysis Statistical process control Fishbone diagrams	Organizational development methods such as the nominal group technique Team-building methods (e.g., role clarification and group feedback)

Source: Dean, J. W., Jr., & Bowen, D. E. (1994). Management theory and total quality: Improving research and practice through theory development. *Academy of Management Review, 19,* pp. 392–418.

Exhibit 16.5
Principles, practices, and techniques of total quality management.

The concept of continuous improvement sometimes confuses students of TQM—how can something be more than 100 percent good? To clarify this, it is helpful to view improvement as a continuum ranging from responding to product or service problems (a reactive strategy) to creating new products or services that please customers (a proactive strategy). Exhibit 16.6 illustrates this continuum. Improvement can occur within each stage as well as between stages.[29]

For example, suppose that you check into a hotel and find no towels in your room. Obviously, a fast and friendly correction of this error is better than a slow and surly response, and cutting response time from 15 minutes to 5 minutes would be a great improvement. Better yet, management will try to prevent missing-towel episodes altogether, perhaps using training to move from 96 percent toward 100 percent error-free towel stocking. Although such error *prevention* is a hallmark of TQM, it is also possible to upgrade the service episode. For example, the hotel might work closely with suppliers to provide fluffier towels at the same price or encourage guests to not use too many towels, thus reducing laundry and room costs. Finally, a new service opportunity might be identified and acted on. For example, the Chicago Marriott hotel discovered (after 15 years of operation) that 66 percent of all guests' calls to the housekeeping department were requests for irons or ironing boards. The manager took funds earmarked to replace black-and-white bathroom TVs with colour sets and instead equipped each room with an iron and ironing board. No one had ever complained about black-and-white TV in the bathroom.[30]

This chain of hotel examples illustrates several features of the continuous improvement concept and TQM in general.[31] First, continuous improvement can come from small gains over time (e.g., gradually approaching 100 percent error-free room servicing) or from more radical innovation (e.g., offering a new service). In both cases, the goal is long-term improvement, not a short-term "fix." Next, improvement requires knowing where we are in the first place. Thus, TQM is very concerned with measurement and data collection—in our examples, we alluded to speed of service, percent of error-free performance, and frequency of

Exhibit 16.6
A continuum of continuous
improvement.

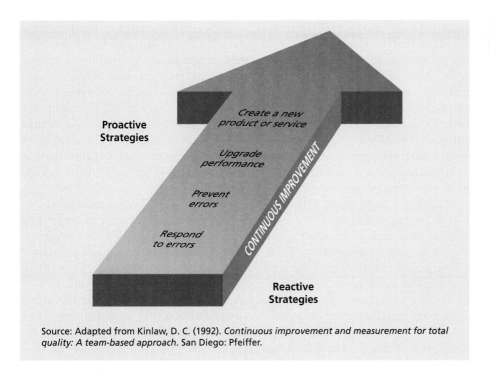

Source: Adapted from Kinlaw, D. C. (1992). *Continuous improvement and measurement for total quality: A team-based approach.* San Diego: Pfeiffer.

customer requests as examples. Next, TQM stresses teamwork among employees and (in the examples given here) with suppliers and customers. Finally, TQM relies heavily on training to achieve continuous improvement.

Although simple job training can contribute to continuous improvement (as in the towel-stocking example), TQM is particularly known for using specialized training in tools that empower employees to diagnose and solve quality problems on an ongoing basis. Some tools, noted in the bottom row of Exhibit 16.5, include:

- *Flowcharts of work processes.* Flowcharts illustrate graphically the operations and steps in accomplishing some task, noting who does what, and when. For instance, what happens when hotel housekeeping receives a guest request for towels?

- *Pareto analysis.* Pareto analysis collects frequency data on the causes of errors and problems, showing where attention should be directed for maximum improvement. For instance, the Marriott data on reasons for calls to housekeeping corresponds to Pareto data.

- *Fishbone diagrams.* Fishbone (cause-and-effect) diagrams illustrate graphically the factors that could contribute to a particular quality problem. Very specific causes ("small bones") are divided into logical classes or groups ("large bones"). In the hotel example, classes of causes might include people, equipment, methods, and materials.

- *Statistical process control.* Statistical process control gives employees hard data about the quality of their own output that enables them to correct any deviations from standard. TQM places particular emphasis on reducing *variation* in performance over time.

These tools to improve the diagnosis and correction of quality problems will not have the desired impact if they fail to improve quality in the eyes of the customer. An essential problem here is that quality has many different and potentially incompatible definitions. For example, ultimate excellence, value for the money, conformance to specifications, or meeting and/or exceeding customer expectations are all potential definitions of quality.³² Although this last definition would seem to be closest to the TQM principle of customer focus, it is not without its weaknesses. For example, customers might have contradictory expectations. Also, they are more likely to have clear expectations about familiar products and services than new or creative products or services. Nevertheless, organizations with a real commitment to TQM make heavy use of customer surveys, focus groups, mystery shoppers, and customer clinics to stay close to their customers. Harley-Davidson holds customer clinics and sponsors bike rallies to learn from its customers. Also, survey feedback programs allow organizations to obtain information about internal customers (such as how the adjacent department views your department's performance).

TQM programs reveal a large number of successes in firms such as Xerox, L.L. Bean, Motorola, and Ritz-Carlton Hotels. However, they have also had their share of problems, all of which ultimately get expressed as resistance. Despite allowing for radical innovation, TQM is mainly about achieving small gains over a long period of time. This long-term focus can be hard to maintain, especially if managers or employees expect extreme improvements in the short term.

Finally, a number of organizations have implemented TQM programs at the same time that they were engaged in radical restructuring or downsizing (e.g., IBM, GM, McDonnell Douglas). Speaking generally, this is not a good recipe for the success of the TQM effort. Employees are likely to be insecure during such periods and unreceptive to calls for initiative and innovation.³³ Cynics may say "the company cares about the customer more than it cares about me."

Despite these problems, the quality movement continues to be one of the most popular of the more elaborate OD efforts.

Reengineering

What does the following mixed bag of companies have in common? Taco Bell, Hallmark Cards, IDS Financial Services, Blue Cross of Washington and Alaska, GTE, Agway, and Bell Atlantic. The answer is that all have experienced reengineering in recent years. Of all the forms of change that we are discussing in this chapter, reengineering is the most fundamental and radical.

Reengineering is the radical redesign of organizational processes to achieve major improvements in factors such as time, cost, quality, or service.³⁴ Reengineering does not fine tune existing jobs, structures, technology, or human resources policies. Rather, it uses a "clean slate" approach that asks basic questions, such as "What business are we really in?" and "If we were creating this organization today, what would it look like?" Then, jobs, structure, technology, and policy are redesigned around the answers to these questions. Reengineering can be applied to an entire organization, but it can also be applied to a major function, such as research and development.

A key word in our definition of reengineering , and one that requires some additional commentary, is *processes*. Processes do not refer to job titles or organizational departments. Rather, **organizational processes** are *activities* or *work* that the organization must accomplish to create outputs that customers (internal or external) value.³⁵ For example, designing a new product is a process that might involve people holding a variety of jobs in several different departments (R&D, marketing, production, and finance). In theory, the gains from reengineering will be greatest when the process is complex and cuts across a number of jobs and departments.

We can contrast reengineering with TQM, in that TQM usually seeks incremental improvements in existing processes rather than radical revisions of processes. However, a TQM effort could certainly be part of a reengineering project.

L.L. Bean
www.llbean.com

Reengineering. The radical redesign of organizational processes to achieve major improvements in factors such as time, cost, quality, or service.

Organizational processes. Activities or work that have to be accomplished to create outputs that internal or external customers value.

What factors have prompted the current interest in reengineering? One factor is "creeping bureaucracy" that is especially common in large, established firms. With growth, rather than rethinking basic work processes, many firms have simply tacked on more bureaucratic controls to maintain order. This leads to over-complicated processes and an internal focus on satisfying bureaucratic procedures rather than tending to the customer. Many corporate downsizings have been unsuccessful because they failed to confront bureaucratic controls and basic work processes.

New information technology has also stimulated reengineering. Many firms were disappointed that initial investments in information technology did not result in anticipated reductions in costs or improved productivity. This is because existing processes were simply automated rather that reengineered to correspond to the capabilities of the new technology. Now, it is commonly recognized that advanced technology allows organizations to radically modify (and usually radically simplify) important organizational processes. In other words, work is modified to fit technological capabilities rather than simply fitting the technology to existing jobs. At Ford Motor Company, for example, a look at the entire process for procuring supplies revealed great inefficiencies.[36] Ford employed a large accounts payable staff to issue payments to suppliers when it received invoices. Now, employees at the receiving dock can approve payment when the *goods* are received. Advanced information technology enables them to tap a database to verify that the goods were ordered and issue a check to the supplier. Needless to say, Ford has radically streamlined the payment process, and the accounts payable department now has fewer employees.

How does reengineering actually proceed? In essence, much reengineering is oriented toward one or both of the following goals:[37]

- The number of mediating steps in a process is reduced, making the process more efficient.
- Collaboration among the people involved in the process is enhanced.

Removing the number of mediating steps in a process, if done properly, reduces labour requirements, removes redundancies, decreases chances for errors, and speeds up the production of the final output. All of this happened with Ford's revision of its procurement process. Enhanced collaboration often permits simultaneous, rather than sequential, work on a process and reduces the chances for misunderstanding and conflict.

Some of the nitty gritty aspects of reengineering include the following practices. You will notice that we have covered many of them in other contexts earlier in the book.[38]

- *Jobs are redesigned, and usually enriched.* Frequently, several jobs are combined into one to reduce mediating steps and provide greater employee control.
- *A strong emphasis is placed on teamwork.* Teamwork (especially cross-functional) is a potent method of enhancing collaboration.
- *Work is performed by the most logical people.* Some firms train customers to do minor maintenance and repairs themselves or turn over the management of some inventory to their suppliers.
- *Unnecessary checks and balances are removed.* When processes are simplified and employees are more collaborative, expensive and redundant controls can sometimes be removed.
- *Advanced technology is exploited.* Computerized technology not only permits combining of jobs, it also enhances collaboration via electronic mail, groupware, and so on.

It is easiest to get a feel for the success of reengineering by considering some of the reductions in mediating steps and improvements in speed that have resulted. CTB Macmillan/McGraw-Hill, a prominent publisher of standardized achievement tests, reduced the steps in its test scoring process from 154 to 68 and its turnaround time for scoring from 21 days to 5. Using software that allows clients to file electronic claims, Blue Cross of Washington and Alaska has handled 17 percent more volume with a 12 percent smaller workforce and halved the time it takes to handle a claim. Using cross-functional teams and advanced technology before its merger with Daimler-Benz, Chrysler cut the design time of its successful Jeep Cherokee from 5 years to 39 months.[39] Such "concurrent engineering" is now common in Detroit, enabling North American car manufacturers to approach the short product development cycle time for which the Japanese are noted. At The Limited, fashions now move from design to store in two months rather that the former two *seasons*. Thus, the firm is much more responsive to fickle swings in trends and taste. Computer technology, flatter structures, fewer "signoffs" on new ideas, and a sense of urgency on the part of management often play a role in such transformations.[40]

Reengineering is most extensive in industries where (1) much creeping bureaucracy has set in, (2) large gains were available with advanced technology, and (3) deregulation increased the heat of competition. These include the insurance, banking, brokerage, and telecommunications industries.

Because reengineering has the goal of radical change, it requires strong CEO support and transformational leadership qualities. Also, before reengineering begins, it is essential that the organization clarify its overall strategy. What business should we really be in? (Do we want to produce hardware, software, or both?) Given this, who are our customers, and what core processes create value for them? If such strategic clarification is lacking, processes that do not matter to the customer will be reengineered. Strong CEO support and a clear strategy are important for overcoming resistance that simply dismisses people who advocate reengineering as "more efficiency experts." Resistance due to self-interest and organizational politics is likely when radical change may lead to layoffs or major change in work responsibilities.

Recent research shows that reengineering must be both broad and deep to have long-lasting, bottom-line results, that is, it should span a large number of activities that cut costs or add customer value, and it should affect a number of elements including skills, values, roles, incentives, structure, and technology.[41] Half-hearted attempts do not pay off.

Does Organizational Development Work?

Does it work, that is, do the benefits of OD outweigh the heavy investment of time, effort, and money? At the outset, we should reemphasize that most OD efforts are *not* carefully evaluated. Political factors and budget limitations might be prime culprits, but the situation is not helped by some OD practitioners who argue that certain OD goals (e.g., making the organization more human) are incompatible with impersonal, scientifically rigorous evaluation.

At the very broadest level, two large-scale reviews of a wide variety of OD techniques (including some we discussed in this chapter as well as job redesign, MBO, and goal setting from Chapters 5 and 6) reached the following conclusions:[42]

- Most OD techniques have a positive impact on productivity, job satisfaction, or other work attitudes.

- OD seems to work better for supervisors or managers than for blue-collar workers.

- Changes that use more than one technique seem to have more impact.
- There are great differences across sites in the success of OD interventions.

The last finding is probably due to differences in the skill and seriousness with which various organizations have undertaken OD projects. In addition, TQM and reengineering programs are most likely to be successful when they are accompanied by a change in organizational culture.[43]

Exhibit 16.7 summarizes the results of a large number of research studies on the impact of OD change efforts on changes in a variety of outcomes. Organizational arrangements included changes in formal structure and some quality interventions. Social factors included the use of team building and survey feedback. Technology changes mainly involved job redesign. Finally, physical setting interventions (which were rare) included things such as changes to open-plan offices.

As you can see, a healthy percentage of studies reported positive changes following an OD effort. However, many studies also reported no change. This underlines the difficulty of introducing change, and it also suggests that variations in how organizations actually implement change may greatly determine its success. The relative lack of negative change is encouraging, but it is also possible that there is a bias against reporting bad outcomes.[44]

Weak methodology has sometimes plagued research evaluations on the success of OD interventions, although the quality of research seems to be improving over time.[45] Some specific problems include the following:[46]

- OD efforts involve a complex series of changes. There is little evidence of exactly which of these changes produce changes in processes or outcomes.
- Novelty effects or the fact that participants receive special treatment might produce short-term gains that really do not persist over time.
- Self-reports of changes after OD might involve unconscious attempts to please the change agent.
- Organizations may be reluctant to publicize failures.

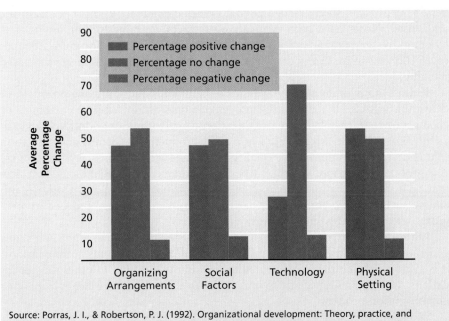

Exhibit 16.7
Organizational change due to organizational development efforts.

Source: Porras, J. I., & Robertson, P. J. (1992). Organizational development: Theory, practice, and research. In M. D. Dunnette & L. M. Hough (Eds.), *Handbook of industrial and organizational psychology* (2nd ed., Vol. 3). Palo Alto, CA: Consulting Psychologists Press.

For these reasons and others, OD continues to be characterized by both problems and promise. Let us hope that promise will overcome problems as organizations try to respond effectively to their increasingly complex and dynamic environments. Speaking of such response, let us turn to innovation.

The Innovation Process

Do you recognize the name Arthur Fry? Probably not. But Arthur Fry is famous in his own way as the inventor of the ubiquitous, sticky Post-its, a top seller among paper office supplies. Fry, a researcher at the innovative 3M Company, developed the product that became Post-its in response to a personal problem—how to keep his place marker from falling out of his church choir hymnal.

What accounts for the ability of individuals such as Arthur Fry and organizations such as 3M to think up and exploit such innovative ideas? This is the focus of this section of the chapter.

What Is Innovation?

American Express
www.americanexpress.com

Innovation. The process of developing and implementing new ideas in an organization.

Innovation is the process of developing and implementing new ideas in an organization. The term *developing* is intentionally broad. It covers everything from the genuine invention of a new idea to recognizing an idea in the environment, importing it to the organization, and giving it a unique application.[47] The essential point is a degree of creativity. Arthur Fry did not invent glue, and he did not invent paper, but he did develop a creative way to use them together. Then 3M was creative enough to figure out how to market what might have appeared to less probing minds to be a pretty mundane product.

It is possible to roughly classify innovations as product (including service) innovations or process innovations.[48] Product innovations have a direct impact on the cost, quality, style, or availability of a product or service. Thus, they should be very obvious to clients or customers. It is easiest to identify with innovations that result in tangible products, especially everyday consumer products. Thus, we can surely recognize that Polaroid cameras, VCRs, fax machines, and Post-it Notes have been innovative products. Perhaps coming less readily to mind are service innovations, such as American Express Travelers Cheques (over 100 years old), FedEx door-to-door courier service, and 24-hour automated banking.

To be a successful innovator, an essential ingredient is creativity. Arthur Fry, the inventor of Post-it® Notes, used his creativity to establish one of the top sellers in office supplies.

Process innovations are new ways of designing products, making products, or delivering services. In many cases, process changes are invisible to customers or clients, although they help the organization to perform more effectively or efficiently. For example, McDonald's new food production system is an innovation that is designed to improve the quality of its sandwiches. Thus, new technology is a process innovation, whether it be new manufacturing technology or a new management information system. New forms of management and work organization, including job enrichment, participation, reengineering, and quality programs, are also process innovations.

Innovation is often conceived of as a stage-like process that begins with idea generation and proceeds to idea implementation. For some kinds of innovations, it is also hoped that the implemented innovation will diffuse to other sites or locations. This applies especially to process innovations that have begun as pilot or demonstration projects:

IDEA GENERATION → IDEA IMPLEMENTATION → IDEA DIFFUSION

In advance of discussing these stages in the following sections, let us note several interesting themes that underlie the process of innovation. First, the beginning of innovation can be pretty haphazard and chaotic, and the conditions necessary to create new ideas might be very different from the conditions necessary to get these ideas implemented. In a related vein, although organizations have to innovate to survive, such innovation might be resisted just like any other organizational change. The result of these tensions is that innovation is frequently a highly political process (Chapter 12).[49] This important point is sometimes overlooked because innovation often involves science and technology, domains that have a connotation of rationality about them. However, both the champions of innovation and the resisters might behave politically to secure or hold onto critical organizational resources.

Generating and Implementing Innovative Ideas

Innovation requires creative ideas, someone to fight for these ideas, good communication, and the proper application of resources and rewards. Let us examine these factors in detail.

Individual Creativity. Creative thinking by individuals or small groups is at the core of the innovation process. **Creativity** is usually defined as the production of novel but potentially useful ideas. Thus, creativity is a key aspect of the "developing new ideas" part of our earlier definition of innovation. However, innovation is a broader concept, in that it also involves an attempt to implement new ideas. Not every creative idea gets implemented.

Creativity. The production of novel but potentially useful ideas.

When we see a company, such as 3M, that is known for its innovations, or we see an innovative project completed successfully, we sometimes forget about the role that individual creativity plays in such innovations. However, organizations that have a consistent reputation for innovation have a talent for selecting, cultivating, and motivating creative individuals. Such creativity can come into play at many "locations" during the process of innovation. Thus, the salesperson who discovers a new market for a product might be just as creative as the scientist who developed the product.

What makes a person creative?[50] For one thing, you can pretty much discount the romantic notion of the naive creative genius. Research shows that creative people tend to have an excellent technical understanding of their domain, that is, they understand its basic practices, procedures, and techniques. Thus, creative chemists will emerge from those who are well trained and up-to-date in their field. Similarly, creative money managers will be among those who have a truly excellent grasp of finance and economics. Notice, however, that having good skills in one's specialty does not mean that creative people are extraordinarily intelligent. Once we get beyond subnormal intelligence, there is no correlation between level of intelligence and creativity.

Most people with good basic skills in their area are still not creative. What sets the creative people apart are additional *creativity-relevant* skills. These include the ability to tolerate ambiguity, withhold early judgment, see things in new ways, and be open to new and diverse experiences. Some of these skills appear to be a product of certain personality characteristics, such as curiosity and persistence. Interestingly, creative people tend to be socially skilled but lower than average in need for social approval. They can often interact well with others to learn and discuss new ideas, but they do not see fit to conform just to get others to like them.

Many creativity-related skills can actually be improved by training people to think in divergent ways and withhold early evaluation of ideas.[51] At Bombardier, employees are learning how to use improvisation as a way to come up with creative ideas and encourage innovation.[52] In addition, some of the methods we discussed in Chapter 11 (electronic brainstorming, nominal group, and Delphi techniques) can be used to hone creative skills. Frito-Lay and DuPont are two companies that engage in extensive creativity training.

Finally, people can be experts in their field and have creativity skills but still not be creative if they lack intrinsic motivation for generating new ideas. Such motivation is most likely to occur when there is genuine interest in and fascination with the task at hand. This is not to say that extrinsic motivation is not important in innovation, as we shall see shortly. Rather, it means that creativity itself is not very susceptible to extrinsic rewards.

Having a lot of potentially creative individuals is no guarantee in itself that an organization will innovate. Let us now turn to some other factors that influence innovation.

Idea Champions. Again and again, case studies of successful innovations reveal the presence of one or more **idea champions,** people who see the kernel of an innovative idea and help guide it through to implementation.[53] This role of idea champion is often an informal emergent role, and "guiding" the idea might involve talking it up to peers, selling it to management, garnering resources for its development, or protecting it from political attack by guardians of the status quo. Champions often have a real sense of mission about the innovation. Idea champions have frequently been given other labels, some of which depend on the exact context or content of the innovation. For example, in larger organizations, such champions might be labeled *intrapreneurs* or *corporate entrepreneurs.* In R&D settings, one often hears the term *project champion; product champion* is another familiar moniker. The exact label is less important than the function, which is one of sponsorship and support, often outside of routine job duties.

For a modest innovation whose merits are extremely clear, it is possible for the creative person who thinks up the idea to serve as its sole champion and push the idea into practice. In the case of more complex and radical innovations, especially those that demand heavy resource commitment, it is common to see more than one idea champion emerge during the innovation process. For example, a laser scientist might invent a new twist to laser technology and champion the technical idea within her R&D lab. In turn, a product division line manager might hear of the technical innovation and offer to provide sponsorship to develop it into an actual commercial product. This joint emergence of a technical champion and a management champion is typical. Additional idea champions might also emerge. For example, a sales manager in the medical division might lobby to import the innovation from the optics division.

What kind of people are idea champions, and what are their tactics? One interesting study examined champions who spearheaded the introduction of expensive, visible new information technologies in their firms (e.g., new management information systems).[54] This research compared "project champions" with nonchampions who had also worked on the same project. The champions tended to exhibit more risk-taking and innovative behaviours. Also, they exhibited clear signs of transformational leadership (Chapter 9), using charisma, inspiration, and intellectual stimulation to get people to see the potential of the innovation. They used a wide variety of influence tactics to gain support for the new system. In short, the champions made people truly *want* the innovation despite its disruption of the status quo.

As we noted earlier, championing an innovation is usually an informal role. Would it be possible to actually *assign* people to be champions as part of their regular job duties? Just ask Progressive Corporation, a successful Cleveland-

Idea champions. People who recognize an innovative idea and guide it to implementation.

based insurance company. Progressive is known for its innovations in specialty vehicle insurance, including selling to risky drivers and insuring recreational vehicles. Several years ago, Progressive switched from a more centralized structure into several decentralized geographical regions. Management was worried that smaller-volume products (such as mobile homes) might be "lost" in the new decentralized structure and lose their innovative edge. To deal with this, they assigned each product a champion to look out for its interests on a total company basis.[55]

Communication. Effective communication with the external environment and effective communication within the organization are vital for successful innovation.

The most innovative firms seem to be those that are best at recognizing the relevance of new, external information, importing and assimilating this information, and then applying it.[56] Experience shows that the recognition and assimilation are a lot more chaotic and informal than one might imagine. Rather than relying on a formal network of journal articles, technical reports, and internal memoranda, technical personnel are more likely to be exposed to new ideas via informal oral communication networks. In these networks, key personnel function as **gatekeepers** who span the boundary between the organization and the environment, importing new information, translating it for local use, and disseminating it to project members. These people tend to have well-developed communication networks with other professionals outside the organization and with the professionals on their own team or project. Thus, they are in key positions to both receive and transmit new technical information.[57] Also, they are perceived as highly competent and a good source of new ideas. Furthermore, they have an innovative orientation, they read extensively, and they can tolerate ambiguity.[58] It is important to note that gatekeeping is essentially an informal, emergent role, since many gatekeepers are not in supervisory positions. However, organizations can do several things to enhance the external contact of actual or potential gatekeepers. Generous allowances for subscriptions, telephone use, and database access might be helpful. The same applies to travel allowances for seminars, short courses, and professional meetings.

Technical gatekeepers are not the only means of extracting information from the environment. Many successful innovative firms excel at going directly to users, clients, or customers to obtain ideas for product or service innovation. This works against the development of technically sound ideas that nobody wants, and it also provides some real focus for getting ideas implemented quickly. For example, Sony requires new employees in technical areas to do a stint in retail sales, and Raytheon's New Products Centre organizes expeditions by technical types to trade shows, manufacturing facilities, and retail outlets.[59] Notice that we are speaking here about truly getting "close to the customer," not simply doing abstract market research on large samples of people. Such research does not have a great track record in prompting innovation; talking directly to users does.

Now that we have covered the importation of information into the organization, what are the requirements of *internal* communication for innovation? At least during the idea generation and early design phase, the more the better. Thus, it is generally true that organic structures (Chapter 14) facilitate innovation.[60] Decentralization, informality, and a lack of bureaucracy all foster the exchange of information that innovation requires. This is one reason why McDonald's has adopted a more decentralized regional-management structure. To this mixture, add small project teams or business units and a diversity of member backgrounds to stimulate cross-fertilization of ideas. For example, the early project design team for Mazda's RX–7 had 29 members, 13 from R&D, 6 from production, 7

Gatekeepers. People who span organizational boundaries to import new information, translate it for local use, and disseminate it.

from sales/marketing, and one each from planning, service, and quality control.[61] There was no room for isolated thinking with that mix! *Fortune* magazine notes a common trend among innovative corporations, including Campbell Soup, 3M, and Apple Computer:

> People in different disciplines are simply not allowed to remain in isolation. Business units are kept small, in part to throw engineers, marketers, and finance experts together into the sort of tight groups most often found in start-up companies. Where the interaction fails to arise naturally, it is engineered: all these companies require their workers to spend a great deal of time at meetings where information is shared and plans are discussed.[62]

In general, internal communication can be stimulated with in-house training, cross-functional transfers, and varied job assignments.[63] One study even found that the actual physical location of gatekeepers was important to their ability to convey new information to co-workers.[64] This suggests the clustering of offices and the use of common lounge areas as a means of facilitating communication. Organizations could also give equal thought to the design of electronic communication media.

One especially interesting line of research suggests just how important communication is to the performance of research and development project groups.[65] This research found that groups with members who had worked together a short time or a long time engaged in less communication (within the group, within the organization, and externally) than groups that had medium longevity. In turn, performance mirrored communication, the high-communicating, medium-longevity groups being the best performers (Exhibit 16.8). Evidently, when

Exhibit 16.8
Group longevity, communication, and performance of research and development groups.

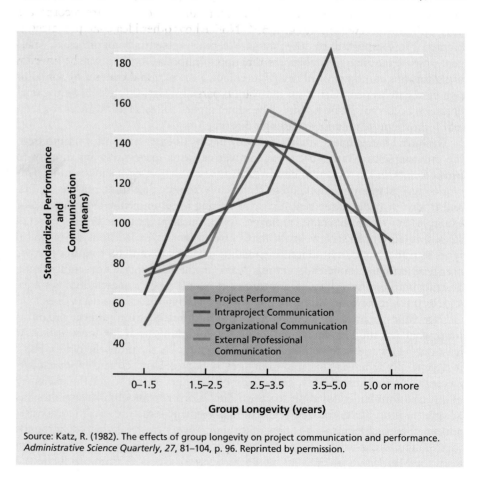

Source: Katz, R. (1982). The effects of group longevity on project communication and performance. *Administrative Science Quarterly, 27,* 81–104, p. 96. Reprinted by permission.

groups are new, it takes time for members to decide what information they require and to forge the appropriate communication networks. When groups get "old," they sometimes get comfortable and isolate themselves from critical sources of feedback. It is important to emphasize that the age of the group is at issue here, not the age of the employees or their tenure in the organization.

Although organic structures seem best in the idea generation and design phases of innovation, more mechanistic structures might sometimes be better for actually implementing innovations.[66] Thinking up new computer programs is an organic task. Reproducing these programs in the thousands and marketing them require more bureaucratic procedures. This transition is important. Although audio and video recording innovations were pioneered in the United States, it was the Japanese who successfully implemented recording products in the marketplace. In part, this stemmed from a recognition of the different organizational requirements for idea generation versus the implementation of ideas.

Resources and Rewards. Despite the romance surrounding the development of innovations on a shoestring using unauthorized "bootlegged" funds, abundant resources greatly enhance the chances of successful innovation.[67] Not only do these resources provide funds in the obvious sense, they also serve as a strong cultural symbol that the organization truly supports innovation. Funds for innovation are seen as an *investment,* not a *cost.* Several observers have noted that such a culture is most likely when the availability of funding is anarchic and multisourced, that is, because innovative ideas often encounter resistance from the status quo under the best of circumstances, innovators should have the opportunity to seek support from more than one source. At 3M, for instance, intrapreneurs can seek support from their own division, from another division, from corporate R&D, or from a new ventures group.[68] (Notice how other idea champions might be cultivated during this process.)

Money is not the only resource that spurs innovation. *Time* can be an even more crucial factor for some innovations. At 3M, tradition dictates that scientists reserve 15 percent of their working time for personal projects. At Chaparral Steel in Midlothian, Texas, supervisors are given "sabbaticals" to work on innovations with customers, suppliers, and universities.[69]

Reward systems must match the culture that is seeded by the resource system. Coming up with new ideas is no easy job, so organizations should avoid punishing failure (see "In Focus: *Shaving to Innovate at Gillette*"). Many false starts with dead ends will be encountered, and innovators need support and constructive criticism, not punishment. In fact, Hallmark puts its executives through a simulation in which they must design a line of greeting cards so that they can better appreciate the frustrations felt by the creative staff.

A survey of research scientists found that freedom and autonomy were the *most* cited organizational factors leading to creativity.[70] Since intrinsic motivation is necessary for creativity, this suggests rewarding good past performance with enhanced freedom to pursue personal ideas. IBM, for example, has a "fellows program" that provides star performers five years of freedom to work on their own projects. In a related vein, many organizations have wised up about extrinsic rewards and innovation. In the past, it was common for creative scientists and engineers to have to move into management ranks to obtain raises and promotions. Many firms now offer dual career ladders that enable these people to be extrinsically rewarded while still doing actual science or engineering.

We have been concerned here mainly with rewarding the people who actually generate innovative ideas. But how about those other champions who sponsor such ideas and push them into the implementation stage? At 3M, bonuses for division managers are contingent on 25 percent of their revenues coming from

in focus → Shaving to Innovate at Gillette

Every working day at a Gillette plant in gritty South Boston, 200 men lather up their faces and scrape away the fifteen-thousandths of an inch their 10,000 whiskers have grown over the previous 24 hours. Peering into side-by-side mirrors, these volunteers are evaluating razors of the future for sharpness of blade, smoothness of glide, and ease of handling. When they are finished, the men punch their judgments of the prototype they used into a computer. In a nearby shower room, women are performing the same exercise on their legs, underarms, and what the company delicately refers to as the "bikini area."

These rituals are carried out in an aging building emblazoned with a quaint sign proclaiming it to be WORLD SHAVING HEADQUARTERS; the whole exercise seems more than a little archaic, like some throwback to a preindustrial age. Yet, the humble facility is operated by one of America's premier corporate innovators, a company that churns out so many cutting-edge products that it has climbed into a select circle of Wall Street superstars. More than 40% of sales have come from new products over the past five years, helping to polish a sparkling overall record. Earnings since 1990 have climbed at an annual rate of 17%, return on equity is nearly 33%, and profit margins are about 12%. Among consumer-products companies, that makes Gillette's return on sales second only to Coca-Cola's 16.6%.

Gillette's commitment to innovation involves pouring hundreds of millions into high-tech research every year. Unlike most consumer companies, whose idea of new products is an endless series of gimmicky line extensions, Gillette prides itself on bringing to market only new products that represent significant improvements. The company has been introducing about 20 new products annually, most of which have succeeded. One of the most successful has been the Sensor family of razors and blades introduced in 1990. Hundreds of millions of Sensor razors and billions of blades have been sold, enough to deliver Gillette 68% of the American market in wet shaving, 73% of Europe, and 91% of Latin America.

Launching Sensor was so complicated and expensive—the company was awarded 29 patents and spent $275 million during design and development—that no competitor has even attempted to knock off an imitation. Gillette's technological prowess is so integral a part of its image that it has even become the stuff of jokes. Quips humorist Dave Barry: "One day soon the Gillette Co. will announce the development of a razor that, thanks to a computer microchip, can actually travel ahead in time and shave beard hairs that don't even exist yet."

Besides spending millions on R&D each year, there are two strategies that contribute to Gillette's success in corporate innovation. First, CEO Alfred Zeien encourages Gillette to eat its young by cannibalizing current products. If they do not bring out a new zinger, they know that someone else will. Second, Zeien assures executives whose prototypes get shelved and never make it to market that they will not be punished. Unlike most companies where executives believe that their careers might be doomed if they do not get a product out, CEO Zeien gives project leaders a chance to be objective.

Source: Excerpted from Grant, L. (1996, October 14). Gillette knows shaving—and how to turn out hot new products. *Fortune*, pp. 207-210.

products that are less than five years old.[71] This stimulates the managers to pay attention when someone drops by with a new idea, and it also stimulates them to turn that new idea into a real product quickly!

Diffusing Innovative Ideas

Many innovations, especially process innovations, begin as limited experiments in one section or division of an organization. This is a cautious and reasonable approach. For example, a company might introduce new automated technology for evaluation in one plant of its multiplant organization. Similarly, an insurance company might begin a limited exploration of job enrichment by concentrating only on clerical jobs at the head office. If such efforts are judged successful, it seems logical to extend them to other parts of the organization. **Diffusion** is the

Diffusion. The process by which innovations move through an organization.

process by which innovations move through an organization. However, this is not always as easy as it might seem!

Richard Walton of Harvard University studied the diffusion of eight major process innovations in firms such as Volvo, Alcan, General Foods, Corning Glass, and Shell U.K. Each effort was rigorous and broad based, generally including changes in job design, compensation, and supervision.[72]

Volvo Group
www.volvo.com

All the pilot projects that Walton studied were initially judged successful, and each received substantial publicity, a factor that often contributes to increased commitment to further change. Despite this, substantial diffusion occurred in only one of the observed firms—Volvo. What accounts for this poor record of diffusion? Walton identified these factors:

- Lack of support and commitment from top management.

- Significant differences between the technology or setting of the pilot project and those of other units in the organization, raising arguments that "it won't work here."

- Attempts to diffuse particular *techniques* rather than *goals* that could be tailored to other situations.

- Management reward systems that concentrate on traditional performance measures, while ignoring success at implementing innovation.

- Union resistance to extending the negotiated "exceptions" in the pilot project.

- Fears that pilot projects begun in nonunionized locations could not be implemented in unionized portions of the firm.

- Conflict between the pilot project and the bureaucratic structures in the rest of the firm (e.g., pay policies and staffing requirements).

Because of these problems, Walton raises the depressing spectre of a "diffuse or die" principle, that is, if diffusion does not occur, the pilot project and its leaders become more and more isolated from the mainstream of the organization and less and less able to proceed alone. As we noted earlier, innovation can be a highly politicized process. Several of the barriers to diffusion that Walton cites have been implicated in limiting the influence that the Saturn project has had on General Motors, including top management changes, union resistance, and competition for resources from old line GM divisions.

One classic study suggests that the following factors are critical determinants of the rate of diffusion of a wide variety of innovations:[73]

- *Relative advantage.* Diffusion is more likely when the new idea is perceived as truly better than the one it replaces.

- *Compatibility.* Diffusion is easier when the innovation is compatible with the values, beliefs, needs, and current practices of potential new adopters.

- *Complexity.* Complex innovations that are fairly difficult to comprehend and use are less likely to diffuse.

- *Trialability.* If an innovation can be given a limited trial run, its chances of diffusion will be improved.

- *Observability.* When the consequences of an innovation are more visible, diffusion will be more likely to occur.

In combination, these determinants suggest that there is considerable advantage to thinking about how innovations are "packaged" and "sold" so as to increase their chances of more widespread adoption. Also, they suggest the value of finding strong champions to sponsor the innovation at the new site.

1. Harley knew that they had a serious product problem, and they had to focus on product quality. Following the purchase of the company from AMF, attention was directed at improving the product. In 1981, management began to examine the management and manufacturing techniques used by the Japanese. A 10-year plan was formulated to improve engines to provide better performance and attract new customers by offering the same quality as the Japanese bikes. They began by designing quality into a new engine configuration and into all the manufacturing processes. To accomplish these goals, Harley adapted three Japanese quality techniques that were seldom used at the time in North America: (1) Intensive employee involvement in decision making, (2) just-in-time inventory control to reduce expensive parts inventories and deliver parts to the assembly when needed, and (3) statistical operator control which enables employees to measure and manage the quality of their own production. Employees were taught how to use statistical tools to monitor and control the quality of their work. In combination, these three techniques formed the Productivity Triad and were responsible for the dramatic improvement in quality and cost reductions that were the foundation of Harley's turnaround. Harley is known today as one of the first victories of the American quality movement and one of the most dramatic. Poor quality almost destroyed the company. Not surprisingly, it has become a poster child for total quality management (TQM).

2. When Harley employees were first told about the plan to convert to a just-in-time inventory program, many laughed out loud and managers reacted with disbelief. It was then decided that employee involvement would be key to the success of any changes. Employees were involved from the start in planning and designing the new system and in working out the details. The company sought the advice of employees on how to solve production problems at the lowest levels. For months, management held meetings with groups of employees from all departments in the company. Changes were implemented only when those involved understood and accepted them. The go-ahead for the change program came only after a consensus decision was made following two months of meetings. Initial resistance was overcome by intensive team building and by sending managers to the University of Tennessee's Institute of Productivity and Quality. The company's employee-involvement commitment and its process for consensus decision making are now part of the Harley culture.

Summary

- All organizations must change because of forces in the external and internal environments. Although more environmental change usually requires more organizational change, organizations can exhibit too much change as well as too little. Organizations can change goals and strategies, technology, job design, structure, processes, culture, and people. People changes should almost always accompany changes in other factors.

- The general change process involves unfreezing current attitudes and behaviours, changing them, and then refreezing the newly acquired attitudes and behaviours. Several key issues or problems must be dealt with during the general change process. One is accurate diagnosis of the current situation. Another is the resistance that might be provoked by unfreezing and change. A third issue is performing an adequate evaluation of the success of the change effort. Many such evaluations are weak or nonexistent.

- Organizational development (OD) is a planned, ongoing effort to change organizations to be more effective and more human. It uses the knowledge of behavioural science to foster a culture of organizational self-examination and readiness for change. A strong emphasis is placed on interpersonal and group processes.

- Four popular OD techniques are team building, survey feedback, total quality management, and reengineering. Team building attempts to increase the effectiveness of work teams by concentrating on interpersonal processes, goal clarification, and role clarification. Survey feedback requires organizational members to generate data that are fed back to them as a basis for inducing change. Total quality management (TQM) is an attempt to achieve continuous improvement in the quality of products or services. Reengineering is the radical redesign of organizational processes to achieve major improvements in time, cost, quality, or service.

- In many OD attempts that received adequate evaluation, positive changes have been observed. Despite this, the careful evaluation of OD programs poses special challenges to researchers.

- Innovation is the process of developing and implementing new ideas in an organization. It can include both new products and new processes.

- Innovation requires individual creativity and adequate resources and rewards to stimulate and channel that creativity. Also, idea champions who recognize and sponsor creative ideas are critical. Finally, internal and external communication are important for innovation. The role of gatekeepers who import and disseminate technical information is especially noteworthy.

- Innovations will diffuse most easily when they are not too complex, can be given a trial run, are compatible with existing practices, and offer a visible advantage over current practices.

Discussion Questions

1. Describe an example of resistance to change that you have observed. Why did it occur?

2. You have been charged with staffing and organizing an R&D group in a new high-technology firm. What will you do to ensure that the group is innovative?

3. What qualities would the ideal gatekeeper possess to facilitate the communication of technical information in his or her firm?

4. Suppose a job enrichment effort in one plant of a manufacturing firm is judged to be very successful. You are the corporate change agent responsible for the project, and you wish to diffuse it to other plants that have a similar technology. How would you sell the project to other plant managers? What kinds of resistance might you encounter?

5. What personal qualities and skills would be useful for an OD change agent to possess? Describe the relative merits of using an internal staff change agent versus an external consultant.

6. Discuss: The best organizational structure to generate innovative ideas might not be the best structure to implement those ideas.

7. Imagine that the U.S. Marine Corps is forming a special hostage rescue unit to aid American hostages around the world. How could team-building principles be used to enhance the formation and functioning of this unit? What are some limitations to using this approach in the military?

8. Debate this statement: Survey feedback can be a problematic OD technique because it permits people who are affected by organizational policies to generate data that speak against those policies.

9. Does leadership, organizational culture, and communication influence the effectiveness of organizational change? Discuss the effect of leadership behaviour, strong cultures, and personal and organizational approaches to communication on the change process and change problems. What should organizations do in terms of leadership, culture, and communication in order to overcome problems and ensure that the change process is effective?

10. How can organizational learning practices, pay, and socialization influence innovation in organizations? Design a program to improve an organization's ability to generate and implement innovative ideas that combines organizational learning practices (Chapter 2), pay systems (Chapter 6), and socialization methods (Chapter 8). What effect does organizational culture have on an organization's ability to innovate?

Experiential Exercise

Measuring Tolerance for Ambiguity

Please read each line of the following statements carefully. Then use the following scale to rate each of them in terms of the extent to which you either agree or disagree with the statement.

Completely disagree			Neither agree nor disagree		Completely agree	
1	2	3	4	5	6	7

Place the number that best describes your degree of agreement or disagreement in the blank to the left of each statement.

_____ 1. An expert who does not come up with a definite answer probably does not know too much.

_____ 2. I would like to live in a foreign country for a while.

_____ 3. The sooner we all acquire similar values and ideals, the better.

_____ 4. A good teacher is one who makes you wonder about your way of looking at things.

_____ 5. I like parties where I know most of the people more than ones where all or most of the people are complete strangers.

_____ 6. Teachers or supervisors who hand out vague assignments give a chance for one to show initiative and originality.

_____ 7. A person who leads an even, regular life in which few surprises or unexpected happenings arise really has a lot to be grateful for.

_____ 8. Many of our most important decisions are based on insufficient information.

_____ 9. There is really no such thing as a problem that cannot be solved.

_____ 10. People who fit their lives to a schedule probably miss most of the joy of living.

_____ 11. A good job is one in which what is to be done and how it is to be done are always clear.

_____ 12. It is more fun to tackle a complicated problem than to solve a simple one.

_____ 13. In the long run, it is possible to get more done by tackling small, simple problems than large and complicated ones.

_____ 14. Often the most interesting and stimulating people are those who do not mind being different and original.

_____ 15. What we are used to is always preferable to what is unfamiliar.

_____ 16. People who insist on a yes or no answer just do not know how complicated things really are.

Scoring and Interpretation

You have just completed the Tolerance for Ambiguity Scale. It was adapted by Paul Nutt from original work by S. Budner. The survey asks about personal and work-oriented situations that involve various degrees of ambiguity. To score your own survey, add 8 to each of your responses to the *odd* numbered items. Then, add up the renumbered odd items. From this total, subtract your score from the sum of the *even* numbered items. Your score should fall between 16 and 112. People with lower scores are tolerant of and even enjoy ambiguous situations. People with high scores are intolerant of ambiguity and prefer more structured situations. In Paul Nutt's research, people typically scored between 20 and 80 with a mean around 45. People with a high tolerance for ambiguity respond better to change. They also tend to be more creative and innovative than those with low tolerance for ambiguity.

Source: Nutt, P. C. (1988). *The tolerance for ambiguity and decision making.* Columbus, Ohio: The Ohio State University College of Business Working Paper Series, WP88–291.

Case Incident

Dandy Toys

Company president George Reed had built a successful toy company called Dandy Toys, which specialized in manufacturing inexpensive imitations of more expensive products. However, with increasing domestic and global competition, he became concerned that his cheap imitations would not be enough to maintain the company's current success. George decided to call a meeting with all the company's managers to express his concerns. He told them that Dandy Toys must change and become more innovative in its products. Rather than just knock off other companies' toys, he told the managers that they must come up with creative and innovative ideas for new and more upscale toys. "By the end of this year," George told the managers, "Dandy Toys must begin making its own in-house designed quality toys." When the managers left the meeting, they were surprised, and some were even shocked, about this new direction for Dandy Toys.

Although a few of the managers suggested some ideas for new toys during the next couple of months, nobody really seemed interested. In fact, business pretty much continued as always at Dandy Toys, and by the end of the year not a single new in-house toy had been made.

1. Comment on the change process at Dandy Toys. What advice would you give the president about how to improve the change process? What are some of the things that might be changed at Dandy Toys as part of the change process?

2. Why wasn't the innovation process more successful at Dandy Toys, and what can be done to improve it?

Case Study

Cableco

Calendarco is a diversified multinational company, which has 135 plants in 16 countries throughout the world. It employs some 69,000 employees and, in 1987, had sales of £5.6 billion, its electrical cable business accounting for some 39 percent of total turnover. Cableco, the electrical cable business of Calendarco, was founded in the U.K. in 1914. It produces a comprehensive range of power and telecommunications cables at four different factories. By 1987, Cableco's turnover had risen to nearly £135 million and the workforce to 2,200 employees. Cableco makes a range of different cables and had been producing building wires, a relatively basic range of "low-tech" electrical cables primarily used for house wiring or domestic appliances at its plant in Southampton. The plant, established in the 1930s, had enjoyed a good relationship with its employees for many years, on the basis of four important elements:

1. Labour segmentation with employees recruited into various grades with little chance of promotion. Manual staff work for 39 hours per week and nonmanual staff work for 35 hours per week. The manual group is made up of process workers (semiskilled), skilled mechanical trades and skilled electrical trades. The nonmanual group is divided between supervisory, clerical, technical, and managerial grades.

2. Job-evaluated payment systems graded by skill, with a productivity bonus paid invariably each month and with overtime working on Saturdays.

3. Recognition of six trade unions covering various grades of manual worker and staff.

4. Nationally agreed terms and conditions of employment determined by the Joint Industrial Council (JIC) for cable making, covering all companies in the industry.

Background to the Case

Overcapacity within the industry and fierce competition from the U.K. and abroad meant that the domestic cable division had been making a loss for some time. In 1984, the company was faced with a choice, should it continue in the business or get out completely? If it was to stay in the business, how could it become more competitive?

The technical director argued that an investment of £20 million in a greenfield site, attracting a development grant from the government and utilizing modern process technology, could produce a profitable return on investment within 24 months if, for the same tonnage, the number of employees could be reduced from 350 to 150. He argued that this was possible with the adoption of new technology, provided there was full flexibility of labour. Calendarco subsequently decided to build a new plant that would house the latest in computer-integrated manufacturing (CIM) systems. The system would be based on three fundamental concepts:

1. A CIM system to plan and direct every phase of the business

2. Flexible manufacturing involving the application of machine technology that allows different areas or zones within the plant to achieve a fast response to varying business needs

3. Just-in-time (JIT) production techniques with computerized monitoring to schedule and sequence the supply of raw material and work-in-progress, thus eliminating expensive stockholding

The main board decided that the project would have a greater chance of success if it was developed away from the company's other sites, and that the new factory should replace the existing plant in Southampton. Furthermore, the board insisted that within the environment of advanced technology and the latest techniques of computer integration, it was essential that the human resources policies of the new factory should also reflect "an equivalent degree of advanced thinking in the human resources area."

The site chosen was in South Wales, some distance from Cableco's other plants and in a development area attracting government financial aid. It was also in an area of high unemployment, promising a plentiful supply of labour.

Devising Appropriate Human Resource Policies

A small project team, consisting of two members of Cableco's divisional human resource department and the new plant general and human resource managers, was given the task of developing the new policies in the human resource area. They began with a period of research, visiting companies the team members believed to be innovators in their field, and taking part in discussions with the Work Research Unit of the Arbitration, Conciliation, and Advisory Services (ACAS).

The new plant human resource manager, recruited from outside the Calendarco organization specifically for the job, had firm views about the way in which employees ought to be managed in the new plant. In particular, he believed that the policies adopted should reflect "best practice" in the U.K.. He was the driving force behind the company's new philosophy. Instead of the rigid job demarcation, repetitive tasks, and traditional supervisory systems in operation at Cableco's other plants, the project team wanted employees in the new factory to work in small, highly adaptable teams. The project team developed plans to create what they called a "model working environment" based on flexibility and involvement, where all employees would be equal, with no distinction between office and factory.

This model working environment was based on the principles of single employee status and cooperative team working, aimed both at motivating employees and ensuring their commitment to the success of the new plant. All staff would enjoy similar terms and conditions of employment, which would include a salary structure based on an annual rather than a weekly-hours contract, and which would reward adaptability and achievement. However, all senior specialists and managerial staff were to be excluded. They would be treated as a corporate rather than a plant resource, liable to be transferred to another part of the Calendarco organization at some time in the future.

The CIM system that had been chosen had certain implications for the type of employee who would be needed to use it. In the first place employees would need to be computer literate. The type of skills they would require were diagnostic rather than motor related, with only a minimal degree of manual skill required. The process was not going to be high speed, but it would involve constant operator attention requiring the application of detailed production schedules as shown on the visual display units with little, if any, supervision. Employees were going to be required to work flexibly not only in relation to the performance of tasks but also in relation to skills (for example, operators carrying out day-to-day maintenance tasks) as well as flexibility in relation to hours worked. From this a profile was developed of the characteristics future employees would be required to possess.

The project team saw recruitment as critical to the successful running of the plant. They endeavoured to select only those employees who would be suited to the different work requirements and ethos of the plant. They wanted employees who had the "right attitude," people who would be flexible, who were anxious to develop their own potential, and who would accept responsibility: they wanted the "best" employees available. The recruitment procedure was time consuming, expensive, and sophisticated. It included the assessment of personality profiles and computer aptitude testing, as well as conventional interviewing techniques. Interviews were held not only by the potential employee's immediate manager within the plant but also with at least two senior members of the management team.

The various functions within the plant (production, maintenance, and administration) were divided up into a number of skill modules, each of which would require a different combination of skills and knowledge. All employees would acquire skill modules across all functions, each skill module requiring between four and eight weeks' training. Employees would be paid a basic salary and an increase of £250 for each skill module they obtained. Calendarco was anxious that pay levels should be kept within reasonable limits and the decision was taken that the level of basic salary should be determined by reference to salaries paid in the local area (a figure that was some £2,000 a year less than at the Southampton plant). Since salaries would increase quite quickly as new skill modules were acquired, Calendarco decided to set levels just below the average for the area.

A key feature of the motivational aspect of the policies was to be comprehensive communication and involvement informally through the free exchange of information, opinions and ideas on operational matters, and formally through joint consultation in the form of the Business Review and Consultative Committee (BRCC). Rather than adopt a nonunion position, the project team was persuaded to main-

tain a policy of union recognition well established in the rest of Calendarco. However, copying other forward-thinking organizations opening new ventures on greenfield sites, they decided to withdraw from the JIC and (after holding a 'beauty contest' where a number of unions were invited to make a presentation to the company as to their suitability for recognition), a single-union, no-strike agreement was signed with the Managerial, Administrative, Technical, and Supervisory Association (MATSA). Among other things, the agreement stressed the importance of operational objectives and arrangements including complete flexibility and active cooperation in all elements of change and an undertaking to accept training, as well as an obligation on the part of the company to provide training as necessary.

The Problem: Implementing the Human Resource Policies

The original time-scale was for the Southampton plant to close by December 1988. The plant was still open in December 1989. The development and design of Cableco's advanced manufacturing technology were fraught with problems that, in turn, had serious implications for the type of employee policies that Cableco had decided to implement. Many of the suppliers had been asked to make significant advances in the development of their equipment, advances that had not been attempted before. They delivered the machinery to the plant only to discover that it did not perform the tasks Cableco required of it. Attempts by Cableco's technicians to modify or repair the new machinery themselves prior to official acceptance by the company would have led to a breach of the manufacturer's warranty. This meant that Cableco employees (who had not been involved in the original design process) were also excluded from the modification process.

Two major factors affected the operation of the company's reward system. The details of the skill modules could only be drawn up once the plant was operating. This could not be done without machinery that worked. In addition, more and more new plants (also attracted by government financial aid and a ready supply of labour) opened up in South Wales, all requiring skilled maintenance workers. The salaries being paid by Cableco quickly became uncompetitive. This led to the introduction of new hierarchical levels within the maintenance department linked to higher salaries, as attempts were made to recruit and retain staff. Twelve months after the opening of the new plant, the union and management were involved in what the management referred to as "conventional and at times fairly confrontational" negotiations, which led to the nominal award of one skill module, regardless of whether the necessary skills had been acquired. In the mind of employees, skill modules became associated with length of service rather than with skill acquisition and flexibility. This distortion of the payment system and infringement of the single-status principle created much resentment among the production workers.

The plant human resources manager, the driving force behind the new policies, left Cableco in October 1988 to pursue a career elsewhere. With his departure, the emphasis on consultation and communication was almost forgotten in the face of the increasing pressures to meet production targets and close down the Southampton factory, and informal communication systems did not develop. The general manager, aware of the substantial difficulties facing the plant, made attempts to keep employees informed but felt that if they knew how serious the plant's position was, they would revert to "traditional adversarial behaviour." The employees argued that they knew things were going badly, and that they did not believe the information they were being given about the plant's performance was accurate. After the human resource manager's departure, the plans for formal communication and information systems were ignored.

Source: Case prepared by Helen Newell. From Gowler, D., Legge, K., & Clegg, C. (Eds.). (1993). *Case studies in organizational behaviour and human resource management* (2nd ed). London, England: Paul Chapman.

1. Describe the environmental changes that prompted the decision to build the new plant, and describe the corresponding internal changes that were proposed. Did these changes constitute reengineering?

2. Evaluate the general concept of the proposed greenfield site plant. Did the proposed organization and policies make sense? Why or why not?

3. Defend this statement: The proposed new Cableco plant constituted organizational innovation.

4. List any observed strengths in the way the change at Cableco was implemented.

5. What were the sources of resistance to change that threatened the new plant?

6. List any observed weaknesses in the way change at Cableco was implemented.

7. How could the change process involved in opening the new plant have been improved? Be sure to consider any relevant organizational development techniques.

Integrative Case: Ace Technology

At the end of Part Three of the text on Social Behaviour and Organizational Processes, you answered a number of questions about the Ace Technology Integrative Case that dealt with issues related to culture, leadership, communication, and decision making. Now that you have completed Part Four of the text and the chapters on The Total Organization, you can return to the Ace Technology Integrative Case and enhance your understanding of some of the main issues associated with the total organization by answering the following questions.

Questions

1. Describe the external environment and its influence on Ace Technology.

2. Describe Ace Technology's response to uncertainty and resource dependence. How effective do you think its response will be, and what are some other strategic responses that it might consider?

3. Consider the concept of organizational change. Does Ace Technology need to change? Why or why not?

4. Discuss the change process and issues in relation to the new programs at Ace Technology. How effectively have the three basic stages been conducted and the main issues managed?

5. Consider the issue of resistance to change at Ace Technology. What factors explain the degree of resistance toward the new strategy and compensation program at Ace Technology?

6. How effective do you think the new compensation program will be for generating and implementing innovative ideas? What else can Ace Technology do to improve innovation?

Research in Organizational Behaviour

Research is a way of finding out about the world through objective and systematic information gathering. The key words here are *objective* and *systematic*, and it is these characteristics that separate the outcomes of the careful study of organizational behaviour from opinion and common sense.

Understanding how researchers conduct their research is important to the study of organizational behaviour for several reasons. First of all, you should be aware of how the information presented in this book was collected. This should increase your confidence in the advantages of systematic study over common sense. Second, you will likely encounter reports, in management periodicals and the popular press, of interventions to improve organizational behaviour, such as job redesign or employee development programs. A critical perspective is necessary to differentiate those interventions that are carefully designed and evaluated from useless or even damaging ones. Those backed by good research deserve the greatest confidence. Occasionally, a manager may have to evaluate a research proposal or consultant's intervention to be carried out in his or her own organization. A brief introduction to research methodology should enable you to ask some intelligent questions about such plans.

Trained behavioural scientists who have backgrounds in management, applied psychology, or applied sociology carry out research in organizational behaviour. While this introduction will not make you a trained behavioural scientist, it should provide an appreciation of the work that goes into generating accurate knowledge about organizational behaviour.

The Basics of Organizational Behaviour Research

All research in organizational behaviour begins with a question about work or organizations. Sometimes, this question might stem from a formal theory in the field. For example, a motivation theory called equity theory (see Chapter 5) is concerned with peoples' reactions to fairness or lack of it. Equity theory suggests the following research question: What do people do when they perceive their pay to be too low in comparison with other people? Other times, a research question

Learning Objectives

After reading the Appendix, you should be able to:

1. Explain what a hypothesis is and differentiate reliability from validity.

2. Understand observational research and distinguish between participant and direct observation.

3. Describe correlational research and explain why causation cannot be inferred from correlation.

4. Explain experimental research and distinguish between independent and dependent variables.

5. Discuss the relative advantages and disadvantages of various research techniques.

6. Explain the Hawthorne effect.

7. State the basic ethical concerns to which researchers must attend.

might stem from an immediate organizational problem. For example, a human resource manager might ask herself: How can we reduce absenteeism among our customer service personnel?

Often, research questions are expressed as hypotheses. A **hypothesis** is a formal statement of the expected relationship between two variables. Variables are simply measures that can take on two or more values. Temperature is a variable, but so are pay, fairness, and absenteeism. A formal hypothesis stemming from equity theory might be: The less fair people perceive their pay to be, the more likely they will be to resign their jobs. Here, a variable that can take on many values, perceived fairness, is linked to a variable made up of two values, staying or leaving. The human resource manager might develop this hypothesis: The introduction of a small attendance bonus will reduce absenteeism. Here, a variable with two values, bonus versus no bonus, is related to one that can take on many values, days of absenteeism.

> **Hypothesis.** A formal statement of the expected relationship between two variables.

Good researchers carefully measure the variables they choose. For one thing, a measure should exhibit high reliability. **Reliability** is an index of the consistency of a research subject's responses. For example, if we ask someone several questions about how fair his or her pay is, the person should respond roughly the same way to each question. Similarly, the person should respond roughly the same way to the same questions next week or next month if there has been no change in pay.

> **Reliability.** An index of the consistency of a research subject's responses.

Measures should also exhibit high validity. **Validity** is an index of the extent to which a measure truly reflects what it is supposed to measure. For instance, a good measure of perceived pay fairness should not be influenced by employees' feelings of fairness about other workplace factors such as supervision. Also, a researcher would expect people who are objectively underpaid to report high pay unfairness and for them to report increased fairness if their pay were increased. Researchers are often able to choose measures with a known history of reliability and validity.

> **Validity.** An index of the extent to which a measure truly reflects what it is supposed to measure.

There are three basic kinds of research techniques—observation, correlation, and experimentation. As you will see, each begins with a research question or questions. Correlation and experimentation are most likely to test specific hypotheses and devote explicit attention to measurement quality.

Observational Techniques

Observational research.
Research that examines the
natural activities of people in an
organizational setting by listening
to what they say and watching
what they do.

Observational research techniques are the most straightforward ways of finding out about behaviour in organizations and thus come closest to the ways in which we develop common-sense views about such behaviour. In this case, *observation* means just what it implies—the researcher proceeds to examine the natural activities of people in an organizational setting by listening to what they say and watching what they do. The difference between our everyday observations and the formal observations of the trained behavioural scientist is expressed by those key words *systematic* and *objective*.

First, the researcher approaches the organizational setting with extensive training concerning the nature of human behaviour and a particular set of questions that the observation is designed to answer. These factors provide a systematic framework for the business of observing. Second, the behavioural scientist attempts to keep a careful ongoing record of the events that he or she observes, either as they occur or as soon as possible afterward. Thus, excessive reliance on memory, which may lead to inaccuracies, is unnecessary. Finally, the behavioural scientist is well informed of the dangers of influencing the behaviour of those whom he or she is observing and is trained to draw reasonable conclusions from his or her observations. These factors help ensure objectivity.

The outcomes of observational research are summarized in a narrative form, sometimes called a *case study*. This narrative specifies the nature of the organization, people, and events studied, the particular role of and techniques used by the observer, the research questions, and the events observed.

Participant Observation

Participant observation.
Observational research in which
the researcher becomes a functioning member of the organizational unit being studied.

One obvious way for a researcher to find out about organizational behaviour is to actively participate in this behaviour. In **participant observation** the researcher becomes a functioning member of the organizational unit he or she is studying in order to conduct the research. At this point you may wonder, "Wait a minute. What about objectivity? What about influencing the behaviour of those being studied?" These are clearly legitimate questions, and they might be answered in the following way: In adopting participant observation, the researcher is making a conscious bet that the advantages of participation outweigh these problems. It is doubtless true in some cases that "there is no substitute for experience." For example, researcher Robert Sutton wanted to find out how employees cope with jobs that require them to express negative emotions.[1] To do this, he trained and then worked as a bill collector. This is obviously a more personal experience than simply interviewing bill collectors.

Another advantage to participant observation is its potential for secrecy—the subjects need not know that they are being observed. This potential for secrecy does raise some ethical issues, however. Sociologist Tom Lupton served as an industrial worker in two plants in England to study the factors that influenced productivity.[2] Although he could have acted in secrecy, he was required to inform management and union officials of his presence to secure records and documents, and he thus felt it unfair not to inform his workmates of his purpose. It should be stressed that his goals were academic, and he was *not* working for the managements of the companies involved. Sometimes, however, secrecy seems necessary to accomplish a research goal, as the following study of "illegal" industrial behaviour shows.

Joseph Bensman and Israel Gerver investigated an important organizational problem: What happens when the activities that appear to be required to get a job done conflict with official organizational policy?[3] Examples of such conflicts include the punch press operator who must remove the safety guard from his machine to meet productivity standards, the executive who must deliver corporate money to a political slush fund, or the police officer who cannot find time to complete an eight-page report to justify having drawn her revolver on a night patrol.

The behaviour of interest to Bensman and Gerver was the unauthorized use of taps by aircraft plant workers. A tap is a hard steel hand tool used to cut threads into metal. The possession of this device by aircraft assemblers was strictly forbidden because the workers could use it to correct sloppy or difficult work such as the misalignment of bolt holes in two pieces of aircraft skin or stripped lock nuts; both these problems could lead to potential structural weaknesses or maintenance problems.

Possession of a tap was a strict violation of company policy, and a worker could be fired on the spot for it. On the other hand, since supervisors were under extreme pressure to maintain a high quota of completed work, the occasional use of a tap to correct a problem could save hours of disassembly and realignment time. How was this conflict resolved? The answer was provided by one of the authors, who served as a participant observer while functioning as an assembler. Put simply, the supervisors and inspectors worked together to encourage the cautious and appropriate use of taps. New workers were gradually introduced to the mysteries of tapping by experienced workers, and the supervisors provided refinement of skills and signals as to when a tap might be used. Taps were not to be used in front of inspectors or to correct chronic sloppy work. If "caught," promiscuous tappers were expected to act truly penitent in response to a chewing out by the supervisors, even if the supervisors themselves had suggested the use of the tap. In short, a *social ritual* was developed to teach and control the use of the tap to facilitate getting the work out without endangering the continued presence of the crucial tool. Clearly, this is the kind of information about organizational behaviour that would be extremely difficult to obtain except by participant observation.

Direct Observation

In **direct observation** the researcher observes organizational behaviour without participation in the activity being observed. There are a number of reasons why one might choose direct observation over participant observation. First, there are many situations in which the introduction of a new person into an existing work setting would severely disrupt and change the nature of the activities in that setting. These are cases in which the "influence" criticism of participant observation is especially true. Second, there are many job tasks that a trained behavioural scientist could not be expected to learn for research purposes. For example, it seems unreasonable to expect a researcher to spend years acquiring the skills of a pilot or banker in order to be able to investigate what happens in the cockpit of an airliner or in a boardroom. Finally, participant observation places rather severe limitations on the observers' opportunity to record information. Existence of these conditions suggests the use of direct observation. In theory, the researcher could carry out such observation covertly, but there are few studies of organizational behaviour in which the presence of the direct observer was not known and explained to those being observed.

   Henry Mintzberg's study of the work performed by chief executives of two manufacturing companies, a hospital, a school system, and a consulting firm provides an excellent example of the use of direct observation.[4] At first glance, this might appear to be an inane thing to investigate. After all, everybody knows that managers plan, organize, lead, and control, or some similar combination of words. In fact, Mintzberg argues that we actually know very little about the routine, everyday behaviour managers use to achieve these vague goals.

Direct observation.
Observational research in which the researcher observes organizational behaviour without taking part in the studied activity.

Furthermore, if we ask managers what they do (in an interview or questionnaire), they usually respond with a variation of the plan-organize-lead-control theme.

Mintzberg spent a week with each of his five executives, watching them at their desks, attending meetings with them, listening to their phone calls, and inspecting their mail. He kept detailed records of these activities and gradually developed a classification scheme to make sense of them. What Mintzberg found counters the common-sense view that some hold of managers—sitting behind a large desk, reflecting on their organization's performance, and affixing their signatures to impressive documents all day. In fact, Mintzberg found that his managers actually performed a terrific amount of work and had little time for reflection. On an average day, they examined 36 pieces of mail, engaged in five telephone conversations, attended eight meetings, and made one tour of their facilities. Work-related reading encroached on home lives. These activities were varied, unpatterned, and of short duration. Half the activities lasted less than nine minutes, and 90 percent less than one hour. Furthermore, these activities tended to be directed toward current, specific issues rather than past, general issues. Finally, the managers revealed a clear preference for verbal communications, by either telephone or unscheduled face-to-face meetings; in fact, two-thirds of their contacts were of this nature. In contrast, they generated an average of only one piece of mail a day.

In summary, both participant and direct observation capture the depth, breadth, richness, spontaneity, and realism of organizational behaviour. However, they also share some weaknesses. One of these weaknesses is a lack of control over the environment in which the study is being conducted. Thus, Mintzberg could not ensure that unusual events would not affect the executives' behaviour. Also, the small number of observers and situations in the typical observational study is problematic. With only one observer there is a strong potential for selective perceptions and interpretations of observed events. Since only a few situations are analyzed, the extent to which the observed behaviours can be generalized to other settings is limited. (Do most executives behave like the five that Mintzberg studied?) It is probably safe to say that observational techniques are best used to make an initial examination of some organizational event on which little information is available and to generate ideas for further investigation with more refined techniques.

Correlational Techniques

Correlational research. Research that attempts to measure variables precisely and examine relationships among these variables without introducing change into the research setting.

Correlational research attempts to measure variables precisely and examine relationships among these variables without introducing change into the research setting. Correlational research sacrifices some of the breadth and richness of the observational techniques for more precision of measurement and greater control. It necessarily involves some abstraction of the real event that is the focus of observation in order to accomplish this precision and control. More specifically, correlational approaches differ from observational approaches in terms of the nature of the data researchers collect and the issues they investigate.

The data of observational studies are most frequently observer notes. We hope that these data exhibit reliability and validity. Unfortunately, because observations are generally the products of a single individual viewing a unique event, we have very little basis on which to judge their reliability and validity.

The data of correlational studies involve interviews and questionnaires as well as existing data. Existing data come from organizational records and include productivity, absence, and demographic information (e.g., age, gender). Variables often measured by questionnaires and interviews include

- subordinates' perceptions of how their managers behave on the job,
- the extent to which employees are satisfied with their jobs, and
- employees' reports about how much autonomy they have on their jobs.

It is possible to determine in advance of doing research the extent to which such measures are reliable and valid. Thus, when constructing a questionnaire to measure job satisfaction, the researcher can check its reliability by repeatedly administering it to a group of workers over a period of time. If individual responses remain fairly stable, there is evidence of reliability. Evidence of the validity of a questionnaire might come from its ability to predict which employees would quit the organization for work elsewhere. It seems reasonable that dissatisfied employees would be more likely to quit, and such an effect is partial evidence of the validity of a satisfaction measure.

In addition to the nature of the data collected, it was pointed out above that correlational studies differ from observational studies in terms of the kinds of events they investigate. Although the questions investigated by observational research appear fairly specific (What maintains an "illegal" behaviour such as tapping? What do executives do?), virtually any event relevant to the question is fair game for observation. Thus, such studies are extremely broad based. Correlational research sacrifices this broadness to investigate the relationship (correlation) between specific, well-defined variables. The relationship between the variables of interest is usually stated as a hypothesis. Using the variables mentioned above, we can construct three sample hypotheses and describe how they would be tested:

- Employees who are satisfied with their jobs will tend to be more productive than those who are less satisfied. To test this, a researcher might administer a reliable, valid questionnaire concerning satisfaction and obtain production data from company records.

- Employees who perceive their supervisor as friendly and considerate will be more satisfied with their jobs than those who do not. To test this, a researcher might use reliable, valid questionnaires or interview measures of both variables.

- Older employees will be absent less than younger employees. To test this, a researcher might obtain data concerning the age of employees and their absenteeism from organizational personnel records.

In each case, the researcher is interested in a very specific set of variables, and he or she devotes effort to measuring them precisely.

A good example of a correlational study is that of Belle Rose Ragins and John Cotton, who studied employees' willingness to serve as mentors to newer organizational members.[5] Mentorship was defined as helping a junior person with career support and upward mobility. The major focus of the study was the relationship between gender and willingness to mentor. The authors reviewed literature that hypothesizes that women may face more barriers to becoming mentors than men because they are in a minority in many employment settings. The authors were also interested in the relationships between age, organizational rank, length of employment, and prior mentorship experience and willingness to mentor.

These variables were measured with questionnaires completed by over 500 employees in three research and development organizations. The researchers found that men and women were equally willing to serve as mentors, although the women perceived more barriers (e.g., lack of qualifications and time) to being a mentor. They also found that higher rank and prior experience as a mentor or a protégé were associated with greater willingness to mentor. Notice that a study such as this could also incorporate existing data from records. For example, we

Exhibit A.1
Hypothetical data from a correlational study of the relationship between supervisory friendliness and subordinate productivity.

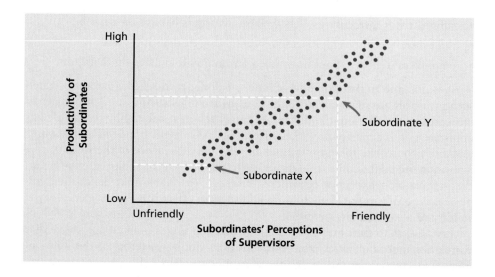

might hypothesize that those with better performance evaluations would be more confident about serving as mentors.

Correlation and Causation

A final important point should be made about correlational studies. Consider a hypothesis that friendly, considerate supervisors will have more productive subordinates than unfriendly, inconsiderate supervisors. In this case, a researcher might have some subordinates describe the friendliness of their supervisors on a reliable, valid questionnaire designed to measure this variable and obtain subordinates' productivity levels from company records. The results of this hypothetical study are plotted in Exhibit A.1, where each dot represents a subordinate's response to the questionnaire in conjunction with his or her productivity. In general, it would appear that the hypothesis is confirmed—that is, subordinates who describe their supervisor as friendly tend to be more productive than those who describe him or her as unfriendly. As a result of this study, should an organization attempt to select friendly supervisors or even train existing supervisors to be more friendly to obtain higher productivity? The answer is *no*. The training and selection proposal assumes that friendly supervisors *cause* their subordinates to be productive, and this might not be the case. Put simply, supervisors might be friendly *if* their subordinates are productive. This is a possible interpretation of the data, and it does not suggest that selection or training to make supervisors friendly will achieve higher productivity. This line of argument should not be unfamiliar to you. Heavy smokers and cigarette company lobbyists like to claim that smoking is related to the incidence of lung cancer because cancer proneness prompts smoking, rather than vice versa. The point here is that *correlation does not imply causation*. How can we find out which factors cause certain organizational behaviours? The answer is to perform an experiment.

Experimental Techniques

Experimental research. Research which changes or manipulates a variable under controlled conditions and examines the consequences of this manipulation for some other variable.

If observational research involves observing nature, and correlational research involves measuring nature, **experimental research** manipulates nature. In an experiment, a variable is manipulated or changed under controlled conditions, and the consequence of this manipulation for some other variable is measured. If all other conditions are truly controlled, and a change in the second variable follows the change that was introduced in the first variable, we can infer that the first change has caused the second change.

In experimental language, the variable that the researcher manipulates or changes is called the **independent variable**. The variable that the independent variable is expected to affect is called the **dependent variable**. Consider the following hypothesis: The introduction of recorded music into the work setting will lead to increased productivity. In this hypothesis, the independent variable is music, which is expected to affect productivity, the dependent variable. Consider another hypothesis: Stimulating, challenging jobs will increase the satisfaction of the workforce. Here, the design of the job is the independent variable and satisfaction is the dependent variable.

Let us return to our hypothesis that friendly, considerate supervisors will tend to have more productive subordinates. If we wish to determine whether friendly supervision contributes to subordinate productivity, the style of supervision becomes the independent variable, and productivity becomes the dependent variable. This means that the researcher must manipulate or change the friendliness of some supervisors and observe what happens to the productivity of their subordinates. In practice, this would probably be accomplished by exposing the bosses to some form of human relations training designed to teach them to be more considerate and personable toward their workers.

Exhibit A.2 shows the results of this hypothetical experiment. The line on the graph represents the average productivity of a number of subordinates whose supervisors have received our training. We see that this productivity increased and remained higher following the introduction of the training. Does this mean that friendliness indeed increases productivity and that we should proceed to train all of our supervisors in this manner? The answer is again *no*. We cannot be sure that *something else* did not occur at the time of the training to influence productivity, such as a change in equipment or job insecurity prompted by rumoured layoffs. To control this possibility, we need a control group of supervisors who are not exposed to the training, and we need productivity data for their subordinates. A **control group** is a group of research subjects who have not been exposed to the experimental treatment, in this case not exposed to the training. Ideally, these supervisors should be as similar as possible in experience and background to those who receive the training, and their subordinates should be performing at the same level. The results of our improved experiment are shown in Exhibit A.3. Here, we see that the productivity of the subordinates whose supervisors were trained increases following training, while that of the control supervisors remains

Independent variable. The variable that is manipulated or changed in an experiment.

Dependent variable. In an experiment, the variable that is expected to vary as a result of the manipulation of the independent variable.

Control group. A group of research subjects who have not been exposed to the experimental treatment.

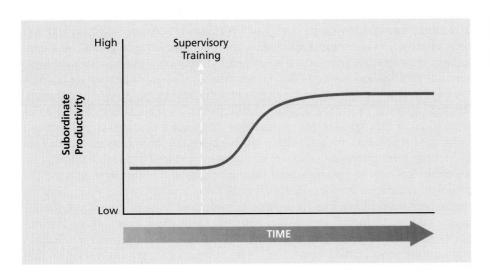

Exhibit A.2
Hypothetical data from an experiment concerning human relations training.

Exhibit A.3
Hypothetical data from an improved experiment concerning human relations training.

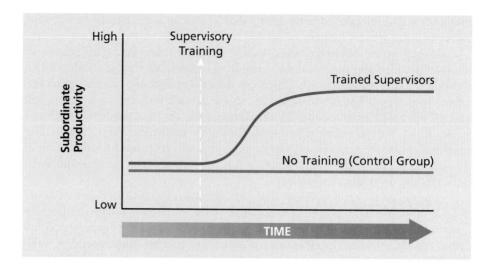

constant. We can, thus, infer that the human relations training affected subordinate productivity.

John Ivancevich and Herbert Lyon conducted an interesting experiment that examined the effects of a shortened workweek on the employees of a company that manufactures food-packaging equipment.[6] The independent variable was the length of the workweek (4 days, 40 hours versus 5 days, 40 hours). Two of the company's divisions were converted to a 4–40 week from a 5–40 week. A third division, remaining on the 5–40 schedule, served as a control group. Workers in the control division were similar to those in the other divisions in terms of age, seniority, education, and salary. The dependent variables (measured one month before the conversion and several times after) included the workers' responses to a questionnaire concerning job satisfaction and stress, absence data from company records, and performance appraisals conducted by supervisors. After 12 months, several aspects of satisfaction and performance showed a marked improvement for the 4–40 workers, when compared with the 5–40 workers. However, at 25 months this edge existed for only one aspect of satisfaction, satisfaction with personal worth. The authors concluded that benefits that had been proposed for the 4–40 workweek were of short-term duration.

A Continuum of Research Techniques

You might reasonably wonder which of the research techniques just discussed is most effective. As shown in Exhibit A.4, these methods can be placed on a continuum ranging from rich, broad-based, and loosely controlled (observation) to specific, precise, and rigorous (experimentation). The method that researchers use to investigate organizational behaviour is dictated by the nature of the problem that interests us. In the writing of this section of the chapter, special pains were taken to choose examples of problems that were well suited to the research techniques employed to investigate them. Bensman and Gerver, as well as Mintzberg, were interested in variables that were not well defined. The variables were thus not easy to isolate and measure precisely, and observation was the appropriate technique. Furthermore, "tapping" was a controversial issue, and the researchers would have had to develop considerable trust to investigate it with questionnaires or formal interviews. Similarly, Mintzberg insists that questionnaires and interviews have failed to tell us what executives actually do. Ragins and Cotton, who studied mentoring, were interested in specific variables that were relatively easily measured. On the other hand, they were not in a position

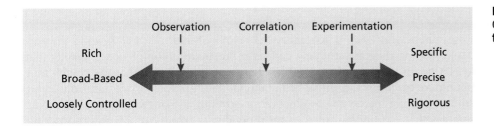

Exhibit A.4
Continuum of research
techniques.

to manipulate the causes of intention to mentor. Ivancevich and Lyon were also interested in a specific set of variables, and they conducted their research on the short workweek in a situation where it was both possible and ethical to manipulate the workweek. In all these cases, the research technique the researchers chose was substantially better than dependence on common sense or opinion.

Combining Research Techniques

Robert Sutton and Anat Rafaeli tested what might seem to be an obvious hypothesis—that friendly, pleasant behaviour on the part of sales clerks would be positively associated with store sales.[7] As obvious as this might seem, it would be a good idea to confirm it before spending thousands of dollars on human relations training for clerks. The study combined correlational and observational methods. In the quantitative correlational part of the study, teams of researchers entered a large North American chain's 576 convenience stores and, posing as shoppers, evaluated the friendliness of the sales clerks on rating scales. They also recorded other factors, such as the length of the line at the register. Existing data from company records provided the total annual sales each store recorded. When the researchers analyzed the data, the results were surprising—the "unfriendly" stores tended to chalk up higher sales!

To understand this unexpected result, the authors resorted to qualitative, observational research techniques. Specifically, each author spent extensive time in many of the convenience stores directly observing transactions between customers and clerks. In addition, each spent time as a participant-observer, actually doing the sales clerk's job. This observation resolved the mystery. The researchers found that when the stores were busy, the sales clerks tended to stop the small talk, concentrate on their work, and process customers as quickly as possible. This behaviour corresponded to customers' expectations for fast service in a convenience store. When business was slow, clerks tended to be friendly and engage in small talk to relieve boredom. Since the busier stores generated higher sales, it is not surprising that their clerks were less friendly. In fact, further analysis of the correlational data showed that clerks were less friendly when the lines were longer.

This study illustrates how two research techniques can complement each other. It also shows that correlation does not imply causation. Although sales were negatively correlated with friendliness, volume of sales affected the expression of friendliness, not the other way around. Of course, these results would probably not generalize to sales settings in which customers expect more personal attention.

Issues and Concerns in Organizational Research

As in every field of study, particular issues confront researchers in organizational behaviour. Three of these issues include sampling, Hawthorne effects, and ethical concerns.

Sampling

Researchers who wish to generalize the results of their research beyond the particular setting they are studying can have the greatest confidence in results that are based on large, random samples. Large samples ensure that the results they obtain are truly representative of the individuals, groups, or organizations being studied and not merely the product of an extreme case or two. Similarly, random samples that ensure that all relevant individuals, groups, or organizations have an equal probability of being studied also give confidence in the generalizability of findings. As was noted earlier, observational studies usually involve small samples, and they are seldom randomized. Thus, generalizing from such studies is a problem. However, a well-designed observational study that answers important questions is surely superior to a large-sample, randomized correlational study that enables one to generalize about a trivial hypothesis.

In experimental research, randomization means randomly assigning subjects to experimental and control conditions. To illustrate the importance of this, we can reconsider the hypothetical study on human relations training. Suppose that instead of randomly assigning supervisors to the experimental and control groups, managers nominate supervisors for training. Suppose further that to "reward" them for their long service, more-experienced supervisors are nominated for the training. This results in an experimental group containing more-experienced supervisors and a control group containing less-experienced supervisors. If supervisory experience promotes subordinate productivity, we might erroneously conclude that it was the *human relations training* that led to any improved results, and that our hypothesis is confirmed. Poor sampling due to a lack of randomization has biased the results in favour of our hypothesis. To achieve randomization, it would be a good idea to ascertain that the subordinates of the experimental and control supervisors were equally productive *before* the training began.

Hawthorne Effects

The Hawthorne effect was discovered as a result of a series of studies conducted at the Hawthorne plant of the Western Electric Company near Chicago many years ago. As explained in Chapter 1, these studies examined the effects of independent variables, such as rest pauses, lighting intensity, and pay incentives, on the productivity of assemblers of electrical components.[8] In a couple of these loosely controlled experiments, unusual results occurred. In the illumination study, both experimental and control workers improved their productivity. In another study, productivity increased and remained high despite the introduction and withdrawal of factors such as rest pauses, shortened workdays, and so on. These results gave rise to the **Hawthorne effect**, which might be defined as a favourable response of subjects in an organizational experiment to a factor other than the independent variable that is formally being manipulated. Researchers have concluded that this "other factor" is psychological in nature, although it is not well understood.[9] Likely candidates include subjects' reactions to special attention, including feelings of prestige, and heightened morale, and so on. The point is that researchers might misinterpret the true reason for any observed change in behaviour because research subjects can have unmeasured feelings about their role in the research.

To return to the human relations training experiment, a Hawthorne effect might occur if the experimental subjects are grateful to management for selecting them for this special training and resolve to work harder back on the job. The supervisors might put in longer hours thinking up ways to improve productivity that have nothing to do with the training they received. However, the researcher could easily conclude that the human relations training itself had improved productivity.

Hawthorne effect. A favourable response by subjects in an organizational experiment that is the result of a factor other than the independent variable that is formally being manipulated.

It is very difficult to prevent Hawthorne effects. However, it is possible, if expensive, to see whether they have occurred. To do so, investigators establish a second experimental group that receives special treatment and attention but is not exposed to the key independent variable. In the human relations experiment, this could involve training that is not expected to increase productivity. If the productivity of the subjects' subordinates in both experimental groups increases equally, the Hawthorne effect is probably present. If productivity increases only in the human relations training condition, it is unlikely to be due to the Hawthorne effect.

Ethics

Researchers in organizational behaviour, no matter who employs them, have an ethical obligation to do rigorous research and to report that research accurately.[10] In all cases, the psychological and physical well being of the research subjects is of prime importance. In general, ethical researchers avoid unnecessary deception, inform participants about the general purpose of their research, and protect the anonymity of research subjects. For example, in a correlational study involving the use of questionnaires, investigators should explain the general reason for the research and afford potential subjects the opportunity to decline participation. If names or company identification numbers are required to match responses with data in personnel files (e.g., absenteeism or subsequent turnover), investigators must guarantee that they will not make individual responses public. In some observation studies and experiments, subjects may be unaware that their behaviour is under formal study. In these cases, researchers have special obligations to prevent negative consequences for subjects. Ethical research has a practical side as well as a moral side. Good cooperation from research subjects is necessary to do good research. Such cooperation is easier to obtain when people are confident that ethical procedures are the rule, not the exception.

Summary

- The systematic study of organizational behaviour, using carefully designed research, represents a useful alternative to reliance only on common sense.

- All research in organizational behaviour begins with a basic question about work or organizations. Frequently, researchers express the question as a hypothesis, a formal statement of the expected relationship between two variables.

- Careful measurement of variables is important in research. Reliability is an index of the consistency of a research subject's responses. Validity is an index of the extent to which a measure truly reflects what it is supposed to measure.

- In observational research, one or a few observers assess one or a few instances of organizational behaviour in its natural setting. In participant observation, the observer actually takes part in the activity being observed. In direct observation, the assessment occurs without the active participation of the researcher.

- Compared with observation, correlational research techniques attempt to measure the variables in question more precisely by using questionnaires, interviews, and existing data. No change is introduced into the research setting. One problem with correlational research is its inability to reveal which variables cause other variables. Researchers use experiments to overcome this problem.

- In experimental research, the investigator actually changes or manipulates some factor in the organizational setting and measures the effect that this manipulation has on behaviour. Causation can be inferred from a carefully designed experiment.

- Proper sampling, attention to Hawthorne effects, and ethical considerations are all components of good organizational research.

References

Chapter 1

1. Gibney, F., Jr. (1999, May 24). World-wide fender blender. Time, pp. 28–32; Taylor, A., III. (1999, January 11). The Germans take charge. *Fortune*, pp. 92–98; Bulkeley, A. (1999, April 1). DaimlerChrysler upbeat on profit. *Financial Post*, p. C11 (Bloomberg News); (1999, April 1). DaimlerChrysler predicts rosy future. *Toronto Star*, p. D3 (Associated Press); McGinn, D., & Theil, S. (1999, April 12). Hands on the wheel. *Newsweek*, pp. 49, 50, 52; Taylor, A., III. (1998, June 8). Gentlemen, start your engines. *Fortune*, pp. 138,140, 142, 144, 146; Coleman, B., & White, G. L. (1998, November 13). War room shapes DaimlerChrysler future. *Globe and Mail.*

2. Katz, D. (1964). The motivational basis of organizational behavior. *Behavioral Science, 9*, 131–146.

3. Peters, T. (1990, Fall). Get innovative or get dead. *California Management Review*, 9–26.

4. Huselid, M.A. (1964). The motivational basis of organizational behaviour. *Behavioural Science, 9*, 131–146.

5. Delancy, J. M.T., & Huselid, M.A. (1996). The impact of human resource management practices on perceptions of organizational performance. *Academy of Management Journal, 39*, 949–969; Delery, J.E., & Doty, D.H. (1996). Modes of theorizing in strategic human resource management: Tests of universalisticv, contingency, and configurational performance predictions. *Academy of Management Journal, 39*, 802–835.

6. Pfeffer, J. (1994). *Competitive advantage through people: Unleashing the power of the work force.* Harvard Business School Press: Boston.

7. Wren, D. (1987). *The evolution of management thought* (3rd ed.). New York: Wiley.

8. For a summary of their work and relevant references, see Wren, 1987.

9. Taylor, F. W. (1967). *The principles of scientific management.* New York: Norton.

10. Weber, M. (1974). *The theory of social and economic organization* (A. M. Henderson & T. Parsons, Transl.). New York: Free Press.

11. See Wren, 1987.

12. Roethlisberger, F. J., & Dickson, W. J. (1939). *Management and the worker.* Cambridge, MA: Harvard University Press; Wrege, C. D., & Greenwood, R. G. (1986). The Hawthorne studies. In D. A. Wren & J. A. Pearce II (Eds.), *Papers dedicated to the development of modern management.* Academy of Management.

13. Argyris, C. (1957). *Personality and organization.* New York: Harper.

14. Likert, R. (1961). *New patterns of management.* New York: McGraw–Hill.

15. Gouldner, A. W. (1954). *Patterns of industrial bureaucracy.* New York: Free Press.

16. Selznick, P. (1949). *TVA and the grass roots: A study in the sociology of formal organizations.* Berkeley: University of California Press.

17. Johns, G. (1993). Constraints on the adoption of psychology–based personnel practices: Lessons from organizational innovation. *Personnel Psychology, 46*, 569–592; Abrahamson, E. (1991). Managerial fads and fashions: The diffusion and rejection of innovations. *Academy of Management Review, 16*, 586–612.

18. Mintzberg, H. (1973). *The nature of managerial work.* New York: Harper & Row. See also Mintzberg, H. (1994, Fall). Rounding out the manager's job. *Sloan Management Review,* 11–26.

19. See Kraut, A. I., Pedigo, P. R., McKenna, D. D., & Dunnette, M. D. (1989, November). The role of the manager: What's really important in different management jobs. *Academy of Management Executive,* 286–293; Gibbs, B. (1994). The effects of environment and technology on managerial roles. *Journal of Management, 20,* 581–604.

20. Luthans, F., Hodgetts, R. M., & Rosenkrantz, S. A. (1988). *Real managers.* Cambridge, MA: Ballinger.

21. Kotter, J. P. (1982). *The general managers.* New York: The Free Press.

22. Simon, H. A. (1987, February). Making management decisions: The role of intuition and emotion. *Academy of Management Executive,* 57–64; Isenberg, D. J. (1984, November–December). How senior managers think. *Harvard Business Review,* 80–90. See also Sims, H. P., Jr., & Gioia, D. A. (Eds.) (1986). *The thinking organization: Dynamics of organizational social cognition.* San Francisco: Jossey-Bass.

23. McGinn & Theil, 1999.

24. Hofstede, G. (1993, February). Cultural constraints in management theories. *Academy of Management Executive,* 81–94.

25. Laabs, J. J. (1993, April). Business growth driven by staff development. *Personnel Journal,* 120–135.

26. Crawford, M. (1993, May). The new office etiquette. *Canadian Business,* 22–31.

27. Kanungo, R.N. (1998). Leadership in organizations: Looking ahead to the 21st century. *Canadian Psychology, 39*

(1–2), pp. 71–82.

28. Jackson, S. E., & Alvarez, E. B. (1992). Working through diversity as a strategic imperative. In S. E. Jackson (Ed.), *Diversity in the workplace: Human resources initiatives.* New York: Guilford.

29. Armstrong–Stassen, M. (1998). Alternative work arrangements: Meeting the challenges. *Canadian Psychology, 39*, pp. 108–123.

30. Meyer, J.P., Allen, N.J., & Topolnytsky, L. (1998). Commitment in a changing world of work. *Canadian Psychology, 39*, pp. 83–93.

31. Shellenbarger, S. (1993, September 3). Work–force study finds loyalty is weak, divisions of race and gender are deep. *Wall Street Journal,* pp. B1, B2.

32. Fisher, A. B. (1991, November 18). Morale crisis. *Fortune,* 70–80.

33. Rigon, J. E. (1992, November 2). Lack of communication burdens restructurings. *Wall Street Journal,* p. B1.

34. See Bureau of Business Practice. (1992). *Profiles of Malcolm Baldrige Award winners.* Boston: Allyn and Bacon.

35. Hitt, M.A., Keats, B. W., & DeMarie, S.M. (1998). Navigating in the new competitive landscape: Building strategic flexibility and competitive advantage in the 21st century. *Academy of Management Executive,* 12, pp. 22–42.

Chapter 2

1. Excerpted from Stamps, D. (1998, January). Learning ecologies. *Training,* pp. 32–38. First paragraph adapted from G. C. Hill & K. Yamada. (1992, December 9) Motorola illustrates how an aged giant can remain vibrant. *Wall Street Journal,* pp. A1, A18.

2. Moses, S. (1991, November). Personality tests come back in I/O. *APA Monitor,* p. 9.

3. Adler, S., & Weiss, H. M. (1988). Recent developments in the study of personality and organizational behavior. In C. L. Cooper & I. Robertson (Eds.), *International review of industrial and organizational psychology.* New York: Wiley.

4. Digman, J. M. (1990). Personality structure: Emergence of the five-factor model. *Annual Review of Psychology, 41*, 417–440; Hogan, R. T. (1991). Personality and personality measurement. In M. D. Dunette & L. M. Hough (Eds.), *Handbook of industrial and organizational psychology* (2nd ed., Vol. 2). Palo Alto, CA: Consulting Psychologists Press; Barrick, M. R., & Mount, M. K. (1991). The big five personality dimensions and job performance: A meta-analysis. *Personnel Psychology, 44*, 1–26.

5. Judge, T.A., Higgins, C.A., Thorensen, C.J., & Barrick, M.R. (1999). The Big Five personality traits, general mental ability, and career success across the life span. *Personnel Psychology*, pp. 52, 621–652.

6. Tett, R. P., Jackson, D. N., & Rothstein, M. (1991). Personality measures as predictors of job performance: A meta-analytic review. *Personnel Psychology*, 44, 703–742; Hough, L. M. et al. (1990). Criterion-related validities of personality constructs and the effect of response distortion on those validities. *Journal of Applied Psychology*, 75, 581–595.

7. Barrick & Mount, 1991.

8. Ones, D. S., Viswesvaran, C., & Schmidt, F. L. (1993). Comprehensive meta-analysis of integrity test validities: Findings and implications for personnel selection and theories of job performance. *Journal of Applied Psychology*, 78, 679–703.

9. Judge, Higgins, Thorensen, & Barrick, 1999.

10. Barrick, M. R., & Mount, M. K. (1993). Autonomy as a moderator of the relationship between the big five personality dimensions and job performance. *Journal of Applied Psychology*, 78, 111–118.

11. Judge, Higgins, Thorensen, & Barrick, 1999.

12. Rotter, J. B. (1966). Generalized expectancies for internal versus external controls of reinforcement. *Psychological Monographs*, 80 (Whole no. 609).

13. Szilagyi, A. D., & Sims, H. P., Jr. (1975). Locus of control and expectancies across multiple organizational levels. *Journal of Applied Psychology*, 60, 638–640.

14. Szilagyi, A. D., Sims, H. P., Jr., & Keller, R. T. (1976). Role dynamics, locus of control, and employee attitudes and behavior., *Academy of Management Journal*, 19, 259–276.

15. Miller, D., Kets de Vries, M. F. R., Toulouse, J. M. (1982). Top executive locus of control and its relationship to strategy-making, structure, and environment. *Academy of Management Journal*, 25, 237–253.

16. Andrisani, P. J., & Nestel, G. (1976). Internal-external control as contributor to and outcome of work experience. *Journal of Applied Psychology*, 61, 156–165.

17. For evidence on stress and locus of control see Anderson, C. R. (1977). Locus of control, coping behaviors, and performance in a stress setting: A longitudinal study. *Journal of Applied Psychology*, 62, 446–451. For evidence on career planning see Thornton, G. C., III. (1978). Differential effects of career planning on internals and externals. *Personnel Psychology*, 31, 471–476.

18. Blau, G. (1993). Testing the relationship of locus of control to different performance dimensions. *Journal of Occupational and Organizational Psychology*, 66, 125–138.

19. Spector, P. E. (1982). Behavior in organizations as a function of employees' locus of control. *Psychological Bulletin*, 91, 482–497.

20. Snyder, M. (1987). *Public appearances/private realities: The psychology of self-monitoring*. New York: W. H. Freeman.

21. Snyder, 1987.

22. Caldwell, D. F., & O'Reilly, C. A., III. (1982). Boundary spanning and individual performance: The impact of self-monitoring. *Journal of Applied Psychology*, 67, 124–127.

23. Kilduff, M. & Day, D.V. (1994). Do chameleons get ahead? The effects of self–monitoring and managerial careers. *Academy of Management Journal*, 37(4), pp. 1047–1060.

24. Ellis, R. J., Adamson, R. S., Deszca, G., & Cawsey, T. F. (1988). Self-monitoring and leader emergence. *Small Group Behavior*, 19, 312–324; Zaccaro, S. J., Foti, R. J., & Kenny, D. A. (1991). Self-monitoring and trait-based variance in leadership: An investigation of leader flexibility across multiple group situations. *Journal of Applied Psychology*, 76, 308–315.

25. Brockner, J. (1988). *Self-esteem at work: Research, theory, and practice*. Lexington, MA: Lexington.

26. Brockner, 1988.

27. Pierce, J. L., Gardner, D. G., Dunham, R. B., & Cummings, L. L. (1993). Moderation by organization-based self-esteem of role condition-employee response relationships. *Academy of Management Journal*, 36, 271–288.

28. Knight, P. A., & Nadel, J. I. (1986). Humility revisited: Self-esteem, information search, and policy consistency. *Organizational Behavior and Human Decision Processes*, 38, 196–206.

29. Brockner, 1988.

30. Tharanou, P. (1979). Employee self-esteem: A review of the literature. *Journal of Vocational Behavior*, 15, 1–29; Pierce, J. L., Gardner, D. G., Cummings, L. L., & Dunham, R. B. (1989). Organization-based self-esteem: Construct definition, measurement, and validation. *Academy of Management Journal*, 32, 622–648.

31. Pierce et al., 1993.

32. For a presentation of operant learning theory, see Honig, W. K., & Staddon, J. E. R. (Eds.). (1977). *Handbook of operant behavior*. Englewood Cliffs, NJ: Prentice-Hall. For a presentation of social learning theory, see Bandura, A. (1986). *Social foundations of thought and action*. Englewood Cliffs, NJ: Prentice-Hall.

33. Day, N. (1998, June). Informal learning gets results. *Workforce*, pp. 31–35.

34. Pfeffer, J. (1994). *Competitive advantage through people: Unleashing the power of the work force*. Boston, MA:

Harvard Business School Press.

35. Pfeffer, 1994.

36. Gordon, A. (February 2000). 35 Best Companies to Work for. *Report on Business Magazine*, 24–32.

37. Farnham, A. (1993, September 20). Mary Kay's lessons in leadership. *Fortune*, pp. 68–77. Ash, M.K. (1984). *Mary Kay on people management*. New York: Warner.

38. Luthans, F., & Kreitner, R. (1975). *Organizational behavior modification*. Glenview, IL: Scott, Foresman.

39. However, more research is necessary to establish the extent of this in organizations. See Arvey, R. D., & Ivancevich, J. M. (1980). Punishment in organizations: A review, propositions, and research suggestions. *Academy of Management Review*, 5, 123–132.

40. Punishment in front of others can be effective under restricted conditions. See Trevino, L. K. (1992). The social effects of punishment in organizations: A justice perspective. *Academy of Management Review*, 17, 647–676.

41. Organ, D. W., & Hamner, W. C. (1982). *Organizational behavior: An applied psychological approach* (Revised ed.). Plano, TX: Business Publications.

42. See Parmerlee, M. A., Near, J. P., & Jensen, T. C. (1982). Correlates of whistle–blowers' perceptions of organizational retaliation. *Administrative Science Quarterly*, 27, 17–34.

43. Bandura, A. (1986). *Social foundations of thought and action: A social cognitive theory*. Englewood Cliffs, NJ: Prentice-Hall.

44. Luthans, F., & Kreitner, R. (1985). *Organizational behavior modification and beyond: An operant and social learning approach*. Glenview, IL: Scott, Foresman; Manz, C. C., & Sims, H. P., Jr. (1981). Vicarious learning: The influence of modeling on organizational behavior. *Academy of Management Review*, 6, 105–113.

45. Bandura, 1986; Goldstein, A. P., & Sorcher, M. (1974). *Changing supervisor behavior*. New York: Pergamon.

46. Bandura, A. (1997). *Self-efficacy: The exercise of control*. New York, NY: W. H. Freeman and Company.

47. Bandura, 1997.

48. Saks, A. M. (1997). Transfer of training and self–efficacy: What is the dilemma? *Applied Psychology: An International Review*, 46, pp. 365–370.

49. Manz, C. C., & Sims, H. P., Jr. (1980). Self-management as a substitute for leadership: A social learning theory perspective. *Academy of Management Review*, 5, 361–367; Hackman, J. R. (1986). The psychology of self-management in organizations. In M. S. Pollack & R. Perloff (Eds.), *Psychology and work*. Washington, DC: American Psychological Association.

50. Kanfer, F. H. (1980). Self-management methods. In F. H. Kanfer & A. P.

Goldstein (Eds.), *Helping people change: A textbook of methods* (2nd ed.). New York: Pergamon.

51. Luthans & Kreitner, 1985; Manz & Sims, 1980.

52. Frayne, C., & Latham, G. (1987). Application of social learning theory to employee self-management of attendance. *Journal of Applied Psychology, 72,* 387–392.

53. Stajkovic, A.D., & Lutans, F. (1997). A meta–analysis of the effects of organizational behavior modification on task performance, 1975–95. *Academy of Management Journal,* 40, pp. 1122–1149.

54. Pedalino, E., & Gamboa, V. U. (1974). Behavior modification and absenteeism: Intervention in one industrial setting. *Journal of Applied Psychology, 59,* 694–698.

55. Komaki, J., Barwick, K. D., & Scott, L. R. (1978). A behavioral approach to occupational safety: Pinpointing and reinforcing safe performance in a food manufacturing plant. *Journal of Applied Psychology, 63,* 434–445. For a similar study, see Haynes, R. S., Pine, R. C., & Fitch, H. G. (1982). Reducing accident rates with organizational behavior modification. *Academy of Management Journal, 25,* 407–416.

56. Wexley, K. N., & Latham, G. P. (1991). *Developing and training human resources in organizations.* New York, NY: HarperCollins.

57. Salas, E., Cannon–Bowers, J. A., & Kozlowski, S. W. J. (1997). The science and practice of training – Current trends and emerging themes. In J. K. Ford (Ed.), *Improving training effectiveness in work organizations.* Mahwah, NJ: Lawrence Erlbaum Associates. pp. 357–367.

58. (1997, February). Bank of Montreal satisfies customers by satisfying employees. *Workforce,* pp. 46–47.

59. Day, 1998.

60. Baldwin, T. T., & Ford, J. K. (1988). Transfer of training: A review and directions for future research. *Personnel Psychology, 41,* 103–105.

61. Day, 1998.

62. Day, 1998.

63. Day, 1998.

64. Stamps, 1998.

65. Tracey, J. B., Tannenbaum, S. I., & Kavanagh, M. J. (1995). Applying trained skills on the job: The importance of the work environment. *Journal of Applied Psychology,* 80, pp. 239–252; Barrett, F. J. (1995). Creating appreciative learning cultures. *Organizational Dynamics,* pp. 36–49.

66. Barrett, 1995.

Chapter 3

1. Sources include Kelly, E. P., Young, A. O., & Clark, L. S. (1993, March–April). Sex stereotyping in the workplace: A manager's guide. *Business Horizons,* 23–29; Lewin, T. (1990, May 16). Partnership in firm awarded to victim of sex bias. *New York Times,* pp. A1, A20; Youngstrom, N. (1990, July). Hopkins wins lawsuit against ex-employer. *APA Monitor,* p. 34.

2. Cox, T., Jr. (1993). *Cultural diversity in organizations: Theory, research, & practice.* San Francisco: Berrett-Koehler.

3. Bruner, J. S. (1957). On perceptual readiness. *Psychological Review, 64,* 123–152.

4. Eagly, A. H., Ashmore, R. D., Makhijani, M. G., & Longo, L. C. (1991). What is beautiful is good, but . . . : A meta-analytic review of research on the physical attractiveness stereotype. *Psychological Bulletin, 110,* 109–128.

5. Stone, E. F., Stone, D. L., & Dipboye, R. L. (1992). Stigmas in organizations: Race, handicaps, and physical unattractiveness. In K. Kelley (Ed.), *Issues, theory and research in industrial/ organizational psychology.* New York: Elsevier.

6. See Krzystofiak, F., Cardy, R., & Newman, J. E. (1988). Implicit personality and performance appraisal: The influence of trait inferences on evaluations of behavior. *Journal of Applied Psychology, 73,* 515–521.

7. Fiske, S. T. (1993). Social cognition and social perception. *Annual Review of Psychology, 44,* 155–194.

8. Secord, P. F., Backman, C. W., & Slavitt, D. R. (1976). *Understanding social life: An introduction to social psychology.* New York: McGraw-Hill. For elaboration, see Wilder, D. A. (1986). Social categorization: Implications for creation and reduction of intergroup bias. *Advances in Experimental Social Psychology, 19,* 291–349.

9. Dion, K. L., & Schuller, R. A. (1991). The Ms. stereotype: Its generality and its relation to managerial and marital status stereotypes. *Canadian Journal of Behavioural Science, 23,* 25–40.

10. For a more complete treatment see Falkenberg, L. (1990). Improving the accuracy of stereotypes within the workplace. *Journal of Management, 16,* 107–118.

11. Kelley, H. H. (1972). Attribution in social interaction. In E. E. Jones et al. (Eds.), *Attribution: Perceiving the causes of behavior.* Morristown, NJ: General Learning Press. For an integrative attribution model, see Medcof, J. W. (1990). PEAT: An integrative model of attribution processes. *Advances in Experimental Social Psychology, 23,* 111–209.

12. Baron, R. A., Byrne, D., & Griffitt, W. (1974). *Social psychology: Understanding human interaction.* Boston: Allyn and Bacon.

13. This discussion of attribution biases draws upon Fiske, S. T., & Taylor, S. E. (1984). *Social cognition.* Reading, MA: Addison-Wesley.

14. Ross, L. (1977). The intuitive psychologist and his shortcomings: Distortions in the attribution process. *Advances in Experimental Social Psychology, 10,* 173–220; Jones, E. E. (1979). The rocky road from acts to dispositions. *American Psychologist, 34,* 107–117.

15. Mitchell, T. R., & Kalb, L. S. (1982). Effects of job experience on supervisor attributions for a subordinate's poor performance. *Journal of Applied Psychology, 67,* 181–188.

16. Watson, D. (1982). The actor and the observer: How are their perceptions of causality divergent? *Psychological Bulletin, 92,* 682–700.

17. Sonnenfeld, J. (1981). Executive apologies for price fixing: Role biased perceptions of causality. *Academy of Management Journal, 24,* 192–198; Waters, J. A. (1978, Spring). Catch 20.5. Corporate morality as an organizational phenomenon. *Organizational Dynamics,* 2–19.

18. Tetlock, P. E. (1985). Accountability: The neglected social context of judgment and choice. *Research in Organizational Behavior, 7,* 297–332; Greenwald, A. G. (1980). The totalitarian ego: Fabrication and revision of personal history. *American Psychologist, 35,* 603–618.

19. Pyszczynski, T., & Greenberg, J. (1987). Toward an integration of cognitive and motivational perspectives on social inference: A biased hypothesis-testing model. *Advances in Experimental Social Psychology, 20,* 197–340.

20. This section relies on Jackson, S. E., & Alvarez, E. B. (1992). Working through diversity as a strategic imperative. In S. E. Jackson (Ed.), *Diversity in the workplace: Human resources initiatives.* New York: Guilford Press.

21. Cox, 1993; Cox, T., Jr. (1991, May). The multicultural organization. *Academy of Management Executive,* 34–47.

22. Crone, G. (1999, Feb. 18). Companies embracing workplace diversity. *Financial Post.*

23. Hartley, E. L. (1946). *Problems in prejudice.* New York: King's Crown Press.

24. Cox, T., Jr., & Nkomo, S. M. (1990). Invisible men and women: A status report on race as a variable in organization behavior research. *Journal of Organizational Behavior, 11,* 419–431; Alderfer, C. P., & Thomas, D. A. (1988). The significance of race and ethnicity for organizational behavior. In C. L. Cooper & I. Robertson (Eds.), *International review of industrial and organizational psychology.* New York: Wiley.

25. Sharpe, R. (1993, September 14). Losing ground. *Wall Street Journal,* pp. A1, 12, 13.

26. Brenner, O. C., Tomkiewicz, J., & Stevens, G. E. (1991). The relationship

between attitudes toward women and attitudes toward blacks in management positions. *Canadian Journal of Administrative Sciences, 8* (2), 80–89.

27. Cox, 1993.

28. Greenhaus, J. H., & Parasuraman, S. (1993). Job performance attributions and career advancement prospects: An examination of gender and race effects. *Organizational Behavior and Human Decision Processes, 55,* 273–297.

29. Powell, G. N. (1992). The good manager: Business students' stereotypes of Japanese managers versus stereotypes of American managers. *Group & Organizational Management, 17,* 44–56.

30. Ragins, B.R., Townsend, B., & Mattis, M. (1998). Gender gap in the executive suite: CEOs and female executives report on breaking the glass ceiling. *Academy of Management Executive,* 12, pp. 28–42.

31. Schein, V. E. (1975). Relationships between sex role stereotypes and requisite management characteristics among female managers. *Journal of Applied Psychology, 60,* 340–344; Brenner, O. C., Tomkiewicz, J., & Schein, V. E. (1989). The relationship between sex role stereotypes and requisite management characteristics revisited. *Academy of Management Journal, 32,* 662–669; Heilman, M. E., Block, C. J., Martell, R. F., & Simon, M. C. (1989). Has anything changed? Current characterizations of men, women, and managers. *Journal of Applied Psychology, 74,* 935–942.

32. Brenner et al., 1989.

33. Rosen, B., & Jerdee, T. H. (1974). Influence of sex role stereotypes on personnel decisions. *Journal of Applied Psychology, 59,* 9–14.

34. Cohen, S. L., & Bunker, K. A. (1975). Subtle effects of sex role stereotypes on recruiters' hiring decisions. *Journal of Applied Psychology, 60,* 566–572. See also Rose, G. L., & Andiappan, P. (1978). Sex effects on managerial hiring decisions. *Academy of Management Journal, 21,* 104–112.

35. Parasuraman, S., & Greenhaus, J. H. (1993). Personal portrait: The life-style of the woman manager. In E. A. Fagenson (Ed.), *Women in management: Trends, issues, and challenge in managerial diversity.* Newbury Park, CA: Sage.

36. Tosi, H. L., & Einbender, S. W. (1985). The effects of the type and amount of information in sex discrimination research: A meta-analysis. *Academy of Management Journal, 28,* 712–723.

37. For a review, see Latham, G. P., Skarlicki, D., Irvine, D., & Siegel, J. P. (1993). The increasing importance of performance appraisals to employee effectiveness in organizational settings in North America. In C. L.Cooper & I. Robertson (Eds.), *International review of industrial and organizational psychology.* New York: Wiley. For a representative study, see Pulakos, E. D., White, L. A., Oppler, S. A., & Borman, W. C. (1989). Examination of race and sex effects on performance ratings. *Journal of Applied Psychology, 74,* 770–780.

38. Fiske, S. T., Beroff, D. N., Borgida, E., Deaux, K., & Heilman, M. E. (1991). Use of sex stereotyping research in Price Waterhouse v. Hopkins. *American Psychologist, 46,* 1049–1060.

39. Sackett, P. R., DuBois, C. L. Z., & Noe, A. W. (1991). Tokenism in performance evaluation: The effects of work group representation on male-female and white-black differences in performance ratings. *Journal of Applied Psychology, 76,* 263–267.

40. Rosen, B., & Jerdee, T. H. (1976). The nature of job-related age stereotypes. *Journal of Applied Psychology, 61,* 180–183. See also Gibson, K. J., Zerbe, W. J., & Franken, R. E. (1992). Job search strategies for older job hunters: Addressing employers' perceptions. *Canadian Journal of Counselling, 26,* 166–176.

41. Gibson et al., 1992.

42. McEvoy, G. M., & Cascio, W. F. (1989). Cumulative evidence of the relationship between employee age and job performance. *Journal of Applied Psychology, 74,* 11–17. For a broader review on age see Rhodes, S. R. (1983). Age related differences in work attitudes and behavior. *Psychological Bulletin, 93,* 328–367.

43. Rosen, B., & Jerdee, T. H. (1976). The influence of age stereotypes on managerial decisions. *Journal of Applied Psychology, 61,* 428–432. Also see Dietrick, E. J., & Dobbins, G. J. (1991). The influence of subordinate age on managerial actions: An attributional analysis. *Journal of Organizational Behavior, 12,* 367–377.

44. Falkenberg, 1990; Fiske et al., 1991.

45. Cox, 1991, p. 40.

46. Shea, G. F. (1992, December). Learn how to treasure differences. *HRMagazine,* 34–37.

47. Caudron, S. (1993, April). Training can damage diversity efforts. *Personnel Journal,* 51–62.

48. Caudron, 1993.

49. Mayer, R. C., & Davis, J. H. (1999). The effect of the performance appraisal system on trust for management: A field quasi–experiment. *Journal of Applied Psychology, 84,* pp. 123–136.

50. Lee, C. (1997, January). Trust. *Training,* pp. 28–37.

51. Mayer & Davis, 1999; Davis, J. H., Mayer, R. C., & Schoorman, F. D. (1995, October). The trusted general manager and firm performance: Empirical evidence of a strategic advantage. Paper presented at the 15th annual meeting of the Strategic Management Society, Mexico City, Mexico. Cited in *Mayer & Davis* (1999).

52. Davis, Mayer, & Schoorman, 1995; Mayer, R. C., Davis, J. H., & Schoorman, F. D. (1995). An integrative model of organizational trust. *Academy of Management Review,* 20, pp. 709–734; Rousseau, D. M., Sitkin, S. B., Burt, R. S., & Camerer, C. (1998). Not so different after all: A cross–discipline view of trust. *Academy of Management Review,* 23, pp. 393–404.

53. Mayer, Davis, & Schoorman, 1995.

54. Mayer & Davis, 1999; Mayer, Davis, & Schoorman, 1995.

55. Lee, 1997.

56. Mayer, Davis, & Schoorman, 1995.

57. McDaniel, M. A., Whetzel, D. L., Schmidt, F. L., & Maurer, S. D. (1994). The validity of employment interviews: A comprehensive review and meta-analysis. *Journal of Applied Psychology, 79,* 599–616; Wiesner, W. H., & Cronshaw, S. F. (1988). A meta-analytic investigation of the impact of interview format and degree of structure on the validity of the employment interview. *Journal of Occupational Psychology, 61,* 275–290. Campion, M.A., Palmer, D.K., and Campion, J.E. (1997). A review of structure in the selection interview. *Personnel Psychology,* 50, pp. 655–702.

58. Hakel, M. D. (1982). Employment interviewing. In K. M. Rowland & G. R. Ferris (Eds.), *Personnel management.* Boston: Allyn and Bacon.

59. Hakel, 1982; Dipboye, R. L. (1989). Threats to the incremental validity of interviewer judgments. In R. W. Eder & G. R. Ferris (Eds.), *The employment interview: Theory, research, and practice.* Newbury Park, CA: Sage.

60. Hollmann, T. D. (1972). Employment interviewers' errors in processing positive and negative information. *Journal of Applied Psychology, 56,* 130–134.

61. Rowe, P. M. (1989). Unfavorable information in interview decisions. In R. W. Eder & G. R. Ferris (Eds.), *The employment interview: Theory, research, and practice.* Newbury Park, CA: Sage.

62. Schmitt, N. (1976). Social and situational determinants of interview decisions: Implications for the employment interview. *Personnel Psychology, 29,* 70–101; Maurer, T. J., & Alexander, R. A. (1991). Contrast effects in behavioral measurement: An investigation of alternative process explanations. *Journal of Applied Psychology, 76,* 3–10; Maurer, T. J., Palmer, J. K., & Ashe, D. K. (1993). Diaries, checklists, evaluations, and contrast effects in measurement of behavior. *Journal of Applied Psychology, 78,* 226–231.

63. For other reasons and a review of the interview literature, see Harris, M. M. (1989). Reconsidering the employment interview: A review of recent literature and suggestions for future research. *Personnel Psychology, 42,* 691–726.

64. Cooper, W. H. (1981). Ubiquitous halo. *Psychological Bulletin, 90,* 218–244; Balzer, W. K., & Sulsky, L. M. (1992). Halo and performance appraisal research: A critical examination. *Journal of Applied Psychology, 77,* 975–985; Murphy, K. R., Jako, R. A., & Anhalt, R. L. (1993). Nature and consequences of halo error: A critical analysis. *Journal of Applied Psychology, 78,* 218–225.

65. Kingstrom, P. D., & Bass, A. R. (1981). A critical analysis of studies comparing behaviorally anchored rating scales (BARS) and other rating formats. *Personnel Psychology, 34,* 263–289; Landy, F. J., & Farr, J. L. (1983). *The measurement of work performance.* New York: Academic Press.

Chapter 4

1. Excerpted from Livesey, B. (1997, March). Provide and conquer. *Report on Business Magazine,* pp. 34–43; Also based on with quotes from: Lush, T. (1998, October 3). Company with a conscience. *The Gazette,* p. C3; Van Alphen, T. (2000, January 22). Good deeds earn equity at Husky. *The Toronto Star,* pp. B1, B8.

2. Hofstede, G. (1980). *Culture's Consequences: International differences in work-related values.* Beverly Hills, CA: Sage, p. 19.

3. Spranger, E. (1928). *Types of men.* New York: Stechat.

4. Rokeach, M. (1973). *The nature of human values.* New York: Free Press.

5. Meglino, B. M., Ravlin, E. C., & Adkins, C. L. (1989). A work values approach to corporate culture: A field test of the value congruence process and its relationship to individual outcomes. *Journal of Applied Psychology, 74,* 424–432.

6. Kristof, A.L. (1996). Person–organization fit: An integrative review of its conceptualizations, measurement, and implications. *Personnel Psychology, 49,* pp. 1–49.

7. Judge, T. A., & Bretz, R. D., Jr. (1992). Effects of work values on job choice decisions. *Journal of Applied Psychology, 77,* 261–271.

8. Black, J. S., & Mendenhall, M. (1990). Cross-cultural training effectiveness: A review and theoretical framework for future research. *Academy of Management Review, 15,* 113–136.

9. MOW International Research Team. (1987). *The meaning of working.* London: Academic Press.

10. Hofstede, 1980. For a critique of this work, see Dorfman, P. W., & Howell, J. P. (1989). Dimensions of national culture and effective leadership patterns: Hofstede revisited. *Advances in International Comparative Management, 3,* 127–150.

11. Hofstede, G. (1991). *Cultures and organizations: Software of the mind.* London: McGraw-Hill; Hofstede, G., & Bond, M. H. (1988). The Confucius connection: From cultural roots to economic growth. *Organizational Dynamics, 16* (4), 4–21.

12. Hofstede, G. (1984). The cultural relativity of the quality of life concept. *Academy of Management Review, 9,* 389–398; Hofstede, G. (1993, February). Cultural constraints in management theories. *Academy of Management Executive,* 81–94.

13. Lazar, E. (1993, February). Values must blend in overseas operations. *Personnel Journal,* 67–70.

14. Young, S. M. (1992). A framework for successful adoption and performance of Japanese manufacturing practices in the United States. *Academy of Management Review, 17,* 677–700.

15. Basadur, M. (1992, May). Managing creativity: A Japanese model. *Academy of Management Executive,* 29–42.

16. Laabs, J. J. (1993, August). How Gillette grooms global talent. *Personnel Journal,* 64–75.

17. Staff reporter. (1992, December 30). Korea's biggest firm teaches junior execs strange foreign ways. *Wall Street Journal,* pp. 1, 4.

18. Jones, E. E., & Gerard, H. B. (1967). *Foundations of social psychology.* New York: Wiley.

19. Janis, I. L., & Mann, L. (1965). Effectiveness of emotional role-playing in modifying smoking habits and attitudes. *Journal of Experimental Research in Personality, 1,* 84–90; Culbertson, F. M. (1957). Modification of an emotionally held attitude through role-playing. *Journal of Abnormal and Social Psychology, 54,* 230–233.

20. Goldstein, A. P., & Sorcher, M. (1974). *Changing supervisor behavior.* New York: Pergamon.

21. For a review and critique, see Mayer, S. J., & Russell, J. S. (1987). Behavior modeling training in organizations: Concerns and conclusions. *Journal of Management, 13,* 21–40. For an example of cross-cultural training see Harrison, J.K. (1992). Individual and combined effects of behavior modeling and the cultural assimilator in cross-cultural management training. *Journal of Applied Psychology, 77,* 952–962.

22. Locke, E. A. (1976). The nature and causes of job satisfaction. In M. D. Dunnette (Ed.), *Handbook of industrial and organizational psychology.* Chicago: Rand McNally. See also Rice, R. W., Gentile, D. A., & McFarlin, D. B. (1991). Facet importance and job satisfaction. *Journal of Applied Psychology, 76,* 31–39.

23. Smith, P. C. (1992). In pursuit of happiness: Why study general job satisfaction? In C. J. Cranny, P. C. Smith, & E. F. Stone (Eds.), *Job satisfaction.* New York: Lexington.

24. Smith, P. C., Kendall, L. M., & Hulin, C. L. (1969). *The measurement of satisfaction in work and retirement.* Chicago: Rand McNally; Smith, P. C., Kendall, L. M., & Hulin, C. L. (1985). *The job descriptive index* (Rev. ed.). Bowling Green, OH: Department of Psychology, Bowling Green State University.

25. Weiss, D. J., Dawis, R. V., England, G. W., & Lofquist, L. H. (1967). *Manual for the Minnesota satisfaction questionnaire: Minnesota studies in vocational rehabilitation.* Minneapolis: Vocational Psychology Research, University of Minnesota.

26. Locke, E. A. (1969). What is job satisfaction? *Organizational Behavior and Human Performance, 4,* 309–336; Rice, R. W., McFarlin, D. B., & Bennett, D. E. (1989). Standards of comparison and job satisfaction. *Journal of Applied Psychology, 74,* 591–598.

27. Adams, J. S. (1963). Toward an understanding of inequity. *Journal of Abnormal and Social Psychology, 67,* 422–436. For a review, see Greenberg, J., & Cohen, R. L. (Eds.) (1982). *Equity and justice in social behavior.* New York: Academic Press.

28. See Kulik, C. T., & Ambrose, M. L. (1992). Personal and situational determinants of referent choice. *Academy of Management Review, 17,* 212–237.

29. Greenberg, J. (1987). A taxonomy of organizational justice theories. *Academy of Management Review, 12,* 9–22.

30. McFarlin, D. B., & Sweeney, P. D. (1992). Distributive and procedural justice as predictors of satisfaction with personal and organizational outcomes. *Academy of Management Journal, 35,* 626–637; Greenberg, J. (1987). Reactions to procedural injustice in payment distributions: Do the means justify the ends? *Journal of Applied Psychology, 72,* 55–61.

31. Cropanzano, R., & Folger, R. (1989). Referent cognitions and task decision autonomy: Beyond equity theory. *Journal of Applied Psychology, 74,* 293–299, p. 293. See also Folger, R. (1987). Reformulating the preconditions of resentment: A referent cognitions model. In J. C. Masters & W. P. Smith (Eds.), *Social comparison, justice, and relative deprivation: Theoretical, empirical, and policy perspectives.* Hillsdale, NJ: Erlbaum.

32. Judge, T. A. (1992). The dispositional perspective in human resources research. *Research in Personnel and Human Resources Management, 10,* 31–72.

33. Judge, T. A., & Hulin, C. L. (1993). Job satisfaction as a reflection of disposition: A multiple source causal analysis. *Organizational Behavior and Human Decision Processes, 56,* 388–421; Judge, T. A., & Locke, E. A. (1993). Effect of dysfunctional thought processes on subjective well-being and job satisfaction.

Journal of Applied Psychology, 78, 475–490.

34. Staw, B. M., & Barsade, S. G. (1993). Affect and managerial performance: A test of the sadder-but-wiser vs. happier-and-smarter hypotheses. *Administrative Science Quarterly, 38,* 304–331.

35. This material draws upon Locke, 1976.

36. Warr, P. B. (1987). *Work, unemployment, and mental health.* Oxford: Oxford University Press; Jamal, M., & Mitchell, V. F. (1980). Work, nonwork, and mental health: A model and a test. *Industrial Relations, 19,* 88–93.

37. Tait, M., Padgett, M. Y., & Baldwin, T. T. (1989). Job and life satisfaction: A reevaluation of the strength of the relationship and gender effects as a function of the date of the study. *Journal of Applied Psychology, 74,* 502–507; Judge, T. A., & Watanabe, S. (1993). Another look at the job satisfaction-life satisfaction relationship. *Journal of Applied Psychology, 78,* 939–948.

38. [add] Lu, V. (1999, August 15). Rising sick days cost billions. *The Toronto Star,* pp. A1, A10.

39. Hackett, R. D., & Guion, R. M. (1985). A reevaluation of the absenteeism-job satisfaction relationship. *Organizational Behavior and Human Decision Processes, 35,* 340–381; Scott, D. D., & Taylor, G. S. (1985). An examination of conflicting findings on the relationship between job satisfaction and absenteeism: A meta-analysis. *Academy of Management Journal, 28,* 599–612; McShane, S. L. (1984). Job satisfaction and absenteeism: A meta-analytic re-examination. *Canadian Journal of Administrative Sciences, 1* (1), 61–77.

40. Nicholson, N., & Johns, G. (1985). The absence culture and the psychological contract—Who's in control of absence? *Academy of Management Review, 10,* 397–407.

41. Farris, G. F. (1971). A predictive study of turnover. *Personnel Psychology, 24,* 311–328. However, the more general relationship between performance and voluntary turnover is negative, as shown by Bycio, P., Hackett, R. D., & Alvares, K. M. (1990). Job performance and turnover: A review and meta-analysis. *Applied Psychology: An International Review, 39,* 47–76 and Williams, C. R., & Livingstone, L. P. (1994). Another look at the relationship between performance and voluntary turnover. *Academy of Management Journal, 37,* 269–298.

42. Steel, R. P., & Ovalle, N. K., 2d. (1984). A review and meta-analysis of research on the relationship between behavioral intentions and employee turnover. *Journal of Applied Psychology, 69,* 673–686.

43. In general, tests of aspects of the Mobley turnover model have been very supportive. However, not all of the steps in the model can be separated em-

pirically. See Hom, P. W., & Griffeth, R. W. (1991). Structural equations modeling test of a turnover theory: Cross-sectional and longitudinal analyses. *Journal of Applied Psychology, 76,* 350–366.

44. Carsten, J. M., & Spector, P. E. (1987). Unemployment, job satisfaction, and employee turnover: A meta-analytic test of the Muchinsky model. *Journal of Applied Psychology, 72,* 374–381.

45. Steel & Ovalle, 1984.

46. Iaffaldano, M. T., & Muchinsky, P. M. (1985). Job satisfaction and job performance: A meta-analysis. *Psychological Bulletin, 97,* 251–273.

47. Lawler, E. E., III (1973). *Motivation in organizations.* Monterey, CA: Brooks/Cole.

48. Organ, D.W., and Ryan, K. (1995). A meta-analytic review of attitudinal and dispositional predictors of organizational citizenship behavior. *Personnel Psychology, 48,* pp. 775–802.

49. Organ, D. W. (1988). *Organizational citizenship behavior: The good soldier syndrome.* Lexington, MA: Lexington. See also Schnake, M. (1991). Organizational citizenship: A review, proposed model, and research agenda. *Human Relations, 44,* 735–759.

50. Organ, 1988.

51. Organ, 1988; Organ, D. W., & Konovsky, M. (1989). Cognitive versus affective determinants of organizational citizenship behavior. *Journal of Applied Psychology, 74,* 157–164.

52. Moorman, R. H. (1991). Relationship betwen justice and organizational citizenship behaviors: Do fairness perceptions influence employee citizenship? *Journal of Applied Psychology, 76,* 845–855.

53. George, J. M. (1991). State or trait: Effects of positive mood on prosocial behaviors at work. *Journal of Applied Psychology, 76,* 299–307.

54. Meyer, J. P., & Allen, N. J. (1991). A three-component conceptualization of organizational commitment. *Human Resource Management Review, 1,* 61–98; Meyer, J. P., Allen, N. J., & Smith, C. A. (1993). Commitment to organizations and occupations: Extension and test of a three-component conceptualization. *Journal of Applied Psychology, 78,* 538–551.

55. Meyer, J. P., Allen, N. J., & Topolnytsky, L. (1998). Commitment in a changing world of work. *Canadian Psychology, 39*(1–2), pp. 83–93.

56. Meyer & Allen, 1991; Mathieu, J. E., & Zajac, D. M. (1990). A review and meta-analysis of the antecedents, correlates, and consequences of organizational commitment. *Psychological Bulletin, 108,* 171–194.

57. Wanous et al., 1992.

58. Mathieu & Zajac, 1990.

59. Mathieu & Zajac, 1990; For a careful study see Jaros, S. J., Jermier, J. M., Koehler, J. W., & Sincich, T. (1993).

Effects of continuance, affective, and moral commitment on the withdrawal process: An evaluation of eight structural equation models. *Academy of Management Journal, 36,* 951–995.

60. Meyer, J. P., Paunonen, S. V., Gellatly, I. R., Goffin, R. D., & Jackson, D. N. (1989). Organizational commitment and job performance: It's the nature of the commitment that counts. *Journal of Applied Psychology, 74,* 152–156.

61. Randall, D. M. (1987). Commitment and the organization: The organization man revisited. *Academy of Management Review, 12,* 460–471.

62. Meyer, Allen, & Topolnytsky, 1998.

63. Cascio, W. F. (1993, February). Downsizing: What do we know? What have we learned? *Academy of Management Executive,* 95–104.

64. Meyer, Allen, & Topolnytsky, 1998.

Chapter 5

1. Based on Starbucks. (1997, September, 29). Making values pay. *Fortune,* 261–272. (Excerpt from Shultz, H., & Yang, D. J. (1997). Pour your heart into it. Hyperion.); Bank, D. (1997, January 21). Starbucks faces growing competition: Its own stores. *Wall Street Journal,* pp. B1, B9. Weiss, N. (1998, August). How Starbucks impassions workers to drive growth. *Workforce,* pp. 61–64; Reese, J. (1996, December 9). Starbucks: Inside the Coffee Cult. *Fortune,* pp. 190–200.

2. Campbell, J. P., Dunnette, M. D., Lawler, E. E., III, & Weick, K. E., Jr. (1970). *Managerial behavior, performance, and effectiveness.* New York: McGraw-Hill. Also see Blau, G. (1993). Operationalizing direction and level of effort and testing their relationship to job performance. *Organizational Behavior and Human Decision Processes, 55,* 152–170.

3. Dyer, L., & Parker, D. F. (1975). Classifying outcomes in work motivation research: An examination of the intrinsic-extrinsic dichotomy. *Journal of Applied Psychology, 60,* 455–458; Kanungo, R. N., & Hartwick, J. (1987). An alternative to the intrinsic-extrinsic dichotomy of work rewards. *Journal of Management, 13,* 751–766. Also see Brief, A. P., & Aldag, R. J. (1977). The intrinsic-extrinsic dichotomy: Toward conceptual clarity. *Academy of Management Review, 2,* 496–500.

4. Vallerand, R. J. (1997). Toward a hierarchical model of intrinsic and extrinsic motivation. *Advances in Experimental Social Psychology, 29,* pp. 271–360.

5. Deci, E. L., & Ryan, R. M. (1985). *Intrinsic motivation and self-determination in human behavior.* New York: Plenum.

6. Deci & Ryan, 1985.

7. Eisenberger, R., & Cameron, J. (1996). Detrimental effects of reward: Reality

or myth? *American Psychologist, 51,* pp. 1153–1166.

8. Wiersma, U. J. (1992). The effects of extrinsic rewards in intrinsic motivation: A meta-analysis. *Journal of Occupational and Organizational Psychology, 65,* 101–114; Guzzo, R. A. (1979). Types of rewards, cognitions, and work motivation. *Academy of Management Review, 4,* 75–86.

9. Based on Campbell, J. P., & Pritchard, R. D. (1976). Motivation theory in industrial and organizational psychology. In M. D. Dunnette (Ed.), *Handbook of industrial and organizational psychology.* Chicago: Rand McNally.

10. See Henkoff, R. (1993, March 22). Companies that train best. *Fortune,* 62–75.

11. The distinction between need (content) and process theories was first made by Campbell et al., 1970.

12. Maslow, A. H. (1970). *Motivation and personality* (2nd ed.). New York: Harper & Row.

13. Alderfer, C. P. (1969). An empirical test of a new theory of human needs. *Organizational Behavior and Human Performance, 4,* 142–175. Also see Alderfer, C. P. (1972). *Existence, relatedness, and growth: Human needs in organizational settings.* New York: The Free Press.

14. McClelland, D. C. (1985). *Human motivation.* Glenview, IL: Scott, Foresman.

15. McClelland, D. C., & Winter, D. G. (1969). *Motivating economic achievement.* New York: The Free Press, pp. 50–52.

16. McClelland, D. C., & Boyatzis, R. E. (1982). Leadership motive pattern and long-term success in management. *Journal of Applied Psychology, 67,* 737–743; McClelland, D. C., & Burnham, D. (1976, March–April). Power is the great motivator. *Harvard Business Review,* 159–166. However, need for power might not be the best motive pattern for managers of technical and professional people. See Cornelius, E. T., III, & Lane, F. B. (1984). The power motive and managerial success in a professionally oriented service industry organization. *Journal of Applied Psychology, 69,* 32–39.

17. Wahba, M. A., & Bridwell, L. G. (1976). Maslow reconsidered: A review of research on the need hierarchy theory. *Organizational Behavior and Human Performance, 15,* 212–240.

18. Schneider, B., & Alderfer, C. P. (1973). Three studies of measures of need satisfaction in organizations. *Administrative Science Quarterly, 18,* 498–505. Also see Alderfer, C. P., Kaplan, R. E., & Smith, K. K. (1974). The effect of relatedness need satisfaction on relatedness desires. *Administrative Science Quarterly, 19,* 507–532. For a disconfirming test, see Rauschenberger, J., Schmitt, N., & Hunter, J. E. (1980). A test of the need hierarchy concept by a

Markov model of change in need strength. *Administrative Science Quarterly, 25,* 654–670.

19. McClelland, 1985; Spangler, W. D. (1992). Validity of questionnaire and TAT measures of need for achievement: Two meta-analyses. *Psychological Bulletin, 112,* 140–154.

20. Herzberg, F. (1966). *Work and the nature of man.* Cleveland: World Publishing.

21. Lawler, E. E., III. (1973). *Motivation in work organizations.* Monterey, CA: Brooks/Cole.

22. Vroom, V. H. (1964). *Work and motivation.* New York: Wiley.

23. Mitchell, T. R. (1974). Expectancy models of job satisfaction, occupational preference, and effort: A theoretical, methodological, and empirical appraisal. *Psychological Bulletin, 81,* 1053–1077. Also see Pinder, C. C. (1984). *Work motivation: Theory, issues, and applications.* Glenview, IL: Scott, Foresman; Kanfer, R. (1990). Motivation theory in industrial and organizational psychology. In M. D. Dunnette & L. M. Hough (Eds.), *Handbook of industrial and organizational psychology* (2nd ed., Vol. 1). Palo Alto, CA: Consulting Psychologists Press.

24. A good discussion of how managers can strengthen expectancy and instrumentality relationships is presented by Strauss, G. (1977). Managerial practices. In J. R. Hackman & J. L. Suttle (Eds.), *Improving life at work: Behavioral science approaches to organizational change.* Glenview, IL: Scott, Foresman.

25. Adams, J. S. (1965). Injustice in social exchange. *Advances in Experimental Social Psychology, 2,* 267–299.

26. Kulik, C. T., & Ambrose, M. L. (1992). Personal and situational determinants of referent choice. *Academy of Management Review, 17,* 212–237.

27. Mowday, R. T. (1991). Equity theory predictions of behavior in organizations. In R. M. Steers & L. W. Porter (Eds.), *Motivation and work behavior,* pp. 111–131. New York: McGraw-Hill; Carrell, M. R., & Dittrich, J. E. (1978). Equity theory: The recent literature, methodological considerations, and new directions. *Academy of Management Review, 3,* 202–210.

28. Mowday, 1987; Carrell & Dittrich, 1978.

29. See Kulik & Ambrose, 1992.

30. The best-developed theoretical position is that of Locke, E. A., & Latham, G. P. (1990). *A theory of goal setting and task performance.* Englewood Cliffs, NJ: Prentice-Hall.

32. Mento et al., 1987; Locke, E. A., Latham, G. P., & Erez, M. (1988). The determinants of goal commitment. *Academy of Management Review, 13,* 23–39.

33. See Erez, M., Earley, P. C., & Hulin, C. L. (1985). The impact of participa-

tion on goal acceptance and performance: A two-step model. *Academy of Management Journal, 28,* 50–66.

34. Latham, G. P., Erez, M., & Locke, E. A. (1988). Resolving scientific disputes by the joint design of crucial experiments by the antagonists: Application to the Erez-Latham dispute regarding participation in goal setting. *Journal of Applied Psychology, 73,* 753–772.

35. Latham, G. P., Mitchell, T. R., & Dosset, D. L. (1978). The importance of participative goal setting and anticipated rewards on goal difficulty and job performance. *Journal of Applied Psychology, 63,* 163–171; Saari, L. M., & Latham, G. P. (1979). The effects of holding goal difficulty constant on assigned and participatively set goals. *Academy of Management Journal, 22,* 163–168.

36. For a discussion of this issue, see Saari & Latham, 1979.

37. Locke, E. A., & Latham, G. P. (1984). *Goal setting—A motivational technique that works.* Englewood Cliffs, NJ: Prentice-Hall.

38. Adapted from Latham, G. P., & Locke, E. (1979, Autumn). Goal setting—a motivational technique that works. *Organization Dynamics,* 68–80; Latham, G. P., & Baldes, J. J. (1975). The "practical significance" of Locke's theory of goal setting. *Journal of Applied Psychology, 60,* 122–124.

39. Kagitcibasi, C., & Berry, J. W. (1989). Cross-cultural psychology: Current research and trends. *Annual Review of Psychology, 40,* 493–531.

40. Hofstede, G. (1980). *Culture's consequences: International differences in work-related values.* Beverly Hills, CA: Sage.

41. For a review, see Kagitcibasi & Berry, 1989.

42. Adler, N. J. (1992). *International dimensions of organizational behavior* (2nd ed.). Belmont, CA: Wadsworth.

43. Kirkman, B. L., & Shapiro, D. L. (1997). The impact of cultural values on employee resistance to teams: Toward a model of globalized self–managing work team effectiveness. *Academy of Management Review, 22,* pp. 730–757.

44. Adler, 1992, p. 159.

Chapter 6

1. Hodgetts, R.M. (1997, Winter). A conversation with Donald F. Hastings of the Lincoln Electric Company. *Organizational Dynamics,* pp. 68–74; *60 Minutes,* Lincoln Electric Company, 1993; Epstein, G. (1989, October). Inspire your team. *Success,* p. 12; Perry, N.J. (1988, December 19). Here come richer, riskier pay plans. *Fortune,* 50–58; Sharplin, A. D. (1990). Lincoln Electric Company, 1989. In A. A. Thompson, Jr., & A. J. Strickland, III. *Strategic management: Concepts and cases.* Homewood, IL: BPI/Irwin.

2. Hodgetts, 1997.

3. For reviews, see Lawler, E. E., III. (1971). *Pay and organizational effectiveness: A psychological view.* New York: McGraw-Hill; Chung, K. H. (1977). *Motivational theories and practices.* Columbus, OH: Grid. For a careful study, see Wagner, J. A., III, Rubin, P. A., & Callahan, T. J. (1988). Incentive payment and nonmanagerial productivity: An interrupted time series analysis of magnitude and trend. *Organizational Behavior and Human Decision Processes, 42*, 47–74.

4. Locke, E. A., Feren, D. B., McCaleb, V. M., Shaw, K. N., & Denny, A. T. (1980). The relative effectiveness of four methods of motivating employee performance. In K. D. Duncan, M. M. Gruneberg, & D. Wallis (Eds.), *Changes in working life.* London: Wiley.

5. Fein, M. (1973, September). Work measurement and wage incentives. *Industrial Engineering,* 49–51.

6. For a general treatment of why firms fail to adopt state-of-the-art personnel practices see Johns, G. (1993). Constraints on the adoption of psychology-based personnel practices: Lessons from organizational innovation. *Personnel Psychology, 46,* 569–592.

7. Posner, B. G. (1989, May). If at first you don't succeed. *Inc.,* 132–134, p. 132.

8. Lawler, 1971.

9. Lawler, 1971; Nash, A., & Carrol, S. (1975). *The management of compensation.* Monterey, CA: Brooks/Cole.

10. Heneman, R. L. (1990). Merit pay research. *Research in Personnel and Human Resources Management, 8,* 203–263; Ungson, G. R., & Steers, R. M. (1984). Motivation and politics in executive compensation. *Academy of Management Review, 9,* 313–323; Tosi, H. L., & Gomez-Mejia, L. R. (1989). The decoupling of CEO pay and performance: An agency theory perspective. *Administrative Science Quarterly, 34,* 169–189.

11. Haire, M., Ghiselli, E. E., & Gordon, M. E. (1967). A psychological study of pay. *Journal of Applied Psychology Monograph, 51,* (Whole No. 636).

12. Ramsay, L. (1999, February 5) Action shifts from salary to incentives. *Financial Post.* p. C18.

13. Lublin, J. S. (1997, January 8) Why more people are battling over bonuses. *The Wall Street Journal,* pp. B1, B7.

14. Meyer, H. H. (1991, February). A solution to the performance appraisal feedback enigma. *Academy of Management Executive,* 68–76.

15. See Zenga, T. R. (1992). Why do employers only reward extreme performance? Examining the relationships among pay, performance, and turnover. *Administrative Science Quarterly, 37,* 198–219.

16. Lawler, E. E., III, (1972). Secrecy and the need to know. In H. L. Tosi, R. J. House, & M. D. Dunnette (Eds.), *Managerial motivation and compensation.* East Lansing, MI: Michigan State University Press.

17. Futrell, C. M., & Jenkins, O. C. (1978). Pay secrecy versus pay disclosure for salesmen: A longitudinal study. *Journal of Marketing Research, 15,* 214–219, p. 215.

18. For a study of the prevalence of these plans see Lawler, E. E. III, Mohrman, S. A., & Ledford, G. E. (1992). *Employee involvement and total quality management: Practices and results in Fortune 1000 companies.* San Francisco: Jossey-Bass.

19. Hays, S. (February 1990). "Ownership cultures" create unity. *Workforce,* 78(2), 60–64.

20. Gordon, A. (February 2000). 35 best companies to work for. *Report on Business Magazine* 24–32.

21. Hays, 1999.

22. Graham-Moore, B., & Ross, T. L. (1990). *Gainsharing: Plans for improving performance.* Washington, DC: Bureau of National Affairs; Markham, S. E., Scott, K. D., & Little, B. L. (1992, January–February). National gainsharing study: The importance of industry differences. *Compensation & Benefits Review,* 34–45; Miller, C. S., & Shuster, M. H. (1987, Summer). Gainsharing plans: A comparative analysis. *Organizational Dynamics,* 44–67.

23. Davis, V. (1989, April). Eyes on the prize. *Canadian Business,* 93–106.

24. Graham-Moore & Ross, 1990; Moore, B. E, & Ross, T. L. (1978). *The Scanlon way to improved productivity: A practical guide.* New York: Wiley.

25. Perry, N. J. (1988, December 19). Here come richer, riskier pay plans. *Fortune,* 50–58; Lawler, E. E. (1984). Whatever happened to incentive pay? *New Management, 1*(4), 37–41.

26. Hammer, T. H. (1988). New developments in profit sharing, gainsharing, and employee ownership. In J. P. Campbell & R. J. Campbell (Eds.), *Productivity in organizations.* San Francisco: Jossey-Bass.

27. Cooper, C. L., Dyck, B., & Frohlich, N. (1992). Improving the effectiveness of gainsharing: The role of fairness and participation. *Administrative Science Quarterly, 37,* 471–490.

28. Lawler, E. E., III, & Jenkins, G. D., Jr. (1992). Strategic reward systems. In M. D. Dunette & L. M. Hough (Eds.), *Handbook of industrial and organizational psychology* (2nd ed., Vol. 3). Palo Alto, CA: Consulting Psychologists Press.

29. Murray, B., and Gerhart, B. (1998). An empirical analyses of a skill-based pay program and plant performance outcomes. Academy of Management Journal, 41, 68–78.

30. Taylor, F. W. (1967). *The principles of scientific management.* New York: Norton.

31. This discussion draws upon Gibson, J. L., Ivancevich, J. M., & Donnelly, J. H., Jr. (1991). *Organizations* (7th ed.). Homewood, IL: Irwin.

32. Hackman, J. R., & Oldham, G. R. (1980). *Work redesign.* Reading, MA: Addison-Wesley.

33. Oldham, G. R., Hackman, J. R., & Stepina, L. P. (1979). Norms for the job diagnostic survey. *JSAS Catalog of Selected Documents in Psychology, 9,* 14. (Ms. No. 1819).

34. Rentsch, J.R., and Steel, R.P. (1998). Testing the durability of job characteristics as predictors of absenteeism over a six–year period. Personnel Psychology, 51, 165–190.

35. See, for example, Johns, G., Xie, J. L., & Fang, Y. (1992). Mediating and moderating effects in job design. *Journal of Management, 18,* 657–676.

36. Tiegs, R. B., Tetrick, L. E., & Fried, Y. (1992). Growth need strength and context satisfactions as moderators of the relations of the Job Characteristics Model. *Journal of Management, 18,* 575–593; Johns et al., 1992.

37. This section draws in part on Hackman & Oldham, 1980.

38. Dumaine, B. (1989, November 6). P&G rewrites the marketing rules. *Fortune,* 34–48, p. 46.

39. Dowling, W. F. (1973). Job redesign on the assembly line: Farewell to the blue collar blues? *Organizational Dynamics,* 51–67.

40. Locke, E. A., Sirota, D., & Wolfson, A. D. (1976). An experimental case study of the successes and failure of job enrichment in a government agency. *Journal of Applied Psychology, 61,* 701–711.

41. Stonewalling plant democracy (1977, March 28). *Business Week.*

42. Good descriptions of MBO programs can be found in Mali, P. (1986). *MBO updated: A handbook of practices and techniques for managing by objectives.* New York: Wiley; Raia, A. P. (1974). *Managing by objectives.* Glenview, IL: Scott, Foresman; Odiorne, G. S. (1965). *Management by objectives.* New York: Pitman;

43. Rodgers, R., & Hunter, J. E. (1991) Impact of management by objectives on organization productivity. *Journal of Applied Psychology, 76,* 322–336.

44. Rodgers & Hunter, 1991.

45. See Rodgers, R., Huner, J. E., & Rogers, D. L. (1993). Influence of top management commitment on management program success. *Journal of Applied Psychology, 78,* 151–155.

46. For discussions of these and other problems with MBO, see Pringle, C. D., & Longenecker, J. G. (1982). The ethics of MBO. *Academy of Management Review, 7,* 305–312; Levinson, H. (1979, July–August). Management by whose objectives. *Harvard Business Review,* 125–134; McConkey, D. D. (1972, October). 20

ways to kill management by objectives. *Management Review*, 4–13.

47. See Ronen, S. (1984). *Alternative work schedules: Selecting, implementing, and evaluating*. Homewood, IL: Dow Jones-Irwin; Ronen, S. (1981). *Flexible working hours: An innovation in the quality of work life*. New York: McGraw-Hill; Nollen, S. D. (1982). *New work schedules in practice: Managing time in a changing society*. New York: Van Nostrand Reinhold.

48. For a good study showing absence reduction see Dalton, D. R., & Mesch, D. J. (1990). The impact of flexible scheduling on employee attendance and turnover. *Administrative Science Quarterly, 35*, 370–387.

49. Baltes, B., Briggs, T.E., Huff, J.W., Wright, J.A., and Neuman, G.A. (1999). Flexible and compressed workweek schedules: A meta–analyses of their effect son work–related criteria. Journal of Applied Psychology, 84, 496–513.

50. Pierce, J. L., Newstrom, J. W., Dunham, R. B., & Barber, A. E. (1989). *Alternative work schedules*. Boston: Allyn and Bacon; Ronen, 1981 and 1984; Golembiewski, R. T., & Proehl, C. W. (1978). A survey of the empirical literature on flexible workhours: Character and consequences of a major innovation. *Academy of Management Review, 3*, 837–853.

51. Baltes et al, 1999.

52. Ronen, 1984; Nollen, 1982.

53. Pierce et al., 1989; Ronen, 1984; Ronen, S., & Primps, S. B. (1981). The compressed workweek as organizational change: Behavioral and attitudinal outcomes. *Academy of Management Review, 6*, 61–74.

54. Pierce et al., 1989; Ivancevich, J. M., & Lyon, H. L. (1977). The shortened workweek: A field experiment. *Journal of Applied Psychology, 62*, 34–37.

55. Johns, G. (1987). Understanding and managing absence from work. In S. L. Dolan & R. S. Schuler (Eds.), *Canadian readings in personnel and human resource management*. St. Paul, MN: West.

56. Ivancevich & Lyon, 1977; Calvasina, E. J., & Boxx, W. R. (1975). Efficiency of workers on the four-day workweek. *Academy of Management Journal, 18*, 604–610; Goodale, J. G., & Aagaard, A. K. (1975). Factors relating to varying reactions to the 4-day workweek. *Journal of Applied Psychology, 60*, 33–38.

57. Baltes et al, 1999.

58. This section relies on Pierce et al., 1989.

59. DeFrank, R. S., & Ivancevich, J. M. (1998). Stress on the job: An executive update. Academy of Management Executive, 12, 55–66.

60. Grensing–Pophal, L. (1997, March). Employing the best people – from afar. Workforce, 76(3), p.30–38; Piskurich, G. M. (1998). *An organizational guide to telecommuting: Setting up and running a successful telecommuter program*. Alexandria, VA: American Society for Training and Development.

61. Grensing–Pophal, 1997.

62. DeFrank & Ivancevich, 1998; Goldsborough, R. (1999, May 14). Make telecommuting work for you. *Computer Dealer News*. P.19–20.

63. Grensing–Pophal, 1997.

64. Hampton, J. (June 14, 1999). Balancing between work and life. *Canadian HR Reporter* (Guide to Employee Benefits), G1, G2.

65. Hill, E. J., Miller, B. C., Weiner, S. P., Colihan, J. (1998). Influences of the virtual office on aspects of work and work/life balance. Personnel Psychology, 51, 667–683.

66. DeFrank & Ivancevich, 1998; Grensing–Pophal, 1997.

67. Goldsborough, 1999.

68. Hill, Miller, Weiner, & Colihan, 1998.

69. Bailey, D. S., & Foley, J. (1990, August). Pacific Bell works long distance. HRMagazine, 50– 52.

70. Brelis, M. (1999, January 20). Telecommuting takes back seat to office life. National Post (The Boston Globe).

71. Grensing–Pophal, 1997.

72. Tenner, A. R., & DeToro, I. J. (1992). *Total quality management: Three steps to continuous improvement*. Reading, MA: Addison-Wesley; Dale, B., & Cooper, C. (1992). *Total quality and human resources: An executive guide*. Oxford: Blackwell; Kinlaw, D. C. (1992). *Continuous improvement and measurement for total quality: A team-based approach*. San Diego: Pfeiffer.

73. Blackburn, R., & Rosen, B. (1993, August). Total quality and human resource management: Lessons learned from Baldrige Award-winning companies. *Academy of Management Executive*, 49–66; George, S. (1992). *The Baldrige quality system*. New York: Wiley.

74. Spendolini, M. J. (1992). *The benchmarking book*. New York: AMACOM.

75. Spendolini, 1992.

76. Blackburn & Rosen, 1993.

77. Waldman, D. A., Ghali, A., & Rancourt, M. (1983). *Performance appraisal and total quality management: An investigation of user preferences*. Paper presented at the annual meeting of the Academy of Management, Atlanta.

78. Shellenbarger, S. (1992, December 7). Managers navigate uncharted waters trying to resolve work-family conflicts. *Wall Street Journal*, pp. B1, B6.

79. DeFrank & Ivancevich, 1998.

80. Oldham et al., 1979.

Chapter 7

1. Excerpted with minor editing from Choquette, K.K. (1998, May 1). Team approach wins points with workers. USA TODAY, p.5B.

2. For a partial review, see Kahn, A., & McGaughey, T. A. (1977). Distance and liking: When moving close produces increased liking. *Sociometry, 40*, 138–144.

3. Byrne, D. (1969). Attitudes and attraction. In L. Berkowitz (Ed.), *Advances in experimental social psychology* (Vol. 4). New York: Academic Press.

4. Shaw, M. E. (1981). *Group dynamics: The psychology of small group behavior* (3rd ed.). New York: McGraw-Hill; Jones, E. E., & Gerard, H. B. (1967). *Foundations of social psychology*. New York: Wiley.

5. Tuckman, B. W. (1965). Developmental sequence in small groups. *Psychological Bulletin, 63*, 384–399; Tuckman, B. W., & Jensen, M. A. C. (1977). Stages of small-group development revisited. *Group & Organization Studies, 2*, 419–427.

6. Harris, S. G., & Sutton, R. I. (1986). Functions of parting ceremonies in dying organizations. *Academy of Management Journal, 29*, 5–30.

7. Seger, J. A. (1983). No innate phases in group problem solving. *Academy of Management Review, 8*, 683–689.

8. Ginnett, R. C. (1990). Airline cockpit crew. In J. R. Hackman (Ed.), *Groups that work (and those that don't)*. San Francisco: Jossey-Bass.

9. Gersick, C. J. G. (1989). Marking time: Predictable transitions in task groups. *Academy of Management Journal, 32*, 274–309; Gersick, C. J. G. (1988). Time and transition in work teams: Toward a new model of group development. *Academy of Management Journal, 31*, 9–41.

10. Gersick, 1989, 1988.

11. Hare, A. P. (1976). *A handbook of small group research*. New York: The Free Press; Shaw, 1981.

12. Hare, 1976; Shaw, 1981.

13. The following discussion relies upon Steiner, I. D. (1972). *Group process and productivity*. New York: Academic Press.

14. Steiner, 1972; Hill, G. W. (1982). Group versus individual performance: Are n+1 heads better than one? *Psychological Bulletin, 91*, 517–539.

15. Jackson, S. E., Stone, V. K., & Alvarez, E. B. (1993). Socialization amidst diversity: The impact of demographics on work team oldtimers and newcomers. *Research in Organizational Behavior, 15*, 45–109; Guzzo, R. A., & Shea, G. P. (1992). Group performance and intergroup relations in organizations. In M. D. Dunnette & L. M. Hough (Eds.), *Handbook of industrial and organizational psychology* (2nd ed., Vol. 3). Palo Alto, CA: Consulting Psychologists Press.

16. Watson, W. E., Kumar, K., & Michaelson, L. K. (1993). Cultural diversity's impact on interaction process and performance: Comparing homoge-

neous and diverse task groups. *Academy of Management Journal, 36,* 590–602.

17. Guzzo, R. A., & Dickson, M. W. (1996). Teams in organizations: Recent research on performance and effectiveness. *Annual Review of Psychology, 47,* pp. 307–338.

18. For an example of the social process by which this sharing may be negotiated in a new group, see Bettenhausen, K., & Murnighan, J. K. (1991). The development of an intragroup norm and the effects of interpersonal and structural challenges. *Administrative Science Quarterly, 36,* 20–35.

19. Kanter, R. M. (1977). *Men and women of the corporation.* New York: Basic Books, p. 37.

20. Leventhal, G. S. (1976). The distribution of rewards and resources in groups and organizations. In L. Berkowitz & E. Walster (Eds.), *Advances in experimental social psychology* (Vol. 9). New York: Academic Press.

21. See Mitchell, T. R., Rothman, M., & Liden, R. C. (1985). Effects of normative information on task performance. *Journal of Applied Psychology, 70,* 48–55.

22. Jackson, S. E., & Schuler, R. S. (1985). A meta-analysis and conceptual critique of research on role ambiguity and role conflict in work settings. *Organizational Behavior and Human Decision Processes, 36,* 16–78. For a methodological critique of this domain, see King, L. A., & King, D. W. (1990). Role conflict and role ambiguity: A critical assessment of construct validity. *Psychological Bulletin, 107,* 48–64.

23. Jackson & Schuler, 1985.

24. O'Driscoll, M. P., Ilgen, D. R., & Hildreth, K. (1992). Time devoted to job and off-job activities, interrole conflict, and affective experiences. *Journal of Applied Psychology, 77,* 272–279.

25. See Latack, J. C. (1981). Person/role conflict: Holland's model extended to role-stress research, stress management, and career development. *Academy of Management Review, 6,* 89–103.

26. Jackson & Schuler, 1985.

27. Treiman, D. J. (1977). *Occupational prestige in comparative perspective.* New York: Academic Press.

28. Shaw, 1981.

29. Kiesler, S., & Sproull, L. (1992). Group decision making and communication technology. *Organizational Behavior and Human Decision Processes, 52,* 96–123.

30. Strodbeck, F. L., James, R. M., & Hawkins, C. (1957). Social status in jury deliberations. *American Sociological Review, 22,* 713–719.

31. Gordon A. (February 2000). 35 Best Companies to Work For. *Report on Business Magazine,* 24–32.

32. Kiesler & Sproull, 1992.

33. For other definitions and a discussion of their differences, see Mudrack, P. E.

(1989). Defining group cohesiveness: A legacy of confusion? *Small Group Behavior, 20,* 37–49.

34. Stein, A. (1976). Conflict and cohesion: A review of the literature. *Journal of Conflict Resolution, 20,* 143–172.

35. Cartwright, D. (1968). The nature of group cohesiveness. In D. Cartwright & A. Zander (Eds.), *Group dynamics* (3rd ed.). New York: Harper & Row.

36. Lott, A., & Lott, B. (1965). Group cohesiveness as interpersonal attraction: A review of relationships with antecedent and consequent variables. *Psychological Bulletin, 64,* 259–309.

37. Anderson, A. B. (1975). Combined effects of interpersonal attraction and goal-path clarity on the cohesiveness of task-oriented groups. *Journal of Personality and Social Psychology, 31,* 68–75. Also see Cartwright, 1968.

38. Seashore, S. (1954). *Group cohesiveness in the industrial workgroup.* Ann Arbor, MI: Institute for Social Research.

39. Blanchard, F. A., Adelman, L., & Cook, S. W. (1975). Effect of group success and failure upon interpersonal attraction in cooperating interracial groups. *Journal of Personality and Social Psychology, 31,* 1020–1030.

40. Aronson, E., & Mills, J. (1959). The effects of severity of initiation on liking for a group. *Journal of Abnormal and Social Psychology, 59,* 177–181.

41. Bowen, D. E., Ledford, G. E., Jr., & Nathan, B. R. (1991, November). Hire for the organization, not the job. *Academy of Management Executive,* 35–51.

42. Bylinski, G. (1993, October 18). How to leapfrog the giants. *Fortune,* p. 80.

43. Cartwright, 1968; Shaw, 1981.

44. Schacter, S. (1951). Deviation, rejection, and communication. *Journal of Abnormal and Social Psychology, 46,* 190–207. See also Barker, J. R. (1993). Tightening the iron cage: Concertive control in self-managing teams. *Administrative Science Quarterly, 38,* 408–437.

45. Mullen, B., & Copper, C. (1994). The relation between group cohesiveness and performance: An integration. *Psychological Bulletin, 115,* pp. 210–227.

46. Podsakoff, P.M., MacKenzie, S.B., & Ahearne, M. (1997). Moderating effects of goal acceptance on the relationship between group cohesiveness and productivity. *Journal of Applied Psychology, 82,* pp. 974–983.

47. Seashore, 1954. Also see Stogdill, R. M. (1972). Group productivity, drive, and cohesiveness. *Organizational Behavior and Human Performance, 8,* 26–43. For a critique, see Mudrack, P. E. (1989). Group cohesiveness and productivity: A closer look. *Human Relations, 42,* 771–785.

48. Gulley, S. M., Devine, D. J., & Whitney, D. J. (In press). A meta-analysis of cohesion and performance:

Effects of level of analysis and task interdependence. *Small Group Research.*

49. Shepperd, J. A. (1993). Productivity loss in small groups: A motivation analysis. *Psychological Bulletin, 113,* 67–81; Kidwell, R. E., III, & Bennett, N. (1993). Employee propensity to withhold effort: A conceptual model to intersect three avenues of research. *Academy of Management Review, 18,* 429–456.

50. Shepperd, 1993; Kidwell & Bennett, 1993; George, J. M. (1992). Extrinsic and intrinsic origins of perceived social loafing in organizations. *Academy of Management Journal, 35,* 191–202.

51. Guzzo & Dickinson, 1996.

52. Guzzo & Dickinson, 1996; Banker, R. D., Field, J. M., Schroeder, R. G., & Sinha, K. K. (1996). Impact of work teams on manufacturing performance: A longitudinal field study. *Academy of Management Journal, 39,* pp. 867–890.

53. Kirkman, B. L., & Shapiro, D. L. (1997). The impact of cultural values on employee resistance to teams: Toward a model of globalized self–managing work team effectiveness. *Academy of Management Review, 22,* pp. 730–757.

54. Guzzo & Dickinson, 1996; Banker, Field, Schroeder, & Sinha, 1996; Kirkman & Shapiro, 1997.

55. Campion, M. A., Papper, E. M., & Medsker, G. J. (1996). Relations between work team characteristics and effectiveness: A replication and extension. *Personnel Psychology, 49,* pp. 429–452.

56. Hackman, J. R. (1987). The design of work teams. In J. W. Lorsch (Ed.), *Handbook of organizational behavior.* Englewood Cliffs, NJ: Prentice-Hall.

57. Campion, M. A., Medsker, G. J., & Higgs, A. C. (1993). Relations between work group characteristics and effectiveness: Implications for designing effective work groups. *Personnel Psychology, 46,* 823–850.

58. Dumaine, B. (1990, May 7). Who needs a boss? *Fortune,* 52–60.

59. Wall, T. D., Kemp, N. J., Jackson, P. R., & Clegg, C. W. (1986). Outcomes of autonomous workgroups: A field experiment. *Academy of Management Journal, 29,* 280–304, p. 283.

60. Parts of this section rely on Hackman, 1987.

61. See Ashforth, B. E., & Mael, F. (1989). Social identity theory and the organization. *Academy of Management Review, 14,* 20–39.

62. Treece, J. (1990, April 9). Here comes GM's Saturn. *Business Week,* 56–62.

63. Wall et al., 1986; Cordery, J. L., Mueller, W. S., & Smith, L. M. (1991). Attitudinal and behavioral effects of autonomous group working: A longitudinal field study. *Academy of Management Journal, 34,* 264–276.

64. Manz, C. C., & Sims, H. P., Jr. (1987). Leading workers to lead themselves:

The external leadership of self-managing work teams. *Administrative Science Quarterly, 32,* 106–128.

65. For reviews of research on self-managed groups, see Chapter 3 of Cummings, T. G., & Molloy, E. S. (1977). *Improving productivity and the quality of working life.* New York: Praeger; Goodman, P. S., Devadas, R., & Hughes, T. L. G. (1988). Groups and productivity: Analyzing the effectiveness of self-managing teams. In J. P. Campbell & R. J. Campbell (Eds.), *Productivity in organizations.* San Francisco: Jossey-Bass; Pearce, J. A., III, & Ravlin, E. C. (1987). The design and activation of self-regulating work groups. *Human Relations, 40,* 751–782.

66. Campion, M. A., Papper, E. M., & Medsker, G. J. (1996). Relations between work team characteristics and effectiveness: A replication and extension. *Personnel Psychology, 49,* pp. 429–452; Campion, M. A., Medsker, G. J. , & Higgs, A. C. (1993). Relations between work group characteristics and effectiveness: Implications for designing effective work groups. *Personnel Psychology, 46,* pp. 823–850.

67. Hyatt, D. E., & Ruddy, T. M. (1997). An examination of the relationship between work group characteristics and performance: Once more into the breech. *Personnel Psychology, 50,* pp. 553–585.

68. Kirkman, B. L., & Shapiro, D. L. (1997). The impact of cultural values on employee resistance to teams: Toward a model of globalized self–managing work team effectiveness. *Academy of Management Review, 22,* pp. 730–757; Banker, R. D., Field, J. M., Schroeder, R. G., & Sinha, K. K. (1996). Impact of work teams on manufacturing performance: A longitudinal field study. *Academy of Management Journal, 39,* pp. 867–890.

69. Farnham, A. (1994, February 7). America's most admired company. *Fortune,* 50–54; Dumaine, B. (1993, December 13). Payoff from the new management. *Fortune,* 103–110.

70. Waterman, R. H., Jr. (1987). *The renewal factor.* New York: Bantam Books; McElroy, J. (1985, April). Ford's new way to build cars. *Road & Track,* 156–158.

71. Pinto, M. B., Pinto, J. K, & Prescott, J. E. (1993). Antecedents and consequences of project team cross-functional cooperation. *Management Science, 39,* 1281–1297; Henke, J. W., Krachenberg, A. R., & Lyons, T. F. (1993). Cross-functional teams: Good concept, poor implementation! *Journal of Product Innovation Management, 10,* 216–229. Mustang examples from White, J. B., & Suris, O. (1993, September 21). How a 'skunk works' kept the Mustang alive— on a tight budget. *Wall Street Journal,* pp. A1, A12.

Chapter 8

1. Excerpted with minor editing from Ramstad, E. (1998, September 21). How Trilogy Software trains its new recruits to be risk takers. *Wall Street Journal,* pp. A1, A10.

2. See Morrison, E. W. (1993). Newcomer information seeking: Exploring types, modes, sources, and outcomes. *Academy of Management Journal, 36,* 557–589.

3. The terms information dependence and effect dependence are used by Jones, E. E., & Gerard, H. B. (1967). *Foundations of social psychology.* New York: Wiley.

4. Festinger, L. (1954). A theory of social comparison processes. *Human Relations, 7,* 117–140; Thomas, J., & Griffin, R. (1983). The social information processing model of task design: A review of the literature. *Academy of Management Review, 8,* 672–682.

5. Kelman, H. C. (1961). Processes of opinion change. *Public Opinion Quarterly, 25,* 57–78.

6. Asch, S. E. (1952). *Social psychology.* Englewood Cliffs, NJ: Prentice-Hall.

7. Hollander, E. P. (1958). Conformity, status, and idiosyncrasy credit. *Psychological Review, 65,* 117–127; Hollander, E. P. (1964). *Leaders, groups, and influence.* New York: Oxford University Press.

8. Van Maanen, J., & Schein, E. H. (1979). Toward a theory of organizational socialization. *Research in Organizational Behavior, 1,* 209–264.

9. Feldman, D. C. (1976). A contingency theory of socialization. *Administrative Science Quarterly, 21,* 433–452.

10. Wanous, J. P. (1992). *Organizational entry: Recruitment, selection, orientation, and socialization of newcomers.* (2nd ed.). Reading, MA: Addison-Wesley.

11. Wanous, J. P. (1976). Organizational entry: From naive expectations to realistic beliefs. *Journal of Applied Psychology, 61,* 22–29.

12. See Breaugh, J. A. (1992). *Recruitment: Science and practice.* Boston: PWS-Kent.

13. Morrison, E. W., & Robinson, S. L. (1997). When employees feel betrayed: A model of how psychological contract violation develops. *Academy of Management Review, 22,* pp. 226–256.

14. Robinson, S. L., & Rousseau, D. M. (1994). Violating the psychological contract: Not the exception but the norm. *Journal of Organizational Behavior, 15,* pp. 245–259.

15. Morrison & Robinson, 1997; Robinson, S. L. (1996). Trust and breach of the psychological contract. *Administrative Science Quarterly, 41,* pp. 574–599.

16. Morrison & Robinson, 1997.

17. Morrison & Robinson, 1997.

18. This discussion draws upon Van Maanen & Schein, 1979, but differs in detail.

19. Wanous, 1992; Breaugh, 1992.

20. Wanous, 1992; Breaugh, 1992.

21. Phillips, J.M. (1998). Effects of realistic job previews on multiple organizational outcomes: A meta–analysis. *Academy of Management Journal, 41,* pp. 673–690.

22. Premack, S. L., & Wanous, J. P. (1985). A meta-analysis of realistic job preview experiments. *Journal of Applied Psychology, 70,* 706–719. See also Wanous, J. P., Poland, T. D., Premack, S. L., & Davis, K. S. (1992). The effects of met expectations on newcomer attitudes and behaviors: A review and meta-analysis. *Journal of Applied Psychology, 77,* 288–297.

23. Premack & Wanous, 1985; McEvoy, G. M., & Cascio, W. F. (1985). Strategies for reducing employee turnover: A meta-analysis. *Journal of Applied Psychology, 70,* 342–353.

24. Morrison & Robinson, 1997.

25. Van Maanen, J., & Schein, E.H. (1979). Toward a theory of organizational socialization. In: B.M. Staw (Ed.), *Research in organizational behavior,* Vol. 1.). Greenwich, CT: JAI Press, pp. 209–264.

26. Ashforth, B.E., & Saks, A.M. (1996). Socialization tactics: Longitudinal effects on newcomer adjustment. *Academy of Management Journal, 39,* pp. 149–178; Jones, G.R. (1986). Socialization tactics, self–efficacy, and newcomers' adjustments to organizations. *Academy of Management Journal, 29,* pp. 262–279.

27. Ashforth & Saks, 1996.

28. This section was written by J. Bruce Prince.

29. Scandura, T. (1992). Mentorship and career mobility: An empirical investigation. *Journal of Organizational Behavior, 13,* 169–174; Fagenson, E. (1989). The mentor advantage: Perceived career/job experiences of protégés versus non-protégés. *Journal of Organizational Behavior, 10,* 309–320; Fagenson, E. (1988). The power of a mentor: Protégés and nonprotégés' perceptions of their own power in organizations. *Group and Organization Studies, 13,* 182–192; Dalton, G. W., Thompson, P. H., & Price, R. (1977, Summer). The four stages of professional careers—A new look at performance by professionals. *Organizational Dynamics,* 19–42.

30. Dreher, G., & Ash, R. (1990). A comparative study of mentoring among men and women in managerial, professional and technical positions. *Journal of Applied Psychology, 75,* 539–546; Whitely, W., Dougherty, T., & Dreher, G. (1991). Relationship of career mentoring and socioeconomic origin to managers' and professionals' early career progress. *Academy of Management Journal, 34,* 331–351.

31. Kram, K. (1985). *Mentoring.* Glenview, IL: Scott, Foresman.

32. Murray, M. (1991). *Beyond the myths and magic of mentoring: How to facilitate an effective mentoring program.* San Francisco, CA: Jossey-Bass; Lawrie, J. (1987). How to establish a mentoring program. *Training & Development Journal, 41*(3), 25–27.

33. Chao, G., Walz, P., & Gardner, P. (1992). Formal and informal mentorships: A comparison on mentoring functions and contrast with nonmentored counterparts. *Personnel Psychology, 45*, 619–636; Noe, R. (1988). An investigation of the determinants of successful assigned mentoring relationships. *Personnel Psychology, 41*, 457–479.

34. Kram & Isabella, 1985. Mentoring alternatives: The role of peer relationships in career development. *Academy of Management Journal, 28*, 110–132.

35. Ragins, B. R. (1989). Barriers to mentoring: The female manager's dilemma. *Human Relations, 42*, 1–22; Noe, R. A. (1988). Women and mentoring: A review and research agenda. *Academy of Management Review, 13*, 65–78; Cox, T., Jr. (1993). *Cultural diversity in organizations: Theory, research, & practice.* San Francisco: Berrett-Koehler.

36. Ragins, B., & McFarlin, D. (1990). Perceptions of mentor roles in cross-gender mentoring relationships. *Journal of Vocational Behavior, 37*, 321–339.

37. Morrison, A., White, R., & Van Velsor, E. (1987). *Breaking the glass ceiling: Can women reach the top of America's largest corporations?* Reading, MA: Addison-Wesley; Burke, R., & McKeen, C. (1990). Mentoring in organizations: Implications for women. *Journal of Business Ethics, 9*, 317–322; Dennett, D. (1985, November). Risks, mentoring helps women to the top. *APA Monitor*, p. 26.

38. Noe, R. (1988). An investigation of the determinants of successful assigned mentoring relationships. *Personnel Psychology, 41*, 457–479; Cox, 1993.

39. Morrison et al., 1987.

40. Cox, 1993; Ibarra, H. (1993). Personal networks of women and minorities in management. *Academy of Management Review, 18*, 56–87.

41. Nkomo, S., & Cox, T. (1989). Gender differences in the upward mobility of black managers: Double whammy or double advantage? *Sex Roles, 21*, 825–839.

42. Thomas, D. (1989). Mentoring and irrationality: The role of racial taboos. *Human Resource Management, 28*, 279–290; Thomas, D. (1990). The impact of race on managers' experiences of developmental relationships: An intraorganizational study. *Journal of Organizational Behavior, 11*, 479–492.

43. Ostroff, C., & Kozlowski, S. W. J. (1992). Organizational socialization as a learning process: The role of information acquisition. *Personnel Psychology, 45*, pp. 849–874.

44. Morrison, E. W. (1993). Newcomer information seeking: Exploring types, modes, sources, and outcomes. *Academy of Management Journal, 36*, pp. 557–589; Morrison, E. W. (1993). Longitudinal study of the effects of information seeking on newcomer socialization. *Journal of Applied Psychology, 78*, pp. 173–183.

45. Ostroff & Kozlowski, 1992.

46. Saks, A.M., & Ashforth, B. E. (1996). Proactive socialization and behavioral self-management. *Journal of Vocational Behavior, 48*, pp. 301–323.

47. Ashford, S.J., & Black, J.S. (1996). Proactivity during organizational entry: The role of desire for control. *Journal of Applied Psychology, 81*, pp. 199–214; Whitely, W.T., Peiró, J.M., Feij, J.A., & Taris, T.W. (1995). Conceptual, epistemological, methodological, and outcome issues in work-role development: A reply. *Journal of Vocational Behavior, 46*, pp. 283–291.

48. Turban, D. B., & Dougherty, T. W. (1994). Role of protégé personality in receipt of mentoring and career success. *Academy of Management Journal, 37*, pp. 688–702.

49. For a more complete discussion of various definitions, theories, and concepts of culture, see Schein, E. H. (1992). *Organizational culture and leadership* (2nd ed.). San Francisco: Jossey-Bass; Smircich, L. (1983). Concepts of culture and organizational analysis. *Administrative Science Quarterly, 28*, 339–358; Allaire, Y., & Firsirotu, M. E. (1984). Theories of organizational culture. *Organization Studies, 5*, 193–226; Hatch, M. J. (1993). The dynamics of organizational culture. *Academy of Management Review, 18*, 657–693.

50. Sackmann, S. A. (1992). Culture and subculture: An analysis of organizational knowledge. *Administrative Science Quarterly, 37*, 140–161.

51. Gregory, K. L. (1983). Native-view paradigms: Multiple cultures and culture conflicts in organizations. *Administrative Science Quarterly, 28*, 359–376.

52. Kilmann, R., Saxton, M. J., & Serpa, R. (1986, Winter). Issues in understanding and changing culture. *California Management Review*, 87–94; Deal, T. E., & Kennedy, A. A. (1982). *Corporate cultures: The rites and rituals of corporate life.* Reading, MA: Addison-Wesley. For a critique, see Saffold, G. S., III. (1988). Culture traits, strength, and organizational performance: Moving beyond "strong" culture. *Academy of Management Review, 13*, 546–558.

53. Raynal, W. (1993, December 20). Down, but not out. *Autoweek*, p. 15.

54. Gordon, G. G., & Di Tomaso, N. (1992). Predicting corporate performance from organizational culture. *Journal of Management Studies, 29*, 783–798. For a critique of such work

see Siehl, C., & Martin, J. (1990). Organizational culture: A key to financial performance. In B. Schneider (Ed.), *Organizational climate and culture.* San Francisco: Jossey-Bass.

55. Sheridan, J. E. (1992). Organizational culture and employee retention. *Academy of Management Journal, 35*, 1036–1056.

56. Lorsch, J. W. (1986, Winter). Managing culture: The invisible barrier to strategic change. *California Management Review*, 95–109.

57. Cartwright, S., & Cooper, C. L. (1993, May). The role of culture compatibility in successful organizational marriage. *Academy of Management Executive*, 57–70.

58. Kets de Vries, M. F. R., & Miller, D. (1984). *The neurotic organization: Diagnosing and changing counterproductive styles of management.* San Francisco: Jossey-Bass.

59. Kets de Vries, M. F. R., & Miller, D. (1984, October). Unstable at the top. *Psychology Today*, 26–34, p. 32.

60. See Schein, 1992.

61. Uttal, B. (1985, August 5). Behind the fall of Steve Jobs. *Fortune*, 20–24.

62. Pascale, R. (1985, Winter). The paradox of "corporateculture": Reconciling ourselves to socialization. *California Management Review*, 26–41; Pascale, 1984; for some research support, see Caldwell, D. F., Chatman, J. A., & O'Reilly, C. A. (1990). Building organizational commitment: A multifirm study. *Journal of Occupational Psychology, 63*, 245–261.

63. Hatch, 1993; Ornstein, S. (1986). Organizational symbols: A study of their meanings and influences on perceived organizational climate. *Organizational Behavior and Human Decision Processes, 38*, 207–229.

64. Nulty, P. (1989, February 27). America's toughest bosses. *Fortune*, 40–54.

65. Trice, H. M., and Beyer, J. M. (1984). Studying organizational cultures through rites and ceremonials. *Academy of Management Review, 9*, 653–669.

66. Martin, J., Feldman, M. S., Hatch, M. J., & Sitkin, S. B. (1983). The uniqueness paradox in organizational stories. *Administrative Science Quarterly, 28*, 438–453.

67. Peters, T., & Austin, N. (1985). *A passion for excellence: The leadership difference.* New York: Random House.

Chapter 9

1. McCartney, S. (1997, April 22). Scrappy Southwest reaches coast in one stop. The Wall Street Journal, p. B1, B10; Walmsley, A. (1999, December). Plane crazy. *Report on Business Magazine*, pp. 62-72; Labick, K. (1994, May 4). Is Herb Kelleher America's best CEO? *Fortune*, 44–52; Veverka,

M. (1994, November 21). Blood and guts Kelleher. Southwest Chief rallies troops against United. *Crains's Chicago Business*, p.3; Barrett, C. (1993, November). Giving customers P.O.S. *Sales & Marketing Management*, p. 52; Bovier, C. (1993, June). Teamwork: The heart of an airline. *Training*, 53–58; Maxon, T. (1994, October 14). Hey Herb, have you checked out this morning's USA Today yet? *The Dallas Morning News*, p. 1D.

2. Smith, V. (1999, April). Leading us on. *Report on Business Magazine*, pp. 90–96.

3. Bass, B. M. (1990). *Bass & Stogdill's handbook of leadership: A survey of research* (3rd ed.). New York: Free Press.

4. This list is derived from Bass, 1990; House, R. J., & Baetz, M. L. (1979). Leadership: Some empirical generalizations and new research directions. *Research in Organizational Behavior*, 1, 341–423; Locke, E. A., et al. (1992). *The essence of leadership: The four keys to leading effectively*. New York: Free Press; Lord, R. G., DeVader, C. L., & Alliger, G. M. (1986). A meta-analysis of the relationship between personality traits and leadership perceptions: An application of validity generalization procedures. *Journal of Applied Psychology*, 71, 402–410.

5. Bottger, P. C. (1984). Expertise and air time as bases of actual and perceived influence in problem-solving groups. *Journal of Applied Psychology*, 69, 214–221.

6. Lewis, G. H. (1972). Role differentiation. *American Sociological Review*, 37, 424–434.

7. Bales, R. F., & Slater, P. E. (1955). Role differentiation in small decision-making groups. In T. Parsons, et al. (Eds.), *Family, socialization, and interaction process*. Glencoe, IL: Free Press; Slater, P. E. (1955). Role differentiation in small groups. *American Sociological Review*, 20, 300–310.

8. For a pessimistic review, see Korman, A. K. (1966). "Consideration," "initiating structure," and organizational criteria—A review. *Personnel Psychology*, 19, 349–361. For an optimistic update, see Kerr, S., & Schriesheim, C. (1974). Consideration, initiating struture, and organizational criteria—An update of Korman's 1966 review. *Personnel Psychology*, 27, 555–568.

9. Kerr, S., Schriesheim, C. A., Murphy, C. J., & Stogdill, R. M. (1974). Toward a contingency theory of leadership based upon the consideration and initiating structure literature. *Organizational Behavior and Human Performance*, 12, 62–82.

10. For a review of the evidence, see Filley, A. C., House, R. J., & Kerr, S. (1976). *Managerial process and organizational behavior* (2nd ed.). Glenview, IL: Scott, Foresman. Also see Larson, L. L., Hunt, J. G., & Osborn, R. N. (1976).

The great hi-hi leader behavior myth: A lesson from Occam's razor. *Academy of Management Journal*, 19, 628–641.

11. Fiedler, F. E. (1967). *A theory of leadership effectiveness*. New York: McGraw-Hill; Fiedler, F. E., & Chemers, M. M. (1974). *Leadership and effective management*. Glenview, IL: Scott, Foresman; Fiedler, F. E. (1978). The contingency model and the dynamics of the leadership process. In L. Berkowitz (Ed.), *Advances in experimental social psychology* (Vol. 11). New York: Academic Press.

12. For a summary, see Fiedler, 1978.

13. See Ashour, A. S. (1973). The contingency model of leader effectiveness: An evaluation. *Organizational Behavior and Human Performance*, 9, 339–355; Graen, G. B., Alvares, D., Orris, J. B., & Martella, J. A. (1970). The contingency model of leadership effectiveness: Antecedent and evidential results. *Psychological Bulletin*, 74, 285–296.

14. Schriesheim, C. A., Tepper, B. J., & Tetreault, L. A. (1994). Least preferred co-worker score, situational control, and leadership effectiveness: A meta-analysis of contingency and performance predictions. *Journal of Applied Psychology*, 79, 561–573; Peters, L. H., Hartke, D. D., & Pohlmann, J. T. (1985). Fiedler's contingency theory of leadership: An application of the meta-analysis procedures of Schmidt and Hunter. *Psychological Bulletin*, 97, 274–285; Strube, M. J., & Garcia, J. E. (1981). A meta-analytic investigation of Fiedler's contingency model of leadership effectiveness. *Psychological Bulletin*, 90, 307–321.

15. House, R. J., & Dessler, G. (1974). The path-goal theory of leadership: Some post hoc and a priori tests. In J. G. Hunt & L. L. Larson (Eds.), *Contingency approaches to leadership*. Carbondale, IL: Southern Illinois University Press; House, R. J., & Mitchell, T. R. (1974, Autumn). Path-goal theory of leadership. *Journal of Contemporary Business*, 81–97. See also Evans, M. G. (1970). The effects of supervisory behavior on the path-goal relationship. *Organizational Behavior and Human Performance*, 5, 277–298.

16. House & Dessler, 1974; House & Mitchell, 1974; Filley, House, & Kerr, 1976; Wofford, J. C., & Liska, L. Z. (1993). Path-goal theories of leadership: A meta-analysis *Journal of Management*, 19, 857–876.

17. See, for example, Greene, C. N. (1979). Questions of causation in the path-goal theory of leadership. *Academy of Management Journal*, 22, 22–41; Griffin, R. W. (1980). Relationships among individual, task design, and leader behavior variables. *Academy of Management Journal*, 23, 665–683.

18. Mitchell, T. R. (1973). Motivation and participation: An integration. *Academy of Management Journal*, 16, 160–179.

19. Maier, N. R. F. (1973). *Psychology in industrial organizations* (4th ed.). Boston: Houghton Mifflin; Maier, N. R. F. (1970). *Problem solving and creativity in individuals and groups*. Belmont, CA: Brooks/Cole.

20. Maier, 1970, 1973.

21. Strauss, G. (1955). Group dynamics and intergroup relations. In W. F. Whyte, *Money and motivation*. New York: Harper & Row.

22. Vroom, V. H., & Jago, A. G. (1988). The new leadership: *Managing participation in organizations*. Englewood Cliffs, NJ: Prentice-Hall; Vroom, V. H., & Yetton, P. W. (1973). *Leadership and decision-making*. Pittsburgh: University of Pittsburgh Press.

23. Vroom & Yetton, 1973, p. 13.

24. See Vroom & Jago, 1988, for a review. See also Field, R. H. G., Wedley, W. C., & Hayward, M. W. J. (1989). Criteria used in selecting Vroom-Yetton decision styles. *Canadian Journal of Administrative Sciences*, 6(2), 18–24.

25. Reviews on participation reveal a complicated pattern of results. See Miller, K. I., & Monge, P. R. (1986). Participation, satisfaction, and productivity: A meta-analytic review. *Academy of Management Journal*, 29, 727–753; Wagner, J. A., III, & Gooding, R. Z. (1987). Shared influence and organizational behavior: A meta-analysis of situational variables expected to moderate participation-outcome relationships. *Academy of Management Journal*, 30, 524–541; Wagner, J. A., III, & Gooding, R. Z. (1987). Effects of societal trends on participation research. *Administrative Science Quarterly*, 32, 241–262.

26. The transformational/transactional distinction is credited to Burns, J. M. (1978). *Leadership*. New York: Harper & Row.

27. Bass, B. M. (1985). *Leadership and performance beyond expectations*. New York: Free Press; Bass, B. M. (1990, Winter). From transactional to transformational leadership: Learning to share the vision. *Organizational Dynamics*, 19–31.

28. House, R. J. (1977). A 1976 theory of charismatic leadership. In J. G. Hunt & L. L. Larson (Eds.), *Leadership: The cutting edge*. Carbondale, IL: Southern Illinois University Press.

29. Conger, J. A., & Kanungo, R. N. (1988). Behavioral dimensions of charismatic leadership. In J. A. Conger & R. N. Kanungo (Eds.), *Charismatic leadership: The elusive factor in organizational effectiveness*. San Francisco: Jossey-Bass; Conger, J. A., & Kanungo, R. N. (1987). Toward a behavioral theory of charismatic leadership in organizational settings. *Academy of Management Review*, 12, 637–647.

30. House, R. J., Woycke, J., & Fodor, E. M. (1988). Charismatic and noncharismatic leaders: Differences in behavior

and effectiveness. In J. A. Conger & R. N. Kanungo (Eds.), *Charismatic leadership: The elusive factor in organizational effectiveness.* San Francisco: Jossey-Bass.

31. Howell, J. M. (1988). Two faces of charisma: Socialized and personalized leadership in organizations. In J. A. Conger & R. N. Kanungo (Eds.), *Charismatic leadership: The elusive factor in organizational effectiveness.* San Francisco: Jossey-Bass; Howell, J. M., & Avolio, B. J. (1992, May). The ethics of charismatic leadership. Submission or liberation? *Academy of Management Executive,* 43–54.

32. Hater, J. J., & Bass, B. M. (1988). Superiors' evaluations and subordinates' perceptions of transformational and transactional leadership. *Journal of Applied Psychology, 73,* 695–702; Avolio, B. J., & Bass, B. M. (1988). Transformational leadership, charisma, and beyond. In J. G. Hunt, B. R. Baglia, H. P. Dachler, & C. A. Schriesheim (Eds.), *Emerging leadership vistas.* Lexington, MA: Lexington Books.

33. Stewart, T. A. (1991, August 12). GE keeps those ideas coming. *Fortune,* pp. 41-49.

34. Bartlett, C., & Ghoshal, S. (1995, May-June). Changing the role of top management: Beyond systems to people. *Harvard Business Review,* pp. 132-142.

35. House, R. J., & Aditya, R. N. (1997). The social scientific study of leadership: Quo vadis? *Journal of Management, 23,* pp. 409-473; Tierney, P., Farmer, S. M., & Graen, G. B. (1999). An examination of leadership and employee creativity: The relevance of traits and relationships. *Personnel Psychology, 52,* 591-620; Gerstner, C. R., & Day, D. V. (1997). Meta-analytic review of leader-member exchange theory: correlates and construct issues. *Journal of Applied Psychology, 82,* pp. 827-844.

36. Gestner & Day, 1997.

37. Manz, C. C., & Sims, H. P. (1989). *Super-leadership.* New York, NY: Prentice-Hall.

38. Cohen, S. G., Chang, L., & Ledford, G. E. Jr. (1997). A hierarchical construct of self-management leadership and its relationship to quality of work life and perceived work group effectiveness. *Personnel Psychology, 50,* pp. 275-308.

39. Conger, J. A. (1998). *Winning 'em over: A new model for management in the age of persuasion.* New York, NY: Simon & Schuster.

40. Hawkins, L., & Hudson, M. (1998, August). Leaders as negotiators. *HR Monthly,* pp. 6-8.

41. Goleman, D. (1998, November-December). What makes a leader? *Harvard Business Review,* pp. 93-102.

42. Conger, 1998.

43. Goleman, 1998.

44. Hawkins & Hudson, 1998.

45. Hitt, M. A., Keats, B. W., & DeMarie, S. M. (1998). Navigating in the new competitive landscape: Building strategic flexibility and competitive advantage in the 21st century. *Academy of Management Executive,* 12, pp. 22-42.

46. Gregersen, H. B., Morrison, A. J., & Black, J. S. (1998, Fall). Developing leaders for the global frontier. *Sloan Management Review,* pp. 21-32.

47. Gregersen, Morrison, & Black, 1998.

48. Ireland, R. D., & Hitt, M. A. (1999). Achieving and maintaining strategic competitiveness in the 21st century: The role of strategic leadership. *Academy of Management Executive,* 13, pp. 43-57.

49. Ireland & Hitt, 1999.

50. Ireland & Hitt, 1999.

51. Ireland & Hitt, 1999.

52. Gregersen, Morrison, & Black, 1998; Church, E. (1999, January 7). Born to be a global business leader. *The Globe and Mail,* p. B8.

53. Eagley, A. H., & Johnson, B. T. (1990). Gender and leadership style: A meta-analysis. *Psychological Bulletin, 108,* 233–256.

54. Kass, S. (September 1999). Employees perceive women as better managers than men, finds five-year study. *ADA Monitor 30(8),* 6.

55. Dorfman, P. (1996). International and cross-cultural leadership. In: B.J. Punnett & O.Shenkar (Eds.), *Handbook for International Management Research.* Cambridge, MA: Blackwell Business, pp. 267-349.

56. Bass, B.M. (1997). Does the transactional-transformational leadership paradigm transcend organizational and national boundaries? *American Psychologist,* 52, pp. 130-139.

57. Adapted from Katz, D., & Kahn, R. L. (1978). *The social psychology of organizations* (2nd ed.). New York: Wiley.

58. For a review of the evidence that concludes that leadership matters, see House & Baetz, 1979. See also Thomas, A. B. (1988). Does leadership make a difference in organizational performance? *Administrative Science Quarterly, 33,* 388–400.

59. Pfeffer, J. (1977). The ambiguity of leadership. *Academy of Management Review,* 2, 104–112. Pfeffer also cites evidence that leadership is less important than other organizational factors.

60. Kerr, S. (1977). Substitutes for leadership: Some implications for organizational design. *Organizational and Administrative Sciences,* 8, 135–146; Kerr, S., & Jermier, J. M. (1978). Substitutes for leadership: Their meaning and measurement. *Organizational Behavior and Human Performance,* 22, 375–403.

61. There is some disagreement about how to actually test this theory. In our opinion, the following research provides partial support for the view of neutralizers and substitutes presented in the chapter. Podsakoff, P. M., MacKenzie, S. B., & Fetter, R. (1993) Substitutes for leadership and the management of professionals. *Leadership Quarterly, 4,* 1–44; Podsakoff, P. M., Niehoff, B. P., Mackenzie, S. B., & Williams, M. L. (1993). Do substitutes for leadership really substitute for leadership? An empirical examination of Kerr and Jermier's situational leadership model. *Organizational Behavior and Human Decision Processes, 54,* 1–44.

Chapter 10

1. Excerpted from: (1997, February). A circus juggles HR worldwide. *Workforce,* 76(2), p. 50; Flynn, G. (1997, August). Acrobats, Aerialists and HR: The big top needs big HR. *Workforce,* 76(8), pp. 38-45.

2. Nobel, B. P. (1993, September 19). Dissecting the 90's workplace. *New York Times,* p. F21.

3. Meissner, M. (1976). The language of work. In R. Dubin (Ed.), *Handbook of work, organization, and society.* Chicago: Rand McNally.

4. Meissner, 1976.

5. Mintzberg, H. (1973). *The nature of managerial work.* New York: Harper & Row.

6. Miller, K. L. (1992, August 17). Honda sets its sights on a different checkered flag. *Business Week,* 45–46.

7. Very few organizations formally institute such policies. See Saunders, D. M., & Leck, J. D. (1993). Formal upward communication procedures: Organizational and employee perspectives. *Canadian Journal of Administrative Sciences,* 10, 255–268.

8. Davis, K. (1968). Success of chain-of-command oral communication in a manufacturing management group. *Academy of Management Journal,* 11, 379–387.

9. Parvanova, T. (1998, September). Bombardier's VP HR: We're the best game in town. *The Canadian Journal of Workplace Issues,* Plans, and Strategies, p. 21.

10. Foltz, R. G. (1985). Communication in contemporary organizations. In C. Reuss & D. Silvis (Eds.), *Inside organizational communication* (2nd ed.). New York: Longman.

11. Snyder, R. A., & Morris, J. H. (1984). Organizational communication and performance. *Journal of Applied Psychology,* 69, 461–465.

12. From an unpublished review by the author. Some studies are cited in Jablin, F. M. (1979). Superior-subordinate communication: The state of the art. *Psychological Bulletin,* 86, 1201–1222. See also Dansereau, F., & Markham, S. E. (1987). Superior-subordinate communication: Multiple levels of analysis. In F. Jablin, L. Putnam, K. H. Roberts, & L. W. Porter (Eds.), *Handbook of*

organizational communication. Newbury Park, CA: Sage; Harris, M. M., & Schaubroeck, J. (1988). A meta-analysis of self-supervisor, self-peer, and peer-supervisor ratings. *Personnel Psychology, 41,* 43–62.

13. Jablin, 1979.

14. Tesser, A., & Rosen, S. (1975). The reluctance to transmit bad news. In L. Berkowitz (Ed.), *Advances in experimental social psychology* (Vol. 8). New York: Academic Press.

15. Read, W. (1962). Upward communication in industrial hierarchies. *Human Relations, 15,* 3–16; For related studies, see Jablin, 1979.

16. Evidence that subordinates tend to suppress communicating negative news to the boss can be found in O'Reilly, C. A., & Roberts, K. H. (1974). Information filtration in organizations: Three experiments. *Organizational Behavior and Human Performance, 11,* 253–265. For evidence that this is probably self-presentational, see Bond, C. F., Jr., & Anderson, E. L. (1987). The reluctance to transmit bad news: Private discomfort or public display? *Journal of Experimental Social Psychology, 23,* 176–187.

17. Ashford, S. J. (1989). Self-assessments in organizations: A literature review and integrated model. *Research in Organizational Behavior, 11,* 133–174; Harris & Shaubroeck, 1988.

18. Lawler, E. E., III, Porter, L. W., & Tennenbaum, A. (1968). Managers' attitudes toward interaction episodes. *Journal of Applied Psychology, 52,* 432–439. For a similar study with similar results, see Whitely, W. (1984). An exploratory study of managers' reactions to properties of verbal communication. *Personnel Psychology, 37,* 41–59.

19. Studies reviewed in Meissner, 1976.

20. Callan, V. J. (1993). Subordinate-manager communication in different sex dyads: Consequences for job satisfaction. *Journal of Occupational and Organizational Psychology, 66,* 13–27.

21. Noon, M., & Delbridge, R. (1993). News from behind my hand: Goosip in organizations. *Organization Studies, 14,* 23–36.

22. Davis, K. (1977). *Human behavior at work* (5th ed.). New York: McGraw-Hill.

23. Davis, K. (1953). Management communication and the grapevine. *Harvard Business Review, 31*(5), 43–49; Sutton, H., & Porter, L. W. (1968). A study of the grapevine in a governmental organization. *Personnel Psychology, 21,* 223–230.

24. Bartlett, C.A., and Ghosal, S. (1995, May-June). Changing the role of top management: Beyond systems to people. Harvard Business Review, pp. 132–142.

25. Rosnow, R. L. (1980). Psychology of rumor reconsidered. *Psychological Bulletin, 87,* 578–591.

26. Rosnow, R. L. (1991) Inside rumor: A personal journey. *American Psychologist, 46,* 484–496.

27. Kanter, R. M. (1977). *Men and women of the corporation.* New York: Basic Books.

28. For reviews, see Heslin, R., & Patterson, M. L. (1982). *Nonverbal behavior and social psychology.* New York: Plenum; Harper, R. G., Wiens, A. N., & Matarazzo, J. D. (1978). *Nonverbal communication: The state of the art.* New York: Wiley.

29. Mehrabian, A. (1972). *Nonverbal communication.* Chicago: Aldine- Atherton.

30. Mehrabian, 1972.

31. DePaulo, B. M. (1992). Nonverbal behavior and self-presentation. *Psychological Bulletin, 111,* 203–243.

32. Edinger, J. A., & Patterson, M. L. (1983). Nonverbal involvement and social control. *Psychological Bulletin, 93,* 30–56.

33. Rasmussen, K. G., Jr. (1984). Nonverbal behavior, verbal behavior, resume credentials, and selection interview outcomes. *Journal of Applied Psychology, 69,* 551–556.

34. Campbell, D. E. (1979). Interior office design and visitor response. *Journal of Applied Psychology, 64,* 648–653. For a replication, see Morrow, P. C., & McElroy, J. C. (1981). Interior office design and visitor response: A constructive replication. *Journal of Applied Psychology, 66,* 646–650.

35. McElroy, J. C., Morrow, P. C., & Ackerman, R. J. (1983). Personality and interior office design: Exploring the accuracy of visitor attributions. *Journal of Applied Psychology, 68,* 541–544.

36. Molloy, J. T. (1993). *John T. Molloy's new dress for success.* New York: Warner; Molloy, J. T. (1987). *The woman's dress for success book.* New York: Warner.

37. Rafaeli, A., & Pratt, M. G. (1993). Tailored meanings: On the meaning and impact of organizational dress. *Academy of Management Review, 18,* 32–55; Solomon, M. R. (1986, April). Dress for effect. *Psychology Today,* 20–28; Solomon, M. R. (Ed.). (1985). *The psychology of fashion.* New York: Lexington.

38. Forsythe, S., Drake, M. F., & Cox, C. E. (1985). Influence of applicant's dress on interviewer's selection decisions. *Journal of Applied Psychology, 70,* 374–378.

39. Solomon, 1986.

40. Tannen, D. (1994). Talking from 9 to 5. New York, NY: William Morrow and Company, Inc.

41. Koonce, R. (1997, September). Language, sex, and power: Women and men in the workplace. Training & Development, pp. 34-39.

42. Tannen, D. (1995, September-October). The power of talk: Who gets heard and why. Harvard Business Review, 73, pp.138-148.

43. Koonce, 1997.

44. Tannen, 1994.

45. Koonce, 1997; Tannen, 1995.

46. Adler, N. J. (1992). *International dimensions of organizational behavior* (2nd ed.). Belmont, CA: Wadsworth, p. 66.

47. Ramsey, S., & Birk, J. (1983). Preparation of North Americans for interaction with Japanese: Considerations of language and communication style. In D. Landis & R. W. Brislin (Eds.), *Handbook of intercultural training* (Vol. III). New York: Pergamon.

48. Ekman, P. (Ed.). (1982). *Emotion in the human face* (2nd ed.). Cambridge: Cambridge University Press. See also Ekman, P. (1993). Facial expression and emotion. *American Psychologist, 48,* 384–392.

49. Furnham, A., & Bocher, S. (1986). *Culture shock: Psychological reactions to unfamiliar environments.* London: Methuen, pp. 207–208.

50. Examples on gaze and touch draw on Furnham & Bocher, 1986; Argyle, M. (1982). Inter-cultural communication. In S. Bochner (Ed.), *Cultures in contact: Studies in cross-cultural interaction.* Oxford: Pergamon.

51. Collett, P. (1971). Training Englishmen in the non-verbal behaviour of Arabs: An experiment on intercultural communication. *International Journal of Psychology, 6,* 209–215.

52. Furnham & Bochner, 1986; Argyle, 1982.

53. Ramsey & Birk, 1983, p. 235.

54. Furnham & Bochner, 1986; Argyle, 1982.

55. Tannen, D. (1995, September-October). The power of talk: Who gets heard and why. *Harvard Business Review, 73,* pp.138-148.

56. Levine, R., West, L. J., & Reis, H. T. (1980). Perceptions of time and punctuality in the United States and Brazil. *Journal of Personality and Social Psychology, 38,* 541–550.

57. Hall, E. T., & Hall, M. R. (1990). *Understanding cultural differences.* Yarmouth, ME: Intercultural Press.

58. Dulek, R. E., Fielden, J. S., & Hill, J. S. (1991, January–February). International communication: An executive primer. *Business Horizons,* 20–25.

59. The following relies in part on Whetten, D. A., & Cameron, K. S. (1991). *Developing management skills* (2nd ed.). New York: HarperCollins; DeVito, J. A. (1992). *The interpersonal communication book* (6th ed.). New York: HarperCollins; Athos, A. G., & Gabarro, J. J. (1978). *Interpersonal behavior.* Englewood Cliffs, NJ: Prentice-Hall.

60. Duleck et al, 1991.

61. Daft, R. L., & Lengel, R. H. (1984). Information richness: A new approach to managerial behavior and organizational design. *Research in Organizational Behavior, 6,* 191–233.

62. Siegel, J., Dubrovsky, V., Kiesler, S., & McGuire, T. W. (1986). Group processing in computer mediated communication. *Organizational Behavior and Human Decision Processes, 37,* 157–187.

63. Lengel, R. H., & Daft, R. L. (1988, August). The selection of communication media as an executive skill. *Academy of Management Executive,* 225–232.

64. Prince, J. B. (1994, January). Performance appraisal and reward practices for total quality organizations. *Quality Management Journal,* 36–46; Newman, R. J. (1993, November 1). Job reviews go full circle. *U.S. News & World Report;* Cardy, B., & Dobbins, G. (1993, Spring). The changing face of performance appraisal: Customer evaluations and 360 appraisals. *Human Resources Division News,* 17–18.

65. Walker, A.G., and Smither, J.W. (1999). A five-year study of upward feedback: What managers do with their results matters. *Personal Psychology, 52,* pp. 393-423.

66. For a good description of how to develop and use organizational surveys, see Dunham, R. B., & Smith, F. J. (1979). *Organizational surveys.* Glenview, IL: Scott, Foresman. See also Rosenfeld, P., Edwards, J. E., & Thomas, M. D. (1993). Improving organizational surveys: New directions and methods (special issue). *American Behavioral Scientist, 36,* 411–550.

67. Lublin, J. S. (1997, June 18). Dear Boss: I'd rather not tell you my name, but... *Wall Street Journal,* pp. B1, B15.

68. Taft, W. F. (1985). Bulletin boards, exhibits, hotlines. In C. Reuss & D. Silvis (Eds.), *Inside organizational communication* (2nd ed.). New York: Longman.

69. Templin, N. (1993, December 7). Companies use TV to reach their workers. *Wall Street Journal,* pp. B1, B10.

70. Burnaska, R. (1976). The effects of behavior modeling training upon managers' behaviors and employees' perceptions. *Personnel Psychology, 29,* 329–335.

71. Capella, J. N. (1981). Mutual influence in expressive behavior: Adult-adult and infant-adult dyadic interaction. *Psychological Bulletin, 89,* 101–132.

Chapter 11

1. Sources include Capers, R. S., & Lipton, E. (1993, November). Hubble error: Time, money, and millionths of an inch. *Academy of Management Executive,* 41–57 (originally published in *Hartford Courant*); Broad, W. J. (1993, December 7). Some feared mirror flaws even before Hubble orbit. *New York Times,* pp. C1, C10; Rosewicz, B. (1993, November 29). Shuttle aims to fix Hubble and more. *Wall Street Journal,* p. B6. Capers, R. S. (1994). NASA post Hubble: Too little, too late? *Academy of Management Executive,* 8, pp. 68-72; Dunn, M. (1999, December 22). Shuttle snares ailing Hubble for repairs. *The Toronto Star,* p. A14.

2. Mintzberg, H. (1979). *The structuring of organizations.* Englewood Cliffs, NJ: Prentice-Hall.

3. MacCrimmon, K. R., & Taylor, R. N. (1976). Decision making and problem solving. In M. D. Dunnette (Ed.), *Handbook of industrial and organizational psychology.* Chicago: Rand McNally.

4. Simon, H. A. (1957). *Administrative behavior* (2nd ed.). New York: Free Press.

5. Bazerman, M. (1990). *Judgment in managerial decision making* (2nd ed.). New York: Wiley.

6. Whyte, G. (1991, August). Decision failures: Why they occur and how to prevent them. *Academy of Management Executive,* 23–31; Russo, J. E., & Schoemaker, P. J. H. (1989). *Decision traps.* New York: Doubleday.

7. The latter two difficulties are discussed by Huber, G. P. (1980). *Managerial decision making.* Glenview, IL: Scott, Foresman. For further discussion of problem identification, see Kiesler, S., & Sproull, L. (1982). Managerial response to changing environments: Perspectives on problem sensing from social cognition. *Administrative Science Quarterly, 27,* 548–570; Cowan, D. A. (1986). Developing a process model of problem recognition. *Academy of Management Review, 11,* 763–776.

8. Whyte, 1991; Russo & Schoemaker, 1989.

9. Tversky, A., & Kahneman, D. (1973). Availability: A heuristic for judging frequency and probability. *Cognitive Psychology, 5,* 207–232. Also see Taylor, S. E., and Fiske, S. T. (1978). Salience, attention, and attribution: Top of the head phenomena. In L. Berkowitz (Ed.), *Advances in experimental social psychology* (Vol. 11). New York: Academic Press.

10. Lichtenstein, S., Fischhoff, B., & Phillips, L. D. (1982). Calibration of probabilities: The state of the art in 1980. In D. Kahneman, P. Slovic, & A. Tversky (Eds.), *Judgment under uncertainty: Heuristics and biases.* Cambridge: Cambridge University Press.

11. Markels, A. (1997, April 8). Memo 4/8/97, FYI: Messages inundate offices. *The Wall Street Journal,* B1, B8.

12. Miller, J. G. (1960). Information input, overload, and psychopathology. *American Journal of Psychiatry, 116,* 695–704.

13. Manis, M., Fichman, M., & Platt, M. (1978). Cognitive integration and referential communication: Effects of information quality and quantity in message decoding. *Organizational Behavior and Human Performance, 22,* 417–430; Troutman, C. M., & Shanteau, J. (1977). Inferences based on nondiagnostic information. *Organizational Behavior and Human Performance, 19,* 43–55.

14. O'Reilly, C. A., III. (1980). Individuals and information overload in organizations: Is more necessarily better? *Academy of Management Journal, 23,* 684–696.

15. Feldman, M. S., & March, J. G. (1981). Information in organizations as signal and symbol. *Administrative Science Quarterly, 26,* 171–186.

16. Kahneman et al, 1982; Tversky, A., & Kahneman, D. (1976). Judgment under uncertainty: Heuristics and biases. *Science, 185,* 1124–1131.

17. Northcraft, G. B., & Neale, M. A. (1987). Experts, amateurs, and real estate: An anchoring-and-adjustment perspective on property pricing decisions. *Organizational Behavior and Human Decision Processes, 39,* 84–97.

18. Simonson, I., & Nye, P. (1992). The effect of accountability on susceptibility to decision errors. *Organizational Behavior and Human Decision Processes, 51,* 416–446.

19. Simon, H. A. (1957). *Models of man.* New York: Wiley; Cyert, R. M., & March, J. G. (1963). *A behavioral theory of the firm.* Englewood Cliffs, NJ: Prentice-Hall. For an example, see Bower, J., & Zi-Lei, Q. (1992). Satisficing when buying information. *Organizational Behavior and Human Decision Processes, 51,* 471–481.

20. Bazerman, 1990, pp. 1–2.

21. Kahneman, D., & Tversky, A. (1979). Prospect theory: An analysis of decision under risk. *Econometrica, 47,* 263–291.

22. Whyte, 1991.

23. Sitkin, S. B., & Pablo, A. L. (1992). Conceptualizing the determinants of risk behavior. *Academy of Management Review, 17,* 9–38.

24. For a detailed treatment and other perspectives, see Northcraft, G. B., & Wolf, G. (1984). Dollars, sense, and sunk costs: A life cycle model of resource allocation decisions. *Academy of Management Review, 9,* 225–234.

25. Brockner, J. (1992). The escalation of commitment to a failing course of action: Toward theoretical progress. *Academy of Management Review, 17,* 39–61; Staw, B. M., & Ross, J. (1987). Understanding escalation situations: Antecedents, prototypes, and solutions. *Research on Organizational Behavior, 9,* 39–78.

26. Staw, B. M. (1981). The escalation of commitment to a course of action. *Academy of Management Review, 6,* 577–587. For the limitations on this view, see Knight, P. A. (1984). Heroism versus competence: Competing explanations for the effects of experimenting and consistent management. *Organizational Behavior and Human Performance, 33,* 307–322.

27. Arkes, H. R., & Blumer, C. (1985). The psychology of sunk cost. *Organizational Behavior and Human Decision Processes, 35,* 124–140.

28. Whyte, G. (1986). Escalating commitment to a course of action: A reinterpretation. *Academy of Management Review, 11,* 311–321.

29. Simonson & Nye, 1992; White, 1991; Simonson, I., & Staw, B. M. (1992). Deescalation strategies: A comparison of techniques for reducing commitment to losing courses of action. *Journal of Applied Psychology, 77,* 419–426.

30. Whyte, G. (1993). Escalating commitment in individual and group decision making: A prospect theory approach. *Organizational Behavior and Human Decision Processes, 54,* 430–455.

31. Hawkins, S. A., & Hastie, R. (1990). Hindsight: Biased judgments of past events after outcomes are known. *Psychological Bulletin, 107,* 311–327.

32. Greenwald, A. G. (1980). The totalitarian ego: Fabrication and revision of personal history. *American Psychologist, 35,* 603–618.

33. Mitchell, T. R., & Beach, L. R. (1977). Expectancy theory, decision theory, and occupational preference and choice. M. F. Kaplan & S. Schwartz (Eds.), *Human judgment and decision processes in applied settings.* New York: Academic Press.

34. Pinfield, L. T. (1986). A field evaluation of perspectives on organizational decision making. *Administrative Science Quarterly, 31,* 365–388.

35. Nutt, P. C. (1989). *Making tough decisions.* San Francisco: Jossey-Bass.

36. Nutt, P. C. (1999). Surprising but true: Half the decisions in organizations fail. *The Academy of Management Executive, 13,* pp. 75-90.

37. Lord, R. G., & Maher, K. J. (1990). Alternative information-processing models and their implications for theory, research, and practice. *Academy of Management Review, 15,* 9–28.

38. Shaw, M. E. (1981). *Group dynamics* (3rd ed.). New York: McGraw-Hill, p. 78.

39. Hill, G. W. (1982). Group versus individual performance: Are n+1 heads better than one? *Psychological Bulletin, 91,* 517–539.

40. Shaw, 1981; Davis, J. H. (1969). *Group performance.* Reading, MA: Addison-Wesley; Libby, R., Trotman, K. T., & Zimmer, I. (1987). Member variation, recognition of expertise, and group performance. *Journal of Applied Psychology, 72,* 81–87.

41. Janis, I. L. (1972). *Victims of groupthink.* Boston: Houghton Mifflin.

42. Esser, J.K. (1998). Alive and well after 25 years: A review of groupthink research. *Organizational Behavior and Human Decision Processes, 73,* pp. 116-141.

43. Aldag, R. J., & Fuller, S. R. (1993) Beyond fiasco: A reappraisal of the groupthink phenomenon and a new model of group decision processes. *Psychological Bulletin, 113,* 533–552; McCauley, C. (1989). The nature of social influence in groupthink: Compliance and internalization. *Journal of Personality and Social Psychology, 57,* 250–260. For another view of causes, see Whyte, G. F. (1989). Groupthink reconsidered. *Academy of Management Review, 14,* 40–56.

44. Janis, 1972.

45. Moorhead, G., Ference, R., & Neck, C. P. (1991). Group decision fiascoes continue: Space shuttle Challenger and a revised groupthing framework. *Human Relations,* 539–550. Esser, 1998.

46. This is our analysis. The data cited is from Capers & Lipton, 1993.

47. Hart, P. (1998). Preventing groupthink revisited: Evaluating and reforming groups in government. *Organizational Behavior and Human Decision Processes, 73,* pp. 306-326.

48. Stoner, J. A. F. (1961). *A comparison of individual and group decisions involving risk.* Unpublished Master's thesis. School of Industrial Management, Massachusetts Institute of Technology.

49. Lamm, H., & Myers, D. G. (1978). Group-induced polarization of attitudes and behavior. In L. Berkowitz (Ed.), *Advances in experimental social psychology* (Vol. 11). New York: Academic Press.

50. Isenberg, D. J. (1986). Group polarization: A critical review and meta-analysis. *Journal of Personality and Social Psychology, 50,* 1141–1151.

51. Nutt, 1999.

52. Maier, N. R. F. (1973). *Psychology in industrial organizations* (4th ed.). Boston: Houghton Mifflin; Maier, N. R. F. (1970). *Problem solving and creativity in individuals and groups.* Belmont, CA: Brooks/Cole.

53. Tjosvold, D. (1985). Implications of controversy research for management. *Journal of Management, 11*(3), 21–37.

54. Schwenk, C. R. (1984). Devil's advocacy in managerial decision-making. *Journal of Management Studies, 21,* 153–168. For a study, see Schwenk, C., & Valacich, J. S. (1994). Effects of devil's advocacy and dialectical inquiry on individuals versus groups. *Organizational Behavior and Human Decision Processes, 59,* 210–222.

55. Osborn, A. F. (1957). *Applied imagination.* New York: Scribners.

56. See for example Madsen, D. B., & Finger, J. R., Jr. (1978). Comparison of a written feedback procedure, group brainstorming, and individual brainstorming. *Journal of Applied Psychology, 63,* 120–123.

57. Delbecq, A. L., Van de Ven, A. H., & Gustafson, D. H. (1975). *Group techniques for program planning.* Glenview, IL: Scott, Foresman, p. 8.

58. Delbecq et al., 1975.

59. Gallupe, R. B., Dennis, A. R., Cooper, W. H., Valacich, J. S., Bastianutti, L. M., & Nunamaker, J. F., Jr. (1992). Electronic brainstorming and group size. *Academy of Management Journal, 35,* 350–369. See also Dennis, A. R., & Valacich, J. S. (1993). Computer brainstorms: More heads are better than one. *Journal of Applied Psychology, 78,* 531–537.

60. The following relies on Kiesler, S., & Sproull, L. (1992). Group decision making and communication technology. *Organizational Behavior and Human Decision Processes, 52,* 96–123.

61. McGuire, T., Kiesler, S., & Siegel, J. (1987). Group and computer-mediated discussion effects in risk decision making. *Journal of Personality and Social Psychology, 52,* 917–930.

Chapter 12

1. Verburg, P. (1999, February, 26). Olympic flameout. *Canadian Business,* p.11, 12; 60 Minutes program, ÒOlympic GoldÓ, aired March 1999; Came, B. (1999, March 29). The games begin again. *Maclean's,* pp.30-33; CBC National Magazine program called ÒReform the RingsÓ, aired on April 22, 1999; (1999, February 10). Salt Lake City condemns its own in ethics report. *National Post* (The Associated Press); (1999, February 3). Nagano showered millions on IOC members. *The Globe and Mail,* S12 (Reuters News Agency, Tokyo); Fisher, M., & Brubaker, B. (1999, January 24). The lords of the rings. *The Toronto Star,* p. A12. (Washington Post); (1999, January 22). Salt Lake offers worth $100,000 probe finds. *National Post,* (The Associated Press and The Canadian Press); Starkman, R. (1999, January 23). IOC bigwigs' heads buried deep in sand. *The Toronto Star,* p. E4.

2. Brass, D. J., & Burkhardt, M. E. (1993). Potential power and power use: An investigation of structure and behavior. *Academy of Management Journal, 36,* 441–470.

3. These descriptions of bases of power were developed by French, J. R. P., Jr., & Raven, B. (1959). In D. Cartwright (Ed.), *Studies in social power.* Ann Arbor, MI: Institute for Social Research.

4. Rahim, M. A. (1989). Relationships of leader power to compliance and satisfaction with supervision: Evidence from a national sample of managers. *Journal of Management, 15,* 545–556; Tannenbaum, A. S. (1974). *Hierarchy in organizations.* San Francisco: Jossey-Bass.

5. Podsakoff, P. M., & Schriesheim, C. A. (1985). Field studies of French and Raven's bases of power: Critique, reanalysis, and suggestions for future research. *Psychological Bulletin, 97,* 387–411.

6. Heider, F. (1958). *The psychology of interpersonal relations*. New York: Wiley.

7. Grossman, L. M. (1993, March 10). As secretaries buy more for their firms, marketers regard them with reverence. *Wall Street Journal*, pp. B1, B8.

8. Podsakoff & Schriesheim, 1985.

9. Ragins, B. R., & Sundstrom, E. (1990). Gender and perceived power in manager-subordinate dyads. *Journal of Occupational Psychology, 63*, 273–287.

10. The following is based upon Kanter, R. M. (1977). *Men and women of the corporation*. New York: Basic Books. For additional treatment see Pfeffer, J. (1992). *Managing with power: Politics and influence in organizations*. Boston: Harvard Business School Press.

11. See Thomas, K. W., & Velthouse, B. A. (1990). Cognitive elements of empowerment: An "interpretative" model of intrinsic task motivation. *Academy of Management Review, 15*, 668–681; Conger, J. A., & Kanungo, R. N. (1988). The empowerment process: Integrating theory and practice. *Academy of Management Review, 13*, 471–482.

12. Tichy, N. M., & Sherman, S. (1993, June). Walking the talk at GE. *Training and Development*, 26–35.

13. Bowen, D. E., & Lawler, E. E., III. (1992, Spring). The empowerment of service workers: What, why, how, and when. *Sloan Management Review*, 31–39.

14. Kipnis, D., Schmidt, S. M., & Wilkinson, I. (1980). Intraorganizational influence tactics: Explorations in getting one's way. *Journal of Applied Psychology, 65*, 440–452; Kipnis, D., & Schmidt, S. M. (1988). Upward-influence styles: Relationship with performance evaluation, salary, and stress. *Administrative Science Quarterly, 33*, 528–542.

15. See Brass & Burkhardt, 1993.

16. Kipnis et al., 1980. See also Keys, B., & Case, T. (1990, November). How to become an influential manager. *Academy of Management Executive*, 38–51.

17. Kipnis & Schmidt, 1988.

18. Kipnis, D. (1976). *The powerholders*. Chicago: University of Chicago Press.

19. McClelland, D. C. (1975). *Power: The inner experience*. New York: Irvington.

20. Winter, D. G. (1988). The power motive in women—and men. *Journal of Personality and Social Psychology, 54*, 510–519.

21. McClelland, D. C., & Burnham, D. H. (1976, March–April). Power is the great motivator. *Harvard Business Review*, 100–110.

22. Ashforth, B. E. (1989). The experience of powerlessness in organizations. *Organizational Behavior and Human Decision Processes, 43*, 207–242.

23. Salancik, G. R., & Pfeffer, J. (1977, Winter). Who gets power—and how they hold on to it: A strategic contingency model of power. *Organizational Dynamics*, 3–21.

24. Salancik, G. R., & Pfeffer, J. (1974). The bases and use of power in organizational decision making: The case of a university. *Administrative Science Quarterly, 19*, 453–473. Also see Pfeffer, J., & Moore, W. L. (1980). Power in university budgeting: A replication and extension. *Administrative Science Quarterly, 25*, 637–653. For conditions under which the power thesis breaks down, see Schick, A. G., Birch, J. B., & Tripp, R. E. (1986). Authority and power in university decision making: The case of a university personnel budget. *Canadian Journal of Administrative Sciences, 3*, 41–64.

25. Hickson, D. J., Hinings, C. R., Lee, C. A., Schneck, R. E., & Pennings, J. M. (1971). A strategic contingency theory of intraorganizational power. *Administrative Science Quarterly, 16*, 216–229; for support of this theory, see Hinings, C. R., Hickson, D. J., Pennings, J. M., & Schneck, R. E. (1974). Structural conditions of intraorganizational power. *Administrative Science Quarterly, 19*, 22–44; Saunders, C. S., & Scamell, R. (1982). Intraorganizational distributions of power: Replication research. *Academy of Management Journal, 25*, 192–200; Hambrick, D. C. (1981). Environment, strategy, and power within top management teams. *Administrative Science Quarterly, 26*, 253–276.

26. Kanter, 1977, pp. 170–171.

27. Hickson et al., 1971; Hinings et al., 1974.

28. Hickson et al., 1971; Hinings et al., 1974; Saunders & Scamell, 1982.

29. Kipnis, 1976, p. 159.

30. Nulty, P. (1989, July 31). The hot demand for new scientists. *Fortune*, 155–163.

31. Nord, W. R., & Tucker, S. (1987). *Implementing routine and radical innovations*. Lexington, MA: Lexington Books.

32. Mayes, B. T., & Allen, R. W. (1977). Toward a definition of organizational politics. *Academy of Management Review, 2*, 672–678.

33. Porter, L. W., Allen, R. W., & Angle, H. L. (1981). The politics of upward influence in organizations. *Research in Organizational Behavior, 3*, 109–149.

34. Porter et al., 1981; Madison, D. L., Allen, R. W., Porter, L. W., Renwick, P. A., & Mayes, B. T. (1980). Organizational politics: An exploration of managers' perceptions. *Human Relations, 33*, 79–100.

35. Geis, F., & Christie, R. (1970). Overview of experimental research. In R. Christie & F. Geis (Eds.), *Studies in Machiavellianism*. New York: Academic Press.

36. Geis & Christie, 1970.

37. Brass, D. J. (1984). Being in the right place: A structural analysis of individual influence in an organization. *Administrative Science Quarterly, 29*, 518–539.

38. Kotter, J. P. (1982). *The general managers*. New York: Free Press.

39. Shellenbarger, S. (1993, December 16). I'm still here! Home workers worry they're invisible. *Wall Street Journal*, pp. B1, B4.

40. What follows relies on Ashforth, B. E., & Lee, R. T. (1990). Defensive behavior in organizations: A preliminary model. *Human Relations, 43*, 621–648.

41. Boeker, W. (1992). Power and managerial dismissal: Scapegoating at the top. *Administrative Science Quarterly, 37*, 400–421.

42. This draws loosely on Glenn, J. R., Jr. (1986). *Ethics in decision making*. New York: Wiley.

43. For reviews, see Tsalikis, J., & Fritzsche, D. J. (1989). Business ethics: A literature review with a focus on marketing ethics. *Journal of Business Ethics, 8*, 695–743; Trevino, L. K. (1986). Ethical decision making in organizations: A person-situation interactionist model. *Academy of Management Review, 11*, 601–617.

44. Tyson, T. (1992). Does believing that everyone else is less ethical have an impact on work behavior? *Journal of Business Ethics, 11*, 707–717.

45. Tsalikis & Fritzsche, 1989.

46. Kaynama, S.A., King, A., and Smith, L.W. (1996). The impact of a shift in organizational role on ethical perceptions: A comparative study. *Journal of Business Ethics, 15*, pp. 581-590.

47. Franke, G.R., Crown, D.F., and Spake, D.F. (1997). Gender differences in ethical perceptions of business practices: A social role theory perspective. *Journal of Applied Psychology, 82*, pp. 920-934.

48. Tsalikis & Fritzsche, 1989.

49. Bird, F., & Waters, J. A. (1987). The nature of managerial moral standards. *Journal of Business Ethics, 6*, 1–13.

50. Trevino, L. K., Sutton, C. D., & Woodman, R. W. (1985). *Effects of reinforcement contingencies and cognitive moral development on ethical decision-making behavior: An experiment*. Paper presented at the annual meeting of the Academy of Management, San Diego; Hegarty, W. H., & Sims, H. P., Jr. (1978). Some determinants of unethical behavior: An experiment. *Journal of Applied Psychology, 63*, 451–457.

51. Levine, D. B. (1990, May 21). The inside story of an inside trader. *Fortune*, 80–89, p. 82.

52. Grover, S. L. (1993). Why profesionals lie: The impact of professional role conflict on reporting accuracy. *Organizational Behavior and Human Decision Processes, 55*, 251–272.

53. Staw, B. M., & Szwajkowski, E. W. (1975). The scarcity-munificence component of organizational environments and the commission of illegal acts.

Administrative Science Quarterly, 20, 345–354.

54. Sonnenfeld, J., & Lawrence, P. R. (1989). Why do companies succumb to price fixing? In K. R. Andrew (Ed.), *Ethics in practice: Managing the moral corporation*. Boston: Harvard Business School Press.

55. Hegarty & Sims, 1978; Hegarty, W. H., & Sims, H. P., Jr. (1979). Organizational philosophy, policies, and objectives related to unethical decision behavior: A laboratory experiment. *Journal of Applied Psychology, 64*, 331–338.

56. Colby, A., & Kohlberg, L. (1987). *The measurement of moral judgment. Volume 1: Theoretical foundations and research validation*. Cambridge: Cambridge University Press; also see Trevino, 1986, and Grover, 1993.

57. Victor, B., & Cullen, J. B. (1988). The organizational bases of ethical work climates. *Administrative Science Quarterly, 33*, 101–125.

58. Baucus, M. S., & Near, J. P. (1991). Can illegal corporate behavior be predicted? An event history analysis. *Academy of Management Journal, 34*, 9–16.

59. Baucus & Near, 1991.

60. Sonnenfeld & Lawrence, 1989. See also Hosmer, L. T. (1987). The institutionalization of unethical behavior. *Journal of Business Ethics, 6*, 439–447.

61. Morgan, R. B. (1993). Self- and coworker perceptions of ethics and their relationships to leadership and salary. *Academy of Management Journal, 36*, 200–214.

62. Luthans, F., Hodgetts, R. M., & Rosenkrantz, S. A. (1988). *Real managers*. Cambridge, MA: Ballinger.

63. O'Hara, J. (1998, May 25). Rape in the military. *Maclean's*, p.14.

64. Peirce, E., Smolinski, C. A., & Rosen, B. (1998). Why sexual harassment complaints fall on deaf ears. *Academy of Management Executive, 12*, pp. 41–54.

65. Seppa, N. (1997, May). Sexual harassment in the military lingers on. *APA Monitor, 28*(5), pp. 40-41.

66. Schneider, K. T., Swan, S., & Fitzgerald, L. F. (1997). Job-related psychological effects of sexual harassment in the workplace: Empirical evidence from two organizations. *Journal of Applied Psychology, 82*, pp. 401–415.

67. Murray, B. (1998, July). Workplace harassment hurts everyone on the job. *APA Monitor, 29*(7), p. 35.

68. Schneider, Swan, & Fitzgerald, 1997.

69. Cleveland, J. N., & Kerst, M. E. (1993). Sexual harassment and perceptions of power: An underarticulated relationship. *Journal of Vocational Behavior, 42*, 49–67.

70. Seppa, 1997.

71. Seppa, 1997.

72. Peirce, Smolinski, & Rosen, 1998; Seppa, 1997.

73. O'Hara, 1998.

74. Peirce, Smolinski, & Rosen, 1998.

75. Peirce, Smolinski, & Rosen, 1998.

76. Peirce, Smolinski, & Rosen, 1998.

77. Flynn, G. (1997, February). Respect is key to stopping harassment. *Workforce, 76*(2), p. 56.

78. Peirce, Smolenski, & Rosen, 1998.

79. Weaver, G.R., Trevi–o, L.K., and Cochran, P.L. (1999). Corporate ethics programs as control systems: Influences of executive commitment and environmental factors. *Academy of Management Journal, 42*, pp. 41–57.

80. This draws on Waters, J. A., & Bird, F. (1988). *A note on what a well-educated manager should be able to do with respect to moral issues in management*. Unpublished manuscript.

81. See Jones, T. M. (1991). Ethical decision making by individuals in organizations: An issue-contingent model. *Academy of Management Journal, 16*, 366–395.

82. Harringotn, S. J. (1991, February). What corporate America is teaching about ethics. *Academy of Management Executive*, 21–30, p. 24.

83. Weber, J. (1990). Measuring the impact of teaching ethics to future managers: A review, assessment, and recommendations. *Journal of Business Ethics, 9*, 183–190.

Chapter 13

1. Sources: Based on the following: White, J. B., & MacDonald, E. (1997, April 23). Generation Gap. *The Wall Street Journal*. p. A1, A13; Berton, L. (1996, July 29). Andersen flap could presage formal split. *The Wall Street Journal*, pp. B1, B7; MacDonald, E., & White, J. B. (1998, February 4). Divorce petition. *The Wall Street Journal*, pp. A1, A10; MacDonald, E. (November 22, 1999). Andersen Worldwide files counterclaim for $14.6 billion against one of its units. *The Wall Street Journal*, p. C26; MacDonald, E. (July 28, 1999). Andersen Consulting's breakup battle with Arthur Andersen nears showdown. *The Wall Street Journal*, p. A2; O'Crockett, R. O. (January 18, 1999). Next stop, splitsville: What a divorce will cost Andersen Consulting. *Business Week*, p. 100;

2. Kolb, D. M., & Bartunek, J. M. (Eds.) (1992). *Hidden conflict in organizations: Uncovering behind-the-scenes disputes*. Newbury Park, CA: Sage.

3. This section relies partly on Walton, R. E., & Dutton, J. M. (1969). The management of interdepartmental conflict: A model and review. *Administrative Science Quarterly, 14*, 73–84.

4. Kramer, R. M. (1991). Intergroup relations and organizational dilemmas: The role of categorization processes. *Research in Organizational Behavior, 13*, 191–228; Messick, D. M., & Mackie, D. M. (1989). Intergroup rela-

tions. *Annual Review of Psychology, 40*, 45–81; Ashforth, B. E., & Mael, F. (1989). Social identity theory and the organization. *Academy of Management Review, 14*, 20–39.

5. Johns, G. (1994). Absenteeism estimates by employees and managers: Divergent perspectives and self-serving perceptions. *Journal of Applied Psychology, 79*, 229–239.

6. See Whyte, W. F. (1948). *Human relations in the restaurant industry*. New York: McGraw-Hill.

7. Moritz, M. (1984). *The little kingdom: The private story of Apple Computer*. New York: Morrow, pp. 246–247.

8. Thomas, K. W. (1992). Conflict and negotiation in organizations. In M. D. Dunnette & L. M. Hough (Eds.), *Handbook of industrial and organizational psychology* (2nd ed., Vol. 3). Palo Alto, CA: Consulting Psychologists Press.

9. Sellers, P. (1991, November 18). A boring brand can be beautiful. *Fortune*, 169–179, p. 179.

10. Moore, M. L., Nichol, V. W., & McHugh, P. P. (1992). Review of no-fault absenteeism cases taken to arbitration, 1980–1989: A rights and responsibilities analysis. *Employee Rights and Responsibilities Journal, 5*, 29–48; Scott, K. D., & Taylor, G. S. (1983, September). An analysis of absenteeism cases taken to arbitration: 1975–1981. *The Arbitration Journal*, 61–70.

11. See Wilder, D. A. (1986). Social categorization: Implications for creation and reduction of intergroup bias. *Advances in Experimental Social Psychology, 19*, 291–349; Sherif, M. (1966). *In common predicament: Social psychology of intergroup conflict and cooperation*. Boston: Houghton Mifflin; Blake, R. R., Shepard, M. A., & Mouton, J. S. (1964). *Managing intergroup conflict in industry*. Houston: Gulf.

12. Thomas, 1992.

13. Seabrook, J. (1994, January 10). E-mail from Bill. *The New Yorker*, 48–61, p. 52.

14. Johnson, D. W., Maruyama, G., Johnson, R., Nelson, D., & Skon, L. (1981). Effects of cooperative and individualistic goal structures on achievement: A meta-analysis. *Psychological Bulletin, 89*, 47–62. See also Tjosvold, D. (1991). *The conflict-positive organization*. Reading, MA: Addison-Wesley.

15. Magnet, M. (1994, February 21). The new golden rule of business. *Fortune*, 60–64.

16. Tjosvold, D., Dann, V., & Wong, C. (1992). Managing conflict between departments to serve customers. *Human Relations, 45*, 1035–1054.

17. Neale, M. A., & Bazerman, M. H. (1992, August). Negotiating rationally: The power and impact of the negotiator's frame. *Academy of Management Executive*, 42–51, p. 42.

18. Wall, J. A., Jr. (1985). *Negotiation: Theory and practice*. Glenview, IL: Scott, Foresman.

19. Walton, R. E., & McKerzie, R. B. (1991). *A behavioral theory of labor negotiations* (2nd ed.). Ithaca, NY: ILR Press.

20. What follows draws on Pruitt, D. G. (1981). *Negotiation behavior*. New York: Academic Press.

21. Wall, J. A., Jr., & Blum, M. (1991). Negotiations. *Journal of Management, 17*, 273–303.

22. Wall & Blum, 1991.

23. Bazerman, M. H. (1990). *Judgment in managerial decision making* (2nd ed.). New York: Wiley.

24. The following draws on Bazerman, M. H., & Neale, M. A. (1992). *Negotiating rationally*. New York: The Free Press.

25. Sherif, 1966; Hunger, J. D., & Stern, L. W. (1976). An assessment of the functionality of the superordinate goal in reducing conflict. *Academy of Management Journal, 19*, 591–605.

26. Pruitt, 1981; Kressel, K., & Pruitt, D. G. (1989). *Mediation research*. San Francisco: Jossey-Bass.

27. Kressel & Pruitt, 1989.

28. Wall & Blum, 1991; Pruitt, 1981.

29. Scott & Taylor, 1983. See also Moore et al., 1992.

30. Robbins, S. P. (1974). *Managing organizational conflict: A nontraditional approach*. Englewood, Cliffs, NJ: Prentice-Hall, p. 20.

31. Brown, L. D. (1983). *Managing conflict at organizational interfaces*. Reading, MA: Addison-Wesley.

32. Robbins, 1974; also see Brown, 1983.

33. Ramsay, L. (1999, March 15). Stress, the plague of the 1990s. *National Post*, p. D10. Best, P. (1999, February). All work (Stressed to the max? Join the club). *Report on Business Magazine*, p.3.

34. Underwood, A., & Kalb, C. (1999, June 14). Stress. *Newsweek*, pp. 54-63.

35. DeFrank, R. S., & Ivancevich, J. M. (1998). Stress on the job: An executive update. *Academy of Management Executive, 12*, pp. 55–66.

36. Xie, J. L., & Johns, G. (1995). Job scope and stress: Can job scope be too high? *Academy of Management Journal, 38*, pp. 1288-1309.

37. Cole, T. (1999, February). All the rage. *Report on Business Magazine*. pp. 50–57.

38. This model has much in common with many contemporary models of work stress. For a comprehensive summary see Kahn, R. L., & Byosiere, P. (1992). Stress in organizations. In M. D. Dunnette & L. M. Hough (Eds.), *Handbook of industrial and organizational psychology* (2nd ed., Vol. 3). Palo Alto, CA: Consulting Psychologists Press.

39. McGrath, J. E. (1970). A conceptual formulation for research on stress. In J. E. McGrath (Ed.), *Social and psychological factors in stress*. New York: Holt, Rinehart, Winston.

40. Roth, S., & Cohen, L. J. (1986). Approach, avoidance, and coping with stress. *American Psychologist, 41*, 813–819.

41. Kahn & Byosiere, 1992. For a recent study see Spector, P. E., & O'Connell, B. J. (1994). The contribution of personality traits, negative affectivity, locus of control, and Type A to the subsequent reports of job stressors and job strains. *Journal of Occupational and Organizational Psychology, 67*, 1–11.

42. Friedman, M., & Rosenman, R. (1974). *Type A Behavior and your heart*. New York: Knopf.

43. Chesney, M. A., & Rosenman, R. (1980). Type A behavior in the work setting. In C. L. Cooper and R. Payne (Eds.), *Current concerns in occupational stress*. Chichester, England: Wiley. For a typical study see Jamal, M., & Baba, V. V. (1991). Type A behavior, its prevalence and consequences among women nurses: An empirical examination. *Human Relations, 44*, 1213–1228.

44. Matthews, K. A. (1982). Psychological perspectives on the Type A behavior pattern. *Psychological Bulletin, 91*, 293–323. Fine, S. & Stinson, M. (2000, February 3). Stress is overwhelming people, study shows. *The Globe and Mail*, pp. A1, A7.

45. Booth-Kewley, S., & Friedman, H. S. (1987). Psychological predictors of heart disease: A quantitative review. *Psychological Bulletin, 101*, 343–362; Williams, R. (1989). *The trusting heart: Great news about Type A behavior*. New York: Random House; Ganster, D. C., Schaubroeck, J., Sime, W. E., & Mayes, B. T. (1991). The nomological validity of the Type A personality among employed adults. *Journal of Applied Psychology, 76*, 143–168.

46. Fine, S. & Stinson, M. (February 3, 2000). Stress is overwhelming people, study shows. *The Globe and Mail*, A1, A7.

47. Parasuraman, S., & Alutto, J. A. (1981). An examination of the organizational antecedents of stressors at work. *Academy of Management Journal, 24*, 48–67.

48. Mintzberg, H. (1973). *The nature of managerial work*. New York: Harper & Row.

49. An excellent review of managerial stressors can be found in Marshall, J., & Cooper, C. L. (1979). *Executives under pressure*. New York: Praeger.

50. Xie, J. L. & Johns, G. (1995). Job scope and stress: Can job scope be too high? *Academy of Management Journal, 38*, pp. 1288-1309.

51. Karasek, R. A., Jr. (1979). Job demands, job decision latitude, and mental strain: Implications for job redesign. *Administrative Science Quarterly, 24*, 285–308. Also see Fox, M. L., Dwyer, D. J., & Ganster, D. C. (1993). Effects of stressful job demands and control on physiological and attitudinal outcomes in a hospital setting. *Academy of Management Journal, 36*, 289–318.

52. Maslach, C., & Jackson, S. E. (1984). Burnout in organizational settings. In S. Oskamp (Ed.), *Applied social psychology annual* (Vol. 5). Beverly Hills, CA: Sage, p. 134.

53. Cordes, C. L., & Dougherty, T. W. (1993). A review and integration of research on job burnout. *Academy of Management Review, 18*, 621–656. For a comprehensive study see Lee, R. T., & Ashforth, B. E. (1993). A longitudinal study of burnout among supervisors and managers: Comparisons of the Leiter and Maslach (1988) and Golembiewski et al. (1986) models. *Organizational Behavior and Human Decision Processes, 54*, 369–398.

54. For a study of burnout among police personnel, see Burke, R. J., & Deszca, E. (1986). Correlates of psychological burnout phases among police officers. *Human Relations, 39*, 487–501.

55. See Pines, A. M., & Aronson, E. (1981). *Burnout: From tedium to personal growth*. New York: The Free Press.

56. Gibb-Clark, M. (1999, June 4). Work v. family: The $2.7-billion crisis. *The Globe and Mail*, p. M1.

57. Gibbs-Clark, 1999.

58. DeFrank, R. S., & Ivancevich, J. M. (1998). Stress on the job: An executive update. *Academy of Management Executive, 12*, pp. 55-66.

59. Jackson, S. E., & Schuler, R. S. (1985). Meta-analysis and conceptual critique of research on role ambiguity and conflict in work settings. *Organizational Behavior and Human Decision Processes, 36*, 16–78. For a critique of some of this research, see Fineman, S., & Payne, R. (1981). Role stress—A methodological trap? *Journal of Occupational Behaviour, 2*, 51–64.

60. Schneider, K. T., Swan, S., & Fitzgerald, L. F. (1997). Job-related and psychological effects of sexual harassment in the workplace: Empirical evidence from two organizations. *Journal of Applied Psychology, 82*, pp. 401-415; Fitzgerald, L. F., Drasgow, F., Hulin, C. L., Gelfand, M. J., & Magley, V. J. (1997). Antecedents and consequences of sexual harassment in organizations: A test of an integrated model. *Journal of Applied Psychology, 82*, pp. 578-589.

61. Schneider, Swan, & Fitzgerald, 1997; Fitzgerald, Drasgow, Hulin, Gelfand & Magley, 1997.

62. Schneider, Swan, & Fitzgerald, 1997.

63. Peirce, E., Smolinski, C. A., & Rosen, B. (1998). Why sexual harassment complaints fall on deaf ears. *Academy of Management Executive, 12*, 41–54; Schneider, Swan, & Fitzgerald, 1997.

64. Fitzgerald, Drasgow, Gelfand, & Magley (1997). Glomb, T. M., Munson, L. J., Hulin, C. L., Bergman, M. E., & Drasgoe, F. (1999). Structural equation models of sexual harassment: Longitudinal explorations and cross-sectional generalizations. *Journal of Applied Psychology, 84*, 14–28.

65. Jamal, M. (1984). Job stress and job performance controversy: An empirical assessment. *Organizational Behavior and Human Performance, 33*, 1–21; Motowidlo, S. J., Packard, J. S., & Manning, M. R. (1986). Occupational stress: Its causes and consequences for job performance. *Journal of Applied Psychology, 71*, 618–629.

66. Johns, G. (1997). Contemporary research on absence form work: Correlates, causes and consequences. *International Review of Industrial and Organizational Psychology, 12*, pp. 115–173.

67. Beehr, T. A., & Newman, J. E. (1978). Job stress, employee health, and organizational effectiveness: A facet analysis, model, and literature review. *Personnel Psychology, 32*, 665–699; Kahn & Byosiere, 1992.

68. Beehr & Newman, 1978. For a later review and a strong critique of this work, see Fried, Y., Rowland, K. M., & Ferris, G. R. (1984). The physiological measurement of work stress: A critique. *Personnel Psychology, 37*, 583–615. See also Fried, Y. (1989). The future of physiological assessments in work situations. In C. L. Cooper & R. Payne (Eds.), *Causes, coping, and consequences of stress at work*. Chichester, England: Wiley & Sons. Fine, S. & Stinson, M. (2000, February 3). Stress is overwhelming people, study shows. *The Globe and Mail*, p. A1, A7.

69. Fine & Stinson, 2000.

70. Cooper, C. L., Mallinger, M., & Kahn, R. (1978). Identifying sources of occupational stress among dentists. *Journal of Occupational Psychology, 61*, 163–174. See also DiMatteo, M. R, Shugars, D. A., & Hays, R. D. (1993). Occupational stress, life stess and mental health among dentists. *Journal of Occupational and Organizational Psychology, 66*, 153–162.

71. Cohen, S., & Williamson, G. M. (1991). Stress and infectious disease in humans. *Psychological Bulletin, 109*, 5–24.

72. Wall, T. D., & Clegg, C. W. (1981). A longitudinal field study of group work redesign. *Journal of Occupational Behaviour, 2*, 31–49.

73. Cohen, S., & Wills, T. A. (1985). Stress, social support, and the buffering hypothesis. *Psychological Bulletin, 98*, 310–357; Kahn & Byosiere, 1992.

74. This section relies on a *Wall Street Journal* special section on Work & Family (1993, June 21) and Shellenbarger, S. (1993, June 29). Work & family. *Wall Street Journal*, p. B1.

75. Ivancevich, J. M., Matteson, M. T., Freedman, S. M., & Phillips, J. S. (1990). Worksite stress management interventions. *American Psychologist, 45*, 252–261; Murphy, L. R. (1984). Occupational stress management: A review and appraisal. *Journal of Occupational Psychology, 57*, 1–15.

76. Ivancevich et al., 1990; Murphy, 1984.

77. Hampton, J. (June 14, 1999). Balancing between work and life. *Canadian HR Reporter* (Guide to Employee Benefits), pp. G1, G2.

78. Faught, L. (1997, April). At Eddie Bauer you can work and have a life. *Workforce, 76*(4), pp. 83-90.

79. Lush, T. (1998, October 3). Company with a conscience. *The Gazette*, p. C3.

80. Weiss, N. (1998, August). How Starbucks impassions workers to drive growth. *Workforce*, pp. 61–64.

81. Gebhardt, D. L., & Crump, C. E. (1990). Employee fitness and wellness programs in the workplace. *American Psychologist, 45*, 262–272; Jex, S. M. (1991). The psychological benefits of exercise in work settings: A review, critique, and dispositional model. *Work and Stress, 5*, 133–147; Falkenberg, L. E. (1987). Employee fitness programs: Their impact on the employee and the organization. *Academy of Management Review, 12*, 511–522.

Chapter 14

1. Corbett, B. (1989, September). A system of non-management. *Canadian*, pp. 14-20; Martin, J. (1998, January 12). So, you want to work for the best.... *Fortune*, pp. 77–78; Anfuso, D. (1999, March). Core values shape W. L. Gore's innovative culture. *Workforce, 78* (3), pp. 48–53; Huey, J. (1994, February 21). The new post-heroic leadership. *Fortune*, 42–50.

2. Mintzberg, H. (1979). *The structuring of organizations*. Englewood Cliffs, NJ: Prentice-Hall.

3. Lawrence, P. R., & Lorsch, J. W. (1969). *Organization and environment: Managing differentiation and integration*. Homewood, IL: Irwin.

4. For an extended treatment of the role of interdependence between departments, see McCann, J., & Galbraith, J. R. (1981). Interdepartmental relations. In P. C. Nystrom & W. H. Starbuck (Eds.), *Handbook of organizational design* (Vol. 2). Oxford, England: Oxford University Press.

5. For a comparison of functional and product departmentation, see McCann & Galbraith, 1981; Walker, A. H., & Lorsch, J. W. (1968, November–December). Organizational choice: Product vs. function. *Harvard Business Review*, 129–138.

6. See Davis, S. M., & Lawrence, P. M. (1977). *Matrix*. Reading, MA: Addison-Wesley.

7. Contemporary treatment of these forms of departmentation can be found in Daft, R. L. (1992). *Organization theory and design* (4th ed.). St. Paul, MN: West; Robey, D. (1991). *Designing organizations* (3rd ed.). Homewood, IL: Irwin.

8. Mintzberg, 1979.

9. See Hall, R. H. (1962). Intraorganizational structural variation: Application of the bureaucratic model. *Administrative Science Quarterly, 7*, 295–308.

10. Lawrence & Lorsch, 1969.

11. Galbraith, J. R. (1977). *Organization design*. Reading, MA: Addison-Wesley.

12. See Birnbaum, P. H. (1981). Integration and specialization in academic research. *Academy of Management Journal, 24*, 487–503.

13. This discussion relies on Galbraith, 1977.

14. Lawrence & Lorsch, 1969.

15. Galbraith, 1977.

16. These definitions of structural variables are common. However, there is considerable disagreement about how some should be measured. See Walton, E. J. (1981). The comparison of measures of organizational structure. *Academy of Management Review, 6*, 155–160.

17. Research on these hypotheses is sparse and not always in agreement. See Dewar, R. D., & Simet, D. P. (1981). A level specific prediction of spans of control examining effects of size, technology, and specialization. *Academy of Management Journal, 24*, 5–24; Van Fleet, D. D. (1983). Span of management research and issues. *Academy of Management Journal, 26*, 546–552.

18. Treece, J. B. (1990, April 9). Here comes GM's Saturn. *Business Week*, 56–62.

19. For a study, see Hetherington, R. W. (1991). The effects of formalization on departments of a multi-hospital system. *Journal of Management Studies, 28*, 103–141.

20. *60 Minutes*, October 17, 1993.

21. Mintzberg, 1979, p. 182.

22. Ritzer, 1993.

23. Personal communication with Food Lion's Brian Peace, April and May 1995.

24. Deutschman, A. (1994, May 2). How H-P continues to grow and grow. *Fortune*, 90–100, p. 98.

25. Daft, 1992.

26. The terms *mechanistic* and *organic* (to follow) were first used by Burns, T., & Stalker, G. M. (1961). *The management of innovation*. London: Tavistock Publications. For a relevant study, see Courtright, J. A., Fairhurst, G. T., & Rogers, L. E. (1989). Interaction patterns in organic and mechanistic systems. *Academy of Management Journal, 32*, 773–802.

27. Snow, C. C., Miles, R. F., & Coleman, H. J., Jr. (1992, Winter). Managing 21st century network organizations. *Organizational Dynamics*, 5–19; Miles,

R. E., & Snow, C. C. (1992, Summer). Causes of failure in network organizations. *California Management Review*, 53–72.

28. Dess, G.G., Rasheed, A.M.A., McLaughlin, K.J., and Priem, R.L. (1995). The new corporate architecture. Academy of Management Executive, 9, 7–20.

29. Miles & Snow, 1992.

30. Tully, S. (1993, February 8). The modular corporation. *Fortune*, pp. 106–114; Dess, G. G., Rasheed, A. M. A., McLaughlin, K. J., & Priem, R. L. (1995). The new corporate architecture. *Academy of Management Executive*, 9, pp. 7–20.

31. Tully, 1993; Dess, Rasheed, McLaughlin, Priem, 1995.

32. Tully, 1993.

33. Berman, D. (1996, September). Car and striver. *Canadian Business*, pp. 92–99.

34. Dess, Rashid, McLaughlin & Priem, 1995.

35. Berman, 1996.

36. Tully, 1993; Dess, Rasheed, McLaughlin, Priem, 1995.

37. Tully, 1993.

38. Dess, Rasheed, McLaughlin, Priem, 1995.

39. (1993, January 25). Jack Welch's lessons for success. *Fortune*, pp.86–93, Excerpt from Control Your Destiny or Someone Else Will, by Noel M. Tichy and Stratford Sherman (1993), Doubleday.

40. Rao, R. M. (1995, April 3). The struggle to create an organization for the 21st century. *Fortune*, pp. 90–99; Jacob, R. (1992, May 18). The search for the organization of tomorrow. *Fortune*, pp. 92–98.

41. Jacob, 1992.

42. Dess, Rasheed, McLaughlin, Priem, 1995.

43. Dess, Rasheed, McLaughlin, Priem, 1995.

44. (1993, January 25). Jack Welch's lessons for success. *Fortune*, pp.86–93, Excerpt from Control Your Destiny or Someone Else Will, by Noel M. Tichy and Stratford Sherman (1993), Doubleday

45. Rao, 1995; Jacob, 1992.

46. For a good general review of size research see Bluedorn, A. C. (1993). Pilgrim's progress: Trends and convergence in research on organizational size and environments. *Journal of Management, 19*, 163–191.

47. Much of this research was stimulated by Blau, P. M. (1970). A theory of differentiation in organizations. *American Sociological Review, 35*, 201–218. For a review and test, see Cullen, J. B., Anderson, K. S., & Baker, D. D. (1986). Blau's theory of structural differentiation revisited: A theory of structural change or scale? *Academy of Management Journal, 29*, 203–229.

48. Dewar, R., & Hage, J. (1978). Size, technology, complexity, and structural differentiation: Toward a theoretical

synthesis. *Administrative Science Quarterly, 23*, 111–136; Marsh, R. M., & Mannari, H. (1981). Technology and size as determinants of the organizational structure of Japanese factories. *Administrative Science Quarterly, 26*, 33–57.

49. Mansfield, R. (1973). Bureaucracy and centralization: An examination of organizational structure. *Administrative Science Quarterly, 18*, 77–88; Hage, J., & Aiken, M. (1967). Relationship of centralization to other structural properties. *Administrative Science Quarterly, 12*, 79–91.

50. DeWitt, R. L. (1993). The structural consequences of downsizing. *Organization Science, 4*, 30–40.

51. Freeman, S. J., & Cameron, K. S. (1993). Organizational downsizing: A convergence and reorientation framework. *Organization Science, 4*, 10–29.

52. Cascio, W. F. (1993, February). Downsizing: what do we know? What have we learned? *Academy of Management Executive*, 95–104.

53. DeWitt, 1993; Sutton, R. L., & D'Aunno, T. (1989). Decreasing organizational size: Untangling the effects of money and people. *Academy of Management Review, 14*, 194–212.

54. Cascio, 1993.

55. Brockner, J. (1988). The effects of work layoffs on survivors: Research, theory, and practice. *Research in Organizational Behavior, 10*, 213–255.

56. Burke, W.W. (1997, Summer). The new agenda for organization development. *Organizational Dynamics*, pp. 7–18.

57. Child, J. (1984). *Organization: A guide to problems and practice*. London: Harper & Row.

58. Presidential Commission. (1986). *The report on the space shuttle Challenger accident*. Washington, DC: U.S. Government Printing Office.

59. Pugh, D. (1979, Winter). Effective coordination in organizations. *Advanced Management Journal*, 28–35.

Chapter 15

1. Sources include: Staff. (1994, October 17). Will it work this time? *Autoweek*, 4–5; Bennet, J. (1994, March 29). Saturn, GM's big hope, is taking its first lumps. *New York Times*, pp. A1, A12; Woodruff, J. (1992, August 17). Saturn. *Business Week*, 86–91; Treece, J. B. (1990, April 9). Here comes GM's Saturn. *Business Week*, 56–62; Taylor, A., III. (1988, August 1). Back to the future at Saturn. *Fortune*, 63–69; Fisher, A. B. (1985, November 11). Behind the hype at GM's Saturn. *Fortune*, 34–49.(add) Austen, I. (1999, March 26). Problem child. *Canadian Business*, 22–31; Vaughn, M. (1999, July 5). Smiling happy people. *Autoweek*, 20–21.

2. Katz, D., & Kahn, R. L. (1978). *The social psychology of organizations* (2nd ed.). New York: Wiley.

3. This list relies upon Duncan, R. (1972). Characteristics of organization environments and perceived environmental uncertainty. *Administrative Science Quarterly, 17*, 313–327.

4. See Khandwalla, P. (1981). Properties of competing organizations. In P. C. Nystrom & W. H. Starbuck (Eds.), *Handbook of organization design* (Vol. 1). Oxford: Oxford University Press.

5. Zachary, G. P. (1994). Consolidation sweeps the software industry; small firms imperiled. *Wall Street Journal*, pp. A1, A6.

6. Volberda, H.W. (1996). Toward the flexible form: How to remain vital in hypercompetitive environments. *Organization Scene, 7*, pp. 359-374.

7. Kirkpatrick, D. (1990, February 12). Environmentalism: The new crusade. *Fortune*, 44–55.

8. Connolly, T., Conlon, E. J., & Deutsch, S. J. (1980). Organizational effectiveness: A multiple-constituency approach. *Academy of Management Review, 5*, 211–217.

9. Fisher, 1985.

10. Duncan, 1972; Just how to measure uncertainty has provoked controversy. See Milliken, F. J. (1987). Three types of perceived uncertainty about the environment: State, effect, and response uncertainty. *Academy of Management Review, 12*, 133–143; Downey, H. K., & Ireland, R. D. (1979). Quantitative versus qualitative: Environmental assessment in organizational studies. *Administrative Science Quarterly, 24*, 630–637.

11. Duncan, 1972; Tung, R. L. (1979). Dimensions of organizational environments: An exploratory study of their impact on organization structure. *Academy of Management Journal, 22*, 672–693. For contrary evidence, see Downey, H., Hellriegel, D., & Slocum, J. (1975). Environmental uncertainty: The construct and its application. *Administrative Science Quarterly, 20*, 613–629.

12. See also Leblebici, H., & Salancik, G. R. (1981). Effects of environmental uncertainty on information and decision processes in banks. *Administrative Science Quarterly, 26*, 578–596.

13. See At-Twaijri, M. I. A., & Montanari, J. R. (1987). The impact of context and choice on the boundary-spanning process: An empirical extension. *Human Relations, 40*, 783–798.

14. Pfeffer, J., & Salancik, G. R. (1978). *The external control of organizations: A resource dependence perspective*. New York: Harper & Row; Yasai-Ardekani, M. (1989). Effects of environmental scarcity and munificence on the relationship of context to organizational structure. *Academy of Management Journal, 32*, 131–156.

15. Castrogiovanni, G. J., (1991). Environmental munificence: A theoreti-

cal assessment. *Academy of Management Review, 16,* 542–565.

16. Pfeffer & Salancik, 1978.

17. Boyd, B. K., Dess, G. G., & Rasheed, A. M. A. (1993). Divergence between archival and perceptual measures of the environment: Causes and consequences. *Academy of Management Review, 18,* 204–226.

18. For an analog, see Miller, D., Dröge, C., & Toulouse, J. M. (1988). Strategic process and content as mediators between organizational context and structure. *Academy of Management Journal, 31,* 544–569.

19. Miles, R. C., & Snow, C. C. (1978). *Organizational strategy, structure, and process.* New York: McGraw-Hill.

20. Lawrence, P. R., & Lorsch, J. W. (1967). *Organization and environment: Managing differentiation and integration.* Homewood, IL: Irwin. For a follow-up study, see Lorsch, J. W., & Morse, J. J. (1974). *Organizations and their members: A contingency approach.* New York: Harper & Row.

21. For a review, see Miner, J. B. (1982). *Theories of organizational structure and process.* Chicago: Dryden.

22. Branch, S. (1997, October 13). What's eating McDonald's? *Fortune,* 122–125; Leonhardt, D. (1998, March 9). McDonald's: Can it regain its golden touch? *Business Week,* pp. 70–77; (1999, February 1). Greenberg serving up a fresher McDonald's. *National Post,* p. C2. (Bloomberg News).

23. Frederickson, J. W. (1986). The strategic decision process and organizational structure. *Academy of Management Review, 11,* 280–297.

24. Romme, A. G. L. (1990). Vertical integration as organizational strategy formation. *Organization Studies, 11,* 239–260.

25. Chatterjee, S., Lubatkin, M., & Schoenecker, T. (1992). Vertical strategies and market structure: A systematic risk analysis. *Organization Science, 3,* 138–156; D'Aveni, R. A., & Ilinitch, A. Y. (1992). Complex patterns of vertical integration in the forest products industry: Systematic and bankruptcy risks. *Academy of Management Journal, 35,* 596–625.

26. D'aveni, R.A., and Ravenscraft, D.J. (1994). Economies of integration versus bureaucracy costs: Does vertical integration improve performance? *Academy of Management Journal, 37*(5), pp. 1167-1206.

27. Pfeffer & Salancik, 1978; Hill, C. W. L., & Hoskisson, R. E. (1987). Strategy and structure in the multiproduct firm. *Academy of Management Review, 12,* 331–341; Lubatkin, M., & O'Neill, H. M. (1987). Merger strategies and capital market risk. *Academy of Management Journal, 30,* 665–684.

28. Kanter, R. M. (1989, August). Becoming PALS: Pooling, allying, and linking across companies. *Academy of Management Executive,* 183–193.

29. Burtt, D. N. (1989, July–August). Managing suppliers up to speed. *Harvard Business Review,* 127–135.

30. Parkhe, A. (1993). Strategic alliance structuring: A game theoretic and transaction cost examination of interfirm cooperation. *Academy of Management Journal, 36,* 794–829. See also Ring, P. S., & Van de Ven, A. H. (1994). Developmental processes of cooperative interorganizational relationships. *Academy of Management Review, 19,* 90–118.

31. Parkhe, A. (1993). Partner nationality and the structure-performance relationship in strategic alliances. *Organizational Science, 4,* 301–324.

32. Schoorman, F. D., Bazerman, M. H., & Atkin, R. S. (1981). Interlocking directorates: A strategy for reducing environmental uncertainty. *Academy of Management Review, 6,* 243–251, p. 244. For a recent study, see Haunschild, P. R., (1993). Interorganizational imitation: The impact of interlocks on corporate acquisition activity. *Administrative Science Quarterly, 38,* 564–592.

33. Schoorman et al., 1981.

34. See Oliver, C. (1991). Strategic responses to institutional processes. *Academy of Management Review, 16,* 145–179; Davis, G. F., & Powell, W. W. (1992). Organization-environment relations. In M. D. Dunnette & L. M. Hough (Eds.), *Handbook of industrial and organizational psychology* (2nd ed., Vol. 3). Palo Alto, CA: Consulting Psychologists Press.

35. Rousseau, D. M. (1979). Assessment of technology in organizations: Closed versus open systems approaches. *Academy of Management Review, 4,* 531–542.

36. Child, J. (1972). Organizational structure, environment and performance: The role of strategic choice. *Sociology, 6,* 2–22.

37. Rousseau, 1979; Gillsepie, D. F., & Mileti, D. S. (1977). Technology and the study of organizations: An overview and appraisal. *Academy of Management Review, 2,* 7–16.

38. Perrow, C. A. (1967). A framework for the comparative analysis of organizations. *American Sociological Review, 32,* 194–208.

39. Thompson, J. D. (1967). *Organizations in action.* New York: McGraw-Hill.

40. Thompson, 1967, p. 17.

41. Miller, C. C., Glick, W. H., Wang, Y. D., & Huber, G. P. (1991). Understanding technology-structure relationships: Theory development and meta-analytic throery testing. *Academy of Management Journal, 34,* 370–399. For information on measurement, see Withey, M., Daft, R. L., & Cooper, W. H. (1983). Measures of Perrow's work unit technology: An empirical assessment and a new scale. *Academy of Management Journal, 26,* 45–63.

42. Cheng, J. L. C. (1983). Interdependence and coordination in organizations: A role-system analysis. *Academy of Management Journal, 26,* 156–162.

43. Van de Ven, A. H., Delbecq, A. L., & Koenig, R., Jr. (1976). Determinants of coordination modes within organizations. *American Sociological Review, 41,* 322–338.

44. Woodward, J. (1965). *Industrial organization: Theory and practice.* London: Oxford University Press.

45. Mintzberg, H. (1979). *The structuring of organizations.* Englewood Cliffs, NJ: Prentice-Hall.

46. Marsh, R. M., & Mannari, H. (1981). Technology and size as determinants of the organizational structure of Japanese factories. *Administrative Science Quarterly, 26,* 33–57; Keller, R. T., Slocum, J. W., Jr., & Susman, G. J. (1974). Uncertainty and type of management in continuous process organizations. *Academy of Management Journal, 17,* 56–68; Zwerman, W. L. (1970). *New perspectives on organizational theory.* Westport, CT: Greenwood.

47. Singh, J. V. (1986). Technology, size, and organizational structure: A reexamination of the Okayma study data. *Academy of Management Journal, 29,* 800–812.

48. Walton, R. E. (1989). *Up and running: Integrating information technology and the organization.* Boston: Harvard Business School Press.

49. Child, J. (1987). Organizational design for advanced manufacturing technology. In T. D. Wall, C. W. Clegg, & N. J. Kemp (Eds.), *The human side of advanced manufacturing technology.* Sussex, England: Wiley.

50. From the Massachusetts Institute of Technology report *Made in America,* as excerpted in *Fortune,* May 22, 1989, p. 94.

51. This table draws in part on Nemetz, P. L., & Fry, L. W. (1988). Flexible manufacturing organizations: Implications for strategy formulation and organization design. *Academy of Management Review, 13,* 627–638; Main, J. (1990, May 21). Manufacturing the right way. *Fortune,* 54–64; Jelinek, M., & Goldhar, J. D. (1986). Maximizing strategic opportunities in implementing advanced manufacturing systems. In D. D. Davis (Ed.), *Managing technological innovation.* San Francisco: Jossey-Bass.

52. Cummings, T. G., & Blumberg, M. (1987). Advanced manufacturing technology and work design. In Wall et al.

53. Zammuto, R. F., & O'Connor, E. J. (1992). Gaining advanced manufacturing technologies' benefits: The roles of organizational design and culture. *Academy of Management Review, 17,* 701–728; Nemetz & Fry, 1988; Child, 1987. The following draws upon Child.

54. Dean, J. W., Jr., Yook, S. J., & Susman, G. I. (1992). Advanced manufacturing

technology and organizational structure: Empowerment or subordination? *Organization Science, 3,* 203–229.

55. Collins, P.D., Ryan, L.V., and Matusik, S.F. (1999). Programmable automation and the locus of decision-making power. *Journal of Management, 25,* pp. 29–53.

56. Wall, T. D., & Davids, K. (1992). Shopfloor work organization and advanced manufacturing technology. *International Review of Industrial and Organizational Psychology, 7,* 363–398.

57. Wall, T. D., Jackson, P. R., & Davids, K. (1992). Operator work design and robotics systems performance: A serendipitous field study. *Journal of Applied Psychology, 77,* 353–362; Wall, T. D., Corbett, J. M., Martin, R., Clegg, C. W., & Jackson, P. R. (1990). Advanced manufacturing technology, work design, and performance: A change study. *Journal of Applied Psychology, 75,* 691–697.

58. Cummings & Blumberg, 1987; Blumberg, M., & Gerwin, D. (1984). Coping with advanced manufacturing technology. *Journal of Occupational Behaviour, 5,* 113–130.

59. From an unpublished paper by C. A. Voss, cited in Child, 1987.

60. Long, R. J. (1987). *New office information technology: Human and managerial implications.* London: Croom Helm.

61. Long, 1987.

62. Dopson, S., & Stewart, R. (1990). What is happening to middle management? *British Journal of Management, 1,* 3–16.

63. See Bloomfield, B. P., & Coombs, R. (1992). Information technology, control and power: The centralization and decentralization debate revisited. *Journal of Management Studies, 29,* 459–484.

64. Huber, G. P. (1990). A theory of the effects of advanced information technologies on organizational design, intelligence, and decision making. *Academy of Management Review, 15,* 47–71.

65. Long, 1987; Hughes, K. D. (1989). Office automation: A review of the literature. *Relations Industrielles, 44,* 654–679.

66. Long, 1987.

67. Medcof, J. W. (1989). The effect and extent of use of information technology and job of the user upon task characteristics. *Human Relations, 42,* 23–41.

68. Medcof, J.W. (1996). The job characteristics of computing and non-computing work activities. *Journal of Occupational and Organizational Psychology, 69,* pp. 199–212.

69. Long, 1987.

Chapter 16

1. Peters, T. J., & Waterman, R. H, Jr. (1982). *In search of excellence.* New York, NY: Warner Books; Moser, P. (1988, July 4). The McDonald's mystique. *Fortune Guide to Managing,* pp. 25-28; Leonhardt, D. (1998, March 9). McDonald's: Can it regain its golden touch? *Business Week,* pp. 70- 77; Horovitz, B., & Strauss, G. (1998, May 1). Fast-food icon wants shine restored to golden arches. *USA Today,* pp. 1B, 2B. (1999, February 1); Greenberg serving up a fresher McDonald's. *National Post,* p. C2. (Bloomberg News); Branch, S. (1996, November 11). McDonald's strikes out with grownups. *Fortune,* pp. 157-162.

2. Nadler, D. A., & Tushman, M. L. (1989, August). Organizational frame bending: Principles for managing reorientation. *Academy of Management Executive,* 194–203.

3. This list relies mostly on Leavitt, H. (1965). Applied organizational changes in industry: Structural, technological, and humanistic approaches. In J. G. March (Ed.), *Handbook of organizations.* Chicago: Rand McNally.

4. Cameron, K. S., & Quinn, R. E. (1999). *Diagnosing and changing organizational culture.* Reading: MA. Addison-Wesley.

5. Lewin, K. (1951). *Field theory in social science.* New York: Harper & Row.

6. See Howard, A. (Ed.) (1994). *Diagnosis for organizational change: Methods and models.* New York: Guilford; Levinson, H. (1972). *Organizational diagnosis.* Cambridge, MA: Harvard University Press.

7. The first five reasons are from Kotter, J. P., & Schlesinger, L. A. (1979, March–April). Choosing strategies for change. *Harvard Business Review,* 106–114.

8. Frank, R. (1994, May 23). As UPS tries to deliver more to its customers, labor problems grow. *Wall Street Journal,* pp. A1, A8.

9. Tichy, N. M., & Devanna, M. A. (1986). *The transformational leader.* New York: Wiley.

10. The following relies partly on Kotter & Schlesinger, 1979.

11. For reviews, see Macy, B. A., Peterson, M. F., & Norton, L. W. (1989). A test of participation theory in a work redesign field setting: Degree of participation and comparison site contrasts. *Human Relations, 42,* 1095–1165; Filley, A. C., House, R. J., & Kerr, S. (1976). *Managerial process and organizational behavior* (2nd ed.). Glenview, IL: Scott, Foresman.

12. Tichy & Devanna, 1986; Yukl, G. A. (1989). *Leadership in organizations* (2nd ed.). Englewood Cliffs, NJ: Prentice-Hall.

13. Catalanello, R. F., & Kirkpatrick, D. L. (1968). Evaluating training programs—The state of the art. *Training and Development Journal, 22,* 2–9.

14. Goodman, P. S., Bazerman, M., & Conlon, E. (1980). Institutionalization of planned organizational change. *Research in Organizational Behavior, 2,* 215–246.

15. Goodman et al., 1980.

16. For a review of various definitions, see Porras, J. I., & Robertson, P. J. (1992). Organizational development: Theory, practice, and research. In M.D. Dunnette & L. M. Hough (Eds.), *Handbook of industrial and organizational psychology* (2nd ed., Vol. 3). Palo Alto, CA: Consulting Psychologists Press.

17. French, W. L., & Bell, C. H., Jr. (1973). *Organization development.* Englewood Cliffs, NJ: Prentice-Hall.

18. Beer, M., & Walton, E. (1990). Developing the competitive organization: Interventions and strategies. *American Psychologist, 45,* 154–161; Beer, M. (1980). Organization change and development: A systems view. Glenview, IL: Scott, Foresman.

19. Beer, M. (1976). The technology of organizational development. In M. D. Dunnette (Ed.) *Handbook of industrial, and organizational psychology.* Chicago: Rand McNally. See also Dyer, W. (1987). *Team building: Issues and alternatives* (2nd ed.). Reading, MA: Addison-Wesley.

20. Kerr, A. (1999, August 23). Compaq Canada climbs the training wall. The Globe and Mail, B8.

21. Wakeley, J. H., & Shaw, M. E. (1965). Management training: An integrated approach. *Training Directors Journal, 19,* 2–13.

22. Bennet, J. (1993, June 23). Team spirit is new message at Olds. *New York Times,* pp. D1, D15; Tarr, S. C., & Juliano, W. J. (1992, October). Leading a team through downsizing. *HRMagazine,* 91–100.

23. This description relies upon Beer, 1980; Huse, E. F., & Cummings, T. G. (1985). *Organization development and change* (3rd ed.). St. Paul, MN: West; Nadler, D. A. (1977). *Feedback and organization development: Using data-based methods.* Reading, MA: Addison-Wesley.

24. Taylor, J., & Bowers, D. (1972). *Survey of organizations: A machine-scored standardized questionnaire instrument.* Ann Arbor, MI: Center for Research on Utilization of Scientific Knowledge, Institute for Social Research, University of Michigan.

25. Read, W. H. (1991, January). Gathering opinion on-line. *HRMagazine,* 51–53.

26. Johnson, R. H., Ryan, A. M., & Schmit, M. (1994). *Employee attitudes and branch performance at Ford Motor Credit.* Presentation at the annual conference of the Society for Industrial and Organizational Psychology, Nashville, Tennessee.

27. For an eclectic view of current TQM concerns, see the Total Quality Special Issue of the July 1994 *Academy of Management Review.*

28. Deming, W. E. (1986). *Out of the crisis*. Cambridge, MA: Massachusetts Institute of Technology Center for Advanced Engineering Study; Crosby, P. B. (1979). *Quality is free*. New York: McGraw-Hill; Juran J. M. (1992). *Juran on quality by design*. New York: Free Press.

29. Kinlaw, D.C. (1992). *Continuous improvement and measurement for total quality: A team-based approach*. San Diego: Pfeiffer.

30. Berry, L. L., Parasuraman, A., & Zeithaml, V. A. (1994, May). Improving service quality in America: Lessons learned. *Academy of Management Executive*, 32–45.

31. Kinlaw, 1992; Bounds, G., Yorks, L., Adams, M., & Ranney, G. (1994). *Beyond total quality management: Toward the emerging paradigm*. New York: McGraw-Hill.

32. Reeves, C. A., & Bednar, D. A. (1994). Defining quality: Alternatives and implications. *Academy of Management Review, 19*, 419-445.

33. Krishnan et al., 1993.

34. Hammer, M., & Champy, J. (1993). *Reengineering the corporation: A manifesto for business revolution*. New York: HarperBusiness; Stewart, T. A. (1993, August 23). Reengineering: The hot new management tool. *Fortune*, 41–48; Greengard, S. (1993, December). Reengineering: Out of the rubble. *Personnel Journal*, 48B–48O.

35. Hammer & Champy, 1993.

36. Hammer & Champy, 1993.

37. Teng, J. T. C., Grover, V., & Fiedler, K. D. (1994, Spring). Business process reengineering: Charting a strategic path for the information age. *California Management Review*, 9–31.

38. Hammer & Champy, 1993; Teng et al., 1994.

39. Examples from Greengard, 1993 and Teng et al., 1994.

40. See Dumaine, B. (1989, February 14). How managers can succeed through speed. *Fortune*, 54–59.

41. Hall, G., Rosenthal, J., & Wade, J. (1993, November–December). How to make reengineering really work. *Harvard Business Review*, 119–131.

42. Neuman, G. A., Edwards, J. E., & Raju, N. S. (1989). Organizational development interventions: A meta-analysis of their effects on satisfaction and other attitudes. *Personnel Psychology, 42*, 461–489; Guzzo, R. A., Jette, R. D., & Katzell, R. A. (1985). The effects of psychologically based intervention programs on worker productivity: A meta-analysis. *Personnel Psychology, 38*, 275–291.

43. Cameron & Quinn, 1999.

44. For a meta-analytic summary, see Robertson, P. J., Roberts, D. R., & Porras, J. I. (1993). Dynamics of planned organizational change: Assessing support for a theoretical model. *Academy of Management Journal, 36*, 619–634. See also Macy, B. A., & Izumi, H. (1993). Organizational change, design, and work innovation: A meta-analysis of 131 North American field studies—1961–1991. *Research in Organizational Change and Development, 7*, 235–313.

45. Porras & Robertson, 1992; Nicholas, J. M., & Katz, M. (1985). Research methods and reporting practices in organization development: A review and some guidelines. *Academy of Management Review, 10*, 737–749.

46. White, S. E., & Mitchell, T. R. (1976). Organization development: A review of research content and research design. *Academy of Management Review, 1*, 57–73.

47. For an attempt to provide some order to this subject see Wolfe, R. A. (1994). Organizational innovation: Review, critique and suggested research directions. *Journal of Management Studies, 31*, 405–431.

48. Tushman, M., & Nadler, D. (1986, Spring). Organizing for innovation. *California Management Review*, 74–92.

49. Frost, P. J., & Egri, C. P. (1991). The political process of innovation. *Research in Organizational Behavior, 13*, 229–295.

50. This three-part view of creativity is from Amabile, T. M. (1988). A model of creativity and innovation in organizations. *Research in Organizational Behavior, 10*, 123–167. See also Woodman, R. W., Sawyer, J. E., & Griffin, R. W. (1993). Toward a theory of organizational creativity. *Academy of Management Review, 18*, 293–321.

51. Basadur, M. (1994). Managing the creative process in organizations. In M. A. Runco (Ed.), *Problem finding, problem solving, and creativity*. Norwood, NJ: Ablex; Kabanoff, B., & Rossiter, J. R. (1994). Recent developments in applied creativity. *International Review of Industrial and Organizational Psychology, 9*, 283–324.

52. Rosenberg, M. (1999, May 17). Improvisation promotes innovative thinking, company flexibility. *Canadian HR Reporter* (Guide to Thinking & Development), pp. G9, G15.

53. Galbraith, J. R. (1982, Winter). Designing the innovating organization. *Organizational Dynamics*, 4–25.

54. Howell, J. M., & Higgins, C. A. (1990). Champions of technological innovation. *Administrative Science Quarterly, 35*, 317–341.

55. Orlicke, J. (1985). *The Progressive Corporation (B)*. Boston: Harvard Business School.

56. Cohen, W. M., & Levinthal, D. A. (1990). Absorptive capacity: A new perspective on learning and innovation. *Administrative Science Quarterly, 35*, 128–152.

57. Tushman, M. L., & Scanlan, T. J. (1981). Characteristics and external orientations of boundary spanning individuals. *Academy of Management Journal, 24*, 83–98; Tushman, M. L., & Scanlan, T. J. (1981). Boundary spanning individuals: Their role in information transfer and their antecedents. *Academy of Management Journal, 24*, 289–305.

58. Keller, R. T., & Holland, W. E. (1983). Communicators and innovators in research and development organizations. *Academy of Management Journal, 26*, 742–749.

59. Kanter, R. M. (1988). When a thousand flowers bloom: Structural, collective, and social conditions for innovation in organization. *Research in Organizational Behavior, 10*, 169–211.

60. Kanter, 1988; Nord, W. R., & Tucker, S. (1987). *Implementing routine and radical innovations*. Lexington, MA: Lexington Books; Damanpour, F. (1991). Organizational innovation: A meta-analysis of effects of determinants and moderators. *Academy of Management Journal, 34*, 555–590.

61. Nonaka, I. (1990, Spring). Redundant, overlapping organization: A Japanese approach to managing the innovation process. *California Management Review*, 27–38.

62. Sherman, S. P. (1984, October 15). Eight big masters of innovation. *Fortune*, 66–84, p. 72.

63. Tushman & Scanlan, 1981, pp. 289–305.

64. Keller & Holland, 1983.

65. Katz, R. (1982). The effects of group longevity on project communication and performance. *Administrative Science Quarterly, 27*, 81–104.

66. For a review, see Nord & Tucker, 1987. However, this prescription is controversial. For other views see Kanter, 1988 and Marcus A. A. (1988). Implementing externally induced innovations: A comparison of rule-bound and autonomous approaches. *Academy of Management Journal, 31*, 235–256.

67. Damanpour, 1991; Kanter, 1988.

68. Galbraith, 1982.

69. Peters, T. (1987). *Thriving on chaos*. New York: Knopf.

70. Amabile, 1988.

71. Galbraith, 1982.

72. Walton, R. E. (1975, Winter). The diffusion of new work structures: Explaining why success didn't take. *Organizational Dynamics*, 3–22.

73. Rogers, E. M. (1983). *Diffusion of innovations* (3rd ed.). New York: Free Press.

Appendix

1. Sutton, R. I. (1991). Maintaining norms about expressed emotions: The case of bill collectors. *Administrative Science Quarterly, 36*, 245–268.

2. Lupton, T. (1963). *On the shop floor*. Oxford: Pergamon.

3. Bensman, J., & Gerver, I. (1963). Crime and punishment in the factory: The function of deviancy in maintain-

ing the social system. *American Sociological Review, 28,* 588–598.

4. Mintzberg, H. (1973). *The nature of managerial work.* New York: Harper & Row.

5. Ragins, B. R., & Cotton, J. L. (1993). Gender and willingness to mentor in organizations. *Journal of Management, 19,* 97–111.

6. Ivancevich, J. M., & Lyon, H. L. (1977). The shortened workweek: A field experiment. *Journal of Applied Psychology, 62,* 34–37.

7. Sutton, R. I., & Rafaeli, A. (1988). Untangling the relationship between displayed emotions and organizational sales: The case of convenience stores. *Academy of Management Journal, 31,* 461–487.

8. Roethlisberger, F. J., & Dickson, W. J. (1939). *Management and the worker.* Cambridge, MA: Harvard University Press; Greenwood, R. G., & Wrege, C. D. (1986). The Hawthorne studies. In D. A. Wren & J. A. Pearce II (Eds.), *Papers dedicated to the development of modern management.* The Academy of Management.

9. Adair, J. G. (1984). The Hawthorne effect: A reconsideration of the methodological artifact. *Journal of Applied Psychology, 69,* 334–345.

10. See Academy of Management. (1992). The Academy of Management code of ethical conduct. *Academy of Management Journal, 35,* 1135–1142; Lowman, R. L. (Ed.). (1985) *Casebook on ethics and standards for the practice of psychology in organizations.* College Park, MD: Society for Industrial and Organizational Psychology.

Index

The page on which a key term is defined is set in boldface.

Photo Credits